Ohio Authors and Their Books

1796–1950

Ohio Authors and Their Books

BIOGRAPHICAL DATA AND SELECTIVE BIBLIOGRAPHIES
FOR OHIO AUTHORS, NATIVE AND RESIDENT,
1796–1950

EDITED BY

WILLIAM COYLE

WITTENBERG UNIVERSITY

PRELIMINARY RESEARCH BY

MR. AND MRS. ERNEST WESSEN

SPONSORED BY
THE MARTHA KINNEY COOPER
OHIOANA LIBRARY ASSOCIATION

THE WORLD PUBLISHING COMPANY

CLEVELAND AND NEW YORK

PUBLISHED BY The World Publishing Company
2231 WEST 110TH STREET, CLEVELAND 2, OHIO
FOR
The Martha Kinney Cooper
Ohioana Library Association

PUBLISHED SIMULTANEOUSLY IN CANADA BY
NELSON, FOSTER & SCOTT LTD.

Library of Congress Catalog Card Number: 62-7594

FIRST EDITION

WP162

Printed in the United States of America.

Contents

Purpose and Scope

A VOLUME DEVOTED to the authors of a single state requires a brief statement of explanation, if not of defense. Its purpose is not to gratify state pride by "claiming" every writer who ever crossed the borders of Ohio or by amassing effusive praise of every Ohioan who ever set pen to paper. It is, rather, to record biographical data and bibliographical check lists that should prove useful to librarians, historians, students of literature, and others interested in Ohio's past and present. Furthermore, the biographies viewed collectively represent one panel in the full expanse of American literature. Detailed examination of a regional segment of a national literature may reveal fresh insights and new emphases. The danger in such a study is exalting the part above the whole. We have tried to avoid making excessive claims for Ohio literature, but it may be said without flourishing the state flag unduly that the quantity and quality of writing by Ohioans should invalidate the impression created by some historians of a cultural desert extending from Massachusetts to Indiana.

At a rough guess, perhaps eighty million people have lived within the borders of Ohio since the state was settled. To include the name of every person who has written something that saw print would make this work too cumbersome to be useful. Although it may seem that we have cast our nets too wide, from a file of more than 15,000 names of authors associated with Ohio we have included only about one-third. We have attempted to devise a sensible formula for inclusion of books and authors, but have made occasional exceptions when they seemed justified by the logic of a particular situation or when they seemed likely to enhance the usefulness of this volume.

The essential problem is contained in two deceptively simple questions suggested by our title: Who is an Ohio author? and What is a book? Our interpretations of these questions, which are much simpler in practice than in statement, are outlined below as briefly as possible.

The apparently simple word *author* is susceptible to various ambiguities. It has been interpreted here as a person who has published at least one original work of general interest. This definition excludes editors, compilers, translators, illustrators, or sponsors of books written by others.

So few Americans spend their lives within a single state that determining who should be considered an Ohioan is more difficult than it might seem. To begin with, an author born in Ohio clearly belongs in a volume of this kind, even though his entire term of residence was spent in a maternity ward. An author who spent a major portion of his life in Ohio also belongs. In addition, we have included, for brief treatment, some authors who spent only a few years in Ohio, especially if they wrote any of their books while living here. We have, however, omitted authors who were in Ohio only while attending college or whose residence was extremely brief. Therefore, we have not included Vachel Lindsay, who spent three years at Hiram College; Mark Twain, who passed a crucial winter in Cincinnati before becoming a river pilot; or Thomas Beer and Clarence Day, who spent boyhood summers in Bucyrus and Painesville.

Our basic definition of an eligible book was that it must be a published work of general interest. This definition does not rule out pamphlets, but it does exclude mimeographed works, unpublished manuscripts, and works written for special groups. The major categories of books that have been excluded are the following:

1. Textbooks and manuals.
2. Single speeches or lectures printed as pamphlets.
3. Single magazine articles reprinted as pamphlets.
4. Graduate theses and dissertations.
5. Technical scientific, legal, and medical works.
6. Publications of fraternal orders.
7. Sermons.
8. State and Federal Government publications.
9. Family histories and genealogical works.
10. Cookbooks, almanacs, atlases, gazetteers, etiquette books, joke books, and similar compilations.

The vast amount of material published in the twentieth century has made a further limitation necessary. We have, therefore, included only those authors who have published at least one eligible work listed in the Library of Congress catalogues of printed cards before December 31, 1950. Since the 232 volumes of printed cards that were searched represent more than six million books, this seemed the most reliable and uniform criterion for twentieth-century books.

The entries for writers who are included are of three general types:

I. A writer who published at least one eligible work before December 31, 1900: a biographical summary and a check list of his writings.

II. A writer who published at least one eligible work between January 1, 1901, and December 31, 1950: a biographical summary, one or more representative titles, and if possible a citation of a biographical reference book.

III. A writer who lived in Ohio for only a brief period: treatment similar to Group II with special emphasis on the subject's Ohio years.

Sketches of some especially notable authors in Groups I and II have been written by contributors. Except that the opening sentences of these sketches have been standardized, they are of great variety. Because most of the subjects are treated in standard biographical encyclopedias, we have encouraged contributors to avoid stereotyped patterns and discuss their subjects from whatever viewpoint seemed appropriate. A list of contributors will be found in Appendix B.

Three groups of authors have been given somewhat out-of-the-ordinary treatment. First, public figures like Ulysses S. Grant and George Armstrong Custer, whose writings were an incidental aspect of their careers and whose lives are fully covered in standard biographical compilations, are treated more briefly than their total accomplishment would seem to merit. Second, we have included biographical sketches, but not bibliographies, of a few major pioneers in the field of textbook writing like William McGuffey, Platt Rogers Spencer, and Joseph Ray. Similarly, writers of dime novels have been included as biographical entries, but their enormous bibliographies and cross-references to their numerous pen names have often been omitted.

ABBREVIATIONS

In the entries themselves, three abbreviations are used frequently:

e.g., for example
O.V.I., Ohio Volunteer Infantry
q.v., which see

After many entries for twentieth-century authors, a biographical reference book is cited. For these citations, the following abbreviations are used:

AATB, *American Authors and Their Books*
AMS, *American Men of Science*
ANT, *American Novelists of Today*
BDCP, *Biographical Dictionary of Contemporary Poets*
CB, *Current Biography*
CWW, *American Catholic Who's Who*
DAB, *Dictionary of American Biography*
DAS, *Directory of American Scholars*
IATB, *Indiana Authors and Their Books*
JBA, *Junior Book of Authors*
LE, *Leaders in Education*
NC, *National Cyclopedia of American Biography*
OBB, *Ohio Blue Book*
OCM, *Ohio Composers and Musical Authors*
RC, *Representative Clevelanders*
RLA, *Religious Leaders of America*
TCA, *Twentieth Century Authors*
WO, *Women of Ohio*
WW, *Who's Who in America*
WWAA, *Who's Who in American Art*
WWAE, *Who's Who in American Education*
WWAW, *Who's Who of American Women*
WWC, *Who's Who in the Clergy*
WWCI, *Who's Who in Commerce and Industry*
WWE, *Who's Who in the East*
WWL, *Who's Who in Labor*
WWLS, *Who's Who in Library Service*
WWMW, *Who's Who in the Midwest*
WWNAA, *Who's Who among North American Authors*
WWO, *Who's Who in Ohio (1930)*

WWT, *Who's Who in the Theatre*
WWW, *Who Was Who in America*
WWWJ, *Who's Who in World Jewry*

MISCELLANEOUS NOTES

1. The form of the bibliographies follows library practices as closely as possible. Long titles have been shortened, and the omission of words has been indicated by an ellipsis. Publication facts not found on the title page of a book are enclosed in square brackets. Unlike library cataloguing procedure, however, the arrangement of titles is chronological rather than alphabetical.
2. In the biographical entries, names beginning with *Mc* or *M'* are alphabetized as though spelled *Mac.*
3. Information given in the text of an entry, such as the name of a collaborator or the use of a pen name, is not repeated in the bibliography.
4. Except for major American cities that have no counterpart in Ohio, all non-Ohio place names are followed by the name of the state or country in which they are located. Ohio counties, townships, towns, and cities are not followed by the name of the state.
5. The terminal date for the bibliographies is 1950. When necessary and possible, biographical information has been extended to 1960. The word "now" in a sketch signifies 1960.
6. Although we have made every effort to collect accurate and complete information on all Ohio authors, some entries are incomplete and some undoubtedly contain errors. Inevitably, many long-sought facts will come to light after this work is in print. At a later time, therefore, we intend to print a sheet of corrections and additions that can be inserted in this volume. Readers who discover mistakes or omissions are invited to send information to the Ohioana Library, Columbus 15, Ohio.

Ohio in American Literature

"AMERICAN LITERATURE," according to Frederick Jackson Turner, "is not a single thing. It is a choral song of many sections." In the Midwestern portion of this song, however, it is difficult to identify a distinctive Ohio voice. Some observers, in fact, have implied that Ohio has not even hummed along with the literary music; according to a history of Allen County (1921), a local educator, when asked to discuss the literature of the area, replied succinctly, "Why write about what ain't?" Actually, as the present volume attests, Ohio has produced a large number of writers, both major and minor; but many seem American authors first and Ohio authors only incidentally. There has never been a homogeneous Buckeye school of literature; one finds little unity of spirit, slight similarity in techniques or materials, and surprisingly little personal acquaintance among Ohio's numerous authors. Major literary figures who have come out of Ohio include William Dean Howells, Sherwood Anderson, James Thurber, and Hart Crane. A more disparate group can scarcely be imagined. Instead of a distinctive regional spirit, the writing of Ohioans shows a surprisingly complete representation of popular taste in the nation as a whole.

Because authors by nature of their calling are solitary and individualistic, the notion of a thoroughly unified regional literature is to some extent an illusion. Perhaps community of purpose and similarity of themes and techniques can be found at only two periods in American literary history: in New England during the second quarter of the nineteenth century, and in the South during the second quarter of the twentieth. In both of these regions, drastic social change, which saw established ways of life being displaced, was accompanied by a literary awakening. Apparently, confrontation of the old and the new in a culture energizes the literary artist. In Ohio, however, and probably in the other states created from the Northwest Territory, social change, though rapid, has been comparatively uncomplicated.

Except in Cincinnati during the 1830s and 1840s, there is no period in Ohio's history when writers engaged in significant collective endeavor. The short-lived literary periodicals described by W. H. Venable in his *Beginnings of Literary Culture in the Ohio Valley,* the literary and discussion societies, and numerous active publishing houses bespeak a concern with literary matters not found elsewhere in Ohio. Enthusiasm and bustle, however, are no substitute for genius; and Cincinnati before the Civil War had no truly great writers.

Although many Cincinnati writers were New Englanders who established a transcendentalist magazine before the famous *Dial* was founded in Massachusetts, most of them agreed that a distinctive regional literature should be developed.

Writers like James Hall, Timothy Flint, and William D. Gallagher expressed an aggressive provincialism typical of the local-color movement a generation later. In 1858 William T. Coggeshall complained that the West was not adequately represented in literature and that writers and lecturers needed a "seaboard indorsement" to be taken seriously in the West. Proponents of a regional literature insisted that the literary scene was dominated by an Eastern clique, that Western vigor was preferable to an effete Eastern culture, and that writers should use Western materials. Unfortunately, a provincial inferiority complex caused writers to look to Eastern authors and to the British romantics for models and to ignore the crude, everyday world around them in favor of an artificial literary make-believe. The combination of valid theory and faulty practice is illustrated by Thomas Peirce's advice to Western writers:

> Be yours the office to describe
> The blooming belles of Flora's tribe.

Although some realistic accounts of frontier Ohio were written by Benjamin Drake and others, much of the early literature was a mixture of melodrama and sentimentality.

The local-color movement after the Civil War, which stressed accurate treatment of regional materials, was essentially retrospective, as writers drew on their own memories of a region. By the 1880s, when local color was popular, however, the frontier was a matter of historical record rather than personal recollection in Ohio, where conquest of the wilderness had been violent but relatively swift.

More impressive than fiction and poetry during Ohio's early years were the numerous almanacs, gazetteers, textbooks, manuals, and handbooks of every description. They reflect a concern with the practical and the matter-of-fact. In medicine, law, and science, there was much less tendency to imitate Eastern models.

A major reason, then, for the lack of a unified regional spirit in Ohio's literature was the rapid growth of the state. Rich soil and other natural bounties attracted a flood tide of settlers and resulted in phenomenally rapid development. Ohio passed quickly from frontier wilderness to an agricultural economy and soon thereafter to an industrial, urban society. Another reason for the absence of regional solidarity was the diversity of the population. Easy access from east and south attracted settlers from New England, Pennsylvania, Kentucky, and Virginia. Industrialization and the rapid growth of cities attracted a variety of ethnic groups. A melting-pot culture may evoke a healthy democratic spirit, but it does not produce a homogeneous literature.

Despite the diversity of Ohio's literary history and the lack of any sustained "Buckeye spirit," some significant generalizations can be abstracted from the biographical and bibliographical data in this volume. The chief danger in such an endeavor is the fallacy of environmental determinism—of assuming that each author wrote as he did because of his birth or residence in Ohio. There is, of course, no way of proving that any individual author would have written differently if he had lived in Maine, Kansas, or Oregon. By concentrating on broad tendencies, however, and by using individual authors as illustration rather than as proof, one can discover interesting reflections of Ohio's social and cultural history.

One obvious characteristic is what Venable called the "exodic" tendency of Ohio authors. There have always been more authors *from* Ohio than *in* Ohio. Since its earliest settlement, the state has attracted a great variety of settlers and has sent them or their children to every corner of the Union. A surprising number of the memoirs by mountain men, gold-seekers, and other pioneers of the Far West were written by men of Ohio origin. The biographical entries in this volume show Ohio-born authors living in almost every state. Howells set the pattern for this "Buckeye exodus" in 1860, when he headed for New England after publishing some poems in the *Atlantic Monthly*. As a Mecca for professional authors, Boston has been supplanted by Broadway and Hollywood, but the tendency to emigrate persists.

For many of these displaced Ohioans, the state has remained a nostalgic image recalled with wistful affection. Pleasant recollections of Ohio can be found in numerous autobiographical books by writers living outside their native state. As he grew older, Howells returned often to memories of his Ohio boyhood, and James Thurber once wrote "The clocks that strike in my dreams are often the clocks of Columbus." Generally speaking, Ohio authors who have left the state have not rejected it. The writer's alienation from his native roots has been a major theme in twentieth-century American literature, but it is not very noticeable in the writing of Ohioans.

The literary output of Ohioans, both in and out of the state, has been large and varied. Religious books undoubtedly outnumber all others. Although sermons are not listed in this volume, the bibliographies contain more books on religion—polemical, devotional, homiletic, and historical—than on any other subject.

A major reason for this productivity in religious books was the close identification of church groups with the educational history of the state. Every major denomination founded at least one college or seminary, and Miami University and Ohio University, both state institutions, were unofficially identified with the Presbyterians and the Methodists respectively. Clergymen who doubled as faculty members were prolific writers on religion as well as other topics. Another reason was that a writer on religious subjects found many receptive publication outlets. At least six denominations published periodicals in Cincinnati during the nineteenth century, and the Methodists conducted a thriving book-publishing firm there, as the United Brethren did in Dayton.

Though seldom stated in so many words, the major causes of religious ferment in early Ohio were the ordinary citizens' desire for an egalitarian religion and the clergy's struggle to adapt Calvinism to frontier conditions. Numerous popular religious movements, more or less devoted to these ends, flourished in Ohio, and the doctrinal disputes and other controversies that some of them engendered resulted in many books and pamphlets. The Baptist, Presbyterian, and Methodist clergy—the largest groups—were highly productive writers, but activities of other sects also resulted in the making of many books. The Shakers, who established communities in Warren, Montgomery, and Cuyahoga Counties, operated their own printing press. The Church of the New Jerusalem prospered, especially in southern Ohio. Kirtland was a way-station for the Mormons in the 1830s.

Akron was a center of Universalism. The Unitarians were ready writers, especially the transplanted New Englanders in Cincinnati. The Disciples of Christ and the United Brethren founded many churches in Ohio, and clergymen of both persuasions were prolific writers. German Methodism was founded in Cincinnati, as was Reform Judaism. Josiah Strong, Washington Gladden, and other leaders of the Social Gospel movement at the turn of the century served Ohio churches. Even the contemporary "peace of mind" tendency in religion is epitomized by Ohio-born Norman Vincent Peale, and the phrase was originated by another Ohioan—Rabbi Joshua Loth Liebman.

The fourth estate has produced nearly as many books as the first. The rapid growth of towns and cities, a literate citizenry, and the importance of politics in Ohio life help account for the numerous newspapers that have flourished in the state. Many writers, like Howells and Thurber, served journalistic apprenticeships before turning to literary careers. Ohio has also known a great many professional journalists: for example, Charles Hammond, Whitelaw Reid, Murat Halstead, David R. Locke, Don Carlos Seitz, George Kennan, William Henry Smith, Charles Merz, Anne O'Hare McCormick, O. O. McIntyre, Percy Hammond, James B. Reston, Fred C. Kelly, Earl Wilson, Herman Fetzer (Jake Falstaff), Hugh S. Fullerton, and Lowell Thomas. These and other Ohio journalists have written a great variety of books.

Even before Ohio was admitted to statehood, a sharp contest ensued between Federalists and anti-Federalists. Politics has been a major activity ever since, partly because of the diversity of the population and partly, perhaps, because of the public's enjoyment of political excitement. The state has seen many rousing political contests and has produced more than its share of major political figures. These leaders and their supporters have turned out many books and pamphlets. Also, Ohioans appear unexpectedly in the political annals of other states: for example, Edmund G. Ross, senator from Kansas who cast a decisive vote against the impeachment of Andrew Johnson, was born in Ashland; James B. Weaver, leader of the Farmers' Alliance, was born in Dayton; John P. Altgeld, governor of Illinois, was reared in Richland County; and George W. Norris, senator from Nebraska, was born in Sandusky County.

Many persons today probably envision Ohio as a bastion of conservatism, but this image is not consistent with the multitude of reformers among the state's authors. Many communal experiments were attempted: Owenite communities in the 1830s, Fourieristic phalanxes in the 1840s, and a variety of others devoted to spiritualism, hydrotherapy, or food fads. Also, the Quakers in the east and south, the abolitionists in the Western Reserve, and the radicals among the Germans in Cincinnati were all cordial to the reforming spirit. Innumerable books and pamphlets were written on abolition, temperance, and women's rights—reforms that now seem rather innocuous because they were successful. Ohio has also seen a host of more radical or more eccentric reformers, such as Josiah Warner, Nathan C. Meeker, and Orson Murray, who founded utopian communities; Victoria and Tennessee Woodhull, fervent advocates of women's rights, free love, and—in their old age—eugenics; John B. Newbrough, who founded the Shalam Community in New Mexico and wrote a bible for its guidance; Elias Longley, proponent of phonetic spelling and other reforms; and Jacob S. Coxey, leader of the Commonweal of Christ, popularly known as Coxey's Army. These reformers and many others promoted their pet projects by means of pamphlets and books.

The mysterious mounds in southern Ohio are probably the chief reason that the state has attracted or produced such distinguished archaeologists as Ephraim G. Squier, Edwin H. Davis, William C. Mills, William Henry Adams, Charles Whittlesey, Warren K. Moorehead, and Henry G. Shetrone. Besides these scholars, many enthusiastic local amateurs have written books and pamphlets, some soberly describing the mounds and others fancifully re-creating the culture of the Mound Builders.

The enormous amount of historical writing is more difficult to explain. Such organizations as the Historical and Philosophical Society, Firelands Historical Society, Western Reserve Historical Society, Ohio Historical Society, and others have encouraged writing and research. An awakening of state pride after the Civil War partially accounts for the abundance of regimental histories and war memoirs. Local semicentennials and centennials, encouragement from commercial publishers, and the gratification early settlers and their descendants found in commemorative chronicles resulted in a spate of community and county histories, especially in the 1880s and 1890s. Besides this essentially amateur historical writing, however, Ohio has also produced such notable professional historians as Hubert H. Bancroft, James Ford Rhodes, Archer B. Hulbert, Albert J. Beveridge, Arthur M. Schlesinger (father and son), Carl F. Wittke, and a number of others. Most of them, though, have pursued their active careers outside the state. Rhodes, for example, left Cleveland for Massachusetts after resolving to devote himself to history, and Bancroft conducted his vast research projects at the opposite side of the continent in California.

Impressive in sheer bulk is the verse turned out by Ohioans. Since the early nineteenth century, the state has abounded in amateur poets. Among the Ohioans in Coggeshall's *Poetry and Poets of the West* (1860), there are few professional writers but many unlikely versifiers, such as Charles Hammond and Salmon P. Chase. If any goddess has presided over Ohio poetry, it has been Vesta, patron of home and hearth. Housewives, students, physicians, lawyers, farmers, and teachers have written verse as an avocation. Outlets for their poems have been religious and educational magazines and, formerly, the "Poet's Corner" featured in many newspapers. Many have gathered their work in self-financed collections, published by a local printer or, more recently, by a "vanity press."

Ohio poets have produced a number of elocutionary favorites: "Rain on the Roof" (Coates Kinney), "The Flag Goes By" (Henry H. Bennett), "Your Flag and My Flag" (Wilbur D. Nesbit), and "Bob White" (Marion F. Ham). Henry Lyden Flash, perhaps the most popular poet of the Confederacy, was born in Cincinnati; and John H. Titus, putative author of "The Face on the Bar Room Floor," was a native of Ashtabula County. The affinity of Ohio poets with popular taste is also shown by single lines that have passed into the folk culture of the familiar: for example, "Sheridan twenty miles away" (Thomas B. Read), "It isn't raining rain to me, it's raining violets" (Robert Loveman), and "Off agin, on agin, gone agin. Finnigin" (Strickland Gillilan).

Nineteenth-century poetry in Ohio, as in America generally, inclined toward the sentimental, the moralistic, the decorous, and the derivative. Poets looked for models to Longfellow, to the British romantics, and, less fortunately, to Mrs. Hemans and other writers of religious or domestic verse. Later, James Whitcomb Riley was widely admired, and amateur poets turned out reams of dialect verse on rustic subjects. Still later, Edgar A. Guest inspired a host of imitators. The turn of the century evoked many commemorative poems, odes to Ohio, and the like, more distinguished for fervent state pride than for poetic quality.

The most notable names among mid-nineteenth-century poets include William D. Gallagher, Alice and Phoebe Cary, Otway Curry, and Coates Kinney. Gallagher was probably the most authentic poet of the time, but his Wordsworthian feeling for nature was often vitiated by moralizing and sentimentality. Poets of the later nineteenth century include John James Piatt, Edith M. Thomas, Edward Rowland Sill, and Paul Laurence Dunbar. No truly first-rank poets appear in the century, but a number of minor poets reflect general taste of their day. Twentieth-century poets include Jean Starr Untermeyer, Ridgely Torrence, and Hart Crane. Crane probably has received the most respectful attention from critics, but he is an admittedly exotic figure in the Ohio landscape.

The achievement of Ohio authors is more distinguished in fiction than in poetry. William Dean Howells, the major author the state has produced, and Sherwood Anderson are probably the most important novelists. Howells' definition and defense of realism and his practice of his theories for more than fifty years represent a major contribution to American literature. The sense of loneliness and frustration in Anderson's masterpiece, *Winesburg, Ohio,* is unique in American fiction. Besides these two, Ohio has known such minor but significant writers of fiction as Albion W. Tourgee, Constance F. Woolson, Mary H. Catherwood, Albert G. Riddle, Ambrose Bierce, John B. Naylor, Charles Chesnutt, and Brand Whitlock.

In fiction written simply as popular entertainment, Ohio writers have also been productive. Although Sandusky-born Orville J. Victor did not invent the dime novel, as is sometimes claimed, he did more than anyone else to popularize the form. While he served as editor of Beadle publications, his wife, Metta F. Victor, was one of the most popular in his corps of writers. Emerson Bennett, who wrote many adventure stories a cut above the Beadle productions, lived in Cincinnati during the 1840s. Other Ohioans who turned out popular novels and stories were Oliver Coomes, Thomas C. Harbaugh, Nathan D. Urner, and Edward S. Ellis.

The all-time American best-seller, *Uncle Tom's Cabin,* evolved from materials collected during Mrs. Stowe's eighteen years in Cincinnati. Best-selling Ohio novelists of the twentieth century include Zane Grey, Fannie Hurst, Ben Ames Williams, Lloyd C. Douglas, Louis Bromfield, Jim Tully, Earl Derr Biggers, and William R. Burnett.

Ohio has also produced a number of outstanding writers of juvenile books, including Martha Finley, creator of the saccharine Elsie Dinsmore series; Sarah C. Woolsey (Susan Coolidge), author of *What Katy Did* and many other books; and Elizabeth W. Champney, author of the Vassar Girls series. Children's favorites created by Ohioans include Seckatary Hawkins, Buster Brown, Little Mary Mixup, Raggedy Ann, and the Teenie Weenies. Twentieth-century writers of books for children include Adèle and Cateau DeLeeuw, Marion Renick, Robert McCloskey, Father Francis J. Finn, and Lois Lenski.

Ohio authors have also shown a decided proclivity for humor. Analyzing sources of humor is not only futile but self-defeating, as the analysis usually destroys its subject; but some possible reasons for the profusion of humorous writing suggest themselves. First, a fairly obvious reason is the large number of newpapers that were receptive to this type of material. Second, a tentative reason is the blending of Southern and New England cultures in Ohio. A mixture of Southern exuberance and dry Yankee understatement was characteristic of the post-Civil War "funny men." Third, still more tentatively, the mark of much humor is incongruity; and even in 1960 the Ohio scene is filled with incongruous contrasts, as, for example, one can drive in ten minutes from a roaring industrial city to a secluded, sleepy village.

Whatever the reasons may be, Ohio literature abounds in humor. Charles Farrar Browne became Artemus Ward while a Cleveland newspaperman, and David Ross Locke (Petroleum V. Nasby) spent almost all of his journalistic career in Ohio. William Tappan Thompson, humorist of middle Georgia, spent his boyhood in the Western Reserve. Wilbur F. Hinman, an Ohio journalist, created Si Klegg, comic Civil War soldier. Although he spent his adult life in Indiana, Frank M. Hubbard (Abe Martin) was born in Bellefontaine. Frederick B. Opper and Richard F. Outcault, each of whom is sometimes credited with inventing the comic strip, were both Ohio natives. James Thurber, whose work cuts much deeper than journalistic humor, drew frequently on his memories of Columbus and Ohio State University.

Ohio, it seems, has produced an extensive literature but a miscellaneous one. It might be represented as a pyramid with a half-dozen major authors at the top, numerous minor authors below, and a broad base of amateur or casual writers. Authors on all levels have shown considerable responsiveness to public taste.

One of the proudest boasts of Ohioans is that they live in the typical American state, the epitome of average America. Manufacturers, it is said, regard Ohio as a median area for testing new products. Although this view of Ohio is debatable, it is consistent with the general impression made by the state's literary history. Ohio writers have reflected popular tastes and interests; few of them have been trail-breakers or iconoclasts; they have turned a mirror rather than a lens on American society. Although Ohio has never fostered a cohesive regional school of writers, it has been a seedbed of popular culture. Best-selling fiction, poetry with popular appeal, religious and reform writing, children's stories, journalistic humor—these are the fields in which Ohio authors have been most productive.

The complexity of modern American society and the concentration of publishing and entertainment in New York City make it unlikely that a unified regional school will develop in Ohio or anywhere else. However, the emergence in the 1950s of talented young novelists like Vance Bourjaily, Bentz Plagemann, Herbert Gold, and James Purdy suggests that Ohio's diversified contribution to American literature is continuing.

Acknowledgments

ASSEMBLING biographical and bibliographical data on more than 4,600 authors, many of them relatively obscure, has of necessity been a massive collaboration. So many persons have generously volunteered information or responded to inquiries that listing them all by name is a literal impossibility. I can, therefore, specify only those whose assistance has been extensive, continuing in some instances throughout the ten years that this project has been under way. My gratitude to the many persons and institutions given only generalized acknowledgment is no less sincere.

Major credit for this volume belongs to the Ohioana Library Association, which has sponsored the research and the publication. Mrs. Depew Head, now Director Emeritus, first conceived of the project more than ten years ago and worked closely with Ernest Wessen, the original editor. My own debt is greatest to Walter R. Marvin, the present Director, who has participated vigorously in the search for data and has patiently borne almost daily requests for assistance of all kinds. I have also received much help from the Ohioana staff, especially Florence J. Kelley and Josephine J. Swinehart, Librarians. I am also indebted to the Ohioana membership and staff over the past thirty years, who collected biographical information on Ohio authors and filed it in the Ohioana Library. While I have worked on the book, I have received help and counsel from the Editorial Committee, composed of officers of the Ohioana Association: Carl Vitz, Mrs. Howard Bevis, Mrs. Depew Head, G. Harrison Orians, and Joseph K. Vodrey. Carl Vitz, chairman of the committee, has been a valued adviser throughout all stages of the research, has read portions of the manuscript, and has worked diligently to discover data on Hamilton County authors. Finally, I am deeply obligated to the current Ohioana county chairmen listed in Appendix A and to their predecessors. Lists of questions were sent them; they consulted court records, visited cemeteries, interviewed relatives of authors, advertised in newspapers, and wrote letters to find the answers.

Much of the research for this project has, of course, been done in libraries. Query-lists were sent to libraries in almost every Ohio county and in cities throughout the United States; hundreds of libraries supplied information, for which I am most grateful. In the libraries where I have worked, I have received much assistance and advice. Among the librarians to whom I am obligated are Yeatman Anderson, III, and Ethel M. Hutchins of Cincinnati Public Library; Donna Root of Cleveland Public Library; Elizabeth Faries, William Hamilton, and Helen H. Santmyer of Dayton Public Library; Alice Hook of Historical and Philosophical Society Library; Elizabeth Martin of Ohio Historical Society

Library; Irene McCreery of Toledo Public Library; Luella Eutsler of Wittenberg University Library; and Margaret Leanhard of the State of Ohio Library, Union Catalogue Division. After checking unidentified titles in the last-named library, I spent a week searching for the remainder in the main catalogue and the union catalogue of the Library of Congress, where I was tendered every facility for research.

A large number of the authors in this volume are not included in any reference books, and many others are found only in county histories or biographical dictionaries published during their lifetimes. This has necessitated a great deal of grass-roots research to discover dates of birth and death, to say nothing of significant events between the two. Paradoxically, it has been most difficult to learn the birth date for a living writer and the death date for a dead one. I have not included the date of birth for any living author who prefers that it remain unspecified, but I have tried to find death dates for all authors known to be deceased. Many such facts have been furnished by the Ohio Department of Vital Statistics, thanks to the co-operation of William H. Viegel, Chief of that department. Also, Colonel William B. Haines, in charge of soldiers' claims for Ohio, permitted me to search the burial records in his office. Some Ohio veterans not listed there have been located in the National Archives, Washington, D. C.

Biographical facts have been collected from numerous other sources to which I can make only blanket acknowledgments. Lists of questions were sent to probate courts, county historical associations, medical societies, and bar associations throughout Ohio. Separate queries were also sent to many cemeteries, newspapers, schools, and churches. The response to these queries was exceptionally good. Also, lists of questions were sent to alumni associations of more than a hundred colleges, and almost all of them responded with the information needed.

The contributors listed in Appendix B have prepared sketches of more than a hundred authors. To these busy persons, who have graciously given the time and work necessary to investigate their subjects, I am deeply obligated.

Annual grants, arranged by Dean John N. Stauffer of Wittenberg University, have supplemented funds from Ohioana to provide student assistance in typing and filing. The students who have worked on the project are Donald E. Bauer, Walter Brumm, Dennis E. Lauman, and Claire M. Crowley. My wife, Charlotte Coyle, has not only assisted with the typing and clerical work during school vacations but has also endured patiently a clutter of file cards, manuscript pages, manila folders, reference books, photostats, clippings, and other accouterments of the research. My children, Mary Joan and Daniel Coyle, have proved to be filial file clerks.

At the risk of omitting names that should be included, I wish to acknowledge special help received from Betty E. Baldwin, Cincinnati; Alice F. Bliss, Ashtabula; Graham Bryson, Xenia; Elizabeth Claflin, Cleveland; Virginia T. Curry, Cincinnati; Kathryn M. Keller, Toledo; Mr. and Mrs. Oliver Kuhn, Hartville; Andrew P. Martin, Cleveland; Melrose Pitman, Cincinnati; Alice C. Redhead, Cleveland; Mary L. Spining, Springfield; Erman D. Southwick, Marietta; Gordon W. Thayer, Cleveland; David K. Webb, Chillicothe; Tessa S. Webb, Columbus; and Kathryn E. Williams, Wilmington.

Last, but most importantly, I want to emphasize my gratitude and admiration for the research and organization done by Mr. and Mrs. Ernest Wessen of Mansfield. Years of bibliographical experience and extensive knowledge of Americana made Mr. Wessen uniquely qualified to edit this work. Before he was compelled by ill health to abandon the project, he planned the basic format, collected masses of data and citations of sources, and wrote many entries. His name is appended to certain longer sketches, but many of the unsigned shorter entries are also the result of his research. Mrs. Wessen searched biographical dictionaries for eligible names and prepared an efficient card-file that has been indispensable. That this book would never have been completed without their tireless labors is a simple statement of fact. Much of the credit for whatever usefulness this work may have belongs to the Wessens; errors of omission and commission are, of course, my own responsibility.

WILLIAM COYLE
Wittenberg University

Ohio Authors and Their Books

1796–1950

The entries for writers who are included are of three general types:

I. A writer who published at least one eligible work before December 31, 1900: a biographical summary and a check list of his writings.

II. A writer who published at least one eligible work between January 1, 1901, and December 31, 1950: a biographical summary, one or more representative titles, and if possible a citation of a biographical reference book.

III. A writer who lived in Ohio for only a brief period: treatment similar to Group II with special emphasis on the subject's Ohio years.

Ohio Authors and Their Books 1796–1950

A

AARONSOHN, MICHAEL (July 5, 1896–), rabbi, born in Baltimore, Md., has lived in Cincinnati for more than forty years. Serving as a sergeant major in the 147th Infantry during World War I, he was wounded and left totally blind. He returned to Cincinnati and graduated from the University of Cincinnati and Hebrew Union College in 1923. He has been field representative of the Union of American Hebrew Congregations, has served as chaplain of several veterans' organizations, and has lectured widely on his victory over blindness and in support of Henry George's theories. He has published two novels, the first of which is largely autobiographical: *Broken Lights,* Cincinnati, 1946.

ABBE, CLEVELAND (Dec. 3, 1838–Oct. 28, 1916), was born in New York City and educated in the schools there and at Michigan Agricultural College. His significant Ohio connection is limited to two years, 1868–70, when he served as director of the Cincinnati Observatory. There he issued storm warnings based on telegraphic reports and drew the first weather maps. Abbe wrote almost three hundred papers on various aspects of weather and climate, many of them issued in pamphlet form.

ABBEY, EVERETT LUCIUS (Oct. 10, 1855–Jan. 1, 1945), educator, was born in Mayfield, Cuyahoga County. After graduating from the University of Wooster in 1880, he was superintendent of schools in Cambridge and later in Euclid. He then served seventeen years as attendance officer in East Cleveland, retiring in 1938.

The Religious Drama of the Tyrol . . . , Cleveland, 1900.

"A Twist of the Lion's Tail," East Cleveland, [1926].

ABDULLAH. Pseud. See Otway Curry.

ABERNETHY, ALONZO (April 14, 1836–Feb., 1915), educator, was born in Sandusky County. He served in the 9th Iowa Volunteers, 1861–65. After graduating from the University of Chicago in 1866, he held various educational posts in Illinois and Iowa. His death occurred in Des Moines. His writings include *A History of Iowa Baptist Schools,* [Osage, Iowa, 1907]. WWW 1

ABERNETHY, WEALTHA VIETH (April 12, 1870–June 19, 1956), was born in Circleville, Pickaway County. She worked there as a court reporter before her marriage to Judge Isaac N. Abernethy, and after his death she worked in the Motor Vehicle Department, Columbus. She published an autobiographical volume: *Odds and Ends,* [Columbus, 1943], which she revised and republished in 1948 as *Yesterdays.*

ABRAMS, LISLE JOSEPH (Nov. 6, 1903–), was born in Cameron, W. Va., but when he was seven his family moved to Lisbon, Columbiana County, where he has since lived. His poems have appeared in magazines and anthologies, and he has published one collection: *Through the Years,* New York, 1944.

ADAMS, ALMEDA C. (Feb. 26, 1865–Sept. 8, 1949), musician, was born in Meadville, Pa., but she lived near Toledo as a child. She lost her eyesight when only six months old, and at the age of seven entered the State School for the Blind at Columbus, and graduated in music. After attending the New England Conservatory of Music for two years, she taught piano and voice at the University of Nebraska. Settling in Cleveland in 1901, she taught music to various local groups, including every social settlement. In 1926 this amazing woman left on a year's travel in Europe as a chaperone for a group of music students. On her return she wrote a book which received wide acclaim: *Seeing Europe through Sightless Eyes,* New York, [1929]. Twice more she toured Europe unaccompanied, after which she enjoyed enthusiastic demand as a lecturer on European travel. She died in Cleveland.

ADAMS, CHARLES JOSIAH (Oct. 31, 1850–July 4, 1924), clergyman, was born in New Lisbon, Columbiana County. After graduating from Mount Union College in 1871, he attended Yale University and Boston University, and was ordained an Episcopal priest in 1875. He served as rector of several churches, including St. Luke's, Rossville, N. Y.

Where Is My Dog? Or, Is Man Alone Immortal? New York, 1892.
How Baldy Won the County Seat, New York, 1902.
Hope Undeferred, and Two Other Poems, New York, 1916.
Reprieve! and Other Poems, New York, 1916.
Awakenings, with In Athens, New York, 1917.
This and That, and That and This, New York, 1919.

ADAMS, EMMA HILDRETH DRAKE (Feb. 18, 1827–c.1900), was born in Perry, N. Y., but lived in Cleveland for a number of years. She graduated from Baldwin University, and in 1852 she married Herman S. Adams of Columbus. Approximately the last twenty years of her life were spent in Los Angeles.

Digging the Top Off and Other Stories, Cincinnati, 1887.
To and Fro in Southern California . . . , Cincinnati, 1887.
John of Wycliffe . . . , Oakland, Calif., [1890].
Jottings from the Pacific . . . , Oakland, Calif., [1890].
The Tonga Islands . . . , Oakland, Calif., [1890].
Two Cannibal Archipelagoes . . . , Oakland, Calif., [1890].
Jottings from the Pacific, No. 2 . . . , Oakland, Calif., [1891].

ADAMS, HARRIET L. (Sept. 6, 1838–Dec. 20, 1913), was a journalist in Cleveland for a number of years. Her death occurred in that city. Besides writing the book below, she assisted Sarah Victor (q.v.) in writing her autobiography.

A Woman's Journeyings in the New Northwest, Cleveland, 1892.

ADAMS, JACOB (March 30, 1842–May 29, 1930), was born in Hancock County. In the Civil War he served as a private in the 21st O.V.I. and was wounded at the Battle of Chickamauga. After the war he attended high school in Findlay, taught school at Van Lue, and bought a farm near Ayersville. At the age of 83 he began copying his Civil War diary and excerpts from his letters. The manuscript was edited by H. M. Povenmire and published by the Ohio Archaeological and Historical Society: *Diary of Jacob Adams . . . ,* Columbus, 1930.

ADAMS, JAMES ALONZO (May 21, 1842–June 4, 1925), educator and clergyman, was born in Ashland, Ashland County. He graduated from Knox College in 1867. He taught at Straight University, New Orleans, 1875–77, edited the Dallas, Texas, *Daily Commercial,* 1877–80, and was ordained a Congregational minister in 1880. He occupied pulpits in St. Louis and Chicago. In addition to being the editor-in-chief of *The Advance* from 1903 until his death, he wrote a large number of religious tracts. His death occurred in Chicago. All three of the titles below were published under the pen name Grapho.

Colonel Hungerford's Daughter. Story of an American Girl, Chicago, 1896.
Victoria; Maid-Matron-Monarch, Chicago, 1901.
A Progressive Teacher, Chicago, 1917.

ADAMS, JAMES BARTON (April 17, 1843–Oct. 22, 1918), was born in Somerset, Jefferson County. He was educated at Richmond, Jefferson County, and at Mt. Pleasant, Iowa, where his parents moved in 1854. He served throughout the Civil War with Iowa troops and after the war was a member of the scouts that protected the construction crews of the Union Pacific. He was at various times a cowboy, a peace officer, a reporter on the Denver *Post,* and a miner. He died at Vancouver, Wash.

Breezy Western Verse, [Denver?], 1898.

ADAMS, RUFUS W. (? – ?), probably an itinerant schoolteacher from Vermont, is believed to have arrived at Marietta about 1810. In 1815 his *Young Gentleman and Lady's Monitor* was published in Zanesville. It is described on the title page as the "Second edition revised and corrected," and was copyrighted in 1814. It filled a great need and won the praise of leading Ohio Valley educators; by 1818 three more editions had been published. It seems quite possible that an edition prior to that printed in Zanesville in 1815 was published in Ohio but no copy is known to exist, and Adams had previously published the same work in Vermont. On the title page of this and other known works Adams refers to himself as the author of *Juvenile Rambler.* No trace of this work has been found.

The Young Gentleman and Lady's Explanatory Monitor . . . , Danville, Vt., 1808.

A Dissertation. Designed for the Yeomanry of the Western Country. Containing a Correct Description of the Best Method of Making Butter and Cheese . . . , Marietta, [1813].

The Farmer's Assistant, Containing a Complete Description of the Best Methods of Raising and Keeping Cows, & Making Butter and Cheese . . . , Marietta, 1814.

ADAMS, SEYMOUR WEBSTER (1815–Sept. 24, 1864), clergyman, was born in Vernon, N. Y. He was pastor of the First Baptist Church, Cleveland, and his death occurred in that city.

Memoirs of Rev. Nathaniel Kendrick, D.D., and Silas N. Kendrick, Philadelphia, 1860.

ADAMS, WILLIAM EDWARD (Oct. 15, 1866–March 14, 1946), educator, was born in Medina, Medina County. He attended Hiram College and the Cleveland School of Expression. He served as head of the department of speech, Hiram College 1893–97. Ordained to the ministry of the Disciples of Christ Church, he served in various states for twenty years and afterward was head of the department of speech at Spokane University, 1921–30, and at Whitworth College, Spokane, 1930–34. He published a volume of verse: *Pegasus and Company, Limited . . . ,* Spokane, Wash., 1939. WW 21

ADAMS, WILLIAM LYSANDER (Feb. 5, 1821–April 26, 1906), was born in Painesville, Lake County. In their search for greener pastures his Vermont parents settled in Galesburg, Ill., where he received his early education. For a time he studied for the ministry under Alexander Campbell at Bethany, Va., but abandoning the idea of becoming a preacher, he went to Oregon in 1848, where he farmed, taught school, and wrote for the newspapers. His first book, *A Melodrame,* published under the pen name Breakspear, was a merciless political satire, wherein he flayed the leading Democrats of the time, imputing to them the treasonable design of detaching Oregon from the United States. Buying the newspaper plant of the defunct Oregon *Spectator* in 1855, he established the Oregon *Argus* at Oregon City, which he continued until President Lincoln appointed him collector of the port of Astoria in 1861. After studying medicine in Philadelphia, he began practicing in Portland in 1873. He then established a sanitarium at Hood River, Ore. He was one of the founders of the Republican Party in Oregon. It has been said that "as a Republican editor he was more feared and more hated than any man of his day in Oregon . . . 'dreaded by his foes and not greatly loved by his friends.' " He died in Portland.

A Melodrame Entitled "Treason, Stratagems, and Spoils," in Five Acts, [Portland, Oreg., 1852].

Oregon As It Is; Its Present and Future . . . , Portland, Oreg., 1873.

History of Medicine and Surgery from the Earliest Times, Portland, Oreg., 1888.

ADDINGTON, SARAH (April 6, 1891–Nov. 7, 1940), was born in Cincinnati, Hamilton County. She graduated from Earlham College in 1912. After marrying Howard C. Reid in 1917, she lived in New York City. She published a number of juvenile books, e.g., *Pudding Lane People,* Boston, 1926. WWW 1

ADDIS, HAROLD AHMED NOUREDDIN (Oct. 6, 1884–Dec., 1958), was born in Washington County. He attended Ohio State University. A resident of California, he was interested in prehistoric man, published short stories in various periodicals, and also published a collection of verse: *Arrow of Flame,* Pasadena, Calif., 1946. WWNAA 7

ADDIS, HUGH (July 6, 1909–), was born in Chesterhill, Morgan County. He was educated in California and now lives in Sierra Madre. His writings include a mystery story: *Dark Voyage,* New York, 1944.

ADDIS, THOMAS. Pseud. See Michael McAlister.

ADLER, FREDERICK HENRY HERBERT (Oct. 3, 1885–Dec. 26, 1959), educator, was born in Chicago. He graduated from Ohio State University in 1909 and the University of Illinois (Ph.D.) in 1913. After teaching English for brief periods at several universities, including Ohio State University and Case Institute of Technology, he joined the Western Reserve University faculty in 1911 and served until 1956. Active in poetry organizations, he published numerous poems in periodicals and also published several collections, e.g., *Leaven for Loaves,* New York, 1927. WW 30

ADNEY, EDWIN TAPPAN (July 13, 1868–Oct. 10, 1950), woodcarver, painter, writer, and adventurer, was born in Athens, Athens

County. He attended the University of North Carolina for a few months in 1881 and studied at the Art Students' League in New York for three years. He wrote a large number of magazine articles on a wide range of subjects—outdoor life, archaeology, the North American Indian, heraldry, and ethnology—and also supplied illustrations for the works of others. His firsthand study of Indians began during a trip to New Brunswick in 1887, and within a few years he became known throughout Canada and the United States as an outstanding authority on the Indians of Canada. Because of his intimate knowledge of the Indians, and their canoes in particular, he was chosen by the Hudson Bay Company to collaborate with Adam Scott in painting the large murals which adorn Hudson Bay House in Winnipeg. He covered the Klondike gold rush in 1897–98 for the London *Chronicle* and *Harper's Weekly*. He designed and carved the superlative overmantels in the Château Frontenac at Quebec. Despite these and many other noteworthy activities he found time to indulge in intensive genealogical research. He died near Upper Woodstock, Canada.

The Klondike Stampede, New York, 1900.
Harper's Outdoor Book for Boys, New York, 1908.

AFFLECK, THOMAS (July 13, 1812–Dec. 30, 1868), agriculturist, born in Dumfries, Scotland, came to America in 1832. From 1840 to 1842 he was junior editor of *Western Farmer and Gardener,* published in Cincinnati. He then moved to Mississippi and subsequently to Texas. As an advocate of diversified farming in the South, he published articles and almanacs. He also wrote *Bee Breeding in the West,* Cincinnati, 1841.

AGATE. Pseud. See Whitelaw Reid.

AGEE, ALVA (Oct. 1, 1858–Dec. 10, 1943), agriculturist and educator, was born in Cheshire, Gallia County. He attended Marietta College and University of Wooster and afterward served in the agriculture departments of Pennsylvania State College and Rutgers University. He lectured widely on farming, contributed numerous articles to agricultural periodicals, and published several books, e.g., *Crops and Methods for Soil Improvement,* New York, 1912. WWW 1

AGGER, EUGENE EWALD (Dec. 4, 1879–), educator, was born in Cincinnati, Hamilton County. After graduating from the University of Cincinnati in 1901 and Columbia University (Ph.D.) in 1907, he taught economics at Columbia, 1907–26, and at Rutgers University, 1926–50. He has written articles and books on economic questions, e.g., *Money and Banking Today,* New York, [1941]. WWNAA 7

AHRENDTS, MARINDA BAINES (Aug. 28, 1877–Jan. 29, 1935), was born near Barnesville, Belmont County, the town in which she spent her life. After her death her husband published a memorial volume of her verse: *Thru the Door and Other Poems,* East Aurora, N. Y., 1935.

AIKEN, SAMUEL CLARK (Sept. 21, 1790–Jan. 1, 1879), clergyman, was born in Windham, Vt. In 1835 he came to Cleveland's famous Old Stone Church as its first permanent pastor. Although occasionally under attack for his conservative attitude on slavery, he became one of the city's outstanding civic leaders. His discourse, "Moral View of Railroads . . . ," delivered upon the completion of the Cleveland and Columbus Railroad in 1851, is a masterpiece of naïveté; for therein he expressed the belief that railroads would prevent war by bringing nations together, that they would not be operated on the Sabbath Day since only Christian gentlemen would be on the directorates, and that no liquor would be sold on them. He resigned his pulpit in 1861. His death occurred in Cleveland.

The Laws of Ohio in Respect to the Colored People, Shown to Be Unequal, Unjust and Unconstitutional, Cleveland, 1845.

AKELEY, MARY JOBE (Jan. 29, 1886–), was born near Tappan, Harrison County. A graduate of Scio College, she has made exploring expeditions to Africa and Canada. Her husband, Carl E. Akeley, died in 1926 while leading an expedition to the Belgian Congo for the American Museum of Natural History; Mrs. Akeley took charge of the expedition after his death. She has lectured widely, has taught at Hunter College, and has operated a summer camp at Mystic, Conn. Her writings include *Restless Jungle,* New York, [1936]. WW 29

AKERS, LEWIS ROBESON (Aug. 25, 1881–), clergyman, was born in Asheville, N. C. He graduated from Asbury College, Wilmore, Ky., in 1903 and was ordained to the Methodist ministry in 1904. He served several Ohio pastorates: Conesville, Nevada, Willard, Sebring, Ashland, and Steubenville. He now lives in Norfolk, Va. He has published, among other books, a collection of lectures: *The Red Road to Royalty . . . ,* New York, [1927]. WW 24

AKERS, WILLIAM JOSEPH (Aug. 2, 1845–March 23, 1917), hotel proprietor, was born in Manchester, England. His family migrated to America in 1847, and his father soon established himself as a leading contractor in Cleveland. His father's fortune dwindled, however, in the panic of 1857, and William was forced to go to work in a blacksmith shop at the age of thirteen. In 1865 he began working in the Union Depot restaurant, and from that time his main interest was the hotel and restaurant business. He is best remembered in Cleveland as proprietor of the Forest City House. He was active in civic affairs and charitable projects. His only published book was a history of Cleveland schools: *Cleveland Schools in the 19th Century,* Cleveland, 1901.

ALBACH, JAMES R. (July 30, 1797–April 20, 1865), was born in Hunterdon, N. J. During the early years of his life, while engaged in the profession of teaching, he traveled through the West. In 1857 he published *Annals of the West,* a substantial enlargement of the work originally written by James H. Perkins (q.v.). In 1850 it had been somewhat enlarged and revised by J. M. Peck, but Albach's travels and observations enabled him to so expand the work that it became a veritable encyclopedia of events connected with the history of the Ohio Valley. He spent the last twelve years of his life in Oxford, Butler County.

Annals of the West: Embracing a Concise Account of the Principal Events Which Have Occurred in the Western States and Territories, from the Discovery of the Mississippi Valley to the Year 1856, Pittsburgh, 1856.

ALBAUGH, BENJAMIN F. (1836–1917), was born in West Milton, Miami County. He was a farmer and horticulturist and for over thirty years lectured on these and allied subjects. He wrote *The Gardenette,* [Piqua], 1912.

ALBAUGH, DOROTHY PRISCILLA (Mrs. Charles B. Stickell) (July 8, 1903–), was born in Columbus, Franklin County. She graduated from Ohio Wesleyan University in 1925 and has also done graduate work at Ohio State University. She now lives in Richwood, Union County. Under her maiden name she has published poems, articles, and short stories in various anthologies, magazines, and newspapers. She has also published three collections of verse, e.g., *By Quill and Candlelight,* [Worthington?, 1947].

ALBAUGH, NOAH H. (May 22, 1834–Aug. 31, 1907), was born in Miami County. He began teaching school in 1851. In 1858 he started a small nursery in Miami County, and within fifteen years he had branch nurseries in Illinois, Kansas, and Wisconsin. The book of poems below is his only publication. He died in Phoneton.

Wayside Blossoms, Dayton, 1885.

ALBEE, HELEN RICKEY (Mrs. John) (March 15, 1864–Oct. 14, 1939), was born in Dayton, Montgomery County, the daughter of James Rickey, the city's leading bookseller. She attended Dayton public schools and studied designing in New York. In 1897 she established the Abnákee Rug Industry, said to have been the first rural industry in America to develop rug-making as a handicraft. She lived in New Hampshire. She contributed many articles to periodicals on subjects relating to handicrafts and horticulture.

Mountain Playmates, New York, 1900.

Abnákee Rugs, Cambridge, Mass., 1901.

Hardy Plants for Cottage Gardens, New York, 1910.

The Gleam, New York, 1911.

A Kingdom of Two, New York, 1913.

ALBERRY, FAXON FRANKLIN DUANE (Dec. 3, 1848–Jan. 18, 1930), lawyer, was born in Franklin County. He attended high school in Columbus and studied law and philosophy in Berlin and Leipzig. He was admitted to the Ohio bar in 1873 and practiced in Columbus. He was professor of law at Ohio State University, 1896–1900. His writings include *Michael Ryan, Capitalist . . . ,* Columbus, 1913.

ALBRIGHT, EVELYN MAY (May 1, 1880–April 19, 1942), educator, was born in Sidney, Shelby County. She graduated from Ohio Wesleyan University in 1898 and the University of Chicago (Ph.D.) in 1915. She served on the faculty of Ohio Wesleyan, 1900–11, and after 1915 taught at the University of Chicago. She published several texts on creative writing, professional articles on Spenser and Shakespeare, and *Dramatic Publication in England, 1580–1640 . . . ,* New York, 1927. WW 6

ALDEN, CARROLL STORRS (March 15, 1876–), educator, was born in Medina, Medina County. He earned a Ph.D. at Yale in 1903 and in 1904 joined the faculty of the U. S. Naval Academy, where he taught until his retirement in 1941. He still lives in Annapolis. He has written textbooks for use at the Academy, historical studies of the navy, and a biography: *Lawrence Kearny, Sailor Diplomat,* Princeton, 1936. WW 26

ALDEN, ISABELLA MacDONALD (Nov. 3, 1841–Aug. 5, 1930), was born in Rochester, N. Y. Following her marriage in 1866 to Gustavus Rosenberg Alden, a young Presbyterian minister, she lived for several years in Cincinnati. Under the pen name Pansy she wrote a multitude of Sunday School books, e.g., *Three People,* Cincinnati, 1871.

ALDRICH, FRED HAMPTON (Sept. 11, 1861–April 27, 1944), lawyer, son of Julia Carter Aldrich (q.v.), was born near Wauseon, Fulton County. After spending three years at Adrian College, he read law and was admitted to the bar in 1883. He practiced in Cadillac, Mich., and served two terms as circuit court judge. In 1900 he moved to Detroit, where he practiced and taught at the Detroit College of Law until his death. He wrote a number of legal treatises and *World Peace or Principles of International Law in Their Application to Efforts for the Preservation of the Peace of the World,* Detroit, 1921.

ALDRICH, JULIA CARTER (Jan. 28, 1834–Aug. 26, 1924), was born in Liverpool, Medina County. She taught in district schools, and in 1854 she married Joseph Aldrich of New York. Much of her life was spent in Wauseon, Fulton County.

Hazel Bloom, Buffalo, 1899.

A Memory of Eighteen Hundred Sixty-five; A Tribute to Abraham Lincoln . . . , Wauseon, 1914.

ALEXANDER, DE ALVA STANWOOD (July 17, 1845–Jan. 30, 1925), was born in Maine but was brought to Ohio when he was seven years old. He enlisted in the 128th O.V.I. when he was sixteen and served throughout the Civil War. At the close of the war he returned to Maine to complete his education and then settled in Indiana. He published a family history, political speeches, and biographical and historical studies, e.g., *A Political History of the State of New York,* New York, 1906.

ALEXANDER, JOHN EDMISTON (June 2, 1815–1901), clergyman and educator, was born near Lewiston, Pa. He graduated from Jefferson College in 1839 and was ordained to the Presbyterian ministry in 1843. He served as a school principal and as a pastor in Ohio during the 1850s and 1860s. He was president of Washington College, Tenn., 1877–83. He wrote a family history and *A Historical Sketch of Washington College, Tennessee,* [Bristol, Tenn.], 1902.

ALEXANDER, JOHN ROMICH (May 23, 1849–April 16, 1940), clergyman and educator, was born in Wooster, Wayne County. After graduating from Ohio Central College in 1871 and Xenia Theological Seminary in 1874, he was ordained to the ministry of the United Presbyterian Church. From 1875 until his retirement in 1917, he was a missionary and teacher in Egypt. His writings include *The Truth about Egypt,* New York, 1911. WWW 3

ALEXANDER, ROBERT (June 15, 1837–Feb. 27, 1901), clergyman, was born in Belmont County. He graduated from Washington College, Pa., in 1855 and studied at Princeton Theological Seminary. After being ordained to the Presbyterian ministry in 1860, he occupied a pulpit in Lancaster County, Pa., until 1866, when he became pastor of the First Presbyterian Church in St. Clairsville, in which capacity he served from 1867 to 1899. He died in Philadelphia.

Historical Sketch of the First Presbyterian Church in St. Clairsville . . . , Wheeling, W. Va., 1869.

ALEXIS. Pseud. See John M. Leavitt.

ALEY, HOWARD C. (Jan. 12, 1911–), educator, was born in Youngstown, Mahoning County. He graduated from Youngstown College in 1935 and has done graduate work at the University of Pittsburgh. He is a teacher in Wilson High School and has edited a number of educational publications for the Youngstown schools. His books include a centennial history of the Mahoning County Agricultural Society: *The First Hundred Years . . . ,* [Youngstown], 1946.

ALGER, RUSSELL ALEXANDER (Feb. 27, 1836–Jan. 24, 1907), was born in Medina County. He attended Richfield Academy, studied law in Akron, and was admitted to the bar in 1859. In the same year he removed to Grand Rapids, Mich., and engaged in the lumber business. In Aug., 1861, he enlisted in the army as a private. He was discharged with the rank of colonel Sept. 20, 1864, subsequently being given the brevet rank of brigadier general and then of major general of volunteers. Resuming his business in Detroit, he acquired a large fortune and served one term as governor of Michigan. In 1889 he became national commander of the Grand Army of the Republic. President McKinley appointed him to his cabinet as Secretary of War on March 5, 1897. His wholly inept administration of this office left a long trail through the newspapers and critical literature dealing with the war with Spain. He resigned under fire in July, 1899, and wrote his *Spanish-American War* by way of an apologia. He became senator from Michigan in 1902, but died before the expiration of his term of office.

Eulogy on the Late General Philip H. Sheridan . . . , Detroit, 1888.

The Spanish-American War, New York, 1901.

ALLARDICE, JAMES BURNS (March 21, 1919–), was born in Canton, Stark County. He graduated from the College of Wooster in 1941. A free-lance writer for motion pictures and television, he now lives in Van Nuys, Calif. He wrote a play which was produced in 1949 and published the following year: *At War with the Army,* New York, [1950].

ALLBECK, WILLARD DOW (Oct. 5, 1898–), theologian, was born in Millville, Pa. He was ordained to the Lutheran ministry in 1922 and since 1937 has been professor of historical theology at Hamma Divinity School, Springfield. He has published numerous articles and reviews and *Theology at Wittenberg* . . . , Springfield, 1946. WW 30

ALLEN, ABEL LEIGHTON (Jan. 25, 1850–Dec. 8, 1927), lawyer, was born in Kenton, Hardin County. He graduated from Ohio Wesleyan University in 1875 and Cincinnati Law School in 1877 and afterward practiced in Chicago. He wrote *The Message of New Thought,* New York, [1914]. WWW 1

ALLEN, ADAM. Pseud. See Beryl Williams.

ALLEN, DON. Pseud. See Hiram L. True.

ALLEN, EMORY ADAMS (1853–1933?), publisher, was born in Cincinnati, Hamilton County. Little is known concerning this rather prolific author and Cincinnati book publisher. He was the junior partner in the Central Publishing House from 1879 through 1915, associated with Smith C. Ferguson. He is reported to have died in Prague, Czechoslovakia.

Golden Gems of Life, (with Smith C. Ferguson), Cincinnati, 1880.

The Prehistoric World: Or, Vanished Races, Cincinnati, 1885.

History of Civilization, 4 vols., Cincinnati, 1887–89.

Scenes Abroad . . . , Cincinnati, 1890.

Labor and Capital . . . , Cincinnati, [1891].

The Life and Public Services of James Bair Weaver . . . , [n.p., 1892].

The Ready Cotton Reckoner, Cincinnati, 1896.

The Planter's Guide . . . , Cincinnati, 1902.

Gems of Immortality . . . , Cincinnati, [1909].

Our Canal in Panama . . . , Cincinnati, 1913.

ALLEN, ETHAN (Jan. 1, 1904–), baseball player and coach, was born in Cincinnati, Hamilton County. In 1927 he graduated from the University of Cincinnati, where he excelled in sports. He was signed by the Cincinnati Reds and also played with several other major league teams before his retirement in 1938. He joined the National League public relations department in 1938, was a sports commentator, and served in Special Services during World War II. In 1946 he became head baseball coach at Yale University. He has published several books on baseball, e.g., *Winning Baseball,* New York, [1942].

ALLEN, FLORENCE ELLINWOOD (March 23, 1884–), lawyer and judge, was born in Salt Lake City, Utah. She attended New Lyme Institute, Ashtabula County, and graduated from Western Reserve University in 1904 and from the law school of New York University in 1913. She was music editor of the Cleveland *Plain Dealer,* 1906–09. In 1914 she began the practice of law in Cleveland. She has served as judge of the Court of Common Pleas, 1920–22, as a justice of the Supreme Court of Ohio, 1922–34, and as a judge of the U. S. Circuit Court of Appeals, 1934–59. She has published numerous articles and two books: *Patris,* Cleveland, 1908, and *This Constitution of Ours,* New York, [1940]. WW 30

ALLEN, FREDERICK DE FOREST (May 25, 1844–Aug. 4, 1897), educator, was born in Oberlin, Lorain County. He graduated from Oberlin College in 1863 and taught school until 1866, when he was appointed professor of Greek and Latin at the University of East Tennessee. In 1874 he was called to the University of Cincinnati, and while there he found time to prepare his excellent edition of the *Medea* of Euripides and his important *Remnants of Early Latin.* He accepted a call to Harvard in 1880 to be professor of classical philology.

Remnants of Early Latin . . . , Boston, 1880.

ALLEN, HANS VAN NES (1914–), was born in Glendale, Hamilton County. At the age of eighteen he went to Africa with a medical missionary. On his return he attended college and worked on the Cincinnati *Times-Star.* He served in World War II and is now an investment broker in Tulsa, Okla. He wrote an account of his African experiences: *I Found Africa,* Indianapolis, [1939].

ALLEN, HORACE NEWTON (April 23, 1858–Dec. 11, 1932), missionary and diplomat, was born in Delaware, Delaware County. He graduated from Ohio Wesleyan University in 1881 and Miami Medical College in 1883. He went to Korea in 1884 as a medical missionary of the Presbyterian Church. After saving the life of a prince and others in a revolution, he became medical officer to the Korean Court. He served as secretary to the U. S. legation, 1890–97, as minister and consul general, 1897–1901, and as envoy extraordinary and minister plenipotentiary, 1901–05. He died in Toledo.

Korean Tales . . . , London, 1889.

A Chronological Index of Korean Foreign Intercourse from the Beginning of the Christian Era to 20th Century, Seoul, 1901.

Things Korean . . . , New York, 1908.

ALLEN, HUGH (July 4, 1882–), journalist, was born in Washington Court House, Fayette County. He was educated at the University of Michigan. He became a journalist and from 1920 to 1926 edited the Akron *Beacon-Journal.* In 1926 he joined the public relations department of Goodrich Tire and Rubber Co. He now lives in St. Louis, Mo. He has written several books, e.g., *Rubber's Home Town. The Real-Life Story of Akron,* New York, 1949.

ALLEN, IRA WILDER (1827–Dec., 1896), educator, was professor of mathematics, astronomy, and civil engineering at Antioch College. He was a member of the original faculty and was a thorn in the side of Horace Mann (q.v.). In 1860 he was living in Sidney, but later moved to Lafayette, Ind. He died in Chicago.

A Collection of Facts. History of the Rise, Difficulties & Suspension of Antioch College . . . , Columbus, 1858.

ALLEN, JAMES TURNEY (Sept. 14, 1873–Sept. 29, 1949), philologist, was born in Cleveland, Cuyahoga County. He graduated from Pomona College in 1895 and Yale University (Ph.D.) in 1898. He served on the faculty of the University of California, 1898–1943. His writings include a Greek textbook, archaeological and philological articles, and *Stage Antiquities of the Greeks and Romans . . . ,* New York, 1927. WWW 2

ALLEN, LEE (Jan. 12, 1915–), journalist, was born in Cincinnati, Hamilton County. He graduated from Kenyon College in 1937, held several publicity and broadcasting positions, and wrote on baseball for *Sporting News.* He is now historian of the National Baseball Hall of Fame and Museum, Cooperstown, N. Y. He has published a history of baseball and a history of the Cincinnati Reds: *The Cincinnati Reds,* New York, [1948].

ALLEN, MARY WOOD. See Mary Wood-Allen.

ALLEN, MAURICE E. (June 22, 1886–), lawyer, was born in Seoul, Korea. He graduated from Massachusetts Institute of Technology in 1908 and the University of Michigan law school in 1911. After completing his legal studies, he came to Toledo and practiced there until his retirement. He now lives in Santa Monica, Calif. He has published a volume of poems: *Mixed Cargo,* San Diego, 1931. OBB

ALLEN, PHILIP. Pseud. See Edmond M. Hamilton.

ALLEN, WILLIAM ALONZO ("Montana Allen") (Sept. 2, 1848–Jan. 27, 1944), was born in Summerfield, Noble County. A crack shot and an outstanding Indian fighter, he was one of the founders of Billings, Mont., and besides being a stock-raiser he served on occasion as dentist, blacksmith, and express messenger. His autobiography is an account of his colorful career: *Adventures with Indians and Game, or Twenty Years in the Rocky Mountains,* Chicago, 1903.

ALLENSWORTH, CARL (July 19, 1908–), was born in Canton, Stark County. He graduated from Canton McKinley High School and Oberlin College and studied drama at Yale University. He now lives in Mamaroneck, N. Y. He has written one-act plays, including *Village Green* produced in 1941 with Frank Craven as star: *Village Green,* [New York, 1941].

ALLING, ETHAN (Aug. 13, 1800–April 22, 1868), was born in North Milford, Conn. He came to the Western Reserve with his father in 1817; they made the first settlement on the site of what is now Twinsburg. He built a hotel, operated a stage line, and later opened a store in Twinsburg. In collaboration with Luman Lane (q.v.), he wrote a splendid account of his pioneer experiences.

Locust Grove Cemetery. Twinsburgh, from 1817, by Ethan Alling, and from 1820, by Luman Lane, Akron, 1861.

ALLISON, DAVID P. (April 8, 1886– ?), journalist, was born in Greenfield, Highland County. He left Ohio while a boy and afterward was a newspaperman in North Carolina for many years. He is deceased, but the date of his death has not been found. He published at least five novels, e.g., *The Fifth of the Medlocks,* Grand Rapids, Mich., 1940.

ALLISON, EDWIN HENRY (March 16, 1847–1919), was born in Macomb County, Mich. He served throughout the Civil War and in 1867 went to Dakota Territory, where he married into the Brule tribe and is said to have had several Sioux wives. He was largely responsible for the surrender of the hostile Indians in 1881 which saved the nation years of bloody border warfare. He was a frequent visitor to Dayton, where his story was published in 1891, and lived in that city for a time. He was appointed a substitute on the Dayton police force, Nov. 20, 1891, was given a regular appointment the following May, and served until Nov. 23, 1892. Subsequently he is recorded in the city directories as an "author" and as a "lecturer." He apparently left Dayton about 1898. His last days were spent in Pierre, S. D.

The Surrender of Sitting Bull, Being a Full and Complete History of the Negotiations Conducted by Scout Allison Which Resulted in the Surrender of Sitting Bull and Entire Band of Hostile Sioux in 1881. A Vivid Description of Indian Life, and Thrilling Adventure . . . , Dayton, 1891.

ALLYN, EUNICE ELOISAE GIBBS (? – ?), journalist, was born near Cleveland, Cuyahoga County. She was Washington correspondent of the Chicago *Inter-Ocean,* a writer for the St. Louis *Globe* and the New York *World,* and also won distinction as an artist and a lecturer.

One Thousand Smiles, [Dubuque, 1898].
The Cats' Convention, New York, 1909.

ALPHA. Pseud. See Sara T. Drukker.

ALTGELD, EMMA FORD (1849–March 29, 1915), was born in Richland County. The daughter of John Ford, a wealthy farmer, she was educated at Oberlin College, where she developed considerable ability as a musician. She married John Peter Altgeld (q.v.) Nov. 21, 1877. The bitterness of the attacks upon her husband following his pardon of the participants in the Chicago Haymarket riot brought on a nervous breakdown. When Altgeld took the stump for re-election, she worried greatly over the bitterness of the campaign. When the returns showed that her husband had been defeated, Mrs. Altgeld became afflicted with a nervous malady from which she never recovered. Following the death of her husband it was learned that his fortune had been dissipated in real-estate speculations. Friends in Illinois took up subscriptions totaling $10,000 to provide for her relief. She died in Chicago.

Sarah's Choice; Or, the Norton Family, Chicago, 1887.

ALTGELD, JOHN PETER (Dec. 30, 1847–March 12, 1902), was born in Nassau, Germany. He was the son of an illiterate and indigent peasant, who brought his family to Richland County in 1848. The Altgelds were one of a number of German families who settled in the vicinity at the time, all of whom prospered. The elder Altgeld became a tenant farmer who in little more than a decade became the owner of one of the better farms in an area noted for its rich farmlands. If the boyhood of John Peter Altgeld was one of drudgery, it was no worse and certainly in some respects better than the lot of the average farmer's son of those days; he not only attended the local country school, but was permitted to attend high school in neighboring Mansfield. He served briefly in an Ohio regiment in 1864, and after returning home studied law and taught school. In 1869 he went to Darke County, then drifted West, finally locating in northwestern Missouri, where he practiced law. In 1874 he was elected state's attorney of Andrew County, Mo., but within a year resigned and moved to Chicago. On Nov. 21, 1877, he married his childhood sweetheart, Emma Ford (see Emma Ford Altgeld), the daughter of a wealthy farmer of Richland County who had recently died. With the settlement of her father's estate Altgeld plunged into real-estate speculation and accumulated a large fortune which he later lost, leaving his wife penniless at the time of his death. In 1886 he was elected to the superior court of Cook County and resigned as chief justice of that court in 1891. He was elected governor of Illinois in 1892; on taking office he lost no time in putting into effect many of the reforms which he had advocated. However, although it outraged public opinion at the time, his reputation as governor is based upon his pardon of the alleged anarchistic agitators who had been convicted of participating in the events which led to the killings in the Chicago Haymarket riot of May 4, 1886. These pardons were granted on June 26, 1893, and his brief of reasons which accompanied them gains weight over the years. It was the consensus of informed observers at the time that, but for his alien birth, Altgeld would have been the Democratic candidate for the Presidency instead of William Jennings Bryan. He was renominated for the office of governor in 1896, and though he ran far ahead of the Democratic Presidential ticket he was defeated. A consummate politician, his career was a complete refutation of his expressed views that the poor and unfortunate had less than a fair chance in American life.

Ernest J. Wessen

Live Questions: Including Our Penal Machinery and Its Victims, Chicago, 1890.
Reasons for Pardoning Felden, Neebe and Schwab, [Chicago, 1893].
Live Questions . . . Comprising His Papers, Speeches and Interviews . . . , Chicago, 1899.
Oratory; Its Requirements and Its Rewards, Chicago, 1901.
The Cost of Something for Nothing, Chicago, 1904.

ALTER, KARL JOSEPH (Aug. 18, 1885–), archbishop of Cincinnati, was born in Toledo, Lucas County. He graduated from St. John's College, Toledo, and from St. Mary's Seminary, Cleveland. After being ordained a Catholic priest, he served churches in Leipsic and Lima, 1910–14, and was director of Catholic Charities, Toledo, 1914–19. He was consecrated bishop of Toledo in 1931 and archbishop of Cincinnati in 1950. He has published a collection of lectures and essays: *A Bishop's Rostrum,* Milwaukee, [1946]. CWW 11

ALTICK, RICHARD DANIEL (Sept. 19, 1915–), educator, was born in Lancaster, Pa. He graduated from Franklin and Marshall College in 1936 and the University of Pennsylvania (Ph.D.) in 1941. He has been a member of the English department, Ohio State University, since 1945. He has written magazine articles, textbooks, and *The Scholar Adventurers,* New York, 1950. DAS 3

ALWOOD, WILLIAM BRADFORD (Aug. 11, 1859–April 13, 1946), horticulturist and educator, was born in Delta, Fulton County. After spending two years (1879–81) teaching in a country school, he attended Ohio State University and Columbian (now George Washington) University. From 1891 to 1904 he was professor of horticulture at Virginia Polytechnic Institute. He also served in the U. S. Department of Agriculture. He wrote many pamphlets and bulletins on horticultural subjects.

AMBLER, CHARLES HENRY (Aug. 12, 1876–Aug. 31, 1957), educator, was born in New Matamoras, Washington County. He graduated from West Virginia University in 1901 and the University of Wisconsin (Ph.D.) in 1905. He taught history at Randolph Macon College, 1908–17, and at West Virginia University, 1917–47. He wrote many articles, several biographies, and textbooks on West Virginia history, and *A History of Transportation in the Ohio Valley . . . ,* Glendale, Calif., 1932. WWW 3

AMBLER, HENRY LOVEJOY (Sept. 10, 1843–June 14, 1924), dentist and educator, was born in Medina, Medina County. He was for many years dean of the Dental School, Western Reserve University.

The Foil and Its Combinations for Filling Teeth, Philadelphia, 1897.
Facts, Fads and Fancies about Teeth, Cleveland, 1900.
Around the World Dentistry, Cleveland, 1910.
History of Dentistry in Cleveland, Ohio, Cleveland, 1911.

AMES, DELANO (May 29, 1906–), was born at Lake Holm near Mount Vernon, Knox County. He attended Kent School, Conn., and Yale University. He now lives in London, England, where he publishes mystery stories and other fiction. He has also published a novel: *Not in Utter Nakedness,* New York, 1932.

AMES, VAN METER (July 9, 1898–), educator, was born in Desoto, Iowa. He graduated from the University of Chicago (Ph.B., 1919; Ph.D., 1924) and has been a member of the philosophy department, University of Cincinnati, since 1925. He has published several books, e.g., a volume of poetry: *Out of Iowa,* New York, [1936], and a study of fiction: *Aesthetics of the Novel,* Chicago, [1928]. DAS 3

AMMEN, DANIEL (May 15, 1820–July 11, 1898), naval officer, was born in Brown County. He was appointed midshipman July 7, 1836, and served in the Wilkes exploring expedition, the Biddle cruise to Japan and China, and other long cruises. At the outbreak of the Civil War he was executive officer of the North Atlantic blockading squadron. He commanded the monitor *Patapsco* in the attack on Fort McAllister, March 3, 1863; suppressed an attempted mutiny on the commercial steamer *Ocean Queen* in 1864; and participated in the two attacks on Fort Fisher in the winter of 1864–65. A boyhood intimacy with U. S. Grant ripened into a close friendship, and through Grant's influence he was placed in charge of the Bureau of Yards and Docks in 1868. He became chief of the Bureau of Navigation in 1871, where he served until his retirement as rear admiral, June 4, 1878. He was secretary of the Isthmian Canal Commission, 1872–76, and became widely known as an advocate of the Nicaragua canal route. He died in Washington, D. C.

The Proposed Inter-oceanic Ship Canal across the American Isthmus between Greytown and Brito, via Nicaragua, [New York], 1878.

The American Inter-oceanic Ship Canal Question, Philadelphia, 1880.

The Atlantic Coast, New York, 1883.

Country Houses and Their Improvement, Washington, D. C., [1885].

The Certainty of the Nicaragua Canal Contrasted with the Uncertainties of the Eads Ship-Railway, Washington, D. C., [1886].

The Errors and Fallacies of the Interoceanic Transit Question . . . , New York, [1886].

The Old Navy and the New . . . , Philadelphia, 1891.

AMSBARY, MARY ANNE (April 20, 1921–) was born in Cleveland, Cuyahoga County. After attending Allegheny College and the University of Michigan, she worked for the World Publishing Company. She married George S. Amsbary, an official of the University of Illinois Press, and moved to Urbana, Ill. In 1952, under her own name, she published a novel on political corruption; she has also published under the pen name Kay Lyttleton a series of books for girls, e.g., *Jean Craig, Graduate Nurse,* Cleveland, [1950]. WWAW 1

AMSTUTZ, PETER B. (June 6, 1846–Jan. 16, 1938), manufacturer of wooden forks and hay rakes, was born in Wayne County. He lived most of his life in Allen County. His writings, published by himself, include *Das Zweite Kommen Christi. Auf Grundlage der Heiligen Schrift,* [Bluffton, 1926].

ANDERSON, BESSIE WAYNE (Mrs. George Y.) (Sept. 2, 1867–Feb. 17, 1955), was born in Cincinnati, Hamilton County. She attended Cincinnati public schools and Ohio State University. A resident of Cleveland for many years, she published many poems in church publications and in Cleveland newspapers. Her death occurred in Clearwater, Fla. She published *Without Fear, and Other Poems,* Philadelphia, [1939].

ANDERSON, DWIGHT (April 13, 1882–Dec. 13, 1953), publicist, was born in Cleveland, Cuyahoga County. After attending Western Reserve Academy and Ohio State University, he graduated in law from Western Reserve University in 1906. He was a public relations director for a number of public health groups. His writings include *What It Means to Be a Doctor,* New York, [1939]. WWW 3

ANDERSON, EDWARD LOWELL (Oct. 4, 1842–March 2, 1916), lawyer, was born in Cincinnati, Hamilton County. With his twin brother, Frederick Longworth Anderson, he attended Phillips Exeter Academy; but both boys left school to enter the army when the Civil War began. Edward was a captain in the 52nd O.V.I., was wounded at Jonesboro, and served on General Sherman's staff. He studied law at the University of Cincinnati after the war and was admitted to the Ohio bar in 1866. His books on horsemanship were highly esteemed. He also wrote a history of the Anderson family. He died in Cincinnati.

Northern Ballads, New York, 1874.

The Skipper's Last Voyage, Cincinnati, 1875.

Six Weeks in Norway, Cincinnati, 1877.

Soldier and Pioneer . . . , Cincinnati, 1878.

How to Ride and School a Horse, London, 1881.

On Horseback, in the School and on the Road, New York, 1882.

The Gallop, Edinburgh, 1883.

Modern Horsemanship . . . , Cincinnati, 1884.

Vice in the Horse and Other Papers on Horses and Riding, Edinburgh, 1886.

The Universality of Man's Appearance and Primitive Man, Edinburgh, 1891.

Curb, Snaffle and Spur . . . , Boston, 1894.

Riding & Driving, (with Price Collier), New York, 1905.

Horses and Riding, Fort Leavenworth, Kan., 1909.

Colonel Archibald Gracie's The Truth about Chickamauga . . . , [Cincinnati?, 1912].

ANDERSON, ETHEL TODD, was born in Mineral Ridge, Trumbull County. She graduated from Oberlin College in 1912. Her husband, Clarence S. Anderson, served on the faculty of Pennsylvania State University, and since his retirement she has lived in Los Altos, Calif. She has published several widely read books for children, e.g., *The Scarlet Bird,* New York, [1948].

ANDERSON, GEORGE WOOD (Dec. 8, 1873–), clergyman, was born in Belle Center, Logan County. After graduating from Ohio Wesleyan University in 1899, he was ordained to the Methodist ministry and served his first pastorate in Lima, 1899–1903. He served churches in Pennsylvania and other states and was an evangelist, 1920–40. In 1940 he began editing the weekly *Minister's Research Letter.* He now lives in New York City. His writings include *Unfinished Rainbows and Other Essays,* New York, [1922]. WW 23

ANDERSON, LARZ (Aug. 15, 1866–April 13, 1937), diplomat, was born in Paris, France. He spent his boyhood in Cincinnati, where his family was one of the most prominent in the society of the city. He was in the U. S. diplomatic service, 1891–1913, and afterward lived in Brookline, Mass., and Washington, D. C. His wife, Isabel Weld Perkins Anderson (1876–1948), whom he married in 1897, wrote a great many travel books, plays, and poems. She also edited the posthumous collection of his papers: *Letters and Journals of a Diplomat,* New York, [1940]. WWW 1

ANDERSON, LEWIS FLINT (July 18, 1866–Nov. 17, 1932), educator, was born in Waterford, Ontario. He graduated from the University of Toronto in 1893 and Clark University (Ph.D.) in 1907. In 1909 he became professor of the history and philosophy of education at Ohio State University. His writings include *History of Common School Education . . . ,* New York, 1909. WWW 1

ANDERSON, MARJORIE (March 8, 1892–Nov. 29, 1954), educator, was born in Sandusky, Erie County. She graduated from Smith College in 1913 and the University of Chicago (Ph.D.) in 1926. She served in the Sandusky library, 1917–20, taught in Bryn Mawr School, 1922–23, and after 1927 taught at Hunter College, where she was head of the English department at the time of her death. She published a book of poems: *A Web of Thoughts,* Boston, 1921. DAS 1

ANDERSON, OLIVE SAN LOUIE (1842–June 5, 1886), educator, was born in Lexington, Richland County. After graduating from the University of Michigan in 1875, she joined the faculty at Santa Barbara College, Calif. She was drowned in the Sacramento River. Her book was published under the pen name Sola.

An American Girl and Her Four Years in a Boys' College, New York, 1878.

ANDERSON, RICHARD CLOUGH (Feb. 22, 1872–Oct. 20, 1916), younger brother of Larz Anderson (q.v.), was born in Cincinnati, Hamilton County. After graduating from Yale University in 1894, he was associated with a number of companies, including the American Book Company, the Hallwood Cash Register Company in Columbus, Standard Plastic Relief Company, and Franklin Motor Car Company. He wrote *Animals in Social Captivity,* Cincinnati, [1914].

ANDERSON, SAMUEL G. (1854–Oct. 9, 1900), clergyman, was born in Minnesota. After graduating from the University of Minnesota and Union Theological Seminary, he was a pastor in St. Paul, Minn., for five years before coming to Toledo, where he served at Westminster Presbyterian Church from 1888 until his death from typhoid fever. Several of his sermons were published in addition to the title below.

Woman's Sphere and Influence, [Toledo, 1898].

ANDERSON, SHERWOOD (Sept. 13, 1876–March 8, 1941), was born in Camden, Preble County. Few writers have evoked such varied critical judgments. When he died, a "special homage number" of *Story* (Sept.–Oct., 1941) commemorated "his personality and work as one of the rare and representative American expressions." Admirers celebrated "the greatest contemporary short-story writer," "the achieved artist," "our Dostoievsky of the corn belts." Yet twelve years earlier the *Sewanee Review* (April–June, 1929) had rung the death knell of a writer who had nothing to say. In 1927 N. B. Fagin wrote a book praising Anderson's greatness as the first American "chronicler of the adventures of the spirit of the inner man." In the same year the *New Republic* announced that Anderson "is dying before our eyes" (Aug. 3, 1927). Introducing *The Sherwood Anderson Reader* (1947), Paul Rosenfeld compared Anderson's prose with the "freshness of clover, buttercups, black-eyed Susans." Of the same prose Lionel Trilling said "it approaches in effect the inadequate use of a foreign language" (*Kenyon Review,* III, 1941). Rosenfeld affirmed that Anderson's "freshness, innocence, fineness steadily maintained themselves" for a quarter-century. It was Trilling's essential criticism that Anderson never progressed from the "simple idea" with which he scored his first success; that he never learned the craft of writing; and that such "stubborn continuance" in immaturity cannot satisfy mature readers. Even so, Horace Gregory claims an "undisputed" place for Anderson's stories and "immortality" for their author (*Portable Sherwood Anderson,* 1949). These extremes of judgment are epitomized, perhaps explained, by Rosenfeld's assertion that Anderson "is no less valuable to our culture than Walt Whitman" and by Trilling's deprecating reference to Anderson's "populist-Whitmanesque tradition." It is a commonplace with adverse critics that Anderson appeals only to adolescents: the substance of his work is vague feeling, deliquescing into sentimentality; his form is a crude shapelessness that reveals his unwillingness and inability to concentrate and clarify. Admiration, looking at the same works, sees a comprehensive sympathy for common folk, especially for the emotionally maimed; it sees a healthy distrust of speculation and an insistence on primary emotions; it sees a brave revolt against sterile literary conventions. Anderson, in short, excites almost the same controversy as Whitman, to whose tradition he belongs rather than to that of Hawthorne and Henry James. Irving Howe (*Sherwood Anderson,* New York, 1951) deplores the influence on Anderson of James Joyce; James Schevill denies the influence (*Sherwood Anderson,* Denver, 1951). D. H. Lawrence, whose "kingship" Anderson announced in a review, is thought to have been an unfortunate influence on his middle years. The influences of George Borrow, Gertrude Stein, and the French impressionist painters have been variously invoked. Howe and Gregory insist on the influence of Mark Twain. Anderson himself, it has been said, influenced Hemingway (whose parody *Torrents of Spring* made him anathema to Anderson's admirers), Faulkner, Thomas Wolfe, and—in a general way—all writers of the short story who have combated commercial slickness. Critical disputants agree upon certain points: his proper medium was the short story, his seven "novels" being expansions thereof. When the high points of his achievement are named, the same titles recur: foremost, *Winesburg, Ohio;* then single stories—"Death in the Woods," "The Triumph of the Egg," "I Want to Know Why," "The Man Who Became a Woman." There is agreement on his essential subject: a lament for the death of the emotional life under the impact of the machine age. He envisioned American life as a vast loneliness over which men and women crawled in vain search for love. He persistently images the house of life, whose doors are closed. "Unused" women, craftsmen broken by the machine, businessmen who see the hollowness of their "success," adolescents bewildered by their new emotions—these are the recurrent characters in a long-continued "fable of American estrangement, whose theme is the loss of love" (Howe). That fable was expressed in 25 volumes in as many years. His early writings were commended by Floyd Dell before they were published, but general acclaim waited upon the publication of his fourth book, *Winesburg.* Unadventurous readers condemned the sexual element of the book, but critics almost unanimously welcomed it as a masterpiece in a new manner. Of all his books only *Dark Laughter* achieved commercial success; not even warmest admirers think that book one of his best. Biographers assert that Anderson had by that time run out of subject matter, was aware of the flagging of his imagination, and knew himself to be in a real crisis. By the time his *Memoirs* appeared, he was generally regarded as a "has-been," and the book got little attention. That book was prepared for posthumous publication by Paul Rosenfeld, whose methods have been severely criticized, and Schevill calls for a new edition. It is not from those *Memoirs* or from the other autobiographical volumes (*Tar; A Story Teller's Story*) that the objective facts of Anderson's life may be learned. He confessed himself bored by literal recounting of detail, felt free only when he could exercise his imagination. He exaggerates the poverty of his youth; is alternately hostile and sympathetic toward his father; overdraws his mother, perhaps from a sense of not having appreciated her in life. On the other hand, his avowed fictions draw freely upon his diurnal experience, and it has been claimed for them as for the autobiographies that they truly represent the spirit if not the facts of his life. Those facts, with markedly different interpretations, may be learned from the biographies by Schevill and Howe. Anderson was the third child of a "shiftless, drifting" family that lived briefly in various small towns. His education was irregular, and when the family broke up after the death of his mother, he drifted from job to job. He served briefly in the army during the Spanish-American War, seeing no combat. He spent a term at Wittenberg Academy, wrote advertising in Chicago, married in 1904, and had three children. He engaged in various businesses, ultimately achieving comfortable success as a manufacturer of paint in Elyria. He was already writing and felt increasingly dissatisfied with his business and with his marriage. He appears to have suffered a nervous breakdown. By his own account he one day said to his secretary, "I have been walking in a long river and my feet are wet." He thereupon walked out of the factory, resumed advertising work in Chicago, but spent most of his time writing. He was shortly separated from his wife. Chicago was at that time the scene of vigorous literary activity—what Anderson later called a "Robin's-egg Renaissance"—and he became the intimate of some of the leading figures, who encouraged him to publish. In 1916 he was married to Tennessee Mitchell; on their honeymoon they visited his first wife. The second marriage was dissolved in 1924, and he immediately married again. The success of *Dark Laughter* enabled him to build a home at Marion, Va., and also to buy two newspapers, one Republican and one Democratic, which he published and edited. Financial pressures forced him to undertake lecture tours, for which he was ill-fitted, and to write potboiler articles for magazines. He traveled widely in America, partly from economic necessity, partly from a restless urgency that prevented him from ever feeling secure in any one place or company. His third marriage was dissolved in 1932; he married again the following year. During the 1930s he was attracted to left-wing political doctrines—more, probably, out of sympathy for the poor than from ideological conviction. Schevill rightly calls that interest "a negative approach." He did, however, sign a manifesto; play an inconspicuous part at a European conference; join a committee of protest over President Hoover's treatment of the Bonus Army. He continued to publish a book a year and to write widely for the magazines, but his fame was eclipsed by the rising stars of Hemingway, Faulkner, and others. He died at Colón, Canal Zone, and was buried at Marion, Va.

Denham Sutcliffe

ANDERSON, THOMAS MACARTHUR (Jan. 21, 1836–May 8, 1917), army officer, was born in Chillicothe, Ross County. He was educated at Mount St. Mary's College, Md., and the Cincinnati Law School. During the Civil War he was a member of the 6th O.V.I., and he subsequently entered the regular army with the rank of major. In 1898 he accompanied General Merritt to Manila. He died in Portland, Ore.

The Political Conspiracies Preceding the Rebellion; Or, the True Stories of Sumter and Pickens, New York, 1882.

On Methods of Meeting Our Military Necessities, [Vancouver, 1888].

Should Republics Have Colonies?, Boston, [1906].

ANDORN, SIDNEY (Sept. 25, 1904–), journalist and radio commentator, was born in Newark, Licking County. He has worked on the Cleveland *Press* and the Cleveland *News* and has been a commentator on Station WGAR. He has written a number of radio scripts and a pamphlet: *The Cleveland Scene; 1936–1946,* Cleveland, 1946.

ANDREWS, CLARENCE EDWARD (Nov. 25, 1883–Dec. 12, 1932), educator, was born in New York City. A graduate of Yale University (A.B., 1906; Ph.D., 1912), he taught English at Ohio State University from 1915 until his death. Besides anthologies and textbooks, he published *The Innocents of Paris,* New York, 1928. WWW 1

ANDREWS, CLARENCE LEROY (Oct. 19, 1862–Aug. 22, 1952), was born in Ashtabula County, but was reared in Oregon. He was an accountant and worked for various state and Federal agencies. He led the campaign for protection of Eskimo-owned reindeer herds. Much of his life was spent in Alaska, the subject of most of his writings, e.g., *The Story of Alaska,* [Seattle, 1931]. WW 24

ANDREWS, EBENEZER BALDWIN (April 29, 1821–Aug. 14, 1880), was born in Danbury, Conn. He graduated from Marietta College in 1842 and Princeton Theological Seminary in 1844. He served in the Congregational ministry until 1851, when he became professor of geology at Marietta College. He became assistant geologist to the Ohio State geological survey in 1861. The last years of his life were spent in Lancaster.

Report to the Purchasers of Coal and Salt Lands on Federal Creek and Marietta Run, Athens County . . . , Marietta, [1854].

An Account of the Fall of Meteoric Stones at New Concord . . . , [n.p.], 1860.

Rock Oil, Its Geological Distribution, [Marietta, 1861].

Report on the Economical Geology of Southern Ohio, Traversed by the Marietta and Cincinnati Railroads . . . , Cincinnati, 1865.

Letter . . . on the Coal and Iron Deposits of the Upper Sunday Creek and Moxahala Valleys, in Perry County . . . , Columbus, 1873.

Report on the Exploration of a Cave, and of the Mounds in Ohio, [Cambridge, Mass.], 1877.

Report of Geological Investigations along the Line of the Cleveland, Canton, Coshocton & Straitsville Railw'y . . . , Cleveland, 1878.

ANDREWS, GERTRUDE NELSON (d.Oct. 10, 1938), was born in Toledo, Lucas County. She graduated from Central High School, Toledo, and began speaking for women's suffrage in that city. She was also gifted as an elocutionist and was associated with an amateur acting company. She married Fred G. Andrews, a reporter on the Toledo *Blade,* and later lived in New York City and California. She died in Carmel, Calif. She wrote scenarios for Frank Keenan, a book on scenario writing, and a biography of Corse Payton: *The Romance of a Western Boy* . . . , Brooklyn, 1901.

ANDREWS, ISRAEL WARD (Jan. 3, 1815–April 18, 1888), educator, was born in Danbury, Conn. After a year at Amherst College he entered Williams College, where he graduated in 1837. The following year he was called to Marietta College, where he spent the rest of his life, serving as president, 1855–88. He became very active in general educational work in Ohio. In an article in the Marietta *Intelligencer,* April 1–8, 1856, he pointed out, "In an institute held in one of the counties of Ohio, the word 'nuisance' was spelled in more than twenty different modes," and made a strong plea for the adoption of a standard dictionary for classroom use, specifically Webster's dictionary as revised by Goodrich. By way of sales promotion the article was reprinted by the publishers of the dictionary and widely circulated. It served to bring the young college president and his little-known college to the attention of educators throughout the country. He became one of the founding members of the National Teachers' Association and a member of the National Council of Education. His *Manual of the Constitution* was widely used as a textbook in colleges and universities for well over half a century.

Webster's Dictionaries, Springfield, Mass., 1856.
Why Is Allegiance Due? and Where Is It Due? . . . , Cincinnati, 1863.
Manual of the Constitution of the United States . . . , Cincinnati, [1874].
Historical Sketch of Marietta College . . . , Cincinnati, 1876.
The Educational Work and Place of Ohio, [n.p., 1877].
Washington County and the Early Settlement of Ohio . . . , Cincinnati, 1877.

ANDREWS, J. CUTLER (Sept. 9, 1908–), educator, was born in Delaware, Delaware County. After graduating from Ohio Wesleyan University, he did graduate work at Harvard. He joined the history faculty of Carnegie Institute of Technology in 1931, and since 1952 has been teaching at Pennsylvania College for Women. He has published *Pittsburgh's Post-Gazette* . . . , Boston, [1936].

ANDREWS, MARTIN REGISTER (April 6, 1842–April 20, 1913), professor of history at Marietta College, was born in Meigs County. After serving in the Civil War, he attended Marietta College and graduated in 1869. He was superintendent of the Steubenville schools, 1870–79, principal of Marietta Academy, 1879–94, and a member of the college faculty, 1894–1910. He wrote *History of Marietta and Washington County* . . . , Chicago, 1902. WWW 1

ANGELL, ERNEST (June 1, 1889–), lawyer, was born in Cleveland, Cuyahoga County. He was admitted to the Ohio bar in 1914 and practiced in Cleveland for four years. After service in World War I he began practice in New York City, where he has since lived. He has written professional and popular articles and *Supreme Court Primer,* New York, [1937]. WW 30

ANGELL, HILDEGARDE (d. July 23, 1933), sister of Ernest Angell (q.v.), was born in Cleveland, Cuyahoga County. She was educated at Hathaway-Brown School, Cleveland, and in France and Germany. Around 1922 she moved to New York City, where she worked for a time on *McClure's Magazine.* She married Granville M. Smith in 1930; they lived in Tampico, Mexico, for two years and moved to Kansas City, Mo., about six months before her death. Her best-known book was a biography: *Simón Bolívar,* New York, 1930.

ANGLE, PAUL McCLELLAND (Dec. 25, 1900–), historian, was born in Mansfield, Richland County. He graduated from Miami University in 1922. He has been associated with the Illinois State Historical Society, 1925–45, and the Chicago Historical Society, 1945– . One of the nation's best-known Lincoln scholars, he has published numerous articles and books in the field of his specialty, e.g., *Lincoln, 1854–1861* . . . , Springfield, Ill., [1933]. WW 30

ANSHUTZ, EDWARD POLLOCK (March 23, 1846–Jan. 1, 1918), was born in Clarington, Monroe County. He was educated in district schools of Virginia and at Heron's Seminary, Cincinnati. He moved to Philadelphia in 1872. He was editor of *New Church Life,* 1880–85, and also served as editor of *Homeopathic Recorder* and of *Homeopathic Envoy.* In addition to writing several technical treatises on homeopathic medicine, he wrote popular books on the subject and compiled a book of remedies. He died in Philadelphia.

Safety in Cholera Time . . . , Philadelphia, [1892].
Sexual Ills and Diseases . . . , Philadelphia, 1896.

Dogs. How to Care for Them in Health and Treat Them When Ill . . ., Philadelphia, 1903.

Therapeutic By-ways . . ., Philadelphia, 1916.

ANSPACHER, LOUIS KAUFMAN (March 1, 1878–May 10, 1947), lecturer and dramatist, was born in Cincinnati, Hamilton County. After graduating from College of the City of New York, he lived in New York City and lectured at various institutions in that city. He published numerous plays and other books, e.g., *This Bewildered Age,* New York, 1935. WWW 2

ANTRIM, DORON KEMP (Aug. 25, 1889–), was born in Germantown, Montgomery County. After graduating from DePauw University in 1913, he was a salesman for Wurlitzer Co., Dayton, 1914, operated a music store in Stevensville, Mont., 1915–18, and served in World War I. He was on the editorial staff of *The Musical Observer* and *Metronome* magazines, 1921–28, and since 1928 has been a free-lance writer. He has published articles in most national magazines and has also written books on music, e.g., *Teaching Music and Making It Pay,* Philadelphia, 1927. WW 26

ANTRIM, ERNEST IRVING (Feb. 21, 1869–Jan. 6, 1953), educator and banker, brother of Doron K. Antrim (q.v.), was born in Germantown, Montgomery County. After graduating from DePauw University in 1889, he taught at Belmont College, Cincinnati, and at other universities. He earned his doctorate at Göttingen University in 1897. He left the teaching profession in 1904 and was an official of the Van Wert National Bank, 1904–28. He wrote *Fifty Million Strong; Or, Our Rural Reserve,* Van Wert, 1916. WWW 3

ANTRIM, GEORGE DOYLE (Jan. 27, 1867–June 4, 1958), was born near Indianapolis, Ind., but came to Montgomery County in 1903, where he was engaged in the ice cream business. He wrote poems as an avocation and published a collection of humorous verse: *A Pig Tale and a Few Others,* Dayton, 1940.

ANTRIM, JOSHUA (c.1820– ?), was born in Clinton County. His family moved to Champaign County in 1831, and he later lived in Middleburg, Logan County.

The History of Champaign and Logan Counties, from Their First Settlement, Bellefontaine, 1872.

APPLETON, ELIZABETH HAVEN (Oct. 16, 1815–Nov. 15, 1890), educator, was born in a suburb of Liverpool, England. Her father came to Baltimore, Md., while she was a small girl; in 1832, after spending three years at Wheeling, Va., he brought his family to Cincinnati. She taught school in Baltimore and the South in the 1840s. After returning to Cincinnati, she taught in a girls' school kept by Lyman Harding, 1849–55, and operated her own school, 1855–75. After retiring from teaching, she annually gave a course of lectures on literature and art. The posthumous collection of her writings was made up largely of these lectures. She was librarian of the Historical and Philosophical Society of Ohio, 1876–86.

In Memory of Elizabeth Haven Appleton . . . , Cincinnati, 1891.

APPLETON, EVERARD JACK (March 24, 1872–Feb. 19, 1931), journalist, was born in Charleston, W. Va. He came to Cincinnati in 1893 and passed the remainder of his life in that city. Using the pen name Ginger Jar, he published poems in various newspapers and magazines; he also published at least one collection: *The Quiet Courage, and Other Songs of the Unafraid,* Cincinnati, [1912].

ARBUTHNOT, MAY HILL (April 27, 1884–), educator, was born in Mason City, Iowa. A graduate of the University of Chicago, she served on the faculty of Western Reserve University, 1922–50. She still lives in Cleveland. She has contributed many articles to educational magazines, prepared school readers, and written other books, e.g., *Children and Books,* Chicago, [1947]. WWAW 1

ARCHBOLD, ANN (c.1820– ?), is said to have been born near New Matamoras, Washington County. She went to Iowa in 1845, traveling overland in a leisurely manner. After teaching school in Iowa for several years, she returned to Ohio chiefly by river steamers on the Missouri and Ohio Rivers. The first book below is a fine relation of her experiences, containing much of interest on the Indians and the Mormons.

A Book for the Married and Single, the Grave and the Gay: and Especially Designed for Steamboat Passengers, East Plainfield, 1850.

A Pamphlet for Gentlemen and Ladies of All Sorts and Sizes, Washington, D. C., 1851.

ARCHER, WILLIAM CLIFFORD (March 30, 1876–Aug. 19, 1950), lawyer, was born in Noble County, where he attended country schools. At the age of eighteen he began teaching school while reading law. After editing newspapers in Caldwell, Hillsboro, and Athens, he became the first Secretary of the Ohio State Liability Board of Awards. His efforts in establishing Ohio's workmen's compensation laws led to his being named deputy commissioner of the New York Workmen's Compensation Bureau, where he served for fifteen years. From 1929 until his death he was insurance consultant to numerous contractors. His family published privately a collection of his verse: *Arrows,* New York, 1931.

AREY, HARRIET ELLEN GRANNIS (April 14, 1819–April 26, 1901), journalist, was born in Cavendish, Vt. She entered Oberlin College in 1837 and received the degree of A.B. in 1845, her studies having been interrupted by eye trouble. She taught school in Cleveland until 1848, when she married Oliver Cromwell Arey and moved to Buffalo, N. Y., where for several years she edited *The Youth's Casket* and later *The Home Monthly.* After teaching school at Brockport, N. Y., Whitewater, Wis., and Yonkers, N. Y., she returned to Ohio in 1879 and settled in Cleveland. There Mrs. Arey edited *The Earnest Worker* in the 1880s and was one of the founders and the first president of the Ohio Women's State Press Association.

Household Songs and Other Poems, New York, 1855.

Home and School Training, Philadelphia, 1884.

ARGOW, WENDELIN WALDEMAR WIELAND (Aug. 9, 1891–), clergyman, was born in Dayton, Montgomery County. He was ordained a Baptist minister in 1914 but became a Unitarian in 1920. He has served churches in Ohio, Iowa, and New York. Since 1941 he has been pastor of the First Unitarian church, Baltimore, Md. He has written many pamphlets and several books, e.g., *Beyond,* Cedar Rapids, Iowa, 1931. WW 28

ARMSTRONG, MOSES KIMBALL (Sept. 19, 1832–Jan. 11, 1906), was born in Milan, Erie County. After completing his education at Western Reserve College, he moved to Minnesota Territory in 1856, where he was employed as a surveyor. In 1858 he moved to the Indian village of Yankton, Dakota Territory. He served in various capacities in the territorial government and was chosen president of the council in 1867. He was elected as territorial delegate to the Forty-second and Forty-third Congresses. In 1874 he went to St. James, Minn., where he engaged in banking and the real-estate business. He died in Albert Lea, Minn.

History and Resources of Dakota, Montana, and Idaho . . . , Yankton, 1866.

Information for Persons Who Propose to Come West, Yankton, 1869.

The Early Empire Builders of the Great West, St. Paul, Minn., 1901.

ARMSTRONG, ROBERT GRENVILLE (Feb. 4, 1888–July 25, 1956), clergyman, was born in Reed City, Mich. After graduating from Oberlin College in 1912, he was pastor of the Congregational church, Amherst, Lorain County, 1913–17. He later served churches in New York State and New England. He died in Hartford, Conn. He wrote *Historic Lebanon . . . ,* Lebanon, Conn., [1950]. RLA 2

ARMSTRONG, WILLIAM JACKSON (1841–1913), was born in Warren County. He graduated from Antioch College in 1862. He was inspector general of U. S. Consulates for twenty years; he then became a lecturer advocating social reforms. He lived in Columbus for many years. His death occurred in Los Angeles. Some of his lectures were published in pamphlet form.

An Artist Historian, Columbus, 1899.

The Greatest Living Man, Columbus, [1902].

The Heroes of Defeat, Cincinnati, 1905.

ARNE, SIGRID (May 9, 1900–), journalist, was born Agnes Holmquist in New York City, but grew up in Cleveland and attended the schools of that city. She changed her name to Sigrid Arne in 1922 when she went to work on the Cleveland *Plain Dealer* after her graduation from the University of Michigan. She worked on various newspapers in Oklahoma and Michigan in the 1920s, was on the Cleveland *News,* 1930–31, and after more than twenty years as an Associated Press correspondent rejoined the *News* in 1957. While covering the United Nations for the Associated Press, she wrote *The United Nations Primer,* New York, [1945].

ARNESON, BEN ALBERT (May 22, 1883–Feb. 13, 1958), educator, was born in Barneveld, Wis. He graduated from Whitewater Normal School in 1908 and the University of Wisconsin in 1913; he completed his doctorate at the University of Wisconsin in 1916. He was professor of political science at Ohio Wesleyan University, 1917–53, and after his retirement continued to live in Delaware. He wrote social studies textbooks and *The Democratic Monarchies of Scandinavia,* New York, 1939. WW 29

ARNOLD, BIRCH. Pseud. See Alice E. Bartlett.

ARNOLD, JAMES OLIVER (Jan 29, 1838–March 16, 1905), was born in Dayton, Montgomery County, and spent his life in that city. He developed a suburban section of Dayton, organized the Dayton and Southeastern Railroad, and was a director of several street railway companies.

Social Science, [Dayton?, 1898?].

Advanced Thought on Electrical and Spiritual Voltage . . . , Dayton, 1902.

ARNOLD, NELSON ESTA (July 23, 1863–May 27, 1932), journalist, was born in Pomeroy, Meigs County. He edited various country newspapers and owned the Marion *Mirror,* 1900–07. He died in Marion. He wrote *Thoughts—In Prose and Poetry,* Lancaster, 1928.

ARPEE, LEON (1877–Nov. 24, 1947), clergyman, was born near Constantinople, Turkey. A Presbyterian minister, he lived in Ohio from 1904 until his death; he spent his last fifteen years in Athens. His writings include *The Atonement in Experience, a Critical Study,* [London, 1932]. OBB

ARTZ, FREDERICK BINKERD (Oct. 19, 1894–), educator, was born in Dayton, Montgomery County. He graduated from Oberlin College in 1916, served in France during World War I, and earned his Ph.D. at Harvard University in 1924. In 1924 he joined the Oberlin history department. A specialist in French history, he has written several books on the subject, e.g., *France under the Bourbon Restoration, 1841–1830,* Cambridge, [Mass.], 1931. WW 30

ASCHAM, JOHN BAYNE (Feb. 12, 1873–Nov. 14, 1950), clergyman, was born in Vanlue, Hancock County. He graduated from Ohio Wesleyan University in 1900 and Boston University (Ph.D.) in 1907. Ordained to the Methodist ministry in 1897, he preached on Ohio circuits, 1897–1902, was pastor of several Ohio churches, 1902–25, and was director of the Children's Home, Cincinnati, 1928–42. His death occurred in Tucson, Ariz., where he had lived since 1946. He wrote several books on religious themes, e.g., *Help from the Hills,* Cincinnati, [1911]. WWW 3

ASHBROOK, WILLIAM ALBERT (July 1, 1867–Jan. 1, 1940), editor and congressman, was born in Johnstown, Licking County. In 1885 he began editing the Johnstown *Independent.* He served the 17th Ohio District as congressman in Washington for nine terms. His intimate diary, which he started in 1886 and kept for over forty years before publishing it privately, is a valuable document: *A Line a Day for Forty Odd Years . . . ,* 2 vols., [Johnstown, 1930–32]. WWW 1

ASHBURN, JOSEPH NELSON (Feb. 6, 1838–Jan. 20, 1919), was born in Ohio, probably in Cleveland, Cuyahoga County. He served in the 86th O.V.I. from June, 1863, to Feb., 1864. After the war he lived in Cleveland, where he was employed as a purchasing agent; he died in that city. He wrote *History of the Eighty-sixth Regiment . . . ,* Cleveland, 1909.

ASHBURN, PERCY MOREAU (July 28, 1872–Aug. 20, 1940), army officer, was born in Batavia, Clermont County, the older brother of Thomas Q. Ashburn (q.v.). He served in the army medical corps, 1898–1932. Besides a textbook on military hygiene, he wrote *A History of the Medical Department of the United States Army,* Boston, 1929. WWW 1

ASHBURN, THOMAS QUINN (Nov. 17, 1874–May 2, 1941), army officer, was born in Batavia, Clermont County. He graduated from the U. S. Military Academy, after which he served in the regular army. His writings include *History of the 324th Field Artillery . . . ,* [New York, 1920]. WWW 1

ASHLEY, BARNAS FREEMAN (Nov. 27, 1833–April 14, 1915), clergyman, was born in Liverpool, Nova Scotia. He was educated by private tutors in Boston and attended Ohio Medical College, Cleveland. For many years he was a pastor of Baptist churches and later of a Dutch Reformed Church, New York City. He retired to Ravenna, Portage County, about 1890, where he wrote a number of books for boys.

A Tan Pile Jim . . . , Chicago, [1894].

Dick and Jack's Adventures on Sable Island, Chicago, [1895].

Air Castle Don . . . , Chicago, [1896].

ASHLEY, CHARLES SUMNER (Jan. 1, 1864–Nov. 25, 1925), son of James M. Ashley (q.v.), was born in Toledo, Lucas County. He was a prominent attorney and real-estate operator in Toledo for many years and was a founder of the Toledo Museum of Art.

The Financial Question . . . , Toledo, 1895.

ASHLEY, FREDERICK WILLIAM (Jan. 12, 1863–June 14, 1942), educator and librarian, was born in Mansfield, Richland County. He graduated from Western Reserve University in 1885. After a year in Missouri he served on the faculty of Western Reserve Academy, 1887–97, and was librarian in Painesville, 1897–98. From 1900 until his retirement in 1936, he was on the staff of the Library of Congress. Besides technical articles and books relating to library work, he published a volume of reminiscences: *"If You're Off for Old Ohio in the Morning,"* [Washington, D. C., 1932]. WWW 3

ASHLEY, JAMES M. (Nov. 14, 1824–Sept. 16, 1896), was born in Allegheny County, Pa.; shortly thereafter the family moved to Portsmouth, Scioto County. Self-educated, he went to work for the *Scioto Valley Republican* at the age of seventeen. He became editor of the *Democrat* at Portsmouth in 1848. Having studied law in his spare time, he was admitted to the bar in 1849. Following his marriage in 1851 he removed to Toledo, where he engaged in the wholesale drug business. Keenly interested in politics he was one of the founding fathers of the Republican Party in the Toledo district. He was elected to Congress and served from Dec. 5, 1859, to March 3, 1869. In 1861 he prepared the first measure for Reconstruction in the Southern states. He also introduced the first proposition to amend the Constitution of the United States to abolish slavery. It was on his initiative that the move for the impeachment of President Johnson was begun, which resulted in his defeat in the ensuing election. President Grant appointed him territorial governor of Montana, but he was removed within a year because of his sharp criticisms of Grant's policies. His speeches represent the radical Republicanism of his day and are now important historical sources; only a few of the major ones are listed below. Following his return to Toledo he built the road which became the Toledo, Ann Arbor and Northern Michigan Railroad, and served as its president from 1877 to 1893.

Success of the Calhoun Revolution . . . , Washington, D. C., 1860.

The Rebellion—Its Causes and Consequences . . . , Toledo, 1861.

The Union of the States: The Majority Must Govern: It Is Treason to Secede . . . , [Washington, D. C., 1861].

"Initiate Emancipation," Washington, D. C., 1862.

The Liberation and Restoration of the South, Washington, D. C., 1864.

Impartial Suffrage the Only Safe Basis of Reconstruction, Washington, D. C., 1866.

Representative Government Can Only Be Maintained by the Subordination of the Executive and Judicial to the Legislative Power . . . , Washington, D. C., [1869].

Reminiscences of the Great Rebellion, [Toledo, 1890].

The Impending Political Epoch, New York, [1891?].

Duplicate Copy of the Souvenir from the Afro-American League of Tennessee to Hon. James M. Ashley of Ohio. Orations and Speeches, Philadelphia, 1894.

ASTER, RAY. Pseud. See John M. Leavitt.

ASTON, HOWARD (c.1844–Nov. 11, 1919), was born in Montgomery County, Miss. He enlisted in the 97th O.V.I. at Zanesville in July, 1862, and was discharged the following February because of physical disability. He apparently later enlisted in the cavalry. He was county clerk, Muskingum County, in the 1870s. He died in California. He wrote a book based on his war diary: *History and Roster of the Fourth and Fifth Independent Battalions and Thirteenth Regiment Ohio Cavalry Volunteers . . . ,* Columbus, 1902.

ATHENS, IDA GERDING (Feb. 23, 1882–), educator, was born in Cincinnati, Hamilton County. She attended Ohio Wesleyan University and the University of Cincinnati and was for many years in the Cincinnati public school system as an attendance officer and a teacher. She published a volume of verse: *Brethren,* Cincinnati, 1940.

ATKINSON, MATTHEW (Jan. 8, 1827–Jan. 17, 1913), was born in Carroll County. His father was Isaac Atkinson, a pioneer known locally as "the father of Carroll County." Isaac built and operated a grist mill, an oil mill, a woolen mill, and a carding machine, all of which were destroyed by fire in 1843. *The Family Director* was probably published as a service to a public thus bereft of those essential local industries.

The Family Director: Designed as a Help to Those, Who Are Supplying Themselves in Whole or in Part, with Woolen Goods of Their Own Manufacture . . . , Carrollton, 1844.

ATKINSON, ROBERT J. (June 20, 1820–Feb. 25, 1871), lawyer, was born in Columbiana County and later lived in Carrollton, Carroll County. He read law and was admitted to the Ohio bar, served in the Ohio Senate for two terms, and was Third Auditor of the Treasury, 1855–64. In 1866 he was appointed attorney and counselor to the Supreme Court. The pamphlet below is his only known publication.

Public Debt! Taxation! Reconstruction! A View of the Situation, Financial and Political, Washington, D. C., 1867.

ATWATER, CALEB (Dec. 25, 1778–March 13, 1867), was born in North Adams, Mass. He graduated from Williams College in 1804 with the degrees of B.A. and M.A. For a while he conducted a school for young ladies in New York and studied for the ministry, later becoming a Presbyterian minister. Giving up the ministry because of ill health, he began to study law and within a few months was admitted to the bar. Impoverished by the failure of a business venture, he moved with his wife and two small children to Circleville, Pickaway County, in 1815. There was no shortage of good lawyers in the district in which he had chosen to settle, and just how he managed to support his family during the next few years does not appear. The astonishing fact is that on March 25, 1819, but a few months less than four years after his arrival in Ohio, he wrote the eminent geologist Parker Cleveland that he had submitted his work on the antiquities of Ohio to the American Antiquarian Society; that he had under preparation a civil and natural history of Ohio; and that he would be glad to aid in preparing a geological map of the Midwest. During the months which followed, he plied Cleveland with a clutter of geological information, some of which, such as the discovery of silver ore in Hocking and of nickel in Columbus, must have amazed that learned gentleman though it did not deceive him; for not a word of it appeared in the second edition of his *Elementary Treatise on Mineralogy and Geology,* which he was preparing. In 1820 the American Antiquarian Society published Atwater's *Descriptions of the Antiquities Discovered in the State of Ohio and Other Western States,* over 260 pages, with a folding map and ten plans. It contained many glaring omissions, the most notable of which was his failure to mention the Serpent Mound; it is manifest that Atwater did not visit all of the sites he claimed to have examined; and there can be little doubt that he leaned heavily upon the work of others. Withal, considering the short time he had been in Ohio and the handicaps under which he must have labored, it was a remarkable production and stands as the first systematic account of the earthworks of the Ohio Valley. In 1821 he was elected to the assembly and was an unsuccessful candidate for Congress in 1822. In Chillicothe he attempted to establish a weekly in 1824. The first number of *The Friend of Freedom* appeared on Feb. 4, and though but three numbers are known to have been published, it is believed that it it struggled along without support until the following April, when the sheriff appeared and levied upon Atwater's personal property to satisfy a creditor. His first real break came in May, 1829, when he was appointed by President Jackson one of three commissioners to treat with the Winnebagos in the vicinity of Prairie du Chien, Wis. Following the conclusion of the treaties Atwater carried them to Washington, and in 1831 published his *Remarks Made on a Tour to Prairie Du Chien; Thence to Washington City, in 1829,* an account of the episode with a description of the country traversed. The book appears to have escaped the attention of the critics until 1833, when he republished it, along with his paper on Western antiquities, under the title of *The Writings of Caleb Atwater.* James Hall devoted six and a half pages of his *Western Monthly Magazine* to a severe criticism of the work, wherein he presented evidence that at least a part of it had been lifted from Timothy Flint's *Condensed Geography and History of the Western States,* ridiculed Atwater's claim that in Illinois he had seen ten thousand acres thickly set with artichokes, jibed at Atwater's steamboats "with their dashing oars, leaving a stream of dense smoke behind them, floating horizontally along in the air," and in general tore the book asunder. But the critics really went to work in 1838, when his *History of the State of Ohio* appeared. The criticism was general and is best summed up, perhaps, by William Davis Gallagher's comment in the *Hesperian:* "As a literary production, Mr. Atwater's book is deplorably deficient." Drawing his material largely from the *Transactions of the Western Literary Institute, and College of Professional Teachers,* he pubpublished his *Essay on Education* in 1841. The sales of his *Remarks Made on a Tour to Prairie du Chien* were disappointing. The title page of unsold copies was removed and a new one reading *The Indians of the Northwest, Their Maners* [*sic*], *Customs, &c* . . . was substituted—a somewhat pretentious title considering that he had spent but little more than a month with those Indians. This and his last book, *Mysteries of Washington City, during Several Months of the Session of the 28th Congress,* Henry Howe found him trying to sell to his neighbors: "A queer talker . . . his life appears to have been a struggle with penury. He did but little, if any law business; he had a large family, six sons and three daughters, and his books were but a meagre source of support, and these he sold by personal solicitation." Already forgotten by most of his contemporaries, he died in Circleville over two decades later in complete obscurity.

Ernest J. Wessen

Descriptions of the Antiquities Discovered in the State of Ohio and Other Western States . . . , Worcester, Mass., 1820.
Remarks Made on a Tour to Prairie du Chien; Thence to Washington City, in 1829. Columbus, 1831.
The Writings of Caleb Atwater, Columbus, [1833].
A History of the State of Ohio, Natural and Civil, Cincinnati, [1838].
An Essay on Education, Cincinnati, 1841.
Mysteries of Washington City, during Several Months of the Session of the 28th Congress, Washington, D. C., 1844.

ATWATER, GEORGE PARKIN (Sept. 8, 1874–Oct. 21, 1932), Episcopal clergyman, was born in Lisbon, Columbiana County. He graduated from Kenyon College in 1895. From 1897 to 1926 he was rector of the Church of Our Saviour in Akron. His writings include *The Episcopal Church; Its Message for Men of Today,* [Akron, 1917]. WWW 1

AUDUBON, JOHN JAMES (April 26, 1785–Jan. 27, 1851), artist and ornithologist, lived in Cincinnati in 1820 while working as taxidermist and curator of the Western Museum. At this time apparently he first conceived of publishing his drawings of birds. In Oct., 1820, he began a trip down the Ohio and Mississippi, thus beginning his lifelong vocation. The first volume of his masterpiece, *The Birds of America,* was published in London in 1827.

AUGHEY, JOHN HILL (May 8, 1828–July 30, 1911), clergyman, was born in New Hartford, N. Y. His family moved to Ohio when he was a small child, and he was reared near Steubenville. After graduating from Franklin College in 1852, he became a Presbyterian minister and served a number of parishes in Mississippi until the Civil War, during much of which he was interned. Later he filled pulpits in Indiana, western Pennsylvania, and Ohio. He served as home missionary in Idaho and Indian Territory, 1887–98. He retired at Newton, N. J., in 1904. His death occurred in that community.

The Iron Furnace; Or, Slavery and Secession, Philadelphia, 1863.
Tupelo, Lincoln, Neb., 1888.

AUGSPURGER, MARIE M. (Aug. 8, 1898–), was born in Middletown, Butler County, and now lives in Warren County. She graduated from Miami University in 1920, taught school for a time, and has been employed by the Middletown Gas and Electric Company since 1924. She has done research on several subjects pertaining to the Far West and has published a book based on data collected during her annual vacations: *Yellowstone National Park, Historical and Descriptive,* Middletown, 1948.

AUMANN, FRANCIS ROBERT (Jan. 21, 1901–), educator, was born in Delaware, Delaware County. He graduated from Ohio Wesleyan University in 1921, studied law for two years, and graduated from the State University of Iowa (Ph.D.) in 1928. He has been on the political science faculty of Ohio State University since 1928. Author of a great many professional articles and reviews, he has also written several books, e.g., *The Changing American Legal System . . . ,* Columbus, 1940.

AUNT FANNY. Pseud. See Frances Dana Barker Gage.

AUSTERLITZ, EMANUEL H. (Dec. 8, 1838–March 29, 1927), publisher, was born in Prague, Austria. He came to America in 1865 and to Cincinnati in 1866. He worked for the Block Publishing Company and also founded the *Freie Press,* a German newspaper which he sold in 1886. He died in Cincinnati at the age of 89.

Cincinnati from 1800 to 1875 . . . , Cincinnati, [1875].

AUSTIN, GEORGE McKENDREE (Aug. 23, 1856–Oct. 25, 1930), physician, was born on a farm in Vernon Township, Clinton County. He practiced medicine in Wilmington for over forty years. He collected and classified the fossils of the Richmond group and presented a collection said to contain over 25,000 specimens to the Smithsonian Institution. He wrote *Surface Geology of Clinton County . . . ,* [Wilmington], 1930.

AVERY, ELROY McKENDREE (July 14, 1844–Dec. 1, 1935), was born in Erie, Mich. During the Civil War he served in the 11th Michigan Cavalry. For a while he was employed on the editorial staff of the Detroit *Tribune.* In 1871 he graduated from the University of Michigan and became superintendent of schools in East Cleveland. He turned to the lecture platform in 1879, and for two seasons he toured the country giving popular lectures on the new electric light. In 1881 he became a pioneer organizer of electric light and power companies. In the meantime he had come into prominence as the author of several successful textbooks on language and physical science. He was a member of the Cleveland city council, 1891–92, and of the Ohio senate, 1893–97. After 25 years spent in preparation, the first volume of his projected sixteen-volume *History of the United States and Its People* was published in 1904. Though intended to be a popular history of the United States, the work is full and critical, even iconoclastic in many respects. With fine discrimination he drew upon the country's leading collections for the thousands of rare prints and documents, reproductions of which were used to illustrate the work—not infrequently in full color and occasionally on folded inserts. The seventh volume was published in 1910, and to this point the cost of the work is said to have run well into six figures. With a ballooning mass of manuscript before him, the publisher suspended the work. Avery spent the last years of his life in Florida.

Shall Our Antiquities Be Preserved?, [Cleveland, 1899?].
A History of the United States and Its People . . . , 7 vols., Cleveland, 1904–10.
John Humfrey, Massachusetts Magistrate . . . , Cleveland, 1912.
A History of Cleveland and Its Environs . . . , 3 vols., Chicago, 1918.

AVEY, ALBERT EDWIN (May 29, 1886–), educator, was born in Hannibal, Mo. He attended high school in Cincinnati. A graduate of Yale University (A.B., 1908; Ph.D., 1915), he served on the Ohio State University philosophy faculty, 1917–54, and since his retirement he has continued to live in Columbus. He has published a number of textbooks and *Re-thinking Religion,* New York, [1936]. WW 28

AYDELOTT, BENJAMIN PARHAM (Jan. 7, 1796–Sept. 10, 1880), clergyman, was born in Philadelphia, Pa. He graduated from the College of Physicians and Surgeons, New York, in 1815, was ordained a deacon of the Protestant Episcopal Church by Bishop Hobart in 1820, and was ordained to the priesthood in 1822. He became rector of Christ Church, Cincinnati, in 1828. Hobart was Bishop Philander Chase's (q.v.) bitter, unrelenting foe, and it is significant that Aydelott was the leader of the faction that succeeded in ousting Chase from Kenyon College in 1831. He resigned from Christ Church on March 22, 1835, the year in which he was elected president of Woodward College, Cincinnati, in which position he served for ten years. In the meantime he had become a Presbyterian, and in 1838 he became pastor of Lane Seminary Church. He died in Cincinnati.

In Answer to the Rt. Rev. P. Chase, Cincinnati, [1832].
Duties of American Citizens, Cincinnati, 1840.
Our Country's Evils and Their Remedy, Cincinnati, 1843.
The Secret of a Sound Judgment . . . , Cincinnati, 1844.
Incidental Benefits of Denominational Divisions, Cincinnati, 1846.
Church's Duties in the Temperance Cause, Cincinnati, 1865.
Ethics for Our Country and the Times, Cincinnati, 1866.
Thoughts for the Thoughtful, Cincinnati, 1866.
Great Question: Sceptical Philosophy Examined, Cincinnati, 1868.
Prejudice against Colored People, Cincinnati, [n.d.].

AYRES, ALFRED. Pseud. See Thomas E. Osmun.

AYRES, ATLEE BERNARD (July 12, 1874–), architect, was born in Hillsboro, Highland County. He studied at the Art Students' League and the Metropolitan School of Architecture in New York City, and since 1899 has practiced in San Antonio, Texas. He has written *Mexican Architecture; Domestic, Civil and Ecclesiastical,* New York, 1926. WW 26

AYRES, LEONARD PORTER (Sept. 15, 1879–Oct. 29, 1946), was born in Niantic, Conn. He joined the Cleveland Trust Company staff in 1920 and resided in Cleveland until his death. He wrote a number of books and articles on education, psychology, and economics, e.g., *The Economics of Recovery,* New York, 1933. WWW 2

B

BABBITT, EDWIN DWIGHT (Feb. 1, 1828–c.1905), father of Irving Babbitt (q.v.), was born in Hamden, N. Y. He attended Knox College, Galesburg, Ill., where his father was in residence as a missionary. He arrived in Dayton in the late 1850s, and in 1860 he established the Miami Commercial College. In 1863 he published *The Babbittonian Sys-*

tem of Penmanship, which became quite popular and was republished in England. He became an active spiritualist in 1869 and commenced his practice as a psychophysician. For a time he appears to have been associated with Joseph Rodes Buchanan (q.v.) in Boston, and he later practiced in Brooklyn and New York City. After 1877 he devoted his time to writing and lecturing.

The Babbittonian System of Penmanship, Dayton, 1863.
The Health Guide; Aiming at a Higher Science of Life and the Life-Forces; Giving Nature's Simple and Beautiful Laws of Cure, New York, 1874.
The Principles of Light and Color; Including among Other Things the Harmonic Laws of the Universe, the Etherio-Atomic Philosophy of Force, Chromo Chemistry, Chromo Therapeutics, and the General Philosophy of the Fine Forces, Together with Numerous Discoveries and Practical Applications . . . , New York, 1878.
The Wonders of Light and Color, Including Chromopathy or the New Science of Color Healing, New York, 1879.
The Health Manual . . . , New York, 1880.
Religion as Revealed by the Material and Spiritual Universe, New York, 1881.
Health and Power . . . , New York, 1893.
Human Culture and Cure, Los Angeles, 1898.

BABBITT, IRVING (Aug. 2, 1865–July 15, 1933), a leading critic of modern thought and literature, proponent of humanism, and one of Harvard's great teachers, was born in Dayton, Montgomery County. Son of Edwin Dwight Babbitt (q.v.) and Augusta Darling, he lived for some years on the Darling farm at Madisonville, graduated from Woodward High School in Cincinnati, and, aided by his uncles, proceeded to Harvard University. At Harvard his study of Horace, Plato, and Aristotle supported the classical bent of his mind. There also and later in Paris he pursued Hindu studies highly influential in the formation of his thought. Through all the rest of his life he found the essential "wisdom of the ages" in the classical authors named above and in the teachings of Buddha and Confucius. The modern writers who contributed most to his thought were Goethe, Joubert, Sainte-Beuve, Arnold, and Emerson, who, whatever new elements they introduced, bore witness to the perennial validity of the old wisdom. Babbitt himself adopted the role of the modern mind—the critical and positive mind—rejecting all external authority. Science he respected like anyone else, but he denounced pseudo-science and the naturalistic philosophies that seemed to him jerry-built on scientific foundations. He held it a fateful violation of practical experience to reduce what is distinctively human to the natural level. He affirmed that man lives on two levels, the natural and the human. There is a "law for man" as well as a "law for thing." In the data of consciousness itself we recognize this dualism, these clashing forces. A man becomes human in proportion as "higher will," the centripetal force, imposes a limit to the centrifugal force of appetite and temperament and makes possible a superior fulfillment. The golden mean is thus the precondition of the insight and happiness appropriate to man. Babbitt humbly granted that there is a reality, or the illusion of a reality, above man. If he could not espouse any one religion (he was closest to Buddhism), he persistently defended the allied traditions of "humanism and religion." To discard these traditions in the common way of modernity is, he held, to throw out the baby with the bath. For nearly forty years—from 1894 until his death—Babbitt lectured at Harvard on the failure of modern thought and literature to maintain vitally what he liked to call the truths of the inner life. Thousands of students came under the spell of his vigorous masculinity, impressive character, and weighty intellect. This side of his work has been well revealed in *Irving Babbitt: Man and Teacher,* edited in 1941 by Frederick Manchester and Odell Shepard. At the same time, through articles and books, Babbitt played a leading role in the remarkable development of American literary and general criticism during the first three decades of the twentieth century. He dealt with education in *Literature and the American College . . . ,* Boston, 1908; with art in *The New Laocoön . . . ,* Boston, 1910; with literature in *The Masters of Modern French Criticism . . . ,* Boston, 1912, and *Rousseau and Romanticism . . . ,* Boston, 1919; and with politics in *Democracy and Leadership . . . ,* Boston, 1924. He was the central figure in the controversy over humanism which held widespread public attention from about 1927 to 1931, taking part with allies and disciples in the manifesto published in 1930: *Humanism and America.* A bibliography of his publications was included in a posthumous volume, *Spanish Character and Other Essays,* Boston, 1940.

Norman Foerster

BABCOCK, BERNIE (April 28, 1868–), journalist, was born in Unionville, Ashtabula County. When she was ten, her family moved to Arkansas. She was educated at Little Rock University. She was on the staff of the Arkansas *Democrat,* later owned and edited *The Arkansas Sketch Book,* and was president of the Arkansas Museum of Natural History and Antiquities. Her home in 1959 was Petit Jean Mountain, Ark.

The Daughter of a Republican, Chicago, 1900.
The Martyr; A Story of the Great Reforms, Chicago, 1900.
Justice to the Woman, Chicago, 1901.
At the Mercy of the State, Chicago, 1902.
An Uncrowned Queen; The Story of the Life of Frances E. Willard Told for Young People, Chicago, 1902.
Mammy; A Drama, New York, 1915.
Yesterday and Today in Arkansas; A Folio of Rare and Interesting Pictures . . . , Little Rock, 1917.
The Soul of Ann Rutledge, Abraham Lincoln's Romance, Philadelphia, 1919.
The Coming of the King, Indianapolis, 1921.
The Soul of Abe Lincoln, Philadelphia, 1923.
When Love Was Bold, [n.p.], 1924.
Booth and the Spirit of Lincoln; A Story of a Living Dead Man, Philadelphia, 1925.
Little Abe Lincoln, Philadelphia, 1926.
Lincoln's Mary and the Babies, Philadelphia, 1929.
Lighthorse Harry's Boy; The Boyhood of Robert E. Lee, Philadelphia, 1931.
The Heart of George Washington, a Simple Story of Great Loves, Philadelphia, 1932.
Little Dixie Devil, New York, 1937.
Hallerloogy's Ride with Santa Claus, [n.p.], 1939.
Other Worlds Than This, [n.p.], 1943.

BACHER, OTTO HENRY (March 31, 1856–Aug. 16, 1909), etcher and illustrator, was born in Cleveland, Cuyahoga County. In 1878 he went to Munich to study, and in 1880 he began working under Duveneck in Venice, where he was friendly with Whistler. In 1883 he returned to America, and except for a trip to London in 1885–86 he spent the remainder of his life in New York City and Bronxville. His only book was *With Whistler in Venice,* New York, 1908; because of objections by the executrix of Whistler's estate, letters by Whistler were withdrawn, and the book was reissued in 1909. DAB 1

BACKUS, EDWIN BURDETTE (Dec. 27, 1888–July 7, 1955), clergyman, was born in Blanchester, Clinton County. He graduated from the University of Michigan in 1909 and Meadville Theological Seminary in 1912, after which he served as pastor of Unitarian churches in various states. His writings include a devotional book, *The Pattern on the Mountain,* Boston, [1939]. WWW 3

BACKUS, EMMA HENRIETTE SCHIERMEYER (Mrs. Henry W.) (Dec. 18, 1877–), was born in Cincinnati, Hamilton County. She attended Cincinnati schools and has been active in civic affairs in that city. She has written pageants for several historical celebrations, an operetta, *Twilight Alley,* and several novels, e.g., *The Rose of Roses,* Boston, 1914. WWNAA 6

BACON, DELIA SALTER (Feb. 2, 1811–Sept. 2, 1859), whose name is associated with the biggest mare's-nest in the history of the English-speaking world, was born in Tallmadge, Summit County. She came from a long line of New England Puritans; her father, a Congregational missionary, had moved to the Western Reserve to found a farming settlement of fellow New Englanders which was to be unsurpassed, as Delia's biographer says, "for comfort, prosperity, intelligence, and morality." The project collapsed almost immediately and the Bacon family returned to Connecticut, where the father died in 1817. Delia was reared in a foster home until adolescence, and then she began a career as schoolmistress, which was as ill-fated as her father's Utopian project. She conducted a series of schools in Connecticut, New Jersey, and western New York State, all of which came to grief with dismaying rapidity. Failing in the schoolroom, she turned to writing as a means of earning a livelihood. In 1831 she entered her tale "Love's Martyr" in a contest conducted by the Philadelphia *Saturday Courier,* and won the first prize of $100. The fact that Edgar Allan Poe had entered five stories in the same contest, none of which won any money, is often recalled, either to illustrate the deplorable condition of taste at that time or to suggest that Miss Bacon was perhaps a better writer than she is usually given credit for being. However, any candid reader of Poe's five stories, which were later printed in the *Saturday Courier,* will admit that Poe, whose genius came only by fits and starts, deserved to lose the prize. Miss Bacon published, in addition to this story, at least two books of fiction: *Tales of the Puritans* and *The Bride of Fort Edward.* Neither work has any but historical interest. During her early womanhood Miss Bacon found a new way to put to practical account the ideas and information she had somehow collected despite an irregular education and frequent ill health. She became a lecturer to adult classes—one of the first women to follow the profession in America, or, for that matter,

England. Successful at first on a small scale, her lectures eventually became so popular that she delivered them in many Eastern cities, to large audiences of both sexes. Her favorite subject was history, with literature running a close second. It is said that she had a fine platform presence and that her lectures, always delivered without notes, brought fascination to even the most commonplace topic. When she concluded her 1852 season of lectures in Boston and Cambridge, the last phase of her life, for all biographical purposes the most important, began. No one seems to know how or when she first conceived the tremendous idea which was to dominate her every thought and action thenceforth. The notion that Shakespeare did not write the plays attributed to him, and that Francis Bacon did or at least helped to, was not original with her; it had been put forth as early as 1769 and again in 1848, and possibly Miss Bacon got her first inspiration from one of these sources. On the other hand, she may, in a fashion by no means unheard-of in intellectual history, have developed her idea independently, in entire ignorance that others had had it too. What *is* certain is that in 1852 she was writing to Emerson concerning her theory, and Emerson, while reserving judgment on the theory itself, was giving her every encouragement to proceed with her arcane researches. The next year, with money given her by a New York lawyer named Charles Butler, she went to England, the scene of the strange plot she was convinced she had uncovered, and with fanatical devotion and ingenuity proceeded to remold all available historical evidence to fit the pattern her theory required. Her theory was, in a few words, this: In the Elizabethan Age there had existed a secret society, composed of many of the most brilliant men of the age, which had worked out an elaborate political philosophy. Since this philosophy was at variance with everything the age stood for, it could not possibly be announced, or its existence even hinted at. Therefore, the members of the society decided to send it down to posterity in a sort of time capsule. The time capsule was the body of plays said to be written by William Shakespeare, who was actually, Miss Bacon asserted, no better than an ignorant lackey. In reality, these plays were composed by the conspirators, who couched their message to future ages in complicated ciphers, double meanings, quibbles, and all the other secretive paraphernalia in which the Elizabethans allegedly delighted. When the time was ripe, someone would be inspired to discover, beneath the seemingly innocent surface of "Shakespeare's" text, the whole revolutionary philosophy which had been too hot to handle in the early seventeenth century. And that foreordained discoverer, Miss Bacon knew, was to be none other than herself. She is commonly credited (if that is the right word) with propagating the so-called Baconian theory, by the terms of which Francis Bacon hid behind the name of Shakespeare, all of whose plays were really his. But the truth is that Miss Bacon did not hold to this idea. She was, of course, uncompromisingly anti-Shakespearean; the historical personage William Shakespeare could not have written those plays, therefore did not, and that was that. But she inclined to the view that it was a syndicate, not a lone individual, that composed the plays. Even Francis Bacon himself, whom she adored, was not man enough to do it single-handed. This interesting thesis is what she set forth to prove during her stay in England. Introduced by Emerson, she visited the Carlyles in Cheyne Row; on her first visit, when she blandly outlined her theory, Carlyle let out a shriek which, on her own authority, could be heard a mile away. But Carlyle liked her none the less; "we find her, with her modest shy dignity, with her solid character and strange enterprise, a real acquisition," he wrote to Emerson, and he did all he could, by counsel and letters of introduction, to further her project, though, he admitted, "truly there can [be] no madder" one. The letter he gave her to present to London publishers is a masterpiece of ambiguity: "She is a person of definite ideas, of conscious veracity in thought as well as word, and . . . probably no book written among us during these two years has been more seriously elaborated, and in all ways made the best of, than this of hers." For three years Miss Bacon lived, as she said, "as much alone with God and the dead as if I had been a departed spirit," and then it was time to proclaim her discovery to the world. She therefore addressed herself to Nathaniel Hawthorne, American consul at Liverpool, whose sister-in-law, Elizabeth Peabody, was among her closest friends back home. Would he read her manuscript, make inquiries among publishers, in short become her unpaid business agent? Hawthorne, retiring man though he was, burdened with his official duties as well as his own writing, replied cordially, and thus let himself in for what must have been, to put it mildly, one of the most trying episodes of his life. Like Emerson and Carlyle, he could not subscribe to her theory; he saw her for what she was—in his own excellent phrase, a "bewildered enthusiast." But either Delia Bacon had an attractive personality—which is seldom the case with monomaniacs of either sex but may well have been true of her—or those three gentlemen were capable of a patient tolerance far beyond the call even of nineteenth-century politeness. Perhaps it was both. Hawthorne, as a consequence, endured a barrage of interminable, repetitious, querulous, hysterical, chaotic letters from Miss Bacon, answered them as a gentleman should, and in the end found a publisher for her book, but only after he himself put up a considerable guarantee. He saw her only once, but the essential story of his contact with her may be read in his essay in *Our Old Home* called "Recollections of a Gifted Woman." While her negotiations with Hawthorne were proceeding, Miss Bacon moved to Stratford-on-Avon in preparation for her *coup de maître.* The ultimate key to the whole mystery, which she had patiently approached from many avenues, lay buried, according to the letters of Francis Bacon correctly interpreted, in Shakespeare's grave. All that was needed now was to open the tomb. The municipal and church officials in whom she confided humored her and gave her free run of the church. There is no weirder picture in English literary annals than that of Delia Bacon spending a whole night inside the dark church, debating whether or not to take the irrevocable step. The upshot was that she could not bring herself to do what she had so long known she must do; for there was a bare possibility that somehow her calculations were wrong, that Bacon was referring not to Shakespeare's grave but to his own, or Spenser's, or Raleigh's. And if this grave, once opened, proved not to contain the papers upon which the whole Gothic structure of her theory rested, she feared the consequences to her sanity. Ironically, she might just as well have gone on to that final act of grave robbery, for within a few months the mayor of Stratford wrote Hawthorne that Miss Bacon's reason had finally gone over the brink upon which it had been tottering so long. She was returned to America in 1858, and on Sept. 2 of the next year she died. Meanwhile, in 1857, her book, *The Philosophy of the Plays of Shakespeare Unfolded,* had been published in London, with a preface by Hawthorne in which he confessed he had not read the book. Nobody will blame him for this, because it is one of the most unintelligible books ever printed. But like many other books that are much oftener spoken of than read, it started a whole new chapter, the end of which is not in sight, in the history of human superstition.

Richard D. Altick

Tales of the Puritans . . . , New York, 1831.
The Bride of Fort Edward, Founded on an Incident of the Revolution, New York, 1839.
The Philosophy of the Plays of Shakespeare Unfolded, Boston, 1857.

BACON, LEONARD (Feb. 19, 1802–Dec. 24, 1881), clergyman, brother of Delia Bacon (q.v.), was born in Detroit, Mich., where his father, David Bacon, was a missionary. In 1804 Rev. Bacon returned to Connecticut. In 1807 he came to Ohio, where he surveyed and platted Tallmadge, Summit County, and erected a church. His dream of founding a Christian community in the wilderness was a failure, however, and he returned once more to Connecticut. Leonard Bacon thus spent about five years of his boyhood on the Ohio frontier. A prolific writer, he published many sermons and addresses. Perhaps his most influential book, however, was *Slavery Discussed in Occasional Essays . . . ,* New York, 1846.

BADGER, JOSEPH (Feb. 28, 1757–April 5, 1846), pioneer preacher, was born in Wilbraham, Mass. He graduated from Yale College in 1785 and was ordained a Congregational minister at Blandford, Mass., in 1787. He served the Blandford church until Oct. 24, 1800. He then "missionated" in the Western Reserve under the Connecticut Missionary Society (Congregational). After traveling 600 miles through unbroken forest, he arrived at Youngstown Dec. 28, 1800. He visited the scattered settlements, consisting of one to eleven families, despite the difficulties of distance and travel. He preached, gave counsel and encouragement and medical aid, distributed books, and promoted education. At Austinburg on Oct. 24, 1801, he organized the first Congregational church in the Reserve. In 1802 he brought his wife and six children to this settlement, and they established their home in a crude cabin. In 1803 his salary of $7 per week was reduced to $6. He continued his visitations, organized churches, and in 1805 preached for eighty days to the Wyandot Indians around Sandusky Bay. He preached, lectured on temperance, urged them to build schools and improve their land, and represented them before government authorities. Returning to the Indians in 1806, sponsored by the Western Missionary Society (Presbyterian), he established a mission and a school. In the winter of 1808–09 he raised $1,117 in New England for the Indian work. He made this cross-country journey on horseback seven times between 1800 and 1820. In 1810 he took his family to Ashtabula, where he gave half of his time to preaching; the other half he spent in nearby settlements. He served as chaplain and postmaster in the War of 1812. He organized the Ashtabula church Dec. 7, 1821; moved to Kirtland in 1822; organized the church in Gustavus in 1825 and remained there until 1835. The last decade of this fruitful life was spent at Maumee, Milton, and Perrysburg, where he died. He is buried in Fort Meigs Cemetery, Perrysburg. Joseph Badger's life portrays the struggle of early life in the Western Reserve—settlements six to fifteen miles apart; no roads, mud and snow often knee-deep; no transportation, no communication or exchange; no physicians; no church buildings, though services were held in cabins, barns, groves; and no schools. Salt and clothing were costly and difficult to obtain. Breadstuff was scarce until gristmills could be started. Cattle hair was used for weaving. Settlers built their own cabins and boats and made furniture, shoes, plows, and saddlebags. Bees furnished honey for sugar and wax for candles. Animals strayed for the lack of enclosure. And ever with these pioneers was the memory of the old settled country now so remote from them. The book below was edited by Henry Noble Day (Aug. 4, 1808–Jan. 12, 1890), member of Western Reserve College faculty, 1840–58, and author of a number of textbooks.

Clarence Stafford Gee

A Memoir of Rev. Joseph Badger; Containing an Autobiography, and Selections from His Private Journal and Correspondence, Hudson, 1851.

BAER, LIBBIE C. RILEY (Nov. 18, 1849–Feb. 27, 1929), was born in Bethel, Clermont County. She graduated from Clermont Academy in 1865. In November, 1867, she married Captain John M. Baer, and they moved to Appleton, Wis. She wrote verse and sketches for various periodicals and published a collection: *In the Land of Fancy, and Other Poems,* New York, [1902].

BAGBY, ARTHUR T. (April 4, 1879–Feb. 2, 1949), was born in St. Paul, Ky. He served in the Spanish-American War. In 1909 he settled in Portsmouth, where he spent the remainder of his life. He worked for more than thirty years as a railroad conductor. He wrote a novel: *Peter Burling, Pirate,* Philadelphia, [1924].

BAGGS, MAE LACY (Sept. 12, 1875–Sept. 9, 1922), was born in Independence, Mo. She was privately educated in the United States and France and traveled widely. In 1916 she married Thomas A. Baggs. Their residence was Toledo. She wrote several books, e.g., *Colorado, the Queen Jewel of the Rockies . . . ,* Boston, 1918. WWW 1

BAHMER, WILLIAM J. (Aug. 1, 1872–Nov. 21, 1953), journalist, was born in Bakersville, Coshocton County. He was editor of the Coshocton *Bulletin* for four years, worked on newspapers in New York and Pittsburgh, was in the advertising department of the Pennsylvania Railroad, and served as assessor of Allegheny County, Pa. He prepared for publication *Centennial History of Coshocton County . . . ,* 2 vols., Chicago, 1909.

BAILEY, HENRY TURNER (Dec. 9, 1865–Nov. 26, 1931), teacher, was born in Scituate, Mass. He was educated in Boston and also studied abroad. In 1917 he came to Cleveland, where he served in various capacities with the Cleveland School of Art, Cleveland Museum of Art, and John Huntington Polytechnic Institute. He edited *School Arts* and wrote a number of textbooks, technical studies of art education, and other books, e.g., *Yankee Notions,* Cambridge, [Mass.], 1929. WWW 1

BAILEY, RAE (July 24, 1879–1958), was born in Savannah, Ashland County. She worked in Washington, D. C., as secretary to Senator Pomerene, 1914–17; attended Palmer School of Chiropractic, Davenport, Iowa, 1917–19; practiced in Savannah, 1919–34; and was employed by the Council of Churches Board of Education, 1935–47. She died in Washington, D. C. She wrote a history of her native village and Clear Creek Township: *Old Keys; An Historical Sketch . . . ,* Washington, D. C., 1941.

BAINBRIDGE, LUCY SEAMAN (Jan. 18, 1842–Nov. 19, 1928), was born in Cleveland, Cuyahoga County. She was educated in Cleveland schools. During the Civil War she worked with the Potomac Division, helping the wounded. In 1866 she married Rev. William Folwell Bainbridge, a Baptist minister. While living in New York City, she was active in the Brooklyn City Mission Society and in the Woman's Branch, New York City Mission Society. Her death occurred in New York City.

'Round the World, Cleveland, 1881.

Round the World Letters, Boston, 1882.

Helping the Helpless in Lower New York, New York, [1917].

Jewels from the Orient . . . , New York, [1920].

Yesterdays, New York, [1924].

BAIRD, SAMUEL JOHN (Sept. 17, 1817–April 10, 1893), clergyman, was born in Newark, Licking County, the son of a Presbyterian clergyman. As a youth he assisted his father in editing *The Christian Herald* at Pittsburgh. He occupied various pulpits, most of them in the South. He is important in the history of Presbyterianism, not as a preacher but as a scholar and ecclesiastical historian. He was a prolific writer, and the following list of his works is selective. The *Collection* became an unofficial statute book of the Presbyterian Church in America. He died in West Clifton Forge, Va.

A Collection of the Acts, Deliverances, and Testimonies of the Supreme Judicatory of the Presbyterian Church from Its Origin in America to the Present Time . . . , Philadelphia, 1856.

The Socinian Apostasy of the English Presbyterian Churches . . . , Philadelphia, 1857.

The First Adam and the Second. The Elohim Revealed in the Creation and Redemption of Man . . . , Philadelphia, 1860.

A Rejoinder to the Princeton Review, upon the Elohim Revealed, Touching the Doctrine of Imputation and Kindred Topics, Philadelphia, 1860.

A History of the New School, and of the Questions Involved in the Disruption of the Presbyterian Church in 1838, Philadelphia, 1868.

BAKER, ALBERT RUFUS (March 24, 1858–April 5, 1911), ophthalmologist, was born in Salem, Pa. He earned an M.D. degree at Western Reserve University in 1879, and he did postgraduate work in medicine in New York and Europe, 1881–83. In 1888 he joined the faculty of the Cleveland College of Physicians and Surgeons. He edited the *Cleveland Medical Gazette,* 1885–96, and published one book: *Coughs, Cold and Catarrh . . . ,* Cleveland, 1904. WWW 1

BAKER, ARTHUR MULFORD (Oct. 11, 1880–Sept. 22, 1941), clergyman, was born in Wapakoneta, Auglaize County. He graduated from Defiance College in 1906, from McCormick Theological Seminary in 1909, and from Indiana University (Ph.D.) in 1928. He served as pastor of various Presbyterian churches, 1909–24, and after 1924 did editorial work on Sunday school publications. He wrote many religious books and articles and *Hoofbeats in the Wilderness; A Tale of the Indiana Territory before the Coming of Permanent Settlers,* New York, 1930. WWW 1

BAKER, CORNELIA (June 16, 1855–March 12, 1930), was born in Jackson County. She was on the editorial staff of the Chicago *Daily News* and contributed stories and verse to various magazines. Her books include *Coquo & the King's Children,* Chicago, 1902. WWW 1

BAKER, JAMES HEATON (May 6, 1829–May 25, 1913), was born in Monroe, Butler County. He grew up in Lebanon and at his grandfather's home near Middletown. After graduating from Ohio Wesleyan University in 1852, he purchased the *Scioto Gazette* in Chillicothe. He was active in the formation of the Republican Party in Ohio and was elected Secretary of State in 1855. In 1857 he emigrated to Minnesota, where he also was prominent in Republican councils, and in 1859 he was elected Secretary of State there. He served during the Civil War as colonel of the 10th Minnesota Volunteers. His regiment took part in the Indian War in Minnesota and later was on provost duty in St. Louis. After the war he held various public posts. His historical studies were largely an avocation which he pursued during his later years in Mankato, Minn. Several of his papers and addresses, published by the Minnesota Historical Society, are not listed below.

A Song of Friendship. An Elegy on the Death of Charles Scheffer . . . , St. Paul, 1877.

Lives of the Governors of Minnesota, St. Paul, 1908.

BAKER, MAGDALENA D. H. (1897–), was born in Washington Court House, Fayette County. She later lived in Ironton and Cincinnati. She published a collection of poems: *Gleanings from Life,* Cincinnati, [1931].

BAKER, MAY ALLREAD (April 17, 1897–), was born in Darke County. She has published numerous poems in farm magazines and religious periodicals and a collection of verse: *Willow Brook Farm,* Elgin, Ill., [1946].

BAKER, MELYN D. (Jan. 11, 1800–March 31, 1852), clergyman, was born in Essex County, N. J. In 1802 his father moved to a farm near Cincinnati and in 1805 to Enon, Clark County. He became a minister of the Christian Church in 1841 and preached in Dayton and the surrounding area. A selection of his writings was edited by John Ellis (q.v.).

Memoir of Melyn D. Baker, with Extracts from His Correspondence and Manuscripts, Springfield, 1853.

BAKER, NAAMAN RIMMON (Feb. 2, 1868–), educator, was born in Lima, Allen County. He was educated at Mt. Morris College, Ill., and Lineville College, Ala. He was principal of Chesterfield Academy, S. C., 1891–95, president of Citronelle College, Ala., 1895–99, and afterward a teacher and school superintendent in the Alabama public schools.

Constancy and Other Poems, Mt. Morris, Ill., 1894.

BAKER, NEWTON DIEHL (Dec. 3, 1871–Dec. 25, 1937), lawyer and public official, was born in Martinsburg, W. Va., but spent much of his life in Cleveland. He was associated with Mayor Tom Loftin Johnson (q.v.) and as city solicitor led the fight against the traction companies. In 1911 and again in 1913 Baker was elected mayor of Cleveland and sought to carry out the aims of his predecessor. In 1916 President Wilson named him Secretary of War. The relationship between these two reserved, idealistic liberals was intimate. In 1920 Baker returned to Cleveland and resumed his law practice. His views grew increasingly conservative, and his opposition to the New Deal during its early years was pronounced. He died at his home in Shaker Heights and is buried in Lake View Cemetery, Cleveland. He published numerous speeches, magazine articles, and one book, *Why We Went to War,* New York, [1936]. DAB 22

BALDUS, SIMON ALEXANDER (1872–Jan. 20, 1957), editor, was born in Cincinnati, Hamilton County, where he attended St. Xavier School and Xavier University. In 1907 he moved to Chicago. He was managing editor of *Extension* magazine, 1907–51. He wrote many articles on economics and one book: *The New Capitalism,* Chicago, 1923.

BALDWIN, ALPHA WRIGHT (1866–1929), was born in Rock Creek, Ashtabula County. His death occurred in Alliance. His avocation was writing poems and songs, which were collected in *The Songs of a Carpenter,* [Alliance, 1929].

BALDWIN, CHARLES CANDEE (Dec. 2, 1834–Feb. 2, 1895), lawyer and judge, was born in Middletown, Conn. His family moved to Elyria when he was five months old but returned to Connecticut in 1847 when the father died. After graduating from Harvard Law School in 1857, Baldwin returned to Cleveland to practice. He was elected circuit court judge in 1884 and served on the bench until his death. He was a founder of the Western Reserve Historical Society and was also a leader in moving Western Reserve College from Hudson to Cleveland. He was a keen student of regional history and archaeology, and wrote many genealogical works, papers, and addresses that are not listed below.

Relics of the Mound Builders, [Cleveland, 1874].

Early Maps of Ohio and the West, Cleveland, 1875.

Notice of Historical and Pioneer Societies in Ohio, Cleveland, 1875.

The Iroquois in Ohio . . . , [Cleveland, 1878?].

Indian Migration in Ohio . . . , [n.p., 1879].

Memorial of Colonel Charles Whittlesey . . . , [Cleveland, 1887].

History of Man in Ohio . . . , [n.p., 1890?].

BALDWIN, CHARLES JACOB (Aug. 10, 1841–April 13, 1921), clergyman, born in Charleston, N. Y., graduated from Madison (Colgate) University in 1864 and Rochester Theological Seminary in 1868. Ordained to the Baptist ministry, he served churches in Chelsea, Mass., and Rochester, N. Y., before coming to Granville in 1886. He published a volume of sermons in 1895 and *The First American and Other Sunday Evening Studies in Biography,* Granville, 1911. OBB

BALDWIN, ELBERT FRANCIS (March 10, 1857–Sept. 26, 1927), journalist, was born in Cleveland, Cuyahoga County. After graduating from Williams College in 1884, he studied at the University of Berlin for two years. He served on the editorial staffs of the *Independent,* New York *Mail and Express,* and *Outlook.* His death occurred in Geneva, Switzerland. He wrote *The World War; How It Looks to the Nations Involved and What It Means to Us,* New York, 1914. WWW 1

BALDWIN, HARMON ALLEN (June 3, 1869–March 11, 1936), clergyman, was born in Pierpont, Ashtabula County. After attending Mount Union College, he became a Methodist evangelist in 1890; he also served churches in Pennsylvania, West Virginia, Ohio, and Georgia. He wrote several books on religious themes, e.g., *Holiness and the Human Element,* Louisville, Ky., [1919]. WWW 1

BALDWIN, WILLIAM HENRY (July 16, 1851–Sept. 26, 1923), was born in Youngstown, Mahoning County. He was associated with First National Bank, Youngstown, 1877–1900, and was also an executive of several steel companies. He retired in 1901 and devoted the rest of his life to social work. After his retirement he lived in Washington, D. C. He published several articles and pamphlets on tuberculosis and family problems and one book: *Family Desertion and Non-support Laws . . .* , Washington, D. C., 1904. WWW 1

BALL, ALICE ELIZA (1867–April 25, 1948), educator, was born in Cincinnati, Hamilton County. She taught at Hathaway-Brown School, Cleveland. Her death occurred in New York City. She wrote several books on ornithology, e.g., *Bird Biographies,* New York, 1923.

BALL, EUSTACE HALE (Nov. 4, 1881–April 20, 1931), was born in Gallipolis, Gallia County. He graduated from the University of Cincinnati in 1903 and later studied at Harvard and the Boston Conservatory of Music. A gifted violinist and painter, he also wrote for the New York *Sun* for several years. He died in Laguna Beach, Calif., where he had moved about three months before. He wrote several syndicated newspaper serials, fictional versions of movies, and *Bubbles from Gotham's Pierian Spring,* New York, 1912.

BALL, FRANK CLAYTON (Nov. 24, 1857–March 19, 1943), manufacturer, was born in Greensburg, Summit County. He settled in Muncie, Ind., in 1888, was president of Ball Bros. Co., and was associated with other industrial firms. His autobiography was privately published: *Memoirs . . .* , Muncie, 1937. WWW 2

BALLANTINE, WILLIAM GAY (Dec. 7, 1848–Jan. 10, 1937), educator, was born in Washington, D. C. He graduated from Marietta College in 1868 and Union Seminary in 1872; he also studied at the University of Leipzig. He served on the Oberlin College faculty, 1878–91, and as president of Oberlin, 1891–96. Besides publishing the titles below and several logic textbooks, he edited *The Oberlin Jubilee* (1883), a collection of speeches and other material relative to the fiftieth anniversary of the college.

Jehovah's Champion . . . , Oberlin, 1890.
Christ in the Gospel of Mark, New York, [1898].
Religious Education for the Coming Social Order, Boston, [1917].
The Young Man for Jerusalem, Boston, 1921.
Understanding the Bible, Springfield, Mass., [1925].
Discovering Jesus, New York, [1927].
Peggy in the Park, Verses . . . , Springfield, Mass., [1933].
Biographical Notes, Together with Selected Addresses, Essays & Miscellaneous Poems, Stamford, Conn., 1939.

BALLARD, HARLAN HOGE (May 26, 1853–Feb. 18, 1934), was born in Athens, Athens County. After graduating from Williams College he made his home in Massachusetts. He served as principal of Lenox High School and of Lenox Academy, and as librarian of the Berkshire Athaneum and Museum. In addition to the titles listed below, he wrote several language and science textbooks and translated Virgil's *Aeneid* into English hexameters.

Pieces to Speak and How to Speak Them, New York, [1879].
Handbook of the St. Nicholas Agassiz Association, Pittsfield, Mass., 1882.
Open Sesame; One Hundred Answers in Rhyme to William Bellamy's Century of Charades, Boston, 1896.
Re-open Sesame. Rhymed Acrostics Answering Bellamy's "Second Century" . . . , Boston, 1897.
The Tiler's Jewel . . . , Boston, 1921.
Adventures of a Librarian, New York, 1929.

BALLARD, WILLIS TODHUNTER (Dec. 13, 1903–), was born in Cleveland, Cuyahoga County. He attended Westtown Preparatory School in Pennsylvania and Wilmington College. After working as an electrical engineer and editing an electrical trade magazine, he shifted to free-lance writing. He now lives in Sherman Oaks, Calif. He has published fiction in almost all national magazines and has written numerous Western stories and mysteries. Some of his mysteries were published under the pen name Harrison Hunt, e.g., *Murder Picks the Jury,* New York, 1947.

BALLOU, ELSIE AULTMAN (April 4, 1894–), was born near Millersburg, Holmes County. After studying at Oberlin College, she taught for five years in Akron and Warren elementary schools. She graduated from the School of Religious Education, Boston University; served as educational director, First Presbyterian Church, Boston; and taught in the Dayton schools, while her husband, Luther Ballou, a Congregational minister, was serving a pastorate in that city. She now lives in Whitesboro, N. Y. She has published poems and articles in various periodicals and has published a collection of verse: *Highways,* Boston, 1931.

BANCROFT, HUBERT HOWE (May 5, 1832–March 2, 1918), historian, publisher, and book collector, was born in Granville,

Licking County. He was born 200 years after his earliest American ancestors landed in Massachusetts. His parents, Azariah Ashley Bancroft and Lucy Howe Bancroft, had come to Ohio from Granville, Mass. In his youth Hubert learned thrift and industry and other good Puritan traits. Lucy was a schoolteacher, but her son's formal education stopped at the local academy. However, he is reported to have read the Bible at the age of three which, as he said, saved him much reading of the book later. He hated household and barnyard chores, but loved the fruit trees, Saturday night nutcracking, and attempts at riding the unbroken colts. In 1847–48 he devoted himself to studies in preparation for college, but soon renounced these endeavors in favor of a business career, which began when, at the age of sixteen, he went to Buffalo, N. Y., to work in the bookstore of his brother-in-law, George H. Derby. He worked in the bindery and the countinghouse and was a salesman on the road, picking up his books at Mansfield and peddling them to country merchants all over Ohio. When the gold fever reached its height in 1852, Bancroft sailed for California to be followed by a shipment of Derby's books worth some $5,000. With his father, who had gone to the gold regions in 1850, Bancroft tried his hand at mining until his books arrived. Then he learned of Derby's death and sold out the entire shipment for the benefit of his sister. He obtained on credit a small stock of books and stationery which he took to Crescent City and enjoyed a modestly successful venture. In 1855 he returned to Granville, but the hurly-burly of the West was now too much a part of him and he soon was back in San Francisco launched on an independent career in bookselling that was to bring him fame and fortune. To replenish his stock of books, he made frequent trips to the East, and on one of these he met and married Emily Ketchum. In 1859 he took into equal partnership his brother Albert L. Bancroft, whose name was used thereafter to designate the firm. During the Civil War a great volume of business developed, and receipts were further increased by a windfall that enabled the firm to buy its books in the East for depreciated paper and sell them in the West for gold. Frequently moving into larger and better quarters, expanding operations in printing and allied fields, and associating with himself capable and dependable assistants, Bancroft achieved great business success. With his wife he journeyed several times to Europe, and whenever opportunity offered he paid visits to Ohio. "Anyone who deals in books runs the risk of becoming a collector," significantly remarks J. W. Caughey, Bancroft's biographer. Few collectors, however, have been privileged to gather books on so grand a scale or to so practical an end. His collection began in 1859, when he was publishing a Pacific Coast handbook. As a convenience he brought together all the items in stock on Western history, expressing surprise to find that they numbered more than half a hundred titles; he would certainly have been incredulous at the thought that during the next quarter-century he would build up a collection of some 60,000 volumes on this subject. Yet to this task he began to devote his energies, almost to the exclusion of business affairs. He searched the bookshops of San Francisco, kept an eye on the auction houses, took over private collections; and later he scoured Boston, New York, Philadelphia, Washington, London, Paris, and other book centers. Books cascaded on cascades of books. At auction he secured large portions of the Andrade, Fischer, Squier, and Ramirez collections, purchases at the latter sale alone amounting to some $30,000. Agents all over the world were responsive to his requests, new books were acquired on publication, and catalogues of antiquarian booksellers yielded many treasures. One of the great additions to the library was the gift of the family of General Mariano G. Vallejo. Continuing his avid interest in books, Bancroft started acquiring vast quantities of manuscripts and newspapers, the latter collection itself finally exceeding 5,000 volumes. In its day and for decades after it was formed, no library existed that could compare with Bancroft's for the history of Western America. He meant to make good use of it. In order to create a history of Western America based on original sources, Bancroft became a reader. But it was soon apparent that to harness the knowledge in his 60,000 volumes would require a dozen Methuselahs; time would not wait, it must be outdistanced. Applying big-business methods to scholarship, he found the way. He employed a corps of readers, note-takers, copyists, indexers, and writers who, some years and $100,000 later, had cubbyholed at finger-tip touch the sum total of recorded knowledge on any given topic at any given time for any given place on Bancroft's half of the American continent. Originally he planned to do all the writing —at least the final writing—of his histories. But again time obtruded. Of the 39 thick volumes of the *Works*—comprising some 30,000 pages, including voluminous documentation in small type—Bancroft outlined and supervised the whole, rewrote considerable portions, and was sole author of approximately ten of the volumes. His librarian, H. L. Oak, wrote an equal number, and William Nemos wrote five volumes, as did Frances Fuller Victor (q.v.). Although the mass production was harshly criticized, there was nothing reprehensible about it unless it was the failure to give credit to the collaborators which, primarily for commercial reasons, was not done. Bancroft had a genius for simple, clear, and exact writing, and his guiding hand can be seen throughout large portions of the volumes that were not his personal assignment. The historian's devotion to his literary task was demonstrated when he declined in 1875 the Republican nomination for Congress, saying that 10,000 stood ready to serve their country, but no one would take up his work should he abandon it. In 1876—Emily having died in 1869—he took a second wife, Matilda Coley Griffing of New Haven, Conn. They had four children—Paul, Griffing, Philip, and Lucy. She was an ideal historian's wife, not tempting him to social frivolity, but providing encouragement in his work. The 39 volumes known as the *Works* comprise the following: *Native Races* (5 vols.), *History of Central America* (3 vols.), *History of Mexico* (6 vols.), *History of North Mexican States and Texas* (2 vols.), *History of Arizona and New Mexico* (1 vol.), *History of California* (7 vols.), *History of Nevada, Colorado, and Wyoming* (1 vol.), *History of Utah* (1 vol.), *History of the Northwest Coast* (2 vols.), *History of Oregon* (2 vols.), *History of Washington, Idaho, and Montana* (1 vol.), *History of British Columbia* (1 vol.), *History of Alaska* (1 vol.), *California Pastoral* (1 vol.), *California Inter Pocula* (1 vol.), *Popular Tribunals* (2 vols.), *Essays and Miscellany* (1 vol.), and *Literary Industries* (1 vol.). The first volume appeared in 1875 and the last in 1890. As perhaps the most gigantic literary undertaking of the nineteenth century, the creation of the histories had been remarkable, but no less so was the marketing of them. Taking on a project that would have seemed to most publishers downright forbidding at best, the historian devised a system of subscription canvassing so effective that scarcely a literate home in the West lacked its volume or set of Bancroft. This success is the more amazing when considered in relation to the cost of the sets, which ran from $175 to $390, depending on the binding. Sales exceeded a quarter-million volumes with a gross return of more than one million dollars. Reception of the monumental series at the hands of the critics and the public was mixed. Many of those who expressed themselves most forcibly against it had no qualifications whatever to judge its value, but unfortunately wielded wide influence. Others, who ordinarily would have been qualified, were animated by animosity or jealousy. Bancroft had not been a fence-straddler, and in taking a stand on controversial matters he laid himself open to the violent jabs of those whose convictions differed from his own. On many points of disagreement a further sifting of the facts has vindicated Bancroft's views, and today it is generally recognized that he rendered a more important service than any other American historian and probably accomplished the greatest feat of historiography since Thucydides. Bancroft continued writing until he was 84, producing the *Chronicles of the Builders* series, *Resources of Mexico* (1893), *The New Pacific* (1900), *The Book of Wealth* (1909–10), *Retrospection, Political and Personal* (1912), and *In These Latter Days* (1917). In all, he turned out more than sixty volumes, mostly on weighty matters, but handled with a charm and twinkling of humor that give us history at once reliable and readable. How much would have been lost to us without him is as incalculable as it would be appalling. For he has left not only his histories, but also his vast collection of source materials—the Bancroft Library of the University of California—an enduring monument to his fame and a living workshop for the scores of successors whose duty it will be to explore further particular avenues of Western history to which Bancroft pointed the way. But, as he prophesied: "He who shall come after me will scarcely be able to undermine my work by laying another and deeper foundation." The bibliography below is, of necessity, extremely selective.

Charles Eberstadt

The Works of Hubert Howe Bancroft . . . , 39 vols., San Francisco, 1882–90.

The Early American Chroniclers, San Francisco, 1883.

The Book of the Fair . . . , Chicago, 1893.

The New Pacific, New York, 1900.

Some Cities and San Francisco, and Resurgam, New York, 1907.

Retrospection, Political and Personal, New York, 1912.

Modern Fallacies . . . , New York, 1915.

Why a World Centre of Industry at San Francisco Bay?, New York, 1916.

In These Latter Days, Chicago, 1917.

BANKS, LOUIS ALBERT (Nov. 12, 1855–June 17, 1933), clergyman, born in Corvallis, Oreg., was pastor of First Methodist Church, Cleveland, in the late 1890s. He published many sermons and religious books, e.g., *Heavenly Trade-Winds,* Cincinnati, 1895.

BANNON, HENRY TOWNE (June 5, 1867–Sept. 6, 1950), lawyer, was born in Scioto County. He graduated from the University of Michigan in 1889, read law, and was admitted to the Ohio bar in 1891. He served in the 59th and 60th Congresses. He practiced law in Portsmouth. A big-game hunter, he contributed many articles to outdoor periodicals. He also published *Scioto Sketches* . . . , Chicago, 1920.

BANTA, MELISSA ELIZABETH RIDDLE (March 27, 1834–1907), was born in Cheviot near Cincinnati, Hamilton County. When she was fourteen, her family moved to Covington, Ky., where she attended the Female Collegiate Institute. At the age of seventeen she married Joseph I. Perrin of Vicksburg; he died of yellow fever the following year. When she returned North, her father moved to Bloomington, Ind., where she married David D. Banta in 1856. They lived in Franklin, Ind.

Songs of Home, Menasha, Wis., 1895.

BARBEE, WILLIAM J. (1816–Oct. 27, 1892), physician, was born in Winchester, Ky. He attended Miami University, studied medicine under Daniel Drake, and later practiced in Cincinnati, 1836–46. After leaving Ohio, he was a schoolteacher and minister of the Christian Church in Kentucky, Tennessee, and Missouri. Besides a book on geology and several on religious themes, he wrote *The Cotton Question,* New York, 1866.

BARDOLY, LOUIS STEPHEN (1893–), physician, born in Hungary, came to Cleveland in 1921. He practiced medicine there until 1945, when he left to become director of a hospital at Roslyn, N. Y. He wrote several plays which were produced in Cleveland, including a play defending mercy-killing: *Personal Tragedy* . . . , Cleveland, 1936.

BARDON, MINNA FEIBLEMAN (July 18, 1900–), was born in Cincinnati, Hamilton County. She attended Cincinnati public schools and the University of Cincinnati. Wife of Emanuel Bardon, a printer, she has written advertising for several Cincinnati department stores and agencies, edited *Writer's Digest,* and published fiction and articles in periodicals. She has also published a number of romances and mystery novels, e.g., *The Case of the Dead Grandmother,* New York, [1937].

BAREIS, GEORGE F. (July 23, 1852–Jan. 7, 1932), was born near Bremen, Fairfield County. In 1854 he removed with his parents to Empire Mills near Canal Winchester. He was educated in district and public schools. In the fall of 1868 he settled in Canal Winchester, where he conducted a successful lumber business. He was an enthusiastic student of history and archaeology; he wrote *History of Madison Township, Including Groveport and Canal Winchester, Franklin County, Ohio,* Canal Winchester, 1902.

BARKER, JOHN MARSHALL (Oct. 1, 1849–Feb., 1928), clergyman and educator, was born in Fredericktown, Knox County. He graduated from Ohio Wesleyan University in 1874 and Boston University (B.D., 1877; Ph.D., 1892) and was ordained a Methodist minister in 1876. He served churches in Massachusetts, 1876–78, Mexico, 1878–85, and New York State, 1885–89. After teaching one year at Ohio Wesleyan, he joined the sociology faculty at Boston University in 1899 and taught there until his retirement in 1921. He died at Newton Centre, Mass.

History of Ohio Methodism; A Study in Social Science, Cincinnati, 1898.

The Saloon Problem and Social Reform, Boston, 1905.

The Social Gospel and the New Era, New York, 1919.

BARKER, LAURA EMILY COOKE (June 9, 1866–April 28, 1927), was born in Sandusky, Erie County. Her father, Pitt Cooke, was associated with the banking firm organized by his brother, Jay Cooke. When Jay Cooke & Co. failed in 1873, Pitt Cooke returned to Sandusky and recouped much of his lost fortune through real estate. Laura Cooke married Franklyn S. Barker. She died in Erie County.

Society Silhouettes . . . , Cleveland, 1898.

Mezzotints, Wausau, 1900.

The Immutable Law, Aurora, N. Y., 1921.

BARKER, MARY LUCRETIA (Mrs. M. L. B. Franklin) (Aug. 5, 1912–), was born in Youngstown, Mahoning County. She attended Ohio Wesleyan University and Youngstown College. Since her marriage in 1946, she has lived in Denver, Colo. Her poems, most of them published under her maiden name, have appeared in various periodicals; and she has also published several collections, e.g., *Voices That Sang,* Cedar Rapids, Iowa, [1940].

BARNARD, WILLIAM FRANCIS (c.1865–May 21, 1947), advertising executive, moved to Cleveland from Chicago in 1917. He published two books on advertising and two collections of poetry, e.g., *The Tongues of Toil, and Other Poems,* Chicago, 1911.

BARNES, FAYE KING. See Faye King.

BARNES, GILBERT HOBBS (March 30, 1889–Aug. 12, 1945), educator, was born in Lincoln, Neb. He attended Ohio Wesleyan University for two years and graduated from the University of Michigan in 1912; he later earned his doctorate at the University of Michigan in 1929. He was professor of economics at Ohio Wesleyan, 1920–45. He edited the letters of Theodore Weld (q.v.) and wrote a book designed to show that the antislavery movement originated in Ohio: *The Antislavery Impulse, 1830–1844,* New York, [1933]. WWW 2

BARNES, JEREMIAH ROOT (1808–1900), clergyman, was born in Stonington, Conn. After graduating from Yale Divinity School in 1836, he served Congregational churches in Indiana and Minnesota until 1886, when he settled in Marietta. The last fourteen years of his life were spent in that community.

Jephthah and His Daughter and Other Poems, New York, 1887.

BARNES, LEMUEL CALL (Nov. 6, 1854–July 18, 1938), clergyman, was born in Kirtland, Lake County. He graduated from Kalamazoo College in 1875 and from Newton Theological Institution in 1878. Ordained a Baptist minister in 1878, he served as a pastor in Minnesota, Pennsylvania, and Massachusetts. He retired from the ministry in 1924. He died in Yonkers, N. Y. A prolific writer, he wrote a number of books and articles on religious and historical subjects, e.g., *Missions to the Heathen,* New York, [1910]. WWW 1

BARNES, WALTER (July 29, 1880–), educator, was born in Barnesville, Belmont County. He graduated from West Virginia University in 1905 and New York University (Ph.D.) in 1930. He taught English in West Virginia and New York colleges, 1907–47. He now lives in West Bradenton, Fla. Besides articles on educational subjects and textbooks on English, he has written *The Photoplay as Literary Art,* Newark, N. J., 1936. WW 27

BARNES, MRS. WILLIAM C. See Faye King.

BARNEY, ELIAM E. (Oct. 14, 1807–1880), was born in Jefferson County, N. Y. After attending Lowville Academy and Union Academy, Belleville, N. Y., he graduated from Union College in 1831. In 1833 he moved to Ohio, where he taught for six months at Granville College, was principal of Dayton Academy, 1834–38, and of Cooper Female Academy, 1845–51. He then entered business and established the Dayton Car Works. Realizing that the forests were rapidly disappearing, he became interested in encouraging the growing of catalpa trees.

Facts and Information in Relation to the Catalpa Tree . . . , Dayton, 1878.

Additional Facts and Information in Relation to the Catalpa Tree . . . , Dayton, [1879?].

BARNITZ, ALBERT TROVILLO SIDERS (March 10, 1833– ?), was born in Everett, Pa. He was brought to Ohio in his infancy when his parents settled in Crawford County. He attended Kenyon College, 1853–54. In the late 1850s he was a clerk in the publishing firm of Mack R. Barnitz, Cincinnati. He must have lived in Cincinnati for some time before the appearance of his volume of verse in 1857, for that work is dedicated to the Cincinnati publisher H. M. Rulison, who is referred to therein as an early friend. According to Coggeshall, Barnitz was teaching elocution and studying law in Cleveland in 1860.

The Mystic Delvings, Cincinnati, 1857.

BARONE, ALLEN G. (Oct. 28, 1867–Nov. 17, 1947), was born in Homer Township, Medina County. He attended district schools and Ohio Business College, Mansfield, after which he taught for a time at Heidelberg College. He wrote *Cosmogony, A Study of the Origin of the World,* Boston, 1937.

BARR, GRANVILLE WALTER (Oct. 25, 1860–March 29, 1939), physician and journalist, was born in Medway, Clark County. He attended Asbury College, 1877–80, Rush Medical College, 1882–83, and Jefferson Medical College, 1883–84. As a student at Asbury he was active in journalism, and in 1880 he and Lucien Stephens compiled *The Songs of Asbury University.* He taught at the College of Physicians and

Surgeons, Keokuk, Iowa, 1890–98, and at Highland Park College of Pharmacy in Des Moines, 1915–16. As a journalist he was on the staff of the Keokuk *Gate City,* 1899–1902, and the Keokuk *Standard,* 1902–10. He wrote many articles and stories for magazines and medical journals. His books include *Shacklett, the Evolution of a Statesman,* New York, 1901. WW 13

BARRETT, BENJAMIN FISKE (June 24, 1808–Aug. 6, 1892), Swedenborgian preacher and writer, was born in Dresden, Maine. He graduated from Harvard Divinity School in 1838 and was ordained as a Unitarian minister. He had already become interested in the New Church Society, and in 1840 he became a New Church preacher in New York City. From 1848 to 1850 he was with the New Church Society in Cincinnati. The remainder of his life was spent in Philadelphia and Germantown. His numerous publications include *Life of Emanuel Swedenborg . . . ,* New York, 1841.

BARRETT, DON CARLOS (April 22, 1868–Jan. 19, 1943), educator, was born in Spring Valley, Greene County. He graduated from Earlham College in 1889 and Harvard University (Ph.D.) in 1901 and also studied in Germany. He served on the faculties of Earlham College, Harvard University, and Haverford College. Besides many articles in journals, he published *The Greenback and Resumption of Specie Payment,* 1862–1879, Cambridge, Mass., 1931. WWW 2

BARRETT, EDNA DUERINGER (Sept. 15, 1896–Nov. 4, 1947), was born in Dennison, Tuscarawas County. A resident of Cleveland for many years, she died in Alliance. She published *Mrs. Colletti, and Other Poems,* Los Angeles, [1936].

BARRETT, FRED W. (Nov. 15, 1858–March 25, 1951), publisher, was born in Oxford, Butler County. His parents moved to Springfield in 1860, and he spent the rest of his life in that community. He was president of Barrett Brothers, publishers of legal forms. He wrote *From a Diary,* Springfield, 1934.

BARRETT, GEORGE (Dec. 6, 1796–Aug. 18, 1875), manufacturer, was born in Danby, Vt. In 1839 he moved to Delaware, where he operated a woolen mill, and in 1843 he moved to Spring Valley, Greene County, where he built a mill. He was a member of the Society of Friends and a firm abolitionist. When his house burned, he determined to erect one that could not burn. Following an account in a New York newspaper and improvising when necessary, he erected a house of concrete, probably the first such building in Ohio. His book describing the construction is certainly one of the first do-it-yourself books.

The Poor Man's Home, and Rich Man's Palace . . . , Cincinnati, 1854.

BARRETT, JOHN PRESSLEY (Feb. 5, 1852–May 1, 1924), clergyman, was born in Isle of Wight County, Va. A minister of the Christian Church, he served churches in Montgomery County, 1903–19, and also edited the *Herald of Gospel Liberty,* published in Dayton. He died in Winston-Salem, N. C. He published his autobiography, *Forty Years on the Firing Line; Or, Scenes, Incidents, and Experiences along the Way of a Soldier of the Cross . . . ,* Dayton, [1914]. OBB

BARRETT, JOSEPH HARTWELL (April 15, 1824–April 9, 1910), journalist, was born in Ludlow, Vt. In 1857 he moved to Cincinnati, where he served on the *Daily Gazette,* 1857–61, and on the *Daily Chronicle and Times,* 1868–79. His biography of Lincoln was enlarged and reissued in 1864 and again in 1865. He died at Loveland.

Life of Abraham Lincoln . . . , Cincinnati, 1860.

Abraham Lincoln and the Presidency, 2 vols., Cincinnati, 1904.

BARRETT, LEONARD ANDREW (Nov. 1, 1874–Feb. 27, 1945), clergyman, was born in Covington, Ky. He graduated from Centre College in 1898 and McCormick Theological Seminary in 1900. Ordained in the Presbyterian ministry, he served a church in Cleveland, 1903–11, and he spent his last years in Wooster. His writings include *Essence of Christianity,* New York, [1929]. WWW 2

BARRETT, SELAH HIBBARD (Feb. 24, 1822–1883), clergyman, was born in Rutland, Meigs County. He joined the Free Will Baptist Church in 1838 and soon afterward, though almost entirely self-educated, he began teaching school. In 1845 he began preaching; although he traveled as an evangelist throughout the Eastern states and Canada, Rutland remained his home. At one time he operated a drugstore there.

The Journal of Selah Hibbard Barrett, Pomeroy, 1847.

Autobiography . . . , Rutland, [1872].

BARRINGER, EDWIN C. (Sept. 19, 1892–), journalist, was born in Sandusky, Erie County, but attended public schools in Fremont, where his parents moved in 1900. He attended Case Institute of Technology and Western Reserve University, worked on Cleveland and Columbus newspapers, 1912–17, was an associate editor of Penton Publishing Co., Cleveland, 1917–38, and in 1938 became executive secretary of the Institute of Scrap Iron and Steel. He published a pamphlet on scrap steel: *The Story of Scrap . . .* , New York, [1939], which he enlarged and republished in 1947. WWCI 8

BARROWS, ELIJAH PORTER (Jan. 5, 1805–Sept. 14, 1888), clergyman and educator, born in Mansfield, Conn., graduated from Yale University in 1826. He was a school principal in Hartford, Conn., 1826–31, was ordained to the Presbyterian ministry in 1832, and served as pastor of the First Free Presbyterian Church, New York City, 1832–37. He served on the faculty of Western Reserve College, 1837–52, Andover Theological Seminary, 1853–66, and Oberlin Theological Seminary, 1871-80.

A View of the American Slavery Question, New York, 1836.
Memoir of Everton Judson, Boston, 1852.
Sacred Geography, and Antiquities . . . , New York, [1872].

BARROWS, JOHN HENRY (July 11, 1847–June 3, 1902), clergyman and educator, born in Medina, Mich., served pastorates in various states before becoming president of Oberlin College in 1898. During his administration he attempted to improve relations between the town and the college. He wrote several books, including a life of Henry Ward Beecher and *The Christian Conquest of Asia . . .* , New York, 1899.

BARSCHAK, ERNA (Sept. 12, 1898–Oct. 12, 1958), educator, born in Berlin, Germany, was a member of the psychology department, Miami University, from 1942 until her death. Besides professional publications, she published *My American Adventure,* New York, 1945. WWAW 1

BARTELLE, JOHN PETER (Oct. 24, 1858–Jan. 8, 1946), was born in Toledo, Lucas County. He was secretary of the Kelsey-Freeman Lumber Co. and associate editor of the Wood Construction Publishing Co. After completing forty years in the lumber business, he wrote a volume of reminiscences: *Forty Years on the Road,* Cedar Rapids, Iowa, 1925.

BARTH, HAROLD BRADSHAW (July 25, 1884–), was born in East Liverpool, Columbiana County. He attended East Liverpool schools, Mercersburg Academy, Pa., and the Byron King School of Oratory. He was secretary of the East Liverpool Chamber of Commerce for twenty years and is now curator of the East Liverpool Historical Society Museum. He prepared for publication *History of Columbiana County . . .* , 2 vols., Indianapolis, 1926.

BARTHOLOMEW, PAUL CHARLES (July 15, 1907–), educator, was born in Salem, Columbiana County. He graduated from the University of Notre Dame in 1929 and the University of Kentucky (Ph.D.) in 1938. He has been on the Notre Dame faculty in the department of political science since 1929. He has published *American Government under the Constitution,* Dubuque, Iowa, 1947. WW 30

BARTLETT, ALICE ELINOR (1848–1920), born in Wisconsin, was a reporter for the Toledo *Blade,* 1872–75. She afterward lived in Chicago, where she wrote a number of novels. She often wrote under the pen name Birch Arnold.

Until the Day Break, Philadelphia, [1877].

BARTLETT, CECIL RICHMOND. See Cecil Jane Richmond.

BARTLETT, EDWIN JULIUS (Feb. 16, 1851–June 10, 1932), educator, was born in Hudson, Summit County. After graduating from Dartmouth College in 1872, he taught school in Illinois and studied medicine. He graduated from Rush Medical College, Chicago, in 1879 but did not practice. He was in the chemistry department, Dartmouth, 1879–1920. Besides textbooks and genealogical works, he published *A Dartmouth Book of Remembrance . . .* , Hanover, N. H., 1922. WWW 1

BARTLETT, WILLARD W. (1884–), educator, was born in New York State. He graduated from Colgate University in 1910 and Ohio State University (Ph.D.) in 1933. He spent the years 1915–25 in the Orient. He returned to the United States to become assistant to the president of Carleton College in Minnesota. He was later president of Rio Grande College in Ohio, and he was head of the Department of Education, Otterbein College, 1936–46. Since his retirement he has lived in Claremont, Calif. He wrote *Education for Humanity, the History of Otterbein College,* Westerville, 1934.

BARTLEY, THOMAS WELLES (Feb. 11, 1812–June 20, 1885), lawyer, was born in Jefferson County. After the close of the War of 1812 his family settled on a farm near Mansfield, Richland County. He attended Jefferson College, Pa., studied law, and was admitted to the Ohio bar in 1833. After long service in the general assembly he was elected speaker of the state senate in 1843, and upon Shannon's resignation he became acting governor from April 15 to Dec. 3, 1844. Elected to the state supreme court, he served from Feb., 1852, to Feb., 1859, serving as chief justice for three years. He practiced law in Mansfield, Cincinnati, and Washington, D. C. from 1859 until his death. Many of his speeches were published separately.

The Rights of the Owners of Private Properties Taken in War, to Just Compensation . . . , Washington, D. C., 1873.

A Review of the Currency Question, with Special Reference to Fiat Money Doctrine, Washington, D. C., 1879.

BARTON, BRUCE (Aug. 5, 1886–   ), advertising executive, born in Robbins, Tenn., spent his early boyhood in Ohio while his father Rev. William E. Barton (q.v.) was attending Oberlin Seminary and serving as a pastor. After graduating from Amherst College in 1907, he edited the *Home Herald, Housekeeper,* and *Every Week* and was an assistant sales manager for P. F. Collier & Son. He became one of the country's leading advertising men and is now chairman of the board of Batten, Barton, Durstine, and Osborn. He has written many articles and a number of books, the best known of which was a best seller for two years: *The Man Nobody Knows; A Discovery of Jesus,* Indianapolis, [1925]. WW 30

BARTON, FRED BUSHNELL (April 30, 1891–   ), was born in Wellington, Lorain County, the son of Rev. William E. Barton and younger brother of Bruce Barton (qq.v.). He graduated from Amherst College in 1912 and has been in the advertising business in Akron since 1918. He was a war correspondent in World War II. He has written several books on hobbies, salesmanship, and similar topics, e.g., *Let Yourself Go . . .* , New York, 1937.

BARTON, THOMAS H. (Dec. 8, 1828–Dec. 28, 1911), was born in Bedford Township, Meigs County. He was educated in local schools and studied medicine under his brother. He began practicing in 1851. During the Civil War he was a hospital steward for three years in the 4th West Virginia Infantry. After the war he returned to the practice of medicine, served a term as justice of the peace, and became a retail druggist. As a full and interesting narrative of his personal experience in the Civil War, his book is important. On the other hand, he has recorded in great detail his experiences as a physician, justice of the peace, and druggist in Meigs County, and his book is also an important contribution to the local history of the county. He died in Syracuse, Meigs County.

Autobiography of Dr. Thomas H. Barton, the Self-made Physician of Syracuse, Ohio . . . , Charleston, W. Va., 1890.

BARTON, WILLIAM ELEAZER (June 28, 1861–Dec. 7, 1930), clergyman, father of Bruce and Fred B. Barton (qq.v.), born in Sublette, Ill., graduated from Oberlin Seminary in 1890 and afterward served Congregational churches in northeastern Ohio until 1899, when he moved to Oak Park, Ill. He wrote a number of biographies and religious books; while in Ohio, he published *Life in the Hills of Kentucky,* Oberlin, 1890.

BASCOM, HENRY BIDLEMAN (May 27, 1796–Sept. 8, 1850), clergyman, born in Hancock, N. Y., spent the formative years of his ministry in Ohio. His family moved first to western New York, then to Maysville, Ky., and in 1813 to Brown County, Ohio. Here at the age of seventeen he was licensed as a Methodist preacher. For three years he preached on circuit in the Ohio Conference. After preaching in Tennessee and Kentucky, he was returned to Ohio for one more year, 1822–23. He later served as chaplain of the U. S. Senate, as president of Transylvania University, and as Bishop of the Methodist Episcopal Church, South. He published *Methodism and Slavery,* [Frankfort, Ky., 1845], and two volumes of sermons, which sold widely. His *Works* were published in four volumes. He was a powerful orator and took an active part in the debates that led to the division of the Methodist churches.

BATES, DAVID HOMER (c.1837–June 15, 1926), telegrapher, was born in Steubenville, Jefferson County. He was a railroad telegrapher at Altoona, Pa., when on April 22, 1861, he became one of the first four operators to form the nucleus of the U. S. Military Telegraph Corps. He was assigned to duty in the telegraph office of the War Department, where he served throughout the Civil War. His duties threw him into intimate contact with President Lincoln. "The bonds were close between Lincoln and David Homer Bates," wrote Carl Sandburg, one of several leading writers on Lincoln who have leaned heavily upon Bates's *Recollections.* After the Civil War Bates worked for Western Union. He wrote *Lincoln in the Telegraph Office. Recollections of the United States Military Telegraph Corps during the Civil War,* New York, 1907.

BATES, ELISHA (c.1779–1861), was born in Virginia. Around 1817 he came to Mount Pleasant, Belmont County, where he became the leader of orthodox Quakers in Ohio and also published several magazines: *The Philanthropist,* 1818–22, *The Moral Advocate,* 1821–22, and *The Miscellaneous Repository,* 1829–36. He spent some years in England.

The Juvenile Expositor . . . , Mount Pleasant, 1821.
The Doctrines of Friends . . . , Mount Pleasant, 1825.
The Retrospect: Or, Reflections of the Goodness of Providence . . . , Mount Pleasant, 1825.
Sermons Preached by Mr. Elisha Bates . . . With Extracts from His Writings . . . , London, England, 1836.
An Examination of Certain Proceedings and Principles of the Society of Friends . . . , St. Clairsville, 1837.

BATES, ERNEST SUTHERLAND (Oct. 14, 1879–Dec. 4, 1939), educator, was born in Gambier, Knox County. He attended University School in Cleveland and graduated from the University of Michigan in 1902 and Columbia University (Ph.D.) in 1908. He taught at Oberlin College, the University of Arizona, and the University of Oregon. Although he wrote on a variety of subjects, he is best known for his books and articles about the Bible, e.g., *Biography of the Bible . . . ,* New York, 1937. WWW 1

BATES, JAMES LAWRENCE (Jan. 4, 1815–May 2, 1890), lawyer and judge, was born in Canandaigua, N. Y. After graduating from Hobart College, Geneva, N. Y., in 1833, he read law. He came to Columbus in 1835 and began to practice. He served as a judge in Franklin County, 1851–66, and as director of the Ohio State Penitentiary, 1866–74. He wrote a life of his father-in-law, Alfred Kelley. His death occurred in Columbus.

Alfred Kelley; His Life and Work, Columbus, 1888.

BATES, MARGARET HOLMES ERNSPERGER (Oct. 6, 1844–1927), was born in Fremont, Sandusky County. After teaching school in Ohio and Indiana, she married Charles A. Bates of Indianapolis. She wrote book reviews, articles, and poems and compiled several collections of recitations and monologues for school use. Around 1890 she moved to New York City; her death occurred in that city. *The Chamber over the Gate* and *A Woman's Love* were published under the pen name Margaret Holmes.

Manitou, Indianapolis, 1881.
The Chamber over the Gate, Indianapolis, 1886.
The Price of the Ring, Chicago, 1892.
Shylock's Daughter, Chicago, 1894.
Jasper Fairfax, New York, [1897].
In the First Degree, New York, 1907.
Silas Kirkendowne's Sons, Boston, 1908.
Paying the Piper, New York, 1910.
Hildegarde, and Other Lyrics, New York, [1911].
Browning Critiques, Chicago, 1921.
A Woman's Love, Chicago, [n.d.].

BATES, MINER SEARLE (May 28, 1897–), clergyman and educator, was born in Newark, Licking County, the son of Miner Lee Bates, Disciples of Christ clergyman and president of Hiram College from 1908 to 1921. After graduating from Hiram in 1916, he was named a Rhodes scholar and studied at Oxford; he later earned a Ph.D. in history from Yale University in 1935. He was on the faculty of Nanking University, 1920–50, and since 1950 has taught at Union Theological Seminary. He has written *Half of Humanity; Far Eastern Peoples and Problems,* New York, [1942]. DAS 3

BATES, RALPH ORR (June 29, 1847–Dec. 27, 1909), was born in Mansfield, Richland County. He enlisted in the 9th Ohio Cavalry in 1862; he subsequently was captured and confined in various prisons in the Confederacy. Upon his release from Andersonville in an incredibly weakened condition, he claimed to have been sent to Washington by General Sherman, as a horrible example of the manner in which Federal prisoners were being treated at Andersonville. He finally returned to his home in Mansfield, where his former neighbors were outraged by his appearance. Afterward he went on the lecture platform and traveled about the United States giving his lecture, "From Andersonville Prison, Georgia, to the White House." A careful search of Mansfield newspaper files and other records, however, reveals nothing to confirm Bates's story; and the directories of Mansfield do not disclose his name or that of his father, Calvin, who is supposed to have been most active in "putting down the rebellion." He died at Santa Cruz, Calif. A posthumous book was published: *Billy and Dick from Andersonville Prison to the White House,* Santa Cruz, Calif., 1910.

BATH, CYRIL JOHN (Dec. 21, 1890–), manufacturer, was born in London, England, but has lived in Cuyahoga County since 1909. President of Cyril Bath Co., Solon, manufacturers of heavy machine tools, he has also published numerous pamphlets on economic and international questions, e.g., *Europe in the Modern Age,* New York, [1948].

BAUDER, LEVI F. (Jan. 28, 1840–Oct. 2, 1913), was born in Cleveland, Cuyahoga County. He attended Oberlin College and later taught school. During the Civil War he served in the 7th O.V.I. and was discharged with the rank of ordnance sergeant. He was auditor of Cuyahoga County, 1879–81, and for several years was a justice of the peace. He was admitted to the bar in 1890. For five years he was a member of the board of the Cleveland Public Library. An inveterate contributor of short poems to Cleveland newspapers, he printed *Passing Fancies* for private circulation.

Passing Fancies: Poems, Cleveland, 1880.

BAUER, MARY T. (March 25, 1885–Aug. 24, 1949), educator, was born in Cleveland, Cuyahoga County. After graduating from Cleveland Kindergarten Training School in 1905, she taught in Cleveland kindergartens until her retirement in 1944. She died in Cleveland at the age of 64. She published *Happy Childhood,* Boston, [1934].

BAUGHMAN, ABRAHAM J. (Sept. 5, 1838–Oct. 1, 1913), journalist and historian, was born in Richland County. He attended district schools, taught school, and studied law. He was connected with the New York *World* and the Chicago *Inter-Ocean* and also worked on a number of Ohio newspapers. His death occurred in Mansfield. He wrote several histories of Ohio counties, e.g., *History of Richland County . . . ,* Chicago, 1908.

BAUSLIN, DAVID HENRY (Jan. 21, 1854–March 3, 1922), clergyman and educator, was born in Winchester, Va. He graduated from Wittenberg College in 1876 and from the seminary in 1878. Ordained a Lutheran minister in 1878, he served as pastor in several Ohio churches, 1878–96; he then became professor of practical theology in Wittenberg Theological Seminary and was made dean in 1911. He was editor of the *Lutheran World,* 1901–12. His death occurred in Bucyrus. His writings on religious subjects include *The Lutheran Movement of the Sixteenth Century; An Interpretation,* Philadelphia, [1919].

BÄUMELER, JOSEPH MICHAEL. See Joseph M. Bimeler.

BAXTER, SAMUEL ALEXANDER (Oct. 26, 1839–Jan. 5, 1908), physician and financier, was born in Lima, Allen County. He collaborated with Charles C. Miller in writing *History of Allen County,* Chicago, 1906.

BAXTER, WILLIAM (July 6, 1820–Feb. 11, 1880), clergyman, was born in Leeds, Yorkshire, and was brought to Allegheny City, Pa., by his parents in 1828. When he was eighteen he joined the Disciples of Christ, and after his graduation from Bethany College in 1845 he devoted the rest of his life to church-related service. He served pastorates in Pennsylvania, Mississippi, and Louisiana, and for three years he was a professor at Newton College, Miss. On March 7, 1854, he married Mrs. Fidelia Vail, the widow of a Mississippi planter but a native of Massachusetts. Presumably she shared her new husband's antislavery views. In 1859 he became president of Arkansas College in Fayetteville, Ark. When the war broke out and the student body disintegrated, Baxter was unable to maintain his pro-Northern views in safety, and the college building, used as a barracks, was burned on March 4, 1862. Baxter and his family fled the state. His *Pea Ridge and Prairie Grove* describes the experiences of a Northern sympathizer in a border state. Baxter wrote war poems which were published in *Harper's Weekly,* other poems, and the popular hymn "Let Me Go." In Cincinnati from 1863 to 1865, he was active as a journalist and preacher. From 1865 to 1875 he was pastor of the Christian church at Lisbon. Some of his temperance speeches were published in pamphlet form. He died in New Castle, Pa.

Pea Ridge and Prairie Grove; Or, Scenes and Incidents of the War in Arkansas, Cincinnati, 1864.

Life of Elder Walter Scott . . . , Cincinnati, 1874.

Life of Knowles Shaw, the Singing Evangelist, Cincinnati, 1879.

BAYER, ELEANOR R. (Oct. 13, 1914–), was born in Cleveland, Cuyahoga County. She graduated from Western Reserve University in 1935. She has published magazine fiction and with her husband, Leo G. Bayer (q.v.), has published several mystery novels under the pen name Oliver Weld Bayer, e.g., *Brutal Question,* New York, 1947.

BAYER, LEO G. (Sept. 6, 1908–), lawyer, was born in Cleveland, Cuyahoga County, and graduated from Western Reserve University (A.B., LL.B.). He began practicing law in Cleveland in 1933. He has collaborated with his wife, Eleanor R. Bayer (q.v.), in writing several mystery stories.

BAYER, OLIVER WELD. Pseud. See Eleanor R. and Leo G. Bayer.

BEACH, ARTHUR GRANDVILLE (Nov. 29, 1870–Jan. 28, 1934), educator, was born in Marietta, Washington County. He graduated from Marietta College in 1891 and Yale Divinity School in 1896. After serving about fifteen years as a Congregationalist minister, he completed his doctorate at the University of Michigan in 1913 and joined the Marietta faculty as professor of English in the same year. He wrote *A Pioneer College; The Story of Marietta . . . ,* [Chicago], 1935. WWW 1

BEACH, EDWARD LATIMER (June 30, 1867–Dec. 20, 1943), naval officer, was born in Toledo, Lucas County. He graduated from the U. S. Naval Academy in 1888 and served in the Regular Navy until 1921. After his retirement he was a lecturer at Stanford University. His death occurred at Palo Alto, Calif. He wrote a number of novels on navy life, e.g., *An Annapolis Plebe,* Philadelphia, 1907. WW 16

BEACH, JOHN NOBLE (Jan. 29, 1829–July 17, 1897), physician, was born in Amity, Madison County. He studied at Ohio Wesleyan University and at Starling Medical College, where he graduated in 1850. He practiced at Unionville Center and Plain City, and after 1858 at Jefferson. He served in the Civil War with the 40th O.V.I.

History of the Fortieth Ohio Volunteer Infantry, London, 1884.

BEADLE, JOHN HANSON (March 14, 1840–Jan. 15, 1897), journalist, was born in Parke County, Ind. In 1867 he was employed on the editorial staff of the Cincinnati *Commercial* and went to the Far West as correspondent of that newspaper in the summer of 1868. He served as correspondent of the *Commercial* for a number of years in the Far West and in Ohio, finally severing the connection when he became owner-editor of the Rockville, Ind., *Tribune* in 1879. He wrote a number of books which had a popular appeal, e.g., *Life in Utah; Or, the Mysteries and Crimes of Mormonism . . . ,* Philadelphia, 1870.

BEALL, EMMA JACOBS REBECCA (July 2, 1865– ?), was born near New Philadelphia, Tuscarawas County. She taught school and afterward studied nursing in Illinois. In 1905 she married Dr. Judson T. Beall of Coshocton. In 1940 she was a resident of Los Angeles, Calif. She wrote *A New Day,* [Los Angeles, 1940].

BEAN, ELIJAH HARRY (April 25, 1875–), osteopathic physician, was born in Guysville, Athens County. After graduating from the American School of Osteopathy, Kirksville, Mo., in 1910, he practiced in Columbus. He now lives in Pensacola, Fla. He has written several medical articles and one book, *Food Fundamentals; A View of Ill-Health as Caused by Wrong Habits of Living . . . ,* [Columbus, 1916]. OBB

BEAR, JOHN W. (1800–Feb. 12, 1880), born in Frederick County, Md., was made a bound boy working in a tavern, but ran away in 1816 and came to Belmont County. He served for a time at the Wyandot Indian Agency at Upper Sandusky and also lived in other parts of the state. At the Whig Convention of 1840 in Columbus, he appeared on the platform wearing his blacksmith's apron and carrying his hammer and tongs. Called the "Buckeye Blacksmith," he was widely known as a political orator and also lectured on temperance. He later served in the customs house in Philadelphia, Pa. In his autobiography he advises his readers to avoid politics and strong drink.

Life and Travels of John W. Bear, "The Buckeye Blacksmith" . . . , Baltimore, 1873.

BEARD, ADELIA BELLE (1857–Feb. 16, 1920), was born in Painesville, Lake County. She was educated in private schools, studied drawing and painting at Cooper Union and the Art Students' League, taught drawing, and was an illustrator for books and magazines. She also invented the "Beard animals" and the "Beard birds." She and her younger sister, Mary Caroline (q.v.), lived in Flushing, Long Island. All of the titles below are collaborations.

How to Amuse Yourself and Others . . ., New York, 1887.
New Ideas for Work and Play . . ., New York, 1902.
Indoor and Outdoor Handicraft and Recreation for Girls, New York, 1904.
Things Worth Doing and How to Do Them, New York, 1906.
Home Mission Handicraft . . ., New York, 1908.
Little Folks' Handy Book, New York, 1910.
The National Organization, Girl Pioneers of America . . ., New York, 1914.
On the Trail; An Outdoor Book for Girls, New York, 1915.
Mother Nature's Toy-Shop, New York, [1918].

BEARD, DANIEL CARTER (June 21, 1850–June 11, 1941), was born in Cincinnati, Hamilton County. His father, James Henry Beard (May 20, 1812–April 4, 1893), had come to Cincinnati from Painesville around 1835; he was a successful portrait painter, and his four sons and two daughters all became artists. Daniel attended school in Covington, Ky. His boyhood spent on the shores of the Ohio River left him with a lifelong love of the outdoors and an interest in pioneer life. While in his late teens, he began work as a surveyor in the office of the Cincinnati city engineer. He became a skillful map-maker. Discovering a gift for drawing animals, he followed the lead of his brothers and sisters in determining to become an artist. He went to New York, studied at the Art Students' League, 1880–84, and worked on various magazines. He taught drawing at the Women's School of Applied Design. He illustrated various books, including Mark Twain's *Connecticut Yankee at King Arthur's Court.* His books and articles for boys were extremely popular, and he organized the Sons of Daniel Boone and Boy Pioneers; but his nation-wide fame began in 1910 when he joined Ernest Thompson Seton and others in forming the Boy Scouts of America. Until his death he was known as Uncle Dan to millions of Boy Scouts. Throughout this period he wrote regularly for *Boys' Life.* Wearing a buckskin costume he lectured to boys' groups. He died at Suffern, N. Y.

What to Do and How to Do It . . ., New York, 1882.
Moonblight and Six Feet of Romance, New York, 1892.
Outdoor Games for All Seasons . . ., New York, 1896.
For Playground, Field and Forest . . ., New York, 1900.
New Ideas for American Boys . . ., New York, 1900.
The Jack of All Trades: Fair Weather Ideas, New York, 1904.
New Ideas for Out of Doors . . ., New York, [1906].
Dan Beard's Animal Book and Camp-fire Stories, New York, 1907.
The Boy Pioneers, Sons of Daniel Boone, New York, 1909.
Boat-building and Boating, New York, 1911.
Shelters, Shacks, and Shanties, New York, 1914.
The American Boys' Book of Bugs, Butterflies and Beetles, Philadelphia, 1915.
Camp Hints for Hike and Bike . . ., [New York, 1916].
The American Boys' Book of Signs, Signals and Symbols, Philadelphia, 1918.
The American Boys' Handybook of Camp-Lore and Woodcraft, Philadelphia, 1920.
The Black Wolf Pack, New York, 1922.
The American Boys' Book of Birds and Brownies of the Woods, Philadelphia, 1923.
Do It Yourself: A Book of the Big Outdoors, Philadelphia, 1925.
Wisdom of the Woods, Philadelphia, 1926.
Buckskin Book for Buckskin Men and Boys, Philadelphia, [1929].
Boy Heroes of Today . . ., New York, 1932.
Hardly a Man Is Now Alive . . ., New York, 1939.

BEARD, FRANK. See Thomas F. Beard.

BEARD, JAMES CARTER (June 6, 1837–Nov. 15, 1913), artist, older brother of Daniel C. Beard (q.v.), was born in Cincinnati, Hamilton County. He read law with Rutherford B. Hayes and was admitted to the bar in 1861, but practiced only briefly. Like his talented brothers and sisters he turned to art and enjoyed great success as an illustrator of books and magazine articles. He was probably best known for his articles on nature in *St. Nicholas* and other national magazines. He served for many years on the staff of D. Appleton and Company. He lived in Brooklyn, N. Y., until around 1910, when he moved to New Orleans, where he spent the last three years of his life.

Little Workers . . ., New York, 1871.
The Artist's Manual . . ., New York, [1877].
Painting on China . . ., New York, [1882].
Curious Homes and Their Tenants, New York, 1897.
Billy Possum, New York, [1909].

BEARD, MARY CAROLINE (Lina) (1853–Aug. 13, 1933), was born in Cincinnati, Hamilton County. She attended a private school in Covington, Ky., and Wesleyan Academy, Cincinnati; and like her sister, Adelia (q.v.), studied art in New York. She founded the Good Citizenship League of Flushing, Long Island, and the Girl Pioneers of America, an organization intended to parallel the Boy Pioneers, founded by her brother, Daniel Carter Beard (q.v.). All of her books were written with her sister, Adelia.

BEARD, THOMAS FRANCIS (Feb. 6, 1842–Sept. 28, 1905), known professionally as Frank Beard, was born in Cincinnati, Hamilton County, the son of James Henry Beard, a portrait painter. At the age of twelve he began submitting sketches to national magazines. While serving with the 7th O.V.I., he drew sketches for *Leslie's Weekly* and *Harper's Weekly*. After the war he lectured widely and developed the chalk talk as his specialty; he also provided illustrations and cartoons for *Judge* and other periodicals. He was professor of esthetics at Syracuse University, 1881–84, and in 1890 he became editor of the *Ram's Horn*, a religious weekly published in Chicago.

The Black-board in the Sunday School, New York, 1877.

Picture Puzzles . . . , Toronto, Ontario, [1899].

Fifty Great Cartoons, Chicago, [189-?].

Bible Symbols . . . , Chicago, [1904].

BEARD, WILLIAM HOLBROOK (April 13, 1825–Feb. 20, 1900), portrait painter, was born in Painesville, Lake County. In 1857 he went abroad to study art, and in 1860 he settled in New York. He was widely known for his allegorical pictures and for the humor portrayed in his pictures of animals. He wrote a textbook, *Action in Art,* in 1893 and also published various magazine articles. He died in New York City.

Humor in Animals . . . , New York, [1885].

BEARDSLEE, JOHN WALTER (1837–March 31, 1921), clergyman and educator, was born in Ottawa County. After graduating from Rutgers University, he served several churches and taught at Western Theological Seminary, Holland, Mich., 1888–1917, and at New Brunswick Seminary, 1917–21.

The Bible among the Nations, Chicago, 1899.

BEARDSLEY, DANIEL B. (May 12, 1832–Sept. 29, 1894), was born in Licking County. His parents moved to Hancock County in 1834. After attending district schools, he began teaching in 1850, read law, and was admitted to the bar in 1856. He served 27 years as justice of the peace for Findlay Township. In 1872 he was elected mayor of Findlay. His death occurred in Findlay.

History of Hancock County . . . , Springfield, 1881.

BEATTY, JOHN (Dec. 16, 1828–Dec. 21, 1914), soldier and banker, was born near Sandusky, Erie County. In 1854 he married Lucy Tupper of Cleveland and settled in Cardington, where he and his brother William organized Beatty Brothers Bank. In 1861 he joined the 3rd O.V.I. as a captain; he was promoted to lieutenant colonel, and in March, 1863, was brevetted brigadier general. In Jan., 1864, he resigned from the army and returned to Cardington. His resignation may have been due to his dislike of West Point officers and his advocacy of total war against the South, or it may have been motivated by his brother William's desire to serve in the army. Throughout his career he was active in the Republican Party; he served in the House of Representatives, 1868–73, and though he held no more elective offices he spoke widely in support of Republican candidates and policies. In 1873 he opened the Citizen's Savings Bank in Columbus; he retired in 1903. He died in Columbus and is buried in Sandusky. His most important book, his war memoirs, was republished in 1946. His three novels have little merit, but *The Acolhuans,* a fantastic story of the Mound Builders, attracted some notice.

The Citizen Soldier; Or, Memoirs of a Volunteer, Cincinnati, 1879.

The Belle O'Becket's Lane . . . , Philadelphia, 1883.

McKinleyism, As It Appears to a Non-Partisan, [Columbus, 1894].

Answer to Coin's Financial School, 1896.

High or Low Tariff, Which? Columbus, 1897.

The Acolhuans . . . , Columbus, 1902.

McLean, a Romance of the War, Columbus, 1904.

BEAUCHAMP, LOU JENKS (Jan. 14, 1851–June 4, 1920), journalist and lecturer, was born in Cincinnati, Hamilton County. Self-educated, he joined the staff of the Cincinnati *Star* while still in his teens. He sold sketches and poems to various newspapers and magazines, became managing editor of the Fort Wayne, Ind., *Gazette,* and later lived in Hamilton. He also delivered over 10,000 lectures on humorous topics and on temperance, some of which were reprinted in pamphlet form.

Sunshine. Written in the Interest of Temperance, Sunshine and Good Humor . . . , Hamilton, 1879.

This, That and the Other; A Collection of Stories Sketches and Poems, Wise and Otherwise, Hamilton, 1882.

What the Duchess and I Saw in Europe . . . , Hamilton, 1896.

BEAUDRY, EVIEN G. (April 11, 1894–), born in Brunswick, Mich., attended Michigan Ferris Institute and Western State Teachers College and taught school for several years in Michigan before coming to Akron in 1925. In 1934 she joined the editorial staff of Saalfield Publishing Company; now retired, she still lives in Akron. She has published poems, articles, and stories in various magazines under the name Goldie Beaudry and has also published books for children, e.g., *Puppy Stories,* New York, 1934.

BEAUDRY, GOLDIE. See Evien G. Beaudry.

BEAVER, ROBERT PIERCE (May 26, 1906–), clergyman and educator, was born in Hamilton, Butler County. He graduated from Oberlin College in 1928 and Cornell University (Ph.D.) in 1933. He has also studied at Yale Divinity School, the University of Munich, and Union Theological Seminary. He has served Evangelical and Reformed churches in Cincinnati and other cities and has taught in several seminaries. Since 1955 he has been a member of the federated theological faculty, University of Chicago. His writings include *The Year of Grace,* St. Louis, [1935]. WW 30

BEAZELL, WILLIAM PRESTON (June 21, 1877–March 12, 1946), journalist, was born in St. Clairsville, Belmont County. He worked on newspapers in Pittsburgh and New York. He published *Account of the Ball Given in Honor of Charles Dickens in N. Y. City, 1842,* [New York, 1908]. WWW 2

BEBENROTH, CHARLOTTA M. (Mrs. Otto C.) (June 1, 1890–), educator, was born in Cleveland, Cuyahoga County. She attended Baldwin-Wallace College and has been for many years a teacher in the Cleveland public schools. She has published stories and poems in juvenile magazines and one book: *On the Farm with Bob and Nancy,* Akron, 1933.

BECK, JOHN CRAFTON (Jan. 19, 1822– ?), physician, was born in Vienna, Ind. After graduating from the Medical College of Ohio, Cincinnati, he returned to Indiana to practice. In 1858 he joined the faculty of Cincinnati College of Medicine and Surgery. He was a surgeon in the Civil War, afterward practiced in Newport, Ky., but in 1870 returned to Cincinnati to practice. He edited *Cincinnati Medical and Surgical News.*

Opiumania . . . , [Cincinnati, 1874].

BECKER, HENRY JACOB (June 19, 1846–Dec. 1, 1934), clergyman, was born in Massillon, Stark County. As a young man he worked in coal mines, attended Heidelberg College, and served in the 188th O.V.I., Feb.–Sept., 1865. He was converted to the United Brethren church after the war and in 1869 was licensed to preach. He served as an itinerant minister in Ohio until 1875, when he went to California as a missionary. In 1905 he became a Presbyterian. He spent his old age in Dayton.

Borachio's Bo-Peep; Or, the Drunkard's Play with Children . . . , [Sacramento?, Calif., 1882].

Dr. Becker's Brownies Rummaging among the Mediums of Modern Spiritualism . . . , [Huntington, Ind.], 1900.

BECKMAN, THEODORE N. (Sept. 3, 1895–), educator, was born in Russia. He graduated from Ohio State University (A.B., 1920; Ph.D., 1924) and has since taught economics and sociology there, specializing in marketing. He has also been a consultant to various state and national agencies. He has written economics textbooks and some studies of economic questions, e.g., *The Chain Store Problem* . . . , New York, 1938. WW 30

BEDELL, GREGORY THRUSTON (Aug. 27, 1817–March 11, 1892), clergyman, born in Hudson, N. Y., served Episcopal churches in New York and Virginia before being elected bishop coadjutor of Ohio in 1859. He served as bishop, 1873–89. Living at Gambier, he also taught some courses at Bexley Seminary, Kenyon College.

A Votive Pillar, New York, 1853.

Personal Presence of God the Holy Ghost . . . , Cleveland, 1874.

The Pastor. Pastoral Theology, Philadelphia, 1880.
Enlightened Public Opinion in the Church . . . , Cleveland, 1881.

BEDELL, MARY CREHORE (March, 1870–), was born in Cleveland, Cuyahoga County. She graduated from Smith College and afterward lived in Ithaca, N. Y. She wrote *Modern Gypsies, the Story of a Twelve Thousand Mile Motor Camping Trip Encircling the United States,* New York, [1924].

BEECHER, CATHERINE ESTHER (Sept. 6, 1800–May 12, 1878), eldest daughter of Lyman Beecher (q.v.), was born in East Hampton, Long Island, N. Y. She attended Miss Pierce's School but also educated herself through wide reading. In 1822 Alexander M. Fisher, a brilliant professor at Yale, to whom she was engaged, was lost at sea—an event later used by her sister, Harriet Beecher Stowe (q.v.), in *The Minister's Wooing.* The loss of her fiancé and the responsibility for younger brothers and sisters imposed on her by the death of her mother confirmed her lifelong character of headstrong, domineering spinsterhood. She conducted Hartford Female Seminary, 1824–32. She accompanied her father on his first visit to Cincinnati, and that city was her nominal home from 1832 to 1850, but she traveled widely in the interests of educational projects in which she was interested. She organized the Western Female Institute in Cincinnati, 1832–37, and was a founder of the Board of National Popular Education. She assisted in the preparation of McGuffey's *Fourth Reader,* and echoed another textbook to such an extent that a charge of plagiarism was made. She established a number of schools and devoted her life to education of women, especially in domestic arts; but she was a determined opponent of women's suffrage. Her old age was spent in the homes of her brothers and sisters. She died in Elmira, N. Y., at the home of her half-brother, Thomas (q.v.). Besides the titles below, she published numerous textbooks, the most important of which treat domestic science for women.

An Essay on Slavery and Abolitionism . . . , Boston, 1837.
A Treatise on Domestic Economy . . . , Boston, 1841.
Letters to Persons Who Are Engaged in Domestic Service, New York, 1842.
The Duty of American Women to Their Country, New York, 1845.
Truth Stranger Than Fiction . . . , Boston, 1850.
The True Remedy for the Wrongs of Women . . . , Boston, 1851.
Letters to the People on Health and Happiness, New York, 1855.
Common Sense Applied to Religion . . . , New York, 1857.
Religious Training of Children . . . , New York, 1864.
The American Woman's Home . . . , Boston, 1869.
Woman Suffrage and Woman's Profession, Hartford, 1871.
Woman's Profession as Mother and Educator . . . , Philadelphia, 1872.
Educational Reminiscences and Suggestions, New York, 1874.

BEECHER, CHARLES (Oct. 7, 1815–April 21, 1900), clergyman, son of Lyman Beecher (q.v.), was born in Litchfield, Conn. After graduating from Bowdoin College in 1834, he came to Lane Seminary, where his father was president. Uncertain of his religious faith, he gave up plans for the ministry and taught music for a time in Cincinnati. He then was a shipping clerk in New Orleans, and his descriptions of Louisiana and of a brutal overseer furnished a setting and the character of Simon Legree for his sister's novel, *Uncle Tom's Cabin.* In 1844 he regained his faith while living in Indianapolis, Ind. He later served as a minister in New Jersey, Massachusetts, and Pennsylvania. He wrote on spiritualism and music and also wrote several books expounding his own peculiar, somewhat mystical theology, e.g., *Redeemer and Redeemed,* Boston, 1864.

BEECHER, EDWARD N. (May 6, 1846–Nov. 2, 1933), druggist, was born in Homer, Licking County, but grew up in Oberlin. He graduated from Oberlin College in 1866 and in 1889 settled in Cleveland, where he operated a drugstore for forty years. He died in Cleveland at the age of 87.

The Lost Atlantis; Or, "The Great Deluge of All." An Epic Poem, Cleveland, 1897.

BEECHER, GEORGE (May 6, 1809–July 1, 1843), clergyman, was born in East Hampton, Long Island, N. Y. After graduating from Yale University in 1828, he taught at Groton, and in 1832 he accompanied his father, Lyman Beecher (q.v.), to Cincinnati. After being ordained to the Presbyterian ministry in 1833, he served churches at Batavia, Rochester, N. Y., and Chillicothe. He died in Chillicothe when a gun with which he intended to frighten birds from his fruit trees discharged accidentally. A posthumous collection of his writings was edited by Catherine Beecher: *The Biographical Remains of Rev. George Beecher . . . ,* New York, 1844.

BEECHER, HENRY WARD (June 24, 1813–March 8, 1887), the most popular clergyman of his day, was born in Litchfield, Conn. Like his brothers, he spent only a short time in Cincinnati, where his father, Lyman Beecher (q.v.), was president of Lane Seminary, 1832–50. He came to Lane Seminary in 1834 after graduating from Amherst College, studied theology intermittently, helped found the Cincinnati Young Men's Temperance Society, published some anonymous anti-Catholic articles in the *Daily Evening Post,* and edited the Cincinnati *Journal* for a few months in 1836. In 1837 he accepted a call to Lawrenceburg, Ind.; two years later he took a church in Indianapolis; and in 1847, he was called to Plymouth Church, Brooklyn, where he remained for the rest of his life. A prolific writer like most of the Beechers, he published many sermons and essays. From a literary point of view his most interesting work is a novel, *Norwood . . . ,* New York, 1868.

BEECHER, LYMAN (Oct., 1775–Jan. 10, 1863), clergyman, was born in New Haven, Conn. After graduating from Yale, he was ordained to the Presbyterian ministry in 1799 and served pastorates in East Hampton, Long Island, 1779–1810, Litchfield, Conn., 1810–26, and Boston, 1826–32. In this latter charge he was a militant opponent of Unitarianism and Catholicism. In 1832 he accepted the presidency of Lane Seminary, Cincinnati, and was also appointed pastor of the Second Presbyterian Church. Almost immediately after he brought his large family to the city, he found himself in difficulties. Conservative Presbyterians, led by Joshua L. Wilson (q.v.), who had secured his appointment to Lane Seminary, attacked him for his theological views. He was acquitted by the local presbytery and by the synod meeting in Dayton, but the bitterness engendered by the controversy did much to harm the Presbyterian cause in the West. The chief difficulty, however, arose within the Lane Seminary student body. Led by Theodore Weld (q.v.), the students formed an antislavery society which scandalized the city. They refused to heed Beecher's pleas for moderation and his advocacy of colonization. While he was in the East raising funds, the students left the seminary, most of them transferring to Oberlin College and a few to Western Reserve College at Hudson. Until his resignation in 1850, Beecher struggled to keep the seminary operating and to induce students to attend. After retiring, he bought a house in Brooklyn, N. Y., to be near his famous son, Henry Ward Beecher, and there he passed the remainder of his days. Besides the titles below, many of his sermons were published.

A Plea for the West, Cincinnati, 1835.
Views in Theology, Cincinnati, 1836.
Autobiography . . . , 2 vols., (Charles Beecher, ed.), New York, 1864.

BEECHER, THOMAS KINNICUTT (Feb. 10, 1824–March 14, 1900), clergyman, was born in Litchfield, Conn. In 1832 he came to Cincinnati with his father, Lyman Beecher (q.v.). After graduating from Illinois College in 1843, he was a high school principal in the East, 1846–52. In 1854 he became pastor of the Independent Congregational Church, Elmira, N. Y. He spent the remainder of his life in Elmira, where his independent, sometimes eccentric behavior made him one of the town's best-known citizens, universally known as "Father Tom" in his old age. He contributed many outspoken editorials to local newspapers, and some of his sermons were printed. After his death a collection of stories for children was published: *In Tune with the Stars,* Elmira, 1901. DAB 2

BEECHER, WILLIS JUDSON (April 29, 1838–May 10, 1912), clergyman and educator, was born in Vinton County. After graduating from Hamilton College in 1858, he taught at Whitestown, N. Y., Seminary, 1858–61; and after graduating from Auburn Theological Seminary in 1864, he was ordained to the Presbyterian ministry. He taught at Knox College, Ill., 1865–69, and was pastor of the First Church of Christ, Galesburg, Ill., 1869–71. He served on the faculty of Auburn Seminary, 1871–1908. His death occurred in Auburn. He wrote a number of works on religious themes, e.g., *The Prophets and the Promise . . . ,* New York, [1905].

BEER, SAMUEL HUTCHISON (July 28, 1911–), educator, was born in Bucyrus, Crawford County. He graduated from the University of Michigan in 1932, was a Rhodes scholar, 1932–35, and completed his doctorate at Harvard in 1943. He was associated with the New York *Post* and *Fortune* magazine before joining the department of government at Harvard in 1938. He served in the army during World

War II. He has published an exposition of liberalism based on the metaphysics of Alfred North Whitehead: *The City of Reason,* Cambridge, Mass., 1949. WW 30

BEERY, JESSE (June 13, 1861–Feb. 22, 1945), was born near Pleasant Hill, Miami County, and spent his life in that area. Applying the principles developed by John S. Rarey (q.v.), he broke horses on his father's farm and acquired considerable renown. He gave public exhibitions and established a correspondence school of horsemanship.

Jesse Beery's Practical System of Colt Training . . . , [Lima, 1890].
The Thoroughbreds, [Piqua, 1912].
The Beery System of Horsemanship . . . , [Dayton, 1914].
Prof. Beery's Saddle-Horse Instructions . . . , [West Carrollton], 1934.

BEHRENDS, ADOLPHUS JULIUS FREDERICK (Dec. 18, 1839–May 22, 1900), clergyman, was born in Nymwegen, Holland. When he was five, his family came to Ohio, where he grew up. In 1862 he graduated from Denison University and in 1865 from Rochester Theological Seminary. In 1873 he became pastor of the First Baptist Church in Cleveland, but in Jan., 1876, he resigned his pulpit because of his opposition to restricted communion. He became a Congregationalist minister, first in Providence, R. I., and after 1883 in Brooklyn, N. Y. He was popular and successful as a minister and as a public lecturer. Numerous sermons, in addition to the titles below, were published.

In Memoriam Harriet E. Hatch . . . , Providence, 1882.
The World for Christ, New York, 1896.
The Old Testament under Fire, New York, 1897.
The Christ of Nineteen Centuries, (William Herries, comp.), Brooklyn, 1904.

BEHRMAN, ETHEL KNAPP (Nov. 9, 1880–June 20, 1943), was born in Cincinnati, Hamilton County. Known as the Story Lady of the Air, she broadcast popular programs over various Cincinnati radio stations. She published a collection of her verse: *Doorways,* Cincinnati, 1936.

BEILER, IRWIN ROSS (Jan. 14, 1883–), clergyman and educator, was born in Lima, Allen County. He graduated from Ohio Wesleyan University in 1907, Boston University School of Theology in 1911, and Boston University (Ph.D.) in 1918. He was on the faculty of Baker University, Kansas, 1913–18, was pastor of a Methodist church in Minneapolis, 1918–20, and was on the faculty of Allegheny College, 1920–48. He is now living in Meadville, Pa. He wrote *Studies in the Life of Jesus,* [Nashville, 1936]. WW 27

BEISTLE, ALDARILLA SHIPLEY (Feb. 13, 1896–Feb. 26, 1949), was born in Pittsburgh, but she grew up in Cleveland, where her family moved when she was three years old. She wrote and conducted a children's radio program on Cleveland radio station WGAR, wrote numerous plays for children, and published several children's books, e.g., *Just Peggy,* Philadelphia, [1939].

BELDEN, GEORGE P. (c.1845– ?), the "White Chief," was born near New Philadelphia, Tuscarawas County. In his book he relates that he ran away from home at the age of thirteen, landed in Brownsville, Nebraska Territory, and promptly wrote and induced his father to come out and establish the *Nemaha Valley Journal.* This is untrue and it is probable that the rest of his narrative is a series of brash fabrications strung on a thin thread of historical fact, although the editor, General James S. Brisbin, vouches for the fidelity of the narrative to the original manuscript. When last heard from, Belden was trapping in hostile Indian country on Medicine Creek.

Belden, the White Chief; Or, Twelve Years among the Wild Indians of the Plains . . . , Cincinnati, 1870.

BELDEN, HENRY S. (July 4, 1840–April 20, 1920), was born in Canton, Stark County. He attended Kenyon and Wittenberg Colleges and graduated from Cincinnati Law School in 1861. He developed the coal and clay resources of the Canton region and manufactured paving brick used in Canton and other cities. Besides articles in religious journals, he wrote *Heaven . . . ,* [Akron, 1912].

BELKNAP, EUGENE McCAMLY (Feb. 1, 1898–Sept. 23, 1949), manufacturer, born in Syracuse, N. Y., lived in Toledo about twenty years while president of American Mat Corp. He published a definitive work, *Milk Glass,* New York, 1949.

BELL, ALVIN EUGENE (April 10, 1882–), clergyman, was born in Mansfield, Richland County. He graduated from Wittenberg College in 1905 and from Hamma Divinity School in 1908. Ordained a Lutheran minister in 1908, he served in Bryan, 1908–13, and at Glenwood Avenue Church, Toledo, 1913–52. Besides articles and books on devotional subjects, he published a book in opposition to the teachings of Mary Baker Eddy: *The Word of a Woman, versus the Word of God . . .* , Burlington, Iowa, 1917. WW 30

BELL, ARCHIE (March 17, 1877–Jan. 27, 1943), drama critic and world traveler, was born in Geneva, Ashtabula County, and later lived in Cleveland. He worked on the Cleveland *World* and was drama critic for the Cleveland *News.* Besides numerous travel books, he wrote *The Clevelanders . . . An Exposé of High Life in the Forest City,* New York, [1907]. WW 20

BELL, BERNARD IDDINGS (Oct. 13, 1886–Sept. 5, 1958), clergyman and educator, was born in Dayton, Montgomery County. He graduated from the University of Chicago in 1907 and was ordained to the Episcopal priesthood in 1910. He served as pastor of various churches and taught at Stephens College, N. Y., 1919–33, and Columbia University, 1930–33. He was consultant to the Bishop of Chicago on educational matters, 1946–55. He published numerous articles, books of sermons, devotional books and others on religious themes, e.g., *Religion for Living, a Book for Postmodernists,* London, 1939. WWW 3

BELL, CORYDON WHITTEN (July 16, 1894–), artist, was born in Tiffin, Seneca County. He attended high school in Sandusky and studied at the University of Michigan and Western Reserve University. He was an advertising and book illustrator in Cleveland, 1922–44. In 1921 he married Thelma Harrington (see Thelma Harrington Bell), whose books he has illustrated. Since moving to Sapphire, N. C., he has published magazine articles and books on the hill regions of his adopted state, e.g., *Come Snow fer Christmas . . .* , Cleveland, 1947.

BELL, FRANK. Pseud. See Mildred W. Benson.

BELL, JAMES MADISON (April 3, 1826–1902), Ohio's first native Negro poet, was born in Gallipolis, Gallia County, where he resided until 1842, when he went to Cincinnati to learn the plasterer's trade. During his twelve years' stay in that city he appears to have been a plasterer and nothing more; an examination of contemporary local publications discloses no contributions from his pen. In 1854 he moved to Chatham, Canada West, where four years later John Brown was to call his "Provisional Constitutional Convention," preparatory to his raid upon Harper's Ferry. During the Congressional investigation that followed the raid, the original records of the Chatham convention were made public, and it was disclosed that Bell had played an active role. He fled to California early in 1860. It was there that his earliest known separately published poem appeared. He returned to Ohio and took up permanent residence at Toledo, probably early in 1866. The year 1865 is usually given, but he was present in San Francisco on Jan. 1, 1866, when he delivered a poem in commemoration of the anniversary of the Emancipation Proclamation at Zion Church. He was a member of the national convention which nominated Ulysses S. Grant for the Presidency in 1868.

A Poem Entitled The Day and the War . . . , San Francisco, 1864.

An Anniversary Poem Entitled The Progress of Liberty . . . , San Francisco, 1866.

A Poem Entitled The Triumph of Liberty . . . , Detroit, 1870.

The Poetical Works of James Madison Bell, Lansing, Mich., [1901].

BELL, MARGARET VAN HORN DWIGHT (Dec. 29, 1790–Oct. 9, 1834), born in Connecticut, was the niece of Timothy Dwight. In 1810 she left New Haven, Conn., to live with cousins in Warren, Trumbull County. In 1811 she married William Bell, Jr., and around 1815 they moved to Pittsburgh, Pa. Her journal kept during her wagon trip to Ohio was edited by Max Farrand: *A Journey to Ohio . . .* , New Haven, 1912.

BELL, THELMA HARRINGTON (July 3, 1896–), was born in Detroit, Mich. She attended Cleveland public schools and graduated from Western Reserve University. She was an advertising copywriter until her marriage to Corydon W. Bell (q.v.) in 1921. She lived in Cleveland, 1910–44, and now lives in Sapphire, N. C. She has written a number of books for juvenile readers, e.g., *Black Face,* New York, 1931.

BELLAW, AMERICUS WELLINGTON (March 17, 1842– ?), was born in Troy, Miami County. At the age of sixteen he was apprenticed to a monument carver in St. Joseph, Mo. In 1867 he moved to Sidney, where he later published a humorous paper, *The Old Man.* Under various pseudonyms (Joe Jot, Washington Whitehorn, Noah Nuff), he wrote verse and fiction for various New York periodicals. He also wrote dime novels in various Beadle series, e.g., *Peter, the Dandy Greenhorn . . .* , New York, 1891.

BENDER, ERIC J. (Aug. 8, 1902–), editor, was born in Cleveland, Cuyahoga County. He graduated from Ohio State University in 1925 and has since been associated with various educational publishers. In 1939 he joined Row Peterson as editor of educational films. He now lives in Wilmette, Ill. His writings include a book on sweepstakes and lotteries: *Tickets to Fortune . . .* , New York, [1938]. WW 28

BENDER, GEORGE H. (Sept. 27, 1896–June 19, 1961), Republican political leader, was born in Cleveland, Cuyahoga County. He served seven terms in Congress and was named to complete the Senatorial term of Robert A. Taft in 1954. He wrote *The Challenge of 1940,* New York, 1940. WW 30

BENDER, JOHN S. (1827–Oct. 9, 1912), born near Carlisle, Pa., was brought to Wayne County when he was eleven years old and lived there until early manhood, when he moved to Indiana. He taught school, practiced law, and operated a newspaper in Plymouth, Ind. He wrote a book on currency and *A Hoosier's Experience in Western Europe . . .* , Plymouth, 1880.

BENEDICT, AGNES ELIZABETH (1889–Jan. 5, 1950), educator, was born in Cincinnati, Hamilton County. She graduated from Vassar College and later studied in Europe and at Columbia University. She was editor of *The American Child,* was a research editor with the National Association of Day Nurseries, and at the time of her death was director of Center Academy, Brooklyn, N. Y. She wrote several books on children and education, including a history of American education: *Progress to Freedom . . .* , New York, [1942].

BENEDICT, ANNE KENDRICK (April 26, 1851–Oct. 24, 1922), wife of Wayland R. Benedict (q.v.), was born in Rochester, N. Y. While her husband was a minister and teacher in Cincinnati, she took an active part in various Cincinnati organizations and in the Ohio State Federation of Women's Clubs. In 1879 she was one of the organizers of the Cincinnati Kindergarten Association. Most of her writings were stories for the American Baptist Publishing Society.

The Fisherman's Daughter, Philadelphia, [1895].
Centa, Child Violinist, Philadelphia, [n.d.].
The Hathaway's Sister, Philadelphia, [n.d.].
Island Story, Philadelphia, [n.d.].
My Wonder Story, Boston, [n.d.].

BENEDICT, HESTER A. (Oct. 2, 1838– ?), was born in Streetsboro, Portage County. She was educated at Western Reserve Seminary. In 1856 she married Hamon Benedict of Streetsboro, and after his death she married P. T. Dickinson of Sacramento, Calif. She afterward lived in Sacramento and Alameda, Calif. Besides the volume of verse listed below, she contributed to various magazines and newspapers.

Vesta, Philadelphia, 1872.

BENEDICT, WAYLAND RICHARDSON (Jan. 9, 1848–July 21, 1915), educator, husband of Anne K. Benedict (q.v.), was born in Rochester, N. Y. He graduated from the University of Rochester in 1865 and Rochester Theological Seminary in 1870. Ordained to the Baptist ministry, he was a pastor at Mt. Auburn, 1873–75, before joining the University of Cincinnati faculty, on which he served from 1875 to 1907. After his retirement he lived in Cambridge, Mass. He wrote a number of textbooks besides the titles listed below.

Theism and Evolution, [n.p.], 1886.
New Studies in the Beatitudes . . . , [Cincinnati, 1894].
World Views and Their Ethical Implications . . . , [Cincinnati], 1902.

BENNETT, EMERSON (March 16, 1822–May 11, 1905), was born on a farm near Monson, Mass. At the age of seventeen he ran away from home and wandered about the East. In 1840 he was in New York City, where he published *The Brigand,* a story in verse which was greeted with derision by the critics. In 1843 he was in Philadelphia. After an unsuccessful love affair, he came to Cincinnati in the spring of 1844; here he was to launch his literary career. For a time he worked soliciting subscriptions to the *Western Literary Journal,* edited by E. C. Z. Judson (Ned Buntline) (q.v.). He began selling stories to the Cincinnati *Commercial.* In 1846 Bennett and J. H. Green (q.v.) published the *Casket* at Lawrenceburg, Ind. He also served as an editor of the *Columbian and Great West.* In the late autumn of 1850 he returned to Philadelphia, where he spent the remainder of his life. He turned out a great many frontier melodramas and some city stories, which were published in twenty-five-cent editions by U. P. James of Cincinnati and T. B. Peterson of Philadelphia. A typical work, written during his Cincinnati years, was *Mike Fink: A Legend of the Ohio,* Cincinnati, 1848. The country around Lancaster is the setting for *The Forest Rose; A Tale of the Frontier,* Cincinnati, 1850.

BENNETT, HENRY HOLCOMB (Dec. 5, 1863–April 30, 1924), brother of John Bennett (q.v.), was born in Chillicothe, Ross County. He graduated from Kenyon College in 1886, after which he studied landscape painting at the Art Students' League, New York City. He then spent several years in the West engaged chiefly in railroading. He served as a reporter and city editor on the *Scioto Gazette* in Chillicothe, 1893–97, retiring from journalism to spend the rest of his days in writing poetry, short stories, and forthright articles on labor relations and in illustrating books. His verse and short stories appeared in leading magazines —*McClure's, Century, Lippincott's, Youth's Companion,* and *St. Nicholas,* among others. Reprinted in many readers and anthologies, his best-known poem, "The Flag Goes By," which was first published in *Youth's Companion,* is a part of the unforgettable poetry to which Ohio poets have contributed so heavily. His death occurred in Chillicothe. Besides a book on army life and an art book, he wrote *The County of Ross . . . ,* Madison, Wis., 1902.
WWW 1

BENNETT, JOHN (May 17, 1865–Dec. 28, 1956), was born in Chillicothe, Ross County; he died in Charleston, S. C., where he had lived for many years. If the many-sided John Bennett had done nothing more than write the graceful verses with which not too many associate his name, his fame would be that of many another poet whose name is embalmed in the more inclusive anthologies of American poetry. Or if he had been content only with his study of the speech and folklore of the Gullah Negro, he would be remembered for that contribution. Or, lacking either of these, he might well be remembered as a composer, as a not unsuccessful playwright, as an illustrator, or as an editor. Yet, for none of these will John Bennett be best and longest remembered: he will be remembered, and for a long and unpredictable time to come, as the author of two of the best juvenile books ever produced in the United States: *Master Skylark* and *Barnaby Lee.* John Bennett was born in 1865, a year that marks (somewhat roughly) the great turning point in American juvenile literature. Virtually everything produced in the United States for children before that year was written with a determined emphasis on "moral improvement" or education (so-called), and with pure entertainment either wholly disregarded or present in minute, perhaps accidental or unconscious, quantity. The middle 1860s saw the advent of such radicals as Edward S. Ellis, Harry Castlemon, Horatio Alger, Jr., Oliver Optic, and Louisa May Alcott who, consciously, wrote with the thought of entertainment first and with moralizing either a secondary quality or almost wholly lacking. These and a few others laid the foundation for what was to come: the golden age of American juvenile literature as exemplified by all that is best in *Our Young Folks, Harper's Round Table, Youth's Companion,* and, above all, *St. Nicholas* of blessed memory. Some authors of the earlier dreary period continued to grind out preachments thinly disguised as juvenile reading, as, for example, Bennett's fellow townswoman Martha Finley Farquharson (q.v.), creator of Elsie Dinsmore. But these less gifted authors were to be consigned to oblivion by succeeding generations of young readers, and our present era sees them as little more than curious period pieces. John Bennett was untouched by the output of these; his work shows none of their influence. John Bennett reached his greatest height with his contributions to *St. Nicholas: Master Skylark* and *Barnaby Lee,* both of which have a quality of timelessness that gives the positive impression that they will be read, reread, and loved long after many (perhaps most) of Bennett's contemporaries are forgotten. To both of these novels he brought so thorough a knowledge and understanding of the periods of which he wrote that as the *Critic* (New York) for Oct. 16, 1897, commented: "*Master Skylark* . . . has a positive educational value, aside from its interest as a story." Or, to quote the austere London *Athenaeum* of Dec. 11, 1897: "the writer knows the Elizabethan age, and his romance is better than many a history lesson." Bennett exhibited a rare talent: the ability to produce a historically accurate atmosphere without sacrifice of action. The dialogue in *Master Skylark* is not pure Elizabethan but is, rather, a skillful and necessary compromise—not a weak imitation liberally besprinkled with *thees* and *thous* in the fatuous hope that these would be sufficient to flavor the whole. As a master storyteller John Bennett never made the mistake of assuming that young readers, being young, are unable to distinguish genuine from counterfeit. Bennett's prose is the happy product of a writer who feels as a poet and sees as a painter. As a conscious poet he wrote:

> These are the hills the Lord hath
>   made
> That man may fear him unafraid.
> Up through the gateway of the
>   skies

Their purple slopes of peace arise
Like sunlit paths to Paradise.

But his poetry often emerges when he is least aware of it. Indeed, not a few of his (if you please) prose passages can be offered in "poetic form" as, for example, the following from *Master Skylark,* which I take the liberty of rearranging:

Beyond was a wood of chestnut-trees
As blue and leafless as a grove of spears;

And when the painter's influence is uppermost we find such splendid splashes of color as:

A cloud of dust was rising from the London road and drifting off across the fields like smoke when the old ricks burn in damp weather—a long, broad-sheeted mist; and in it were bits of moving gold, shreds of bright colors vaguely seen, and silvery gleams like the glitter of polished metal in the sun. And as he looked the shifty wind came down out of the west again and whirled the cloud of dust away, and there he saw a long line of men upon horses coming at an easy canter up the highway. Just as he had made this out the line came rattling to a stop, the distant drumming of hoofs was still, and as the long file knotted itself into a rosette of ruddy color amid the April green, a clear, shrill trumpet blew and blew again.

But above all John Bennett is a teller of tales, and so skilled in the art that he can cause Nick Atwood to say "I'd rather be my mother's boy" and not have his young readers think Nick a milksop. In the hands of a lesser writer the passage could be mawkish; but John Bennett, being a master of his craft, causes it to be natural and realistic. John Bennett's place in literature is secure. He had the rare privilege of seeing at least one of his books become a classic—and more than that cannot be given to any teller of tales.

Jacob Blanck

Master Skylark; A Story of Shakespeare's Time, New York, 1897.

Barnaby Lee, New York, 1902.

The Treasure of Peyre Gaillard . . . , New York, 1906.

Songs Which My Youth Sung, Charleston, S. C., 1914.

Madame Margot; A Grotesque Legend of Old Charleston, New York, 1921.

Apothecaries' Hall, a Unique Exhibit at the Charleston Museum; An Ancient Drug-shop Whose Business Survived Plagues, Wars, Great Fires and Earth Quakes for One Hundred and Forty Years . . . , Charleston, S. C., 1923.

The Pigtail of Ah Lee Ben Loo . . . , New York, 1928.

Blue Jacket, War Chief of the Shawnees, and His Part in Ohio's History, Chillicothe, 1943.

The Doctor to the Dead; Grotesque Legends & Folk Tales of Old Charleston, New York, [1946].

BENNETT, R. KING. Pseud. See Richard N. Taneyhill.

BENSON, HENRY CLARK (1815– ?), clergyman, was born near Xenia, Greene County. He became a Methodist minister in 1842, taught Greek at Asbury University, 1850–52, and in 1852 moved to the West, where he was a missionary to the Choctaw Indians and also edited religious papers in California and Oregon.

Life among the Choctaw Indians . . . , Cincinnati, 1860.

BENSON, MILDRED WIRT (July 10, 1905–), born in Ladora, Iowa, has lived in Toledo since 1923. She is the widow of George A. Benson, former editor of the Toledo *Times,* a paper on which she has also worked as courthouse reporter. A prolific author of well over a hundred books for children, she has written under various pen names, e.g., John M. Foster, *Ruth Darrow in the Fire Patrol . . . ,* New York, [1930]; Joan Clark, *Penny Nichols Finds a Clue,* Chicago, [1936]; Dorothy West, *Dot and Dash at Happy Hollow,* New York, [1938]; Frank Bell, *Flash Evans, Camera News Hawk,* New York, [1940]; and Fred C. Rotsvald, *Linda,* New York, [1940].

BENTLEY, WILLIAM PRESTON (April 13, 1862–April 16, 1941), clergyman, was born in Wilmington, Clinton County. After graduating from Bethany College in 1890, he studied agriculture at Ohio State University. Under the auspices of the Disciples of Christ Church, he went to China as a missionary. In 1898 he established the College of Science in Central China; he wrote several textbooks for use there and translated books into Chinese. After returning to the United States he served a church in San Francisco and was on the faculty of Chapman College. He published a collection of verse: *Where Fountains Play,* New York, 1938.

BENTON, ARIEL (Feb. 13, 1792–Nov. 7, 1883), who came to Chardon from New England in 1815, spent his life in Geauga County. His recollections of pioneer life in the Western Reserve were published for the family by his nephew, Ira E. Benton of Peoria, Ill.

Life and Times of Ariel Benton . . ., Peoria, Ill., 1882.

BENTON, ELBERT JAY (March 23, 1871–March 28, 1946), educator, was born in Dubuque, Iowa. He earned his Ph.D. at Johns Hopkins University in 1903. After teaching in Kansas and Indiana, he joined the faculty of Western Reserve University, where he remained until his retirement in 1941. He published several scholarly historical studies, collaborated in the writing of several American history textbooks, and wrote concerning Cleveland, e.g., *Cultural Story of an American City, Cleveland*, Cleveland, 1943. WWW 2

BENTON, GUY POTTER (May 26, 1865–June 28, 1927), educator, was born in Kenton, Hardin County. He served as president of several institutions: Upper Iowa University (1899–1902), Miami University (1902–11), and University of Vermont (1911–19). From 1921 to 1924 he was chief educational consultant to the president of the University of the Philippines. He wrote *The Real College*, Cincinnati, [1909]. WWW 1

BENTON, WALTER J. (Oct. 27, 1907–), was born Walter Potashnik in Austria. His family came to America in 1922 and settled in Warren, Trumbull County, where he attended public schools. After graduating from Ohio University in 1933, he worked for five years as an investigator for the Department of Welfare, New York City, served in the Signal Corps during World War II, and now lives in New York City. He has published poems in many national magazines; his first collected volume was published during the war: *This Is My Beloved*, New York, 1943.

BERDAN, JOHN MILTON (July 9, 1873–April 3, 1949), educator, was born in Toledo, Lucas County. After graduating from Yale in 1896, he taught in Toledo for a time before joining the Yale faculty. He retired from teaching in 1941. His advice was valued by Sinclair Lewis and numerous other writers who were his students at Yale. He published several textbooks and *Early Tudor Poetry*, New York, 1920. WWE 1

BERGEN, FANNY DICKERSON (Feb. 4, 1846– ?), educator and folklorist, was born in Mansfield, Richland County. She graduated from Antioch College in 1875. She taught school in Mansfield, in Cleveland, and at Antioch College. The first two titles below were written in collaboration with her husband, Joseph Y. Bergen (q.v.); the last two were prepared under the sponsorship of the American Folklore Society.

The Development Theory . . ., Boston, 1884.

Glimpses at the Plant World, New York, 1892.

Current Superstitions . . ., New York, 1896.

Animal and Plant Lore . . ., New York, 1899.

BERGEN, JOSEPH YOUNG (Feb. 22, 1851–Oct. 10, 1917), was born in Red Bank, Maine. After graduating from Antioch College in 1872, he worked for a time on the Ohio Geological Survey. He collaborated with his wife, Fanny D. Bergen (q.v.), in writing two books and also wrote a number of science textbooks.

BERGER, DANIEL (Feb. 14, 1832–Sept. 12, 1920), clergyman, was born near Reading, Pa. In 1838 the family moved to Springfield, where Daniel grew up on a farm. After two years' attendance at the Ohio Methodist Conference high school, he spent three years teaching at an academy in New Carlisle and afterward became principal of a school in Springfield. In 1853 he married Mary Frances Merry (c.1833–Feb. 10, 1915), a cousin of Cardinal Merry del Val. A convert to Protestantism before her marriage, she published in 1913 a widely read pamphlet: *In and Out of Catholicism*. Daniel became a minister of the United Brethren Church in 1854, served as a pastor until 1858, edited the *Religious Telescope* in Dayton, 1858–69, and was editor of the Sunday School literature of the United Brethren Church, 1869–95.

History of the Church of the United Brethren in Christ, New York, 1894.

BERGER, ELMER (May 27, 1908–), rabbi, was born in Cleveland, Cuyahoga County. He attended Cleveland public schools and graduated from the University of Cincinnati in 1930 and Hebrew Union College in 1932. He was a rabbi in Pontiac, Mich., 1932–36, and Flint, Mich., 1936–43. He is executive director of the American Council for Judaism and has written several books, e.g., *The Jewish Dilemma*, New York, 1945.

BERING, JOHN A. (1839–1922), was born in Highland County. He served in the 48th O.V.I. from Oct., 1861, to June, 1865. He was taken prisoner in April, 1864, and was imprisoned until the end of the war. He collaborated with Thomas Montgomery in writing the regimental history listed below.

History of the Forty-eighth Ohio Veteran Volunteer Infantry . . . , Hillsboro, 1880.

BERKMAN, JACK N. (Feb. 12, 1905–), laywer, born in London, England, was brought when two years old to Canton, where he grew up. After graduating from the University of Michigan in 1926, he attended Harvard Law School and on completing his work began practice in Steubenville. He has published *Playing God, a Heroesque Comedy . . .* , Boston, [1931].

BERNARD, FLORENCE SCOTT (July 19, 1889–May 27, 1948), was born in Clyde, Sandusky County. She attended the public schools of Tiffin and after 1914 lived in Toledo. She published short stories in magazines and one book, *Diana of Briarcliffe,* Boston, [1923]. WW 16

BERRY, ELWOOD SYLVESTER (Feb. 3, 1879–July 1, 1954), Catholic priest, was born near Morganville, Morgan County. A graduate of Mount Saint Mary's College, Emmitsburg, Md., he taught in country schools in Morgan County, 1896–99, studied at Mount Saint Mary's of the West, Cincinnati, 1901-06, served various parishes in Ohio, 1906–22, and taught philosophy and theology at Mount Saint Mary's, Md., from 1922 until his death. He published several books on religious themes, e.g., *The Apocalypse of St. John,* Columbus, 1921.

BESSE, HENRY (1823–1901), physician, was born in Licking County. He read medicine for two years, took a term of lectures at Starling Medical College, and began practicing in East Liberty in 1847. In 1857 he graduated from Western Reserve Medical College, and in 1863 he moved to Delaware, where he practiced until 1899. In March, 1871, he became agent and physician to Mina and Minnie, Siamese twins born the year before in Morrow County. The "double babe" was exhibited in several Ohio cities but died in July soon after the exhibition reached Boston. About one-third of Dr. Besse's curious book is devoted to a description of the united babies.

Diploteratology; Or, a History of Some of the Most Wonderful Human Beings That Have Ever Lived in Double Form . . . , Delaware, 1874.

BEST, NOLAN RICE (April 9, 1871–July 20, 1930), editor, was born in Rich Hill, Knox County. He graduated from Otterbein College in 1892. After a year with the United Brethren Publishing House, Dayton, and six years with the Zanesville *Daily Courier,* he joined the staff of *The Interior* (later *The Continent*); he was associated with this periodical from 1901 until 1924, when he became executive secretary of the Baltimore Federation of Churches. His death occurred in Baltimore, Md. His books, written on religious and inspirational themes, include *The College Man in Doubt,* Philadelphia, 1902. WWW 1

BEST, SUSIE MONTGOMERY (Aug. 4, 1869–March 13, 1944), educator, was born in Cincinnati, Hamilton County, and spent her entire life in that city. A teacher in the elementary schools, she published articles and poems in various periodicals and also composed valentine verses for a commercial publisher. She also wrote several titles in a series, *World Famous Stories in Historic Settings.*

The Fallen Pillar Saint, and Other Poems, New York, 1890.

Altar Candles, Boston, [1927].

Leaves from Life's Tree, a Book of Verse, Philadelphia, [1947].

BETTAN, ISRAEL (Jan. 16, 1889–Aug. 5, 1957), rabbi, was born in Lithuania. He graduated from the University of Cincinnati in 1910 and was ordained a rabbi in 1912. He served a synagogue in Charleston, W. Va., 1912-22, and was on the faculty of Hebrew Union College, 1922–55. He published several books on religious subjects, e.g., *The Five Scrolls; A Commentary . . .* , Cincinnati, 1950.

BETTEN, FRANCIS SALES (Salesius) (April 16, 1863–Dec. 8, 1942), clergyman and educator, born in Wocklum, Germany, came to America in 1898. A member of the Society of Jesus, he taught in several Catholic universities, including St. Ignatius (John Carroll) in Cleveland, 1909–28. He wrote several history textbooks and some religious works, e.g., *St. Boniface and St. Virgil . . .* , [Washington, D. C., 1927]. WWW 2

BETTY, MRS. WILLIAM H. See Gladys E. Toon.

BEUM, ROBERT LAWRENCE (Aug. 20, 1929–), was born in Mount Vernon, Knox County, but moved to Columbus at an early age. He attended Ohio State University and in 1960 is studying for his doctorate at the University of Nebraska. While a student at Ohio State, he published a collection of poems under the pen name Robert Lawrence: *The Ninth Hour,* New York, [1948].

BEVERIDGE, ALBERT JEREMIAH (1862–April 27, 1927), lawyer, historian, and U. S. Senator, was born in Highland County, but lived only the first three years of his life in Ohio. When he was three, his parents moved to Illinois, and throughout his mature life he was a resident of Indiana. He graduated from Asbury University, Greencastle, Ind., in 1885, read law and was admitted to the bar in 1887, practiced in Indianapolis, and took an active part in Indiana Republican politics. He served in the Senate, 1899–1910, noted chiefly as an exponent of imperialism. His joining the Progressive movement in 1912 probably was the cause of his subsequent failures to win public office. As a historian and biographer, his masterpiece was *The Life of John Marshall,* 4 vols., New York, 1916–19. His biography of Lincoln, which is probably better known, was left incomplete at the time of his death. DAB 2

BEVIS, ALMA DARST MURRAY (Feb. 4, 1888–), was born and educated in Cincinnati, Hamilton County. She graduated from the University of Cincinnati in 1909 and later did graduate work in several universities and taught school in Iowa and Ohio. She has lived in Columbus since 1940, when her husband, Howard L. Bevis, became president of Ohio State University. Mrs. Bevis has published a historical study of Harvard: *Diets and Riots . . . ,* Boston, 1936. WWAW 1

BEVIS, SOPHIA CORTOULDE HAZLETT (July 17, 1846– ?), was born in Zanesville, Muskingum County. After working on New York newspapers for some years, she came to Cincinnati around 1883 to work on the *Penny Post.* She married Henry M. Bevis, a Cincinnati printer and publisher. She was one of the founders of the Woman's Press Club in Cincinnati.

Poems, Cincinnati, 1890.

BICKHAM, WILLIAM DENISON (March 30, 1827–March 29, 1894), journalist, was born in Cincinnati, Hamilton County. He attended Cincinnati schools and Bethany College. At the age of twenty he became city and commercial editor of the Louisville *Daily Courier.* In 1850 he joined the rush to the gold fields of California; after working in various capacities on San Francisco newspapers, he returned to Ohio in 1854. He wrote his book on Rosecrans' campaign while in the field as a war correspondent for the Cincinnati *Commercial.* When the Dayton *Journal* was destroyed by a mob on May 5, 1863, he was invited to take charge and re-establish the newspaper. He assumed proprietorship, a position he held until his death in Dayton over thirty years later.

Rosecrans' Campaign with the Fourteenth Army Corps, or the Army of the Cumberland: A Narrative of Personal Observations . . . , Cincinnati, 1863.

From Ohio to the Rocky Mountains . . . , Dayton, 1879.

BICKLEY, GEORGE W. L. (1823–1867), born in Russell County, Va., was left an orphan at the age of twelve. He went to Europe, where he spent a number of years trying to trace his family. Wherever he happened to be, he attended medical lectures—Paris, London, Edinburgh, New York, Philadelphia. Later, though apparently lacking an academic degree, he is believed to have taught in medical schools in the South; meanwhile his mind was occupied with grandiose schemes. At one time he is said to have toyed with the idea of overthrowing the Mexican government and establishing himself as emperor, while on another occasion he promoted a project for buying the entire coal output of the Dominican Republic. He turned up at Jeffersonville, Tazewell County, Va., about 1850, opened an office in the Union Hotel, and began practicing medicine there. It was during this lull in his otherwise eventful career that he took time out—a scant seven weeks—to gather the materials and write a creditable history of the county. He turned up at Cincinnati in 1851 with the manuscript, found a publisher, and the following year began teaching materia medica at the Eclectic Medical Institute. Declaring that his work as a lecturer was eminently satisfactory, Dr. Otto Juettner said: "He was the equal of any medical writer in the West at that time. His style reminds one of Drake, rhetorical and of classic purity." In 1853 he published a popular novel, *Adalaska,* which was translated into German and French. In April of that year—airily denying pecuniary considerations—he founded the *West American Review* "to elevate and purify the tone of American literature by a critical examination of its defects and merits." A serial feature was included "to meet a morbid appetite which has manifested itself in the constant and ever increasing demand for popular Magazines in the United States." The following November the *Review* absorbed the *Parlor Magazine,* of which Alice Cary was editor, and continued until Oct., 1854, under the title *American Monthly.* Shortly after its suspension Bickley went underground. Little is actually known of Bickley's movements during the next two years. He is said to have toured the South, where he espoused the cause of the Southern Rights Clubs, and to have organized "castles" of his subversive Knights of the Golden Circle. His only known portrait, believed to have been taken at this time, shows him wearing the insignia of the order. As quietly as he had slipped away, he returned to the practice of medicine in Cincinnati and to the faculty of the Eclectic Medical Institute in 1857. The next year he became editor of the *Scientific Artisan,* and in conjunction with Dr. R. S. Newton he established the *Cincinnati Eclectic and Edinburgh Review.* With secession almost an accomplished fact in 1860, he again went underground and began organizing the Knights in the border states. He emerged long enough in May, 1861, to address a defiant "Open Letter to the Kentucky Legislature" wherein he boasted of 8,000 Knights scattered through every county of that state. He could hardly have chosen a more inopportune moment, for this was the very month in which that implacable foe of the Knights, the Union Club, was organized in Louisville, and that was the last heard of him in Kentucky. With a glib story of having been caught in the deep South at the outbreak of hostilities and forced to serve in the Confederate army, he turned up at General Rosecrans' headquarters in July, 1863, seeking a pass to Cincinnati. Long since he had become a marked man in the North, and it was probably with tongue in cheek that the General granted him the pass, accompanied by the injunction that he must travel direct to Cincinnati with no stops between. He made the mistake of stopping at New Albany, Ind., where he found a military reception committee awaiting him, and then and there he went out of circulation for the duration of the war. Afterward he toured Europe lecturing and sightseeing. He died in Baltimore, Md.

Ernest J. Wessen

History of the Settlement and Indian Wars of Tazewell County, Virginia . . . , Cincinnati, 1852.
Adalaska: Or, the Strange and Mysterious Family of the Cave of Genreva, Cincinnati, 1853.
Physiological and Scientific Botany, [Cincinnati, 1853].
Principles of Scientific Botany, Cincinnati, 1853.
Concentrated Preparations, Cincinnati, 1855.

BICKNELL, EMELINE LARKIN (Feb. 19, 1825–May 29, 1916), was born on her father's farm at Great Bend, Meigs County. In 1846 she was married to Isaac Cowdery, but in 1854 she obtained a divorce and reassumed her maiden name. She taught school in Meigs County, was superintendent of a Methodist home for the aged in New York State, and returned to Ohio to become matron of the Meigs County Children's Home. After retiring she lived in Pomeroy, where she died at the age of 91. Throughout her life she published poetry in various periodicals, but the volume below is her only collection.

Violets, and Other Poems, New York, 1897.

BIDDLE, HORACE PETERS (March 27, 1811–May 13, 1900), lawyer and judge, was born in a log cabin in what is now Hocking County. He attended district schools, read law in Lancaster under Hocking H. Hunter, and was admitted to the Ohio bar in 1839. In the same year he left Ohio for Indiana, and the remainder of his life was spent in that state. He practiced in Logansport, served as circuit court judge, and also served on the State Supreme Court, 1874–81. In his home on Biddle's Island in the Wabash River, he maintained the largest private library in the state, translated works from several European languages, and entertained a wide circle of friends. An edition of the first title below is said to have appeared in 1849, but no copy has been located.

A Few Poems, Cincinnati, 1858.
The Musical Scale, Cincinnati, 1860.
Poems, New York, 1868.
Biddle's Poems, New York, 1872.
The Definition of Poetry . . . , Cincinnati, 1873.
Glances at the World, [n.p.], 1873.
My Scrap Book, Logansport, 1874.
American Boyhood, Philadelphia, 1876.
The Analysis of Rhyme . . . , Cincinnati, 1876.
An Essay on Russian Literature, Cincinnati, 1877.
The Tetrachord . . . , Cincinnati, 1877.
Amatories by an Amateur, Cincinnati, 1878.
The Elements of Knowledge, Cincinnati, 1881.
Prose Miscellany, Cincinnati, 1881.
Last Poems, Cincinnati, 1882.
The Eureka . . . , Logansport, 1886.
Life and Services of John B. Dillon, (with John Coburn), Indianapolis, 1886.

BIDDLE, JACOB ALBERT (Dec. 24, 1845–Sept. 24, 1914), was born in Rochester, Lorain County. He was president of Philomath College, Oreg., and later served as pastor in Milford and South Norwalk, Conn. His death occurred in South Manchester, Conn.

Social Regeneration, Hartford, 1896.
The Perfect Life, Boston, [1915].

BIDWELL, JOHN (Aug. 5, 1819–April 4, 1900), was born in Chautauqua County, N. Y. His family moved to Ashtabula County in 1831 and later moved on to Darke County. In 1836 young Bidwell walked the nearly 300 miles back to Ashtabula in order to enter Kingsville Academy. There he made such progress that he was elected principal of the institution for 1837. He taught school in Darke County in 1838 and then decided to seek his fortune in the West. In May, 1841, he joined the Bartleson party at Independence, Mo., and thus became a member of the first emigrant train to make the journey to California from Missouri. From his arrival until his death—from the Bear Flag revolt of 1846 to his candidacy for Governor of California in 1890 on the Prohibition ticket—he played an active role in shaping the history of California. In 1849 he acquired the extensive Rancho Chico of 22,000 acres, which he brought to such a high state of development that he was recognized as the outstanding agriculturist of the state. He was one of the early regents of the University of California and a benefactor of the State Normal School.

John Bidwell's Trip to California, 1841, [St. Louis, Mo., 1842].

Echoes of the Past: An Account of the First Emigrant Train to California, Fremont in the Conquest of California, the Discovery of Gold and Early Reminiscences, Chico, Calif., [1900].

BIERBOWER, ELSIE JANIS. See Elsie Janis.

BIERCE, AMBROSE GWINNETT (June 24, 1842–1914?), remembered principally for the macabre short stories in *Tales of Soldiers and Civilians* and *Can Such Things Be?,* and *The Devil's Dictionary,* was born in Meigs County. His father, Marcus Aurelius Bierce, and his mother, Laura Sherwood, were both born in Cornwall, Conn. The families migrated to Portage County, where Marcus married Laura in 1822. In 1840 the family moved to Horse Cave, Meigs County. The reticence of Bierce about his early childhood and the scarcity of family records prevent our knowing much about his early life. It is said that the father had an unusually large number of books and that he had a taste for poetry. In 1846 they left Ohio for Walnut Creek, Ind. The uncle of Ambrose Bierce was Lucius Verus Bierce (q.v.), whose flamboyant career was of the sort which would have attracted the nephew. Family tradition has it that Ambrose visited Lucius at various times in Akron and that Lucius sent him to the Kentucky Military Institute for a period. Bierce's inclination to say little about his youth prevents our knowing what his associations with his uncle were. Nor is information from Lucius available on this interesting subject. Early after the outbreak of the Civil War, Bierce joined Company C of the Ninth Regiment of Indiana Volunteers. His war years proved him a good soldier, and he was to receive citations for bravery in action and for excellence of service. He fought at Girard Hill, Carrick's Ford, Shiloh, Chickamauga, Missionary Ridge, and Kennesaw Mountain, where he was wounded in the head. He received a discharge early in 1865. His war experiences provided him with material for most of his memorable short stories and for some of his finest sketches. In 1866 he became attached to the staff of General William B. Hazen (q.v.), under whom he had served in the army. Bierce's job was mapping and topographical studies. When the expedition reached California, Bierce was disappointed to learn that his conscientious service was ill rewarded by a second lieutenancy. He resigned. He was to remain in California for the next five years. In 1867 he began contributing to the journals and magazines on the West Coast, the *Californian* printing his earliest poems. Soon he was appearing in the *News Letter, The Golden Era,* and other publications. December 25, 1871, he was married to Mollie Day. The bride's father gave the young couple a trip to England as a wedding gift. They were to remain in England until the autumn of 1875. Bierce worked on the staff of *Fun,* edited the short-lived *Lantern* for the Empress Eugénie, and contributed to *Hood's Comic Annual.* He made various acquaintances among London's literary figures, including George Augustus Sala, W. S. Gilbert, and Thomas Hood. His mordantly humorous sketches (observed in his early books, *The Fiend's Delight* and *Nuggets and Dust Panned out in California*) earned for him the sobriquet "Bitter Bierce." In 1876 the Bierces were back in San Francisco. Bierce worked on the *Wasp* and the *Argonaut* until William Randolph Hearst took over *The Examiner* in 1887. As conductor of the column "Prattle," which appeared on the editorial page, Bierce made himself the literary dictator of the Pacific coast; his satirical and witty mots were widely quoted. His first volume of stories, *Tales of Soldiers and Civilians* (1891), however grim and vivid, was not a publishing success. In 1892 he revised and rewrote G. A. Danziger's

The Monk and the Hangman's Daughter. Can Such Things Be? (1893) contained some of his memorable stories, dealing with supernatural occurrences and weird episodes. It was in the early years of this decade that Bierce achieved his greatest work. Hearst sent Bierce to Washington in 1896 to write against Huntington's proposed refunding bill; the following year he was again in the East, this time as correspondent of the New York *American.* In 1906 appeared *The Cynic's Word Book,* later titled *Devil's Dictionary,* remembered for its sardonic definitions and its devastating disillusionment. His best work was now over; there remained principally his garnering of fugitive pieces. He edited his *Collected Works* (1909–12) in a dozen volumes. This was an ill-advised undertaking, for the material republished was largely inferior; Bierce was unwilling to omit patently immature work or stuff better left hidden. His reputation gained nothing by the pretentious row of volumes. By 1913 he felt lonely and tired. He had been disappointed in the publishing fiasco of his *Collected Works;* moreover, many of his friends were now dead. He made a nostalgic tour of the battlefields upon which he had fought and remembered the old excitement. The political disturbances in Mexico attracted him, and he decided to cross the border. From time to time word was heard from him; but after December 26, 1913, there was only silence. The various myths concerning his death have remained unresolved, but he found what he sought, "the good, kind darkness." He remains an important though not a key figure in American literature. While his work may suggest the manner and material of Poe, it is actually not very much like Poe's. No doubt he learned method from Poe and from Bret Harte. In turn he seems to have anticipated such unlike writers as Stephen Crane and O. Henry.

Charles Duffy

Nuggets and Dust Panned Out in California, (by Dod Grile, Collected and loosely arranged by J. Milton Sloluck), London, [1872].
The Fiend's Delight, (by Dod Grile), New York, 1873.
Cobwebs from an Empty Skull, (by Dod Grile), New York, 1874.
Tales of Soldiers and Civilians, San Francisco, 1891.
Black Beetle in Amber, San Francisco, 1892.
The Monk and the Hangman's Daughter, Chicago, 1892.
Can Such Things Be?, New York, [1893].
Fantastic Fables, New York, 1899.
Shapes of Clay, San Francisco, 1903.
The Cynic's Word Book, New York, 1906.
A Son of the Gods and a Horseman in the Sky, San Francisco, 1907.
The Collected Works . . . , 12 vols., New York, 1909–12.
The Shadow on the Dial, and Other Essays, San Francisco, 1909.
Write It Right . . . , New York, 1909.
The Letters of Ambrose Bierce . . . , (Bertha C. Pope, ed.), San Francisco, 1922.
Twenty-one Letters . . . , (Samuel Loveman, ed.), Cleveland, 1922.

BIERCE, CHLOE B. CONANT (Oct. 30, 1802–Dec. 31, 1846), was born in Beckett, Mass. Her parents brought her to Portage County in 1811. She taught school in Pennsylvania during the summers of 1819 and 1821 and married H. N. Bierce in 1823. Twenty-three years after her death from tuberculosis, her son, Rev. D. E. Bierce, discovered, edited, and published her journals.

Journal and Biographical Notice . . . , Cincinnati, 1869.

BIERCE, LUCIUS VERUS (Aug. 4, 1801–Nov. 11, 1876), youngest of the seven children of William and Abigail (Bell) Bierce, was born in Cornwall Bridge, Conn. His father was a Revolutionary War veteran who, as a farmer and shoemaker, kept his family in "comfortable circumstances." Aside from the modest fame that Lucius enjoyed, none of the family achieved distinction. His eldest brother, Marcus Aurelius, was the father of Ambrose Bierce (q.v.), and, according to family legend, young Ambrose modeled himself somewhat on his favorite uncle, Lucius. Soon after the death of Abigail in Sept., 1815, the family migrated to Nelson, Portage County, in the Connecticut Reserve of Ohio. There were no advanced schools in the newly settled Western Reserve, so young Bierce enrolled in the Academy of Ohio University in Dec., 1817. His Roman name suited him well, for the college's classical curriculum left a decided mark upon his mind, and his participation in the weekly debates of the Athenian Literary Society introduced him to a lifelong interest in forceful oral expression. In Sept., 1822, he graduated from the University with an A.B. degree. One month later Bierce started what might be described as the American frontier's "Grand Tour." In company with a college chum he set forth on foot on a year-long, 1,800-mile "ramble" through the South. He stayed briefly at Lancaster, S. C., where he "played pedagogue" and read law. In May, 1823, having walked on to Athens, Ala., he completed his legal reading and was licensed as an attorney. Upon his return to Ohio, Bierce continued his study of law and was licensed to practice in Ohio. He settled in the Western Reserve, where in 1826 he commenced his career of public service as prosecuting attorney for Portage County and justice of the peace of Ravenna Township, offices which he held for eleven years. Commissioned a captain in the Ohio Militia in 1832, he attained the rank of brigadier general five years later. That same year Bierce moved a few miles west to the young canal town of Akron, where he lived until his death. Here he practiced law, served six terms as mayor, was president of the Akron School Board at a time when the influential Akron School Law was promulgated, and was elected state senator. He was a founder of Akron Lodge, Free and Accepted Masons, and its Master for many years. In 1853 he became Grand Master of the Grand Lodge of Ohio. Bierce supported the Washingtonian temperance movement, urged local resistance to the Fugitive Slave Act of 1850, extolled the virtues of John Brown and aided him in his Kansas ventures. On patriotic occasions he came to be the unofficial public orator of the city and its surrounding areas. Most colorful of his many undertakings was the abortive military foray that he led into Windsor, Ontario, during the Canadian Rebellion of 1837–38. As a leading spirit in the Hunters or Patriot movement, Bierce was commissioned Major General and Commander in Chief of the Patriot forces in Canada, and in Dec., 1838, he personally led the western forces across the Detroit River. His "army," variously estimated at 147 to 400 men, was routed by Canadian militia, and most of his force was captured, but Bierce and a few followers made good their escape to Michigan. Bierce was twice indicted in Federal court for violating American neutrality laws, but both indictments were dropped. Too old for active campaigning in the Civil War, Bierce raised a company of volunteers for the Union armies and two companies of Marines which he delivered at his own expense to the Washington Navy Yard. He served as assistant adjutant general of Volunteers in Ohio, as inspector for Ohio, and, near the war's end, as a commandant of Camp Washburne and Camp Randall, Wis. Throughout his life Bierce was a keen observer of people and places. On his long Southern walk he kept notes that he expanded into a journal which he later edited, evidently with an eye toward publication. Despite his pretentious style, one feels the force of Bierce's convictions, the slash of his caustic wit. This is evident in his description of his first encounter with Negro slavery, his assessment of Indians and half-breeds, and his description of eccentric characters such as the Kentuckian who claimed to be Jesus Christ. This journal was one of the items Bierce donated to the library of the recently established Buchtel College, now the University of Akron. Though never properly published, poorly edited portions of the journal were serialized in the *Akron Alumni Quarterly* (1919–22). Local history, specifically the history of the Western Reserve, was the subject of most of Bierce's published writing. Sometime in the ante-bellum period he determined to record the story of this region he had claimed for his own. Soon after he settled in Akron he began collecting historical material which he organized into sketches of the various townships of Summit County. In 1854 the Canfield brothers of Akron published eighteen of these sketches in a collection called *Historical Reminiscences of Summit County*. Between 1855 and 1868, seventeen similar sketches of Portage County townships appeared in the *Portage County Democrat* under the title "Home Reminiscences." They were intended to be part of a history of the Western Reserve which never materialized. Bierce had published an introductory essay for this proposed history in the Akron *Argus* (1873–74). This essay and the sketches form a substantial basis for such a history. Numerous other historical articles and orations were printed in newspapers and pamphlets, and had Bierce been able to gather all his writings in one publication, it would have constituted the most extensive material yet compiled about the history of the Western Reserve. Bierce was not a great stylist. His histories are not analytical nor do they deal with the broad sweep of events, but they do represent a detailed account of the lives of the people who first settled the Reserve. He has properly labeled his writings "reminiscences"—reminiscences of Indians, of big hunts, of pioneer hardships. He was much concerned, as were the pioneers, with "firsts," and the first settler, the first child born in an area, the first church were accounted for whenever possible. By preserving and recording the recollections of early settlers he performed an important historical function. Only a small portion of Bierce's writings concern subjects other than the Reserve. In 1855 he published his revision of Sir Roger L'Estrange's abstract of Seneca's *Morals*. In 1868 he tried his hand at biography with a brief assessment of Asaph Whittlesey of Tallmadge. He also left a number of unpublished essays on science and religion. Bierce regretted his lack of surviving heirs. In 1836 he married Frances C. Peck, who bore him a son. The infant's death in Feb., 1839, was followed in six months by his mother's. In 1840 Bierce married Sophronia Ladd. She survived him by six years, but their daughter died when nineteen. On Nov. 11, 1876, in the Centennial Year, "General" Bierce, as he was respectfully called, died quietly at his Akron home.

George W. Knepper

Historical Reminiscences of Summit County . . . , Akron, 1854.

BIGELOW, MAURICE ALPHEUS (Dec. 8, 1872–Jan. 6, 1955), educator, was born in Milford Center, Union County. He graduated from Ohio Wesleyan University in 1894 and from Harvard University (Ph.D.) in 1901. He served on the biology faculty, Columbia University, 1899–1939. He published a number of textbooks and a series of lectures: *Sex Education . . .* , New York, 1916. WWW 3

BIGGER, DAVID DWIGHT (May 18, 1849–Feb. 3, 1932), clergyman, born in Pittsburgh, Pa., was pastor of First Presbyterian Church, Tiffin, 1878–96. His death occurred in St. Petersburg, Fla. He wrote at least two biographies, e.g., a life of General William H. Gibson: *Ohio's Silver-Tongued Orator . . .* , Dayton, 1901.

BIGGERS, EARL DERR (Aug. 26, 1884–April 5, 1933), was born in Warren, Trumbull County. After graduating from Harvard in 1907, he wrote for the Boston *Traveler.* His first popular success came in 1913 with *Seven Keys to Baldpate,* which was fairly successful as a novel but spectacularly so as a play starring George M. Cohan. Biggers' best-known character, Charlie Chan, appeared first in *The House Without a Key,* Indianapolis, [1925]. The suave, sagacious Chinese detective caught the public's fancy and has been reincarnated in a comic strip, motion pictures, and television plays. Altogether, Biggers wrote six Charlie Chan novels, all of them first serialized in the *Saturday Evening Post* and all immensely popular. The amiable, patient Chinese is one of the half-dozen best-known fictional detectives. DAB 21

BIGGS, LOUISE OGAN (July 24, 1882–Oct. 28, 1958), educator, was born in Elk Township, Vinton County. After graduating from Ohio University, she taught school in McArthur and also in Wisconsin and West Virginia. She published a book of Bible stories and *A Brief History of Vinton County,* Columbus, 1950.

BILES, ROY EDWIN (May 12, 1888–March 3, 1941), was born in Cincinnati, Hamilton County. After he became interested in gardening, he lectured widely on the subject and published articles in the Cincinnati *Enquirer* and other newspapers. He published two books, the first of which was *The Book of Garden Magic,* [Cincinnati, 1935].

BILLINGS, JOHN SHAW (April 12, 1838–March 11, 1913), physician and librarian, was born in southeastern Indiana. He attended Miami University and Medical College of Ohio during the 1850s and practiced in Cincinnati during 1860–61. He was a prolific and influential writer of articles, pamphlets, and books on medicine, statistics, hospital construction, libraries, and related subjects.

BILLINGS, JOSH. Pseud. See Henry W. Shaw.

BILLINGSLEY, AMOS STEVENS (Nov. 14, 1818–Oct. 12, 1897), clergyman, was born near East Palestine, Columbiana County. He graduated from Jefferson College in 1847 and Allegheny Theological Seminary in 1850. He served as pastor of several churches, as a missionary in Nebraska and Colorado, and as an army chaplain. The first title below was also published as *From the Flag to the Cross. . . .* He died in Statesville, N. C.

Christianity in the War . . . , Philadelphia, 1872.

The Life of the Great Preacher, Reverend George Whitefield . . . , Philadelphia, 1878.

BIMELER, JOSEPH MICHAEL (c.1778–Aug. 27, 1853), was the leader of the German Separatists who founded the village of Zoar in Tuscarawas County from the time of their migration from Württemberg in 1817 until his death. The colony was organized on 5,500 acres of land purchased with the aid of Quakers in Philadelphia, where the colonists landed on their arrival in America. Little is known of Bimeler's early life, but he is said to have been a schoolteacher in Munich as a young man. His interests were broad; he had a professional knowledge of weaving and had more than a passing interest in music, he had read widely in the fields of medicine, chemistry, astronomy, and history. The outstanding success of the Zoar experiment in communal living is sufficient proof of his acumen as a businessman. His guiding hand was sadly missed after his death, although the village continued to prosper and, even as late as the 1890s, was described by city dwellers as a rural paradise. The three volumes listed below, containing more than 2,500 pages, are adequate testimony both of Bimeler's mastery of Separatist theology and of his recognition by the villagers as their spiritual guide. The volume *Etwas Fürs Herz!*, which was the last to be printed, covers the period 1822–29 and therefore antedates the material in the two volumes of *Die Wahre Separation*. These addresses (they were never referred to as sermons), more than 500 in all, represent approximately one-third of those delivered by Bimeler in the course of thirty years. Herr Bimeler did not write these sermons. He spoke extemporaneously Sunday after Sunday, believing along with his listeners that the Holy Spirit was speaking through him. The addresses were preserved under circumstances that might be described as fortuitous. Johannes Neef, a young member of the Society and for a time the village schoolmaster, began in 1822 to make notes of Bimeler's remarks in order that his father, who was deaf, might know what the leader was saying. His early efforts, preserved in *Etwas Fürs Herz!*, were in the nature of summaries, but his skill increased with the years, and *Die Wahre Separation* apparently contains the lectures almost as they were delivered. Neef continued his labor of love until his untimely death in 1832, and all save Part Four of *Die Wahre Separation* may be attributed to him. Another amanuensis appeared in 1834, but his name has been lost. The Separatists had a passion for anonymity; Bimeler's name does not appear in these volumes, and it is only by tradition that Jacob Sylvan is identified as the editor of the volumes and the author of the valuable introduction. Bimeler's death was a tragic blow to the Society, for there was no obvious successor in either secular or religious leadership. For a time the regular Sunday service consisted of reading from religious literature, but this did not appeal to the congregation. It then occurred to some of the villagers that Neef's manuscripts might be printed as a source of spiritual guidance. After an unsuccessful experiment with a small press, they purchased adequate equipment and hired an experienced printer. The press was sold after the single project was completed. Aside from these volumes and two hymnals, no Zoar imprints of this period have been identified. The communal life at Zoar has attracted perennial interest because of its economic program, but to the villagers themselves the religious beliefs that they held in common were of transcendent importance. Bimeler's writings are the source for the study of those beliefs and are therefore of interest to the specialist. The reader will seek in vain for more than passing reference to the daily life of these unique Ohioans.

William T. Utter

Die Wahre Separation, Oder die Wiedergeburt, Dargestellet in Geistreichen und Erbaulichen Versammlungs-reden und Betrachtungen . . ., 4 parts in 2 vols., Zoar, 1856–60.

Etwas Fürs Herz! Oder Geistliche Brosamen von des Herrn Tisch Gefallen . . ., 2 parts in 1 vol., Zoar, 1860–61.

BINKLEY, ROBERT CEDRIC (Dec. 10, 1897–April 11, 1940), educator, was born in Mannheim, Pa. He was educated at Stanford University (A.B., 1922; Ph.D., 1927). From 1929 until his death he was a member of the history department of Western Reserve University. Besides technical books and articles on historical research, he wrote *Responsible Drinking*, New York, [1930]. WWW 1

BINKLEY, WILFRED ELLSWORTH (July 29, 1883–), educator, was born in Allen County. He graduated from Ohio Northern University in 1907 and Ohio State University (Ph.D.) in 1936. He taught in Ohio public schools, 1900–21, after which he joined the faculty of Ohio Northern. His books include *The Powers of the President; Problems of American Democracy*, New York, 1937. WW 30

BIRD, ANNA M. PENNOCK (June 28, 1855–Oct. 10, 1946), was born in Lancaster, Pa., where she was reared a Quaker and where she began teaching school at the age of eighteen. She moved to Toledo in 1894 and spent the remainder of her life in that community. Her lectures on applied psychology led to the formation of mothers' and teachers' clubs, which are said to have been the first Parent-Teachers Association in Toledo. In 1903 she married C. L. Bird, a civil engineer. She was a Theosophist and was president of Harmony Lodge, Toledo, for 36 years. She was also a vegetarian and conducted classes in preparing vegetable meals. She wrote articles for *New Thought* and other magazines and published many letters and articles in Toledo newspapers.

Creative Force in the Vegetable, Animal and Human World . . ., Toledo, [1897].

Inside of Our Own Doors, Toledo, [1897].
The Thought Circle, Toledo, [1898].

BIRD, HELEN LOUISA BOSTWICK (Jan. 5, 1826–Dec. 20, 1907), was born in North Charlestown, N. H. In 1838 she removed with her family to Bucyrus and, shortly after, to Ravenna. She began contributing verse to the press in 1844, the year in which she married Edwin Bostwick. Within a few years her verse was appearing in many leading periodicals. "I bestow upon Mrs. Bostwick a sincere praise that need not waste itself in compliment. Her poems betray study of the best authors of our language, without being the less original. If her faculty does not amount to genius, it is at least transcendent talent." Thus wrote William Dean Howells in 1860. Yet, her best work was to follow the death of Mr. Bostwick, on Sept. 9, 1860. Her contributions appeared in the *National Era,* the *New York Independent,* the *Atlantic Monthly,* and other periodicals. Her "Drafted" was one of the best-known poems of Civil War days; it won its place in public school repertories, where it remained until protests against the draft became unfashionable. So too with the rest of the work of this once very popular poet; it has since been obscured by the vagaries of fashion. Following her marriage to Dr. John F. Bird in 1875 she moved to Philadelphia, where she spent the remainder of her life.

Buds, Blossoms, and Berries, Columbus, 1861.
Four O'Clocks. Poems, Philadelphia, 1880.

BIRINYI, LOUIS KOSSUTH (April 19, 1887–Sept. 3, 1941), lawyer, was born in Hungary. He came to the United States in 1903 and, after graduating from Franklin and Marshall College in 1913, settled in Cleveland. He graduated from Western Reserve University law school in 1916 and afterward practiced in Cleveland. He published both articles and books on his native country, e.g., *The Tragedy of Hungary; An Appeal for World Peace,* Cleveland, [1924].

BIRKHIMER, WILLIAM EDWARD (March 1, 1848–June 10, 1914), army officer, was born in Somerset, Perry County. After serving as a private in the 4th Iowa Volunteer Cavalry, 1864–65, he attended the U. S. Military Academy, where he graduated in 1870. He rose to the rank of brigadier general and retired, at his own request, after forty years' service in 1906. His death occurred in Washington, D. C.

The Law of Appointment and Promotion in the Regular Army of the United States . . . , New York, 1880.
Historical Sketch of the Organization, Administration, Matériel and Tactics of the Artillery, United States Army, Washington, D. C., 1884.
Military Government and Martial Law . . . , Washington, D. C., 1892.

BISHOP, JESSE P. (June 1, 1815–Oct. 28, 1881), lawyer, was born in New Haven, Vt. After coming to Ohio in 1836, he entered Western Reserve College, where he graduated the following year. He read law, was admitted to the Ohio bar, and practiced in Cleveland.

Presidential Question. A Legal View of the Presidential Conflict of 1876, [Cleveland, 1876?].
The Southern Question. A View of the Policy and Constitutional Powers of the President . . . , Cleveland, 1877.

BISHOP, JOSIAH GOODMAN (Sept. 14, 1833–March 23, 1922), clergyman, was born in St. Clair Bottom, Va. Ordained to the ministry of the Christian Church in 1856, he preached in several states. From 1890 until 1915 he devoted himself to the missionary endeavors of his church. He founded and edited the *Christian Missionary,* published in Dayton. He died in Watertown, Mass. He wrote a volume on missionary activities of his church: *The Christians and the Great Commission . . . ,* Dayton, 1914.
OBB

BISHOP, ROBERT HAMILTON (July 26, 1777–April 29, 1855), clergyman and educator, was born near Edinburgh, Scotland. He was licensed to preach by the presbytery of Perth in 1802 and sailed for America the same year. After serving for two years as a missionary in southern Ohio, he was made professor of philosophy at Transylvania University, where he remained until 1824. He was the first president of Miami University, 1824–41, and taught history and political science there, 1841–44. He taught at Farmers' College, Pleasant Hill, from 1845 until his death. His theories regarding the influence of society on the individual make him a pioneer in the development of sociology. He opposed slavery, a stand which led to his leaving Miami, but he also opposed the extreme measures of the abolitionists. Besides the titles below, he published sermons, pamphlets, and textbooks in logic and government.

An Apology for Calvinism, Lexington, 1804.
A Legacy to Vacant Congregations, Lexington, 1804.
An Outline of the History of the Church in the State of Kentucky . . . , Lexington, 1824.

Sketches of the Philosophy of the Bible . . . , Oxford, 1833.

Addresses Delivered at Miami University 1829–1834, Hamilton, 1835.

BISSELL, WALTER LEWIS (Feb. 5, 1879–May 6, 1957), educator, was born in Rootstown, Portage County. A graduate of Western Reserve University in 1903, he taught in the Cleveland schools for many years. He wrote a family history, articles on education and literature, and a number of plays, e.g., *When Marble Speaks, a Dream of World Peace,* Cleveland, [1934].

BITTINGER, LUCY FORNEY (Aug. 29, 1859–1907), was born in Cleveland, Cuyahoga County. She compiled a book of prayers, wrote genealogical works, and published a valuable historical study: *The Germans in Colonial Times,* Philadelphia, 1901.

BLACK, EFFIE SQUIER (March 4, 1866–April 18, 1906), was born in Sulphur Springs, Crawford County. After her marriage to Thomas B. Black in 1885, she lived in Kenton, Hardin County. She is said to have written articles for magazines and composed hymns which were used by leading evangelists.

Heart-Whispers, Cleveland, [1900].

BLACK, FORREST REVERE (Nov. 3, 1894–Sept. 21, 1943), educator, was born in Tiffin, Seneca County. He was admitted to the Ohio bar in 1920 and practiced for one year in Tiffin, after which he entered college teaching. He served on the faculties of several universities and spent ten years in government service. He published numerous magazine articles, both professional and popular; his books include *Ill-Starred Prohibition Cases . . . ,* Boston [1931]. WWW 2

BLACK, GLENN G. (May 6, 1888–), was born in Bedford, Cuyahoga County, but spent much of his life in Lucas County. Since his retirement in 1956 as sales manager for the Dog Food Division, Kasco Mills, Toledo, he has lived in Tryon, N. C. Deeply interested in hunting and field sports, he has written numerous articles for outdoors magazines and one book, *American Beagling,* New York, [1949].

BLACK, JAMES RUSH (March 3, 1827–Nov. 19, 1895), physician, born in Lanark, Scotland, came to America in 1841. He studied at Denison University and the College of Physicians and Surgeons, New York City. After practicing a few years in Linville and Hebron, he went to California. During the Civil War he served as surgeon of the 113th O.V.I. and afterward practiced medicine in Newark, Licking County, and taught at Columbus Medical College. He wrote a number of scientific and medical articles, both professional and popular.

Alcohol as Medicine, and How It Affects the Temperance Cause, Syracuse, N. Y., 1870.

The Ten Laws of Health . . . , Philadelphia, 1872.

BLACK, MARGARET SHAFER (Nov. 17, 1859–Oct. 17, 1913), was born in Dayton, Montgomery County. After teaching school for a time in Indianapolis, Ind., she moved to Mansfield in 1890. Her death occurred in Ann Arbor, Mich.

Hadassah; Or, Esther, Queen to Ahasuerus, Chicago, 1895.

BLACK, ROBERT LOUNSBURY (Sept. 15, 1881–Jan. 24, 1954), lawyer and railroad president, was born in Norwood, Hamilton County. He graduated from Yale University in 1903 and Harvard Law School in 1906. He practiced in Cincinnati and also served as president of the Little Miami Railroad. He wrote *The Little Miami Railroad,* Cincinnati, [1940]. WWW 3

BLACK, SAMUEL CHARLES (Sept. 6, 1869–July 25, 1921), Iowa-born clergyman, was pastor of Collingwood Avenue Presbyterian Church in Toledo, 1910–19. While living in Ohio, he wrote *Progress in Christian Culture,* Philadelphia, 1912. WWW 1

BLACKLEDGE, CELIZE FOOTE (Oct., 1857–1937), was born on a farm near Fredericktown, Knox County. In 1936 she was living in Bellville. She published a novel: *Who Knows . . . ,* [Mt. Vernon, 1926], and as Cella Foote Blackledge, a collection of verse: *The Minstrel's Inspiration . . . ,* Fredericktown, 1915.

BLACKMORE, SIMON AUGUSTINE (Feb. 24, 1849–Sept. 5, 1926), clergyman and educator, was born in Milwaukee, Wis. He was ordained a Roman Catholic priest in 1885 and taught at St. Xavier's College, Cincinnati, from 1886 to 1888 and at St. Ignatius' College, Cleveland, from 1917 until his death. His writings include several studies of Shakespeare and *Spiritism, Facts and Frauds,* New York, 1924. WWW 1

BLACKWELL, ELIZABETH (1813–March 3, 1897), was born in England. In the 1860s she came to Toledo, where she gave music lessons and was active in the cultural life of that city.

Poems, [Toledo, 1884].

BLACKWELL, ELIZABETH (Feb. 3, 1821–May 31, 1910), pioneer woman doctor and sister of Henry B. Blackwell (q.v.), spent about four years in Cincinnati (1838–42). In 1849, despite serious obstacles she became a physician; and in 1857 with her sister Emily she founded the New York Infirmary and College for Women and devoted her life to the cause of women's practicing medicine. She wrote numerous books on medical, educational, and social questions.

BLACKWELL, HENRY BROWN (May 4, 1825–Sept. 7, 1909), editor and reformer, was born in Bristol, England. In 1832 the family came to New York and in 1838 moved to Cincinnati. The father died soon after they arrived in Cincinnati, leaving his widow with nine children to support. Henry worked at various jobs before becoming a hardware dealer. Like the other members of his family he was a vigorous opponent of slavery and just as vigorous a proponent of women's rights. In 1855 he married Lucy Stone, Oberlin graduate and reformer. Having pledged himself to the cause of women's suffrage, he devoted his life to this and other humanitarian causes. His proposal that the South institute women's suffrage to offset the effects of Negro suffrage illustrates his single-minded commitment to the cause of women's rights. An excellent businessman, he made enough money from various ventures to support the causes in which he and his wife were interested. He published pamphlets and edited the *Women's Journal.* His death occurred in Dorchester, Mass.

What the South Can Do. How the Southern States Can Make Themselves Masters of the Situation, [New York, 1867].

Reciprocity, a Republican Issue, Boston, [1904?].

BLAINE, HARRY G. (Nov. 25, 1858–Jan. 31, 1930), physician, was born in Wheeling, Va., but in 1861 he was brought to Attica, Seneca County, and grew up there. At sixteen he began teaching school. After studying medicine with an Attica doctor, he attended Indiana Eclectic Medical College, Indianapolis, where he graduated in 1882. He practiced in Reedstown for a year and afterward in Attica and Toledo. In 1884 he established a monthly magazine, *Medical Compend.* He also taught at Toledo Medical College.

The Physician: His Relation to the Law . . . , Toledo, 1893.

BLANCHARD, CHARLES ELTON (Aug. 29, 1868–Jan. 16, 1945), physician, was born in Orwell, Ashtabula County. After graduating from Western Reserve University Medical School in 1902, he practiced in Cleveland and Youngstown. He published the *Letters* (1931) and the *Diary* (1934) of a Dr. Amos Betterman (1825–1910), an old-style country doctor. All evidence indicates that he was an imaginary character invented by Blanchard to exemplify virtues he admired. Besides numerous pamphlets, verse, and medical works, he published *Our Unfinished Revolution,* Youngstown, 1933.

BLANCHARD, FERDINAND QUINCY (July 23, 1876–   ), clergyman, was born in Jersey City, N. J. He graduated from Amherst College in 1898 and Yale Divinity School in 1901. He was pastor of Euclid Avenue Congregational Church, Cleveland, 1915–51. After retiring he continued to live in Cleveland. He has written hymns and religious books, e.g., *For the King's Sake,* East Orange, N. J., 1909. WW 28

BLANCHARD, JONATHAN (Jan. 19, 1811–May 14, 1892), clergyman, was born in Rockingham, Vt. He attended Lane Theological Seminary, and was installed as pastor of the Sixth Presbyterian Church, Cincinnati, in 1838. He was a vigorous opponent of slavery and of the Masons and Odd Fellows. A record of his debate with N. L. Rice (q.v.) was reprinted at least twice: *A Debate on Slavery . . . ,* Cincinnati, 1846.

BLANCHARD, LUCY MANSFIELD (March 6, 1869–April 23, 1927), educator, born in Boston, Mass., graduated from Belmont College, Cincinnati, in 1888 and served on its faculty as professor of Greek and Latin, 1888-94. She later taught at Bartholomew's School for Girls, Cincinnati. She spent her later life in Salt Lake City, Utah. She wrote several books for juvenile readers, e.g., *Chico; The Story of a Homing Pigeon,* Boston, [1922]. WWW 1

BLANEY, CHARLES E. (c.1875–Oct. 21, 1944), dramatist and producer, was born in Columbus, Franklin County. He wrote his first play at 21 and rapidly became successful as a writer and producer of melodramas. He was associated with various theatrical chains, and at the time of his retirement from the theatrical business in 1919 he owned several theaters. In the last

25 years of his life he was in the real-estate business in New Canaan, Conn. Of the more than 180 plays that he wrote and produced, few were committed to print, although a few novels were printed that were based on his more popular melodramas, e.g., *The Child Slaves of New York . . .*, New York, 1904.

BLEDSOE, ALBERT TAYLOR (Nov. 9, 1809–Dec. 8, 1877), studied at Kenyon College after his graduation from the U. S. Military Academy in 1830. He was on the Kenyon faculty, 1833–34, and that of Miami University, 1835–36. A militant controversialist, he is best known for his defense of secession: *Is Davis a Traitor; Or, Was Secession a Constitutional Right Previous to the War of 1861?,* Baltimore, 1866.

BLISS, DANIEL (Aug. 17, 1823–July 27, 1916), founder of the American University, Beirut, was born in Georgia, Vt. After the death of his mother when he was nine, he lived with relatives near Painesville and Kingsville. He graduated from Kingsville Academy in 1848, after which he entered Amherst College. His *Reminiscences . . .*, New York, 1920, was edited by his son Frederick. DAB 2

BLISS, PHILEMON (July 28, 1813–Aug. 24, 1889), congressman and judge, was born in North Canton, Conn. He resided in Ohio for twenty years (1841–61). He practiced law in Elyria, served as judge of the 14th district from 1849 to 1852, and served in Congress from 1854 to 1856. In 1861 he moved to the Dakota Territory and in 1863 to Missouri. He published several of his speeches in the House of Representatives and a treatise on legal pleading.

Of Sovereignty, Boston, 1885.

BLISS, SYLVIA HORTENSE (Dec. 13, 1870–), was born in Toledo, Lucas County. She attended the schools of Toledo and Des Moines, Iowa. After studying music at Syracuse University, she was a church organist and music teacher in Vermont. She now lives in Rochester, Vt. She has written *Quests; Poems in Prose,* Montpelier, Vt., 1920, and a book of verse: *Sea Level,* North Montpelier, Vt., 1933. WWNAA 7

BLOOM, SAMUEL STAMBAUGH (March 11, 1834–Aug. 1, 1902), lawyer, was born in Perry County, Pa. He taught school, farmed, and read law before coming to Ohio in 1856. He served as mayor of Shelby, 1858–63, and in 1864 began the practice of law. He edited the Shelby *News,* 1868–89. He was active in Democratic politics and served in the state legislature, 1864–68 and 1878–82. He moved to Columbus in 1891 but returned to Shelby before his death.

Why Are You a Democrat? . . ., Cincinnati, 1880.

Why We Are Democrats . . ., Cincinnati, [1884].

One Hundred Years of Platforms, Principles and Policies of the American Democracy, Shelby, 1900.

BLOOMER, JAMES M. (1842–Sept. 22, 1923), journalist, was born in Zanesville, Muskingum County, and attended the schools of that community. He attended business college in Cincinnati and also learned the machinist's trade. He settled in Toledo in 1873 and while serving as principal of St. Mary's School studied law; he was admitted to the bar in 1878. Around 1880 he and J. P. Coates took over the Toledo *News,* which had been founded by the Knights of Labor, and operated it as a Democratic, pro-labor paper. It was later merged with the Toledo *Bee.* He lived in Los Angeles, Calif., 1913–19, but returned to Toledo four years before his death.

The Co-operative Educator. A Key to the Mines of Wealth Accessible to Honest Producers . . ., [Toledo, 1888].

D'Mar's Affinity . . ., New York, [1903].

BLOSS, GEORGE MANOR DAVIS (May 2, 1827–May 28, 1876), lawyer and journalist, was born in Irisburg, Vt., but grew up in Watertown, N. Y., where his father moved in 1830, and in Oswego, N. Y. In 1850 he was admitted to the New York bar, and in 1852 he moved to Cincinnati to practice. In 1866 he moved to Branch Hill, Clermont County, and commuted to Cincinnati every day. He began writing for the *Enquirer* and remained on the editorial staff of that newspaper until his death in a railway accident.

Life of George H. Pendleton, Cincinnati, 1868.

Historic and Literary Miscellany, Cincinnati, 1875.

BLOUGH, ELIZABETH R. D. See Elizabeth D. Rosenberger.

BLUE, GUY. Pseud. See Rollin J. Britton.

BLUE, HERBERT TENNEY ORREN (Sept. 9, 1887–), educator, was born in Ada, Hardin County, but was reared in Kenton. He graduated from Ohio Northern University in 1913 and Hiram College in 1918.

He was a teacher and principal in Hardin County schools for nine years and a teacher in Canton, 1919–54. In summer he served on the staff of the Kenton *Times* and now writes historical feature stories for that newspaper. He still lives in Canton. He has written two county histories: *History of Stark County . . .* , Chicago, 1928, and *Centennial History of Hardin County . . .* , [Canton, 1933].

BLYMYER, WILLIAM H. (March 4, 1864–April 15, 1939), lawyer, was born in Mansfield, Richland County. He lived in Pelham Manor, N. Y., but returned to Mansfield to spend his summers. Besides legal works he wrote *Doctrine and Discipline; Or, the Failure of the American Educational System,* [Poughkeepsie, N. Y., 1927].

BOARDMAN, MABEL THORP (c.1861–March 17, 1946), American Red Cross official, was born in Cleveland, Cuyahoga County. She was educated in private schools of Cleveland and New York and in Europe. In 1896 her family moved to Washington, D. C. Her service with the Red Cross won her many decorations and honors from foreign governments. Her death occurred in Washington, D. C. Her writings include *Under the Red Cross Flag at Home and Abroad,* Philadelphia, 1915. WWW 2

BODLE, ALAN. Pseud. See Emory Norris.

BODLEY, RACHEL LITTLER (Dec. 7, 1831–June 15, 1888), educator, was born in Cincinnati, Hamilton County. She graduated from Wesleyan College, Cincinnati, in 1849 and taught there until 1860. In 1865 she was appointed professor of chemistry and toxicology at Women's Medical College of Pennsylvania. She died in Philadelphia. Besides the title below, she prepared a catalogue of Joseph Clark's herbarium which was published in Cincinnati in 1865.

The College Story, Philadelphia, 1881.

BOGEN, BORIS D. (1869–June 30, 1929), was born in Moscow, Russia, and came to the United States in his early twenties. He served as librarian at the Jewish Educational Alliance, New York City, and as superintendent of an agricultural school in Woodbine, N. J. He was named superintendent of United Jewish Charities, Cincinnati, was a field agent of National Jewish Social Service during World War I, and in 1925 became executive secretary of B'nai B'rith with headquarters in Cincinnati. He wrote *Jewish Philanthropy,* New York, 1917, and an autobiography, published posthumously: *Born a Jew,* New York, 1930.

BOGGESS, ARTHUR CLINTON (March 2, 1874–Sept. 5, 1955), educator, was born in Catlin, Ill. From 1910 to 1915 he taught history and economics at Lucknow Christian College, India, and afterward taught at Baldwin-Wallace College, 1916–41. He wrote a book describing his experiences in India: *First Days in India,* Cincinnati, [1912]. WW 20

BOHN, FRANK (Sept. 26, 1878–), author and lecturer, was born in Cuyahoga County. He graduated from Ohio State University in 1900 and the University of Michigan (Ph.D.) in 1904. He has lectured and written on the labor movement, economic questions, and international relations. He collaborated with Richard T. Ely in writing *The Great Change; Work and Wealth in the New Age,* New York, 1935. WW 30

BOLLES, JAMES AARON (1810–Sept. 19, 1894), clergyman, was born in Norwich, Conn. He graduated from Trinity College in 1830 and General Seminary in 1833. After serving as assistant rector or rector of several churches, he was rector of Trinity Church, Cleveland, 1853–59. After living twelve years in Boston, he returned to Cleveland in 1871 to spend the remainder of his life.

The Episcopal Church Defended: With an Examination into the Claims of Methodist Episcopacy . . . , Batavia, N. Y., [1843].

Holy Matrimony, New York, 1870.

Connecticut and Bishop Seabury . . . , Cleveland, 1890.

BOLTON, AQUILA MASSEY (1773–May 13, 1857), was born in Philadelphia, Pa. On July 22, 1806, he was received into the Concord Meeting of Friends on a certificate from the Philadelphia Meeting dated May 30, 1806. He established a school in Belmont County and supplemented his income by selling books. On Sept. 26, 1811, he was disowned by the Short Creek Monthly Meeting of Friends, to which he had transferred, for marrying contrary to discipline. What little is known of his career does not indicate that he was amenable to any discipline. All of his known writings were in verse and, for the most part, on highly controversial subjects. Sometime before 1827 he became affiliated with the Shakers. In 1832 in his reply to "sundry defamatory letters written by A. M. Bolton," Richard

McNemar (q.v.) referred to him as "late a catechumen in the United Society, at Union Village (Ohio)." By this time Bolton had probably moved on to neighboring Dayton, where in 1841 he was elected recorder of the city council. He was reelected in 1842. His death occurred in Dayton.

The Independency of the Mind, Affirmed. A Poem, in Two Parts. With Occasional Notes, Wheeling, 1807.

The Art of Domestick Happiness, and Other Poems, Pittsburgh, Pa., 1817.

The Whore of Babylon Unmasked; Or, a Cure for Orthodoxy . . . , Philadelphia, 1827.

Present Prospects . . . , Dayton, 1841.

Some Lines in Verse about the Shakers. Not Published by Authority of the Society So-called, New York, 1846.

BOLTON, CHARLES EDWARD (May 16, 1841–1901), was born in South Hadley Falls, Mass., and graduated from Amherst College in 1865. After marrying Sarah K. Bolton (q.v.), he lived in Cleveland, where he was active in a number of industries and mercantile firms. He also patented several inventions. He traveled frequently in Europe and lectured about his trips.

Notes from Letters of Charles E. Bolton . . . , Cambridge, Mass., 1892.

A Model Village of Homes, and Other Papers, Boston, 1901.

Travels in Europe and America, New York, [1903].

The Harris-Ingram Experiment, Cleveland, 1905.

BOLTON, CHARLES KNOWLES (Nov. 14, 1867–Nov. 19, 1950), antiquarian, son of Sarah K. and Charles E. Bolton (qq.v.), was born in Cleveland, Cuyahoga County. After graduating from Harvard University in 1890, he served on the staffs of the Harvard Library, 1890–93, Brookline, Mass., Library, 1894–98, and the Boston Athaneum, 1898–1933. He died at Ayer, Mass. In addition to the titles below, he wrote numerous articles and compiled a bibliography of heraldry and a family history.

The Gossiping Guide to Harvard and Places of Interest in Cambridge . . . , Cambridge, Mass., 1892.

Saskia, the Wife of Rembrandt, New York, 1893.

On the Wooing of Martha Pitkin; Being a Versified Narrative of the Time of the Regicides . . . , Boston, 1894.

The Love Story of Ursula Wolcott, Being a Tale in Verse . . . , Boston, 1895.

Brookline; The History of a Favored Town, Brookline, Mass., 1897.

The Private Soldier under Washington, New York, 1902.

Scotch Irish Pioneers in Ulster and America, Boston, 1910.

The Elizabeth Whitman Mystery at the Old Bell Tavern in Danvers . . . , Peabody, Mass., 1912.

The Founders; Portraits of Persons Born Abroad Who Came to the Colonies in North America before the Year 1701 . . . , 3 vols., [Boston], 1919–26.

The Real Founders of New England . . . , Boston, 1929.

Terra Nova: The Northeast Coast of North America before 1602 . . . , Boston, 1935.

BOLTON, SARAH KNOWLES (Sept. 15, 1841–Feb. 21, 1916), was born in Farmington, Conn. Precocious and gifted, she was a publishing poet at fifteen. After graduating from Hartford Female Seminary in 1860, she taught in Natchez, Miss., until forced by the outbreak of war to return north. In 1866 she married Charles E. Bolton (q.v.) and afterward, except for rather extensive traveling, lived in Cleveland. She served on the editorial staff of the *Congregationalist,* 1878–81, and traveled in Europe, studying women's education and labor conditions, 1881–83. She was active in the temperance movement and in various humanitarian reforms, especially those opposing cruelty to animals. She was also a prolific writer, especially in the area of biography.

Orlean Lamar, and Other Poems, New York, 1864.

The Present Problem, New York, 1874.

Facts and Songs for the People. Prepared Specially for Use in the Blaine and Logan Campaign, Cleveland, 1884.

How Success Is Won, Boston, [1885].

Lives of Poor Boys Who Became Famous, New York, [1885].

Lives of Girls Who Became Famous, New York, [1886].

Social Studies in England, Boston, [1886].

Stories from Life, New York, [1886].

Famous American Authors, New York, [1887].

From Heart and Nature, (with Charles K. Bolton), New York, 1887.

Famous American Statesmen, New York, [1888].

Successful Women, Boston, [1888].

Famous Men of Science, New York, [1889].

Famous English Authors of the Nineteenth Century, New York, [1890].

Famous European Artists, New York, [1890].

Famous English Statesmen of Queen Victoria's Reign, New York, [1891].
Famous Types of Womanhood, New York, [1892].
Famous Voyagers and Explorers, New York, [1893].
Famous Leaders among Men, New York, [1894].
Famous Leaders among Women, New York, [1895].
The Inevitable, and Other Poems, New York, [1895].
Nuggets; Or, Secrets of Great Success, (with F. T. Wallace), Cleveland, 1895.
Famous Givers and Their Gifts, New York, [1896].
The Story of Douglas, Cleveland, 1898.
Every-day Living, Boston, 1900.
Our Devoted Friend, the Dog, Boston, 1902.
Charles E. Bolton; A Memorial Sketch, Cambridge, 1907.
Sarah K. Bolton; Pages from an Intimate Autobiography, Edited by Her Son, Boston, 1923.

BOND, BEVERLEY WAUGH, JR. (July 31, 1878–), educator, was born in Blacksburg, Va. He served in the history department of the University of Cincinnati, 1920–49, and has lived in Cincinnati since his retirement. He was also associated with the Historical and Philosophical Society (curator, 1939–42; president, 1942–45). He has written several articles and books on historical subjects, e.g., *The Quit-rent System in the American Colonies,* New Haven, Conn., 1919. WW 26

BOND, LEWIS HAMILTON (July 28, 1838–Aug. 11, 1912), lawyer, was born in Nelsonville, Athens County. He was admitted to the Ohio bar in 1859 and, except for his Civil War service, practiced in Cincinnati until 1907. In 1862 he superintended recruiting in Ohio, and in 1863 he was placed in command of a battalion of the Third Ohio Infantry and sent in pursuit of Morgan. He received Morgan's surrender at Salinesville, July 26, 1863. In 1866 he was appointed U. S. district attorney in Cincinnati. Besides the titles below, he published two volumes of legal reports.

One Year in Briartown, Cincinnati, 1879.
The Capture and Trial of a Confederate Spy Sent to Ohio by Jefferson Davis . . . , Cincinnati, 1887.

BONE, JOHN HERBERT ALOYSIUS (Oct. 31, 1830–Sept. 17, 1906), journalist, was born in Cornwall, England. He was a reporter in London and Liverpool before coming to Cleveland in 1851. In 1857 he joined the staff of the Cleveland *Herald,* where he had been publishing articles since his arrival in the city. When the *Herald* was acquired by the *Plain Dealer* in 1885, Bone became chief editorial writer and literary editor. His comments were often signed "Spectacles." An authority on Elizabethan literature and owner of one of the largest libraries in Ohio, he was an intimate friend of James Russell Lowell. He published articles on literary and historical subjects in leading magazines of the day. One of his major exploits was publishing the story of Matthew Brayton (q.v.). Highly respected in journalistic circles, he continued to send his pieces to the *Plain Dealer* even while on his deathbed.

Stories and Legends; With Other Poems, Boston, 1852.
Petroleum and Petroleum Wells . . . , Philadelphia, 1865.

BONNER, DAVID FINDLEY (April 2, 1842– ?), clergyman, was born in Greenfield, Highland County. He graduated from Muskingum College in 1860 and from Pittsburgh Theological Seminary in 1865. As a Presbyterian minister, he served pastorates in various states. Besides articles and pamphlets, he wrote *Saving the World; What It Involves and How It Is Being Accomplished,* Middletown, N. Y., 1902. WWW 3

BONSER, THOMAS ATHELSTAN (Sept. 21, 1860–Aug. 4, 1935), educator and museum curator, was born in Dayton, Montgomery County. After graduating from Otterbein College in 1899, he taught in Spokane, Wash.; in 1918 he became curator of the Spokane Museum. The Ohio State Academy of Science published his *Ecological Study of Big Spring Prairie, Wyandot County, Ohio,* Columbus, 1903. WWW 1

BONTE, GEORGE WILLARD (May 16, 1873–March 13, 1946), writer and artist, was born in Cincinnati, Hamilton County. He worked in various capacities in journalism and in the motion-picture industry; he was art manager of Warner Brothers, 1923–31. In a single year he published three books of nursery rhymes, e.g., *The Sandman Rhymes,* New York, [1904]. WWW 2

BOOKWALTER, JOHN W. (1837–Sept. 26, 1915), was born in Rob Roy, Ind. Studious and possessed of a strong original mind, he early grappled with such problems as the steam or mist which arose from the waters that fell over a dam near his father's farm. About 1865 he went to Springfield, Clark County, where he was employed by James Leffel, the manufacturer of a famous water wheel. He became Leffel's partner, married his daughter, and upon Leffel's death succeeded to his business, which had attained world-wide proportions. Seeking to increase the sale of his product in foreign lands, in 1870 he became a globe-trotter. In 1881 he permitted himself to become the Democratic nominee for Governor of Ohio. Shocked by the demand made on him by the State Executive Committee for $25,000, Bookwalter sent his check for $5,000 and conducted his campaign without the Committee. He was defeated by the incumbent, Charles Foster. In 1898 he made a trip through Siberia and Central Asia, often living with the peasants. His superb, detailed account of this journey, published the following year for private circulation among his friends, has been accepted as an outstanding source. His death occurred in San Remo, Italy.

Canyon and Crater; Or, Scenes in California and the Sandwich Islands, Springfield, 1874.
Mill Dams, Springfield, 1874.
Home and International Trade . . . , New York, 1886.
If Not Silver, What?, Springfield, 1896.
Siberia and Central Asia, Springfield, 1899.
Rural versus Urban; Their Conflict and Its Causes . . . , New York, 1910.

BOOKWALTER, LEWIS (Sept. 18, 1846–Nov. 30, 1935), clergyman and educator, was born in Hallsville, Ross County. After graduating from Western College, Toledo, Iowa, in 1872, he was licensed to preach by the United Brethren Church. He taught at several colleges and was a pastor in Dayton, 1886–94. He was president of Western College, 1894–1904, and Otterbein College, 1904–09. After his retirement he lived in Oberlin.

The Family; Or, the Home and the Training of Children, Dayton, 1894.
Repentance, Dayton, 1902.

BOOLE, ELLA ALEXANDER (July 26, 1858–March 13, 1952), temperance advocate, was born in Van Wert, Van Wert County. She graduated from the University of Wooster in 1878. Active throughout her life in Presbyterian missions work and temperance causes, she was president of the World W.C.T.U., 1931–47. She died in New York City at the age of 93. Her writings include *Give Prohibition Its Chance,* Evanston, Ill., [1929]. WWW 3

BOONE, RICHARD GAUSE (Sept. 9, 1849–April 8, 1923), educator, born in Spiceland, Ind., earned a Ph.D. at Ohio University in 1889 and was superintendent of Cincinnati schools, 1899–1903. He published several books on education, e.g., *A History of Education in Indiana,* New York, 1892.

BOOTH, EMMA SCARR (April 25, 1835–July 9, 1927), was born in Hull, England. When she was nine years old, her parents brought her to a farm outside Cleveland. She married a mill-owner of Twinsburg, and after his mill burned in 1865 she moved to Painesville and did needlework to support herself. Her husband deserted her to go to the Titusville oil fields, and she moved to Cleveland, where she lived with her mother and made her living by giving music lessons. She wrote songs and composed instrumental music. The first book below, a humorous account of an eccentric spinster, was published under the pseudonym Miss Karan Kringle of Klodsville, Ohio.

Karan Kringle's Journal . . . , Philadelphia, 1885.
A Wilful Heiress, Buffalo, 1892.
The Family of Three, Iesuina, and Other Poems, Buffalo, 1893.

BOOTH, EMMONS RUTLEDGE (March 4, 1851–Jan. 5, 1934), osteopath, born in Franklin County, Ind., attended National Normal University, Lebanon, 1871–74, and afterward taught school in Missouri and Cincinnati. He graduated from the University of Wooster in 1896 and the American School of Osteopathy, Kirksville, Mo., in 1900. He afterward practiced osteopathy in Cincinnati. He published *History of Osteopathy . . . ,* Cincinnati, [1905]. WWO

BOSTWICK, HELEN LOUISA. See Helen L. B. Bird.

BOSWORTH, EDWARD INCREASE (Jan. 10, 1861–July 1, 1927), clergyman and educator, was born in Dundee, Ill. He attended Oberlin College, 1879–81, and graduated from Yale University in 1883. After graduating from Oberlin Theological Seminary in 1886, he was ordained a Congregational minister, served for one year in Mt. Vernon, and in 1887 joined the Oberlin Seminary faculty. He was associated with the college and seminary as professor, dean, and acting president until his death. His scholarship, teaching, and administrative ability did much to strengthen the program of the college and the seminary.

Studies in the Acts and Epistles . . . , New York, 1898.

Studies in the Teaching of Jesus & His Apostles, New York, 1901.
Studies in the Life of Jesus Christ, New York, 1904.
The Present Crisis in the Kingdom of God . . . , New York, [1907].
New Studies in Acts . . . , New York, 1908.
Working Together . . . , (with Reno Hutchinson), New York, 1908.
The Modern Interpretation of the Call to the Ministry, New York, 1909.
The Story of Paul's Life . . . , Philadelphia, 1909.
The Weak Church and the Strong Man . . . , New York, 1909.
Christ in Everyday Life . . . , New York, 1910.
Can Prayer Accomplish Anything apart from the Man Who Prays?, New York, [1916].
Thirty Studies about Jesus, New York, 1917.
The Master's Way . . . , (with John L. Lobingier), New York, 1918.
What It Means to Be a Christian . . . , Boston, [1922].
The Life and Teaching of Jesus . . . , New York, 1924.
The Christian Religion and Human Progress . . . , (Ernest Pye, ed.), New York, [1948].

BOSWORTH, FRANCKE HUNTINGTON (Jan. 25, 1843–Oct. 17, 1925), physician, was born in Marietta, Washington County. He attended local schools and Marietta College and graduated from Yale University in 1862. During the Civil War he served with West Virginia troops, and afterward he settled in New York City, where he became one of the world's outstanding laryngologists. He published three textbooks on the diseases of the nose and throat. Art was his hobby, and he was widely known in literary circles.

Taking Cold, Detroit, 1891.
The Doctor in Old New York, New York, 1898.

BOTELER, MATTIE M. (Aug. 28, 1859–Aug. 28, 1929), was born in Jamestown, Greene County. After completing her education in Greene County schools, she spent the remainder of her life in Cincinnati. She was on the editorial staff of the Standard Publishing Company for 37 years and for sixteen years edited the magazine *Lookout.* Active in the Christian Church, she compiled a book of religious songs and published sermon outlines and Sunday school lessons in addition to the titles below.

Shut-in; A Story of the Cross . . . , Cincinnati, [1895].
The Conversion of Brian O'Dillon, Cincinnati, [1896].
Side Windows; Or, Lights on Scripture Truths, Cincinnati, 1901.
The Evolution of Juliet, Cincinnati, [1903].
Joe Binder's Wild Westing, Cincinnati, [1903].
Like As We Are, Cincinnati, [1903].

BOTKIN, CHARLES WILLOUGHBY (Jan. 26, 1859–Nov. 15, 1927), journalist, was born in Circleville, Pickaway County. Much of his life was spent in Gothenburg, Neb., where he published a newspaper, the *Independent.* He published a book of poems and prose paragraphs from the newspaper: *The Sense and Nonsense of One Man,* and a book of verse: *My Ohio,* Gothenburg, Neb., 1925.

BOUGHTON, WILLIS (April 17, 1854–June 16, 1942), educator, born in Victor, N. Y., came to Cincinnati in 1889 as an instructor in the technical school. He next taught at Ohio University, 1889–91; 1892–99. From 1900 until his retirement in 1924, he taught English at Erasmus Hall High School, Brooklyn, N. Y. He wrote words for several songs, edited literature textbooks, and published *Mythology in Art,* Chicago, 1891.

BOURJAILY, BARBARA WEBB. See Barbara Webb.

BOURJAILY, VANCE NYE (Sept. 17, 1922–), born in Cleveland, Cuyahoga County, spent his early boyhood years in Ohio and later lived in Pennsylvania and Virginia. He graduated from Bowdoin College and served in World War II. He was writer-in-residence at the University of Iowa, 1956–59. Since the publication of his novel *The Violated* in 1958, he has been widely regarded as one of the most promising of America's younger writers. His first novel was *The End of My Life,* New York, 1947.

BOURNE, ALEXANDER (1786–Aug. 5, 1849), born in Wareham, Mass., was trained as a civil engineer, and came to Ohio in 1810. In 1813 he was drafted into the Ohio militia, was soon appointed adjutant to Colonel Mills Stephenson, and appears to have served with some distinction in the War of 1812. Upon receiving his discharge he returned to the practice of his profession in Chillicothe. He will be remembered longest for the superb map of Ohio which he prepared in collaboration with B. Hough and which was published in Philadelphia in 1814. Between 1825 and 1840 he rendered valuable services to the Canal Commission. An observant scientist he contributed a number of valuable articles to Silliman's *American Journal of Science.* He retired sometime after 1845 and returned to Massachusetts. He died at Wareham.

The Surveyor's Pocket-book . . . , Chillicothe, 1834.

BOUTON, EMILY ST. JOHN (Feb. 13, 1837–Feb. 8, 1927), educator and journalist, was born in New Canaan, Conn. Her parents came to Sandusky when she was a child, and she attended the schools of that community. She later taught in high schools at Milan, Tiffin, Toledo, and Chicago. From 1879 to 1907 she was literary and household editor of the Toledo *Blade.* After 1907 she devoted herself to writing and lecturing. She published etiquette and hygiene books in addition to the titles below.

Pretty Is As Pretty Does . . . , Toledo, 1888.
Life's Gateways: Or, How to Win Real Success, Boston, 1896.
The Life Joyful, 1910.

BOUTON, JOHN BELL (March 15, 1830–Nov. 18, 1902), born in Concord, N. H., was editor of the Cleveland *Plain Dealer,* 1851–57. He left Cleveland for New York City, where he was a journalist until 1889, when he moved to Cambridge, Mass. He wrote several books, including a novel published anonymously: *Round the Block . . . ,* New York, 1864.

BOW, FRANK TOWNSEND (Feb. 20, 1901–), lawyer and congressman, was born in Canton, Stark County. He was admitted to the Ohio bar in 1923 and has since practiced in Canton. He was elected to the House of Representatives in the 82nd–85th Congresses. He has written *Independent Labor Organizations and the National Labor Relations Act,* New York, 1940. WW 30

BOWEN, DANA THOMAS (March 6, 1896–), born in Cleveland, Cuyahoga County, attended Cleveland schools. He was at one time a sailor on the Great Lakes, and has collected historical material relative to Lakes shipping and has published three books on this subject, e.g., *Lore of the Lakes . . . ,* Daytona Beach, Fla., 1940.

BOWERSOX, CHARLES A. (Oct. 16, 1846–Jan. 4, 1921), lawyer and judge, was born in St. Joseph's Township, Williams County. After teaching several terms in district schools, he entered Otterbein College, where he graduated in 1874. He was superintendent of Edgerton schools, read law, and was admitted to the bar in 1879. He practiced until 1917, when he was elected judge of common pleas court. He wrote *A Standard History of Williams County . . . ,* 2 vols., Chicago, 1920.

BOWMAN, JAMES CLOYD (Jan. 18, 1880–Sept. 28, 1961), educator, was born in Leipsic, Putnam County. After graduating from Ohio Northern University in 1905, he taught English in several Midwestern colleges and later lived in Chapel Hill, N. C., where he wrote a number of books for boys, e.g., *Mystery Mountain,* Chicago, 1940. WW 28

BOYD, ELLEN B. (July 8, 1855–Oct. 16, 1922), was born in Marietta, Washington County. She wrote under the name Nellie Boyd. She died in Marietta.

Vagabond Rhymes by an Idler, Boston, 1892.
A Passing Voice, Boston, 1907.

BOYD, LOUISE ESTHER VICKROY (Jan. 22, 1827–July 25, 1909), was born in Urbana, Champaign County. When she was four years old, her family moved to Johnstown, Pa. In 1865 she married Dr. Samuel S. Boyd; they lived in Dublin, Ind., but she returned to Ohio some years before her death, which occurred in Ada. From the middle of the nineteenth century until her death, she contributed to the New York *Tribune,* the Cincinnati *Gazette, Century* magazine, and other popular periodicals.

Twilight Stories for Little People, Philadelphia, 1869.
Poems, (Esther Griffin White, ed.), Richmond, Ind., 1911.

BOYD, ROBERT (April 5, 1792–July 1, 1880), clergyman, was born in Westmoreland County, Pa. A Methodist minister, he came to Steubenville in 1832 and about 1868 went to Barnesville, where he spent the remainder of his life.

Personal Memoirs: Together with a Discussion upon the Hardships and Sufferings of Itinerant Life . . . , Cincinnati, 1867.

BOYD, THOMAS ALEXANDER (July 3, 1898–Jan. 27, 1935), was born in Defiance, Defiance County. His father having died shortly before his birth, his mother became a nurse to support the family. He was sent to Woodward High School, Cincinnati, and Elgin Academy in Illinois. In May, 1917, he enlisted in the U. S. Marine Corps; he served in France, received the *croix de guerre,* and was discharged in 1919. After working on the St. Paul, Minn., *News* for a time, he opened a bookstore in St. Paul, which became a meeting place for writers of the area, including F. Scott Fitzgerald and Sinclair Lewis. At their urging he set down his war experiences in *Through the Wheat,* New York, 1923. It was widely praised as one of the first realistic novels of World War I. Interested from boyhood in frontier history, he also wrote a number of historical and biographical books, e.g., *Simon Girty the White Savage,* New York, 1928. He settled in Vermont in 1929. Attracted to the political left during the Depression of the early 1930s, he ran for governor of Vermont on the Communist Party slate in 1934. He died of a cerebral hemorrhage at the age of 37. DAB 21

BOYESEN, HJALMAR HJORTH (Sept. 23, 1848–Oct. 4, 1895), born in Frederiksvarn, Norway, came to America in 1869. After a brief period in Chicago he came to Urbana, where from 1870 to 1873 he headed the department of Latin and Greek. Homesick for his native Norway, he wrote *Gunnar; A Tale of Norse Life,* Boston, 1874. The success of the book, first serialized by Howells in the *Atlantic,* encouraged Boyesen to remain in America.

BOYLAN, MARGUERITE THERESA (July 9, 1887–), social worker, was born in Columbus, Franklin County. She graduated from Ohio State University in 1909 and Fordham University (Ph.D.) in 1939. She has been active in Catholic charities and social work organizations. Her writings include magazine articles and an account of the National Catholic War Council after World War I: *They Shall Live Again* . . . , New York, 1945. CWW 11

BOYLAND, GEORGE HALSTEAD (Jan. 19, 1845–Jan. 16, 1919), physician, was born in Cincinnati, Hamilton County. After graduating from Andover Academy in 1862, he attended Yale University but did not graduate. He served with the surgical corps of the French army during the Franco-Prussian War. He graduated in medicine from University of Leipzig in 1874. His experiences with the French army are the subject of his only book.

Six Months under the Red Cross with the French Army, Cincinnati, 1875.

BOYLE, JAMES (Nov. 28, 1853–June 11, 1939), journalist, was born in Essex, England. He came to America in 1870 and was on the staff of the Cincinnati *Commercial Gazette,* 1871–91. He was private secretary to Governor William McKinley, 1892–96, and American consul at Liverpool, England, 1897–1905. Some of his writings were published first in the Cincinnati *Enquirer.* His last years were spent in Columbus.

Life of William McKinley . . . , (with Robert P. Porter), Cleveland, 1897.

The Initiative and Referendum: Its Folly, Fallacies, and Failures, Columbus, [1912].

What Is Socialism? An Exposition and a Criticism . . . , New York, 1912.

BOYNTON, CHARLES BRANDON (June 12, 1806–April 27, 1883), clergyman, was born in West Stockbridge, Mass. After a career in business and law, he was ordained a Presbyterian minister in 1840. He served as pastor of the Sixth Presbyterian Church, Cincinnati, 1846–56. He became a vigorous opponent of slavery and was a member of a party sent to Kansas in 1854 to discover its possibilities for settlement by Northerners. Several of his sermons and public orations were published. He served twice again (1857–65 and 1873–77) in the pulpit of the Sixth Presbyterian (later Vine Street) Church and died in Cincinnati at the home of a daughter.

A Journey through Kansas . . . , (with T. B. Mason), Cincinnati, 1855.

The Russian Empire . . . , Cincinnati, 1856.

English and French Neutrality and the Anglo-French Alliance in Their Relations to the United States & Russia . . . , Cincinnati, 1864.

The History of the Navy during the Rebellion, 2 vols., New York, 1867–68.

BOYNTON, HENRY VAN NESS (July 22, 1835–1905), journalist, was born in West Stockbridge, Mass., the son of Charles B. Boynton (q.v.). He came to Ohio in 1846, when his father became minister of the Sixth Presbyterian Church, Cincinnati. He graduated from Woodward High School in 1855 and afterward attended military school in Kentucky. In 1861 he was commissioned major in the 35th O.V.I.; he commanded the regiment during the Chickamauga and Missionary Ridge battles, after which he was breveted brigadier general. After the war he became Washington correspondent of the Cincinnati *Gazette.* He engaged in some of the postwar controversies that developed as generals began to publish their memoirs. He aroused considerable excitement by his criticism of Sherman's *Memoirs.* Some of his orations and addresses were published separately as pamphlets.

Sherman's Historical Raid. The Memoirs in the Light of the Record . . . , Cincinnati, 1875.
The National Military Park, Chickamauga-Chattanooga . . . , Cincinnati, 1895.
Was General Thomas Slow at Nashville? . . . , New York, 1896.
Errors in School Histories Compared with the Official Record, Washington, D. C., 1903.

BRACKETT, EDWARD AUGUSTUS (Oct. 1, 1818–March 15, 1908), sculptor, was born in Vassalboro, Maine. From 1835 to 1841 he lived in Cincinnati, where he worked for a printer and began the study of sculpture. He was best known for his portrait busts of notable men. He also wrote considerable verse and several books on spiritualism, e.g., *Materialized Apparitions . . .* , Boston, 1886.

BRACKETT, LEIGH. See Edmond M. Hamilton.

BRADBURY, HARRIET BOWKER (Dec. 23, 1863–April 7, 1945), reformer, born in Brooklyn, N. Y., lectured widely on women's rights and other subjects. She settled in Ohio around 1912.
The New Philosophy of Health, Boston, 1897.
The Light That Is in Thee . . . , New York, 1899.
Voices of Earth and Heaven, New York, 1899.
The Gospel of Beauty, London, 1900.
Civilization and Womanhood, Boston, [1916].

BRADEN, ALTA TAYLOR. See Alta Taylor.

BRADEN, CLARK (Aug. 8, 1831–1915), clergyman, was born in Gustavus, Trumbull County. He taught in district schools, attended Farmers' College, and served in the Civil War with the 127th Illinois Volunteer Infantry. As a minister of the Disciples of Christ Church, he served 35 different churches, most of them in Ohio and Illinois. He frequently debated against members of other denominations, and some of these debates were also published.
The Problem of Problems . . . , Cincinnati, 1877.

BRADEN, JAMES ANDREW (July 10, 1872–June 28, 1955), a prolific writer of juvenile books, was born in Greensburg, Summit County. He attended Warren public schools. When he was seventeen, he started as a reporter on the Canton *Repository;* he spent three years there and eight years on Akron newspapers before entering industry and public relations work. He published a number of books, including the Auto Boys series, between 1902 and 1913. He resumed his writing in the late 1920s. In 1936 he moved to Michigan, but he returned to Ohio in 1940 to marry Alta Taylor (q.v.). They lived near West Richfield. He died in Grosse Pointe, Mich., while visiting a daughter. Under the pen name Hugh McAllister, he published *Steve Holworth of the Oldham Works,* New York, 1930. WWW 3

BRADFORD, GEORGE WINTHROP (July 4, 1895–Feb. 16, 1960), educator, was born in Clyde, Sandusky County. After graduating from the College of Wooster in 1921, he studied at Western Reserve University, taught at Case Institute of Technology, 1923–26, and did graduate work at the University of Wisconsin, 1926–28. He was a member of the Wooster Engli h faculty from 1928 until his death. He published a collection of poems, *Wayside Lyrics,* Boston, 1921. DAS 1

BRADFORD, GERTRUDE YERGIN (Oct. 1, 1881–Feb. 19, 1930), was born in Fremont, Mich., but spent the greater part of her life in Youngstown. She moved to Los Angeles in 1924 but returned to Youngstown two months before her death. She lectured on psychology and New Thought, wrote numerous magazine articles, and published two books, e.g., *The Subconscious Mind, How to Reach and Arouse,* Holyoke, Mass., 1924.

BRADFORD, WARD (1809– ?), was born in Portage County. He later lived in Indiana, Illinois, and Iowa. In 1849, after operating a Mormon hotel in Iowa, he went to California. In 1852 he moved to Oregon, and ten years later he settled in Nevada. He seems to have visited or lived in a dozen or more mining towns in the West.
Biographical Sketches of the Life of Major Ward Bradford . . . , [Fresno?, Calif., 1891?].

BRADLEY, GLENN DANFORD (April 12, 1884–Jan. 4, 1930), educator, was born in Kinderhook, Mich. He graduated from the University of Michigan (A.B., 1907; Ph.D., 1915). From 1916 until his death he was a member of the University of Toledo history faculty. His writings, which deal chiefly with the Southwest, include *The Story of the Pony Express . . .* , Chicago, 1913. WWW 1

BRADLEY, RAMONA KAISER. See Ramona Kaiser.

BRADSHAW, MARION JOHN (Dec. 14, 1886–), clergyman, was born in Salem, Columbiana County. He graduated from Hiram College in 1911 and was ordained to the ministry in the Disciples of Christ Church the following year. He served several churches and was for brief periods on the faculties of Union Theological Seminary, Hiram College, and Grinnell College. He joined the faculty of Bangor Theological Seminary in 1925, became a Universalist, and preached at several churches in Maine. He has published books on Maine and on religious themes, e.g., *Philosophical Foundations of Faith . . .*, New York, 1941. WW 30

BRADY, CYRUS TOWNSEND (Dec. 20, 1861–Jan. 24, 1920), clergyman, was born in Allegheny, Pa. He was an Episcopal rector in Toledo, 1905–09. He was a prolific writer of adventure novels, historical works, biographies, sermons, and juvenile books. Books published during his Toledo years include *The Patriots; The Story of Lee and the Last Hope,* New York, 1906. DAB 2

BRAGDON, CLAUDE FAYETTE (Aug. 1, 1866–Sept. 17, 1946), artist and author, was born in Oberlin, Lorain County. As an architect in Rochester, N. Y., he designed several important buildings. He also was art director for a number of Walter Hampden's plays. He lectured often on theosophy and architecture. At the time of his death, he was living in New York City.

The Golden Person in the Heart, Gouverneur, N. Y., 1898.
A Brief Life of Annie Besant . . ., Rochester, N. Y., 1909.
The Beautiful Necessity . . ., Rochester, N. Y., 1910.
Episodes from an Unwritten History, Rochester, N. Y., 1910.
The Small Old Path, Rochester, N. Y., 1911.
A Primer of Higher Space (The Fourth Dimension), Rochester, N. Y., 1913.
Projective Ornament, Rochester, N. Y., 1915.
Four-Dimensional Vistas, New York, 1916.
Old Lamps for New; The Ancient Wisdom in the Modern World, New York, 1925.
The New Image, New York, 1928.
Merely Players, New York, 1929.
The Eternal Poles, New York, 1931.
The Frozen Fountain, New York, 1932.
An Introduction to Yoga, New York, 1933.
More Lives Than One, New York, 1938.
The Secret Springs; An Autobiography, London, [1938].
The Arch Lectures, New York, [1942].
Yoga for You, New York, 1943.

BRAIN, BELLE MARVEL (Aug. 4, 1859–May 25, 1933), educator, was born in Springfield, Clark County. After graduating from Springfield High School, she served as supervisor of drawing in the Springfield public schools, 1878–95. She was prominent in various educational and religious societies. She later lived in Schenectady, N. Y.

Fuel for Missionary Fires, Boston, 1894.
The Morning Watch, [n.p.], 1897.
Weapons for Temperance Warfare . . ., Boston, [1897].
Quaint Thoughts of an Old-time Army Chaplain, [n.p.], 1898.
The Transformation of Hawaii; How American Missionaries Gave a Christian Nation to the World; Told for Young Folks, New York, [1898].
Holding the Ropes; Missionary Methods for Workers at Home, New York, 1904.
The Redemption of the Red Man; An Account of Presbyterian Missions to the North American Indians of the Present Day, New York, 1904.
All about Japan; Stories of Sunrise Land Told for Little Folks, New York, [1905].
Adventures with Four Footed Folk . . ., New York, 1908.
Love Stories of Great Missionaries, New York, 1913.
From Every Tribe and Nation . . ., Chicago, 1927.

BRAINE, ROBERT D. (May 20, 1861–July 24, 1943), musician, was born in Springfield, Clark County. He operated a music conservatory in Springfield, contributed articles on music to various magazines, and for 25 years was violin editor of *Étude.* His death occurred in Springfield.

Messages from Mars by the Aid of the Telescope Plant, New York, 1892.

BRAINERD, THOMAS (June 17, 1804–Aug. 21, 1866), Presbyterian minister, was born in Leyden, N. Y. He was in Cincinnati from 1831 to 1837, first as minister of the Fourth Church and then as Lyman Beecher's associate in Second Church. He remained loyal to Beecher during the latter's heresy trial. Many of his sermons were published, but he is remembered chiefly for his biography of John Brainerd, missionary to the Indians: *The Life of John Brainerd . . .*, Philadelphia, [1865].

BRANCH, EDWARD PAYSON (May 26, 1844–Dec., 1937), was born in Ohio, probably in Lake County. He attended Madison Seminary and engaged in the lumber business until 1906, when he retired. He afterward lived in Portland, Oreg., and Melbourne, Fla. He died in Florida.

Plain People; A Story of the Western Reserve, New York, 1892.

BRAND, JAMES (Feb. 26, 1834–April 11, 1899), clergyman, was born in Three Rivers, Quebec, Canada. After entering Yale University in 1861, he withdrew to serve throughout the Civil War with Connecticut troops. He graduated from Yale in 1866 and Andover Theological Seminary in 1869. After four years at Danvers, Mass., he was called to First Congregational Church, Oberlin. Here he preached until his death. He was an active advocate of temperance. An address outlining the history of First Church was published in 1877.

James Brand, Twenty-Six Years of the First Congregational Church, Oberlin; Some Chapters from His Life . . . Written by Himself for His Family, Shortly before His Death, Oberlin, 1899.

BRANDT, HERBERT W. (1882–March 8, 1955), born in Cleveland, Cuyahoga County, was a 1907 graduate of Case Institute of Technology, where he starred in football; he operated a hotel and restaurant supply company in Cleveland. His hobby of ornithology took him on 42 expeditions and led to his writing three books on bird life, e.g., *Texas Bird Adventures . . . ,* Cleveland, 1940.

BRANDT, JOHN LINCOLN (Oct. 26, 1860–March 27, 1946), clergyman, was born in Somerset, Perry County. A minister in the Christian Church, he served as pastor in Ohio, Colorado, Indiana, Missouri, Oklahoma, Australia, and California. He traveled widely and wrote numerous articles for religious journals. He died in Los Angeles.

The Lord's Supper, Cincinnati, 1888.
Turning Points; Or, Great Questions for Young Men and Women, Cincinnati, 1890.
Christian Science Examined and Exposed . . . , Denver, 1891.
Marriage and the Home, Chicago, 1892.
The False and the True, [n.p.], 1893.
America or Rome, Christ or the Pope, Toledo, 1895.
Anglo-Saxon Supremacy . . . , Boston, [1915].
Finding Christ, New York, 1930.
The Origin of Churches, Melbourne, Australia, [n.d.].
What about the Modern Dance?, Cincinnati, [n.d.].
Why Am I a Christian? [n.p., n.d.].

BRANHAM, CHARLES ALLEN (Jan. 18, 1904–), poet, was born in Cincinnati, Hamilton County. He has written greeting card verses and advertising copy, was an advertising manager for several Cincinnati firms, and is now an advertising executive in Rochester, N. Y. He has published poems in various newspapers; his first collection was *Life's Journey,* Indianapolis, 1929.

BRANNAN, WILLIAM PENN (March 22, 1825–Aug. 9, 1866), self-educated poet and painter, was born in Cincinnati, Hamilton County, and was reared on a farm near the city. He operated a portrait studio in Cincinnati and for a time in Chicago and Louisville, Ky. His poems and humorous prose sketches, most of them published under the pen name VanDyke Brown, appeared in leading periodicals. His burlesque sermon "The Harp of a Thousand Strings" was widely popular with amateur and professional elocutionists. He died in Cincinnati.

The Hardshell Baptist Strikes Ile, New York, 1865.
Vagaries of VanDyke Brown; An Autobiography in Verse, Cincinnati, 1865.

BRAUN, OSCAR C. (April 22, 1859–April 26, 1945), educator, was born in Germany, but came to the United States when he was seventeen and lived in Cincinnati until his death at the age of 86. Until his retirement in 1941, he taught German and served as registrar at Ohio Mechanics Institute. He was active in the German Literary Society of Cincinnati and dedicated to its members a book of poems: *Wir Deutsch-Amerikaner,* Cincinnati, 1911.

BRAVERMAN, LIBBIE LEVIN (Mrs. Sigmund) (Dec. 20, 1900–), was born in Boston, Mass., and has lived in Cleveland since about 1924. She has taught in the Cleveland public schools and has served as educational director of Euclid Avenue Temple. She has written articles on Jewish education and with Nathan Brilliant has produced several pageants for use in Jewish schools. She has also written a book about Palestine: *Children of the Emek,* New York, [1937].

BRAY, FRANK CHAPIN (May 7, 1866–March 24, 1949), journalist, was born in Salineville, Columbiana County. After graduating from Wesleyan University, Conn., in 1890, he served on the editorial staff of *Literary Digest* and other periodicals. His books include *Headlines in American History,* [New York, 1937]. WWW 2

BRAYTON, MATTHEW (April 7, 1818–1862), was born in Sandusky County. In 1821 he was taken by his family to Tymochtee Township, Wyandot County, where on Sept. 20, 1825, the little boy was snatched up by a party of Canadian Indians and carried off into captivity. Either the fear of being discovered with a white captive in their possession or their love for whisky caused one tribe after another to trade their captive. With his origin completely forgotten, he finally wound up with the Copperheads and married into that tribe in 1851. He was positively identified as a white man in 1859 and, informed that he had been captured in Ohio, he set out for that state in an effort to find a trace of his family. In Cleveland he was introduced to J. H. A. Bone (q.v.), who wrote and published Brayton's story in the Cleveland *Herald.* The narrative aroused wide interest, with the result that on Nov. 18, 1859, he was identified by the presence of two scars incident to childhood mishaps as the missing Matthew Brayton. The following year the narrative of the captivity was published in book form. This important "captivity" has been the subject of no little controversy. It has been charged that it would not have been possible for Brayton to have made some of the movements described among the tribes named. These critics have overlooked the fact that Brayton was taken captive at the age of seven, had lived with the Indians for 34 years, could not read or write, and spoke English with great difficulty. Though Bone sought to preserve the simplicity of Brayton's account, in padding out the story he introduced the inaccuracies which have aroused doubt as to the authenticity of the entire narrative. There exists ample evidence to prove that the "captive" was indeed Matthew Brayton. The best sources are the files of Upper Sandusky *Union* and the *Seneca Advertiser* (Tiffin) for the year 1859. At the outbreak of the Civil War, Brayton enlisted in an Indiana regiment. While in the service he was taken dangerously ill, and after a short sickness he died at Pittsburgh Landing.

Ernest J. Wessen

The Indian Captive. A Narrative of the Adventures and Sufferings of Matthew Brayton, in his Thirty-Four Years of Captivity among the Indians of North-western America, Cleveland, 1860.

BREAKSPEAR. Pseud. See William L. Adams.

BRECKLING, GRACE JAMISON (Feb. 5, 1900–), was born in Stillman Valley, Ill., and has lived in Cleveland since 1925. She graduated from Rockford College and has taught English in Cleveland high schools. She has published several novels since her first: *Dream without End,* Philadelphia, [1950].

BRENNAN, JOHN PATRICK (Dec. 24, 1866–Oct. 30, 1932), clergyman, was born in Napoleon, Henry County. Becoming a telegrapher when he was fifteen, he worked for three years before determining to become a Roman Catholic priest. He studied at Canisius College, Buffalo, N. Y., and Xavier College, Cincinnati. He completed his studies for the priesthood at St. Mary's Seminary, Cleveland, and after being ordained in 1894 served churches in Youngstown and Cleveland. He published stories in Catholic periodicals, a book of prayers, and the play listed below.

Esther, the Persian Queen, Youngstown, [1897].

BRENNEMAN, HENRY B. (Aug. 12, 1831–Sept. 28, 1887), who was born in Fairfield County, was a deacon in the Mennonite Church for 23 years and conducted a column in the *Herald of Truth* for several years. He died in Elkhart, Ind., where he spent the greater part of his adult life.

Gems of Truth for Children . . . , Elkhart, Ind., 1873.

BRENNER, ROBERT WILLIAM (June 22, 1904–July 17, 1959), engineer, was born in Maineville, Warren County. He was employed as a draftsman at the American Laundry Machine Company, was active in the Methodist Church, and was a member of the Lebanon Symphony Orchestra. He wrote numerous historical articles for various area newspapers and also published a local history: *Maineville, Ohio, History . . . ,* Cincinnati, 1950.

BRENT, LORING. Pseud. See George F. Worts.

BRENTFORD, BURKE. Pseud. See Nathan D. Urner.

BREUER, ELIZABETH (Bessie) (Oct. 18, 1892–), was born in Cleveland, Cuyahoga County. She was educated in the public schools of St. Louis and attended the school of journalism, Missouri State University. After serving as a reporter on the St. Louis *Times* and the New York *Tribune,* she began publishing magazine articles. Her serious writing began during the 1920s while she was living in France. Her fiction is notable for its intense awareness of feminine psychology and for its experimental technique. Her short stories, which have appeared in *Story, The New Yorker, Harper's Bazaar,* and other magazines, have been awarded several prizes. Her most successful novel was *Memory of Love,* New York, 1934. TCA

BREWBAKER, CHARLES WARREN (Oct. 18, 1869–), clergyman, was born in State Line, Pa. Ordained to the ministry of the United Brethren Church in 1893, he served churches in various states and in Canton, 1898–1904. He was general secretary of Sunday School and Brotherhood Work, 1913–29; director of the Bureau of Evangelism, 1929–33; and pastor of Fairview Church, Dayton, 1933–39. He now lives in Dayton. He has written *Evangelism and the Present World-Order,* New York, 1932. WW 26

BREWER, ABRAHAM TITUS (Sept. 20, 1841–April 17, 1933), lawyer, was born in Monroe County. After serving in the Civil War with the 61st Pennsylvania Volunteers, he studied law and was admitted to the Ohio bar in 1869. He lived and practiced in Cleveland. With G. A. Laubscher, he wrote a legal treatise on Ohio corporations which attained five editions.

How to Make the Sunday School Go, Cincinnati, [1897].
True War Stories, 1907.
History of Sixty-First Regiment, Pennsylvania Volunteers, [Pittsburgh, Pa., 1911].

BREWER, ANNETTE FITCH (Jan. 31, 1870–Oct. 29, 1960), was born in Ashtabula, Ashtabula County, a descendant of one of the pioneer county families. After graduating from Lake Erie Seminary in 1890, she was active in the movement for women's suffrage. She married Isaac C. Brewer in 1893 and lived in the state of Washington for some time. After returning to Ohio, she married a Mr. Nelson and lived in Jefferson, where she published numerous historical feature stories in the Jefferson *Gazette.* She also broadcast historical programs over the Ashtabula radio station in the late 1930s. Her only book was published under the name Annette Fitch-Brewer: *The Story of a Mother Love,* [Akron, 1913]. OBB

BREWSTER, GEORGE (1800–1865), educator, arrived in Cleveland in 1831. He was a school principal there in 1837 and later taught in Columbus. He published the *Western Literary Magazine* at Detroit, Columbus, and Lawrence, Kan.

Lectures on Education, Columbus, 1833.
A New Philosophy of Matter . . . , Boston, 1843.
Lectures on the Origin of the Globe . . . , Columbus, 1850.

BREWSTER, H. POMEROY (March 7, 1831–1906), was born in Ravenna, Portage County, but soon after his birth his parents moved to Rochester, N. Y., where he spent most of his life. After a period of study and travel abroad, he was an importer in England, 1851–58. Returning to Rochester, he was in the banking business until 1870, when he retired to devote himself to writing.

The Coffee Houses and Tea Gardens of Old London, Rochester, 1888.
The Story of a Welsh Girl, [Rochester?], 1888.
England and Its Rulers . . . , Chicago, 1892.
The Cross in Iconography, Archaeology, Architecture . . . , Rochester, [1894].
Saints and Festivals of the Christian Church, New York, [1904].

BREWSTER, STANLEY FARRAR (Aug. 22, 1889–), lawyer, was born in Cincinnati, Hamilton County. He graduated from University of Cincinnati in 1910 and Harvard Law School in 1913. He practiced in New York City, 1922–29, and was on the faculty of Washington College of Law. His books include legal texts and *Twelve Men in a Box,* Chicago, 1934. WW 30

BREWSTER, WILLIAM NESBITT (Dec. 5, 1862–Nov. 22, 1916), missionary, was born in Highland County. He graduated from Ohio Wesleyan University in 1883 and Boston University School of Theology in 1886. He served for many years as a Methodist missionary in India and China. His books include *The Methodist Man's Burden,* New York, 1913. WWW 1

BRICKER, GARLAND ARMOR (March 20, 1881–), educator, was born in Etna, Licking County. He attended Lima College and graduated from Ohio University in 1918. He taught in Ohio public schools, the agriculture department of Ohio State University, and other universities. In 1937 he became manager of the Youngstown Book Store, and he is now president of Pennsylvania-Ohio University, Youngstown. Besides a number of agriculture textbooks, he has written *The Church in Rural America,* Cincinnati, [1919]. WW 21

BRINKERHOFF, HENRY R. (Oct. 9, 1836– ?), soldier, was born in Medina County. He enlisted in the U. S. Army Aug. 19, 1861, and served until his retirement as a lieutenant colonel in 1900. During his service he had many experiences among the Indian tribes, which he used in the novel listed below.

Nah-Nee-Ta, a Tale of the Navajos, Washington, D. C., 1886.

BRINKERHOFF, ROBERT MOORE (May 4, 1880–Feb. 17, 1958), cartoonist and illustrator, was born in Toledo, Lucas County. He worked as a cartoonist on the Toledo *Bee,* the Toledo *Blade,* the Cleveland *Leader,* and later for United Features Syndicate. His death occurred in Minneapolis, Minn. He illustrated stories for many magazines. His cartoon character, Little Mary Mixup, is the subject of his book, *Little Mary Mixup in Fairyland,* New York, 1926. WWW 3

BRINKERHOFF, ROELIFF (June 28, 1828–June 4, 1911), lawyer and journalist, was born in Owasco, N. Y. He was educated in local schools and neighboring academies. After teaching two years in district schools, he drifted to Tennessee, where he served as tutor in the family of Andrew Jackson, Jr., at the Hermitage. Inheriting a substantial fortune on the death of his father, he came to Mansfield, studied law under his kinsman Jacob Brinkerhoff, and was admitted to the bar in 1851. He soon switched from the practice of law to journalism, and in 1855 he bought from J. R. Locke (q.v.) and associates the Mansfield *Herald,* which he edited until 1861, when he entered the army as quartermaster. After the war he returned to Mansfield and became a conspicuous figure in state politics. His wealth left him leisure to devote to philanthropy, genealogical research, and penology. In 1893 he became president of the National Prison Association, and he was vice-president of the International Prison Congress which met in Paris in 1895. He was a founder and the first president of the Ohio Archaeological Society and for fifteen years was president of its successor, the Ohio State Archaeological and Historical Society. Though highly personal his *Recollections* is an entertaining and valuable commentary on men and events of the last three quarters of the nineteenth century. He also wrote two family histories. His death occurred in Mansfield.

The Volunteer Quartermaster, New York, 1864.

Recollections of a Lifetime, Cincinnati, 1900.

BRITTON, ROLLIN JOHN (Dec. 9, 1864–March 28, 1931), lawyer, was born in Akron, Summit County. In 1877 his parents moved to Constantine, Mich., and a few years later to Gallatin, Mo. He attended Normal School at Stanberry, Mo., and taught school and read law in Gallatin. He participated in the land rush to the Cherokee Strip in 1889, but returned to Missouri because of ill health. He practiced law in Gallatin until 1910 and afterward in Kansas City, Mo. Especially interested in the history of the Mormons in Missouri, he wrote many historical and biographical articles. He also published fiction, and under the pen name Guy Blue he wrote considerable poetry for newspapers. At least two collections of his poetry were published, e.g., *Stuff, Effused by Guy Blue,* Gallatin, Mo., 1912.

BROADBECK, CAPTAIN. Pseud. See James W. Gazlay.

BROBECK, FLORENCE (July 19, 1895–), journalist, born in Ashville, Pickaway County, graduated from Ohio State University in 1917 and has lived in New York City since 1921. She was women's editor of the New York *Herald Tribune* for seven years and for a number of years was associate editor of *McCall's.* As a free-lance writer she has published articles in various magazines and newspapers. She has also written several popular cookbooks and a book about cats: *The Cat on the Mat,* New York, 1935. WWNAA 7

BROCKIE, JOHN MEIKLE (April 27, 1879–Jan. 3, 1949), clergyman and journalist, was born in Glasgow, Scotland. After graduating from the University of Maine and Bangor Theological Seminary, he served pastorates in New England and New York, 1905–28. He was editor of the Mt. Sterling *Tribune,* 1929–49. He published several books of prose and verse, e.g., *What's It All About?,* [Mt. Sterling, 1933]. BDCP

BROMFIELD, ANNETTE MARIA COULTON (April 29, 1863–Jan. 7, 1947), mother of Louis Bromfield (q.v.), was born in Monroe Township, Richland County. She died in Springfield Township in the same county. She wrote a book about a dog belonging to her son: *Laddie Boy; The Autobiography of a Dog,* New York, 1936.

BROMFIELD, LOUIS (Dec. 27, 1896–March 19, 1956), was born in Mansfield, Richland County. In the nineteenth century Mansfield was one of those sleepy little Middle Western towns described by Sherwood Anderson as "devoted to the practice of the old trades, to agriculture and merchandising." It was the seat of Richland County, where early settlers had found the land productive and stayed on it to produce large and established families like the Bromfield clan. The town's personality began to change in the 1870s and 1880s when the smoke of factories and foundries claimed the rural skies. With it came wealth and poverty, company owners and common laborers, dreadful architecture and ugly slums, and a sense of urgency and hurry. In the midst of these lived the heirs of the old families who had been reared in the quiet and simplicity of the rural community. To two of them, Charles and Annette Bromfield, a son Louis was born two days after Christmas in 1896. Throughout his sixty years he retained a nostalgia for the pleasant life of his ancestors, a trait that marked his philosophy and his writings. The large and lovable Bromfield family also provided him with many of the best characters of his novels and short stories. Near-poverty dogged the Bromfields while Louis was growing up. In the place of money, however, his parents and his grandfather Coulter gave him a romantic spirit, a love of life, an appreciation of beauty and of just plain fun, and an affection for the land and for nature. His mother, a persevering woman, guided his education and provided him with a library of the great English authors. He remained a voracious reader throughout his life, though he reacted to her domination with a desire for personal freedom. Hard times drove the Bromfields to the Coulter farm when Louis was about sixteen, and he decided to go to Cornell University to study agriculture. After a semester he returned when his grandfather became ill; he worked on the farm for a year and a half before he decided upon a different life. In Sept., 1916, he left for Columbia University to enter journalism. This time the war intervened, and in 1917 he joined the ambulance service and served two years in France. New York City became his home after the war. There he married Mary Appleton Wood, an aspiring young writer, in 1921. Between 1919 and 1925 he worked as a reporter, became foreign editor of *Musical America,* served as dramatic and book critic of the *Bookman,* wrote a monthly column called "The New Yorker" for *Bookman,* was music critic on the original staff of *Time,* and was advertising manager of G. P. Putnam's Sons. Meanwhile he spent his spare time writing four novels which were never to see print and in 1924 *The Green Bay Tree,* which launched him as a successful novelist. The following year *Possession* also hit the best-seller lists. After it appeared in the fall, the Bromfields sailed for a visit to Paris. They found France attractive and less expensive than the United States, and made their home near Paris for fourteen years. With his first two novels Bromfield began a panel of four books on the "ungainly, swarming, glittering spectacle of American life," the next two being *Early Autumn* (1926), which won him the Pulitzer Prize, and *A Good Woman* (1927). The setting for *Early Autumn* was a New England town, and for each of the other three, in which the characters were members of his own family, it was "the town," presumably Mansfield, and New York and Paris. In each the story unfolds in the changing American scene of the last decade of the nineteenth century and the first two decades of the twentieth century. In these novels Bromfield displayed a genuine talent for telling stories and creating memorable characters. He suggested that they might be brought together under the title "Escape." The first two deal with the rebellion of the "new woman," the third with a struggle for release from an old and decaying New England family, and the fourth with a son's reaction to his mother's domination. Novels continued to come from his pen at a rapid rate: *The Strange Case of Annie Spragg* (1928), *Twenty-Four Hours* (1930), and *A Modern Hero* (1932), weaker stories in which he experimented with new forms and new ideas. In 1929 he published *Awake and Rehearse,* his first volume of short stories. In *A Modern Hero* he moved from his concern for escape from social restrictions and personal inhibitions to a recognition that the individual must control his drives if he is to have happiness. In *The Farm* (1933) he celebrated the conscience and integrity of the individual in rural America. For this book he returned to the Richland County scene and his family to produce a significant study of the "good way of life" which industrialism had displaced. It remained one of his favorites among his own writings. It also restored him to the literary position he had won with his first four novels. In *Here Today and Gone Tomorrow* (1934), four short novels reprinted from *Cosmopolitan,* Bromfield slipped into mediocrity. *The Man Who Had Everything* (1935) was significant only for his analysis of his own restlessness in the 1930s, when success began to pall on him and he began talking of returning to a farm in Ohio. Several trips to India, beginning in 1932, resulted in *The Rains Came* (1937), a very popular story in which he compared the faith of a rising people with that of the West, where he saw life "drooping and dying." In 1938 the threat of war drove the Bromfields home, where they bought three adjoining farms near Mansfield and settled down to farm. In 1939 he issued a sharp attack on Neville Chamberlain and the men in power in England in a pamphlet entitled *England, a Dying Oligarchy*. In the same year *It Takes All Kinds* appeared, containing four short novels and five short stories from *Cosmopolitan*. J. P. Marquand called the volume "a case book of literary craftsmanship which anyone in the profession will be the better for studying." For several years he wrote stories without much substance, including *Night in Bombay* (1940); *Wild Is the River* (1941), a romantic historical novel of New Orleans under Yankee occupation; and *Until the Day Break* (1942), a tale about Paris during the German occupation in World War II. *Mrs. Parkington* (1943) was a model in construction, but it lacked strong characters. *What Became of Anna Bolton* (1944) proved exciting but lacked depth and integrity and represented a considerable drop in quality from *Mrs. Parkington*. *The World We Live In* (1944), a collection of fascinating short stories from *Cosmopolitan*, dealt with Americans and Europeans in the prewar and war years. After his return from France, the farm called "Malabar" and agriculture dominated Bromfield's interest. He turned Malabar into a pilot farm of experimentation which soon attracted thousands of visitors a year from all over the world. His success in reviving worn-out land and his other experiments led a group of citizens of Wichita Falls, Texas, to invite him to start a second Malabar near that town, and some years later, at the request of Brazilian officials, he set up a third Malabar in Brazil. His most effective writings now concerned the farm and farming. *Pleasant Valley* (1945), the story of an amateur farmer trying to operate a large farm, opened a series of four books on the subject. It also restored Bromfield to a high rank in American letters. It was followed by *Malabar Farm* (1948), aimed particularly at people who desired practical information on reclamation and general farming; *Out of the Earth* (1950), concerned primarily with new techniques in agriculture; and *From My Experience* (1955), which dealt with later operations at Malabar and at Malabar-do-Brazil. Bromfield interspersed his farm books with *A Few Brass Tacks* (1946), a disapproving analysis of American materialism and a criticism of the New Deal; *Kenny* (1947), a weak collection of short stories; *Colorado* (1947), a satirical novel on Westerns and Westerners; and *The Wild Country* (1948), a piece of psychological fiction about a growing boy. With *Mr. Smith* (1951), a story in which a small American businessman analyzes the purposelessness and hypocrisy of his own life in terms of the emptiness of our society, Bromfield once more won the plaudits of the critics. His concern with the problems of this nation and of civilization in general led to *A New Pattern for a Tired World* (1954), a nonfiction criticism of American policy and a plan for more effective leadership in the world. His writing career concluded with *Animals and Other People* (1955), a volume of stories about people who were "teched" that they were loved by animals. Bromfield's books had tremendous sales. His first novel, *The Green Bay Tree*, is said to have earned him about $1,500,000. Several books, including *The Rains Came*, were translated into sixteen languages. Before his death over 400,000 copies of *The Rains Came* had been printed in the German translation alone. A dozen of his books were translated into ten or more languages each, and all but the last three were translated into at least one language. Virtually all of his books have been frequently reprinted in English. Before his death his five farm books had sold over 300,000 copies, and they have continued to sell. His popularity was achieved without the help of book clubs, with which he refused to have anything to do. To Bromfield the primary purpose of literature was to entertain. Writing on a sweeping canvas, he built his stories around exciting adventure and plenty of sex. His exceptional ability to tell a story was his forte; his second strength probably lay in his talent for character portrayal, but in this area he served his female figures better than his male ones. Finally, he was a literary craftsman whose technique was sometimes better than his stories. He did his most effective writing on the problems of personal escape from inhibitions and family and social restrictions in his first four books, and on the hollowness of modern life and the virtues of rural America in later works. It is apparent that he was a prodigious writer. Besides fiction, the volumes on the farm, and the books on the state of the prewar and postwar world, he produced numerous articles, many parts of books, several plays and movie scripts, and a syndicated newspaper column. He was constantly in demand as a speaker on literary subjects, farming and conservation, and international affairs, and for a time conducted a Saturday afternoon broadcast on a national radio hook-up. At the same time, he brought up three daughters and maintained a large home that was always filled with visitors. He had great personal charm, a deep understanding of people, and a warm sympathy for the unfortunate. He has been characterized as one of the most independent of Americans, and he gave his blessing to those characters in his books who fought for their personal rights. Until his return to the farm, Bromfield actually was not sure of himself or of his purpose in life. At Malabar he finally achieved a "sense of *belonging,* of being a small and relatively unimportant part of something vast but infinitely friendly."

James H. Rodabaugh

BRONSON, SHERLOCK ANSON (April 21, 1807–May 7, 1890), clergyman and educator, was born in Waterbury, Conn. In the same year his family moved to Lorain County. He graduated from Kenyon College in 1833 and was ordained an Episcopal priest in 1835. He served churches in Granville, 1837–45, Sandusky, 1850–66, and Mansfield, 1872–89. He was president of Kenyon College, 1845–50, and served on the seminary faculty there, 1866–72. The first title below is an important financial history of Kenyon College. His death occurred in Mansfield.

A Memento of the Donors and Founders of the Theological Seminary of the Protestant Episcopal Church in the Diocese of Ohio, and Kenyon College, Cincinnati, 1860.

John Sherman; What He Has Said and Done . . . , Columbus, 1880.

BROOKE, JOHN THOMPSON (Feb. 4, 1800–Aug. 19, 1861), clergyman, was born in Frederick, Md. After reading law with Roger B. Taney, he was admitted to the bar and practiced for two or three years. He then studied at a theological seminary in Alexandria, Va., and was ordained an Episcopal priest in 1826. He served three years in Martinsburg, Va., and nine years in Georgetown, Washington, D. C., before coming to Christ Church, Cincinnati, where he was rector, 1835-47. He was later a professor at Kenyon College and rector of Christ Church, Springfield, 1854–60. Besides the titles below, several of his sermons and addresses were published.

Union: How Far Consistent or Justifiable in View of the Present Differences between Churchmen, Cincinnati, 1859.

Short Notes on the Dred Scott Case, Cincinnati, 1861.

BROOKE, MARY GOULD (May 22, 1858–Jan. 22, 1946), was born in Eaton, Preble County. She married an Eaton banker and spent her life in that community. She was actively interested in local history. She wrote *Historic Eaton and Fort St. Clair,* Eaton, 1930.

BROOKER, LOUISA JONES (1869–Dec. 20, 1955), educator, taught in Cleveland elementary schools, 1902–38. She published a collection of verse for children, *Half-past Five . . . ,* New York, [1938].

BROOKS, ALDEN (Feb. 8, 1883–), was born in Cleveland, Cuyahoga County. After attending schools in France and England, he graduated from Harvard University in 1905. He was a teacher in the United States and a newspaperman in France; during World War I he served in the French Foreign Legion. In 1935 he settled in Maryland as a tobacco farmer and writer; he now lives in Topango, Calif. He has published several books, e.g., a novel, *Escape,* New York, 1924.

BROOKS, CHARLES STEPHEN (June 25, 1878–June 29, 1934), was born in Cleveland, Cuyahoga County. After graduating from Yale University in 1900, he conducted a printing and stationery business in Cleveland until 1915, when he moved to New York. He returned to Cleveland to live a few years before his death. He published plays, fiction, several collections of essays, e.g., *Chimney-Pot Papers,* New Haven, [Conn.], 1919, and a book of boyhood memories: *Prologue,* New York, [1931]. WWW 1

BROOKS, CHATTY. Pseud. See Rosella Rice.

BROOKS, ELIPHALET (? – ?), was born in Ohio, probably in Wakeman, Huron County. He was probably the son of John Brooks, a pioneer settler of that community. His book "advocating the personal coming of Christ" was privately printed.

The Harmony of Prophecy, Wakeman, 1863.

BROOKS, JENNIE (April 23, 1853–Feb. 15, 1934), was born in Cincinnati, Hamilton County. She graduated from Oxford College for Women in 1871. She published

many articles and stories on nature in national magazines. She also published two books on nature study, e.g., *Quests of a Bird Lover,* Boston, [1922]. OBB

BROOKS, LAKE. Pseud. See Arthur R. Harding.

BROOKS, NELLIE SUMNER (1867–), poet, born in Dayton, Montgomery County, of New England parents who returned to Connecticut to reside after her birth, graduated from Oberlin College and returned to take up permanent residence in Dayton in 1894 after her marriage to Virgil L. Brooks, a Dayton plumbing contractor. She wrote *Maple Mansion Melodies,* Dayton, 1930.

BROOKS, ROBERT CLARKSEN (Feb. 7, 1874–Feb. 2, 1941), educator, was born in Piqua, Miami County. He graduated from Indiana University in 1896 and Cornell University (Ph.D.) in 1903. He served on the faculties of several universities, including the University of Cincinnati (1908–12); at the time of his death he was teaching at Swarthmore College. His writings include *Corruption in American Politics and Life,* New York, 1910. WWW 1

BROOKS, WILLIAM KEITH (March 25, 1848–Nov. 12, 1908), zoologist, was born in Cleveland, Cuyahoga County, the son of a prosperous merchant. His interest in science developed early. In 1866 he entered Hobart College, where he spent two years, and in 1870 he graduated from Williams College. His graduate work was done at Harvard University. From 1876 until his death he was a member of the biological department of Johns Hopkins University. In addition to the books listed below, he wrote numerous scientific papers and technical works.

The Law of Heredity . . . , Baltimore, 1883.
The Oyster, a Popular Summary of a Scientific Study, Baltimore, 1891.

BROSANUS, MATTHEW. Pseud. See Harry M. Brown.

BROTHERTON, ALICE WILLIAMS (April 4, 1848–Feb. 9, 1930), was born in Cambridge City, Ind. In her girlhood she accompanied her parents to Cincinnati, where, except for short periods of residence in her native state and in St. Louis, Mo., she spent the rest of her life. Her education was received mainly in Cincinnati, where she graduated from Woodward High School in 1870. As early as 1872 she began to write for the press, and she contributed to various leading periodicals, including *Century, Scribner's, Atlantic Monthly, St. Nicholas,* and the New York *Independent.* She died in Cincinnati.

Beyond the Veil, Chicago, 1886.
The Sailing of King Olaf and Other Poems, Chicago, 1887.
What the Wind Told the Treetops, New York, 1888.
The Orchard Path and Other Poems, 1917.

BROTHERTON, JOHN WILLIAMS, son of Alice W. Brotherton (q.v.), was born in Cincinnati, Hamilton County, and still lives in that city. He graduated from the University of Cincinnati in 1939. He has published poems in Cincinnati newspapers and in a collection: *Airs and Graces,* Cincinnati, 1931.

BROWDER, URIAH MARION (1846–1907), clergyman, was born in Jamestown, Greene County. A minister of the Disciples of Christ Church, he served as an evangelist and pastor in Illinois and Ohio. He died in Dayton.

The Ministry of Reconciliation . . . , St. Louis, Mo., 1879.
The Process of Regeneration, Litchfield, Ill., 1884.
Browder's Pulpit . . . , St. Louis, Mo., 1887.

BROWN, ALBERT M. (Aug. 28, 1901–), social worker, was born in Cleveland, Cuyahoga County. He attended the University of Pittsburgh and Western Reserve University. Since 1924 he has been in social work in New York, Cleveland, and Toledo. He has published several volumes of plays for boys, e.g., *A Collection of Boys' Plays,* Boston, [1933].

BROWN, DAVID LESLIE (Sept. 9, 1885–), was born in Buffalo, N. Y. After graduating from Ohio Wesleyan University, he was a Methodist minister, a lecturer at the St. Louis World's Fair, and a teacher. He was an executive of Goodyear Tire and Rubber Company, Akron, 1916–29. After retiring he lived in Florida and in Europe; he now lives in New York City. He has written poems and articles for various magazines and two books on business, e.g., *On Setbacks . . . ,* New York, 1919.

BROWN, EDWARD (Nov. 1, 1814– ?), clergyman, was born in Colebrook, Ashtabula County. No details concerning his life have been found except that he became pastor of the Wadsworth Congregational Church in 1874. His pamphlet is valuable for its history of Medina County.

Wadsworth Memorial . . . , Wadsworth, 1875.

BROWN, FREDERIC (Oct. 29, 1906–), writer of mystery stories, was born in Cincinnati, Hamilton County, and lived there until he was 23 years old. His home at present is Tucson, Ariz. His numerous mystery novels include *The Dead Ringer,* New York, 1948. WW 30

BROWN, GEORGE (Jan. 29, 1792–Oct. 25, 1871), clergyman and educator, was born in Washington County, Pa. He was brought to Steubenville in 1800 and grew up in that town. In 1814 he became an itinerant Methodist preacher and traveled throughout Ohio, Virginia, and western Pennsylvania. He served for a time as president of Madison College, Uniontown, Pa., and also lived in Xenia and Cincinnati. On becoming editor of the *Western Methodist Protestant* in 1860, he moved to Springfield, where he wrote his recollections. His book provides an important account of pioneer life in Steubenville and of his service during the War of 1812. He describes an otherwise unrecorded march across Ohio and a description of the harrowing experience of "short-term" men, discharged at Lower Sandusky and turned loose to find their way to their homes through trackless swamps and forests. His death occurred in Springfield.

Recollections of Itinerant Life; Including Early Reminiscences, Cincinnati, 1866.
The Lady Preacher: Or, the Life and Labors of Mrs. Hanna Reeves . . . , Springfield, 1870.

BROWN, HALLIE QUINN (March 10, 1860–Sept. 16, 1949), educator, was born in Pittsburgh, Pa. Her parents moved to Ohio in the year of her birth. After graduating from Wilberforce University in 1873, she was a school principal in Dayton for two years; dean of Allen University, Columbia, S. C., 1885–87; and dean of Tuskegee Institute, 1892–93. In 1902 she joined the English faculty of Wilberforce University. She lectured and gave readings and published several books, e.g., *Pen Pictures of Pioneers of Wilberforce . . .* , [Xenia, 1937].

BROWN, HARRY MATTHEW (Jan. 24, 1921–), educator, was born in Newark, Licking County. He graduated from Baldwin-Wallace College in 1946 and Western Reserve University (Ph.D.) in 1955. He taught English at Baldwin-Wallace, 1946–50, and since 1950 has been on the faculty of West Virginia University. Under the pen name Matthew Brosanus, he has published a volume of poetry: *Sea-Rock and Coral,* Prairie City, Ill., [1950]. DAS 3

BROWN, JESSIE HUNTER. See Jessie H. B. Pounds.

BROWN, JOE EVAN (July 28, 1892–), comedian, was born in Holgate, Henry County. Beginning as a circus acrobat in 1902, he became one of America's best-loved comedians in musical comedies and motion pictures. His tours of the war zone during World War II resulted in his writing *Your Kids and Mine,* New York, 1944. WW 30

BROWN, JOHN FRANKLIN (May 1, 1865–Feb. 15, 1940), educator and editor, was born in Springboro, Warren County. He graduated from Earlham College in 1889 and Cornell University (Ph.D.) in 1896. After about twenty years in educational work, he joined Macmillan Company as an editor in the secondary school department. He wrote several books on education, e.g., *The American High School,* New York, 1909.

BROWN, JOHN PORTER (Aug. 17, 1814–April 28, 1872), diplomat and Oriental scholar, was born in Chillicothe, Ross County, the son of a tanner. In 1832 he joined his uncle, David D. Porter, American minister in Constantinople. Brown held various posts in the American legation. During his forty years of diplomatic service, the actions that brought him to public notice were his trip to America in 1850 with Amin Bey, the first Turkish mission to visit this country, and his implusive demand in 1853 that an Austrian ship surrender Martin Koszta, a Hungarian patriot who had announced his intention of becoming an American citizen. Brown translated several Turkish works into English, including a collection of fairy tales, *Turkish Evening Entertainments* (1850). He died in Constantinople.

History of the Dervishes; Or, Oriental Spiritualism, Philadelphia, 1868.

BROWN, KENNETH IRVING (April 27, 1896–), educator, was born in Brooklyn, N. Y. After serving as president of Hiram College (1930–40) and Denison University (1940–50), he became director of the Danforth Foundation. His writings include *A Campus Decade; The Hiram Study Plan of Intensive Courses,* Chicago, [1940]. WW 30

BROWN, MARCUS MONROE (c.1855–Oct. 16, 1915), was born in Batavia, Ill. He practiced law in Chicago before coming to Cleveland in 1896, where he successfully engaged in home-building and real estate. Under the sponsorship of Euclid Avenue Baptist Church, he published a eulogistic biography of John D. Rockefeller and an attack on Ida M. Tarbell's account of Standard Oil and its founder: *A Study of John D. Rockefeller . . .* , Cleveland, 1905.

BROWN, MARY ELIZABETH ADAMS (March 13, 1844–Aug. 17, 1917), was born in Champaign County. She lived in Cincinnati for much of her life. She was a genealogist and also wrote a study of book dedications.

Ellice Larrabee, a Tale of the Olden Time, Cincinnati, 1889

The Story of John Adams, a New England Schoolmaster, New York, 1900.

BROWN, MOSES TRUE (March 4, 1827–Sept. 11, 1900), educator, was born in Deerfield, N. H. He graduated from Tufts College in 1866. He was superintendent of schools in Toledo for six years and an editor with Van Antwerp, Bragg & Co., Cincinnati, for two years. He joined the Tufts faculty and taught there until his retirement in 1890. In 1894 he moved to Sandusky, where he spent the remainder of his life. He was widely known as a lecturer and as an interpreter of Dickens.

The Synthetic Philosophy of Expression, as Applied to the Arts of Reading, Oratory, and Personation, Boston, 1886.

BROWN, ORIL (Sept. 16, 1908–), psychologist, was born in Maumee, Lucas County. He graduated from Northwestern University in 1930 and is at present a research psychologist at George Washington University. He has written magazine articles and one book: *Youth under Dictators,* Evanston, Ill., 1940.

BROWN, PERCY WHITING (Jan. 21, 1887–), investment broker, was born in Concord, Mass. He graduated from Harvard University in 1908 and has been a resident of Cleveland since 1923. He has published privately a collection of papers: *Middlesex Monographs,* Cleveland, 1941. WW 30

BROWN, ROLLO WALTER (March 15, 1880–Oct. 13, 1956), writer and lecturer, was born near Crooksville, Perry County. He read law for a time in Zanesville, but gave it up to attend Ohio Northern University (1899–1903) and Harvard University (1903–05). In 1924, after a career in college teaching, he devoted himself to lecturing and writing. He stayed often at the MacDowell Colony in Peterborough, N. H., where he knew Edward Arlington Robinson, subject of his book *Next Door to a Poet,* New York, 1937. He wrote several novels and books about writing, but he was most successful with short interpretative biographical sketches, as in *Lonely Americans,* New York, 1929. His autobiography, *The Hills Are Strong,* appeared in 1953. TCA

BROWN, SARA LOWE (Nov. 10, 1870–Jan. 28, 1957), was born in Groveport, Franklin County. She was reared in the locally famous Rarey Mansion, which had been the home of her great-uncle, John Solomon Rarey (q.v.), the world-famous horse-tamer, who was immortalized by Robert Browning in "A Likeness." Mrs. Brown's earliest recollections were of her uncle's horse Cruiser. The horse, whose comfort had been amply provided for in his master's will, survived Rarey by nine years, dying July 6, 1875, at the age of 23. Keeping green the memory of her illustrious uncle and the horse who shared his fame was a lifetime labor of love with Mrs. Brown. Those interested in the vast literature on the horse have long since accepted Mrs. Brown's book as the basic source on the subject: *The Horse Cruiser and the Rarey Method of Training Horses,* Columbus, 1925.

BROWN, VANDYKE. Pseud. See William P. Brannan.

BROWN, WILLIAM KENNEDY (Aug. 3, 1834–Oct., 1915), clergyman and educator, was born in Fayette County, Pa. After entering the Methodist ministry in 1856, he served in the Pittsburgh Conference and later in the Cincinnati Conference. He published the *Monitor* in Alliance, 1869–76. He was president of Cincinnati Wesleyan Woman's College, 1882–92. His death occurred in Cincinnati.

Guenethics; Or, the Ethical Status of Woman, New York, 1887.

BROWN, WILLIAM MONTGOMERY (Sept. 4, 1855–Oct. 31, 1937), clergyman, was born near Orrville, Wayne County. Left an orphan after the Civil War, he was bound out to a farmer near Cleveland. A wealthy woman, Mrs. Mary S. Bradford, became interested in him and financed his education at Kenyon. In 1885 he married her daughter, Ellen Bradford. He became a deacon in the Episcopal Church in 1883 and was ordained to the priesthood the following year. He was rector of the Galion Church, 1883–91, and later a missionary and archdeacon for the Diocese of Ohio. He was consecrated bishop of Arkansas in 1898, but resigned because of ill health in 1912. In 1925 he was tried for heresy, largely on the basis of his book, *Communism and Christianity,* and he was deposed from the office of bishop. He spent his last years in Galion. He left a half million dollars to foster communism in America.

The Church for Americans, New York, 1895.

The Crucial Race Question . . . , Little Rock, Ark., 1907.

The Level Plan for Church Union . . . , New York, 1910.

Communism and Christianity . . . , Galion, [1920].

My Heresy: The Autobiography of an Idea, New York, 1926.

The Human Meaning of Christian Doctrines, New York, [1928].

Heresy; "Bad Bishop Brown's" Quarterly Lectures . . . , [Galion, 1930].

Teachings of Marx for Girls and Boys, Galion, 1935.

BROWNE, CHARLES FARRAR (April 26, 1834–March 6, 1867), humorist, was born in Waterford, Maine, of pioneer stock and of parents well placed in the community. He was born Charles F. Brown, but added the final "e" in later life. Leaving home at thirteen with a minimum of schooling, he became a roving printer, drifted from one town to another, setting type and occasionally trying his hand at writing short pieces for his own amusement. Although only six years of his short life were spent in Ohio, it was here that he developed his distinctive style of humor. At twenty, tiring of his employment in Boston, he accepted Greeley's suggestion and turned his restless steps toward the West. He seems to have had no particular destination in mind, but in the course of a few weeks turned up in Cincinnati, where he worked for a time. He soon moved on to Dayton and then to Springfield for brief stays; then to Tiffin, where he remained nearly a year; and finally to Toledo. In Oct., 1857, he took a job on the news desk of the Cleveland *Plain Dealer.* The *Plain Dealer* was a four-page evening daily in its sixteenth year of publication, a pugnacious Democratic organ in a stoutly Republican community. It habitually carried a chip on its shoulder, and the defender of the chip was peppery little J. W. Gray, founder and proprietor of the paper. Always alert for fresh talent to brighten his columns, Gray observed Browne's work on the Toledo *Commercial* and invited him down the lake to the Cuyahoga metropolis. Browne went to the *Plain Dealer* as commercial and local news editor. The duties of the job were dully routine to a mind as effervescent as his, and, as he had sometimes done at Toledo, he found relief by presenting his news of the city in whimsical terms to the delight of his readers. A *bon vivant* and a born raconteur, he became popular in the night life of the city, and his pranks were part of contemporary history. Artemus Ward emerged from the chrysalis of Browne in Jan., 1858, when under this curious pseudonym he began writing of his wholly imaginary "show bizniss." The stunt was popular from the first. The name Browne dropped into disuse; that of Artemus Ward was on many tongues. His friends and admirers were myriad. Ward left Cleveland in mid-November, 1860, in response to a "louder call," as Gray wrote in farewell to his distinguished employee. He joined the staff of *Vanity Fair* in New York City and soon afterward became editor of this periodical, in whose columns originally appeared much of his work, later gathered in book form. During the six years that remained to him, he wrote industriously, lectured widely, and achieved recognition as one of the foremost of American humorists. The Lincoln cabinet found the President chuckling over Ward's "High Handed Outrage in Utica" when it assembled on special call in Sept., 1862, to hear for the first time the Emancipation Proclamation. Artemus Ward went to London in June, 1866, for an extended lecture tour. He was invited to write for *Punch* and was well received among men of letters. His popularity was marked from the first, but his days were to be few and he never saw America again. A frail physique, long overtaxed, finally gave way. He died of tuberculosis at Southampton, less than 33 years of age. It has been said that he founded a new school of American humor. His friend Bret Harte called it "the humor of audacious exaggeration—of perfect lawlessness—a humor that belongs to the country of boundless prairies and stupendous cataracts." Thus defined, Harte declared, Artemus Ward was "*the* American humorist par excellence." His works appeared in various editions after his death, and several spurious pieces were published under his name.

Archer H. Shaw

Artemus Ward, His Book . . ., New York, 1862.

Artemus Ward; His Travels . . ., New York, 1865.

Artemus Ward in London, and Other Papers, New York, 1867.

Artemus Ward's Panorama . . ., New York, 1869.

BROWNE, JUNIUS HENRI (Oct. 14, 1833–April 2, 1902), journalist, was born in Seneca Falls, N. Y., but was reared in Cincinnati, where his father was a banker. When he was eighteen, he became a reporter and worked on several Cincinnati newspapers. During the Civil War he served as correspondent for the New York *Tribune.* In May, 1863, he was captured by Confederate troops and imprisoned. For a year and a half he was held in various Southern prisons, until he escaped in 1864. This experience is the subject matter of his *Four Years in Secessia.* After the war he was associated with the New York *Tribune* and the *Times;* he also wrote numerous magazine articles. His death occurred in New York City.

Four Years in Secessia . . ., Hartford, Conn., 1865.

The Great Metropolis; A Mirror of New York . . ., Hartford, Conn., 1869.

Sights and Sensations in Europe . . ., Hartford, Conn., 1871.

BROWNING, CHARLES HENRY (Aug. 5, 1846–June, 1926), genealogist, was born in Cincinnati, Hamilton County. After operating a coal mining and shipping company in Covington, Ky., he moved to Philadelphia in 1873. He was Philadelphia correspondent for the New York *Herald* for 45 years. He published elaborate genealogical works, notably *Americans of Royal Descent . . .*, which was first published in 1883 and subsequently appeared in numerous new editions. He also published *Welsh Settlement in Pennsylvania,* Philadelphia, 1912. WWW 1

BROWNLEE, JANE A. (1851–Dec. 27, 1941), educator, was born in Toledo, Lucas County. She served as principal of Lagrange School in Toledo for many years before retiring in 1906. While she served in this capacity, some of her ideas on character building in public schools won wide recognition. Her death occurred in San Diego, Calif. Her books on educational topics include *Character Building in School,* New York, [1912].

BROWNLOW, WILLIAM GANNAWAY (Aug. 29, 1805–April 29, 1877), journalist, politician, and clergyman of Tennessee, spent a short time in Ohio. Arrested and expelled from the Confederacy in the spring of 1862 for his Unionist activities, he came to Ohio to recover his health. While recuperating, he wrote *Sketches of the Rise, Progress, and Decline of Secession; With a Narrative of Personal Adventures among the Rebels,* Philadelphia, 1862.

BRUCE, MARY LELIA HOGE, was born in Dungannon, Va., and has lived in Cincinnati since 1925. A graduate of George Washington University, she has published articles and poems in various periodicals and has been active in the Cincinnati Woman's Press Club and other literary organizations. She has also published a collection of verse: *This High Hour,* Cincinnati, 1950.

BRUCKER, MARGARETTA (Dec. 27, 1883–Nov. 11, 1958), was born in Saginaw, Mich., and was brought to Shelby when she was six months old. She later spent her summers in Harbor Springs, Mich., and her winters in Shelby and Akron. She died at the age of 74. She wrote a number of popular novels, both juveniles and mysteries, e.g., *Sue Ellen,* New York, [1941]; *Poison Party,* New York, [1938].

BRUDNO, EZRA SELIG (June 5, 1878–Dec. 12, 1954), lawyer, was born in Lithuania. He attended Western Reserve University, 1896–97, and Yale University, 1898–1900. He practiced law in Cleveland, 1900–49. He wrote a number of books, e.g., *The Tether,* Philadelphia, 1908. WW 21

BRÜHL, GUSTAVUS (May 31, 1829–Feb. 16, 1903), physician and archaeologist, was born in Herdorf, Prussia. He studied medicine, philosophy, and history in European universities and in 1848 came to America, intending to join an uncle in Missouri. Low water in the Ohio River compelled him to stop over in Cincinnati, where he decided to remain permanently and practice medicine. A successful doctor, he was also active in the cultural and civic life of the community. He published numerous scientific articles in medical journals. His study of American archaeology led him to travel in the western United States, Central America, South America, and Mexico and resulted in lectures, articles, and books. Under the pen name Kara Giorg (Serbian for Black George), he contributed considerable poetry to the monthly magazine published in Cincinnati, *Der Deutsche Pionier.* The subjects were usually nature, Indians, or German pioneers in the American colonies.

Poesien des Urwalds, New York, 1871.
Die Culturvolker Alt-Amerika's, 4 vols., New York, 1875–87.
Aztlan-Chicomoztoc . . . , New York, 1879.
Charlotte: Eine Episode aus der Colonialgeschichte Louisianas, Cincinnati, 1883.
Zwischen Alaska und Feuerland . . . , Berlin, 1896.
Abendblocken, Chicago, [1897].
Standerbeg, Cincinnati, 1903.

BRUNSON, ALFRED (Feb. 9, 1793–Aug. 3, 1882), clergyman, was born in Danbury, Conn. Converted to Methodism at an early age, he moved to a farm in Trumbull County in 1812. He preached in the Western Reserve and in northwestern Pennsylvania before moving farther west. He died in Prairie du Chien, Wis.

Prairie du Chien . . . , Milwaukee, 1857.
A Western Pioneer . . . , Cincinnati, 1872.

BRUSH, ALBERT MOOREHEAD (Jan. 2, 1897–Dec. 16, 1954), was born in Zanesville, Muskingum County, the son of Edmund Cone Brush (q.v.). He attended Zanesville schools, Cincinnati Dramatic School, and Muskingum College. An antique dealer specializing in Japanese and French prints, he lived in New York, Paris, and Los Angeles. He published a volume of poems: *The Waxen Leaf,* Mill Valley, Calif., 1938.

BRUSH, DOROTHY HAMILTON (March 14, 1894–), was born in Cleveland, Cuyahoga County. After attending Hathaway-Brown School, Cleveland, she graduated from Smith College in 1917. A founder of the Cleveland Maternal Health Association, she has been active in working for eugenics and birth control and is at present field advisor for the International Planned Parenthood Federation. She is also president of the Brush Foundation, Cleveland. She has written numerous articles and book reviews and several plays, e.g., a play about Pueblo Indians: *The Poor Little Turkey Girl . . . ,* New York, [1928].

BRUSH, EDMUND CONE (Oct. 22, 1852– ?), physician, was born in Zanesville, Muskingum County. He graduated from Starling Medical College, in 1875. He practiced in Perry County and after 1884 in Zanesville. He contributed many articles to professional publications and wrote a useful pamphlet on first aid.

How to Care for the Injured, Zanesville, [1888].

BRUSH, KATHERINE INGHAM (Aug. 15, 1902–June 10, 1952), was born in Middletown, Conn. From 1920 to 1927, while married to Thomas Stewart Brush, she lived in East Liverpool. During her Ohio years, she began selling short stories, most of them to *College Humor,* and published her first book: *Glitter,* New York, 1926. TCA

BRYAN, JENNIE MOORE (July 10, 1854–June 7, 1931), educator, was born in Batavia, Clermont County. After attending the Batavia schools, she studied at Columbia University and the Sorbonne. She taught in the schools of Batavia, Madisonville, and Mount Washington until her retirement in 1914. She died in Cincinnati at the age of 77. She published a volume of poems: *High Tower,* Cincinnati, [1929].

BRYAN, JOHN (Aug. 18, 1853–Dec. 9, 1918), was born in Auglaize County. According to legend, while traveling in Europe as a young man he fell in love with a young Swiss girl, and when his suit proved unsuccessful, he declared himself an unbeliever. He entered business in Cincinnati, owned a physician's supply house which produced a highly popular brand of soap, and patented a number of inventions. In 1893 he purchased a 500-acre estate in Greene County, where he erected a huge barn that he proclaimed to be larger than Solomon's temple. Calling himself "the sage of Riverside," he expressed his opinions, most of them iconoclastic, very freely. He opposed American participation in World War I and was a determined opponent of organized religion. After his death it was found that his will left Riverside Farm to Greene County or to the State of Ohio, provided no religious worship be permitted there. The county promptly refused the bequest; the legislature followed suit but later reversed its decision and accepted the tract, now John Bryan Park, as a game preserve and park.

Fables and Essays, New York, 1895.

BRYANT, LORINDA MUNSON (March 21, 1855–Dec. 13, 1931), was born in Granville, Licking County. She studied at Granville Female College, Chicago College of Pharmacy, Denison University, and Cornell University. In 1877 she became the first woman registered pharmacist in Ohio. In 1905, after fifteen years of teaching school in New Jersey, she devoted her time to writing and turned out a great many books for children, e.g., *American Painters and Their Pictures,* New York, 1917. WWW 1

BUCHANAN, JOHN JENKINS (1855–Aug. 24, 1937), physician, was born in Wellsville, Columbiana County. He graduated from Western University of Pennsylvania in 1877 and the University of Pennsylvania Medical School in 1881. He afterward practiced in Pittsburgh and taught at the University of Pittsburgh Medical School. He wrote a travel book, *Take Your Own Car Abroad and Find Your Own Europe . . .*, Pittsburgh, [1930]. WWW 1

BUCHANAN, JOSEPH RODES (Dec. 11, 1814–Dec. 26, 1899), was born in Frankfort, Ky. He was the son of that versatile genius Joseph Buchanan, who has been referred to as the earliest native physiological psychologist and who founded Cincinnati's first purely literary periodical, *The Literary Cadet,* in 1819. He was the earliest exponent of the Pestalozzian system of education in the Ohio Valley. With such a father it is hardly surprising that the boy was an infant prodigy. Before he was twelve years old, he had "mastered the outlines of grammar, geography, history, mathematics, astronomy, chemistry, natural philosophy, mental philosophy, political economy," and was dipping into Blackstone's *Commentaries.* After his father died in 1829, he earned his living as a printer and later as a teacher. Believing that "every individual aspiring to a liberal education should attend a course of lectures in a medical college," he entered Transylvania University in 1834. Here he acquired a deep-seated interest in phrenology and cerebral physiology. His studies were interrupted by lecture tours in the South, where he conducted experiments in phrenology. He received his M.D. degree at Louisville Medical Institute in 1841. A year later he issued his basic work, *Sketches of Buchanan's Discoveries in Neurology.* He claimed to have developed two sciences—psychometry and sarcognomy—to a point where the trained psychometer could diagnose any disease at sight, while the sarcognomist could heal all diseases by making passes over the body. A brilliant speaker, he made several lecture tours which attracted large crowds. Truculent and opinionated, he joined the faculty of the Eclectic Medical Institute of Cincinnati in 1846 and became a dominant figure in the turbulent history of that institution. He was forced out in 1856 and opened a rival institution, the Eclectic College of Medicine. From 1849 to 1856 he published and edited *The Journal of Man,* a well printed and ably edited monthly in which he promulgated his extraordinary views. At loggerheads with his colleagues at the Eclectic College of Medicine, he resigned and moved to Louisville, Ky., where in 1863 he was an unsuccessful candidate for Congress on the Copperhead ticket. There followed an interlude during which he was engaged in the manufacture of salt at Syracuse, N. Y., and then in 1867 he became professor of physiology at the Eclectic Medical College in New York City. He resigned in 1881 and went to Boston, where he established his own school of therapeutics and published a new series of *The Journal of Man,* 1887-90. In failing health he moved to San Jose, Calif., to spend the remainder of his life. Besides the titles below, some of his separate lectures were published in pamphlet form.

Ernest J. Wessen

Sketches of Buchanan's Discoveries in Neurology, Louisville, Ky., 1842.

Report of Three Lectures in Defense of Neurology . . ., Cincinnati, 1848.

Eclecticism and Exclusivism, Cincinnati, 1851.

Outlines of Lectures on the Neurological System of Anthropology . . ., Cincinnati, 1854.

Manual of Psychometry: The Dawn of a New Civilization, Cincinnati, 1855.

Moral Education: Its Laws and Methods . . ., New York, [1882].

Periodicity: The Absolute Law of the Entire Universe, San Jose, Calif., 1897.

Primitive Christianity . . ., 2 vols., San Jose, Calif., 1898.

BUCHANAN, ROBERT (Jan. 15, 1797–April 23, 1879), born in western Pennsylvania, was educated at Meadville Academy, and taught there for a time. In 1820 he came to Cincinnati, where he established himself as a grocer and pork packer. He also opened a cotton factory and invested in river steamboats. He was a director of several insurance companies and was an official in Cincinnati banks. As a hobby he experimented with grape culture and wrote newspaper articles on horticulture. The second edition of the book below contains an appendix by Nicholas Longworth (q.v.) on the cultivation of the strawberry.

A Treatise on the Cultivation of the Grape in Vineyards, Cincinnati, 1850.

BUCK, JIRAH DEWEY (Nov. 4, 1838–Dec. 13, 1916), physician, was born in Fredonia, N. Y. In 1864 he graduated from Cleveland Homeopathic College, and from 1866 to 1871 he served on the faculty. He then moved to Cincinnati, where he called a meeting of doctors that led to the organization of Pulte Medical College. He taught there, 1872–80, and in 1880 he became dean. He lectured widely on Masonry, psychology, hypnotism, Christian Science, and

New Thought. His death occurred in Cincinnati.

The Perfect Man Is the Anthropomorphic God . . . , [Chicago, 1888].
The Nature and Aim of Theosophy, Cincinnati, 1889.
A *Study of Man and the Way to Health,* Cincinnati, 1889.
Mystic Masonry . . . , Cincinnati, 1896.
Browning's Paracelsus and Other Essays, Cincinnati, 1897.
The Crusade of Freemasonry . . . , Chicago, 1907.
Constructive Psychology; Or, the Building of Character by Personal Effort, Chicago, 1908.
The Lost Word Found in the Great Work (Magnum Opus), Chicago, 1908.
The New Avatar and the Destiny of the Soul . . . , Cincinnati, 1911.
The Soul and Sex in Education, Morals, Religion, and Adolescence . . . , Cincinnati, 1912.
Modern World Movements; Theosophy and the School of Natural Science . . . , Chicago, 1913.

BUCK, PAUL HERMAN (Aug. 25, 1899–), educator, was born in Columbus, Franklin County. He graduated from Ohio State University in 1921 and Harvard University (Ph.D.) in 1935. He joined the history faculty at Harvard in 1926, became dean in 1942, provost in 1945, and since 1955 has been director of libraries. He received the Pulitzer Prize in history in 1938 for *The Road to Reunion, 1865–1900,* Boston, 1937. WW 30

BUCKMASTER, HENRIETTA. Pseud. See Henrietta Henkle.

BUDGETT, FRANCES ELIZABETH JANES (c.1873–Feb. 5, 1928), was born in New Philadelphia, Tuscarawas County. She was educated in private schools and at the University of Michigan. She lived in Japan, Europe, and various parts of the United States. She published short stories and novelettes in various magazines and also published several books under the pen name of Elizabeth DeJeans, e.g., *The Winning Chance,* Philadelphia, 1909.

BUEHRING, PAUL HENRY (July 5, 1880–Aug. 16, 1958), clergyman and educator, was born in Elkhorn, Wis. He graduated from Wartburg College, Iowa, in 1898 and Lutheran Seminary, Columbus, in 1905. He served as a pastor in St. Mary's, 1905–11, was a teacher in Nebraska, 1911–19, and was a member of the Capital Seminary faculty, 1919–46. He died in Columbus. He wrote *The Spirit of the American Lutheran Church,* Columbus, 1940. WWW 3

BUGBEE, LUCIUS HATFIELD (April 29, 1874–Feb. 22, 1948), clergyman, was born in Glendale, Hamilton County. He graduated from Boston University (A.B., 1897; S.T.B., 1899). After his ordination he served pastorates in several states and served on editorial boards of the Methodist Church. His writings include *Living Leaders, Judged by Christian Standards,* New York, [1923]. WWW 2

BULKLEY, LORENZO HILL (Nov. 24, 1856–Feb. 20, 1949), was born in West Groton, N. Y. He became a book agent in Cincinnati in 1880, and in 1888 he moved to Columbus. He was a salesman for American Art Works, Coshocton, for 35 years. Known as the "salesman poet," he lectured widely and published several books, e.g., *In Tune with Time,* New York, [1945].

BULLARD, FREDERIC LAURISTON (May 13, 1866–Aug. 3, 1952), journalist, was born in Wauseon, Fulton County. He graduated from the University of Wooster in 1891 and Yale Divinity School in 1903. After ten years in the Presbyterian and Congregational ministry, he entered journalism. From 1907 to 1943 he was with the Boston *Herald.* He won the Pulitzer Prize for editorials in 1926. In addition to numerous articles and pamphlets on Abraham Lincoln, he wrote *Famous War Correspondents,* Boston, 1914. WWW 3

BUNDY, ROY DALTON (May 12, 1887–), educator, born in Carthage, Ill., has lived in Cleveland since 1924. He was associated with the Cleveland public schools until his retirement in 1957. After 1946 he was supervisor of vocational education. He has written a number of books and pamphlets, most of them related to industrial and educational questions, e.g., *Collective Bargaining,* New York, 1937. RC 27

BUNKER, JOHN JOSEPH LEO (April 11, 1884–), was born in Cincinnati, Hamilton County. After graduating from Xavier University in 1905, he was engaged in the real-estate business and advertising in Cincinnati. He conducted his own advertising agency, 1925–48. He has published verse and prose in many national periodicals and has compiled several anthologies of Catholic literature. He has also published a collection of poems: *Shining Fields and Dark Towers,* New York, 1919. CWW 9

BUNTLINE, NED. Pseud. See Edward Z. C. Judson.

BUNTS, FRANK EMORY (June 3, 1861–Nov. 28, 1928), surgeon, was born in Youngstown, Mahoning County. He graduated from U. S. Naval Academy in 1881, after which he served two years in the navy. He then undertook the study of medicine and graduated from Western Reserve Medical College in 1886; seven years later he became professor of surgery in the same institution. He published a collection, *The Soul of Henry Harrington, and Other Stories,* Cleveland, 1916. WWW 1

BURBA, GEORGE FRANCIS (May 4, 1865–Aug. 6, 1920), editor, was born in Hodgenville, Ky. Though educated as a lawyer, he never practiced. From 1901 until his death, which occurred in Columbus, he edited newspapers in Springfield, Dayton, and Columbus. He wrote *Our Bird Friends . . . ,* New York, 1908. WWW 1

BURDETTE, ROBERT JONES (July 30, 1844–Nov. 19, 1914), journalist, humorous lecturer, and clergyman, was born in Greensboro, Pa., but spent a part of his boyhood in Ohio. His parents later took him to Peoria, Ill., where he grew up. Known as the "Hawkeye Man," he was popular as a lecturer and journalist. In 1888 he became a Baptist preacher. He published several books, e.g., *Hawk-eyes,* New York, 1879.

BURGESS, PERRY (Oct. 12, 1886–), born in Joplin, Mo., has lived for a number of years at Geneva-on-the-Lake. His work in the medical campaign against leprosy furnished material for a novel, *Who Walk Alone,* New York, [1940]. WW 30

BURGHEIM, MAX (Aug. 23, 1848–April 8, 1918), was born at Minden on the Weser, Germany. In 1863 he came to Cincinnati, where he opened a bookstore. He served in the army during the Civil War. In 1890 he acquired the Cincinnati *Freie Press* and the *Abend Presse.* He became police commissioner of Cincinnati in 1899 and later served as president of the Board of Public Service.

Der Führer von Cincinnati. Ein Vollständiger und Zuverlässiger Wegweiser durch die Stadt und Ihre Umgebung . . . , Cincinnati, [1875].

Reiseskizzen aus Europa, Cincinnati, [1883].

Cincinnati in Wort und Bild . . . , Cincinnati, [1888].

Die Katholischen Kirchen, Klöster, Institute und Wohlthätigkeits . . . , Cincinnati, [1890].

BURKETT, CHARLES WILLIAM (Jan. 3, 1873–), agriculturist, was born in Thornville, Perry County. After graduating from Ohio University in 1895, he taught agriculture in several universities, edited *The American Agriculturist,* 1908–22, and was on the editorial staff of the McFadden Book Company, 1923–32. He lectured often to farmers' institutes and published a number of agriculture textbooks. He now lives in Miami Beach, Fla.

History of Ohio Agriculture . . . , Concord, N. H., 1900.

Between Two Lives; A Drama of the Passing of the Old and the Coming of the New in Rural Life, New York, 1914.

BURKHARDT, FRANKLIN ALPHUS (Dec. 29, 1872–Dec. 5, 1945), was born near Lima, Allen County. His writings, which consist mainly of genealogical works, include a biography: *Pioneer Days of George H. A. Burkhardt,* [Los Angeles], 1935.

BURKHART, ROY ABRAM (Aug. 28, 1895–), clergyman, was born in Newville, Pa. He graduated from Otterbein College and the University of Chicago (M.A., Ph.D.). He was director of youth work for the United Brethren and Evangelical churches of Dayton, 1923–27, was ordained to the ministry of the Congregational Christian Church in 1929, and was minister of the First Community Church, Columbus, 1935–58. As a minister he devoted much of his attention to pastoral counseling, and he has written articles and books related to various phases of this subject, e.g., *Thinking about Marriage,* New York, 1934. WW 30

BURNELL, WILLIAM PERCIVAL (Jan. 19, 1857– ?), clergyman, was born in Bridgton, Maine. After attending St. Lawrence College, he was ordained a Universalist minister in Cleveland in 1874. He preached in Cleveland, Clyde, and Margaretta in Ohio and also served churches in other states. He spent two years as a canvasser for Buchtel College, an experience that was the subject of his book, which was published anonymously.

Recollections of a College Beggar, Cleveland, 1882.

BURNET, FRANK DANA (July 3, 1888–), great-grandson of Judge Jacob Burnet (q.v.), was born in Cincinnati, Hamilton County. He attended public schools in Cincinnati and graduated from Cornell University in 1911. He afterward was on the staff of the New York *Evening Sun* and

Life. He wrote for various magazines and also wrote some movie scenarios. He now lives in Stonington, Conn. His numerous books include a volume of verse, *Poems*, New York, [1915], and several plays, e.g., *It Is a Strange House*, Boston, 1925. WW 19

BURNET, JACOB (Feb. 22, 1770–May 10, 1853), born in Newark, N. J., was the son of William Burnet, member of the Continental Congress. After graduating from Princeton College in 1791, he studied law and was admitted to the bar. He arrived at the frontier settlement of Cincinnati in 1796. He was one of the three judges appointed to hold court in Cincinnati, Vincennes, and Detroit, and was a member of the territorial councils, 1799–1802. After the organization of the state government in 1803 he was called upon to play a leading role in shaping the basic laws in the Ohio code. He was a member of the state legislature, 1812–16, and he was a judge of the Supreme Court of Ohio from 1821 to 1828, when he resigned in order to fill the vacancy in the U. S. Senate caused by the resignation of William Henry Harrison. He was not a candidate for renomination upon the expiration of his term in 1831. In this year the legislature of Kentucky elected him one of the commissioners to settle its territorial disputes with Virginia. The last notable act of his political career was his speech at the Harrisburg Convention in 1839 which nominated William Henry Harrison for the Presidency. The speech was published in pamphlet form. He was one of the founders of the Cincinnati College, served as its first president, and in many other ways took a leading part in the intellectual and social movements of Cincinnati. In 1837 at the insistence of his niece's husband, John Delafield (q.v.), he wrote a series of letters relating to the early settlement of the Northwestern Territory, which appeared in the *Transactions of the Historical and Philosophical Society of Ohio* in 1839. These he enlarged and published as *Notes on the Early Settlement of the North-western Territory* in 1847—an autobiographical sketch upon which the aged judge draped his informative reminiscences of incidents relating to the early settlement of the Territory. It remains one of the most important sources for the period covered. His death occurred in Cincinnati.

Ernest J. Wessen

Notes on the Early Settlement of the North-western Territory, Cincinnati, 1847.

BURNET, WHITTIER (Jan. 27, 1876–Jan. 30, 1945), educator, was born on a farm near Lytle, Warren County. After graduating from Waynesville High School, he attended Ohio State University and the University of Cincinnati. He taught in county schools, at Ohio State, and at Oklahoma A. and M. College. He died in Seymour, Mo., where he spent his last years. His short stories appeared in various periodicals, and he also published a collection of verse: *Trail of Song*, [n.p.], 1937.

BURNETT, ALFRED (Nov. 2, 1824–April 4, 1884), confectioner, poet, monologist, tragedian, journalist, was born in Bungay, Suffolk, England. The versatile "Alf" Burnett was one of the most colorful and popular characters of ante-bellum Cincinnati. When he was but four years old, he was sent to New York to live with an aunt, the mother of General Ward B. Burnett. In 1832 he was put in an academy at Utica, N. Y., where he remained until 1836, when he was taken from school and sent to Cincinnati. Within a very few years he was proprietor of a confectionery business so successful that it allowed him leisure to dabble in amateur theatricals and to take a somewhat militant part in the antislavery movement. He seems to have been the only victim of the "Scanlon Mob" of 1843. It was Burnett who supplied the arms to householders who stood off the mob trying to catch a ten-year-old slave girl, with the result that his own house was stoned. He collected the stones in barrels and passed them out in later years as "proslavery" arguments. He was already contributing comic verse to local newspapers under the pen name "Squibs" and touring in nearby states giving his popular monologues. He made his debut as Hamlet in the American Theatre in Cincinnati in 1849. In 1850 he became editor of the *Warning Bell*, a literary magazine which he founded in partnership with Enos B. Reed, but which was soon suspended because of a European tour. According to Reed, who later served as his manager, this tour was undertaken at the suggestion of Edwin Forrest. The two men later started the Cincinnati *Home Journal*. Burnett was the author of several songs which became popular. Although he seems to have given more and more of his time to the stage, his Cincinnati business was not neglected, and by 1860 he was operating three confectionery establishments in that city. At the commencement of the Civil War he joined the 6th O.V.I. and served as a sergeant throughout the campaign in West Virginia. He was subsequently engaged as a war correspondent by several Cincinnati papers. His letters from the front enjoyed considerable popularity, and a number of them were published in *Incidents of the War.* Coggeshall credits Burnett with having published "a little volume of poems and recitations" in 1859, but no record of it can be found. He made a number of professional tours in the Middle West after the war, and for a time he was employed by a press association.

Ernest J. Wessen

Magnetism Made Easy; Or, Instructions in Magnetism for the Many, Cincinnati, 1847.

Incidents of the War; Humorous, Pathetic and Descriptive, Cincinnati, 1863.

Alf. Burnett's Comic Faces, Facially Illustrated, Intermingled with Poetic Gems, Cincinnati, [1867].

BURNETT, CHARLES C. (April 21, 1843–Sept. 1, 1898), was born on a farm near Chagrin Falls, Cuyahoga County. While he was a boy, his parents moved to Vincennes, Ind. He enlisted in an Indiana regiment in 1861 and was discharged for disability two years later after recovering from typhoid fever. He returned to Ohio in 1869, manufactured cane chairs in Toledo for a short time, and in 1870 became a lumber dealer in Cleveland. The book below was published under the pen name Ash Slivers. He is said to have written a book about the Hawaiian Islands, but no copy has been located.

The Land of the O——O. Facts, Figures, Fables and Fancies, Cleveland, 1892.

BURNETT, DAVID STAATS (July 6, 1808–July 8, 1867), clergyman, was born in Dayton, Montgomery County. He became the first pastor of the Baptist Church in Dayton in 1827. He was converted to the teachings of Alexander Campbell in 1829; his church became a Campbellite organization, only a few of the old members refusing to stay. He wrote a number of articles for various church publications. His death occurred in Baltimore, Md.

The Pastorate, Cincinnati, [n.d.].

The Poverty of Jesus, the Wealth of the Saints, Cincinnati, [n.d.].

BURNETT, HENRY LAWRENCE (Dec. 26, 1838–Jan. 4, 1916), lawyer, was born in Youngstown, Mahoning County. He graduated from Ohio State National Law School in 1859. At the outbreak of the Civil War he joined the 2nd Ohio Cavalry, saw active service, and in 1863 was appointed major in the judge advocate department and assigned to the Department of Ohio. At the request of Governor Morton of Indiana he was sent to that state in 1864 to prosecute the members of the subversive Knights of the Golden Circle. He took part in other treason trials and was associated with John A. Bingham in the prosecution of the assassins of Lincoln. Some of his legal arguments were published. After the war he practiced law in Cincinnati until 1872, when he moved to New York, where he acquired an outstanding reputation as an advocate. McKinley appointed him federal district attorney for the southern district of New York in 1898, and on the completion of his four-year term he was reappointed by Roosevelt.

Some Incidents in the Trial of President Lincoln's Assassins . . . , New York, 1891.

BURNETT, WILLIAM RILEY (Nov. 25, 1899–), was born in Springfield, Clark County, the son of a veterinary. He also lived in Dayton and Columbus. He attended public schools in Springfield, Dayton, and Columbus and Miami Military Institute, Germantown. He attended Ohio State University in 1919, was an insurance salesman, and worked for six years in the Department of Industrial Relations. During this period he wrote constantly, but sold none of his writings for the first eight years. He has never surpassed the success of his first novel: *Little Caesar,* New York, 1929, the first realistic gangster novel and the basis of a notable motion picture. Several of his subsequent novels have been made into motion pictures, and he has written numerous movie scripts. His home is in southern California. Of his many books, some with an Ohio setting are *Goodbye to the Past . . . ,* New York, 1934, *The Goodhues of Sinking Creek,* New York, 1934, *King Cole,* New York, 1936. ANT

BURNS, JAMES JESSE (Oct. 26, 1838–1911), educator, was born in Brownsville, Licking County. He began teaching in Titusville on the Ohio River in 1857. The next year he was principal of an academy in Natchez, Miss., and also read law. After returning to Ohio he served as a principal and superintendent in a number of cities and also was state commissioner of common schools, 1877–80. He wrote several textbooks. His death occurred in Defiance.

Our Schools and School Systems, [n.p.], 1878.

The Story of English Kings, According to Shakespeare, New York, 1899.

Educational History of Ohio . . . , Columbus, 1905.

BURNS, WILLIAM JOHN (Oct. 19, 1861–April 14, 1932), detective, was born in Baltimore, Md. When he was a child, his parents moved to Zanesville and soon afterward to Columbus. His father, a tailor, was named Columbus police commissioner; William assisted him in his investigations. He won considerable attention by clearing up an election fraud case in 1885 and four years later joined the U. S. Secret Service. In 1909 he founded the William J. Burns Detective Agency in New York City. He resigned as president of the agency in 1921 to become head of the F.B.I., a position he held until 1924. He died in Sarasota, Fla. The best-known detective of his generation, he wrote a novel in collaboration with Isabel Ostrander: *The Crevice,* New York, [1915], and several books on his detective work, e.g., *Stories of Check Raisers . . . ,* Chicago, [1923]. DAB 21

BURR, ARIL BOND (Oct. 23, 1880–Dec. 29, 1955), was born in Shelby City, Ky., but lived most of his life in Cincinnati. He was for many years postmaster in East End station, Cincinnati. He wrote a novel based on his memories of early life in Kentucky: *Panther Rock,* Cincinnati, [1931].

BURRELL, GEORGE ARTHUR (Jan. 23, 1882–Aug. 16, 1957), engineer, was born in Cleveland, Cuyahoga County. A graduate of Ohio State University, he was a chemist with the U. S. Geological Survey, 1904–08, and did research for the U. S. Bureau of Mines, 1908–16. After World War I, in which he served as a colonel, he was an executive of several refining companies. He wrote a number of technical articles and books. He spent a year in Russia, when he was engaged by the Russian government to modernize the natural gas industry, and wrote *An American Engineer Looks at Russia,* Boston, [1932]. WWW 3

BURRIS, MARCUS LINDSAY (March 9, 1872–May 26, 1934), educator, was born on a farm near Catlettsburg, Ky. He graduated from Hiram College in 1896 and afterward lived in Ohio from 1911 until his death. He was for many years a teacher at South High School, Youngstown. His poems were published in various periodicals, and he also published a collection: *The Run of the Mine,* New York, [1931].

BURROWS, MILLAR (Oct. 26, 1889–   ), educator and clergyman, was born in Cincinnati, Hamilton County. He graduated from Cornell University in 1912, Union Theological Seminary in 1915, and Yale University (Ph.D.) in 1925. He served on the faculties of Tusculum College, 1920–23, and Brown University, 1925–29, and began teaching at Yale in 1934. He has published numerous magazine articles and books on religious subjects, e.g., *Palestine Is Our Business,* Philadelphia, [1949]. WW 30

BURSON, WILLIAM (Nov. 24, 1833–Jan. 16, 1880), was born in Salineville, Columbiana County. A farmer and a carpenter, he was residing in Wellsburgh at the beginning of the Civil War. He was a member of Company A, 32nd O.V.I., at the time of his capture in the movements near Atlanta. Among narratives of personal adventure in the Civil War his little book assumes highest rank. Ryan refers to it as an account of adventures which would make fiction pale, while Coulter rates it as a valuable account of travel in the Confederacy.

A Race for Liberty; Or, My Capture, Imprisonment, and Escape, Wellsville, 1867.

BURSTEIN, ABRAHAM (Oct. 25, 1893–   ), rabbi, was born in Cleveland, Cuyahoga County. He graduated from Columbia University in 1913 and became a rabbi in 1923. Since 1923 he has served in New York City, where he has also edited a number of Jewish magazines. He has published many plays, stories, and biographies, e.g., *The Boy Called Rashi,* New York, 1940. BDCP

BURT, JOHN STRUTHERS June 25, 1880–   ), educator, was born in Struthers, Mahoning County. He attended Westminster College and Princeton University, served in World War I, and taught at Rayen High School, Youngstown, 1924–44. In 1944 he moved to Phoenix, Ariz., where he now lives. He wrote *History of Northeastern Ohio,* 3 vols., Indianapolis, 1935.

BURT, NATHANIEL CLARK (April 23, 1825–March 4, 1874), clergyman, was born in Fairton, N. J. He served as a Presbyterian clergyman in Cincinnati and elsewhere in Ohio.

Hours among the Gospels . . . , Philadelphia, 1865.

The Far East . . . , Cincinnati, 1869.

The Land and Its Story . . . , New York, 1869.

BURT, PITTS HARRISON (May 6, 1837–Aug. 16, 1906), broker, was born in Cincinnati, Hamilton County. After graduating from Yale University in 1859, he became a broker in Cincinnati. He was one of the organizers of the Cincinnati Stock Exchange. Active in the cultural life of the city, he was one of the first subscribers to the May Music Festivals and was a director of the Rookwood Pottery. His only book was the novel listed below. He died in Cincinnati.

Regret of Spring; A Love Episode, New York, 1898.

BURT, RICHARD WELLING (April 23, 1823–July 7, 1911), was born in Warwick, N. Y. When he was a child, his family moved to a farm in Coshocton County. He served in the Mexican War; taught school; published a newspaper, the *Progressive Age,* in Coshocton, 1853–56; and operated a coal business in Newark. He enlisted as a private in the 76th O.V.I. in Nov., 1861, and was discharged as a captain in July, 1865. He was wounded at the battle of Resaca. After the war he settled in Peoria, Ill. He operated a grocery business, was internal revenue storekeeper, 1875–85, and manufactured soap. From his youth he composed poems and songs for political or patriotic occasions.

Historical Centennial Poem, Peoria, Ill., 1876.

War Songs, Poems and Odes . . . , Peoria, Ill., 1906.

BURTOFT, LAVINA ADALINE HOLLINGSWORTH JUDKINS (March 2, 1849–March 27, 1929), was born in Harrison County. Frank Judkins, whom she married in 1869, died in 1893, and in 1912 she married Thomas Burtoft. Her death occurred in St. Clairsville. She published travel sketches in newspapers and at least two books of poems, and with her son, Clyde H. Judkins, she wrote a memoir of her brother, a Civil War general and political figure: *Biographical Sketch of Hon. David A. Hollingsworth . . . ,* [Cleveland, 1920].

BURTON, CHARLES EMERSON (March 19, 1869–Aug. 27, 1940), clergyman, was born in Poweshiek County, Iowa. Ordained a Congregational minister in 1898, he became associate pastor with Washington Gladden (q.v.) in 1909; from 1911 to 1914 he was pastor of Euclid Avenue Church in Cleveland. His writings include *Finding a Religion to Live By,* Boston, [1936]. WWW 1

BURTON, ERNEST DE WITT (Feb. 4, 1856–May 26, 1925), theologian, was born in Granville, Licking County. He graduated from Denison University in 1876 and Rochester Theological Seminary in 1882 and also studied in Germany. In 1892 he was appointed professor of New Testament literature at the University of Chicago. He published a number of textbooks. A bibliography of his writings can be found in *Christianity in the Modern World . . . ,* Chicago, [1927]. WWW 1

BURTON, GIDEON (Aug. 11, 1811–May 1, 1903), merchant, was born in Sussex County, Del. As an agent for a Philadelphia merchant, he made his first trip to Ohio at the age of twenty, and in 1848 he settled in Cincinnati, where he established a silk store. During the next half-century he had broad experience in business affairs and was active in the cultural life of Cincinnati. His privately printed book is a valuable collection of anecdotes and reminiscences. He died in Cupalo, Pa., at the age of 92.

Reminiscences of Gideon Burton. Written by Himself in His Eighty-fifth Year, Cincinnati, 1895.

BURTON, HAROLD HITZ (June 22, 1888–), Supreme Court justice, was born in Jamaica Plain, Mass. He graduated from Bowdoin College in 1909. In 1912 he began to practice law in Cleveland. He was mayor of Cleveland, 1935–40; U. S. Senator, 1940–45; and an associate justice of the U. S. Supreme Court, 1945–58. He compiled the history of the 361st Infantry Regiment in World War I: *600 Days Service . . . ,* [Portland, Oreg., 1921]. WW 30

BURTON, KATHERINE (March 12, 1887–), was born in Cleveland, Cuyahoga County. A graduate of Western Reserve University, she has served on the editorial staff of *McCall's, Redbook,* and other magazines, and now lives in Bronxville, N. Y. She was converted to Roman Catholicism in 1930 and has written articles for the *Sign* and other religious magazines. She has published several books, most of them biographies, e.g., a life of Mrs. Rose Hawthorne Lathrop: *Sorrow Built a Bridge . . . ,* New York, 1937. CWW 11

BURTON, THEODORE ELIJAH (Dec. 20, 1851–Oct. 28, 1929), lawyer and legislator, was born in Jefferson, Ashtabula County. After graduating from Oberlin in 1872, he taught there for two years while reading law. He was admitted to the Ohio bar in 1875 and practiced in Cleveland. He served both in the House of Representatives (1886–88, 1894–1909, and 1920–28) and in the Senate (1909–14 and 1928–29). His writings on historical and economic subjects include a biography: *John Sherman,* Boston, 1906. DAB 21

BURTON, THOMAS WILLIAM (May 4, 1860–March 23, 1939), physician, was born of slave parents in Madison County, Ky. A graduate of Indiana Medical College, he practiced in Zanesville, Xenia, and Springfield. He wrote an autobiographical book, *What Experience Has Taught Me,* Cincinnati, 1910.

BUSBEY, HAMILTON (April 1, 1840–Aug. 1, 1924), journalist, was born in Clark County and lived for many years in South Vienna. He was editor of *Turf, Field and Farm* for nearly forty years. He published several books on horses and horse racing, e.g., *The Trotting and Pacing Horse in America,* [New York, 1904]. WWW 1

BUSBEY, L. WHITE (Nov. 22, 1852–Oct. 31, 1925), journalist, younger brother of Hamilton Busbey (q.v.), was born in Vienna, Trumbull County. He was Washington correspondent of the Chicago *Inter-ocean,* 1879–1905, and secretary to Joseph G. Cannon, Speaker of the House of Representatives, 1904–11. His death occurred in Washington, D. C. He wrote a biography, *Uncle Joe Cannon; The Story of a Pioneer American* . . . , New York, [1927]. WWW 1

BUSH, MRS. EDWARD G. W. See Rosemary Sprague.

BUSH, HAROLD MONTFORT (Nov. 14, 1871–Aug. 7, 1945), mechanical engineer, was born in Dansville, N. Y. He moved to Columbus in 1893 and thereafter was associated with various Columbus industries and railroads. He published articles on military subjects in addition to recollections of his service in the Spanish-American War: *The Diary of an Enlisted Man,* Columbus, 1908. WWO

BUSHNELL, EDWARD (May 18, 1865–Nov. 17, 1944), lawyer, was born in Fremont, Sandusky County. He graduated from Western Reserve University in 1887 and was admitted to the bar in 1891. He practiced in Cleveland. He wrote an account of a trip to England: *The Truthful Traveller* . . . , Cleveland, 1936. WWW 2

BUSHNELL, HENRY (Jan. 31, 1824–Nov. 19, 1905), clergyman, was born in Granville, Licking County. Educated at Marietta College, Lane Seminary, and Andover Seminary, he entered the ministry. He served churches in Ohio, and for a time was principal of Central College Academy. His death occurred in Westerville.

The History of Granville, Licking County . . . , Columbus, 1889.

Following the Star . . . , Philadelphia, 1894.

BUSSENIUS, LUELLEN TETERS (Feb., 1872–), was born in Caldwell, Noble County, but spent only the first seven years of her life in that community. She is a sister of Wilbertine T. Worden (q.v.). A graduate of the University of Colorado, she has served on the editorial staff of the *Delineator* and other fashion magazines. She now lives in Chicago. Besides stories in numerous periodicals, she has written a novel, *The Honorable Miss Cherry Blossom* . . . , New York, 1924.

BUTLER, HENRY A. (Oct. 8, 1872–April 26, 1934), industrialist, was born in Youngstown, Mahoning County. He graduated from Harvard University in 1897. He wrote a book which is based on a journal of his experiences in service with the American Red Cross in France during World War I: *Overseas Sketches* . . . , [Cleveland, 1921].

BUTLER, JAY CALDWELL (Sept. 3, 1844–July 13, 1885), was born in Venice, Erie County. He served in the Civil War from June, 1862, to June, 1865, as a captain in the 101st O.V.I. After the war he was a manufacturer of doors and window blinds in Sandusky. His son, Watson H. Butler, published *Letters Home by Jay Caldwell Butler* . . . , [Binghamton, N. Y.], 1930.

BUTLER, JOSEPH GREEN, JR. (Dec. 21, 1840–Dec. 19, 1927), was born in Temperance Furnace, Pa. He became a successful ironmaster while in his early twenties and moved to Youngstown in 1863, where he played a prominent role in almost every enterprise of note in the Mahoning Valley. He erected and presented to the city of Youngstown the Butler Art Institute. He wrote a number of books, e.g., *First Trip across the Continent,* Cleveland, 1904, and *Recollections of Men and Events* . . . , [Youngstown, 1925].

BUTLER, JOSEPH MARION (Aug. 18, 1858–March 23, 1913), was born in New Rochester, Wood County. He was later engaged in business in Youngstown, where he was an active worker in the Protestant Episcopal Church.

History of St. John's Parish, [Youngstown, n.d.].

BUTLER, MARGARET MANOR (Mrs. Clyde H.) (March 1, 1898–), was born in Cleveland, Cuyahoga County, but lived most of her life in Lakewood. She is a graduate of Smith College. She was an organizer of the Lakewood Historical Society and now is curator of the museum. She has written numerous articles on local history and one book, *The Lakewood Story,* New York, 1949.

BUTTENWEISER, ELLEN CLUNE (Aug. 12, 1870–July 22, 1933), was born in Warkworth, Ontario, Canada. She attended Queens University, Kingston, Ontario, University of Leipzig, and University of Heidelberg, earning a doctorate from the latter institution. Wife of Moses Buttenweiser (q.v.), she lived in Cincinnati from 1897 until her death, was active in club work, and contributed to various literary magazines. She also wrote *The Obstinate Child,* Philadelphia, [1912?]. OBB

BUTTENWEISER, MOSES (April 5, 1862–March 11, 1939), theologian, was born in Beerfelden, Germany. He was educated in Germany and after coming to America was appointed to the faculty of Hebrew Union College, Cincinnati, in 1897. He served there for more than forty years. His death occurred in Palo Alto, Calif. Besides translations and texts, his books include *The Prophets of Israel . . .* , New York, 1914. WWW 1

BUTTERFIELD, CONSUL WILLSHIRE (July 28, 1824–Sept. 25, 1899), historian, was born in Oswego County, N. Y. His family moved to Melmore, Seneca County, in 1834. Educated at Normal School, Albany, N. Y., he became a teacher. He was superintendent of Seneca County schools, 1848–49. He was admitted to the bar in 1855 and practiced law at Bucyrus until 1875. His *Historical Account of the Expedition against Sandusky* (1873) served to distinguish him as a historian of importance. An outstanding contribution to Revolutionary history, the work was a readable, attractive story and enjoyed a good sale. Spurred on by the success of this book Butterfield abandoned the practice of law in 1875 and moved to Madison, Wis., where he would enjoy ready access to the great Lyman C. Draper collection of source materials. An attempt to collaborate with Draper met with failure, and their book was never printed. In 1877 he became a staff historian with a Chicago concern engaged in publishing county histories. From 1886 to 1889 he served in an editorial capacity on the *Magazine of Western History,* a periodical in which some of his best work appears. He moved to South Omaha, Neb., in 1888, where he was again engaged in editing local histories.

History of Seneca County . . . , Sandusky, 1848.

A Comprehensive System of Grammatical and Rhetorical Punctuation, 1854.

An Historical Account of the Expedition against Sandusky under Col. William Crawford in 1872 . . . , Cincinnati, 1873.

The Washington-Crawford Letters, Cincinnati, 1877.

History of the University of Wisconsin . . . , Madison, 1879.

Washington-Irvine Correspondence, Madison, 1882.

A Short Biography of John Leith . . . , Cincinnati, 1883.

Journal of Capt. Jonathan Heart on the March of His Company from Connecticut to Fort Pitt . . . , Albany, N. Y., 1885.

The History of the Girtys . . . , Cincinnati, 1890.

History of Brulé's Discoveries and Explorations . . . , Cleveland, 1898.

History of Lieutenant-Colonel George Rogers Clark's Conquest of the Illinois and of the Wabash Towns . . . , Columbus, 1903.

BUTTLES, JOEL (Feb., 1787–Aug., 1850), was born in Grandby, Conn. His father was one of the original proprietors of Worthington, where he settled with his family in 1804. Joel Buttles taught school at Worthington until Aug. 21, 1811, when, in partnership with one George Smith, he bought the weekly newspaper *Western Intelligencer.* Because of a disagreement between the two men, the partnership was dissolved in Dec., 1812, and Buttles moved to Franklinton. In 1814 he was appointed postmaster in Columbus, a position which he held until 1829. In 1814 the *Western Intelligencer* was moved to Columbus and Buttles again acquired an interest in it, which he retained until June 27, 1817. He became a successful businessman in Columbus, held many offices of trust, and was president of the City Bank for several years. The extracts from his diary, which were privately published by his descendants, provide a superb account of pioneer life in central Ohio. His death occurred in Urbana.

Extracts from the Diary of Joel Buttles, [Newport, R. I., 1889].

BYER, HERBERT (Oct. 31, 1899–), was born in Cincinnati, Hamilton County. He graduated from Ohio State University. He was associated with the Columbus *Citizen,* 1921–24. He is chairman of the board of Byer and Bowman advertising agency in Columbus. He has published articles in trade papers and business journals and a novel about an imaginary American university: *To the Victor,* New York, 1936.

BYERS, JOSEPH PERKINS (Sept. 23, 1868–Aug. 11, 1950), social worker, was born in Columbus, Franklin County. His father was secretary of the Ohio Board of State Charities; and Joseph served as his assistant, 1888–90, and as his successor, 1890–92. He afterward was superintendent of various institutions and social agencies in Indiana, New York, New Jersey, and Kentucky. After his retirement in 1938 he returned to live in Delaware County. He wrote *The Village of Happiness, the Story of the Training School,* [Vineland, N. J., 1934]. WW 21

BYERS, WILLIAM NEWTON (Feb. 22, 1831–March 25, 1903), was born in Madison County. Self-educated, he became a surveyor, and in 1852 he crossed the continent in the employ of the Federal government. He married and lived for a time in Omaha, Neb. In 1859 he moved to Denver, Colo., where he spent the remainder of his life. He published Colorado's first newspaper, *Rocky Mountain News,* at Cherry Creek, April 23, 1859. Printing his paper for a time in the attic of Uncle Dick Wootton's cabin and later in a printing office located on stilts in Cherry Creek itself, he guided his newspaper through great obstacles and finally retired from publishing in 1878. On his arrival in the Territory he plunged into public affairs. He was a leading advocate of statehood for Colorado, served as postmaster of Denver, and was president of the Chamber of Commerce.

A Handbook to the Gold Fields of Nebraska and Kansas, (with John H. Kellom), Chicago, 1859.

Encyclopedia of Biography of Colorado; History of Colorado, Chicago, 1901.

BYFORD, WILLIAM HEATH (March 20, 1817–May 21, 1890), physician and educator, was born in Eaton, Preble County. His family left Ohio when he was four years old, and he grew up in Indiana and Illinois. He returned to Ohio to study at Ohio Medical College, where he graduated in 1845. He later taught at Evansville Medical College, Rush Medical College, and Woman's Medical College, Chicago. Besides the title below, he published a number of medical works on gynecology and obstetrics.

The Philosophy of Domestic Life, Boston, 1869.

BYINGTON, CYRUS (March 11, 1793–Dec. 31, 1868), missionary, was born in Massachusetts. Trained as a lawyer, he became a missionary and spent his life among the Choctaws, except for the two years following his retirement to Belpre, Ohio, in 1866. Byington's lifework was the preparation of a dictionary and grammar of the Choctaw language. He also translated parts of the Bible into Choctaw.

BYRNE, THOMAS SEBASTIAN (July 29, 1841–Sept. 4, 1924), clergyman, was born in Hamilton, Butler County. He graduated from St. Mary's of the West in 1868 and afterward spent three years at the American College in Rome. He was ordained a Roman Catholic priest in 1869. From 1887 to 1894 he was president of St. Mary's of the West. He was appointed bishop of Nashville, Tenn., in 1894. Besides the title below, he wrote religious pamphlets.

Man from a Christian Point of View, Cincinnati, 1893.

C

CABLE, JOHN LEVI (April 15, 1884–), lawyer and former congressman, was born in Lima, Allen County. He graduated from Kenyon College in 1906 and the law school of George Washington University in 1909. Since being admitted to the bar, he has practiced in Lima. He served in the U. S. House of Representatives, 1921–25 and 1929–33. His writings, chiefly of a legal nature, include *Loss of Citizenship, Denaturalization, the Alien in Wartime,* Washington, D. C., 1943. WW 30

CACKLER, CHRISTIAN (June 27, 1791–July 5, 1878), was born in Washington County, Pa. He came to Portage County with his parents May 10, 1804. Throughout his long life in this area he bore a splendid reputation for probity. His rambling *Recollections,* which contains a first-hand account of John Brown, is one of the most valuable accounts extant of pioneer life in northern Ohio.

Recollections of an Old Settler . . . , [Kent, 1874].

CADMUS. Pseud. See John C. Zachos.

CADWELL, CLARA GERTRUDE (? – ?), was born in Jefferson, Ashtabula County, where her family were close friends of the Howells family. Except that she later lived in Cleveland, nothing else is known of her life.

De Barr's Friends; Or, Number Seventeen . . . , Cleveland, 1881.

CADY, JOHN HENRY (1846–1927), was born in Cincinnati, Hamilton County. He saw some intermittent service during the early days of the Civil War and in 1864 joined the 11th Ohio Volunteer Cavalry. He was in a detachment which went up the Platte River to the Pike's Peak gold fields in 1865. After being discharged he went to Arizona. At Tucson he built the largest dance hall and saloon in the Territory, presided over his own gambling layouts, operated what he was pleased to call a "hotel" at Patagonia, "figured in many lynchings," and lived to tell his story in an autobiographical volume: *Arizona's Yesterdays . . . ,* [Patagonia, Ariz.], 1915.

CALDWELL, DAVID S. (Dec. 22, 1820–Sept. 6, 1889), was born in Hagerstown, Md., but grew up in western Crawford County, where his parents moved when he was a child. At the time of the organization of the 123rd O.V.I., he was made first lieutenant of Company H, which was organized by Captain John Newman of Crestline. He was promoted to captain Feb. 3, 1863. He was captured at Winchester, Va., on June 15, 1863, when his regiment was surrendered by Colonel Ely of the 18th Connecticut, who was temporarily in command. He wrote one of the most thrilling accounts of escape from a Confederate prison.

Incidents of War, and Southern Prison Life, Dayton, 1864.

CALDWELL, HOWARD WALTER (Aug. 26, 1853–March 2, 1927), educator, was born in Bryan, Williams County. In 1883 he was appointed to the history department of the University of Nebraska, his alma mater. He wrote a number of articles and textbooks. His home was Lincoln, Neb., and his death occurred in that city.

Henry Clay, the Great Compromiser . . . , Milwaukee, Wis., [1899].

CALISCH, EDWARD NATHANIEL (June 23, 1865–Jan. 7, 1946), rabbi, was born in Toledo, Lucas County. He attended Hughes High School in Cincinnati, the University of Cincinnati, and Hebrew Union College. He was a rabbi in Peoria, Ill., 1887–91, and in Richmond, Va., 1891–1945. He published religious textbooks for children and teachers, a collection of his addresses, and *The Jew in English Literature . . . ,* Richmond, Va., [1909]. WWW 2

CALLAGHAN, J. DORSEY (Jan. 3, 1895–   ), was born in Dennison, Tuscarawas County, and attended the schools of that community. After serving in World War I, he was a merchant in Columbus and Cincinnati, and in Mt. Clemens, Mich. While recovering from an illness, he wrote poems for the Detroit *Free Press* and later joined the staff as music critic. He is still with that paper and lives in Highland Park, Mich. He has published a volume of poems: *Music Off Stage,* [Detroit, 1945].

CALLAGHAN, JAMES F. (March 28, 1839–Dec. 12, 1899), priest, born in Trenton, N. J., was brought to Cincinnati by his parents in 1845. He graduated from Mount St. Mary's of the West in 1859, was ordained to the Roman Catholic priesthood in 1863, and afterward served at All Saints University and St. Peter's Cathedral. A selection of his writings was published posthumously by his sister, Emily A. Callaghan: *Memoirs and Writings . . . ,* Cincinnati, 1903.

CAMPBELL, DAISY RHODES (May 23, 1854–May 11, 1927), was born in Delaware, Delaware County, and spent her life in that community. She attended Ohio Wesleyan University. She wrote articles, stories, and books for children, e.g., *The Violin Lady,* Boston, 1916. WW 12

CAMPBELL, EDWIN R. (1787–1857), was born in Butler County. He worked on the Cincinnati *Daily Times* and *Daily Dispatch* before emigrating to California.

The Heroine of Scutari, and Other Poems, New York, 1857.

CAMPBELL, ELSIE JANE COSLER (Oct. 22, 1887–   ), was born in Miami Township, Greene County. She attended a business college and Columbia University, was employed as a public stenographer, and is now a resident of Dayton. Her poems have appeared in various periodicals and anthologies, and she has published a collection: *The Book of Thrills,* Dayton, 1934. BDCP

CAMPBELL, JAMES EDWIN (Jan. 26, 1867–Jan. 30, 1896), was born in Pomeroy, Meigs County. He attended public schools and Miami University. He worked on several Chicago newspapers and also taught school in Rutland, Ohio, Charleston, W. Va., and Oberlin, Ohio. He was one of the first Negroes to write dialect poetry. His death occurred in Pomeroy.

Echoes from the Cabin and Elsewhere, Chicago, [1895].

CAMPBELL, JOHN BUNYAN (1820–1904), "vitapathic" physician, was born at Little Pine Creek, Pa. He opened a school in Fairmount, the American Health College, to teach vitapathy, which Otto Juettner (q.v.) described as "a mongrel mixture of half-digested science, brazen assurance and medical and religious quackery." Juettner acknowledged that many of Campbell's students went on to study medicine elsewhere and became effective physicians. His books were not sold, and his students were sworn not to reveal their contents.

Encyclopedia of Nature, Containing the Full and Complete Vitapathic System of Medical Practice . . . , Cincinnati, 1878.

Spirit Vitapathy; A Religious Scientific System of Health and Life for Body and Soul . . . , [Cincinnati, 1891].

Life! Physical and Spiritual . . . , Cincinnati, [18– ?].

CAMPBELL, JOHN POAGE (1767–Nov. 4, 1814), clergyman, was born in Augusta County, Va. He preached in various towns in southern Ohio. His death occurred in Chillicothe.

The Doctrine of Justification by Imputed Righteousness Considered . . . , Danville, [Ky.], 1805.

Strictures on the Letters Published by Barton W. Stone . . . , Lexington, Ky., 1805.

Vindex . . . , Lexington, Ky., 1806.

The Pelagian Detected . . . , Lexington, Ky., 1811.

CAMPBELL, JOHN WILSON (Feb. 23, 1782–Sept. 24, 1833), lawyer and judge, was born in Augusta County, Va., of Irish parents. His family moved to Kentucky in 1791 and shortly afterward to Ohio, where he earned money for his education by clearing timberlands and by teaching school. In 1808 he was admitted to the bar and began to practice in West Union, Adams County. He served in Congress, 1817–27. After the election of Andrew Jackson, whom he had supported, he was appointed U. S. district judge. In 1826 he settled on a Brown County farm, and in 1831 he moved to Columbus. He died at Delaware Sept. 24, 1833, in the cholera epidemic that struck Ohio that year. His writings and a sketch of his life were compiled by his widow, Eleanor W. Campbell.

Biographical Sketches; With Other Literary Remains of the Late John W. Campbell . . . , Columbus, 1838.

CAMPBELL, LILY BESS (June 20, 1883–), educator, was born in Ada, Hardin County. She graduated from the University of Texas in 1905 and the University of Chicago (Ph.D.) in 1921. She served on the faculty of the University of Wisconsin, 1911–18, and the University of California at Los Angeles, 1922–50. Besides scholarly articles and monographs, her writings include several books on Shakespeare and the English theater, e.g., *Shakespeare's Tragic Heroes, Slaves of Passion,* Cambridge, England, 1930. WW 30

CAMPBELL, LOUIS WALTER (May 17, 1899–), ornithologist, was born in Toledo, Lucas County. He has been a columnist for the Toledo *Times* and is active in various nature study and conservation organizations. Besides articles and pamphlets on nature, he has published a book, *Birds of Lucas County,* Toledo, [1940].

CAMPBELL, MARION (d.1944), was born in Bellefontaine, Logan County. In 1927 she married Alexander Winton, Cleveland automobile manufacturer, from whom she was divorced a few years later. She lived in Los Angeles for a number of years. Her death occurred in Florida. Interested in American Indians, she wrote an opera, *The Seminole,* which was produced in Cleveland, and also organized the Women's National League for Justice to the Indians. She wrote another opera, poems, and a book: *The Boyhood of Tecumseh . . . ,* Philadelphia, [1940].

CAMPBELL, MARY ELIZABETH (Feb. 11, 1903–), educator, was born in Cambridge, Guernsey County. She graduated from Radcliffe College in 1925 and Yale University (Ph.D.) in 1937. She has been a member of the English Department, Indiana University, since 1927 except for service with the American Red Cross during World War II.

A specialist in eighteenth century British literature, she has written a number of articles on Daniel Defoe and has also published popular novels, e.g., *The White Hand Murder Mystery,* New York, 1936. DAS 3

CAMPBELL, MARY REBECCA (July 26, 1881–Oct. 11, 1939), was born in Youngstown, Mahoning County. She died in New York City. She wrote a biography of her father, Walter L. Campbell (q.v.): *The Life of Walter Campbell,* New York, 1917.

CAMPBELL, OSCAR JAMES, JR. (Aug. 16, 1879–), educator, was born in Cleveland, Cuyahoga County. He graduated from Harvard University (A.B., 1903; Ph.D., 1910) and afterward taught English at the University of Wisconsin, 1911–21, the University of Michigan, 1921–35, and Columbia University, 1936–50. In addition to a number of widely used textbooks, his writings include *Shakespeare's Satire,* New York, 1943. WW 30

CAMPBELL, WALTER L. (Nov. 13, 1842–Jan. 25, 1905), lawyer and journalist, was born in Salem, Columbiana County. When he was five years old, an accident left him blind for life. From nine to sixteen, he attended the School for the Blind at Columbus. He became a skilled organist. After attending Salem High School, he entered Western Reserve College in 1863 and graduated with honors in 1867. He read law in Salem and spent a year at Harvard Law School. In 1869 he went to the Wyoming Territory, of which his brother had just been appointed governor. On returning to Ohio, he was admitted to the bar in 1873. He owned and edited the *Mahoning Register* in Youngstown. From 1884 to 1886 he served as mayor of the city. Though totally blind, he moved freely about the city with no assistance, and he followed successfully his professions of law and journalism.

Our Sovereign's Characteristics, Washington, D. C., 1876.

Civitas: The Romance of Our Nation's Life, New York, 1886.

CANFIELD, DWIGHT R. (March 29, 1872–April 20, 1956), physician, was born in Scotch Ridge, Wood County. He attended district schools and later taught school to finance his medical education. After graduation from Toledo Medical College in 1907, he practiced at Perrysburg, and his death occurred in that community. Local history was his hobby, and he published a number of articles on that subject, and *Poems of the Maumee Valley,* [Fostoria, 1943].

CANFIELD, FLAVIA CAMP (1844–Aug. 12, 1930), mother of Dorothy Canfield Fisher (q.v.), was born in Michigan. In 1873 she married James H. Canfield (q.v.) and lived in Ohio while he was president of Ohio State University. She died in Arlington, Vt. She wrote several books, e.g., *Around the World at Eighty,* Rutland, Vt., 1925.

CANFIELD, JAMES HULME (March 18, 1847–March 29, 1909), librarian and university president, was born in Delaware, Delaware County, the son of an Episcopal clergyman, but much of his boyhood was spent in Brooklyn, N. Y., where his father was rector of Christ Church. After graduating from Williams College in 1868, he spent two years in railroad-building in Iowa and Minnesota. He then read law and was admitted to the Michigan bar in 1872. While practicing in St. Joseph, Mich., he married Flavia A. Camp (see above). Canfield entered educational work in 1877, when he accepted a professorship at the University of Kansas. From 1891 to 1895 he was chancellor of the University of Nebraska and from 1895 to 1899 was president of Ohio State University. He resigned to become librarian of Columbia University, a a post he held until his death. He was extremely popular as a speaker and was a prolific writer of articles for magazines.

Taxation; A Plain Talk for Plain People, New York, 1883.

Local Government in Kansas, Philadelphia, [1885].

History and Government of Kansas, Philadelphia, [1894].

The Ohio State University as a School of Post-Graduate Instruction Only . . . , Columbus, 1898.

The College Student and his Problems, New York, 1902.

The Spirit of '76 . . . , [New York?, 1907].

Report on Certain Educational Characteristics in England and France, [New York, 1908].

CANFIELD, MARY GRACE WEBB (July 12, 1864–July 26, 1946), was born in Springfield, Clark County. A graduate of Buchtel College, Akron, she was active in the women's suffrage movement and the Universalist Church. In 1891 she married Rev. Harry L. Canfield, a Universalist minister. Her last years were spent in Brattleboro and Woodstock, Vt. She published articles in various periodicals, edited a three-volume collection of hymns, and wrote *The Valley of the Kedron . . .*, South Woodstock, Vt., 1940.

CANFIELD, SILAS SPRAGUE (March 13, 1824–June 30, 1902), was born in Hamburg, N. Y. He taught school and operated a sawmill in New York State before coming to Milan in 1852. In 1857 he settled in Wood County. He was mustered into the service, Sept. 19, 1861, as captain of Company K, 21st O.V.I. He was captured Sept. 20, 1863, at Chickamauga, and was exchanged March 20, 1865. Though lacking in personal narrative, his history of his regiment is a valuable and well-documented account of its otherwise unrecorded participation in the Chickamauga battle. After his discharge from the army he operated a sawmill and a farm, and taught school near Scotch Ridge.

History of the 21st Regiment Ohio Volunteer Infantry, in the War of the Rebellion, Toledo, 1893.

CANIFF, MILTON ARTHUR (Feb. 28, 1907–), cartoonist, was born in Hillsboro, Highland County. He graduated from Ohio State University in 1930 and worked as a cartoonist on the Dayton *Journal-Herald* and the Columbus *Dispatch* before achieving syndication with his comic strip "Terry and the Pirates." A story based on the comic strip has been published: *April Kane and the Dragon Lady . . .*, Racine, Wis., [1942]. WW 30

CANTWELL, JOHN SIMON (1837–1907), clergyman, was pastor of Universalist churches in Columbus, Camden, Fairfield, and Cincinnati. He moved to Massachusetts in 1881.

Thirty Days over the Sea . . ., Cincinnati, 1873.

CAREY, CHARLES. Pseud. See Charles C. Waddell.

CAREY, CHARLES HENRY (Oct. 27, 1857–Aug. 26, 1941), lawyer, was born in Cincinnati, Hamilton County. After graduating from Denison University in 1881, he studied law in Cincinnati and afterward practiced in Portland, Oreg., 1883–1932. He published a volume of legal digests in 1888, edited *The Journals of Theodore Talbot . . .* (1931) and Lansford W. Hastings' *Emigrants' Guide to Oregon and California* (1932), and wrote a state history: *History of Oregon*, Chicago, 1922. WWW 1

CARLISLE, WALTER EWING (Jan. 6, 1877–Oct. 5, 1956), journalist, was born in Hillsboro, Highland County. He was on the staff of the *Ohio State Journal*, 1909–55, working as a proofreader and also conducting a column, "Poetry and Rhyme." He died in Columbus. Besides poems and articles in various periodicals, he published a collection of verse: *Lights and Shadows*, Columbus, [1941].

CARLTON, FRANK TRACY (Dec. 22, 1873–), educator, was born in Mantua, Portage County. He graduated from Case Institute of Technology in 1895 and the University of Wisconsin (Ph.D.) in 1906. After teaching at Albion College, 1906–19, and at DePauw University, 1919–27, he joined the Case faculty as professor of economics. He retired in 1944 and since that time has continued to live in Cleveland. Besides articles in professional journals and textbooks, his writings include several books on organized labor, e.g., *Organized Labor in American History*, New York, 1920. WW 26

CARNES, SIDNEY CECIL (Sept. 11, 1909–Feb. 14, 1953), journalist, was born in Fairview, Guernsey County, but his parents moved to Barnesville in 1910. After attending Muskingum College for a time, he transferred to Ohio State University and graduated in journalism in 1932. He worked on the Columbus *Star* and the New York *World-Telegram*, wrote many radio shows, and was a correspondent for the *Saturday Evening Post*. After World War II he lived in Laredo, Texas. One of the original Citizens for Eisenhower, he was en route to Washington to take a post in the State Department when he died near Lawrenceville, Ind. He wrote a life of John L. Lewis, several books on World War II, some travel books, and a biography: *Jimmy Hare: News Photographer*, New York, 1940. WWW 3

CARNEY, AUBREY TOULMIN (Jan. 12, 1921–), was born in Dayton, Montgomery County, and was educated in Dayton schools. After graduating from Smith College, she worked for a year on the Dayton *Daily News*. Since her marriage to Fletcher B. Carney she has lived in Birmingham, Ala. She has written considerable fiction. Her first novel was *No Certain Answer*, New York, 1947.

CARPENTER, FLORA LEONA (Feb. 15, 1877–), educator, was born in Marysville, Union County. She attended high school in Wichita, Kan., graduated from City Normal School, Toledo, in 1901, studied art in New York and Chicago, and taught in the Toledo schools, 1901–07 and 1911–42. She is now living in Toledo. She has published a work in eight volumes for children: *Stories Pictures Tell . . .*, Chicago, [1918].

CARPENTER, FRANK GEORGE (May 8, 1855–June 18, 1924), traveler and journalist, was born in Mansfield, Richland County. He graduated from University of Wooster in 1877. In 1879 he became Columbus correspondent of the Cleveland *Leader.* Representing newspaper syndicates, he traveled to all parts of the world. A by-product of his travels was a series of geographical readers, the first of which (Asia) appeared in 1897. His textbooks were widely popular and appeared in many editions. Besides his geographical readers, the chief series are Carpenter's world travels and readers on commerce and industry. His death occurred in Nanking, China.

South America, Social, Industrial, and Political . . ., Akron, 1900.

CARPENTER, MATILDA GILRUTH (Aug. 12, 1831–March 23, 1923), was born in Philadelphia, Pa. She lived in Fayette County, 1867–84. She was the acknowledged leader of a group of Washington Court House women who, on Christmas Eve, 1873, fired by a lecture by Dio Lewis on "Our Girls," vowed to close every saloon in the community within a week's time. On Christmas morning, the movement was organized, and it is claimed locally that this was the beginning of the "Woman's Crusade" from which emerged the Woman's Christian Temperance Union. The fact is that the basic idea was Dr. Lewis', and that he had presented it on December 23 to the good ladies of Hillsboro, who had lost not a moment in organizing. According to Francis E. C. Willard (q.v.), "The whirlwind of the Lord began in the little town of Hillsboro on the 23rd of December, 1873." Mrs. Carpenter's death occurred in Columbus.

The Crusade; Its Origin and Development at Washington Court House and its Results . . ., Columbus, 1893.

CARR, MICHAEL W. (1851–April 30, 1922), journalist, born in Ireland, was brought to Toledo in 1861. He attended Toledo schools and University of Notre Dame. He edited the *Toledo Review,* 1873–79, and from 1881 until his death he lived in Indianapolis, Ind., where he wrote for various newspapers and magazines. He published several volumes on the Catholic Church in Indiana, e.g., *A History of the Catholicity in Richmond and Wayne Co. Ind. . . .*, Indianapolis, 1889.

CARR, ROBERT SPENCER (March 26, 1909–), was born in Washington, D. C., but was brought to Columbus when he was one year old and lived there until 1925. When he was fifteen, he received national publicity when a reporter discovered that he wrote horror and adventure stories for pulp magazines. He attended East High School in Columbus except for his senior year, which was completed at Ashley. While living in Ashley, he wrote *The Rampant Age,* New York, 1928. This frank portrayal of high school youth created a sensation, especially among his former Columbus classmates. At the age of eighteen he was writing for a Hollywood studio. He abandoned motion pictures and wandered about the United States for three years. In 1932 he arrived in Russia, where he lived for five years. He married a Russian girl, graduated from a Moscow university, and worked for Russian movie studios. In 1938 he returned to the United States, where he has occasionally worked in Hollywood and has written several mystery novels and fantasies.

CARREL, CORA GAINES (May 7, 1860–Oct. 23, 1927), was born in Lake County. She was active in the Eastern Star and in civic activities. A few years before her death she moved to Los Angeles.

Buckeye Ballads, Cincinnati, 1900.

CARREL, MINNIE E. BUTLER (April 14, 1862–Sept. 14, 1938), was born in Lake County. She married Fred Carrel around 1882 and lived in Willoughby. Besides poems in periodicals and anthologies, she published a collection: *Fireside Poems,* [Madison, Wis.], 1923.

CARRIER, WARREN PENDLETON (1918–), was born in Cheviot, Hamilton County. Educated at Wabash College, Miami University, and Harvard University, he has taught English at the University of Iowa and Bard College. He now lives in Sweet Briar, Va. His publications include a book of poems: *Desire for Death,* [Chapel Hill, N. C., 1942].

CARRIGAN, M. J. See James Emmitt.

CARRIGHAR, SALLY, was born in Cleveland, Cuyahoga County. She has written for various motion-picture companies, 1923–28, and for radio, 1928–38. Since 1938 she has been a free-lance writer, specializing in natural history. Her home now is in Lyme, N. H. She has written several books, e.g., *One Day at Teton Marsh,* New York, 1947.

CARRINGTON, HENRY BEEBEE (March 2, 1824–Oct. 26, 1912), soldier, was born in Wallingford, Conn. He graduated from Yale in 1845, and for a year and a half he taught in Irving Institute, Tarrytown, N. Y., where he was encouraged by Washington Irving to write his *Battles of the American Revolution.* After a course of study in the Yale Law School, he moved to Columbus in 1848. There he practiced law for twelve years, nine of which were spent in partnership with William Dennison, subsequently governor of Ohio. He was one of the founders of the Republican Party in Ohio and a warm friend of Salmon P. Chase, who, as governor, appointed him to a position on his staff in 1857. Carrington's specific task was the reorganization of the Ohio militia, the successful accomplishment of which led to his appointment as adjutant general. He was reappointed by Chase's successor, Governor Dennison. Following President Lincoln's first call for troops, Carrington demonstrated his ability by organizing and mustering in nine regiments of Ohio militia. He was appointed colonel in the 18th U. S. Infantry, and, at the request of Governor Oliver P. Morton, he was detached from his command and sent to Indiana, where he superintended the recruiting of more than 100,000 volunteers. He was promoted to brigadier general, and under his direction the disloyal Knights of the Golden Circle and other subversive organizations were uncovered. When mustered out of the volunteers he rejoined the 18th Regiment, then serving in the Army of the Cumberland. Late in 1865 he was ordered to the Indian service in Nebraska, where he built Fort Kearny, and participated in the Red Cloud War and several independent engagements. Suffering from a severe wound, he was granted a year's leave of absence in 1869, and retired from the army in 1870. He was professor of military science and tactics at Wabash College, Ind., 1870–73. He contributed many articles to leading periodicals, and many of his addresses were published separately.

Ernest J. Wessen

Ocean to Ocean. Pacific Railroad and Adjoining Territories . . . , Philadelphia, 1869.
Military Education in American Colleges, [Indianapolis, 1870].
Battles of the American Revolution, 1775–1781 . . . , New York, 1876.
Crisis Thoughts, Philadelphia, 1878.
Ohio Militia and the West Virginia Campaign, 1861, [Marietta?], 1879.
Battle Maps and Charts of the American Revolution . . . , New York, [1881].
The Strategic Relations of New Jersey to the War for American Independence, Newark, N. J., 1885.
The Obelisk and Its Voices. The Inner Facings of Washington Monument with Their Lessons, Boston, 1887.
Patriotic Reader . . . , Philadelphia, [1888].
Kristopherus, the Christbearer, Boston, [1892].
Beacon Lights of Patriotism . . . , New York, 1894.
Military Movements in Indiana, [Boston?, 18– ?].
Theodore D. Weld and a Famous Quartette . . . , [Hyde Park?, Mass., 1904].
The New Center of Gravity, the World-Reapers of the Grand Army Harvest . . . , [Boston?, 1905].
Dream and Story, Boston, [1908].
Washington the Soldier, Boston, 1908.
Winfield Scott . . . , [Boston?, 1910].

CARRINGTON, MARGARET IRVIN SULLIVANT (1831–1870), was born in Columbus, Franklin County, the granddaughter of the founder of that city. She married General Henry Beebee Carrington (q.v.), whom she accompanied to the West when he was assigned to the command of Fort Kearny, Neb., in 1866. *Ab-sa-ra-ka, Home of the Crows,* is an account of her experiences. Thomas W. Field was of the opinion that Mrs. Carrington had had little personal experience among the Indians; however, there is in existence a letter from General Carrington in which he states that over half of the Indian demonstrations described by her "were under her own eye."

Ab-sa-ra-ka Home of the Crows: Being the Experience of an Officer's Wife on the Plains . . . , Philadelphia, 1868.

CARSON, JULIA MARGARET HICKS (Mrs. William J.), born in Columbus, Franklin County, was graduated from Ohio State University in 1921 and from the School of Law, Yale University, in 1926. She has directed research for the League of Women Voters in several cities and now lives in Philadelphia, Pa. She has written a history of the U.S.O. and several biographies, e.g., *Son of Thunder, Patrick Henry,* New York, 1942. WWAW 1

CARTER, ALFRED GEORGE WASHINGTON (March 4, 1819–Feb. 21, 1885), lawyer and judge, was born in Cincinnati, Hamilton County. After attending Alexander Kinmont's school and Miami University, he read law with Judge Timothy Walker and was admitted to the bar. He was elected prosecuting attorney of Hamilton County and later served two terms as judge of the common pleas court. Besides the volume of reminiscences listed below, he wrote articles on drama for the press and also wrote several plays, including a dramatization of *Les Miserables* which was presented at Pike's Opera House.

The Old Court House . . . , Cincinnati, 1880.

CARTER, JOHN HENTON (May 3, 1832–March 2, 1910), journalist, was born in Marietta, Washington County. After his father died, his mother took the family to her former home in Liverpool, England, but after two years they returned to Marietta. From 1846 to 1870 he worked on steamboats in various capacities, usually supervising the galleys. One of the many legends concerning him is that on the first day of a voyage he would serve such rich, tempting food that many passengers became ill and ate little for the rest of the trip. During the Civil War he lived in Columbus, Ky., and other river towns. In 1866 he moved to Cairo, Ill., and in 1870 to St. Louis, where he was river editor of the *Globe-Democrat.* Around 1871 he began publishing annual almanacs, *Commodore Rollingpin's Almanac.* In Chapter XVI of *Life on the Mississippi,* his friend Mark Twain quoted speed records from one of the almanacs. In 1883 he went to New York with Joseph Pulitzer to write for the *World.* He returned to St. Louis about six years later as a freelance writer and lecturer. He spent the last five years of his life at the home of a daughter in Marietta, and he died in that community. He is still remembered there for his colorful personality and flamboyant costumes. *Thomas Rutherton,* which is based on his early life, *Ozark Postoffice,* and *Mississippi Argonauts* were published under his own name; the others appeared under the pen name Commodore Rollingpin.

The Log of Commodore Rollingpin . . . , New York, 1874.
Thomas Rutherton. A Novel, New York, [1890].
Duck Creek Ballads, New York, [1894].
Log Cabin Poems, St. Louis, 1897.
The Impression Club; A Novel, New York, 1899.
The Man at the Wheel . . . , St. Louis, 1899.
Ozark Postoffice . . . , St. Louis, 1899.
Out Here in Ol' Missoury, St. Louis, 1900.
Mississippi Argonauts; A Tale of the South, New York, 1903.

CARTWRIGHT, PETER (Sept. 1, 1785–Sept. 25, 1872), frontier Methodist preacher, preached in Ohio in 1805–06 on the Scioto and Hohocking circuits and the following year on the Marietta circuit. A vivid account of the frontier is found in his autobiography (1857).

CARVER, GEORGE (Dec. 19, 1888–Oct. 29, 1949), educator, was born in Cincinnati, Hamilton County. He graduated from Miami University in 1916. From 1923 until his death, he was on the English faculty of the University of Pittsburgh. Besides a number of textbooks and articles, he wrote a book of biographical sketches: *Alms for Oblivion . . .* , Milwaukee, [1946]. WWW 3

CARY, ALICE (April 26, 1820–Feb. 12, 1871), poet, was born near Mount Healthy, Hamilton County. Her introduction to poetry came largely from her school readers and the "Poet's Corner" in a Universalist paper to which her parents subscribed. Her mother died in 1835, and two years later Robert Cary married again. The stepmother considered the reading and writing of poetry a waste of time, and Alice and her younger sister, Phoebe (q.v.), found the home atmosphere uncongenial until their father built a separate house for himself and his wife. Alice's first poem appeared in the Cincinnati *Sentinel* in 1838, and soon her verse was appearing in Cincinnati periodicals, the *National Era, Graham's Magazine,* and others. Her poem "Pictures of Memory" was praised highly by Poe. The two sisters came to the attention of Rufus P. Griswold, who supervised the publication of *Poems of Alice and Phoebe Cary,* New York, 1849. In 1850 the sisters visited New York and New England. The highlight of the trip was a visit to Whittier. In November, Alice moved to New York, and in April of the following year, Phoebe joined her. They established themselves in a small cottage, where they held open house each Sunday evening. Horace Greeley was perhaps their most regular visitor, but others included George Ripley, P. T. Barnum, Thomas Bailey Aldrich, and Whitelaw Reid. Although both sisters sympathized with the women's rights movement, they were not militant reformers. Alice was named first president of the Woman's Club (later the Sorosis), the first women's club in the United States. An invalid in her last years, Alice continued to receive friends and admirers until her death. Her novels are melodramatic and reflect her somewhat restricted experience. *Clovernook,* based on memories of her childhood on a farm, contains some elements of realism, but the general tone is sentimental. Her poetry, highly esteemed during her lifetime, suffers also from an excess of sentimentality.

Poems of Alice and Phoebe Cary, New York, 1849.
Clovernook; Or, Recollections of Our Neighborhood in the West, 2 vols., New York, 1852–53.
Hagar; A Story of Today, New York, 1852.
Lyra, and Other Poems, New York, 1852.
Clovernook Children, Boston, 1855.
Poems, Boston, 1855.
Married, Not Mated . . . , New York, 1856.
Ballads, Lyrics, and Hymns, New York, 1866.
The Bishop's Son, New York, 1867.
Snow-Berries. A Book for Young Folks, Boston, 1867.
A Lover's Diary, Boston, 1868.
The Last Poems of Alice and Phoebe Cary, (Mary Clemmer Ames, ed.), New York, 1873.
Ballads for Little Folks, New York, 1874.
The Poetical Works of Alice and Phoebe Cary . . . , New York, 1877.
Early and Late Poems of Alice and Phoebe Cary, Boston, 1887.

CARY, PHOEBE (Sept. 4, 1824–July 31, 1871), younger sister of Alice Cary (q.v.), was born on the family farm at Mount Healthy, Hamilton County. She shared Alice's interest in reading and writing poetry and published her first poem in a Boston newspaper at the age of fourteen. In April, 1851, she and her younger sister, Elmina, who died in 1862, joined Alice in New York City. More robust than Alice, she assumed most of the domestic duties in the New York home. Visitors who left written records of the social evenings with the Cary sisters invariably commended her flashing wit. She was a firm believer in spiritualism during her last years. Overshadowed by her older sister during her lifetime, she was chiefly admired for the hymn "Nearer Home." She was also, however, a skillful parodist and a clever writer of light verse. She died at Newport, R. I., five months after the death of her older sister. For collections of the verse of both sisters, see the sketch of Alice Cary.

Poems and Parodies, Boston, 1854.
Poems of Faith, Hope and Love, New York, 1868.

CARY, SAMUEL FENTON (Feb. 18, 1814–Sept. 29, 1900), was born in Cincinnati, Hamilton County. He was a first cousin of Alice and Phoebe Cary (qq.v.). After graduating from Miami University in 1835 and Cincinnati Law School in 1837, he practiced law until 1845, when he abandoned his practice to devote himself to the cause of temperance. He edited various temperance papers. He served in the 40th Congress and in 1876 was the candidate for vice-president on the Greenback ticket.

Cary Memorials . . . , Cincinnati, 1874.
General Samuel F. Cary on the Aims of the Independent Greenback Party . . . , [New York, 1876].

CASE, ALDEN BUELL (July 25, 1851–Oct. 27, 1932), clergyman, was born in Gustavus, Trumbull County. He graduated from Tabor College in 1878 and Yale Divinity School in 1881. Ordained a Congregational minister in 1881, he filled various missionary posts in South Dakota, California, and Mexico until his retirement in 1925. He died in Pomona, Calif. He wrote *Thirty Years with the Mexicans . . . ,* New York, [1917].

CASE, LEONARD (June 27, 1820–Jan. 6, 1880), philanthropist and occasional writer, was born in Cleveland, Cuyahoga County, the second son of Leonard Case, a prominent lawyer and land agent. After graduating from Yale University in 1842 and studying law for two years at Cincinnati Law School, he opened a law office in Cleveland. His practice was highly selective, being largely limited to his father's land business. He and his brother William organized a group of young men who called themselves "Arkites," an organization that later became the Rowfant Club. Following an illness contracted while touring Europe, Case was a partial invalid. He never married. After his father's death in 1864, he devoted himself to travel, writing, and philanthropy. He endowed the Cleveland Library Association and assisted in the founding of the Western Reserve Historical Society. His major benefaction, however, was the establishment of the Case School of Applied Science (Case Institute of Technology), which opened its doors in 1881. Case wrote long descriptive letters to his friends while traveling and published numerous poems. In 1860 the *Atlantic Monthly* printed his "Treasure Trove," a mock-heroic narrative poem, which was published in book form late in 1872, dated 1873.

Treasure Trove, Boston, 1873.

CASS, LEWIS (Oct. 9, 1772–June 17, 1866), soldier and statesman, was an Ohio resident from 1800, when he came to Marietta to study law, until 1813, when he was appointed governor of Michigan. He published numerous political and historical speeches. While minister to France (1836–42), he wrote a series of essays: *France; Its King, Court, and Government,* New York, 1840.

CASSELMAN, ARTHUR VALE (July 20, 1874–May 1, 1957), clergyman, was born in Minerva, Stark County. He graduated from Heidelberg College in 1895 and from Heidelberg Seminary in 1898. Ordained in the Reformed Church, he served a pastorate in Columbiana, 1898–1902, another in Reading, Pa., 1906–21, and held various executive positions associated with the missionary work of his church. His writings include *The End of the Beginning; A Narrative of the Missionary Enterprise of the Reformed Church,* Philadelphia, 1936. WWW 3

CATHCART, WALLACE HUGH (April 2, 1865–Sept. 6, 1942), was born in Elyria, Lorain County. He graduated from Denison University in 1890 and served as librarian during his attendance there. He was secretary of the Taylor Austin Co., 1890–97, and general manager of Burrows Brothers, 1897–1914. His writings include a bibliography of Hawthorne and *The Association in Baptist History,* [Cleveland?, 1911?]. WW 21

CATHERWOOD, MARY HARTWELL (Dec. 16, 1847–Dec. 26, 1902), was born in Luray, Licking County. Out of her many writings and activities comes the necessity to mention her in several small ways whenever the story of American fiction between 1875 and 1900 is recounted. Fred Lewis Pattee has pointed out, for example, that she was the first American woman novelist of any significance born west of the Appalachians; furthermore, she was the first woman writer of any prominence to acquire a college education and to be graduated not from a school in the East but from a new college sprung up in Ohio. Such "firsts," of course, are scarcely more than the curiosities of time and geography and would not alone warrant much special mention of Mrs. Catherwood. Another peripheral reason for recalling her is that during the hot debate raging in the 1880s and 1890s over the "new realism," Mrs. Catherwood was chief spokesman for Middle Western conservatism when the controversy reached the clashing point at the Chicago World's Fair in the summer of 1893. Young Hamlin Garland, who appeared at the literary conference there as the chief apostle for the new faith, has recorded his flurry with Mrs. Catherwood as one of the minor episodes in the history of American criticism. Somewhat more directly important in the literary story is the negative fact that Mrs. Catherwood's greatest fame in her own lifetime came from her numerous historical romances, beginning with *The Romance of Dollard* (1889), which led in the revival of this reactionary and decadent phenomenon in the 1890s. Though these artificially romantic novels gave her national acclaim, they are very nearly dead now and hold little respect in later critical evaluations of her work. More positive is the fact that, a decade earlier, Mrs. Catherwood had been experimenting with little excursions into the critically realistic reporting of life as she knew it in the Corn Belt farm and village communities where she had lived in Ohio, Indiana, and Illinois. Her chronicling of the sordidness and bitterness she recognized there had appeared first in local sketches and stories in local Indiana papers, such as the novelette, "A Little God," printed in the Kokomo *Weekly Dispatch* (1878–79). These culminated in the novel *Craque-O'-Doom,* based upon the provincial barrenness of the Ohio town of Hebron, where she had spent her girlhood, at the intersection of the Ohio Canal and the Old National Road. This critical vein in American fiction, which fifty years later was to be commonly rated as important, is usually dated from E. W. Howe's *The Story of a Country Town* (1883) and Joseph Kirkland's *Zury: The Meanest Man in Spring County* (1887). Mrs. Catherwood's *Craque-O'-Doom,* though not so well written as either of these, antedated both and was the forerunner of all the later *Winesburgs*. Although Mrs. Catherwood did not elect to develop this line of frank reportage, out of it grew her two groups of best writings. Had she stuck to it, Professor Pattee has said, she might have become the Mary E. Wilkins of the West. As it was, she was the pioneer and only exploiter during the 1880s of old Corn Belt regional material in the established local-color tradition. The June, 1882, issue of William Dean Howells' *Atlantic Monthly,* for example, included her short story "Serena," a thinly plotted but well-integrated little tale packed full of the manners, customs, folk beliefs, and people that Mrs. Catherwood remembered from the Buckeye Lake farm communities of central Ohio in the 1850s and 1860s.

Other stories descriptive of the same sort of life in Ohio, Indiana, and Illinois were appearing in *Lippincott's, Ladies' Repository, Harper's Bazaar,* and elsewhere. They continued to appear throughout Mrs. Catherwood's life. Through sheer vitality of realistic color combined with a pleasant romanticism, such stories as "The Stirring-Off" and "The Queen of the Swamp" (both from the Hebron–Buckeye Lake–Kirkersville swamp country of the 1850s) continue to appear in anthologies and are the best reporting that the "local-color" era saw from this oldest part of the Cornlands culture belt. During the 1890s, Mrs. Catherwood produced a second notable group of regional tales, which are now her best-known works. These dealt with French life, particularly that which was to be found along the Canadian border. Although nearly all of these French tales contain some period material reflecting the historical interpretations of Francis Parkman and the long romances that were now Mrs. Catherwood's major literary effort, they are essentially regional in quality, taking their central interest from the vivid minutiae of speech, manners, personalities, and action that the author delighted in. These stories, which follow the St. Lawrence and the Great Lakes all the way from Acadia (as in "The Chase of Saint-Castin") to primitive Sault Sainte Marie (as in "The Windigo"), or to nineteenth century Mackinac Island (as in "The Mothers of Honore"), represent the best integration of Mrs. Catherwood's particular narrative powers. They are the portions of her writing most frequently reprinted today. Their greatest strength lies in an ability to combine more or less idealistic, but simple and often hauntingly charming, plots with a wealth of memorable local-color detail. Throughout her long writing career Mrs. Catherwood also wrote many juvenile works, one of which, *Rocky Fork,* is still in print and is probably the best firsthand fictional reflection of a central Ohio rural school district in the 1860s. With this résumé of her literary importance as a background, her life story takes on considerable interest. The daughter of Dr. Marcus and Phoebe Thompson Hartwell, Mrs. Catherwood was born Dec. 16, 1847, in Luray, on the Old National Road, in Licking County. When she was about nine, the Hartwells, in a group of Ohio families, migrated to Milford, Iroquois County, Ill. In 1857, a year after moving to Milford, the father died, and the mother one year later, leaving eleven-year-old Mary with a younger sister and brother. The three orphans were returned to Ohio and reared by maternal grandparents in Hebron. The Hebron years that ensued Mrs. Catherwood reported in later years as very unhappy. She often returned to this neighborhood in her stories, usually reporting Hebron unpleasantly, as in *Craque-O'-Doom.* On the other hand, she often used the neighboring farm region of Luray, George's Chapel, the pigeon swamps, and Buckeye Lake, where many of her relatives lived, as a land of idyllic escape, as in "The Stirring-Off" and "The Queen of the Swamp." At the age of fourteen, she began teaching in various country schools of Licking County. Then two years later she was publishing her first poems and sketches in the Newark, Ohio, *North American,* and in 1865 at the age of eighteen, with the aid of M. L. Wilson (q.v.), editor of the *North American,* was admitted to Granville Female College, where in 1868 she finished a four-year course at the end of three years. She later used the Granville setting for various short stories, the novel *A Woman in Armor,* and the juveniles *Rocky Fork* and *Bony and Ban.* While teaching in Granville and in Danville, Ill., 1868–74, she developed her free-lance writing skills and in April, 1871, won a $100 prize for a short story published in *Wood's Household Magazine.* She immediately became a regular contributor to *Wood's* and to other periodicals and was encouraged by these successes to leave teaching in the autumn of 1874 and go to Newburgh, N. Y., the home of *Wood's,* to support herself by free-lance writing. It was a rather daring venture for a young Middle Western woman in the 1870s, but Mary Hartwell seems to have succeeded fairly well for a time. In May, 1875, she moved to Cincinnati along with Helen Osborne (later Mrs. Henry Edward Krehbiel) to write for *Golden Hours, Ladies' Repository,* and other publications. Her first novel, *A Woman in Armor,* appeared in 1875. In 1876, she was forced by the economic depression to return to the help of friends and relatives in Illinois. The Cincinnati years are reflected in a juvenile, *The Dogberry Bunch,* which is said to have inspired the writing of *Five Little Peppers.* In 1877, she married James Steele Catherwood of Hoopeston, Ill., and resided for a time in Oakford (Fairfield), Ind. Here she became a regular contributor to local papers, established an important friendship with James Whitcomb Riley, and was soon seeking the national field again through a voluminous output of stories, articles, and juveniles. From 1879 to 1882, the Catherwoods resided in Indianapolis, where she was dramatic reviewer for the *Saturday Review,* published her second novel, *Craque-O'-Doom,* and was at the center of the literary group that included Riley, Benjamin Parker, and other young Hoosiers. Oakford and other Indiana rural scenes appear in numerous sketches, stories, and serials during these years in *Lippincott's, Harper's Bazaar,* and elsewhere. In 1882, the Catherwoods moved to Hoopeston, Ill., which was to be their home the rest of her life except for summers on Mackinac Island, and a Chicago residence from 1897 to 1902. A son was born and died in 1883. Her daughter Hazel (Mrs. Donald P. Cameron) was born in 1884. In 1886, Mrs. Catherwood with Riley, Maurice Thompson, and other authors from the Middle West organized, at Indianapolis, the Western Association of Writers, which continued for two decades to be an important though conservative literary force in the middle states. Mrs. Catherwood, now under the influence of Parkman, became absorbed in the *ancien régime* of French-America. Many stories and novels resulted in rapid succession, most of which appeared first in the *Century, Harper's* or the *Atlantic.* Books dealing with the Western Corn Belt during the same period were *The Spirit of an Illinois Town,* and *The Queen of the Swamp,* and *Other Plain Americans.* There was a flood also of juveniles and miscellaneous material. *Lazarre,* her last novel, was based upon the popular tradition of the "Lost Dauphin." In addition to enjoying a best-seller run, it was given a successful dramatization by Otis Skinner. It has some small continuing value today in the fact that a fictional episode between the Dauphin and Johnny Appleseed soon broke away from the novel and has become firmly established in the Appleseed folk canon of the Middle West. Out of the tremendous bulk of her rapid output, a few Corn Belt and French border local-color short stories have shown the vitality of true art and deserve now to be collected into a standard volume. Some of the best of the Ohio-Indiana-Illinois tales are to be found scattered through various periodicals of the 1880's and in the little collection *The Queen of the Swamp.*

Robert Price

A Woman in Armor . . . , New York, 1875.
Craque-O'-Doom. A Story, Philadelphia, 1881.
Rocky Fork, Boston, [1882].
Old Caravan Days, Boston, [1884].
The Romance of Dollard, New York, [1889].
The Story of Tonty, Chicago, 1890.
The Lady of Fort St. John, Boston, 1891.
Old Kaskaskia, Boston, 1893.
The White Islander, New York, 1893.
The Chase of Saint-Castin and Other Stories of the French in the New World, Boston, 1894.
The Days of Jeanne d'Arc, New York, 1897.
The Spirit of an Illinois Town, and the Little Renault . . . , Boston, 1897.
Bony and Ban, The Story of a Printing Venture, Boston, [1898].
Heroes of the Middle West; The French, Boston, 1898.
Mackinac and Lake Stories, New York, 1899.
The Queen of the Swamp, and Other Plain Americans, Boston, 1899.
Spanish Peggy; A Story of Young Illinois, Chicago, 1899.
Lazarre, Indianapolis, [1901].

CAULKINS, DANIEL (July 24, 1824–1902), physician, was born in Sullivan County, Vt. After attending Bancroft Academy and the Troy Conference Seminary, he served in the Mexican War. He studied medicine and afterward practiced and taught school in Farmer and Williams Center. In 1896 he moved to Toledo, where he spent his last years. His book describes a flying machine to be driven by "electric-magnetic power." The principle, he said, he discovered through study of the nervous system. Although he threatened to turn his invention over to a foreign power unless it was promptly accepted by the United States, it seems to have made no greater impact than his earlier discovery of the "circulation of the nerves."

Aerial Navigation; The Best Method, Toledo, 1895.

CAVANAUGH, JOHN WILLIAM (May 21, 1870–March 22, 1935), Roman Catholic priest and president of the University of Notre Dame, 1905–19, was born in Leetonia, Columbiana County. He graduated from Notre Dame in 1890 and was ordained to the priesthood in 1894.

St. Paul, the Apostle of the World, New York, 1895.
The Priests of Holy Cross, Notre Dame, [1904].
Conquest of Life, Notre Dame, [n.d.].
The Modesty of Culture, Notre Dame, [n.d.].

CHAFER, LEWIS SPERRY (Feb. 27, 1871–Aug. 22, 1952), clergyman, was born in Rock Creek, Ashtabula County. He graduated from Oberlin College in 1892 and was ordained as a Presbyterian minister in 1900.

After a career as a traveling evangelist, 1900–24, he founded Dallas Theological Seminary. His death occurred in Seattle, Wash. His writings were religious in nature, e.g., *Grace,* [Philadelphia, 1922]. WWW 3

CHALLEN, JAMES (Jan. 29, 1802–Dec. 9, 1878), clergyman, was born in Hackensack, N. J. After attending Transylvania College, he came to Cincinnati in 1825, and that city remained his home for the rest of his life. As pastor of Enon Baptist Church, he led his congregation in forming the First Church of Disciples of Christ. He was active in forming new churches and traveled widely throughout the United States as a Disciples missionary. A prolific writer, he published many essays and poems in periodicals, prepared question books on the Bible, edited several magazines and annuals, and also edited the Juvenile Library in 41 volumes (1859).

The Cave of Machpelah and Other Poems, Philadelphia, 1854.

The Gospel and Its Elements, Philadelphia, 1856.

Christian Evidences, Philadelphia, 1857.

Frank Eliott; Or, Wells in the Desert, Philadelphia, 1859.

Igdrasil; Or, the Tree of Existence, Philadelphia, 1859.

Island of the Giant Fairies, Philadelphia, 1868.

CHALMERS, ALLEN KNIGHT (June 30, 1897–), clergyman and educator, was born in Cleveland, Cuyahoga County. He graduated from Johns Hopkins University in 1917 and Yale Divinity School in 1922. Ordained a Congregational minister in 1922, he served a church in New York City until 1948, when he joined the faculty of Boston University School of Theology. His books include *Candles in the Wind,* New York, 1941. WW 30

CHALMERS, JEAN (d. Sept. 28, 1939), was born in Michigan, but lived in Toledo after her marriage to W. W. Chalmers, who served in the U. S. House of Representatives, 1920–30. During her stay in Washington she published a volume of poems: *Washington People, Places and Other Poems,* [Toledo, 1928].

CHAMBERLAIN, ERNEST BARRETT (Jan. 22, 1883–), editor and school consultant, was born in Oberlin, Lorain County. He graduated from Oberlin College in 1904 and from the seminary in 1910. He taught English and music in several institutions before devoting himself to public relations in the field of education. Since his retirement, he has lived in Oberlin. His writings include *Our Independent Schools . . . ,* [New York, 1944]. LE 3

CHAMBERLAIN, JACOB (April 13, 1835–March 2, 1908), missionary, born in Sharon, Conn., was reared in Hudson, where his family moved in 1838. He graduated from Western Reserve College in 1856 and continued his education in the fields of theology (Union Seminary and Rutgers) and medicine (New York University and Western Reserve College). In 1859 he was ordained a missionary of the Dutch Reformed Church and sailed for India, where he devoted his life to evangelistic and medical endeavors. He mastered the Telugu and Tamil languages, preached widely, and established several hospitals.

The Bible Tested in India, New York, 1878.

In the Tiger Jungle and Other Stories of Missionary Work among the Telugus of India, New York, [1896].

The Religions of the Orient, 1896.

The Cobra's Den, and Other Stories of Missionary Work among the Telugus of India, New York, [1900].

The Kingdom in India, Its Progress and Its Promise, New York, [1908].

CHAMBERLAIN, WILLIAM ISAAC (Feb. 11, 1837–June 30, 1920), brother of Jacob Chamberlain (q.v.), was born in Sharon, Conn., and was brought to Hudson when he was a year old. He received an M.A. degree from Western Reserve College in 1861. He taught Latin and Greek at Western Reserve, 1859–66, was Ohio State Secretary of Agriculture, 1880–86, and was president of Iowa Agricultural College, 1886–90. He also served in editorial capacities on the *Ohio Farmer* and *The National Stockman and Farmer.*

Tile Drainage, [n.p.], 1891.

CHAMBERLIN, WILLIAM FOSDICK (Feb. 20, 1870–July 28, 1943), businessman, was born in Randolph, N. Y., but his family moved to Dayton when he was three years old, and he grew up in that city. After graduating from Denison University in 1890, he entered the insurance business. He was active in musical activities in Dayton. Besides a history of his college fraternity, Phi Gamma Delta, he wrote an autobiographical book: *I Remember,* Newark, 1942.

CHAMBERLIN, WILLIAM HENRY (Oct. 19, 1833–March 11, 1912), was born in Ross County. He was commissioned first lieutenant in the 81st O.V.I., Oct. 1, 1861, and resigned with the rank of major, Sept. 15, 1864. His faithful chronicle of the services of the 81st O.V.I. was one of the first Ohio regimental histories written after the war. From 1895 to 1898 he was recorder of the Ohio commandery of the Military Order of the Loyal Legion of the U. S., in which capacity he edited volumes IV and V of the splendid *Sketches of War History* published by that organization. For a time he was head of the Associated Press bureau in Cincinnati.

History of the Eighty-first Regiment . . ., Cincinnati, 1865.

CHAMBERS, JAMES JULIUS (Nov. 21, 1850–Feb. 12, 1920), journalist, was born in Bellefontaine, Logan County. After graduating from Cornell University in 1870, he became a reporter on the New York *Tribune*. Two years later, at the height of the controversy over the source of the Mississippi River, he explored its headwaters and discovered Elk Lake and the connecting stream which bears his name. Returning to New York he contrived to have himself committed to the Bloomingdale Asylum; gaining his release after ten days, he published disclosures which resulted in the liberation of twelve sane persons and a revision of New York's lunacy laws. In 1873 he joined the staff of the New York *Herald,* serving as correspondent in various parts of the world; he became managing editor in 1886, and the following year he launched the Paris *Herald.* He was managing editor of the New York *World,* 1889–91. His remaining years were spent in travel and writing.

A Mad World and Its Inhabitants, London, 1876.
On a Margin . . ., New York, 1884.
Lovers Four and Maidens Five . . ., Philadelphia, 1886.
"In Sargasso" . . ., New York, 1896.
A Woman's Mistake, London, 1896.
The Rascal Club, London, [1897].
The Destiny of Doris . . ., New York, 1901.
The Mississippi River and Its Wonderful Valley . . ., New York, 1910.
The Book of New York; Forty Years' Recollections . . ., New York, [1912].
News Hunting on Three Continents, New York, 1921.

CHAMBERS, MERRITT MADISON (Jan. 26, 1899–), educator, was born in Knox County. He graduated from Ohio Wesleyan University in 1922 and Ohio State University (Ph.D.) in 1931. He has operated Lafayette Farms, Mt. Vernon, since 1951. He has edited or written a variety of books and bibliographies pertaining to education, e.g., *"Every Man a Brick!" The Status of Military Training in American Universities,* Bloomington, Ill., [1927]. WW 30

CHAMPNEY, ELIZABETH WILLIAMS (Feb. 6, 1850–Oct. 13, 1922), was born in Springfield, Clark County. She graduated from Vassar College in 1869. In her later years she chose to forget that she had written the once very popular "Vassar Girls" series, yet today the name of "Lizzie" Champney is remembered only as the author of that landmark in American juvenile literature. In 1873 she married the distinguished painter James Wells Champney, who illustrated many of her books. Her death occurred in Seattle, Wash.

In the Sky Garden, Boston, 1877.
All around a Palette, Boston, 1878.
Bourbon Lilies, Boston, 1878.
Entertainments, Boston, [1879].
Rosemary and Rue, Boston, 1881.
Three Vassar Girls Abroad, Boston, 1883.
Three Vassar Girls in England, Boston, 1884.
Three Vassar Girls in Italy, Boston, 1885.
Three Vassar Girls in South America, Boston, 1885.
Great Grandmother's Girls in New France, Boston, [1887].
Three Vassar Girls in Tyrol, Boston, 1887.
Three Vassar Girls on the Rhine, Boston, 1887.
Great Grandmother's Girls in New Mexico, Boston, [1888].
Three Vassar Girls at Home, Boston, 1888.
Three Vassar Girls in France, Boston, [1888].
Three Vassar Girls in Russia and Turkey, Boston, [1889].
Witch Winnie; The Story of a "King's Daughter," New York, [1889].
Three Vassar Girls in Switzerland, Boston, [1890].
Witch Winnie's Mystery, New York, [1891].
Three Vassar Girls in the Holy Land, Boston, [1892].
Witch Winnie's Studio, New York, [1892].
Six Boys, Boston, [1893].
Witch Winnie in Paris, New York, [1893].
Witch Winnie in Shinnecock, New York, [1894].
Paddy O'Learey and His Learned Pig, New York, 1895.
Witch Winnie at Versailles, New York, [1895].
Witch Winnie in Holland, New York, 1896.
Pierre and His Poodle, New York, 1897.
Witch Winnie in Venice, New York, 1897.
Witch Winnie in Spain, New York, 1898.

Patience, a Daughter of the Mayflower, New York, 1899.
Anneke; A Little Dame of New Netherlands, New York, 1900.
The Romance of the Feudal Chateaux, New York, 1900.
A Daughter of the Huguenots, New York, 1901.
Romance of the Renaissance Chateaux, New York, 1901.
Margarita; A Legend of the Fight for the Great River, New York, 1902.
Romance of the Bourbon Châteaux, New York, 1903.
Romance of the French Abbeys, New York, 1905.
Romance of the Italian Villas, New York, 1906.
Romance of the Roman Villas, New York, 1908.
Romance of Imperial Rome, New York, 1910.
Romance of Old Belgium, (with Frère Champney), New York, 1915.
Romance of Old Japan, (with Frère Champney), New York, 1917.
Romance of Russia, (with Frère Champney), New York, 1921.

CHANCELLOR, WILLIAM ESTABROOK (Sept. 25, 1867–), educator, was born in Dayton, Montgomery County. He graduated from Amherst College in 1889. After teaching in high schools in the East, he joined the faculty of the College of Wooster in 1914. In 1927 he became professor of economics at Xavier University, Cincinnati. His residence in 1960 was a rest home in Wooster. The author of many textbooks, he also wrote a notorious attack on President Harding's ancestry: *Warren Gamaliel Harding, President of the United States. A Review of Facts Collected from Anthropological, Historical and Political Researches,* [Wooster, 1922]. A less dubious claim to remembrance is the book *Our Presidents and Their Office . . . ,* New York, 1912. WW 26

CHANDLER, ALBERT RICHARD (May 25, 1884–March 22, 1957), educator, born in Norwich, Conn., was a member of the Ohio State University philosophy department, 1914–51. He graduated from Dartmouth in 1908 and from Harvard (Ph.D.) in 1913. He died in Worthington. He edited an anthology, published a bibliography on esthetics, and a book entitled *Rosenberg's Nazi Myth,* Ithaca, N. Y., 1945. WW 27

CHANDLER, CHARLES DeFOREST (Dec. 24, 1878–May 18, 1939), army officer, was born in Cleveland, Cuyahoga County. He served in the U. S. Army, 1898–1920, and was chief of the balloon section of the Air Service in France during World War I. In addition to several technical books and manuals, a book written with Frank P. Lahm was published posthumously: *How Our Army Grew Wings; Airmen and Aircraft before 1914,* New York, [1943]. WWW 1

CHANDLER, FRANK WADLEIGH (June 16, 1873–June 13, 1947), educator, was born in Brooklyn, N. Y. He graduated from Brooklyn Polytechnic Institute in 1891 and Columbia University (Ph.D.) in 1899. In 1910 he became professor of English and comparative literature at the University of Cincinnati. He retired in 1943. Besides a number of textbooks he wrote several critical studies, e.g., *Modern Continental Playwrights,* New York, 1931. WWW 2

CHANDLER-TUCKER, GERTRUDE LEE (Dec. 23, 1872–March 23, 1953), was born in Chandlerville, Ill. She spent part of her girlhood in Cleveland, and after her marriage to Stanley Tucker she lived in Willoughby. Under the name Gertrude Lee she published at least three collections of verse, e.g., *Scattered Gems,* Boston, [1930].

CHANNING, WILLIAM ELLERY (Nov. 29, 1818–Dec. 23, 1901), nephew of the founder of American Unitarianism, lived for a brief period in Cincinnati, where his uncle, James H. Perkins (q.v.), was a Unitarian minister. After deciding to discontinue his Harvard course of study, Channing went to Illinois in 1839, where he lived in a log hut for a time. He then went to Cincinnati, where he read law and wrote for the *Gazette.* He left in 1842 to settle in Concord, Mass., so that he could be near Emerson. Channing was a prolific and undisciplined poet. His best-known work is probably *Thoreau, the Poet-Naturalist,* Boston, 1873.

CHANNING, WILLIAM HENRY (May 25, 1810–Dec. 23, 1884), Unitarian minister, served as pastor of a Unitarian church in Cincinnati from 1839 to 1841. During the same period he edited the *Western Messenger.* A fairly prolific writer, he is best known for a three-volume biography of his uncle, William Ellery Channing: *The Life of William Ellery Channing,* Boston, 1848.

CHAPIN, HENRY DWIGHT (Feb. 4, 1857–June 27, 1942), physician and educator, was born in Steubenville, Jefferson County. He graduated from Princeton University in

1877 and the New York College of Physicians and Surgeons in 1881. He practiced in New York City and taught at the New York Post-Graduate Medical School and hospital. Besides his well-known *Diseases of Infants and Children* and other professional works, he wrote several books for popular consumption. His death occurred in Bronxville, N. Y.

Diphtheria, [New York, 1890].
Vital Questions, New York, [1905].
Health First, the Fine Art of Living, New York, 1917.
Heredity and Child Culture, New York, [1922].

CHAPMAN, ERVIN S. (June 23, 1838–Aug. 30, 1921), clergyman, was born in Defiance County. He entered the United Brethren ministry in 1870 and transferred to the Presbyterian Church in 1883; he served as a pastor in Ohio, Wyoming, and California. An active temperance advocate, he wrote many articles against liquor and *Latest Light on Abraham Lincoln, and War-Time Memories . . . ,* New York, [1917]. WWW 1

CHAPMAN, LEE JACKSON (Dec. 22, 1867–Feb. 14, 1953), physician, was born in central Texas and was named for Confederate generals. He studied at Lebanon University and Starling Medical College, Ohio State University. He lived and practiced in Columbus and in Lancaster. After losing his sight in a blasting accident in 1925, he began writing poems, a collection of which was published privately: *Human Sunshine,* Lancaster, 1930.

CHAPMAN, ROSE WOODALLEN (June 25, 1875–Oct. 27, 1923), writer and lecturer, daughter of Mary Wood-Allen (q.v.), was born in Lakeside, Ottawa County. She was active in the W.C.T.U. and in the American Social Hygiene Association. She lectured widely and wrote several books on child training, e.g., *The Moral Problem of the Children,* New York, [1911]. WWW 1

CHARLES, JOAN. Pseud. See Charlotte W. Underwood.

CHARLESWORTH, RUBY HUGHES (May 27, 1905–), was born in Greenville, Darke County. She attended public schools in Greenville and graduated from Asbury College, Wilmore, Ky. She has published a novel, *Rain on the Roof,* Philadelphia, [1947].

CHASE, JESSIE MacMILLAN ANDERSON (May 6, 1865–June 28, 1949), was born in Cincinnati, Hamilton County. After graduating from Smith College in 1886, she was a tutor in Latin and Greek at Milton Academy. After marrying Robert S. Anderson, an artist, she made her home in Boston. Besides the titles below, she wrote several textbooks.

Three Freshmen; Ruth, Fran, and Nathalie, Boston, 1898.
Mayken; A Child's Story of the Netherlands in the Sixteenth Century, Chicago, 1902.
A Daughter of the Revolution, Boston, 1910.
Chan's Wife; A Story, Boston, 1919.
The Story of Paul Revere, Junior; Revolutionary Days in Old Boston, Boston, [1932].

CHASE, JOHN A. (c.1828–May 13, 1907), lawyer, was born in Trenton, Mich. During the Civil War he raised ten companies for service and was colonel of the 14th O.V.I. He afterward practiced law in Toledo, and his death occurred in that city.

History of the Fourteenth Ohio Regiment . . . , Toledo, 1881.

CHASE, PHILANDER (Dec. 14, 1775–Sept. 20, 1852), the first bishop of the Protestant Episcopal Church in Ohio and, later on, in Illinois, founder of Kenyon College at Gambier, was born at Cornish, N. H., as the fifteenth child of a Congregational family. While studying at Dartmouth College (1791–96), he joined the Episcopal Church. After graduation, a year and a half of theological study under an Anglican clergyman equipped him with what was considered sufficient for ordination in those days; already married since 1796, he was ordained deacon in 1798 and priest in 1799. An enthusiastic missionary all through his life, he started his career with missions work in upper New York State. After having been rector in Poughkeepsie, N. Y. (1799–1805), New Orleans (1805–11), and Hartford, Conn. (1811–17), he came to Ohio in 1817 as one of the first missionaries of his church to minister to a sparse population of Episcopalians. His feverish and adventurous activity in preaching and organizing parishes in widely scattered places all over the new state made him conspicuous at once among the few clergymen in Ohio, and in 1818 he was elected bishop of the newly established diocese. The task of organizing the diocese in a half-wilderness which had just been opened up to settlement, with new settlers coming in great numbers, appealed to his pioneer instincts. Strong in will and body;

unafraid of any kind of work, whether clerical, manual, or agricultural; enjoying hardships rather than avoiding them; entirely free of fear and unshakable in his belief in God's providence, he defied the difficulties of his missionary work. Since no salary was connected with his position as a bishop, he made a living by running a farm at Worthington, sometimes without help, and for one year (1821–22) by directing Cincinnati College as its president. At the same time he provided, off and on, the parishes at Delaware, Berkshire, Worthington, and Columbus with his ministrations, and traveled widely on horseback over the state in his episcopal visitations. The development of the diocese depended on additions to its clerical personnel. Disappointed in his expectations of receiving missionary help from the East, Chase conceived the plan of educating his own clergy in a school to be established within the diocese. Ohio was too poor to finance his plan and solicitations in the East did not help; Chase, an enterprising and untiring traveler, went to England in 1823 to collect money for his plan. The idea met with strong disapproval and active opposition, even from the American episcopate. Chase nevertheless succeeded in finding sponsors among the English nobility and moneyed church people. The idealistic sincerity of his appeal and the unceasing flow of his eloquence, combined with a shrewd utilization of personal contacts as soon as they were established, brought him the considerable result of about $30,000, enough to make at least a start. Meanwhile, his plan for a theological seminary, for which there were no satisfactorily prepared candidates in the Middle West, had broadened into the idea of an institution able to give preparatory education, as well as theological training. Originally incorporated in 1824 as the Theological Seminary of the Protestant Episcopal Church in Ohio and beginning its activities at Chase's farm at Worthington, the school developed quickly into a grammar school and college in which theological training played only a minor part. In 1826, Chase found a location which he considered ideal: a hill in the wilderness, five miles from Mt. Vernon; a "retreat of virtue in seclusion from the vices of the World." There he built his school, named Kenyon College for his foremost English benefactor, and founded a village which he gave the name of another English sponsor, Lord Gambier. Old Kenyon, the oldest hall of the college and the first attempt at Collegiate Gothic in America, was built in 1827–29. It was destroyed by fire in 1949 and has since been rebuilt. For a few years, Chase ruled his college on the strict principles of what he called "patriarchal" government, largely with the assistance of his efficient second wife, Sophia Ingraham Chase. She and a few other members of the family were the only collaborators who ever possessed his full confidence. A born autocrat, compared by one of his biographers to Wellington and Czar Nicholas of Russia, Chase alienated both his college faculty and the diocesan clergy and laity by his domineering ways and his lack of regard for other people's feelings. He demanded unqualified submission to his will from everybody. In 1831, in consequence of a "conspiracy," he rashly resigned his episcopacy and retired to a farm in Michigan. Four years later, he accepted the election as bishop of the new diocese of Illinois, where he spent the rest of his life doing once more what he had done in his Ohio years: preaching, organizing, traveling, but on an even larger scale; he even begged another diocesan school (Jubilee College, near Peoria: founded 1838, now extinct). In 1843, he succeeded, by seniority, to the position of Presiding Bishop of the Protestant Episcopal Church. Generally respected rather than beloved, he died by an accident at Jubilee College on Sept. 20, 1852. The Church, both in Ohio and in Illinois, owes much to his vision and energy. He was entirely unselfish and capable of great sacrifice; his whole life was devoutly dedicated to what he considered God's will, which, however, as forceful characters of his type will do, he occasionally identified with his own intentions. It remains true for the whole of his career that, as his parishioners at Hartford stated in 1818: "His zeal may sometimes have transcended the limits of prudence." As a monument to Chase, the Chase Tower, in which a series of stained-glass windows by J. C. Connick presents his life story in a most original style, was erected at Kenyon College in 1927. Chase's literary activity was subordinated to his missionary and educational aims. Besides his utterances in official capacity—episcopal addresses and pastoral letters—he published some sermons, and numerous appeals, broadsides, and pamphlets for his cause. This material is partly polemical in character and not always pleasant. Often the good intentions of the fund-raiser and the controversialist get the better of a due sense of proportion. In 1841–44 Chase published his only large work, the *Reminiscences* (Seven issues: 1–4, Peoria, 1841–42; 5–7, New York, 1843–44). A second, enlarged, edition in two volumes appeared in Boston in 1848. Describing life in New England before 1800, in New Orleans at the beginning of the nineteenth century, in Ohio and Illinois between 1817 and 1848, the book will retain a certain value as a source; some chapters give vivid pictures of genuine adventure. For the most part, however, the unctuous and flowery style, the frequent stress on the author's "sufferings" and unmeasured breadth, make the work hard reading even as a period piece. For long stretches, the narrative is interrupted by a printed file of Chase's enormous correspondence, with little discrimination between wheat and chaff. The *Motto,* a journal which Chase published and, for the greater part, wrote himself in his last years at Jubilee College (1847–52), is a miscellany of tracts, correspondence, diocesan notes, and polemics.

R. G. Salomon

The Star in the West, or Kenyon College . . . , [Columbus?, 1828].

Bishop Chase's Defence of Himself against the Late Conspiracy at Gambier . . . , [Steubenville, 1831].

Defence of Kenyon College, Columbus, 1831.

The Reminiscences of Bishop Chase . . . , New York, 1844.

Bishop Chase's Defence against the Slanders of the Rev. G. M. West, [n.p., n.d.].

CHASE, SALMON PORTLAND (Jan. 13, 1808–May 7, 1873), lawyer and statesman, was born in Cornish, N. H. In 1820, with his brother and H. H. Schoolcraft, he came to Ohio. He spent three years in Worthington and Cincinnati, living with his uncle, Philander Chase (q.v.). In 1823, he entered Dartmouth and later read law in Washington, D. C., with William Wirt. In 1830, he returned to Cincinnati to practice and soon acquired a reputation as an antislavery man. His *Statutes of Ohio* was a milestone in the development of Ohio law. The *Sketch* listed below was originally published as an introduction to the first volume of the larger work. Chase was elected to the Senate in 1849; he also served for a time as Lincoln's Secretary of the Treasury and as Chief Justice of the Supreme Court during the Reconstruction period. Many of his political speeches and letters were published separately.

A Sketch of the History of Ohio, Cincinnati, 1833.

Statutes of Ohio, 3 vols., Cincinnati, 1833–35.

CHEFFEY, JESSIE ANN (July 24, 1895–), nurse, born in Waterford, Washington County, still lives in that community. A graduate of Washington County Normal School and the Chautauqua School of Nursing, she has taught in elementary schools and done private nursing. Her poems have appeared in many periodicals and anthologies, and she has published a collection: *Jewels by the Wayside,* New York, [1942].

CHENEY, FRANK J. (March 16, 1851–Oct. 30, 1919), who was born in Conneaut, Ashtabula County, was president of the Cheney Medicine Co., Toledo, and lived in that city for many years before his death. He published two collections of stories, e.g., *A Life of Unity and Other Stories,* Toledo, 1901.

CHERRINGTON, ERNEST HURST (Nov. 24, 1877–March 13, 1950), editor and temperance advocate, was born in Hamden, Vinton County. A graduate of Ohio Wesleyan University in 1897, he was active in the Anti-Saloon League and worked on newspapers in various cities. At the time of his death he lived in Westerville. His writings, all relating to the temperance movement, include *The Evolution of Prohibition . . . ,* Westerville, [1920]. WWW 2

CHERRY, PETER PATTERSON (Sept. 17, 1848–April 11, 1937), was born in Neshanic, N. J.; his parents moved to Sharon, Medina County, in 1856. A lifelong cripple, he was driving a stage between Akron and Cleveland at the age of twelve. He taught school in Wadsworth Township and edited the Sharon *Tidal Wave,* the *Young Folks' Gem,* and other papers. In 1880 he moved to Akron, where he worked in the offices of B. F. Goodrich Co. for many years. He was deeply interested in local history and archaeology and published articles on those subjects, in addition to the titles below.

The Grave-Creek Mound . . . , Wadsworth, 1877.

Curious Stones from the Stone Age, Wadsworth, 1878.

The Portage Path, Akron, 1911.

The Western Reserve and Early Ohio, Akron, 1921.

CHESELDINE, RAYMOND MINSHALL (April 4, 1892–Dec. 24, 1954), army officer, was born in London, Madison County. He graduated from Ohio Wesleyan University and from the Washington College of Law. He served in the army in both World Wars and retired as a colonel in 1951. During World War II he was an aide to Gen. Lucius D. Clay. He also served on the Federal Reserve Board. His death occurred in Corona, Calif. He contributed a number of military papers to professional publications and published *Ohio in the Rainbow: Official Story of the 166th Infantry, 42nd Division, in the World War,* Columbus, 1924.

CHESLEY, MARTIN. Pseud. See Chesley M. Hutchings.

CHESNUTT, CHARLES WADDELL (June 20, 1858–Nov. 15, 1932), novelist, was born in Cleveland, Cuyahoga County, the year after the Dred Scott decision and the year before the South made its last aggressive attempt to reopen the slave trade. It was a period of mounting national tension and the tension was to strike deeply into the imagination of the growing boy. While Charles was still an infant, the family moved for a short time to Oberlin, then an important station in the Underground Railroad. His father participated in the famous Oberlin-Wellington Rescue and, when the Civil War broke out, enlisted in the Union Army and served throughout the war. Long after, Chesnutt was to recall these formative years and to realize how they had impressed him and molded his character and career. He was to relate to his family how he had listened with awe to the singing of the new "Battle Hymn of the Republic." The vision of the Lord trampling out the vintage from the "grapes of wrath" was a vision of reality and eternal justice. He was to recall, too, holding his mother's hand and, with thousands of other Cleveland citizens, filing in deep silence past the bier of the martyred President lying in state in Cleveland's Public Square. Child though he was, he somehow caught the emanation of greatness and was moved and influenced by it. The year after the close of the Civil War, the Chesnutt family returned to their home in Fayetteville, N. C., which they had left a decade earlier in their search for a fuller life in the North. Here Charles attended the Howard School, at fourteen became a pupil-teacher, and at sixteen went to Charlotte as a regular teacher. In the summer, teaching in small ungraded country schools, he was moved with compassion as daily he faced his little group of ignorant but poignantly eager children. Young Chesnutt started a journal in which he recorded the intimate details of his life. Intent on his own education, he devoured history and biography, read the English classics, memorized vast amounts of poetry, gave himself a course in higher mathematics, and, entirely by himself, learned Latin, French, and German. Fortunately for him, a noted language teacher, Professor Neufeld, had come to Fayetteville to hold classes in French and German for those wealthy enough to take advantage of such opportunity. Neufeld, a German Jew by birth and a former student of T. H. Huxley, consented to give Chesnutt private lessons although friends had warned him that, in doing so, he would lose some of his white pupils. Chesnutt wrote in his journal: "A fellow-feeling makes us wondrous kind," for Neufeld had declared that he was "quite able to lose twenty pupils without experiencing any inconvenience." Neufeld, impressed by young Chesnutt's obvious zeal and accomplishments, "broke the color line"; Chesnutt, in turn, with such expert help made French and German an integral part of his equipment as a writer and student of society. At nineteen Chesnutt was appointed assistant principal of the New Fayetteville State Normal School, established to train teachers for the colored schools. Three years later he became its principal. Alone with his journal in the evenings, Chesnutt poured out his inmost thoughts and aspirations: "I think I must write a book. If I do write I shall write for a purpose, a high, holy purpose, and this will inspire me to greater effort. The object of my writing would not be so much the elevation of the colored people, as the elevation of the whites—for I consider the unjust spirit of caste which is so insidious as to pervade a whole nation, and so powerful as to subject a whole race to scorn and social ostracism—I consider this a barrier to the moral progress of the American people." In 1878, Chesnutt married. Two daughters were born of the union. Considering their future as well as his own, Chesnutt wrote in the spring of 1882: "I shudder to think of exposing my children to the social and intellectual proscription to which I have been a victim." To escape these circumstances, he needed a means of support. He set himself to master stenography, the art which held the promise of independence for him and his family. He studied and practiced assiduously, calling upon his wife for dictation until, as he relates in his journal, he almost worried Susan into a "positive dislike" for him. By the following spring Chesnutt had succeeded. He could write two hundred words a minute. To the regret of all his friends and associates, he left Fayetteville for New York City. He found work as a reporter for a Wall Street news agency and later wrote a daily column called "Wall Street Gossip" for the New York *Mail and Express.* His real opportunity, however, came some months later in Cleveland, the city of his birth, where in the law office of Judge Samuel E. Williamson, he worked as a stenographer and studied law. Established now, Chesnutt sent for his family, settled them in a comfortable home, and began to write in earnest. The *Atlantic Monthly* published the first of his "conjure" stories in 1887. In the same year he was admitted to the Ohio bar, standing at the head of his class. In 1890 he set up in business as a court reporter, a business which he followed for the rest of his life. During the decade of the 1890s he spent all his spare time in writing. In 1900 and 1901, he even closed his business office in order that nothing might stand between him and his ambition to bridge the race problem, to make some contribution to what Myrdal was to describe later as The American Dilemma. Chesnutt's contribution was at once simple and profound. He wrote about Negroes as human beings, as persons, not as types or subtypes. This was indeed a new departure in literature, for no white writer had done this and the colored race in this country had, as yet, no recognized literary spokesman. Chesnutt was fortunate in having Houghton, Mifflin and Company as his publishers. The members of the firm were deeply interested in the "Negro problem." Walter Hines Page, literary adviser for the firm and editor of the *Atlantic Monthly,* approved Chesnutt's approach to the problem and greatly admired his literary skill and art in presenting it. They became warm friends. The year 1899 was outstanding for Chesnutt. Two volumes of his short stories were published by Houghton, Mifflin and Company. *The Conjure Woman,* published in March, is a collection of stories in Negro dialect told by "Uncle Julius." They are simple, moving tales about the days of slavery and the activities of old Aunt Peggy, the plantation conjure woman. This book, widely acclaimed, headed the list of best-sellers in Cleveland during the month of April. The Rowfant Club, of which Chesnutt later became a member, persuaded Houghton, Mifflin to issue a special numbered edition of 150 copies for which members of the club and of the Cleveland bar subscribed. *The Wife of his Youth and Other Stories of the Color Line,* published in Dec., 1899, contains stories about people of mixed blood living mainly in the North. Chesnutt's aim in these stories was to put understanding and tenderness for the Negro into the hearts of his readers. Two of the greatest literary critics of the period wrote essays about these books: Hamilton Wright Mabie, in the *Outlook* of Feb. 24, 1900, and William Dean Howells, in the *Atlantic Monthly* of May, 1900. Both of these critics placed Chesnutt in the top rank of American short story writers. In this same year, Chesnutt wrote a biography of the great abolitionist Frederick Douglass for the series called *The Beacon Biographies of Eminent Americans,* published by Small, Maynard and Company of Boston. The *Encyclopaedia Britannica* lists this as one of the standard works on the life of Douglass. *The House behind the Cedars,* Chesnutt's most popular novel, was published in Oct., 1900. This is a love story, romantic and tragic, touching upon the theme of intermarriage, which up to that time had been considered untouchable in American literature. It was called by the critics "the most notable novel of the month," and had gone into its fourth printing by April, 1901. *The Marrow of Tradition* was published in Oct., 1901, just after Theodore Roosevelt had invited Booker T. Washington to dinner at the White House to discuss the Negro problem and its bearing on the political situation. This act by the President aroused great indignation in the South and produced an avalanche of bitter condemnation of Roosevelt and his policy of "social equality." This novel, written at white heat after a visit to the South, presents for the first time in American literature the conflict between the white leaders of the South and the educated, cultured colored people there. The story is told with extraordinary skill and with great dramatic power. The Northern papers expressed unqualified praise for it; the critics acclaimed it as the most important book on the Negro since *Uncle Tom's Cabin;* but the Southern press denounced it as a bitter and libelous attack upon the white people in their relations with the Negro. It was an acknowledged literary success and was rated by the *Outlook* among the twenty-five books of the year. But the South had gained a hearing in the North and, to the astonishment and bitter disappointment of Chesnutt and his publishers, *The Marrow of Tradition* was not the financial success that they had expected. Chesnutt's last book, *The Colonel's Dream,* was published by Doubleday, Page and Company in Sept., 1905, and was issued in England by Archibald Constable and Company. This was written with the avowed purpose of exposing peonage and the convict lease system which were making the lives of the Negro masses far more wretched than in the days of slavery. Many people thought it his best book and gave it great praise, but America was tired of reading about the wrongs done to the Negro, and it was not as popular as his other books. The Southern press, as usual, denounced it bitterly and claimed that his stories of cruelty and injustice to the Negro were not only "false but impossible!" In Dec., 1905, Colonel George Harvey, president of Harper and Brothers, invited Chesnutt along with one hundred and fifty of America's most distinguished writers of imaginative literature to attend Mark Twain's seventieth birthday party at Delmonico's in New York City. This party, proclaimed as one of the most important events in the history of American literature, was considered by Chesnutt as the peak of his literary career. His days as a novelist and writer of short stories were practically over by then. He had thoroughly alienated the greater part of the white reading public by his outspoken stand for recognition of the Negro as a human being and an American citizen, and by his demand for civil rights and equality of opportunity. Once again, business and civic matters claimed his full time. In Cleveland and throughout the country, Chesnutt was recognized as the champion of the Negro. As president of the Council of Sociology (from which organization the Cleveland Welfare Federation was developed) and as a member of the Cleveland Chamber of Commerce, his opportunities to work for the advancement of the Negro were, of course, greatly increased. He wrote many articles and lectured frequently in various cities on the problems of the colored citizens of our country. In 1928 he was awarded the Spingarn Medal for his "pioneer work as a literary artist depicting the life and struggles of Americans of Negro descent, and for his long and useful career as scholar, worker, and freeman of one of America's greatest cities."

Helen M. Chesnutt

The Conjure Woman, Boston, 1899.
Frederick Douglass, Boston, 1899.
The Wife of His Youth, and Other Stories of the Color Line, Boston, 1899.
The House behind the Cedars, Boston, 1900.
The Marrow of Tradition, Boston, 1901.
The Colonel's Dream, New York, 1905.

CHESTER, GEORGE RANDOLPH (1869–Feb. 26, 1924), was born in Ohio (according to one account, his birthplace was in Cincinnati, Hamilton County). Although he achieved considerable celebrity, few specific details regarding his early life are available. He left home at an early age and worked at various jobs throughout the country. He was a reporter on the Detroit *News* for several years before returning to Cincinnati, where he worked on the *Enquirer,* 1901–08. "The Strike Breaker," a story in *McClure's,* was his first work to attract national attention. He wrote stories for *Cosmopolitan* and other national magazines and also worked for various motion-picture companies as a writer and director. His best-known work was *Get-Rich-Quick Wallingford,* New York, [1908], which was also the basis of a play by George M. Cohan. Chester died in New York City and is buried in Cincinnati. DAB 4

CHEYFITZ, EDWARD THEODORE (Sept. 13, 1913–), labor union official, was born in Montreal, Canada. After graduating from the University of Michigan in 1934, he was an official of the Mine, Mill and Smelter Workers, C.I.O., in Toledo until 1946. He resigned to take a position with the Moving Picture Association of America, which he resigned in 1951 to study law. He has written pamphlets and magazine articles on labor questions and a book: *Constructive Collective Bargaining,* New York, 1947. WWL

CHIDLAW, BENJAMIN WILLIAMS (July 14, 1811–July 14, 1892), clergyman, was born in Bala, Wales. In 1821 his parents emigrated to Delaware County, where the boy received his primary education in a log schoolhouse; he later attended Philander Chase's academy at Worthington. He graduated from Miami University in 1833. Ordained by the Presbytery of Oxford in 1835, he settled over a Welsh Congregational Church at Paddy's Run, Butler County, where he preached and taught in Welsh and English, 1836–43. He was employed by the American Sunday School Union in Cincinnati; during this association, which was continued for many years, he established many Sunday schools. While on a visit to Wales in 1840, he published an account in Welsh of his trip from Ohio, a history of the Welsh settlements in America, and advice to those about to emigrate to the United States. During the Civil War he served for a time as chaplain of the 39th O.V.I. His autobiography contains a splendid account of his early days in Ohio. He died in Wales while visiting his birthplace.

Yr American, Yr Hwn Sydd yn Cynnwys Nodau ar Daith o Ddyffryn Ohio I Gymru, Golwg ar Dalaeth Ohio; Hanes Sefydliadau Cymreig yn America; Cyfarwyddiadau I Ymofynwyr Cyn y Daith, ac yn y Wlad, Llanrwst, Wales, 1840.
The Story of My Life, Philadelphia, [1890].

CHIPMAN, H. G. (1827–1852), journalist, was born in Cincinnati, Hamilton County. He began his literary career by writing for the *Great West*. He served as a volunteer in the Mexican War, and after his return he published a series of sketches that were extensively copied and highly commended. Other series, published in the *Enquirer* and the *Commercial*, also attracted considerable attention. He worked as a printer, and in 1850 was one of the proprietors and editors of the *Nonpareil*.

Lilly of Senora, Cincinnati, 1849.

CHIPMAN, NORTON PARKER (March 7, 1838–Feb. 1, 1924), lawyer and judge, was born in Milford, Clermont County. After graduating from Cincinnati Law School in 1859, he practiced in Iowa. He served throughout the Civil War, rising to the rank of brigadier general. From 1871 to 1875 he was delegate to Congress from the District of Columbia; many of his speeches in the House were printed as pamphlets. In 1875 he went to California, where he became presiding justice of the District Court of Appeals, San Francisco. As president of the California Board of Trade, he wrote articles and pamphlets on the industries and resources of the state.

The Horrors of Andersonville Rebel Prison . . . , San Francisco, 1891.

The Tragedy of Andersonville; Trial of Captain Henry Wirz, the Prison Keeper, [Sacramento?, Calif.], 1911.

CHISHOLM, BELLE V. (Aug. 30, 1843– ?), was born in Beaver County, Pa. In 1863 she moved with her parents to New Concord, Muskingum County. She attended Muskingum College, and after teaching school for a time she married Dr. Isaac W. Chisholm of Zanesville. Besides the titles below, she published fiction in various periodicals.

Who Wins? . . . , Philadelphia, 1888.

In Search of a Home, Philadelphia, 1890.

Stephen Lyle, Gentleman and Philanthropist, Cincinnati, 1891.

Consecrated Anew . . . , Philadelphia, [1893].

CHRISTY, DAVID (1802– ?), journalist, was editor of the *Harrison Telegraph*, published in Cadiz, from 1824 until 1836. While in Cadiz, he edited the *Historical Family Library* (1835–36) and began editing the five-volume *Calvinistic Family Library* (1835–44). After leaving Cadiz, he lived in Oxford for a time and then moved to Cincinnati, where, according to tradition, his printing outfit was thrown into the Ohio River because of his antislavery tendencies. In 1848 he was appointed agent of the American Colonization Society and undertook to raise money to purchase a tract of land in Africa to be known as "Ohio in Africa" and to be used as a site for a free settlement for Negroes. He appeared before the Ohio Legislature in 1849, when that body was engaged in a hot debate over the repeal of the "Black Laws," which were designed to prevent the immigration of Negroes into Ohio. Christy delivered lectures on colonization before the legislature which were later published as a pamphlet. His *Lectures on African Colonization* was republished in 1857 as *Ethiopia: Her Gloom and Glory*. His most important work, *Cotton Is King*, which was published anonymously, was intended to convince abolitionists of the failure of their efforts. It is said to have been consulted by Lincoln. Christy had a natural aptitude for science; he reported on geological observations in periodicals and for a time held a position with a mineral company.

H. B. McConnell

Letters on Geology . . . , Rossville, 1848.

The Spirit Rappings, Mesmerism, Clairvoyance, and Psychometry . . . , Cincinnati, 1851.

Republic of Liberia. Facts for Thinking Men . . . , [Cleveland], 1852.

Lectures on African Colonization and Kindred Subjects, Columbus, 1853.

Cotton Is King . . . , Cincinnati, 1855.

The Southern Highlands, As Adapted to Pasturage and Grape Culture, Cincinnati, 1858.

Pulpit Politics; Or, Ecclesiastical Legislation on Slavery, in Its Disturbing Influence on the American Union, Cincinnati, 1862.

CHRISTY, WILBUR A. (1845–1928), clergyman, was born in Kinsman, Trumbull County. He wrote at least two books on religious themes, e.g., *The Theory of Immersion Considered* . . . , Louisville, Ky., [1926].

CHRONIQUEUSE. Pseud. See Olive Logan.

CHUBB, EDWIN WATTS (Aug. 25, 1865–July 23, 1959), educator, was born in Lebanon, Pa. He graduated from Lafayette College in 1887 and later studied at the University of Berlin. After teaching at Schuylkill Seminary, California State Normal School, and Platteville State Normal School, he joined the faculty of Ohio University in 1900. He taught English there, served as dean, and twice was acting president. Besides a number of textbooks, he wrote *Stories of Authors, British and American,* New York, 1910. WW 21

CHURTON, HENRY. Pseud. See Albion W. Tourgee.

CIRACI, NORMA (June 11, 1922–), novelist, born in Cleveland, Cuyahoga County, attended public schools in that city. She attended Northwestern University, 1940–42, dropped out of school to work as a waitress, factory hand, and taxi driver, then returned to Northwestern and graduated in 1945. The result of her experiences in Florida and elsewhere was a vivid first novel: *Detour,* New York, 1947.

CIST, CHARLES (April 24, 1793–Sept. 8, 1868), born in Philadelphia, Pa., was the son of Charles Cist (1738–1805), a noted Philadelphia printer and publisher who, during the administration of John Adams, was the first public printer. The boy was educated in Philadelphia. After the War of 1812, he moved first to Pittsburgh and then to Harmony, Pa., where he operated a store and served as postmaster. He moved to Cincinnati in 1827. He compiled the Cincinnati directories of 1842 and 1843 and, in the latter year, established a family journal, *The Weekly Advertiser.* Intensely interested in the early history of Ohio, he encouraged competent writers to submit authentic articles on the early history and statistics of the state. With slight changes in its masthead, the *Advertiser* was continued until 1853. In Oct., 1845, he began publishing the monthly *Cincinnati Miscellany,* in which appeared not only much of the best historical material which had been printed in the *Advertiser* but a number of new contributions, the most important of which was Colonel J. Johnston's superb serial, *Recollections of the Last Sixty Years.* The *Miscellany* was suspended with the issue of March, 1846. Cist's best-known works are his annals of Cincinnati: *Cincinnati in 1841; Sketches and Statistics of Cincinnati in 1851;* and *Sketches and Statistics of Cincinnati in 1859.* In the first of these is a review of the early annals of the city drawn from contemporary newspapers and a full, graphic letter written by John Cleves Symmes to his partner, Jonathan Dayton, in 1789. Fortified with the priceless material which he had collected for the *Advertiser,* he devoted over 150 pages of the issue of 1859 to the city's early annals, a most important supplement to his earlier account. Cist's works are invaluable sources. His death occurred in Cincinnati.

Ernest J. Wessen

Cincinnati in 1841: Its Early Annals and Future Prospects, Cincinnati, 1841.
Sketches and Statistics of Cincinnati in 1851, Cincinnati, 1851.
Sketches and Statistics of Cincinnati in 1859, [Cincinnati, 1859].

CIST, HENRY MARTYN (Feb. 20, 1838–Dec. 17, 1902), born in Cincinnati, Hamilton County, was the son of Charles Cist (q.v.). He graduated from Farmers' College, Cincinnati, in 1858 and then studied law. In 1861 he enlisted as a private in the O.V.I.; he saw much service and advanced through the ranks to the brevet of brigadier general. After the war he returned to the practice of law in Cincinnati and assumed the office of corresponding secretary of the Society of the Army of the Cumberland. He contributed many articles on the Civil War to periodicals and edited the reports of the Society of the Army of the Cumberland, which extended to seventeen volumes. His death occurred in Rome, Italy.

The Army of the Cumberland. New York, 1882.
The Romance of Shiloh, [Cincinnati, 1895?].

CIST, LEWIS JACOB (Nov. 30, 1818–March 30, 1885), born in Harmony, Pa., was the eldest son of Charles Cist (q.v.). When he was nine years old, his parents moved to Cincinnati, where the boy attended school. After studying at Hanover College he was employed by the Commercial Bank of Cincinnati and later became teller of the Ohio Life and Trust Company. He was engaged in the banking business in St. Louis, 1850–70. In 1870 he returned to Cincinnati, where he spent the rest of his days. He was for many years secretary of the Cincinnati Zoological Gardens. Before going to St. Louis he wrote considerable verse, which appeared in the *Western Monthly Review,* the *Hesperian,* and his father's *Weekly Advertiser.* He became widely known as a leading collector of autographs. In America, his collection was excelled only by the great William E. Sprague collection. It was sold in New York in 1886 and 1887.

Trifles in Verse; A Collection of Fugitive Poems, Cincinnati, 1845.

CLAFLIN, TENNIE. Pseud. See Tennessee C. C. Cook.

CLARK, ALEXANDER (March 10, 1834–July 6, 1879), clergyman, was born near Wellsville, Jefferson County. After teaching school for five years, he was ordained to the Methodist ministry in 1861, and served churches in Pennsylvania and Ohio. He became editor of the *Methodist Recorder* in 1870. His death occurred in Atlanta, Ga., while he was making a Southern trip.

The Old Log Schoolhouse . . ., Philadelphia, 1859.
The Red Sea Freedman, Philadelphia, 1864.
The Gospel in the Trees . . ., Philadelphia, 1868.
Memory's Tribute to the Life Character and Work of the Rev. T. H. Stockton, New York, 1869.
Workaday Christianity . . . , New York, 1870.
Starting Out: A Story of the Ohio Hills, Philadelphia, 1875.
Summer Rambles in Europe, New York, 1877.

CLARK, CHARLES THEODORE (Jan. 17, 1845–April 19, 1911), who was born in Dalton, Wayne County, served as a captain in the 125th O.V.I. from Sept., 1862, to Sept., 1865. Ryan described his book as "one of the best" regimental histories. Clark also lived in Trumbull County; his death occurred in Franklin County.

Opdycke Tigers, 125th O.V.I. . . . , Columbus, 1895.

CLARK, CYNTHIA CHARLOTTE MOON (Aug. 10, 1829–Nov. 20, 1895), Confederate spy, lecturer, author, and newspaperwoman, was born in Danville, Va. Her father, Robert S. Moon, was one of "the Albemarle Moons" of Virginia. In the early 1830s, Robert Moon and his wife (Cynthia A. Sullivan) came to Oxford, Butler County, to live. At the age of five, their third child and eldest daughter, Cynthia Charlotte, was memorizing selections from the best English poets and studying the Latin language. Under the tutelage of her scholarly father, she became well grounded in languages, history, and literature. As a young woman, "Lottie" Moon was not beautiful, but she was a dainty little sprite, with rosy cheeks, sparkling deep-set gray eyes, a wealth of soft brown hair, and beautiful hands. She was a brilliant conversationalist, a wit, a superb mimic, an unconscionable flirt and prankster. One of her maddest pranks was the jilting of young Ambrose E. Burnside at the altar, in Brownsville, Ind. The patient Burnside, however, courted her until she married James Clark, a graduate of Miami University and the Cincinnati Law School. Charlotte Moon met her match in James Clark. On the evening of Jan. 30, 1849, he arrived at the Moon home determined not to suffer the fate of Burnside. When he met "Lottie" at the head of the stairs to go down to the parlor to be married, he pulled a small revolver from his pocket and whispered, "There will be a wedding here tonight or a funeral tomorrow." There was a wedding. The Clarks established their home at Jones Station, near Hamilton, the county seat of Butler County. James was a rising young attorney in Hamilton. On an independent ticket, he was elected judge of the common pleas court in 1855. In the exciting campaign of 1856, "Mrs. Judge Clark" organized the women of Butler County to take an active part in the campaign. With enthusiasm they made a silken banner to be offered as a prize to the township having the largest attendance at a Democratic rally. Mrs. Clark made the first presentation with a short but stirring patriotic speech. Throughout the Civil War, the Clarks ardently supported Clement L. Vallandigham (q.v.). Judge Clark was a strict Constitutionalist and boldly declared his views. He was considered "the brains of the Butler County Copperheads." The Clarks and Virginia Moon, youngest sister of Mrs. Clark, played important roles in the Great Northwest Conspiracy in which the Knights of the Golden Circle plotted with the Confederate government to join forces and bring the war to a close on Northern soil. The Clark home at Jones Station was a supply base for the Confederacy and hiding place for Confederate spies and soldiers in need of help. Mrs. Clark performed many perilous missions for the Knights of the Golden Circle and the Confederacy. She and her sister Virginia were intimate friends of Jefferson Davis. Posing as an English invalid traveling for her health, she once tricked Secretary of War Stanton, President Lincoln, and George B. McClellan into passing her through Union lines. She was carrying important dispatches to Jefferson Davis. In Richmond, she was known as "the embassadress of the North." In April, 1863, upon her return to Cincinnati from one of these missions, she found her mother and sister in the custody of General Ambrose E. Burnside at his headquarters at the Burnet House. They had been arrested on board the *Alice Dean* as they were about to sail for Memphis, Tenn., with medical supplies and mail for the South. With a stout heart, Charlotte faced the General, pretending not to know him, and asked for a pass to the South. She was quietly placed under guard and confined to the fashionable Spencer House for a time. After her release, she disappeared from Ohio. In 1864, the Knights of the Golden Circle became the Sons of Liberty, and Vallandigham was their Supreme Commander. The crushing defeat of Vallandigham by John Brough in the race for the governorship of Ohio in that year shattered the grandiose plans of those involved in the Great Northwest Conspiracy. Early in December, Judge Clark left Butler County forever. The Clarks went to New York City, a Copperhead stronghold, to live. Judge Clark practiced law and wrote regularly for the New York *Ledger,* a literary magazine having a weekly circulation of more than 400,000. Mrs. Clark wrote for the New York *World,* an important Copperhead paper. In poetry, Charlotte Clark could express deep emotions with great power. After the war was over, her poem "Peace" appeared in Southern newspapers and magazines under her own name. It was a moving lamentation for the Lost Cause. In 1870, Charlotte was sent to Paris as a correspondent of the New York *World* during the Franco-Prussian War. She was presented at court by the American Minister. From Paris, she went to London, where she became identified with an artistic and literary set. One night, at a card party in the stately home of Edward Bulwer-Lytton, she was challenged to write a book in which a woman would be the wielder of power. Lord Lytton said to her, "It is a gallant battle cry, 'Place aux Dames.' You will succeed." Charlotte replied, "In such a combat and with such a cause, Lord Lytton, there is no such word as fail." Upon her return to the United States, Mrs. Clark lectured in the principal cities of the North with much success under the *nom de plume* of "Chalk Level." Her lectures dealt with social and economic conditions in France, England, and the United States. A lecture on literature was entitled "Literary Bohemia." The work promised Lord Lytton and his friends appeared in 1878 under the name of Charles M. Clay. The initials of Mrs. Clark's pseudonym matched her own, and Clay was the name of her maternal grandmother. The book was published under the title of *How She Came into Her Kingdom.* One critic wrote that this was the "maddest book of the season," but fascinating because of the author's "unrivalled powers of expression." Others compared her to Jules Verne, George Eliot, and Charlotte Brontë in imagination and dramatic power. A second edition of this sensational novel was published in 1880. White and Stokes brought out a third edition entitled *A Daughter of the Gods* in 1883. A fourth edition was published under the same title in Dodd's Dollar Novels series in 1885. A second novel, *Baby Rue,* appeared in the No Name series. Mrs. Clark's two-volume work, *The Modern Hagar,* was published in the Kaaterskill series in 1882. The New York *Times* found it "easy to praise and easy to find fault with . . . but impossible to ignore." The next year, a one-volume edition was issued. The author's wide acquaintance with politics and economics supported the assumption that "Charles M. Clay" was a man. Even Jefferson Davis was deceived. A popular book which went through several editions—*More True Than Truthful* (1887)—has been incorrectly ascribed to her. It was written by Mrs. Charles Montague Clay. After the death of her husband in 1881, Charlotte Clark, aided by her son, earned her living by translating French novels. At one time she undertook to write a guide to all the waterways of America. So far as is known, only a small pamphlet on the Mississippi River was published. She did not live to complete a novel based on her experiences in Paris. Charlotte Moon Clark died in Philadelphia at St. George's Rectory, the home of her only child, the Rev. Franklin Pinckney Clark (1852–1910).

Ophia D. Smith

How She Came into Her Kingdom; A Romance . . . , Chicago, 1878.
Baby Rue . . . , Boston, 1881.
The Modern Hagar. A Drama, 2 vols., New York, 1882.

CLARK, DAVIS WASGATT (Feb. 1812–May 23, 1871), clergyman, was born in Mount Desert, Maine. He graduated from Wesleyan University, Conn., in 1836. He became a Methodist clergyman in 1843 after teaching in New York State for several years. In 1852 he became editor of the *Ladies' Repository* in Cincinnati and continued in that position until he was chosen bishop in 1864. As bishop he worked chiefly in Kentucky and Tennessee. He died in Cincinnati. Besides the titles below, he published a mathematics textbook, sermons, and numerous pamphlets.

Death-bed Scenes . . . , New York, 1851.
Life and Times of Rev. Elijah Hedding . . . , New York, 1855.
Historical Sketches . . . , Cincinnati, 1856.
Traits and Anecdotes of Birds and Fishes . . . , Cincinnati, 1856.

CLARK, DAVIS WASGATT (July 28, 1849–July 25, 1935), clergyman, son of Bishop D. W. Clark (q.v.), was born in New York City. He graduated from Ohio Wesleyan University in 1871 and Boston University

School of Theology in 1875. Among the cities where he served as a Methodist minister were Columbus, Dayton, and Cincinnati. He was district superintendent, Cincinnati, 1900–05. He published articles and books on social questions, e.g., *Child Labor and the Social Conscience . . .* , [New York, 1924]. WWW 1

CLARK, EDNA MARIA (Mrs. James E.) (June 1, 1874–June 18, 1961), art historian and authority on early American crafts, was born in Woodstock, Champaign County. A graduate of Ohio State University, she also studied at Harvard University and toured European art galleries during several summers. She wrote many articles on American crafts for periodicals, lectured on art in various cities, superintended the restoration of historic houses, and compiled a valuable book: *Ohio Art and Artists,* Richmond, [Va.], 1932.

CLARK, FRED GEORGE (Nov. 2, 1890–), industrialist, was born in Cleveland, Cuyahoga County. He attended Kenyon College, 1909–13. He held various positions in the petroleum industry before becoming chairman of the American Economic Foundation in 1939. He has directed numerous radio forums and written newspaper articles on economic issues. His books, several of which were written in collaboration with Richard S. Rimanoczy, include *Magnificent Delusion,* New York, [1940]. WW 30

CLARK, GEORGE GERLAW (March 3, 1857–Dec. 19, 1931), clergyman, was born in Casstown, Miami County. After graduating from Wittenberg College in 1887 and the Seminary in 1890, he was ordained to the Lutheran ministry. He served churches in Kentucky, Ohio, Kansas, and Colorado. At the time of his death he was pastor of a Lutheran church in Canon City, Colo. He is buried in Dayton.

History of Wittenberg College . . . , Springfield, 1887.

CLARK, GEORGE RAMSEY (March 20, 1857–Dec. 14, 1945), naval officer, was born in Monroe, Butler County. With several other naval officers he wrote *The Navy 1775 to 1910,* 2 vols., Baltimore, 1910, which was reissued several times in revised and enlarged editions. WWW 2

CLARK, GERTRUDE THERESA (1868–Aug. 9, 1905), born in Pekin, Ill., was brought to Toledo while a young girl and spent her life in that city. Her poems appeared in newspapers and magazines, and she published one collection: *Heart Songs,* Toledo, 1901.

CLARK, HAROLD TERRY (Sept. 4, 1882–), lawyer, was born in Derby, Conn. He graduated from Yale University in 1903 and Harvard Law School in 1906, in which year he was admitted to the Ohio bar. He practiced in Cleveland, has been active in civic and humanitarian enterprises, and has written several pamphlets and books relating to these interests, e.g., *Talking Gloves for the Deaf and Blind,* [Cleveland, 1917]. WW 30

CLARK, JOAN. Pseud. See Mildred W. Benson.

CLARK, MAZIE EARHART (Feb. 16, 1874–Jan. 10, 1958), poet, born in Glendale, Hamilton County, was married to George Clark. A beauty operator and a chiropodist, she wrote poetry as a pastime. Her poems appeared in various periodicals, and she published a collection: *Garden of Memories,* Cincinnati, 1932.

CLARK, NATALIE LORD RICE (Dec. 20, 1867–Dec. 16, 1932), was born in Danvers, Mass. She was assistant editor of *Living Age,* 1897–1900. In 1900 she married Frank L. Clark and in 1908 came with him to Miami University, where he served as professor of Greek. Some of her writings were published under the pen name Hobart Clear.

The Green Garnet, Boston, 1895.

Blake Redding: A Boy of To-day, Boston, 1903.

Bacon's Dial in Shakespeare; A Compass-Clock Cipher, Cincinnati, 1922.

Bacon's Drama Dial in Shakespeare; A Puppet Stage in the Plays . . . , Mansfield, 1924.

Hamlet on the Dial Stage, Paris, 1931.

CLARK, NEIL McCULLOUGH (Dec. 13, 1890–), was born in Croton, Licking County. He attended Croton public schools and East High School, Cleveland, and graduated from Harvard University in 1912. He did editorial work for A. W. Shaw Company, Chicago, 1912–20, and has since been a free-lance writer. His home is in South Strafford, Vt. He has published poems, articles, and short stories in many national magazines, and he has written several biographies and other books, e.g., *An Inside Story of Success . . .* , New York, 1929. WWNAA 7

CLARK, WALTER ERNEST (June 9, 1873–May 1, 1955), educator, was born in Defiance, Defiance County. He graduated from Ohio Wesleyan University in 1896 and Columbia University (Ph.D.) in 1903. He taught political science at the University of Nevada, 1907–17, and served as president, 1917–38. He published a number of pamphlets and books on economic questions, e.g., *The Cost of Living,* Chicago, 1915. WWW 3

CLARKE, EDWIN LEAVITT (May 21, 1888–Sept. 15, 1948), educator, was born in Westboro, Mass. He graduated from Clark University in 1909 and Columbia University (Ph.D.) in 1916. He taught sociology at Ohio State University, 1919–23, and Oberlin College, 1927–30. His works include a textbook, a doctoral study of American authors, and *Petting, Wise or Otherwise?,* New York, 1938. WWW 2

CLARKE, JOHN HESSIN (Sept. 18, 1857–March 22, 1945), lawyer and judge, was born in Lisbon, Columbiana County. After graduating from Western Reserve University in 1877, he read law and was admitted to the Ohio bar. He served as associate justice of the U. S. Supreme Court, 1916–22. His death occurred in San Diego, Calif. He wrote *America and World Peace,* New York, 1925. WWW 2

CLARKE, PETER H. (? – ?), educator, was born in Cincinnati, Hamilton County. A teacher in the Cincinnati schools, he was instrumental in securing the establishment of Gaines High School and served as its principal, 1866–87. He conducted classes after school hours to train teachers for Negro schools. He taught in St. Louis, Mo., 1895–1908.

The Black Brigade of Cincinnati . . . , Cincinnati, 1864.

CLARKE, ROBERT (May 1, 1829–Aug. 27, 1899), book dealer, publisher, and bibliophile, was born in Annan, Dumfreeshire, Scotland. Coming with his parents to Cincinnati in 1840, he was educated locally and had a short try at bookkeeping. Then, following his inclinations, he became interested in a small secondhand bookshop in the city. This he developed into Robert Clarke and Company, which in addition succeeded H. W. Derby & Co. in 1858 as a new book outlet. Thence into publishing where finally the firm became incorporated in 1894 as the Robert Clarke Company. The bookstore's stock was accurately described in a series of seven catalogues, *Bibliotheca Americana,* issued from 1875 to 1893, recommended by such authorities as Justin Windsor and John Fiske. Clarke was responsible for a most interesting and discriminating series of publications. Although his law publications were then the most important in the West, his historical reprints are of the greatest interest today. Drawing from an extensive personal library, he began in 1868 by issuing reprints of four rare pamphlets such as "The Court Sermon, 1674." His best-known publications are the seven volumes of the Ohio Valley Historical Series issued between 1868 and 1871. These books, published against the advice of his partners, were purchased by the more important libraries and historical societies. *Bouquet's Expedition* (Cincinnati, 1868) was the first of this series which was hailed by critics and students as an important contribution to American history. However, local support was wanting and this valuable project was brought to a close with the seventh volume. These books and others related to the history and culture of the Ohio Valley were all bound in the same green pebbled cloth which soon became recognized as distinctive of the Clarke publications. W. H. Venable's *Beginnings of Literary Culture in the Ohio Valley* (1891) is now one of the most useful and valuable of the firm's publications. Clarke himself edited for the Historical Series George Rogers Clark's *Campaign in Illinois, 1778–79* (1869), James McBride's *Pioneer Biographies* (1869), and Captain James Smith's *Captivity with the Indians* (1870). His own published productions are very slight: a record of the distribution and sale of lots in the town of Losantiville 1789 to 1790, *Information Wanted with Reference to the Early Settlers of Losantiville (Now Cincinnati),* (1870), *The Ancient of Days* (1873), and an explanation of the authenticity of an aboriginal artifact, *The Prehistoric Remains Which Were Found on the Site of the City of Cincinnati, Ohio, with a Vindication of the "Cincinnati Tablet"* (1876). His home in Glendale, a suburb of Cincinnati, was famous for its library, which W. H. Venable said could not be duplicated in the West. A carefully chosen collection of 7,000 volumes of Americana was purchased from it by William A. Procter a few years before Clarke's death to be presented to the University of Cincinnati, where it now forms an important part of the University Library. An earlier collection of about 4,000 volumes of Americana had been purchased in 1874 by Rutherford B. Hayes to form the nucleus of his personal library now in the Hayes Memorial Library at Fremont. A collection of Clarke's books on fishing is in the Field Museum of Chicago while his personal copies, uniformly bound in dull green three-quarter leather, of the books printed by the Clarke firm are in the library of the Historical and Philosophical Society of Ohio. Clarke was never married, contentedly spending his life in constant reading and study. He was a bibliophile as well as a connoisseur of printing. His own books are attractive productions, most legible, being reminiscent of the more subtle typography of William Pickering from the early part of the century. Clarke was one of the first life members of the Ohio Archaeological and Historical Society, being elected a trustee in Feb., 1899. He was beloved in Glendale and was specially known as the founder of the Lyceum. He raised the money to build this unique social center and presented it with a library of nearly 5,000 volumes. He died suddenly in the library of his home, having devoted a good life to publishing books of quality in the West.

Wyman W. Parker

Information Wanted with Reference to the Early Settlers of Losantiville (Now Cincinnati), Cincinnati, 1870.

The Ancient of Days, Cincinnati, 1873.

The Prehistoric Remains Which Were Found on the Site of the City of Cincinnati, Ohio, with a Vindication of the "Cincinnati Tablet," Cincinnati, 1876.

The Founders of Ohio, Cincinnati, 1888.

CLAY, CHARLES M. Pseud. See Cynthia C. M. Clark.

CLEAR, HOBART. Pseud. See Natalie L. R. Clark.

CLEAVELAND, CHARLES H. (1820–1863), physician, was born in Lebanon, N. H. He graduated from Dartmouth Medical School in 1843. In 1854 he came to Cincinnati to teach in the Eclectic Medical Institute. A dispute with other faculty members led Cleaveland to attempt to gain control of the school. Unable to buy sufficient stock, he barricaded himself and some friends in the building but was driven out. Despite repeated attempts until stopped by the police, he was unable to retake the beleaguered building. He and some friends, including Joseph Rodes Buchanan (q.v.), thereupon organized the College of Eclectic Medicine to compete with the Institute. Besides the book below, Cleaveland published a medical lexicon, a book on diseases of the feet, and several medical articles.

Galvanism; Its Application as a Remedial Agent, New York, 1853.

CLEAVELAND, MOSES (Jan. 29, 1754–Nov. 16, 1806), founder of Cleveland, led the survey party in 1796 that laid out the city. After returning to Connecticut in the fall of 1796, Cleaveland never returned to the Western Reserve. Though not an author in the usual sense of the word, he published *An Oration Commemorative of the Life and Death of General George Washington,* Windham, Conn., 1800.

CLEMANS, SARAH ISABELLA CHAFFIN (July 27, 1840–Nov. 5, 1885), was born near Jamestown, Greene County. She taught in the Jamestown schools before her marriage to William Clemans, then superintendent of schools and after 1866 a Methodist minister. After her death her husband compiled a volume of her poems, letters, and excerpts from her journal.

Flowers from the Pathways of a Consecrated Life . . . , Columbus, 1886.

CLEMENS, WILLIAM MONTGOMERY (Jan. 16, 1860–Nov. 25, 1931), journalist, was born in Paris, Stark County. He was educated in Akron schools and at Buchtel College. From 1879 until 1908 he served on the editorial staffs of a number of metropolitan newspapers, including the Pittsburgh *Dispatch,* Cleveland *Plain Dealer,* San Francisco *Chronicle,* and New York *World.* A prolific writer and a tireless researcher in the field of genealogy, he not only founded several short-lived periodicals, but also edited genealogical records for a number of families and compiled lists of early wills and marriage records. His death occurred in Somerset, Bermuda.

Famous Funny Fellows; Brief Biographical Sketches of American Humorists, Cleveland, 1882.

Mark Twain; His Life and Work . . . , San Francisco, 1892.

Life of Admiral George Dewey . . . , New York, [1898].

A Ken of Kipling; Being a Biographical Sketch of Rudyard Kipling . . . , New York, 1899.

Theodore Roosevelt, the American, New York, [1899].

The Gilded Lady; Being the True Story of a Crime against the United States Government as Recorded by Henry Chardon, Late of the Secret Service, New York, [1903].

Benjamin Franklin; A Biographical Sketch, Akron, 1904.

American Unclaimed Money Index . . . , New York, 1914.

The Ancestry of Theodore Roosevelt . . . , New York, 1914.

Button Gwinnett, Man of Mystery . . . , Pompton Lakes, N. J., 1921.
Famous Virginians . . . , Pompton Lakes, N. J., 1921.
The Ancestry of Mary Baker Eddy . . . , Pompton Lakes, N. J., 1924.
Life and Times of John Brown, [n.p., n.d.].

CLERINIC. Pseud. See Milton G. Nicola.

CLESS, GEORGE HENRY (Dec. 6, 1892–), was born in Columbus, Franklin County. He graduated from Ohio State University in 1914 and New York State School of Forestry, Syracuse, in 1916. He served in World War I, published the Barnesville *Enterprise,* 1922–24, held various positions in Virginia and New York State, and is now managing editor of Christian Economic Publications, New York. He has published a book on world peace: *The Eleventh Commandment,* New York, 1938. WW 24

CLEVELAND, GRACE ELIZABETH MATTHEWS (June 30, 1864–June 30, 1933), was born in Glendale, Hamilton County. A daughter of Stanley Matthews, Supreme Court justice and the wife of Harlan Cleveland, a Cincinnati attorney, she wrote *Mother Eva Mary C. T. . . . ,* Milwaukee, Wis., [1929].

CLEVELAND, KATE. Pseud. See Mrs. Rebecca S. R. Nichols.

CLIFTON, JOHN LEROY (June 13, 1881–April 24, 1943), educator, was born in Etna, Licking County. He taught in Ohio public schools, 1898–1911, graduated from Ohio University in 1913, was an official in the Ohio Department of Education, 1911–15, and joined the faculty of Ohio State University in 1915. His writings include *Ten Famous American Educators,* Columbus, [1933]. WWW 3

CLINTON, ALTHEA L. Pseud. See Alta Taylor.

CLOPPER, EDWARD NICHOLAS (Jan. 1. 1879–Dec. 1, 1953), social worker, was born in Cincinnati, Hamilton County. He graduated from Bethany College, W. Va., in 1897 and the University of Cincinnati (Ph.D.) in 1912. He served with a number of state and Federal social agencies and taught social work at the University of Cincinnati and Ohio State University. Child welfare, his major interest, was the subject of a wide variety of articles, reports, and books, e.g., *Society and the Child,* Boston, [1929]. WWW 3

CLYMAN, JAMES (1792–Dec. 27, 1881), frontiersman, was born in Virginia. His flaming career of adventure started in Stark County in 1811, the year in which his family settled there. Commencing with the Indian outbreaks which followed the Battle of Tippecanoe, he served as ranger until the close of the War of 1812. The next few years he spent with surveying parties. He joined Ashley's second expedition to ascend the Missouri in 1823. He was a member of the party of four who were the first to circumnavigate the Great Salt Lake. He was a soldier in the Black Hawk War, 1832–34. While serving with General Henry Dodge in Wisconsin, he was severely wounded in an encounter with an Indian. He crossed the plains to Willamette, Oreg., in 1844 and the following year went to California. He guided a group of disappointed emigrants back to Independence, Mo., in 1846 and guided another party westward in 1848, settling down that year in Napa. Bernard DeVoto has referred to Clyman's journals, which were edited by Charles L. Camp, as one of the half-dozen classics in the field. His death occurred at Napa, Calif. His journals were published as *James Clyman; American Frontiersman . . . ,* San Francisco, 1928.

CLYMER, ALBERT (Dec. 10, 1827–1897), was born in Fairfield County, where he operated a farm throughout his life. He wrote poetry as an avocation.

Echoes from the Woods . . . , Cedar Rapids, Iowa, 1888.

COAN, CHARLES FLORUS (April 30, 1886–Sept. 19, 1928), educator, was born in Dayton, Montgomery County. He graduated from the University of Washington in 1908 and the University of California (Ph.D.) in 1920. He taught at the University of New Mexico and other schools. Besides professional articles he published *A History of New Mexico,* 3 vols., [Chicago, 1925]. WWW 1

COATES, ARCHIE AUSTIN (Oct. 21, 1891–), was born in Dayton, Montgomery County, where his father was on the staff of the Dayton *Journal.* He was educated in Dayton and New York City schools and graduated from Columbia University in 1913. He was associated with various periodicals including the New York *Tribune, Literary Digest,* and the original *Life.* He was a staff writer at C.B.S. radio for four years. He is now employed in the Department of Motor Vehicles, California. His poems have appeared in various magazines, and he has published a collection: *City Tides,* New York, [1918].

COATES, WILLIAM R. (Nov. 17, 1851–Feb. 20, 1935), was born in North Royalton, Cuyahoga County. Soon after his birth the family moved to Brecksville, where he attended public schools. After studying at Oberlin College, he taught school in Brecksville and Independence for twelve years. A leader in the Republican Party in Cleveland, he served as county clerk and was mayor of Brooklyn village before it was annexed to the city in 1894. He published *A History of Cuyahoga County and the City of Cleveland,* 3 vols., Chicago, 1924. WWO

COCHRAN, JOHN SALISBURY (Sept. 9, 1841–March 26, 1926), judge, was born in Colerain Township, Belmont County. From his memories of his native county, he wrote a series of sketches, many dealing with Civil War days: *Bonnie Belmont . . . ,* [Wheeling, W. Va., 1907].

COCHRAN, NEGLEY DAKIN (Dec. 20, 1863–April 13, 1941), journalist, was born in Martins Ferry, Belmont County. He attended Lindsley Institute, Wheeling, W. Va., and the University of Michigan. In 1883 he entered journalism in Toledo, where he worked for all of the major newspapers at various times; in 1897 he became editor of the *News-Bee.* He published a biography, *E. W. Scripps,* New York, [1933]. OBB

COCHRAN, WILLIAM C. (March 29, 1848–Sept. 19, 1936), lawyer, was born in Oberlin, Lorain County. In 1869 he graduated from Oberlin College, where his father was a member of the faculty. After studying law he was admitted to the bar; he practiced in Cincinnati, 1872–1915. He continued to live in Cincinnati after his retirement and died in that city. He compiled a law lexicon, published a valuable account of the early life of Gen. Jacob D. Cox, first delivered as an address, and wrote *The Western Reserve and the Fugitive Slave Law . . . ,* Cleveland, 1920. OBB

COE, DOUGLAS. Pseud. See Beryl Williams.

COE, KATHERINE HUNTER (Jan. 17, 1886–May 12, 1950), poet, born in Indiana, married Dr. Oliver P. Coe of Cincinnati and thereafter lived in that city until her death. She was active in Cincinnati poetry groups and published a collection of verse: *Sundial Shadows,* Dawlish, England, [1938]. WWNAA 7

COFFEEN, HENRY ASA (Feb. 14, 1841–Dec. 9, 1912), was born near Gallipolis, Gallia County. He moved with his parents to Indiana and thence to Illinois in 1853. Following his graduation from Abingdon College he became a teacher, and for a time he was a member of the faculty of Hiram College. He moved to Sheridan, Wyo., in 1884; there he became prominent in politics and was elected to the 53rd Congress.

Vermillion County (Illinois), Historical, Statistical, and Descriptive . . . , Danville, Ill., [1871?].

COFFIN, ELIJAH (Nov. 27, 1830–April 19, 1910), who was born on a farm in Harmony Township, Clark County, learned the shoemaking trade as a boy and was a shoemaker in South Charleston for fifteen years. Elected sheriff of the county in 1868, he settled in Springfield, where he also engaged in farming and the real estate business. He served four terms as sheriff and later was warden of the Ohio Penitentiary, 1886–90 and 1896–1900.

Speeches and Essays on Prison Reform . . . , Columbus, 1899.

COFFIN, LEVI (Oct. 28, 1798–Sept. 16, 1877), was born in New Garden, N. C., of Quaker parentage. Although his education was slight, he taught school at intervals. His efforts to conduct a Sunday school for Negroes were unappreciated by neighboring slave-owners, and in 1826 he moved to Newport (Fountain City), Ind. Here for twenty years he was very active in assisting Negroes escaping from the South. In 1847 he went to Cincinnati, where he opened a wholesale free-labor store, supported by Indiana Quakers. During and after the Civil War he worked zealously for the welfare of freedmen.

Reminiscences of Levi Coffin, the Reputed President of the Underground Railroad . . . , Cincinnati, [1876].

COFFINBERRY, ANDREW (Aug. 20, 1788–May 12, 1856), lawyer, was born in Martinsburg, Va. He came with his parents to Chillicothe in 1806 and moved to Lancaster the following year. After serving two years in the navy, he read law in Mansfield, where he later practiced. In 1836 he was at Perrysburg and served as one of Governor Lucas's advisors during the boundary dispute with Michigan. He went to California in 1849 but returned to Ohio before his death, which occurred at Findlay. He dressed in Colonial costume as late as 1855 and because of his polished manners and meticulous appearance was known among his legal colleagues as Count Coffinberry. His long poem describing the wilderness frontier and Indian warfare apparently was written by 1825. It was published in 1842 by the Ohio Bar Association "as a compliment to the author."

The Forest Rangers; A Poetic Tale of the Western Wilderness in 1794 . . . , Columbus, 1842.

COGGESHALL, WILLIAM TURNER (Sept. 6, 1824–Aug. 2, 1867), editor and librarian, was born in Lewistown, Pa. In 1842 he came to Akron, where he edited a temperance paper; in 1847 he moved to Cincinnati to work on the *Gazette.* He edited or wrote for a variety of magazines, the most important of which was *The Genius of the West,* a monthly, 1854–56. He served as state librarian, 1856–62. During the Civil War he was on Governor Dennison's staff and is said to have done secret service work in Virginia, during which service he contracted the tuberculosis which caused his death. He owned the Springfield *Republic,* 1862–65, wrote for the *Ohio State Journal,* 1865–66, and served as private secretary to Governor Jacob D. Cox early in 1866. He was named American minister to Ecuador in the hope that a warm climate would restore his health, but he died in Quito. His fiction, which was quite popular during his lifetime, is too moralistic and sentimental for modern taste. His major contribution to literary history was his continuation of the thesis of W. D. Gallagher (q.v.) that Western writers were ignored because of the domination of publishing and critical circles by an Eastern clique. Coggeshall expressed his belief in an address, "The Protective Policy in Literature," delivered in 1859. He planned a series of anthologies to illustrate the merit of Western writers, but only the first was completed, the invaluable collection, *The Poets and Poetry of the West.*

The Signs of the Times: Comprising a History of the Spirit-Rappings, in Cincinnati and Other Places . . . , Cincinnati, 1851.

Easy Warren and His Contemporaries: Sketched for Home Circles, New York, 1854.

Oakshaw; Or, the Victims of Avarice: A Tale of Intrigue, Cincinnati, 1855.

The Newspaper Record . . . , Philadelphia, 1856.

Home Hits and Hints, New York, 1859.

The Poets and Poetry of the West . . . , Columbus, 1860.

Stories of Frontier Adventure in the South and West, Columbus, 1860.

Ohio's Prosperity, Social and Material . . . , [n.p., 1863?].

Lincoln Memorial . . . , Columbus, 1865.

COHEN, ARMOND E. (June 5, 1909–), rabbi, was born in Canton, Stark County. He graduated from New York University in 1930 and Jewish Theological Seminary in 1934. Since 1934 a rabbi of Park Synagogue, Cleveland, he has written *All God's Children; A Jew Speaks,* New York, 1945. WWWJ

COHON, SAMUEL SOLOMON (March 22, 1888–), rabbi, born in Lohi, Russia, came to America in 1904 and graduated from the University of Cincinnati in 1911. He served as rabbi of several congregations in Ohio and Illinois before joining the Hebrew Union faculty, where he taught Jewish theology, 1923–56. His writings include *What We Jews Believe,* Cincinnati, 1931. WW 30

COIT, STANTON (Aug. 11, 1857–Feb. 15, 1944), religious lecturer, was born in Columbus, Franklin County. He attended Amherst College, Columbia University, and the University of Berlin. A leader in the Ethical Religion movement, he lectured at the West London Ethical Society, was a settlement worker in New York City, and preached at the Ethical Church, London, England. Besides the titles below, he compiled a hymnbook and books of "ethical scriptures." He died in England.

Neighborhood Guilds; An Instrument of Social Reform, London, 1891.

National Idealism and a State Church . . . , London, 1907.

National Idealism and the Book of Common Prayer . . . , London, 1908.

Woman in Church and State, London, 1910.

The Soul of America . . . , New York, 1914.

Is Civilization a Disease?, Boston, 1917.

COLBY, HENRY FRANCIS (Nov. 25, 1842–May 8, 1915), clergyman, was born in Roxbury, Mass., and was ordained to the ministry in the Baptist Church in 1868. He served as pastor of First Baptist Church, Dayton, until his retirement in 1903, and after retiring continued to live in Dayton until his death.

A Tribute to the Memory of Eliam E. Barney, Cincinnati, 1881.

A Tribute to the Memory of Ebenezer Thresher, Dayton, 1886.

A Tribute to the Memory of Charles H. Crawford, Dayton, 1888.

History of the First Baptist Church . . . , Dayton, 1914.

Under Caesar's Shadow, New York, 1918.

COLBY, JUNE ROSE (June, 1856–May 11, 1940), educator, was born in Cherry Valley, Ashtabula County. She graduated from the University of Michigan in 1878 and earned her Ph.D. there in 1886. After teaching in high schools, 1879–92, she taught at Illinois State Normal University, 1892–1931, published numerous professional works, and wrote *Literature and Life in School,* [Boston, 1906]. WWW 1

COLE, ARTHUR CHARLES (April 22, 1886–), educator, was born in Ann Arbor, Mich. He served in the history departments of Ohio State University, 1920–30, and Western Reserve University, 1930–44. He retired at Brooklyn College in 1958 and has since lived in Florida. He has written numerous articles and several books related to American history, e.g., *The Irrepressible Conflict, 1850–1865,* New York, 1934. WW 29

COLE, MERL BURKE (Mrs. Homer Lee Kimsey) (d. June 4, 1959), was born in Nevada, Wyandot County. She was educated in private schools, later lived in Placerville, Calif., and wrote *Six Days on a Mule in Mexico,* Boston, 1928. WWAW 1

COLE, RALPH DAYTON (Nov. 30, 1873–Oct. 15, 1932), lawyer and congressman, was born in Vanlue, Hancock County. He practiced law in Findlay and served in the House of Representatives, 1905–11. He was a founder of the American Legion. He served as lieutenant colonel in the division whose history he wrote with William C. Howells: *The Thirty-seventh Division in the World War . . . ,* Columbus, 1926. WWW 1

COLEMAN, MRS. AUGUSTUS T. See George Elliston.

COLEMAN, MARY LOUISE RANDOLPH Nov. 28, 1890–), was born in Springfield, Clark County. She attended Massachusetts schools and studied art in New York, Chicago, and Europe. A practicing landscape and interior architect in Westport, Conn., she has published numerous magazine articles and a book on beekeeping: *Bees in the Garden and Honey in the Larder,* New York, 1939.

COLER, CYPHRON SEYMOUR (Feb. 18, 1858–Jan. 6, 1944), educator, was born in Malta-McConnelsville, Morgan County. He graduated from Ohio University in 1883 and did graduate work at Johns Hopkins University. He was a Federal land agent in the Dakota Territory, taught in the public schools of Ohio, North Carolina, and New Jersey, and lectured at various institutes. He died in West Lafayette, where he spent the last 25 years of his life.

Character Building . . . , New York, 1897.

COLERICK, EDWARD FENWICK (1822–1905), lawyer, was born in Mount Vernon, Knox County. His family moved to Fort Wayne, Ind., in 1828, and he spent his life in that state. He practiced law in Fort Wayne and Indianapolis. Besides the title below, he published many articles in periodicals.

Adventures of Pioneer Children; Or, Life in the Wilderness . . . , Cincinnati, 1888.

COLLETT, MARY STOKES TIBBALS (Nov. 5, 1876–Sept. 19, 1933), poet, born in Clear Creek Township, Warren County, married Howard Collett and lived in Wilmington. She published a pamphlet collection of her verse: *Home Poems,* [Roswell, N. M., 1917].

COLLINS, CHARLES H. (April 15, 1832–Dec. 28, 1904), lawyer, was born in Maysville, Ky., the brother of William Armstrong Collins (q.v.). In 1850 he moved to a farm at Horse Shoe Bend on the east fork of the Little Miami River in Clermont County, which had been his father's home. He was admitted to the Ohio bar at Batavia in 1854. He lived in Waverly, Mo., 1858–64, but then settled in Hillsboro, where he spent the rest of his life. His play, *Wibbleton to Wobbleton,* was written at sea to divert the passengers of a ship that broke its shaft and drifted for 21 days until repairs were made; the play was later printed for his family.

Echoes from the Highland Hills, Cincinnati, 1884.

Wibbleton to Wobbleton . . . , Hillsboro, 1885.

From Highland Hills to an Emperor's Tomb . . . , Cincinnati, 1886.

The New Year Comes, My Lady, Buffalo, N. Y., 1895.

Here and There in Verse and Prose, Norwalk, 1897.

Past and Present, Hillsboro, 1899.

COLLINS, CLINTON (Nov. 15, 1863–Jan. 25, 1940), was born in Cincinnati, Hamilton County. After graduating from Woodward High School and Harvard University, he published a Democratic newspaper in Cincinnati and was active in local politics. He was assistant editor of reports and statutes of the State Supreme Court, Columbus, 1912–37.

Poems, Sketches of Moses Traddles, Cincinnati, 1890.

COLLINS, ELIJAH THOMAS (Jan. 12, 1818–Oct. 21, 1901), physician, was born in Clark County. After studying medicine, he practiced for nearly sixty years in South Charleston. He wrote *The Soul . . . ,* Cincinnati, [1901].

COLLINS, JAMES H. (April 25, 1904–March 22, 1935), aviator, was born in Warren, Trumbull County. Left an orphan at the age of eleven, he was reared in Cuyahoga Falls by an uncle and aunt. He graduated from high school in Akron and attended the University of Akron for a time while working nights at Goodyear Rubber Company. In 1925 he graduated from the Army Advanced Flying School, Kelly Field, Texas. After four years of intermittent service as an Air Corps lieutenant, he became a free-lance pilot. An article in the *Saturday Evening Post* on his experiences gained him a post as aviation columnist for the New York *Daily News.* He planned to give up flying after filling a contract with Grumman Aircraft Corporation. He died when a biplane he was testing crashed near Farmingdale, Long Island. He had just completed a book which was published posthumously: *Test Pilot,* New York, [1935].

COLLINS, MARY CATHERINE LOVE (June 3, 1882–), was born in Loveville, Pa., but has lived in Cincinnati since 1924. After graduating from Dickinson College and the University of Kentucky Law School, she was admitted to the bar in 1911. She was national president of Chi Omega Sorority, 1910–52. She has written numerous magazine articles and a play, *The Thrill to Power,* New York, [1929]. WO 2

COLLINS, PEARL (PAUL) VALOROUS (July 22, 1860–March 8, 1931), journalist, was born in Camden, Preble County. He studied at the University of Minnesota, University of Toulouse, and the Art Students' League. After working as a reporter on the Dayton *Herald* and the Cincinnati *Commercial Gazette,* he went to Paris to study art, but became cable correspondent for the New York *Tribune* and other American newspapers. He interviewed de Lesseps when he returned from his Panama inspection and Pasteur when he first announced the successful treatment of hydrophobia. He was editor and proprietor of the St. Peter, Minn., *Tribune,* 1887–90, and principal owner of the *Northwestern Agriculturist,* Minneapolis, 1893–95. He was the Progressive Republican nominee for governor of Minnesota in 1912. He then became manager of the Paul V. Collins International Newspaper Syndicate, Washington and London. He also wrote for magazines and interviewed Benito Mussolini for *Outlook* in 1927. His death occurred in Washington, D. C.

A Baton for a Heart, Chicago, 1888.
A Country Romance, Milwaukee, 1896.
Canadian Reciprocity vs. American Manufacturers as Well as Farmers . . . , Minneapolis, [1910?].

COLLINS, MRS. VIVIAN. See Marjorie M. Wing.

COLLINS, WILLIAM ARMSTRONG (Feb. 21, 1834–Nov. 4, 1898), lawyer and journalist, was born in Maysville, Ky., the brother of Charles H. Collins, (q.v.). In 1850 he moved to Cincinnati, where he studied law and was admitted to the bar. He practiced in Cincinnati, New Orleans, and Memphis, and later was associated in an editorial capacity with various newspapers, including the Cleveland *Plain Dealer,* Pittsburgh *Chronicle,* and the Cincinnati *Saturday Night.* In 1874 he moved to Florida; his last years were spent in Hagerstown, Md.

At Long and Short Range, Philadelphia, 1893.

COLLISON, WILSON (Nov. 5, 1893–May 4, 1941), who was born in Gloucester, Adams County, wrote a number of successful plays, including *Getting Gertie's Garter* (1921), in collaboration with Avery Hopwood (q.v.), and numerous mystery novels, e.g., *A Woman in Purple Pajamas,* New York, 1931, published under the pen name Willis Kent. WWW 1

COLT, CLEM. Pseud. See Nelson C. Nye.

COLTON, OLIVE A. (Sept. 2, 1873–), was born in Toledo, Lucas County. She wrote and lectured on women's suffrage, the American Red Cross, and other topics. She has published a number of pamphlets and booklets and a travel account: *Rambles Abroad,* Toledo, [1904].

COLVER, ANNE (Mrs. S. Stewart Graff) (June 20, 1908–), born in Cleveland, Cuyahoga County, now lives in Westchester County, N. Y. She has written mysteries under the pen name Colver Harris, e.g., *Murder in Amber,* New York, 1938, and several biographies and historical novels, e.g., *Mr. Lincoln's Wife,* New York, [1943].

COLVIN, DAVID LEIGH (Jan. 28, 1880–Sept. 7, 1959), was born in South Charleston, Clark County. He graduated from Ohio Wesleyan University in 1900 and Columbia University (Ph.D.) in 1913. He lectured widely on the subject of prohibition and served as an officer of various temperance and reform organizations. His writings include *Prohibition in the United States . . .*, New York, 1926. WWW 3

COLVIN, MARY MILES (Aug. 16, 1871–Sept. 5, 1956), educator, was born in Mineral Ridge, Trumbull County. After attending National Normal University, she taught in the schools of Youngstown. She married Curtis P. Colvin of Scranton, Pa. After his death she returned to Youngstown, where she conducted a private school and lectured. She published a collection of verse: *My Tapestry and Other Poems*, [Youngstown, 1931].

COLWELL, STEPHEN (March 25, 1800–Jan. 15, 1871), industrialist and economist, studied law in Steubenville and practiced for a time in St. Clairsville before he left the state to become an iron manufacturer. He wrote widely on both economic and religious themes, including *New Themes for the Protestant Clergy . . .*, Philadelphia, 1851.

COLYTON, HENRY JOHN. Pseud. See Sarah A. Zimmerman.

COMAN, KATHARINE (Nov. 23, 1857–Jan. 11, 1915), educator, was born in Newark, Licking County. She graduated from the University of Michigan in 1880 and was on the faculty of Wellesley College, 1883–1913. Besides history textbooks she wrote *Economic Beginnings of the Far West . . .*, 2 vols., New York, 1912. WWW 1

COMEGYS, CHARLES GEORGE (July 30, 1865–July 28, 1943), lawyer, was born in Cincinnati, Hamilton County, the youngest child of Cornelius George Comegys (q.v.). He graduated from the University of Cincinnati in 1878, studied at Cincinnati Law School, and was admitted to the bar in 1880. He practiced in Cincinnati, and his death occurred in that city.

Cornelius G. Comegys, M.D.; His Life and Career in the Development of Cincinnati for Nearly Half a Century . . ., Cincinnati, 1896.

COMEGYS, CORNELIUS GEORGE (July 23, 1816–Feb. 10, 1896), physician, was born in Cherbourg, Del. He was educated at Dover Academy. Failing in an attempt to establish a business in Indiana, he began the study of medicine and graduated from the University of Pennsylvania in 1848. He came to Cincinnati in 1849, where his zest for writing was first disclosed; *Etiology and Treatment of Phthisis Pulmonalis* appeared in the transactions of the Cincinnati Medico-Chirurgical Society for 1849, and Matthew Simpson (q.v.), editor of the *Western Christian Advocate*, employed him as assistant editor. While abroad in 1851 for a year of study in London and Paris, he served as European correspondent of the *Advocate*. He became professor of anatomy in the Cincinnati College of Medicine in 1852, resigning to accept the chair of the institutes of medicine in the new Miami Medical College. This was united with the Medical College of Ohio in 1857, and Comegys retained his chair until 1869. He became lecturer on clinical medicine in the Cincinnati hospital in 1857. For many years he was director of the board of education, and he played an active role in developing the Cincinnati Public Library. He assisted in the organization of the University of Cincinnati in 1869. Up to the time of his death, he fought persistently for the creation of a department of public health. On Oct. 3, 1839, he married Rebecca Turner Tiffin, daughter of Edward Tiffin, the first governor of Ohio. His *Reminiscences of the Life and Public Services of Edward Tiffin* was published in 1869. Written as a reply to a derogatory article by William N. Anderson in the Circleville *Democrat*, it has become a recognized source on the life of the governor. His most ambitious literary work was the translation from the French of Renouard's *History of Medicine*. He was the author of a great many papers published in the medical press—two of them especially attracted much attention: *On the Pathology and Treatment of Phthisis* (1854), which was referred to in the American editions of *Watson's Practice* and *Copeland's Dictionary*, and *On Cool Bathing Treatment of (Infantile) Enterocolitis* (1875). His death occurred in Cincinnati.

Ernest J. Wessen

The Discouragements and Encouragements of the Medical Student, Cincinnati, 1856.

Reminiscences of the Life and Public Services of Edward Tiffin, Ohio's First Governor, Chillicothe, 1869.

Cincinnati; A Plea for an Institute, Cincinnati, 1889.

COMMONS, JOHN ROGERS (Oct. 13, 1862–May 11, 1944), economist, was born in Hollandsburg, Darke County. He graduated from Oberlin College (A.B., 1888; A.M., 1890). After teaching for brief periods in several universities, he joined the faculty of the University of Wisconsin in 1904 and remained on the staff until his retirement in 1932. He also served on many state and Federal agencies. He was an influential teacher and a prolific writer. He produced many articles, pamphlets, and textbooks in addition to the titles listed below.

The Distribution of Wealth, New York, 1893.
Social Reform and the Church, New York, [1894].
Proportional Representation, New York, [1896].
Social Problems, New York, 1898.
Representative Democracy, New York, [1900].
Races and Immigrants in America, New York, 1907.
Documentary History of the American Industrial Society, Cincinnati, 1910.
Labor and Administration, New York, 1913.
History of Labour in the United States, (with others), 4 vols., New York, 1918–35.
Industrial Goodwill, New York, 1919.
A Reconstruction Health Program, [Madison, Wis., 1920].
Legal Foundations of Capitalism, New York, 1924.
Institutional Economics: Its Place in Political Economy, New York, 1934.
Myself, New York, 1934.

COMPTON, ARTHUR HOLLY (Sept. 10, 1892–), physicist, was born in Wooster, Wayne County. His father, Elias Compton, was a Presbyterian minister and a professor in the college. Arthur graduated from the College of Wooster in 1913 and went to Princeton for graduate study (A.M., 1914; Ph.D., 1916). After a year of teaching at the University of Minnesota and two years with Westinghouse, he went to Cambridge University, England, where he worked under the great British scientist, Ernest Rutherford. Compton became professor of physics at Washington University, St. Louis, 1920–23, and then the University of Chicago, 1923–45. He returned to Washington University as chancellor, 1945–53, and is now distinguished service professor. He was awarded the Nobel Prize for Physics in 1927 for his work with X-rays and has received many other honors. During World War II he directed the Metallurgical Laboratory of the Manhattan Project. He has published technical scientific articles, lectures on science and education, and his story of the Manhattan Project, *Atomic Quest: A Personal Narrative,* New York, 1956. A volume of his lectures is entitled *The Freedom of Man,* New Haven, 1935. CB 58

COMPTON, KARL TAYLOR (Sept. 14, 1887–June 22, 1954), physicist, was born in Wooster, Wayne County, eldest son in a distinguished family of scientists. He graduated from the College of Wooster in 1908 and Princeton (Ph.D.) in 1912. After teaching two years at Reed College and serving in France during World War I, he was professor of physics at Princeton, 1919–30. From 1930 to 1948 he was president of Massachusetts Institute of Technology. He also served as an adviser or an official of many governmental research projects. The essence of many of his lectures and speeches published separately can be found in *A Scientist Speaks . . . ,* Cambridge, [Mass.], 1955. WWW 3

COMPTON, WILSON MARTINDALE (Oct. 15, 1900–), educator, was born in Wooster, Wayne County, the brother of Arthur H. and Karl T. (qq.v.). Like his brothers he graduated from the College of Wooster (1911) and earned a Ph.D. at Princeton (1915). After a year as an instructor at Dartmouth College and two years with the Federal Trade Commission, he became secretary of the National Lumber Manufacturers Association, 1918–44. He was also professor of economics at George Washington University, 1934–41, and president of Washington State College, 1944–51. Since 1953 he has been president of the Council for Financial Aid to Education. He has published articles and speeches on economics, forestry, and science, e.g., *Conservation: The Form or the Substance: Which?* [Chicago, 1919]. WW 30

COMSTOCK, DANIEL WEBSTER (Dec. 16, 1840–May 19, 1917), lawyer and judge, was born in Germantown, Montgomery County. After graduating from Ohio Wesleyan University in 1860, he began the study of law in New Castle, Ind. In 1866 he settled in Richmond, Ind., and in 1867 he married Josephine A. Rohrer of his native town. He practiced law in Richmond, served in the Indiana State Senate, and was judge of the Seventh Judicial Circuit.

Ninth Cavalry: One Hundred and Twenty-first Regiment Indiana Volunteers, Richmond, Ind., 1890.

CONARD, HOWARD LOUIS (1853-Dec. 7, 1925), who was born in Hartford, Licking County, attended Kenyon College and Ohio Wesleyan University. After two years as State Librarian (1883–85) and a few years as a hack writer, Conard learned during a trip in the West that one of the last and most colorful of the "mountain men," the famous "Uncle Dick" Wootton, was still living in his adobe house high in the Raton Mountains. Seeking him out, Conard took down the old fellow's narrative of his eventful past. Therein lies Conard's claim to fame. He had the good sense to let the old trapper tell his story in his own rambling style—his story that touched virtually every outstanding incident in the opening of the Rocky Mountain region. The book achieved immediate recognition as a classic in the literature of the Rocky Mountain West. Conard's death occurred in Columbus.

"Uncle Dick" Wootton, the Pioneer Frontiersman of the Rocky Mountain Region . . . , Chicago, 1890.

Reconstructing Eden, Columbus, 1909.

CONDON, FRANK (1882–Dec. 19, 1940), was born in Toledo, Lucas County. He began his career as a reporter in his native city, moved to New York City to work as an advertising man, and in 1925 moved to Hollywood. He died in Beverley Hills, Calif. A highly successful writer for motion pictures and for national magazines, he also published *Once in a Blue Moon,* New York, [1929].

CONE, MARY (? – ?), was born in Marietta, Washington County. She never married and spent most of her life in the vicinity of Marietta.

Two Years in California, Chicago, 1876.

Life of Rufus Putnam . . . , Cleveland, 1886.

CONE, ORELLO (Nov. 16, 1835–June 23, 1905), educator, was born in Lincklaen, N. Y. In 1864 he became a Universalist minister. A liberal, painstaking scholar, he aroused controversy within and outside his church. From 1880 to 1897 he was president of Buchtel College, now the University of Akron. During his stay in Akron he published some of his most important studies of the New Testament.

Salvation, Boston, 1889.

Gospel-Criticism and Historical Christianity . . . , New York, 1891.

The Gospel and Its Earliest Interpretations . . . , New York, 1893.

Paul; The Man, the Missionary, and the Teacher, New York, 1898.

The Epistles . . . , New York, 1901.

Rich and Poor in the New Testament . . . , New York, 1902.

CONE, STEPHEN DECATUR (Feb. 12, 1840–Aug. 11, 1908), journalist, was born near Crosby, Hamilton County. He learned the printing trade on the *Intelligencer* in Hamilton. During the Civil War he served in the 167th O.V.I., after which he became a foreman-printer in various establishments in Cincinnati, Columbus, Fort Wayne, Ind., and Hamilton. He edited the Oxford *Citizen,* 1885–91, and the Paulding *Democrat,* 1892–97. His last years were spent in Hamilton.

Biographical and Historical Sketches; A Narrative of Hamilton . . . , Hamilton, [1896].

A Concise History of Hamilton . . . , Middletown, 1901.

CONGER, ARTHUR LATHAM (Jan. 30, 1872–Feb. 22, 1951), army officer, was born in Peninsula, Summit County, and was reared in Akron. He graduated from Harvard University in 1894, enlisted in the army in 1898, and retired as a colonel in 1928. After his retirement he joined an automobile brokerage business in Akron. His death occurred in Pasadena, Calif. He wrote *The Rise of U. S. Grant,* New York, [1931].

CONGER, EMILY BRONSON (May 7, 1843–May 31, 1917), wife of Arthur L. Conger, Akron industrialist, was born in Peninsula, Summit County. Active in Akron cultural and social activities, she also studied osteopathy and was one of the first women to earn a degree in that field. She published an account of her travels in the Orient and of two years spent with her son, Colonel A. L. Conger (q.v.), in the Philippines: *An Ohio Woman in the Philippines* . . . , [Akron, 1904].

CONGER, SARAH PIKE (July 24, 1842– ?), was born in Painesville, Lake County. She graduated from Lombard College in 1863. In 1866 she married Edwin Hurd Conger, a lawyer, congressman, and diplomat. When her husband was appointed minister to Brazil in 1891, she accompanied him to his post, as she did when he was transferred to China in 1898. The latter experience provided her with material for books on China, e.g., *Old China and Young America,* Chicago, 1913. WW 6

CONKLIN, EDWIN GRANT (Nov. 24, 1863–Nov. 27, 1952), educator, was born in

Waldo, Marion County. He graduated from Ohio Wesleyan University in 1885 and Johns Hopkins University (Ph.D.) in 1891. He served on the faculties of Ohio Wesleyan, 1891–94, Northwestern University, 1894–96, the University of Pennsylvania, 1896–1908, and Princeton University, 1908–33. He wrote a great many scientific articles and monographs and numerous books on evolution, heredity, and education, e.g., *The Direction of Human Evolution,* New York, 1921. WWW 3

CONNELLEY, CELIA LOGAN (Dec. 17, 1837–June 18, 1904), daughter of Cornelius Ambrosius Logan (q.v.), was born in Philadelphia, Pa. She came to Cincinnati when her family settled there in 1840; there she attended school and at an early age began appearing on the stage. Her first husband was the Cincinnati artist Miner Kilbourne Kellogg (q.v.), with whom she lived in Europe while serving as a correspondent for American newspapers. During the Civil War she translated the war news for the newspapers of Milan, Italy, where she was then a resident. Afterward she was associate editor of *The Capital* in Washington, D. C. Divorced from Kellogg, she married James F. Connelley in 1872. Most of her novels and plays were published under the pen name L. Fairfax.

The Elopement; A Tale of the Confederate States of America, London, 1863.
An American Marriage, [n.p., 1883].
"Maryland," An Original Drama . . . , [n.p., 1884].
Her Strange Fate. A Novel, New York, [1888].

CONNELLY, THOMAS W. (Sept. 21, 1839–Jan. 29, 1908), was born near Bradyville, Adams County. He was educated in the public schools of Manchester. On Oct. 14, 1861, he enlisted in the 70th O.V.I. and served with this regiment, a part of Sherman's forces, throughout the war. He was discharged in Aug., 1865. After the war he made his home in Manchester, holding the offices of marshal, notary public, and constable. He was an active member of the G.A.R. and the Republican Party. He wrote a regimental history: *History of the Seventieth Ohio Regiment . . . ,* Cincinnati, 1902.

CONNER, ELIZA ARCHARD (Jan. 4, 1838–1912), journalist, was born in Clermont County. She graduated from Antioch College in 1861, taught in the schools of Indianapolis, Ind., and in 1869 married Dr. George Conner of Cincinnati. In 1865 she became a regular contributor to the *Saturday Evening Post* under the nom de plume "Zig," and later to the Cincinnati *Commercial* under the initials "E. A." She became literary editor of the New York *World* in 1884, and the following year, joined the American Press Association in an editorial capacity.

"E. A." Abroad. A Summer in Europe, Cincinnati, 1883.

CONNER, JACOB ELON (Oct. 21, 1861– ?), was born in Wilmington, Clinton County. He graduated from the University of Iowa (A.B., 1891; Ph.D., 1903). After teaching in several universities, he entered government service. He was American consul at Saigon, 1907–09, and St. Petersburg, Russia, 1909–14.

Uncle Sam Abroad, Chicago, [1900].
Christ Was Not a Jew . . . , New York, 1936.

CONNER, JAMES RYAN (Sept. 21, 1839–June 30, 1930), clergyman, was born in Crossenville, Perry County. He graduated from Ohio Wesleyan University in 1867. He served as a Methodist and later as a Congregational clergyman. He wrote *Mistaken Views of Scripture,* Cincinnati, 1923.

CONOVER, CHARLOTTE REEVE (June 14, 1855–Sept. 23, 1940), historian, was born in Dayton, Montgomery County. She attended Dayton schools and the University of Geneva, Switzerland. She married Frank Conover (q.v.) of Dayton in 1874. She taught private classes, lectured on historical subjects, wrote feature stories for the Dayton *Journal,* and served as historical secretary to J. H. Patterson, president of National Cash Register Company. She published a number of useful historical and biographical works, e.g., *Some Dayton Saints and Prophets,* [Dayton], 1907, and *Dayton and Montgomery County . . . ,* 4 vols., New York, 1932, and an autobiographical work: *On Being Eighty . . . ,* Yellow Springs, 1938. OBB

CONOVER, FRANK (May 29, 1853–Oct. 24, 1912), was born in Dayton, Montgomery County. In 1875 he graduated from Massachusetts Institute of Technology, but he practiced engineering for only a short time. He turned to law and was admitted to the bar in 1878. In 1879 he married Charlotte Elizabeth Reeve (see above), daughter of a Dayton physician. He wrote editorials and poems for Dayton newspapers and delivered many public addresses, chiefly on libraries and education. He died in Dayton.

Centennial Portrait and Biographical Record of the City of Dayton and of Montgomery County . . . , [Logansport, Ind.], 1897.

CONRARD, GEORGE HARRISON ALOYSIUS (Sept. 21, 1869–June 15, 1930), who was born in Hardin County, went to Arizona in the early 1890s, and there he became a successful businessman. During the latter years of his life he followed writing as a profession. He was a classical scholar whose poems ranked high in poetic technique. In addition to poetry he wrote stories, novels, and plays.

A Junior's Poems, Cincinnati, 1891.
Idle Songs and Idle Sonnets, Cincinnati, 1897.
Quivira, Boston, 1907.
The Golden Bowl, New York, 1925.
The Ogre of Bandit Roost, New York, 1927.
Peggy of Lone Peak, New York, 1927.
Desert Madness, New York, [1928].

CONROY, JACK (Dec. 5, 1899–), born in Moberly, Mo., spent several years as a migratory worker and lived four years in Toledo (1927–31) before publishing his autobiographical first novel: *The Disinherited,* [New York, 1933].

CONTEUR. Pseud. See Edwin Henderson.

CONVERSE, JULIUS ORRIN (May 1, 1834–Sept. 2, 1902), editor, was born in Chardon, Geauga County. He began working in the local printing shop when he was sixteen, and in 1859 he became editor of the *Jeffersonian Democrat,* renamed in 1872 the Geauga *Republican.* He edited this newspaper until 1902. He was active in politics and was a popular speaker. His address on James A. Garfield, reprinted as a pamphlet, was widely circulated.

Garfield, the Ideal Man . . . , Cleveland, 1882.

CONWAY, MONCURE DANIEL (March 17, 1832–Nov. 15, 1907), clergyman, was born in Virginia and was minister of First Congregational Church, Cincinnati, 1856–62. Slaves from his father's plantation made their way north, and he settled them near Yellow Springs. He took an active part in Cincinnati cultural life; he founded and edited *The Dial,* where he published contributions from Emerson, Howells, and others. A prolific writer, he contributed to the *Atlantic Monthly* and other periodicals while living in Ohio and also published an appeal for abolition: *The Golden Hour,* Boston, 1862. Acquainted with most of the American and British writers of his day, he wrote a valuable record of the literary world in his autobiography, *Autobiography . . . ,* Boston, 1904.

COOK, TENNESSEE CELESTE CLAFLIN (Oct. 26, 1845–Jan. 18, 1923), was born in Homer, Licking County. She and her sister, Victoria C. Woodhull Martin (q.v.), are two of the most flamboyant characters Ohio has produced. Tennessee married a John Bartels but never used his name. Although both sisters lived in England after 1877, they visited the United States frequently, always managing to stir some controversy that kept them in the public eye. In 1885 Tennessee married a wealthy Englishman, Francis Cook, who later was made a baronet. As Lady Cook she settled down in semirespectability. She collaborated with her sister in writing *The Human Body the Temple of God.* Like her sister she lectured frequently, and some of her talks were issued separately as pamphlets. Before going to England she usually signed herself Tennie C. Claflin.

Constitutional Equality a Right of Women . . . , New York, 1871.
What Was Her Crime? . . . , [New York, 1876].
Talks and Essays, 4 vols. in 2, London, [1897].
Essays on Social Topics, London, [1898].
Illegitimacy, [London, 1909?].
Who Rules? [n.p., 191-?].

COOKE, EDMUND VANCE (June 5, 1864–Dec. 18, 1932), poet, born in Port Dover, Ontario, Canada, was educated in the public schools of Cleveland and spent his life in that city. A popular lecturer and a nonconformist, he advocated the single tax, practiced vegetarianism, and opposed vaccination.

A Patch of Pansies, New York, 1894.
Rimes to Be Read, Chicago, [1897].
Impertinent Poems, New York, 1903.
Chronicles of the Little Tot, New York, [1905].
The Biography of Our Baby, New York, [1906].
Told to the Little Tot, New York, [1906].
A Morning's Mail, Philadelphia, 1907.
Just Then Something Happened, New York, 1909.
Little Songs for Two, New York, [1909].
I Rule the House, New York, [1910].
Baseballology, Chicago, 1912.
The Story Club, New York, [1912].
The Uncommon Commoner . . . , New York, [1913].
Cheerful Children, Chicago, [1923].

Companionable Poems, Chicago, 1924.
From the Book of Extenuations . . . , New York, [1926].

COOKE, FLORA JULIETTE (d.Feb., 1953), educator, was born in Bainbridge, Ross County. She attended public school in Youngstown and then studied at Chicago Normal School. She taught in Francis W. Parker School, Chicago, 1891–1900, and served as principal, 1900–34. The book below was revised several times. She also published articles on education.

Nature Myths and Stories for Little Children, Chicago, [1895].

COOKE, GRACE MacGOWAN (Sept. 11, 1863–1944), who was born in Grand Rapids, Wood County, spent her girlhood in Chattanooga, Tenn., where her father was editor of the Chattanooga *Times.* She married William Cooke of Chattanooga, from whom she was later divorced. She began contributing to magazines in 1888 and was the first president of the Tennessee Women's Press Club. With her sister, Alice MacGowan (q.v.), she joined Upton Sinclair at Helicon Hall, his experimental community in New Jersey, and followed him to California when the hall burned. She lived for many years at Carmel, Calif., where her home was a gathering place for artists and writers. She wrote a number of novels, e.g., *The Power and the Glory,* New York, 1910. Several of her books were collaborations with her sister Alice. WW 19

COOKSON, CHARLES W. (July 6, 1861–Nov. 14, 1947), educator, was born in Redfield, Perry County. He attended Fultonham Academy, College of Wooster, and Ohio University. After serving as superintendent of schools in various Ohio communities, he settled in Troy, where he wrote his autobiography, *After Fifty Years, a Pleasant Memory,* [Troy, 1942]. OBB

COOLIDGE, SUSAN. Pseud. See Sarah C. Woolsey.

COOMES, OLIVER (Aug. 26, 1845–June 27, 1921), was born near Newark, Licking County. In 1856 his parents moved to Iowa, and he spent most of his life in that state. He operated a farm in Cass County from 1870 until a few years before his death, when he retired to Atlantic. He served in the Iowa legislature, 1877–80. In 1870 he began to write dime novels; some were detective stories but most were stories of the Midwest frontier and the Indian. A few appeared under the pen name Will Dexter, but most he published as Oll Coomes. Altogether he wrote more than 75 stories in various Beadle series. A few representative titles are *Antelope Abe, the Boy Guide . . . ,* New York, 1872; *Foghorn Phil, the King of the Border . . . ,* New York, 1874; *Jabez Dart, Detective . . . ,* New York, 1887; *Dandy Bill's Doom . . . ,* New York, 1891.

COOMES, OLL. See Oliver Coomes.

COOPER, DOROTHY (1902–1939), educator, was born in Lockland, Hamilton County. A graduate of the University of Cincinnati, she taught English in Hughes High School, Cincinnati, for fifteen years. Her poems appeared in various periodicals, and after her death her father published a collection: *Bedrock,* Prairie City, Ill., [1943].

COOPER, JACOB (Dec. 7, 1830–Jan. 21, 1904), educator, was born near Somerville, Butler County. He graduated from Yale University in 1852 and from the University of Berlin (Ph.D.) in 1854. He also studied theology at Halle and Edinburgh. In 1855 he became professor of Greek at Centre College, Danville, Ky. Here he soon found himself the leader of a group of educators who were intent on supporting the Federal cause and who established the *Danville Review,* of which Cooper was the editor, 1861–65. He joined the faculty of Rutgers College in 1866, where for 27 years he was professor of Greek and from 1893 until his death was professor of philosophy and logic. He served as an editor of *Bibliotheca Sacra,* 1897–1903. His published writings were chiefly articles contributed to scholarly periodicals and later issued as pamphlets. His death occurred in New Brunswick, N. J.

The Loyalty Demanded by the Present Crisis, Philadelphia, 1864.

COOPER, WILLIAM COLBY (1835–Dec. 7, 1914), physician, was born in North Bend, Hamilton County. According to Otto Juettner (q.v.), he was without formal education when he became a schoolteacher at the age of twenty, and in twelve years he rose to be principal of a high school. After studying medicine for a short while under a local practitioner, he entered the Eclectic Medical Institute, from which he graduated in 1867. He practiced for twelve years in Indianapolis, where he edited a small professional journal, the *Medical Review.* In 1880 he took up his permanent residence in Cleves. His death occurred in that community. For twelve years he was associated with W. E. Bloyer in the editorial management of the *Medical Gleaner.* He was a gifted writer with a delightful sense of humor and was a forcible critic and observer.

The Primitive Fundamental, Cleveland, 1897.
Tethered Truants; Being Essays, Sketches and Poems, Cincinnati, 1897.
Immortality . . . , Cleves, 1904.
Preventive Medicine . . . , Cleves, 1905.
Mind and Matter, Cleveland, [n.d.].

COOPERRIDER, GEORGE T. (March 20, 1852–Aug. 8, 1916), clergyman, was born in Licking County. After graduating from Capital University in 1875 and Columbus Theological Seminary in 1877, he served various pastorates, 1877–1901. He also edited the *Lutheran Standard,* 1898–1909. He died in Columbus.

Be True, Columbus, 1890.
The Lamb of God, Columbus, 1902.
The Last Things, Columbus, 1911.
In His Service, Columbus, 1913.

COPELAND, THOMAS WELLSTED (July 10, 1907–), educator, was born in East Cleveland, Cuyahoga County. A graduate of Yale University (A.B., 1928; Ph.D., 1933), he taught English at his alma mater, 1934–49, and since 1949 has been a member of the University of Chicago faculty. His writings include *Our Eminent Friend Edmund Burke . . . ,* New Haven, 1949. DAS 3

COPPENS, CHARLES (May 24, 1835–Dec. 14, 1920), Jesuit educator, was on the faculty of St. Xavier's College, Cincinnati, 1860–62. He published numerous articles, textbooks, and devotional works.

COQUINA. Pseud. See George O. Shields.

CORBIN, CHARLES RUSSELL (Dec. 21, 1893–Feb. 19, 1950), journalist, was born in Zanesville, Muskingum County. He worked on newspapers in Zanesville, Toledo, and Minneapolis; the last city was his residence at the time of his death. His books include *Why News Is News,* New York, [1928]. WWW 2

COREY, HERBERT (June 28, 1872–Dec. 28, 1954), journalist, was born in Toledo, Lucas County. He spent a number of years in Colorado and Wyoming before joining the Cincinnati *Enquirer* in 1900. He was later traveling correspondent for the Cincinnati *Times-Star.* He died in Washington, D. C. He wrote numerous magazine articles and several books on topics of current public interest, e.g., *The Truth about Hoover,* New York, 1932. WWW 3

COREY, LEWIS (1894–Sept. 16, 1953), educator, was born Louis C. Traina in Italy, but was brought to the United States when a child of three. He grew up in San Francisco, was director of the Bolshevist Bureau in New York, and was one of the organizers of the Communist Party in the United States in 1919. In 1922 he broke with the party, the first of its major leaders to do so; for the rest of his career he was one of the most vigorous leaders of the anti-Communist liberal movement. He was associate professor of political economy, Antioch College, 1942–51. He wrote a number of books on social and economic issues, e.g., *The House of Morgan,* New York, 1930.

CORINNE. Pseud. See Sarah M. N. G. Dahlgren.

CORLETT, WILLIAM THOMAS (April 15, 1854–June 11, 1948), physician, was born in Orange, Coshocton County. He graduated from the medical department of University of Wooster in 1877, studied in Europe, and served on the faculties of Wooster, 1883–85, and Western Reserve University, 1885–1924. Besides a number of medical articles on diseases of the skin, he wrote *The Medicine-Man of the American Indian and His Cultural Background,* Springfield, Ill., [1935]. WWW 2

CORNE, MOLLY E. Pseud. See Mrs. Clifford B. Sturgeon.

CORNELL, ANNETTE PATTON, poet, born in Knoxville, Tenn., lived in Cincinnati for fifteen years. She is now a resident of Fort Mitchell, Ky., and she is still active in Cincinnati literary activities. She attended the University of Cincinnati, University of Tennessee, and Schuster Martin School of Drama. In 1920 she married Dr. Josiah H. Cornell. Since 1928 she has published poems in more than a hundred periodicals and in many anthologies. In 1936 she was cofounder with B. Y. Williams (q.v.) of *Talaria,* a poetry quarterly, and she is now editor of Talaria publications. She has published several collections of verse, among them, a collaboration with Frank Hartman (q.v.): *Golden Feather,* Ludlow, Ky., 1938, and *The Forbidden Woman,* Cincinnati, 1939.

CORNETET, NOAH E. (June 2, 1867–Nov. 13, 1931), clergyman and educator, was born in Mowrystown, Highland County. He was educated at Otterbein College. After being ordained a United Brethren minister in 1890, he served parishes in Hallsville, Cynthiana, Newark, and Logan. From 1901 until his death he was on the faculty of Otterbein College. He wrote *Prayer, a Means of Spiritual Growth,* Dayton, [1904]. WWW 1

CORNWELL, DOROTHEA GRAFF (Mrs. Donovan C.) (Nov. 17, 1925–), who was born in Pittsburgh, Pa., lived in Youngstown and Painesville for eighteen years, moved to Louisville, Ky., after her marriage, and now lives in Philadelphia. She has written book reviews and feature stories for various newspapers and has published short stories. Her novel *They Dare Not Go A-hunting,* New York, 1944, was awarded the Dodd Mead prize for fiction in 1944.

CORSON, ELLA MAY JACOBY (Aug. 2, 1861–Jan. 25, 1953), wife of Oscar T. Corson (q.v.), was born in Camden, Preble County. She was active in the cultural life of Columbus, where her husband served as commissioner of common schools. Her writings include *Glimpses of Longfellow,* Columbus, 1903.

CORSON, OSCAR TAYLOR (May 3, 1857–April 14, 1928), educator, was born near Camden, Preble County. He served as principal of several Ohio schools and was state commissioner of common schools, 1892-98. He lectured widely and wrote articles and books on educational and other subjects, e.g., *Abraham Lincoln; His Words and Deeds,* Dansville, N. Y., [1937]. WWW 1

CORWIN, JANE HUDSON (Oct. 6, 1809–March 6, 1881), born in County Down, Ireland, was the daughter of a Presbyterian clergyman who came to the United States in 1818. In 1829 she married Jesse Corwin, brother of Thomas Corwin (q.v.), and resided near Hamilton. She contributed many sketches and poems to various periodicals and newspapers. These were collected, and 500 copies were published at the solicitation of her friends.

The Harp of Home; Or, the Medley, Cincinnati, 1858.

CORWIN, THOMAS (July 29, 1794–Dec. 18, 1865), lawyer and public official, was born in Bourbon County, Ky., but grew up in Lebanon, where his father moved in 1798. Largely self-educated, he was admitted to the bar in 1818. He served in the Ohio legislature, 1822–29, in the U. S. House of Representatives, 1830–40 and 1858–61, as governor of Ohio, 1840–42, in the U. S. Senate, 1844–50, as Secretary of the Treasury, 1850–53, and as minister to Mexico, 1861–64. At the time of his death in Washington, D. C., he was practicing law in that city. His vigorous opposition to the Mexican War probably handicapped his political advancement. He was a witty, eloquent orator, and many of his speeches were published separately.

Speeches of Thomas Corwin, with a Sketch of His Life, (Isaac Strohm, ed.), Dayton, 1859.

COSGROVE, MAYNARD GILES (June 5, 1895–), engineer, was born in Sylvania, Lucas County. After graduating from the University of Michigan in 1917, he was a valuation engineer for Chicago Commonwealth Edison Company and was on field duty with the Federal Power Commission, 1939–59. He has written a number of historical pamphlets, e.g., *A History of Sylvania for the First Hundred Years . . . ,* [Sylvania, 1933].

COTTER, JAMES HENRY (Aug. 19, 1858–Dec. 9, 1947), clergyman, was born in Tipperary, Ireland. Educated at Mt. St. Mary's, Md., he edited the *Catholic Columbian,* published in Columbus, and from 1889 until his death was pastor of St. Lawrence Church, Ironton. In 1904 he began lecturing on Ireland and Shakespeare. He published a book about his native town: *Tipperary,* New York, [1929]. CWW 7

COTTINGHAM, WALTER HORACE (Jan. 8, 1866–March 12, 1930), was born in Ounenice, Ontario, Canada. In 1898 he was made general manager of the Sherwin Williams Company in Ohio, and in 1908 he became president of the company. He resigned as president in 1922 and retired to England, where he spent the remainder of his life. He published a widely distributed book, *Business Success,* [Cleveland?, 1907]. OBB

COTTON, JAMES HARRY (June 9, 1896–), clergyman, born in Stephens, Minn., graduated from the College of Wooster in 1921 and served on the Wooster faculty, 1926–28. He was pastor of Broad Street Presbyterian Church, Columbus, 1928–40. Since leaving Ohio he has been president of McCormick Theological Seminary, 1940–47, and professor of philosophy, Wabash College. He has written *The Christian Experience of Life,* New York, [1933]. WW 30

COTTON, WILLIA DAWSON (Sept. 2, 1868–June 7, 1942), librarian, was born in Marietta, Washington County. She became librarian of Marietta Public Library in 1901, and spent her entire life in that community. She wrote *Sketch of Mound Cemetery . . .*, Marietta, 1904.

COULTER, ERNEST KENT (Nov. 14, 1871–May 1, 1952), lawyer, was born in Columbus, Franklin County. After graduating from Ohio State University in 1893, he worked on New York newspapers and studied law. He was one of the organizers of the Children's Court, New York City, founded the Big Brother Movement in 1904, and was active in other children's protective movements. He practiced law, 1912–37, and after his retirement lived in California. His writings include *The Children in the Shadow*, New York, 1913. WW 26

COVERT, JOHN CUTLER (Feb. 11, 1837–Jan. 14, 1919), founder and first president of the Rowfant Club of Cleveland, was born in Norwich, N. Y. His parents brought him to Cleveland while he was a boy, and, after serving a three-year apprenticeship, he worked as a printer in Cleveland and other cities. He became a reporter on the Cleveland *Leader* in 1868 and in 1890 was made editor. He lived in France, 1897–1909, serving as American consul in Lyons and Marseilles and teaching English. His death occurred in Cleveland.

The A.B.C. of Finances . . ., Akron, 1896.

COVEY, MRS. ARTHUR S. See Lois Lenski.

COWDEN, ROBERT (May 24, 1833–Sept. 27, 1922), was born in Leesville, Crawford County. Educated in local schools, he became a carpenter and worked at this trade until Sept. 9, 1861, when he enlisted as a private in Company B, 56th Illinois Volunteer Infantry. His service career was a most active one. He was promoted to lieutenant by reason of meritorious service at the battle of Shiloh, and on July 29, 1863, he was promoted to major of the 59th U. S. Colored Infantry. He was discharged Jan. 31, 1866, with the rank of lieutenant colonel. He served as postmaster at Galion, 1878–82. For a great many years he was a member of the general board of the Ohio Sunday School Association and became known throughout Ohio and the United Brethren Church as "The Sunday School Man." He wrote a family history in addition to the regimental history cited below.

A Brief Sketch of the Organization and Services of the Fifty-ninth Regiment of United States Colored Infantry, and Biographical Sketches, Dayton, 1883.

COWEN, BENJAMIN RUSH (Aug. 15, 1831–1908), who was born in Moorefield, Harrison County, was a journalist and also held various political appointments. During the Civil War he rose from private to brigadier general of volunteers. He died in Cincinnati.

Our Beacon Light . . ., Columbus, 1884.

The Miracle of the Nineteenth Century. Do Missions Pay?, Cincinnati, 1891.

Abraham Lincoln; An Appreciation by One Who Knew Him, Cincinnati, 1909.

COWLES, HENRY (April 24, 1803–Sept. 6, 1881), clergyman and educator, was born in Norfolk, Conn. He graduated from Yale University in 1826, and after attending the theological seminary for two years, he was ordained a home missionary in 1828. He came to Ohio, where he labored in missionary work for two years, chiefly in Ashtabula and Sandusky. He was on the faculty of Oberlin College, 1835–48, edited the *Oberlin Evangelist*, 1848–62, was general agent of the College, 1860–63, and was a lecturer there, 1869–78. He was an active antislavery man.

The Revelation of John . . ., New York, 1871.

The Pentateuch . . ., New York, 1874.

Hebrew History . . ., New York, 1875.

The Gospel and Epistles of John . . ., New York, 1876.

The Epistle to the Hebrews . . ., New York, 1878.

The Shorter Epistles . . ., New York, 1879.

The Longer Epistles of Paul . . ., New York, 1880.

Luke . . ., New York, 1881.

Matthew and Mark . . ., New York, 1881.

A Defence of Ohio Congregationalism and Oberlin College, [n.p., n.d.].

COWLES, JULIA DARROW (Jan. 6, 1862–Sept. 6, 1919), was born in Norwalk, Huron County. She graduated from Central High School, Buffalo, N. Y., in 1880 and studied at the University of Minnesota and Northwestern Conservatory, Minneapolis. She was department editor of the *Housekeeper*, 1903-06, and specialized in literature for children and storytelling to children. Her death occurred in Minneapolis, Minn.

Artistic Home Furnishing for People of Moderate Means, New York, [1898].

Jim Crow's Language Lessons, and Other Stories of Birds and Animals, New York, [1903].

Our Little Athenian Cousin of Long Ago; Being the Story of Hiero, a Boy of Athens, Boston, 1913.

Our Little Roman Cousin of Long Ago; Being the Story of Marcus, a Boy of Rome, Boston, 1913.

The Art of Story Telling, with Nearly Half a Hundred Stories, Chicago, 1914.

Our Little Spartan Cousin of Long Ago; Being the Story of Chartas, a Boy of Sparta, Boston, 1914.

Favorite Fairy Tales Retold; The First of a Series of Children's Classics Adapted for Story-telling, Chicago, 1915.

Our Little Macedonian Cousin of Long Ago; Being the Story of Nearchus, a Boy of Macedonia and Companion of Alexander, Boston, 1915.

Favorite Folk Tales Retold; The Second of a Series of Children's Classics Especially Adapted for Story-telling, Chicago, 1916.

Our Little Saxon Cousin of Long Ago; Being the Story of Turgar, a Boy of Anglo-Saxons, in the Time of Alfred the Great, Boston, 1916.

Going to School in Animal Land, Chicago, [1917].

Indian Nature Myths, Chicago, [1918].

The Children's Story Hour, (with Ethelyn Abbott), Chicago, 1924.

The Child's Own Fairy Book, Chicago, 1924.

Favorite Tales for Story-telling, Chicago, 1924.

Myths from Many Lands, Chicago, 1924.

Twilight Folk Tales, Chicago, 1924.

COX, GEORGE CLARKE (May 17, 1865–Dec. 17, 1943), clergyman, educator, and investment counselor, was born in Columbus, Franklin County. He graduated from Kenyon College in 1886 and Harvard University (Ph.D.) in 1910. He served as an Episcopal priest, 1888–1908. After resigning from the ministry in 1908, he was on the Harvard faculty until 1911, and he then taught at Dartmouth until 1915. After 1915 he was an insurance analyst and an economic advisor. Besides many magazine and newspaper articles, he wrote *The Public Conscience . . . ,* New York, [1922]. WWW 2

COX, JACOB DOLSON (Oct. 27, 1828–Aug. 4, 1900), was born in Montreal, Canada, of American parents, who moved to New York City the year after his birth. He attended private schools. He moved to Lorain in 1846 and three years later married Helen C. Finney, the daughter of Charles G. Finney (q.v.), president of Oberlin College. He graduated from Oberlin in 1851, studied law in Warren while serving as superintendent of schools, and was admitted to the bar in 1853. He was a member of the state senate in 1860 and 1861. During the Civil War he entered the Union Army as a brigadier general of Ohio Volunteers, April 23, 1861, and was promoted to major general, Oct. 6, 1862. Having been elected governor of Ohio in 1865, he resigned from the army Jan. 1, 1866. He served as governor, 1866–68, then moved to Cincinnati, where he resumed the practice of law. He was Secretary of Interior in the first Cabinet of President Grant, resigning Nov. 1, 1870, and again resuming the practice of law in Cincinnati. While president of the Wabash Railroad, 1873–78, he lived in Toledo. He was elected to the 45th Congress, but declined to be a candidate for renomination. He served as dean of the Cincinnati Law School, 1881–97, and as president of the University of Cincinnati, 1885–89. He died at Magnolia, Mass., and was interred at Spring Grove Cemetery, Cincinnati. From 1874 until his death he reviewed military books for the *Nation,* and he also wrote several important military histories. Many of his addresses were published separately as pamphlets.

Reconstruction and the Relation of the Races in the United States, Columbus, 1865.

Atlanta, New York, 1882.

The March to the Sea. Franklin and Nashville, New York, 1882.

The Second Battle of Bull Run . . . , Cincinnati, 1882.

The Battle of Franklin, Tennessee . . . , New York, 1897.

Military Reminiscences of the Civil War, 2 vols., New York, 1900.

COX, JACOB DOLSON (Nov. 1, 1881–Feb. 16, 1953), industrialist, was born in Cleveland, Cuyahoga County, the grandson of Jacob D. Cox (q.v.). He graduated from Williams College in 1903. After spending eight years in the lumber business in Oregon and Washington, he began as a mechanic in the Cleveland Twist Drill Co., founded by his father, and rose to the presidency in 1919. He wrote *The Economic Basis of Fair Wages,* New York, [1926]. WWW 3

COX, JAMES MIDDLETON (March 31, 1870–July 15, 1957), newspaper publisher, was born in Jacksonburg, Butler County. He grew up on a farm, learned the printing business, taught school, and worked on the Cincinnati *Enquirer.* In 1898 he bought the Dayton *Daily News,* to which he later added papers in Canton, Springfield, Atlanta, Ga., and Miami, Fla. He was a member of Congress, 1909–13, served three terms as governor of Ohio, 1913–15, 1917–21, and was the Democratic candidate for President in 1920. He published an autobiography, *Journey through My Years,* New York, 1946. WWW 3

COX, JOSEPH (Aug. 4, 1822–Oct. 13, 1900), lawyer and judge, was born in Chambersburg, Pa., but his parents brought him to Cincinnati in 1830. He read law, was admitted to the bar, and practiced in Cincinnati. He also served fifteen years as judge of common pleas court and fourteen years as judge of the circuit court. Besides the booklet below, several of his addresses were published as pamphlets.

United States Supreme Court: Its Organization and Judges to 1835, [Cincinnati, 1890].

COX, KENYON (Oct. 27, 1856–March 17, 1919), artist, was born in Warren, Trumbull County, the son of General Jacob Dolson Cox (q.v.). His paintings, mostly portraits, hang in many galleries. Though tolerant of other styles, he was a traditionalist in his own paintings. Several of his lectures and articles on painting were reprinted. He also wrote *Mixed Beasts, Rhymes and Pictures,* New York, 1904. DAB 4

COX, SAMUEL SULLIVAN (Sept. 30, 1824–Sept. 10, 1889), journalist and congressman, was born in Zanesville, Muskingum County, where his father, Ezekiel T. Cox, was editor of the *Muskingum Messenger.* After spending two years at Ohio University, he transferred to Brown University, where he graduated in 1846. He read law and practiced for two years in Cincinnati. A trip to Europe resulted in his writing *A Buckeye Abroad.* He became editor of the *Ohio Statesman* in Columbus in 1853 and from that time took an increasingly active part in politics. In 1856 he was first elected to the House of Representatives, where he served a total of twenty years, though not continuously. A vivid description of a sunset written for his newspaper gave him the nickname "Sunset" Cox, which remained with him throughout his life. During the Civil War he supported the government war effort, but he favored a swift peace, and he maintained his friendship with Clement L. Vallandigham (q.v.). In 1866 he moved to New York City, where he practiced law and continued his participation in Democratic politics. Many of his speeches were published separately, and he was a prolific contributor to newspapers and magazines.

A Buckeye Abroad; Or, Wanderings in Europe, and in the Orient, New York, 1852.

Ohio Politics. Cox after Giddings . . . , [Washington, 1859].

Eight Years in Congress, from 1857 to 1865. Memoir and Speeches, New York, 1865.

Search for Sunbeams in the Riviera, Corsica, Algiers and Spain, New York, 1870.

Why We Laugh, New York, 1876.

Free Land and Free Trade. The Lessons of the English Corn Laws Applied to the United States, New York, 1880.

Arctic Sunbeams: Or, from Broadway to the Bosphorus, by Way of the North Cape, 2 vols., New York, 1882.

Memorial Eulogies . . . , Washington, 1883.

Union—Disunion—Reunion. Three Decades of Federal Legislation . . . , Providence, R. I., 1885.

Diversions of a Diplomat in Turkey, New York, 1887.

The Isles of the Princes . . . , New York, 1887.

COX, WILLIAM VAN ZANDT (June 12, 1852–July 24, 1923), was born near Zanesville, Muskingum County. A graduate of Ohio Wesleyan University in 1874, he was admitted to the Ohio bar in 1877. He served in the U. S. Museum and was an official of many expositions. He became president of Second National Bank, Washington, D. C., in 1901. He wrote and lectured on historical and biographical subjects and with Milton H. Northrup wrote a life of his uncle, Samuel S. Cox (q.v.).

Life of Samuel Sullivan Cox, Syracuse, N. Y., 1899.

Biography of Matthew Gault Emery . . . , Washington, D. C., 1904.

COXE, MARGARET (1800– ?), was born in Burlington, N. J. Her personal life is quite obscured by her activity in behalf of the feminist movement. She apparently became effective in Ohio in the 1840s, reaching Cincinnati by 1845. There she taught in and probably helped to found the Cincinnati Female Seminary, being its director from 1849 to 1851. Her pious pen was very busy exhorting action and admonishing conduct of the righteous ladies of the day. Her moral strictures, *The Young Lady's Companion,* now as dull and old hat as the cause itself, received from clergymen what would be termed "rave" notices today. Isaac E. Whiting of Columbus was her enterprising publisher and sent out the manuscript for separate printings both in Gambier and in Boston, Mass. A third edition in gift format (1846) included "Token of Affection" on the gaudy title page and appended a recommended "List of books for female readers." The enormous success of this conduct book led to a similar book whose title is but a variant to intrigue a wider audience: *Claims of the Country on American Females.* Her *Floral Emblems; Or, Moral Sketches from*

Flowers is as juvenile and as saccharine as the decade itself when sentimentality was the convention. She was earlier responsible for several religious juveniles all published anonymously in New York: *Botany of the Scriptures, Wonders of the Deep, The Infant Brother,* and *Visit to Nahant.* These have sunk into an obscurity from which it is only kindness and good taste not to rescue them.

Wyman W. Parker

The Young Lady's Companion; In a Series of Letters, Columbus, 1839.
The Life of John Wycliffe, D.D., Columbus, 1840.
Claims of the Country on American Females, 2 vols., Columbus, 1842.
Floral Emblems; Or, Moral Sketches from Flowers, Cincinnati, 1845.
The Young Lady's Companion, and Token of Affection . . . , Columbus, 1846.
Woman: Her Station Providentially Appointed . . . , Columbus, 1848.

COXEY, JACOB SECHLER (April 16, 1854–May 18, 1951), reformer, was born in Selingsgrove, Pa., but lived most of his mature life in Massillon. Though wealthy from sandstone quarries, scrap iron, patent medicines, and a variety of other enterprises, he led bands of unemployed to Washington in 1894 and again in 1914 to urge loans of fiat money to local governments to finance public works. Though designated the Commonweal of Christ, his followers were familiarly known as Coxey's Army. He was a perennial candidate for political office. He wrote an analysis of his panacea: *The Coxey Plan . . . ,* Massillon, 1914. WWW 3

COY, MARTIN (April 8, 1863–Oct. 17, 1949), was born in Louisville, Stark County. He moved to Alliance in 1916 and was employed at the Alliance Machine Company and the First National Bank. In 1905 he became treasurer of the East Ohio Classis of the Reformed Church. He published a volume of religious sayings: *Gems of Wisdom,* New York, [1941].

COYLE, ROBERT McCURDY (July 17, 1860–Feb. 24, 1936), was born in Cincinnati, Hamilton County, but made his home in Philadelphia, Pa., where he was an insurance broker. He published privately *Fenceless France; The Story of an Automobile Ride,* Philadelphia, [1908]. WWW 1

CRABTREE, JAMES WILLIAM (April 18, 1864–June 9, 1945), educator, was born in Scioto County. After graduating from State Normal School, Peru, Neb., he taught in Nebraska and Wisconsin. He was secretary of the National Education Association, 1917–35. Besides numerous articles on educational subjects, he wrote his autobiography: *What Counted Most,* Lincoln, Neb., 1935. WWW 2

CRAFTS, SARA JANE (d. 1930), religious educator, was born in Cincinnati, Hamilton County. She was active in the temperance movement, was a Chautauqua lecturer, and founded the International Primary Union of Sunday School Teachers. With her husband, Wilbur F. Crafts, she wrote a number of lesson books for use in Sunday Schools and pleas for temperance.

The Infant Class . . . , (Edward Eggleston, ed.), Chicago, 1870.
A Tour around the World among the Temperance Brownies . . . , New York, [1896].

CRAIG, CLARENCE TUCKER (June 7, 1895–Aug. 20, 1953), clergyman and educator, was born in Benton Harbor, Maine. He graduated from Morningside College, Iowa, in 1915 and Boston University (S.T.B., 1919; Ph.D., 1924). He was professor of New Testament at Oberlin Graduate School of Theology, 1928–46. During his Ohio years he published *One God, One World . . . ,* New York, 1943. WWW 3

CRAIG, JOHN DAVID (April 28, 1903–), was born in Cincinnati, Hamilton County. From 1924 to 1941 he served as cameraman and director on various expeditions. He has specialized in the production of adventure motion pictures and television films that require underwater or jungle scenes. His experiences are described in *Danger Is My Business,* New York, 1938. WW 30

CRAMER, MICHAEL JOHN (Feb. 6, 1835–Jan. 23, 1898), clergyman and diplomat, was born near Schaffhausen, Switzerland. In 1845 his family came to America and settled in Cincinnati, where Michael learned the printing trade. After graduating from Ohio Wesleyan University in 1859, he became a Methodist minister. In 1863 he married Mary Frances Grant, sister of U. S. Grant. He served in diplomatic posts in Leipzig, 1867–70, Denmark, 1871–81, and Switzerland, 1881–85. He died in Carlisle, Pa., while serving as professor of philosophy at Dickinson College. He published many theological articles, but only one book.

Ulysses S. Grant: Conversations and Unpublished Letters, New York, [1897].

CRANE, GABRIEL (1783– ?), was born in New Jersey. After coming to Ohio, he lived in Warren County, and died in Waynesville sometime after 1850. Except for his authorship of the pamphlet below, nothing is known of his life.

A Review of the Writings of Philo Pacificus against War . . . , Lebanon, 1818.

CRANE, HART (July 21, 1899–April 27, 1932), poet, was born in Garrettsville, Portage County. His father, Clarence A. Crane, was an energetic businessman, owner of a chain of confectionery stores and a candy manufacturer. His mother was an ardent Christian Scientist. Their incompatibility culminated in divorce in 1916, and Crane later attributed the unhappiness of his personal life to "the curse of sundered parentage." Throughout his parents' domestic difficulties, he sided with his mother and was constantly at odds with his father, whose chief concern was that he should enter the family business. He attended public schools of Warren and Cleveland. He was writing verse at the age of thirteen, but found little encouragement except from a few little magazines, which were to remain his chief publishing outlet. In 1916, after a bitter quarrel with his father, he went to New York City to stay with Carl Schmitt, an Ohio-born painter. He wrote for the *Pagan* and other *avant-garde* periodicals and drifted into the irregular habits which culminated in homosexuality and alcoholism. From 1916 to 1925 he alternated between Ohio and Greenwich Village, working intermittently as a reporter, a warehouse helper, a salesman, and a shipyard worker. His only congenial companionship in Ohio he found at Herbert Fletcher's bookshop next to his father's store in Akron. In the early 1920s he produced his first major poems, "For the Marriage of Faustus and Helen" and "At Melville's Tomb." Publication of *White Buildings* in 1926 led to two grants from Otto Kahn, wealthy patron of the arts, and enabled him to work on his ambitious long poem, *The Bridge*. This poem, a conscious effort to refute the spirit of Eliot's *Wasteland,* attempted to express the myth of America, its vitality and strength. The central symbol of the poem is Brooklyn Bridge. His wish to identify himself with American life resembles the poetic aims of Whitman. A subjective mysticism renders the poem highly obscure and robs it of organic unity, but it is filled with vivid images. The critical success of *The Bridge* in 1930 resulted in Crane's receiving a Guggenheim fellowship to go to Mexico to write a long poem on Cortes and Montezuma. Feeling that he had failed and had wasted his fellowship time in Mexico, he leaped to his death from the ship on which he was traveling back to New York. *Collected Poems,* edited by Waldo Frank, was published in 1933. His genuine poetic talents, which were never fully realized, and the pathos of his personal life won him a circle of admirers; but the obscurity and inconclusiveness of his verse have kept that circle small. DAB 21

CRANMER, GIBSON LAMB (1826–1903), lawyer, was born in Cincinnati, Hamilton County. After graduating from Woodward College in 1847, he read law; he practiced in Wheeling, W. Va., and also served for eight years as judge of Wheeling municipal court. He wrote *History of Wheeling City and Ohio County, West Virginia,* Chicago, 1902. WWW 1

CRANSTON, EARL (June 27, 1840–Aug. 2, 1932), clergyman, was born in Athens, Athens County, and was reared in Jackson County. After attending Ohio University, he served with Ohio and West Virginia troops in the Civil War. Converted to Methodism after the war, he joined the Ohio Conference in 1867, and after preaching in several states was made bishop in 1896. He was a founder of the Methodist Book Concern, Cincinnati. He died in New Richmond. He published numerous books and addresses, including a plea for the reuniting of Northern and Southern branches of the Methodist Church: *Breaking Down the Walls,* New York, [1915]. DAB 21

CRANSTON, LUCIE MASON (July 6, 1857–Oct. 23, 1937), wife of Bishop Earl Cranston (q.v.), was born in Cincinnati, Hamilton County. She attended Ohio Wesleyan Female Seminary. After her husband's retirement in 1912, they lived near New Richmond, Clermont County, and her death occurred in that community. She published an anonymous collection of poetry: *Some Little Verses (Mostly Reverses) by an Unversed Author,* Cincinnati, [1928].

CRAPSEY, ALGERNON SIDNEY (June 28, 1847–Dec. 31, 1927), clergyman, father of the poet Adelaide Crapsey, was born in Hamilton County. After spending two years in the army during the Civil War, he entered business. From 1869 to 1872 he studied at St. Stephen's College and Seminary, after which he was ordained an Episcopal priest. After serving as rector of St. Andrew's Church, Rochester, N. Y., 1879–

1906, he was deposed for heresy for questioning the divinity of Jesus Christ. His death occurred in Rochester.

Five Joyful Mysteries, New York, 1888.
The Story of a Simple Life . . . , New York, 1900.
The Greater Love, New York, [1902].
Religion and Politics, New York, [1905].
The Re-birth of Religion . . . , New York, 1907.
Did Jesus Really Live? A Debate . . . , Chicago, [1908].
The Rise of the Working Class, New York, 1914.
International Republicanism, the Way to Permanent Peace, Philadelphia, 1918.
The Ways of the Gods, New York, 1920.
The Last of the Heretics . . . , New York, 1924.

CRARY, CHRISTOPHER GORE (Jan. 22, 1806–March 13, 1895), born in Becket, Mass., was brought to Kirtland by his parents in 1811. They were among the first settlers of that community. When past eighty, he wrote his reminiscences for the Willoughby *Independent.* They were later published in an edition of 100 copies. He died in Lamoile, Iowa, at the home of a son.

Pioneer and Personal Reminiscences, Marshalltown, Iowa, 1893.

CRAVATH, PAUL DRENNAN (July 14, 1861–July 1, 1940), lawyer, was born in Berlin Heights, Erie County, where his father was Congregational minister. His father was chaplain of the 101st O.V.I. during the Civil War, and afterward the family lived in Cincinnati (1866–70). He graduated from Oberlin in 1882 and Columbia Law School in 1886. Practicing in New York City, he became one of the nation's first modern corporation lawyers. Besides legal works, he published several accounts of his travels, including *Letters Home from the Far East and Russia,* [New York, 1931]. DAB 22

CRAVENS, MARY J. (1825–Feb. 5, 1912), born in Pavilion, N. Y., lived in Toledo for nearly thirty years. She came there in 1873, when her husband, Charles Cravens, became pastor of the Unitarian church. She was active in the cultural life of the city, worked for the cause of women's suffrage, and published poems in various periodicals. The volume listed below was written in memory of a daughter who died in childhood.

Story of Daisy . . . , Toledo, 1898.

CRAWFORD, BENJAMIN F. (May 12, 1881–), clergyman, was born near London, Madison County. He graduated from Ohio Wesleyan University in 1906 and also studied at Boston University and the University of Pittsburgh. He retired from the Methodist ministry in 1945 and now lives in Delaware. He has published several books on religious themes, e.g., *Religious Trends in a Century of Hymns,* Carnegie, Pa., [1937]. RLA 2

CRAWFORD, CHARLES (1866–Dec. 28, 1945), army officer, was born in Coshocton, Coshocton County. He graduated from the U. S. Military Academy in 1889 and served in the army until his retirement as a brigadier general in 1919. After retiring from the army, he lived in Paola, Kan. His death occurred in that community. He wrote a book on economics and at least two books on military subjects, e.g., *Six Months with the 6th Brigade,* Kansas City, Mo., [1928]. WWW 3

CRAWFORD, LYDIA BENEDICT, poet, was born in New Orleans. In 1900 she married Wilmer Crawford, and in 1908 they moved to Cincinnati, where she lived until 1955, when she returned to New Orleans. She has published a collection of poems: *The Afterglow,* Columbus, 1937.

CRAWFORD, MARY (Oct. 23, 1861–May 17, 1946), missionary, was born in Madison Township, Columbiana County. She attended Mount Hope Academy, Mount Union College, and Moody Bible Institute, Chicago. In 1895 she joined her aunts Sue and Kate McBeth, Presbyterian missionaries to the Nez Percé Indians. After her formal retirement, she continued to teach music and recreation among the Indians. She died in the West and is buried at Spalding, Idaho. She wrote *The Nez Percés Since Spalding . . . ,* [Berkeley, Calif.], 1936.

CRAWFORD, THOMAS ROBB (March 8, 1821–June 24, 1898), clergyman, was born near New Athens, Harrison County, but grew up near Steubenville, where his parents moved when he was a few months old. He graduated from Franklin College in 1844, taught there for two years, and was ordained by the Steubenville Presbytery in 1846. He was pastor of Nottingham Presbyterian Church, Moorefield, 1847–86.

Historical Narrative of the Presbyterian Church of Nottingham . . . , Wheeling, W. Va., 1871.
Forty Years Pastorate and Reminiscences, Wheeling, W. Va., 1887.

CREAGER, CHARLES E. (April 28, 1873–), was born in Farmersville, near Dayton, Montgomery County. While attending Northern Indiana University, he taught school; he later worked on various newspapers in Dayton, Columbus, Cincinnati, and Marietta. He served with the 4th O.V.I. during the Spanish-American War. In 1904 he moved to Muskogee, Okla., and still lives in that community. He served in the 61st Congress, was in the U. S. Indian Service, and was in the oil business until his retirement in 1934.

The 14th Ohio National Guard . . ., Columbus, 1899.

CRECRAFT, EARL WILLIS (Jan. 27, 1886–March 30, 1950), educator, was born in Brookville, Ind. He graduated from Franklin College in 1907 and Columbia University (Ph.D.) in 1911. He was professor of political science at the University of Akron, 1919–38, and professor and dean at Kent State University, 1938–47. His writings include *Freedom of the Seas,* New York, 1935. WWW 3

CREHORE, WILLIAM WILLIAMS (Feb. 3, 1864–Sept. 13, 1918), civil engineer, was born in Cleveland, Cuyahoga County. He graduated from Yale University in 1886 and Sheffield Scientific School in 1888. He lived in New Jersey. Besides technical articles, he wrote *Protection's Brood; A Presentation of the Direct and Indirect Consequences of the Continuance of a Protective Tariff System . . .*, New York, 1912. WWW 1

CRESSEY, GEORGE BABCOCK (Dec. 15, 1896–), educator, was born in Tiffin, Seneca County. He graduated from Denison University in 1919 and the University of Chicago (Ph.D.) in 1921. He joined the faculty of the University of Syracuse in 1931. Widely known as a geographer and geologist, he has written numerous textbooks and books on current problems, e.g., *The Basis of Soviet Strength,* London, [1944]. WW 29

CRESSLER, ALFRED MILLER (Sept. 19, 1877–Nov. 19, 1939), banker, born in Fort Wayne, Ind., lived in Cincinnati from 1914 until his death. An executive of Central Trust Company, he published *Vignettes of Writers and Artists,* [San Francisco], 1946.

CRETCHER, MACK (Dec. 9, 1868–June 20, 1946), journalist, was born in Springhills, Champaign County. In 1871 his parents moved to Kansas. After attending the schools of Sedgwick, Kan., he operated a farm and then published the Sedgwick *Pantagraph,* 1892–1913. After eight years in the Philippines as assistant director of agriculture, he edited the Newton *Journal,* 1925–40. He wrote *The Kansan; A Novel,* Philadelphia, [1923]. WWNAA 7

CREW, FLEMING H. (May 21, 1882–), lawyer, was born in McConnelsville, Morgan County. After graduating from Ohio State University (A.B.; LL.B), he began the practice of law in Cleveland in 1907. He was assistant attorney general in Puerto Rico, 1910–11. He retired from active practice in 1930 and now lives in Beverly. With his sister, Alice Crew Gall (q.v.), he wrote several hundred stories for children and a number of books, e.g., *The Royal Mimkin,* New York, 1934.

CREWSON, EVANDER A. (Dec. 8, 1849– ?), was born in Washington County. No details concerning his life have been found, but he apparently moved to Missouri, where his only book was published.

Old Times, a Collection of Poems, Kansas City, Mo., 1893.

CRILE, GEORGE WASHINGTON (Nov. 11, 1864–Jan. 7, 1943), physician, was born in Chilli, Coshocton County. He graduated from Ohio Northern University in 1886 and University of Wooster (M.D.) in 1887. He was a member of the Wooster faculty, 1899–1900, and of the Western Reserve University faculty, 1900–24. One of the world's great surgeons, he was a founder of the Cleveland Clinic. He wrote a great many professional articles and books, as well as books for the general reader, e.g., *A Mechanistic View of War and Peace,* New York, 1915. WWW 2

CRILE, GRACE McBRIDE (Jan. 23, 1876–Aug. 23, 1948), was born in Cleveland, Cuyahoga County. She married the distinguished surgeon George W. Crile (q.v.), Feb. 7, 1900. She accompanied her husband on a scientific expedition to Africa and kept a day-by-day journal of her adventures, which she published as *Skyways to a Jungle Laboratory,* New York, [1936]. She also edited a two-volume autobiography of her husband, drawing on his diaries and other records and adding sidelights written by herself.

CRIPPEN, WILLIAM G. (July 4, 1820–April, 1863), journalist, was born in Cincinnati, Hamilton County. At the age of sixteen, he became a printer working for J. A. James. In 1840 he was one of the founders of the

Cincinnati *Times* and served for many years on its editorial staff. In the early years of the Civil War he served as a correspondent. Many of his newspaper pieces were written under the pen name Invisible Green. Although his humorous sketches appear to have attracted wide attention, little is known about him.

Green Peas, Picked from the Patch of Invisible Green, Esq., Cincinnati, [1856].

CRISPIN, WILLIAM FROST (Nov. 14, 1833–Jan. 20, 1916), clergyman, was born near New Martinsburg, Fayette County, and spent his boyhood on a farm in Highland County. After graduating from National Normal University in 1860, he taught school for several terms and then entered the drug and grocery business. In the early 1880s he was employed by Buchtel College as a fund-raiser. He was an ardent prohibitionist. He preached for a number of years before his ordination as a Universalist minister in 1890, after which he organized a church in Mansfield and also preached in Springfield. His death occurred in Akron. Besides the title below, he published a family history and a lecture on Abraham Lincoln.

Universalism and Problems of the Universalist Church, Akron, 1888.

CRONBACH, ABRAHAM (Feb. 16, 1882–), educator and rabbi, was born in Indianapolis, Ind. He graduated from the University of Cincinnati in 1902 and Hebrew Union College in 1906. After serving as rabbi in various cities, including Akron (1917–19), he joined the faculty of Hebrew Union College, where he served as professor of social studies, 1922–50. His writings include *The Quest for Peace,* Cincinnati, 1937. WW 28

CROOK, ALJA ROBINSON (June 17, 1864–May 30, 1930), educator, was born in Circleville, Pickaway County. He graduated from Ohio Wesleyan University in 1887. After 1892 he lived in Illinois, where he taught at Wheaton College and Northwestern University and served as curator of the State Museum of Natural History, 1906–17. His writings include technical articles and monographs and *A History of the Illinois State Museum of Natural History,* Springfield, Ill., 1907. WWW 1

CROOK, GEORGE (Sept. 23, 1829–March 21, 1890), army officer, was born near Dayton, Montgomery County. After graduating from the U. S. Military Academy in 1848, he served in the Northwest until the outbreak of the Civil War. His service during the war was commendable though unspectacular, and he rose to the brevet grade of major general. After the war until his death, Crook served in the West, fighting against the Sioux in 1876 and against the Apaches in the early 1880s. His general attitude toward the Indians, however, was humane and enlightened. Except for letters on the Indian question and official reports, he published nothing during his lifetime. His autobiography was edited by Martin F. Schmitt in 1946: *General George Crook. His Autobiography,* Norman, Okla., 1946. DAB 4

CROOK, ISAAC (Dec. 10, 1833–Feb. 20, 1916), clergyman and educator, was born in Crossenville, Perry County. He graduated from Ohio Wesleyan University in 1859. Ordained to the ministry of the Methodist Church in 1864, he served pastorates in Ohio, Illinois, Michigan, Minnesota, and Kentucky. He also served as president of the University of the Pacific, 1891–92, chancellor of Nebraska Wesleyan University, 1892–96, and president of Ohio University, 1896–98. His death occurred in Spokane, Wash.

Hon. C. C. White. A Character Sketch, Cincinnati, 1896.

Jonathan Edwards, Cincinnati, [1903].

The Earnest Expectation, Cincinnati, [1905].

John Knox: The Reformer, Cincinnati, [1906].

The Great Five; The First Faculty of the Ohio Wesleyan University, Cincinnati, [1908].

CROOKS, JAMES (Oct. 6, 1825–Feb. 1, 1908), physician, was born in Butler County, a native Ohioan by the length of a hallway. His parents' home was on the state line, and he was born on the Ohio side. The following year the family moved to Indiana, where he spent his life except during his attendance at Eclectic Medical College, Cincinnati, where he graduated in 1859.

The Autobiography of James Crooks . . . , Terre Haute, Ind., 1900.

CROSS, DAVID WALLACE (Nov. 17, 1814–April 9, 1891), was born in Richland, N. Y. After attending Hamilton Seminary, he moved to Cleveland in 1836. He practiced law for a while, but in 1835 with Oliver Hazard Perry (q.v.) he engaged in coal mining in the Mahoning Valley—a business in which he acquired a substantial fortune so that he could retire in 1867. He was one of the founders of the renowned Winous

Point Shooting Club on Sandusky Bay and became well known for his articles on gunnery and angling.

Fifty Years with the Gun and Rod . . . , Cleveland, 1880.

CROSS, NELSON (1820–March 13, 1897), lawyer and judge, was born in Lancaster, N. H. Before the Civil War he practiced law in Cincinnati, where he was a founder of the Literary Club and also served as judge of common pleas court in 1854. During the Civil War, he served in the 1st Long Island Volunteers and the 67th New York Infantry. He was cited for gallantry at Gettysburg, and in 1867 he was promoted to the brevet rank of major general. After the war he practiced law in New York City until 1894. He died in Dorchester, Mass.

Life of General Grant . . . , New York, [1872?].

CROSS, ROSELLE THEODORE (Aug. 21, 1844–Nov. 18, 1924), clergyman, was born in Richville, N. Y. He entered Oberlin College in 1861, and while in college he taught in several Ohio schools. He attended Union Theological Seminary and was ordained to the ministry of the Congregational Church in 1869. After serving as principal of the preparatory department, Oberlin College, 1869–74, he served numerous pastorates in the West. He was a pastor in Cleveland, 1910–12, and in Twinsburg, 1912–17. After retiring from the ministry, he continued to live in Twinsburg until his death. Besides the titles below, he published a rhetoric manual and a family history.

Home Duties . . . , Chicago, [1886].
Clear as Crystal . . . , Chicago, [1887].
Crystals and Gold, York, Neb., 1903.
My Mountains, Boston, 1921.

CROSS, STEWART. Pseud. See Harry S. Drago.

CROTHERS, SAMUEL (Oct. 22, 1783–July 22, 1856), clergyman, was born near Chambersburg, Pa. He accompanied his father to Lexington, Ky., in 1787. In 1809 he was licensed to preach by the Kentucky Presbytery, and in 1810 he began preaching in Greenfield and Chillicothe. As a result of his opposition to closed communion, he resigned in 1818 and moved to Winchester, Ky., but he returned to Greenfield in 1820 and organized a church that he served until his death. He was a vigorous opponent of slavery and wrote a series of letters on abolition in the Cincinnati *Journal,* 1827–31. He died in Oswego, Ill., while visiting his son. Besides the title below, a number of his sermons were published.

The Life and Writings of Samuel Crothers, D.D., (Andrew Ritchie, ed.), Cincinnati, 1857.

CROTHERS, SAMUEL DICKEY (April 20, 1883–July 19, 1916), clergyman, was born in Greenfield, Highland County, the son of Samuel Crothers (q.v.). He studied at Centre College, Princeton University, and Danville Seminary. In 1863 he became pastor of the Greenfield church, where his father had served for more than 35 years. He resigned his pastorate in 1900 because of ill health.

Centennial Historical Sketches of Greenfield, Ohio, and Vicinity, (with W. H. Irwin), Greenfield, 1876.

CROUSE, DAVID ELDRIDGE (Oct. 7, 1882–), electrical engineer, was born in Kingston, Ross County, and attended the schools of that community. He was chief engineer of several electric railway companies in Maryland and New York. After retiring in 1932, he returned to Kingston, where he now lives. In 1934 he prepared a centennial history of the town. He has also published *The Ohio Gateway,* New York, 1938.

CROUSE, RUSSEL (Feb. 20, 1893–), the son of Hiram Powers and Sarah (Schumacher) Crouse, is said to have been born in Findlay, Hancock County. No other city in or out of Ohio has claimed to be his birthplace, but Findlay has never taken the trouble to deny it. Thus the Ohioana Library has been placed in the delicate position of listing Mr. Crouse among its *Ohio Authors and Their Books.* His father was a newspaperman and for many years was the publisher of the Toledo *News-Bee.* This forms the basis of the assertion that Russel Crouse was educated in the public schools of Toledo. He did attend the public schools of Toledo. This must be said in all fairness to Crouse, even if it is not fair to Toledo. He was a loving son, however, and did learn enough to read newspapers—his father's and others. It is not strange, therefore, that when he reached the age of earning a living (this was expected of boys around the turn of the century) he turned to newspaper work. In 1910 he started as a reporter on the Cincinnati *Commercial-Tribune.* The next we hear of the subject of this dossier is that he had become a reporter on the Kansas City *Star.* The year was 1911. He was later promoted (?) to sports writer and managed to hold his job on this paper for five years. During his tenure as sports writer there was a prize fighter in the Middle West who fought under the name of Buck Crouse. This quickly settled the question of how his intimates would address our hero. You can hardly call a sports writer Russel, so he was called Buck, an appellation that has stuck to him ever since. In 1916 Buck approached the management of the Kansas City *Star* for a small raise. He was turned down and removed himself from that paper. He has said since that had he received this paltry raise he might have spent the rest of his life on the Kansas City *Star*. Thus are dramatists made. He next went to the Cincinnati *Post* as a political reporter. And in 1918 he enlisted in the Navy. When his children say to him: "Daddy, what did you do in the great war?", being a truthful man, he has to answer: "'I was on recruiting duty." He was also managing editor of the *Great Lakes Bulletin*. After the war the evidence in the files shows that he came to New York and was a reporter on the New York *Globe*, the New York *Evening Mail*, and the New York *Evening Post*. Of these three papers, only the latter survived Mr. Crouse's services. He became a columnist, publishing paragraphs of his own devising, besides light verse and pieces of wit which were contributed. Through this column he gained a reputation in New York of being a most amusing fellow. On June 17, 1923, he married Alison Smith (now deceased), a newspaperwoman with whom he had worked on the *Evening Globe*. During his stints on New York newspapers he eked out his salary by serving as press agent for various people in the entertainment field, such as Ruth Draper, Edward Johnson of the Met, and a string of prize fighters. In 1932 he obtained a leave of absence from the New York *Post* and became the press agent for the Theatre Guild. This organization was at that time the most active and distinguished management producing plays in the city of New York. Press agentry brought Mr. Crouse into the theater, an institution of which he had been a devotee since he first went to burlesque shows. In 1931 Mr. Crouse took a fling at writing the libretto of a musical comedy. It was called *The Gang's All Here*. Several collaborators were called in to contribute ideas, among them being Oscar Hammerstein, II. This is worth mentioning because in 1959 Mr. Crouse again found himself working with Oscar Hammerstein, II. *The Gang's All Here* did not attract any great public attendance and collapsed after a few weeks. In 1933, in collaboration with Corey Ford, Mr. Crouse wrote the libretto of *Hold Your Horses* for Joe Cook. This was his first success in the theater. It ran an entire season. In 1934 Mr. Crouse was looking out of the window of his office in the Guild Theatre on 52nd Street. Looking out of an office window of the Alvin Theatre, exactly across the street, was the producer, Vinton Freedley, who called across to Crouse to come over and see him. It turned out Freedley had been trying to reach Mr. Crouse all day, it not occurring to him that his quarry was just across the street. When they met, Mr. Freedley said, "How would you like to write a musical comedy with Howard Lindsay?" Mr. Crouse answered, "When do we start?" They started that night, and this collaboration has lasted ever since—a matter of 25 years as of now. To list their joint efforts: *Anything Goes*, 1934; *Red, Hot and Blue*, 1936; *Hooray for What?*, 1937; *Life with Father*, 1939; *Strip for Action*, 1942; *State of the Union*, 1945 (Pulitzer Prize Play, 1946); *Life with Mother*, 1948; *Call Me Madam*, 1950; *Remains to Be Seen*, 1951; *The Prescott Proposals*, 1953 (starring Katharine Cornell); *The Great Sebastians*, 1955 (starring Alfred Lunt and Lynn Fontanne); *Happy Hunting*, 1956; *Tall Story*, 1959; *The Sound of Music*, 1959 (with Rodgers and Hammerstein and starring Mary Martin). *Life with Father* holds the record of the longest consecutive run of any play in New York City. Not content with writing plays this team also produced plays written by other dramatists: *Arsenic and Old Lace*, by Joseph Kesselring (1941), *The Hasty Heart*, by John Patrick (1945), and *Detective Story*, by Sidney Kingsley (1949). The only play they both wrote and produced was *The Great Sebastians*. Mr. Crouse's success as an author is not limited to plays. He wrote the following books: *Mr. Currier and Mr. Ives* (1930), *It Seems like Yesterday* (1931), *Murder Won't Out* (1932), *The American Keepsake* (1932). Besides these, he has been a contributor of articles to magazines; and both alone and in collaboration with Howard Lindsay has written many screenplays, and together Mr. Crouse and Mr. Lindsay adapted for television *Arsenic and Old Lace* and *State of the Union*. On June 28, 1945, Mr. Crouse married Anna Erskine, the daughter of the distinguished author and educator, John Erskine. They have two children—Timothy, born 1947, and Lindsay Ann, born 1948. Mr. Crouse and his wife have collaborated on two Landmark books for children: *Peter Stuyvesant* and *Alexander Hamilton and Aaron*

Burr. The Crouses have a house at 151 East 61st Street in New York City and another at Annisquam, Mass., where they spend the summer months. Mr. Crouse is active in the Dramatists' Guild and its parent body, The Authors' League of America, which he served at one time as president. He is a member of The Players. In 1951 Mr. Crouse was given an honorary degree of Doctor of Fine Arts by Ohio Wesleyan. The humorist who is the subject of this biography thereupon stated that this answered the question "Is there a doctor in the Crouse?" This anecdote is included as an encouragement to all young Ohioans who someday hope to be writers.

Howard Lindsay

CROWELL, BENEDICT (Oct. 21, 1869–Sept. 8, 1952), mining engineer, was born in Cleveland, Cuyahoga County. He graduated from Yale University in 1891. During World War I he was assistant secretary of war and director of munitions, and in World War II he was defense consultant to Secretary of War Henry L. Stimson. With Robert F. Wilson (q.v.), he wrote a six-volume World War I history: *How America Went to War,* New Haven, 1921. WW 26

CROWELL, CHESTER THEODORE (Oct. 14, 1888–Dec. 26, 1941), was born in Cleveland, Cuyahoga County. He worked on various newspapers in the Southwest and on the New York *Evening Post.* He was a special assistant to the Secretary of the Treasury in the early years of the New Deal, an experience that led to his writing *Recovery Unlimited; The Administration's Monetary Policy and the Current Boom,* New York, [1936]. WWW 1

CROWNFIELD, GERTRUDE (Oct. 26, 1867–June 3, 1945), was born in Baltimore, Md., and became a schoolteacher in Urbana at the age of seventeen. She also attended Urbana University for a time. She later taught school in Wisconsin and was a nurse in New York City. She wrote many historical novels for young readers, e.g., *Freedom's Daughter,* New York, 1930. AATB

CROZIER, ALFRED OWEN (Aug. 10, 1863–Sept. 26, 1939), lawyer and banker, was born in Grand Rapids, Mich., and lived there until 1909, when he moved to Cincinnati. He was an active supporter of Theodore Roosevelt in the Bull Moose campaign of 1912. His death occurred at Harbor Springs, Mich. He wrote a number of technical works dealing with finance and international law and also published a novel, *The Magnet; A Romance of the Battles of Modern Giants,* New York, 1908. OBB

CRUMLEY, JOHN JACKSON (Feb. 10, 1863–Jan. 1, 1952), state forester and educator, was born in Carter County, Tenn. He earned his Ph.D. at Johns Hopkins University in 1904. After serving as professor of Latin at Antioch College, he became a state forester at the Ohio Experiment Station, Wooster, in 1909. In 1912 he moved to Athens. He established a number of parks in southern Ohio. His writings on forestry include *Constructive Forestry for the Private Owner,* New York, 1926.

CULBERTSON, ANNE VIRGINIA (Nov. 16, 1864–Dec. 7, 1918), was born in Zanesville, Muskingum County. She attended public and private schools in Wisconsin, Missouri, and Kentucky, and graduated from Putnam Seminary, Zanesville. She contributed verse and stories to magazines and also gave readings from her own works. She lived in Zanesville. Most of her writing is in Negro dialect.

Lays of a Wandering Minstrel, Philadelphia, 1896.

At the Big House Where Aunt Nancy and Aunt 'Phrony Held Forth on the Animal Folks, Indianapolis, [1904].

Banjo Talks, Indianapolis, [1905].

CULBERTSON, HENRY COE (July 11, 1874–March 2, 1933), clergyman, was born in Cincinnati, Hamilton County, the son of James Coe Culbertson (q.v.). After graduating from the University of Cincinnati in 1895 and Columbus Law School in 1898, he earned a bachelor of divinity degree at the University of Chicago and in 1902 was ordained a Presbyterian minister. He served widely scattered pastorates throughout the United States. Among his writings is *Evolution Helps Christianity . . . ,* [Chicago, 1925]. WWW 1

CULBERTSON, HUGH EMMETT (April 15, 1882–   ), lawyer and judge, was born in Havana, Huron County. He attended Milan schools, read law in Sandusky, and graduated from the law school of Ohio State University in 1905. In the same year he began practicing in Sandusky and also became an editor on the staff of the Laning Law Book Company, Norwalk. He was a writer on the staff of the Lawyers' Co-operating Publishing Company, Rochester, N. Y., 1908–12. He resumed the practice of law at Loudonville in 1912. He has served as judge of the court of common pleas and now lives in Ashland. His writings include *Medical Men and the Law . . .*, Philadelphia, 1913. WW 8

CULBERTSON, JAMES COE (Dec. 19, 1840–1908), physician, was born at Culbertson's Mills, Miami County. He entered the Civil War as a private, became a hospital steward, and was promoted to assistant surgeon. He served with the 5th O.V.I. and the 137th O.V.I. After the war he began practicing medicine in Cincinnati, where he edited the *Lancet and Clinic.* In 1893 he was named to the faculty of Cincinnati College of Medicine and Surgery.

Luke: The Beloved Physician . . ., Cincinnati, 1899.

CULLER, ARTHUR JEROME (March 14, 1883–Nov. 27, 1946), clergyman, was born at Hartville, Stark County. He graduated from Juniata College in 1908, Union Theological Seminary in 1911, and Columbia University (Ph.D.) in 1912. A minister of the Disciples of Christ, he was dean of Hiram College, 1921–29, and pastor of Heights Christian Church in Cleveland, 1930–45. His writings include *Creative Religious Literature; A New Literary Study of the Bible,* New York, 1930. WWW 2

CULLER, LUCY YEEND (Feb. 25, 1849–Oct. 10, 1924), was born in Cheltenham, England. When she was three, her family came to Claridon Township, Geauga County. She attended district schools until she was fifteen and then became a country schoolteacher. She entered Oberlin College and graduated in 1873. She afterward taught in the Cleveland public schools for four years. In 1877 she married Rev. Jacob H. Culler, a Lutheran minister. They lived in Williams County, Iowa, and Bucyrus, Wapakoneta, and Springfield.

Europe, through a Woman's Eye, Philadelphia, 1883.

Violet, Burlington, Iowa, 1889.

Lectures. Addresses, Dayton, 1905.

A Retrospect and Other Poems, Dayton, 1914.

CUNNINGHAM, ALBERT BENJAMIN (June 22, 1888–), educator, was born in Linden, W. Va., but grew up in Ohio. He graduated from Muskingum College in 1913, Drew Theological Seminary in 1915, and New York University (Ph.D.) in 1926. He was dean of Lebanon University, 1916–17, and taught English at several other institutions before joining the staff of Texas Technical College in 1929. He has written educational articles and numerous mystery novels, some of them under the pen name Garth Hale, e.g., *Murder at Deer Lick,* New York, 1939. WW 30

CUNNINGHAM, AUBURN S. (May 15, 1884–), industrial engineer, was born in Lafayette, Ind., and attended the public schools of Frankfort, Ind., and Bucyrus. He later lived in Cleveland and Canton. He has written a Presidential history which has been issued in several revised editions: *Everything You Want to Know about the Presidents,* [Cleveland, 1928].

CUNNINGHAM, VIRGINIA (June 20, 1909–), was born in Dayton, Montgomery County. After graduating from Ohio State University in 1931, she taught at Wilbur Wright High School, Dayton, until 1938, when she resigned to do free-lance writing. She has also done editorial work for Scott, Foresman Company, 1940–46, and Saalfield Publishing Company, 1946–47. In 1949 she married Lloyd E. Holmgren, a mining engineer, and until 1954 she lived in South America. She is now a resident of Portland, Oreg. She has published many articles and stories in children's magazines and more than twenty books, e.g., *Paul Laurence Dunbar and His Song,* New York, 1947.

CUNNINGHAM, WALLACE McCOOK (March 23, 1881–Nov. 10, 1945), educator, was born in Lisbon, Columbiana County. He graduated from Roanoke College in 1902 and the University of Pennsylvania (Ph.D.) in 1922. He taught at Wharton School of Finance, 1908–09 and 1917–21. He was engaged in ranching and real estate in British Columbia, 1909–17, and taught at a number of universities including New York University, 1921–24, University of Southern California, 1924–27, and the University of Georgia, 1931–33. He also was president of the California Stock Exchange. He wrote a book to prove that a group of Freemasons headed by Francis Bacon wrote Shakespeare's plays: *The Tragedy of Francis Bacon, Prince of England . . .*, Los Angeles, 1940. WW 21

CUNNINGHAM, WILLIAM M. (March 9, 1829–Aug. 16, 1909), was born in Newark, Licking County. A merchant and insurance agent in Newark, he published several manuals and handbooks on Freemasonry and a historical work: *History of Freemasonry in Ohio from 1791 . . .*, 3 vols., Cincinnati, 1909–14.

CURRAN, GEORGE EDWIN (May 10, 1892–), was born in Zanesville, Muskingum County, where he attended St. Thomas school until he was fourteen. After learning telegraphy, he was employed by the Pennsylvania Railroad. His last known address was Los Angeles. His poems appeared in various periodicals, and he also published a collection: *The Last Judgment,* Zanesville, [1924].

CURRAN, GRACE WICKMAN (1865–Sept. 26, 1946), was born in Norwalk, Huron County. Her husband, Charles C. Curran, was an artist, and she was for a number of years librarian at the National Academy of Design, New York City. She edited monthly books for art-lovers, 1908–10, and wrote a novel, *A Seventh Daughter,* Boston, 1904.

CURRIER, ALBERT HENRY (Nov. 15, 1837–Nov. 11, 1927), clergyman and educator, was born in Skowhegan, Maine. He graduated from Bowdoin College in 1857 and Andover Theological Seminary in 1862. Ordained a Congregational minister in 1862, he served churches in Massachusetts, 1862–81, and served on the faculty of Oberlin Theological Seminary, 1881–1907.

The Life of Constans L. Goddell, D.D., New York, [1887].
Where Is Charley? 1905.
Nine Great Preachers, Boston, 1912.
The Present Day Problem of Crime, Boston, 1912.
Biographical and Literary Studies, Boston, [1915].
Robert Leighton, the Apostolic Anglican Prelate of Scotland; A Biographical Sketch, Oberlin, [1923].

CURRY, OTWAY (March 26, 1804–Feb. 17, 1855), poet, was born in Greenfield, Highland County. In 1823 he went to Lebanon, where he learned the carpenter's trade, at which he worked until 1829. He was a farmer in Union County until 1839 and served in the legislature, 1836–37. He was associated with William Davis Gallagher (q.v.) in publishing the *Hesperian* in 1838. He began to study law in 1839, and with the exception of the years 1843–45, when he edited the *Torch-Light* at Xenia, and 1853–54, when he edited the *Scioto Gazette* at Chillicothe, he practiced law until his death, which occurred at Marysville. In the summer of 1827 a number of poetical contributions signed "Abdullah" appeared in the newspapers of Cincinnati in quick succession, which, according to William D. Gallagher, were so much superior to the ordinary run of such things as to excite general attention. Gallagher, enamored of one of the productions entitled "The Minstrel's Home," determined to find out the author if it were possible to do so. After a time he found "Abdullah" among a group of young carpenters engaged in building a business structure in Cincinnati; thus began a lifelong friendship between these distinguished poets.

The Lore of the Past, Cincinnati, 1838.

CURRY, WILLIAM LEONTES (June 25, 1839–April 27, 1927), was born in Union County. He was the nephew of Otway Curry (q.v.). He entered Otterbein College in 1860, but withdrew in Jan., 1861, to study law. He served in the 1st Ohio Cavalry until Dec. 30, 1864, when he was discharged for disability. He was a merchant in Union County until 1875, served three terms as county auditor, and held various state and county posts. He died in Columbus, where he lived in his old age. Besides the titles below, he published articles on historical and military subjects. His regimental history is highly praised by Ryan.

War History of Union County . . . , Marysville, 1883.
Four Years in the Saddle, History of the First Regiment, Ohio Volunteer Cavalry . . . , Columbus, 1898.
History of Jerome Township, Union County . . . , Columbus, 1913.
Ohio, the Buckeye State, Columbus, 1915.
History of Union County . . . , Indianapolis, 1915.

CURTIS, ALVA (June 3, 1797–Oct., 1881), physician, was born in Columbia, N. H. He practiced medicine in Cincinnati and served as dean of the Physio-medical College there.

Lectures on Midwifery . . . , Columbus, 1837.
A Fair Examination and Criticism of All the Medical Systems in Vogue, Cincinnati, 1855.
The Provocation and the Reply . . . , Cincinnati, 1870.
Lectures on the Philosophy of Language, of Grammar and Composition, Cincinnati, 1874.
The Physio-medical Family Book . . . , New York, 1875.

CURTIS, ANNA LOUISA (Aug. 15, 1882–), was born in Waite Hill, Lake County. Although her family moved to New York City while she was a child, she spent her summer vacations with her grandparents in Ohio. She graduated from Swarthmore College in 1904. An original member of the Friends Service Committee, organized in 1917, she was active in its work. She was secretary of the Island Press, 1940–56. She now lives in New York City. She has published many stories, poems, and articles in periodicals for young people, including a collection: *Stories of the Underground Railroad,* New York, 1941.

CURTIS, MATTOON MONROE (Oct. 19, 1858–Sept. 19, 1934), educator, was born in Rome, N. Y. He graduated from Hamilton College in 1880 and Union Theological Seminary in 1883; he also studied for two years at University of Leipzig. Ordained a Presbyterian minister in 1883, he preached at Beckwith Memorial Church in Cleveland until 1888, when he joined the Western Reserve University faculty. Besides a number of works in his professional field of philosophy, he wrote *The Story of Snuff and Snuff Boxes,* New York, 1935.

CURTIS, WILLIAM ELEROY (Nov. 5, 1850–Oct. 5, 1911), journalist and world traveler, was born in Akron, Summit County. He graduated from Western Reserve College in 1871. He was on the staff of the Chicago *Inter-Ocean,* 1873–87; he then became Washington correspondent of the Chicago *Record,* a connection which continued until the end of his days. He traveled through South America as special commissioner of the United States and in 1889 remained as the first director of the Bureau of American Republics. As director of the bureau he began publication of handbooks, several of which he wrote himself. Well launched on his career as a globe-trotter, for which he became best known, he resigned from the bureau in 1893. His brilliant letters describing important incidents and picturing foreign lands brought him wide recognition. He was a prime favorite in Chicago newspaper circles and a soft touch for the impecunious members of the fraternity. Eugene Field, who owed him money, once wrote in his column in the Chicago *Daily News:* "W. E. Curtis is in town to look after his permanent investments." He died of apoplexy in Philadelphia.

Tibbelses' Folks, Chicago, 1875.
Zachariah Chandler, an Outline Sketch of His Life and Public Services, 1880.
Children of the Sun, Chicago, 1883.
A Summer Scamper along the Old Santa Fe Trail . . . , Chicago, 1883.
The Capitals of Spanish America, New York, 1888.
The Land of the Nihilist. Russia . . . , Chicago, 1888.
Trade and Transportation between the United States and Spanish America, Washington, D. C., 1889.
Handbook of the American Republics, Washington, D. C., 1890.
Costa Rica, Washington, D. C., 1891.
Ecuador, Washington, D. C., 1891.
Guatemala, Washington, D. C., 1891.
Venezuela—a Land Where It Is Always Summer, Washington, D. C., 1891.
The United States and Foreign Powers, Meadville, Pa., 1892.
The Relics of Columbus . . . , Washington, D. C., 1893.
Venezuela . . . , New York, 1896.
The Yankees of the East . . . , Chicago, 1896.
Today in France and Germany, Chicago, 1897.
Between the Andes and the Ocean . . . , Chicago, 1900.
The True Thomas Jefferson, Philadelphia, 1901.
Abraham Lincoln, Philadelphia, 1902.
Denmark, Norway and Sweden, Akron, 1903.
The True Abraham Lincoln, Philadelphia, 1903.
The Turk and His Lost Provinces . . . , Chicago, 1903.
To-day in Syria and Palestine, Chicago, 1904.
Egypt, Burma and British Malaysia, Chicago, 1905.
Modern India, Chicago, 1905.
One Irish Summer, New York, 1909.
Around the Black Sea . . . , New York, 1911.
Letters on Canada, [n.p.], 1911.
Turkestan; "The Heart of Asia," New York, 1911.

CURTISS, GEORGE LEWIS (Nov. 21, 1835–March 30, 1898), clergyman, was born in Columbia, Lorain County. After graduating from Baldwin University in 1854, he taught mathematics at Moore's Hill College, Ind. He afterward served as pastor of various Methodist churches in Indiana. Besides the titles below, he published several textbooks in theology and church history.

History of the Methodist Episcopal Church in Shelbyville . . . , Shelbyville, Ind., 1878.
Tragic Trio, Indianapolis, 1882.
Sketches from the Romance of American History, [Jeffersonville, Ind., 1886].
Arminianism in History . . . , Cincinnati, 1894.

CURTISS, PHEBE A. (Aug. 2, 1856–Aug. 23, 1936), was born in Cleveland, Cuyahoga County. She graduated from Cleveland Normal School and taught in the Cleveland public schools. After her marriage to Frank Curtiss in 1881, she lived in Painesville. She was superintendent of the Children's Division of the Ohio Sunday School Association. She died in Chicago. She published a number of programs and texts for use in Sunday schools and a pamphlet on childhood: *The Child You Used to Be,* Cincinnati, [1916].

CURWEN, MASKELL E. (Feb. 9, 1825–July 11, 1868), lawyer, was born near Villanova, Pa. After coming to Dayton in 1844, he was admitted to the Ohio bar and practiced law in that city. He was also a part-time editor of the Dayton *Transcript.* In 1850 he became professor of law at the University of Cincinnati and in 1858 was made dean of the law school. He published several legal works besides the title below. His history of Dayton is the first full-length history of the city; it was first written as an introduction to Odell's business directory. He died in London, England, while on a European trip intended to renew his health.

A Sketch of the History of the City of Dayton, Dayton, 1850.

CUSHING, GEORGE HOLMES (May 3, 1873–Dec. 3, 1953), was born near Goshen, Clermont County. He was educated in Springfield and worked on the editorial staffs of various Ohio newspapers until 1907, when he moved to Chicago and became editor of the *Black Diamond.* He edited this magazine until 1918, operated a laboratory in Washington, D. C., and became a public speaker in behalf of the coal industry. In 1937 he became editor of the *Retail Coalman.* He wrote *The Human Story of Coal,* Washington, D. C., 1923. WW 16

CUSHING, HARVEY WILLIAMS (April 8, 1869–Oct. 8, 1939), surgeon, was born in Cleveland, Cuyahoga County. He graduated from Yale University in 1891 and completed his medical training at Harvard University in 1895. He was a practicing surgeon from 1895 to 1933 and also served on the faculties of Johns Hopkins, Harvard, and Yale. He died at New Haven Hospital and is buried in Lakeside Cemetery, Cleveland. Besides writing a number of technical medical works, he won the Pulitzer Prize for his biography, *The Life of Sir William Osler,* 2 vols., Oxford, 1925. DAB 22

CUSHMAN, CLARISSA WHITE FAIRCHILD (Jan. 13, 1889–), was born in Oberlin, Lorain County. She graduated from Oberlin College in 1911. She now lives in Arlington, Va. She has published a number of novels, both as magazine serials and as books, e.g., *The Other Brother,* Boston, 1939. WWAW 1

CUSHMAN, CORINNE. Pseud. See Metta V. F. Victor.

CUSTER, GEORGE ARMSTRONG (Dec. 5, 1839–June 25, 1876), soldier, was born in New Rumley, Harrison County. He attended local schools until he was ten years old, after which he spent part of his time with his half-sister, Lydia Reed, in Monroe, Mich. At the age of seventeen he was appointed to U. S. Military Academy, where he was graduated without distinction in 1861. Despite his mediocre record at West Point, he attracted the attention of several generals, most notably George B. McClellan, rose rapidly in rank, and served with distinction in numerous engagements. He was named major general of volunteers at the close of the Civil War. In 1866, after toying with the idea of joining the army of Juárez in Mexico, he joined the 7th Cavalry as lieutenant colonel. His victory over Cheyennes at the Battle of Washita in 1868 kept him in the public eye. He was stationed in Kentucky, 1871–73, and then was sent to the Dakota Territory. In 1874 he led an exploring expedition through the Black Hills which resulted in miners flocking into the area and in the unrest among the Sioux which culminated at Little Big Horn two years later. Custer's testimony against Indian agents caused Grant to remove him from his command, and he was restored just in time to join the expedition against the Sioux in May–June, 1876. The events of June 25 continue to be debated by military historians, but the annihilation of Custer and his entire force is one of the most familiar legends of American history. His only book, which first appeared in the *Galaxy,* sold widely and helped create the image of a flamboyant hero that still persists in the public mind.

My Life on the Plains . . . , New York, 1874.

CUTLER, CARROLL (Jan. 31, 1829–Jan. 24, 1894), clergyman and educator, was born in Windham, N. H. He graduated from Yale University in 1854 and was licensed to preach in 1858. In 1860, after a year of study in Germany, he joined the faculty of Western Reserve College at Hudson. In 1871 he became president of the college; in 1886, four years after the college had been moved to Cleveland, he resigned, but continued to serve until 1888 and then taught for an additional year. After leaving Western Reserve, he taught at Negro colleges in the South until his death.

A History of Western Reserve College . . . , Cleveland, 1876.

The Beginnings of Ethics, New York, 1889.

CUTLER, JAMES ALBERT (Jan. 24, 1876–), educator, was born in Princeville, Ill. He graduated from the University of Colorado in 1900 and Yale University (Ph.D.) in 1903. He served on the sociology faculty of Western Reserve University, 1916–46. He wrote numerous articles and reviews and, with Maurice R. Davie, *A Study in Professional Education at Western Reserve University . . .* , Cleveland, [1930]. WW 30

CUTLER, JERVIS (Sept. 19, 1768–June 25, 1846), son of Rev. Manasseh Cutler (q.v.), secretary of the Ohio Company, was born in Martha's Vineyard, Mass. In his teens he was placed in Boston to acquire a mercantile education, but dissatisfied with a merchant's life, he soon gave it up and went to Europe, where he visited France and Denmark. When the Ohio Company was organized, Jervis' adventuring spirit was aroused and he joined the original party that left his father's parsonage at Ipswich to found a settlement at Marietta. As the boats carrying the settlers neared the confluence of the Muskingum and Ohio Rivers, young Jervis was the first to leap ashore. He spent most of the rest of his life in the Western country, so that he wrote from firsthand knowledge of the section and its inhabitants. In 1807 he was elected major in Colonel McArthur's Ohio regiment. When troops were wanted to take possession of Louisiana, he was appointed captain and raised a full company of men with which in 1809 he was ordered to New Orleans. In 1812 at New Orleans, probably while recuperating from a severe attack of yellow fever, he wrote his *Topographical Description.* In 1823 he moved his family from Ohio to Nashville, Tenn., where he was an engraver. Later he settled in Evansville, Ind., where his death occurred. He was the last survivor of the Ohio Company.

Mary Hoge Bruce

A Topographical Description of the State of Ohio, Indiana Territory, and Louisiana . . . , Boston, 1812.

CUTLER, JULIA PERKINS (Jan. 24, 1814–Dec. 18, 1904), was born in Constitution, Washington County. In 1854 she moved to Marietta to live with her brother, William P. Cutler (July 12, 1812–April 11, 1889). In addition to the titles below, she published poems in various periodicals; and with her brother she edited the papers of her grandfather, Manasseh Cutler.

The Founders of Ohio . . . , Cincinnati, 1888.

Life, Journals and Correspondence of Manasseh Cutler, 2 vols., Cincinnati, 1888.

Life and Times of Ephraim Cutler . . . , Cincinnati, 1890.

CUTLER, MANASSEH (May 13, 1742–July 28, 1823), versatile Congregational clergyman, who was instrumental in persuading Congress to make favorable terms for the land purchase of the Ohio Company, was in Ohio for only a year (1788–89). His most important publication from an Ohio viewpoint is *An Explanation of the Map Which Delineates That Part of the Federal Lands, Comprehended between Pennsylvania West Line, the Rivers Ohio and Scioto, and Lake Erie . . .* , Salem, [Mass.], 1787. This important document, published anonymously, contains a description of the Ohio country.

CUTTER, ORLANDO PHELPS (1824–July 1, 1884), was born in Cleveland, Cuyahoga County, and spent his life in that city. His only publication was an account of his Civil War service.

Our Battery; Or, the Journal of Company B, 1st O.V.A., Cleveland, 1864.

D

DABNEY, CHARLES WILLIAM (June 19, 1855–June 15, 1945), president of the University of Cincinnati, 1904–20, was born in Hampden-Sydney, Va. He graduated from Hampden-Sydney College in 1873 and the University of Göttingen (Ph.D.) in 1880. The Department of Agriculture published some of his addresses and reports before 1901, and he wrote many articles, but his major work was *Universal Education in the South,* 2 vols., Chapel Hill, N. C., [1936]. WWW 2

DABNEY, WENDELL PHILLIPS (Nov. 4, 1865–June 3, 1952), editor, was born in Richmond, Va., where his father, a former slave, was a successful caterer. He taught school for several years, attended Oberlin College, and arrived in Cincinnati in 1894. He operated a hotel for a time, was assistant city paymaster, 1897–1923, and edited the *Union* for nearly fifty years. He published *Cincinnati's Colored Citizens; Historical, Sociological and Biographical,* Cincinnati, [1926].

DAGGETT, MARY STEWART (May 30, 1856–March 9, 1922), was born in Morristown, Belmont County. She graduated from Steubenville Seminary in 1873. In addition to the titles below, she wrote several plays that were produced but not published. She died in Pasadena, Calif.

Mariposilla; A Novel, Chicago, 1895.
The Broad Aisle; A Realistic Tale of Ohio, New York, [1899].
The Higher Court, Boston, [1911].
The Yellow Angel, Chicago, 1914.

DAHLGREN, SARAH MADELINE VINTON GODDARD (July 13, 1825–May 28, 1898), born in Gallipolis, Gallia County, was the daughter of Samuel F. Vinton, who represented his district in Congress for more than twenty years. She attended the Convent of the Visitation, Georgetown, D. C., and when she reached maturity, became her father's hostess in Washington. In 1846 she married Daniel C. Goddard of Zanesville. He died in 1862, and three years later she married the distinguished authority on naval ordnance, Admiral John A. Dahlgren. A scholarly and versatile writer, she edited her husband's *Memoir of Ulric Dahlgren,* wrote the preface to his *Notes on Maritime and International Law,* and produced noteworthy translations of French and Spanish religious works. Her first book, a volume of poems and sketches published under the pen name Corinne, appeared in 1859. Although she devoted her life in Washington to literature and religion, she managed to become an acknowledged social leader. Her *Etiquette of Social Life in Washington,* though not her most distinguished literary production, was her most influential one, for it became the *vade mecum* of Washington society and ran through many editions. She founded the Washington Literary Society in 1873, and her home became a salon for a large circle of literary acquaintance.

Idealities, Philadelphia, 1859.
Thoughts on Female Suffrage . . . , Washington, 1871.
Etiquette of Social Life in Washington, Washington, 1873.
South Sea Sketches . . . , Boston, 1881.
Memoir of John A. Dahlgren . . . , Boston, 1882.
South Mountain Magic . . . , Boston, 1882.
A Washington Winter, Boston, 1883.
The Lost Name; A Novelette, Boston, 1886.
Divorced. A Novel, Chicago, 1887.
Lights and Shadows of a Life; A Novel, Boston, 1887.
Chim: His Washington Winter, New York, 1892.
The Secret Directory . . . , Philadelphia, [1896].
The Woodley Lane Ghost, and Other Stories, Philadelphia, 1899.

DAILEY, WILLIAM MITCHELL (1812–Feb. 5, 1877), educator, was born in Coshocton, Coshocton County, but spent most of his life in Indiana. He graduated from Indiana University in 1836. He was president of Indiana University, 1853–59. Besides the titles below, many of his speeches and sermons were published.

The Powerful Pen and the Eloquent Tongue . . . , Bloomington, Ind., 1859.
The Great Rebellion, Madison, Ind., 1862.

DALE, CHRISTOPHER (Feb. 9, 1917–), was born in Dayton, Montgomery County. After serving four years in the Marine Corps, he published a short book: *Hypnosis Is Yours. Use It!,* Dayton, 1944.

DALE, EDGAR (April 27, 1900–), educator, was born in Benson, Minn., and has been a member of the department of education at Ohio State University since 1929. He has written a number of books on newspapers and motion pictures, e.g., *The Content of Motion Pictures,* New York, 1935. WW 30

DALE, HARRISON CLIFFORD (March 7, 1885–), educator, born in Lynn, Mass., was on the faculty of Miami University, 1928–37. He was afterward president of the University of Idaho, 1937–46, and comptroller of Reed College, 1946–50. He now lives in Santa Barbara, Calif. He has published a study of the fur trade: *The Ashley-Smith Exploration,* Cleveland, 1918. WW 29

DALE, REBECCA VAN HAMM (c.1894–May 28, 1948), was born in New York City, the daughter of Caleb Van Hamm, a journalist of New York and Cincinnati. After her marriage she lived in Cincinnati, where she was active in cultural activities.

She was killed in an automobile accident at the age of 54. She wrote several plays, e.g., *The Girls' Finesse . . .* , Franklin, 1928.

DALE, SOPHIA DANA (Jan. 28, 1853–May 1, 1932), was born in Marietta, Washington County, and spent her life in that community. She was active in the cultural life of Marietta, and her interest in local history is indicated by the pamphlet listed below.

Historical, Picturesque and Appropriate Names for Streets and Public Properties, Marietta, 1897.

DALES, GEORGE S. (June 29, 1879–), jeweler, was born in Akron, Summit County. He attended Akron public schools and Buchtel College. He was a jeweler in Akron for many years; now retired, he spends his summers in Akron and his winters at Vero Beach, Fla. He has traveled widely and is an enthusiastic amateur photographer. His wife, Lotta E. Dales, edited notes from his travel diaries: *Intimate Glimpses of Many Lands . . .* , Akron, [1928].

DALEY, EDITH (Jan. 1, 1876–Jan. 13, 1948), librarian and journalist, was born in Fostoria, Seneca County. She worked on several newspapers and was city librarian, San Jose, Calif., 1922–43. Her short stories and poems appeared in various periodicals, and she published a volume of poetry: *The Angel in the Sun . . .* , San Jose, [1917]. WWNAA 7

DALLAS, RICHARD. Pseud. See Nathan W. Williams.

DALTON, VAN BROADUS (July 25, 1885–), oral surgeon, was born in Burkesville, Ky. He graduated from the Ohio College of Dental Surgery, Cincinnati, in 1907 and the following year joined the faculty. He taught until 1917 and afterward practiced privately in Cincinnati. Besides numerous professional articles, he has published *The Genesis of Dental Education in the United States,* Cincinnati, 1946. WW 30

DALZELL, JAMES McCORMICK (Sept. 3, 1838–Jan. 29, 1924), was born in Pittsburgh, Pa. His parents moved to Noble County in 1845. He served as a private in the 116th O.V.I. throughout the Civil War, and following his discharge he became a clerk in the Treasury Department in Washington, D.C. He graduated from Columbian Law College in 1868 and afterward practiced law for over thirty years at Caldwell and served a number of terms in the Ohio General Assembly. He contributed many articles to leading newspapers over the signature "Private Dalzell." His death occurred in Washington, D.C.

John Gray, of Mount Vernon . . . , Washington, 1868.

Private Dalzell, His Autobiography, Poems, and Comic War Papers . . . , Cincinnati, 1888.

DANDRIDGE, RAYMOND GARFIELD (1882–Feb. 24, 1930), was born in Cincinnati, Hamilton County. Stricken with paralysis in 1912, he was an invalid for the remainder of his life. He published his poetry in several collections, e.g., *Penciled Poems,* Cincinnati, 1917.

DANFORD, HARRY EDMUND (Aug. 31, 1879–), journalist and educator, was born in Sharon, Noble County. He published a weekly newspaper there, edited newspapers in other communities, taught school, and for fifteen years was a junior high school principal in Huntington, W. Va. Now retired, he lives in Huntington. He has written a number of biographical and historical studies, and two historical novels, e.g., *The West Virginian,* New York, 1926.

DANIELS, WINTHROP MORE (Sept. 30, 1867–Jan. 2, 1944), educator, was born in Dayton, Montgomery County. After graduating from Princeton University in 1888, he taught at Princeton, served on the New Jersey Public Utility Commission, 1911–14, was a member of the Interstate Commerce Commission, 1914–23, and was on the Yale University faculty, 1923–40. Besides magazine articles, a finance textbook, and a memoir of Woodrow Wilson, he wrote *American Railroads; Four Phases of Their History,* Princeton, N. J., 1932. WWW 2

DANNER, JOHN (March 10, 1823–April 12, 1918), manufacturer, was born in Canton, Stark County. After several years as a merchant, he invented a revolving bookcase in 1874. He organized a factory to produce these bookcases, which were used throughout the world. He was active in Canton civic affairs, and for several years before his death at 95 was the oldest citizen of the city. He published a large, useful volume of local history: *Old Landmarks of Canton and Stark County . . .* , Logansport, Ind., 1904, some portions of which were written by Lewis Slusser (Jan. 21, 1820–Dec. 23, 1892), a Canton physician.

DANTON, GEORGE HENRY (May 31, 1880–), educator, was born in New York City, taught German at Western Reserve University, 1905–07, and headed the German department at Oberlin College, 1927–35. He now lives in Berkeley, Calif. Besides numerous textbooks and professional articles, he has published *Germany Ten Years After,* Boston, 1928. WW 26

DARBY, WILLIAM (Aug. 14, 1775–Oct. 9, 1854), geographer, born in eastern Pennsylvania, lived in Ohio for eighteen years, 1781–99. His distinguished career as a surveyor, map-maker, and geographer, however, has little relation to the Ohio country. He lived in Louisiana, Pennsylvania, Maryland, and Washington, D. C. He published textbooks, gazetteers, and maps in addition to the titles listed below.

A Geographical Description of the State of Louisiana . . . , Philadelphia, 1816.

The Emigrant's Guide to the Western and Southwestern States and Territories . . . , New York, 1818.

A Tour from the City of New-York, to Detroit . . . , New York, 1819.

Memoir on the Geography, and Natural and Civil History of Florida . . . , Philadelphia, 1821.

Lectures on the Discovery of America . . . , Baltimore, 1828.

View of the United States, Historical, Geographical, and Statistical . . . , Philadelphia, 1828.

Mnemonika; Or, the Tablet of Memory . . . , Baltimore, 1829.

The Northern Nations of Europe . . . , Chillicothe, 1841.

Remarks on the Tendency of the Constitution of the United States to Give Legislative Control to the President, [n.p., 1842].

DARRAH, DAVID HARLEY (May 27, 1894–), foreign correspondent, was born in Loydsville, Belmont County, and was educated at the University of Akron. After army service in France during World War I, he joined the Paris staff of the Chicago *Tribune.* In 1935 he was expelled from Italy by Mussolini; the following year he published a study of Italy under dictatorship: *Hail Caesar,* Boston, 1936. During World War II he was interned by the Germans, 1942–44. WW 30

DARROW, BENJAMIN HARRISON (July 13, 1889–Jan. 28, 1950), educator, was born near Mechanicsburg, Champaign County. A pioneer in educational radio, he founded the Ohio School of the Air in 1925 and conducted it until 1937. The history of the school is covered in *Radio Trailblazing . . .* , Columbus, [1940].

DARROW, CLARENCE (April 18, 1857–March 13, 1938), lawyer, was born in Kinsman, Trumbull County. In 1898 Brand Whitlock, then a young journalist undecided about following a career in politics or letters, wrote this revealing comment in a personal letter:

> Last January, when I was in Chicago for a day or two, I called upon my old friend Clarence Darrow, the lawyer of more than local fame. He is deeply interested in letters, and should have devoted himself to literature. . . .

Nearly 25 years later Edgar Lee Masters, one-time law partner of the "Man from Kinsman," made allusion to the literary propensities of Darrow:

> He was always a poet too,
> And a poet is the barometer of the world,
> And a vicarious sufferer for all sufferers.
> He was poet who found clay for his modeling
> In those who were martyred for striving
> For the weak, the despoiled. . . .

Thus two established men of letters during two distinct epochs in American literature bore testimony to the creative talent of Clarence Darrow, the transplanted Ohioan who, while a successful attorney in the hectic Chicago of the 1880s—the seething town of Railroad Combine, Beef Trust, and Haymarket—revealed to a close friend a surprising dilemma: "The one thing I want most of all to be is a writer." True to his desire, the former Ashtabula lawyer late in the 1890s took some faltering steps in the ascent of Parnassus, and by 1905 Darrow had published most of the literary work emanating from this initial creative impulse. His writings categorize themselves as criticism, *A Persian Pearl: And Other Essays* (1899); short stories, "Easy Lessons in Law," in the Chicago *American* (July-August, 1902); and novels, *Farmington* (1904) and *An Eye for an Eye* (1905). As a literary critic, Darrow reinforced the vigorous stances of his idol, Col. Robert Ingersoll, by singing the praises of Fitzgerald, Burns, and Whitman—poets who throbbed as a "great universal heart" in sharp contrast to a sordid "commercial, money-getting age." The attorney also lined up behind William Dean Howells, his friend and fellow Ohioan, in the crusade for realism in fiction and integrity in art; he believed, too, with his beloved counselor John P. Altgeld (q.v.) that:

> The greatest artists of the world today are telling facts and painting scenes that cause humanity to stop and think and ask why one should be a master and another be a serf; why a portion of the world should toil and spin, should wear away its strength and life that the rest should live in idleness and ease.

Thus Clarence Darrow embraced an aesthetic that was solidly founded on ethical principles; the social content of literature, artistry based on the cult of love, and reality painted with the orientation of a congenital pessimist became the critical pivots in his creative system. And when William Randolph Hearst invited this curious lawyer to contribute some fiction to the newly founded Chicago *American,* Darrow happily responded with a series of bizarre tales excoriating contemporary jurisprudence and its inequities. The "Easy Lessons" to which Darrow's perhaps unsuspecting readers were introduced generally involved tales of helpless immigrants victimized by the "Doctrine of Assumed Risk." Minorities, competing for jobs on the lowest levels in factories and railroad yards, exposed themselves to unbelievable physical danger, encouraged by the penny-pinching negligence of ruthless employers. Thus, when John Swanson loses his arm in a buzz saw that had no guard, and when Tony Salvador has his leg amputated by a train rolling through faulty signals, no compensation is owed the suffering families of these unfortunate laborers, who realized the dangers under which they worked but who, nevertheless, to avoid starvation, continued "at their own risk" to hold such hazardous jobs. Indeed, Darrow, who was later to earn considerable fame as a labor lawyer, revealed clearly his profound sympathy for the workingman and his union even in these early sketches. Corporation lawyers, thoughtless magistrates, and general legal incompetence are pilloried in "Easy Lessons"; one aspect of Darrow's fiction, then, would link him with the Muckrakers. *Farmington* might well have been given the subtitle "A Grotesque Idyl of Trumbull County," for in this nearly forgotten novel Darrow dissects the Kinsman area of the "brown decades" during the post-Civil War period and in so doing contributes to American letters as poignant a "revolt from the village" document as Anderson's *Winesburg, Ohio,* or Whitlock's *J. Hardin & Son.* The 23 chapters of the novel recount the observations of one John Smith, a gentleman who wandered and blundered, so he tells, "in a zigzag path through childhood" within the "narrow shade of the stubborn little town" of Farmington. Quickly introduced into the real world of "selfishness and greed," Smith was at length initiated into the life of passive despair endured by his fellow townsfolk:

> All my life [the narrator records] I have been planning and hoping and thinking and dreaming and loitering and waiting. All my life I have been getting ready to begin to do something, something worth the while. I have been waiting for the summer and waiting for the fall; I have been waiting for the winter and waiting for the spring; waiting for the night and waiting for the morning; waiting and dawdling and dreaming, until the day is almost spent and the twilight close at hand.

Episodic in structure, *Farmington* also deals with "life and action, and boys and girls, and men and women," people Smith calls "the weird fantastic troop." Darrow gives detailed character analyses of various local *isolatoes* who, standing aside from the passing parade of life, deliberately choose to inhabit a sphere not ruled by the ethical strictures imposed by the unyielding social dogma that epitomized life in Farmington. In short, Clarence Darrow—while he does intersperse pleasant accounts of baseball, holidays, and fishing—paints a grim picture of this nineteenth-century Buckeye "Gopher Prairie," a wasteland dominated by the specter of village puritanism. Darrow's next novel shifts in geography from the rural environs of northeastern Ohio to a jail in Chicago, where Jim Jackson, protagonist of *An Eye for an Eye,* awaits execution for the murder of his wife. The book is mainly polemical in nature and allows the lawyer to air his views on capital punishment and on social complicity: a society that tolerates squalor and poverty will continue to spawn criminals which it must coldly execute. Jackson, in telling his story, confesses to having struck and killed his wife during a frenzied moment when "If there'd been forty scaffolds right before my eyes I'd have brought down that poker just the same." This murderer, incapable of positive reflective action, was driven to his deed by the unseen forces in this "rudderless universe"; irrational man, lacking personal agency, is marked as if by Election for his bitter destiny. Darrow points out that the doomed man possesses a tragic awareness both of his hopeless plight and of the stark altruism that humanity is bound together in a universal brotherhood of sin. With no subplots to hinder the action of the narrative, *An Eye for an Eye* is a cogent embodiment of literary Darwinism. At this point in his glamorous career, Clarence Darrow was sidetracked almost permanently from pursuits literary, but he always remained an interested and able dabbler in letters. His writings belaboring prohibition, his essay explaining agnosticism, and his tracts legal and evolutionary appeared during the 1920s and early 1930s in the most popular periodicals of the day (*Liberty, The Saturday Evening Post*), as well as in the more esoteric and iconoclastic (*The Debunker, The American Mercury*). In 1932 he published his well-known autobiography, *The Story of My Life,* a work as spellbinding as a panorama of newspaper headlines. Unfortunately, in this self-portrait Darrow avoids mention of his literary ambitions and achievements. He does, however, paint the picture of Kinsman with somewhat more roseate colors than he had utilized for Farmington, its fictional counterpart, some 25 years earlier. Rather than that contemporary criticism should dismiss Darrow as a literary indiscretion, an artless amateur, or a curious dilettante, historians of our letters should regard him as a minor American author whose nonacademic, undisciplined critical and fictional broadsides, coupled with his national prestige, gave aid and sustenance to the literature of realism during the crucial years when it struggled for intellectual recognition. Although he has attained almost mythical stature as an American hero for his legal achievements, Clarence Darrow's contributions to the area of arts and letters are far from insignificant.

Abe C. Ravitz

A Persian Pearl: And Other Essays, East Aurora, N. Y., 1899.

Realism in Literature and Art, Chicago, [1899].

Resist Not Evil, Chicago, 1903.

Farmington, Chicago, 1904.

"The Open Shop," Chicago, 1904.

An Eye for an Eye, New York, 1905.

Crime; Its Cause and Treatment, New York, [1922].

The Prohibition Mania . . . , New York, 1927.

The Story of My Life, New York, 1932.

DARROW, JASON (1787–March 31, 1868), was born in Connecticut. He is believed to have been an early member of the Shaker colony in Warren County, but to have left it in 1824, after which he lived east of Lebanon.

The New Light on the Christian Church, Covington, Ky., 1846.

DARSIE, CHARLES (Feb. 9, 1872–Sept. 23, 1948), clergyman, was born in Warren, Trumbull County. A graduate of Bethany College, W. Va., he was ordained to the ministry of the Disciples of Christ Church. His Ohio pastorates included North Eaton, Collingwood, Paulding, Uhrichsville, and Cleveland. He died at Burton, Geauga County. He wrote several books on religion and family life and *The Art of Winning Folks,* St. Louis, 1922.

DARST, LILLIE C. (1846–1883), was born in Circleville, Pickaway County, and attended the public schools of that community. In 1875 she was editor and owner of the Circleville *Herald,* and in 1881 she became engrossing clerk of the Ohio Senate. She published poems in magazines and newspapers which were collected in the posthumous volume *The Chained Angel of the Afterthought and Other Poems,* [Circleville], 1932.

D'ARUSMONT, FRANCES WRIGHT PHIQUEPAL (Sept. 6, 1795–Dec. 13, 1852), reformer, was born in Dundee, Scotland. In Cincinnati's Spring Grove Cemetery, a simple granite shaft marks the grave of Frances Wright Phiquepal D'Arusmont. Few people who visit the cemetery are aware that the monument marks the grave of one of the nineteenth-century's most brilliant women, Frances Wright. Lecturer, writer, and champion of the oppressed, she counted among her friends Jeremy Bentham, Thomas Jefferson, Robert Owen, and General Lafayette. Her parents were moderately wealthy but left her an orphan at an early age. Until she and her sister Camilla came into possession of the estate left by their parents, they made their home with their maternal grandfather, General Duncan Campbell of the British Army. In spite of the conservative family surroundings, Frances early became a champion of liberal doctrine. This interest turned her attention to America, which she felt, as did other European liberals, to be the land of hope. Accordingly, Fanny and Camilla Wright set out in 1818 for a visit to the New World, arriving in New York in September of that year. There they were received in the best social circles. An event of note during their New York stay was the production at the Park Theatre of *Altdorf,* a tragedy written by Fanny. In May, 1820, the Wright sisters returned to England, and Fanny began work on a book describing her American trip. In 1821 she published *Views of Society and Manners in America.* The book was widely read in Europe and brought an invitation to the young author to visit General Lafayette. A close friendship developed and when the elderly statesman revisited the United States in 1823, the Wright sisters followed and joined him. During his triumphal trip through the country, the Wrights were often with him and never far behind. As a result of this trip, Frances Wright met several leading liberals including Robert Owen, who shortly afterward founded New Harmony. Appalled by Negro slavery, Miss Wright conceived the idea of setting up a colony where slaves might earn their freedom. A site was purchased near the present city of Memphis, Tenn., and in 1827 the colony Nashoba was established. After two difficult years, like so many other utopian ventures the project failed. After the failure of her colony, Miss Wright came to Cincinnati and in July, 1828, delivered a series of lectures in the Hamilton County Court House. A number of years later, Miss Wright took up residence in Cincinnati. In 1831 she had married a French physician, Guillaume Jervis Casimir Phiquepal D'Arusmont, whose adopted son had established himself as a brewer in Cincinnati. Here the husband settled down to write and manage his wife's business affairs. Frances found little time to spend at home but continued her lecture tours throughout the Eastern seaboard. Domestic life, often interrupted, finally came to a complete break in 1847. Residence in Cincinnati had been broken by a period in Scotland and France, but in 1848 Fanny returned to Cincinnati to spend the remainder of her days. In January of 1852, she broke her hip in a fall on the ice. From this accident she did not recover, but died Dec. 13, 1852. She was, as previously stated, buried in the Spring Grove Cemetery. A monument was raised on the grave by her daughter. On it is carved a bibliography of Mrs. D'Arusmont's published writings.

Ernest I. Miller

Altdorf, a Tragedy . . . , Philadelphia, 1819.

Views of Society and Manners in America . . . , New York, 1821.

A Few Days in Athens . . . , London, 1822.

Course of Popular Lectures, New York, 1829.

Fables, New York, 1830.

Biography, Notes, and Political Letters . . . , 2 vols, New York, 1844.

England, the Civilizer . . . , London, 1848.

DAUGHERTY, HARRY MICAJAH (Jan. 26, 1860–Oct. 12, 1941), attorney general of the United States, was born in Washington Court House, Fayette County, where he began the practice of law in 1881. He moved to Columbus in 1893 and in 1921 was named attorney general by President Harding. A central figure in the Harding administration, he continued to serve after Harding's death but resigned under fire March 28, 1924. With the assistance of Thomas Dixon, he wrote his account of the Harding regime: *The Inside Story of the Harding Tragedy,* New York, 1932. WWW 1

DAUGHTERS, CHARLES G. (Feb. 24, 1897–), born in Moore's Hill, Ind., moved to Milford, Clermont County, in 1906. He attended Milford public schools and Ohio State University, and taught school in Van Wert. He was employed by the Van Wert Manufacturers' Association, 1919–27, was associated with various manufacturing concerns, and headed the Small Business Research Bureau in Washington, D. C. He now lives in Washington, but Milford remains his legal residence. He has written many articles on business and economics and a book on chain stores: *Wells of Discontent* . . . , New York, [1937].

DAULTON, AGNES WARNER McCLELLAND (April 29, 1867–June 5, 1944), was born in New Philadelphia, Tuscarawas County. She attended Oberlin College. She contributed serials and stories to *St. Nicholas* and other magazines and lectured on literature and children. Among her books is *The Gentle Interference of Bub,* New York, 1912. WWW 2

DAVEY, JOHN (June 6, 1846–Nov. 8, 1923), tree surgeon, was born in Somersetshire, England. He came to Warren in 1873 and moved to Kent in 1881. He lectured throughout the country on the preservation of trees. Besides technical books and articles on tree surgery, he published *Gloryville or Hellburg, Which?,* [Akron], 1908. DAB 5

DAVIDSON, HENRY M. (c.1839–1900), was born in Freedom, Portage County. In August, 1862, he enlisted in the 1st Ohio Light Artillery, and was discharged in July, 1865. His *History of Battery A* is a terse and accurate account of an organization that saw hard service throughout the war. His *Fourteen Months in Southern Prisons* is a superior account of his experiences as a prisoner in Danville, Va., and Andersonville, Ga. It was republished in 1890 as *Experience in Rebel Prisons.* After the Civil War he operated a drugstore in Ogdensburg, N. Y., and he died in that community.

Fourteen Months in Southern Prisons . . . , Milwaukee, 1865.

History of Battery A, First Regiment of Ohio Vol. Light Artillery, Milwaukee, 1865.

DAVIDSON, WILBUR LEROY (April 3, 1853–Sept. 17, 1912), clergyman and lecturer, was born in Woodsfield, Monroe County. He graduated from Scio College in 1870 and Drew Theological Seminary in 1876. He was ordained to the Methodist ministry in 1876, served various pastorates, 1876–86, and was field agent of the Sunday School Union, 1886–89. He was superintendent of several Chautauquas, 1887–1911; field agent of the Chautauqua Literary and Scientific Circle, 1895–1902; and manager of the National Chautauqua Bureau after 1908.

Over the Sea; And What I Saw, Cincinnati, 1885.

DAVIE, OLIVER (July 15, 1857–May 11, 1911), naturalist and poet, was born in Xenia, Greene County. In 1860 his father moved to Columbus and opened a variety store. As a boy Oliver opened a shop above his father's store, dealing in Indian relics, mineral specimens, and curios. He studied taxidermy and published a useful manual on the art. He also wrote poetry and essays on nature. He was the subject of a poem by James Whitcomb Riley, "The Naturalist."

The Naturalist's Manual . . . , Columbus, 1882.

Methods in the Art of Taxidermy, Columbus, 1894.

Reveries and Recollections of a Naturalist, Columbus, 1898.

Odds and Ends of Prose and Verse, Columbus, 1902.

DAVIES, ARTHUR ERNEST (March 18, 1867–Dec., 1954), educator, was born in England. After graduating from Yale University, he was a Congregational minister, 1892–1900. He taught philosophy at Ohio State University, 1900–19, and at Colorado College, 1919–25, and wrote a textbook on logic and *The Moral Life . . . ,* Baltimore, 1909. WW 14

DAVIES, JOHN T. (Aug. 14, 1869–June 22, 1953), was born in Jackson County. He taught in Jackson schools before moving to Columbus, where he served for 35 years as an executive of a drug company. His home was in Worthington. He wrote verse as a hobby and published a collection of his poems: *Golden Milestones,* [Jackson, 1945].

DAVIS, ARTHUR NEWTON (Jan. 1, 1879–), dental surgeon, was born in Piqua, Miami County. He lived in Berlin, Germany, and practiced dentistry there, 1903–18. The Kaiser and his family were among his patients, and he wrote *The Kaiser As I Know Him,* New York, [1918]. He now lives in Los Angeles. WW 22

DAVIS, EDWIN HAMILTON (Jan. 22, 1811–May 15, 1888), archaeologist, was born in Hillsboro, Highland County. As early as 1831, while attending Kenyon College, he became interested in the many Indian mounds in the vicinity and commenced research upon them. The results were incorporated in an oration, "The Antiquities of Ohio," given at the Kenyon graduation exercises, Sept. 4, 1833. He was "more influenced and encouraged" to continue such studies by the interest expressed by Daniel Webster, who was visiting in the West in 1833. Young Davis was presented to Webster in company with the Kenyon College president and, hearing Webster urge with great earnestness the importance of preserving these fast-disappearing monuments, "resolved to carry it out in the only practical way which suggested itself to me, *viz:* By procuring accurate surveys of the various works and recording them with full descriptions of the same." Although graduation from the Cincinnati Medical College (c.1838) and practice in Chillicothe intervened, he persisted in his resolve and together with E. G. Squier (q.v.) and at his own expense surveyed nearly one hundred groups of earthworks and opened two hundred mounds. The great resultant work by Squier and Davis, *Ancient Monuments of the Mississippi Valley,* was published by the Smithsonian Institution as Volume I of *Smithsonian Contributions to Knowledge.* A classic of American archaeology, it is today of decided value for its accurate surveys and descriptions of mounds long plowed under just as Webster had predicted. The book, according to A. Morlot, the Swiss archaeologist, is "as glorious a monument of American science, as Bunker's Hill is of American bravery." Squier, who monopolized most of the glory of this publication, went on to wider archaeological fields, leaving Davis with a collection of thousands of specimens to show for the $5000 he had expended in the explorations. His largest collection of mound relics was described by J. J. Ampère, whose trip to Ohio in 1851 included visits to the mounds. Ampère saw Davis in New York for the express purpose of examining his collection and devoted to it an enthusiastic chapter of his book. Failing to interest the Smithsonian in the purchase of these artifacts, Davis sold a large collection of these items to the Blackmore Museum of Salisbury, England, and deposited a smaller collection in the American Museum of Natural History in New York City. He remained a doctor in Chillicothe until 1850, when he was called to teach at the New York Medical College, where he occupied the chair of materia medica and therapeutics till 1860. In 1854, he gave a course of lectures on archaeology at the Lowell Institute of Boston, later repeating it in Brooklyn and New York. Like many people of devoted purpose, he was imposed upon easily, and he was virtually unrecognized for his archaeological endeavors. Author of "Report of the Committee on the Statistics of Calculous Disease in Ohio" (in the *Transactions* of the Ohio Medical Society, Columbus, 1850), he was also an editor of the *American Medical Monthly.*

Wyman W. Parker

Ancient Monuments of the Mississippi Valley, (with Ephraim G. Squier), [Washington, 1848].

On Ethnological Research . . . , [Washington, 1867].

DAVIS, HAROLD EUGENE (Dec. 3, 1902–), educator, was born in Girard, Trumbull County. He graduated from Hiram College in 1924 and Western Reserve University (Ph.D.) in 1933. From 1927 to 1947 he was professor of history and political science at Hiram College; since 1947 he has been on the faculty of American University, Washington, D. C. Besides textbooks and professional articles, he has published *Latin American Leaders,* New York, 1949. WW 30

DAVIS, HARRIET RIDDLE (Nov. 15, 1849–Dec. 13, 1938), daughter of A. G. Riddle (q.v.), was born in Janesville, Wis. She lived in Cleveland and Toledo; her death occurred in the latter city. Besides the novel below, she published *In Sight of the Goddess* in *Lippincott's* (1895), but it apparently was not issued as a book.

Gilbert Elgar's Son, New York, 1890.

DAVIS, HARRY E. (Dec. 26, 1882–Feb. 4, 1955), lawyer, was born in Cleveland, Cuyahoga County. A graduate of Hiram College and Western Reserve University, he practiced law in Cleveland and served in both houses of the state legislature. He wrote *A History of Freemasonry among Negroes in America,* [Cleveland?, 1946].

DAVIS, LEMUEL CLARKE (Sept. 25, 1835–Dec. 14, 1904), journalist, was born near Sandusky, Erie County. After a common school education, he became a reporter. He was editor of the Philadelphia *Inquirer,* 1869–87, and of the *Public Ledger* after 1887. Besides the novel below, he published a number of magazine articles. On March 4, 1863, he married Rebecca Blaine Harding, widely known as a writer of fiction; their son, Richard Harding Davis, was far better known than either of his parents as a novelist and journalist.

A Stranded Ship: A Story of Sea and Shore, New York, 1869.

DAVIS, LYMAN EDWYN (Dec. 28, 1854–Aug. 13, 1930), clergyman, was born in Perrysburg, Lucas County. After graduating from Adrian College in 1877, he was ordained to the ministry of the Methodist Protestant Church. He served several pastorates in New York and Pennsylvania, and was for many years editor of the *Methodist Recorder.* He wrote *Democratic Methodism in America . . . ,* New York, [1921]. WWW 1

DAVIS, THOMAS KIRBY (Feb. 11, 1826–Dec. 24, 1918), clergyman, was born in Chambersburg, Pa. He graduated from Yale University in 1845 and Princeton Theological Seminary in 1849. Ordained to the Presbyterian ministry, he served churches in Pennsylvania, Ohio, and California. While serving as librarian of University of Wooster, 1876–1904, he also served as pastor of eight Presbyterian churches in north central Ohio. He wrote for newspapers and religious periodicals throughout his ministerial career. He published sermons, a family history and *Mind and Spirit; A Study in Psychology,* Boston, 1914. OBB

DAVIS, WILLIAM BRAMWELL (July 22, 1832–Feb. 17, 1893), physician, was born in Cincinnati, Hamilton County. He graduated from Ohio Wesleyan University in 1852 and from Miami Medical College in 1855. He served in the Civil War as surgeon of the 137th O.V.I., and from 1873 until his death he was on the faculty of Miami Medical College. Besides the title below, he published a number of medical papers and reports.

Observations on Revaccination during the Epidemic of Smallpox in Cincinnati in November and December, 1875, Cincinnati, 1876.

DAWES, CHARLES GATES (Aug. 27, 1865–April 23, 1951), banker, diplomat, vice-president of the United States, 1925–29, was born in Marietta, Washington County, the son of Gen. Rufus R. Dawes (q.v.). He graduated from Marietta College in 1884. He practiced law in Nebraska, 1887–94, and was comptroller of the currency during the McKinley administration. From 1902 to 1921 he was president of the Central Trust Company of Illinois, which he had organized. In World War I he was general purchasing agent for the A.E.F., and his colorful testimony before a postwar Congressional committee first brought him national prominence. He served as director of the budget, as chairman of the Reparations Commission, as vice-president, and as ambassador to Great Britain, 1929–32.

The Banking System of the United States . . ., Chicago, 1894.
Essays and Speeches . . ., Boston, 1915.
A Journal of the Great War, Boston, 1921.
The First Year of the Budget of the United States, New York, 1923.
Notes as Vice President, 1928-29, Boston, 1935.
How Long Prosperity?, Chicago, 1937.
Journal as Ambassador to Great Britain, New York, 1939.
A Journal of Reparations, London, 1939.
A Journal of the McKinley Years, (Bascom N. Timmons, ed.), Chicago, 1950.

DAWES, RUFUS CUTLER (July 30, 1867–Jan. 8, 1940), was born in Marietta, Washington County, the son of Gen. Rufus R. Dawes (q.v.) and the younger brother of Charles G. Dawes (q.v.). A graduate of Marietta College (1886), he went to Chicago in 1897, where he organized and managed various public utility companies. He was president of the Chicago World's Fair of 1933–34. He died in Evanston, Ill., and was buried in Marietta. After World War I. he served as advisor to the committee which prepared a plan of reparations settlements and wrote *The Dawes Plan in the Making,* Indianapolis, [1925]. DAB 22

DAWES, RUFUS R. (July 4, 1838–Aug. 1, 1899), father of Charles G. and Rufus C. Dawes (qq.v.), was born in Malta, Morgan County. He spent his boyhood in Malta and Constitution. He studied at the University of Wisconsin, but spent his last two years at Marietta College, from which he graduated in 1860. He was in Juneau County, Wis., when the Civil War began and organized a company which was incorporated into the 6th Wisconsin, the regiment he commanded at Gettysburg. He was promoted to colonel and was breveted brigadier general. After the war he was engaged in the lumber business in Marietta and served in Congress, 1880–82.

Service with the Sixth Wisconsin Volunteers, Marietta, 1890.

DAWSON, MOSES (1768–1844), professional Irishman and polemical writer, arrived in Philadelphia at the age of 49 from Belfast. He had left behind him two jail sentences and a reward for his arrest offered by the provost marshal of Glasgow, where he had sojourned for a time. In the United States his bellicose career, spent principally in Cincinnati, was to continue as he became a "Jackson Man" and the determined enemy of Charles Hammond (q.v.) and all Whigs. The son of a linen draper, he was born in the small port of Carrickfergus, in Northern Ireland, received a basic classical education in Belfast, and then followed his father's trade. But his real vocation was Irish independence, for which he barely escaped the gallows alongside other members of the United Irishmen. About 1817 Dawson came to Cincinnati and soon opened a Lancastrian school on Water Street, devoted to education divorced from religion. Within two years the school closed its doors, and Dawson's rough-and-tumble newspaper career in Cincinnati opened up with his column in the *Inquisitor and Cincinnati Advertiser.* Shortly thereafter he became proprietor, and he remained with the paper, published under various titles, until old age brought his retirement in 1841. The *Advertiser* in those years became the sounding board for Dawson's prolific opinions on economic, political, social, and religious questions. In the first number of the paper under the new proprietor (Jan. 27, 1823) there appears an attack on John Quincy Adams. Why not? Dawson's creed and prophet were Democracy and Jackson, though with some later modification in regard to the voice of the people. The Monroe Doctrine, America free from European influence, secularized education, private enterprise (including privately owned city waterworks), abolition of public debt, encouragement of museums and theaters, the advancement of science, revolutionary patriots in Europe, the celebration of St. Patrick's Day in Cincinnati, a canal around the falls of the Ohio, and many another project and cause found eager champions in Dawson and his *Advertiser.* Dawson's admiration for William Henry Harrison dated from the Congressional election of 1822. By 1824 he had published his biography of Harrison. But admiration turned to opposition as Dawson saw, or thought he saw, less and less "Democratic edge" on the old warrior. Clay, Webster ("the Yankee Crow"), John Q. Adams, and Harrison in politics were not Dawson's style. "When this old hat was new the people used to say, the best of all the democrats were Harrison and Clay." That they never were such was Dawson's eventual opinion. In the election of 1828 Jackson's candidacy was cried up by Dawson as editor of *The Friend of Reform and Corruption's Adversary* in bitter debate with Charles Hammond's *Truth's Advocate and Anti-Jackson Expositor.* The fight was not in the genteel tradition on either side. Thereafter Hammond of the *Gazette* and Dawson of the *Advertiser* were in almost continual verbal warfare, until darkness intervened. In dress and manners Dawson's habits were simple republican (old style) like Benjamin Franklin's. He was solid, square-built, and florid; he wore an olive-green coat, nankeen pants, and broad-brimmed hat. A serviceable cane completes the picture of what he wanted to be—an honest citizen with no airs. Thus he must have looked when, three years before his death, he sold his share of the paper and dismounted forever from the editorial tripod.

Virginius C. Hall

A Historical Narrative of the Civil and Military Services of Major-General William H. Harrison . . . , Cincinnati, 1824.

Sketches of the Life of Martin Van Buren . . . , Cincinnati, 1840.

DAWSON, WILLIAM LEON (Feb. 20, 1873–April 30, 1928), clergyman and ornithologist, was born in Leon, Iowa. He graduated from Oberlin College in 1897 and from the seminary in 1899. He was ordained to the Congregationalist ministry in 1899, and he served as pastor of North Church, Columbus, 1900–02. His death occurred in California. He wrote studies of bird life in several states, e.g., *The Birds of Ohio,* Columbus, 1903. WWW 1

DAY, ALBERT EDWARD (Nov. 18, 1884–), clergyman and lecturer, was born in Euphemia, Preble County. After graduating from Taylor University in 1904, he was ordained as a Methodist minister and served churches in Bellefontaine, Cincinnati, Delaware, and Canton. He also served churches in other states and lectured widely. He published several books on religious themes, e.g., *Present Perils in Religion,* New York, [1928]. WW 30

DAY, HENRY NOBLE. See Joseph Badger.

DAY, LEWIS W. (Dec. 1, 1839–March 16, 1899), was born in Richland County. He enlisted in the 101st O.V.I. on Aug. 6, 1862, and was discharged in Dec., 1863, for disability. He lived in Hillsdale, Mich., for a time after his discharge. He taught in the schools of Marion, Galion, and Cleveland. He was superintendent of schools in Canton at the time of his death.

Story of the One Hundred and First Ohio Infantry . . . , Cleveland, 1894.

DAY, SARAH J. (Nov. 5, 1860–May 11, 1940), was born in Cincinnati, Hamilton County. In 1872 her family moved to Brooklyn, N. Y., and after 1907 she lived in Englewood, N. J. She graduated from Packer Collegiate Institute, Brooklyn, in 1879. She won a prize at the Brooklyn Institute of Arts and Sciences for a poem, "Battle of Long Island," in 1913. The last title below is a biography of her father, Timothy C. Day.

From Mayflowers to Mistletoe; A Year with the Flower Folk, New York, 1900.

Fresh Fields and Legends Old and New, New York, 1909.

Wayfarers and Wings, New York, 1924.

The Man on a Hill Top, Philadelphia, [1931].

DAY, STEPHEN A. (July 13, 1882–Jan. 5, 1950), lawyer, was born in Canton, Stark County. He graduated from the University of Michigan in 1905, read law, and was admitted to the bar in 1907. He practiced in Cleveland and Chicago and was a member of Congress, 1941–45. He wrote *The Constitutionalist,* Boston, [1936]. WWW 2

DEAN, CORINNE, educator, was born in Toledo, Lucas County. After graduating from the University of Chicago, she studied at the Sorbonne and at Columbia University. She has taught in the schools of Puerto Rico, worked as a government translator, and now lives in Brazil. She has published *Cocoanut Suite; Stories of the West Indies,* Boston, [1944].

DEASY, MARY MARGARET (May 20, 1914–), was born in Cincinnati, Hamilton County. She graduated from Cincinnati Conservatory in 1935 and appeared for a time as a concert pianist. She abandoned music for literature and published several short stories in the late 1940s that were included in the annual collections of "best" stories. A careful craftsman with an experimental viewpoint toward her art, she turned to the novel after achieving success in the short story. Between 1948 and 1957 she published seven novels, receiving highest critical acclaim perhaps for *Cannon Hill,* her second, Boston, 1949. WWAW 1

DeBECK, WILLIAM LOOMIS (Aug. 25, 1835– ?), was born in New Jersey but spent much of his life in Cincinnati, where he attended Woodward High School. He worked as a teacher and as a clerk and also was a reporter for the *Enquirer*. Around 1883 he moved to Chicago. The book listed below, an account of spectacular crimes in Cincinnati, was published under the pen name "An Old Citizen."

Murder Will Out. The First Step in Crime Leads to the Gallows. The Horrors of the Queen City . . . , Cincinnati, 1867.

DeCAMP, ELLIS O. (April 4, 1874–May 16, 1938), was born in Cincinnati, Hamilton County. When he was three years old, his family moved to Hartwell, where he spent his boyhood. He graduated from Ohio Wesleyan University in 1896, taught school for six years, and then joined the Williamson Heater Company, of which he was vice-president at the time of his death. A small volume of his verse, *A Bouquet of Verse,* Cincinnati, 1938, was published by his wife.

De CAPITE, MICHAEL (April 13, 1915–Jan. 17, 1950), was born and reared in Cleveland, Cuyahoga County. He attended Cleveland schools and in 1938 graduated from Ohio University. He worked as a laborer and as a reporter, studied architecture, served in the army during World War II, and was a press officer with the United Nations. His second novel, *No Bright Banner,* New York, [1944], deals with the son of an Italian immigrant growing up on Cleveland's South Side and attending Claremont College, a school that somewhat resembles Ohio University. ANT

De CHAMBRUN, CLARA LONGWORTH (1873–June 1, 1954), was born in Cincinnati, Hamilton County. If there were one word to describe her, it is "ardent." She loved her birthplace passionately and wrote about it often. She glowed with affection for her family, back to early ancestors, and for the friends of her childhood at "Rookwood" on Grandin Road. Even against the pressure of public opinion, she championed her French intimates. For the land of her birth her patriotism never faltered. She adopted with equally warm embrace the country of her soldier-diplomat-banker husband, Count Aldebert de Chambrun, rejoicing that, as a direct descendant of Lafayette, he held American as well as French citizenship. They maintained close relationships with both countries. Most of the Countess's mature years were spent in France, but they returned to Cincinnati for their golden wedding. They chose to remain in France through both World Wars. The Countess died there in 1954 and lies buried in French soil. If nothing great was ever achieved without enthusiasm, Clara de Chambrun's lifetime researches and writings on Shakespeare can lay claim to greatness. In the days of the Bacon-Shakespeare controversy she took up the cudgels for the Bard, and deep was her scorn for his doubters. She had learned to read from a Shakespeare picture book, and her love for the poet deepened with time. It led to years of research which produced some dozen works on him in both English and French, including a play and a fictionalized biography. *Shakespeare, Actor-Poet* (1927), published in both languages, brought her the Bordin Prize of the French Academy. Reviewing it in the New York *Times,* Richard Le Gallienne pronounced the work "on the whole the most convincing and complete life of Shakespeare yet written." Because life seemed zestful to her, the Countess recorded her experiences in detail. Two of her books, *Shadows like Myself* (1936) and *Shadows Lengthen* . . . (1949), are autobiographical. Two more, *The Making of Nicholas Longworth* (1933), a memoir of her brother, who served as Congressman and Speaker of the House, and *Cincinnati: The Story of the Queen City* (1939), are family books. In her eyes, Cincinnati was a Longworth city. Her personality shines out against a panorama of distinguished intellectuals, diplomats, and political, military, and social leaders in whose society she circulated. She was an aristocrat, with the strength and weakness which the label implies. During two World Wars in France she accepted hardship lightly, took daring chances, bowed down to no man, and regarded physical fear, even the danger of death, as lese majesty. Toward humanity in the mass she was an onlooker. The sight of fleeing refugees crowding the roads with their meager belongings, children, old people, and animals evoked words of pity, but obviously no empathy: "Once again we had to face the heart-rending spectacle of fleeing population. Except for this blot on the peaceful landscape, nothing more lovely could be imagined than the valley of Coulommiers wrapped in the fairy veils of a dewy September dawn." The education of Clara brings a groan of envy in this television era. Her grandfather, Joseph Longworth, whose home the family shared, believed that young people who live in the country learn more from nature than from academic instruction. He also held a theory that adults should never talk down to children. Walking through the beech woods on their estate, he recited Shakespeare to the four-year-old. From her mother she learned composition, arithmetic, and American history. The wife of the French consul came to give language lessons. In the evening, around the library lamp, the children listened to readings from Dickens, Thackeray, Scott, and Pope's translations of the *Iliad* and the *Odyssey*. They were taken to the best plays and operas. In the little playhouse on the grounds they presented their own renditions of classical drama. Later, young Miss Longworth attended a small private school. It was not until years after her marriage that the Countess was made to feel aware of the need for a formal degree. When the Count de Chambrun was serving as military attaché at the French Embassy in Washington, his intellectually eager wife spent much time at the Library of Congress. There she unearthed the translations of John Florio, which explained Shakespeare's knowledge of French and Italian source materials. "I worked hard over my discovery," she says, "thrilled that a girl from Cincinnati with little scholastic training and no university studies whatever had made it." For just this lack she was unable to attract the attention of either Shakespeare scholars or publishers. Eventually, her book was privately printed. As her studies into the sources of Shakespeare's work deepened, she determined to acquire a degree. At forty, she achieved the difficult Doctor of Letters at the Sorbonne. Friendship, according to the standards of Clara de Chambrun, demanded consistent loyalty against all odds. Since little-girl days she had been devoted to the family friend, William Howard Taft. She dedicated one of her early novels to him. Letters passed between them frequently. When Theodore Roosevelt took his Bull Moose followers out of President Taft's Republican Party organization, the Longworths were confronted with a dilemma: Nicholas Longworth was married to Alice Roosevelt. Their decision, though difficult, was typical. Clara, and brother Nick as well, stood by their old friend, Taft, against Nick's father-in-law. It would have been unthinkable for the de Chambruns to leave France during wartime. By World War II the Count's military days were over and he headed the American Hospital. The Countess kept the American Library going. Under its sign hung the name "C. Longworth Chambrun, Doctor of the University of Paris." "This formula proved completely boche-proof," she said, until June, 1944, when the Gestapo took over and created trouble. They could not down the cocky little Cincinnatian. Because of their broad affiliations, the de Chambruns were in a unique position to know what was going on on both sides. Their pro-Americanism and devotion to democratic France were not doubted. The marriage of their only son, René, to Josée Laval, daughter of Pierre Laval, premier during the occupation, placed them close to the workings of the Vichy Government. The Countess expressed bitterness at the distorted view which the U. S. Government representatives and press implanted concerning the officials who preferred to stay in France and try to keep the nation alive. At considerable length in *Shadows Lengthen* she explains the difficulties of the Vichy Government in its struggle to protect the French people and preserve an organization. "He [Marshal Pétain] was there as Chief of State to maintain the dignity of France, leaving the interior government in the hands of one [Pierre Laval] who had given full proof of competence in many spheres, and who at the same time was the most convinced upholder of democratic institutions." She regarded Laval as a murdered martyr. "A complete revision of popular opinion will have to be made in order to approach historical truth," she concludes. Characteristically, the Countess took what action she could. Shortly before her death she made arrangements to have Laval's body exhumed from its potter's field grave and buried in the plot of Lafayette and de Chambrun. John Hollister, who knew the Countess, described her as "dynamic, with great dignity and poise and a good sense of humor!" "She rode her hobbies hard," he said. Though born a Protestant, she became a devout Catholic and tried to prove her beloved Shakespeare a Catholic, too.

Iphigene Bettman

DEERING, IVAH EVERETT (April 28, 1889–), was born in Stewartsville, Mo. She attended the University of Washington and later taught in Washington elementary schools. She lived in Cincinnati from 1932 to 1946, while her husband, Tam Deering, was city recreation director. She now lives in Marysville, Wash., and teaches part time at Everett Junior College. Her writings include a collection of poems: *Stormy Petrel*, Philadelphia, [1949].

De FORD, SARA WHITCRAFT (Nov. 9, 1916–), educator, was born in Youngstown, Mahoning County. After graduating from Mount Holyoke College in 1936, she had intended to study law, the profession of her father, but she transferred her interest to literature and earned a doctorate from

Yale University in 1942. She has taught at Barnard College, 1942–46, and since 1946 at Goucher College. Her poems have appeared in various periodicals, and she has published three collections, e.g., *The Return to Eden,* [New York, 1940]. DAS 3

DEINDÖRFER, JOHANNES (July 28, 1828–May 14, 1907), clergyman, was born in Bavaria. He came to Michigan as a Lutheran missionary in 1851, moved to Iowa in 1853 after a doctrinal dispute, and with others organized the Evangelical Lutheran Synod of Iowa. He served as pastor of Lutheran churches in Toledo, 1865–70, and Defiance, 1870–89, though retaining his connection with the Iowa Synod.

Geschichte der Evangel.-Luth. Synode von Iowa und Anderen Staaten . . . , Chicago, 1897.

DeJEANS, ELIZABETH. Pseud. See Frances E. J. Budgett.

DELAFIELD, JOHN, JR. (Oct. 12, 1812–1865), was born in Uxbridge, England. He was the son of an American father who, though held a prisoner throughout the War of 1812, had been permitted to carry on a lucrative banking business in London. The fortune so acquired was swept away in a financial crisis in 1819. It was then that the father's intimate friend, Washington Irving, wrote of the Delafields' experiences in that graceful story "The Wife," which appears in the *Sketch Book.* The family returned to New York in 1820, where Delafield senior became cashier and president of the Phoenix Bank and was soon on his way to acquiring a second and much larger fortune. The Phoenix Bank was closely affiliated with a number of Midwestern banking institutions, one of which was the bank of Marietta, of which Arius Nye was cashier. Upon young Delafield's graduation from Columbia University in 1830, he served as librarian of the New York Historical Society for a time. In 1831 he was sent to Marietta, where he commenced the study of law under Nye. Shortly after his arrival in Marietta, an impressionable young woman—herself newly arrived from the East—described him as "the only dandy here . . . an elegant young man from New York and an Episcopalian. He is studying law here and is a teacher of music at the Institute." He was admitted to the bar in 1833, and on April 20, 1833, in partnership with Edward W. Nye, he bought the newspaper *American Friend and Marietta Gazette.* Two months later he married Edith Wallace, the niece of Judge Jacob Burnet (q.v.). At this time the great Ohio land boom was at its peak. Eastern speculators were being showered with elegantly colored maps, pamphlets, and books descriptive of the various localities in which lands were being offered for sale. Out of this clutter of promotional literature a few items have survived to acquire some degree of respect as historical sources. Such a one is young Delafield's *Brief Topographical Description of the County of Washington, State of Ohio,* published in New York early in 1834. It was the first history of an Ohio county to be published. On Oct. 18, 1834, Delafield announced his withdrawal from the editorial office of the *Gazette* and his election as cashier of the newly organized Clinton Bank in Columbus. In its early years the Clinton Bank was the only United States depository west of the Ohio River. It made the payments on such government works as the National Road, the mails, military posts, Indian annuities, and other governmental services. In guarded wagons, its deposits came from as far away as the land office in the village of Chicago. For a youngster of 22, it was a position of tremendous responsibility, yet he seems to have been equal to it; letters from contemporary Midwestern bankers indicate that he had their respect and esteem. He resigned from the bank in 1838 to devote his time to the completion of a work on archaeology. In 1837 Delafield induced Jacob Burnet to begin writing a series of letters, in which the aged judge recounted his recollections of incidents relating to the early settlement of the Northwestern Territory. The series of seven leters, an important historical work, was published in Part Second, Volume I, of the *Transactions of the Historical and Philosophical Society of Ohio* in 1839. The result of Delafield's own archaeological research was published in 1839: *The Origin of the Antiquities of America.* The book was enthusiastically received by European as well as American reviewers. In the *North American Review,* John Gorham Palfrey said: "A quarto volume, from what when we studied geography, used to be known by the instructive name of the 'territory northwest of the Ohio,' is something to attract attention, and when we open it and find it printed in a style which emulates the London press, and is seldom even attempted in America, we turn to the title page again to see if we did not mistake its birthplace. That one of the community in that great pork-mart should write a book upon a subject requiring long study and deep thought, is to us a pleasing fact." Not the least impressive feature of the work was a folded color engraving of Mexican paintings eighteen feet in length, engraved from drawings by the versatile author. It was, so far as is known, Delafield's final literary effort. Early in the 1840s he removed to Memphis, Tenn., and became a partner in the law firm of Delafield and Massey. He gained considerable recognition throughout the Mississippi Valley as a specialist in land cases. He removed to St. Louis, Mo., in 1849, but continued to maintain an office in Memphis. He died in Liverpool, England.

Ernest J. Wessen

A Brief Topograhpical [sic] Description of the County of Washington, in the State of Ohio, New York, 1834.

An Inquiry into the Origin of the Antiquities of America, Cincinnati, 1839.

DeLEEUW, ADÈLE LOUISE (Aug. 12, 1899–), was born in Hamilton, Butler County, attended schools there and in Cincinnati, and now lives in Plainfield, N. J. She traveled throughout the world with her parents, lived for a time in New York City, and then became a librarian in Plainfield. She has written many books for adults and for children and a volume of poems: *Berries of the Bittersweet,* Boston, 1924. WWAW 1

DeLEEUW, CATEAU (Sept. 22, 1903–), was born in Hamilton, Butler County. She studied painting in New York and Paris and has exhibited her work in various cities. She has illustrated a number of books written by her sister, Adèle (q.v.), and they have collaborated on children's books. Sometimes using the pen names Jessica Lyon and Kay Hamilton, she has published a number of books in her own right, e.g., *Love Is Where You Find It,* Philadelphia, 1947. WWAW 1

DELLENBAUGH, FREDERICK SAMUEL (Sept. 13, 1853–Jan. 30, 1935), artist and author, was born in McConnelsville, Morgan County. He was artist and topographer with Major Powell's second expedition to explore the Colorado and Green Rivers and was a member of several other exploring expeditions to Alaska and Siberia, Iceland, the American Southwest, and South America. He wrote a number of books, including studies of Frémont and Custer; but he is best known for two books about the Powell expedition: *The Romance of the Colorado River . . . ,* New York, 1902, and *A Canyon Voyage . . . ,* New York, 1908. DAB 21

DeLONG, ARTHUR HAMILTON (March 23, 1862–Dec. 17, 1919), clergyman, was born in Napoleon, Henry County. A graduate of Northwestern University and Garrett Biblical Institute, he served as a Methodist minister in northwestern Indiana. He wrote *It Is Not Lawful; A Romance,* New York, [1913].

DELP, IRWIN W. (Sept. 21, 1889–), educator, was born in Dayton, Montgomery County. After graduating from Miami University, he entered the Canton school system, where he served in various administrative capacities until his retirement in 1949. He now lives in Canton. His writings include *The Santa Fe Trail to California . . . ,* Boston, 1933.

DEMING, KIRK. Pseud. See Harry S. Drago.

DEMING, WILLIAM CHAPIN (Dec. 6, 1869–April 9, 1949), Kentucky-born journalist, lived in Ohio for seven years, 1894–1901, while he edited the Warren *Tribune.* From 1910 until his death he lived in Cheyenne, Wyo. He published a number of books and pamphlets. Agnes W. Spring edited his *Collected Writings and Addresses . . . ,* 4 vols., Glendale, Calif., 1946–47.

DEMORET, ALFRED (Feb. 7, 1843–May 21, 1931), was born in Butler County. He served as a private in the 93rd O.V.I. from Aug., 1862, to June, 1865. His regimental history was first published in the Venice *Gazette* and was then revised and published as a book.

A Brief History of the Ninety-Third Regiment . . . , [Ross, 1898].

DENTON, FRANKLIN EVERT (Nov. 22, 1859–May 28, 1947), journalist, was born in Chardon, Geauga County. At the age of seven he learned to set type in the office of the *Jeffersonian Democrat,* published by his uncle, Julius O. Converse (q.v.). He edited the Geauga *Leader* at Burton, 1884–87, and from 1887 to 1902 worked on several Cleveland newspapers. He later edited the Ravenna *Republican.* His last years were spent in Chardon and Cleveland. His death occurred in Cleveland.

The Early Poetical Works of Franklin E. Denton, Cleveland, 1883.

DENTON, SHERMAN FOOTE (Sept. 24, 1856–June 17, 1937), naturalist, son of William Denton (q.v.), was born in Dayton, Montgomery County. He attended school in Massachusetts, and in 1880 he visited Nevada and California on his first collecting trip. In 1883 he went to Australia and New Guinea in search of specimens. He also worked in the Smithsonian Institution for several years. He perfected methods of mounting fish and butterflies and supplied specimens to museums throughout the country. He died at Weston, Mass.

Incidents of a Collector's Rambles in Australia, New Zealand, and New Guinea, Boston, 1889.

As Nature Shows Them: Moths and Butterflies of the United States East of the Rocky Mountains . . . , 2 vols., Boston, 1900.

DENTON, WILLIAM (Jan., 1823–1883), reformer, was born in Darlington, England. Soon after his conversion to Methodism at the age of sixteen, he was a popular lecturer on temperance. In 1848 he came to the United States. After spending a short time in Cincinnati, he went to Dayton, where he taught school and served as a principal. He married Elizabeth Foote of Cincinnati, who collaborated on the second book listed below. His interest in geology led him to adopt unpopular ideas regarding creation, and on a few of his lecture trips he was threatened with mob violence. His debate with James A. Garfield (q.v.) drew a large crowd. In the 1850s he moved to Massachusetts. He died in New Guinea while on a world speaking and exploring tour.

Poems for Reformers, Dayton, 1856.

The Soul of Things; Or, Psychometric Researches and Discoveries, Boston, 1863.

Our Planet, Its Past and Future . . . , Boston, [1868].

The Irreconcilable Records; Or, Genesis and Geology, Boston, 1870.

Radical Discourses on Religious Subjects . . . , Boston, 1872.

What Was He? Or, Jesus in the Light of the Nineteenth Century, Wellesley, Mass., 1877.

Is Darwin Right? . . . , Wellesley, 1881.

DENVER, DRAKE C. Pseud. See Nelson C. Nye.

DENVER, JANE CAMPBELL (Feb. 8, 1821–Dec. 7, 1847) and **MARY CAROLINE DENVER** (Feb. 8, 1821–Oct. 16, 1860), twin sisters, were born near Winchester, Va. When they were about ten years old, the family moved to a farm near Wilmington, Clinton County. Mary commenced writing poetry at the age of eleven, and Jane began writing some years later. Identical twins of great beauty, their personal resemblance was extraordinary. Mary wrote rapidly, without effort, while Jane wrote with less ease but perhaps with more vigor of expression. To both, their gift was a source of great happiness. Both died at Wilmington, and they are buried there. In 1875 their distinguished brother, James W. Denver (q.v.), published their poems.

Poems, New York, 1875.

DENVER, JAMES WILLIAM (Oct. 23, 1817–Aug. 9, 1892), lawyer, was born in Winchester, Va. His parents moved with their family to Wilmington, Clinton County, in 1830. He graduated from Cincinnati Law School and was admitted to the bar in 1844. He commenced practice at Xenia, where he also edited a newspaper, the *Thomas Jefferson.* He soon moved to Platte City, Mo., where he bought and edited the *Platte Argus* and practiced law, with a bit of schoolteaching on the side. He served in the Mexican War, and in 1850 he went to California and engaged in trading. An unfortunate controversy with Edward Gilbert, editor of the *Daily Alta California,* resulted in a duel in which Gilbert was killed. Denver was elected without difficulty to the 34th Congress, but in later years political adversaries made effective use of distorted versions of the duel. In Congress he proposed that three transcontinental railroads be built; though none was authorized, a continuing study of the subject made him one of the leading railroad attorneys in Washington in later years. In 1857 he was appointed Commissioner of Indian Affairs by President Buchanan and went to the West to negotiate treaties with the Indians. Needing a strong arm in the turbulent Kansas Territory, Buchanan appointed him secretary of the Territory in Dec., 1857, and governor the following May. Having restored law and order, he returned to Washington in 1859, where, in association with Albert Pike, he became active in prosecuting the claims of the Cherokee and Choctaw Indians. On the outbreak of the Civil War, he entered the Federal army and served two years with the rank of brigadier general. Resigning in the spring of 1863 he returned to Washington and reopened his offices. The fact that he was employed in the defense of the infamous Captain Henry Wirz, prison keeper at Andersonville, seems to have escaped the attention of those Union veterans who endorsed him for the Presidency at the Soldiers' Convention in Cleveland in 1866. From 1860 until his death he maintained his legal residence at Wilmington, though he spent most of his time in Washington, where he served as attorney for a number of western railroads, specialized in the prosecution of Indian claims, and more particularly negotiated the famous and complex California land cases, on which he became an outstanding authority. His briefs, hundreds of which were printed, demonstrate tireless research and are of no little value to the historian. He was an unsuccessful candidate for Congress from Ohio in 1870. At the Democratic conventions of 1876 and 1884, he was mentioned in connection with the Democratic nomination for the Presidency, but rumors of his association with the Wirz case and the twisted versions of the duel with Gilbert presented hurdles which he could not hope to clear.

Ernest J. Wessen

DeQUILLE, DAN. Pseud. See William Wright.

DeRAN, EDNA SMITH (Nov. 7, 1870– ?), was born in Pyrmont, Montgomery County. She attended National Normal University, Lebanon, and Cincinnati Conservatory of Music. She lived in New Orleans, La., and Detroit, Mich. She is deceased, but the date of her death has not been learned. She published several collections of verse, e.g., *Muted Melodies,* Kalamazoo, Mich., 1926. BDCP

DERBY, ROSWELL, JR. (Feb. 4, 1854–Oct. 28, 1927), lawyer, was born in Fulton County. After reading law, he was admitted to the bar and practiced in Milan. He published *Poems of Friendship, Love, and Hope,* Boston, 1917.

DeSCHWEINITZ, EDMUND ALEXANDER (1825–1887), clergyman, served a brief pastorate at Dover about 1847–48. He wrote *The Life and Times of David Zeisberger . . . ,* Philadelphia, 1871.

DESSAR, LEO CHARLES (1847–1924), lawyer, was born in Cincinnati, Hamilton County. He was admitted to the Ohio bar and later practiced in New York City.

A Royal Enchantress; The Romance of the Last Queen of the Berbers, New York, 1900.

DETWEILER, FREDERICK GERMAN (March 4, 1881–), clergyman and educator, was born in Louisville, Ky. He was ordained a Baptist minister in 1908 and served churches in Oberlin, 1908–11, Dayton, 1912–15, and Galion, 1915–17. He earned an A.B. at Denison University in 1917 and a Ph.D. from University of Chicago in 1922. From 1917 until his retirement in 1949, he was on the faculty of Denison University. He now lives in Dallas, Texas. His writings include *The Negro Press in the United States,* Chicago, [1922]. WW 26

DEUTSCH, ALEX TOM, engineer, born in Vienna, Austria, lived in Cincinnati for fifteen years. He now lives in Washington, D. C. He has published technical books and papers and a collection of prose and poetry: *Beach of Life . . . ,* Cincinnati, [1949].

DEUTSCH, GOTTHARD (Jan. 31, 1859–Oct. 14, 1921), educator, was born in Kanitz, Austria, and came to the United States in 1891 to join the faculty of Hebrew Union College. He spent the remainder of his life in Cincinnati.

Die Symbolik in Cultus . . . , Brünn, 1886.
Theory of Oral Tradition, 1895.
Andere Zeiten . . . , Berlin, 1897.
Philosophy of Jewish History, Cincinnati, 1897.
Unlösbare Fesseln . . . , Frankfort, 1902.
Four Epochs of Jewish History, 1905.
Israel Bruna; An Historical Tragedy in Five Acts, Boston, 1908.
The History of the Jews, New York, 1910.
Der Glaube on Hobelspaene, 1915.
Scrolls; Essays on Jewish History and Literature . . . , 3 vols., Cincinnati, 1917–20.

DeVELLING, CHARLES THEODORE (June 25, 1842–Jan. 14, 1923), was born in Athens, Athens County, and attended school in Lancaster. He studied dentistry with his brother-in-law and, after the Civil War, settled in Zanesville to practice. He later dealt in real estate and lived in Washington, D. C., for several years but returned to Zanesville before his death.

History of the Seventeenth Regiment, First Brigade, Third Division, Fourteenth Corps, Army of the Cumberland . . . , Zanesville, 1889.

DEVINE, GEORGE BURNETT (Oct. 22, 1892–), was born in Miamisburg, Montgomery County. Though deaf since 1904 and blind since 1932, he mastered the art of reading and writing Braille and has also made carpentry his hobby. Since 1941 he has lived in Dayton. He has published a volume of homespun verse: *Everyday Poems in Everyday English,* Miamisburg, 1937.

DEVOL, GEORGE H. (Aug. 1, 1829– ?), was born in Marietta, Washington County. In the preface to his book it is stated that "He [the author] belongs to the celebrated Devol family of Marietta." This is confirmed by an inscription on the flyleaf of a copy of the book in the Stimson Collection, Marietta College Library, where Rodney M. Stimson (q.v.) wrote "George H. Devol, the author of this 'work,' was born in Marietta, and was always, and is yet a 'bad egg.'

His father, Barker Devol, was known to [me] many years as a quiet citizen of not bad reputation . . . this book is worthless, even as a record of Devol's worthless life and adventures." Devol's book is now a sought-after classic in its field. He was still living in 1889, but the exact date of his death has not been found. It is interesting to note that Devol may not be the only famous double-dealer from Marietta to write of his skullduggery; it is probable that Jonathan Harrington Green (q.v.), "The Reformed Gambler," was also born in that community.

Forty Years a Gambler on the Mississippi, Cincinnati, 1887.

DE WEESE, TRUMAN ARMSTRONG (June 19, 1860–March 19, 1936), was born near Troy, Miami County. After graduating from high school in Dayton, he studied medicine for two years before turning to journalism. He was an editorial writer for the Chicago *Times-Herald,* 1894–1904, director of special publicity for the St. Louis Exposition, 1904, and after 1906 director of publicity for the Shredded Wheat Company.

The Young Man with Nothing but Brains, [n.p.], 1896.
The Principles of Practical Publicity . . . , Buffalo, 1906.
The Bend in the Road and How a Man of the City Found It, New York, 1913.
Keeping a Dollar at Work . . . , [New York], 1915.

DEXTER, CHARLES (Jan. 17, 1830–Sept. 12, 1893), was born in Cincinnati, Hamilton County, the son of an Englishman who operated a wholesale grocery and liquor business in the city. After graduating from Harvard University in 1851, he entered his father's business. The volume below consists partly of original verses and partly of translations from German poetry.

Versions and Idle Measures, Cincinnati, 1865.

DEXTER, WILL. Pseud. See Oliver Coomes.

DICE, CHARLES AMOS (Nov. 5, 1878–), educator, was born in Strasburg, Tuscarawas County. He graduated from Ohio Northern University in 1905, Drew Theological Seminary in 1908, and the University of Wisconsin (Ph.D.) in 1924. He served on the faculty of Ohio State University, 1919–49, and since his retirement has continued to live in Columbus. He has published *The Stock Market,* London, England, 1926. WW 20

DICK, GERTRUDE McCONNELL (Mrs. Karl W.) (March 22, 1899–), was born in Massillon, Stark County. She now lives in Cleveland, where she gives readings with musical background. She has written a story of an Alsatian boy living during World War II in an Ohio mining town: *Kaleidoscope,* Philadelphia, [1944].

DICK, SAMUEL MEDARY (April 4, 1857–March 5, 1938), clergyman, was born in Pickaway County. He graduated from Ohio Wesleyan University in 1887 and the University of Michigan (Ph.D.) in 1891. After being ordained to the Methodist ministry in 1895, he served churches in New England and Minnesota and later lived in Pasadena, Calif. He patented various devices, including an instantaneous carbonator. Besides the titles below, he edited a collection of patriotic talks in 1895.

The Principle of Synthetic Unity in Berkeley and Kant, Lowell, Mass., 1898.
Psychotherapy . . . , [Minneapolis, 1909].
Analysis and Interpretation of Old Age Revolving Pensions as Outlined by F. E. Townsend, Chicago, 1934.

DICKERSON, ROY ERNEST (April 3, 1886–), social worker and lawyer, was born in Versailles, Ind. He practiced law in Colorado, 1910–16, entered Y.M.C.A. and De Molay work, and came to Cincinnati in 1941 as associate director of the American Institute of Family Relations and as a teacher at the University of Cincinnati. He has written numerous books on social problems, e.g., *Growing into Manhood,* New York, 1933. WW 30

DICKEY, JAMES H. (1780–1856), clergyman, was born in Virginia. He was licensed to preach by the Presbyterian Church in 1808; served as a domestic missionary in Tennessee, Kentucky, and Ohio; and was pastor of South Salem Church, Ross County, 1810-36. In 1837 he moved to Union Grove, Ill., where he spent the remainder of his life. Like his brother-in-law, Samuel Crothers (q.v.), he was an outspoken opponent of slavery. His book is a refutation of the Scriptural defense of slavery.

A Review of a Summary of Biblical Antiquities . . . , Ripley, 1834.

DICKINSON, CORNELIUS EVARTS (April 23, 1835–March 7, 1925), clergyman, was born in Heath, Mass. He graduated from Amherst College in 1860 and Chicago Theological Seminary in 1863. After serving several Congregational churches in Illinois, he came to Marietta in 1883 and remained an Ohio resident for the rest of his life. His *History of Belpre* was largely a republication of material drawn from the works of Samuel Prescott Hildreth (q.v.).

The First Church Organization in Marietta . . . , Columbus, 1888.
A Century of Church Life, Marietta, 1896.
A History of Belpre, Washington County, Ohio, Parkersburg, W. Va., [1920].

DICKINSON, EDWARD (Oct. 10, 1853–Jan. 25, 1946), musician and educator, was born in West Springfield, Mass. He graduated from Amherst College in 1876 and studied music in Boston and Berlin. From 1893 to 1922 he was a member of the Oberlin College faculty, and after his retirement he continued to live in Oberlin. He published several books on music, e.g., *Music in the History of the Western Church . . .* , New York, 1902. WWW 3

DICKMAN, JOSEPH THEODORE (Oct. 6, 1857–Oct. 23, 1927), army officer, was born in Dayton, Montgomery County. During World War I he commanded a division, a corps, and finally the Third Army. He retired as a major general in 1921. He wrote an account of military operations in France: *The Great Crusade,* [New York, 1927]. DAB 5

DICKORÉ, MARIE (Aug. 15, 1883–), was born in Cincinnati, Hamilton County. She graduated from the University of Cincinnati in 1907 and has done graduate work in history at the University of Wisconsin and Ohio State University. She has written historical feature articles for the *Times-Star* and the *Enquirer* and books and pamphlets on historical subjects, e.g., *The Order of the Purple Heart . . .* , Cincinnati, 1943. WWMW 6

DICKSON, ARTHUR PARKINSON (1888–c.1940), was born in Dayton, Montgomery County. He studied art in New York City and for more than twenty years was art director of Fox Films. His writings include a novel published posthumously: *Death for the Corners,* Boston, [1941].

DICUS, M. E. Pseud. See Charles Gatchell.

DIEBOLD, JANET HART (July 8, 1917–), lawyer, was born in Cincinnati, Hamilton County. She graduated from Swarthmore College in 1937 and Duke University School of Law in 1954. Admitted to the bar in the District of Columbia in 1955, she is now an assistant counsel, Board of Governors, Federal Reserve System, and lives in Washington, D. C. She has been married twice, and as Janet Diebold published a novel about a young American girl studying in Denmark: *Mandrake Root,* New York, [1946]. Under her present name, Janet Hart Sylvester, she has published legal articles and some poems.

DIEHL, HENRY ARCHER (Aug. 26, 1876–Nov. 1, 1952), educator, was born in West Farmington, Trumbull County. After attending Hiram College, he taught school in Trumbull and Mahoning Counties and for 25 years was superintendent of West End schools in Ashtabula. He spent 36 years in educational work before retiring to become a public lecturer in Ohio and other states. He wrote epigrams, short stories, and poems which appeared in various magazines. One collection of his verse was published: *Three Dozen Poems by the Way, Three Dozen Poems Sad and Gay,* Cleveland, 1906.

DIEHL, MICHAEL (1819–April 20, 1869), clergyman and educator, was born in Franklin County, Pa. In 1846 after his graduation from Gettysburg College and Seminary and his ordination as a Lutheran minister, he was called to Wittenberg College as professor of ancient languages. While teaching in Springfield, he served as pastor of several churches in the vicinity of the city. He retired from teaching in 1868 and died in Springfield the following year.

Biography of Rev. Ezra Keller, D.D., Founder and First President of Wittenberg College, Springfield, 1859.

DIETZ, DAVID HENRY (Oct. 6, 1897–), writer and lecturer on scientific subjects, was born in Cleveland, Cuyahoga County. He graduated from Western Reserve University in 1919. He has been on the editorial staff of the Cleveland *Press* since 1915, science editor for Scripps-Howard newspapers since 1921, and lecturer at Western Reserve since 1927. He has written numerous articles and books since his first: *The Story of Science,* New York, [1931]. WW 30

DIFFENDORFER, RALPH EUGENE (Aug. 15, 1879–Jan. 31, 1951), clergyman, was born in Haysville, Ashland County. He graduated from Ohio Wesleyan University in 1902 and Drew Theological Seminary in 1907. He served in various executive positions in educational and missionary organizations of the Methodist Church. He died in Madison, N. J. He edited and wrote a number of books on the missionary movement, e.g., *China and Japan?,* New York, [1938]. WWW 3

DILLON, JOHN BROWN (c.1807–Feb. 27, 1879), journalist and historian, was born in Wellsburg, Va. Soon after his birth his parents moved to Belmont County, where he spent his boyhood. His father died in 1816, and a year later the boy was apprenticed to the Wellsburg printer John Berry. In 1824 he went to Cincinnati, where he was employed as a printer, working for some time on the Cincinnati *Gazette* under his former Belmont County neighbor, the brilliant Charles Hammond (q.v.). Like so many other young Cincinnati littérateurs of that day, he read law in his spare time. His first published poem of which we have record, "The Burial of the Beautiful," appeared in the *Gazette* in 1826. He contributed to Timothy Flint's *Western Review* in 1827, and published "The Orphan's Lament" in James Hall's *Western Souvenir* in 1829. During the rest of his stay, and for some years after leaving the city, he was a regular contributor to Cincinnati publications. In 1834 he went to Logansport, Ind., where with Stanislaus Lassell he founded the *Canal Telegraph.* He was admitted to the bar in Logansport. He had long been interested in local history, and within a year after his arrival in Indiana he had become a member of the newly organized Indiana Historical Society, an organization in which he served with distinction in various offices until the end of his days. While he was in Logansport, he began his projected *History of Indiana,* the first volume of which appeared in 1843. This scholarly and readable book was a commercial failure. Claiming without apparent justification that the text had been substantially revised, he permitted it to be reissued in 1859 with scanty material, supposedly bringing the history of the state down to 1859. He appears to have engaged but little in legal practice. After holding several minor state offices, he was appointed in 1863 as ex-officio Superintendent of Documents and Librarian to the Department of the Interior in Washington, D. C. Under political pressure he resigned in 1871 to become Clerk to the Committee on Military Affairs in the House of Representatives. In 1875 he moved to Indianapolis, where he remained until his death. His *Oddities of Colonial Legislation* was completed by Ben Douglass (q.v.) of Ohio.

Ernest J. Wessen

The History of Indiana, from Its Earliest Exploration by Europeans, to the Close of the Territorial Government in 1816 . . . , Indianapolis, 1843.

Notes on Historical Evidence in Reference to Adverse Theories of the Origin and Nature of the Government of the United States of America, New York, 1871.

Oddities of Colonial Legislation in America . . . , Indianapolis, 1879.

The National Decline of the Miami Indians, Indianapolis, 1897.

DILWORTH, HIRAM POWERS (May 19, 1878–), was born in Hicksville, Defiance County. After graduating from the Cincinnati College of Music and studying abroad, he became a concert pianist and toured the United States. In 1904 he became a guard at the Art Institute of Chicago; now retired, he still lives in Chicago. He has written poetry since he was eleven years old and has donated manuscript volumes of verse to many libraries. He has also published several volumes, e.g., *Seven Sonnets and Ode to the Merry Moment,* [Chicago, 1916].

DIMMETTE, CELIA PUHR (Mrs. Charles L.) (Sept. 26, 1896–), was born in Brookings County, S. D., but has lived in Summit County for more than forty years. She has published poems in various magazines and newspapers, and one collection of her verse: *Toward the Metal Sun,* Boston, 1950.

DINWIDDIE, ELIZABETH McMURTIE (Jan. 26, 1886–), was born in Charlottesville, Va. She was a social worker in the South for several years before moving to Cleveland in 1923. She is married to Lewis L. Holladay. Under her maiden name, she published a volume of verse: *Creeds and Byways,* Boston, [1923].

DITTRICK, HOWARD (Feb. 14, 1877–July 11, 1954), physician, born in St. Catherine's, Ontario, Canada, came to the United States in 1900. He studied medicine at the University of Toronto and Lakeside Hospital, Cleveland. He practiced in Cleveland until 1943, and after his retirement he directed the editorial department of Cleveland Clinic. He was widely known as a writer of historical and medical articles and also published one book, *Pioneer Medicine in the Western Reserve,* Cleveland, 1932. WWW 3

DIX, FRED KELLER (1891–Feb. 5, 1944), journalist, was born in Prospect, Marion County. He attended Prospect public schools, and in 1924 he bought the Prospect *Monitor.* He also broadcast programs over a Marion radio station. He published poems in various periodicals and a collection, *Poems,* Prospect, [1921].

DIXON, J. M. (c.1820– ?), journalist, son of Jacob Dixon (q.v.), was born in southeastern Ohio. Between 1850 and 1867 he apparently served on the editorial staffs of several Iowa newspapers. He was associate editor of the *Iowa State Register* in Oct., 1867, when he was stricken with blindness. Shortly afterward he returned to Harrison, Hamilton County, where he spent the rest of his life.

The Valley of the Shadow: Comprising the Experiences of a Blind Ex-Editor, New York, 1868.

Centennial History of Polk County, Iowa, Des Moines, 1876.

DIXON, JACOB (May 20, 1793–Sept., 1849), clergyman and physician, was born in Virginia. In 1805 he moved with his family to Washington County. He became a Methodist minister in 1825 and served in various Ohio conferences until 1834, when he began to practice medicine at Frankfort, Ross County. He practiced in that area until his death at Marshall. He published poems in the *Western Christian Monitor,* Chillicothe, and other periodicals. The volume below contains a four-part epic, "Divination Overruled."

The Poetical Works of Jacob Dixon . . . , Columbus, 1833.

DOAN, EDWARD NEWELL (Oct. 8, 1904–), educator, was born in West Carrollton, Montgomery County. A graduate of Ohio Wesleyan University in 1926, he has taught political science and journalism at several universities and now lives in Miamisburg. His interest in the Progressive movement led to his writing *The La Follettes and the Wisconsin Idea,* New York, 1947.

DOAN, FRANK CARLETON (Feb. 13, 1877–May 14, 1927), clergyman and educator, was born in Nelsonville, Athens County. He graduated from Ohio State University in 1898 and Harvard University (Ph.D.) in 1904. He taught at Ohio University, 1900–04, and Meadville Theological Seminary, Pa., 1904–14. After 1914 he served as pastor of Unitarian churches in New Jersey, Iowa, and New York. His writings include *Religion and the Modern Mind . . . ,* Boston, 1909. WWW 1

DOANE, ROBERT RUTHERFORD (March 10, 1889–Oct. 20, 1960), economist, was born in Wilmington, Clinton County. He attended Wilmington College and Ohio Wesleyan University and did graduate work at several universities. He served as an economist with several industrial firms and was also a member of many conferences on economic questions. He lived in New York City and wrote magazine articles and books on economic questions, e.g., *The Anatomy of American Wealth . . . ,* New York, 1940.

DOBBS, CATHERINE ROSE BIGGS (Jan. 30, 1908–), was born in Barberton, Summit County. She has lectured widely and is active in civic and cultural activities in Summit County. She has served in the state senate and has been mayor of Barberton since 1956. She has written an account of the Zoar community: *Freedom's Will: The Society of Separatists of Zoar . . . ,* New York, 1947.

DOBYNS, FLETCHER (1872–Dec. 13, 1942), lawyer, was born near Columbus, Franklin County. After graduating from Harvard University in 1898 and Northwestern University Law School in 1901, he was admitted to the Illinois bar and afterward practiced in Chicago. His writings include *The Underworld of American Politics,* New York, [1932]. WWW 2

DODD, HENRY MARTYN (Aug. 6, 1839–June 28, 1925), clergyman, was born in Ridgeville, Lorain County. After graduating from Hamilton College in 1863, he taught school for four years. He graduated from the Theological Seminary, Auburn, N. Y., in 1870 and was ordained to the Presbyterian ministry in 1873. He served several churches in New York State, and after his retirement he lived at Clinton, N. Y. He wrote a family history, several books on religious themes, and a church history: *Centennial History of the Old Congregational Church,* Windham, N. Y., 1903. WWW 1

DODD, THOMAS J. (Aug. 4, 1837– ?), born in Harper's Ferry, Va., came to Cincinnati in 1887 to establish Dodd Classical High School. A Methodist clergyman, he served several churches in Kentucky. He published *Miracles: Were They, or Were They Not Performed by Jesus? . . . ,* Cincinnati, 1899.

DODDS, SAMUEL (Feb. 28, 1858–Dec. 26, 1947), educator, was born in Prospect, Pa. He graduated from Grove City College in 1881 and Pittsburgh Theological Seminary in 1889. He joined the faculty of the College of Wooster in 1918 and lived in Ohio for the remainder of his life. He wrote *Friendship's Meaning . . . ,* [Butler, Pa., 1919]. WWW 2

DODGE, HOMER JOSEPH (June 1, 1891–May 3, 1960), journalist, was born in Auburn Geauga County. In 1909 his family moved to Maryland, and soon afterward he became a reporter on the Washington *Post.* He also worked on the Washington *Herald* and was a correspondent for International News Service. In 1913 he founded Bankers' Information Service, and he also was a founder of Editorial Research Reports. One of the best-known figures in Washington journalistic circles, he was a member of the National Press Club for fifty years. He wrote numerous magazine articles and one book: *The Pursuit of a Whisper,* [New York, 1925].

DODGE, JACOB RICHARDS (Sept. 28, 1823–Oct. 1, 1902), statistician, was born in New Boston, N. H. He lived in Springfield between 1857 and 1861, while editing the *American Ruralist,* and wrote numerous articles and bulletins on agricultural subjects, and the book *Red Men of the Ohio Valley . . . ,* Springfield, 1860.

DODGE, MARTIN HERBERT (Aug. 27, 1892–Nov. 25, 1957), public relations executive, was born in Auburn, Geauga County. He graduated from Oberlin College in 1915 and Columbia University (Ph.D.) in 1918. After serving as manager of the Industrial Bureau of the Merchants' Association of New York, 1918–27, he was an executive of a number of companies and was a labor consultant with the Department of Commerce, 1946–53. He wrote a number of articles, pamphlets, and books on economics, labor, and public relations, e.g., *Know Your Isms,* New York, 1950. WWW 3

DOERNENBURG, EMIL (April 28, 1880–March 20, 1935), educator, was born in Langenberg, Germany. He taught at Ohio University, 1911–17, the University of Pennsylvania, 1917–30, and LaSalle College, 1931–33. Besides textbooks and magazine articles, he wrote *Sturm und Stille,* [New York, 1916]. OBB

DOERNER, CELIA (March 6, 1853–April 18, 1918), educator, was born in Pomeroy, Meigs County. She taught at Hughes High School, Cincinnati, in the 1880s and 1890s. In 1904, because of ill health, she retired from teaching and moved to Daytona, Fla., and thence to Denver, Colo. From 1909 until her death, she lived in Grant's Pass, Oreg. She compiled a textbook for the Eclectic Series in 1881, and wrote *Little Ripples of Song,* Boston, 1914.

DOGGETT, HENRY S. (Oct. 15, 1837–c.1885), lawyer and educator, was born in Hillsboro, Highland County. After studying in Hillsboro Academy under Professor Isaac Sams, whose biography he later wrote, he read law and was admitted to the bar in 1858. He published the Hillsboro *Gazette,* 1861–62, was a war correspondent for a time, and in 1866 was made superintendent of Hillsboro schools. He died while traveling in the South.

A Sketch of the Life and Professional Services of Isaac Sams . . . , Cincinnati, 1880.

DOGGETT, LAWRENCE LOCKE (Dec. 22, 1864–Nov. 13, 1957), educator, was born in Manchester, Iowa. He graduated from Oberlin College in 1886 and was active in Y.M.C.A. work in Ohio until 1896, when he became president of International Y.M.C.A. College, Springfield, Mass., a position he held until 1936. He published, among other books, *History of the Young Men's Christian Association,* 2 vols., New York, 1896–1919. WW 25

DOHERTY, HENRY LATHAM (May 15, 1870–Dec. 26, 1939), engineer and financier, was born in Columbus, Franklin County. Beginning as an office boy in the Columbus Gas Company, he rose to chief engineer, and after he came to the attention of New York bankers controlling the firm his rise was rapid. In 1905 he formed his own company to serve utility companies, and in 1910 he organized Cities Service. He wrote several technical papers, but his most characteristic writings are in a collection of his addresses and letters compiled by Glenn Marston: *Principles and Ideas for Doherty Men . . . ,* 6 vols., [New York], 1923. DAB 22

DONAHEY, JAMES HARRISON (April 8, 1875–June 1, 1949), cartoonist on the Cleveland *Plain Dealer,* brother of Vic and William Donahey (qq.v.), was born in West Chester, Tuscarawas County. He attended the Cleveland School of Art. His books, which consist largely of drawings, include *Romance of the Great Lakes,* [Cleveland?, 1936?]. WWW 2

DONAHEY, MARY AUGUSTA DICKERSON (Sept. 22, 1876–   ), was born in New York City. She lived in Ohio, 1876–92 and 1898–1914. From 1898 to 1905 she wrote for the Cleveland *Plain Dealer.* In 1905 she married William Donahey (q.v.). She now lives in Chicago. She has compiled a cookbook and written a number of stories for young people, e.g., *Marty Lu,* New York, 1925. WWAW 1

DONAHEY, VIC (July 7, 1873–April 8, 1946), political leader, brother of James and William Donahey (qq.v.), was born in West Chester, Tuscarawas County. After serving in various local and county offices, he was state auditor, 1912–20, served three terms as governor, 1922–28, and served in the U. S. Senate, 1935–41. His political views are expressed in *The Beak and Claws of America,* Waynesfield, [1931]. WWW 2

DONAHEY, WILLIAM (Oct. 19, 1883–), younger brother of Vic and James Donahey (qq.v.), was born in West Chester, Tuscarawas County. He studied at the Cleveland School of Art and in 1903 began working on the Cleveland *Plain Dealer.* His characters the Teeny Weenies were enormously popular as a newspaper feature and as the subject of a series of books, e.g., *Adventures of the Teeny Weenies,* Chicago, [1920]. WW 20

DONALDSON, THOMAS CORWIN (Dec. 27, 1843–Nov. 18, 1898), lawyer, was born in Columbus, Franklin County. He attended Columbus public schools and Capital University. In the Civil War he served with the 19th O.V.I. and the 199th Pa. V.I. He was admitted to the Ohio bar in 1867 and moved to Boise City, Idaho Territory, in 1869. He held a number of official posts in Idaho before moving to Philadelphia in 1875. He wrote several reports, most of them relating to land laws or Indian affairs. In 1879 he discovered many of George Catlin's Indian relics stored in Philadelphia; he catalogued them and published *The George Catlin Indian Gallery* in 1887. The book was sponsored by the Smithsonian Institution and was printed by the Government Printing Office. A mass of manuscript relative to his six years in Idaho was edited by his son, Thomas B. Donaldson, and published in 1941. While living in Philadelphia he was a friend of Walt Whitman and frequently called on Whitman at his home in Camden, N. J. He kept notes on their meetings, and his book contains many personal touches describing Whitman in his last years. In 1885 Donaldson raised money to buy Whitman a phaeton, which was manufactured especially for the poet in Columbus.

Walt Whitman the Man, New York, 1896.
The House in Which Thomas Jefferson Wrote the Declaration of Independence, Philadelphia, 1898.
Idaho of Yesterday, (Thomas B. Donaldson, ed.), Caldwell, Idaho, 1941.

DONAVIN, SIMPSON K. (1831–1902), journalist, was born in Shippensburg, Pa. In 1859 he was a reporter in Baltimore, Md., and was one of the first reporters to reach Harper's Ferry after John Brown's raid; he also was present at Brown's execution. In 1868 he came to Delaware, and he also lived in Columbus. In 1883 he was made editor of the Columbus *Times.* A friend of Samuel J. Tilden, he was active in Democratic politics. Besides the title below, he wrote at least two magazine articles on John Brown that were also issued as pamphlets. He died in Columbus.

Where Will This Path Lead? . . . , Norwalk, 1898.

DONEY, CARL GREGG (July 24, 1867–Nov. 5, 1955), clergyman and educator, was born in Columbus, Franklin County. A graduate of Ohio State University (B.Sc., 1891; Ph.D., 1902), he was ordained to the Methodist ministry in 1893 and served churches in several Ohio communities and in Washington, D. C. He was president of West Virginia Wesleyan College, 1907–15, and of Willamette University, 1915–34. He wrote several books on religious themes, e.g., *God Answers Prayer,* New York, [1924]. WWW 3

DONNAVAN (DONOVAN), CORYDON (c.1816– ?), was born in Ohio. Left an orphan at an early age, he learned the printing trade in Cincinnati and in 1837 became an itinerant printer and newspaperman in the South. Returning to Cincinnati, he bought and edited the *Daily Morning Message* for a time and then moved to Lafayette, Ind., where he established a printing office and founded the *Wabash Standard* in 1845. The next year he was serving as clerk on the Ohio River steamboat *Ontario* when that vessel was sent to the Gulf of Mexico to transfer troops from the Brazos to Matamoros. While a member of a small hunting party, he was captured by Mexican irregulars in Oct., 1846. He escaped from the Mexicans and returned to Cincinnati in the spring of 1847. His adventures in Mexico proved so successful that he employed several artists to paint a panorama of Mexico with which he toured the country lecturing to large audiences and selling many thousands of copies of his graphic narrative.

Adventures in Mexico: Experiences during a Captivity of Seven Months in the Interior . . . , Cincinnati, 1487 [1847].

DONOVAN, CORYDON. See Corydon Donnavan.

DONOVAN, JOSEPH WESLEY (March 2, 1839–June 17, 1933), lawyer and judge, was born in Toledo, Lucas County. After attending Jonesville Academy, Hillsdale College, and Ohio School of Law, he was admitted to the bar in 1870. He practiced in Detroit and also served as circuit court judge, 1894–1912. He died in Detroit at the age of 94. Besides the title below, he published legal works and books on public speaking.

Secrets of Success . . . , New York, [1887].

DORNBLASER, IRENE LaWALL (May 30, 1882–), missionary and teacher, was born in Wheeling, W. Va. She graduated from Wittenberg College and was a missionary-teacher in China for sixteen years. Since retiring she has lived in Springfield. Under the pen name Irene LaWall, she published a study of youth under Hitler: *Land That I Love,* Columbus, 1945.

DORNBLASER, THOMAS FRANKLIN (June 27, 1841–Dec. 22, 1941), clergyman, born in Mackeyville, Pa., graduated from Wittenberg College in 1871 and from the Seminary in 1872. Ordained to the Lutheran ministry, he served churches in Lucas, 1872–74, and Bucyrus, 1891–95, as well as in Illinois and Kansas. He served with the Pennsylvania Cavalry in the Civil War and later published his memoirs: *Sabre Strokes of the Pennsylvania Dragoons . . .* , Philadelphia, 1884.

DORR, NELL BECKER (Mrs. John Van Nostrand) (Aug. 27, 1893–), photographer, was born in Cleveland, Cuyahoga County, and later lived in Massillon. She learned the art of photography from her father, John Jacob Becker. A resident of New York City since 1933, she has exhibited photographs in many cities and has directed several documentary moving pictures. Her books include *In a Blue Moon,* New York, 1939. WWAW 1

DORSEY, GEORGE AMOS (Feb. 6, 1868–March 29, 1931), anthropologist, was born in Hebron, Licking County. He graduated from Denison University in 1888 and Harvard University (Ph.D.) in 1894. He was curator of the Field Museum of Natural History, Chicago, and was on the staff of Northwestern University and the University of Chicago. Besides technical books and articles, he wrote several popular books on science, e.g., *Why We Behave like Human Beings,* New York, 1925, and a novel, *Young Low,* New York, [1917]. DAB 21

DOUD, HARRIET EBERLY (1841–Nov. 7, 1944), was born near Bowling Green, Wood County. After attending a normal school in Michigan, she taught school in Warsaw, Ind., for a time before settling in Norwalk in 1875. A book about pioneers along the Portage River, which she had written in 1893, was published in 1938, when she was 97: *Hoof-Beaten Trails,* [Binghamton, N. Y., 1938].

DOUGLAS, LLOYD CASSEL (Aug. 27, 1877–Feb. 13, 1951), clergyman, was born in Columbia City, Ind. After graduating from Wittenberg College in 1900 and Hamma Divinity School in 1903, he was ordained to the Lutheran ministry. He later became a Congregationalist, and in the last years of his ministry served nondenominational churches. After completing his seminary training, he lived in Ohio for two periods—as a Lutheran minister in Lancaster, 1905–08, and as a Congregational minister in Akron, 1921–26. Perhaps the most popular religious writer America has known, he consciously or unconsciously sensed the temper of the public mind and produced books that found millions of readers. His first writing was nonfiction that reflects dissatisfaction with dogma and perhaps his own struggle on changing his affiliation, e.g., *Those Disturbing Miracles,* New York, 1927. In the late 1920s and early 1930s, he wrote several best-selling novels, e.g., *Magnificent Obsession,* New York, 1929. These he followed with historical novels dealing with Biblical times, e.g., *The Robe,* Boston, 1942. WWW 3

DOUGLAS, MARY BUTLER (d. Jan. 9, 1858), was born in Onondaga County, N. Y. Her father moved to Lancaster, Fairfield County, where she met and married Richard Douglas, a lawyer of Chillicothe. The volume below was published under the pseudonym "A Lady."

On the Conservative Elements of the American Republic, Chillicothe, 1842.

DOUGLASS, BEN (Aug. 13, 1836–July 24, 1909), lawyer, was born in Plain Township, Wayne County. After attending Vermillion Institute, Hayesville, he went to Cleveland Law School, where he graduated in 1861. He practiced law in Wooster, served in the postmaster general's office, Washington, D. C., and edited the *Jacksonian* in Wooster. During the Presidential campaign of 1868, he was sent to California and Nevada to speak in support of the Republican ticket. (On the second book listed below, his last name is spelled with one *s.*)

History of Wayne County . . . , Indianapolis, 1878.

History of the Lawyers of Wayne County, Ohio, from 1812 to 1900, Wooster, 1900.

DOWD, QUINCY LAMARTINE (July 8, 1848–April 15, 1936), clergyman, was born in Seville, Medina County. After graduating from Oberlin College in 1870, he attended Yale Divinity School. He was ordained to the ministry, served churches in various states, and died at Lombard, Ill. His writings include *Increasing Values in Jesus,* Boston, 1925. WWNAA 7

DOWLER, BENNET (April 16, 1797–1879), physician, was born in Ohio. In 1854 he founded the *Medical and Surgical Journal* in New Orleans. He was noted for his experiments upon the human body soon after death. He wrote a number of medical articles and reports which are not listed below.

Contributions to the Natural History of the Alligator . . . , New Orleans, 1846.

Researches upon the Necropolis of New Orleans . . . , New Orleans, 1850.

Experimental Researches, Illustrative of the Functional Oneness, Unity, and Diffusion of Nervous Action . . . , New Orleans, [1851].

Contributions to Experimental Physiology . . . , New Orleans, 1852.

Tableaux of New Orleans, [New Orleans, 1853?].

Tableaux of the Yellow Fever of 1853 . . . , New Orleans, 1854.

Critical Researches in Medical Terminology . . . , [New Orleans, 1858?].

DOWLING, GEORGE THOMAS (June 2, 1849–1928), clergyman, was born in New York City, the son of a Baptist clergyman. After studying at the College of the City of New York, he abandoned plans for the ministry and entered business; a phrenological reading, however, convinced him that he should fulfill his parents' dreams. He completed his education at Colgate University and Crozier Theological Seminary. After successful pastorates in New Jersey, Rhode Island, and Syracuse, N. Y., he was called to Euclid Avenue Baptist Church, Cleveland, where he served for twelve years. In 1895 he became an Episcopal priest and served churches in California and in Brooklyn, N. Y. Other than sermons his chief literary production was *The Wreckers,* which was written to refute the antilabor novel by John Hay (q.v.), *The Breadwinners.* Dowling's book is prolabor but idealistic and condescending.

The Wreckers. A Social Study, Philadelphia, 1886.

DOWLING, LEVI H. (May 18, 1844–Aug. 13, 1911), clergyman, was born in Belleville, Richland County. A minister of the Disciples of Christ Church at the age of sixteen, he was a chaplain in the Civil War. After the war he practiced medicine and devoted himself to the cause of prohibition. He compiled song books and wrote at least one book: *The Aquarian Gospel of Jesus the Christ* . . . , Los Angeles, 1908.

DOWNES, RANDOLPH CHANDLER (July 26, 1901–), educator, born in South Norwalk, Conn., has been in the history department, University of Toledo, since 1946. He graduated from Dartmouth College in 1923 and Ohio State University (Ph.D.) in 1929. He has written a number of books on Indians in Ohio and other historical subjects, e.g., *Council Fires on the Upper Ohio* . . . , [Pittsburgh], 1940. DAS 3

DOWNING, EDWARD COLLINS (Feb. 24, 1862–Sept. 18, 1948), educator, was born in Wooster, Wayne County, and graduated from University of Wooster in 1885. He taught at Macalester College, 1891–1912, and was also on the staff of Webb Publishing Co., St. Paul, Minn. Besides a Latin textbook, he published a collection of poems: *Stairways of the Years,* Minneapolis, 1946.

DOWNING, LAURA CASE (July 26, 1843–Sept. 27, 1914), was born in Ohio, but spent much of her life in Phoenix, Ariz., where she served as a school principal and as a librarian and became a very popular clubwoman. She wrote *Poem Pictures,* Boston, 1904.

DOWNS, EDWARD (c.1829–March 15, 1884), was born in Ohio, probably in Muskingum County. He enlisted as a captain in the 20th O.V.I. in Oct., 1861, was promoted to major, and was discharged because of illness on April 1, 1864. After the war he was a minister in Iowa and Dakota Territory. His book, which is an account of C. L. Ruggles, a Northern agent, was republished as *The Great American Scout and Spy* in 1868 and as *Perils of Scout Life* in 1873.

Four Years a Scout and Spy . . . , Zanesville, 1866.

DOYLE, EDWIN ADAMS (Jan. 13, 1867–Nov. 26, 1941), was born in Winchester, Adams County, of a pioneer family. He attended school in Winchester and for a time edited the Winchester *Visitor.* His entire life was spent in his native community.

Poems and Lyrics Relating to the Spanish and Cuban War, Winchester, 1898.

Phocion. A Dramatic Poem, and Other Poems, Winchester, 1910.
Poems Descriptive, Narrative and Reflective . . . , Winchester, 1915.
Troezene: A Masque of the Gods . . . , Winchester, 1916.
War Pieces, Winchester, 1920.
Mariana: A Monologue, Boston, 1935.
Poems on Various Occasions, Boston, 1935.

DOYLE, JOHN HARDY (April 23, 1844–March 24, 1919), lawyer and judge, was born in Perry County. He attended Denison University and was admitted to the bar in 1865. He practiced law in Toledo and served as judge of common pleas court and of the state supreme court. He wrote *A Story of Early Toledo . . . ,* Bowling Green, [1919]. WWW 1

DOYLE, JOSEPH BEATTY (Sept. 10, 1849–Dec. 12, 1927), lawyer and journalist, was born in Steubenville, Jefferson County. He attended Iron City Commercial College, Pittsburgh, Pa., studied law, and was admitted to the bar in 1870. He became city editor of the Steubenville *Daily News,* Sept. 11, 1871, and remained with that paper and the Steubenville *Herald* as managing editor until 1905. He was also librarian of the Jefferson County Library. His writings on historical subjects include *20th Century History of Steubenville and Jefferson County, Ohio, and Representative Citizens,* Chicago, 1910.

DRAGO, HARRY SINCLAIR (March 20, 1888–), was born in Toledo, Lucas County, where he attended public schools and the University of Toledo and for a time worked on a newspaper. He has lived for a number of years in White Plains, N. Y. He is a prolific author of adventure novels, most of them Western stories. Some indication of his productivity can be found in the fact that in one year (1950) he published five novels: under the pen name of Will Ermine, *Apache Crossing, My Gun Is My Law,* and *Watchdog of Thunder River,* and under the pen name of Bliss Lomax, *The Fight for the Sweetwater* and *The Law Busters.* He has also used as pen names J. Wesley Putnam, Kirk Deming, Sinclair Drago, and Stewart Cross.

DRAGO, SINCLAIR. Pseud. See Harry S. Drago.

DRAKE, BENJAMIN (1795–April 1, 1841), was born in Mayslick, Ky. In 1814 he came to Cincinnati to work in a drugstore owned by his elder brother, Daniel (q.v.). He later was a partner in a dry goods store operated by his father, Isaac Drake, but financed by Daniel. He read law and after the store failed he began practicing in Cincinnati. He had already become known as a writer for his contributions to the Cincinnati *Literary Gazette.* His "Bass-Island Cottage" in the first issue (Jan. 1, 1824) is the first Western short story. He helped establish the Cincinnati *Chronicle and Literary Gazette* and edited it, 1826–34, with the assistance of E. D. Mansfield (q.v.). He also founded and edited *The Western Agriculturist* in 1830. *Cincinnati in 1826* was republished in England and Germany and encouraged emigration to Cincinnati. The pieces in *Tales and Sketches of the Queen City* describe frontier life in realistic, vivid detail and represent his major achievement as a pioneer regional writer.

Cincinnati in 1826, (with E. D. Mansfield), Cincinnati, 1827.
The Life and Adventures of Black Hawk . . . , Cincinnati, 1838.
Tales and Sketches of the Queen City, Cincinnati, 1839.
Sketches of the Civil and Military Services of William Henry Harrison, (with C. S. Todd), Cincinnati, 1840.
Life of Tecumseh, and of His Brother the Prophet . . . , Cincinnati, 1841.

DRAKE, CHARLES DANIEL (April 11, 1811–April 1, 1892), son of Daniel Drake (q.v.), was born in Cincinnati, Hamilton County. From 1827 to 1830 he was a midshipman in the navy. He was admitted to the Ohio bar in 1833 and moved the following year to St. Louis, Mo., where he practiced. He lived in Cincinnati again from 1847 to 1850. He was active in Missouri politics and was elected to the U. S. Senate in 1867, where he allied himself with extremists among the Radical Republicans. He resigned from the Senate in 1870 to become chief justice of the U. S. Court of Claims, where he served until 1885. He published a number of separate speeches and a legal treatise and edited autobiographical letters written by his father: *Pioneer Life in Kentucky.*

Union and Anti-Slavery Speeches Delivered during the Rebellion, Cincinnati, 1864.

DRAKE, DANIEL (Oct. 20, 1785–Nov. 5, 1852), physician, author, educator, philanthropist, and civic leader, was a native of New Jersey but, by adoption, an Ohioan. The second child of Isaac and Elizabeth (Shotwell) Drake, he was born on a farm now a part of Plainfield, N. J. When Daniel was less than three years of age, his father and his father's two brothers with their families moved to Kentucky. Here the Drakes founded the settlement of Mayslick. Their homes were one-room log cabins with single doors but without windows. Daniel's early schooling was desultory. He was taught in small, single-room log schoolhouses by itinerant and poorly trained teachers. At the age of fifteen with barely more than a smattering of reading, writing, and arithmetic, he was apprenticed as a student of medicine to Dr. William Goforth (1766–1817) of Cincinnati. Young Drake was indefatigable and possessed an eager mind with a retentive memory as is shown by progress so rapid that his preceptor, Dr. Goforth, took him into full partnership at the end of four years. It was then that Dr. Goforth gave his pupil a "diploma," the first issued west of the Allegheny Mountains, which attested to Drake's knowledge of "physics, surgery and midwifery." A year later (1805) Drake rode horseback over the mountains and on to Philadelphia, where he attended his first course of medical lectures at the University of Pennsylvania. Returning to Kentucky he practiced for a year at Mayslick near his father's home. Here he observed an epidemic, possibly typhoid fever, the report of which represented his first venture into the field of medical literature: *Some Account of the Epidemic Diseases Which Prevail at Mays-lick in Kentucky.* In 1807, Drake moved to Cincinnati, which became his home for the remainder of his life. Although occupied with a large practice, he was constantly writing. The rarest of his publications, *Notices Concerning Cincinnati,* published in 1810, dealt with the topography, meteorology, botany, and medical conditions found in the city and described for the first time a hitherto unknown local malady, "milk-sickness." This book contained the first comprehensive account of a Midwestern town and was also the first with a medical section to be published west of the Alleghenies. In 1812, Drake led in the establishment of a public library and of a Lancastrian seminary. He was also instrumental in forming the "School of Literature and Arts," before which he delivered the presidential address in 1814. This discourse, widely acclaimed, was reprinted in *The National Intelligencer* (Washington, D. C.). Shortly before returning to Philadelphia in 1815, to attend a second course of lectures and to obtain his medical degree, he completed a book which gave him an international reputation: *Natural and Statistical View, or Picture of Cincinnati and the Miami Country.* When the medical department of Transylvania University at Lexington, Ky.—the first west of the Allegheny Mountains—opened in 1817, Drake became professor of materia medica and medical botany. He remained in Lexington only one term. Returning to Cincinnati, he inaugurated courses of medical instruction which culminated in the incorporation (1819) of the Medical College of Ohio, of which he was president. His important *Inaugural Discourse on Medical Education* in 1820 received much laudatory comment and has been reprinted (1951). Dissension arose in the faculty, and Drake was expelled by vote of those who owed their positions to him. His description of these events, *A Narrative of the Rise and Fall of the Medical College of Ohio* (1822), is a much sought-after item of medical Americana. He taught at Transylvania University from 1823 to 1827 and then returned to Cincinnati. Here, with Dr. Guy W. Wright (d. 1831) he established *The Western Medical and Physical Journal, Original and Eclectic.* In this journal were published his essays on medical education, which have been termed "far and away, the most important contributions ever made to the subject in this country." These essays were first published in book form in 1832 and were reprinted in 1952. Ever interested in the cause of temperance, Drake delivered the first of his published addresses on this subject in 1828: *A Discourse on Intemperance . . . Before the Agricultural Society of Hamilton County.* With the appearance of cholera in many parts of the world in 1832, Drake began an exhaustive investigation of the disease. This study culminated in the publication of a book on the subject: *A Practical Treatise on the History, Prevention, and Treatment of Epidemic Cholera* (1832). At the 45th anniversary celebration of the founding of Cincinnati, held Dec. 26, 1833, Dr. Drake in response to a toast extolled the virtues of the buckeye and wove the history of the Ohio Valley into his speech. He suggested that this was a suitable emblematic tree for the state, with the result that since that time Ohio has been termed "the Buckeye State." Space does not permit discussion of Dr. Drake's various professorships, but it is important to mention that he was the leader in the establishment of the medical department of Cincinnati College (1835), which had the most distinguished faculty ever assembled in the West. At this time Drake's writings were almost entirely confined to pamphlets issued in reply to attacks made on him by his enemies in the Medical College of Ohio. He has been accused of quarrelsomeness, but no record can be found of any controversies in which he was the aggressor. Once attacked, however, he showed no quarter and argued so logically and often so persistently that he was almost invariably victorious. When the medical department of Cincinnati College closed in 1839 because of lack of endowment and hospital facilities, Drake accepted the Chair of Clinical Medicine and Pathological Anatomy in the Louisville Medical Institute, now the School of Medicine of the University of Louisville. This chair had been especially created in order to induce him to come to Louisville. Here he was happy lecturing to the largest classes of medical students that the West had known until then. His professorial duties occupied about four months of the year, and the remainder was spent at his home in Cincinnati, where he was engaged in writing, or in travel throughout the Mississippi Valley for the purpose of collecting facts to be included in a monumental work on diseases of that region. Drake's three earliest contributions to medical literature constitute the germ plasm of his later impressive volumes. It is evident from the first announcement made in 1822 of his projected work that it was based upon the broadest possible foundation, including sociological studies in relation to diseases as well as topographical, geological, meteorological, and botanical relationships. Despite wretched accommodations and modes of travel, "in skiffs, on rail roads, in stages, buggies, common wagons, on horse back, mule back and on foot, by day and by night . . . ," he covered fully 30,000 miles in quest of information. We are fortunate in having accounts of many of the places visited, since Drake embodied some of his observations in editorials—"Traveling Memoranda," "Traveling Editorials"—which appeared in his medical journal. His alertness to every phase of human activity is clearly revealed by these 25 letters. Although hurriedly written, their flowing style and clearness of presentation make them models. While busily engaged in preparing his book throughout the 1840s, Drake wrote many scientific papers and addresses. During the winter of 1847 he wrote a series of ten letters for his children in which he graphically described his boyhood. With some deletions by his son, Charles D. Drake (q.v.), these letters were published in Cincinnati in 1870 with the title *Pioneer Life in Kentucky*. These letters were reprinted in 1907. Re-edited from the original manuscript, they were again published under the previous title in 1948. Termed "the greatest of all Kentucky books," it is a vivid portrayal of family, farm, and social life in the frontier settlement of Mayslick. Against the background of a "forest-born" democracy, we see, forged on the anvil of necessity, the earliest form of institutions and traditions that we today take for granted. Had Daniel Drake written nothing else, his fame as a writer would be secure. On April 24, 1850, in Cincinnati, was published the first volume of a work which was to make the name of Daniel Drake immortal: *A Systematic Treatise, Historical, Etiological and Practical, on the Diseases of the Interior Valley of North America as They Appear in the Caucasian, African, Indian, and Esquimaux Varieties of Its Population.* This book was immediately recognized as a classic, receiving enthusiastic reviews not only in the United States but also in England and on the Continent. Some of the contemporary opinions are as follows; the book "belongs to the very highest rank of our medical literature, and may probably come to be regarded as the most original work published in America"; "the contents of the book are so varied and extensive as to defy analysis"; "the profession are much indebted to Dr. Drake for his indefatigable exertions in producing a work of such magnitude and importance." Recently a distinguished medical historian (Garrison) stated that "there was nothing like this book in literature" and another equally famous medical historian (Sigerist) called it "one of the greatest masterpieces of medico-geographic research." The second volume was published posthumously in 1854. Drake deplored slavery but at the same time strongly disapproved of the actions of rabid abolitionists which he realized would lead to sectional strife if they continued. In an effort to alleviate the situation, he wrote three letters on slavery which were published (April, 1851) in *The National Intelligencer* (Washington, D. C.). In 1940 these remarkable letters were published in book form. The last book published during Drake's lifetime was *Discourses Delivered by Appointment, before the Cincinnati Medical Library Association* (Cincinnati, 1852). These essays furnish an interesting description of the physicians, medical conditions, and medical journalism found in early Cincinnati. Drake's total extant writings—books, essays, editorials, book reviews, etc.—amount to over 3,000 items. Only major works are listed below. He continued to teach and to write until a few days before his death. During the funeral services in Cincinnati, Nov. 10, 1852, all stores were closed, the streets silent, and the mourners crowded into Christ Church, where the Rev. Dudley A. Tyng (1825–58) closed his sermon with these words: "May God in mercy grant that this death we so much mourn may be the seed of Life to many souls; and that all who feel his loss may follow his example."

Emmet Field Horine

Notices Concerning Cincinnati, Cincinnati, 1810.

Natural and Statistical View, or Picture of Cincinnati and the Miami Country . . . , Cincinnati, 1815.

The People's Doctors; A Review by 'The People's Friend' . . . , Cincinnati, 1829.

Practical Essays on Medical Education and the Medical Profession in the United States, Cincinnati, 1832.

A Practical Treatise on the History, Prevention, and Treatment of Epidemic Cholera . . . , Cincinnati, 1832.

Report on the Subject of the Education of the Blind . . . , Columbus, 1835.

A Systematic Treatise, Historical, Etiological and Practical, on the Principal Diseases of the Interior Valley of North America . . . , New York, 1850.

Discourses Delivered by Appointment before the Cincinnati Medical Library Association . . . , Cincinnati, 1852.

A Systematic Treatise . . . , 2nd series, Philadelphia, 1854.

Pioneer Life in Kentucky, (Charles D. Drake, ed.), Cincinnati, 1870.

DRAKE, EMILY HOPKINS (May, 1877–), educator, was born in Columbus, Franklin County. After graduating from Normal School, Fredonia, N. Y., she taught in the schools of Brooklyn, N. Y. Her writings include *Natalie and the Brewsters,* Boston, [1931]. WWNAA 6

DRAKE, WILLIAM A. (Dec. 9, 1899–), was born in Dayton, Montgomery County. He has worked on various newspapers and was managing editor of *Vanity Fair,* 1922–24. He has also been a writer for various motion-picture companies in Hollywood and still lives there. He has translated numerous works by European authors and has written *Contemporary European Writers,* New York, 1928. WW 26

DRAPER, ANDREW SLOAN (June 21, 1848–April 27, 1913), educator and prolific writer and lecturer on education, born in Westford, N. Y., was superintendent of schools in Cleveland from 1892 to 1894. Several of his addresses delivered during this period were published.

DREES, CHARLES WILLIAM (Sept. 13, 1851–Aug. 31, 1926), missionary, was born in Xenia, Greene County. He graduated from Ohio Wesleyan University in 1871 and the School of Theology, Boston University, in 1874. Immediately after his graduation he was sent to Mexico as a missionary. While on leave in 1877, he married Ada M. Combs of Clermont County. In 1887 he was sent to South America, where he lived until his retirement in 1924. His wife edited his letters from Mexico, adding some biographical notes: *Thirteen Years in Mexico . . . ,* New York, [1915]. WWW 2

DRENNAN, MARIE (Aug. 30, 1890–Nov. 4, 1950), educator, was born in Swanton, Fulton County. After graduating from Ohio Wesleyan University in 1915, she began teaching school; she taught English at Ohio Wesleyan from 1917 until her death. She published poetry and a pageant, *The Age of the Sun . . . ,* New York, 1928. BDCP

DRUKKER, SARA TOBIAS (July 31, 1852–March 4, 1914), born in New York City, lived in St. Louis, Mo., and Cincinnati for more than 25 years. She was active in civic affairs. Using the pen names Edwina Rowe and Alpha, she wrote for various periodicals. A selection of her writings was published by her four daughters: *A Literary Find,* Philadelphia, 1914.

DRURY, AUGUSTUS WALDO (March 21, 1851–Feb. 18, 1935), clergyman and educator, was born in Madison County, Ind. In 1877 he graduated from Bonebrake Theological Seminary, Dayton, and in 1880 he became a member of the faculty. He was also a trustee of the United Brethren Publishing House in Dayton.

Life of Rev. Philip William Otterbein . . . , Dayton, 1884.

Life of Bishop J. J. Glossbrenner . . . , Dayton, 1889.

Disciplines of the United Brethren in Christ, Dayton, 1895.

Baptism, Its Place in the Church Visible . . . , Dayton, 1902.

History of the City of Dayton and Montgomery County, 2 vols., Chicago, 1909.

Outlines of Doctrinal Theology . . . , Dayton, 1914.

History of the Church of the United Brethren in Christ, Dayton, 1924.

Otterbein Birthday Book, Dayton, [?].

DuBOIS, CONSTANCE GODDARD (c.1855–1911 ?), anthropologist, was born in Zanesville, Muskingum County. She attended Putnam Female Seminary. Although she maintained a residence in Waterbury,

Conn., she spent most of her mature years in firsthand study of the Indians of California, from whom her manifest sympathy permitted her to learn things regarded as sacred and almost never communicated by them. She was one of the founders of the American Anthropological Association. A scholarly associate described her as an enlightened amateur untainted by academic training, with instincts for strict scholarly accuracy. She was on the staff of *Out West* (Los Angeles) and was editor of the *Asa Gray Bulletin,* 1893–1900.

Martha Corey; A Tale of the Salem Witchcraft, Chicago, 1890.
Columbus and Beatriz: A Novel, Chicago, 1892.
A Modern Pagan; A Novel, New York, [1895].
A Soul in Bronze; A Novel of Southern California, Chicago, 1900.
The Condition of the Mission Indians of Southern California, Philadelphia, 1901.
The Religion of the Luiseño Indians of Southern California, Berkeley, Calif., [1908].

DuBOIS, FRANCES HULME (Oct. 4, 1889–), was born in Madisonville, Hamilton County. After graduating from Madisonville High School in 1906, she studied horticulture and landscape design at the University of Cincinnati. She was an active partner in a landscape nursery business operated by her family and also wrote a weekly garden column for the Cincinnati *Post* for eighteen years. With Gertrude DuBois she wrote *Peter and Penny Plant a Garden,* New York, 1936.

DUCDAME. Pseud. See Henry Hooper.

DUCKWORTH, SOPHIE HAGEMANN (Dec. 21, 1870–Dec. 13, 1951), was born in Waverly, Pike County, the daughter of a Lutheran minister. She attended Waverly schools and after finishing high school taught in Pike County rural schools. In 1900 she married James A. Duckworth, an Englishman. She lived in England for a time and later in Fort Thomas, Ky. While living in Fort Thomas, she was a member of the Cincinnati Woman's Press Club and other literary groups. She published a romance in verse: *The Love of Quintell . . . ,* Boston, 1922.

DUDLEY, LUCY MAY BRONSON (May 1, 1848–May, 1920), was born in Peninsula, Summit County, and attended the Episcopal Female Seminary in Granville. She served as organist of churches in Warren and Cleveland.

Contributions to the Knowledge of the Semites, [n.p.], 1893.
Letters to Ruth, New York, [1896].
A Royal Journey, New York, 1901.
"A Writer's Inkhorn," New York, 1910.

DUFF, MRS. DAVID. See Ethel H. Miller.

DUFF, WILLIAM ALEXANDER (Oct. 16, 1872–Oct. 7, 1950), journalist, was born in Ashland, Ashland County. After attending Wittenberg College and Ohio Wesleyan University, he worked on newspapers in Galion, Mansfield, Cleveland, and Sandusky. He then bought a farm near Ashland and edited the Ashland *Times-Gazette.* Besides a play about Johnny Appleseed (1929), he wrote *History of North Central Ohio . . . ,* Topeka, Kan., 1931. OBB

DUFFEE, MAY MARGARETTA, was born in Washington Court House, Fayette County, and has spent her entire life in that community. For many years she assisted her father, James W. Duffee, in the operation of his store. She began writing poems and songs in 1917 and has since written more than 1,200 poems, which have appeared in various periodicals and anthologies. She has published several collections of verse, e.g., *Poems That Are Real, That Appeal, That You Feel,* [Washington Court House], 1917. BDCP

DUFFY, HERBERT SMITH (Feb. 25, 1900–Dec. 29, 1956), lawyer, was born in New Lexington, Perry County, but grew up in Columbus. After serving in the Naval Air Service in World War I, he attended Ohio State University and Dartmouth College. He graduated from Harvard Law School in 1924 and began practice in Cleveland the same year. He served as attorney general of Ohio, 1937–39 and 1949–51. From 1951 until his death he practiced in Columbus. He wrote a biography: *William Howard Taft,* New York, 1930. WWO

DUKE, JOHN KLINE (Aug. 20, 1844–Nov. 27, 1903), was born in Piketon, Pike County. During the Civil War he served in Company F, 53rd O.V.I. After the war he taught school in Illinois for a year, and in 1866 he moved to Portsmouth, where he worked in the First National Bank and later was engaged in the insurance and real-estate business.

History of the Fifty-Third Regiment Ohio Volunteer Infantry . . . , Portsmouth, 1900.

DUKES, HARRIET ELIZABETH GROSS (Aug. 11, 1855–June 21, 1939), was born in Findlay, Hancock County. She was married to P. C. Dukes and lived in Findlay. Her poems appeared in *Christian Witness*, the Findlay *Morning Republican*, and various other periodicals. She published a collection of verse: *Sunlit Heights*, Boston, [1928].

DULAC, GEORGE. Pseud. See George Perkins.

DULL, PAUL PHELLIS (May 30, 1907–), lawyer and judge, was born in Celina, Mercer County. He graduated from Ohio Wesleyan University in 1929, was in educational work, 1931–33, and graduated from Ohio State University Law School in 1937. He began practice in Celina in 1937, served in the U.S. Air Force, 1944–45, and has been judge of common pleas court, Mercer County, since 1947. He has published at least three collections of verse, e.g., *Sprouts from a Small Potato*, New York, [1940]. WWMW 6

DULLES, FOSTER RHEA (Jan. 24, 1900–), educator, born in Englewood, N. J., has been a member of the Ohio State University history faculty since 1941. He has written numerous professional articles, several books on American relations with the Orient, and *Lowered Boats: A Chronicle of American Whaling*, New York, [1923]. WW 30

DUMOND, DWIGHT LOWELL (Aug. 27, 1895–), educator, was born in Kingston, Ross County. He graduated from Baldwin-Wallace College in 1920 and the University of Michigan (Ph.D.) in 1929. He has been a member of the Michigan history faculty since 1930. He has published a history of the United States, professional articles, and a collection of lectures first delivered at University College, London: *Antislavery Origins of the Civil War in the United States*, Ann Arbor, Mich., 1939. WW 30

DUMONT, JULIA LOUISE CORRY (Oct., 1794–Jan. 2, 1857), the earliest native Ohioan whose writings have been preserved, was born in Waterford, Washington County. Her father was one of the first settlers at Marietta in 1788. The family returned to Rhode Island while she was a child. After the death of her father her mother remarried, and they moved to Saratoga County, N. Y., where she attended Milton Academy, taught school for several years, and married John Dumont in Aug., 1812. The following October the young couple moved to Cincinnati, where they lived until March, 1814, when they settled in Vevay, Ind. Mrs. Dumont resumed teaching in 1820; among her students were Edward and George C. Eggleston, both of whom paid her high tribute in their writings. Her literary reputation is based upon her short stories and poems, most of which were contributed to Cincinnati, periodicals—the Cincinnati *Literary Gazette*, Cincinnati *Mirror*, *Western Literary Journal*, and *Ladies' Repository*. Her "Theodore Harland" was the prize-winning story in a contest conducted by the Cincinnati *Chronicle* in 1827. "Ashton Grey" and other short stories, contributed to the *Western Literary Journal* and the *Ladies' Repository*, were collected and published in 1856. No collection of her verse was ever published, though some of her poems achieved great popularity.

Life Sketches from Common Paths: A Series of American Tales, New York, 1856.

DUN, JOHN DAVIS (Oct. 10, 1891–), journalist, was born in Columbus, Franklin County. In his early teens he joined the staff of the Columbus *Citizen* and worked on that newspaper while attending high school and Ohio State University. After graduating in 1914 he joined the Toledo *Times* and edited that newspaper, 1918–39. During World War II he was an ambulance driver in the American Field Service attached to the French Foreign Legion in North Africa. After his retirement he moved to Tucson, Ariz., and since 1950 he has lived in La Jolla, Calif. He published *Eleven Stories . . .*, East Aurora, N. Y., [1938]. WW 16

DUNBAR, PAUL LAURENCE (June 27, 1872–Feb. 10, 1906), poet, was born in Dayton, Montgomery County, and spent most of his short lifetime in that community. The first twenty years sped by for him much as for any boy, white or black, in a typical Midwestern small town. His first four adult years stretched out discouragingly as he struggled to make a living, find himself, realize his well-defined ideals and hopes and aims. The last ten saw recognition in good measure, but an uphill fight on a rocky road as he strove to keep mind and body fit for the steady and welcome market demand on his pen. From boyhood days he had the divine afflatus of the poet, the constant urge to find listeners to his message—all this alongside the mental reactions of his race. Early in his twenties he wrote to a friend, "I did once want to be a lawyer, but that ambition has long since died out before the all-absorbing desire to be a worthy singer of the songs of God and nature. To be able to interpret my own people through song and story, and to prove to them that after all we are more human than African." A singer first, he was an interpreter of his people next—always a message-bearer, a poet, a creator in the Greek sense. I remember speaking to him once about the rhythm and cadence in one of his poems. Sharp and prompt came his comment: "Yes, all right, but I surely hope and trust you find it something more than just that!" A poet, no mere rhymester. Both of Paul L. Dunbar's parents had been slaves in Kentucky, owned by different masters. His father, Joshua, born in 1816, had escaped to Canada. He came back to enlist in 1863 in Company F, 55th Massachusetts; was discharged Oct. 28, 1863, because of injuries; re-enlisted Jan. 9, 1864, in the 5th Massachusetts Cavalry as a sergeant; and was discharged Oct. 31, 1865. He settled in Dayton, worked as a plasterer, and in 1871 married Matilda J. Murphy (born Borton in 1845). Matilda had then two sons by an earlier marriage. She had come to Dayton to work as a laundress. Joshua entered the Soldiers' Home near Dayton in 1882 and died there Aug. 16, 1885. Matilda survived Paul, dying Feb. 24, 1934, in the home he had provided for her. Paul went through school in due course, graduating in 1891 from Central High School. He wrote the class poem; was president of the boys' debating society, the Philomathean; and was editor of the *High School Times,* the students' monthly magazine. With high school days finished and no prospect of college, he spent his next four years in search of work. He worked as an elevator man in the Callahan office bulding and as a judge's messenger in the county court house. Day's work came first, of course, but with it then, as ever, was the constant drive for self-expression. Newspapers printed a poem now and then, but pay was scant. At his own expense he printed in Dayton a book of poems, *Oak and Ivy,* dated 1893 but off the press late in 1892. Thanks to the interest of Dayton friends he gave readings before such groups as the Western Association of Writers in Dayton and elsewhere in Ohio, Michigan, and Indiana. A Toledo friend not only arranged for readings in that city, but also helped print *Majors and Minors,* another collection of poems, in 1895. This friend gave a copy of the book to James A. Herne when he was playing in his *Shore Acres* in Toledo. Herne sent the copy to William Dean Howells. This kindly soul and acute critic, possibly mindful of his own days in Hamilton and Columbus, reviewed the book in *Harper's Weekly,* June 27, 1896, warm in praise of "this unknown but not ungifted poet." Introduction like that brought prompt results, setting Dunbar for the rest of his life in the public eye with the natural satisfactions and troubles. *Lyrics from Lowly Life* came out in 1896 with an introduction by Howells. Chapman and Hall brought out an English edition in 1897. Demand for copy, prose or poetry, came quickly, with of course the drain on nerves and physique. Eighteen volumes of poetry and fiction came from his pen before death laid its hand on him. Six volumes were published after his death. Hundreds of separate poems, short stories, and articles stand to his credit. His songs were set to music; his contributions to dramatic sketches and similar pieces number several score. After 1896 he lived mainly in New York and Washington, D. C., the latter residence beginning with his appointment Sept. 20, 1897, to the staff of the Library of Congress, where he served as reading room assistant and stack deck attendant until 1898. On March 6, 1898, he married in New York City Alice Ruth Moore of New Orleans and Boston. They separated in 1902. Early in the 1900s tuberculosis set in. He vainly hunted for relief in the Catskills, in the Rockies, and elsewhere—all to no avail. He spent his last three years with his mother in Dayton in the house he had bought at 219 North Summit Street. Three years after his death, on the anniversary of his birth, his grave in Woodland Cemetery was marked by a granite memorial set there by public subscription led by the Dunbar Memorial Association. His home was bought by the State of Ohio in 1936 as a historical memorial, and since then it has been maintained and administered by the Ohio State Historical Society and has been kept in much the same condition as when the poet died. Paul L. Dunbar stood about five feet, nine inches tall. Rather slight, he weighed perhaps 140 pounds. He had a nervous and responsive temperament, was kindly in nature, quick to anger or to pleasure, but held no resentments. Heights of joy alternated with depths of despondency. Hungry for friends, he delighted in companionship. He might have agreed that in the abstract a peaceful solitude invited poetic joy, but he would never have thought of seeking that solitude as a pioneer in unexplored territory. Thoroughly happy in urban life and sights and sounds, he was an equally keen observer and delighter in all forms of outdoor life and scenery at a comfortable distance. Once he said he would like to be a farmer, but his was certainly not the temperament for the routine and exacting demands on the patience and persistence of the farmer. His poetry is essentially of his own day and generation. It is sentimental, rhymed, emotional but never mawkish. It would find no place in our present annual "Poetry Awards." He was none the less a poet first and foremost, a Negro poet, eager to set forth the varied emotions of his race. In that respect he is unquestionably the first of our Negro writers as to the time he played his role, also the first with any appreciable output of lasting literary quality. Aside from race or color it is Time that will settle his place in our American literature.

Harry M. Lydenberg

Lyrics of Lowly Life, New York, 1896.
Folks from Dixie, New York, 1898.
The Uncalled, a Novel, New York, 1898.
Lyrics of the Hearthside, New York, 1899.
Poems of Cabin and Field . . . , New York, 1899.
The Love of Landry, New York, [1900].
The Strength of Gideon, and Other Stories, New York, 1900.
Uncle Eph's Christmas; A One Act Negro Musical Sketch, [n.p.], 1900.
Candle-Lightin' Time, New York, 1901.
The Fanatics, New York, 1901.
The Sport of the Gods, New York, 1902.
In Old Plantation Days, New York, 1903.
Lyrics of Love and Laughter, New York, 1903.
When Malindy Sings, New York, 1903.
The Heart of Happy Hollow, New York, 1904.
Li'l Gal, New York, 1904.
Howdy, Honey, Howdy, New York, 1905.
Lyrics of Sunshine and Shadow, New York, 1905.
Joggin' Erlong, New York, 1906.
The Life and Works of Paul Laurence Dunbar . . . , (Lida Keck Wiggins, ed.), Naperville, Ill., [1907].
The Complete Poems . . . , New York, 1913.
Speakin' o' Christmas, and Other Christmas and Special Poems, New York, 1914.

DUNBAR, SEYMOUR (1866–April 18, 1947), was born in Cincinnati, Hamilton County. After attending high school in Terre Haute, Ind., he worked on the Cincinnati *Post* and newspapers in St. Louis and New York City. He soon retired from journalism, however, to devote himself to historical research. In 1921 he identified the Fort Sutter papers covering the Bear Flag revolt in 1846; he edited them in 39 volumes. He spent more than twenty years on his monumental work, *A History of Travel in America . . . ,* 4 vols., Indianapolis, [1915].

DUNCAN, JOHN ALLISON (Dec. 20, 1903–), lawyer, was born in Cleveland, Cuyahoga County. He graduated from Princeton University in 1925 and Western Reserve Law School in 1929. He has since practiced in Cleveland. He wrote, illustrated, and published privately a collection of legal oddities: *In the Name of the Law!,* [Cleveland, 1937].

DUNCAN, JOHN BROWN (Jan. 16, 1883–Dec. 26, 1945), born in Brigdon, Ontario, Canada, was reared in Detroit. He lived in Toledo, 1942–45, while working with the procurement division of the Air Force; during his Ohio residence he published a novel: *Heather Heritage,* New York, [1943].

DUNCAN, MARION HERBERT (Jan. 17, 1896–), was born in Celina, Mercer County. He graduated from Hiram College in 1918. He served in Tibet as a missionary, 1921–34, and was a member of the second Brooke Dolan expedition to eastern Tibet, 1934–36. Now a resident of Alexandria, Va., he has served various governmental agencies as a consultant on the Far East and was stationed in Japan, 1947–51 and 1955. He has written articles and books on Tibet, e.g., *The Mountain of Silver Snow,* Cincinnati, [1929].

DUNCAN, NORMAN (July 2, 1871–Oct. 18, 1916), author of children's stories and travel books, was born in Brantford, Ontario, Canada, and spent his last years in Willoughby, Lake County. He is best known for *Doctor Luke of the Labrador,* [New York, 1904]. WWW 1

DUNCAN, WALTER WOFFORD TUCKER (Oct. 29, 1869–Aug. 2, 1945), clergyman, was born in New Brunswick, Canada. He came to the United States in 1887, was ordained to the Methodist ministry in 1900, and, after serving churches in various states, became pastor of Lakewood Methodist Church, Cleveland, in 1931. He was an Ohio resident for the remainder of his life. He published sermons and *The Preacher and Politics . . . ,* New York, [1930]. WWW 2

DUNDASS, SAMUEL RUTHERFORD (June 30, 1820–Oct. 6, 1850), was born in Jefferson County. On March 24, 1849, the Steubenville Company, a hopeful band of sixty persons, set out for the Promised Land in California. At the Kansas River the large company broke up into groups of ten, and Dundass with a few companions went on independently from this point. There were no particularly dramatic adventures, and perhaps their desperate stages of a few miles a day—from one waterhole to the next—were commonplace experiences, but nowhere are such experiences recorded with greater fidelity than in Dundass' very full journal, which he kept from day to day. Arriving in California and finding little gold, he moved on to San Francisco, Nov. 15, 1849, where he became Inspector of the Port, at which point his journal ends. He died in Buffalo, N. Y.

Journal of Samuel Rutherford Dundass . . . , Steubenville, 1857.

DUNHAM, CHESTER FORRESTER (May 19, 1891–Feb. 22, 1959), clergyman, lecturer, and art collector, was born in Chicago, Ill. He attended Yale University, Oberlin College, and the University of Chicago. Except for an interval devoted to graduate study, he was pastor of Park Congregational Church, Toledo, 1928–52, and after his retirement he continued to live in that city. He published *Christianity in a World of Science,* New York, 1930.

DUNLAP, E. K. (1853–1885), was born in Cedarville, Greene County, and attended school there. As a young man he went to California, where he lived until 1884, when he returned to Cedarville. He died the following year and is buried in Cincinnati. His only known publication is an account of the vicissitudes of a legless veteran. It was published in pamphlet form by a G.A.R. post.

Corporal John, [San Jose, Calif.?, 1879?].

DUNLAP, MAURICE PRATT (Dec. 9, 1882–), journalist and diplomat, was born in Toledo, Lucas County. His family moved to St. Paul, Minn., around 1890. He graduated from Princeton University in 1912. After several years in editorial work, he entered the diplomatic service and between 1915 and 1942 served in American consulates in various cities. He now lives in Dell Rapids, S. Dak. He has published numerous articles, has also lectured on Norse civilization, the subject of his book *Stories of the Vikings,* Indianapolis, [1923]. WW 26

DUNLEVY, ANTHONY HOWARD (Dec. 21, 1793–Dec. 1, 1881), lawyer, was born in Cincinnati, Hamilton County, but lived in Lebanon, Warren County, from 1797 until his death. Interested in local history, he wrote articles for the *Western Star* and other newspapers.

History of the Miami Baptist Association . . . , Cincinnati, 1869.

DUNLEVY, JOHN (1769–Sept. 16, 1826), clergyman, was born near Winchester, Va. His parents moved to Washington, Pa., in the same year. He went to Kentucky, where he taught school and was ordained to the Presbyterian ministry in 1797. In 1800 he became minister of the Presbyterian Church at Eagle Creek, Adams County. After he was converted to Shakerism by Richard McNemar (q.v.) in 1806, most of his congregation followed him into the Shaker faith. He died at West Union, Ind., while visiting the Shaker community there.

A Manifesto, or a Declaration of the Doctrines and Practice of the Church of Christ, Pleasant Hill, Ky., 1818.

DUNN, WALDO HILARY (Oct. 4, 1882–), educator, was born in Rutland, Meigs County. He graduated from Yale University in 1906. From 1907 to 1934 he was a member of the English department, College of Wooster, and from 1934 to 1952 he was on the faculty of Scripps College, Claremont, Calif. His residence now is Wooster. He has written a number of biographies and scholarly studies, and *The Vanished Empire, a Tale of the Mound Builders,* Cincinnati, 1904. WW 30

DUNNE, GERALD W. E. (Nov. 9, 1886–Jan. 29, 1953), clergyman, was born in Lima, Allen County. After graduating from the University of Dayton in 1916 and Mount St. Mary's of the West Seminary, Cincinnati, in 1922, he was ordained to the Roman Catholic priesthood. He was a teacher at Central Catholic High School, Toledo, 1923–52. He published four books of verse, e.g., *Songsmith,* Toledo, 1935. CWW 9

DUNTON, JAMES GERALD (Nov. 10, 1899–), was born in Circleville, Pickaway County. He was an ambulance driver in World War I and graduated from Harvard University in 1923. He taught school for a time, then did editorial work and freelance writing. He served in the army, 1942–55, and since 1957 has been Director of Office of Public Services, Department of Defense. He has published numerous articles and books, including a novel, *Wild Asses,* Boston, [1925]. WW 28

DURHAM, E. SAMUEL (Aug. 3, 1853–July 30, 1944), was born near Newtown, Hamilton County. He was employed in Cincinnati as a streetcar conductor and was active in the I.O.O.F. lodge. The volume below was prepared at the request of his family. He died in Cincinnati.

The Pioneer Settlers of the Lower Little Miami Valley, [n.p., 1897?].

DUSTIN, CHARLES. Pseud. See John U. Giesy.

DUTCHER, ADDISON PORTER (Oct. 11, 1818–Jan. 30, 1884), physician and lecturer, was born in Durham, N. Y. He was educated in the school of Benjamin Romaine, where Washington Irving had also been a pupil. In 1839 he was granted an M.D. degree by the New York College of Physiology and Surgery. After practicing in New York and Pennsylvania, he accepted the chair of Principles and Practices of Medicine at Charity Hospital Medical School, Cleveland. He taught and practiced medicine in Cleveland for the remainder of his life. He was a prolific writer on medical subjects. He also wrote and lectured on abolition of slavery and on temperance.

Pulmonary Tuberculosis: Its Pathology, Nature, Symptoms, Diagnosis, Prognosis, Causes, Hygiene, and Medical Treatment, Philadelphia, 1875.

Sparks from the Forge of a Rough Thinker, Cleveland, 1880.

Two Voyages to Europe, Cleveland, 1884.

DUVALL, TRUMBULL GILLETTE (March 20, 1861–May 9, 1951), educator, was born in Indianapolis, Ind. He graduated from DePauw University in 1888 and the School of Theology, Boston University, in 1889. He studied in Germany, 1890–92, and after three years at DePauw he joined the faculty of Ohio Wesleyan University. After his retirement he continued to live in Delaware until his death. He wrote *Great Thinkers; The Quest of Life for its Meaning,* New York, 1937. WW 21

DWIGGINS, WILLIAM ADDISON (June 19, 1880–Dec. 25, 1956), book designer, was born in Martinsville, Clinton County. After studying art in Chicago, he settled in Hingham, Mass., which remained his home for the rest of his life. Until the end of the 1920s he worked mostly in advertising. He began designing books for Alfred A. Knopf, Inc., and was also associated with Mergenthaler Linotype Company. A prolific pamphleteer, he wrote many discussions of advertising and typography, some under the pen name Hermann Püterschein, e.g., *Paraphs,* New York, 1928. WWW 3

DYAR, MURIEL CAMPBELL (Dec. 31, 1876–), was born in Marietta, Washington County. She graduated from Marietta College in 1899. In 1915 she moved to California, where her residence now is El Cajon. She wrote stories for *Harper's* and published *Davie and Elizabeth, Wonderful Adventures,* New York, 1908.

DYER, ADA MAY (Mrs. Amos) (April 18, 1876–), educator, was born in Winterport, Maine. In 1915 she came to Columbus, where she taught in public schools and conducted a piano school. She is still living in Columbus. Besides composing music, she has published a volume of poems: *Echoes from Forestside,* Columbus, [1949].

DYER, JOHN LEWIS (March 16, 1812–June 16, 1901), clergyman, was born in Franklin County. After being converted to Methodism in 1830, he became a zealous religious worker. He began preaching in Wisconsin in 1849. One of the last of the great circuit riders of the Methodist Episcopal Church, he became an integral part of the westward-moving frontier. The year 1861 found him at Denver, determined to go to the mining camps in the mountains. Oro, Buckskin Joe, Fairplay, Cache Creek, California Gulch—no camp was too rough or too remote for Dyer. He earned his living carrying the mails across the mountains, often traveling on a pair of homemade skis which he called snowshoes. He labored for many years, extending his circuit into New Mexico. His *Snow-shoe Itinerant* is an unpretentious, factual account of his experiences. After retiring in 1889, he lived with his daughter, Mrs. Abbie Streeter, in Denver until his death. He was affectionately known as "Father Dyer" in the rough mining camps of Colorado.

The Snow-shoe Itinerant. An Autobiography . . . , Cincinnati, 1891.

DYKSTRA, CLARENCE ADDISON (Feb. 25, 1883–May 6, 1950), educator, was born in Cleveland, Cuyahoga County. After graduating from the University of Iowa in 1903, he did graduate work at the University of Chicago. He taught at Ohio State University, 1907–09, and the University of Kansas, 1909–18. He was executive secretary of the Cleveland Civic League, 1918–20, held similar posts in other cities, and was city manager of Cincinnati, 1930–37. He was president of the University of Wisconsin, 1937–45, and provost of the University of California, 1945–50. Several of his addresses were published separately, and he also wrote a pamphlet, *Lip Service or Civil Service?*, [Chicago], 1936. WWW 3

DYKSTRA, GERALD OSCAR (May 13, 1906–), educator, was born in Allegan, Mich., and was educated at the University of Michigan. He practiced law in Cleveland, 1930–35, and was a member of the faculty at Ohio University, 1936–50. Since 1950 he has been professor of business law at the University of Michigan. He has published textbooks and articles, e.g., *A Belated Rebuttal on Russia*, Allegan, Mich., [1928]. WW 28

E

EAGLESON, HODGE MacILVAIN (June 11, 1895–), clergyman, was born in Cambridge, Guernsey County, the son of a Presbyterian minister. After graduating from Ohio State University in 1916, he was ordained to the Methodist ministry; he has preached in British Columbia and California and is now a pastor in Pittsburgh, Pa. He has published an autobiographical volume: *Laughing into Glory*, New York, [1947].

EAKES, MILDRED (Jan. 13, 1894–), educator, was born in Oxford, Ga. She graduated from LaGrange College in 1913 and Cincinnati Conservatory of Music in 1926. She was a music supervisor, choir director, and organist in the South until 1925, when she moved to Cincinnati, where she served on the Conservatory faculty. In 1951 she retired, and she now lives in Decatur, Ga. She has published a collection of poems: *Women Are That Way*, New York, [1950].

EALY, LAWRENCE ORR (Sept. 17, 1915–), lawyer and educator, was born in Ocean City, N. J., but his family moved to Steubenville in 1920. He graduated from Temple University in 1934 and the University of Pennsylvania (LL.B., 1937; Ph.D., 1947). He practiced law in Steubenville, 1937–40, served in the navy during World War II, has taught at Temple and Rutgers Universities, and is now provost of Hobart and William Smith Colleges, Geneva, N. Y. He has written several articles on Latin America and a historical novel: *Under the Puppet's Crown*, Boston, 1939. DAS 3

EARHART, WILL (April 1, 1871–April 23, 1960), educator, was born in Franklin, Warren County. He taught music in Richmond, Ind., 1900–12, and was director of music in the schools of Pittsburgh, Pa., 1912–40. He also lectured at the University of Pittsburgh and Carnegie Institute of Technology. His death occurred in Portland, Oreg. He wrote many articles on music education, textbooks, and several books on music, e.g., *Music to the Listening Ear*, New York, [1932]. DAS 2

EASTMAN, EPHRAIM RICHARD (May 6, 1854–Feb. 14, 1931), lawyer, was born in Woodstock, Champaign County. He attended school in Union County, studied languages, and read law. After teaching school from 1872 to 1883, he began the practice of law, and lived in Ottawa. He published *Eastman's Poems, Original and Translated*, Toledo, 1902. OBB

EASTMAN, FRED (July 11, 1886–), clergyman, was born in Lima, Allen County. After graduating from University of Wooster in 1908 and Union Theological Seminary in 1911, he was ordained to the Presbyterian ministry. He served a church in Locust Valley, N. Y., 1912–17, and was in educational and editorial work for the American Red Cross and the Presbyterian Church, 1917–26. His writings include numerous magazine articles, plays, pageants (some published under the pen name Richard Morse), and *Unfinished Business of the Presbyterian Church in America*, [Philadelphia, 1921]. WW 30

EASTMAN, LINDA ANNE (July 17, 1867–), librarian, was born in Oberlin, Lorain County, and attended Oberlin College. She taught in the Cleveland schools, 1885–92, and joined the staff of the Cleveland Public Library in 1892. Except for a year at the Dayton Public Library (1895–96), she remained on the Cleveland library staff until her retirement in 1938. She was head librarian, 1918–38. Besides professional articles, she published *Portrait of a Librarian, William Howard Brett*, Chicago, 1940. WW 26

EATON, JEANNETTE (Nov. 30, 1886–), was born in Columbus, Franklin County. She graduated from Vassar College and did graduate work at Ohio State University, earning an M.A. degree in 1911. She has worked on nation-wide educational surveys and has written for several major magazines. She has published a number of books, largely biographies for young readers, e.g., *Young Lafayette,* New York, 1932. WWAW 1

EATON, JOHN (Dec. 5, 1829–Feb. 9, 1906), clergyman and educator, born in Sutton, N. H., lived in Ohio about ten years. After graduating from Dartmouth in 1854, he was principal of Ward School, Cleveland, 1854–56, and superintendent of schools in Toledo, 1856–59. In 1861 he became chaplain of the 27th O.V.I., and the following year General Grant directed him to organize freed Negroes. After the war he founded the Memphis *Post* in 1865, worked with the Freedmen's Bureau, and in 1870 became Commissioner of the Bureau of Education in Washington, D. C. He returned to Ohio to serve as president of Marietta College, 1886–91. His death occurred in Washington, D. C. Several of his addresses were published as pamphlets, and he also wrote *Grant, Lincoln and the Freedmen . . . ,* New York, 1907. WWW 1

EBERLE, EDITH (Oct. 29, 1889–), was born in West Unity, Williams County; she has also lived in Toledo and Cleveland. After graduating from Transylvania College in 1914, she taught school for three years, was a missionary in the Philippines, 1917–23, and was an executive of the United Christian Missionary Society, 1923–57. In 1953 she married Rev. Cyrus M. Yocum, who died in 1958. She now lives in Indianapolis, Ind. She has published many pamphlets and magazine articles and at least three books, e.g., *Palm Tree and Pine; Stories of the Philippine Islands,* Cincinnati, [1927].

ECKERT, JOSEPHINE PAULINE. See Josephine P. E. Gill.

ECKSTEIN, GUSTAV (Oct. 26, 1890–), physiologist, was born in Cincinnati, Hamilton County. He earned a D.D.S. degree at the University of Cincinnati in 1911, practiced dentistry for several years, and earned an M.D. in 1924. In 1922 he was made a member of the University of Cincinnati faculty. A close friend of Alexander Woollcott, he was the basis for one of the minor characters in *The Man Who Came to Dinner.* Eckstein has published studies of animals, a novel, and several plays. He has traveled often in Europe and Japan and wrote a biography of the Japanese bacteriologist, Hideyo Noguchi: *Noguchi,* New York, 1931. WW 28

ECLAIR, LYDEN. Pseud. See Henry L. Flash.

EDDY, THOMAS MEARS (Sept. 7, 1823–Oct. 7, 1874), clergyman, was born in Newton, Hamilton County. He was educated in the seminary, Greensborough, Ind., and from 1842 to 1853 was a Methodist circuit rider in Indiana. He held pastorates in Illinois, Maryland, and Washington, D. C., and edited the *Northeastern Christian Advocate* in Chicago. He published a number of speeches and sermons. His death occurred in New York City.

The Patriotism of Illinois . . . , 2 vols., Chicago, 1865–66.

EDGAR, JOHN FARIS (Oct. 29, 1814–Aug. 15, 1905), was born in Dayton, Montgomery County. A building contractor by profession, he was also superintendent of Mad River and Lake Erie Railroad. His only book is a study of early Dayton. He died in Philadelphia.

Pioneer Life in Dayton and Vicinity, 1796–1840, Dayton, 1896.

EDGERTON, JAMES ARTHUR (Jan. 30, 1869–Dec. 3, 1938), journalist, was born in Plattsville, Shelby County. He graduated from National Normal University, Lebanon, in 1887 and also studied at Marietta College. He edited county and state papers for several years, was on the editorial staff of the Denver *News,* 1899–1903, and was affiliated with the American Press Association for a number of years. He was the Prohibition Party nominee for vice-president of the United States in 1928. His death occurred in Alexandria, Va.

Poems, Marietta, [1889].
A Better Day, Lincoln, Neb., [1891].
Populist Handbook for Nebraska, Denver, 1895.
Songs of the People, Denver, 1895.
Voices of the Morning, Chicago, 1898.
Glimpses of the Real, Denver, 1903.
In the Gardens of God, New York, 1904.
History of New Thought, New York, 1917.
My Personal Adventures in Truth, Holyoke, Mass., 1919.
The Philosophy of Jesus, the Basis of a New Reformation, Boston, [1928].
Invading the Invisible, Washington, D. C., [1931].

EDGERTON, JESSE (July 12, 1845–1929), Quaker poet, was born near Barnesville, Belmont County, the youngest of fifteen children. Like his brothers and sisters, he was active in the Society of Friends throughout his life. For a number of years he was a harness maker and manager of a handle factory in Columbiana. From 1901 to 1905 he was superintendent of Friends Boarding School at Barnesville and from 1905 until his death he lived at Damascus.

Why Am I a Friend?, Salem, 1893.
A Brook by the Way, Damascus, 1913.
Militarism, the Curse of the Nations, Damascus, 1915.

EDGERTON, WALTER (Oct., 1806–1879), was born in Ohio, but in 1829 moved to Henry County, Ind., where he farmed and taught school. He was an active abolitionist and opposed changes in the Quaker faith and practice. He died in Minneapolis, Minn.

A Brief Review of Certain Phrenological Works of O. S. Fowler, Newport, Ind., 1848.
A History of the Separation in Indiana Yearly Meeting of Friends; Which Took Place in the Winter of 1842 and 1843 on the Anti-Slavery Question . . . , Cincinnati 1856.
Modern Quakerism Examined . . . , Indianapolis, 1876.

EDWARDS, DONALD EARL (Feb. 7, 1916–), was born in East Liberty, Logan County. He served in the army in World War II and afterward lived in Marion and Gambier. His last address in Ohioana files (1951) was Columbus. His poems have appeared in various periodicals and he has published a collection: *Who Walks with Dreams,* Dallas, Texas, [1947].

EDWARDS, ELEANOR LEE. Pseud. See Metta V. F. Victor.

EDWARDS, SAMUEL E. (March 22, 1810–1895), was born in Armstrong County, Pa. In 1812 his parents came to Washington County, and soon afterward they moved to Cincinnati. From boyhood he hunted bear and deer and was widely known for his hunting exploits, especially in the Maumee Valley. He lived in Napoleon, Henry County, where he reared eighteen children. Despite the protests of his first wife, who was a Lutheran, he became a Campbellite, and in 1855 he became a medium despite the objections of his minister; but he later gave up spiritualism. His autobiography is somewhat rare and is a valuable account of the Ohio frontier.

The Ohio Hunter; Or, a Brief Sketch of Samuel E. Edwards, the Great Bear and Deer Hunter of the State of Ohio, Battle Creek, Mich., 1866.

EELLS, HASTINGS (June 9, 1895–), educator, was born in Absecon, N. J., and has been a member of the history department at Ohio Wesleyan University since 1925. He has published textbooks, articles, and *Martin Bucer,* New Haven, 1931. WW 30

EFFLER, LOUIS ROBERT (Dec. 9, 1888–), physician, was born in Toledo, Lucas County. He practiced medicine in Toledo and still lives in that city. A prolific writer, he has published many articles and books on medical and historical topics. He has also published a number of travel booklets, e.g., *My Flight to Hopi-Land . . . ,* [Toledo, 1941].

EGGLESTON, BENJAMIN (Jan. 2, 1747–1832), was born in Middlefield, Mass. He came to Aurora, Portage County, in 1807 and spent the rest of his life in that community. A former Revolutionary War soldier, he is the probable author of the book below, although it may have been written by his son and namesake. The book was announced for three volumes, but only the first was published.

An American Field of Mars . . . , Cleveland, 1839.

ELAM, CHARLES MILTON (July 10, 1882–Nov. 7, 1944), was born in Cincinnati, Hamilton County. He was employed by the Baltimore and Ohio Railroad, 1919–32, and also operated the Open Sesame Press, which published his own poems and those of other writers. His published works include a pamphlet, *The Case for an A Priori Language,* Cincinnati, [1932].

ELBERT, JOHN ALOYSIUS (March 15, 1895–), Catholic priest and educator, was born in Brooklyn, N. Y., and has lived in Ohio at several times since graduating from the University of Dayton in 1915. He taught at the University of Dayton Preparatory School, 1918–21, was professor of philosophy, University of Dayton, 1926–28 and 1947–48, was principal of Purcell High School, Cincinnati, 1928–31, and served as president of University of Dayton, 1938–44. Since 1948 he has been Provincial Superior, Society of Mary, Province of Cincinnati. He has written a number of religious articles and books, e.g., *Prayer in a Modern Age,* Ozone Park, N. Y., 1941. WW 30

ELDRIDGE, CHARLOTTE BLAKLEY (June 14, 1910–), was born in Dayton, Montgomery County. After graduating from Steele High School, Dayton, she attended Ohio State University and the Dayton Art Institute and worked as a fashion designer in Dayton and Cincinnati. She was married to Harry C. Eldridge, Jr., of Franklin, now deceased; now Mrs. Burr Sutter, she lives in Phoenix, Ariz. She has been a columnist for the Franklin *Chronicle,* the Dayton *Journal-Herald,* and the *Arizonian,* published in Scottsdale, Ariz. She was on the staff of *Arizona Highways Magazine,* 1951–56, and also produced a television show in Phoenix. She has written several plays, e.g., *Holiday House!* . . . , Franklin, [1938].

ELDRIDGE, ETHEL JONES (June 20, 1880–), was born in Tampa, Fla. After her marriage to Harry C. Eldridge (q.v.), publisher of Franklin, she made her home in that community. Now an invalid she still lives in Franklin. She adapted Chinese stories for American children and also wrote *Children's Pantomimes for Special Days,* Franklin, 1936.

ELDRIDGE, HARRY CARLETON (June 10, 1872–Sept. 12, 1946), publisher, was born in Franklin, Warren County. He established the Eldridge Entertainment House, which published songs, plays, and operettas, most of them intended for performance by schools and churches. He died in Franklin. Some of the entertainments he published were written by himself, e.g., *Billy Brown's Christmas Stunt* . . . , Franklin, 1934.

ELLARD, HARRY G. (Dec. 12, 1864–Jan. 2, 1913), was born in Cincinnati, Hamilton County. As a boy he suffered from incipient tuberculosis, and his parents sent him to live in the West for several years. He recovered his health and later played on one of the early Cincinnati Red Stockings baseball teams. His father, who operated a sporting goods store, was one of the organizers of the team. He wrote a valuable history of the Cincinnati baseball club and also traveled widely in Europe, South America, and Asia. Besides the titles below, he published considerable poetry in periodicals under the pen names the Poet Lariat and the Cowboy Poet.

Ranch Tales of the Rockies, Canon City, Colo., 1899.

Baseball in Cincinnati; A History, Cincinnati, 1908.

ELLARD, VIRGINIA G. (Jan. 22, 1839–Oct. 14, 1912), was born in Cincinnati, Hamilton County. Her husband operated a sporting goods store; and her son, Harry G. Ellard (q.v.), was a baseball star and author of a history of the Cincinnati Reds. Mrs. Ellard was active in Cincinnati organizations and wrote a number of poems, especially sonnets, many of which were published in the Cincinnati *Commercial Tribune* and some of which were collected in the second book below.

Grandma's Christmas Day, Cincinnati, 1880.

The Unity of Life and Spirit, New York, [1906].

ELLIOTT, BLANCHE (1890–Oct. 1, 1959), educator, was born in Mill Creek Township, Coshocton County. A graduate of Kent State University, she taught in the Coshocton schools for thirty years before retiring in 1942. She published poems in various periodicals and also wrote a book for young readers: *Timothy Titus,* New York, 1937.

ELLIOTT, CHARLES (May 16, 1792–Jan. 8, 1869), Methodist clergyman and educator, was born in Ireland. Soon after coming to America in 1814 he was preaching in Ohio. In 1822 he was missionary to the Wyandots. After a number of years in Pennsylvania, he returned to Ohio and was presiding elder of the Dayton District, 1850–51. In his last years he was president of Iowa Wesleyan University. He wrote a vigorous anti-Catholic polemic: *Delineation of Roman Catholicism* . . . , 2 vols., New York, 1841, and several books opposing slavery, e.g., *The Bible and Slavery* . . . , Cincinnati, 1859.

ELLIOTT, CHARLES BURKE (Jan. 6, 1861–Sept. 18, 1935), lawyer, was born in Morgan County. He attended district schools and spent a year in the preparatory department of Marietta College. When his family moved to Iowa, he attended the law school of the University of Iowa and graduated in 1881. While practicing law in Minneapolis, he did graduate work at the University of Minnesota, wrote a dissertation on American policy regarding fisheries that attracted wide attention, and in 1888 was awarded the first Ph.D. granted by the university. He filled various judicial posts and from 1910 to 1912 was a member of the Philippine Commission. From 1913 until his death, he practiced law in Minneapolis. He published a number of legal works and two books on the Philippines: *The Philippines to the End of the Military Regime* . . . , Indianapolis, [1917] and *The Philippines to the End of the Commission Government* . . . , Indianapolis, [1917]. DAB 21

ELLIOTT, FRANKLIN REUBEN (April 27, 1817–Jan. 10, 1878), horticulturist, was born in Guilford, Conn., and in 1844 moved to Cleveland, where he spent the remainder of his life. He wrote numerous articles for horticultural periodicals.

Elliott's Fruit Book . . . , New York, 1854.
Popular Deciduous Evergreen Trees and Shrubs . . . , New York, 1868.
Hand-book for Fruit Growers . . . , Rochester, N. Y., 1876.
Hand Book for Practical Landscape Gardening . . . , Rochester, N. Y., 1877.

ELLIOTT, GEORGE (Dec. 14, 1851–Nov. 2, 1930), clergyman, was born in Licking County. After attending Otterbein University, he graduated from Cornell College, Iowa, in 1872. He served as pastor of Methodist churches in Maryland, Pennsylvania, and Michigan, and was for some time editor of the *Methodist Review.* He spent his last years in New York City.

The Abiding Sabbath, [New York], 1884.
The Beauty of Jesus, Cincinnati, 1904.
Biblical Criticism and Preaching, New York, 1912.
The Christmas Canticles, New York, 1922.

ELLIOTT, HARRISON SACKET (Dec. 13, 1882–June 27, 1951), educator, was born in St. Clairsville, Belmont County. He graduated from Ohio Wesleyan University in 1905, Drew Theological Seminary in 1911, and Yale University (Ph.D.) in 1940. He held various administrative positions in the Methodist Church, 1905–10, was in Y.M.C.A. work, 1910–25, and taught at Drew Seminary, 1921–23, and Union Theological Seminary, 1922–50. He died in Rhinebeck, N. Y. He published numerous articles and books on religion and psychology, e.g., *How Jesus Met Life Questions,* New York, 1920. WWW 3

ELLIOTT, HENRY WOOD (Nov. 13, 1846–May 25, 1930), artist and naturalist, was born in Cleveland, Cuyahoga County, the son of Franklin R. Elliott (q.v.). He was educated in Cleveland schools. In 1862 he became private secretary to Joseph Henry, Secretary of the Smithsonian Institution; he was associated with the Smithsonian as an artist and explorer for the rest of his life. He was a member of the Western Union Telegraph Expedition to Alaska, 1865–67. He was sent to the Seal Islands of Alaska by the Treasury Department in 1872–74 and in 1880; and he drew up the 1905 treaty regarding fur seals. He wrote several monographs and magazine articles.

Our Arctic Province, Alaska and the Seal Islands, New York, 1886.

ELLIOTT, JOSEPH TAYLOR (Jan. 24, 1837–Aug. 4, 1916), was born in Butler County. His family moved to Indianapolis, Ind., when he was thirteen, and he spent the remainder of his life in Indiana. He served in the Civil War and was one of the survivors of the sinking of the *Sultana* near Memphis, Tenn., in April of 1865, an experience he described in his only publication: *The Sultana Disaster,* Indianapolis, 1913. IATB

ELLIOTT, WALTER HACKETT ROBERT (Jan. 6, 1842–April 18, 1928), missionary, born in Detroit, Mich., came to Cincinnati in the late 1850s to study law and was admitted to the Ohio bar in 1861. He served throughout the Civil War with the 5th O.V.I. In 1867 he was converted to Catholicism, and in 1872 he was ordained a priest. He wrote numerous devotional books and biographies, e.g., *Life of Father Hecker,* New York, 1891.

ELLIS, ALSTON (Jan. 26, 1847–Nov. 14, 1920), educator, was born in Kenton County, Ky., and was educated at Miami University. He taught in the public schools of Kentucky and was superintendent of schools in Hamilton, 1871–79, and Sandusky, 1880–87. After some years in Colorado, he was named president of Ohio University in 1901 and served in that capacity until his death.

Some Phases of Popular Education, [n.p., 18– ?].

ELLIS, EDGAR WILLIAM (Jan. 29, 1864– ?), was born in West Sonora, Preble County. He held various offices in the Knights of Pythias and was a clerk in the Department of State, Columbus. He wrote *Just a Bit of Verse,* [Columbus, 1931].

ELLIS, EDWARD SYLVESTER (April 11, 1840–June 20, 1916), was born in Geneva, Ashtabula County, and spent part of his boyhood in the town of Ashtabula. He attended the State Normal School of New Jersey, began teaching when in his teens, and in his early thirties was superintendent of schools in Trenton, N. J. After 1876 he devoted himself to writing. He lived in Upper Montclair, N. J. He wrote for so many publishers under such a variety of pen names that a complete bibliography of his work is probably impossible, but he undoubtedly deserves to be designated as Ohio's most prolific writer. He turned out well over 200 adventure novels, biographies, and textbooks. Some idea of his productivity may be gained from a list of his publications in a single year (1893): *Across Texas, The Campers Out, The Great Berwyck Bank*

Robbery, Lena-Wingo, The Mohawk, The River Fugitives, The Third Man, Through Apache Land, and *The Wilderness Fugitives.* Among his many pen names were the following: Capt. J. F. C. Adams, Boynton Belknap, M.D., J. G. Bethune, Capt. Latham C. Carleton, Frank Faulkner, Col. H. R. Gordon, Capt. R. M. Hawthorne, Lieut. Ned Hunter, Lieut. R. H. Jayne, Charles E. LaSalle, Seward D. Lisle, E. S. St. Max, Capt. H. R. Millbank, Billex Muller, Lieut. J. H. Randolph, Seelin Robins, and Emerson Rodman.

ELLIS, JOHN (Aug. 26, 1812–1894), clergyman, was born in Albany County, N. Y. He became affiliated with the New York Christian Conference and began to preach around 1832. In 1852 he brought his family to Enon, Clark County. With Ohio as his headquarters he became a traveling minister and preached extensively in Texas and elsewhere in the West. His last years were spent in Yellow Springs. His autobiography was prepared for publication by his wife.

Autobiography and Poems of Eld. John Ellis . . . , Springfield, 1895.

ELLISTON, GEORGE (Mrs. Augustus T. Coleman) (1883–Oct. 6, 1946), poet, was born in Mt. Sterling, Ky., but attended high school in Cincinnati and spent the remainder of her life in that city. While still in her teens she began working as a reporter; in 1909 she became society editor of the *Times-Star,* and she remained on the staff until her death. She published poems in numerous periodicals; many of them were set to music and translated into several languages. She published a number of collections under her maiden name, e.g., *Everyday Poems,* Cincinnati, [1921]. WWW 2

ELLS, BENJAMIN FRANKLIN (1805–Jan. 12, 1874), publisher, was born in Concord, Conn. In 1818 his father brought his family to Wheeling, Va., and in 1827 came to Newark, where he lived until his death in 1865. The first book to bear the imprint of B. F. Ells was *The Dialogue Grammar; Or, Book Instructor to Teach the Science of English Grammar without a Teacher . . . ,* South Hanover, Ind. Printed at the Hanover College Press, 1834. The preface is dated New Lexington, Dec. 1, 1834. New Lexington lies about 25 miles south of Newark in an adjoining county. No residential connection of any sort can be verified with either New Lexington or Hanover. Ells was neither a student nor a teacher at Hanover; that he was a Presbyterian is his only possible connection with the college. One other book, *History of the Romish Inquisition, Compiled from Various Authors,* was issued with a Hanover imprint in 1835. Besides his individual imprints and a brief connection with his brother, G. W. Ells, the following firm names appear on the record: Ells & Strong, Ells & McGregor, Ells & Claflin, Ells, Claflin & Co., L. F. Claflin & Co., More, Clarke & Co., Osborn & Ells, Ells, Marquis & Co., Burrows & Ells—in all, eleven combinations in 33 years. At the end of such a record, it is difficult to decide whether to list him as an author, an editor, a compiler, an artist with scissors and paste, a publisher, or a promoter. He was all of these, yet died without reaping renown or financial security. Only the rarity of the little books that bear his name on their title pages arouses our interest. Though his early school readers were of the time of McGuffey, it is for publishing interest rather than for subject matter, style, or originality that these imprints are collected. Appropriating and adapting the brain children of other men—snatches here and snatches there—was at most a venial sin in a day when copyright meant little; but we note that Ells was usually careful to avail himself of what small protection he could obtain by copyrighting materials in his own name. In 1835 appeared a somewhat abbreviated edition of the *Dialogue Grammar,* published in Dayton by B. F. Ells and E. M. Strong. Thereafter until his death, Ells was a resident of Dayton. From cemetery records, old bill heads, newspaper advertisements, reminiscences of a lady who lived in the former Ells home around 1870, and county court records, a fragmentary story can be pieced together showing the alternate progress and mortgage-ridden difficulties of a man whose memory lacks even a gravestone reminder. A reported gift to Dayton still exists on Euclid Avenue between Third and Fifth Streets, a tiny green strip of park, but it does not bear his name and there is no absolute proof that it was his donation. Of his publications, eighteen were schoolbooks—grammars, readers, spellers, arithmetic and algebra texts. Ninety were gay, tiny toy books of different sizes, priced from one to ten cents; only 34 of these toy books have been located. Ells' remaining publications were of great variety—historical, biographical, practical, and devotional; compilations of tales and songs and recipes. His final imprint was a Dayton city directory for 1856. The last years of Ells' life were darkened by financial worries. During the 1850s there was a wild flurry of dealing in real estate on the west side of

Dayton, in which Ells and his various partners engaged in buying and subdividing land. Apparently, many titles were transferred without clearing previous mortgages. A crazy, wildcat situation developed which was bound to collapse. Ells gave numerous mortgages between 1847 and 1858; in 1858 the record stops, apparently because there was nothing more to mortgage. The final showdowns came in 1863 and 1864, when there were numerous court sales of his land and printing equipment. Ells died suddenly while attending church with one of his adopted daughters. The neighbors said he was "very strict, a very religious man, somewhat irascible." The newspaper obituary stated, "He was a very peculiar man in many respects. At one time he had accumulated considerable property, but he was unfortunate, and during the last years of his life was in reduced circumstances. He was regarded as a man of exemplary moral character." The record of the final sale of his personal property in April, 1874, in Montgomery County probate court is a sad one. The total amount received from the sale of pamphlets, unbound books, and other effects was $130.14; the expenses of probate were $125.42, leaving proceeds of $4.72 to turn over to the heirs.

William Hamilton

ELSER, DONALD (Jan. 15, 1915–), educator, was born in North Lima, Mahoning County. A graduate of Youngstown University, he has done graduate work at several universities. Before joining the Air Corps in World War II, he taught in the schools of Mahoning and Trumbull Counties. He has been a member of the English Department, Youngstown University, since 1948. He has written a number of plays, e.g., *Special Guest,* Evanston, Ill., 1948.

ELSON, HENRY WILLIAM (March, 1857–Jan. 29, 1954), educator, was born in Muskingum County. After attending Ohio State University, he graduated from Thiel College in 1886 and Lutheran Theological Seminary, Philadelphia, in 1889. He served several Lutheran churches in Pennsylvania, taught at Ohio University and New York University, and was president of Thiel College, 1916–21. He died in Plainfield, N. J. Besides the books below, he wrote several widely used history textbooks, notably *Modern Times and the Living Past* (1921), which sold over a million copies.

The Story of a Great General, Ulysses S. Grant, Philadelphia, [1899].

The Story of a Noble Woman, Frances E. Willard, Philadelphia, [1899].

The Story of a Wonderful Hunter, Daniel Boone, Philadelphia, [1899].

The Story of "Old Hickory," Andrew Jackson, Philadelphia, [1899].

Through the Years with Our Constitution, Boston, [1937].

ELWELL, JOHN JOHNSON (June 22, 1820–March 13, 1900), physician and lawyer, was born near Warren, Trumbull County. He attended Western Reserve University and graduated from Cleveland Medical College in 1846. He also studied law and was admitted to the Ohio bar in 1854. His pioneer work on malpractice established him as an authority on medical jurisprudence. He served in the Civil War as a quartermaster, rising to the brevet rank of brigadier general. After the war he practiced law in Cleveland. He wrote numerous articles.

A Medico-Legal Treatise on Malpractice and Medical Evidence . . . , New York, 1860.

ELY, CHARLES ARTHUR (May 2, 1829–Sept. 30, 1864), was born in Elyria, Lorain County. He was educated by private tutors. A chronic disease of his eyes prevented him from attending college. Upon the death of his father, Heman Ely, the founder of Elyria, he traveled extensively in Europe and became interested in breeding Devon cattle. He imported the first herd of this breed into Lorain County in 1855. On the advice of his physician he set out on a world tour in 1858. Arranging to send a herd of his prize Devons overland to San Francisco, he set out for the same point via the Cape of Good Hope and China. He had so timed the departure of his herd that he and his cattle arrived in San Francisco within a few weeks of each other. In California, where he arrived in Aug., 1858, he wrote a series of articles for the *Alta California* and delivered a series of scientific lectures to the students of California College at Oakland. He returned to Elyria in Oct. 3, 1860. A chronic illness rendered him an invalid for the rest of his days. His death occurred in Columbus.

Science the True Basis of Education . . . , San Francisco, 1860.

EMENY, BROOKS (July 29, 1901–), educator, was born in Salem, Columbiana County. He graduated from Princeton University in 1924, studied international law in European universities as a Carnegie fellow, 1924–27, was on the Yale faculty, 1927–31, and taught at Western Reserve University, 1935–47. He has published numerous magazine articles and several books on international politics, e.g., *Mainsprings of World Politics . . . ,* New York, 1943. WW 30

EMERSON, JOHN (May 29, 1874–March 8, 1956), actor and playwright, was born in Sandusky, Erie County. He studied at Oberlin College, Western Reserve University, and University of Chicago. He was general stage director for Charles Frohman, 1910–14, and afterward wrote and produced motion pictures for Paramount, Metro-Goldwyn-Mayer, and other companies. On June 15, 1919, he married Anita Loos, author of *Gentlemen Prefer Blondes.* They collaborated on two books about motion pictures and a number of movies and plays, e.g., *The Whole Town's Talking . . . ,* New York, 1925. WWW 3

EMERSON, MRS. M. FARLEY (? – ?), truculent advocate of women's rights, was born in Ohio, judging from the very little that is known about her career. She lectured at Eaton on "the rights of man and the duties of woman" on April 3, 1855. In the broadside advertising that lecture, a number of testimonials from Ohio, Indiana, Illinois, and Iowa newspapers appear, indicating that she had been lecturing in the area for a number of years. In her book, which contains not a little libelous matter directed largely against Kentucky, Ohio, western Virginia, and western Pennsylvania hotel and tavern owners, she mentions her Ohio relatives. Because of a long list of Ohio correspondents found in her possession by Southern authorities, she was suspected of being an antislavery agitator. Her book appeared under the pen name "An American Woman."

Woman in America: Her Character and Position as Indicated by Newspaper Editorials, and Sustained by American Social Life, Cincinnati, 1857.

EMERSON, OLIVER FARRAR (May 24, 1860–March 13, 1927), educator, was born in Iowa. He graduated from Grinnell College in 1882, taught school for several years, and began graduate study at Cornell University, where he received his Ph.D. in 1891. He was professor of English at Western Reserve University, 1896–1927. He died in Ocala, Fla., where he was recuperating from a physical breakdown. Highly respected in the world of philological and literary scholarship, he published textbooks, editions of Gibbon and Chaucer, and many valuable articles and monographs.

The History of the English Language, New York, 1894.

A Brief History of the English Language, New York, 1896.

An Outline History of the English Language, New York, 1906.

Chaucer: Essays and Studies; A Selection from the Writings of Oliver Farrar Emerson, Cleveland, 1929.

EMERSON, RICHARD WIRTZ (May 13, 1925–), born in Watertown, N. Y., came to Columbus in 1942. He graduated from Ohio State University in 1948, was a director of Golden Goose Press, and presented a poetry program over WOSU, the Ohio State University radio station. He now lives in Sausalito, Calif. He has published fiction and poetry in national magazines and several collections of poems, e.g., *The Central Thread,* Philadelphia, [1947].

EMERSON, WILLIAM DANA (July 9, 1813–Jan., 1891), was born in Marietta, Washington County. He graduated from Ohio University in 1833 and taught at Marietta College and in Kentucky and Illinois for a time. Returning to Ohio in 1839, he studied law, was admitted to the bar in 1841, and opened an office in Cincinnati. He began contributing verse to the *Herald of Truth* in 1847.

Occasional Thoughts in Verse, Springfield, 1851.

Rhymes of Culture, Movement and Repose, Cincinnati, 1874.

History and Incidents of Indian Corn and Its Culture . . . , Cincinnati, 1878.

EMMITT, JAMES (Nov. 6, 1806–1895), was born in Armstrong County, Pa. After coming to southern Ohio as a boy, he worked as a farmhand, blacksmith, and teamster. In 1828 he began operating a grocery store in Waverly, and three years later he was made postmaster. He prospered and extended his interests gradually so that in his later years he owned a bank, a store, a sawmill and grist mill, a distillery, and a furniture factory in Waverly, and also owned considerable property in Chillicothe and in Iowa and Missouri. He served in the state senate, 1867–70. During a tour of Europe, 1865–66, he purchased many statues and paintings for his mansion in Waverly. His memoirs were prepared with the assistance of M. J. Carrigan of Chillicothe.

Life and Reminiscences of Hon. James Emmitt as Revised by Himself, Chillicothe, 1888.

ENGLE, TRALL (Aug. 15, 1881–), farmer, was born near Ohio City, Van Wert County. He attended Van Wert schools, and after teaching for nine years he operated a farm near Van Wert. He now lives in Lima. He has published poems, which are described as "interpretations of revelations," e.g., *Self Beautiful,* Van Wert, 1930.

ENGLEHARDT, ZEPHYRIN (Nov. 13, 1851–April 27, 1934), German-born Franciscan missionary to the Indians and author of several historical studies of the Catholic Church in the Southwest, attended school and seminary in Cincinnati, while his parents lived in Covington, Ky. After his ordination he was in Cleveland for two brief periods (1879; 1890–92). His books include *The Franciscans in California,* Harbor Springs, Mich., 1897.

ENGLEMAN, JAMES OZRO (Sept. 13, 1873–Sept. 15, 1943), educator, was born in Jeffersonville, Ind. After teaching in several Indiana schools, he attended Indiana University. He was a school superintendent in Illinois, Wisconsin, and Indiana, did graduate work at Ohio State University, 1927–28, and was president of Kent State University, 1928–38. He died while on a fishing trip at Middle Bass Island, Lake Erie. He wrote several textbooks and *Moral Education in School and Home,* Chicago, 1918. WWW 2

ENGLISH, JOSIAH GIBERTON (Dec. 13, 1833–Aug. 1, 1916), was born in New Jersey. He served as a Union soldier during the Civil War and subsequently filled a pastorate in Xenia. He also worked as a carpenter and contractor. He moved to Clermont County, where he lived near Felicity. His volume about Fort Ancient is in verse. His *Origin and End of Civil Government* was inspired by an encounter between Henry Eckerle, a white man, and Lewis Clay, a Negro policeman.

Poems, Xenia, 1888.

Fort Ancient in Warren County, Ohio, Dayton, 1889.

The Origin and End of Civil Government, [Xenia, 1892].

ENN, C. C. Pseud. See C. C. Neibling.

ENSIGN, SAMUEL JAMES RUSSELL (April 1, 1898–), clergyman, born in Marcus, Iowa, was a Presbyterian missionary in China and Siam, 1924–29. In 1930 he became minister of First Presbyterian Church, Huron. He now lives in Whittier, Calif. He presents dramatic impersonations of Biblical characters in costume and has published *I Am: A Series of Bible Autobiographies,* Huron, 1939.

EPP, PETER (1894–Jan. 10, 1959), educator, was born in Petershagen, Russia, the son of Dutch colonists. Educated in Russia, Germany, and Switzerland, he taught in Russia for twelve years before coming to the United States in 1924. He taught German and Russian at Bluffton College, 1924–34, and Ohio State University, 1934–51. His writings include *Eine Mutter,* Bluffton, 1932.

EPPSE, MERL R. (Jan. 17, 1893–), educator, was born near Greenville, Darke County, and lived in Ohio until he was twenty years old. He returned to Ohio to teach in 1919 and was a clerk in the Columbus Post Office, 1920–24. He graduated from Drake University in 1927 and in 1928 joined the faculty of Tennessee State University, where he is now chairman of the department of history and geography. He has written several books on race relations and Negro history, e.g., *The Negro, Too, in American History,* Chicago, 1938. DAS 3

EPSTEIN, BERYL WILLIAMS. See Beryl Williams.

ERDMANN, MYRTLE HILL (July 27, 1872–July 14, 1949), was born in Chillicothe, Ross County. She was married to Frank R. Erdmann of that community. Active in Chillicothe musical activities, she published verse in various periodicals. She died in Boston, but is buried in Chillicothe. She published a collection: *Mother's Book of Verse,* Columbus, [1941].

ERMINE, WILL. Pseud. See Harry S. Drago.

ERRETT, ISAAC (Jan. 2, 1820–Dec. 19, 1888), clergyman, was born in New York City, the son of an Irish immigrant, Henry Errett, a convert to the Disciples of Christ, who died in 1825. In 1832 Isaac's mother, who had remarried, took her family to Pittsburgh, Pa. Young Isaac worked on a farm, in a bookshop, and in a printing office; he studied at night to gain an education. In 1840 he began preaching in Pittsburgh. After three years there, he served Ohio churches at New Lisbon, North Bloomfield, and Warren. In 1849 he was one of the founders of Western Reserve Eclectic Institute, which became Hiram College eighteen years later. He opposed slavery at a time when many members of his faith were opposed to war, and when the Civil War began he sought a colonel's commission. Meanwhile, in 1856 he had moved to Michigan with a group of Disciples who were in the lumber business. He spent eight years there, organizing new churches and preaching widely. After two years in Chicago he came to Cleveland, where he edited the newly established *Christian Standard.* In 1868 he was named the first president of Alliance College, but he resigned the following year because college administration interfered with his editorial duties. In 1869 the *Standard* offices were moved to Cincinnati. As an editor Errett was a spokesman for the liberal wing of the Disciples church. He favored interdenominational co-operation and active missionary efforts. He devoted considerable time to missionary organizations. On controversial questions within the church, he was usually aligned with James A. Garfield (q.v.). He was chosen to preach Garfield's funeral sermon in Cleveland in Sept., 1881. Besides the titles below, he published sermons and addresses and also edited the writings of George Edward Flower.

Modern Spiritualism Compared with Christianity, a Debate between Joel Tiffany, Esq., of Painesville and Rev. Isaac Errett of Warren, Warren, 1855.
A Brief View of Missions: Ancient and Modern, 1857.
First Principles . . . , Cincinnati, [1868?].
Walks about Jerusalem: A Search after the Landmarks of Primitive Christianity, Cincinnati, 1871.
Talks to Bereans, Cincinnati, 1872.
Letters to a Young Christian, Cincinnati, 1877.
Evenings with the Bible, Old Testament Studies, 3 vols., Cincinnati, 1884–89.
Why Am I a Christian?, Cincinnati, 1889.
Our Position: A Brief Statement of the Distinctive Features of the Plea for Reformation Urged by the People Known as Disciples of Christ, Cincinnati, [188?].
Linsey-Woolsey and Other Addresses, Cincinnati, 1893.
The Querists' Drawer, a Discussion of Difficult Subjects and Passages of the Scriptures . . . , (Z. T. Sweeney, ed.), Cincinnati, [1910].

ERSKINE, DOROTHY BLISS (Sept. 11, 1906–), was born in Steubenville, Jefferson County. She attended Ohio State University and has held a variety of positions —as an advertising writer, a hotel manager, and a medical clerk in Baltimore. In 1957 she collaborated with Patrick Dennis in writing *The Pink Hotel;* she has also written at least two other books, e.g., *Miss Pettinger's Niece,* New York, 1949.

ESPY, JAMES POLLARD (May 9, 1785–Jan. 24, 1860), meteorologist, born in Pennsylvania, studied law and taught school in Xenia from 1808 to 1812. He published numerous reports and articles and a book: *Philosophy of Storms,* Boston, 1841. As a government meteorologist, he lived in Washington, D. C., but his death occurred in Cincinnati.

ESTEVEN, JOHN. Pseud. See Samuel Shellabarger.

ETAN, RAYMOND. Pseud. See Nathan R. Melhorn.

EUBANK, EARLE EDWARD (March 20, 1887–Dec. 17, 1945), educator, born in Columbia, Mo., served on the sociology faculty of the University of Cincinnati, 1921–45. He died in Florida while on sick leave from the university. He published professional articles and textbooks, but his best-known publication contained the life story of a convict, Charles L. Clark, and an analysis by Professor Eubank: *Lockstep and Corridor . . . ,* Cincinnati, [1927].

EULALIE. Pseud. See Mary Eulalie F. Shannon.

EUSTIS, HELEN (Dec. 31, 1916–), was born in Cincinnati, Hamilton County. She attended Hillsdale School and Smith College, where she graduated in 1938. She now lives in New York City. She has published numerous articles and short stories in national magazines. Her first novel was a psychological thriller with its setting on the campus of a women's college: *The Horizontal Man,* New York, [1946].

EVANGELINE. See Evangeline Ink.

EVANS, BERGEN (Sept. 19, 1904–), educator, was born in Franklin, Warren County. He graduated from Miami University in 1924, was a Rhodes scholar from 1928 to 1931, and earned his doctorate from Harvard University in 1932. He has been on the English faculty of Northwestern University since 1932. He has published many articles in national magazines and is widely known as a moderator of various television programs. Among his books is *The Natural History of Nonsense,* New York, 1946. WW 30

EVANS, DANIEL LUTHER (April 2, 1895–), educator, was born in Columbus, Franklin County. He graduated from Ohio State University (A.B., 1917; Ph.D., 1923), served in the Medical Department in World War I, and has been a member of the Ohio State philosophy faculty since

1922. His writings include numerous professional articles and *New Realism and Old Reality . . .*, Princeton, N. J., 1928. WW 28

EVANS, FREDERICK NOBLE (July 26, 1881–Nov. 30, 1946), landscape architect, was born in Youngstown, Mahoning County. He studied at Harvard University and in Germany. He practiced in Cleveland, 1910–14, was on the faculty of University of Illinois, 1914–20, and was city landscape architect of Sacramento, Calif., from 1920 until his death. He lectured on garden design and wrote *Town Improvement . . .*, New York, 1919. WWW 2

EVANS, JOHN (March 9, 1814–July 3, 1897), was born in Waynesville, Warren County. After graduating from Lynn Medical College, Cincinnati, he began the practice of medicine. A year later he moved to Indiana, where he led the movement to establish a state hospital for the insane and in 1845 became its first superintendent. Three years later he resigned to accept a professorship of obstetrics at Rush Medical College, Chicago. Although he gained prominence at Rush and served as one of the editors of the *Northwestern Medical and Surgical Journal,* his rapidly expanding business interests led him to give up his profession in 1859. He was one of the founders of Northwestern University and resided in the suburb later named for him, Evanston. On March 26, 1862, President Lincoln appointed him territorial governor of Colorado. His summary treatment of the Cheyenne Indians achieved its purpose but brought him under considerable criticism, which resulted in his writing the *Reply,* one of the rarest of all Western books, and his only known publication aside from medical articles and official documents. He resigned the governorship in 1865. As a philanthropist, real-estate operator, and railroad builder, he became the outstanding figure in the young state. When he died, Colorado honored him with a state funeral.

Reply of Governor Evans, of the Territory of Colorado, to That Part Referring to Him, of the Report of "The Committee on the Conduct of the War," Headed "Massacre of Cheyenne Indians," Denver, 1865.

EVANS, LAWRENCE BOYD (Feb. 3, 1870–Oct. 30, 1928), lawyer, was born in Radnor, Delaware County, but spent little of his life in Ohio. When he was a year old, his parents moved to Noblesville, Ind., where he grew up. After serving on the faculty of Tufts College, 1900–12, he studied law at Harvard University. He published handbooks on American government and important legal case books. He was state librarian of Massachusetts, 1917–19, and counselor of the Brazilian Embassy in Washington, D. C., 1919–28. Besides his scholarly and legal works, he published a biography: *Samuel W. McCall, Governor of Massachusetts,* Boston, 1916. DAB 6

EVANS, LLWELLYN IOAN (June 27, 1833–July 25, 1892), clergyman and educator, was born in Wales. He came to America in 1850 and for a short time lived in Newark, where his father was a minister. He went to Wisconsin, where he graduated from Racine College in 1856. The next year he came to Cincinnati to attend Lane Seminary. He graduated in 1860, was pastor of Lane Seminary Church, 1860–63, and served on the seminary faculty, 1863–92. A few months before his death he resigned to join the faculty of Bala Theological Seminary, Wales. Besides the title below, he published sermons and Biblical commentaries.

Poems, Addresses and Essays, New York, 1893.

EVANS, NELSON WILEY (June 4, 1842–May 27, 1913), lawyer, was born in Sardinia, Brown County. He attended Miami University from Jan., 1861, to June, 1863, and after a brief tour of duty with the 129th O.V.I., he returned to Miami and graduated in 1864, after which he became assistant adjutant of the 173rd O.V.I. After being discharged as a captain in 1865, he entered the Cincinnati Law School. Admitted to the Ohio bar in April, 1866, he practiced in Portsmouth.

A History of Adams County . . ., (with Emmons B. Stivers), West Union, 1900.

A History of Scioto County . . ., Portsmouth, 1903.

A History of Taxation in Ohio . . ., Cincinnati, 1906.

A Model Constitution for the State of Ohio, [Portsmouth?], 1912.

The Federal Constitution of 1797 Rewritten According to the Ideas of Alexander Hamilton . . ., Columbus, [1913].

EVANS, VIRGINIA MORAN (Mrs. Albert R.) (March 2, 1909–), was born in Dayton, Montgomery County, and still lives in that city. She graduated from Miami Jacobs Business College and has attended the University of Dayton and Miami University. Her poems have appeared in many national magazines and in anthologies, and she has published a collection of verse which won the American Weave Award for 1946: *When March Sets Free the River . . . ,* Cleveland, 1946.

EVANS, WILL (June 27, 1910–), was born in Parkersburg, W. Va., and has lived most of his life in Jackson County. He attended Rio Grande College and now operates a farm near Oak Hill. His poems have appeared in many magazines and newspapers, and he has published one collection: *The Bitter Bread,* New York, [1947].

EVANS, WILLIAM R. (Jan. 24, 1845–Sept. 23, 1913), clergyman, was born in Gallia County. He was admitted to the Presbyterian ministry in 1876. For the rest of his life he operated a farm near Peniel and preached on the circuit of Welsh churches in Gallia and Jackson Counties. He wrote many articles and letters, both in English and in Welsh, for magazines and newspapers.

Welshmen as Civil, Political and Moral Factors in the Formation and Development of the United States Republic, Utica, N. Y., 1894.

Autobiography of Rev. W. R. Evans . . . , Columbus, 1913.

EVATT, HARRIET TORREY (June 24, 1895–), was born in Knoxville, Tenn. She came to Ohio with her parents at the age of sixteen. She studied at Columbus Academy of Fine Arts. Her husband, William S. Evatt, is a lawyer in Columbus; their residence is Worthington. She has written a number of mysteries for children, most of them laid in the French-Canadian Indian country of Canada. She has illustrated all of her books. She published many poems and stories for children before publishing her first book: *The Red Canoe,* Indianapolis, [1940]. WWAW 1

EVENS, JOSEPH (March 8, 1765–Feb. 7, 1849), was born in New Jersey. He was a pioneer settler in Clearcreek Township, Warren County. He spent much of his life fighting for constitutional reform. His first pamphlet was printed by Looker, Palmer & Reynolds, in Cincinnati in 1816; no copy is known to exist. His last effort was published when he was 83 and appears to have received considerable editorial notice.

Propositions Respecting Government, Cincinnati, 1816.

New Mode of Petitioning, Instructing Our Representatives, or Voting for Propositions to Become Law, Warren County, 1831.

A New Mode of Government, Wherein the People Would Govern Themselves by Laws, Originating with Individuals in the Form of Bills . . . , [Warren County], 1847.

EVERETT, HOMER (Jan. 30, 1813–June 22, 1888), was born near Milan, Erie County. After attending school at Lower Sandusky, he read law and was admitted to the Ohio bar in 1841. He practiced for several years and operated a farm near Fremont, Sandusky County. He was postmaster at Lower Sandusky, was mayor of Fremont, was county sheriff and county auditor, and served as state senator, 1867–71. He died at Osborne, Kan., while visiting a daughter.

The History of Sandusky County . . . , Fremont, 1878.

EVERS, CHARLES W. (July 22, 1837–July 29, 1909), journalist, was born in Miltonville, Wood County. After working as a carpenter and teaching school, he entered Oberlin College, but gave up his studies to enlist in the 2nd Kentucky Infantry. He was captured, imprisoned, and after his exchange was discharged in 1864. On his return to Wood County he was elected sheriff. In 1870 he founded the *News* at Bowling Green, a paper later merged with the *Sentinel.* He published *Adventures of Alf Wilson* by John A. Wilson (q.v.) in his newspaper and wrote the introduction to the printed volume. He died in Toledo. A volume of local history was completed after his death by F. J. Oblinger: *Many Incidents and Reminiscences of the Early History of Wood County . . . ,* Bowling Green, 1910.

EVERSON, FLORENCE McCLURG (May 22, 1887–), was born in Vermilion, Erie County. She attended Oberlin College, Cleveland School of Art, and Western Reserve University. Her husband, Howard Farrar Everson, was born Feb. 10, 1888, in Brighton, Lorain County. They now live near Wellington. They have collaborated on several books for young readers, e.g., *The Secret Cave,* New York, [1930].

EVERSON, HOWARD FARRAR. See Florence M. Everson.

EVERSULL, HARRY KELSO (Sept. 20, 1895–Sept. 13, 1953), clergyman and educator, was born in Cincinnati, Hamilton County. He graduated from Wabash College in 1919 and Yale Divinity School in 1922. He was pastor of Walnut Hills Church, Cincinnati, 1924–37 and 1946–53, president of Marietta College, 1937–42, and executive secretary of Cincinnati Council of Churches, 1942–46. His writings include *The Evolution of an Old New England Church . . .* , East Haven, Conn., 1924. WWW 3

EVERTS, ORPHEUS (Dec. 18, 1826–June 19, 1903), physician, was born in Salem, Ind. He studied medicine under his father and received his degree from the Medical College of Indiana in 1846. He began to practice in St. Charles, Ill., devoting his spare time to editing a country newspaper. For a time he served as registrar of the U. S. Land Office at Hudson, Wis. During the Civil War he was surgeon of the 20th Regiment of Indiana Volunteers. Afterward he returned to his practice, giving special attention to psychiatry and neuropathology. He was appointed superintendent of the Indiana Hospital for the Insane in 1868. In 1880 he assumed the management of the Cincinnati Sanitarium and remained its head until his death. He was an alienist of great ability and had a vast reputation as an expert in medico-legal cases. He was called in the trial of Charles J. Guiteau, the murderer of President Garfield. His death occurred in Cincinnati.

O-Na-We-Quah, and Other Poems, LaPorte, Ind., 1856.
The Spectral Bride and Other Poems, LaPorte, Ind., 1857.
Giles & Co.; Or, Views and Interviews Concerning Civilization, Indianapolis, 1878.
Constancy, a Midsummer Night's Idyl, Indianapolis, 1881.
What Shall We Do for the Drunkard? . . . , Cincinnati, 1883.
Facts and Fancies (Light and Heavy). A Metrical Melange, Cincinnati, 1896.
The Cliffords; Or, "Almost Persuaded," Cincinnati, 1898.
Lost Poet, Cincinnati, 1901.
Insanity and the Insane, [Cincinnati?, 1902].

EWART, FRANK CARMAN (Sept. 4, 1871–Sept. 28, 1942), educator, was born in Marietta, Washington County. He graduated from Denison University in 1892 and did graduate work at the University of Chicago and in Europe and Cuba. He taught at Granville Academy, 1893–95, Denison University, 1896–97, Kalamazoo College, 1897–99, and Colgate University, 1899–1939. He annotated Rostand's *L'Aiglon.* His death occurred in Hamilton, N. Y. He wrote *Cuba y las Costumbres Cubanas,* Boston, [1919]. WWNAA 7

EWING, ELMORE ELLIS (Feb. 16, 1840–Oct. 20, 1900), was born in Ewington, Gallia County. He entered Ohio University in 1860, but two years later he enlisted as a private in the 91st O.V.I. He was discharged Dec. 4, 1864, on account of wounds and settled in Portsmouth, where he became a merchant and lived until 1895, when he moved to the Pacific coast. His death occurred in San Francisco.

The Story of the Ninety-first . . . , Portsmouth, 1868.
Bugles and Bells, or Stories Told Again . . . , Cincinnati, 1899.

EWING, HUGH BOYLE (Oct. 31, 1826–June 30, 1905), was born in Lancaster, Fairfield County. He attended the U. S. Military Academy, but did not graduate. In the gold rush of 1849 he made his way to California via New Orleans, Texas, and Mexico. He was ordered by his father, Thomas Ewing, then Secretary of the Interior, to join an expedition to rescue emigrants trapped in the high Sierras. He began the practice of law in St. Louis in 1856 and then moved to Leavenworth, Kan., to practice with his younger brother Thomas, his foster-brother William Tecumseh Sherman (q.v.), and Dan McCook. In 1858 he returned to Ohio to take charge of his father's saltworks. He was commissioned in the Ohio Volunteers on May 6, 1861, and served brilliantly throughout the war. He was breveted major general March 13, 1865, for "meritorious services" and was discharged a year later. He served as U. S. Minister to Holland, 1866–70, and practiced law in Washington, D. C., until 1874, when he retired and returned to Ohio. His death occurred in Lancaster. Besides the titles below he published numerous magazine articles and stories.

A Castle in the Air, New York, 1888.
The Black List; A Tale of Early California, New York, 1893.

EWING, MAX ANDERSON (April 7, 1903–June 16, 1934), was born in Pioneer, Williams County. While attending the University of Michigan, 1920–23, he was music critic for the Ann Arbor *Times-News.* He studied piano in New York, 1924–27, and afterward lived in Europe. His residence abroad furnished the background for a novel, *Going Somewhere,* New York, 1933.

EWING, THOMAS (May 21, 1862–Dec. 7, 1942), lawyer, was born in Leavenworth, Kan., of a family distinguished in Ohio history. His grandfather had been a Senator from Ohio and a cabinet officer under three Presidents; his father distinguished himself in the Civil War and served in Congress as a Representative from Ohio, 1877–81. The third Thomas lived in Lancaster, 1870–81; during this period he studied for two years at University of Wooster. When his father moved to New York City to practice law, he accompanied him and completed his education at Columbia University. He became a successful patent lawyer. He published some poems and translations of Horace, a family history, and *Jonathan; A Tragedy,* New York, 1902. WWW 2

EYSSEN, MARGUERITE FOLSOM (July 25, 1893–), was born in Cleveland, Cuyahoga County, but grew up in Wooster. After graduating from the College of Wooster in 1914, she taught in high schools in Salem, Akron, and Wooster. A resident of Bradford, Pa., she has published fiction in many national magazines and a novel about the development of the petroleum industry in western Pennsylvania: *Go-Devil,* New York, 1947.

F

FAGLEY, FREDERICK LOUIS (May 8, 1879–Aug. 25, 1958), clergyman, was born in Bethel, Clermont County. He graduated from Evansville College, Ind., in 1905, and Oberlin Seminary in 1910. He was pastor of Plymouth Congregational Church, Cincinnati, 1911–14, and executive secretary of the Cincinnati Federation of Churches, 1914–18. He afterward held various executive positions in the Congregational Church. He published several books on religious education and church history, e.g., *Story of the Congregational Christian Churches,* Boston, 1941. WWW 3

FAIRCHILD, EDWARD HENRY (1816–1889), clergyman and educator, brother of James H. and George T. Fairchild (qq.v.), was born in Massachusetts, but was brought to Lorain County in his childhood. Before his graduation from Oberlin College in 1838, he worked in Cincinnati for the education of Negroes—a cause he championed all his life. He was a pastor until 1853, was principal of the Oberlin Preparatory Department, 1853–69, and was president of Berea College, Ky., 1869–89. Some of his addresses were reprinted as pamphlets.

Historical Sketch of Oberlin College, Springfield, 1868.

Berea College, an Interesting History, Berea, Ky., 1875.

FAIRCHILD, GEORGE THOMPSON (Oct. 6, 1838–March 16, 1901), educator and clergyman, brother of James H. and Edward H. Fairchild (qq.v.), was born in Brownhelm, Lorain County. He graduated from Oberlin College in 1862 and the Theological School in 1865. He taught at Michigan Agricultural College, 1865–79, where he was ordained to the Congregational ministry in 1871, was president of Kansas State Agricultural College, 1879–97, and was vice-president of Berea College, 1898–1901. He died in Columbus.

Rural Wealth and Welfare . . . , New York, 1900.

FAIRCHILD, JAMES HARRIS (Nov. 25, 1817–March 19, 1902), educator, brother of Edward H. and George T. Fairchild (qq.v.), was born in Stockbridge, Mass. When James was a year old, his father migrated to the Western Reserve. In 1834, the year after Oberlin College was founded, he entered the freshman class. The remainder of his life was associated with that institution: as a tutor, 1838–42, as professor of languages, of mathematics, and later of moral philosophy and theology, 1842–66 and 1889–98, and as president, 1866–89. He published numerous sermons and articles in addition to the titles below.

The Joint Education of the Sexes. A Report . . . , Oberlin, 1852.

Early Settlement and History of Brownhelm . . . , Oberlin, 1867.

Moral Philosophy; Or, the Science of Obligation, New York, 1869.

Woman's Right to the Ballot, Oberlin, 1870.

Oberlin: The Colony and the College, 1833–1883, Oberlin, 1883.

Elements of Theology, Natural and Revealed, Oberlin, 1892.

FAIRCHILD, LUCIUS (Dec. 27, 1831–May 23, 1896), soldier and diplomat, was born in Kent, Portage County, where his parents had migrated from New England. In 1846 the family moved to Wisconsin, and Lucius' later career is associated chiefly with that state. In 1849 he joined the gold rush to California and remained until 1855. His letters, published in 1931, are his only claim to literary distinction. He served with Wisconsin troops during the Civil War, was governor of Wisconsin for six years, filled various diplomatic posts abroad, and was active in the affairs of the G.A.R.

California Letters of Lucius Fairchild, (Joseph Schafer, ed.), Madison, Wis., 1931.

FAIRFAX, L. Pseud. See Celia L. Connelley.

FAIRFIELD, EDMUND BURKE (Aug. 7, 1821–Nov. 17, 1904), clergyman and educator, was born in Parkersburg, Va., but had several terms of residence in Ohio. He graduated from Oberlin College in 1842 and the seminary in 1845. He was pastor of the Congregational church in Mansfield from 1859 to 1875 and again, after a rather stormy educational career in various states, from 1896 to 1900. He died in Oberlin. He published numerous sermons, addresses, and articles. His review of the Beecher-Tilton case was first published in the Mansfield *Herald: Wickedness in High Places . . . ,* [Mansfield], 1874.

FAISON, MABEL HUBBARD (May 10, 1884–July 3, 1946), educator, was born in Cincinnati, Hamilton County. She graduated from the University of Cincinnati. She married Sherwood B. Faison, a Cincinnati contractor. She was a teacher in the Cincinnati schools for twenty years. She collaborated on several books with Mamie L. Hammel (q.v.), using the pen name Hammel Johnson, and also wrote a book for children: *Scalawag the Scottie,* New York, [1940].

FALCONBRIDGE. Pseud. See Jonathan F. Kelley.

FALKNER, LEONARD (July 7, 1900–), journalist, was born in Cleveland, Cuyahoga County. He attended public schools there and also studied briefly at Ohio State University. He has worked on the New York *Post* and is now feature editor for the New York *World-Telegram & Sun.* He has also been a staff writer for *American Magazine* and has published stories and articles in numerous other magazines. His first novel was a mystery story: *Murder Off Broadway,* New York, [1930]. WWNAA 6

FALSTAFF, JAKE. Pseud. See Herman Fetzer.

FARBER, MILTON L. (July 14, 1902–), lawyer, was born in Philadelphia, but has lived in Ohio since 1910. He graduated from Ohio State University in 1923 and the Law School in 1926. He practices in Columbus. He has written a humorous account of the legal profession: *Blackstone and White Rock,* New York, 1948.

FARGO, LUCILE FOSTER (Oct. 18, 1880–), librarian, born in Lake Mills, Wis., was associated with the school libraries in Akron, 1929–30, and was a member of the Library School faculty, Western Reserve University, 1937–45. She now lives in Berkeley, Calif. In addition to articles and books on library work, she has written *Prairie Girl,* New York, 1937. WW 28

FARIS, LILLIE ANNE (Nov. 13, 1868–March 6, 1945), educator, was born in Lynchburg, Highland County. She graduated from Lynchburg High School at the age of fourteen and afterward taught in the county schools. She taught also in Marietta and in the training school, Ohio University. She was on the editorial board of Standard Publishing Company, Cincinnati, and prepared many texts and manuals for use in Sunday schools. She also published a book about Longfellow: *A Study of the Children's Poet,* Dansville, N. Y., [1904].

FARMER, ELIHU JEROME (1836–Dec. 27, 1900), businessman, was born in Cleveland, Cuyahoga County. In 1864 he married Lydia Hoyt (see Lydia H. F. Painter). An advocate of free silver, he published a book of statistics in addition to the titles below.

The Resources of the Rocky Mountains . . . , Cleveland, 1883.

The Conspiracy against Silver . . . , Cleveland, 1886.

FARMER, JAMES EUGENE (July 5, 1867–May 31, 1915), educator, was born in Cleveland, Cuyahoga County, the son of Lydia H. and Elihu J. Farmer (qq.v.). He graduated from Yale University in 1891 and afterward was a teacher in St. Paul's School, Concord, N. H., 1894–1908. He died in New York City.

Essays on French History . . . , New York, 1897.

The Grenadier; A Story of the Empire, New York, 1898.

The Grand Mademoiselle . . . , New York, 1899.

Brinton Eliot from Yale to Yorktown, New York, 1902.

Versailles and the Court under Louis XIV, New York, 1905.

FARMER, LYDIA HOYT. See Lydia H. F. Painter.

FARNY, HENRY F. (July 15, 1847–Dec. 23, 1916), artist, was born in Alsace-Lorraine. Best known for his paintings of the Indian and the Far West, he seems out of place in this galaxy of writers, great and near great. Yet his claim to inclusion, though tenuous, is none the less authentic, not so much for his one book as for his association with two other Ohio authors. With Lafcadio Hearn (q.v.) he was co-editor of the short-lived and strangely named *Ye Giglampz,* which aspired to be the American *Punch.* For nine weeks during the summer of 1874 these two young men, Farny 27 and Hearn 24, struggled to produce this magazine. Hearn's annotations in his own file, now in the Cincinnati Public Library, show that Farny contributed articles, illustrations, and cartoons. William H. McGuffey (q.v.) and his readers are inseparable from the literary history of the Midwest. For many years they enjoyed a tremendous vogue. Sales, however, were lagging in the 1860s and 1870s, as Eastern competition was capturing the Western market. Farny comes into the picture as illustrator for the edition of 1879. The complete series was revised with Farny as *de facto* art editor. He drew many of the illustrations in the Primer, the six Readers, and the Speller, including title pages, tailpieces, and text illustrations. Of a total of over 300, more than a fourth are by him, and he is the only artist to appear in each of the series. They are authentic McGuffey, in keeping with the elevated moral tone, as they picture the everyday life and familiar activities of the rural Midwest. Leadership was recaptured and all previous sales records were exceeded. That Farny took pride in his share of the work we learn from his statement that he had "introduced a new and decent kind of school book illustration." His one recorded book (probably only twelve copies were issued) would be classed by bookmen as "Curiosa" or "Facetiae."

Carl Vitz

The Lady and the Flea, [Cincinnati, c.1896].

FARNY, MARGARET WITHROW (July 12, 1898–), was born in Cincinnati, Hamilton County. She graduated from Wellesley College. She married Eugene Farney and now is living in San Rafael, Calif. She has written a biography of her father, John Murphy Withrow, Cincinnati surgeon and educator: *Sevenmile Harvest . . . ,* [Caldwell, N. J., 1942].

FARQUHAR, ROBERT. See Ross Farquhar.

FARQUHAR, ROSS (Oct. 30, 1883–July 1, 1938), publisher, was born in Gratis, Preble County. In 1901 he settled in Franklin, where he was associate editor of the Franklin *Chronicle* and in 1928 established the Farquhar Play Bureau, which specialized in plays for amateur groups. He wrote a number of skits, monologues, and plays, some in collaboration with his son, Robert Farquhar (Sept. 20, 1908–), e.g., *Hurricane Hal . . . ,* Franklin, 1928.

FARQUHARSON, MARTHA. Pseud. See Martha Finley.

FAULEY, WILBER FINLEY (Oct. 15, 1872–Dec. 21, 1942), journalist, was born in Fultonham, Muskingum County. He graduated from Fultonham Academy in 1890 and afterward studied music in Philadelphia. He contributed historical articles to the *Bookman* and other national magazines, and served on the staff of several New York newspapers, 1900–09. In 1909 he joined the staff of the New York *Times.* He wrote several melodramas and novels, some of which he published under the name Wilber Fawley, e.g., *Jenny Be Good,* New York, [1919], and *Virginity, a Novel,* New York, [1931].

FAULKNER, EDWARD H. (July 31, 1886–), was born in Lot, Ky. He became a county agent in Ohio in 1918, was in the insurance business, 1926–40, and was farm editor of radio station WTAM, Cleveland, 1943–44. He now lives in Elyria. He has published at least four books on agriculture, including a study of its economic aspects: *Uneasy Money,* Norman, Okla., 1946.

FAUST, SAMUEL D. (Nov. 24, 1852–July 12, 1929), clergyman, was born near Roxbury, Pa. He graduated from Bonebrake Theological Seminary in 1884 and Lebanon Valley College in 1889. Ordained to the ministry of the United Brethren in Christ Church in 1888, he served churches in Pennsylvania and Colorado, 1884–93, and afterward taught at Bonebrake Seminary and was also on the staff of the United Brethren Printing Establishment, Dayton. His writings include *Regeneration,* Dayton, 1902. WWW 1

FAWCETT, MARY HUESTIS (May, 1843–?), was born in Ohio. She attended Mount Pleasant Seminary. For many years she contributed both prose and verse to periodicals.

Poems, Cincinnati, 1880.

Marguerite; Or, the Quaker Minister's Daughter, Chicago, 1906.

FAWLEY, WILBER. See Wilber F. Fauley.

FEATHER, WILLIAM (Aug. 25, 1889–), publisher, was born in Jamestown, N. Y. He graduated from Western Reserve University in 1910, was a reporter on the Cleveland *Press,* 1910–15, and organized his own printing and publishing company in 1916. He published *William Feather's Magazine* and a number of books and pamphlets, e.g., *The Ideals and Follies of Business,* Cleveland, [1927]. WW 30

FEE, WILLIAM INGRAM (Feb. 15, 1817–1900), clergyman, was born in Felicity, Clermont County, a town founded by his father and grandfather. After graduating from Augusta College, Ky., in 1842, he was licensed to preach by the Methodist church. He served on circuits in southern Ohio, West Virginia, and Kentucky, 1842–52, and afterward served churches in Hillsboro, Cincinnati, Dayton, Springfield, Piqua, and other communities. Both of the books listed below are autobiographical.

Bringing the Sheaves . . . , Cincinnati, 1896.
Garnered Sheaves . . . , Cincinnati, 1900.

FELCH, WILLIAM FARRAND (Aug. 30, 1855–June 8, 1930), journalist, was born in Columbus, Franklin County. He was educated in the public schools of Columbus and Salem. He wrote *Memorial History of the Felch Family in America,* which is said to have been published in five parts, but only two are known to exist. In 1884 he founded the *Western Critic* in Columbus, which expired after the appearance of a few numbers; equally short-lived was the *Inland Monthly,* which appeared the following year.

Legends and Lyrics, Columbus, 1882.

FELL, FREDERICK. Pseud. See Edmond M. Hamilton.

FELTER, HARVEY WICKES (June 15, 1865–Oct. 27, 1927), physician, was born in Rensselaerville, N. Y. He received his M.D. degree from Eclectic Medical Institute, Cincinnati, in 1888, began practice in Cincinnati in 1889, and joined the Institute faculty in 1891. He wrote a number of medical books, including *History of the Eclectic Medical Institute . . . ,* Cincinnati, 1902. WWW 1

FENN, PERCY THOMAS (Oct. 23, 1892–), educator, was born in Yonkers, N. Y. He graduated from Hobart College in 1915 and from Harvard University (Ph.D.) in 1922. He has been on the political science faculty of Oberlin College since 1927. Besides professional articles, he has published *The Development of the Constitution,* New York, [1948]. WW 30

FENNELL, MARK (May 6, 1844–April 30, 1931), was born in England. He worked in a Cleveland rolling mill and died in that city. His book, copies of which are now extremely scarce, maintains that the steam engine was seen by Biblical prophets in their visions.

The Steam Engine Fulfilling Prophecy . . . , Cleveland, 1891.

FENNEMAN, NEVIN M. (Dec. 26, 1865–July 4, 1945), geologist, was born in Lima, Allen County. He graduated from Heidelberg College in 1883 and the University of Chicago (Ph.D.) in 1901. He was a member of the University of Cincinnati faculty from 1907 to 1937. He wrote numerous government bulletins, professional articles, and textbooks, and *Geology of Cincinnati and Vicinity,* Columbus, 1916. WWW 2

FENNER, CORNELIUS GEORGE (Dec. 20, 1822–Jan. 4, 1847), clergyman, was born in Providence, R. I. He was a Unitarian minister, and for a time before his death in Cincinnati he occupied the pulpit of James Handasyd Perkins (q.v.). He published *Poems of Many Moods,* Boston, 1846.

FENNER, MRS. JESSE A. See Marian W. Wildman.

FENTON, FRANK E. (Feb. 13, 1904–), was born in Liverpool, England, and lived in Columbus for 22 years. He attended Columbus schools, graduated in journalism from Ohio State University in 1927, and afterward became a scenario writer in Hollywood. He now lives in Los Angeles. He has published stories and articles in various magazines and a novel: *A Place in the Sun,* New York, [1942].

FERGUSON, CHARLES D. (1832– ?), was born in Aurora, Portage County. In 1849 he crossed the plains to California, where he worked in the gold fields until 1852, when he went to Australia. There he drifted from one mining camp to another. With the exploits of the horse-tamer John T. Rarey (q.v.) in England filling the newspapers, Ferguson set himself up as an "Australian Rarey" in 1857 and appears to have had considerable success. After drifting from one job to another, he finally returned to Ohio in 1883 and was living in Farmington in 1888. His narrative of his experiences, though a bit disjointed, is entertaining and valuable.

The Experiences of a Forty-niner during Thirty-four Years Residence in California and Australia, (Frederick T. Wallace, ed.), Cleveland, 1888.

FERGUSON, JOHN BOHN (June 10, 1879–), clergyman, was born in Camden, Preble County. After graduating from Miami University in 1903 and from Princeton Theological School in 1907, he was ordained to the Presbyterian ministry and served churches in Ohio, Indiana, and the Philippine Islands. Now retired, he lives in Indianapolis, Ind. He has written an account of his service with the Y.M.C.A. during World War I and articles and books on religious topics, e.g., *Worship in the Church . . . ,* [Philadelphia, 1938].

FERGUSON, JOHN DELANCEY (Nov. 13, 1888–), educator, born in Scottsville, N. Y., was a member of the English departments of three Ohio colleges: Heidelberg, 1914–18, Ohio Wesleyan, 1918–30, and Western Reserve, 1930–44. He has published a number of articles, textbooks, and biographies, e.g., *Mark Twain: Man and Legend,* Indianapolis, [1943]. WW 29

FERM, VERGILIUS TURE ANSELM (Jan. 6, 1896–), educator, was born in Sioux City, Iowa. He has been on the philosophy faculty of the College of Wooster since 1927. A prolific writer, he has published many articles and books, e.g., *What Can We Believe?,* New York, [1948]. WW 30

FERNALD, JAMES CHAMPLIN (Aug. 18, 1838–Nov. 10, 1918), clergyman and editor, was born in Portland, Maine. After graduating from Harvard University in 1860 and Newton Theological Institution in 1863, he was ordained to the Baptist ministry. He served Ohio churches in Clyde, McConnelsville, Galion, Springfield, and Garretsville, 1876–89. He was an ardent prohibitionist, and his writings in this field caught the attention of Isaac K. Funk (q.v.), who took him to New York as an assistant editor of the *Homiletic Review.* He later served on the staff of the *Standard Dictionary;* he also compiled a number of English textbooks.

The Economics of Prohibition, New York, 1890.
The New Womanhood, New York, 1891.
English Synonyms and Antonyms . . . , New York, 1896.
The Imperial Republic, New York, 1898.
The Spaniard in History, New York, 1898.
True Motherhood, New York, 1900.
Scientific Sidelights . . . , New York, 1903.

FERRIL, HELEN RAY (Oct. 31, 1897–), journalist, was born in Columbus, Franklin County, the daughter of Franklin A. Ray, an engineering professor at Ohio State University for over fifty years. She graduated in music from Denison University in 1918 and completed nurse's training at St. Luke's Hospital, Chicago, in 1921. She and her husband, Thomas H. Ferril, own and publish the *Rocky Mountain Herald* in Denver, Colo. A column that she wrote for that newspaper led to the publication of a humorous volume: *The Indoor Birdwatcher's Manual,* New York, [1950].

FERRIS, THEODORE N., JR. (Feb. 28, 1920–), editor, was born in Cleveland, Cuyahoga County. He graduated from Western Reserve University in 1946 and served for a time as associate editor of *American Fruit Grower.* He is now editor of publications, Fenn College. He has published a volume of poems: *Man's World,* Chicago, 1948.

FESS, SIMEON DAVIDSON (Dec. 11, 1861–Dec. 23, 1936), educator and legislator, was born near Harrod, Allen County. Supporting himself by teaching country schools, he attended Ohio Northern University. Immediately after his graduation in 1889, he was appointed professor of American history. He graduated from the Ohio Northern law school in 1894 and from 1896 to 1900 was dean of the school. From 1907 to 1917 he was president of Antioch College. He was a member of the House of Representatives, 1912–22, and the Senate, 1922–34. He was nationally prominent as a spokesman for the conservative wing of the Republican Party and for the most uncompromising prohibitionists. He published several textbooks, many of his Congressional speeches, and *The History of Political Theory and Party Organization in the United States . . . ,* Dansville, N. Y., [1907]. DAB 22

FETTERMAN, JOSEPH L. (March 20, 1897–April 12, 1953), physician and educator, born in Russia, was brought to Cleveland by his parents in 1904. He attended Cleveland schools and graduated from Western Reserve University in 1918 and the School of Medicine in 1921. He served on the Western Reserve faculty and during World War II was a major in the Medical Corps. He published two books on neuropsychiatry and *The Spinal Column, a Series of Medical Sayings,* Cleveland, 1940.

FETZER, HERMAN (Jake Falstaff) (June 24, 1899–Jan. 17, 1936), was born in Summit County. The rich black muck of the celery swamps around Copley produced Jake Falstaff, whose enduring love for that good earth distilled itself into poetry and prose that have the authentic mark of rightness and permanence. To Swiss and Alsatian parents he was born Herman Fetzer on a farm in Maple Valley, now part of Akron. In elementary school at Maple Valley there was fortunately a wise teacher who advised the boy who wrote poems about death at the age of six to write instead about the steamy summer sun on the celery beds, the frosty creak of a barn door in winter, and the local tales of Dick Johnson and Tecumseh in the neighborhood mingling with echoes of central European folklore around the farm firesides. "I elected in the wisdom of my boyhood to be a peasant," he wrote. And his later writing career as Jake Falstaff he considered a peasant accomplishment, "for it consists in the telling of tales." The boy went to school at Akron's South and West High Schools, but spent less than a month at the University of Akron, deliberately deciding to go directly to books for his education, as he went directly to newspaper work to earn a living. After normal reportorial apprenticeship, he began in 1920 to write a column on the Akron *Times,* "Pippins and Cheese." Except for a brief interlude in Florida, he wrote this column for the *Times* for ten years and continued it for four more in the *Beacon-Journal.* He also wrote a portion of the *Centennial History of Akron* (1925). His literary stature and reputation steadily increased, and Franklin P. Adams invited him to New York to write a column in the *World* replacing his famous "Conning Tower" during F.P.A.'s vacation. This was the period of the publication of Falstaff's first full-length books: *The Book of Rabelais* (1928) and *Reini Kugel, Lover of This Earth* (1929). Together with the immediate success of his column in the *World,* these brought many offers of a New York career. Jake refused to consider them. "Forgive me, hearty and amiable city," his poem "Valedictory" began, "if, having beheld your beauty, I go back to my own places." Back he went, this time to the Cleveland *Press* to resume his column "Pippins and Cheese" and to do rewrites and special features. There his associates knew him as a superlative newspaper craftsman who enjoyed the rough and tumble of the city room. While he was writing his books, his column, and a series of poems and articles for *The New Yorker, Collier's,* the *Nation,* the *Ladies' Home Journal,* and other magazines, he always did his share of the routine production of the newsroom as well. While still in Akron on the *Times,* he married Hazel Stevenson, a fellow staff-member. He died suddenly on Jan. 17, 1936, of pneumonia, just over 35 years old. Carl Sandburg was only one of many who felt that Falstaff's writing career, fruitful and authentically productive though it was, had really only begun—that his poems were "the real thing," with "a curious finality about them." His last books were posthumous, largely made up from his newspaper and magazine writing collected and edited by his widow. They stand as proof of the abiding excellence of the whole body of that work, and of even greater promise cut off by death. Posthumous publications were *Alice in Justice-land* (1937), *The Bulls of Spring: The Selected Poems of Jake Falstaff* (1937), *How Reini Kugel Went to Meet the Spring* (1938), *Jacoby's Corners* (1940), *The Big Snow, Christmas at Jacoby's Corners* (1941), and *Come Back to Wayne County* (1942).

Willis Thornton

FEUER, LEONI (May 23, 1903–), rabbi, born in Hazelton, Pa., attended Cleveland public schools, the University of Cincinnati, and Hebrew Union College. Ordained a rabbi in 1927, he served in Cleveland until 1935 and since then at Collingwood Avenue Temple, Toledo. He has written several books on the Jewish religion, e.g., *On Being a Jew,* New York, 1947.

FICK, HENRY H. (Aug. 16, 1849–March 23, 1935), educator, was born in Leubeck, Germany. He came to America in 1864. He received his Ph.D. at Ohio University in 1891. He served as a teacher in the Cincinnati public schools, 1870–92, as principal of the Sixth District School, 1892–1901, as assistant superintendent of public schools, 1901–03, and as supervisor of German from 1903 until his retirement in 1915. He wrote a number of textbooks relating to the teaching of history and literature and drawing. He edited *Erziehungsblaetter,* 1889–1900, and *Jung Amerika,* 1901–06.

Aesthetic Culture. An Essay, [Cincinnati?], 1881.

The Dance of Death. A Dissertation, New York, 1887.

In Freud und Leid, Cincinnati, 1914.

FIEBERGER, GUSTAVE JOSEPH (May 9, 1858–Oct. 18, 1939), army officer, was born in Akron, Summit County. As an instructor at the U. S. Military Academy from 1896 to 1922, he wrote a number of textbooks and manuals for use by cadets, e.g., *Campaigns of the American Civil War,* [West Point, N. Y., 1914]. WWW 1

FIELD, ALFRED GRIFFITH (Nov. 7, 1850–April 3, 1921), actor, was born Alfred G. Hatfield in Leesburg, Va. He was reared in Brownsville, Pa., and at an early age he became a minstrel show performer and actor and changed his last name to Field. In the 1880s he settled in Columbus, where he spent the remainder of his life. He was manager of Al G. Field's Greater Minstrels and also operated a farm. He wrote an account of his life: *Watch Yourself Go By . . .* , Columbus, 1912. OBB

FIELD, HOPE (Mrs. Richard P.) (Aug. 5, 1905–), was born in Baltimore, Md., and lived in Cincinnati from 1923 until 1942. Under the pen name Field Williamson, she published *I Cried All Night,* New York, [1942]. Under her own name she published other novels, including one that has part of its action in Cincinnati: *Stormy Present,* New York, 1942.

FIELD, JASPER NEWTON (March 25, 1855–March 21, 1929), clergyman and educator, was born in Union County. After graduating from Denison University, he served as pastor of Baptist churches in Canton and in other states. A founder of Redlands University in California, he served as its first president, 1909–14. Besides magazine articles and separate addresses, he published a collection of talks: *Isms, Fads & Fakes . . .* , Indianapolis, [1904].

FIELD, LOUISE A. See Adah L. Saalfield.

FIELD, SARA BARD (Sept. 1, 1882–), was born in Cincinnati, Hamilton County, but her family moved to Detroit, Mich., when she was three years old. After graduating from Western Reserve University, she married Rev. Ehrgott, a Baptist minister, and with him went to Burma. After returning to the United States, her husband was a pastor in Cleveland. When she and her husband became Socialists, the congregation's dismayed protests led to their moving to Portland, Oreg. Here she met and later married the poet Charles Erskine Scott Wood, whose poems she has edited. She also lectured on women's suffrage and other subjects. She is living in Los Gatos, Calif. She has published several books of poems, e.g., *Darkling Plain,* New York, 1936. TCA

FILLER, LOUIS (May 2, 1912–), educator, was born in Odessa, Russia. After graduating from Temple University in 1934 and from Columbia University (Ph.D.) in 1943, he worked for the War Department for two years. He has been a member of the history department, Antioch College, since 1946. He has published several books, e.g., *Crusaders for American Liberalism,* New York, [1939]. DAS 3

FILLMORE, JOHN COMFORT (Feb. 4, 1843–Aug. 14, 1898), pioneer musical educator, was born in Connecticut. He graduated from Oberlin College in 1865 and after a year's study in Leipzig was an instructor in the Oberlin music department, 1867–68. He wrote several books about music history and education, including *Pianoforte Music: Its History, with Biographical Sketches and Critical Estimates of Its Greatest Masters,* Chicago, 1883.

FILLMORE, PARKER HOYSTED (Sept. 21, 1878–June 5, 1944), was born in Cincinnati, Hamilton County. He graduated from the University of Cincinnati in 1901. He was a teacher in southern Luzon, Philippine Islands, 1901–04, and a member of the bankinghouse of W. H. Fillmore and Co., Cincinnati, 1904–18. Moving to New York City, he lived in a Czech settlement and began collecting Czechoslovakian legends and fairy tales. He died in Amherst, Va. He wrote a number of books for children, including several volumes of fairy tales from various nations, e.g., *Czechoslovak Fairy Tales,* New York, 1919. WW 21

FILSON, DAVIDSON (June 5, 1829–March 8, 1899), was born in Franklin County, Pa., and came to Steubenville in 1843. There he conducted a book and periodical store until 1863, when he became interested in photography and established himself in that business. He wrote his history of the local schools while serving as a member of the Steubenville Board of Education. His death occurred in Steubenville.

Steubenville Public Schools . . . , Steubenville, 1892.

FILSON, JOHN (c.1741– ?), was born in Pennsylvania. Around 1782 he journeyed down the Ohio River to Kentucky. While teaching school in Lexington, he wrote a life of Daniel Boone, which was published as an appendix to the book listed below and later republished in many editions. He traveled throughout Kentucky gathering material for his book and also working as a surveyor. Around 1788 he became a partner of Matthias Denham of New Jersey, who had purchased from John Cleves Symmes 800 acres north of the Ohio River. Filson laid out the streets of a town and also supplied its name—Losantiville. The town he mapped and helped to found became Cincinnati. While exploring the Symmes Purchase, he disappeared; the belief on the frontier was that he had been killed by Indians.

The Discovery, Settlement and Present State of Kentucke . . . , Wilmington, [Del.], 1784.

FINDLEY, SAMUEL (Oct. 26, 1818–Nov. 2, 1889), clergyman and educator, was born in West Middletown, Pa. His father made a missionary trip into Ohio in 1818 to establish churches in Guernsey County, and in 1824 he moved his family to Washington, Guernsey County. After graduating from Franklin College in 1839, Samuel studied in the seminary at Meadville, Pa. In 1841 he was licensed by the Second Presbytery of Ohio. He was president of Madison College, Antrim, and served as a school principal and as pastor in Troy, Dayton, Chillicothe, and several other Ohio communities. At the time of his death he was pastor of Roxabell Presbyterian Church. Besides the title below, several of his sermons were published.

Rambles among the Insects, Philadelphia, 1878.

FINDLEY, SAMUEL (Dec. 1, 1831–May 7, 1908), educator, was born on a farm near New Concord, Muskingum County. He attended Muskingum College and taught in the schools of Xenia, Columbus, and Cleveland. In 1868 he was named superintendent of Akron public schools, a position he held for fifteen years. He also edited the *Ohio Educational Monthly,* 1882–96.

The Teacher and His Work, Akron, 1899.

FINGER, CHARLES JOSEPH (Dec. 25, 1869–Jan. 8, 1941), was born in Willesden, England, and came to America in 1887. He traveled in South America, Africa, the Klondike, and Mexico. From 1913 to 1920 he was general manager of a group of Ohio railways. A prolific writer, he published adventure stories, juvenile books, and several Haldeman-Julius Little Blue Books. An example of his 35 publications is *David Livingstone; Explorer and Publisher,* New York, 1927. WWW 2

FINK, BRUCE (Dec. 22, 1861–July 10, 1927), botanist, was born in Blackberry, Ill. He became professor of botany at Miami University in 1906. His writings include numerous technical articles and books on lichens, textbooks, and a widely read discussion of the tobacco problem: *Tobacco,* New York, [1915]. WWW 1

FINK, OLLIE E. (July 30, 1898–), educator, was born in Irville (Nashport), Muskingum County. After graduating from Muskingum College in 1922, he was a teacher and principal in Zanesville and was curriculum supervisor in charge of conservation, State Department of Education. Now retired, he lives at Hidden Acres Farm, Zanesville. He has written articles and reports on conservation and collaborated with Homer L. Royer (q.v.) in writing *Buckeye Tales,* Chicago, [1945].

FINKELSTEIN, LOUIS (June 14, 1895–), rabbi and educator, was born in Cincinnati, Hamilton County. He graduated from the College of the City of New York in 1915 and Columbia University (Ph.D.) in 1918. He was rabbi of a New York City synagogue, 1919–31, and since 1920 has been associated with Talmud Jewish Seminary—its president from 1940 to 1951 and its chancellor since 1951. He has published numerous articles, reviews, and books, e.g., *Jewish Self-government in the Middle Ages,* New York, 1924. WW 30

FINLAYSON, GRACE McCONAHY REININGER (June 17, 1885–), was born in Van Wert, Van Wert County, and now lives in Los Angeles. She graduated from Van Wert High School and later attended the University of Arizona and the University of California. Under the pen name Grace Reini, she has published plays, poems, articles, and stories, e.g., a one-act comedy, *Vines Keep Out the Sun . . .* , Boston, [1938]. WWAW 1

FINLEY, JAMES BRADLEY (July 1, 1781–Sept. 6, 1856), clergyman, was born in North Carolina, the son of a Methodist missionary and teacher. The family later settled near Chillicothe. Though he studied medicine to please his father and was admitted to practice in 1800, James was determined to be a hunter. His conversion to Methodism in 1801, however, led him into the ministry. He entered the Ohio Conference in 1809 and rode long, difficult circuits. He was a missionary to the Wyandots, 1821–29, and chaplain of the Ohio penitentiary, 1845–49. The intervening and subsequent periods were devoted to the active ministry. His books were drawn chiefly from his journals. He died in Cincinnati.

History of the Wyandot Mission, at Upper Sandusky . . . , Cincinnati, 1840.

Memorials of Prison Life, (B. F. Tefft, ed.), Cincinnati, 1851.

Autobiography of Rev. James B. Finley . . . , (W. P. Strickland, ed.), Cincinnati, 1853.

Sketches of Western Methodism . . . , (W. P. Strickland, ed.), Cincinnati, [1854].

Life among the Indians; Or, Personal Reminiscences and Historical Incidents Illustrative of Indian Life and Character, (D. W. Clark, ed.), Cincinnati, 1857.

FINLEY, JEAN. Pseud. See Ella D. Lee.

FINLEY, JOHN (Jan. 11, 1797–Dec. 23, 1866), "the father of western humorous poetry," was born in Brownsburg, Va. He came to Cincinnati around 1816 and apparently moved to Indiana in 1820, although he was married in Yellow Springs in 1826. He held several public offices in Indiana, wrote many poems for newspapers, and published one book: *The Hoosier's Nest, and Other Poems,* Cincinnati, 1860.

FINLEY, MARTHA (April 26, 1828–Jan. 30, 1909), was born in Chillicothe, Ross County. Around 1834 her parents moved to South Bend, Ind., where she was educated. In 1854 the family moved to the East, where she taught school and wrote Sunday school books, some under the name Farquharson, the Gaelic version of Finley. In 1876 she moved to Elkton, Md., where she passed the remainder of her life. It would be extraordinarily simple to dismiss all of her books by baldly stating that as literature they were and are utterly and completely worthless; that they are mawkish, bigoted, maudlin, and untrue; unreadable, boring, and (this above all) incredibly unfair to the children who, by parental injunction or other necessity, were obliged to read them. And by "other necessity" I mean specifically the lack of other, superior, reading matter designed for the juvenile mind. It would be simple, and not unfashionable, if you please, so to dismiss one of the most read of our native American nineteenth-century authors; it would also be unjust. For, to be as angelically reasonable as Miss Finley's own immortal Elsie Dinsmore, one must not condemn Miss Finley but rather her era; if her output wasn't what those times demanded (and the demand for her books was huge and still continues but in a far lesser degree) the Elsie Dinsmore series couldn't have survived. If Martha Finley had been born not in 1828 as she was, but in 1898 instead, she would have risen to an eminence no less than the one she achieved. For the later generation she might have turned her talent to the creation of soap operas or inspirational novels, or both, which, whether the present era chooses to believe it or not, are no less shoddy than Miss Finley's *Clouds and Sunshine; Or, the Faith Brightened Pathway* and *Willie Elton, the Little Boy Who Loved Jesus,* both of which, with other titles, flowed from the Finley pen before Martha Finley hit the mother lode in 1867 and came up with Elsie Dinsmore. Unless one is prepared to condemn virtually every American juvenile author of (more or less) the pre-1865 period, one may not in justice sneer at Martha Finley, who was, after all, nothing more than the reflection of her generation's avowed, not actual, attitude toward life. This is not to say that Martha Finley's books are therefore and of themselves worth reading; they are not, at least not now. But they are, and should be preserved as, manifestations of a common adult attitude toward children in the mid-nineteenth century; and, further, as concrete examples of what a not unimportant section of the adult American mind considered the ideal approach to the spiritual life both now and hereafter. The Finley books, in a real sense, were intended as moral guides for the young. As to whether or not the adults of that period felt themselves obliged to point up the preachment by personal example need not concern us here and now; that is a question for the social historians and, more to the point, too close an examination may embarrass the shades of our elders. The fact of the matter is that there was painfully little nondidactic or nonmoralizing reading matter for the juvenile when Martha Finley first broke into print; and by comparison with much that was then current and accepted, her output wasn't too bad—which is the faintest sort of praise where no praise is intended. It wasn't until the 1860s that there was even the suggestion of the richness that was to come. Until that time the material produced specifically for the young was generally of such an impossible nature that children were swift to turn to books written not as juveniles but, rather, as adult books. It is no accident that such adult works as *The Last of the Mohicans, Two Years before the Mast,* and *The California and Oregon Trail* found ready acceptance among the young—for whom they were not written, and that a child of that period read these and their like by choice and not by compulsion. The child also read, and these fall into the same category, *Robinson Crusoe, The Adventures of Gil Blas,* and *The Autobiography of Baron Trenck.* We have this on the authority of one who was there: no less an observer than Thomas Bailey Aldrich, who, in his autobiographical *The Story of a Bad Boy* (1870) declared that as a boy the latter three were on his preferred reading list. Nor was it an accident that such publications as the Beadle Dime Novels, which, too, were intended for adults and not children, found so wide a market among eager young readers. So far as the youngsters were concerned, there was nothing else to read save a rare juvenile book such as Goulding's *The Young Marooners* (1852) and pitifully few others written with the accent on entertainment and with moral education either wholly lacking or well concealed. It was an age in which masses of juvenile books were issued by the American Sunday-School Union, the Presbyterian Board of Publication, and other worthy organizations. No great imagination is needed to sense the type of material these organizations were prepared to sponsor; but if imagination fails, herewith are the guiding principles as adopted by the American Sunday-School Union. (Incidentally, appearance of this notice on the copyright page of the Union's publications must have been taken as fair enough warning by many a nineteenth-century youngster.) The notice:

> No books are published by the American Sunday-School Union without the sanction of the Committee of Publication, consisting of fourteen members, from the following denominations of Christians, viz. Baptist, Methodist, Congregational, Episcopal, Presbyterian, Lutheran, and Reformed Dutch. Not more than three of the members can be of the same denomination, and no book can be published to which any [*sic!*] member of the Committee shall object.

With shackles such as these the wonder is not that Martha Finley wrote as she did, but that she wrote at all. However, it was under such sterile auspices that her first book was produced: *Ella Clinton; Or, by Their Fruits Ye Shall Know Them,* issued in Philadelphia by the Presbyterian Board of Publication in 1856. The Board, we may be certain, operated in the same antiseptic vacuum set up by the Union with (perhaps) a few embellishments of its own. One may argue that with the passage of time and the emerging example of the *St. Nicholas* group of juvenile authors, Martha Finley might have been inspired to do something better than her Elsie Dinsmore series; but this is to suggest that she had an ability which her books indicate she did not have. Or it might be that having established a market (and a large market it was) for her particular brand of pap, she saw no reason to change her formula. Martha Finley, like the bustle, was the product of her time. She is to be ridiculed no more, or less, than the authors of the slush currently found acceptable by no small portion of our adult population which develops callouses listening to soap operas or grows purblind absorbing the immeasurable spate of trash spewed forth by certain presses. Martha Finley is the spiritual ancestor of some our most popular writers. It seems fitting to append a few extracts from Martha Finley's work—a few will be ample, more than that would work a cruel and unusual punishment. The first, most naturally, is from one of the Elsie books, *Mildred's Married Life and a Winter with Elsie Dinsmore* (1882):

> One stormy afternoon as the little girls sat together in Elsie's dressing-room, pleasantly busied in millinery and mantua-making for the family of dolls, Annie said, "I read *Oliver Twist* while we were at Holly Hall."
>
> Elsie looked up in surprise. "Did you? Would your father and mother let you read such books?"
>
> "Well," returned Annie, blushing, "I never heard them mention *Oliver Twist,* at all, and I peeped into it one day and found it so interesting I just couldn't help going on and reading the whole story. I thought why shouldn't I read what Milly and Brother Charlie and Cousin Horace and Cousin Rose do?"
>
> "Papa says," returned Elsie slowly, "that I might as well ask why baby may not eat everything that we older ones do."
>
> "I suppose he means that our minds haven't cut their teeth yet," said Annie, laughing. "But don't you wish you were grown up enough to read novels?"
>
> "I don't know; I'd like to read them dearly well, but I love to be papa's little girl and sit on his knee."
>
> "You'll do that when you're grown up," remarked Annie with a wise nod of her pretty head. "I'll tell you the story of *Oliver Twist* if you want me to."
>
> The offer was a tempting one, Elsie did want so very much to know what became of Oliver finally, and all about several of the other characters in whom she had become interested; for one minute she hesitated; then said firmly, "It wouldn't be right for me to hear it, Annie dear, without papa's leave, and that I shouldn't even dare to ask. But I thank you all the the same."
>
> "Elsie, you are so good and obedient that you often make me feel ashamed of myself," Annie said, with a look of hearty,

affectionate admiration into her cousin's face.

The fair face crimsoned . . .

The observant reader might be permitted to inquire how, without reading *Oliver Twist,* Elsie came to know so much about Oliver and the "other characters in whom she had become interested"; but let us not inquire and take a brief passage from *Elsie Dinsmore* (1867), the first of the whole noble series:

> " 'Man looketh upon the outward appearance, but the Lord pondereth the heart,' " said [seventeen-year-old] Rose, gently. "No, dear Adelaide, you are mistaken; for I can truly say 'mine iniquities have gone over my head as a cloud, and my transgressions as a thick cloud.' Every duty has been stained with sin, every motive impure, every thought unholy. From my earliest existence, God has required the undivided love of my whole heart, soul, strength, and mind; and so far from yielding it, I lived at enmity with Him, and rebellion against His government, until within the last two years. For seventeen years He has showered blessing upon me, giving me life, health, strength, friends, and all that was necessary for my happiness; and for fifteen of those years I returned Him nothing but ingratitude and rebellion. For fifteen years I rejected His offers of pardon and reconciliation, turned my back upon the Saviour of sinners, and resisted all the strivings of God's Holy Spirit, and will you say that I am not a great sinner?" Her voice quivered . . .

In 1870 Louisa May Alcott issued her successful *An Old-Fashioned Girl.* Soon thereafter Martha Finley published *An Old-Fashioned Boy* and thereby, in spite of her moral preachments, gave a curious demonstration of an ability to cut an occasional corner. In format the Finley book was a frank imitation of the Alcott production, even to the tooling of the binding. Miss Alcott was properly incensed and promptly and publicly protested. But imitation or not, herewith an extract from *An Old-Fashioned Boy.* The speakers are Fred Landon, age seventeen, and his sister Elena, age fourteen, who thus discuss the second marriage of their widowed mother:

> He dashed away a tear with the back of his hand as he spoke. "But," he went on, "I think you mistake in fancying that this sudden second marriage proves her love to our father to be less than we believed. Our father was like a strong, sturdy oak, our mother a beautiful vine clinging lovingly to him for support; and when death tore them rudely asunder, the lovely tendrils, reaching out in their blind helpless agony, laid hold of a tree of a less noble kind, vainly hoping to find in it another oak. No, it was only because she could not live without what she had lost in being separated from my [*sic!*] father, that she did this which has brought such grief to us."
>
> "And yet we ought not to grieve if it has added to her happiness," murmured Elena.
>
> "If!" sighed Fred, turning away his face; "ah, that doubt is the thorn whose sting is the sharpest with me now, sister. The more I see of Mr. Rush, the more thoroughly convinced I am that he is not the sort of man to make a gentle, sensitive, refined woman like my [*sic!*] mother, happy; and—I fear she is beginning to find it out. I have been with her half the afternoon, and I am sure she is not happy; and we, sister, must do all we can to supply to her all that she finds lacking in her husband—the tender protecting love and care our father ever lavished upon her."
>
> "Oh, Fred, it breaks my heart to think of the possibility of what you suspect!" cried Elena, with a fresh burst of tears. "Flowers could as well live without sunshine as our precious mother without love. But she shall never be without it while her son and daughter live. Ah, if she had only been satisfied with what they could give! We were so happy here together; and now the dear home must be forsaken, and all for what?"

Curtain!

Jacob Blanck

Ella Clinton . . . , Philadelphia, 1856.

Marion Harvey . . . , Philadelphia, [1857].

Clouds and Sunshine . . . , Philadelphia, 1859.

Mysie's Work and How She Did It . . . , Philadelphia, [1864].

Willie Elton, the Little Boy Who Loved Jesus . . . , Philadelphia, [1864].

Black Steve, or the Strange Warning . . . , Philadelphia, [1865].

Elsie Dinsmore . . . , Philadelphia, [1867].

Elsie's Holidays at Roselands . . . , New York, [1868].

Casella . . . , Philadelphia, [1869].

Lilian; Or, Did She Do Right? . . . , Philadelphia, [1871].

An Old-Fashioned Boy . . . , Philadelphia, [1871].

Wanted—A Pedigree . . . , Philadelphia, [1871].

Elsie's Girlhood . . . , New York, [1872].

Our Fred . . . , New York, [1874].
Elsie's Womanhood . . . , New York, [1875].
Elsie's Motherhood . . . , New York, [1876].
Signing the Contract, and What It Cost . . . , New York, [1879].
Elsie's Widowhood . . . , New York, [1880].
Mildred and Elsie . . . , New York, [1881].
Grandmother Elsie . . . , New York, [1882].
Mildred's Married Life . . . , New York, [1882].
Elsie's New Relations . . . , New York, [1883].
Elsie at Nantucket . . . , New York, [1884].
Mildred at Home . . . , New York, [1884].
The Two Elsies . . . , New York, [1885].
Elsie's Kith and Kin . . . , New York, [1886].
Mildred's Boys and Girls . . . , New York, [1886].
The Thorn in the Nest . . . , New York, [1886].
Elsie's Friends at Woodburn . . . , New York, [1887].
Christmas with Grandma Elsie . . . , New York, [1888].
Elsie and the Raymonds . . . , New York, [1889].
Elsie Yachting with the Raymonds . . . , New York, [1890].
Elsie's Vacation and After Events . . . , New York, [1891].
Elsie at Viamede . . . , New York, [1892].
Elsie at Ion . . . , New York, [1893].
The Tragedy of Wild River Valley . . . , New York, [1893].
Elsie at the World's Fair . . . , New York, [1894].
Mildred's New Daughter . . . , New York, [1894].
Elsie's Journey on Inland Waters . . . , New York, [1895].
Elsie at Home . . . , New York, [1897].
Elsie on the Hudson and Elsewhere . . . , New York, [1898].
Twiddledetwit; A Fairy Tale . . . , New York, [1898].
Elsie in the South . . . , New York, [1899].
Elsie's Young Folks in Peace and War . . . , New York, [1900].
Elsie's Winter Trip . . . , New York, [1902].
Elsie and Her Loved Ones . . . , New York, [1903].
Elsie and Her Namesakes . . . , New York, [1905].

FINLEY, RUTH EBRIGHT (Mrs. Emmet) (Sept. 25, 1884–Sept. 24, 1955), was born near Akron, Summit County. She attended Oberlin College and Buchtel College. She worked in an editorial capacity on numerous periodicals, including the Cleveland *Press,* 1911, Scripps-Howard newspapers, 1912–18, Washington, D. C., *Herald,* 1919, and others. She died in Glen Cove, N. Y. Her publications include numerous articles and a biography: *The Lady of Godey's, Sarah Josepha Hale,* Philadelphia, 1931. WWW 3

FINN, FRANCIS JAMES (Oct. 4, 1859–Nov. 2, 1928), educator, was born in St. Louis, Mo. He entered the Society of Jesus in 1879 and was ordained a priest in 1891. In 1897 he was appointed professor of literature at St. Xavier's College, Cincinnati, where he had taught earlier for a brief period. After two years because of poor health he was reassigned to St. Xavier's Church. He directed the parish school for the remainder of his life. He produced a series of books for boys, most of them laid in Jesuit boarding schools and colleges. His first novel, *Percy Wynn,* was published under the pen name Neenah.

Percy Wynn; Or, Making a Boy of Him, Chicago, [1889].
Tom Playfair; Or, Making a Start, New York, 1892.
Claude Lightfoot; Or, How the Problem Was Solved, New York, 1893.
Harry Dee: Or, Making It Out, New York, 1893.
Mostly Boys. Short Stories, New York, 1895.
Ada Merton, St. Louis, Mo., 1896.
Ethelred Preston; Or, the Adventures of a Newcomer, New York, 1896.
New Faces and Old; Short Stories, St. Louis, Mo., 1896.
Echoes from Bethlehem. A Christmas "Miracle," St. Louis, Mo., 1897.
My Strange Friend, New York, 1897.
That Football Game: And What Came of It, New York, 1897.
The Best Foot Forward, and Other Stories, New York, 1900.
His First and Last Appearance, New York, 1900.
"But Thy Love and Thy Grace," New York, 1901.
The Fairy of the Snows, New York, 1913.
That Office Boy, New York, 1915.
Cupid of Campion, New York, 1916.
Lucky Bob, New York, 1917.
His Luckiest Years . . . , New York, 1918.
Facing Danger, New York, 1919.
Bobbie in Movieland, New York, 1921.
On the Run, New York, 1922.
Lord Bountiful, New York, 1923.
The Story of Jesus, [Chicago, 1924].
Sunshine and Freckles, New York, 1925.
Candles' Beams, New York, 1926.
Father Finn, S. J., the Story of His Life Told by Himself . . . , (Daniel A. Lord, ed.), New York, 1929.

FINNEY, BURNHAM (Dec. 22, 1899–), editor, was born in Portsmouth, Scioto County. He graduated from the University of Cincinnati in 1921, was associated with the City Club and the Planning Commission, 1925–29, and was Cincinnati editor of *Iron Age.* He lived in Detroit, 1930–38, and has since lived in New York City. He has written many articles for magazines and a book: *Arsenal of Democracy . . . ,* New York, [1941]. WW 30

FINNEY, CHARLES GRANDISON (Aug. 29, 1792–Aug. 16, 1875), evangelist and educator, was born in Warren, Conn., and grew up in Oneida County, N. Y. He taught school and studied law, but after his conversion in 1821 he studied theology and was ordained in 1824. For the next ten years he conducted highly successful revivals in Eastern cities. In 1832 his admirers bought the Chatham Street Theater, New York City, and remodeled it into the Broadway Tabernacle for his use. In 1836 he left the presbytery and became a Congregationalist. When a group of students from Lane Seminary rebelled in 1835 and left the institution for Oberlin, Finney was invited to form a theological department at the college. With the financial support of Arthur Tappan, he undertook the task. For the rest of his life he was intimately associated with Oberlin, serving as president of the college from 1851 to 1866 and as pastor of the First Congregational Church from 1835 to 1872. Although he occasionally conducted revivals in the East and in England, the college was the center of his interest. He advocated abolition and strict abstinence and opposed Masonry. His theology, however, was considered dangerously liberal by many right-wing Calvinists. He died in Oberlin at the age of 83. He published sermons and lectures in addition to the titles listed below.

Lectures on Revivals of Religion, New York, 1835.

Lectures to Professing Christians, Oberlin, 1836.

Lectures on Systematic Theology, 2 vols., Oberlin, 1846–47.

The Reviewer Reviewed: Or, Finney's Theology and the Princeton Review, Oberlin, 1847.

The Character, Claims, and Practical Workings of Freemasonry, Cincinnati, [1869].

Memoirs of Rev. Charles G. Finney . . . , New York, 1876.

FIPPIN, ELMER OTTERBEIN (Sept. 18, 1879–Dec. 26, 1949), agriculturist, was born in Columbus, Franklin County. He graduated from Ohio State University in 1900 and did graduate work at Cornell University. He served as an assistant in the soil survey conducted by the United States Bureau of Soils, 1900–04, was on the Cornell faculty, 1905–19, was director of agricultural experiment stations in Haiti, and an advisor to the Tennessee Valley Authority. He wrote several books on agriculture, e.g., *Rural New York,* New York, 1921. WWW 3

FIRESTONE, CLARK BARNABY (Sept. 10, 1869–June 3, 1957), journalist, was born in Lisbon, Columbiana County. After graduating from Oberlin College in 1911, he worked on the New York *Mail and Express,* 1892–99, and the New York *World,* 1899–1912. He returned to Lisbon in 1913 to work in a bank, and in 1921 he joined the staff of the Cincinnati *Times-Star.* He retired in 1954. He wrote several travel books and books about the Ohio River, e.g., *Flowing South,* New York, [1941], also three volumes of poems, e.g., *The Winding Road,* Cincinnati, 1937. WWW 3

FIRESTONE, HARVEY SAMUEL (Dec. 20, 1868–Feb. 7, 1938), manufacturer, was born in Columbiana, Columbiana County. He was educated in a rural school and in the local high school. While working as a salesman for his uncle's buggy company, he decided to enter the rubber business. A company he established in Chicago in 1896 was sold for a profit after three years, and Firestone moved to Akron, where he organized the Firestone Tire and Rubber Company in 1900. The firm prospered, especially after orders from Henry Ford began in 1906. A civic leader in Akron and a major figure in the world rubber industry, Firestone found time to write or assist in the writing of three books, e.g., *Rubber, Its History and Devolopment,* [Akron, 1922]. He died in Miami Beach, Fla., and was buried in Columbiana Cemetery. DAB 22

FIRESTONE, HARVEY SAMUEL, JR. (April 20, 1898–), executive, was born in Chicago, Ill., the son of Harvey S. Firestone (q.v.). Since graduating from Princeton in 1920, he has been associated with the Firestone Rubber Company, Akron. A series of his radio talks was published in book form: *The Romance and Drama of the Rubber Industry,* [Akron, 1932]. WW 30

FIREY, MILTON JACOB (Aug. 16, 1839–Dec. 27, 1908), clergyman, was born in Clearspring, Md. He graduated from Wittenberg College in 1862 and was ordained to the Lutheran ministry in 1864. He later served churches in Ohio, Pennsylvania, and Kansas. He died in Philadelphia. He wrote several theological works, e.g., *Infant Salvation . . .* , New York, 1902.

FISCHER, MARTIN HENRY (Nov. 10, 1879–), physician and educator, was born in Kiel, Germany, and was brought to America in 1885. He taught at Rush Medical College, Chicago, and the University of California before joining the University of Cincinnati faculty, where he served from 1910 to 1950. He has written and translated a number of professional books and articles in medicine and chemistry. He has also written *In Praise of Man,* Springfield, Ill., 1943. Howard Fabing has compiled three volumes of his "divers utterances": *Fischerisms . . .* , Cincinnati, 1930–44.

FISH, WILLISTON (Jan. 15, 1858–Dec. 19, 1939), lawyer, was born in Berlin Heights, Erie County. He spent his youth in that town except for three years near Burr Oak, Mich. In 1876 he entered Oberlin, but the following year he was appointed to the U. S. Military Academy. After graduating in 1881, he spent six years in the army and then read law. He was admitted to the Illinois bar in 1893 and practiced law and engaged in the traction business in Chicago until his retirement in 1923. Besides his two novels, the first of which was published under the pseudonym Fush, he wrote a great many technical and popular magazine articles. His most famous publication was "A Last Will," first printed in *Harper's Weekly* in 1898 and reprinted in newspapers all over the country.

Won at West Point . . . , Chicago, 1883.

Short Rations, New York, 1899.

FISHBACK, WILLIAM PINCKNEY (Nov. 11, 1831–Jan. 15, 1901), lawyer and journalist, was born in Batavia, Clermont County. After studying at Miami University and Farmers' College, Cincinnati, he read law with his father and was admitted to the bar. In 1857, however, he moved to Indianapolis, Ind., where he practiced law until his death. He was a journalist for four years: on the staff of the Indianapolis *Journal,* 1870–72, and St. Louis *Democrat,* 1872–74. Besides the titles below, he compiled a legal manual.

A Plea for Honest Elections, Indianapolis, 1886.

The Lawyer in Literature, Indianapolis, 1892.

Recollections of Lord Coleridge, Indianapolis, 1895.

FISHER, BENJAMIN FRANKLIN (Dec. 22, 1873–Oct. 26, 1916), manufacturer, was born in Steubenville, Jefferson County. He studied at DePauw University and Oberlin College. He spent most of his life in Canton and died in that city. Besides a volume of essays on Francis Thompson, he published at least two volumes of verse, e.g., *Life Harmonies,* Canton, [1914].

FISHER, DOROTHY CANFIELD (Feb. 17, 1879–Nov. 9, 1958), daughter of James H. and Flavia C. Canfield (qq.v.), was born in Lawrence, Kan. She lived in Columbus, 1895–99, while her father was president of Ohio State University. After graduating from Ohio State in 1899, she earned a doctorate in romance languages from Columbia University. After her marriage to John R. Fisher in 1907, she lived on a farm near Arlington, Vt. She wrote a number of distinguished short stories and novels, the best of them portraying rural Vermont, e.g., *Seasoned Timber,* New York, [1939]. WW 30

FISHER, E. BURKE (1799?–1859?), lawyer, practiced law in Cleveland during the 1840s. He apparently came to the city from Pittsburgh, where he was editing *The Literary Examiner and Western Monthly Review* in 1839. Under the pen name Timothy Jenkins he wrote two satires: *The Bench and Bar of Cuyahoga County. A Modern Epic,* Cleveland, 1843, and *Wars of the Barn-Burners of Cuyahoga County. An Epic Extraordinary,* Cleveland, 1844. He was later a journalist in Columbus and reportedly died in South Bend, Ind.

FISHER, GEORGE ADAMS (July 10, 1835–Jan. 20, 1904), was born near Calcutta, Columbiana County. In 1853 he began teaching school, but in 1857 with an older brother he went to Texas to enter the cattle business. In 1862, according to his book, he was conscripted into the Confederate army. He ran away within a few weeks and reached Arkansas, where he was captured and compelled to join the army again. His next attempt to escape was successful, and he reached St. Louis safely, returned to Ohio, and resumed the profession of school teaching in St. Clair Township. His death occurred in Cleveland.

The Yankee Conscript: Or, Eighteen Months in Dixie, Philadelphia, 1864.

FISHER, GEORGE CLYDE (May 22, 1878–Jan. 7, 1949), naturalist, was born near Sidney, Shelby County. He graduated from Miami University in 1905 and Johns Hopkins University (Ph.D.) in 1913. He taught in Ohio public schools and in various colleges before joining the staff of the Museum of Natural History, New York City, in 1913. He led numerous scientific expeditions. He wrote articles and textbooks on astronomy and nature study and *The Life of Audubon,* New York, [1949]. WWW 2

FISHER, GEORGE JOHN (April 2, 1871–), Boy Scout executive, was born in Cincinnati, Hamilton County. He graduated from Cincinnati College of Medicine in 1898. He was associated with the Y.M.C.A., 1892–1919, and with the Boy Scouts of America from 1919 to the present. Besides a volume of talks on scouting, he wrote, in collaboration with Elmer Berry, *The Physical Effects of Smoking . . . ,* New York, 1917. WW 30

FISHER, LENA LEONARD (Nov. 27, 1870–March 1, 1930), was born in Pittsburgh, Pa., daughter of Adna B. Leonard (q.v.). She lived in Springfield, Dayton, and Cincinnati, where her father served Methodist churches; after her marriage to Rev. John F. Fisher in 1896, she lived for a time in Cleveland. She lectured throughout the country on religious subjects, and was professor of comparative religions at the University of Southern California, 1921–30. She wrote numerous articles for religious and general magazines and also published three books on Methodist missions, e.g., *Lantern Stories . . . ,* New York, [1913].

FISHER, SAMUEL WARE (April 5, 1814–Jan. 18, 1874), clergyman, was born in Morristown, N. J. He was called in 1847 to succeed Lyman Beecher (q.v.) in the pulpit of Second Presbyterian Church, Cincinnati. He left Ohio in 1858 when he became president of Hamilton College. Many of his sermons and addresses were published separately as pamphlets, and a collection appeared in 1860: *Occasional Sermons and Addresses,* New York, 1860.

FISHER, STOKELY S. (Aug. 8, 1865–May 30, 1924), clergyman and educator, was born near Graysville, Monroe County. He served as pastor of a number of Methodist churches between 1883 and 1913. He was also president of West Lafayette College, 1904–06, and from 1913 until his death was a member of the faculty of Kansas City University.

Lelia Lee, and Other Poems, Cambridge, 1885.

Fanny Fay, and Other Poems, Wellsville, 1886.

Poems of Life, Kansas City, Kan., 1925.

FISHER, WILLIAM HUBBELL (Jan. 2, 1837–Oct. 6, 1909), lawyer, was born in Albany, N. Y., but after he was three years old lived in Cincinnati, where his father was a Presbyterian minister. He graduated from Hamilton College in 1864, studied law at Columbia University, and was admitted to the bar in 1867. He practiced in Utica, N. Y., 1867–70, and thereafter in Cincinnati. His death occurred in Cincinnati.

Poems on Mont Blanc and Switzerland, Cincinnati, [1898].

FISK, GEORGE MYGATT (July 16, 1864–April 29, 1910), educator, was born in Canfield, Mahoning County. He graduated from the University of Michigan in 1890 and afterward studied at several European universities, earning a Ph.D. at the University of Munich in 1896. He was on the faculty of the University of Illinois, 1902–08. He wrote technical books and articles in the fields of economics and politics, a textbook, and *Continental Opinion Regarding a Proposed Middle European Tariff-Union,* Baltimore, 1902. WW 6

FISKE, ASA SEVERANCE (March 2, 1833–July 30, 1925), clergyman, was born in Strongsville, Cuyahoga County. He graduated from Amherst College in 1855, studied at Andover and Yale Seminaries, and was ordained to the Congregational ministry in 1860. He served as pastor of churches in Minnesota, Connecticut, New York, California, Washington, Pennsylvania, and Louisiana. Besides the titles below, he contributed articles to secular and religious papers.

Reason and Faith, Washington, D. C., 1900.

Ruth; An Idyll of the Olden Time, Washington, D. C., 1900.

FISKE, GEORGE WALTER (June 3, 1872–Oct. 10, 1945), clergyman and educator, was born in Holliston, Mass. He graduated from Amherst College in 1895 and Hartford Theological Seminary in 1898. He served as minister of several Congregational churches, 1898–1907, and was a member of the Oberlin College faculty, 1907–37. He wrote a large number of books on religion and religious education, including *The Christian Family,* New York, [1929]. WW 24

FITCH, FLORENCE MARY (Feb. 17, 1875–June 2, 1959), educator, born in Stratford, Conn., grew up in Cincinnati and Buffalo, N. Y. After graduating from Oberlin College in 1897, she taught in Buffalo for three years, studied in Germany, and received her Ph.D. from the University of Berlin in 1903. She was on the Oberlin faculty, 1903–40, and after her retirement continued to live in Oberlin. She published several books on religious subjects, e.g., *One God; The Ways We Worship Him,* New York, [1944]. WWAW 1

FITCH-BREWER, ANNETTE. See Annette F. Brewer.

FITE, EMERSON DAVID (March 3, 1874–May 10, 1953), educator, was born in Marion, Marion County. He graduated from Yale University in 1897 and Harvard University (Ph.D.) in 1905. He was a member of the Yale faculty, 1906–13, and Vassar College faculty, 1913–44. He wrote a number of books on American politics and history, e.g., *Government by Cooperation,* New York, 1932. WWW 3

FITZGERALD, PITT LOOFBOURROW (Oct. 3, 1893–   ), was born in Waterloo, Fayette County. He attended the schools of Washington Court House, and afterward he studied at the Pennsylvania Academy of Fine Arts and had private study under the late N. C. Wyeth. He served in the 308th Engineers in World War I. He is now publisher and art director of *American Creative,* Prescott, Ariz. He has written a number of historical novels for teen-age boys, e.g., *The Black Spearman,* Philadelphia, 1934, concerning the Mound Builders, and *Drovers East,* Philadelphia, [1940].

FLAGG, WILLIAM JOSEPH (April 15, 1818–April 15, 1898), was born in New Haven, Conn. After studying law and being admitted to the bar in New York City, he came to Cincinnati, where he married a daughter of the elder Nicholas Longworth (q.v.). In 1852 he bought a tract of land on the Ohio River on which to raise grapes; he also toured France to study grape-raising and wine-making. In 1855 he built a cottage of peeled white poplar logs, known as Buckhorn Cottage, near Buena Vista. He and his wife lived there for several years, and his book *Wall Street and the Woods* describes the wild hilly country around the cottage. He died in New York City.

Abuses in the Navy. Case of Lieutenant Flagg, [Cincinnati, 1851].
Three Seasons in European Vineyards . . . , New York, 1869.
A Good Investment . . . , New York, 1872.
Wall Street and the Woods, New York, 1885.
Yoga; Or, Transformation . . . , New York, 1898.

FLANNERY, M. JAY (Aug. 25, 1857–Jan. 20, 1920), educator, was born in Dayton, Montgomery County. After teaching school for a number of years, he graduated from Heidelberg College in 1901. He afterward taught Latin in Hamilton High School. He published a volume of verse: *Songs under Open Skies,* Cincinnati, [1912].

FLASH, HENRY LYDEN (Jan. 20, 1835–1914), once popular Southern poet, was born in Cincinnati, Hamilton County. His parents were native Jamaicans, both of whom had been educated in England. In 1839 the family moved from Ohio to New Orleans. Henry graduated from the Western Military Institute in Kentucky in 1852. He was on the staff of the Mobile, Ala., *Register* for a while, but in 1857 he went to Italy, where he spent a year and served as correspondent to the New Orleans *Delta* and the Montgomery, Ala., *Mail.* His first volume of poems was published in the summer of 1860 and is said to have sold out in two months. Another edition of his poetry was published in 1906. During his service in the Confederate army, he served as aide to Gen. W. J. Hardee, and also served on the staff of Gen. Joe Wheeler. Toward the close of the war, he became editor of the Macon, Ga., *Telegraph,* and it was during this period that he wrote three war poems which achieved great popularity throughout the Confederacy—"Zollikoffer," "Jackson," and "Polk." Many of his poems were published under the pen name Lyden Eclair and under the nickname "Harry" Flash. After spending three years in Galveston, Texas, following the war, he returned to New Orleans and became a successful businessman. He retired in 1886 and moved to Los Angeles, where he spent the remainder of his life.

Poems, New York, 1860.
Poems, New York, 1906.

FLEISCHMANN, JULIUS (April 29, 1900–   ), was born in Cincinnati, Hamilton County. He was educated at Franklin School, Cincinnati, and Hotchkiss School, Conn., and graduated from Yale University in 1920. During World War II he served in Canada and England as a naval attaché. He has published an account of a world cruise: *Footsteps in the Sea,* New York, [1935].

FLEISCHMANN, MAXIMILIAN CHARLES (Feb. 26, 1877–Oct. 16, 1951), was born in Riverside, Montgomery County, and was educated in Cincinnati public schools and Ohio Military Institute. At the age of eighteen he entered the manufacturing department of the Fleischmann Company and rose to the chairmanship of the board. After his retirement he lived in Nevada. He wrote for private circulation *After Big Game in Arctic and Tropic; A Sportsman's Notebook . . .*, Cincinnati, 1909. WWW 3

FLEMING, DANIEL JOHNSON (Jan. 30, 1877–), clergyman and educator, was born in Xenia, Greene County. He graduated from University of Wooster in 1898 and Union Theological Seminary in 1903. Ordained to the Presbyterian ministry, he served on the faculty of Forman Christian College, Lahore, India, 1904–13. In 1914 he earned a Ph.D. at the University of Chicago. From 1918 to 1944 he was on the faculty of Union Theological Seminary. His residence in 1960 was in Claremont, Calif. He has written many books on missions and on the art of Asia and Africa, e.g., *Building with India,* New York, [1922]. WW 26

FLEMING, WALLACE BRUCE (Nov. 22, 1872–June 30, 1952), clergyman and educator, was born in Cambridge, Guernsey County. He graduated from Muskingum College in 1894, from Drew Theological Seminary in 1897, and from Columbia University (Ph.D.) in 1914. He was ordained to the Methodist ministry in 1897 and served as a pastor in New Jersey, 1897–1911. He was on the faculty of Drew Seminary, 1911–15, was president of West Virginia Wesleyan College, 1915–22, president of Baker University, 1922–36, and vice-president of West Virginia Wesleyan College, 1937–44. His writings include *Guide Posts to Life Work . . .*, New York, [1924]. WWW 3

FLETCHER, ROBERT HOWE (July 21, 1850–1936), was born in Cincinnati, Hamilton County. After graduating from the U. S. Naval Academy, he transferred to the army and served on the Indian frontier and in California until 1886, when he was retired for disabilities. He was director of the Mark Hopkins Institute of Art, 1899–1915, and of the San Francisco Institute of Art, 1907–15.

A Blind Bargain, a Novel, Chicago, [1889].
The Johnstown Stage, and Other Stories, New York, 1891.
Marjorie and Her Papa, How They Wrote a Story and Made Pictures for It, New York, 1891.
Ten Drawings in Chinatown . . ., San Francisco, [1898].
Annals of the Bohemian Club, San Francisco, 1900.

FLETCHER, ROBERT SAMUEL (Nov. 20, 1900–Dec. 14, 1959), educator, was born in Forestville, N. Y., He graduated from Oberlin College in 1920 and Harvard University (Ph.D.) in 1939. He was a member of the Oberlin history department, 1927–59. His writings include *A History of Oberlin College from Its Foundation through the Civil War,* 2 vols., Oberlin, 1943. DAS 3

FLICK, ALEXANDER CLARENCE (Aug. 16, 1869–July 30, 1942), educator, was born in Galion, Crawford County. He graduated from Otterbein College in 1894 and Columbia University (Ph.D.) in 1901. He was on the history faculty of Syracuse University, 1899–1923, and was New York state historian and director of archives, 1923–39. Besides the title below, he published several textbooks and numerous articles and wrote *The Decline of the Medieval Church . . .*, [London, 1930]. WWW 2

FLICKINGER, DANIEL KUMLER (May 25, 1824–Aug. 29, 1911), clergyman, was born at Seven Mile, Butler County. He grew up on his father's farm and in 1850 joined the Miami Conference of the United Brethren Church. He preached on the circuit and in Cincinnati. In 1855 he made the first of twelve missionary trips to Africa. He was secretary of the missionary society, 1857–85, and missionary bishop, 1885–89. He died in Columbus and is buried at Oxford. He wrote many articles for church publications and also published some sermons and a family history.

Offhand Sketches of Men and Things in Western Africa, Dayton, 1857.
Ethiopia, or Twenty Years of Missionary Life in Western Africa, Dayton, 1877.
The Church's Marching Orders . . ., Dayton, 1879.
Our Missionary Work from 1853–1889, Dayton, 1889.
Fifty-five Years of Active Ministerial Life, Dayton, 1907.

FLINT, MICAH P. (c.1807–1830), son of Timothy Flint (q.v.), was born in Lurenberg, Mass. He was admitted to the Mississippi bar but did not practice law. He accompanied his father on his travels and contributed to his magazine, the *Western Review.*

The Hunter, and Other Poems, Boston, 1826.

FLINT, TIMOTHY (July 11, 1780–Aug. 16, 1840), was born in Reading, Mass. He is probably less frequently mentioned as a writer than as the one man in Cincinnati Mrs. Trollope thought worthy of favorable notice. Yet for several years (1827–33), he was without a doubt the leading literary figure in Cincinnati if not in the whole Western country. When Flint came to Ohio in the fall of 1815 as a missionary, he was not without literary ambitions. In his letter to the Missionary Society of Connecticut requesting the western appointment, he suggested the possibility of establishing, at some central point, a religious publication that would give attention to literature, charities, and institutions. The project did not materialize immediately, however. The family rented a house in Cincinnati, and for four months Flint made a circuit of Kentucky, Indiana, and Ohio. His monthly salary of $25.00, paid by the Mission Board, was insufficient to support his family and in the spring of 1816 he moved westward again, to St. Louis. For six years Flint tried to make a living by preaching and farming in Missouri. His health failed and, in 1822, he went South for his health and spent the next four years in Louisiana. In 1826 he went back to New England by sea. Early in the following year he returned to Cincinnati to begin the literary work to which he had looked forward twelve years before. The first issue of the *Western Monthly Review,* containing, in the main, articles by Flint, appeared in May, 1827. It was published by his son, E. H. Flint, who had established a bookstore and publishing house at 160 Main Street. Cincinnati city directories give two residences occupied by the Flint family: in 1829, George Street north of Elm; and in 1839, Fifth between Race and Elm. In 1826, prior to his return to Cincinnati, Flint's *Recollections of the Last Ten Years* was published in Boston. The book was cordially received, as was the novel *Francis Berrian,* also published in Boston in 1826. A year after he had re-established himself in Cincinnati, Flint's chief contribution to literature, *The History and Geography of the Western States,* was published by his son. A second novel, *The Life and Adventures of Arthur Clenning,* appeared the same year, published in Philadelphia. A third novel, *The Shoshone Valley,* was published in 1831 by E. H. Flint. In 1833 appeared *A Biographical Memoir of Daniel Boone.* Fourteen editions of this work appeared. All bore Cincinnati imprints. All of Flint's work until this time had been well received, but his *Lectures upon Natural History, Geology, Chemistry, the Application of Steam, and Interesting Discoveries in the Arts,* published in Boston in 1833, was criticized in Eastern journals. Very sensitive to criticism, Flint confined his writing thereafter to magazine contributions. During his Cincinnati period, in addition to the *Western Monthly Review,* Flint edited *The Personal Narrative of James O. Pattie of Kentucky.* This appeared in 1831 with a Cincinnati imprint. As translator, Flint issued *The Art of Being Happy* by Joseph Droz. This work was published in Boston in 1832. In 1833, an offer to become editor-in-chief of the *Knickerbocker* was made to Flint. He therefore went to New York in the late summer, leaving his family in Cincinnati. However, his health was such that he remained only long enough to edit one issue, that of October, 1833, and returned to Cincinnati in 1834. His residence in Cincinnati was short and he removed to Alexandria, La., to reside with his family, where he spent his remaining days. He wrote nothing except an unpublished *Second Part of Recollections of the Mississippi Valley* after his Cincinnati period. He died while on a visit to Salem, Mass.

Ernest I. Miller

The Columbian Harmonist, Cincinnati, 1816.

Francis Berrian, or the Mexican Patriot, Boston, 1826.

Recollections of the Last Ten Years, Passed in Occasional Residences and Journeyings in the Valley of the Mississippi . . . , Boston, 1826.

A Condensed Geography and History of the Western States, or the Mississippi Valley, Cincinnati, 1828.

The Life and Adventures of Arthur Clenning . . . , Philadelphia, 1828.

George Mason, the Young Backwoodsman; Or, "Don't Give Up the Ship." A Story of the Mississippi, Boston, 1829.

The Lost Child, Boston, 1830.

The Shoshone Valley; A Romance, Cincinnati, 1830.

The History and Geography of the Mississippi Valley. To Which Is Appended a Condensed Physical Geography of the Atlantic United States, and the Whole American Continent, 2 vols., Cincinnati, 1832.

Biographical Memoir of Daniel Boone, the First Settler of Kentucky. Interspersed with Incidents in the Early Annals of the Country, Cincinnati, 1833.

Indian Wars of the West; Containing Sketches of Those Pioneers Who Headed the Western Settlers in Repelling the Attacks of the Savages, Cincinnati, 1833.

Lectures upon Natural History, Geology, Chemistry, the Application of Steam, and Interesting Discoveries in the Arts, Boston, 1833.

Journal of the Rev. Timothy Flint, from the Red River to the Ouachitta or Washita, in Louisiana, in 1835. [Alexandria, La., 1835].

FLOWER, GEORGE (1788–Jan. 15, 1862), co-founder of Albion, Ill., while living in Mt. Vernon with one of his children wrote *History of the English Settlement in Edwards County, Ill. . . . ,* Chicago, 1882.

FLOWERS, MONTAVILLE (Jan. 7, 1868–Nov. 10, 1934), lecturer, was born in Cincinnati, Hamilton County. He graduated from Ohio Northern University in 1890, was superintendent of schools, Norwood, 1890–96, and operated the Flowers Academy of Music and Dramatic Arts, 1903–07. A popular lyceum lecturer on drama, world problems, and the Orient, he published *The Japanese Conquest of American Opinion,* New York, [1917]. WWW 1

FOGG, FAGIN. Pseud. See Ralf C. Kircher.

FOGG, WILLIAM PERRY (July 27, 1826–1909), was born in Exeter, N. H. In 1851 he established himself in the pottery and chinaware business in Cleveland, and in 1868 he retired from active business to gratify his desire to travel. He was the first American granted permission to travel in the interior of Japan. His letters from foreign lands were published in the Cleveland *Leader* and other newspapers. He was proprietor and editor of the Cleveland *Herald* for a few months in 1877. He lived in Roselle, N. J., 1901–08, and spent the last year of his life in Morris Plains, N. J. His travel books were well written and enjoyed considerable popularity. *Arabistan,* with an introduction by Bayard Taylor, went into several editions.

"Round the World." Letters from Japan, China, India, and Egypt, Cleveland, 1872.

Recent Donations . . . , [Cleveland, 1874].

Arabistan; Or, the Land of "The Arabian Nights" . . . , Hartford, Conn., 1875.

FOGLE, RICHARD HARTER (March 8, 1911–), educator, was born in Canton, Stark County. He graduated from Hamilton College in 1933 and the University of Michigan (Ph.D.) in 1944 and has been a member of the English department, Tulane University, since 1946. He has published articles and a book of criticism: *The Imagery of Keats and Shelley . . . ,* Chapel Hill, N. C., [1949]. DAS 3

FOISEL, JOHN (Sept. 12, 1894–), clergyman, was born in Petersdorf, Transylvania (Romania). He graduated from the theological seminary in Hermanstadt, Transylvania, served in the Austrian army during World War I; and came to the United States in 1921. After a year at Philadelphia Lutheran Seminary, he became pastor of St. John's Lutheran Church, Cleveland, and now lives in that city. He has written historical plays in German and has published a book, *Saxons through Seventeen Centuries . . . ,* [Cleveland, 1936].

FOLEY, LOUIS (Aug. 23, 1892–), educator, was born in Zanesville, Muskingum County. He graduated from Ohio State University in 1915 and has also studied at several French universities. He taught at Ohio State, was an official of Near East Relief in Turkey and Syria, 1919–22, and was on the faculty of Western Michigan College, 1923–46. Since 1946, he has been chairman of the English department, Babson Institute, Mass. He has written numerous professional articles and several books, e.g., *The Greatest Saint of France,* Milwaukee, Wis., [1931].

FOLLET, MARGARET WHIPPLE (1907–), was born in Toledo, Lucas County. After graduating from Scott High School, she spent a year at the University of Wisconsin. At the age of 24, she published a novel with a Toledo setting: *The Kilbys,* New York, 1931. She afterward went to New York City, where she was employed by the publisher Alfred A. Knopf. She now lives in Norwich, Vt.

FOLLETT, ELIZA G. WARD (Sept. 17, 1801–April 29, 1876), was born in Albany, N. Y. She married Oran Follett (q.v.) in Fairport, N. Y., in 1832, and two years later they settled in Sandusky. She was long remembered for her beauty and graciousness, her help to the poor and needy of the town, and her fearless ministrations to the victims of cholera in the epidemic of 1848.

The Young Housekeeper's Assistant, Sandusky, 1874.

FOLLETT, ORAN (Sept. 4, 1798–Oct. 14, 1894), journalist, banker, and railroad president, was born in Gorham, N. Y. His father died when he was small, and after his mother remarried he rebelled against his stepfather's control and ran away from home. At the age of eleven he was a printer's devil in Canandaigua, N. Y. At fourteen he apparently was a powder monkey on the sloop *Jones* on Lake Ontario. After the War of 1812 he returned to the Canandaigua printing office. In 1817 he was an editor in Rochester, N. Y., and in 1819 he owned a paper of his own at Batavia, *The Spirit of the Times.* When he was only 25, he was elected to the New York State Legislature. He moved to Buffalo, where he edited the *Journal* and operated a bookstore until he came to Ohio. In 1834 he came to Sandusky, where he had bought a large tract of land, firmly believing that Sandusky Bay would be the most important harbor on the Great Lakes. He became an influential citizen of the town and took an active part in its commercial and civic life. He was prominent in the Whig Party, edited the Sandusky *Whig* for a time, and served on the State Board of Public Works, 1845–49. He edited the *Ohio State Journal* at Columbus for a few months in 1840, again in 1844, and on a third occasion, 1853–56. He played an important part in the growth of the new Republican Party in Ohio. After leaving the *Journal* in 1856, he founded a publishing firm, Follett, Foster & Co., which issued the Lincoln-Douglas debates. He was also president of a Sandusky bank and of the Sandusky, Dayton & Cincinnati Railroad. His contribution to the Shakespeare-Bacon controversy was privately published.

The Shakespeare Plays. The Theatre, &c. "Who Wrote Shakespeare?" Sandusky, 1879.

FOLMER, HENRY DANIEL (June 18, 1852–Jan 15, 1930), was born in Janesville, Wis., but when he was three years old his family came to Madison County. He taught school in Madison and Franklin Counties before turning to farming. He made a special study of alfalfa and published *Alfalfa on Wildwood Farm . . . ,* Columbus, 1911.

FOLWELL, WILLIAM WATTS (Feb. 14, 1833–Sept. 18, 1929), educator, born in Romulus, N. Y., came to Venice near Sandusky in 1865 to enter the milling business owned by his father-in-law. In 1868 he joined the faculty of Kenyon College, and the next year he left Ohio to become the first president of the University of Minnesota. He wrote *A History of Minnesota,* 4 vols., St. Paul, 1921–30. DAB 6

FOOTE, ALLEN RIPLEY (Jan. 26, 1842–1921), was born in Olcott, N. Y. He served in the Civil War with the 3rd Michigan Infantry. A resident of Columbus, he was editor of *Public Policy,* 1899–1905, commissioner (1901–09) and president (1909–13) of the Ohio State Board of Commerce, and president of the National Tax Association, 1907–13. He edited a three-volume digest of economic legislation, 1892–93, delivered many addresses that were reprinted in pamphlet form, and wrote many articles on economic reform.

Economic Value of Electric Light and Power, Cincinnati, 1889.

Prosperity and Politics, Washington, D. C., 1893.

A Sound Currency and Banking System . . . , New York, 1895.

The Money of the Constitution, New York, 1896.

Powers of Municipalities . . . , [Indianapolis], 1898.

Municipal Public Service Industries, Chicago, 1899.

Ownership and Regulation of Public Service Utilities . . . , Chicago, 1903.

A Practical Solution of the Public Utility Problem . . . , Chicago, [1903].

Compensation for Industrial Injuries, Columbus, [1913].

The Injustice of the Federal Farm Loan Law, Columbus, [1916].

A Model Farm Management and Credit System, Washington, D. C., [1917].

The United Democratic Nations of the World . . . , Washington, D. C., 1917.

The Right to Strike, [Columbus, 1921].

FOOTE, EDWARD BLISS (Feb. 20, 1829–Oct. 5, 1906), physician, was born in Collamer near Cleveland, Cuyahoga County. His father, Herschel Foote, opened the first bookstore in Cleveland in 1819 and later operated a general store at Euclid Avenue and Noble Road. In the 1850s his wife's social ambitions and her strictness with household maids led to a boycott of the store and its failure. The family moved to Saratoga Springs, N. Y. Edward learned the printing trade in the office of the Cleveland *Herald,* was an itinerant printer, and edited newspapers in Connecticut and Brooklyn, N. Y. He graduated from Pennsylvania Medical University in 1860 and afterward practiced in New York. He published popular medical books and was widely known as a reformer and freethinker.

Medical Common Sense . . . , New York, 1859.

Cold Feet: The Cause, Prevention, and Cure . . . , New York, 1867.

Plain Home Talk about the Human System . . . , New York, 1870.

Science in Story. Sammy Tubbs, the Boy Doctor, and "Sponsie," the Troublesome Monkey, New York, 1874.

A Step Backward . . . , New York, 1875.

The Physical Improvement of Humanity . . . , New York, 1876.

Physiological Marriage . . . , New York, 1876.
Dr. Foote's Hand-Book of Health-Hints and Ready Recipes . . . , New York, 1881.
Dr. Foote's Home Cyclopedia of Popular Medical, Social, and Sexual Science . . . , New York, 1901.

FOOTE, EDWARD BOND (Aug. 15, 1854–Oct. 12, 1912), physician, son of Edward Bliss Foote (q.v.), was born in Cleveland, Cuyahoga County. After graduating from the College of Physicians and Surgeons, New York City, he practiced in that city. The second title below, a manual of vegetarianism, included a reprint of the *Health Primer.*

Everybody's Health Primer . . . , New York, 1891.
Food. "What's Best To Eat" . . . , New York, 1891.

FOOTE, GASTON (Sept. 6, 1902–), clergyman, born in Comanche County, Texas, was pastor of Grace Methodist Church, Dayton, 1945–52. His other pastorates have been in the South; he now lives in Fort Worth, Texas. He has published books on religious themes, e.g., *Just Plain Bread . . .* , [Nashville, Tenn.], 1938. WWC 1

FOOTE, JOHN PARSONS (1783–1865), was born in Connecticut. Brother-in-law of Lyman Beecher (q.v.), he came to Cincinnati around 1820. He operated a bookstore at 14 Lower Market Street, 1820–28. In 1824 he published the *Literary Gazette,* whose motto was "Not to display learning but to create a taste for it." Though short-lived, this periodical published important articles by Benjamin Drake and others. Foote also organized the Cincinnati Type Foundry, from which he retired in 1823, and he and his brother operated the city waterworks, 1824–40. His brother, Samuel Edmond Foote (1787–1858), a retired sea captain, followed him to Cincinnati and built a large home at Third and Vine Streets, where the Semi-Colon Club met weekly; he returned to Connecticut in the early 1840s to operate a farm. John remained in Cincinnati, where he became president of the General Board of Underwriters. He was extremely active in civic life. He was an organizer of the Ohio Mechanics Institute in 1828, was active in the Horticultural Society, and was president of the board of trustees of the Medical College of Ohio.

The Schools of Cincinnati and Its Vicinity, Cincinnati, 1855.
Memoirs of the Life of Samuel E. Foote . . . , Cincinnati, 1860.

FOOTE, JOHN TAINTOR (March 29, 1881–Jan. 29, 1950), was born in Leadville, Colo.; but in 1887 his parents moved to Gambier, Knox County, where he attended Kenyon Academy. He married Ada Curtis of Mount Vernon and lived in that community for about twelve years. He later lived in New York and Los Angeles. He wrote plays, motion pictures, and many novels and short stories, e.g., *Pocono Shot; A Dog Story,* New York, 1924, and *Fatal Gesture,* New York, 1933. WWW 2

FOOTE, JULIA A. J. (1823– ?), was born in Schenectady, N. Y., the child of slaves. When she was young, her parents moved to Albany, the home of her future husband, George Foote, who purchased her freedom. After traveling as an evangelist, she moved to Cleveland in 1851 and continued her activities as an evangelist and antislavery lecturer. Her life story describes her experiences in moralistic terms and urges sinners to repent and be saved.

A Brand Plucked from the Fire, Cleveland, 1879.

FOOTE, LUCIUS HARWOOD (April 10, 1826–June 4, 1913), lawyer and diplomat, born in Winfield, N. Y., spent part of his boyhood in northeastern Ohio, where his father served as a Congregational minister. He also attended Western Reserve University, but did not graduate. In 1853 he went to California, read law, practiced in Sacramento, and then entered the diplomatic service. He was the first American minister to Korea. After his retirement in 1885 he lived in San Francisco. He published several books, e.g., *A Red-Letter Day, and Other Poems,* Boston, 1882.

FORAKER, JOSEPH BENSON (July 5, 1846–May 10, 1917), soldier, lawyer, judge, governor of Ohio, and U. S. Senator, was born on a farm near Rainsboro, Highland County. He was the son of Thomas Stacey and Margaret (Reece) Foraker. On both sides, his family was English and Scotch-Irish; his paternal grandfather, John Fouracre, had emigrated from Devonshire, England, to Delaware County in the early eighteenth century. During his first fifteen years Joseph lived the life typical of an Ohio farm lad: many chores about the farm, a few months' schooling annually, Sunday school, and church services at the Methodist Episcopal church, and the boyish pleasures of fishing and swimming. At the age of sixteen he enlisted in Company "A," 89th O.V.I. With this unit he saw action in West Virginia and Tennessee, and in 1864, as a lieutenant under General W. T. Sherman, marched through the Carolinas to Virginia. In mid-June, 1865, he was mustered out a captain. Determined to become a lawyer upon his return to civilian life, he set out to complete his education. After a year at Salem Academy, he attended Ohio Wesleyan University for two years and then transferred to the newly opened Cornell University, from which institution he was graduated in 1869. He was admitted to the Cincinnati bar in 1869, and after several lean years, became a successful attorney. Long interested in politics, he ran for judge of the superior court of Cincinnati in 1879 and was in office two years. In 1883 he was a candidate for governor of Ohio on the Republican ticket but lost because of dissension in party ranks. Two years later, after a second contest with Governor George Hoadly, he was elected governor. Foraker served capably as governor during his two administrations, 1886–90, but his efforts to bring about needed reforms were only partially successfully. Among his accomplishments were the passage of laws requiring registration of voters and the formation of nonpartisan election boards in Ohio's larger cities; the creation of a state board of health; and the establishment of a board of managers for all state penal institutions. Investigation of Cincinnati's corrupt politics and the need for additional state revenues were his constant concerns. His second administration was marked by centennials at Marietta, Cincinnati, and Columbus in 1888. His attempt for a third term was unsuccessful. Although a strong Republican, he did not always go with the party leaders in Ohio; he frequently played the lone wolf. He came to have his own faction, which in the late 1880s and 1890s consistently opposed the John Sherman-Hanna-McKinley group. Because of this opposition, he was accused in 1884 and 1888 of attempting to snatch the Republican Presidential nomination from John Sherman. His opposition reached its height in 1892, when he openly contested the senatorship with the venerable Sherman. After this unsuccessful campaign, he quietly built up his organization for the next one, when the state's other senator came up for reelection in 1896. Foraker's election was assured at the Zanesville convention of 1895 by the masterful organization of his forces. A strong partisan, he was leader in the Bloody Shirt movement of the 1880s. He learned early in his political career that his audiences thrived on Civil War antipathies and, as he later asserted, "I gave them what they wanted." His loud booming voice, his dramatic gestures, and his stinging verbal barbs earned him the name "Fire Alarm Foraker." Later he quieted down, becoming one of the leading orators of his day. He spoke in virtually every Eastern and Midwestern state. While governor, his uncompromising Republicanism led him to taunt President Cleveland publicly, and in reply to the latter's order to return captured Confederate battle flags then hanging in the state capitol, he dramatically announced to the nation that "No battle flags will be surrendered while I am governor." As senator (1897–1909), his oratorical and debating skills earned him a ranking position in the Senate. During the McKinley administration he was a leader of those interested in the Spanish-American War and in imperialism. As chairman of the Senate committee on Pacific Islands and Puerto Rico, he sponsored and pushed through to adoption the Foraker Act, the organic law for Puerto Rico. He was also a member of the powerful Foreign Relations Committee. When Theodore Roosevelt became President, Foraker failed to retain his position as an "administration senator." He could not go along with Roosevelt's program, with its measures of social justice. His opposition reached its climax over the Hepburn Act of 1906. During the Senate debate over this bill to regulate railroads, he took the lead against such proposals. He was the only Republican senator to vote against it. His opposition to Roosevelt ripened into open battle over the complex Brownsville case, in which Foraker took the side of a Negro regiment summarily discharged by a hasty and ill-considered Presidential order. Foraker was retired from politics in 1908 as the result of the Hearst-published Archbold-Foraker letters. These letters disclosed that during his first term as senator he had been employed as a special counsel for the Standard Oil Company. This relationship, not uncommon in the preceding era, was accounted unethical by the nation in 1908. After his political retirement he continued his law practice in Cincinnati, representing many large corporations. His practice had been lucrative since the 1890s. In 1914 he was, he later stated, "wheedled" into running for senator in the primaries; his younger political follower, Warren G. Harding, won the nomination and the seat. During his last years he reviewed his active life as he wrote his *apologia pro vita sua: Notes of a Busy Life* (1916). Many of his speeches were published separately. Foraker's constant companion and adviser was his wife, Julia Bundy Foraker (June 17, 1847–July 21,

1933), whom he had married on October 4, 1870. The daughter of Hezekiah S. Bundy of Jackson County, she reared a "stepladder" of children (three daughters and two sons), managed the governor's mansion and the senator's home, and accompanied her husband on most of his extensive tours. An account of her experiences in Columbus, Cincinnati, and Washington is delightfully presented in her book, *I Would Live It Again,* New York, 1932.

Everett Walters

Speeches of J. B. Foraker, 1869–1917, 7 vols., [n.p., 1869–1917].

Notes of a Busy Life, 2 vols., Cincinnati, 1916.

FORAKER, JULIA BUNDY. See Joseph B. Foraker.

FORAN, MARTIN AMBROSE (Nov. 11, 1844–June 28, 1921), lawyer and judge, was born in Susquehanna County, Pa. After attending St. Joseph's College, he taught school for two years and served in the 4th Pennsylvania Volunteer Cavalry, 1864–65. He worked in Cleveland as a cooper, 1866–69, and edited the *Coopers' Journal,* 1870–74. He was active in organizing international and state unions. In 1874 he was admitted to the Ohio bar. He served in Congress, 1883–89, practiced law in Cleveland, 1889–1910, and served as judge of common pleas court from 1910 until his death. His only novel, a defense of the laboring man, was intended as a reply to *The Breadwinners* by John Hay (q.v.).

The Other Side. A Social Study Based on Fact, Cleveland, 1886.

FORCE, MANNING FERGUSON (Dec. 17, 1824–May 8, 1899), lawyer and judge, was born in Washington, D. C., son of the historian, Peter Force. He graduated from Harvard University in 1845 and from the law school in 1848. The next year he moved to Cincinnati. He was admitted to the bar in 1850 and practiced in Cincinnati. In the Civil War he joined the 20th O.V.I. as a major, commanded a division in Sherman's army during its march to the sea, and rose to the brevet rank of major general. He served as judge of common pleas court in Cincinnati, 1866–76, and as judge of the superior court, 1877–87. From 1888 until his death he was commandant of the Ohio Soldiers' and Sailors' Home at Sandusky. Several of the works below are pamphlets.

Pre-Historic Man. Darwinism or Deity. The Mound Builders, Cincinnati, 1873.

Some Early Notices of the Indians of Ohio. To What Race Did the Mound Builders Belong? Cincinnati, 1879.

From Fort Henry to Corinth, New York, 1881.

Personal Recollections of the Vicksburg Campaign, Cincinnati, 1885.

Some Observations on the Letters of Amerigo Vespucci, Cincinnati, 1885.

General Sherman, New York, 1899.

FORD, CLARA ANNE (Dec. 17, 1893–), born in Alvarado, Texas, has lived in Cleveland since 1922. She has published several stories for children, e.g., *The Little Girl Who Waved . . . ,* New York, 1937.

FORD, COLLIN (Aug. 14, 1889–April 5, 1924), was born in Toledo, Lucas County. After graduating from Yale University in 1910, he lived in Cincinnati, where he engaged in the insurance business. His death occurred in that city. Under the pen name Washington Jefferson Van Buren Pipp, he wrote a pamphlet published posthumously: *The Atrocities of Book-Collecting and Kindred Afflictions,* Cincinnati, 1943.

FORD, MARY A. McMULLEN (1841–April, 1876), spent her girlhood in Brown County. *Snatches of Song* is dedicated to her friends at St. Martin's. Her poems were published under the pen name Una.

Poems, Cincinnati, 1863.

Snatches of Song, St. Louis, 1874.

FOREMAN, DENNIS WALDEN (Sept. 11, 1900–), clergyman, born in West Columbia, W. Va., has lived in Ohio since 1929. Ordained a minister of the United Brethren Church in 1927, he served a church in New Rumley, Harrison County, 1929–31, and St. Paul's Church, Canton, since 1931. He has published numerous articles in religious periodicals and *They That Take the Sword,* New York, 1945. RLA 2

FORNSHELL, MARVIN E. (Aug. 13, 1872–Jan. 23, 1924), was born in Camden, Preble County. After attending the Camden schools, he worked on the Camden *Gazette,* which he edited, 1898–99. He was superintendent of printing at the Ohio State Prison, 1900–16, and also conducted his own business, the Fornshell Printing Co., which he founded in Columbus in 1903. He wrote *The Historical and Illustrated Ohio Penitentiary . . . ,* [Columbus?, 1903].

FORREST, ALBERTINA MAY ALLEN (May 14, 1872–April 27, 1904), was born near Akron, Summit County. She was an active worker in the Disciples of Christ

Church. Her death occurred in Sea Breeze, Fla. A selection of her writings, *Essays on Philosophy and Life,* Indianapolis, 1904, was edited by her husband, Jacob D. Forrest.

FORTUNE, ALONZA WILLARD (June 29, 1873–Dec. 26, 1950), clergyman and educator, was born in Holmes County. He graduated from Hiram College in 1898, graduated in theology from the University of Chicago in 1905, and earned a Ph.D. at Chicago in 1915. A minister in the Disciples Church, he served pastorates in Ohio, New York, and Kentucky. He was on the faculty of the Church of the Bible, Lexington, Ky., 1912–22, and served as a pastor in Lexington, 1922–44. He wrote several books on religion and on the history of the Disciples, e.g., *Origin and Development of the Disciples,* St. Louis, Mo., 1924. WWW 3

FOSDICK, WILLIAM WHITEMAN (Jan. 28, 1825–March 8, 1862), was born in Cincinnati, Hamilton County. He graduated from Transylvania University in 1845, studied law, and practiced for a time in Covington, Ky., Cincinnati, and New York City. In 1858 he returned to Cincinnati and edited the *Sketch Club.* Moncure Daniel Conway (q.v.) described him as a lovable man without enterprise, one who could have accomplished something in literature had he been less fond of the time-consuming game of chess. His rather rococo novel *Malmiztic* met with extravagant praise at the hands of some critics and was openly ridiculed by others, yet all conceded its historical accuracy. His death occurred in Cincinnati.

Malmiztic, the Toltec; And the Cavaliers of the Cross, Cincinnati, 1851.
Ariel, and Other Poems, New York, [1855].
Progress of Liberty . . . , Cincinnati, 1861.

FOSTER, CAROLINE HOLCOMB WRIGHT (Dec. 19, 1864–May 28, 1929), was born in Greenfield, Highland County. She lived in Los Angeles, where she was a social worker and a journalist for many years. Some of her short stories were published in magazines under the pen name Amy Elizabeth Leigh. A posthumous collection of her poetry was edited by Caroline H. S. Wright: *Winds of the World,* Boston, [1934]. WWNAA 3

FOSTER, CHARLES JAMES (Nov. 24, 1820–Sept. 12, 1883), journalist, born in Bicester, England, lived in Cincinnati and Columbus during most of the 1850s. He was editor of the *Ohio Statesman,* 1857–60, and after 1860 worked on New York magazines. He is buried in Columbus. Widely recognized as an authority on racing and other sports, he also wrote a novel: *The White Horse of Wooton . . . ,* Philadelphia, [1878].

FOSTER, EDWIN J. (1847– ?), lawyer, brother of Hanna A., Henry E., and Leonard G. Foster (qq.v.), was born in Strongsville, Cuyahoga County. After graduating from the law school of Boston University, he practiced in Cleveland until his retirement in 1885. He published a collection of verse: *A Pasture Stroll,* [Cleveland, 1914].

FOSTER, ETHEL FIELD (Dec. 11, 1883–), was born in Granville, Licking County. She attended the preparatory department of Denison University, 1899–1902, and H. Thane Miller School for Girls, Cincinnati, 1902–04. She published a number of stories and articles in various magazines and one novel: *A Lamp in the Window,* Los Angeles, [1937].

FOSTER, FINLEY MILLIGAN (c.1854–Jan. 10, 1948), clergyman, was born in Cedarville, Greene County. He held degrees from Indiana University, Reformed Presbyterian Seminary, Pittsburgh, Pa., and New York University (Ph.D.). He was pastor of a church in Bellefontaine, 1880–87, and of Third Reformed Presbyterian Church, the Bronx, N. Y., 1887–1942. He died in Hackensack, N. J. He wrote *Church and State, Their Relations Considered,* [New York, 1940].

FOSTER, FRANK HUGH (June 18, 1851–Oct. 20, 1935), theologian, born in Springfield, Mass., was a resident of Oberlin for two periods totaling eighteen years. A graduate of Harvard University (1873), Andover Theological Seminary (1877), and University of Leipzig (Ph.D., 1882), he taught church history at Oberlin from 1884 to 1892. He was on the faculties of Pacific Seminary, Berkeley, Calif., 1892–1902, and Olivet College, Mich., 1904–16. In 1925 he returned to Oberlin, where he taught Greek and Hebrew until 1933. He translated a number of German works and published many reviews and articles in religious periodicals.

The Seminary Method of Original Study in the Historical Sciences . . . , New York, 1888.
The Fundamental Ideas of the Roman Catholic Church . . . , Philadelphia, 1899.
Christian Life and Theology . . . , New York, [1900].
The Teaching of Jesus Concerning His Own Mission, New York, [1903].
A Genetic History of the New England Theology, Chicago, 1907.

A Brief Doctrinal Commentary on the Arabic Koran . . . , London, [1932].
The Life of Edward Amasa Parks . . . , New York, [1936].
The Modern Movement in American Theology . . . , New York, [1939].

FOSTER, HANNA ALICE (Jan. 27, 1837–March 27, 1926), was born in Strongsville, Cuyahoga County, the sister of Henry E., Edwin J., and Leonard G. Foster (qq.v.). She graduated from Baldwin College in 1866 and afterward lived in Cleveland and Berea. She was active in the temperance movement. Besides the two long narrative poems listed below, she published poetry in various magazines and newspapers. She died in Berea at the age of 89.

Hilda. A Poem, Philadelphia, 1879.
Zululu, the Maid of Anahuac, New York, 1892.

FOSTER, HENRY E. (April 28, 1845–Sept. 15, 1915), lawyer, was born in Strongsville, Cuyahoga County, the brother of Edwin J., Hanna A., and Leonard G. Foster (qq.v.). He attended Baldwin College and studied law at Boston University. After working on newspapers in Toledo and Rochester, N. Y., he practiced law and dealt in real estate in Cleveland. The pamphlet below was published anonymously.

William McKinley and the G.O.P. under the X-ray . . . , Cleveland, [1900].

FOSTER, JAMES (Jan. 27, 1798–Dec. 28, 1876), served in the War of 1812 as a soldier in the First Regiment. He was captured and imprisoned at Detroit. His pamphlet, signed "By an Ohio Volunteer," condemns General Hull for his surrender. Foster died in Troy, Miami County.

The Capitulation, or a History of the Expedition Conducted by William Hull . . . , Chillicothe, 1812.

FOSTER, JOHN M. Pseud. See Mildred W. Benson.

FOSTER, JOHN WELLS (March 4, 1815–June 29, 1873), geologist, was in Ohio from 1835 to 1844. He came to Zanesville to study law, was admitted to the bar, but devoted much of his time to geology. He worked on the geological survey in 1837. He later published a number of important reports on mineral resources, numerous articles, and a book on the Mound-Builders: *Pre-Historic Races of the United States of America,* Chicago, 1873.

FOSTER, LEONARD GURLEY (Sept. 10, 1840–Dec. 13, 1937), was born in Brooklyn, now a part of Cleveland, Cuyahoga County. He graduated from Berea College, taught school, and served in the 8th Ohio Battery during the Civil War. He was for many years a Chautauqua speaker. Like his sister and brothers—Hanna A., Edwin J., and Henry E. (qq.v.)—he wrote poetry as an avocation. At the time of his death, he was said to have written nearly 80,000 poems. He presented the Western Reserve Historical Society with fifty volumes of his verse, 47 of them in manuscript.

Whisperings of Nature, Cleveland, 1893.
Blossoms of Nature, Cleveland, 1908.
The Early Days; A Pioneer Idyl, [Cleveland], 1911.

FOSTER, RANDOLPH SINKS (Feb. 22, 1820–May 1, 1903), clergyman, was born in Williamsburg, Clermont County, where his father was jailer. He grew up in Kentucky, where the family moved, and attended Augusta College. In 1837 he was admitted to the Ohio Conference of the Methodist Episcopal Church, and he preached in Ohio until 1850, serving churches in Hillsboro, Portsmouth, Lancaster, Springfield, and Cincinnati. He served churches in New York City, 1850–57; was president of Northwestern University, 1857–60; returned to the New York area, 1860–68; was on the faculty of Drew Seminary, 1868–72; and was elected bishop in 1872. He retired in 1902. His theological writings were widely discussed and made him a leader in the Methodist Church of his day.

Objections to Calvinism As It Is . . . , Cincinnati, 1849.
Nature and Blessedness of Christian Purity, New York, 1851.
Beyond the Grave . . . , New York, 1879.
Centenary Thoughts for Pew and Pulpit, New York, 1884.
Evidences of Christianity . . . , New York, 1889.
Prolegomena . . . , New York, 1889.
Studies in Theology, 6 vols., New York, 1889–99.
Theism . . . , New York, 1889.
Union of Episcopal Methodisms, New York, 1892.
Creation, God in Time and Space, New York, 1895.
God, Nature and Attributes, New York, 1897.
Sin, New York, 1899.

FOURÉ, HÉLÈNE SELTER (April 11, 1889–), educator, was born in Paris, France. Educated in France, she served on the Ohio State University faculty, 1920–37. She and her husband also taught in the summers at

Western Reserve University, 1923–35. She has returned to Paris to live. She has written numerous articles and books on French civilization, e.g., *The French Cathedrals . . .* , Boston, [1931].

FOUT, HENRY HARNESS (Oct. 18, 1861–1947), clergyman, was born in Grant County, W. Va. He was licensed to preach by the United Brethren Virginia Conference in 1885. The following year he graduated from Shenandoah Collegiate Institute. In 1890 he graduated from Union (Bonebrake) Seminary in Dayton, after which he spent nine years as pastor of Oak Street Church, Dayton, and was presiding elder of the Miami Conference, 1899–1901. During this period he toured the Holy Land and wrote the account listed below. He supervised Sunday school literature for the United Brethren Church, 1901–13 and was elected bishop in 1913. He died in Indianapolis, Ind.

The 1900 Pilgrimage to Egypt and the Holy Land, Dayton, 1900.

FOWKE, GERARD (June 25, 1855–March 5, 1933), archaeologist, was born Charles Mitchell Smith in Maysville, Ky. In 1887 he adopted the name of a maternal ancestor. After a period of schoolteaching, he entered Ohio State University as a special student in 1881. He later participated in archaeological and geological expeditions in the United States and in other parts of the world. He published many articles and reports. His major work is *Archaeological History of Ohio; The Mound Builders and Later Indians,* Columbus, 1902. DAB 21

FOWLER, JOSIAH (Feb., 1800–July 11, 1891), was born in Westfield, Mass. In 1830 he settled in Margaretta, Erie County, where he operated a farm and was a founder of Castalia Congregational Church in 1835. He was an active abolitionist.

An Analysis of Texts of Scripture, Castalia, 1881.

FOWLER, MARY BLACKFORD (Feb. 20, 1892–), was born in Findlay, Hancock County. After graduating from Oberlin College in 1913, she studied sculpture at Demetrios School of Sculpture in Massachusetts. With her husband, the late Harold North Fowler, a professor at Western Reserve University, she wrote a book for children: *Picture Book of Sculpture,* New York, 1929.

FOX, HENRY CLAY (Jan. 20, 1836–Nov. 22, 1920), lawyer, was born near West Elkton, Preble County. His parents moved to Indiana, in which state he grew up and spent his life. He was admitted to the bar in 1861, served in the Civil War with the 57th Indiana Volunteer Infantry, and was appointed county judge in 1896.

Adventures of a Philosopher, a Dun Mule and a Brindle Dog. By an Indiana Man, Richmond, Ind., 1888.

Uncle Zeek and Aunt Liza; A Tale of Episodes, Boston, [1905].

Memoirs of Wayne County and Richmond . . . , 2 vols., Madison, Wis., 1912.

FRAME, NATHAN T. (July 15, 1840–March 27, 1915), clergyman, was born in Morgan County, Pa., but spent his boyhood in Iowa. He and his wife, a native of Indiana, were members of the Society of Friends and traveled throughout the country holding revivals. They usually conducted their meetings in Methodist churches. In 1871 they settled in Clinton County; they later lived in Harveysburg, Warren County, and other Ohio communities. From 1881 until 1914, Rev. Frame was pastor of a church in Jamestown, Greene County.

Under the Lindens. Poems, [Cleveland], 1885.

Reminiscences of Nathan T. Frame and Esther G. Frame, [Cleveland], 1907.

FRANCE, LEWIS BROWN (Aug. 8, 1833–1907), lawyer, was born in Washington, D. C., and spent his youth in Cincinnati, where he learned the printing trade. The city directory for 1856 lists him as a printer; in that year he moved on to Illinois, where he studied law. He later practiced in Colorado, the locale of most of his writings, e.g., *Over the Old Trail: A Novel,* Boston, 1895.

FRANKENBERG, THEODORE THOMAS (Sept. 24, 1877–July 26, 1958), publicist, was born in Franklin County. He was educated in the Columbus public schools. He worked on the Columbus *Dispatch,* 1898–99, on the Columbus *Citizen,* 1899–1903, on the *Ohio State Journal,* 1903–07 and 1908–16, and on the Toledo *Times,* 1908. He lectured widely on journalism and was a publicity counselor for various organizations. He also prepared booklets and brochures for colleges raising funds. His writings include *Spectacular Career of Rev. Billy Sunday . . .* , Columbus, [1913]. OBB

FRANKENSTEIN, GUSTAVUS (c.1829–Dec. 11, 1893), younger brother of John P. Frankenstein (q.v.), was born in Germany, but grew up in Cincinnati, where his parents settled in 1831. He also lived for many years in Springfield. He died in Cincinnati, where he had returned to live with his sisters a few weeks earlier. His only publications that have been discovered were discussions of mathematics.

Magic Reciprocals . . . , Cincinnati, 1875.
Gustavus Frankenstein's Great Principle of Reciprocal Identity, New York, 1878.

FRANKENSTEIN, JOHN PETER (c.1816–April 16, 1881), painter and sculptor, was born in Germany in 1816 or 1817. He was the oldest member of a remarkable family of artists that came to Cincinnati in 1831. Of his three brothers and two sisters, who were all painters and teachers of art, the best known was Godfrey, first president of the Cincinnati Academy of Fine Arts, and —with several of his brothers and sisters— creator of a panorama of Niagara Falls. John began painting at fifteen; he studied in Philadelphia, 1839–44, returned to Cincinnati, and then moved with the rest of the family to Springfield in 1849. From 1856 until about 1865 he maintained a studio in Cincinnati. He spent his last years in New York City, living in apparent poverty, although considerable money was found in his cluttered East Side room after his death. His only literary production was a pamphlet of doggerel verse, satirizing Cincinnati residents who bought foreign art and disregarded local talent. His satire is directed particularly at Nicholas Longworth (q.v.). He also devotes two pages to an attack on Edgar Allan Poe, whom he may have known in Philadelphia. The tone of the pamphlet is suggested by the motto on its title page:

American artists, ah!
American patrons, pshaw!!
American critics, BAH!!!

American Art: Its Awful Altitude, Cincinnati, 1864.

FRANKLIN, MARY LUCRETIA BARKER. See Mary L. Barker.

FRASER, HERBERT (March 3, 1890–Feb. 9, 1953), educator, was born in Mansfield, Richland County. He taught at Phillips Andover Academy and at King's College, Aberdeen, Scotland, and was on the economics faculty of Swarthmore College for 27 years. Internationally recognized as a specialist on monetary systems, he was an adviser to the West German government after World War II. He published numerous technical articles and several books, e.g., *Great Britain and the Gold Standard,* London, 1933. DAS 2

FRAYER, IHNA THAYER (April 13, 1873–), artist and designer, was born in Cleveland, Cuyahoga County. He attended Cleveland School of Art and in 1894 became a designer for various furniture and decorating companies. In 1914 he opened his own studio; he also taught for a number of years at Cleveland Museum of Art. He lived in Hudson for many years and now lives in Florida. He lectured on Ohio history and architecture and published several books on the same subjects, e.g., *Early Homes of Ohio,* Richmond, Va., [1936], and *Ohio in Homespun and Calico,* Richmond, Va., [1942]. WWO

FRAZIER, IDA MAY HEDRICK (Mrs. Robert) (May 14, 1860–March 2, 1943), educator, was born in Fort Recovery, Mercer County, and was a lifelong resident of that community. She taught in the schools of Fort Recovery and vicinity for 42 years. She published *Fort Recovery . . . ,* Columbus, 1948.

FREASE, HARRY (1865–May 14, 1953), lawyer, was born in Canton, Stark County. As a young man he was an engineer on several Ohio railroad construction projects. Admitted to the bar in 1886, he practiced in Canton, was active in a variety of business enterprises, and was an officer of the Ohio National Guard for many years. He published a book on the New Deal: *A Political Paradox . . . ,* Philadelphia, [1934].

FRÉCHETTE, ANNIE THOMAS HOWELLS (March 29, 1844–June 17, 1938), daughter of William C. Howells and sister of William D. Howells (qq.v.), was born in Hamilton, Butler County. In 1877 she married Achille Fréchette, a translator in the Canadian House of Commons. For a time she was literary editor of the Chicago *Inter-Ocean.* She died in San Diego, Calif.

The Farm's Little People, Philadelphia, [1897].
On Grandfather's Farm, Philadelphia, [1897].

FREEMAN, ALBERT DU BOIS (Nov. 2, 1850–June 28, 1943), was born in Richmonddale, Ross County. He lived in California after 1903 and died in Alhambra, Calif. He wrote several booklets, e.g., *Aurelia and the Professor,* [Monterey Park?, Calif., 1923].

FREEMAN, JULIA SUSAN WHEELOCK (Oct. 7, 1833–1900), was born in Avon, Lorain County, but grew up in Erie County, Pa. In 1855 she moved to Michigan. She attended Kalamazoo College and was teaching in Ionia, Mich., when her brother was wounded at Second Bull Run. She went to his bedside, and after his death she served as a nurse throughout the war. She then worked as a clerk in the Treasury Department from 1865 until her marriage to Porter C. Freeman in 1873, after which she lived in Michigan and Springfield, Mo.

The Boys in White: The Experience of a Hospital Agent in and around Washington, New York, 1870.

FREEMAN, MARTIN J. (May 17, 1899–), educator, was born in Ada, Hardin County. He graduated from Ohio Northern University in 1925 and the University of Chicago (Ph.D.) in 1934. He has taught at Iowa State College, University of Chicago, and Hunter College and is now living in Chappaqua, N. Y. He has written several mystery novels, e.g., *The Murder of a Midget,* New York, [1931].

FREEMAN, WILLIAM A. (Aug. 28, 1880–), clergyman, born near Louisville, Ill., was licensed to the ministry of the Christian Church in 1900. He served churches in several states and after 1920 settled in Covington, Miami County. He now lives in Frankfort, Ross County. Besides articles on religious topics, he has published a volume of poems: *Gray Skies and Chuckles,* Covington, [1944].

FREEMAN, WINFIELD (Jan. 3, 1848–July 5, 1926), lawyer, was born in London, Madison County, attended public schools in Winchester, read law, and was admitted to the Ohio bar in 1869. After practicing in Preble County, he moved to Kansas around 1880. He was active in politics and in the Methodist church. He was librarian of the Kansas State Library from 1919 until his death. His writings include *The Prodigal Son,* Topeka, Kan., 1921. WWW 1

FREESE, ANDREW (Nov. 1, 1816–Sept. 5, 1904), educator, was born near Bangor, Maine. He came to Cleveland in 1839 and taught school until 1846, when he was named the first principal of Central High School. In 1854 he was elected the first superintendent of schools in the city and served for ten years. He returned to teaching, 1864–68, and served another year as principal of Central High School, 1868–69, before retiring. He died in Cleveland at the age of 88.

Early History of the Cleveland Public Schools, Cleveland, 1876.

FREITAG, GEORGE (Sept. 26, 1909–), was born in Canton, Stark County, and spent part of his boyhood on a farm near Robertsville. He worked in Canton as a sign painter for a number of years and now lives in San Bernardino, Calif. He has published a number of short stories in national magazines and a novel: *The Lost Land,* New York, [1947].

FRENCH, ASEL BELDEN (Sept. 13, 1838– ?), spiritualist, was born in Farmington, Trumbull County. He attended Western Reserve Seminary. In 1859 he moved to Clyde, where he operated a nursery business. He spent one year at the law school of the University of Michigan and was admitted to the bar in 1872. He practiced in Tiffin until his health failed, and he then returned to the nursery business. He experienced his first trance at the age of sixteen, and throughout his life he was nationally known as a speaker on spiritualism.

Gleanings from the Rostrum, 1892.

FRENCH, ELSIE JANET (Nov. 16, 1861–Jan. 3, 1952), was born in Wakeman, Huron County, and she lived for many years in Berlin Heights, Erie County. Her poems appeared in various periodicals, and she also published a collection: *May Festival and Other Poems,* Berlin Heights, 1925.

FRENCH, HERBERT GREER (Jan. 17, 1872–June 25, 1942), was born in Covington, Ky. He spent much of his life in Cincinnati, where he was a vice-president of Procter & Gamble Company. A collection of his poems was privately published: *Songs of the Shore & Others,* [Cincinnati], 1925.

FREY, JOHN PHILIP (Feb. 24, 1871–Nov. 29, 1957), labor leader, born in Mankato, Minn., came to Cincinnati as editor of the *Molders' Journal.* He was secretary-treasurer of the Metal Trades Union, A.F. of L., 1927–34, and president, 1934–50. His last years were spent in Washington, D. C., where he died at the age of 86. Sometimes referred to as "the scholar of the labor movement," he wrote many articles and several books, e.g., *The Labor Injunction . . . ,* Cincinnati, [1923?]. WWW 3

FRIEDEL, FRANCIS JOSEPH (Aug. 9, 1897–Feb. 12, 1959), clergyman and educator, was born in Cleveland, Cuyahoga County. He graduated from the University of Dayton in 1917, the University of Fribourg, Switzerland, in 1925, and the University of Pittsburgh (Ph.D.) in 1950. Ordained to the Roman Catholic priesthood in 1927, he served on the University of Dayton faculty, 1927–43 and 1950–53. He was president of Trinity College, Sioux City, Iowa, 1943–49. He wrote religious articles and pamphlets and *The Mariology of Cardinal Newman,* New York, 1928. WWW 3

FRIEDLAND, ABRAHAM HYMAN (July 1, 1892–Aug. 3, 1939), educator, was born in Gorodok, Vilna, Russia, and came to the United States in 1907. He was superintendent of Hebrew schools in Cleveland from 1921 until his death. He published poems, articles, and bilingual stories, many of them for use in schools. His books include *Dovid'l,* [New York, 1944].

FRIEDRICH, RALPH (April 17, 1913–), was born in Cincinnati, Hamilton County. He graduated from the University of Cincinnati in 1933 and served on the faculty, 1933–43. After teaching English in the Cincinnati public schools, 1943–47, he was commissioned a second lieutenant in the U. S. Army. Since 1949 he has served in various capacities with the military government in Japan; he has been a military intelligence analyst in Tokyo and Camp Zama since 1958. He has published poems, short stories, and book reviews in various periodicals. He has also published a collection of poems: *Boy at Dusk . . . ,* New York, [1941].

FRINGS, KETTI, was born Katherine Hartley in Columbus, Franklin County. She also lived in Dayton, Akron, and Cleveland. After attending Principia College, St. Louis, she worked for several New York advertising agencies and wrote radio scripts and magazine articles. While living in southern France, she married Kurt Frings, now an actor's representative in Hollywood. She has written numerous screenplays and two novels: *Hold Back the Dawn,* New York, [1940], and *God's Front Porch,* New York, 1944. Her greatest success came, however, with her dramatization of Thomas Wolfe's *Look Homeward, Angel,* for which she received the Pulitzer Prize for Drama in 1958.

FRISBIE, ROBERT DEAN (April 16, 1896–Nov. 19, 1948), was born in Cleveland, Cuyahoga County. After attending schools in Connecticut and California, he served in the army and also was a reporter in California. After 1920 he was a trader and navigator in the South Pacific. He died in Rarotonga, Cook Islands. He wrote short stories, novels, and nonfiction about the South Seas, e.g., *My Tahiti,* Boston, 1937. WWW 2

FRITCHMAN, STEPHEN HOLE (May 12, 1902–), clergyman, was born in Cleveland, Cuyahoga County. He graduated from Ohio Wesleyan University in 1924 and Union Theological Seminary in 1927. He has served on the faculties of several universities, and since 1948 has been pastor of First Unitarian Church, Los Angeles. He has written for various magazines and newspapers, and his books include *Men of Liberty; Ten Unitarian Pioneers,* Boston, 1944. WW 30

FRITZ, JOHN HENRY CHARLES (July 30, 1874–April 12, 1953), clergyman, was born in Martins Ferry, Belmont County. He graduated from Concordia Seminary, Fort Wayne, Ind., in 1897. After serving several Lutheran pastorates, he served as dean of Concordia Seminary, 1920–40. His writings include *Pastoral Theology,* St. Louis, Mo., 1932. WWW 3

FRIZELL, MARTHA G. SINKS (1893–July 15, 1956), wife of William G. Frizell (q.v.), was born in Dayton, Montgomery County. A graduate of Ohio Wesleyan University, she taught in Dayton schools. She published poems in various periodicals and in a collected volume, *A Stranger and Afraid . . . ,* New York [1941]. BDCP

FRIZELL, WILLIAM GIVENS (Aug. 31, 1866–Dec. 14, 1943), lawyer, was born in Dayton, Montgomery County. After graduating from Ohio Wesleyan University in 1887, he read law and was admitted to the bar in 1889. He practiced in Dayton and served in the state legislature, 1903–08. He traveled widely, frequently lectured about his trips, and wrote at least three travel books, e.g., *Out of the Way Places,* Dayton, 1909.

FROHMAN, DANIEL (Aug. 22, 1851–Dec. 26, 1940), was born in Sandusky, Erie County. As a sort of ghost-author, he may have contributed far more to literature than as author of four books and many newspaper and magazine articles. The theater, rather than written literature, has known the Frohman name, and the stage indelibly records its influence. It is difficult to mention any one of the three Frohman brothers—Daniel, Gustave or Charles—without including the other two. Their lives reflect the wisdom of one of Daniel's observations: "The nearer the bottom one begins, the more firmly grounded, deeply rooted he will be. Nature doesn't allow seeds to flower away up in the air; why then should actors be expected to do so?" Daniel Frohman's father, Henry Frohman, came from Darmstadt, Germany, in 1845, and after several stops, settled in Sandusky, where he manufactured cigars and conducted a bar and restaurant. Here the family lived for almost twenty years, and here Daniel was born. The father's histrionic activities were displayed at home, at work, and on the local amateur stage. Play-reading as a boy started Daniel on the literary side of the stage, for he accompanied his father in wagon trips to nearby towns to sell cigars and on the way acted as prompter to his father for his then-current role. Daniel went to school in Sandusky until he was about twelve years old and was then sent to New York City in 1863, where he continued his grammar school education for about another year. His family followed him to New York City in 1864. Daniel has recalled the prison for Confederate officers which was built on Johnson's Island in Sandusky Bay during 1862. It was in Sandusky that he received practically all of his formal education. In this slender warp of education must be woven a woof of experience and observations, beginning with work in the New York *Tribune* offices, where he soon met, and translated the hieroglyphics of, Horace Greeley, and continuing along the never-ending theatrical history of New York's Broadway. The earliest record of a Daniel Frohman article is his contribution on the "Personal Habits of Horace Greeley," published in the Sandusky *Register* of Oct. 26, 1869, a fact which shows, in itself, that Daniel Frohman's thoughts returned to his birthplace even against New York's attractions. Daniel received the usual "Annie Oakleys" through newspaper associates and came in contact with the theater through the *Tribune's* famous critic-author, William Winter, but he undoubtedly had greater impressions and opportunities from contacts in and about his father's cigar store at 708 Broadway, then in the heart of the theatrical district. The original Brentano's bookstore was next door; the Academy of Music, Niblo's Garden, and the Rialto, Union Square, Wallack's and Olympia Theaters were all close by. All three Frohman boys began their theatrical careers as advance agents for theatrical troupes in the days of one-night stands, makeshift theaters, poor transportation, and survival-of-the-fittest business methods. Daniel began in 1874 with the Georgia Minstrels, and with his experience over the next five years, he knew every opera house, theater, and lodge hall in the country. His first management job was with Steele MacKaye at the Madison Square Theatre in 1879. He was joined by his two brothers, and the New York story of the Frohman management began in earnest. The name "Lyceum" is synonymous with Daniel Frohman in the theatrical world. In 1886, he undertook the management of the Old Lyceum and brought forth E. H. Sothern, who starred in *The Highest Bidder* and who continued to make stage history for many years to come. At about that time, David Belasco joined the Frohmans in their after-theater round tables, where menus and tabletops became the stage; table silver and pencils, the players. The friendships and influences that these dream-sessions founded lasted throughout their lives, and each of the participants reported most lively discussions, full of idea interchange, mutual criticism, and stage-technique development. In later life, these early foundations developed into a knowledge of "good theater" and "bad theater" that was well-nigh automatic. The intense interest of the group in those early days made possible the presentation of plays by many famous authors in later years. In 1887, Daniel Frohman began to assemble his famous "Lyceum Stock Company." The key to Daniel Frohman's real contribution to literature as a ghost writer may have been unwittingly given in connection with his comments on the stock company's first play, which he asked Belasco to write. Belasco cooperated with Henry C. DeMille, play reader for Daniel Frohman, and together they wrote *The Wife*. Of this team, "D. F." said: "DeMille had been successful in writing plays alone, but he was primarily a literary person, while Belasco, with his strong natural sense of drama, worked less with lines and situations than with action and stage effect. He saw human nature only from the footlights." The Old Lyceum gave way, after the turn of the century, to the new Lyceum Theatre on 45th Street, and it was opened with E. H. Sothern starring in *The Proud Prince* on Nov. 2, 1903. And the plays went on; but Daniel turned over many interests to his brother Charles, who later met his death with the sinking of the *Lusitania,* May 7, 1915, with those oft-repeated words: "Why fear death? It is the most beautiful adventure in life." It is in this connection that Daniel's philosophy is unscreened: "My own impression about Charles' death is that it occurred at just about the right time. He had reached the climax of his management career. Had he continued he would have been affected by the tremendous reverses that have since affected all industries. He would have had trouble financially and otherwise. As it was, he died while he was at the top and left behind him a splendid record of theatrical achievements." In 1912 Daniel Frohman became a director of Famous Players Film

Company, and, during a period of about five years, the caption "Daniel Frohman Presents" was flashed on screen releases throughout the country. Undoubtedly the most intense activity in which Daniel Frohman engaged was the Actors' Fund, of which he was a charter member from its foundation in 1882 and its first secretary. The Fund provided relief for needy players and operated a home for their retirement. "D. F.," as he was known to the theatrical world, became the sixth president in 1904 and served in that capacity, without compensation and with great activity, until his death. Still the producer, he predicted "The last curtain is falling," and undoubtedly believed that his own life play, like those plays that he staged, should "reflect life, not as it is, but as it should be." He wrote four books: *Memories of a Manager . . .*, New York, 1911, *Charles Frohman, Manager and Man,* (with I. F. Marcosson), New York, 1916, *Daniel Frohman Presents: An Autobiography,* New York, 1935, and *Encore . . .*, New York, 1937.
Charles E. Frohman

FROST, STANLEY (Oct. 26, 1881–June 14, 1942), journalist, was born in Oberlin, Lorain County. He graduated from Berea College in 1902. He worked as a reporter on the New York *Tribune,* 1902 and 1915–20, on the Berea *Citizen,* 1907–10, and on the Detroit *News,* 1910–14. He was also a contributor to several national magazines. His residence at the time of his death was Richmond, Va. His books include *The Challenge of the Klan,* Indianapolis, [1924]. WWW 3

FROST, WESLEY (June 17, 1884–), diplomat, was born in Oberlin, Lorain County. He graduated from Oberlin College in 1907. From 1909 until his retirement in 1944, he served the Department of State in various capacities: as U. S. consul in several cities, as a foreign trade advisor, and as ambassador to Paraguay, 1942–44. His residence in 1960 was Oberlin. During World War I he lectured on submarine warfare and published *German Submarine Warfare . . .*, New York, 1918. WW 24

FRY, BENJAMIN ST. JAMES (June 16, 1824–Feb. 5, 1892), clergyman, was born in Rutledge, Tenn. He attended Woodward College, Cincinnati, and began contributing to the Cincinnati *Times* in 1840. He edited the *Western Rambler.* In 1847 he became a Methodist clergyman, and for a few years he was president of Worthington College for Women. He also served as chaplain of the 63rd O.V.I., 1861–64. In 1865 he moved to St. Louis to take charge of the Methodist Book Concern. He became editor of the St. Louis *Central Christian Advocate* in 1872. His death occurred in St. Louis.

Lives of Bishops Whatcoat, McKendree & George, New York, 1852.

The Life of Robert R. Roberts . . ., New York, 1856.

Property Consecrated; Or, Honoring God with Our Substance . . ., New York, 1856.

An Appeal to Facts . . ., New York, 1890.

FRY, JOSEPH REESE (1811–June, 1865), born in Philadelphia, Pa., lived a few years in Cincinnati, where he edited the *Western Monthly Magazine and Literary Journal* in 1836 and published the *Daily Express,* 1837–39. He was later a banker in Philadelphia and wrote at least two books, e.g., *Our Battles in Mexico . . .*, Philadelphia, 1850.

FRY, SUSANNA MARGARET DAVIDSON (Feb. 4, 1841–Oct. 10, 1920), educator, was born in Burlington, Lawrence County. She was educated at Western College for Women, Oxford, studied at Ohio Wesleyan University, and earned a Ph.D. at Syracuse University. She married the Rev. James D. Fry in 1868, taught in Burlington and Ironton schools, and served on the faculty of Illinois Wesleyan University, 1876–90. She was corresponding secretary of the national W.C.T.U., 1898–1908. She died in Bloomington, Ill., and is buried in Ironton.

A Paradise Valley Girl, Chicago, 1899.

FRYE, BURTON JAMES CONRAD (Aug. 28, 1920–), was born in Huron, Erie County. He graduated from Miami University in 1943 and later studied in Naples. He lived in Lorain while employed by the National Tube Co. and is now living in Lake Geneva, Wis. He has published poems in various magazines and in several collections, e.g., *Castalia,* Prairie City, Ill., [1948].

FULLER, EMILY GUILLON (1860–1927), was born in Bellefontaine, Logan County. She married E. J. Howenstein, an attorney in Bellefontaine. She wrote *The Prize Watch . . .*, Akron, 1901.

FULLER, HUBERT BRUCE (June 15, 1880–Feb. 9, 1957), lawyer, was born in Derby, Conn. He graduated from Yale University in 1901 and from Yale Law School in 1903. In 1903 he began the practice of law in Cleveland. He was secretary to Senator Theodore Burton, 1909–15. He published numerous articles and several books on legal, historical, and political subjects, e.g., *The Speakers of the House,* Boston, 1909. WW 26

FULLERTON, HUGH STUART (Sept. 10, 1873–Dec. 27, 1945), journalist, was born in Hillsboro, Highland County. He began newspaper writing in Hillsboro in 1888, attended Ohio State University, 1891–93, and worked on various newspapers in Cincinnati, Chicago, New York, and Columbus. In 1906 he was the first sports writer to publish predictions on a World Series. He was on the staff of *Liberty* magazine, 1923–28, and also wrote many articles for the *Saturday Evening Post.* He wrote a series of novels for boys describing the baseball exploits of the hero, Jimmy Kirkland. His other books, mostly on racing and other sports, include *Racing Yarns,* New York, [1924]. WW 21

FULLERTON, KEMPER (Nov. 29, 1865–March 24, 1940), educator, was born in Cincinnati, Hamilton County. He graduated from Princeton University in 1888 and from Union Theological Seminary in 1891. He taught at Lane Seminary, Cincinnati, 1893–1904, and was on the faculty of Oberlin Graduate School of Theology, 1904–34. After his retirement, he continued to live in Oberlin until his death. He wrote *Prophecy and Authority . . . ,* New York, 1917. WWW 1

FULMER, CHESTA HOLT (March 18, 1900–Sept. 11, 1957), journalist, was born in Nashville, Tenn., and attended the schools of that city. She married E. Porter Fulmer of Dayton in 1920; during her residence in Dayton she was a reporter and columnist for the Dayton *Herald.* She published a volume of verse and prose: *Far Pastures,* Yellow Springs, [1940].

FULTON, JUSTIN DEWEY (March 1, 1828–April 16, 1901), clergyman, born in Earlville, N. Y., was a Baptist minister in Sandusky, 1855–59. He was a vigorous opponent of slavery, alcohol, the theater, women's suffrage, and Catholicism. While in Sandusky he published the first of his anti-Catholic polemics: *Outlook of Freedom: Or, the Roman Catholic Element in American History,* Cincinnati, 1856.

FUNK, CHARLES EARLE (April 4, 1881–April 16, 1957), editor and lexicographer, was born in Springfield, Clark County. He served as an editor of the *New Standard Dictionary* and numerous other compilations. His death occurred in Mount Dora, Fla. He wrote studies of word-origins, e.g., *A Hog on Ice, and Other Curious Expressions,* New York, [1948]. WWW 3

FUNK, ISAAC KAUFFMAN (Sept. 10, 1839–April 4, 1912), editor and publisher, was born in Clifton, Greene County. He graduated from Wittenberg College in 1860 and was ordained a Lutheran pastor the following year. He served churches in Indiana, in Carey, Ohio, and in Brooklyn, N. Y. As an aid to preachers in search of sermon themes, he founded the *Metropolitan Pulpit* in 1876, which after several changes in its name emerged in 1885 as the *Homiletic Review* and continued under this name until its suspension in 1934. In the same year he began supplying books, pictures, and other materials to ministers. In 1877 he took as a partner Adam W. Wagnalls. The firm of Funk & Wagnalls specialized in reference books for ministers. A temperance paper, the *Voice,* begun in 1885, was highly successful, but the company's most prosperous venture was the *Literary Digest,* begun in 1890. Funk was editor-in-chief of the *Standard Dictionary,* published by his firm. In his declining years he wrote several books on religion and spiritualism, e.g., *The Psychic Riddle,* New York, 1907. DAB 7

FUNKHOUSER, GEORGE A. (June 7, 1841–July 30, 1927), clergyman, was born in Shenandoah County, Va. After serving in the Civil War, 1862–65, he graduated from Otterbein College in 1868 and from Western Theological Seminary, Pittsburgh, in 1871, and was ordained to the ministry of the United Brethren Church. He served on the faculty of Union (Bonebrake) Seminary, 1871–1912. After his retirement, he directed seminary extension work until his death. He died in Dayton. He wrote many articles on religious subjects and *The Divinity of Our Lord,* Dayton, 1902.

FUNSTON, FREDERICK (Nov. 9, 1865–Feb. 19, 1917), army officer, was born in New Carlisle, Clark County, but grew up on a farm in Kansas, where his family moved when he was ten years old. After fighting as a member of the Cuban insurrectionists, he joined the U. S. Army and fought in the Philippines. In 1901 he was promoted to the rank of brigadier general. He wrote *Memories of Two Wars; Cuban and Philippine Experiences,* [New York, 1911]. DAB 7

FURBAY, JOHN HARVEY (Sept. 23, 1903–), educator, was born in Mount Gilead,

Morrow County. He attended Otterbein College, 1921–23, graduated from Asbury College, Wilmore, Ky., in 1924, and earned a Ph.D. from Yale University in 1931. He taught biology in several colleges and universities before joining the U. S. Department of Education in 1943. He has traveled widely in the interests of education and international understanding. He has written for magazines and newspapers and has published several books, e.g., *Nature Chats . . .*, Lancaster, Pa., 1933. WW 30

FURNAS, BOYD EDWIN (June 21, 1848–June 2, 1897), was born in Pleasant Hill, Miami County. At an early age he began contributing poetry to periodicals. He was auditor of Miami County, 1889–96. He compiled an atlas-directory of the county in 1883. Some of his poems were published posthumously.

Poems of Heart and Home, Columbus, 1898.

FUSH. Pseud. See Williston Fish.

G

GABRIEL, JOEL C. (Aug. 21, 1830–April 2, 1891), was born in Muskingum County. He enlisted in the 175th O.V.I. in Sept., 1864, and on Nov. 29 he was captured at Spring Hill, Tenn. He escaped Dec. 22, 1864. The pamphlet recounting his experiences was published by his sister, Mrs. W. W. Ramsay. Its cover title is *Joel C. Gabriel's Escape from the Rebels.* He died at Carlisle, Brown County.

Joel C. Gabriel . . ., Boston, 1894.

GADDIS, MAXWELL PIERSON (Sept. 9, 1811–Sept. 8, 1888), clergyman, born in Lancaster County, Pa., was brought to Ohio in 1817. He was converted at a Methodist camp meeting in 1824. While teaching school in 1830, he was given a license to exhort, and five years later he was licensed as a local preacher. He preached on the circuit in southwestern Ohio, conducted many revivals, and served churches at Fulton, Piqua, Yellow Springs, and other towns. He died in Dayton.

Foot-prints of an Itinerant, Cincinnati, 1855.
The Sacred Hour . . ., Cincinnati, 1856.
Brief Recollections of the Late Rev. George W. Walker, Cincinnati, 1857.
The Conversion of a Skeptic . . ., Cincinnati, 1858.
Last Words and Old-time Memories . . ., New York, 1880.

GAGE, FRANCES DANA BARKER (Oct. 12, 1808–Nov. 10, 1884), reformer and writer, was born in Marietta, Washington County, of New England ancestry. In 1829 she married James L. Gage, a lawyer of McConnelsville. She was an active advocate of abolition, temperance, and women's rights, and in 1851 she presided over a large women's rights convention in Akron. In 1853 the family moved to St. Louis, Mo., where her antislavery views subjected them to threats of violence. Her husband failed in business, and they returned to Ohio, where she edited an agricultural paper in Columbus. When the Civil War broke out, she went South to work with the freedmen and later became an unsalaried agent of the Sanitary Commission. In Sept., 1864, she was injured in a carriage accident in Galesburg, Ill., but she continued to lecture on temperance and the needs of the freedmen until Aug., 1867, when she suffered a paralytic stroke. Though an invalid for the rest of her life, she wrote stories and verses for children, using the pen name Aunt Fanny. She died in Greenwich, Conn.

Elsie Magoon . . ., Philadelphia, 1867.
Poems, Philadelphia, 1867.
Gertie's Sacrifice . . ., New York, 1868.
Steps Upward: A Temperance Tale, Philadelphia, 1870.
Six Mitten Books, 6 vols., New York.
Take Heed and Other Stories, New York.

GAINES, GARRY. Pseud. See Ann V. S. Patterson.

GALAIDA, EDWARD (July 27, 1906–), was born in Youngstown, Mahoning County, and still lives in that city. He attended Harvard University, 1925–29, was a reporter on the Youngstown *Vindicator* for a time, edited a tourist magazine, *Visit,* in California, was a district supervisor, Federal Writers' Project, 1935–41, served in the Air Force during World War II, and is now an interviewer with the Ohio State Employment Service. He has written *Mill Creek Park,* Cleveland, 1941.

GALBRAITH, ROBERT CHRISTY (Nov. 30, 1832–Nov. 18, 1916), clergyman, was born in Frankfort, Ross County. He graduated from Miami University in 1853, was ordained to the Presbyterian ministry in 1857, and served as chaplain at the State Reform Farm for four years. He served Presbyterian churches in Frankfort, Lancaster, Concord, and Chillicothe.

The History of the Chillicothe Presbytery . . . , Chillicothe, 1889.

GALBREATH, CHARLES BURLEIGH (Feb. 25, 1858–Feb. 23, 1934), librarian, was born near Leetonia, Columbiana County. He graduated from New Lisbon High School and in 1882 from Mount Union College. He was superintendent of schools at Wilmot, 1884–86, and East Palestine, 1886–93, and was on the faculty of Mount Hope College, 1893–96, serving the last few months as its president. He resigned, however, to become state librarian, a post he held until 1911 and which he filled again, 1915–18. He did much to expand the resources and services of the library. From 1920 until his death he edited the *Quarterly* of the Ohio Archaeological and Historical Society. He published many biographical and historical studies in the *Quarterly* which were later issued in pamphlet form. Besides numerous articles and monographs, he published a volume of verse: *The Crimson Flower . . .* , Columbus, 1919, and *The History of Ohio,* 5 vols., Chicago, 1925. DAB 22

GALL, ALICE CREW (July 11, 1878–Aug. 20, 1949), was born in McConnelsville, Morgan County. In 1902 she married Henry Ross Gall, a newspaperman; they lived in Cleveland, where her husband worked on the *Leader,* and in 1915 they moved to New York City. After working as a literary agent and publisher's reader in New York, she returned to McConnelsville in 1946. With her brother, Fleming H. Crew (q.v.), she wrote a number of children's stories and books; their collaboration was conducted by correspondence. She also wrote *In Peace and War . . .* , New York, 1941. JBA

GALLAGHER, WILLIAM DAVIS (Aug. 21, 1808–June 27, 1894), was born in Philadelphia, Pa. His lifelong characteristics were energy and impetuousness, qualities inherited in full measure from his father, who was excommunicated on his deathbed for refusing to reveal the secrets of Freemasonry. In 1816 his mother brought her family of four sons to Ohio and settled near what is now Mount Pleasant in Hamilton County. Young William's early education was obtained between the beautiful, truant-inviting countryside and a log schoolhouse. Later he attended the Lancastrian Seminary in Clermont County. He published his first verse at the age of sixteen. A few years later, in 1826, he became the general assistant to the founder of *The Western Tiller,* an agricultural magazine published in Cincinnati; and thereafter, for much of the remainder of his active life, he was associated with various Western newspapers and magazines, chiefly in Cincinnati, Xenia, and Columbus. By any standard, Gallagher's devotion and energy were enormous. He was determined to become the literary apostle of the West and he worked untiringly to that end. He founded or supported at least fourteen periodicals and slaved on them as editor, publisher, and contributor. It must be admitted that most of his ventures were financial failures, the profit from some not even paying for the magazine covers; Ohio in the 1830s and 1840s was not a favorable soil for literature, polite or crude. But the seed Gallagher sowed so lavishly, if it did not sprout well, turned into humus. He introduced many outstanding Eastern writers to Ohio readers, and at least one of his poems, "The Revelers," may have influenced Edgar Allan Poe. In 1831 Gallagher married Miss Emma Adamson, a steady and inspiring helpmate until her death in 1867. Nine children were born to the couple. While writing on a variety of topics—social, political, geographical—Gallagher nevertheless found time to compose a great deal of verse, which was popular in his day. Many of his lyrics were set to music and sung on the stage. In 1835–1837 he published three volumes of his verse under the title *Erato.* Perhaps his most significant journalistic effort was undertaken about this time, when he edited with Otway Curry (q.v.) *The Hesperian, or Western Monthly Magazine,* which ran from May, 1838, to Nov., 1839. In 1841 he brought out a small volume entitled *Selections from the Poetical Literature of the West,* representing the work of 38 poets. The opening selection was a long poem of his own, "Miami Woods," which with some alterations and enlargements later became Part One of his most important poem, bearing the same title. Gallagher was twice elected president of the Historical and Philosophical Society of Ohio, and in 1850 published his President's Address, read before the Society, "Progress in the Northwest." In it he praised the greatness of the Ohio country, the strength of united labor, and "Anglo-Saxonism"—which was Gallagher's term for white domination. His racial principles, however, were not narrow; and in the trying days preceding the Civil War he was an outspoken antislavery man in a region where popular opinion was violently opposed. A new era of public life opened for him in 1850, when he was called to Washington as the private secretary of Thomas Corwin, the Secretary of the Treasury. During the Civil War he held a similar post under Salmon P. Chase. As an appointee of President Lincoln, he performed many valuable services for the Union cause. Gallagher published *Miami Woods and Other Poems* in 1881. His last years were spent in the care of his children, in his picturesque house in Peewee Valley, near Louisville, Ky., where he died. His reputation as a poet rests mainly on "Miami Woods," which finally appeared as a serial in seven parts written from 1839 to 1856. The heart of the poem is the lament of the poet-father over the death of a beloved daughter. The form (blank verse) and the didactic tone of the poem are strongly reminiscent of the eighteenth- and nineteenth-century British nature poets, particularly Wordsworth; and the themes of the poem —the beauty of nature, the sustaining power of religion, and the dignity of the common man—are often tritely managed. But the feeling of bereavement breaks the restraints of artificiality and finds language worthy of it in the latter two parts of the poem and lifts it to the level of the minor elegiac poems of the language.

Tom Burns Haber

Erato, Number I, Cincinnati, 1835.
Erato, Number II, Cincinnati, 1835.
Erato, Number III, Cincinnati, 1837.
Selections from the Poetical Literature of the West . . . , Cincinnati, 1841.
Facts and Conditions of Progress in the North-west . . . , Cincinnati, 1850.
Miami Woods, a Golden Wedding, and Other Poems, Cincinnati, 1881.

GALLAHER, JAMES (Oct. 8, 1792–1853), clergyman, born in Washington County, Tenn., was ordained to the Presbyterian ministry in 1815. After serving churches in Tennessee, he was pastor of Third Presbyterian Church, Cincinnati, 1830–35. After leaving Cincinnati he taught at Marion College, Mo., 1835–39, and served churches in Missouri. He was chaplain of the House of Representatives, 1852–53. He wrote *The Pilgrimage of Adam and David . . . ,* Cincinnati, 1846.

GALLAHER, WALLACE W. (Nov. 20, 1861–June 27, 1959), educator, was born in Mead Township, Belmont County. He was a teacher and principal in Ohio and Missouri. He settled in Dilles Bottom, Belmont County, in 1930. His writings about fishing include *Black Bass Lore,* New York, 1937.

GALLAND, ISAAC (1790–1858), physician and adventurer, was born near Chillicothe, Ross County. He went on a filibustering expedition into Mexico, spent a year in a Spanish prison, and later lived with several Indian tribes. In the 1820s he was practicing medicine in Illinois and, allegedly, supplementing his earnings by counterfeiting. In 1829 he was practicing in Iowa. He was later associated with Joseph Smith in Nauvoo, Ill., and was one of the regents of the Mormon university there. He died in Iowa. His *Iowa Emigrant* is highly prized by collectors of Western Americana. Galland also issued five numbers of *Chronicles of the North American Savages.*

Galland's Iowa Emigrant . . . , Chillicothe, 1840.

GALLIZIER, NATHAN (Feb. 8, 1866–Jan. 14, 1927), was born in Ludwigsburg, Germany, studied for the priesthood, and spent several years with the Benedictine Monks in the upper valley of the Danube. He made a special study of medieval European history. In 1882 he came to the United States. A resident of Cincinnati, he wrote a number of novels dealing with Italian history, e.g., *The Hill of Venus,* Boston, 1913.

GALLOWAY, JULIA REBECCA (Sept. 8, 1874–Jan. 29, 1955), was born in Tippecanoe City, Miami County. She lived in Xenia for a time and moved to Cincinnati while in her teens. She was on the editorial staff of the *Western Christian Advocate* for a number of years. She published numerous poems in magazines and newspapers, and in 1905 she published a collection: *When the Lilacs Bloom, and Other Poems,* Boston, 1905.

GALLOWAY, WILLIAM ALBERT (April 8, 1860–Nov. 7, 1931), physician, was born in Xenia, Greene County, of a pioneer family. He attended Antioch College and graduated from Medical College of Ohio in 1890. He practiced in Xenia. His interest in local history and archaeology led to his writing *The History of Glen Helen,* [Columbus, 1932].

GALLY, JAMES WELLESLEY (Dec. 8, 1828–Oct. 5, 1891), born in Wheeling, Va., lived in Zanesville, 1853–64. He practiced dentistry there and edited the *Aurora,* 1857–60. He later lived in Nevada and

California and wrote for Western magazines. His death occurred in Watsonville, Calif. He wrote *Sand, and Big Jack Small,* Chicago, 1880.

GAMBIER, KENYON. Pseud. See Lorin A. Lathrop.

GAMBLE, SIDNEY DAVID (July 12, 1890–), was born in Cincinnati, Hamilton County. He graduated from Princeton University in 1912. He has served as a Y.M.C.A. official in China, 1918–19 and 1924–27, and has written several books about that country, e.g., *Peking, a Social Survey . . . ,* New York, [1921]. WW 30

GAMERTSFELDER, SOLOMON JACOB (Oct. 10, 1851–Aug. 6, 1925), clergyman and educator, was born in Coshocton County. He graduated from Northwestern College in 1878 and Evangelical Theological Seminary, Naperville, Ill., in 1881. Ordained to the ministry of the Evangelical Association in 1881, he served as pastor of several Ohio churches, 1879–87, was associate editor of the *Evangelical Messenger,* Cleveland, 1887–95, and was professor of systematic theology (1895–1911) and president (1911–19) of Evangelical Theological Seminary, Naperville. His writings include *A Bible Study on Prayer,* Cleveland, [1907].

GANO, LOUISE HEINKE (Dec. 31, 1885–Jan. 1, 1949), was born in Philadelphia, Pa., and lived in Cincinnati from 1925 until her death. She published poetry in the *Times-Star* and other newspapers and also brought out a collection of verse: *From My Muse to You,* Portland, Maine, 1948.

GANTVOORT, ARNOLD JOHANN (Dec. 6, 1857–May 18, 1937), musician, was born in Amsterdam, Holland. He came to America in 1876 and operated a College of Music in Cincinnati until 1921, when he moved to Los Angeles. He wrote a number of music textbooks and *Familiar Talks on the History of Music,* New York, 1913. WWW 1

GARBER, CLARK McKINLEY (June 22, 1891–), educator and lecturer, was born in Butler, Richland County, and at present is living in that community. He graduated from Wittenberg College in 1916 and did graduate work at Ohio State University. He taught at Capital University, 1916–22, was a school principal and superintendent of Eskimo education in Alaska, 1925–34, lectured widely on the Eskimos, 1934–43, and taught in Ohio high schools. He has published a number of articles on Eskimo customs and several books, e.g., *Stories and Legends of the Bering Strait Eskimos,* Boston, [1940].

GARDENER, HELEN HAMILTON (Jan. 21, 1853–July 26, 1925), novelist and reformer, born in Winchester, Va., received much of her education in Ohio. She attended high school in Cincinnati, graduated from Ohio State Normal School in 1872, and was principal of the Ohio Branch State Normal School, 1873–74. After moving to New York City, she lectured and wrote on sociological and humanitarian subjects and wrote several novels, e.g., *An Unofficial Patriot,* [Boston, 1894].

GARDINER, FREDERIC (1822–1889), educator, born in Gardiner, Maine, served on the Kenyon College faculty, 1865–69. He wrote *The Island of Life: An Allegory,* Boston, 1851.

GARDNER, MATTHEW (Dec. 5, 1790–Oct. 10, 1873), clergyman, was born in Stephentown, N. Y. In 1800 his family came to Ohio and purchased a farm near Ripley. As a hand on a flatboat to New Orleans, he was converted temporarily to Universalism. Back in Ohio on his father's farm in 1810, he was baptized in the Christian Church, which he served as a minister throughout the remainder of his life. He organized churches and preached in southern Ohio. Besides the titles below, he published a hymnbook that went into four editions. Both conservative and combative by nature, he sturdily opposed Universalism, Unitarianism, and Freemasonry. Despite threats of violence he attacked Freemasonry at every opportunity.

A Concise History of the United Persecutions against the Church of Christ . . . , Georgetown, 1828.

Twelve Years' Observation and Examination of Mr. Alexander Campbell's Theory and Practice of the Reformation, Cincinnati, 1835.

An Exposure of Masonry . . . , 1849.

The Autobiography of Elder Matthew Gardner . . . , (N. Summerbell, ed.), Dayton, 1874.

GARDNER, ROBERT EDWARD (May 13, 1891–), was born in Columbus, Franklin County. He attended Columbus public schools and Columbus Art School. After serving 28 years in the U. S. Army, he is now retired and lives in Columbus. An expert on weapons, both ancient and modern, he has published numerous magazine articles on the subject and several books, e.g., *American Arms and Arms Makers,* Columbus, 1938. WWMW 54

GAREY, THOMAS ANDREW (July 7, 1830–Aug. 20, 1909), horticulturist, was born in Cincinnati, Hamilton County, but little of his life was spent in Ohio. He lived in Hagerstown, Md., as a boy, moved to Iowa in 1847, and settled in California in 1852. Here he was a pioneer in the citrus fruit industry, and his book on orange culture was the first on the subject in California.

Orange Culture in California . . . , San Francisco, 1882.

GARFIELD, JAMES ABRAM (Nov. 19, 1831–Sept. 19, 1881), soldier, congressman, and twentieth President of the United States, was born in Orange, Cuyahoga County. His father died in 1833, leaving four small children. James worked on the farm, attended school in the winter, and worked as a driver and steersman on the Ohio Canal. He studied at Geauga Seminary, 1849, Western Reserve Eclectic Institute (Hiram College), 1851–54, and Williams College, 1854–56. While teaching at Hiram, 1856–57, and serving as its president, 1857–59, he read law and was admitted to the bar in 1859. During the Civil War he served as lieutenant colonel of the 42nd O.V.I. and rose to the rank of major general. He resigned his commission in Dec., 1863, to take his seat in the House of Representatives, to which his home district had elected him in 1862. He was re-elected to the House eight times. He served with distinction and took part in every major debate during his tenure. In Jan., 1880, the Ohio legislature elected him to the Senate. In June, however, the Republican National Convention ended a long struggle for the nomination by nominating him for the Presidency on the 36th ballot. He was elected in November, and his Senate seat went to John Sherman, whom he had originally supported for the Presidency. On July 2, 1881, while in the Baltimore and Potomac station in Washington, D. C., on his way to Williams College, he was shot by Charles J. Guiteau, a disappointed office-seeker. For eleven weeks he lingered between death and life. He died at Elberon, N. J. Not primarily a literary man, Garfield was an effective orator, especially adept at extemporaneous speaking. His speeches in the House are said to constitute a political history of the period. A taste for florid rhetoric in his early speeches gradually gave way to simplicity and clear-cut statement. Many of his speeches were published as separate pamphlets, and many memorial volumes after his tragic death contained selections from his addresses. Only major collections are listed below. The two-volume *Life and Letters* (1925), edited by Theodore C. Smith, contains selections from his diaries and letters.

General Garfield as a Statesman and Orator . . . , New York, 1880.

James A. Garfield. His Speeches at Home. 1880, Oneonta, N. Y., 1880.

The Works of James Abram Garfield, (Burke A. Hinsdale, ed.), 2 vols., Boston, 1882–83.

Garfield-Hinsdale Letters . . . , (Mary L. Hinsdale, ed.), Ann Arbor, Mich., 1949.

GARIS, LILLIAN C. (1873–April 19, 1954), was born in Cleveland, Cuyahoga County. She studied in private schools and at Columbia University. She began writing verse for newspapers in 1890 and worked on the Newark, N. J., *Evening News,* 1895–1900. She was active in the women's suffrage movement and in Girl Scout work; she did relief work during World War I. Her husband, Howard R. Garis, was the originator of the Uncle Wiggily stories for children. She wrote many stories for children, e.g., *Sally for Short,* New York, 1930, and *The Hermit of Proud Hill,* New York, [1940]. WWW 3

GARLICK, THEODATUS (March 30, 1805–Dec. 9, 1884), sculptor, surgeon, and scientist, was born in Middlebury, Vt. At the age of eleven he walked with an older brother to Erie County, Pa., where he learned blacksmithing. In 1818 he moved to Cleveland and worked as a stonecutter. In 1823 he brought his father and family to Brookfield, Trumbull County, where he worked as a stonecutter and blacksmith in the morning and studied medicine in the afternoon. After graduating from the University of Maryland in 1834, he practiced in Youngstown for eighteen years and afterward in Cleveland. He was renowned as a plastic surgeon. He made medallions and busts of many public figures, was a pioneer photographer, and experimented with fish culture. He wrote technical papers on pisciculture that were published in pamphlet form.

A Treatise on the Artificial Propagation of Certain Kinds of Fish . . . , Cleveland, 1857.

Biography of Ephraim Kirby . . . , Cleveland, 1883.

GARRARD, LEWIS HECTOR (June 15, 1829–July 7, 1887), was born in Cincinnati,

Hamilton County. His baptismal name was Hector Lewis Garrard, but he signed his books Lewis H. In 1846 he made a trip into the West, traveled the Santa Fe Trail, and lived at Bent's Fort for three months. He visited Cheyenne villages with William Bent and also observed the trappers and traders in the area. His account of this experience, *Wah-To-Yah,* A. B. Guthrie has compared favorably with Parkman's *Oregon Trail.* In 1858 he moved to a farm in Minnesota, and in 1870 he settled in Lake City, Minn., where he was president of a bank for three years. In 1880 he returned to Cincinnati. Besides the titles below, he edited a memoir of his grandmother.

Wah-To-Yah, and the Taos Trail . . . , New York, 1850.

Chambersburg in the Colony and the Revolution . . . , Philadelphia, 1856.

GARRETSON, ARTHUR SAMUEL (Nov. 7, 1851–Feb. 20, 1917), was born in Morgan County. In 1874 he settled in Sioux City, Iowa, where he played a leading role in the industrial development of the community. He was cashier of the Sioux National Bank, was one of the builders of the Sioux City and Northern Railroad, helped establish the Union Stockyards in Sioux City, and constructed several important buildings. He died at his ranch at Vilas, S. Dak. A prominent Baptist layman, he wrote *Primitive Christianity and Early Criticisms . . . ,* Boston, 1912.

GARRISON, CURTIS W. (June 29, 1901–), born in Chemung, N. Y., and educated in Richmond, Va., was director of research at Hayes Memorial Library, Fremont, 1937–46. He wrote *The History of Birchard Library,* Fremont, 1941.

GARRISON, ELISHA ELY (Aug. 16, 1871–March 26, 1935), financier, was born in Cincinnati, Hamilton County, the son of a Presbyterian minister. He graduated from Yale University in 1897, studied law at Yale and New York School of Law, and served in the army in 1898 and during World War I. He was an official of several public utility companies in New York City, 1922–27. His death occurred in St. Petersburg, Fla. He published books on accounting and economics and *Roosevelt, Wilson and the Federal Reserve Law . . . ,* Boston, [1931].

GARST, LAURA DELANY (Mrs. Charles E.) (1861–April 8, 1925), was born in Hopedale, Harrison County. She was the wife of a Disciples of Christ missionary. After his death in Japan in 1898, she settled in Des Moines, Iowa, where she lived until her death. She wrote at least two books based on her experiences in the Far East, e.g., *In the Shadow of the Drum Tower,* Cincinnati, [1911].

GARVEY, MOTHER MARY (Aug. 6, 1845–Nov. 11, 1932), was born in County Cavan, Ireland, but was brought to America in 1852. She was educated at the Convent of the Sacred Heart in New York City and Kenwood in Albany, N. Y. She took her first vows as a Roman Catholic nun in 1864, after which she taught in Philadelphia and New York City. In 1889 she came to Cincinnati as Mother Superior of Clifton and Reverend Mother Vicar of the Central Vicariate. In 1898 she was sent to Boston, Mass., and in 1916 she returned to Eden Hall, Philadelphia, where she spent the remainder of her life. She published anonymously a biography of the Mother Superior who supervised her education and inspired her early life: *Mary Aloysia Hardey . . . ,* New York, 1910.

GARVIN, HUGH CARSON (1842–July 12, 1918), educator, was born in Chillicothe, Ross County. He attended Bethany College and Ohio University and also studied in Germany. With two of his brothers he started a college at Wilmington in 1865; when pledges of support were not fulfilled, the school was taken over by the Society of Friends. A clergyman in the Disciples of Christ Church, he served on the faculty of Butler University, 1880–97. He died at Eldon, Mo. He wrote *What the Bible Teaches,* [St. Louis, Mo., 1908].

GARWOOD, IRVING (Nov. 28, 1883–June 8, 1957), educator, was born in Ada, Hardin County. He graduated from Ohio Northern University in 1912 and the University of Chicago (Ph.D.) in 1922. He taught in public schools until 1916 and in several colleges, 1916–24. He was a member of the English faculty, Western Illinois State Teachers College, 1924–46. He published several textbooks and literary studies, e.g., *American Periodicals from 1850–1860,* Macomb, Ill., 1931. WWW 3

GASKILL, JOSEPH W. (March 22, 1843–Aug. 31, 1932), was born in Marlboro, Stark County. He enlisted in the 104th O.V.I. in July, 1862, and was discharged as a corporal in June, 1865. After the war he was a merchant in Iowa until 1874, when he returned to Marlboro to live. He died in Alliance. Besides a booklet on Abraham

Lincoln (1924), he wrote an account of his Civil War experiences: *Footprints through Dixie . . .*, Alliance, 1919.

GASS, SHERLOCK BRONSON (Oct. 17, 1878–Aug. 31, 1945), was born in Mansfield, Richland County. After graduating from the University of Chicago he taught for a year at University High School and in 1906 joined the English department at the University of Nebraska. He wrote several books, e.g., a collection of essays: *The Criers of the Shops,* Boston, 1925, and a volume describing his family's financial difficulties in Chicago in the early 1890s: *Family Crisis,* New York, 1940. WWW 2

GASTON, JOSEPH (1833–July 20, 1913), lawyer and journalist, was born in Ohio. In 1862 he emigrated to Oregon, where he spent the remainder of his life. He practiced law in Jacksonville, edited the *Oregon Statesman* and other papers, promoted railroads, and operated a farm near Gaston. He wrote a history of Oregon and *Portland, Oregon, Its History and Builders . . .*, 3 vols., Chicago, 1911.

GATCHELL, CHARLES (1851–Jan. 26, 1910), physician, was born in Cincinnati, Hamilton County. After graduating from Pulte Medical College, Cincinnati, in 1874, he practiced in Michigan as a homeopathic physician. In 1881 he moved to Chicago, where he practiced and also taught at Hahnemann Medical College. He died in Los Angeles. The second title below was published under the pen name M. E. Dicus, and *Haschisch* under that of Thorold King. He wrote other fiction and also edited *Medical Era,* 1883–1903.

"Doctor, What Shall I Eat?" . . ., Milwaukee, 1880.

"Bless Thee, Bully Doctor!", New York, 1883.

The Key Notes of Medical Practice, Chicago, 1884.

The Treatment of Cholera . . ., Chicago, 1884.

Haschisch; A Novel, Chicago, 1886.

What a Woman Did, Chicago, 1900.

GATES, ARNOLD FRANCIS (Sept. 12, 1914–), born in Johnstown, Pa., lived in Ashtabula and Cuyahoga Counties for more than 25 years. He now lives in New York City. He has been a student of Abraham Lincoln's life; his pamphlets on the subject include *Amberglow of Abraham Lincoln and Ann Rutledge,* West Leisenring, Pa., [1939].

GATES, ELMER (1859–Dec. 3, 1923), psychologist, was born near Dayton, Montgomery County. He taught at the Pennsylvania School of Industrial Art, Philadelphia. An experimental psychologist, he evolved a system of mind-building by systematic means and published a number of works advocating his system, e.g., *The Relation and Development of the Mind and Brain,* [New York, 1912]. WWW 1

GATES, ERRETT (March 2, 1870–May, 1951), clergyman, was born in Cortland, Trumbull County. He graduated from Ohio Normal University in 1887, Union Theological Seminary in 1894, and the University of Chicago (Ph.D.) in 1902. He was a Disciples of Christ minister in Grand Rapids, Mich., and Chicago. He also served as secretary of the Disciples Divinity House, instructor in church history at the University of Chicago, and a member of the editorial staff of the *Christian Century.* His writings include *The Disciples of Christ,* New York, [1905].

GATES, JOSEPHINE SCRIBNER (Sept. 12, 1859–Aug. 21, 1930), was born in Mt. Vernon, Knox County. She attended the public schools of Toledo. In 1881 she married Charles H. Gates and spent the remainder of her life in Toledo. She wrote at least 25 books for children, e.g., *Nannette and the Baby Monkey,* Boston, 1914.

GATES, LAWRENCE GIBSON (Aug. 9, 1858–Dec. 3, 1939), was born in Tipp City, Miami County, and spent his entire life in that community. He was a rural mail carrier for a number of years.

Musings, Troy, 1886.

GATES, WILLEY FRANCIS (March 18, 1865–Dec. 25, 1941), musician, was born in Zanesville, Muskingum County. He graduated from Ohio Wesleyan University in 1888 and later studied music under several instructors. He lived in Los Angeles, 1900–41. He contributed to *Étude* magazine and wrote musical criticism for the Los Angeles *Times.* A teacher of voice and piano, he compiled *Musical Mosaics* and other musical anthologies and wrote a piano textbook.

Anecdotes of Great Musicians, Philadelphia, 1895.

Pipe and Strings, Cincinnati, 1895.

GAUL, AVERY. See Harriette L. A. Gaul.

GAUL, HARRIETTE LESTER AVERY (June 25, 1886–), was born in Youngstown, Mahoning County. She studied at

Hathaway-Brown School, Cleveland, and Smith College. She lived in Painesville, Canton, and Cleveland until 1908, when she married Harvey B. Gaul, a composer and organist. She lived in Pittsburgh, Pa., for 35 years and now lives in Forest Hills, Long Island, N. Y. She has written song lyrics and stories and articles for various magazines. She has also published under the pen name Avery Gaul a suspense novel: *Five Nights at the Five Pines,* New York, 1922. WWNAA 6

GAULT, FRANKLIN BENJAMIN (May 2, 1851-March 16, 1918), educator, was born in Wooster, Wayne County. He graduated from Cornell College, Iowa, in 1877. He served as a school superintendent in Iowa and Colorado, 1877–88, and organized the Tacoma, Wash., school system. He was president of the University of Idaho, 1892–98, Whitworth College, Tacoma, 1899–1906, and the University of South Dakota, 1906–13. He wrote *Should Bible Courses Be Given in State Universities?,* [Vermillion, S. Dak., 1907]. WWW 1

GAUSE, ISAAC (Dec. 9, 1843–April 23, 1920), was born in Green Township, Trumbull County. He served in the 2nd Ohio Volunteer Cavalry from Aug., 1861, until Sept., 1865. After the war he lived in New Mexico and Texas. He died in National Soldiers' Home, Va. In 1916 he was awarded the Medal of Honor for gallantry in capturing the colors of the 8th South Carolina Infantry on Sept. 13, 1864. He wrote *Four Years with Five Armies . . . ,* New York, 1908.

GAVIN, FRANK STANTON BURNS (Oct. 31, 1890–March 20, 1938), clergyman and educator, was born in Cincinnati, Hamilton County. He graduated from the University of Cincinnati in 1912, General Theological Seminary in 1915, and Columbia University (Ph.D.) in 1922. He was ordained an Episcopal priest in 1915 and served churches in Cincinnati and Boston. He joined the faculty of General Theological Seminary in 1923. He published several books on religious topics, e.g., *The Jewish Antecedents of the Christian Sacraments,* New York, 1928. WWW 1

GAY, ELINOR. Pseud. See Mary G. Humphreys.

GAYLER, CHARLES (April 1, 1820–May 28, 1892), author of at least 200 popular plays, spent about thirteen years in Ohio. In 1836 he was teaching school and reading law in Dayton. After being admitted to the bar, he practiced for a time and campaigned for Henry Clay. After a brief stint as editor of the Cincinnati *Evening Dispatch,* he turned to acting on the James W. Bates circuit. His first play, *The Buckeye Gold Hunters,* was produced in Cincinnati in 1849, and the next year he moved to New York City, where he lived for the rest of his life.

GAZE, HARRY (June 13, 1878–Nov. 4, 1959), was born near London, England. After coming to the United States in 1898, he lectured on reincarnation and rejuvenation. He was leader of the New Thought Temple, Cincinnati, 1909–12, and later lived in Connecticut and California. His writings include *How to Live Forever . . . ,* Chicago, [1904].

GAZLAY, ALLEN W. See James W. Gazlay.

GAZLAY, JAMES WILLIAM (July 23, 1784–June 8, 1874), lawyer, was born in New York City. Admitted to the bar in 1809, he moved to Cincinnati in 1813. He practiced law in Cincinnati and served two years as editor of the weekly *Western Tiller.* The first title below, portions of which may have been written by his son, Allen W. Gazlay, was published under the pen name Captain Broadbeck. His death occurred in Cincinnati.

Races of Mankind: With Travels in Grubland, Cincinnati, [1856].

Sketches of Life and Social Relations, with Other Poems, Cincinnati, 1860.

Political Questions, Cincinnati, 1861.

Reconstruction of the Southern States, Cincinnati, 1865.

Scraps from Laws of New Creation . . . , Cincinnati, 1867.

GEER, JOHN JAMES (June 1, 1833–Aug. 23, 1867), clergyman, was born in Rockbridge County, Va., but grew up in Shelby County. A Methodist minister in Cincinnati, he enlisted in the 48th O.V.I. and was wounded and captured at Shiloh. He was imprisoned in Montgomery, Ala., and Macon, Ga. He escaped, was recaptured, and later was exchanged. After the war he served as a pastor in Springfield, where he died as the result of his war injuries.

Beyond the Lines: Or, a Yankee Prisoner Loose in Dixie, Philadelphia, 1863.

GEER, NEY N. (July 26, 1895–), was born in Ashtabula, Jefferson County. He lived for a number of years at Grant's Pass, Oreg. He wrote several Western novels, e.g., *Smoke beyond the Rim,* [New York, 1939].

GEER, WILLIAM CHAUNCEY (June 17, 1876–), chemist, was born in Ogdensburg, N. Y. He graduated from Cornell University (A.B., 1902; Ph.D., 1905). He lived in Akron from 1907 to 1925 while associated with B. F. Goodrich. Upon retiring, he moved to Ithaca, N. Y. He has published several scientific works and *The Reign of Rubber,* New York, 1922. WW 26

GEHRING, ALBERT (March 21, 1870–Feb. 25, 1926), was born in Cleveland, Cuyahoga County. He graduated from Harvard University in 1894. He was a lecturer at the College for Women, Cleveland, and a member of the Cleveland School Council.

Gedichte, Cleveland, 1899.
Racial Contrasts; Distinguishing Traits of the Graeco-Latins and Teutons, New York, 1908.
The Basis of Musical Pleasure . . . , New York, 1910.
Mozart, New York, 1911.
The Appreciation of Music, Cleveland, [1913].
The Religion of Thirty Great Thinkers . . . , Boston, [1925].

GEHRING, JOHN GEORGE (July 4, 1857–Sept. 1, 1932), physician, was born in Cleveland, Cuyahoga County. After graduating from Western Reserve University School of Medicine in 1885, he began to practice in Cleveland. In 1895 he moved to Bethel, Maine, and specialized in functional nervous diseases. He was also president of Gould's Academy, Bethel. His writings include *The Hope of the Variant,* New York, 1923. WWW 1

GEHRING, MABEL GREY (Mrs. Carl W.) (March 14, 1882–), was born in Glasgow, Scotland, but has lived in Ohio since 1908. She was educated at a private school in Paisley, Scotland, and at Scottish Athaneum College. She has lived in Cleveland and Lakewood and is now living in Sandusky. An honorary member of Composers, Authors, and Artists of America, she has written many articles on antiques and other subjects for the *Christian Science Monitor.* A series of articles on Scottish Islands became the basis of her book *On a Scottish Island,* Cleveland, [1949].

GEIGER, GEORGE RAYMOND (May 8, 1903–), educator, born in New York City, has been in the philosophy department, Antioch College, since 1937. He has published several books on social and philosophical questions, e.g., *The Theory of the Land Question,* New York, 1936. WW 30

GEISER, KARL FREDERICK (June 18, 1869–April 1, 1951), educator, was born in Fairbank, Iowa. He graduated from Upper Iowa University in 1893 and Yale University (Ph.D.) in 1900. In 1908 he joined the Oberlin College faculty. His books include *Democracy versus Autocracy . . . ,* Boston, [1918]. WWW 3

GEISSINGER, JAMES ALLEN (Oct. 14, 1873–Oct. 21, 1935), clergyman, was born in Burbank, Wayne County. He attended Ohio Wesleyan University and Capital University and graduated from Ohio State University in 1895. He was ordained to the Methodist ministry in 1895 and served as pastor of churches in Ohio, Texas, Arizona, and California. His writings include *The Democracy of Methodism,* New York, [1920]. WWW 1

GEIST, EDNA EVELYN (Feb. 8, 1878–July 13, 1953), educator, was born in South Webster, Scioto County. She attended Ohio University and Ohio Northern University and graduated from Oskaloosa State College, Iowa. She taught in the New Boston schools for 25 years. She published a collection of verse: *Hearthstone,* New York, [1947].

GENIN, SYLVESTER (Jan. 22, 1822–April 4, 1850), artist and poet, was born in St. Clairsville, Belmont County. He received his education from his father, Thomas H. Genin (q.v.), who wished to relieve him of the boredom of school attendance. The boy began early to copy pictures and was ambitious to become an artist. In 1840–41 he toured the East to learn "what were the prospects of artists." On his return to St. Clairsville he began the study of law. His paintings were chiefly of Biblical and historical subjects. He died in Jamaica, where he had gone in the hope of recovering from tuberculosis. His father published a posthumous collection of his prose pieces, poems, and engravings.

Selections from the Works of the Late Sylvester Genin, Esq., in Poetry, Prose, and Historical Design, New York, 1855.

GENIN, THOMAS HEDGES (March 23, 1796–Oct. 18, 1868), abolitionist, lawyer, and poet, was born in Suffolk County, Long Island, N. Y. Orphaned at the age of fourteen, he lived for a time with William Woodhull, an uncle, who was a graduate of Princeton University. He studied with his uncle and then read law in a New York office. Here he became acquainted with DeWitt Clinton. In 1815 Genin wrote

The Napolead, an epic in blank verse, covering Napoleon's career from the Russian campaign until his departure for Elba. Extracts were published in New York newspapers, but the entire work remained unpublished until 1833. In 1816 he was admitted to the New York bar. In 1817 he married Ann Hillard of Randolph, N. J., and migrated to St. Clairsville, where he spent the remainder of his life. He lived on a farm near the town, practiced law, and served for 26 years as master commissioner in chancery. From his arrival in Ohio he was associated with Benjamin Lundy (q.v.) in the Union Humane Society, a pioneer abolition group. He spoke and wrote against slavery. His incidental writings also advocated a protective tariff and opposed Jackson's bank policy.

The Napolead, in Twelve Books, St. Clairsville, 1833.

Selections from the Writings of the Late Thomas Hedges Genin . . . , New York, 1869.

GEORGE, ANDREW McINTYRE (1857–Sept. 22, 1927), was born in Cedarville, Greene County. He graduated from Geneva College in 1888. His death occurred in Cedarville. He published a collection of verse: *A Leaf of Song,* [Urbana], 1902.

GERARD, CLINTON W. (c.1842–Sept. 25, 1894), lawyer, was born in Newtown, Hamilton County. He served as a sergeant in the 83rd O.V.I. from Aug., 1862, to July, 1865. After the war, he was admitted to the bar and practiced law. He died in Cincinnati.

A Diary. The Eighty-third Ohio Volunteer Infantry in the War, 1862–1865, [Cincinnati, 1889].

GERHART, EMANUEL VOGEL (June 13, 1817–May 6, 1904), theologian, was in Ohio from 1849 to 1854. He was first sent as pastor of the First Reformed Church in Cincinnati; in 1851 he was named president of the newly opened seminary at Heidelberg College. He left in 1854 to become president of Franklin and Marshall College. He was a frequent contributor to religious periodicals and wrote several theological works, e.g., *Prolegomena to Christian Dogmatics,* Lancaster, Pa., 1891.

GERIG, ORIE BENJAMIN (Jan. 18, 1894–), State Department official, was born in Smithville, Wayne County. He graduated from Goshen College in 1917 and the University of Geneva, Switzerland, (D.Sc.) in 1929. He has taught in several universities, was on the staff of the League of Nations, 1930–40, and since 1942 has been a member of the Department of State. He has written *The Open Door and the Mandates System . . . ,* London, [1930]. WW 30

GERMAIN, WILLIAM McKEE (Jan. 16, 1892–), physician and educator, was born in Pittsburgh, Pa., and lived in Cincinnati, 1941–57. He was on the faculty of the University of Cincinnati Medical School and was pathologist of Good Samaritan Hospital. He now lives in Florida and is on the faculty of the University of Miami Medical School. His writings include *Doctors Anonymous . . . ,* New York, [1941].

GERWIG, GEORGE WILLIAM (Jan. 18, 1867–Nov. 11, 1950), writer on educational, literary, and religious topics, was born in Paris, Stark County. He graduated from the University of Nebraska in 1889 and the University of Pittsburgh (Ph.D.) in 1904. From 1892 to 1929 he was secretary of the board of education in Allegheny, Pa., and later in Pittsburgh. He wrote most of his numerous books for children, e.g., *Washington. The Young Leader,* New York, [1923]. WWW 3

G.E.X. Pseud. See Lydia E. H. F. Painter.

GIBSON, KATHERINE. See Katherine Gibson Wicks.

GIDDINGS, JOSHUA REED (Oct. 6, 1795–May 27, 1864), militant abolitionist and congressman, was born in Bradford County, Pa. The family moved to Canandaigua, N. Y., when he was a baby and to Ashtabula County when he was ten years old. He grew up on his father's farm with only intermittent opportunities for schooling. After reading law at Canfield with Elisha Whittlesey, he was admitted to the Ohio bar in 1821 and practiced in Jefferson until 1838, when he was elected to the House of Representatives. Here he served for twenty years, vigorously opposing every measure that seemed to favor slavery and urging free debate on the question. He is thought to have written much of the first Republican platform in 1856. He campaigned for Lincoln in 1860 and was appointed consul general in Canada after the election. He died at Montreal and is buried in Jefferson. Many of his speeches and letters were printed separately as ammunition in his never-ending battle against slaveholding. The first title below consists of articles first published in the *Western Reserve Chronicle* under the pen name Pacificus.

The Rights and Privileges of the Several States in Regard to Slavery . . . , [Warren?, 1843?].

Speeches in Congress, 1841–1852, Boston, 1853.

The Exiles of Florida . . . , Columbus, 1858.

History of the Rebellion: Its Authors and Causes, New York, 1864.

GIDDINGS, LUTHER (c.1823– ?), was a lawyer in Dayton in the 1840s. He joined the 1st Ohio Volunteers as a captain in May, 1846, and was discharged as a major in New Orleans in June of the following year. He was still living in Dayton in 1850, when he applied for a land warrant, but he left the city and no further details have been found. His book appeared anonymously.

Sketches of the Campaign in Northern Mexico . . . , New York, 1853.

GIESY, JOHN ULRICH (Aug. 6, 1877–Sept. 8, 1947), physician, was born in Chillicothe, Ross County. After graduating from Starling Medical College, Columbus, 1898, he practiced at Salt Lake City, Utah. He served in the Medical Corps of the U. S. Army in 1918. He contributed fiction and detective stories to magazines and science articles to medical journals. He also wrote several novels, e.g., *The Valley of Suspicion,* New York, 1927, and under the pen name Charles Dustin, several Western novels, e.g., *Bronco Men,* New York, [1940]. WWW 1

GIESY, SAMUEL HENSEL (Aug. 26, 1826–May 27, 1888), clergyman, was born in Lancaster, Fairfield County. After attending Marshall College and Seminary, he was ordained in 1849 as a minister of the Evangelical and Reformed Church. He served pastorates in Hagerstown, Md., and Philadelphia. He became an Episcopalian in 1870 and was ordained to the priesthood in 1873, after which he was rector of a church in Norwich, Conn. He died in Washington, D. C. Besides the title below, he published a number of sermons.

The I AMs of Christ . . . , New York, [1884].

GIFFEN, JOHN KELLY (June 3, 1853–April 6, 1932), clergyman, was born in St. Clairsville, Belmont County. He graduated from Franklin College in 1879 and Presbyterian Theological Seminary, Allegheny, Pa., in 1881. In 1881 he was ordained to the Presbyterian ministry and was sent as a missionary to Africa. He wrote *The Egyptian Sudan,* New York, [1905]. WWW 1

GIFFORD, FANNIE STEARNS DAVIS (March 6, 1884–), was born in Cleveland, Cuyahoga County. She graduated from Smith College in 1904 and taught English for a time in Kenosha, Wis. Following her marriage to Augustus M. Gifford in 1914, she lived in Pittsfield, Mass. Her poems appeared in national magazines, and she published several collections, e.g., *Myself and I,* New York, 1913. WW 16

GILBERT, AMOS (? – ?), was a prominent schoolteacher in Lancaster, Pa., where in June, 1833, he began publishing an educational monthly called the *Inciter.* The magazine was discontinued in May, 1834, because of want of patronage, and Gilbert moved with his printing press to Salem, Columbiana County. There he is said to have continued publishing the *Inciter* for a while, but no copies have survived. He taught school in Salem, 1834–36, specializing in natural philosophy. Unsuccessful in an attempt to introduce the Pestalozzian system, he dropped from sight before 1840. However, W. T. Coggeshall (q.v.), who reviewed Gilbert's *Memoir of Frances Wright* in the *Genius of the West,* Nov., 1855, stated that Gilbert was still a resident of Columbiana County.

Memoir of Frances Wright, the Pioneer Woman in the Cause of Human Rights, Cincinnati, 1855.

GILBERT, LEVI (Aug. 23, 1852–Dec. 24, 1917), clergyman, was born in Brooklyn, N. Y. He graduated from Wesleyan University in 1874, studied at Drew Theological Seminary, and was ordained to the Methodist ministry in 1878. He graduated from Drew Theological Seminary in 1902. He served as a Methodist minister in Minnesota, Washington, Ohio, and Connecticut. He also edited the *Western Christian Advocate.* He published poetry and prose in various periodicals and also wrote several books, e.g., *Visions of the Christ,* Cincinnati, [1903]. WWW 1

GILCHRIST, MARIE EMILIE (Jan. 4, 1893–), was born in Vermilion, Erie County. She graduated from Smith College in 1916, worked in the Cleveland Public Library, and was an associate editor of the *Reader's Digest,* 1934–52. She has published several books for children and a collection of poems: *Wide Pastures,* New York, 1926. BDCP

GILCHRIST, ROSETTA LUCE (April 11, 1851–Feb. 19, 1921), physician, was born in Kingsville, Ashtabula County. She attended Kingsville Academy, Oberlin College, and Homeopathic Hospital College in Cleveland. In 1890 she began the practice of medicine in Ashtabula. She was active in the women's suffrage movement. Besides her published books, she wrote articles and stories.

Apples of Sodom; A Story of Mormon Life, Cleveland, 1883.

Tibby, a Novel Dealing with Psychic Forces and Telepathy, New York, 1904.

GILES, CHAUNCEY (May 11, 1813–Nov. 6, 1893), Swedenborgian clergyman, was reared in New England. He was teaching in Pomeroy in 1853 when he determined to become a minister. From 1853 to 1864 he was pastor of the Church of the New Jerusalem in Cincinnati. He published numerous lectures and religious books, stories for children, e.g., *The Magic Spectacles,* New York, 1868, and many magazine articles. After leaving Ohio, he lived in New York City and Philadelphia.

GILL, JOSEPHINE PAULINE ECKERT (Dec. 22, 1921–), was born in Nuremberg, Germany, but was brought to America when she was two months old. She attended the schools of Ottawa, Putnam County, and graduated from the University of Michigan in 1943. She taught in Michigan schools until her marriage to William J. Gill in 1948. She has published two novels, the first of them under her maiden name, Josephine P. Eckert: *The Practicing of Christopher,* New York, 1947.

GILL, WILSON LINDSLEY (Sept. 12, 1851–Sept. 12, 1941), educator, was born in Columbus, Franklin County. A lawyer and an industrialist, he turned his interest to education in the 1890s and developed the idea of a school as a miniature republic to train children in democracy. At various times he applied his theories to the schools of New York City, Cuba, Indian reservations, Washington, D. C., and Madison, Wis. He wrote many books, pamphlets, and articles on his theories, e.g., *The School City,* Philadelphia, 1903. WWW 1

GILLESPIE, SAMUEL LOVEJOY (Jan. 12, 1838–March 10, 1909), clergyman, was born near Washington Court House, Fayette County. He enlisted in Company A, 1st Ohio Cavalry, Aug. 6, 1861, and served three years, during which time he was for a short while an inmate of Libby Prison. He later graduated from Princeton Theological Seminary, served as a missionary in West Africa, and was a Presbyterian minister in several states until his death in Los Angeles. His regimental history was published under the pen name Lovejoy.

A History of Co. A, First Ohio Cavalry, 1861–1865. A Memorial Volume . . . , Washington C. H., 1898.

GILLIAM, CHARLES FREDERICK (1853–1915), physician, was born in Columbus, Franklin County. He was superintendent of the State Hospital, Columbus, at the time of his death in an automobile accident.

Love and Medicine. A Novel, Washington, D. C., 1886.

A Victorious Defeat; The Story of a Franchise, Boston, [1906].

GILLIAM, DAVIS TOD (April 3, 1844–Oct. 2, 1923), surgeon and educator, was born in Hebron, Licking County. He served with West Virginia cavalry during the Civil War, was wounded and captured, but escaped to Ohio. In 1863 he was discharged for medical reasons. He later enrolled in the Medical College of Ohio and graduated in 1871. He practiced in Nelsonville, 1871–77; he then became pathologist at Columbus Medical College. In 1879 he was made professor of physiology at Starling Medical College. In his practice and his teaching, he came to concentrate on gynecology and obstetrics. He wrote a number of articles on medical subjects. His Civil War novel, *The Rose Croix,* is signed David T. Gilliam.

The Essentials of Pathology, Philadelphia, 1883.

A Text-book of Practical Gynecology . . . , Philadelphia, 1903.

The Rose Croix, New York, [1906].

Dick Devereux; A Story of the Civil War, Cincinnati, 1915.

GILLILAN, JAMES DAVID (May 19, 1858–Feb. 27, 1935), clergyman, brother of Strickland Gillilan (q.v.), was born in Jackson County. He was a Methodist minister in the West for 45 years, fifteen of them as a missionary in Utah. He published articles in various newspapers and magazines, sometimes using the pen name Dr. Scholae. He also published a life of Thomas C. Iliff and *Trail Tales,* New York, [1915].

GILLILAN, STRICKLAND (1869–April 25, 1954), was born in Jackson County. After attending Ohio University, he worked on the Jackson *Herald,* 1887, the Athens *Herald,* 1888–92, and other newspapers in Richmond, Ind., Marion, Ind., Los Angeles, and Baltimore. In 1905 he gave up journalism for free-lance writing and lecturing. Although he published much, he is best remembered for his poem about an Irish railroad man's report of an accident: "Flannigan: Off agin, on agin, gone agin. Finnigin." The poem, written in Richmond on a day when news was scarce, was reprinted and quoted for many years.

McKinley and Hobart Campaign Glees, [Richmond, Ind., 1896].
Including Finnigan; A Book of Gillilan Verse, Philadelphia, [1908].
Including You and Me, Chicago, 1916.
Sunshine and Awkwardness, Chicago, 1918.
A Sample Case of Humor, Chicago, 1919.
Laugh It Off, Including Songs of Sanity, Chicago, 1924.
Danny and Fanny, the Laurel Cliff Twins, New York, [1928].
Danny and Fanny and Spot, the Fox Terrior Hero, Chicago, 1939.
Gillilan, Finnigan & Co.; Waif Gems Selected from the Writings . . . , (Homer Rodeheaver, comp.), Chicago, [1941].

GILLILAND, THADDEUS STEPHENS (Oct. 27, 1834–Dec. 30, 1909), was born in Adams County, Pa., but his parents moved to a farm in Van Wert County shortly after his birth. He served as a captain in the 15th O.V.I. from Sept., 1861, to April, 1862. He contracted typhoid fever while in the army and was discharged as a result of the aftereffects. He later conducted a grain and produce business in Van Wert. He prepared a historical work: *History of Van Wert County . . . ,* Chicago 1906.

GILLMORE, QUINCY ADAMS (Feb. 28, 1825–April 7, 1888), soldier, was born at Black River, Lorain County. He grew up on his father's farm and attended Norwalk Academy and Elyria High School. Appointed to the U. S. Military Academy, he graduated at the head of the class of 1849. He served with the engineers in various capacities. He was chief engineer of the Port Royal expedition and directed the artillery fire that destroyed Fort Pulaski, which had been considered impregnable. He rose to major general of volunteers and to colonel in the regular army. He served on various commissions and engineering boards and wrote numerous technical books and reports, many of them published by the Government Printing Office.

Practical Treatise on Limes, Hydraulic Cements and Mortars . . . , New York, 1863.
Engineer and Artillery Operation against the Defences of Charleston Harbor in 1863 . . . , New York, 1865.
A Practical Treatise on Roads, Streets, and Pavements, New York, 1876.
Galveston, New York, 1879.

GILMAN, CHANDLER ROBBINS (Sept. 6, 1802–Sept. 26, 1865), physician, was born in Marietta, Washington County. His father moved to Philadelphia, where Chandler attended the University of Pennsylvania and graduated in medicine in 1824. He spent his entire professional life in New York City, practicing and teaching medicine. From 1835 to 1837 he assisted his relative Charles Fenno Hoffman in editing the *American Monthly Magazine.* Gilman published many medical articles and lectures. The two books on the West were published anonymously and have been at various times attributed to Margaret Fuller, Charles Lanman, and Thomas Bangs Thorpe; but the Library of Congress and most other authorities recognize Gilman's authorship. He also wrote a biographical sketch of Dr. J. B. Beck. He died in Middletown, Conn.

Legends of a Log Cabin, by a Western Man, New York, 1835.
Life on the Lakes . . . , 2 vols., New York, 1836.

GILMAN, NICHOLAS PAINE (Dec. 21, 1849–Jan. 23, 1912), was born in Quincy, Ill. A Unitarian minister and educator, he was on the faculty of Antioch College, 1875–78. He published a number of books, e.g., *Socialism and the American Spirit,* Boston, 1893.

GILMORE, ELSIE L. (Dec. 28, 1869–May 24, 1956), was born in Toledo, Lucas County, and spent her life in that city. She published stories for children in various magazines and a volume of verse: *Our Flag, and Other Verse,* [Toledo], 1918.

GILMORE, FLORENCE (Feb., 1880–Sept. 13, 1945), was born in Columbus, Franklin County. She was educated at Sacred Heart convents in Omaha, Neb., and St. Louis, Mo. For many years she was on the staff of the *Catholic Columbian,* published in Columbus; and her death occurred in that city. She published numerous stories and articles in the *Columbian* and other Catholic magazines and also wrote three novels, e.g., *The Parting of the Ways,* St. Louis, Mo., 1914.

GILMORE, WILLIAM EDWARD (Nov. 3, 1824–Jan. 7, 1908), lawyer, was born in Chillicothe, Ross County. After attending Ohio University, 1838–43, he began to study law. He graduated from Lane Theological Seminary in 1846, but again turned to law and graduated from Cincinnati Law School in 1848. He was a student of literature and had a large fund of general information. He contributed many poems and historical and political sketches to various magazines and newspapers. After a torrid legal and political career in Missouri, 1866–73, he returned to Chillicothe, where he lived until his death.

Life of Edward Tiffin, First Governor of Ohio, Chillicothe, 1898.

GILSON, JOHN H. (1841–March 27, 1916), was born in Washington Township, Columbiana County. He served as a private in the 126th O.V.I., Aug., 1862–June, 1865. He afterward operated a farm in Columbiana County.

Concise History of the One Hundred and Twenty-Sixth Regiment . . . , Salem, 1883.

GINGER JAR. Pseud. See Everard J. Appleton.

GIORG, KARA. Pseud. See Gustavus Brühl.

GITTINGS, ELLA PAMELA BEECHER (Feb. 18, 1852–Dec. 11, 1935), was born in Oberlin, Lorain County. She attended the preparatory department of Oberlin College and also attended school in Iowa. She was a poet and a writer of stories.

Margery's Vacation, Boston, [1891].

GIVEN, WELKER (May 17, 1853–March 6, 1938), journalist, was born in Millersburg, Holmes County. In 1868 he moved to Des Moines, Iowa, and most of his life was spent in that state. After attending Columbian University, Washington, D. C., he worked on the Iowa City *Republican,* the Des Moines *Register,* and other newspapers. He was also editor and publisher of the Marshalltown, Iowa, *Times-Republican.* He held various political appointments: he was secretary to Governor Sherman of Iowa, a translator in the U. S. Treasury, commissioner of settlements in the Philadelphia Mint, and secretary of the Iowa Employers Liability Commission. He spent the last 21 years of his life in Clinton, Iowa.

The Tariff Riddle . . . , Philadelphia, 1892.

A Further Study of the Othello . . . , New York, [1899].

A Pagan's Christian Hymn, [Clinton, Iowa], 1916.

A Luxemburg Idyll in Early Iowa, [Clinton, Iowa, 1922].

The Light of the Sierra, Boston, [1928].

GLADDEN, WASHINGTON (Feb. 11, 1836–July 2, 1918), prophet of Applied Christianity and the Social Gospel, was born in Pottsgrove, Pa., the son of a New England schoolmaster and a New York farmer's daughter. Following the death of his father when Washington Gladden was six, he was reared by an uncle on a farm in Tioga County, N. Y. He attended the district school and helped with the work of the farm. At the age of sixteen he was apprenticed to a village newspaper editor and for four years worked at all the jobs found in the printshop. While working for the newspaper, Washington Gladden fell under the influence of a young Congregational minister who pointed out to him the road toward a life of service in the church. A year's intensive work in the local academy prepared Gladden to enter the sophomore class at Williams College, from which he graduated in 1859. In the spring of 1860, following a few months of schoolteaching, Gladden spent six weeks preaching at a revival meeting at Le Raysville, Pa. This experience convinced him that the ministry was to be his life's work. His first charge was in Brooklyn, N. Y., but he soon moved to Morrisania, now part of the Bronx, New York City. In 1866 Gladden went to North Adams, Mass., only to leave in 1871 to become religious editor of the *Independent,* an interdenominational religious journal published in New York City. He resigned this position because of a disagreement over business ethics and became pastor of the North Church, Springfield, Mass., in 1875. At Christmastime, 1882, Gladden became pastor of the First Congregational Church, Columbus. After 32 years he retired, continuing to live in Columbus till his death. Washington Gladden made his reputation in large measure by contributing to the popular journals of the day. In college he was Williamstown correspondent for the Springfield *Republican* and thus came to know the assistant editor, Josiah Holland. When Holland began to edit *Scribner's Monthly* (later *Century*), Gladden became a trusted writer, and between 1870 and 1895 almost every issue contained something from his pen. Around the turn of the century the *Outlook* frequently called upon Gladden for contributions. Naturally Gladden contributed to the religious press of the day. For many years in the 1860s and 1870s the *Independent* published his writings, to be succeeded by *Bibliotheca Sacra* and the *Andover Review.* The *Congregationalist,* the *Alliance,* and the *Christian Union* all received frequent articles from the busy pen of Washington Gladden. Between 1878 and 1881 Gladden edited *Sunday Afternoon,* a magazine published in Springfield, Mass., designed to provide inspirational family reading for the long Sabbath afternoons. Washington Gladden's publications in the periodical press coupled with his sermons and lectures, often published in book and pamphlet form, placed before the public the ideas of a mediating teacher who was constantly trying to make religion comprehensible to a people shaken by the advances of the Industrial Revolution and the resulting rising influence of science and secularism. Gladden taught a religion which was of a loving, helpful nature, aware of the social injustices abroad in the land and willing to reach out a helpful hand so that the Kingdom of God might come to earth.

David W. Lattimer

Songs of William, New York, 1859.
Amusements: Their Uses and Their Abuses, North Adams, Mass., 1866.
Plain Thoughts on the Art of Living . . . , Boston, 1868.
From the Hub to the Hudson . . . , Boston, 1869.
Being a Christian: What It Means and How to Begin, Boston, 1876.
Working People and Their Employers, Boston, 1876.
The Christian Way: Whither It Leads and How to Go On, New York, 1877.
Was Bronson Alcott's School a Type of God's Moral Government? . . . , Boston, 1877.
Things Old and New in Discourses of Christian Truth and Life, Columbus, 1883.
Young Men and the Churches . . . , Boston, 1885.
Applied Christianity . . . , New York, 1886.
Parish Problems . . . , New York, 1887.
Burning Questions of the Life That Now Is and of That Which Is to Come, New York, 1890.
Santa Claus on a Lark and Other Christmas Stories, New York, 1890.
Who Wrote the Bible? . . . , New York, 1891.
Tools and the Man . . . , New York, 1893.
The Church and the Kingdom, New York, 1894.
Francis Charles Sessions, Columbus, 1895.
Ruling Ideas of the Present Age, New York, 1895.
The Relations of Capital and Labor, Cincinnati, 1896.
The Relations of Art and Morality, New York, 1897.
Seven Puzzling Bible Books . . . , New York, 1897.
Social Facts and Forces . . . , New York, 1897.
The Christian Pastor and the Working Church, New York, 1898.
England and America . . . , Columbus, 1898.
Our Nation and Her Neighbors, Columbus, 1898.
How Much Is Left of the Old Doctrines? . . . , New York, 1899.
Straight Shots at Young People . . . , New York, 1900.
Practice of Immorality, Columbus, 1901.
Victoria, Columbus, 1901.
Social Salvation, New York, 1902.
Witnesses of the Light . . . , New York, 1903.
Where Does the Sky Begin?, New York, 1904.
Christianity and Socialism, Cincinnati, 1905.
The New Idolatry and Other Discussions, New York, 1905.
The Church and Modern Life, New York, 1908.
Recollections, New York, 1909.
Fifty Years in the Ministry, Columbus, 1910.
The Labor Question, New York, [1911].
The School of Life, New York, [1911].
Ultima Veritas and Other Verses, Boston, [1912].
Present-day Theology, Columbus, [1913].
Federation for Service, Philadelphia, [1914].
Live and Learn, New York, 1914.
A Plea for Pacifism, Columbus, 1915.
The Forks of the Road, New York, 1916.
The Life Unfailing, Columbus, 1916.
If I Were a Boy; If I Were a Girl, Columbus, 1917.
Religion after the War, [Columbus?, 1917?].
Calendar Verses, Columbus, 1918.
The Interpreter, Chicago, 1918.
The Followers of the Star, [n.p., n.d.].
The Negro's Southern Neighbors and His Northern Friends, New York, [n.d.].
Our First Love. Have We Lost It?, Boston, [n.d.].
The Perfect Law of Charity, [n.p., n.d.].
The Shepherd's Story, Columbus, [n.d.].

GLADDING, EFFIE PRICE (1865–1947), was born in Bellefontaine, Logan County. In 1889 she graduated from Ohio Wesleyan University, where she later served as dean of women. She was associated for many years with the Y.W.C.A. and lectured widely on its work. She died in Easton, Md. She wrote *Across the Continent by the Lincoln Highway,* New York, 1915.

GLADWIN, MARY ELIZABETH (Dec. 24, 1861–Nov. 22, 1939), nurse, was born in Stoke-upon-Trent, England. She was brought to the United States as a child. After graduating from Buchtel College, Akron, in 1887, she taught in Norwalk for six years before beginning her nursing career. Although she served with the American Red Cross in several countries and worked briefly in various states, Akron remained her home, and she died in that city. She wrote several nursing textbooks and *The Red Cross and Jane Arminda Delano,* Philadelphia, 1931. WWW 1

GLASIER, JESSIE (July 9, 1865–Dec. 18, 1955), was born in Bellaire, Belmont County. She graduated from Hiram College and Oberlin Conservatory of Music. In the 1890s she wrote society news for the Cleveland *Plain Dealer;* she was women's club editor, 1905–27, and in 1909 she also became the paper's art critic. The historical novel below was serialized in several newspapers and was widely read. After her retirement she married Myron Fowler Near. She died in De Leon Springs Heights, Fla.

Gaining the Heights, Cincinnati, 1890.

GLASS, FRANCIS (1790–Aug. 23, 1824), educator, was born in Londonderry, Ireland. His parents brought him to America in 1798. He graduated from the University of Pennsylvania when he was nineteen. Having married young, he emigrated with a brood of small children to Ohio in 1817. Here adversity seemed to dog his every footstep. He went from place to place, conducting schools at various times in Warren, Miami, and Montgomery Counties. Although the fame of the young classical scholar, who was to be known as "the Erasmus of the West," spread over the frontier, it brought him few pupils and none of the comforts of life. Seeking a tutor, Jeremiah N. Reynolds (q.v.) found him at the head of a country school in Warren County in 1823. Reynolds had been with Glass but three months when he discovered his teacher's overwhelming desire to write a life of George Washington in Latin prose. In feeble health and living in extreme poverty, he seemed unlikely to accomplish his project. But arrangements were made by Reynolds for his relief, and in 1823 Glass moved to Dayton, where he finished his book. He did not live to learn that his work had been approved by some of the ripest scholars in the country. Proposals to publish the book were inserted in Cincinnati and Dayton papers without response. Glass died in Dayton, and when Reynolds came to Ohio again after ten years he could not locate any of his family. Through the instrumentality of Reynolds, *Washingtonii Vita* was published by Harper Brothers in 1835.

Washingtonii Vita, New York, 1835.

GLASSER, OTTO (Sept. 2, 1895–), biophysicist, was born in Saarbrücken, Germany. He came to the United States in 1922 and has been head of the department of biophysics, Cleveland Clinic, since 1927. He has written professional articles and books as well as *Dr. W. C. Roentgen,* Springfield, Ill., 1945. WW 30

GLAZIER, WILLIAM BELCHER (June 29, 1827–Oct. 25, 1870), lawyer, was born in Hallowell, Maine. After graduating from Harvard University in 1847, he read law and practiced for a short time. He lived in Cincinnati, 1854–70. He was for many years a deputy surveyor of customs.

Poems, Hallowell, Maine, 1853.

GLEASON, SELINA GASCOIGNE (Jan. 23, 1884–May 14, 1957), born in Byfield, England, was brought to Worcester, Mass., in 1894 and was educated in that city. She and her husband, Elmer F. Gleason, a typographical designer, moved to Cincinnati in 1915. She published a collection of essays: *Going Home and Other Selections,* Cincinnati, 1936.

GLEASON, WILLIAM J. (June, 1846–Jan. 20, 1905), was born in County Clare, Ireland, but when he was six months old, his parents emigrated to America, settling first in Vermont. Later in the same year, they came to Cleveland, where he grew up. He learned the printer's trade and in 1860 was employed by the Cleveland *Plain Dealer.* Except for service with the 150th O.V.I. during the Civil War, he was with that newspaper until 1882. He suggested the erection of the Soldiers' and Sailors' Monument, was a member of the monument commission named in 1879, and took an active interest in the monument, which was finally dedicated in 1894. As first secretary of the Cleveland board of elections, organized in 1886, he prepared maps and data which are still in use. He also served as city comptroller and was active in the affairs of the G.A.R.

History of the Cuyahoga County Soldiers' and Sailors' Monument . . . , Cleveland, 1894.

Historical Sketch of the 150th Regiment Ohio Volunteer Infantry . . . , Cleveland, 1899.

GLENN, EMMA LEE PATTERSON (March 25, 1869–May 18, 1942), was born near Cambridge, Guernsey County. Her poems appeared in numerous magazines and anthologies, and she also published two collections, the first of which was dedicated to her husband, Judge James Glenn of Coshocton: *Like a Meteor,* Dallas, Texas, [1938].

GLENN, JAMES SPAHR (June 5, 1875–), was born in Columbus, Franklin County, where he has resided throughout his life. He has published a number of pamphlets, most of them on historical subjects, e.g.,

The Dispossession of British Sovereigns, Columbus, 1945.

GLOCAR, EMILIAN (July 11 1906–), clergyman, born in Moravia, has lived in Ohio since 1939. He was educated at Sarajevo, Yugoslavia, and studied at the Universities of Belgrade and Prague. He was pastor of St. Savo Serbian Orthodox Church, Cleveland, 1939–43, and since 1943 has been pastor of St. Demetrius Church, Akron. He published novels and poems in Prague before coming to America, and he has published several novels since. One of his novels has a Cleveland setting: *A Man from the Balkans,* (Fern Long, trans.), Philadelphia, [1942].

GLUECK, NELSON (June 4, 1900–), president of Hebrew Union College since 1947, was born in Cincinnati, Hamilton County. He graduated from Hebrew Union College in 1918 and the University of Jena (Ph.D.) in 1926. He joined the Hebrew Union faculty in 1929 and has also been a member of several major archaeological expeditions. He has written articles on archaeology and the Bible and also several books, e.g., *The Other Side of the Jordan,* New Haven, Conn., 1940. WW 30

GODDARD, HENRY HERBERT (Aug. 14, 1866–June 18, 1957), educator, was born in Vassalboro, Maine, and lived in Ohio about twenty years. He was director of the State Bureau of Juvenile Research, 1918–22, and a member of the Ohio State University psychology department, 1922–38. After his retirement he lived in Santa Barbara, Calif. He coined the modern usage of the word *moron* and published several important psychological studies, e.g., *The Kallikak Family* . . . , New York, 1912. WW 28

GODLEY, ROBERT F. (March 14, 1908–Aug. 2, 1957), journalist, was born in McKinney, Texas, but lived in Cleveland for most of his life. He graduated from the University of Wisconsin in 1930, wrote a sports column for the Cleveland *Press* for fifteen years, broadcast various types of radio programs over a Cleveland station, and worked as a free-lance writer and public relations adviser. Around 1947 he moved to New York City. Under the pen name Franklin James, he published a mystery novel: *Killer in the Kitchen,* New York, [1947].

GODMAN, JOHN DAVIDSON (Dec. 20, 1794–April 17, 1830), anatomist, was in Cincinnati, 1821–22. On the invitation of Dr. Daniel Drake (q.v.), he joined the staff of the Medical College of Ohio, but the dissension on the faculty led him to resign after one term. While in Cincinnati, he edited the first medical journal published west of the Alleghenies: *Western Quarterly Reporter of Medical, Surgical and Natural Science.* Godman published numerous nature essays, medical works, and an anonymous poem praising a work by his father-in-law, Rembrandt Peale: *Ode Suggested by Rembrandt Peale's National Portrait of Washington,* Philadelphia, 1824.

GODWIN, BLAKE-MORE (Jan. 13, 1894–), museum director, was born in Clinton, Mo. He joined the Toledo Museum of Art staff in 1916 as curator and has been director since 1927. His description of the museum was translated into French and published by an adjunct of the League of Nations, the International Institute of Intellectual Co-operation: *Le Toledo Museum of Art,* [Paris, 1935]. WW 30

GOFF, ALICE CHARLOTTE (Feb. 28, 1894–), engineer, born in Oakfield, N. Y., graduated from the University of Michigan with a degree in civil engineering in 1915. She was a structural engineer at Republic Steel in Youngstown, 1915–59. Highly successful in her profession, she also specialized in designing reinforced concrete buildings and wrote a book based on her own experiences: *Women Can Be Engineers,* Youngstown, 1946.

GOHDES, CONRAD BRUNO (March 19, 1866–Dec. 6, 1952), clergyman, and educator, was born in Pomerania, Germany. He came to Columbus around 1881 and entered Capital University. After graduating in 1885, he entered the seminary and was ordained to the Lutheran ministry in 1888. For 24 years he served churches in various states; in 1912 he joined the Capital history faculty. He published several books on religious themes, e.g., *Does the Modern Papacy Require a New Evaluation?* Burlington, Iowa, 1940. WWW 3

GOLDEN, JOHN (June 27, 1874–June 17, 1955), playwright and producer, born in New York City, was brought up in Wauseon, Fulton County, where his parents moved in 1875. He went to New York City at the age of fourteen to become an actor. He wrote songs and studied law at New York University. He produced over 150 successful Broadway plays and musical comedies, e.g., *Lightnin', Seventh Heaven,*

Claudia, and *The Male Animal.* He also wrote or collaborated in writing many plays, e.g., *Salt Water, a Fresh Play,* New York, 1930. WWW 3

GOLDER, CHRISTIAN (Oct. 18, 1849–Aug. 5, 1922), clergyman, was born in Württemberg, Germany. In 1867 he came to Columbus, Ind., where he was converted to Methodism. Licensed to preach in 1870, he served pastorates in Michigan, Pennsylvania, and Ohio, was associate editor of the *Apologist,* 1890–1908, and was general superintendent of deaconess work, 1908–22. With his sister, Louise, he was a pioneer in the establishment of hospitals and deaconess houses, and he wrote many articles and at least three books on the subject, e.g., *History of the Deaconess Movement . . . ,* Cincinnati, [1903].

GOLDSBOROUGH, ROBERT. Pseud. See John R. Palmer.

GOLUB, JACOB SOLOMON (Nov. 11, 1895–), born in Poland, lived in Cincinnati, 1928–35, while serving as executive director of the Bureau of Jewish Education. He is now librarian for the Jewish Education Committee, New York City. He has published several books on Jewish history, e.g., *The Golden Dawn,* Cincinnati, 1942.

GOOD, JAMES ISAAC (Dec. 31, 1850–Jan. 22, 1924), clergyman and educator, was born in York, Pa. He held various pastorates in Pennsylvania and served on the faculty of Ursinus School of Theology until 1907, when he joined the faculty of Central Theological Seminary, opened in that year at Dayton. Until his death he spent a portion of each year in Dayton and the remainder at Ursinus. Widely recognized as a conservative theologian and church historian, he published many articles and books on religious and historical subjects, e.g., *The Origin of the Reformed Church in Germany,* Reading, Pa., 1887.

GOODENOW, JOHN MILTON (1782–July 20, 1878), was born in Westmoreland, N. H., where he was educated in the public schools, studied law, and was admitted to the bar. He moved to Bloomfield, Jefferson County, in 1812. Sometime before coming West he married Mrs. Sallie Campbell, a sister of John C. Wright, another of whose sisters had married Benjamin Tappan. At this time Wright and Tappan were located in Steubenville, and it would have been difficult to find two more influential men in eastern Ohio. Perhaps it would be incorrect to say that Goodenow joined them there in 1813, for within a very short time after his arrival in Steubenville he found himself embroiled in a bitterly contested slander suit with Tappan. Though he won the suit, the encounter must have been a serious handicap, yet Goodenow appears to have made friends rapidly. In 1828 he ran against his other brother-in-law, Wright, and was elected to the 21st Congress. He resigned his seat on April 9, 1830, having been elected a judge of the supreme court of Ohio. Within a few months he was forced to resign from the supreme court because of ill health. He moved to Cincinnati in 1832 and a year later was appointed presiding judge of the court of common pleas. He was a brilliant scholar. His *Historical Sketches of the Principles and Maxims of American Jurisprudence* was a masterly attack on the viewpoint of Benjamin Tappan and a work on the common law by Philadelphia's William Duane. Printed in Steubenville in 1819 and containing 426 pages, it was the most imposing work to be published in eastern Ohio up to that time; yet he issued but sixty copies, all of which he gave away to lawyers and legislators. He died in New Orleans and is buried in Cincinnati.

Ernest J. Wessen

Historical Sketches of the Principles and Maxims of American Jurisprudence, in Contrast with the Doctrines of the English Common Law on the Subject of Crimes and Punishments . . . , Steubenville, 1819.

Historical Record of the Proceedings of the Court of Common Pleas, and "the Bar" of Hamilton County, Ohio, in Reference to the Appointment of Clerk of Said Court, 1833, 1834, Cincinnati, 1834.

GOODHUE, WILLIS MAXWELL (1873–Nov. 22, 1938), was born in Akron, Summit County. He lived in New York City, where he wrote a number of plays, most of them intended for amateur groups, e.g., a comedy: *"Hello Bill" . . . ,* New York, 1926. AATB

GOODMAN, ALFRED THOMAS (Dec. 15, 1845–Dec. 20, 1871), was born in Washington, Pa. He graduated from Cleveland High School in 1863 and served in the 150th O.V.I. in 1864. He became secretary of the Western Reserve and Northern Historical Society in 1868. An indefatigable research worker, he edited Captain William Trent's journal from the original manuscript, a work rendered doubly valuable by his elaborate notes. His death occurred in Cleveland.

Judges of the Supreme Court of Ohio, under the First Constitution, 1803–1852, Cleveland, 1870.
First White Children in Ohio, [Cleveland], 1871.
Journal of Captain William Trent from Logstown, to Pickawillany, A.D. 1752, Cincinnati, 1871.
Papers Relating to the First White Settlers in Ohio . . . , [Cleveland, 1871].
Memoranda and Notes by the Late Alfred T. Goodman, [Cleveland, 1877].

GOODMAN, JOHN (? – ?), was born in England. Beyond the information drawn from the rather full date lines of his various poems, nothing is known concerning this Cleveland poet. He operated a store at 256 Superior Street, 1860–72. From 1873 to 1875, his poems are dated "Northern Ohio Lunatic Asylum."

Poems and Selections with an Address, Cleveland, 1877.
Long-lost Chronicles of Solomon, and Poems . . . , Cleveland, 1884.

GOODMAN, MAE WINKLER (May 25, 1911–), born in New Orleans, has lived in Cleveland since 1916. She graduated from Western Reserve University and is married to Eli Goodman. Her poems have appeared in numerous periodicals, and she has published at least three collections, e.g., a sonnet sequence: *The Single Flame,* Cleveland, [1948].

GOODRICH, CALVIN (Feb. 22, 1874–Nov. 7, 1954), journalist and scientist, born in Englewood, Ill., lived in Ohio about twenty years. He worked on the Cleveland *Leader* for a time and was with the Toledo *Blade,* 1908–16. In 1924, after working on various newspapers, he joined the University of Michigan zoology faculty. He published various technical works on zoology and *The First Michigan Frontier,* Ann Arbor, Mich., 1940.

GOODWIN, ELIJAH (Jan. 16, 1807–Sept. 4, 1879), clergyman, was born in Champaign County and died near Cleveland, but spent few of the intervening years of his life in Ohio. While he was a child, his family moved westward, finally settling in Daviess County, Ind., where he grew up. Converted to the Christian Church, he preached on the circuit in southern Indiana. He was one of the founders of North Western Christian University (Butler) in Indianapolis, edited church papers, and served churches in Indiana, Kentucky, and Iowa. He published a volume of sermons in 1856. The book below, compiled by James M. Mathes from his diaries and papers, is in effect an autobiography.

Life of Elijah Goodwin . . . , St. Louis, Mo., 1880.

GORDON, JOSEPH (Sept. 28, 1819–Feb. 28, 1858), clergyman, was born near Washington, Pa. After graduating from Washington College in 1840, he attended Allegheny Seminary and became a Presbyterian minister. He served Ohio churches at Ashland, New Philadelphia, and New Athens, was a member of the Franklin College faculty, 1845–50, and published the *Free Presbyterian,* 1854–57. He died in Washington, Pa., where he had returned in the fall of 1857. The posthumous collection of his writings contains numerous articles on various subjects, the greater part of them antislavery.

Life and Writings . . . , Cincinnati, 1860.

GORDON, MAY E. (Dec. 21, 1840–Aug. 23, 1921), educator, was born in Allegheny County, Pa., but lived in Wayne County after 1855. She was a public school teacher for many years. Her death occurred in Wooster.

Easter, the Dawn. A Story of the Resurrection in Verse, [Wooster, 1892].

GORDON, SAMUEL DICKEY (Aug. 12, 1859–June 26, 1936), born in Philadelphia, Pa., was state secretary of the Y.M.C.A. in Ohio, 1886–95. He published a series of inspirational books, e.g., *Quiet Talks on Prayer,* New York, [1904]. WWW 1

GORDON, WILLIAM STEWARD (April 21, 1868–May 8, 1948), clergyman, was born in Danville, Ill., but spent his boyhood in Brown County near Georgetown. In 1880 his parents moved to Oregon, where he attended Willamette University, taught school, and served as a Methodist minister. He retired from the ministry in 1933. He wrote many poems and hymns, which were published in several collections, e.g., *The Western Spirit; A Bunch of Breezy Poems,* New York, [1914].

GORDON, WILMER INGALLS (1860–March 7, 1943), physician, came to Cleveland in 1900, after practicing in New York City and the West. For more than thirty years he practiced in Cleveland and also operated a sanitarium and nurses' training center. An advocate of health without medication, he stressed proper living habits and abstinence from tobacco and alcohol. He published several books on vegetarianism, mental suggestion, New Thought, and similar subjects, e.g., *How to Live 100 Years; Or, the New Science of Living,* Cleveland, [1905].

GORDY, JOHN PANCOAST (Dec. 21, 1851–Dec. 31, 1908), educator, was born near Salisbury, Md. He graduated from Wesleyan University in 1878 and the University of Leipzig (Ph.D.) in 1884. From 1886 to 1896 he was professor of philosophy and pedagogy at Ohio University, and from 1896 to 1900 he was on the faculty of the Ohio State University. In 1901 he accepted a professorship at New York University, where he was teaching at the time of his death by suicide in 1908. Besides the titles below, he published textbooks in psychology and numerous professional articles. His history of political parties was several times revised.

A History of Political Parties in the United States . . . , 3 vols., Athens, 1895.
A Broader Elementary Education, New York, 1903.

GOSS, CHARLES FREDERIC (June 14, 1852–May 7, 1930), clergyman, was born in Meridian, N. Y. He graduated from Hamilton College in 1873 and Auburn Theological Seminary in 1876. Ordained to the Presbyterian ministry, he served several churches before coming to Avondale Church, Cincinnati, where he was pastor, 1894–1912. After his retirement he continued to live in Cincinnati and was an editorial writer for the *Enquirer.* He published sermons in addition to the listed titles. He died in Cincinnati.

The Optimist, Cincinnati, 1897.
The Philopolist; Or, City Lover, Cincinnati, 1898.
The Redemption of David Corson, Indianapolis, [1900].
Little Saint Sunshine, Indianapolis, [1902].
The Loom of Life, Indianapolis, [1902].
Dr. Goss' New Book, Philadelphia, [1905].
Husband, Wife and Home, Philadelphia, [1905].
Just a Minute! Moment-Readings on Scripture Passages . . . , Philadelphia, 1905.
That Other Hand upon the Helm, Cincinnati, [1910].
Cincinnati the Queen City, 1788–1912, 4 vols., Chicago, 1912.
Just a Minute! Moment Readings on Scripture Passages, and a Few on the Great War, Cincinnati, 1918.

GOULD, CHARLES NEWTON (July 22, 1868–Aug. 13, 1949), geologist, was born in Lower Salem, Columbiana County. He graduated from Southwestern College, Winfield, Kan., in 1899 and the University of Nebraska (Ph.D.) in 1906. He was in the geology department of the University of Oklahoma, 1900–11, and directed several geologic surveys for both the Federal and the Oklahoma governments. He published several articles and books on geology and geography, e.g., *Oklahoma Place Names,* Norman, Okla., 1933. WWW 2

GOULD, CLARENCE PEMBROKE (Nov. 1, 1884–), educator, was born in Church Hill, Md. He graduated from Johns Hopkins University (A.B., 1907; Ph.D., 1911) and served on the faculties of several Ohio colleges and universities: Wooster, 1911–18, Western Reserve, 1924–33, Kenyon, 1933–39, and Youngstown, 1939–. He has written numerous professional articles and reviews, and books dealing with the history of Maryland, e.g., *Money and Transportation in Maryland, 1720–1765,* Baltimore, 1915. WW 30

GOULD, DAYTON THOMAS (Feb. 3, 1847–March 9, 1943), was born in Twinsburg, Summit County. His family moved to Geauga County while he was small, and in 1858 they moved to Berea. He attended Baldwin College and graduated from Cleveland College of Physicians and Surgeons in 1870. For more than fifty years he operated a pharmacy in Berea. At the age of eighty, he published a volume of poems: *The Eight-Barred Gate,* Boston, 1927.

GOULD, GEORGE MILBRY (Nov. 8, 1848–Aug. 8, 1922), physician, was born in Auburn, Maine. In 1856 his father moved to Salina, Athens County, where he attended school. He was a drummer boy with the 63rd O.V.I. and after being discharged for ill health enlisted in the 141st O.V.I. He graduated from Ohio Wesleyan University in 1873, spent a year at Harvard Divinity School, and became pastor of a Unitarian church in Chillicothe, where he subsequently opened a bookstore. In 1885 he entered Jefferson Medical College, and after graduating in 1888 he began to practice in Philadelphia, specializing in ophthalmology. His truculent insistence on the relation of eyestrain to physical and mental ill-health involved him in many controversies. He published numerous articles, addresses, and medical dictionaries. In 1887 he opened a correspondence with Lafcadio Hearn (q.v.), who was then in the West Indies; two years later Hearn was a guest in his home. Gould's attempts to reform his exotic house guest were fruitless, and Hearn's *Karma* was the unsatisfactory product of this relationship. Gould died in Atlantic City, N. J.

The Meaning and the Method of Life; a Search for Religion in Biology, New York, 1893.

Borderline Studies; Miscellaneous Addresses and Essays . . . , 2 vols., Philadelphia, 1896–1908.

An Autumn Singer, Philadelphia, 1897.

Suggestions to Medical Writers, Philadelphia, 1900.

Biographic Clinics, 6 vols., Philadelphia, 1903–09.

Concerning Lafcadio Hearn . . . , Philadelphia, [1908].

Fifty-seven Varieties of Medical and Ophthalmic Blunders, Ithaca, N. Y., 1909.

The Infinite Presence, New York, 1910.

GOULD, JEAN R. (May 25, 1909–), was born in Greenville, Darke County, but since 1916 has lived in Toledo. She studied for two years at the University of Michigan, 1927–29, and completed her college work at the University of Toledo in 1937. She has published numerous stories for children and several fictional biographies of writers, e.g., one based on the life of Emily Dickinson: *Miss Emily,* New York, 1946.

GOUSHA, MRS. JOSEPH R. See Dawn Powell.

GOUVY, GERTRUDE (Nov. 21, 1899–Oct. 17, 1960), was born in Cleveland, Cuyahoga County. She was a statistical secretary at Cleveland Trust Company, 1922–37, and afterward was a secretary in Chicago. She was active in the Ohio Poetry Society before moving to Chicago. In 1955 she moved to St. Augustine, Fla. She published articles on business, poems, and a children's book about astronomy: *Speaking of Earth,* Boston, [1941].

GRABIEL, ZEPHANIAH ORLAND (April 20, 1860–1902), was born on a farm near Rushsylvania, Logan County. After attending district schools, he operated a farm and was local correspondent for the Bellefontaine *Examiner* and the *Ohio State Journal.* He also wrote for the press a number of humorous poems on rural life, many of which are included in the volume below. About 1900 he moved to Seattle, Wash., where he spent the last two years of his life.

Nature, [Ada], 1896.

GRAEBNER, WALTER A. (Dec. 16, 1909–), was born in Prairie Township near Columbus, Franklin County, the son of a Lutheran minister. He attended high school in Wauseau, Wis., and the University of Wisconsin, but left a few months before graduation to join the staff of *Time.* In 1937 he was assigned to the London office, where he worked until 1945. He is now managing director of an advertising agency in London. He has written several books, some in collaboration with other reporters. Six months in Russia provided the material for *Round Trip to Russia,* Philadelphia, [1943]. WW 30

GRAFF, MRS. S. S. See Anne Colver.

GRAHAM, ABBIE (May 28, 1889–), born in Lagarto, Texas, has lived in Cleveland since 1934. She graduated from Southwestern University in 1910 and also studied at Columbia University. She was director of adult education at the Cleveland Y.W.C.A. Her writings include a book on the struggle for women's rights: *Ladies in Revolt,* New York, 1934.

GRAHAM, ALBERT ADAMS (Sept. 19, 1848–Feb., 1896), historian and publisher, was born in Franklin County. Left an orphan at an early age, he lived with a brother in Illinois until 1861, when the family settled near Iberia, Morrow County, where he attended Ohio Central College. He wrote the histories of three Ohio counties and later organized a firm for the publication of similar works. He lived in Columbus, 1881–93, and afterward moved to the Southwest.

History of Richland County . . . , Mansfield, 1880.

History of Fairfield and Perry Counties . . . , Chicago, 1883.

Know Your State. The Land and Township System of Ohio Explained . . . , Tiffin, 1906.

GRAHAM, EDWARD P. (July 1, 1862–March 15, 1944), Catholic monsignor, was born in Enniskillen, Ireland. After being ordained to the priesthood at Cleveland in 1890, he served churches in Shelby, Akron, Sandusky, and Canton. He published numerous religious articles, a prayer book for children, and *The Mystery of Naples,* St. Louis, Mo., 1909.

GRAHAM, JOHN. Pseud. See David G. Phillips.

GRAHAM, LUCILE (Jan. 19, 1887–), educator, was born in Portsmouth, Scioto County, and has spent most of her life in that community. A graduate of Goucher College in 1908, she taught English in

Portsmouth High School, 1918–38, and conducted women's programs on local radio stations. She has published three books of verse, e.g., *Hills and Valleys,* New York, [1936].

GRANDIN, RUTH T. Pseud. See Ruth L. Thompson.

GRANGER, ALFRED HOYT (May 31, 1867–Dec. 3, 1939), architect, was born in Zanesville, Muskingum County. He graduated from Kenyon College in 1887 and afterward studied architecture at Boston Technical Institute (M.I.T.) and in Paris. He practiced in Cleveland, 1893–98, during which time he laid out the Euclid Heights development. He afterward practiced in Chicago and Philadelphia. He published several books, including a biography of Charles R. McKim and *The Spirit of Vienna,* New York, [1935]. He created considerable stir with his pamphlet defending the Kaiser in 1915: *By Their Works Ye Shall Know Them,* [Chicago?, 1915], and his book opposing any support of the Allies in 1916: *England's World Empire . . . ,* Chicago, 1916. DAB 22

GRANGER, MOSES MOORHEAD (Oct. 22, 1831–April 29, 1913), lawyer and judge, was born in Zanesville, Muskingum County. After graduating from Kenyon College in 1850, he read law and practiced in Zanesville, 1853–61. During the Civil War he served with the 18th and the 122nd O.V.I., and he left the army as a brevet brigadier general. He returned to his law practice in Zanesville, and in 1866 he became judge of the court of common pleas. He died in Zanesville.

Washington vs. Jefferson; The Case Tried by Battle . . . , Boston, 1898.

A Fair Answer to the Confederate Appeal at Richmond, [n.p., 1907].

The Official Record of the 122nd Regiment . . . , Zanesville, 1912.

GRANT, MAJOR A. F. Pseud. See T. C. Harbaugh.

GRANT, CHARLES ROLLIN (Oct. 23, 1846–Dec. 22, 1933), lawyer and judge, was born in Orange, Conn., the son of a shoemaker. He learned his father's trade and worked on the family farm. He enlisted in the 12th Connecticut Volunteers at the age of fifteen and was discharged in 1863. He came to Cuyahoga Falls, where he worked on a farm for three years and then entered Western Reserve College, graduating in 1872. He studied law in Akron and was admitted to the Ohio bar in 1874. He served as probate judge of Summit County, 1882–91, and judge of the court of appeals, 1912–19. In 1897 he became part-owner of the Akron *Times* and until 1916 wrote numerous editorials for that paper.

Illustrated History of Summit County . . . , Akron, 1891.

GRANT, JAMES J. (April 27, 1908–), was born in Van Wert, Van Wert County, and still lives in that community, where he operates a sign-painting business. He served in the Air Force during World War II. His hobby of gun collecting has supplied subject matter for a number of articles and two books, e.g., *Single-shot Rifles,* New York, 1947.

GRANT, ULYSSES SIMPSON (April 27, 1822–July 23, 1885), Civil War general and eighteenth President of the United States, was born in Point Pleasant, Clermont County. When he was a year old, his father moved to Georgetown, Brown County, where the boy grew up on a farm. He disliked the tanning trade followed by his father, but showed little preference for any other profession. He did develop a love of animals and skill in horsemanship which remained with him throughout his life. He spent two terms at Maysville Seminary, Ky., and one term at the academy in Ripley. In 1839 his father secured his appointment to the U. S. Military Academy. His career after his graduation in 1843 is too familiar to require detailed treatment here: service in the Mexican War, garrison duty until 1854, when he resigned from the army to escape court martial, the years of obscurity in Missouri and Galena, Ill., the victories in the West that brought him national recognition, his appointment as lieutenant general and supreme commander in March, 1864, and the smashing blows against Lee in the Wilderness, and the bewildered stubbornness and blindness to corruption that marked his two terms as President. In a sense, his tenacity and courage were shown more admirably in his last years than at any other time of his life. Encouraged by the ebullient Mark Twain, he persisted in writing his memoirs, though he knew himself to be dying of throat cancer. The two-volume memoirs, which some critics recklessly compared to Caesar's *Gallic Wars,* were sold by subscription. So successful was the sales campaign that Mark Twain paid the Grant family nearly $450,000 in royalties.

Speeches . . . , Washington, D. C., 1868.

Personal Memoirs . . . , 2 vols., New York, 1885–86.
General Grant's Letters to a Friend, 1861–80, New York, 1897.
Letters . . . to His Father and His Youngest Sister . . . , New York, 1912.

GRAPHO. Pseud. See James A. Adams.

GRAVENGAARD, HANS PETER (June 5, 1896–), insurance executive, was born in Brayton, Iowa. He served in World War I and graduated from the University of Nebraska in 1920. In 1926 he came to Ohio, where he has been engaged in the insurance business: in Columbus, 1926–31, Toledo, 1931–43, and Cincinnati, 1943–. He is now vice-president of National Underwriter Company and is editor of *Diamond Life Bulletins.* Besides numerous textbooks and brochures on insurance and selling, he has written a novel about a Danish family in America: *Christmas Again!* Boston, [1936].

GRAVES, ADELIA CLEOPATRA SPENCER (March 17, 1821–1894), was born in Kingsville, Ashtabula County. After graduating from Kingsville Academy, she taught in Kingsville. In 1849 she and her husband, Zwinglas C. Graves, founded Mary Sharp College in Winchester, Tenn., where she taught literature for 31 years. She compiled a number of Sunday school books and contributed stories and poems to various periodicals.
Old Testament Catechism in Rhyme, Nashville, 1859.
Jephthah's Daughter. A Drama in Five Acts, Founded on the Eleventh Chapter of Judges . . . , Memphis, 1867.
Seclusaval, or the Arts of Romanism, Memphis, 1870.

GRAY, ELISHA (Aug. 2, 1835–Jan. 21, 1901), scientist, was born in Barnesville, Belmont County. By working as a carpenter, he was able to attend Oberlin College for two years. His chief interest was in science, especially electricity. He patented several improvements on the telegraph and in 1872 moved to Chicago, where he spent the remainder of his life, devoting most of his time to electrical research. He made preliminary plans for a telephone, which later involved him in protracted legal battles with the Bell Telephone Company. He invented numerous electrical devices, including the telautograph for sending writing or drawing to distant points. Besides the title below, he published a number of technical articles.
Nature's Miracles; Familiar Talks on Science, 3 vols., New York, 1899–1900.

GRAY, JOSEPH M. M. (Aug. 31, 1877–Jan. 9, 1957), clergyman, born in Montgomery, Pa., was pastor of Bexley Methodist Church, 1941–50. He wrote a number of books on religious themes, e.g., *The Contemporary Christ,* New York, [1921]. WW 27

GRAY, OLIVER CROMWELL (Jan. 1, 1821–July 31, 1871), was born in Steubenville, Jefferson County. He attended Grove Academy and taught school at Knoxville. He later studied law in Cincinnati. He served in the Jefferson Greys in the Mexican War. His poems enjoyed local popularity and were collected and edited by his nephew, David Gray Fickes. His death occurred in Steubenville.
Oliver Cromwell Gray. A Sketch of His Life; With His Fragmentary Writings . . . , Philadelphia, 1872.

GRAY, ROBERTSON. Pseud. See Rossiter W. Raymond.

GRAY, WILLIAM CUNNINGHAM (Oct. 17, 1830–Sept. 29, 1901), journalist, was born in Butler County. He grew up on a farm, taught school, and graduated from Belmont College in 1849. He was admitted to the bar in 1852 but did not practice. He established the Tiffin *Tribune* in 1853, was an editorial writer for the Cleveland *Herald* in 1862, and was editor of the Newark *American,* 1863–71. He edited the *Interior* in Chicago from 1871 until his death.
Life of Abraham Lincoln. For the Young Man and the Sabbath School, Cincinnati, 1867.
Campfire Musings, Life and Good Times in the Woods, New York, 1894.
Musings by Camp-fire and Wayside, Chicago, 1902.
Keweenaw . . . , [Berkeley, Calif., 1905].

GRAYDON, THOMAS HETHERINGTON (March 30, 1881–Oct. 14, 1949), was born in Cincinnati, Hamilton County. He was educated at Franklin School, Cincinnati, and graduated from Harvard University in 1903. While at Harvard he starred in football and was chosen an All-American fullback. He later was an executive of a shoe manufacturing company, served in a machine gun battalion during World War I, and after a year in Cincinnati lived in Texas, New York, and California. He was killed in an automobile accident near Indianapolis, Ind., while driving East from his home in

Santa Monica, Calif. He published a book arguing that gravitation can be explained by repulsion as well as by attraction: *New Laws for Natural Phenomena,* [Belmore, N. Y., 1937].

GREEN, ASA T. (Sept. 11, 1846–Oct. 6, 1917), was born in Troy, Miami County. He was self-educated. In his book he describes himself as a "school visitor." He also lectured.

"Eureka"; Or, the Golden Door Ajar, the Mysteries of the World Mysteriously Revealed, Cincinnati, 1883.

GREEN, BERIAH (March 24, 1795–May 4, 1874), clergyman, advocate of abolition and temperance, was on the faculty of Western Reserve College, 1830–33. His sermons against slavery delivered in the college chapel attracted wide attention and led to his being chosen president of the Antislavery convention in 1833. He published a number of sermons and antislavery pamphlets, including a discourse on Elijah P. Lovejoy: *The Martyr . . . ,* [New York], 1838.

GREEN, CHARLES RANSLEY (Nov. 8, 1845–1915), was born in Milan, Erie County. He served in the Civil War, Aug., 1862–June, 1865. Returning to Milan he attended normal school for two years and then saw several years of service with surveying parties on the Union Pacific and Santa Fe railroads. From 1873 to 1880 he lived on a farm near Clarkfield. He went to Kansas in 1880, finally settling in Olathe. He died there in 1915, leaving a clutter of crudely printed pamphlets which cannot be wholly ignored by the historian and which will be the despair of bibliographers for years to come. He also published several family histories.

Patriotic Lyndon . . . , Lyndon, Kan., 1897.

History of the Christian Church, Lyndon, Kansas . . . , Lyndon, Kan., 1901.

History of the Methodist Episcopal Church, Lyndon, Kansas . . . , Lyndon, Kan., 1901.

History of the Presbyterian Church, Lyndon, Kansas . . . , [Lyndon, Kan.], 1901.

"Us" and "Our Neighbors," a Historical Genealogical Directory of . . . Lyndon . . . , [Lyndon?, Kan., 1901].

1861–1911, Fifty Years after We Volunteered to Put Down the Great Rebellion . . . , Olathe, Kan., 1911.

Pioneer Narratives of the First Twenty-five Years of Kansas History . . . , Olathe, Kan., 1912.

Early Days in Kansas . . . , Olathe, Kan., 1913.

Annals of Lyndon, Olathe, Kan., [1914].

A Historical Pamphlet. Wakeman, Ohio. Lives of the Volunteers in the Civil War . . . , [Olathe, Kan.], 1914.

Sac and Fox Indians in Kansas . . . , Olathe, Kan., 1914.

Tales and Traditions of the Marias des Cygnes Valley . . . , [Olathe, Kan.], 1914.

Volunteer Service in the Army of the Cumberland, [Olathe?, Kan., 1914].

GREEN, FRANCIS MARION (Sept. 28, 1836–Feb. 17, 1911), clergyman, was born in Norton, Summit County. After attending Western Reserve Eclectic Institute, Hiram, he taught in Ohio schools, 1855–63. He was ordained to the ministry of the Disciples of Christ Church in 1863. He served in an editorial capacity on various church periodicals. His death occurred in Akron.

A Royal Life; Or, the Eventful History of James A. Garfield . . . , Chicago, 1882.

Christian Missions, and Historical Sketches of Missionary Societies among the Disciples of Christ, St. Louis, Mo., 1884.

Church Minister's Manual, St. Louis, Mo., 1884.

The Life and Times of John Franklin Rowe, Cincinnati, 1899.

Hiram College and Western Reserve Eclectic Institute. Fifty Years of History, 1850–1900, Cleveland, 1901.

GREEN, INVISIBLE. Pseud. See William G. Crippen.

GREEN, JAMES ALBERT (Dec. 1, 1862–Feb. 18, 1955), born in Richmond, Quebec, Canada, was brought to Cincinnati in 1871 and spent the remainder of his life in that city. After attending Farmers' College, Cincinnati, he became a reporter on the *Gazette.* He was city editor of the *Times-Star,* 1884–90. From 1892 until 1924 he was active in iron and steel manufacturing and banking. A civic leader in Cincinnati, he was for many years a trustee of the Public Library. He published several pamphlets on historical subjects and three volumes of verse, e.g., *Cedar and Spruce . . . ,* [Cincinnati, 1918]; but his major work, for which he collected material for over forty years, was *William Henry Harrison, His Life and Times,* Richmond, Va., [1941].

GREEN, JONATHAN HARRINGTON (c. 1812– ?), was born in southern Ohio, possibly in Marietta, Washington County. He was one of the most verbose of that quick-fingered gentry who, having worn out their welcome on Mississippi steamboats, reformed and turned to the lecture platform for their livelihood. He was a gambler on the river steamboats from 1833 to 1842, after which he reformed and entered Augustana College in Kentucky. While there he wrote his first book. At Cincinnati in 1846, he started the magazine the *Casket,* with Emerson Bennett (q.v.) as editor. Typographically and editorially it was a surprisingly creditable production, but according to W. T. Coggeshall: "when the publisher had officiated as cashier of its finances for one year, he declared emphatically that literary enterprise was not justly seconded in the west," and the *Casket* was interred. It was then that he turned to the lecture platform. He proved to be a good showman and attracted large audiences. In 1847 he engaged in an argument with an avowed gambler named Freeman in Philadelphia, which was protracted over a period of three days, the entire argument being reported in most of the newspapers and some of the periodicals of that date. He was living in Philadelphia in 1887.

An Exposure of the Arts and Miseries of Gambling . . . , Philadelphia, 1843.
The Gambler's Mirror . . . , Baltimore, 1844.
Gambling Unmasked! . . . , New York, 1844.
The Secret Band of Brothers . . . , Philadelphia, 1847.
A Report on Gambling in New York . . . , New York, 1851.
Twelve Days in the Tombs . . . , New York, 1851.
The Reformed Gambler; Or, the History of the Later Years of Jonathan H. Green . . . , Philadelphia, [1858].

GREEN, WILLIAM (March 3, 1870–Nov. 21, 1952), labor leader, was born in Coshocton, Coshocton County, the town which he considered home throughout his life. After finishing the eighth grade, he worked for two years on railroad construction, and at sixteen he began working in the mines. Two years later, he was secretary of the local union. In 1906 he was elected president of the Ohio district of the United Mine Workers, and in 1912 he became secretary-treasurer of the national union. In 1924 he was elected president of the American Federation of Labor, succeeding Samuel Gompers. He died in Coshocton. He published numerous articles on the labor movement and several books, e.g., *Labor and Democracy,* Princeton, N. J., 1939. WWW 3

GREENE, JAMES HERVEY (1834–May 30, 1890), was born in Middletown, Butler County. He served in the 8th Wisconsin Regiment from July, 1861, to March, 1865. His death occurred in Medina.

Reminiscences of the War . . . , Medina, [1886].

GREENE, JOHN W. (April 11, 1836–Aug. 12, 1908), merchant, was born in Greensburg, Sandusky County. In 1857 he went to Wisconsin, where he taught school for one term before joining two other men for the trip to Pike's Peak. He returned the following year and worked in a gristmill in Indiana. When the Civil War broke out, he enlisted in the 26th Indiana Volunteers. He was promoted to captain in 1864. He was captured near Morganza, La., and imprisoned near Tyler, Texas. With John A. Whitsit he escaped and made his way to Natchez, Miss. The account of his escape is his only published book. He settled in Toledo in 1871 and sold sewing machines and pianos. He later added other musical instruments and established a prosperous music store in Toledo.

Camp Ford Prison and How I Escaped . . . , Toledo, 1893.

GREENWALD, EMANUEL (Jan. 13, 1811–Dec. 21, 1885), Lutheran pastor, born in Frederick, Md., came to Ohio in 1831. Living in New Philadelphia, he preached throughout the surrounding country. In 1851 he moved to Columbus and established an English Lutheran congregation. Controversy over the question of services held in English and over the administration of Capital University induced him to move to Pennsylvania, where he lived for the remainder of his life. Though an Ohio resident for over twenty years, he published no books while living in the state. In the latter part of his life he published a number of devotional books and pamphlets, e.g., *The Baptism of Children,* Philadelphia, 1872.

GREENWALD, LEOPOLD (Sept. 26, 1889–April 11, 1955), rabbi, was born in Marmaros, Hungary. He was educated in Germany and became a rabbi at eighteen. He came to the United States in 1924, and from March, 1925, until his death he was rabbi of Beth Jacob congregation in Columbus. He wrote more than 500 articles and 44 books dealing with Jewish law and history, e.g., *Oh Le-t Sarah,* St. Louis, Mo., [1939].

GREENWOOD, GERTRUDE SHISLER (Dec. 6, 1899–), born in Akron, Summit County, and now a resident of Canton, has contributed poems to a number of magazines and has published several volumes of verse, e.g., *Each Spring Returning,* Mill Valley, Calif., 1949.

GREER, CARL RICHARD (Feb. 29, 1876–June 28, 1946), journalist and advertising man, was born in Oxford, Butler County. He graduated from Miami University in 1894 and afterward worked as city editor of the Hamilton *Republican News* and as publicity director of Beckett Paper Co., Hamilton. He published books on advertising and a travel account: *The Glories of Greece,* Philadelphia, 1936. OBB

GREGG, FRANK MOODY (Dec. 25, 1864–Jan. 5, 1937), was born in Ripley, Brown County. He attended Ripley public schools. He was a reporter for the Cleveland *Press,* 1891–95, and afterward was an official of the Cleveland Worm & Gear Co. and other manufacturing companies in Cleveland. His later years were spent in New York City.

Andrews Raiders, or the Last Scenes and the Final Chapter of the Daring Incursion into the Heart of the Confederacy, Chattanooga, Tenn., [1891].

The Founding of a Nation; The Story of the Pilgrim Fathers . . . , Cleveland, 1915.

The Voice of the Nation, and Other Verse, New York, [1918].

GREGG, THOMAS, (Dec. 14, 1808–Feb. 11, 1892), journalist, was born in Union Township, Belmont County. As a young man he went to Illinois, where he published newspapers in Carthage, Hamilton, and other towns.

Ruth; A Poem for the Times, Warsaw, Ill., 1864.

History of Hancock County, Illinois . . . , Chicago, 1880.

The Prophet of Palmyra; Mormonism Reviewed and Examined . . . , New York, 1890.

GREGOR, EMMY S. (Mrs. Franklin R.) (Oct. 15, 1892–), born in Scranton, Pa., has lived in Cleveland since 1943. She has published a book for children: *The Elephant Who Came to Tea,* [Cleveland, 1947].

GREGORY, CHESTER ARTHUR (Jan. 24, 1880–Dec. 4, 1956), educator, was born in Shelbyville, Ind., but lived in Cincinnati from 1924 until his death. He was professor of school administration at the University of Cincinnati, 1924–37. He published a number of textbooks and discussions of education, e.g., *"Muddling Along"; Commentaries on the Teaching Profession, Mass Education, Politicians, and Preachers,* Cincinnati, [1940]. WWW 3

GREGORY, DANIEL SEELYE (Aug. 21, 1832–April 14, 1915), Presbyterian clergyman, born in Carmel, N. Y., was on the faculty of University of Wooster, 1871–78. Author of a number of textbooks and religious books, he wrote while in Ohio *Why Four Gospels? . . . ,* New York, 1877. He was later associated with Isaac K. Funk (q.v.) in editing the *Standard Dictionary* and the *Homiletic Review.*

GREINER, CLARK NEWTON (June 10, 1878–June 20, 1957), lumber salesman, was born in Ashville, Pickaway County. He graduated from Ohio Northern University and taught for a time in Circleville. He was associated with the W. M. Ritter Lumber Co. in Columbus for more than fifty years. He published verse in local newspapers and in a collection: *Gin and Took; Letters in Verse from a Travelling Philosopher to His Family and Friends,* Columbus, [1939].

GREINER, HENRY CLAY (1827–June 12, 1908), was born in Ohio, probably in Perry County, because he spent his boyhood in Somerset and practiced dentistry there before and after the Civil War. In 1899 he was living in Chicago, and he died in that city. He served in the 31st O.V.I. from Sept., 1861, to May, 1863, and also was a captain in the 160th Ohio National Guard for 100 days' service in 1864. He wrote *General Phil Sheridan As I Knew Him, Playmate—Comrade—Friend,* Chicago, 1908.

GREVE, CHARLES THEODORE (Jan. 3, 1863–Sept. 4, 1930), lawyer, was born in Cincinnati, Hamilton County, and practiced law in that city from 1885 until his death. He graduated from Harvard University in 1884 and Cincinnati Law School in 1885. He was professor of law at the University of Cincinnati law school, 1904–17. He wrote the historical portions of *Centennial History of Cincinnati and Representative Citizens,* 2 vols., Chicago, 1904. WWW 1

GREVE, JEANETTE S. (July 21, 1860–April 4, 1932), was born in Circleville, Pickaway County. She wrote for various newspapers and magazines and was on the editorial staff of *McCall's* magazine for a number of years. She wrote *The Story of Gatlinburg . . . ,* Strasburg, Va., [1931].

GREY, ZANE (Jan. 31, 1875–Oct. 23, 1939), was born at 705 Convers Avenue, Zanesville, Muskingum County. His father, Dr. Lewis M. Gray, was the grandson of Irish immigrants who settled in Muskingum County. Dr. Gray married Alice Josephine

Zane, daughter of Colonel Ebenezer Zane, who founded Wheeling, Va., and opened Zane's Trace across Ohio in 1797. Named Pearl Zane Gray by his parents, the novelist adopted the English spelling of his family name and dropped his given name when he was mistaken for a woman by readers of his early books. In Zanesville High School Grey gave less attention to academic subjects than to hunting, fishing, and baseball. After the family moved to Columbus, a scout lured him to the University of Pennsylvania to study his father's profession of dentistry and to play baseball. He was graduated in 1896, and he spent four years in unsuccessful dental practice on Thirty-first Street in New York. Feeling an urge to write, Grey produced *Betty Zane,* a novel about his brave great-great-aunt, who saved Fort Henry during the Revolution by carrying an apron full of powder through a hail of enemy bullets. After publishers rejected the manuscript, he borrowed money and had it printed at his own expense in 1903. A year later he married Miss Lina Elsie Roth and moved to Lackawaxen, Pa. He wrote two more books about the Middle West—*The Last Trail* (1909) and *The Spirit of the Border* (1906). His universal popularity, however, grew out of such successful novels about the Far West as *Riders of the Purple Sage* (1912), *Desert Gold* (1913), *The Call of the Canyon* (1924), and *The Thundering Herd* (1925). When fame and fortune came to Grey, he bought a permanent home at Altadena, Calif. In search of adventure he acquired a schooner and sailed on deep-sea fishing expeditions. Among his books on these experiences were *Tales of Fishing Virgin Seas* (1925) and *Tales of Swordfish and Tuna* (1927). As headquarters for hunting trips, Grey owned two ranches in Arizona. He lived close to nature so that he could portray faithfully the background of his stories. He said: "My inspiration to write has always come from nature. Character and action are subordinate to setting." Perhaps that characteristic of his writing helps to explain the cleavage between the opinions of the public and those of the critics. By purchasing 28,000,000 copies of his sixty-nine titles, the public made him the most popular author in the world. Movie versions of his stories further increased his popularity. The extreme view of the critics was expressed by Burton Rascoe in his judgment that Grey had no merit whatsoever "in either style or substance." More temperate critics recognized his lack of humor, improbable plots, unrealistic view of life, and "tedious" style, but they admitted that he had some merits. John Farrar said, ". . . first, he had a genius for storytelling, and second, his philosophies and ideals are identically those of the great mass of the American people." T. K. Whipple wrote this estimate of Zane Grey: "We turn to him not for insight into human nature and human problems nor for refinements of art, but simply for crude epic stories, as we might to an old Norse skald, maker of the sagas of the folk." Zane Grey died at Altadena, Calif.

Norris F. Schneider

GRILE, DOD. Pseud. See Ambrose Bierce.

GRIMES, EDWARD BREENE (May 12, 1859–June 3, 1942), was born in Wayne Township, Montgomery County. He graduated from Otterbein University in 1883. One of the incorporators of the Herald Publishing Company, he was editor of the Dayton *Herald* from 1886 to 1906, and subsequently was assistant to the president of the Ohmer Fare Register Company until 1915. His death occurred in Dayton.

Poems, Dayton, 1883.

Kettle of Coin, Dayton, 1901.

Poems for All the Family, [Greenfield, 1929].

GRIMKÉ, FREDERICK (Sept. 1, 1791–March 8, 1863), lawyer and judge, was born in Charleston, S. C., the brother of the reformers Thomas Smith and Sarah Moore Grimké, who lectured in Ohio but did not reside in the state. He graduated from Yale University in 1810 and moved to Chillicothe in 1818, where he began practicing law. He was judge of the common pleas court in 1829, and in 1836 became a member of the supreme court of Ohio, serving until 1841. A bachelor, he lived in seclusion in Chillicothe hotels and acquired a local reputation of being on the one hand a woman-hater and on the other the fountainhead from which flowed much of the local gossip. His ponderous and monotonous *The Nature and Tendency of Free Institutions,* which was published in 1848, is said by those who profess to have read it to be "full of learning and good sound sense." His death occurred in Chillicothe.

Considerations upon the Nature and Tendencies of Free Institutions, Cincinnati, 1848.

The Works of Frederick Grimké, Columbus, 1871.

GRIMM, HAROLD JOHN (Aug. 16, 1901–), educator, was born in Saginaw, Mich. He graduated from Capital University in 1924, Lutheran Seminary in 1927, and Ohio

State University (Ph.D.) in 1932. He served on the Capital history faculty, 1925–37, at Ohio State University, 1937–54, and at Indiana University, 1954–58. In 1958 he returned to Ohio State University as chairman of the history department. He has written a number of history textbooks and *Martin Luther as a Preacher,* Columbus, [1929]. WW 30

GRIMSHAW, IVAN GEROULD (April 17, 1900–), librarian, was born in Yorkshire, England. He lived in Akron from 1907 to 1920. He graduated from Hiram College in 1924, Yale University (B.D.) in 1925, and the University of Edinburgh (Ph.D.) in 1932. He was for a number of years director of education, Fairmont Presbyterian Church, Cleveland Heights. He was director of the library, Youngstown College, 1947–50, head librarian at Beloit College, 1950–53, and has been on the staff of Fort Wayne, Ind., Public Library since 1954. His writings include *When I Was a Boy in England,* Boston, [1931]. WWAE 19

GRISMER, FRANK A. (July 28, 1899–), was born in Indianapolis, Ind. A graduate of DePauw University and Ohio State University, he has lived for more than thirty years in Akron, where he operates the Catholic Book Shop. His writings include a play, *A Rumor in Paradise . . . ,* New York, 1934.

GRISMER, KARL H. (July 20, 1895–March 13, 1952), journalist, was born in Akron, Summit County. He graduated from the University of Akron in 1916. He worked on the Akron *Evening Times,* on the *Leader* and the *Plain Dealer* in Cleveland, and on the New Orleans *Times-Picayune.* He returned to Akron to work in the public relations department of B. F. Goodrich Co.; lived in Florida, where he produced several local histories; came back to Ohio in 1928 to work for Davey Tree Expert Co., Kent; and was on the Akron *Beacon-Journal,* 1941–45. In 1945 he returned to Florida, where he had nearly completed a valuable history of Akron and Summit County at the time of his death. Another example of his historical writings is *History of St. Petersburg . . . ,* St. Petersburg, Fla., [1924].

GRISSO, FORREST WILBIE (Aug. 5, 1872–), was born in Clark County. After graduating from Ohio Northern University in 1893, he worked as a pharmacist for a number of years and later was employed in Dayton Public Library and Dayton Museum. In 1915 he was ordained a minister in the Church of God. His residence is now in Dayton. He has published a volume of poems: *Sailing the Silver Sea,* [Yellow Springs, 1938].

GRISWOLD, LATTA (Feb. 4, 1876–Aug. 16, 1931), clergyman, was born in Lancaster, Fairfield County. After graduating from Princeton University in 1901 and General Theological Seminary in 1905, he was ordained to the Episcopal priesthood; he served churches in Newport, R. I., New York City, and Lenox, Mass. Besides sermons and doctrinal works, he published several novels, e.g., *Deering at Princeton: A Story of Princeton Life,* New York, 1913. WWW 1

GROESBECK, TELFORD (Aug. 5, 1854–Jan. 14, 1936), lawyer, was born in Cincinnati, Hamilton County. He graduated from Princeton University in 1874 and Harvard Law School in 1877. After being admitted to the Ohio bar in 1878, he practiced in Cincinnati. His death occurred in Cincinnati. His only publication appears to have been the long poem listed below.

The Incas, the Children of the Sun, New York, 1896.

GROFF, WILLIAM N. (May 4, 1857–Dec. 4, 1901), Egyptologist, was born in Cincinnati, Hamilton, County. He left America in the 1880s and is said to have attended the Sorbonne. Although little known in his native land, he is said to have been hailed in Europe as the successor of George Ebers, the famous German Egyptologist. He contributed numerous articles to the *Revue Égyptologique.* He died in Athens, Greece.

Les Deux Versions Démotiques du Décret de Canope. Paris, 1888.

Étude Sur Le Papyrus D'Orbiney, Paris, 1888.

Origins of Art; On the Religious Significance of Sculpture and Painting among the Ancient Egyptians, Cincinnati, 1899.

Oeuvres Égyptologiques, Paris, 1908.

GROOM, CHARLOTTE LOUISE (July 20, 1908–), was born in Cincinnati, Hamilton County. She graduated from the University of Cincinnati in 1929. She has written on art for several newspapers and has published considerable poetry. Four collections of her poems have been published, e.g., *The Street of Women, a Ballad, and Other Poems,* Philadelphia, [1936].

GROSE, PARLEE C. (July 27, 1889–), farmer, was born near Findlay, Hancock County. He graduated from Findlay College in 1907, served in World War I, and operated the General Publishing Company, in McComb. He also operated a farm in Hancock County for many years and now lives in McComb. Technical experiments have been his avocation, and his writings include *The Problem of Vertical Flight,* McComb, [1931].

GROSE, WILLIAM (Dec. 16, 1812–July 30, 1900), soldier and public official, was born near Dayton, Montgomery County. While he was still young, his family moved to Indiana, where he grew up and spent his life. He served with distinction throughout the Civil War, being commissioned brigadier general in July, 1864. His only book is a record of the 36th Indiana Volunteer Infantry, which he commanded at the outset of the war. He was active in Republican circles and served Indiana in various public capacities.

The Story of the Marches, Battles and Incidents of the 36th Regiment Indiana Volunteer Infantry . . . , New Castle, Ind., 1891.

GROSS, SAMUEL DAVID (July 8, 1805–May 6, 1884), surgeon, born on a farm near Easton, Pa., came to Ohio in 1833 as demonstrator of anatomy in the Medical College of Ohio. In 1835 he was named professor of pathological anatomy in the Cincinnati Medical College, where he remained until 1840. He wrote a number of significant medical manuals and treatises while in Cincinnati, e.g., *Elements of Pathological Anatomy,* Boston, 1839.

GROSSCUP, PETER STRENGER (Feb. 15, 1852–Oct. 1, 1921), judge, was born in Ashland, Ashland County. After graduating from Wittenberg College in 1872 and Boston Law School in 1873, he practiced law in Ashland for ten years. In 1883 he moved to Chicago, where he took part in a number of major civil and criminal cases. He served as district judge in Illinois, 1892–99, and as judge of the circuit court of appeals, 1899–1911. His opinions on and off the bench involved him in many controversies; he reversed the heavy penalty levied against Standard Oil of Indiana by Judge Kenesaw M. Landis, for example, and he spoke in favor of Germany in the early years of World War I. He wrote a number of magazine articles on social and economic issues, and many of his speeches were printed. His interest in traction problems and his sympathy with consolidation of industries and utilities can be seen in a pamphlet, *A Simple and Sure Solution of the Transportation Problem,* New York, 1905. DAB 8

GROSSMANN, LOUIS (Feb. 24, 1863–Sept. 21, 1926), rabbi, was born in Vienna, Austria. In 1873 he was brought to America. He graduated from the University of Cincinnati and Hebrew Union College in 1884. After serving as a rabbi in Detroit, 1884–98, he returned to Cincinnati as rabbi of Congregation B'nai Yeshurun and as professor of ethics and pedagogy at Hebrew Union College, 1898–1922. He published a number of textbooks and handbooks on Jewish religion and history, some of them in the nineteenth century. His other works include *The Real Life,* New York, 1914. DAB 8

GROSVENOR, CHARLES HENRY (Sept. 20, 1833–Oct. 30, 1917), lawyer and congressman, was born in Pomfret, Conn. When he was five, his family brought him to Athens County. Educated by his own efforts, he was admitted to the bar in 1857. In the Civil War he enlisted as a private in the 18th O.V.I. and rose to brevet brigadier general. Entering politics in 1873 as a Republican, he was elected to the Ohio House of Representatives. From 1885 to 1907 with the exception of one term, he served in the U. S. House of Representatives. His views were conservative. Highly effective as a campaign orator, he was known as "Old Figgers" for his ability to quote statistics to prove his points. During the last years of his life he practiced law in Athens. Many of his speeches in Congress were separately published. He also wrote *William McKinley, His Life and Work,* Washington, D. C., 1901, and *The Book of the Presidents, with Biographical Sketches . . . ,* Washington, D. C., 1902. DAB 8

GROVE, HARRIET PYNE (Mar. 6, 1866–April 23, 1939), educator, was born in Marysville, Union County. She graduated from Ohio Wesleyan University in 1886 and taught Latin there for ten years. She married Professor John H. Grove of the Ohio Wesleyan faculty. She later taught in the Cincinnati schools; her death occurred in that city. She wrote many books for girls, including the Betty Lee series, the Greycliff Girls series, the Adventurous Allens series, and the Ann Sterling series, e.g., *Ann Sterling,* New York, [1926].

GROVER, DELO CORYDON (May 29, 1869–Jan. 25, 1955), clergyman and educator, was born in Hartsgrove, Ashtabula County. He graduated from Oberlin College in 1891, earned a degree in law at the University of Michigan in 1893, and graduated in theology from Boston University in 1898. He served on the faculties of Mount Union and Baldwin-Wallace Colleges. His major book is *The Volitional Element in Knowledge and Belief . . .* , Boston, 1911. WWW 3

GROVER, EULALIE OSGOOD (June 22, 1873–Dec. 18, 1958), was born in Mantorville, Minn., and grew up in New England. She lived in Oberlin, 1906–26, with her brother, Frederick O. Grover, professor of botany at Oberlin College. In 1926 she moved to Winter Park, Fla. She was the author of numerous popular books for children, including the Sunbonnet Babies series and the Overall Boys series. She also wrote *Robert Louis Stevenson, Teller of Tales,* New York, 1940. WW 21

GROVES, MRS. JAMES A. See Cecil J. Richmond.

GRUELLE, JOHN BARTON (1880–Jan. 9, 1938), cartoonist, born in Arcola, Ill., and reared in Indianapolis, Ind., was working on the Cleveland *Press* when he occupied some idle time in the office by writing a children's story in verse. Rewritten in prose, it became *Raggedy Ann Stories,* New York, [1918], one of the most popular children's books ever written. He was later on the staff of the New York *Herald* and published a great many Raggedy Ann books and other stories. He died in Miami Springs, Fla. IATB

GRUMBINE, HARVEY CARSON (May 1, 1869–Dec. 24, 1941), educator, was born in Fredericksburg, Pa. He graduated from Albright College in 1888 and the University of Munich (Ph.D.) in 1900. He was professor of English at the College of Wooster, 1902–16. His books include *Love, Faith and Endeavor,* Boston, 1909. WWW 2

GUEST, MOSES (Nov. 7, 1755–March 22, 1828), was born in Brunswick, N. J. After serving during the Revolution as an ensign and as a captain in Middlesex regiments, he became a shipowner and captain. His journal, published with his poems, contains descriptions of coastal trips in the 1790s. He came to Cincinnati in 1817 and spent the remainder of his life in that community. A second edition of his poems was published in 1824.

Poems on Several Occasions. To Which Are Annexed Extracts from a Journal . . . , Cincinnati, 1823.

GUILD, ELLA JUNE PURCELL (1887–), social worker, was born in Toledo, Lucas County. Her husband, Arthur A. Guild, served on the University of Toledo faculty, and she was a social worker in Toledo for a number of years. Her latest (1957) address in Ohioana files was San Clemente, Calif. She has written articles and books on social issues, e.g., *Think on These Things; Some Black-White Problems as Seen by a Group of Negro Southerners,* Santa Barbara, Calif., [1947].

GUILFORD, LUCINDA (Linda) **T.** (Nov. 23, 1823–March 1, 1911), educator, was born in Massachusetts. She came to Cleveland in Oct., 1848, the year after her graduation from Mt. Holyoke Female Seminary. Two days after her arrival she founded a Young Ladies Seminary, which was merged in 1854 with the Cleveland Female Seminary under Dr. Samuel St. John of Western Reserve College. After a trip to Europe she opened Cleveland Academy in 1861. Her school was intended for young ladies, but men students were permitted. She stressed discipline and accuracy. Among her pupils were Charles C. Bolton (q.v.), Mrs. Samuel Mather, and Mrs. John Hay. Best known from a literary viewpoint was Constance Fenimore Woolson (q.v.), who remained her lifelong friend and who once wrote her in a letter, "It was from you that I first learned how to write." Miss Guilford was active in the cause of temperance and in Cleveland charities.

The Use of a Life: Memorials of Mrs. Z. P. Grant Banister . . . , New York, 1885.

The Story of a Cleveland School from 1848 to 1881, Cambridge, 1890.

Margaret's Plighted Troth, Cleveland, 1899.

GUILFORD, NATHAN (July 19, 1786–Dec. 18, 1854), educator, was born in Spencer, Mass. He graduated from Yale University in 1812, and in 1814, after studying law, he moved to Kentucky, where he taught school and practiced law. In 1816 he settled in Cincinnati. In 1828 he and his brother George bought Foote's Book Store. An earnest advocate of free public education, he campaigned for tax-supported schools. He established a publishing house that issued annual educational almanacs, edited by Guilford under the pen name Solomon Thrifty. Each page contained a statement regarding the need for public schools. He later brought out a popular speller in 1831 and an arithmetic in 1836. From 1843 to 1847 he edited the Cincinnati *Daily Atlas.* Elected superintendent of Cincinnati schools in 1850, he was forced to resign two years later because of his opposition to the use of the Bible in the schools.

GUISE, CEDRIC HAY (July 25, 1890–), educator, was born in Findlay, Hancock

County. After studying at the University of Michigan and Cornell University, he served on the Cornell faculty, 1915–54. He has written many articles and several books on conservation and forestry, e.g., *The Management of Farm Woodlands,* New York, 1939. AMS 9

GUITTEAU, WILLIAM BACKUS (Nov. 27, 1877–), educator and businessman, was born in Toledo, Lucas County. He graduated from Ohio State University in 1897 and the University of Pennsylvania (Ph.D.) in 1904. He began teaching in the Toledo schools in 1898 and served as superintendent, 1909–21. He was executive secretary of Ohio Crushed Stone Producers, 1933–47. He has written a number of books and pamphlets on history and government, e.g., *Democracy on Trial in the World War,* [Toledo], 1918. WW 30

GUNCKEL, JOHN ELSTNER (Aug. 14, 1846–Aug. 16, 1915), was born in Germantown, Montgomery County. He attended Oberlin College. He was in business with his father in Dayton for a few years and in 1870 moved to Toledo, where he was employed on the Lake Shore and Michigan Southern Railroad. He retired in 1906 and devoted the rest of his life to work among the boys on Toledo's streets, a work for which he became widely known. His death occurred in Toledo. He wrote a history of the Maumee Valley and *Boyville, History of Fifteen Years' Work among Newsboys,* Toledo, 1905. WWW 1

GUNDRY, FRANCES RUTH GILCHRIST (Sept. 18, 1875–Oct. 16, 1933), was born in Alpena, Mich. She graduated from Oberlin College and also studied at the Cleveland School of Art and the Sorbonne. She married John M. Gundry of Cleveland, and afterward lived in that city. Under the pen name of Martha Kean, she published *A Transplanted Nursery: Being the Simple Chronicle of a Summer Sojourn in Brittany . . . ,* New York, 1904.

GUNN, ALEXANDER (Dec. 7, 1837–July 6, 1901), was born in Cleveland, Cuyahoga County. Wealthy by inheritance, he was a familiar figure in European watering places. In 1879 he left his home in Cleveland and went to the community of Zoar to find "sanctuary from the clamors and empty ambitions of the world." For a time he lived at the hotel, but he finally persuaded the trustees to sell him a small log house which became "home" to him for the rest of his days—his beloved "Hermitage." After his death his friends discovered that he had kept a sketchy record of his days at Zoar—random entries in three small notebooks covering the years 1889 to 1901. His random notes possessed great charm. He had captured in simple beautiful prose the cadence and nuances of the tranquil scene. Under the editorial supervision of Don Carlos Seitz (q.v.) *The Hermitage-Zoar Note-Book* and a volume of *Letters* were privately printed in 1902. The first edition, limited to twelve copies, closely followed Gunn's original text. In the second edition, limited to 500 copies, the reference to members as "comrades" was dropped, and other minor textual changes were made. Gunn died at Bad Nauheim, Germany, and is buried at Zoar.

GUNNING, WILLIAM D. (1830–March 8, 1888), educator and clergyman, was born in Bloomingburg, Fayette County. A graduate of Oberlin College, he taught at Hillsdale College, Mich. He died in Greeley, Colo., where he was serving as Unitarian pastor.

Life History of Our Planet, Chicago, 1876.

GUNSAULUS, FRANK WAKELEY (Jan. 1, 1856–March 17, 1921), clergyman and educator, was born in Chesterville, Morrow County. He graduated from Ohio Wesleyan University in 1875 and was ordained to the Methodist ministry in the same year. After preaching for four years he entered the Congregational ministry. He was pastor of the Eastwood Church, Columbus, 1879–81, and of other churches in Massachusetts and Maryland. From 1887 until 1889 he was pastor of Plymouth Congregational Church in Chicago, after which he went to the independent Central Church, where for twenty years he drew great crowds. With the financial support of Philip Danforth Armour he established Armour Institute of Technology in 1893 and served as president until his death. The proceeds from his highly lucrative summer lectures were devoted to forming outstanding art and book collections. The Gunsaulus Collection of Incunabula was later presented to the University of Chicago. His collection of Wedgwood in the Gunsaulus Wing of the Chicago Art Institute is perhaps the finest in existence.

November at Eastwood, Columbus, 1880.
The Transfiguration of Christ, Boston, 1886.
Loose Leaves of Song, Chicago, 1888.
Monk and Knight: An Historical Study in Fiction, Chicago, 1891.
Phidias, and Other Poems, Chicago, 1891.
Songs of Night and Day, Chicago, 1896.

William Ewart Gladstone. A Biographical Study, Chicago, [1898].
Young Men in History, Chicago, 1898.
The Man of Galilee . . . , Chicago, [1899].
Paths to the City of God, New York, [1906].
The Higher Ministries of Recent English Poetry, New York, [1907].
The Minister and the Spiritual Life, New York, [1911].
Martin Luther and the Morning Hour in Europe . . . , Chicago, [1917].
Prayers, New York, [1922].

GURLEY, LEONARD B. (March 10, 1804–March 26, 1880), clergyman, was born in Norwich, Conn. In the fall of 1811 he was brought to the Firelands of Ohio by his parents. He served as pastor of various Methodist churches in Ohio. His poems appeared in the *Ladies' Repository, Western Christian Advocate,* Delaware *Gazette,* and other periodicals. He published a poem in the fourth number of the Sandusky *Clarion* which probably was the first poem published in northwestern Ohio. The last three chapters of his memoir of his father, a silversmith and Methodist minister, contain a valuable account of pioneer life in the Firelands. He died in Delaware.

Memoir of Rev. William Gurley, Late of Milan . . . , Cincinnati, 1850.

GUTHRIE, WILLIAM NORMAN (March 4, 1868–Dec. 9, 1944), clergyman, born in Dundee, Scotland, lived in Ohio for about ten years. After graduating from the University of the South in 1889, he studied for the Episcopal priesthood and was ordained in 1893. He taught modern languages at Kenyon, 1892–93, and served a Cincinnati church, 1893–1900. He was rector of St. Mark's-in-the-Bouwerie, New York, 1911–37. His books include *Songs of American Destiny . . . ,* Cincinnati, 1900.

H

HAAS, WILLIAM HERMAN (June 20, 1872–), educator, was born in Bellevue, Huron County. After studying at Ohio Northern University, he graduated from the University of Chicago (A.B., 1903; Ph.D., 1922). He taught in the geography department, Northwestern University, 1914–37, and still lives in Evanston. His writings include *Outposts of Defense,* Chicago, [1942]. WW 20

HACK, GWENDOLYN DUNLEVY KELLEY (Nov. 10, 1877–), was born in Columbus, Franklin County. She studied art in New York City, Paris, and Chicago. In 1905 she married Dr. Charles W. Hack. Ohioana files contain no recent data concerning her. She wrote *Modern Psychic Mysteries . . . ,* London, [1929]. WW 7

HACK, ROY KENNETH (July 3, 1884–Aug. 25, 1944), educator, was born at Ballston Spa, N. Y. He graduated from Williams College in 1905 and was a Rhodes Scholar, 1905–08. After teaching at Williams College, 1908–12, and at Harvard University, 1912–18, he joined the classics faculty of the University of Cincinnati, where he taught until his death. His writings include *God in Greek Philosophy to the Time of Socrates,* Princeton, N. J., 1931. WWW 2

HADLEY, CHALMERS (Sept. 3, 1872–May 11, 1958), librarian, was born in Indianapolis, Ind. He graduated from Earlham College in 1896. He was librarian of the Public Library of Cincinnati and Hamilton County, 1924–45, and after his retirement continued to live in Cincinnati. He published a number of articles and pamphlets on library work and fund raising and *John Cotton Dana, a Sketch,* Chicago, 1943. WWW 3

HAFFORD, FERRIS S. (March 23, 1857–1916), educator, was born in Fremont, Sandusky County. He taught at Battle Creek College, Mich., at Milton Academy, Oreg., and at the College of Healdsburg, Calif.

The Revellers; A Poem, Healdsburg, Calif., 1893.

HAGERTY, JAMES EDWARD (Aug. 1, 1869–Nov. 10, 1946), educator, was born in La Porte, Ind. He graduated from Indiana University in 1892 and the University of Pennsylvania (Ph.D.) in 1900. He also studied in European universities. He lived for many years in Columbus, where he was on the Ohio State University faculty, 1901–40. Besides technical works and articles, he wrote *Twentieth Century Crime; Eighteenth Century Methods of Control,* Boston, [1934]. WWW 2

HAHN, BENJAMIN DAVIESE (Aug. 21, 1856–May 5, 1938), clergyman, was born in Todd Township, Marion County. After graduating from University of Wooster in 1877 and Rochester Theological Seminary in 1882, he was ordained to the Baptist ministry. He served churches in New England and in Greenville, S. C. He wrote *Organ and Function; A Study of Evolution,* Boston, 1911. WWNAA 7

HAIG, ROBERT MURRAY (Oct. 3, 1887–June 9, 1953), educator, was born in Columbus, Franklin County. He graduated from Ohio Wesleyan University in 1908 and Columbia University (Ph.D.) in 1914. He taught political economy and economics at Columbia University, 1912–43, and also served on many state and federal commissions and bureaus. He published numerous articles and books, especially on the subject of taxation, and *Financing Total War,* New York, 1942. WWW 3

HAIL, WILLIAM JAMES (Nov. 16, 1877–), educator, was born in Osaka, Japan. He graduated from Missouri Valley College in 1899, from Yale Divinity School in 1904, and from Yale University (Ph.D.) in 1921. He was a member of the history department, College of Wooster, 1928–46, and still lives in Wooster. He published *Tseng Kuo-Fan and the Taiping Rebellion . . . ,* New Haven, Conn., 1927. WW 26

HAILMANN, WILLIAM NICHOLAS (Oct. 20, 1836–May 13, 1920), educator, was superintendent of schools in Dayton, 1898–1904. A pioneer advocate of kindergarten training for children and of the doctrines of Friedrich Froebel, he wrote many textbooks and books on elementary education, e.g., *Kindergarten Culture in the Family and Kindergarten . . . ,* Cincinnati, [1873].

HAINES, ELWOOD LINDSAY (March 12, 1893–Oct. 29, 1949), clergyman, was born in Philadelphia, Pa. After graduating from the University of Pennsylvania in 1916 and Philadelphia Divinity School in 1920, he was ordained to the priesthood of the Episcopal Church. He was rector of Christ Church, Glendale, 1931–37, and dean of Christ Church, Louisville, Ky., 1937–44; in 1944, he became Bishop of Iowa. He published *Poems of the African Trail,* Milwaukee, Wis., [1928]. WWW 2

HAIR, ADELBERT (Dell) (Nov. 4, 1871–March 21, 1932), policeman-poet, was born in Morrice, Mich. While still a boy, he served as a drummer with the army at Fort Sill, Okla. He later operated a hotel in Perry, Mich., and a saloon in Jackson, Mich. He came to Toledo around 1900 and served on the Toledo police force, 1906–09. For about twenty years after his resignation from the police force, he was a private detective employed by downtown Toledo merchants. Styling himself Dell Hair, the policeman-poet, he wrote many poems on various subjects, including the lot of a policeman.

Songs of Darkness, Light, and Death, [Lansing, Mich.], 1895.

Echoes from the Beat . . . , Toledo, 1908.

Violets and Thorns from a Dell . . . , Toledo, [1912].

Nature Beautiful, a Collection of Poems, Toledo, [1928].

HALE, GARTH. Pseud. See Albert B. Cunningham.

HALE, WILLIAM JAY (Jan. 5, 1876–Aug. 8, 1955), chemist, was born in Ada, Hardin County. He graduated from Miami University in 1897 and Harvard University (Ph.D.) in 1902. He studied in Germany, 1902–03. After teaching at several universities, he joined the staff of Dow Chemical Co. in 1919 as director of organic chemical research; he became a research consultant in 1934. He published textbooks and technical works in the field of chemistry, and several books relating to farming and chemistry, e.g., *The Farm Chemurgic; Farmward the Star of Destiny Lights Our Way,* Boston, [1934]. WWW 3

HALL, CHARLES FRANCIS (1821–Nov. 8, 1871), explorer, was born in Rochester, N. H., where he became a blacksmith and a most restless one. Drifting westward, he finally settled in Cincinnati about 1850 and established himself as a steel engraver and stationer. Despite an interest in Arctic exploration which amounted to an obsession, he seems to have prospered. He followed with intense interest the efforts of Sir John Franklin to discover the Northwest Passage and studied with avidity the reports of those who sought to determine Franklin's fate. Though a wife and children were housed in the modest home he had built on Mount Adams, he made an unsuccessful attempt to organize an American expedition, which he proposed to lead. Perhaps with a view toward enlisting public support, he started a small daily newspaper, the *Occasional,* Aug. 5, 1858, which he suspended late in the following December. His second newspaper, the daily *Penny Press* (the forerunner of the Cincinnati *Press*), was established in Feb., 1858. Then came McClintock's report of the fate of Franklin. Hall sold his newspaper and went to New York, where, at a meeting of the Geographical Society, he proposed to go in search of the retreating party under Crozier, some of whom he believed might be living as castaways among the Eskimos. A subscription was raised, and he was landed alone at Frobisher Bay, July 30, 1860, with a whaleboat and a few supplies. With the aid of the Eskimos he explored the coasts, discovered relics of the sixteenth-century Frobisher expedition, and in 1862 returned to Cincinnati with his loyal Eskimo aides, Joe and Hannah. He spent the next two years writing an account of his expedition, which was published in London in 1864 as *Life with the Esquimaux* and in New York, the following year, as *Arctic Researches and Life among the Esquimaux.* He shipped on a second expedition July 30, 1864, from which he returned in 1869, intent upon reaching the Pole itself if possible. He succeeded in getting the aid of Congress, and an act was passed appropriating $50,000 and authorizing the use of a naval vessel, the steamer *Polaris.* On Aug. 10, 1871, he reached 82° 11′ north, the most northerly point then reached by any vessel. Turning south, the *Polaris* anchored and Hall made a sledge trip to Cape Brevoort. Soon after his return to the vessel he died of apoplexy. Concerning his Arctic explorations, General Adolphus W. Greely said, "With similar limited resources no man has surpassed Charles Francis Hall in Arctic explorations."

Ernest J. Wessen

Life with the Esquimaux, London, 1864.
Narrative of the Second Arctic Expedition Made by Charles F. Hall . . . , Washington, D.C., 1879.

HALL, CHARLES GILBERT (1866–Nov. 4, 1947), was born in Amelia, Clermont County. He attended the public schools of Cincinnati and the University of Pennsylvania. He was engaged in railroad work until 1903 and afterward was an assistant advertising manager for Curtis Publishing Company. He became a free-lance writer, wrote numerous radio scripts, and also published several books for children, e.g., *Skyways,* New York, 1938.

HALL, EDWARD HENRY (April 16, 1831–Feb. 22, 1912), clergyman, was born in Cincinnati, Hamilton County. He graduated from Harvard University in 1851 and Harvard Divinity School in 1855. Ordained a Unitarian minister, he served in the Civil War as a chaplain with Massachusetts troops. After the war, he was minister of various Massachusetts churches. He prepared several Sunday school lesson books that are not included below.

Ten Lectures on Orthodoxy and Heresy in the Christian Church, Worcester, [Mass.], 1874.
Papias and His Contemporaries . . . , Boston, 1899.
Paul, the Apostle, as Viewed by a Layman, Boston, 1906.

HALL, FRANCIS JOSEPH (Dec. 24, 1857–March 12, 1932), clergyman and educator, was born in Ashtabula, Ashtabula County. He graduated from Racine College in 1882, and after studying at General and Western Theological Seminaries, he was ordained to the Episcopal priesthood in 1886. He was on the faculty of Western Theological Seminary, 1886–1913, and of General Theological Seminary, 1913–28. His death occurred in Onekama, Mich.

Theological Outlines, 3 vols., Milwaukee, Wis., 1892–95.
Historical Position of the Episcopal Church, Milwaukee, Wis., 1896.
The Kenotic Theory . . . , New York, 1898.
Introduction to Dogmatic Theology, New York, 1907.
Authority, Ecclesiastical and Biblical, New York, 1908.
The Being and Attributes of God, New York, 1909.
Evolution and the Fall, New York, 1910.
The Trinity, New York, 1910.
Creation and Man, New York, 1912.
The Bible and Modern Criticism, Milwaukee, Wis., 1915.
The Incarnation, New York, 1915.
The Passion and Exaltation of Christ, New York, 1918.
The Church and the Sacramental System, New York, 1920.
The Sacraments, New York, 1921.
Eschatology . . . , New York, 1922.
Christianity and Modernism, New York, 1924.
Moral Theology, (with Rev. Frank H. Hallock), New York, 1924.
Christian Reunion in Ecumenical Light, New York, 1930.

HALL, GRANVILLE STANLEY (Feb. 1, 1844–April 24, 1924), educator, was born in Ashfield, Mass. He graduated from Williams College in 1867 and Harvard University (Ph.D.) in 1878. He was on the faculty of Antioch College, 1872–76, and during his stay in Ohio preached in Unitarian churches around Yellow Springs. In the course of his distinguished career, he taught at Harvard, Williams, and Johns Hopkins. He was president and professor of psychology at Clark University, 1888–1920. A bibliography of his writing will be found in his autobiography, *Life and Confessions of a Psychologist,* New York, 1923. WWW 1

HALL, HARLAN PAGE (Aug. 27, 1838–April 9, 1907), journalist, was born in Ravenna, Portage County. After graduating from Ohio Wesleyan University in 1861, he settled in St. Paul, Minn. He worked on various newspapers there and founded at least two, the *Dispatch* and the *Globe.* He published the St. Paul *Trade Journal,* 1897–1903. He collected some of his writings in *H. P. Hall's Observations* . . . , St. Paul, 1904.

HALL, HERSCHEL SALMON (Oct. 22, 1874–Feb. 6, 1921), was born in Danville, Ind. He came to Cleveland in 1905 and worked for the American Steel and Wire Company. From 1912 until his death, he lived on a farm near Ashland. He wrote numerous stories on the steel industry for national magazines, poems, and a novel: *Steel Preferred,* New York, [1920].

HALL, JAMES (Aug. 19, 1793–July 5, 1868), born in Philadelphia, Pa., illustrates admirably the versatility which life in the early Middle West seemed to demand. Soldier, lawyer, judge, editor, politician, writer, and banker, he experienced several careers before he was thirty and only in the closing years of his life, in Cincinnati, combined permanence of residence with singleness of occupation. Throughout an active and diversified life, he held one conviction to be basic: his faith in the future of the Ohio Valley and the West. And this he manifested in many ways, through his perennial interest in the religion, education, journalism, history, and literary culture of the region. He was descended from English and Scotch-Irish stock long established in America. His father, John Hall, was associated with the Pennsylvania land office and served as U. S. marshal for the district of Pennsylvania. His mother, Sarah Ewing Hall, was the daughter of a prominent Presbyterian clergyman in Philadephia and inherited from her father a strong interest in literature and philosophy. Indeed, James Hall was by no means the only member of his family to evince literary skill: his mother wrote on religious and philosophical subjects; a brother, John Elihu, became the editor of the distinguished early American magazine the *Portfolio;* and another brother, Harrison, was well known as a Philadelphia publisher. James Hall attended a Philadelphia academy, but his studies were interrupted by the War of 1812, and he served through various campaigns as a lieutenant of artillery, seeing action at Chippewa and Fort Erie. At the end of the war he did not leave the service but retained his commission. He resigned from the army in June, 1818, and immediately commenced the study of law at Pittsburgh. After a short period of somewhat desultory legal reading, he was admitted to the Pittsburgh bar, but in 1820 he set out for the western country and journeyed in a keelboat down the Ohio River as far as Shawneetown, Ill. Many of his vivid travel impressions of this voyage are recorded in one of his earliest books, *Letters from the West.* Illinois was his residence from 1820 to 1833. At first he tried to support himself as a practicing lawyer in Shawneetown. But he shortly was appointed prosecuting attorney for a number of southern Illinois counties, and from 1825 to 1827 he was a judge in the state's Fourth Judicial Circuit. He also found time to devote to journalism and was associated with Henry Eddy in the publication of the *Illinois Gazette* from May 27, 1820, to late 1822. In the winter of 1827 the Illinois legislature elected Hall as state treasurer, a post which he held for four years and which necessitated the removal of his residence from Shawneetown to Vandalia, then the capital of the state. In addition to his political activities at Vandalia, Hall bought a half interest in the *Illinois Intelligencer,* a weekly newspaper which he helped to edit; he was instrumental in organizing the first Illinois state historical society; he edited the first literary annual to appear west of the Alleghenies, the *Western Souvenir,* 1829; and he founded the *Illinois Monthly Magazine,* the first literary periodical west of Ohio. Hall was not re-elected after the expiration of his term in 1831, and he found that lack of both capital and supplies hindered his publishing activities. Early in 1833 he resolved to leave Illinois for Cincinnati, which he described flamboyantly as the Athens of western America. Cincinnati remained his home until his death. The *Illinois Monthly Magazine* did not succumb because of its editor's change of residence; it was rechristened, and as the *Western Monthly Magazine* it survived until 1836. During his early years in Ohio, Hall's activities were as numerous as they had been in Illinois. He continued to practice law and to be active as a writer; he participated in the social life of the city and was one of the main sponsors of the Semi-Colon Club (to which Dr. Daniel Drake, Edward Mansfield, Harriet and Catharine Beecher, and Calvin Stowe also belonged); and he was cashier and subsequently president (until 1865) of the Commercial Bank. Hall married twice. His first wife, who died in 1832, was Mary Harrison Posey, granddaughter of the Revolutionary soldier and territorial governor, whose biography Hall later wrote. His second wife was Mary Louise Anderson Alexander, a young widow when he married her in 1839. James Hall died in Cincinnati and was buried in Spring Grove Cemetery. Hall's writings are numerous, although the bibliographer quickly discovers that much of his work was republished under different titles. His interest in both the economic and political history of the western country induced him to publish a number of works which are essentially descriptive and statistical. Among these should be noted his *Sketches of History, Life, and Manners in the West; Statistics of the West; Notes on the Western States;* and *The West, Its Commerce and Navigation.* More readable because it combines factual background with narrative interpretation is the *Romance of Western History.* Hall was also the author of biographies of William Henry Harrison and Thomas Posey, and he furnished the letterpress for the sumptuous volumes which he and Thomas L. McKenney brought out between 1836 and 1844 in Philadelphia: *History of the Indian Tribes of North America.* For European readers a small edition of portraits of Indians was published: *Photographien nach Color. Portraits aus dem Werk: "History of the Indian Tribes . . ."* (2 vols., Philadelphia, 1838). Hall's more purely literary work took the form of poetry, numerous short stories, and one novel. Hall's verse is scattered through the periodicals he edited and has never been collected, though his poem "Wedded Love's First Home" has been frequently anthologized. He contributed at least one story to the volume entitled *Winter Evenings* and published four volumes of shorter narratives: *Legends of the West; The Soldier's Bride and Other Tales; Tales of the Border;* and *The Wilderness and the Warpath.* His one novel, *The Harpe's Head; A Legend of Kentucky,* was published in Philadelphia in 1833; in England it appeared as *Kentucky: A Tale.* Hall's fiction, his most distinctive literary achievement, was handicapped somewhat by the conventional standards of the age in which he lived. He had fresh and vital material on which to draw, extensive personal experience in unsettled country, and a warm interest in the people and scenes which he knew so well. His awareness of these facts is apparent in his preface to *Legends of the West,* in which he sets down his attitude to his material in some detail. But often the stilted plots and implausible portraiture of the current romantic novels find imitations in his work. He was generally much better when he tried to report the speech that he heard and described landscapes familiar from long experience. Among his short stories, several stand out especially. The three tales that reflect life in the French settlements along the Kaskaskia and Mississippi Rivers are charming narratives: "Michel de Coucy," "A Legend of Carondelet," and "The French Village." No other romancer has captured quite so memorably the quality of this life and the attitude of the indolent villagers, indifferent to manual toil but always eager for a fandango or a shivaree. Hall's Indian tales, such as "The Black Steed of the Prairie" and "The Dark Maid of Illinois," are based on legendary material and do not seem very authentic. Several of his frontier stories are memorable, notably "Pete Featherton," "The Seventh Son," "The Pioneer," and "The Indian Hater"—the last especially because of Herman Melville's later use of the title and theme in his novel *The Confidence Man.* Some of these tales have been widely reprinted and still appear in collections of American short stories. Hall's literary faults were often the faults of his age—prolixity, excessive moralizing, authorial intrusions into the story, and sentimentality. He seldom told a story objectively and he rarely plunged immediately into his narrative. Yet Hall was close to the realistic trend which was developing by the middle of the century and which may be observed in his own treatment of dialogue, in his frontier characters, and particularly in his backgrounds. Moreover, like Edward Eggleston's later novels, Hall's work is rich in social history. Several orations and letters were published separately. As a spokesman for the western country Hall had no superior. Profoundly convinced of its great destiny, he worked indefatigably to advance it in many ways. He urged the older citizens to preserve and record western history. He attempted to improve education and to advance religion. He was interested in science and gave many pages of his periodicals to accounts of the mineral and agricultural wealth of the region. Above all, he urged his readers to write about the West and to support western projects. No chauvinist and certainly no partisan of Great Britain, James

Hall promoted an intelligent regionalism. The cultural development of the Ohio Valley is permanently indebted to him.

John T. Flanagan

Trial and Defense of First Lieutenant James Hall, of the Ordnance Department, United States' Army, Pittsburgh, 1820.

Letters from the West; Containing Sketches of Scenery, Manners, and Customs and Anecdotes Connected with the First Settlements of the Western Sections of the United States, London, 1828.

The Western Souvenir, Cincinnati, 1828.

Winter Evenings. A Series of American Tales, Philadelphia, 1830.

Legends of the West, Philadelphia, 1832.

The Harpe's Head. A Legend of Kentucky, Philadelphia, 1833.

Selections from the Writings of Mrs. Sarah Hall. (With a Memoir by James Hall), Philadelphia, 1833.

The Soldier's Bride; And Other Tales, Philadelphia, 1833.

The Western Reader, Cincinnati, 1833.

Sketches of History, Life, and Manners in the West, Cincinnati, 1834.

Tales of the Border, Philadelphia, 1835.

History of the Indian Tribes of North America, with Biographical Sketches and Anecdotes of Their Principal Chiefs, (with Thomas L. McKenney), Philadelphia, 1836–44.

A Memoir of the Public Services of William Henry Harrison, Philadelphia, 1836.

Statistics of the West at the Close of the Year 1836, Cincinnati, 1836.

The Catholic Question, Cincinnati, 1838.

Notes on the Western States; Containing Descriptive Sketches of Their Soil, Climate, Resources, and Scenery, Philadelphia, 1838.

Plea for the Sabbath; Addresses to the Legal Profession, Baltimore, 1845.

Life of Thomas Posey, Major-General and Governor of Indiana, Boston, 1846.

The West: Its Commerce and Navigation, Cincinnati, 1848.

The West: Its Soil, Surface, and Productions, Cincinnati, 1848.

The Wilderness and the War Path, New York, 1849.

The Romance of Western History: Or Sketches of History, Life, and Manners in the West, Cincinnati, 1857.

HALL, JOHN ANDREW (Aug. 17, 1852–March 28, 1925), clergyman, was born in Morrow County. He graduated from Wittenberg College in 1875 and from the Seminary in 1877. After being ordained to the Lutheran ministry, he served churches in Mifflin, Cincinnati, Canton, and Mansfield. He died in Mansfield. He wrote several books on religious themes, e.g., *The Nature of God . . .* , Philadelphia, [1910].

HALL, MARSHALL RENWOOD (Sept. 13, 1889–April 9, 1947), journalist, was born in Sherman, W. Va., and grew up in Idaho. He began his journalistic career with the Pittsburgh *Dispatch,* edited the Cleveland *Times,* and from 1926 until his death was on the staff of the *Ohio State Journal.* He published considerable adventure fiction, some of it under the pen name of Barry Renwood. Most of his novels deal with the West, e.g., *The Valley of Strife,* Boston, [1925].

HALLE, RITA SULZBACHER. See Rita S. H. Kleeman.

HALSEY, LEWIS (1843–Dec. 25, 1914), clergyman, was born in Trumansburg, N. Y. A graduate of Colgate-Rochester Divinity School, he was a Baptist minister in Interlaken, N. Y., and in Cincinnati. His death occurred in Cincinnati.

The Falls of Taughannock . . . , New York, 1866.

History of the Seneca Baptist Association . . . , Ithaca, N. Y., 1879.

HALSTEAD, MURAT (Sept. 2, 1829–July 2, 1908), journalist, was born on a farm near Paddy's Run, Butler County. On May 18, 1860, Norman B. Judd of Illinois stood on the speaker's platform in the Wigwam, a rambling frame building in Chicago where the Republican Party was in convention to nominate a candidate for President. He offered the name of Abraham Lincoln. Tumultuous cheering shook the building. In the press gallery, swiftly moving pencils noted the demonstration. One reporter wrote: "Imagine all the hogs ever slaughtered in Cincinnati giving their death squeals together." That reporter was Murat Halstead, dark-haired, handsome, thirty years old, of the Cincinnati *Commercial.* His reference to squealing pigs struck fire in Cincinnati, known then as "Porkopolis," center of the pork-packing industry. Halstead rode a train through the night back to Ohio. In every village, guns were booming, tar barrels burning, drums beating. He noted that the people were "delighted with the idea of a candidate for the presidency who thirty years ago split rails on the Sangamon River—classic stream now and forevermore—and whose neighbors called him 'honest'." Halstead's story of the convention has long been source material for Civil War historians and Lincoln scholars. It has been said he wrote a million words a year for forty years. But never again did he rise to such heights. His five words about the Sangamon alone have made him a journalistic immortal. His father was Griffin Halstead, whose parents had brought him to Ohio from North Carolina. His mother was Clarissa Willits Halstead, daughter of Pennsylvanians who settled in the lower Scioto Valley. Murat attended country school, then entered Farmers' College at College Hill. While in college, he wrote for the Hamilton *Intelligencer* and the Rossville *Democrat.* Upon graduation in 1848, he worked on Cincinnati newspapers: the *Daily Atlas,* the *Columbian and Great West,* and the *Enquirer,* before joining the *Commercial* in 1853 under M. D. Potter. During the Civil War, he wrote political news, was a war correspondent, and virtually ran the newspaper. The *Commercial* stood squarely behind the Lincoln administration. Upon Potter's death in 1866, Halstead became chief stockholder and publisher. Halstead left the Republican Party in 1872 to support Horace Greeley for President, but soon returned to the fold. An outspoken foe of corruption in public office, he charged that seats in the U. S. Senate were sold. The Senate got its revenge when it rejected his nomination as minister to Germany by President Harrison in 1889. Halstead, meanwhile, had covered the Franco-Prussian War and conducted a campaign newspaper in New York. Gradually, due to poor financial management, the *Commercial* slipped from his hands, and in 1890, he became editor of the Brooklyn (N. Y.) *Standard Union,* where he wound up his career in journalism. Turning to authorship, he produced a succession of quickly forgotten books. Compiled mainly with scissors and paste pot, they were sold by subscription. Twelve children were born to him and his wife, the former Mary Banks, whom he had married in 1857. When he fell dead at his home, 643 West Fourth Street, Cincinnati, July 2, 1908, the headline in his old newspaper, then the *Commercial-Tribune,* said: "Grand old man of journalism passes away." Among those who sent regrets was his former reporter on the Cincinnati courthouse beat, William Howard Taft.

Robert S. Harper

Caucuses of 1860. A History of the National Political Conventions of the Current Presidential Campaign . . . , Columbus, 1860.

The War Claims of the South. The New Southern Confederacy, with the Democratic Party as Its Claim Agency, Demanding Indemnity for Conquest . . . , Cincinnati, 1876.

Life of Jay Gould, How He Made His Millions, (with J. Frank Beale, Jr.), [Philadelphia], 1892.

One Hundred Bear Stories . . . , New York, [1895].

The White Dollar . . . , Philadelphia, [1895].

The Story of Cuba . . . , Chicago, 1896.

The History of American Expansion and the Story of Our New Possessions . . . , [n.p., 1898].

Our Country in War Relations with All Nations . . . , [n.p., 1898].

Our New Possessions . . . , Chicago, 1898.

Full Official History of the War with Spain . . . , Chicago, 1899.

Life and Achievements of Admiral Dewey . . . , Chicago, 1899.

Briton and Boer in South Africa . . . , [Philadelphia?, 1900].

Galveston: The Horrors of a Stricken City . . . , [Chicago, 1900].

Victorious Republicanism and Lives of the Standard-bearers, McKinley and Roosevelt . . . , [Chicago?, 1900].

Aguinaldo and His Captor . . . , Cincinnati, 1901.

The Illustrious Life of William McKinley, Our Martyred President . . . , [Chicago, 1901].

The Life of Theodore Roosevelt, Twenty-fifth President of the United States, Akron, 1902.

The World on Fire . . . , [n.p., 1902].

Pictorial History of the Louisiana Purchase and the World's Fair at St. Louis . . . , Philadelphia, [1904].

The War between Russia and Japan . . . , Philadelphia, [1904].

HAM, MARION FRANKLIN (Feb. 18, 1867–July 23, 1956), clergyman, was born in Harveysburg, Warren County. In 1885 he left Ohio for Chattanooga, Tenn., where he worked for a newspaper and in a bank. He entered the Unitarian ministry in 1897 and afterward served churches in Tennessee, Texas, and Massachusetts. One of his poems, "Bob White," was reprinted in newspapers throughout the country; William Dean Howells (q.v.) wrote that "it brought back my boyhood in southern Ohio." In addition to his poetry he composed numerous hymns, compiled song books, and wrote a number of stories in Negro dialect. A collected edition of his poems was published in 1954. His death occurred in Arlington, Mass.

The Golden Shuttle, New York, 1896.

Songs of the Spirit, Boston, 1932.

HAMILTON, EDMOND MOORE (Oct. 21, 1904-), was born in Youngstown, Mahoning County, and now lives in Kinsman, Trumbull County. He attended Westminster College, New Wilmington, Pa. A free-lance writer since 1926, he has published many short stories and novels, most of them in the field of science fiction, e.g., *The Star Kings,* New York, [1949]. He has used various pseudonyms, e.g., Philip Allen and Frederick Fell. His novels have been published in England and in Europe. His wife, who writes mystery stories as Leigh Brackett, has lived in Ohio since 1951.

HAMILTON, EDWARD JOHN (Nov. 29, 1834–Nov. 21, 1918), clergyman and educator, spent two periods in Ohio. While his father was a pastor in Cincinnati, he attended preparatory school in that city, 1847–50; he was later pastor of the Presbyterian church in Hamilton, 1866–68. Among his most important works is *The Human Mind . . . ,* New York, 1883.

HAMILTON, EDWIN TIMOTHY (June 5, 1898-), was born in Cleveland, Cuyahoga County. He is the brother of Dorothy Hamilton Brush (q.v.). He attended Cleveland public schools and Roswell Military Academy in New Mexico. During World War I, he left Dartmouth College to serve in the Canadian Royal Air Force, where he attained the rank of captain. He also served in World War II and became a brigadier general. After World War I he worked for the Cleveland Hardware Company. He now lives in Ontario, Canada. He has published several books on handicraft for children, e.g., *Popular Crafts for Boys,* New York, 1935.

HAMILTON, FLORA DESHLER BRENT (Dec. 23, 1872–July 7, 1933), was born in Cheyenne, Wyo., the granddaughter of David Deshler of Columbus. When her father died in 1880, her mother took her abroad for her education. Later, they returned to Columbus. In 1897 she married Thomas B. Hamilton of Columbus, where they lived for some time. She died at her summer home in Culver, Ind. She published essays, translations, and original poems. An essay on the sonnet and sonnets in French and English are included in the posthumous volume *Sonnets,* Boston, 1934.

HAMILTON, FRANKLIN ELMER ELLSWORTH (Aug. 9, 1866–May 5, 1918), clergyman, was born in Pleasant Valley, Muskingum County. He graduated from Harvard University in 1887 and Boston University School of Theology in 1892, was ordained to the Methodist ministry in 1892, and served churches in Massachusetts. He was chancellor of American University, Washington, D. C., 1908–16, and in 1916 was elected bishop of the Methodist Episcopal Church. His writings include *The Cup of Fire,* Cincinnati, [1914].

HAMILTON, GILBERT VAN TASSEL (Jan. 15, 1877–Dec., 1943), physician and psychiatrist, was born in Frazeysburg, Muskingum County. He graduated from Ohio Wesleyan University in 1898 and Jefferson Medical College in 1901. He practiced as a physician and psychiatrist in Pennsylvania, Massachusetts, Ohio, New York, and California. His residence at the time of his death was Santa Barbara, Calif. His writings include *A Research in Marriage,* New York, 1929. WWW 2

HAMILTON, JAY BENSON (Dec. 19, 1847–Jan. 19, 1920), clergyman, was born in West Chester, Butler County. After graduating from Mount Union College, he was ordained to the Methodist ministry in 1872, served various churches in New England, and was president of Walden University, Nashville, Tenn., 1901–04. During his later life he served several churches in New York City.

Empty Churches, and How to Fill Them, New York, 1879.

From the Pulpit to the Poor-House, and Other Romances of the Methodist Itinerancy, Cincinnati, 1892.

HAMILTON, KAY. Pseud. See Cateau deLeeuw.

HAMILTON, WILLIAM DOUGLAS (May 24, 1832 Jan. 22, 1916), lawyer, was born in Scotland, but was brought to the United States at an early age. He graduated from Cincinnati Law School in 1858 and began practice in Zanesville in 1859. He served throughout the Civil War in the 32nd O.V.I. and in the 9th Ohio Cavalry. After the war he practiced in Columbus. He published *Recollections of a Cavalryman . . . ,* Columbus, 1915.

HAMLIN, HOWARD ELROY (July 9, 1888–), educator, was born in North Baltimore, Wood County. He graduated from Ohio Wesleyan University in 1913 and did graduate work at Harvard University. He taught physical education in several colleges and universities, and from 1938 until his retirement was an official of the Ohio Department of Education. He now lives in Columbus. He has published several pamphlets similar to his first publication, *Alcohol Talks to Youth . . .* , [Columbus, 1935].

HAMLINE, LEONIDAS LENT (May 10, 1797–March 23, 1865), clergyman, was born in Burlington, Conn. Noted for his mental precocity, he was teaching school before he was eighteen. He is believed to have arrived in Ohio about 1820; however, the earliest record of him in the state is as a member of the bar in Zanesville in 1825. Though raised as a Congregationalist, he fell under Methodist influences and was licensed to preach in 1829. He joined the Ohio Conference, on probation, in 1832 and was ordained an elder in 1836—the year in which he became assistant editor of the *Western Christian Advocate.* Upon his recommendation, the *Ladies' Repository* was founded in 1841, and he served as editor of this, the Midwest's first successful periodical, until 1844. He was elected bishop in 1844, but was forced by a heart condition to relinquish active service in 1852. Before his death he gave $25,000 to establish what is now Hamline University, St. Paul, Minn. His death occurred in Mount Pleasant, Iowa.

Sermons and Miscellaneous Works, (F. G. Hubbard, ed.), 2 vols., New York, 1869–71.

HAMMEL, MAMIE L. (March 29, 1867–July, 1943), was born in Cincinnati, Hamilton County. Wife of a Cincinnati attorney, Samuel B. Hammel, she wrote many short stories and poems for children which were published in the Cincinnati *Enquirer* and other periodicals. Also, she and Mabel H. Faison (q.v.) collaborated on three novels, published under the pen name Hammel Johnson, e.g., *Prydehurst,* New York, 1926.

HAMMOND, CHARLES (Sept. 19, 1779–April 3, 1840), lawyer and journalist, was born near Baltimore, Md., but grew up in Wellsburg, Va., where his father moved in 1785. Admitted to the Virginia bar in 1801, he practiced in Wellsburg and Wheeling and contributed articles and satirical poems to the press. A series of articles defending Arthur St. Clair, published in the *Scioto Gazette,* won him recognition as a Federalist spokesman. He settled in Belmont County to practice law in 1801, returned to Wheeling in 1804, and five years later came back to Belmont County. He lived on a farm near St. Clairsville until 1822, when he moved to Cincinnati. He edited the Cincinnati *Gazette* from 1825 until his death. He served in the Ohio Legislature, 1813–21, and was reporter of the Ohio Supreme Court, 1823–40. He published the first nine volumes of supreme court reports. In general, he favored the principles of Henry Clay and opposed those of Andrew Jackson. Some of his legal arguments were printed, and some of his newspaper polemics were issued in pamphlet form.

An American System for the Protection of American Industry, [Cincinnati, 1824].

HAMMOND, PERCY HUNTER (March 7, 1873–April 25, 1936), drama critic, was born in Cadiz, Harrison County, the son of Alexander J. and Charlotte Hunter Hammond. He was proud that the Hunters as well as the Hammonds were of Scotch-Irish stock and that he had ancestors who fought in both the Revolutionary and Civil Wars. His ancestors were also engaged in the printing business, and his cousin, Dard Hunter (q.v.), is the world's leading authority on paper-making. He chose to enter the office of the Cadiz *Republican* rather than graduate from high school, and within a year after entering the office as a printer's devil, he was able to set by hand 10,000 ems a day. He saw his first show at the Cadiz Fair. It was held in a tent. He was fascinated and thereafter passed show bills for the local theater and acted as an usher to gain a free seat. He secured a typesetting job in the Government Printing Office, Washington, D. C., where he remained for four years. After returning to Harrison County, he attended Franklin College, 1892-96, served two years on the Chillicothe *News-Advertiser,* owned by his uncle, and then moved to Chicago, where he worked as a police reporter and later became a drama critic. His caustic criticism made him many enemies; he was refused admission to the Shubert theaters for two years. He joined the Chicago *Tribune* in 1908. During World War I he was sent to France as a roving correspondent, and he later reported sports events. Following his habit while on the Cadiz *Republican,* he carried Hart's *Rhetoric* around with him and usually had Roget's *Thesaurus,* Webster's, and Crabb's *English Synonyms* in his suitcase. In 1921 he transferred to the New York *Tribune* and his column was syndicated, so that for several years he was the most influential drama critic in the country. Some of his criticism has been collected in *But—Is It Art?,* New York, 1927, and *This Atom in the Audience . . .* , New York, 1940.

H. B. McConnell

HANCOCK, JOHN (Feb. 18, 1825–June 1, 1891), educator, was born near Point Pleasant, Clermont County. He attended district schools and began teaching at the age of nineteen. Upon the recommendation of Dr. Joseph Ray (q.v.), he was appointed first assistant at the Upper Race Street School, Cincinnati, in 1850 and became principal in 1853. In 1866, he was employed by the publishers of the famous McGuffey Readers—Wilson, Hinkle & Co.—to collect material for a new series of readers. He began his long career as a superintendent of public schools upon his election to that office in Cincinnati in 1867. He served in Cincinnati, 1867–74, in Dayton, 1874–85, and in Chillicothe, 1885–89. In 1889 he was appointed state school commissioner. Throughout his professional career, he was a prolific contributor to educational journals. In 1860 he became chief editor of Elias Longley's short-lived *Journal of Progress in Education and Social Improvement.* His death occurred in Columbus.

Selections from Wordsworth, with a Brief Sketch of His Life, Cincinnati, 1886.

HANDERSON, HENRY EBENEZER (March 21, 1837–April 23, 1918), physician and historian, was born in Orange, Cuyahoga County, and was reared in Cleveland by Lewis Handerson, his uncle. He graduated from Hobart College, Geneva, N. Y., in 1858 and afterward lived in Tennessee and Louisiana. He fought with the Confederacy throughout the Civil War, rising to the rank of major. He studied medicine after the war and practiced in New York City until 1885, when he returned to Cleveland. He was on the medical faculty at University of Wooster, 1894–96, and taught at Ohio Wesleyan University, 1896–1906. About two years before his death he became totally blind. He was a leader in Cleveland medical circles and had a wide reputation as a historian of medicine, publishing many articles and translations. He wrote *Gilbertus Angelicus, Medicine of the Thirteenth Century,* Cleveland, 1918. DAB 8

HANDY, WILLIAM HENRY (Feb. 14, 1843–July 23, 1929), was born in Cincinnati, Hamilton County. He graduated from Gaines High School. Blind throughout much of his life, he dictated the poems and essays in his book *Truths in Rhyme, and Miscellaneous Prose Compositions,* [New York, 1928].

HANFORD, BEN (1861–1910), printer, was born in Cleveland, Cuyahoga County. He learned the printing trade in Marshalltown, Iowa, and later lived in Chicago, Philadelphia, and New York. He devoted three months of each year to lectures favoring socialism and was a perennial candidate for public office on the socialist ticket. He published *Fight for Your Life! Recording Some Activities of a Labor Agitator,* New York, 1909. WWW 1

HANFORD, HELEN ELLWANGER (Jan. 26, 1882–Jan. 9, 1944), was born in Grandview, Washington County, but was reared in Rochester, N. Y., where she married J. Holly Hanford (q.v.). She lived in Cleveland, 1928–44. She wrote stories and articles for various magazines and also published a book on child-rearing: *Parents Can Learn,* New York, [1940].

HANFORD, JAMES HOLLY (March 19, 1882–), educator, was born in Rochester, N. Y. He graduated from the University of Rochester in 1904 and Harvard University (Ph.D.) in 1909. He was professor of English at Western Reserve University, 1928–52, and, during the last five years of this period, also taught at Antioch College. An internationally known scholar in the field of seventeenth-century literature, he first published his widely used *Milton Handbook* in 1926. He has also written *John Milton, Englishman,* New York, [1949]. WW 30

HANKINS, FRANK HAMILTON (Sept. 27, 1877–), educator, was born in Willshire, Van Wert County. He graduated from Baker University in 1901 and Columbia University (Ph.D.) in 1908. He served on the faculties of Clark University, 1906–22, and Smith College, 1922–46. His residence in 1960 was in Northampton, Mass. He has produced a number of sociology textbooks, professional articles, and *The Racial Basis of Civilization . . . ,* New York, 1926. WW 26

HANLEY, HUGH. Pseud. See Emerson Price.

HANNA, CHARLES AUGUSTUS (Dec. 28, 1863–May 19, 1950), banker, was born in Cadiz, Harrison County. He attended the Cadiz public schools, and after graduating from high school he spent several years in his father's bookstore, where he installed a small printing press and in 1882 began printing an amateur paper. He was soon printing ornamental post cards with the reverse side adapted for stamping and addressing. He married Elizabeth Fleming Harrison of Wheeling, W. Va. Possessing unusual ability, he sought his fortune in the West, and after 1885 he made his home in Lincoln, Neb., where he became a close friend of Charles G. Dawes (q.v.). He served as vice-president of Lincoln First National Bank and as treasurer of the Nebraska Stock Yards. He was appointed a national bank examiner and served in New York, 1899–1911. From 1911 to 1940 he was chief examiner of the New York Clearing House. On his death, the New York *Herald-Tribune* pronounced him the leading banker of New York City and described him as a "man of invincible silence." In addition to his duties in connection with billions of dollars, he was an avid student of history. He compiled and published the *Historical Collections of Harrison County,* which has come to be regarded throughout the country as an outstanding county history. In compiling this work, he had records examined in the courthouses of eastern Ohio, southern Pennsylvania, Maryland, and Virginia. He collected names of settlers to whom land grants were made, marriages up to 1850, inscriptions on tombstones up to 1890, histories of churches and early settlements, attestations of wills, and many genealogies of families that settled in Harrison County. The book is in constant demand and has long been out of print. His other main contributions to the book world were *The Scotch-Irish* and *The Wilderness Trail.* His thoroughness as an author was equal to the knowledge and high standards he maintained in his chosen profession as a banker. As an instance of loyalty to one's home community and of interest in its history, there is no better example than Charles A. Hanna.

H. B. McConnell

Historical Collections of Harrison County . . . , New York, 1900.

The Scotch-Irish; Or, the Scot in North Britain, North Ireland, and North America, 2 vols., New York, 1902.

The Wilderness Trail; Or, the Ventures and Adventures of the Pennsylvania Traders on the Allegheny Path . . . , 2 vols., New York, 1911.

HANNA, MARCUS ALONZO (Sept. 24, 1837–Feb. 15, 1904), capitalist and political leader, was born in New Lisbon, Columbiana County. After the family moved to Cleveland in 1852, he advanced rapidly in the business and social life of the city. From his father's grocery and commission business, young Mark Hanna turned to lake transportation, coal and iron, banking, and journalism. He devoted himself to the political fortunes of John Sherman and William McKinley (qq.v.), and his success in procuring McKinley's Presidential nomination in 1896 won him the chairmanship of the Republican National Committee. In 1897 he was named Senator from Ohio. An ardent protectionist and supporter of industrial combinations, Mark Hanna was able to persuade businessmen to contribute heavily to Republican Party campaign funds. His policy of "Stand-pattism" led many to classify him as a reactionary. A man of action rather than a scholar, Hanna wrote little. His only book was published posthumously by an admirer, Joseph Mitchell Chapple: *Mark Hanna: His Book,* Boston, 1904. DAB 8

HANNA, WILLARD A. (Aug. 3, 1911–), educator, was born in Cross Creek, Pa., but spent his boyhood in Loudonville, where his father was a Presbyterian minister. After graduating from the College of Wooster in 1932, he taught English in Shanghai and Hangchow, 1932–36, and afterward taught in American universities. He earned his Ph.D. at the University of Michigan in 1940. He now lives in New York City. He has written a novel about China: *Destiny Has Eight Eyes,* New York, [1941].

HANNAFORD, EBENEZER (March 24, 1840–Jan. 10, 1905), publisher, was born in Devonshire, England, but was brought to the United States when he was four years old. He grew up in Hamilton and Cincinnati. He served throughout the Civil War with the 6th O.V.I. and later wrote the regimental history. He was associated with publishing firms in Cincinnati, Philadelphia, St. Louis, and Springfield, and wrote a book of instructions for book agents. He lived in Springfield from 1896 until his death.

The Story of a Regiment: A History of the Campaigns, and Associations in the Field, of the Sixth Regiment . . . , Cincinnati, 1868.

The Handy War Book . . . , Springfield, [1898].

Eight Poems, Springfield, 1900.

History and Description of the Picturesque Philippines . . . , Springfield, 1900.

HANNAH, IAN CAMPBELL (Dec. 16, 1874–July 7, 1944), educator, was born in Brighton, England. He graduated from Cambridge University in 1895 and afterward studied law. He taught in China, South Africa, and London. He was professor of church history at the Graduate School of Theology, Oberlin College, 1917–25.

A Brief History of Eastern Asia, London, 1900.
The Sussex Coast, London, 1912.
The Berwick and Lothian Coasts, London, [1913].
Capitals of the Northlands, Tales of Ten Cities, London, [1914].
Arms and the Map; A Study of Nationalities and Frontiers, London, [1915].
Quaker-Born; A Romance of the Great War, New York, 1916.
Christian Monasticism; A Great Force in History, New York, 1925.
Voadica; A Romance of the Roman Wall, New York, 1928.
Story of Scotland in Stone, Edinburgh, 1934.
A History of British Foreign Policy, London, 1938.

HANNUM, ALBERTA PIERSON (Aug. 3, 1905–), was born in Condit, Delaware County. When she was seven, her parents moved to Columbus, where she attended the public schools. She graduated from Ohio State University in 1927, and in 1929 she married Robert Fulton Hannum. They live near Moundsville, W. Va. Since her first novel, *Thursday April* (1931), she has published noteworthy short stories and novels about the hill people of West Virginia, Kentucky, and North Carolina, and a novel, based on the Hatfield-McCoy feud: *Roseanna McCoy,* [New York, 1947]. ANT

HANSCOM, ALICE E. (June 3, 1848–Oct. 24, 1932), educator, was born in Gates Mills, Cuyahoga County. After graduating from Willoughby College in 1866, she taught in several Ohio and Kentucky communities. She taught in a private school in New York City, 1880–84, and in the Hathaway-Brown School, Cleveland, 1884–95. She lived in Willoughby during her last years and, despite her failing eyesight, took an active part in the cultural life of the community. Her volume of prose and nature poems was privately published.
Perennia, Cleveland, 1898.

HANTHORN, ALICE (1885–), educator, born in Superior, Neb., has lived in Ohio since 1923. She was a school principal in Cleveland for a number of years and afterward was supervisor of student teaching in Cleveland for Ohio State University. She has published educational articles, readers, primers, and *Billy Boy on the Farm,* Chicago, 1929.

HARBAUGH, HENRY (Oct. 28, 1817–Dec. 28, 1867), clergyman of the German Reformed Church, came to Ohio in 1836 and remained until about 1840, living in Stark, Tuscarawas, and Carroll Counties. He worked as a carpenter, taught school, and wrote poetry. Later a prolific writer of books on religious themes, he also published considerable poetry, much of it in dialect, e.g., *Poems,* Philadelphia, 1860.

HARBAUGH, THOMAS CHALMERS (Jan. 13, 1849–Oct. 28, 1924), was born in Middletown, Md. In 1851 his parents moved to Piqua, and five years later they moved to Casstown, where he spent the remainder of his life. As a boy he worked with his father, a house painter. In 1867 he began writing for local newspapers, and soon he was publishing poems and stories in national magazines and newspapers. Highly prolific, he wrote at least 125 novels for various Beadle series. Some of his dime novels were published under the pen names Capt. Howard Holmes, Capt. Charles Howard, and Major A. F. Grant. His output can be suggested by the titles published in a single year, 1882: *Bel Bravo and his Bear Pards . . .* ; *The Boy Detectives . . .* ; *The Boy Exiles of Siberia . . .* ; *The Buckskin Detective . . .* ; *Captain Apollo, the King-Pin of Bowie . . .* ; *The Condor Killers . . .* ; *The Girl Detective . . .* ; *The Lost Boy Whalers . . .* ; *The Mystery of One Night; Old Winch, the Rifle King . . .* ; *The Pampas Hunters . . .* ; *Snow-Shoe Tom . . .* ; and *The Snow-Trail.* Harbaugh never married but lived with a brother in Casstown. In his last years he was paralyzed and was confined to a wheel chair. He was unable to adapt his style to new tastes in popular fiction, and a year before his death his belongings were sold at sheriff's auction. He died in the Miami County Infirmary.
Maple Leaves. Poems, Cincinnati, 1883.
Bugle Notes of the Blue . . . , [n.p., 1892].
Centennial History. Troy, Piqua and Miami County . . . , Chicago, [1909].
Middletown Valley in Song and Story, [n.p., 1910].
Lyrics of the Gray, [n.p., n.d.].

HARDIN, WILLETT LEPLEY (Dec. 8, 1868–), was born in Coshocton County. He graduated from Buchtel College in 1893 and the University of Pennsylvania (Ph.D.) in 1896. After teaching at Buchtel College and the University of Pennsylvania, he was an executive of coal and gas companies and a consultant chemist. He also edited the *Quarterly Journal of Science, Religion and Philosophy.* His last residence in Ohioana files is Los Angeles. His writings include *Democracy; Its Prob-*

lems and Its Strength, Los Angeles, [1938]. WW 20

HARDING, ARTHUR ROBERT (July 17, 1871–March 3, 1930), journalist, was born in Gallia County. He was editor of the Gallia *Times* and also founded and edited several outdoors magazines. He wrote many articles and books on hunting, fishing, and trapping, some under the pen name Lake Brooks, e.g., *Science of Fishing . . .*, Columbus, [1912].

HARDING, JOHN MILBURN (1873–March 24, 1934), lawyer, was born in Harrison County and also lived in Noble County for a time. After reading law and being admitted to the bar, he practiced in Lorain. He published a narrative in verse: *Lourell, the Indian Maid,* Lorain, [1916].

HARDING, WARREN GAMALIEL (Nov. 2, 1865–Aug. 2, 1923), 29th President of the United States, was born on a farm in Morrow County. After attending district schools, he studied at Ohio Central College, Iberia, 1879–82. In 1882 his family moved to Marion, where he read law for a short time, sold insurance, and worked on the *Democratic Mirror.* In 1884 with a friend, Jack Warwick (q.v.), as partner, he purchased the bankrupt Marion *Star.* He soon bought out Warwick, and as the *Star* prospered he took an increasingly active part in Marion business life. In 1891 he married Florence Kling DeWolfe, widow of a Marion banker. Elected to the Ohio Senate in 1898 and to the lieutenant governor's chair in 1902, he gradually drew the attention of Ohio Republican leaders for his dependability, affability, and conservatism—qualities that were to carry him to the Presidency. He was elected to the U. S. Senate in 1914, and in 1916 delivered the keynote address at the Republican Party convention. Harry M. Daugherty (q.v.) and others began working for his nomination early in 1919, and he was named on the tenth ballot. His administration, though some of its more sensational aspects are still subjects of disagreement, is generally familiar. The extent to which he was the dupe of his subordinates is a matter for debate. His numerous editorials in the Marion *Star* have never been reprinted, and perhaps a later generation will have an opportunity to judge him as a journalist. As a public figure he developed a florid, Senatorial style, marked by a fondness for coined words and alliteration. Collections of many of his speeches were published, e.g., *Rededicating America . . .*, Indianapolis, [1920], and *Our Common Country . . .*, Indianapolis, [1921].

HARDING, WARREN GAMALIEL II (Nov. 2, 1905–), surgeon, nephew of President Harding (q.v.), was born in Columbus, Franklin County. He graduated from Ohio State University. From 1933 to 1941 he practiced medicine in Sydney, Australia. He now lives in Worthington. He has published *An American Looks at Australia,* Washington, D. C., [1943].

HARGRAVE, CATHERINE PERRY (Aug. 13, 1884–Feb. 25, 1953), was born in Cincinnati, Hamilton County. She graduated from Walnut Hills High School in 1901 and also attended the University of Cincinnati. She was for some years librarian of the Cincinnati Art Museum. She published a number of articles in periodicals, and under the sponsorship of John Omwake (q.v.), president of the U. S. Playing Card Co., she wrote *A History of Playing Cards . . .*, Boston, 1930.

HARKNESS, DONNA J., was born in Fultonham, Muskingum County. Her family moved to Indianapolis, Ind., when she was ten years old, and she attended schools in that city. Around 1920 she moved to Cincinnati, where she worked in the public relations department of the New York Central Railroad. In 1958 she moved to Zanesville. Her poems have appeared in numerous magazines, newspapers, and anthologies, and she has published a collection: *The Weather Vane,* [Cincinnati], 1940.

HARPER, FOWLER VINCENT (July 21, 1897–), lawyer and educator, was born in Germantown, Montgomery County. He graduated from Ohio Northern University in 1922, took his law degree in 1923, and completed his doctorate at the University of Michigan in 1926. He has taught at several universities and is now on the faculty of Yale University School of Law. He has published legal books and articles and *Give Me Liberty,* Chicago, [1942]. WW 26

HARPER, MRS. LATHROP COLGATE. See Mabel H. Urner.

HARPER, ROBERT STORY (Oct. 30, 1899–), journalist and novelist, was born in Greenfield, Highland County. He served on the staffs of the Washington Court House *Herald,* 1919–24, the Columbus *Dispatch,* 1924–27, the New York *World,* 1927, and the *Ohio State Journal,* 1928–46. He was managing editor of the *Journal* in 1946 when he retired to devote his full time to writing. He has published nonfiction books on Lincoln and several successful historical novels, e.g., a story of the War of 1812: *Trumpet in the Wilderness,* New York, [1940]. WW 30

HARPER, WILLIAM RAINEY (July 24, 1856–Jan. 10, 1906), author, teacher, and administrator, was born in a log house in the village of New Concord, Muskingum County. His birthplace is now owned by Muskingum College and is open to the public on certain occasions. It contains some of his books and correspondence and suggests the romance of the Harper story. Standing in its front door and looking north up the hill, one can see the older buildings of the college from which he was graduated in 1870, after delivering a commencement oration in Hebrew. Genius cannot be explained, but one can note the early influences affecting it. Harper's grandmother Rainey was known for her accurate knowledge of the Bible. His mother was a woman of remarkable mentality. From her collection of books, she gave him Book No. 1 for his own library: *Intellectual Philosophy* by Abercrombie. Muskingum College was largely a training school for young men wishing to enter the ministry, so its curriculum centered around ancient languages, religion, philosophy, and psychology. From this background young Harper became the foremost Hebrew scholar of his time and found his intellectual interests and writing turning to religion and education. His father owned the village store, still standing on the opposite side of the street and east of the birthplace. What business training he had he gained from working in this store, where he soon learned that "he could sell anybody anything." Beside the store is the house to which the family later moved and in which "Willie" lived as he was growing up. He organized and led the village band and courted young Ella Paul, the daughter of the president of the college. Dr. Paul recognized his linguistic genius and encouraged him to continue his studies at Yale. By the time he was nineteen, he had earned his Ph.D., and married Miss Paul, and was serving as principal of Masonic College in Macon, Tenn. After a year there, he came to Granville as a tutor in the preparatory department at Denison. At that time, he joined the Baptist church; until then, his inquiring mind had prevented his final commitment to any denomination. His affiliation with the Baptist Church in time brought him in contact with John D. Rockefeller, whose millions made possible the founding of the new University of Chicago. Plans for such an institution had been forming in Harper's mind for several years while he was teaching at the Baptist Theological Seminary at Morgan Park, near Chicago, and at Yale. Harper was made the first president of the great new university, and the Harper Memorial Library on its campus is his material monument. Harper's writing career was forced upon him. As a young teacher of Hebrew, it was necessary for him to compose the texts for his large correspondence classes. His first book *Elements of Hebrew* (42 pages) was privately printed in Chicago in 1881. The twentieth edition (200 pages) was published by Scribner's in 1902. It is now published by the University of Chicago Press. A bibliography of his works, published in Goodspeed's *William Rainey Harper,* contains titles of eighteen books of which he was the author, thirteen textbooks of which he was the general editor, nine volumes of Bible Studies and Ancient Records which he edited, and official bulletins of the university, president's reports, and 66 articles in religious and literary journals. He was also the founder and editor of *The Biblical World* and *The American Journal of Semitic Languages and Literature.* His *Commentary on Amos and Hosea* (1905) was long considered the standard work on the prophets. In a letter written shortly before his death, he expressed the wish that this Commentary "might stand as evidence of my life work." Two of his books, *Religion and the Higher Life* (1904) and *The Trend in Higher Education* (1905), are still of interest to the general reader. Two years before his death from cancer he wrote, "I have had for the past thirty days the best time that I can recall in thirty years absolutely without exception. It has consisted in uninterrupted opportunity to read and write." The author had won over the teacher and administrator.

Gladys Forsythe Hazen

The Prospects of the Small College, Chicago, 1900.

The Priestly Element in the Old Testament . . . , Chicago, 1902.

Religion and the Higher Life; Talks to Students, Chicago, 1904.

A Critical and Exegetical Commentary on Amos and Hosea, New York, 1905.

The Prophetic Element in the Old Testament . . . , Chicago, 1905.

The Trend in Higher Education, Chicago, 1905.

HARPSTER, HILDA THANKFUL (1905–), entomologist, was born in Toledo, Lucas County, and attended public school in that city. She graduated from Sweet

Briar College in 1927 and the University of Michigan (Ph.D.) in 1939. She has taught at Michigan State Normal, at Women's College, Greensboro, N. C., and at other schools. Besides technical articles on entomology, she has published *The Insect World,* New York, 1947.

HARRIS, ADAH MAY GLASENER (Sept. 4, 1881–), was born in Nashville, Holmes County. She studied music at McDowell Institute, Columbus, and taught school for several years. In 1899 she married Joseph E. Harris, a Dayton businessman, now deceased. She lives in Dayton. She has published a novel about five generations in an Ohio community: *Clipped Wings,* Philadelphia, [1943].

HARRIS, COLVER. Pseud. See Anne Colver.

HARRIS, LAURA (1894–), born in Rising Sun, Ind., has lived in Cleveland since 1910. A graduate nurse, she worked in Cleveland and Detroit health agencies before her marriage in 1934 to John M. Harris, a Cleveland attorney. She began writing in 1946 and published a novel about life in an Ohio River town at the turn of the century: *Ring in the New,* New York, 1950.

HARRIS, LEON R. (Nov. 18, 1881–Jan. 27, 1960), was born in Cambridge, Guernsey County. He attended Tuskegee Institute and was a founder of the National Federation of Colored Farmers. He edited the Richmond, Ind., *Blade,* 1918–21, and the *Modern Farmer,* 1928–39. After living in Des Moines, Iowa, for a number of years, he moved to Los Angeles, where his death occurred. He wrote poetry and fiction which appeared in various periodicals, and he published at least three books, including a collection of poems about railroads: *Locomotive Puffs from the Back Shop,* Boston, [1946].

HARRIS, MERRIMAN COLBERT (July 9, 1846–May 8, 1921), Methodist missionary and bishop of Japan and Korea, was born in Beallsville, Monroe County. He served with the 12th Ohio Volunteer Cavalry, 1863–65, studied theology after the war, taught school in Fairview, and preached for a time at Uhrichsville. In 1873 he and his wife went to northern Japan as missionaries. Except for the years 1886–1904, he spent his life in Japan, where he came to be deeply loved and respected by the Japanese people. He died and is buried at Ayoyama. He published *Christianity in Japan,* Cincinnati, [1907]. DAB 8

HARRIS, NORMAN DWIGHT (Jan 25, 1870–Sept. 4, 1958), educator, was born in Cincinnati, Hamilton County. He graduated from Yale University in 1892 and the University of Chicago (Ph.D.) in 1901. He was on the faculty of Northwestern University, 1906–29. He wrote numerous magazine articles; his books include *Moving On; The Romance of Travel,* Chicago, 1939. WW 26

HARRIS, WILLIAM LOGAN (Nov. 14, 1817–Sept. 2, 1887), clergyman and educator, was born near Mansfield, Richland County. After his conversion at a camp meeting when he was seventeen, he determined to be a minister. He studied at Norwalk Seminary, preached on the northern circuit and in Delaware, and was principal of Baldwin Institute, Berea. He was professor of chemistry and natural history at Ohio Wesleyan University, 1851–60. He served as a secretary of the Methodist Missionary Society from 1860 until 1872, when he was elected bishop. He opposed the admission of slave-owners to church membership. He died in Brooklyn, N. Y.

The Relation of the Episcopacy to the General Conference, New York, 1888.

HARRISON, BENJAMIN (Aug. 20, 1833–March 13, 1901), 23rd President of the United States, was born on a farm adjoining the estate of his grandfather, William Henry Harrison (q.v.), at North Bend, Hamilton County. After graduating from Miami University in 1852, he read law in Cincinnati for two years and in 1854 settled in Indianapolis, Ind., which remained his home thereafter. He was active in the Republican Party from its formation. In 1862 he helped raise the 70th Indiana Infantry and later commanded a brigade under Sherman. In March, 1865, he was made a brevet brigadier general. After the Civil War he returned to the practice of law. He was elected to the U. S. Senate in 1880, but was defeated for re-election in 1886. He was elected to the Presidency in 1888, but his views on civil service and other issues soon set him at odds with party leaders, who showed little enthusiasm for his renomination in 1892. He won the nomination but was defeated by Grover Cleveland. After leaving the White House, he resumed the practice of law. Most of his publications were collections of addresses, but *This Country of Ours* was written for the *Ladies' Home Journal* at the suggestion of Edward Bok.

Public Papers and Addresses . . . , Washington, 1893.

The Constitution and Administration of the United States of America, London, 1897.
This Country of Ours, New York, 1897.
Views of an Ex-President . . . , (Mary Lord Harrison, comp.), Indianapolis, [1901].

HARRISON, CHARLES JAMES (Aug. 20, 1828–Feb. 15, 1915), educator, was born in New Brunswick, Canada. In 1848, after receiving a certificate from Sunbury Grammar School, he came to Clermont County, where he spent the remainder of his life. He taught school in Owensville, was county school examiner, and was a principal in Owensville and Perintown. He was county auditor, 1874–76. The volume below is a collection of verse and prose.

Tracadie and Other Writings. Cincinnati, 1894.

HARRISON, JOHN POLLARD (1796–1849), physician, born in Louisville, Ky., came to Cincinnati in 1835 at the invitation of Daniel Drake (q.v.) to teach in his medical school. He remained after the school closed in 1839, and in 1841 he joined the faculty of the Medical College of Ohio. He published, in addition to the title below, a two-volume *Materia Medica.* He died of cholera.

Essays and Lectures on Medical Subjects, Philadelphia, 1835.

HARRISON, JOHN SMITH (Feb. 3, 1877–), educator, born in Orange, N. J., and educated at Columbia University (A.B., 1899; Ph.D., 1903), served on the English faculty of Kenyon College, 1903–16. He later taught at Butler University, 1916–46, and now lives in Louisville, Ky. His writings include *The Teachers of Emerson,* New York, 1910. WW 26

HARRISON, JONATHAN BAXTER (1835–1907), clergyman, was born in Ohio. He was ordained as a Unitarian minister in 1860. His residence was in Franklin Falls, N. H.

Certain Dangerous Tendencies in American Life, and Other Papers, Boston, 1880.
The Condition of Niagara Falls . . . , New York, 1882.
Notes on Industrial Conditions, Franklin Falls, N. H., 1886.
The Latest Studies on Indian Reservations, Philadelphia, 1887.
The Colleges and the Indians, and the Indian Rights Association, Philadelphia, 1888.

HARRISON, JOSEPH T. (May 1, 1853–Nov. 28, 1940), lawyer, was born in Scio, Harrison County. He taught school while attending Scio College, from which he graduated in 1875, and while studying in the law school of Cincinnati College, from which he graduated in 1878. After his admission to the bar, he practiced in Cincinnati. He wrote an account of life in the valleys of eastern Ohio: *The Story of the Dining Fork,* Cincinnati, 1927.

HARRISON, THOMAS (Jan. 19, 1813–April 18, 1903), was born in Yorkshire, England. Around 1825 he was brought to Springfield, where he was employed as a printer, a tutor, and a music teacher. In 1837 he bought a part interest in the Springfield *Pioneer,* which he edited for a number of years. He taught in the Ohio Conference High School in Springfield and was one of the founders of the Linden Hill Academy in nearby New Carlisle. When that institution was closed during the Civil War, he moved to Indiana. He died in Shelbyville, Ind.

Music Simplified: Or a New System of Music . . . , Springfield, 1839.
A New Mode of Illustrating Elocution . . . , Shelbyville, Ind., 1874.

HARRISON, WILLIAM HENRY (Feb. 9, 1773–April 4, 1841), ninth President of the United States, was born in Charles City County, Va. He studied medicine briefly in 1790, and the following year he entered the army as an ensign. He served under Anthony Wayne at the Battle of Fallen Timbers. In 1795, while on garrison duty at North Bend, Hamilton County, he married Anna Symmes, daughter of Judge John C. Symmes. He resigned from the army in 1798 and was appointed secretary of the Northwest Territory. In 1800 he was made governor of Indiana and negotiated numerous treaties with the Indians. In October of 1811, at Tippecanoe, he led a body of soldiers against Indians who had been roused to action by Tecumseh. During the War of 1812 he commanded the Army of the Northwest, and in October of 1813, defeated a force of British and Indians at the Battle of the Thames. In 1814 he resigned from the army and returned to North Bend to operate his large farm. He served in the House of Representatives, 1817–19, and in the Senate, 1825–28. He was appointed minister to Colombia, but was recalled by President Jackson after a few months. The resultant controversy was the occasion of the publication listed below. In 1839 he also prepared *A Discourse on the Aborigines of the Ohio Valley . . .* for the Historical and Philosophical Society of Ohio; it was reprinted in 1883. The Presidential campaign of 1840, which extolled the wealthy farmer of North Bend as the log cabin and hard cider candidate, is often considered the beginning of modern political campaigning. Exhausted by the rigors of the campaign, President Harrison died a month after his inauguration.

Remarks of General Harrison . . . , Washington, D. C., 1830.

HARROLD, CHARLES FREDERICK (Sept. 22, 1897–July 10, 1948), educator, was born in Barnesville, Belmont County. He graduated from Ohio State University in 1920 and from Yale University (Ph.D.) in 1925. After teaching at Michigan State Normal School, 1925–43, he joined the Ohio State faculty. He was engaged in an extensive study of John Henry Newman at the time of his death. He also wrote *Carlyle and German Thought . . .* , New Haven, Conn., 1934. DAS 1

HARRY, JOSEPH EDWARD (Oct. 1, 1863–Aug. 12, 1949), was born in Hartford County, Md. He graduated from Johns Hopkins University (A.B., 1886; Ph.D., 1889). He was professor of Greek, 1900–16, and dean of the Graduate School, 1906–16, at the University of Cincinnati. Besides magazine articles, translations, and textbooks, he published *Dogs and Dogs,* New York, 1927. WWW 2

HARSHMAN, SAMUEL RUFUS (Nov. 30, 1841–Sept. 19, 1912?), clergyman, was born in Trumbull County. He attended Allegheny College and Illinois College. He taught school, 1856–64, and was a Methodist clergyman, 1864–69. In 1869 he became an evangelist. He published at least two volumes of sermons and a Biblical commentary. His autobiography was published posthumously: *Memoirs of Samuel Rufus Harshman . . .* , [Akron], 1914.

HART, ALBERT BUSHNELL (July 1, 1854–June 16, 1943), educator and historian, was born in Clarksville, Pa. His parents moved to Cleveland shortly after his birth. He graduated from Harvard University in 1880 and from the University of Freiburg (Ph.D.) in 1883. He served on the history faculty at Harvard, 1883–1926. A highly prolific writer, he wrote a number of textbooks and compiled many source books that are not listed below.

The Coercive Powers of the Government of the United States of America, Eisenach, 1885.

Plans of the Union, 1696–1780, New York, 1894.

Proposals to Amend the Articles of Confederation, New York, 1896.

Salmon Portland Chase, Boston, [1899].

Colonial Children, (with Blanche E. Hazard), New York, 1901.

The Foundations of American Foreign Policy . . . , New York, 1901.

How Our Grandfathers Lived, (with Annie Bliss Chapman), New York, 1902.

Actual Government As Applied under American Conditions, New York, 1903.

The Romance of the Civil War, (with Elizabeth Stevens), New York, 1903.

Slavery and Abolition . . . , New York, 1906.

National Ideals Historically Traced, 1607–1907, New York, 1907.

The Southern South, New York, 1910.

The Obvious Orient, New York, 1911.

School Books and International Prejudices, New York, 1911.

The War in Europe, Its Causes and Results, New York, 1914.

The Monroe Doctrine, an Interpretation, Boston, 1916.

America at War . . . , New York, 1918.

George Washington, Chicago, 1927.

In Our Times, (with John Gould Curtis), New York, 1927.

Washington as President, Washington, D. C., 1931.

Washington, the Man of Mind, Washington, D. C., 1931.

Race Elements in Washington's Time, Boston, 1932.

We and Our History; A Biography of the American People . . . , New York, 1933.

HART, CYRUS WADSWORTH (? – ?), was born in Kensington, Conn., but was long a resident of Fox Township, Carroll County. "The peddler, the preacher, the lawyer, a lover of music, a philosopher, and an admirer of the fair sex"; thus did G. D. Hunt (q.v.) describe this picturesque character, concerning whom very little else is known. The texts of his pamphlets and many articles in Salem newspapers disclose that he was a frequent and unsuccessful office-seeker, one who bombarded the voters with copies of his essays in lieu of the more common types of campaign literature. The third title below was published under the pen name "A member of the bar."

Political Dissertations and Essays, and a Third and Concluding Epistle to a Departed Spirit . . . , New Lisbon, 1819.

Colloquy on the Immortality of the Soul, with an Essay on Prudence, to Which Is Added a Love Touch, Steubenville, 1830.

Essay on Industry, and Biographical

Sketches of Theophilus Radcliff and Emma Jones, Steubenville, 1833.

Imaginary Philosophical Debate, on the Question Which Has the Greater Influence over Human Kind, Money or Love?, [Steubenville], 1843.

Selections from the Philosophical, Polemical, Amatory, Moral, and Other Works of Cyrus Wadsworth Hart, the Lawyer, and the Preacher. Partly in Prose, and Partly in Verse, Cincinnati, 1844.

HART, HASTINGS HORNELL (Dec. 14, 1851–May 9, 1932), social worker, was born in Brookfield, Trumbull County. He graduated from Cleveland Institute in 1867, from Oberlin College in 1875, and from Andover Seminary in 1880. After three years in the Congregational ministry, he turned to social work and served as director of or consultant to various institutions and foundations. His major interest was penology. His writings include *The Restoration of the Criminal,* Boston, [1923]. DAB 21

HART, JAMES MORGAN (Nov. 2, 1839–April 18, 1916), philologist, was on the faculty of the University of Cincinnati, 1876–90. Although most of his writing was in the form of book reviews, articles, and textbooks, he published a recollection of his two years' study abroad: *German Universities: A Narrative of Personal Experience . . . ,* New York, 1874.

HARTER, JOSEPH (March 24, 1837–Oct. 23, 1913), was born in Baden, Germany. In 1855 he came to Tiffin, Seneca County, where he operated a stonecutting and marble shop for many years. He published a small volume expressing his philosophy of life: *The World's Career; Or, a Journey with the World,* Tiffin, [1903].

HARTMAN, FRANK (Feb. 1, 1881–April 25, 1945), clergyman, was born in Nappanee, Ind. He served as pastor of Presbyterian churches in Indiana, Kentucky, Tennessee, Wisconsin, and Ohio. While at New Richmond, Clermont County, he was a founder of the Writers' League of Greater Cincinnati. He published his own poems and those of others on a press that he operated himself. His collections of verse include *The Wine of Life,* New Richmond, 1928.

HARTMAN, HENRY G. (1877–Jan. 3, 1952), educator, was born in Woodhaven, Long Island, N. Y. He graduated from the Polytechnic Institute of Brooklyn and from Columbia University (Ph.D.). He served on the philosophy faculty, University of Cincinnati, 1912–45. His death occurred in Miami, Fla. His writings include *Aesthetics . . . ,* Columbus, 1919.

HARTMANN, RAYE (March 15, 1876–), educator, was born in Mansfield, Richland County, and attended the public schools of that community. She taught in Ohio schools for a number of years before moving to the West. Her last address in Ohioana files is Portland, Oreg. She specialized in "name-psychology," and wrote a book on the subject: *Your Name and Your Personality,* Boston, [1936].

HARTNESS, JAMES (Sept. 3, 1861–Feb. 2, 1934), tool designer, born in Schenectady, N. Y., lived in Cleveland from 1863 to 1882. A gifted tool builder, he later lived in Vermont, where he served as governor, 1921–23. He wrote numerous technical articles and several books, e.g., *The Human Factor in Works Management . . . ,* New York, 1912. DAB 21

HARTWELL, MRS. DICKSON JAY. See Ruth Adams Knight.

HARTWELL, JESSE (1772–Nov. 21, 1860), clergyman, was converted to the Baptist church at the age of sixteen and began preaching when he was eighteen. In 1815 he was sent to Ohio and Pennsylvania as a missionary, and in 1827 he came from New Marlboro, Mass., to settle in Perry, Lake County. In 1836 he donated the site for a Baptist church in Perry, and, though never formally chosen its pastor, he often preached there. His book, which turns a portion of the Bible into iambic pentameter, was probably circulated only among members and friends of the Perry Church and is now exceedingly rare.

The Wars of Michael and the Dragon: Or, a Succinct Versification of the Bible . . . , Painesville, 1845.

HARTZELL, JOSIAH (Sept. 7, 1833–Nov. 11, 1914), lawyer and journalist, was born in Deerfield, Portage County. After graduating from Amherst College in 1854, he read law in Toledo and in Davenport, Iowa. He was admitted to the bar in Iowa, practiced for two years, and came to Canton in 1858 to conduct the *Republican,* a newspaper that became the Canton *Repository and Republican* in 1868. In 1874 he sold his newspaper and became manager of advertising and printing for Aultman and Company. He also served as postmaster of

Canton, 1865–69, and as a member of the Ohio Board of Health. Besides the title below, he wrote numerous magazine articles.

Sketch of the Life of Mrs. William McKinley, Washington, D. C., 1896.

HARTZLER, JOHN ELLSWORTH (Feb. 2, 1879–), clergyman and educator, was born in Ligonier, Ind. He served as a Mennonite minister and was president of Witmarsum Theological Seminary, Bluffton, 1921–31. He published *Education among the Mennonites of America,* [Danvers, Ill., 1925]. His residence is now in Goshen, Ind. WWNAA 7

HARTZOG, WILLIAM BENJAMIN (May 29, 1863–July 12, 1945), clergyman, was born in Willshire Township, Van Wert County. A graduate of Ohio Northern University and Union Bible Seminary, he was ordained to the ministry of the Baptist Church in 1887 and served a number of pastorates in Ohio and Michigan until his retirement in 1926. He died at Mason, Mich. He wrote numerous pamphlets and books on religious themes, e.g., *Ancient Masters and Jesus,* Cleveland, [1905].

HARVEY, MARION (July 16, 1900–), lawyer, born in Rio de Janeiro, Brazil, lived in Cleveland for 22 years. A graduate of Hunter College and Cleveland Law School, she was admitted to the Ohio bar in 1931. She now lives in Los Angeles. She has published a number of mystery stories, e.g., *The Clue of the Clock,* New York, [1929].

HARVEY, ORLANDO EMERY (Nov. 14, 1887–Nov. 27, 1952), physician, was born in Monroeville, Ind. After graduating from Starling Medical College in 1912, he practiced in Ohio City and Van Wert. A specialist in tuberculosis and respiratory diseases, he was superintendent of the state sanitarium at Lima, 1931–38, and lived in Lima after his retirement. He published *Bouquets of Rhyme: Variegated Nuances of Lyrical Diapason,* New York, 1938. BDCP

HARVEY, THOMAS WADLEIGH (Dec. 18, 1821–Jan. 20, 1892), educator, was born in London, N. H., but grew up in Lake County, where his parents moved in 1833. After attending Western Reserve College in Hudson, he taught in Chardon, Massillon, and Painesville. He also served as state school examiner and as commissioner of common schools. After the publication of his first textbook, *Harvey's English Grammar* in 1868, he wrote a number of others, which were widely used. He died in Painesville.

HARVEY, WILLIAM HOPE (Aug. 16, 1851–Feb. 11, 1936), reformer and promoter, was born in Virginia but practiced law in Ohio for two brief periods: in Cleveland, 1876–79, and in Gallipolis, 1881–84. He acquired mining interests in the West and became an advocate of free silver. In 1893 he began *Coin's Financial Series* in Chicago. His most widely read pamphlet was *Coin's Financial School,* Chicago, [1894].

HARVEY, WILLIAM PENN (Nov. 16, 1828–Sept. 17, 1917), was born in Ogden, Clinton County. A member of the Society of Friends, he operated a farm in Clinton County and also worked with the Salvation Army in Columbus. Some of his sermons were published, as well as *Harvey's Poems,* Columbus, 1907.

HASKELL, HENRY JOSEPH (March 8, 1874–Aug. 20, 1952), journalist, was born in Huntington, Lorain County. He graduated from Oberlin College in 1896 and joined the staff of the Kansas City, Mo., *Star* two years later. In 1928 he was named editor of the *Star,* and in 1933 he won the Pulitzer Prize for editorial writing. He published *The New Deal in Old Rome . . . ,* New York, 1939. WWW 3

HASSAUREK, FREDERICK (Oct. 8, 1832–Oct. 3, 1885) was born in Vienna, Austria. He came to Cincinnati in 1849, where he was employed on the *Ohio Staatszeitung,* and the following year established the weekly *Der Hochwachter,* which he sold after several years of successful management. He was admitted to the bar in 1857, built up a substantial practice, and took a deep interest in the politics of the day. Politically he was considered something of a flaming radical, but he became one of the founding fathers of the Republican Party in Cincinnati and was one of its most sought-after speakers; as he grew older, his early socialism virtually disappeared. He served as minister resident to Ecuador, 1861–65. On returning to Cincinnati he became a partner in the *Tägliches Volksblatt.*

Four Years among Spanish-Americans, New York, 1867.

Gedichte, Cincinnati, [1877].

The Secret of the Andes: A Romance, Cincinnati, 1879.

HASTINGS, JAMES SYME (June 3, 1870–June 3, 1921), journalist, was born in Lowell, Mass. After attending McGill University, he went to Cumberland, Md., where he edited a small newspaper called *Uncle*

Sam. He served as a correspondent for the Washington *Times* during the Spanish-American War, and in 1900 was sent to Cincinnati by John R. McLean (q.v.) to be exchange editor for the Cincinnati *Enquirer.* His humor in editing exchange material soon won for him a column of his own composition, and as "Luke McLuke" he became a widely known and widely read newspaper humorist. His column "Bits of Byplay," started in December of 1911, was syndicated and appeared in papers throughout the country. His death occurred in Cincinnati. At least three collections of his humorous writings were published, e.g., *Luke McLuke's Philosophy,* [Cincinnati], 1914.

HASTINGS, LANSFORD WARREN (c.1818–1870), author of one of the rarest books published in Ohio and historically one of the most important, was probably born in Knox County. Some yet-inconclusive evidence indicates that he may have been in Durham, N. C., at an early age; at any rate, he comes within Clio's sharp purview in 1842, when the records show him as a personable, energetic, and ambitious youth of 24, residing in Mount Vernon, and a member of the Ohio bar. His mind was filled with grandiose ideas, and he saw in the Far West his land of opportunity. He may have attended the public lectures on Oregon given by Indian agent Elijah White in Milan, and certainly he had no immunity to the Oregon fever that was in its incipiency in the Ohio country. Hastings threw in his lot with the 1842 overland migration, consisting of some 160 persons under the leadership of Dr. White. After only a few days on the trail White was deposed as captain of the train, and Hastings was elected in his stead. At Fort Laramie, Thomas Fitzpatrick, an experienced mountain man, was engaged as guide. When, at Independence Rock, Hastings was captured by a large band of Sioux, Fitzpatrick adroitly secured his release. Hastings reached Oregon early in October and promptly found scope for his talents by collaborating with Dr. John McLaughlin, the "Father of Oregon." For him Hastings laid out Oregon City—the first American town on the Pacific coast—and performed various legal services in connection therewith. During the winter he proposed before the Pioneer Lyceum the resolution: "It is expedient for the settlers on this coast to establish an independent government." Plainly Hastings had filibustering activities in mind, and he won the debate; but in the spring the Provisional Government was erected, and our adventurer, seeing more fertile fields to the south, led a party of Oregon emigrants into California, where he was cordially received by Captain Sutter. The Texas Revolution and the independent republic established there gave Hastings' schemes a precedent: Could not California, too, be wrested from Mexico? In 1843 there was a meager population of disaffected Americans; if the number could be sufficiently increased, a revolution might readily establish an independent government with himself at its head. Hastings set about writing the first guidebook to California and became that region's first press agent. It is doubtful that the state has ever had a more able proponent. Hastings returned to Ohio in the summer of 1844. To raise the necessary funds to put his book in print, he lectured on California and on temperance. His work appeared as *The Emigrants' Guide to Oregon and California.* It had a ready sale, and subsequent editions, some under variant titles, appeared in 1847, 1848, 1849, 1852, and 1857. A facsimile of the original 1845 edition was published in 1932 with a splendid introduction by C. H. Carey. Hastings' purpose was to induce a large emigration to California in 1846. He succeeded eminently. Meanwhile, late in 1845, he had led a small party to the coast, arriving at Sutter's Fort on Christmas day. In January of 1846 he joined John Bidwell in laying out Sutterville, part of present Sacramento. He also had a connection with the Mormons through Sam Brannan, and laid out Montezuma. Fearing the Oregon settlements might attract the oncoming emigration, he decided to meet the emigrants on the trail at Fort Bridger and turn them from Oregon into California. Kit Carson had led Frémont across the Salt Desert the year before—a shorter but horrendous route—and Hastings determined to try it. He was accompanied by Hudspeth and Clyman and got through to the Oregon Trail, there to encourage the emigrants to follow the shortcut that took his name, Hastings' Cutoff. It had never been traveled by wagons before and was seldom traveled again. Hudspeth guided the Bryant company, and Hastings took in charge the Harlan-Young train. But members of the Donner party who followed along behind picked at the bones of their loved ones in the frozen Sierras. The new California settlers insured the end of the Mexican regime, but Hastings' dream of ruling a new republic faded in the light of on-coming events. He joined the volunteers under Frémont, and soon California was in American hands. In 1847–48 Hastings practiced law at San Francisco, where he bought town lots. He married Charlotte Catherine Toler, daughter of Hopeful Toler. In 1849 he was elected a delegate to the State Constitutional Convention, taking part in the debates and utilizing his geographical knowledge in establishing the boundaries. In the 1850s he continued his law practice in California, notably at Sacramento, and was involved in land projects in Mexico. In 1860 he went with his family to Yuma, Ariz., where he lived several years. According to Arizona census records, in 1860 he gave his age as 42, his profession as lawyer, the value of his real estate as $6,000, and the place of his birth as Ohio. At this time his wife was 31, and they had five children: William W., Isabel V., Irving B., Amelia L., and Henry T., all born in California. Always grasping at the distant star, Hastings espoused the Confederate cause during the War between the States. He conceived a grand military plan to seize Arizona and New Mexico for the Confederacy with troops he would raise in California. Although he went to Richmond to lay the project before President Davis, he failed to win the necessary support. His wife died, and he left his daughter Isabel at a convent in Benicia. After the war he went to Brazil to locate lands for a Confederate colony. Upon his return to Mobile, Ala., in 1867, he published his *Emigrant's Guide to Brazil,* also now an extremely rare volume. He successfully conducted one shipload of colonists to the new haven. In 1870, the day before sailing with another group, he remarried, and his wife accompanied him on the second voyage, during the course of which L. W. Hastings died. The Brazilian colony did not long survive him.

Charles Eberstadt

The Emigrants' Guide to Oregon and California, Containing Scenes and Incidents of a Party of Oregon Emigrants . . . , Cincinnati, 1845.

The Emigrant's Guide to Brazil, [Mobile?, 1867?].

HASTINGS, ROSETTA BUTLER (Aug. 5, 1844–July 16, 1934), was born in Fairfield County, but spent most of her life in Kansas, where her father, a Disciples of Christ minister and an abolitionist, moved around 1850. She graduated from Manhattan State Agricultural College, taught school, and married Rev. Z. S. Hastings, a Disciples minister. She died in Atchison, Kan. She published poems in various periodicals and *Coffin Nails, the Story of Jane McGregor,* Clay Center, Kan., [1908].

HATCH, WILLIAM STANLEY (1789–Dec. 9, 1872), was born in Tolland, Conn. He came to Cincinnati in 1804 to live with an uncle, William Stanley, a merchant. He later became a partner in the business. He served in the War of 1812 from May to September, 1812.

A Chapter of the History of the War of 1812 in the Northwest . . . , Cincinnati, 1872.

HATCHER, HARLAN HENTHORNE (Sept. 9, 1898–), educator, was born in Ironton, Lawrence County. When he became president of the University of Michigan in 1951, his succession to this high office was significant not only for the state of Michigan but also for the state of Ohio. Prior to that time, his life and work had been so closely integrated with his native state as to have become a part of its educational and cultural fabric. Throughout Ohio he was chiefly known as a man of letters. Yet for nearly a quarter of a century he had ably filled the responsibilities of professor, dean, and vice-president at Ohio State University. A descendant of pioneer stock in southern Ohio, he had as a boy roamed the hills on either side of the Beautiful River and watched with fascination the steamers and barges that plied its waters. He attended public schools in Ohio and Kentucky before enlisting as a private in the army in 1918. Mustered out at the end of World War I, he entered Ohio State University, where he graduated in 1922. He received his M.A. in 1923 and his Ph.D. in 1927 from the same institution. Immediately after his graduation in 1922 he was appointed instructor in English at Ohio State. In the same year he married Frank Wilson Colfax, who died after several happy years. He was an excellent teacher, and his work earned him recognition. In 1928 he was made assistant professor, and in 1932 he acquired his full professorship at the age of 34. But in addition to his love of teaching he had the urge to write. In 1928 he published *The Versification of Robert Browning.* This was followed in 1931 by his first novel, *Tunnel Hill,* and in 1934 by another novel, *Patterns of Wolfpen.* Three years later came *Central Standard Time.* In the main these works reflected his love for and his increasing knowledge of his native state. During his graduate study he had traveled in Europe, but Ohio was his field, and year by year he absorbed its legends and traced its geography until he had become a living encyclopedia of Buckeye lore. After publishing a study, *Creating the Modern American Novel,* he turned his attention to writing about Ohio itself; *The Buckeye Country, A Pageant of Ohio* appeared in

1940. By this time, however, the United States had gone to war again, and again Harlan Hatcher put on the uniform, the uniform of the Navy. He continued on active duty until 1944 when, by special arrangement, he was placed on inactive duty in order that he might assume the deanship of the College of Arts and Sciences at Ohio State. The postwar problems of the universities were beginning to loom large in 1944, so the assumption of this post continued his war service in a very significant way. Recognition of his effectiveness came in 1948 when he was made vice-president of the University in charge of faculty. In the early years of the war he married Anne Gregory Vance; two children, Robert Leslie and Anne Linda, now contribute to a delightful family life. Anne Gregory's easy competence has added greatly to the effectiveness of the family team in his administrative capacities. Heavy as his administrative duties were during the postwar period, Harlan Hatcher's zeal for creative writing drove him on to continued productivity. He wrote *The Great Lakes* in 1944 and *Lake Erie* (Great Lakes Series) in 1945. *The Western Reserve, the Story of New Connecticut in Ohio* appeared in 1949. A year later he published *A Century of Iron and Men.* These, to date, are his major literary works. He has, besides, published many articles, both fictional and factual, and has performed a vast amount of editorial labor. He was editor of *The Ohio Guide* in 1940, editor of *Modern Continental, British and American Dramas,* and book editor of the Columbus *Citizen.* He still publishes occasionally, but the duties of a university president are usually heavy, and the University of Michigan is no exception. He performs these duties with zest and distinction and honors the institution which honors him. Honors indeed have come to Harlan Hatcher from many sources. Nearly a score of colleges and universities have conferred upon him honorary doctorates. He has been decorated Commander of the Netherlands Order of Orange-Nassau. Thailand made him a Companion of the Most Exalted Order of the White Elephant. He is a Kentucky Colonel. Certain rivalries between the University of Michigan and Ohio State have long been observed. To be taken from the vice presidency of Ohio State to the presidency of Michigan was recognition indeed. With no abatement in his regard for Ohio State, Harlan Hatcher has proudly carried the banner for Michigan. Both schools and both states take pride in his achievement.

Howard L. Bevis

HATHAWAY, MAURINE, lived for several years in Cincinnati, where she was an active member of the Cincinnati Pad and Pen Club. She was a secretary in the narcotics division of the U. S. Treasury Department, where she heard a number of stories that she recounted in *Fire Castle,* Cincinnati, 1922. She also published several books of verse, e.g., *Affinity,* New York, [1914].

HATHAWAY, WILLIAM E. (Aug. 23, 1844– ?), was born in Milan, Erie County. He attended district schools and the Normal School at Milan. In the 1860s he lived in Chicago, where he operated a grocery store and edited a Quaker magazine, *Herald of Peace.* After the Chicago fire, he settled in Cincinnati, where he edited a monthly publication for the Children's Home and lectured on temperance and other subjects. The book below was published under the pen name Reisenden.

My Grandfather's Old Coat: A Political Allegory, Cincinnati, 1873.

HAVENS, MUNSON ALDRICH (March 24, 1873–Jan. 15, 1942), was born in Washington, D. C. After graduating from Oberlin College in 1893, he was a journalist for five years, and in 1898 became an official of the Cleveland Chamber of Commerce, an organization with which he was associated for many years. He died at Delroy, Fla. He published a life of Horace Walpole and a novel: *Old Valentines . . . ,* Boston, 1914. WWO

HAVIGHURST, MARION BOYD, was born in Marietta, Washington County, and now lives in Oxford, where her husband, Walter Havighurst (q.v.), is a member of the English faculty. A graduate of Smith College, she taught English at Miami, 1926–33. She has published a mystery novel: *Murder in the Stacks,* Boston, 1934, and a collection of poetry: *Silver Wands,* New Haven, [Conn.], 1923. She has recently collaborated with her husband on several books for young readers, e.g., *Song of the Pines,* Philadelphia, [1949]. WO 1

HAVIGHURST, WALTER (Nov. 28, 1901–), was born in Appleton, Wis., and grew up there and in Decatur, Ill. An Ohioan by choice, he has won the rewards of distinguished achievement in three fields of writing, in addition to those of his profession as a university teacher. He entered Ohio's field of magnetism when he became a student at Ohio Wesleyan University in 1919. He took his bachelor's degree at the University of Denver in 1924, and did graduate work at King's College, University of London, and at Columbia University; but he returned to Ohio in 1928 to become a teacher at Miami University, where he is now a professor of English. He married Marion Boyd in 1930 (see Marion B. Havighurst). Havighurst's first novel, *Pier 17* (1935), treated material representative of the economic conflict of the 1930s—a strike on the Seattle waterfront. It was remarkable as a first novel for its breadth of sympathetic characterization and for its power in depicting violent action. The year 1937, however, marked Havighurst's entry into the two literary fields in which he has won highest distinction, by the publication of two books: a novel rich in Ohio history, and a piece of historical writing with a wider, but still regional, theme. Ohio's Lake Erie shore is in the title of *The Quiet Shore* and in the tissue of the novel as a setting significant and warmly realized. The story is that of a family through three generations. Truly memorable characterization—especially of the vigorous founder of the clan and of his mentally afflicted spinster daughter—and a rich sense of the regional past are elements which make this book well worth rereading. *The Upper Mississippi* was one of the first written in the now extensive and well-known "Rivers of America Series." As originally projected by Constance Lindsay Skinner, the "Rivers" books were widely varied in plan and content. In Havighurst's hands, the story of the Upper Mississippi became essentially that of the occupation of the Upper Mississippi region by settlers from the Scandinavian countries. This story he told with much richness of concrete detail and with deep perception of the human drama which marked in all its phases the westward movement of which this migration was a part. In 1944 Havighurst published a second version of *The Upper Mississippi,* revised and amplified "to make this volume fit the shape of the series as it has evolved." Meanwhile he had used fruits of his researches in preparation of this first work of history in the substance of his third and one of his finest novels: *The Winds of Spring* (1940). The story begins in Sweden and carries a nobly-born amateur scientist and artist, and the fisherman's daughter whom he marries, through their long lives as settlers in a community of Scandinavian farmers on the Wisconsin frontier. Though its wide range of firmly realized characters tends to weaken the unity of this book, it is a work of persuasive richness and unquestionable integrity. Havighurst's next novel, *No Homeward Course* (1941), is his least satisfying. In a way, it, too, exemplifies his characteristic fusion of history and fiction: the action occurs on board a Nazi raider in the Caribbean in the first years of World War II, but the demands of a complicated plot and conventional characters of a romantic type combine to rob the book of real validity. The greater part of Havighurst's "extracurricular activity"—his work as a writer—during the first half of the decade of the 1940s lay in the field of regional history and found issue in two of his finest books: *The Long Ships Passing* (1942), and *Land of Promise* (1946). The first is a highly successful attempt to bring to the reader's imaginative experience something of the richness and variety, the drama and color and meaning, of the history of the Great Lakes—a field of the highest importance, and in 1942 one almost untouched by social historians. There are chapters on missionaries and fur traders, on ships and cities, on contemporary commerce and forgotten tragedies. In *Land of Promise,* Havighurst applied a similar method to the historical background of a broadened field, the whole of the old Northwest Territory. Its dramatic presentations of historical characters are especially fine. I find it hard to write with restraint of these two books. They seem to me to warrant most enthusiastic commendation for their boldness and clarity of design, their vitality of style, their unfailing human quality. Havighurst's finest novel is *Signature of Time* (1949). Here again Ohio history is projected in the dramatic terms of family experience and relationships. The setting is fictional Hazard Island in Lake Erie, and four generations of Hazards afford the most interesting and convincing of the novel's characters. To measure Havighurst's growth as a writer, it is only necessary to compare this work with the structurally similar *The Quiet Shore,* published twelve years earlier. The historical flashbacks are introduced more smoothly and have more body and drive. The contemporary scene is more movingly rendered. The style has gained in flexibility and force. As a specialist, of sorts, in the field of "regional literature" for many years, I count *Signature of Time* one of the finest and most satisfying regional novels of the last quarter-century. Distinguished achievements in his professional field of the teaching of English, and in the difficult and important one of fiction for young readers (in which he has produced admirable books, combining history and character development, with the able collaboration of his wife), round out the career of Walter E. Havighurst—a career which has established his position not only as a major contributor to the literature of his adopted state, but as an American writer of integrity, creative vision, and steadily growing power.

John T. Frederick

HAWES, GEORGE EDWARD (Jan. 27, 1864–Sept. 22, 1937), clergyman, was born in Fair Haven, Preble County. He graduated from Washington and Jefferson College in 1885 and Pittsburgh Theological Seminary in 1888. After being ordained to the ministry of the United Presbyterian Church in 1888, he served churches in Pennsylvania, Oregon, and Florida. He published a number of articles and booklets, e.g., *The Fresh Air Child,* New York, [1914]. WW 21

HAWKINS, THOMAS L. (1783–April 18, 1862), serio-comic poet, was born near Carrolton, Ky. In 1817 he came to Sandusky County, where he was one of the incorporators of Fremont. General R. P. Buckland noted that when he opened his first law office in Fremont in 1837, Hawkins had made his office sign. In 1846 Henry Howe (q.v.) found him "an elderly gentleman" and drew upon him for much of his information on the siege of Fort Meigs, where Hawkins had served as keeper of the magazine. In Fremont he preached at the local Methodist church and operated a cabinetmaker's shop. As a cabinetmaker he specialized in the manufacture of washboards and mops, to each of which was attached a card bearing a poetic advertisement:

The wife that scrubs without a mop
Must bend her back full low,
And on her knees mop up the slop
And little comfort know.
And he who loves a cleanly wife,
And wants to keep her clean,
Would make her smile and end all strife
By buying this machine.

In 1856 he moved to Vinton, Iowa, where he spent the remainder of his life.

The Poetic Miscellany, and World's Wonder, Columbus, 1853.

HAY, JOHN MILTON (Oct. 8, 1838–July 1, 1905), born in Salem, Ind., and reared in Warsaw, Ind., was a nominal resident of Cleveland for almost ten years. After acting as one of Lincoln's secretaries during the Civil War and serving in the diplomatic service in Paris and Vienna, on Jan. 8, 1874, Hay married Clara L. Stone, daughter of Amasa Stone, wealthy Cleveland industrialist and railroad builder. All the evidence suggests that Hay was unhappy in the home that Amasa Stone built for his daughter on Euclid Avenue; in *The Breadwinners,* New York, 1884, he describes a pretentious, artificial society surrounded by a vicious mob. Hay built a house in Washington in 1878 and lived there for two years while serving as assistant secretary of state. His father-in-law died May 11, 1883, and soon afterward Hay left Cleveland forever. His anonymous novel apparently had its origin in the summer of 1877 while his father-in-law was in Europe; a railroad strike and the danger of mob violence aroused the suspicion of labor leaders which permeated *The Breadwinners.* The story was first published in *Century Magazine,* and although some readers guessed at the identity of the author and the obvious Cleveland setting would appear to indicate it clearly, Hay never acknowledged the book.

HAYDEN, AMOS SUTTON (Sept. 17, 1813–Sept. 10, 1880), clergyman, was born in Youngstown, Mahoning County. In 1828 he was converted to the Disciples of Christ by the preaching of Walter Scott (q.v.), and at the age of nineteen he became an evangelist. One of the founders of Western Reserve Eclectic Institute, later Hiram College, he served as its principal, 1850–57. He was principal of McNeely Normal School, Hopedale, in 1858, and the next year he moved to Collamer, where he spent the remainder of his life. He composed several hymns and compiled collections for use in churches and camp meetings.

The Vision of Peace on Earth and Good Will among Men, Eureka, Ill., 1869.

Early History of the Disciples in the Western Reserve . . . , Cincinnati, 1875.

HAYDEN, MORGAN PARRITT (June 7, 1845–Nov. 17, 1928), clergyman, was born in Deerfield, Portage County. After graduating from Hiram College in 1872, he was ordained to the ministry of the Disciples of Christ Church. After serving as a minister for a number of years, he joined the faculty of Minneapolis Bible College, where he also served as dean. His death occurred in Minneapolis.

The Bible Key, Cincinnati, 1891.

Facts about Baptism, Cincinnati, [1899?].

The Bible and Woman . . . , Cincinnati, 1902.

The Higher Criticisms . . . , Minneapolis, 1924.

HAYDEN, WARREN LUCE (May, 1835–July) 27, 1918), clergyman, was born in Deerfield, Portage County. After graduating from Williams College in 1861, he became a minister in the Disciples of Christ Church. He served a church in Canton, but most of his pastorates were in Pennsylvania. He died in Indianapolis, Ind. Some of his sermons were published in addition to the titles listed below.

What Is the Christian Church?, [n.p., 1887].
Church Polity . . . , Chicago, 1894.
Centennial Addresses Delivered in 1909, Indianapolis, 1909.

HAYDN, HIRAM COLLINS (Dec. 11, 1831–July 31, 1913), clergyman and educator, was born in Pompey, N. Y. He graduated from Amherst College in 1856 and from Union Theological Seminary in 1859. He was ordained to the Congregational ministry in 1862 and served churches in Meriden, Conn., 1862–66, Painesville, 1866–71, and Cleveland, 1872–1902. He was president of Western Reserve University, 1887–90, and afterward taught in the women's college of Western Reserve. In addition to the titles below, he published a number of sermons and edited a collection of biographies of missionaries.

Lay Effort; Its Range and Methods, New York, [1877].
Death and Beyond, New York, 1878.
Amusements in the Light of Reason and Scripture, New York, [1880].
The Blessed Man of the First Psalm, Cleveland, 1887.
American Heroes in Mission Fields . . . , New York, [1890].
Brightening the World, New York, [1893].
The History of Presbyterianism in Cleveland, Cleveland, 1893.
Western Reserve University, from Hudson to Cleveland . . . , [Cleveland], 1905.
The Face Angelic, Boston, 1908.

HAYDN, HIRAM COLLINS (Nov. 3, 1907–), was born in Cleveland, Cuyahoga County. His father, Howell M. Haydn, was a professor at Western Reserve University, and his grandfather, Hiram Collins Haydn (q.v.), once served as president of the university. He graduated from Amherst College in 1928 and Columbia University (Ph.D.) in 1942. He taught at Hawken School, Cleveland, 1928–41, at the University of North Carolina, 1942–44, and at the New School for Social Research. He has worked in an editorial capacity for numerous publishers and was editor-in-chief of Random House before joining the new Atheneum Publishers in 1960. He has edited several anthologies and has written a number of novels, e.g., *By Nature Free,* Indianapolis, [1943]. WW 30

HAYES, DOREMUS ALMY (May 17, 1863–May 21, 1936), clergyman and educator, was born in Russellville, Brown County. After graduating from Ohio Wesleyan University in 1884 and from Boston University School of Theology in 1887, he was ordained to the Methodist ministry. He published numerous books, most of them Scriptural commentaries, e.g., *The Resurrection Fact,* [Nashville, Tenn., 1932]. WWW 1

HAYES, ELLEN (Sept. 23, 1851–Oct. 27, 1930), educator, was born in Granville, Licking County. She graduated from Oberlin College in 1878. She was a teacher of higher mathematics and astronomy at Wellesley College, 1880–1916. Her long career in Massachusetts but intensified her devotion to her native village of Granville, as is manifested by her *Wild Turkeys and Tallow Candles,* Boston, 1910, a book of great charm and a substantial contribution to the local history of Ohio. She published several other books, including a novel: *The Sycamore Trail,* Wellesley, Mass., 1929. WWW 1

HAYES, HARRY GORDON (March 22, 1883–), educator, was born in Prairie City, Iowa. A graduate of the University of Michigan (A.B., 1910; Ph.D., 1914), he was on the Hiram College faculty, 1910–12, and taught economics at Ohio University, 1920–52. After retiring at Ohio State, he taught at Tulane University and now lives in New Orleans. He has written economics textbooks and *Spending, Saving, & Employment,* New York, 1945. WW 28

HAYES, JEFF W. (March 30, 1858–1917), was born in Cleveland, Cuyahoga County. At the age of fourteen he learned telegraphy, and in 1877 he went to Virginia City, Nev., as a telegraph operator. He worked at the same profession in Portland, Oreg., 1882–94. In 1894 he lost his sight and turned to writing for a livelihood. He returned to Cleveland briefly to work on the *Plain Dealer* and edited the *American Telegrapher* in Los Angeles, but most of his later life was passed in Oregon.

Tales of the Sierras, Portland, 1900.
Looking Backward at Portland . . . , Portland, 1911.
Portland, Oregon, A.D. 1999 . . . , Portland, 1913.
Autographs and Memoirs of the Telegraph, Adrian, Mich., 1916.
Pleiades Club . . . , Portland, 1917.

HAYES, MRS. MEREDITH. See Mary K. Schumann.

HAYES, PHILIP CORNELIUS (Feb. 3, 1833–July 13, 1916), journalist and congressman, was born in Granby, Conn., and spent most of his life in Illinois, where his parents moved soon after his birth. He graduated from Oberlin College in 1860 and afterward enlisted as a private in the 103rd O.V.I. and rose to the brevet rank of brigadier general. He published a volume of war poetry (1914) and a history of his Civil War regiment: *Journal-History of the Hundred and Third Ohio Volunteer Infantry,* Bryan, 1872.

HAYES, RUTHERFORD BIRCHARD (Oct. 4, 1822–Jan. 17, 1893), nineteenth President of the United States, was born in Delaware, Delaware County. After graduating from Kenyon College in 1842, he read law in Columbus and also studied at Harvard Law School. In 1845 he began practice in Lower Sandusky, the home of his uncle, Sardis Birchard. In 1850 he moved to Cincinnati, where he practiced successfully, joined the Literary Club, and married Lucy Webb in 1852. During the Civil War he was a major in the 23rd O.V.I. and later served as judge advocate. He was promoted to brigadier general in October of 1864, and was breveted major general of volunteers in March of 1865. His political career began in 1864, when he was elected to the House of Representatives, but he did not take his seat until the following year. He was re-elected in 1866 but resigned from the House the following year to run for governor. He was elected governor in 1867 and again in 1869 and in 1875. He was named Republican nominee for the Presidency at the party's 1876 convention, held in Cincinnati. Disputed elections in three Southern states required the appointment of an electoral commission to investigate the vote, and on March 2, 1877, he was named President. His term as President resulted in several overdue actions, such as the removal of troops from the South and some reforms in the Civil Service, but these reforms alienated party leaders and made his nomination for a second term an impossibility. He spent his last years at Spiegel Grove near Fremont, devoting himself to prison reform and other humanitarian movements. During his lifetime numerous separate speeches and Presidential messages were published.

Letters and Messages . . . , Washington, D. C., 1881.

Diary and Letters . . . , (Charles R. Williams, ed.), 5 vols., [Columbus], 1922–26.

HAYMAN, LEE RICHARD (Oct. 21, 1922–), born in Indianapolis, Ind., lived in Cleveland after 1924. Since 1951 he has lived in Mexico City, Mexico, where he has served on the faculty of Mexico City College. He graduated from Western Reserve University in 1947. While a student at Cleveland College, he published a collection of verse: *Solid Shadow; A Collection of First Poems,* Cleveland, 1941.

HAYNES, ROY ASA (Aug. 31, 1881–Oct. 20, 1940), was born in Hillsboro, Highland County. He edited the Hillsboro *Dispatch* for several years. An active member of prohibition campaigns, he was federal prohibition commissioner, 1921–27. He was also an executive of the Economy Fire Insurance Co., National Thrift Corp., and Air-way Electric Appliance Corp. He published *Prohibition Inside Out,* New York, 1923. WWW 1

HAYNES, WILLIAM BARBER (May 29, 1881–), was born in Akron, Summit County. He attended Buchtel College, Akron, and operated an Akron real estate firm for many years. An authority on fishing and hunting, he has contributed articles to many outdoors magazines and has written three books on hunting, e.g., *Ducks and Duck Shooting,* Chicago, 1924. WW 30

HAYS, EBENEZER ZANE (Dec. 10, 1837–Dec. 21, 1909), lawyer, was born in Belmont County. His family moved to a farm near Warsaw, Coshocton County, in 1854. After reading law, he was admitted to the bar in 1859. He enlisted in the 32nd O.V.I. in Aug., 1861, and was discharged as a captain in Nov., 1864. After the war he resumed the practice of law and lived in Columbus, Cadiz, Circleville, and Warsaw. He was a member of the Ohio Vicksburg Battle Commission, whose reports he helped compile in 1906.

History of the Thirty-Second Regiment . . . , Columbus, 1896.

HAYWOOD, HARRY LEROY (Nov. 1, 1886–1955), clergyman, was born in Clermont County. He attended Bonebrake Seminary, Dayton, 1906–07, and Lawrence College, 1908–09. He was a pastor in several Midwestern churches and also edited Masonic magazines and wrote on the history of Masonry, e.g., *A Story of the Life and Times of Jacques De Molay,* St. Louis, Mo., [1925]. WWW 3

HAZEN, WILLIAM BABCOCK (Sept. 27, 1830–Jan. 16, 1887) was born in West Hartford, Vt. When he was three years old his parents moved to Huron, Erie County, where he attended local schools. He graduated from the U. S. Military Academy in 1855, and during the next few years he served against the Indians in California, Oregon, and Texas. In 1859 he was severely wounded in an encounter with the Comanches. In 1861 he organized the 41st O.V.I., of which he became colonel. He served with distinction throughout the Civil War, taking command of the Fifteenth Corps in 1865. In 1866 he became colonel of the 38th Infantry. He served as an observer during the Franco-Prussian War and was military attaché at Vienna during the Russo-Turkish War. In the interval between these assignments he became involved in the first of several controversies which distinguished his military career and marked him as a fearless, forthright officer. While stationed in North Dakota he made charges of fraud against post-traders which culminated in damaging revelations against W. W. Belknap, Secretary of War, with the direct result that Belknap was impeached by the House of Representatives and tried before the Senate. Following a quarrel with the volatile Gen. George A. Custer (q.v.) in 1875, he privately published *Some Corrections of "Life on the Plains,"* a detailed, painstaking, and convincing criticism of Custer's book. He was appointed Chief Signal Officer on Dec. 8, 1880. Under his administration, the foundation of the present weather bureau was established by the Signal Corps. Lieutenant A. W. Greely's expedition was sent to Lady Franklin Bay to make meteorological and other observations. When the second of two relief expeditions returned without having reached Greely, Hazen urged the Secretary of War to dispatch a sealer immediately to rescue Greely and his men. When his recommendation was not acted upon, he censured the Secretary, in consequence of which he was court-martialed and reprimanded. His death occurred in Washington, D. C.

Ernest J. Wessen

The School and the Army in Germany and France, with a Diary of Siege Life at Versailles, New York, 1872.

Barren Lands of the Interior of the United States, Cincinnati, 1874.

Some Corrections of "Life on the Plains," St. Paul, Minn., 1875.

The Growth of an Idea, Cincinnati, 1885.

A Narrative of Military Service, Boston, 1885.

General Hazen's Reply to the Second Comptroller . . . , Washington, 1886.

HEADLAND, ISAAC TAYLOR (Aug. 16, 1859–Aug. 2, 1942), clergyman and educator, was born in Freedom, Pa. He graduated from Mount Union College in 1884 and Boston University School of Theology in 1890. Ordained to the Methodist ministry, he sailed as a missionary to Peking in 1890 and served on the faculties of Peking University and Foochow Anglo-Chinese College. He was on the faculty of Mount Union College, 1914–37. He wrote magazine articles on Chinese subjects and lectured on Chinese life, art, language, literature, and history. His death occurred in Alliance. Besides the titles below, he published translations of Chinese poems, a guide to Peking, and a book of Chinese picture puzzles.

Midnight Items and Spare-Moment Scraps, Cincinnati, 1886.

The Chinese Boy and Girl, New York, [1901].

Chinese Heroes; Being a Record of Persecutions Endured by Native Christians in the Boxer Uprising, New York, [1902].

Our Little Chinese Cousin, Boston, 1903.

Court Life in China: The Capital, Its Officials and People, New York, [1909].

The China Hunters; A Trip to China by a Class of Juniors in 1912, West Medford, Mass., [1912].

China's New Day; A Study of Events That Have Led to Its Coming, West Medford, Mass., [1912].

Some By-products of Missions, Cincinnati, [1912].

Home Life in China, New York, 1914.

HEALD, EDWARD THORNTON (Sept. 20, 1885–), was born in Portland, Oreg. He was graduated from Oberlin College in 1907 and immediately entered Y.M.C.A. work. He was Y.M.C.A. Secretary in Canton, 1929–45, and since his retirement has continued to live in that city. He has written a monumental four-volume *Stark County Story,* the chapters of which were originally presented as radio broadcasts, and *Taconic Trails,* Albany, N. Y., 1929.

HEARN, LAFCADIO (June 27, 1850–Sept. 26, 1904), was born on one of the Ionian Isles to an Irish major in the British army and a Greek mother; nevertheless Ohio may lay legitimate claim to being the birthplace of his lustrous career as an author. Losing his parents in early infancy through separation and death, he spent an unhappy boyhood with relatives in the British Isles. Physically handicapped by his small stature, swarthy complexion, and myopic vision, the child was unable to adapt himself to his alien surroundings and quickly became eccentric and antisocial. An accident in a schoolyard game caused him to lose the sight of one eye, leaving him further disfigured and making him feel repulsive to others, especially to women. After his unfortunate boyhood in the British Isles, at the age of nineteen he was dismissed by his semiguardians as incorrigible and was sent to Cincinnati. For three years he lived in that city as a vagrant waif, sleeping in stables or packing boxes and supported by odd jobs. An old sympathetic English printer named Henry Watkins employed Hearn in his Cincinnati shop and encouraged him in a course of self-education. Ambitious to become a writer, he submitted some of his manuscripts to the office of the Cincinnati *Enquirer.* Colonel John A. Cockerill, then editor, described him as "a quaint dark-skinned little fellow, strangely diffident, wearing glasses of great magnifying power, and bearing evidence that he and fortune were scarce on nodding terms." However, the excellence of the manuscripts offered by the trembling little man aroused the editor's admiration. There followed for Hearn three years on the staff of the *Enquirer* and three more years as a reporter for the *Commercial Tribune.* Cockerill wrote of him in later years: "He was poetic, and his whole nature seemed attuned to the beautiful, and he wrote beautifully of things which were neither wholesome nor inspiring. . . . He loved to write of things in humble life. He prowled about the dark corners of the city, and from gruesome places he dug out charming, idyllic stories." After the lapse of over fifty years, Hearn's exploits as a news reporter are still remembered in Cincinnati, as indicated by frequent references to them in the local press. His eccentricities, however, finally outraged the respectable citizens to such an extent that he was forced to leave the city. From Cincinnati he went to New Orleans and subsequently to Japan. The unique literary talent which flowered in New Orleans and came to full fruition in Japan, attracting first national and then world-wide interest, was merely an expansion of the elements which featured his newspaper work in Cincinnati. He applied to the reporting of his own observations and the retelling of old tales a sheen of artistry and a craftsmanship rarely surpassed. While Lafcadio Hearn has undeniably an assured place in the stream of literature, he can never be rated with the great masters. As one of the minor literary artists, his strength rests in his genius as a first-class reporter of all that he observed and in his faithful renditions of West Indian and Japanese folklore. Most of his important pieces can be found in the collected edition: *The Writings . . . ,* 16 vols., Boston, [1922]. Hearn was venerated in Japan, and when he died his funeral was conducted with all of the elaborate ceremony of the Buddhist services for the dead. In an obituary comment, a noted Japanese poet and author, in an effort to express the depth of Japan's bereavement, said of him: "Surely we could lose two or three battleships at Port Arthur rather than Lafcadio Hearn."

W. R. Keagy

HEATON, DAVID (March 10, 1823–June 25, 1870), was born in Hamilton, Butler County. He completed preparatory studies, studied law, and was admitted to the bar. In 1855 he was elected to the Ohio senate. He moved to St. Anthony Falls, Minn., in 1857, and became a member of the Minnesota senate the following year, and served until 1863, when he was appointed special agent of the Treasury Department and the United States depository in New Bern, N. C. He became president of the National Bank at New Bern in 1865. He was a member of the constitutional convention of North Carolina in 1867 and the author of the so-called Raleigh platform. Upon the readmission of North Carolina to representation, he was elected to the 40th Congress and was re-elected to the 42nd Congress at the time of his death, which occurred in Washington, D. C.

Summary Statement of the General Interests of Manufacture and Trade Connected with the Upper Mississippi, Minneapolis, 1862.

HEBBLE, CHARLES R. (Oct. 7, 1874–Dec. 26, 1933), was born in Fairfield County. He graduated from Ohio State University in 1897. He served as manager of Civil and Industrial Departments and later as executive secretary of the Cincinnati Chamber of Commerce. He died in Cincinnati. With Frank P. Goodwin, he wrote a history and description of Cincinnati: *The Citizens' Book,* Cincinnati, 1916.

HECK, EARL LEON WERLEY (July 14, 1896–), was born in Arcanum, Darke County. He attended Arcanum and Greenville schools, was a student at Miami University, 1915–17, served in World War I, and graduated from Harvard University in 1920. He was on the staff of Harvard Library, served in the Ohio General Assembly, and was postmaster of Englewood, Montgomery County, 1940–59. Since retiring he has continued to live in Englewood. He has written a family history and a number of biographical and historical works, e.g., *Augustine Herrman, Beginner of the Virginia Tobacco Trade . . .*, [Richmond], 1941.

HECKEWELDER, JOHN GOTTLIEB (March 12, 1743–Jan. 31, 1823), Moravian missionary to the Indians, was born in Bedford, England. His home after he came to America with his parents in 1754 was Bethlehem, Pa., but he was twice in Ohio for extended periods. From 1771 to 1786 he was in mission service as assistant to David Zeisberger (q.v.). His marriage to Sarah Ohneberg in 1780 at Salem was the first marriage of a white couple performed in Ohio. From 1801 to 1810 he lived at Gnadenhutton, administering the estates of the descendants of the victims of the massacre. His most important writing published during his lifetime was *An Account of the History, Manners, and Customs, of the Indian Nations . . .*, published in *Transactions* of the American Philosophical Society in 1819. Other writings from his journals have been published by various historical societies.

HEDBROOK, ARTHUR. Pseud. See Edward R. Sill.

HEFLEBOWER, CLARA KECK (Aug. 7, 1871–Sept. 6, 1937), was born in Chicago; two months after her birth her parents moved to Cincinnati. She assisted Mrs. Martha K. Cooper in the formation of the Ohioana Library. Her poems appeared in various periodicals, and she also published a book of epigrams: *Winged Arrows,* New York, [1928].

HEINDEL, AUGUSTA FOSS (Jan. 27, 1865–May 9, 1949), was born near Mansfield, Richland County. After her marriage in 1910 to Max Heindel, she lived at Oceanside, Calif., where she and her husband founded the Rosicrucian Fellowship of Mt. Ecclesia. She lectured and wrote on Rosicrucian mysticism and collaborated with her husband in writing a number of books, e.g., *The Message of the Stars . . .*, Oceanside, Calif., [1913]. WWW 2

HEINER, JESSIE MARGARETHE (Feb. 10, 1874–Aug. 15, 1960), educator, was born in Guernsey County. A graduate of Ohio State University in 1927, she taught in the schools of Toledo and Columbus. Her death occurred in Columbus. She published stories and poems in periodicals, some of them under the pen name Margarethe McCrea, and a collection of verse: *This Flowering Branch,* Mill Valley, Calif., 1950.

HEINER, MARIE HAYS (Jan. 13, 1907–), was born in Cleveland, Cuyahoga County, where she graduated from Laurel School in 1924. During her second year at Simmons College, she awoke one morning unable to hear. She has devoted herself to those similarly afflicted and is chairman of the board of trustees of Cleveland Hearing and Speech Center. She has described her own disability and her adjustment to it in *Hearing Is Believing,* Cleveland, [1949].

HEISER, ALTA HARVEY (Oct. 9, 1877–), was born in Wilmington, Clinton County. After her marriage to Karl W. Heiser (q.v.) in 1900, she moved to Hamilton. She was for a number of years a columnist for the Hamilton *Journal-News*. Her special interests are nature and local history. She has published, among other historical studies, *Hamilton in the Making,* Oxford, 1941.

HEISER, KARL WILLIAM (March 4, 1878–April 4, 1939), was born in Hamilton, Butler County, and spent his entire life in that community. In 1900 he married Alta Harvey (see above). He worked on the Hamilton *Daily News* as a young man and also taught school and operated a garden store and floral shop.

Hamilton in the War of '98 . . ., Hamilton, 1899.

HEISTAND, HENRY OLCOTT SHELDON (April 30, 1856–Aug. 8, 1924), army officer, was born on a farm near Richwood, Union County. After graduating from the U. S. Military Academy in 1878, he served in the army until his death. He was President McKinley's military aide.

The Territory of Alaska . . ., Kansas City, Mo., 1898.

HELMS, ELMER ELLSWORTH (Nov. 8, 1863–Feb. 28, 1955), clergyman, was born at Ada, Hardin County. He graduated from Ohio Northern University in 1886; was superintendent of schools in Hutchinson, Kan., 1888–90; was a traveling Y.M.C.A. secretary, 1890–91; and was ordained in the Methodist Episcopal church in 1891. He served pastorates in various states, his last charge being First Church, Los Angeles, 1920–33. After his retirement he continued to live in Los Angeles. He wrote many pamphlets and books on inspirational and religious themes, e.g., *Life Stories,* New York, [1937]. WWW 3

HELSER, ALBERT DAVID (July 10, 1897–), missionary, was born in Thornville, Perry County. He graduated from Manchester College in 1919, was ordained in the Church of the Brethren in 1922, and since 1922 has served as a missionary in Nigeria. He has published several books about Africa, including one on Nigerian folklore: *African Stories,* New York, [1930]. WW 30

HELWIG, JOHN B. (March 6, 1833–July 25, 1904), clergyman and educator, was born on a farm near Canal Dover, Tuscarawas County. After teaching in district schools and working as a blacksmith, he graduated from Wittenberg College in 1861. Ordained to the Lutheran ministry in 1862, he served several pastorates in Ohio and was president of Wittenberg College, 1874–80. After resigning the college presidency, he was pastor of First Lutheran Church, Springfield, and of First Presbyterian Church, Urbana. He died at Bellefontaine.

Lectures. The Rise of the Romish Church. Its Results in Europe, and Its Designs upon the Institutions of America . . . , Dayton, 1876.

HEMINGER, ISAAC NEWTON (Jan. 30, 1868–March 8, 1941), journalist, was born in Allen Township, Hancock County. He attended Findlay College. He worked on the Findlay *Morning Republican,* 1890–92, the Bluffton *News,* 1892–1900, and the Findlay *Morning Republican,* 1900–41. He wrote *Animal Anecdotes, and Other Animal Stories,* Philadelphia, [1929]. WWNAA 7

HEMLER, OPAL TAFE (July 9, 1890–), a concert and operatic singer, was born in Coshocton, Coshocton County. She has been an advertising writer for the Central Press Syndicate and now lives in Cleveland Heights. She has published verse in newspapers and magazines, and two collections, e.g., *Vista Through,* Dallas, Texas, [1940].

HEMPSTEAD, GILES SAMUEL BOOTH (June 8, 1794–July 9, 1883), physician, was born in New London, Conn., but in 1802 his parents brought him to Marietta. He studied at Muskingum Academy and Ohio University, read law in the office of Governor Return J. Meigs, and studied medicine with a Marietta doctor. He practiced in Portsmouth and Hanging Rock, 1816–65. Historical research was his avocation, and he published articles in addition to the pamphlet below.

Antiquities of Portsmouth and Vicinity . . . , Portsmouth, 1875.

HENDERSON, ALGO DONMYER (April 26, 1897–), educator, born in Solomon, Kan., was on the Antioch College faculty, 1922–48, serving as president, 1936–48. With Dorothy Hall he published *Antioch College: Its Design for Liberal Education,* New York, [1946]. WW 30

HENDERSON, EDWIN (July 6, 1844–April 14, 1926), journalist, was born in northern Vermont. He attended Dartmouth College. He was on the staff of the Cincinnati *Commercial,* 1862–80. Entering politics, he was clerk of the city council, 1880–1910, except for two years (1885–86), when he was city editor of the *Commercial Gazette.* He joined the staff of the Cincinnati *Enquirer* in 1920. Under the pen name of Conteur he wrote a series of articles on early days in Cincinnati. His death occurred in Florida.

Cincinnati City Hall, 1806–1896, [n.p., 1896].

HENDERSON, ELLIOTT BLAINE (Oct. 6, 1877–Aug. 3, 1944), was born in Springfield, Clark County. He attended Springfield schools but spent most of his life in Columbus. Concerning his poems, E. G. Burkram, editor of the Columbus *Dispatch,* wrote, "They breathe the most fascinating and admirable characteristics of a race that can sing most effectively and simply the songs of nature, sound the humble heart-beat of contentment, and play upon the lyre of native philosophy and mellow wit." He published nine volumes of poems, e.g., *Plantation Echoes . . . ,* Columbus, 1904.

HENDERSON, HOWARD ANDREW MILLET (Aug. 15, 1836–Jan. 2, 1912), clergyman, was born in Paris, Ky. A graduate of Ohio Wesleyan University, he was ordained to the Methodist ministry and served churches in Alabama, 1857–61. In the Civil War he served in the Confederate Army, and after the war he was a minister in various states. He served a Cincinnati church, 1888–1903, was chaplain of the 1st O.V.I. during the Spanish-American War, and after retiring from the ministry lived in Hartwell. He published sermons and addresses and *Diomede the Centurion . . . ,* [Cincinnati], 1901. WWW 1

HENDERSON, JOSEPH FRANKLIN (1852–Oct. 6, 1916), journalist, was born in Hollansburg, Darke County. In 1856 his family moved to Chester, Ind., and in 1860 to Richmond, Ind. He edited *Gleason's Home Circle and Literary Companion* in Boston, 1877–80; worked on several New York and Chicago newspapers, 1881–90; and edited *Woman's Home Companion* in Springfield, 1896–1913. He died in Kankakee, Ill.

Though chiefly a writer for periodicals, he wrote a few novels in various Beadle series, e.g., *Larry O'Lynn's Dash . . .* , New York, 1891.

HENDERSON, MARC ANTONY, JR. Pseud. See George A. Strong.

HENDRYX, JAMES BEARDSLEY (Dec. 9, 1880–), born in Sauk Center, Minn., was a newspaperman in Springfield, 1905–10. He married Hermione Flagler of Cincinnati in 1915 and lived in that city for about five years while working as a special writer for the *Enquirer.* He has written a number of popular adventure novels about the West and Alaska, e.g., *The Gun-Brand,* New York, 1917. WW 30

HENKEL, ANDREW (Oct. 21, 1790–April 23, 1870), clergyman, was born in Newmarket, Va. He first came to Ohio in 1812 and served as pastor of several Lutheran churches until 1826, when he became pastor of Germantown Evangelical Lutheran Church. He remained in this community until his death. Besides the title below, which was published anonymously, he is said to have written other pamphlets on baptism and on secret societies; he also translated sermons and other works from the German.

Dialogue between Orion Van Lickenthall and Jonathan Screenwell, on Christian Baptism . . . , Dayton, 1865.

HENKLE, HENRIETTA (1909–), was born in Cleveland, Cuyahoga County, where her father, Rae D. Henkle, was drama critic on the *Plain Dealer.* The family moved to New York City when he became foreign editor of the *Herald.* She attended Friends' Seminary and the Brearley School in New York. She began writing for magazines and newspapers while still in her teens. Mrs. Peter J. Stephens in private life, she now lives in New York City. Under the pen name Henrietta Buckmaster, she has written several historical and contemporary novels and a history of the underground railroad: *Let My People Go . . .* , New York, [1941]. ANT

HENKLE, MOSES MONTGOMERY (March 23, 1789–1864), clergyman, was born in Pendleton County, Va., and became an itinerant Methodist minister in Ohio in 1819. He preached among the Wyandots for a time and also preached in Pennsylvania, Tennessee, Kentucky, and Alabama. His writings include *Primary Platform of Methodism . . .* , Louisville, [Ky.], 1851.

HENNI, JOHN MARTIN (June 15, 1805–Sept. 7, 1881), Roman Catholic priest in Cincinnati, 1829–44, was born in Switzerland. He taught philosophy at the Atheneum (St. Xavier's University). In 1834, appointed vicar general of Cincinnati, he served as pastor to German Catholics. In 1837 he founded *Wahrheitsfreund,* the first German Catholic newspaper in the United States. In 1844 he left Ohio for Wisconsin, where he served as bishop and after 1875 as archbishop. He published *Ein Blick in's Thal des Ohios,* Munich, 1836.

HENRI, ROBERT (June 25, 1865–July 12, 1929), artist, was born in Cincinnati, Hamilton County. His family moved to Nebraska in 1878 and soon afterward to Atlantic City, N. J. He attended Chickering Institute in Cincinnati and in 1886 entered the Pennsylvania Academy of Fine Arts in Philadelphia. In 1888 he went to Paris, where he studied at the École des Beaux Arts for two years. He taught for a time in Philadelphia and conducted classes in Paris in the late 1890s. Returning to New York in 1900, he taught in art schools in that city for many years. It is as an inspiring teacher that he will be best remembered; among those strongly influenced by him were George Bellows, Rockwell Kent, John Sloan, and George Luks. In 1929, when the Arts Council of New York polled a great many competent authorities as to the "hundred most important living artists," Henri's name was found among the three who were given first place. A selection from his criticism and class talks was compiled by Margery Ryerson: *The Art Spirit . . .* , Philadelphia, 1923. WWW 1

HENRY, DANIEL, JUN. Pseud. See Daniel H. Holmes.

HENRY, FREDERICK AUGUST (June 16, 1867–Jan. 11, 1948), lawyer and judge, was born in Bainbridge, Geauga County. He graduated from Hiram College in 1888 and earned his master's and law degrees from the University of Michigan. He practiced law in Cleveland for 57 years and from 1905 to 1912 was judge of the Circuit Court. Considerable history of Geauga County is included in his biography of his father: *Captain Henry of Geauga . . .* , Cleveland, 1942. OBB

HENRY, JOHN FLOURNOY (1793–1873), physician, born in Henry's Mills, Ky., came to Cincinnati in 1831 on the invitation of Daniel Drake (q.v.) to join the faculty of Miami University. When the medical department was merged with the Medical College of Ohio, he was made professor of obstetrics. Dissension among the faculty and trustees and Henry's loyalty to Drake led to his removal in 1832. He published medical articles and pamphlets, e.g., *The Cholera in Cincinnati in 1832,* Cincinnati, 1832.

HENRY, MARTIN MALOUSHA (Aug. 12, 1867–1943), optometrist, was born near Ladoga, Ind. As a young man he was a schoolteacher, reporter, and lecturer. After graduating from Northern Illinois School of Optometry, he practiced in Cleveland, Dayton, and Bucyrus. His poems appeared in the Cleveland *Plain Dealer* and other periodicals, and he published one collection: *To Fair Lucille, Love Poems and Other Poems,* Dayton, 1939.

HENRY, WILLIAM ARNON (June 16, 1850–Nov. 24, 1932), agriculturist and educator, was born near Norwalk, Huron County. He attended Ohio Wesleyan University for a year and then taught school to earn money so that he could enter Cornell University. After his graduation in 1880, he was made professor of botany and agriculture at the University of Wisconsin. He developed various agricultural services at the University and profoundly influenced teaching and research in the field. His book on livestock feeding passed through many editions. After retiring in 1907 he lived in Florida and California. He died in San Diego.

Northern Wisconsin, a Hand-book for the Homeseeker, [Madison, Wis., 1896].

Feeds and Feeding . . . , Madison, Wis., 1898.

HENSEY, ANDREW FITCH (June 1, 1880–April 21, 1951), clergyman, was born in Bedford, Cuyahoga County. After attending Hiram College for a time, he graduated from the University of Kentucky in 1904. He preached for a brief period in Brown County and in 1905 left for Africa as a missionary. He was sponsored there by Euclid Avenue Christian Church, 1905–28. After retiring from the mission field, he taught at the School of Missions, Indianapolis, Ind., until 1935. He later lived in Texas and at Sardinia, Brown County. He published a book on African missions: *My Children of the Forest,* New York, [1924].

HENSHALL, JAMES ALEXANDER (Feb. 29, 1836–April 4, 1925), physician and fisherman, was born in Baltimore, Md. He graduated from Eclectic Medical Institute, Cincinnati, in 1860. In 1864 he married Hester S. Ferguson of Cincinnati, and he practiced medicine in that city, 1864–96. His love of fishing led him to enter the U. S. Fisheries Bureau; and he served at stations in Bozeman, Mont., 1896–1909, and Tupelo, Miss., 1909–17. After his retirement he returned to Cincinnati, where he lived until his death. He published a number of technical articles on fish-culture.

The Book of the Black Bass . . . , Cincinnati, 1881.

Camping and Cruising in Florida, Cincinnati, 1884.

More about the Black Bass . . . , Cincinnati, 1889.

Ye Gods and Little Fishes; A Travesty on the Argonautic Expedition in Quest of the Golden Fleece, Cincinnati, 1900.

Bass, Pike, Perch, and Others, New York, 1903.

Favorite Fish and Fishing, New York, 1908.

HENTZ, CAROLINE LEE WHITING (June 1, 1800–Feb. 11, 1856), prolific writer of popular novels, plays, and poetry, lived in Cincinnati, 1832–34, while her husband conducted a school in that city. Her play *Lamorah or the Western Wild* was produced in Cincinnati in 1832, and she also wrote a novel during her Ohio years: *Lovell's Folly,* Cincinnati, 1833. The novel was suppressed because the characters resembled actual persons too closely and Mrs. Hentz was threatened with a libel suit.

HENTZ, JOHN P. (May 5, 1832–Aug. 23, 1915), clergyman, was born in Bevern, Germany. After coming to the United States in 1852, he studied at Gettysburg College and Seminary and was ordained to the ministry of the Lutheran Church in 1864. His longest pastorate was at Evangelical Lutheran Church, Germantown, and he died in that community.

History of the Evangelical Lutheran Congregation in Germantown . . . , Dayton, 1882.

Twin Valley; Its Settlement and Subsequent History . . . , Dayton, 1883.

HENTZ, NICHOLAS MARCELLUS (1797–1856), French refugee, husband of Caroline Lee Whiting Hentz (q.v.), conducted a school in Cincinnati, 1832–34. Besides a monograph on spiders and French textbooks, he wrote a novel: *Tadeuskund, the Last King of the Lenape,* Boston, 1825.

HERBRUCK, EDWARD (May 11, 1849–Dec. 8, 1934), clergyman, was born in Canton, Stark County, and attended Canton schools. After graduating from Heidelberg

College in 1868, he served as a pastor in Akron, 1868–72, and in Canton, 1872–80. He was associate editor of the *Christian World,* 1881–94, and in 1894 he joined the faculty of Central Theological Seminary, Dayton. The book below is an account of a trip to the Holy Land.

Under Eastern Skies . . . , Dayton, 1889.

HERBRUCK, EMIL PETER (Jan. 5, 1856–Dec. 25, 1940), clergyman, was born in Canton, Stark County. He graduated from Heidelberg College and afterward was pastor of Reformed churches in Akron and Canton. He published an autobiographical volume: *Early Years and Late Reflections,* Cleveland, [1923]. OBB

HERGET, JOHN FRANCIS (Oct. 7, 1873–Sept. 27, 1960), clergyman and educator, was born in St. Louis, Mo. He graduated from William Jewell College in 1895 and Rochester Theological Seminary in 1898. He was pastor of Ninth Street Baptist Church, Cincinnati, 1904–28; was president of the Ohio Baptist Convention, 1911–16; and during World War I was senior chaplain of the 37th Division. He served as president of William Jewell College, 1928–42, and after his retirement returned to Cincinnati to live. He wrote two volumes of verse and a small book: *Questions Evolution Does Not Answer,* Cincinnati, [1923]. OBB

HERMAN, WILLIAM (May 10, 1915–), was born in Cleveland, Cuyahoga County. He is president of Argy Powell and Associates and of Herwell Publishing Co. and also conducts Will Herman's School of Writing. Besides a great many stories and articles in national magazines, he has published a book: *Hearts Courageous; Twelve Who Achieved,* New York, 1949.

HERMS, WILLIAM BRODBECK (Sept. 22, 1876–May, 16, 1949), entomologist, was born in Portsmouth, Scioto County. He graduated from Baldwin-Wallace College in 1902. He served on the faculties of Baldwin-Wallace, 1902–05, Ohio State University, 1905–06 and 1907–08, and Ohio Wesleyan University, 1906–07. From 1908 until his retirement in 1946, he was on the faculty of University of California. He published textbooks and technical treatises as well as *Malaria; Cause and Control,* New York, 1913. WWW 3

HERON, MRS. ANNE J. See Anne M. Jacobs.

HERON, HENRIETTA (c.1874–April 12, 1944), born probably in Illinois, graduated from Cincinnati Bible Seminary and was for many years on the staff of Standard Publishing Company, Cincinnati. At the time of her death she was with the Baraca-Philathea Union in Washington, D. C. Her writings include *New Life for the Young People's Bible Class,* Cincinnati, [1921].

HERRICK, CHARLES JUDSON (Oct. 6, 1868–), educator and neurologist, born in Minneapolis, Minn., graduated from Denison University in 1889, was an instructor in Granville Academy, 1891–92, and was on the Denison faculty, 1898–1907. From 1907 to 1934 he taught at the University of Chicago. He now lives in Grand Rapids, Mich. He wrote many technical articles and monographs and *Fatalism or Freedom; A Biologist's Answer,* New York, [1926]. LE 2

HERRICK, CLAY (July 17, 1867–March 4, 1935), banker, was born in Whitehall, Ky., but lived in Ohio for 57 years. After graduating from Western Reserve University (A.B,. 1890; M.A., 1894), he was vice president of Berea College, 1894–97, and headmaster of Western Reserve Academy, 1897–1901. Turning from education to banking, he was vice president of Cleveland Trust Company, 1904–15, and of Guardian Trust Company, 1915–35. He wrote numerous articles on banking and finance and at least two books, e.g., *Trust Companies; Their Organization, Growth and Management,* New York, 1909.

HERRICK, CLAY, JR. (Dec. 15, 1911–), son of Clay Herrick (q.v.), was born in Cleveland, Cuyahoga County, and still lives in that city. He graduated from Western Reserve University in 1934. He is vice president of Carpenter Advertising Co. and a part-time instructor in journalism at his alma mater. He has published *But It's So! A Collection of Historical Sketches of Western Reserve,* Cleveland, [1934].

HERRICK, FRANCIS HOBART (Nov. 19, 1858–Sept. 11, 1940), educator and ornithologist, was born in Woodstock, Vt. After graduating from Dartmouth College in 1881 and Johns Hopkins University (Ph.D.) in 1888, he was a member of Western Reserve University faculty until 1929. After his retirement he continued to live in Cleveland. He wrote textbooks, scientific works, books about birds, and *Audubon the Naturalist . . . ,* 2 vols., New York, 1917. WWW 1

HERRICK, MYRON TIMOTHY (Oct. 9, 1854–March 31, 1929), lawyer, banker, and ambassador to France, was born in Huntington, Lorain County. He studied at Oberlin Academy and Denison University, read law in Cleveland, and was admitted to the bar in 1878. He prospered in several banking and railroad ventures and rose to a position of leadership in the Republican Party. He was governor of Ohio, 1903–05, and ambassador to France, 1912–14 and 1921–29. With R. Ingalls he wrote *Rural Credits, Land and Cooperative,* New York, 1914. DAB 8

HERRICK, SOPHIA McILVAINE BLEDSOE (March 26, 1837–Oct. 9, 1919), daughter of Albert Taylor Bledsoe (q.v.), was born in Gambier, Knox County. She attended a boarding school in Cincinnati and Cooper Female Institute, Dayton. Her later life has no particular relation to Ohio. She married James B. Herrick, an Episcopal clergyman, but left him in 1868 because of his involvement with the Oneida Community. She assisted her father in writing and editing the *Southern Review,* a militant journal dedicated to the unreconstructed Southern viewpoint. A series of articles in *Scribner's,* "Hours with a Microscope," led to a position as editorial assistant, and she was with the magazine from 1879 to 1906. She wrote many articles for the magazine and illustrated them with her own drawings. She also compiled a collection of sonnets in 1902.

The Wonders of Plant Life under the Microscope, New York, 1883.
Chapters on Plant Life, New York, 1885.
The Earth in Past Ages, New York, 1888.
Thoughtful Hours; A Book of Poems, Cincinnati, 1899.
Public School Physiology; Perversion of Truth and Science in the Name of Temperance, [New York, 1908].

HERRIMAN, ABBIE FRANCES SAMPSON (Nov. 25, 1854– ?), educator, was born in Ohio. She attended Oberlin Conservatory of Music and graduated from the Cleveland School of Art in 1891. She afterward taught music and art in Cleveland at the Cleveland School of Art, University School, and Miss Mittleburger's School. She wrote a travel book: *Pencil Sketches; Or, Europe As I Saw It,* Cleveland, 1902. OBB

HERSHEY, SCOTT FUNK (1852–Jan. 10, 1931), Indiana-born clergyman, graduated from Heidelberg College in 1875 and later served two Ohio churches: Middletown, 1884–87, and Wooster, 1905–08. Besides a family history, he wrote *The Science of National Life . . . ,* Burlington, Iowa, 1884.

HERSKOVITS, MELVILLE JEAN (Sept. 10, 1895–), anthropologist, was born in Bellefontaine, Logan County. He graduated from the University of Chicago in 1920 and Columbia University (Ph.D.) in 1923. He has been on the faculty of Northwestern University since 1927, has done field study in various parts of the world, and has published several significant books on anthropology, e.g., *Life in a Haitian Valley,* New York, 1937. WW 30

HERVEY, HENRY MARTYN (Oct., 1838–Sept. 1, 1875), clergyman, was born in Martinsburg, Knox County. After graduating from Kenyon College and Western Theological Seminary, Pittsburgh, he was ordained to the Presbyterian ministry in 1863. He was a pastor in Newark, 1863–75. The pamphlet below was one of the Licking Pioneer Pamphlets.

Historical Sketches of the Presbyterian Churches (O.S.) in Licking County . . . , Newark, [1869].

HERZOG, MARGARET GUION, was born in Cincinnati, Hamilton County, and later lived in Mt. Kisco, N. Y. She began writing for magazines in 1932 and afterward wrote fiction for most of the major national magazines. Her books include *Three to Get Ready,* New York, 1938. WW 21

HESING, WASHINGTON (May 14, 1849–Dec. 18, 1897), journalist, was born in Cincinnati, Hamilton County, but grew up in Chicago, Ill., where his parents moved during his childhood. After graduating from Yale University in 1870 he joined the staff of the *Illinois Staats Zeitung,* owned by his father, and in 1880 he became managing editor. His death occurred in Chicago.

Neunzig Tage in Europa . . . , Chicago, 1887.

HESSLER, IOLA O. (Aug. 15, 1911–), was born in Cincinnati, Hamilton County. She graduated from University of Cincinnati and is married to William H. Hessler (q.v.), foreign editor of the Cincinnati *Enquirer.* She is executive director of Hamilton County Research Foundation and of Hamilton County Good Government League. She is active in civic affairs and has published *Cincinnati, Then and Now,* [Cincinnati], 1949.

HESSLER, WILLIAM HENRY (Aug. 23, 1904–), journalist, was born in Connersville, Ind. He graduated from Ohio Wesleyan University in 1925 and has been on the staff of the Cincinnati *Enquirer* since

1930. He has written articles on public affairs for national magazines and two books, e.g., *Our Ineffective State,* New York, [1937]. WW 30

HEXTER, MAURICE BECK (June 30, 1891–), was born in Cincinnati, Hamilton County. He graduated from University of Cincinnati in 1912 and Harvard University (Ph.D.) in 1924. He now lives in New York City and has been an official of the Federation of Jewish Philanthropies since 1938. He has published a pamphlet, *The Jews in Mexico,* New York, 1926. WW 30

HEYWARD, DOROTHY KUHNS (June 6, 1890–Nov. 19, 1961), was born in Wooster, Wayne County. She attended Columbia University and Radcliffe College and in 1923 married Dubose Heyward, playwright and novelist. She wrote novels, e.g., *The Pulitzer Prize Murders,* New York, [1932], but she was best known for her collaborations with her husband, especially *Porgy; A Play in Four Acts,* (New York, 1927). WW 30

HIATT, VERNA WHINERY (May 26, 1886–), was born in Morrisville, Clinton County. She graduated from Wilmington College in 1909, married Edwin J. Hiatt, and she now lives in Wilmington. Sometimes using pen names Verna Whinery or Marian Morris, she has written many pageants and plays, most of them for schools or Sunday schools, e.g., *My Song and My Star, a Christmas Pageant . . . ,* Dayton, 1934.

HIBBARD, DAVID SUTHERLAND (Oct. 31, 1868–), clergyman and educator, was born in Hamden, Vinton County. After graduating from the College of Emporia in 1893 and Princeton Theological Seminary in 1896, he was ordained to the Presbyterian ministry. He served a pastorate in Kansas for three years and afterward was stationed in the Philippines, serving as president of Silliman Institute, 1901–29. Since his retirement he has lived in Pasadena, Calif. He wrote *Making a Nation; The Changing Philippines,* New York, [1926]. WW 21

HIBBEN, FRANK CUMMINGS (Dec. 5, 1910–), educator, was born in Lakewood, Cuyahoga County. He graduated from Princeton University in 1933 and Harvard University (Ph.D.) in 1940. He worked as an assistant in the Ohio State Museum, 1928–29, and the Cleveland Museum of Natural History, 1930–33. Since 1934 he has been a member of the anthropology faculty, University of New Mexico. He has published a number of professional articles and books and some for the general reader, e.g., *Hunting American Lions,* New York, [1948]. AMS 9

HIBBEN, WILLIAM W. (? – ?), clergyman, born in Uniontown, Pa., was brought to Hillsboro as a child. Licensed as a Methodist minister at Hillsboro in 1832, he moved to Indiana three years later and spent the rest of his life in that state, serving pastorates at Lafayette, Indianapolis, and elsewhere.

Rev. James Havens, One of the Heroes of Indiana Methodism, Indianapolis, 1872.

HICKENLOOPER, ANDREW (Aug. 10, 1837–May 12, 1904), engineer, was born in Hudson, Summit County. As a boy he lived in Circleville and in Cincinnati, where he attended Woodward College. He was city surveyor of Cincinnati before the Civil War. He served with distinction throughout the war and was breveted brigadier general on May 20, 1865. He was U. S. Marshall for southern Ohio, 1866–71, city engineer of Cincinnati, 1871–77, and president of the Cincinnati Gas Light & Coke Company, 1877–1904. Besides the titles below, several of his addresses and technical papers were published.

Fuel-Gas for Cincinnati, Cincinnati, 1896.
The Coming Revolution in the Generation of Power, Cincinnati, 1898.
The Battle of Shiloh, Cincinnati, 1903.

HICKERNELL, WARREN F. (May 31, 1885–), economist, was born in Lafayette, Madison County. Now a resident of New York City, he has published several books on financial topics, e.g., *What Makes Stock Market Prices?,* New York, 1932.

HICKOK, LAURENS PERSEUS (Dec. 29, 1798–May 6, 1888), philosopher, born in Bethel, Conn., and through most of his long life a resident of New England, was professor of Christian theology at Western Reserve College, 1836–44. His writings include *Rational Psychology . . . ,* Auburn, [N. Y.], 1849.

HICKS, FREDERICK CHARLES (Jan. 1, 1863–Sept. 7, 1953), educator, was born in Capac, Mich. He graduated from the University of Michigan (A.B., 1886; Ph.D., 1890). After teaching at the University of Missouri, 1892–1900, he joined the faculty of the University of Cincinnati, where he taught economics and commerce and was president, 1920–29. He was research professor in economics, 1929–53.

The Government of the People of the State of Missouri, Philadelphia, 1897.

Lectures on the Theory of Economics, Cincinnati, 1901.

Competitive and Monopoly Price . . . , Cincinnati, [1911].

HICKS, LEWIS EZRA (March 10, 1839–Nov. 20, 1921), educator, was born in Kalida, Putnam County. He served in the 69th O.V.I., 1861–65, and graduated from Denison University in 1868. He taught at Denison, 1870–84, and at University of Nebraska, 1884–1905; and was president of Rangoon Baptist College, Burma, 1905–11. He died in Atlanta, Ga.

A Critique of Design-Arguments . . . , New York, 1883.

HIGHT, JOHN J. (Dec. 4, 1834–Dec. 18, 1886), born in Bloomington, Ind., graduated from Indiana University in 1854. He died in Cincinnati, where he had been associate editor of the *Western Christian Advocate* for eleven years. A regimental history was published posthumously: *History of the Fifty-eighth Regiment of Indiana Volunteer Infantry . . . ,* Princeton, [Ind.], 1895.

HIGLEY, CHARLES (Oct. 11, 1866–Aug. 2, 1943), lawyer, born in South Bend, Ind., lived in Cleveland from 1868 until his death. He graduated from the University of Michigan law school in 1890 and afterward practiced in Cleveland. He published privately *People Governed and Who Govern,* Cleveland, 1940.

HIGLEY, LOUIS ALLEN (Sept. 8, 1871–April 12, 1955), educator, was born in Wilmot, Stark County. He graduated from Ohio Northern University in 1896 and the University of Chicago (B.S., 1900; Ph.D., 1907). He taught at New Mexico College, Wheaton College, and Kings College in Delaware. He was also dean of Kings College, 1939–47. He died in Bridgeport, Conn., where he lived after his retirement in 1950. He wrote *Science and Truth,* New York, [1940]. AMS 9

HILDRETH, EZEKIEL (July 18, 1784–March 15, 1856), educator, was born in Westford, Mass. After graduating from Harvard in 1814, he taught in Ohio and Virginia until his death. He wrote a textbook, *Logopolis, or, City of Words . . . ,* Pittsburgh, Pa., 1842.

HILDRETH, SAMUEL PRESCOTT (Sept. 30, 1783–July 24, 1863), physician and historian, was born in Methuen, Mass. Throughout his long life he maintained a zest for unbounded inquiry and a diligence for recording his findings. Consequently, he accumulated and preserved copious stores of information from which others might draw. Citations of his writings are abundant in historical and scientific works in current use. If followed back to their source, these references lead to a treasury of early Ohioana and to a writer who found the world too full of fascinating things to confine himself by specialization. Hildreth became an Ohioan by choice. On his arrival alone in Marietta, Oct. 4, 1806, after three weeks of horseback travel, the 23-year-old doctor knew no one in Ohio. His only contact had been established by correspondence with Jabez True, Ohio's first physician. Within a year, Hildreth had met and married another migrant from Massachusetts, Miss Rhoda Cook of Belpre. Four years after his arrival, he was serving in the Ohio General Assembly as its youngest member. During the next half-century, he earned recognition not only in the West but also in his native East and Europe. Hildreth was on the scene early enough to gain personal acquaintance with many of Ohio's pioneer settlers, and long enough to note with concern that a new generation was growing up in ignorance of the facts connected with the beginnings of the state. For years he had been collecting bits of local history—as well as insects, shells, fossils, botanical and mineral specimens. At the age of 58, he started a major history project that would preserve in documented story the proof that much of importance happened in Ohio long before 1803. Five years later, he had two manuscripts, each of which made a book of more than 500 pages. The first, *Pioneer History,* appeared in 1848. While it does not ignore secondary sources, it is primarily a narrative fashioned from selective extracts of journals, diaries, and letters which the author feared would otherwise be lost to future historians, from earliest official records pertaining to Ohio, and from recollections of pioneers and sons of pioneers. What must have been a strong recommendation to readers of the time was the statement of the reviewer in the *New Englander*—that Hildreth's "stories are not less thrilling than the fictions of Cooper." *Memoirs of Early Settlers,* the companion book whose publication had depended on the success of *Pioneer History,* came out in 1852. It presents 37 biographies plus related material on the pioneer residents of southeastern Ohio. A 240-page book, *Contributions to the Early History of the North West,* was published posthumously in 1864, although some of its stories had been written by Hildreth as early as 1836. There is a still later book bearing the Hildreth byline. It was privately published about 1916 by a great-grandson, B. B. Putnam of Marietta, from manuscripts which came into his possession upon the death of the author's bachelor son, Dr. George O. Hildreth, in 1903. This 334-page work contains sketches of family history and an autobiography up to 1840 which includes journals of Hildreth's first journey to Ohio and his Eastern travels with Mrs. Hildreth in 1839. *Pioneer History* was not the first of Hildreth's writings to appear in book form. Editor John S. Williams (q.v.) in 1844 produced a 144-page volume of Hildreth contributions to the short-lived Ohio magazine *American Pioneer.* A volume of 520 pages could be made of his contributions to Professor Silliman's *American Journal of Science and Arts* between 1826 and 1863. As Hildreth mixed history and travel notes with scientific observations, there is much of general interest in these articles. Two of the longer ones are accounts of Ohio travels. Hildreth articles, varying in subject, appeared in many other contemporary periodicals. His first published writing was in print before he was 25, and was prompted by his experience of fighting an epidemic during his first year in Ohio. This is "Remarks on the Weather and Diseases in Some Parts of the State of Ohio, during 1805–6–7; With Topographic Facts on the Country in the Neighbourhood of Bellepre," in the *Medical Repository* (New York, 1808). Elated with "the favourable manner in which my production of last year was received," he submitted in 1809 "A Concise Description of Marietta, in the State of Ohio; With an Enumeration of Some Vegetable and Mineral Productions in Its Neighbourhood," which filled another five pages in the *Repository*. Because of his literary ability, Hildreth could leave an ineffaceable pioneer's imprint on medicine and natural science in Ohio. His writings in Silliman's *Journal* and the first volume of the Ohio Geological Survey have provided starting points for studies by Ohio geologists who followed him. His medical thinking is expressed in two speeches which he put into writing—first, that given in Athens in 1829 before the district medical society of which he was president, published in the *American Journal of the Medical Science* (Philadelphia, 1830), and then his speech as president of the Medical Convention of Ohio in Cleveland in 1839, which takes up most of the pages of the published convention proceedings. Enthusiasm for his subject shows in his writing, whether it concerns remembered New England customs, or what the "all-wise and beneficent Creator . . . has deposited in the rocky strata of the earth," or the rugged life of pioneer Ohioans, or the effects on health of "indolence and the refinement of modern life." He took time out for numerous civic endeavors, but accomplished his voluminous writing during what he termed the "odds and ends of time" found in 55 years of practicing medicine in Ohio. He retired in 1861 but remained a busy citizen up to the brief illness that preceded his death. The home in which Samuel and Rhoda Hildreth reared their three sons and three daughters, and which the doctor substantially enlarged in 1824–25, stands beside the courthouse in Marietta, and—despite twentieth-century adaptation to commercial use—reflects something of the life in an early period of Ohio history.

Erman D. Southwick

Original Contributions to the American Pioneer, Cincinnati, 1844.

Pioneer History: Being an Account of the First Examinations of the Ohio Valley, and the Early Settlement of the Northwest Territory . . . , Cincinnati, 1848.

Biographical and Historical Memoirs of the Early Pioneer Settlers of Ohio, with Narratives of Incidents and Occurrences in 1775, Cincinnati, 1852.

Contributions to the Early History of the North West . . . , Cincinnati, 1864.

HILDRETH, THOMPSON F. (Nov. 29, 1826–March 6, 1911), clergyman, born in Tompkins County, N. Y., was brought to Fairfield Township, Huron County, in 1833. He attended Norwalk Seminary and Ohio Wesleyan University; after being admitted to the bar, he decided that he preferred the ministry. After serving Methodist churches in Ohio and other states, he retired to Norwalk in 1891. His poems appeared in the local newspaper and elsewhere, and he published two collections, the first of which was *Poems of the Heart,* Norwalk, 1903.

HILL, GEORGE WILLIAM (April 22, 1823–Oct. 19, 1884), physician and journalist, was born in Marshall County, Va. In 1824 his father moved to Muskingum County, where George grew up and where he learned the tanner's trade. After attending Ashland Academy, he studied medicine at Georgetown, D. C., receiving his degree in 1859. He practiced in Ashland and also owned and edited the Ashland *Union.* Besides a county history he wrote "Ancient Earthworks of Ashland County," published in the report of the Smithsonian Institution for 1878.

History of Ashland County . . . , [Cleveland], 1880.

HILL, HARRY GRANISON (Sept. 15, 1874–Feb. 15, 1951), clergyman, was born in Union City, Ind., graduated from Bethany College, W. Va., in 1897 and was ordained a minister of the Disciples of Christ Church in the same year. He served a church in Cincinnati, 1899–1902, and returned to that city in 1927 to become consulting psychologist and pastor of the nondenominational City Temple in Cincinnati and conducted a Life Adjustment Clinic there. He was in great demand as a speaker and also published several books and pamphlets on religious themes, e.g., *Paradox and Principle,* Cincinnati, 1938. WWW 3

HILL, JOHN WESLEY (Jan. 1831–Jan. 2, 1913), clergyman, father of John W. Hill (q.v.), was born in Fayette County. He was a Methodist minister for more than fifty years. He died in New York City. He wrote an autobiographical volume: *Life Sketches. Fifty Years in the Itineracy,* Ada, 1904.

HILL, JOHN WESLEY (May 8, 1863–Oct. 12, 1936), clergyman, son of John W. Hill (q.v.), was born in Kalida, Putnam County. After graduating from Ohio Northern University in 1887, he was ordained to the Methodist ministry and served pastorates in various states. He was also chancellor of Lincoln Memorial University, 1916-36. A very popular lecturer, he may have established a marathon record for nonpolitical oratory on July 4, 1917, when he delivered ten addresses in various parts of New York City. He died in Washington, D. C. His writings include *Abraham Lincoln, Man of God,* New York, 1920.

HILL, LAWRENCE FRANCIS (Nov. 19, 1890–), educator, born in Cass County, Texas, was a member of the history faculty, Ohio State University, 1922–59. Besides professional articles, he has written *The Confederate Exodus to Latin America,* [Austin?, Texas], 1936. WW 28

HILL, THOMAS (Jan. 7, 1818–Nov. 21, 1891), clergyman and educator, was born in New Brunswick, N. J. A graduate of Harvard University in 1843 and the Divinity School in 1845, he was a Unitarian minister in Waltham, Mass., until 1859, when he was chosen to succeed Horace Mann as president of Antioch College. When the college was closed by the Civil War, he became president of Harvard. He published a geometry textbook, several addresses, and a book of poems: *In the Woods, and Elsewhere,* Boston, 1888.

HILLER, ROBERT HENRY (May 4, 1864–June 13, 1944), educator, was born in German Valley, N. J. He graduated from Wittenberg College in 1899 and was professor of Greek there, 1911–43. He died in Cooperstown, N. Y. He published a volume containing translations from the Greek and a number of original poems: *Along the Way, and Other Poems,* New York, [1940].

HILLES, FREDERICK WHILEY (June 1, 1900–), educator, was born in Lancaster, Fairfield County. He studied at Yale University (A.B., 1922; Ph.D., 1926) and has been a member of the Yale English faculty since 1926, except for four years' service in the army during World War II. He has published articles and books on the eighteenth century, e.g., *The Literary Career of Sir Joshua Reynolds,* New York, 1936. WW 30

HILLES, HOWARD (Sept. 12, 1877–March 1, 1952), was born near Alliance, Stark County. He attended the public schools of Alliance and spent two years at Mount Union College. In 1906 he settled on a farm near Bourbon, Ind. His verse appeared in local newspapers, and he published a collection: *Untravelled Trails,* Boston, 1916. IATB

HILLS, NORMAN EDWIN (Jan. 4, 1868–Dec. 20, 1944), was born in Cleveland, Cuyahoga County. He was employed by Dolphin Paint and Varnish Co., Toledo, until his retirement in 1929. He died in Willoughby. For some years he lived on Kelleys Island, the subject of his book, *A History of Kelleys Island . . . ,* Toledo, 1925.

HILLS, OSCAR ARMSTRONG (Dec. 13, 1837–Jan. 9, 1919), clergyman, was born in Brownsville, Ind. He served Presbyterian churches in Cincinnati, 1865–78, and Wooster, 1885–1907; and after his retirement in 1907, he continued to live in Wooster. He published a number of sermons not listed below.

Companion Characters: A Series of Studies in Bible Biography . . . , New York, [1883].

Carmina Subsecvia: Songs from Near and Far, New York, [1900].

New Shafts in the Old Mine; An Exposi-

tion of Some Classic Passages of Holy Scripture, Philadelphia, 1906.
The Testimony of the Witnesses; A Devotional and Homiletical Exposition of the Acts of the Apostles, New York, [1913].
Familiar Talks on Sermon Building, New York, [1918].

HIMES, CHESTER BOMAR (July 29, 1909–), born in Jefferson, Mo., lived in Cleveland from 1924 until 1941. After graduating from East High School in 1926, he attended Ohio State University for one year. He worked at various jobs around Cleveland and sold his first short story to *Esquire* magazine in 1934. While associated with the Ohio Writers' Project, he worked on a history of Cleveland. For a time in the early 1940s he worked at Malabar Farm, owned by Louis Bromfield. He has published several realistic and significant studies of race problems since the publication of his first novel: *If He Hollers Let Him Go,* New York, 1945. ANT

HINE, LUCIUS ALONZO (Feb. 22, 1819–1906), reformer, was born in Berlin, Erie County, a community in which the seeds of social unrest were even then sprouting and which would become known for the number of its communitarian experiments, from communities based on purely Fourieristic principles to the love cult that aroused the risibilities of Artemus Ward. He became an open-minded, nonconformist editor and publisher whose philosophy placed him somewhere in the middle ground between his friends, the gentle Fourierist John O. Wattles, and the fanatical Orson Murray (q.v.). Indoctrinated in the new social ideas abroad in the land, Hine studied law in Cincinnati and, for a time, served on the faculty of Woodward College. In Nov., 1844, he started the *Western Literary Journal and Monthly Magazine* in association with E. Z. C. Judson (Ned Buntline) (q.v.). Hine was to furnish $1,000, while Judson was to serve as editor and produce $500. As it turned out, Judson furnished little more than his name, and Hine was forced to supply not only much more than the original $1,500, but to serve as editor as well. Thus a really promising journal folded up after the appearance of the April, 1845, number. Among its contributors were William D. Gallagher, Donn Piatt, Mrs. R. S. Nichols, Mrs. Lee Hentz, Albert Pike, Otway Curry, L. C. Draper, Emerson Bennett, and W. Gilmore Simms. The following January he established *The Quarterly Journal and Review,* which was published through the year 1846. Devoting considerable space to his views on political and social economy, Hine continued to give prominence to literary topics. It contained contributions from most of the writers already mentioned, and several scientific papers on "Geology" by David Dale Owen. In the meanwhile Hine had become identified with John O. Wattles, J. P. Cornell, Paschal B. Smith, and others, who had established a spiritualistic "Brotherhood" or community on the remains of the old Clermont Phalanx, near Rural, Clermont County. The organ of this brotherhood was the *Herald of Progression,* which Wattles published in Cincinnati from April, 1845, to Dec., 1846. In Jan., 1847, the *Herald of Progression* and *The Quarterly Journal and Review* were merged into the *Herald of Truth,* a merger which did not, however, result in the *Herald of Truth* becoming the organ of the "Brotherhood" as Venable asserts. On the contrary, aside from an article in the second number by J. P. Cornell, "The New Philosophy," in which is set forth what is obviously the dogma of the "Brotherhood," there are no references to that organization. Wattles contributed two articles quite in keeping with the general content of the magazine, and dropped out of the picture after March, 1847. Hines edited volume two in absentia, while he was away for six months assisting David Dale Owen in the geological survey of "the far northwestern territories." Well printed, retaining some of the flavor of the *Quarterly Journal,* but much superior in literary style, the *Herald of Truth* was by far the best of Hine's publications. Sandwiched in between articles on social and political reform were poems by Coates Kinney, Sarah T. Bolton and Emerson Bennett and nearly thirty contributions by the Cary sisters. His editorials were few and were, for the most part, blistering attacks aimed at obviously slanted judicial opinions. In July, 1848, he suspended the *Herald of Truth* and turned his attention to spelling and writing reform. He joined hands with the Fourierists, Elias and Alcander Longley (qq.v.), and served as one of the editors of *Type of the Times* from 1848 to 1859. In 1849, one J. S. Hitchcock started in Cincinnati the *Quarterly Review* with Hine as editor. It was suspended after the publication of the second number, Hitchcock having mysteriously disappeared while canvassing for subscribers in Chicago. For a short time in 1850 Hine edited the Cincinnati daily *Nonpareil.* He made his final attempt to establish a magazine in 1869, when he published three numbers of *Hine's Quarterly: Devoted to Political, Financial, Labor and Moral Reforms.* Possessed of a striking personal appearance and a splendid voice, he turned to the lecture platform, where he enjoyed considerable popularity as a lecturer on reforms and educational topics. He spent the last years of his life in seclusion at his home near Loveland.

Ernest J. Wessen

Hine's Political and Social Economy, Cincinnati, 1852.

Priz Esa on Muni-getting and Munispending, Cincinnati, 1854.

Plea for Harmonic Education . . . , Cincinnati, 1856.

The Highest Steeple . . . , Cincinnati, 1858.

The Money-changer: Or, the Law and the Profits. A Drama of Land and Educational Reform, Cincinnati, 1860.

HINMAN, WALTER FISK (c.1841–March 21, 1905), journalist, was born in Ohio, probably in Richland County. In Oct., 1861, he enlisted in the 65th O.V.I. as a private; he served throughout the war, was wounded at Chickamauga, and was discharged in Victoria, Texas, as lieutenant colonel on Nov. 30, 1865. He edited the Alliance *Review,* worked on the Cleveland *Herald* and the *Leader,* and was county clerk of Cuyahoga County. His last years were spent in Washington, D. C., where he worked in the Census Bureau. The prototype of his Si Klegg is said to have been Israel Gaskill, a Civil War soldier from Marlboro. The name was also used for a series of humorous books by John McElroy (q.v.). It has been suggested that Hinman's *Si Klegg and His "Pard"* may have influenced Stephen Crane in writing *The Red Badge of Courage.*

Si Klegg and His "Pard" . . . , Cleveland, 1887.

Camp and Field. Sketches of Army Life . . . , Cleveland, [1892].

The Story of the Sherman Brigade . . . , [Alliance], 1897.

HINSDALE, BURKE AARON (March 31, 1837–Nov. 29, 1900), minister, author, historian, educator, was born in Wadsworth, Medina County. The Hinsdales were one of the first 23 families to settle at Wadsworth. Elisha Hinsdale, the grandfather, a Revolutionary War veteran with experience at Valley Forge, had pioneered to this part of Ohio in 1817. His son Albert was eight years old at the time. Albert eventually married Clarinda Elvira Eyles, daughter of Judge William and Polly Eyles, who resided at Clark's Corners, northwest of Wadsworth. Burke Aaron Hinsdale was the second child and eldest son of this marriage. Young Hinsdale grew up in the midst of pioneer hardship and struggle in this Western Reserve community. He attended the district school and was an eager student, more fond of books than outdoor activities. He particularly enjoyed participating in the popular local debating societies. His mother's family had identified itself very early with the religious movement known as the Disciples of Christ. In fact, many protracted meetings were held in Judge Eyles's barn. Alexander Campbell preached there in 1833 and was well known to the family. It is no wonder that when Burke Aaron Hinsdale was ready to go away to school at the age of sixteen he chose Western Reserve Eclectic Institute, a new Disciples institution at Hiram. He enrolled at the institute on Nov. 21, 1853. It was at Hiram that he met James Abram Garfield (q.v.) and became a devoted admirer and lifelong friend of this man who was destined to become President of the United States. For the following eight years he pursued studies at the "Eclectic" with his academic work being interrupted many times by teaching various terms in district and select schools in and around Hiram. He married Mary Eliza Turner in 1862 when he was operating a select school at Sharon Center. That same year he received an appointment as professor of English at the Hiram institute. This experience was followed by a five-year interval in the preaching ministry. During this period he served Disciples churches at Hiram, Solon, and Cleveland. When he closed his ministry at Franklin Circle Church of Christ in Cleveland in 1868, he would never again hold a regular pastorate. Apparently he discovered that preaching was not his best field. He was not a popular minister, his sermons being too cold and intellectual for the congregations of his day. In 1869 he was on the faculty of Alliance College, a new Disciples school destined to be short-lived. His ability as an educator was recognized by the trustees of Hiram College, and he was elected to the presidency of this school (the successor of Western Reserve Eclectic Institute) on July 1, 1870. He was 34 years old at the time. He came into his own as a teacher, school administrator, and writer in the twelve years that followed at Hiram College. The school had reached college rank only three years before, had been administered by able men, including James Abram Garfield, but it was Hinsdale who really raised the school to college stature. Though not popular as a preacher, he was very successful as a speaker for teachers' associations and as a leader in educational conferences. He had many reasons for being discouraged with his religious brethren at this time because many considered Hiram College a sinking ship, but he kept faith with his constituency in spite of little financial support. During his presidency at Hiram he wrote three major religious books and three of a political nature. His religious writings were *The Genuineness and Authenticity of the Gospels* (1872), *The Jewish-Christian Church* (1878), and *Ecclesiastical Tradition* (1879). He also was a frequent contributor of articles to the *Christian Quarterly,* the *Christian Standard,* and the *Christian-Evangelist,* periodicals of his denomination. He served the Ohio Christian Missionary Society (state organization of the Disciples) as recording secretary (1870–78), as a member of the board of managers (1867–70, 1883), and as president (1878–82), During this time he was a member of the East Ohio Ministers' Association (Disciples) and served a term as president. When James Abram Garfield was nominated by his party as a candidate for the office of the Presidency of the United States, he turned to his friend Hinsdale for help. They were intimate friends, each sharing the confidence of the other. Hinsdale left his classes and took the stump for Garfield, making political speeches in Ohio and Indiana. His most important contribution, however, was his acceptance of a commission to write the official *Republican Text-book for the Campaign of 1880.* Garfield was a dark horse nominee and voters outside Ohio knew little about him. Hinsdale's campaign book interpreted Garfield the *man* to the public and presented him as a type of person that would be popular with the American voters. The book was used extensively during the campaign. Following the untimely death of President Garfield, Hinsdale authored the volume *President Garfield and Education* (1882) as a Hiram College memorial. Later, he edited a two-volume edition of Garfield's speeches, entitled *The Works of James Abram Garfield* (1882–83). These books were all well written and gave Hinsdale an insight into political history which served him well in later years. His intimate friendship with the President was demonstrated by a comment he made at Garfield's death when he told a friend that he must begin the readjustment of himself to the world, since Garfield was no longer in it. By this time Hinsdale had become well known in educational circles, and he was elected superintendent of the public schools at Cleveland, serving from 1882 to 1886. The Cleveland schools were in a textbook squabble at this period as well as being plagued with local patronage scandals. These factors probably prevented his administration from being very significant; at least they contributed to his failure of re-election in 1886. Though he was appreciated by the educators, he could not cope with the local politicians. His annual reports as superintendent and his contributions to educational journals, however, gave him recognition outside of Cleveland. While superintendent he produced one major book, *Schools and Studies* (1884). After leaving the Cleveland school system he did free-lance writing for educational journals and authored another major book, *The Old Northwest* (1888), which was popular for many years. In 1888 he was offered the Chair of Science and Art of Teaching at the University of Michigan. It was in this position, which he held to the time of his death, that he became nationally known as an outstanding educator. The books written while on the university faculty were significant, useful, and widely studied in schools and colleges throughout the nation. He was a pioneer in the field of educational textbooks. Among the better known of these books are *The American Government* (1891), *How To Study and Teach History* (1894), *Jesus as a Teacher* (1895), *Teaching the Language Arts* (1896), *Studies in Education* (1896), and *The Art of Study* (1900). His manuscript *History of the University of Michigan* (1906) was edited by I. N. Demmon and published after Hinsdale's death. He was a member of the Michigan State Teachers Association, the Michigan Schoolmasters Club, the American Council on Education, the National Educational Association, the Historical and Archeological Society of Ohio, the Old Northwest Genealogical Society, and the American Historical Association, and was an honorary member of the Historical Society of Virginia. His monograph *The Training of Teachers* won a medal at the Paris Exposition. Though he never received an earned academic degree, he held honorary Master of Arts degrees from both Bethany and Williams Colleges, an honorary Ph.D. degree from Ohio State University, and honorary LL.D. degrees from Hiram College and Ohio University. When he died at Atlanta, Ga., President Angell of the University of Michigan wrote of him:

> He was generous in his judgments of others, but independent and fearless in forming and expressing his opinions of measures, whether educational, political, or religious. There was a noble manliness in him, an upright and downright integrity of make, an inspiring devotion to whatever is uplifting for men, which commanded universal respect and esteem, and

which will make his memory ever dear to all of us who had the good fortune to know him.

Henry K. Shaw

The Genuineness and Authenticity of the Gospels . . . , Cincinnati, 1872.
Hiram College . . . , [Cleveland?, 1876].
The Jewish-Christian Church . . . , Cincinnati, 1878.
Our Common Schools . . . , Cleveland, 1878.
Arabella Mason Rudolph: Her Ancestry, Life, and Character, Cleveland, 1879.
Ecclesiastical Tradition: Its Origin and Early Growth . . . , Cincinnati, 1879.
The Life and Character of James A. Garfield, [New York?, 1880].
The Republican Text-book for the Campaign of 1880 . . . , New York, 1880.
President Garfield and Education . . . , Boston, 1882.
Schools and Studies, Boston, 1884.
The Old Northwest . . . , New York, 1888.
Jesus as a Teacher and the Making of the New Testament, St. Louis, Mo., 1895.
Studies in Education: Science, Art, History, Chicago, [1896].
Horace Mann and the Common School Revival in the United States, New York, 1898.
History of the University of Michigan . . . , Ann Arbor, 1906.

HINSDALE, WILBERT B. (May 25, 1854–July 25, 1944), physician and educator, was born in Wadsworth, Medina County. He graduated from Hiram College in 1875 and Cleveland Homeopathic Medical College in 1887. From 1895 until his retirement he was on the faculty of the University of Michigan, and after retiring he was associated with the University museum. He wrote a number of books on archaeology, e.g., *The First People of Michigan,* Ann Arbor, [1930]. WWW 2

HINTON, WALTER (Nov. 10, 1889–), aviator, was born in Van Wert, Van Wert County. He entered the navy in 1907 and was a pioneer airplane pilot, participating in many major flights, including a trans-Atlantic flight, May 31, 1919. He now lives in Fort Lauderdale, Fla. He has written *Opportunities in Aviation,* New York, [1929]. WW 27

HIPSHER, EDWARD ELLSWORTH (March 28, 1871–March 7, 1948), musician, was born in Caledonia, Marion County. He graduated from Valparaiso University in 1890 and later studied abroad. He served on the music faculties of several institutions and was associate editor of *Étude,* 1920–40, during which period he lived in Marion. His books on music include *American Opera and Its Composers . . .* , Philadelphia, [1927]. WWW 2

HIRSCH, ARTHUR HENRY (May 21, 1878–), educator, born in Le Mars, Iowa, was a member of the history faculty, Ohio Wesleyan University, 1919–34. He now lives in Detroit, Mich. He has published many professional articles and *The Huguenots of Colonial South Carolina,* Durham, N. C., 1928. WW 30

HITCHCOCK, EMBURY ASBURY (June 26, 1866–April 29, 1948), engineer and educator, born in Henrietta, N. Y., was on the faculty of Ohio State University, 1893–1912 and 1920–36, during the latter period as dean of the school of engineering. After his retirement he continued to live in Columbus. Besides technical and professional articles, he wrote with the assistance of Merrill Weed an autobiographical volume: *My Fifty Years in Engineering,* Caldwell, Idaho, 1939. WWW 2

HITTELL, JOHN SHERTZER (Dec. 25, 1825–March 8, 1901), statistician and author, brother of Theodore H. Hittell (q.v.), was born in Jonestown, Pa. The family moved to Hamilton in 1831, where the father practiced surgery. John graduated from Miami University in 1843 and studied law in Hamilton for a time. The gold rush of 1849 drew him to California, where he spent the remainder of his life and wrote numerous historical works and books on more controversial subjects, e.g., *The Evidences against Christianity,* [San Francisco, 1856].

HITTELL, THEODORE HENRY (April 5, 1830–Feb. 23, 1917), author and lawyer, was born in Marietta, Pa. His father moved to Hamilton in 1831, and here he was educated and practiced law from 1852 to 1855. In 1855 he followed his brother John (q.v.) to California. After a period in San Francisco journalism, he began the practice of law. His most admirable literary work is his four-volume *History of California,* [San Francisco, 1885–97].

HOCHWALT, ALBERT FREDERICK (Dec. 24, 1869–July 24, 1938), publisher, was born in Dayton, Montgomery County, which remained his lifelong home. He established a publishing firm to bring out works dealing with nature. Besides many books on dogs and field sports, he wrote a novel: *Greymist . . .* , New York, [1925]. WWW 1

HOCKING, WILLIAM ERNEST (Aug. 10, 1875–), educator, was born in Cleveland, Cuyahoga County. He graduated from Harvard University (A.B., 1901; Ph.D., 1904) and was on the Harvard faculty as professor of philosophy, 1914–43. He has published textbooks and other books on religion and philosophy, e.g., *Morale and Its Enemies,* New Haven, [Conn.], 1918. WW 30

HODDER, ALFRED (Sept. 18, 1866–March 4, 1907), was born in Celina, Mercer County. He attended school in Cincinnati, studied at home, read law, and was admitted to the Colorado bar in 1889. He did graduate work at Harvard University and after 1898 devoted himself to writing. Using the pen name Francis Walton, he collaborated with Josiah Flint Willard (pen name, Josiah Flint) in writing a book about New York, *The Powers That Prey.*

The Powers That Prey, (with Josiah Flint), New York, 1900.
The New Americans, New York, 1901.
A Flight for the City, New York, 1903.

HODGE, ORLANDO J. (Nov. 25, 1828–April 16, 1912), journalist, was born in Hamburg, N. Y. He worked his passage on a lake boat to Cleveland in 1842, and after serving in the Mexican War he attended Geauga Seminary. During the Civil War he lived in Litchfield, Conn., and served two terms in the Connecticut legislature. In 1867 he returned to Cleveland, where he held various political positions and was owner-editor of the *Sun and Voice,* 1878–89. He compiled a family history, and under the initials O.J.H. published his autobiography: *Reminiscences,* 2 vols., Cleveland, 1902–10.

HODGE, T. SHIRBY. Pseud. See Russel L. Tracy.

HODGSON, RALPH (1871–), was born in Yorkshire, England. After working as a draftsman on the pictorial staff of a London newspaper and as editor of *Fry's Magazine,* he taught English literature at Sendai University, Japan, and Imperial University, Tokyo. In Japan he married a missionary-teacher who had been born in Canton, and in 1941 they settled on an isolated farm, which he has named "Owlairee," in northern Carroll County seven miles from Minerva. In twenty years he has left his rural home on only two occasions. A recluse throughout most of his life, he has given few interviews, and few biographical details are known. In 1946 he received an award from the National Institute of Arts and Letters, and in 1954 he was awarded the Queen's Medal for Poetry. Most of his major poems were published between 1907 and 1913, but he has published *Poems,* New York, 1924, and also three small collections since settling in Ohio. TCA

HODSON, JOSEPH (Feb. 20, 1822–Nov. 3, 1912), was born in Staffordshire, England. He came to America in 1846, and after a year in Philadelphia he settled in Steubenville. He later moved to East Liverpool, where he died at the age of ninety. Apparently only one of the two volumes of the title below was actually published.

Miscellaneous Poems, in Two Volumes, Wellsville, 1866.

HOECK, LOUIS GEORGE (June 30, 1863–Dec. 15, 1952), clergyman, born in Paisley, Scotland, graduated from the University of Glasgow and practiced law in Scotland for ten years, After coming to America he became a pastor in the Church of the New Jerusalem. He came to Cincinnati in 1908 and served as general pastor for the Ohio Association. He retired from the ministry in 1938. He was active in the musical life of Cincinnati. He published several books on the Swedenborgian religion, e.g., *My Church,* Minneapolis, Minn., [1913].

HOEHLER, FRED KENNETH (June 6, 1893–), born in Shenandoah, Pa., lived in Cincinnati, 1915–40. He was director of public welfare, 1927-35, and director of safety, 1933–35. He left Cincinnati to become welfare director of Illinois. He has written numerous articles and books on social questions, e.g., *Europe's Homeless Millions,* [New York, 1946]. WW 30

HOFF, EMANUEL BUECHLEY (Dec. 21, 1860–Dec. 28, 1928), clergyman and educator, was born in Wooster, Wayne County. Ordained a minister of the Church of the Brethren in 1884, he served various churches in the Middle West and taught at Manchester College and Bethany Bible School. His books include *The Message of the Book of Revelation,* Chicago, [1919]. WWW 1

HOFFMAN, ALBERT FRANK (Feb. 3, 1867–May 24, 1950), mailman, was born in Millersburg, Ky., but when he was four his family moved to Cincinnati. At the age of twelve he left school to work for the Cincinnati Street Railway Company. He also worked as a tailor and as a janitor in the Cincinnati schools. He was a mailman from 1891 to 1928. He published numerous poems in Cincinnati newspapers, many of which were reprinted in the two collections below.

Of the Tribe of Judah, and Other Poems, [Cincinnati, 1891].

Driftwood, Cincinnati, 1907.

HOFFMAN, CHARLES W. (July 31, 1870–), lawyer and judge, was born in Glendale, Hamilton County. He studied at National Normal University, 1887–88, taught school for a few years, and studied law at the University of Cincinnati. Admitted to the bar in 1893, he practiced in Cincinnati until 1915, when he became judge of juvenile and domestic relations courts; he later served as judge of the common pleas court. He retired in 1956.

Oak Hill . . . , Norwood, [1896].

The Story of a Country Church, [Cincinnati, 1902].

HOGE, WILLIAM JAMES (1821–July 5, 1864), Presbyterian clergyman, born in Hampden Sydney, Va., spent a few years of his boyhood in Ohio while his father, Samuel Davies Hoge, was serving churches in Hillsborough and Rock Spring and was a member of the Ohio University faculty. He was taken back to Virginia in 1826, when his father died. He was a pastor in New York, a teacher at Union Theological Seminary, and a pastor in Petersburg, where he died of fever during the siege. He achieved considerable success with a story based on the Biblical character Bartimeus: *Blind Bartimeus . . . ,* New York, 1859.

HOLBROOK, ALFRED (Feb. 17, 1816–April 16, 1909), pioneer in the professional training of teachers, was born in Derby, Conn. He came to the Western Reserve in the early 1840s and became a teacher at the lyceum in Berea and later was principal of Baldwin University. On Nov. 24, 1855, he became principal of the normal school at Lebanon, which had been established by the Southwestern Normal School Association. After the first year he operated it as a private enterprise and introduced innovations that so reduced living expenses as to bring a college education within reach of many who could not otherwise obtain it. He wrote a grammar textbook and two education texts: *The Normal: Or, Methods of Teaching the Common Branches . . .* (1859) and *School Management* (1871). Despite the popularity of National Normal University, a steadily increasing enrollment, and the employment of several members of Holbrook's family as teachers, the school encountered financial difficulties and was forced into receivership in 1895. Alfred Holbrook died fourteen years later in Lebanon.

Reminiscences of the Happy Life of a Teacher, Cincinnati, 1885.

HOLBROOK, JOSIAH (1788–June 17, 1854), educator, father of Alfred Holbrook (q.v.), was born in Derby, Conn. An active organizer of lyceums for adult education, he was invited to Berea by John Baldwin in 1837. The Lyceum Village he established there failed in 1842, but Holbrook remained in Berea until 1852, manufacturing globe maps. Throughout his life he published a great many pamphlets on education and textbooks in geology and mathematics.

HOLBROOK, MARTIN LUTHER (Feb. 3, 1831–Aug. 12, 1902), medical writer and publisher, was born in Mantua, Portage County. He studied at Ohio University and at an institution known as the Normal School of Physical Culture. He was associate editor of the *Ohio Farmer,* 1859–61. In 1864 he began as a medical publisher in New York City. He edited the *Herald of Health* and was a prolific writer of books on medical subjects for laymen.

Eating for Strength . . . , New York, 1875.

Liver Complaint, Nervous Dyspepsia, and Headache . . . , New York, [1877].

Hygiene of the Brain and Nerves . . . , New York, 1878.

Marriage and Parentage . . . , New York, 1882.

How to Strengthen the Memory . . . , New York, [1886].

The Hygienic Treatment of Consumption . . . , New York, [1893?].

Chastity, Its Physical, Intellectual, and Moral Advantages, New York, [1894].

Stirpiculture; Or, the Improvement of Offspring through Wiser Generation, New York, 1897.

HOLBROOK, REGINALD HEBER (April 10, 1845–1910), educator, was born in Berea, Cuyahoga County, where his father, Alfred Holbrook (q.v.), was principal of Baldwin University. In 1855 Alfred Holbrook became president of Normal University, and Reginald spent the rest of his boyhood in Lebanon. He served in the Civil War in the 35th O.V.I. and in the Signal Corps. After two years as superintendent of schools in Vineland, N. J., he joined the faculty of Normal University and served as professor and vice president. Besides the title below, he published a number of textbooks in history, literature, and natural philosophy.

An Outline of the Life of Jesus the Christ, [Lebanon, 1874].

HOLCOMB, CARLYSLE HENRY (June 1, 1888–), clergyman, was born in Pierpont, Ashtabula County. He attended Ashtabula public schools, Bethany College, and Kansas City University. Ordained to the ministry in the Disciples of Christ Church, he served pastorates in Croton and Barberton in Ohio and in other states. He now lives in Kansas City, Kan. He has written *By This I Conquer,* Cynthiana, Ky., 1945.

HOLCOMBE, RETURN IRA (Feb. 24, 1845–1916), journalist, was born in Gallia County. He served in the 10th Missouri Regiment, 1861–65, worked on various newspapers in Iowa and Missouri, and after 1888 lived in St. Paul, Minn. Besides the title below, he contributed to various local and county histories.

An Account of the Battle of Wilson's Creek . . . , Springfield, Mo., 1883.

HOLCOMBE, WILLIAM HENRY (May 29, 1825–Nov. 28, 1893), homeopathic physician, was born in Virginia and spent most of his life in the South. He practiced medicine in Cincinnati, 1850–52; while there he observed the success of homeopathic methods in treating cholera and for the rest of his life was a zealous advocate of homeopathy. He wrote a number of medical books, and after his conversion to Swedenborgianism in 1852 he wrote several books on religious themes. His writings include *How I Became a Homeopath,* Chicago, 1869.

HOLDING, CARLISLE B. (Feb. 1, 1849–May 27, 1929), clergyman, was born in Georgetown, Ky. In 1890 he entered the Ohio Conference of the Methodist Episcopal Church; he preached in Toledo and in other Ohio towns until his retirement in 1919. During the 1890s he published a number of popular stories and novels. He died in Akron.

"Cash," Or, Number 19 . . . , New York, 1888.

Her Ben: A Tale of Royal Resolves, Cincinnati, 1889.

Reuben, a Prince in Disguise, Cincinnati, 1890.

The Colonel's Charge . . . , Cincinnati, 1891.

The Little Corporal . . . , Cincinnati, 1891.

An Odd Fellow; A Tale of To-day, Cincinnati, 1895.

HOLLADAY, MRS. LEWIS L. See Elizabeth M. Dinwiddie.

HOLLIDAY, CARL (March 2, 1879–Aug. 16, 1936), was born on a farm near Hanging Rock, Lawrence County. He graduated from the University of Tennessee in 1901 and the American University (Ph.D.) in 1922. After teaching English in a number of Southern schools and colleges, he was a member of the University of Toledo faculty, 1917–29, serving as dean, 1918–29. He was on the faculty of California State College, San Jose, 1929–36. He published textbooks, fiction, e.g., a collection of short stories: *The Old Man of the Woods,* Los Angeles, [1932], and several collections of poetry, e.g., *The Cotton-Picker and Other Poems,* New York, 1907. WWW 1

HOLLIDAY, GEORGE H. (Dec. 11, 1847–June 10, 1919), was born in Pomeroy, Meigs County. He enlisted in the 4th West Virginia Cavalry in Aug., 1863, transferred to the 6th Cavalry, and served until his discharge in May, 1866. In 1878 he was living in Hanging Rock, Lawrence County, and listed his occupation as stove-mounter. He died in Knoxville, Tenn. His book is one of the few narratives of the Powder River Indian Expedition ever published.

On the Plains in '65 . . . Twelve Months in the Volunteer Cavalry Service among the Indians . . . , [n.p., 1883].

HOLLINGTON, RICHARD DEMING (May 21, 1870–Aug. 7, 1944), clergyman, was born in Toledo, Lucas County. He graduated from Ohio Wesleyan University in 1892 and was ordained to the Methodist ministry in 1895. After serving churches in Fostoria, Kenton, Toledo, and elsewhere, he joined the faculty of Garrett Biblical Institute. A popular lecturer on art and psychology, he also published three books on the latter subject, e.g., *Psychology Serving Religion* . . . , New York, [1938]. WWW 2

HOLLISTER, MARY BREWSTER (Aug. 31, 1891–), was born in Foochow, China, the daughter of Ohio-born missionaries. After spending her girlhood in China, she graduated from Ohio Wesleyan University in 1913. She and her husband, George W. Hollister, were in educational and social work in China, 1914–28. In 1930 he joined the faculty of Ohio Wesleyan University. They are now missionaries in Malaya. She has written considerable fiction about China, most of it for children, e.g., *Bright Sky Tomorrow,* New York, [1940]. WWNAA 7

HOLLOWAY, EPHRAIM S. (July 27, 1833–1895), was born in Fairfield Township, Columbiana County. He was a farmer and a carpenter before the Civil War. In Oct., 1861, he enlisted in the 41st O.V.I. as a private and rose through the ranks to command the regiment in 1864. After the war he worked as a carpenter, edited the *Independent Register,* read law, and after 1877 practiced in Columbiana. With Robert L. Kimberley (q.v.), also an officer of the 41st, he prepared the regimental history listed below.

The Forty-first Ohio Veteran Volunteer Infantry . . . , Cleveland, 1897.

HOLLYDAY, ROBERT H. (Sept. 1, 1815–Oct. 30, 1905), clergyman, was born in Ross County. He served Presbyterian churches in various communities, including Bellefontaine, Bellaire, Upper Sandusky, and Findlay. He died in Findlay.

Centennial History of the Presbyterian Church in Northwestern Ohio . . . , Ada, 1888.

HOLMAN, MARY VELORA (March 31, 1901–), educator, was born in Circleville, Pickaway County. She graduated from the University of Vermont in 1924 and has done graduate work in education at Columbia University. She has been a psychiatric social worker, a high school teacher, and director of travel groups in Europe; she now is director of guidance in the Orange, N. J., schools. She has written *How It Feels to Be a Teacher,* New York, 1950.

HOLMES, ARTHUR (May 5, 1872–), clergyman and educator, was born in Cincinnati, Hamilton County. He graduated from Hiram College in 1899, was ordained in the Disciples of Christ ministry the same year, and received his Ph.D. at the University of Pennsylvania in 1908. He served pastorates in several states and was on the faculty of various colleges before joining the Butler University faculty in 1933. His residence is now Norwood, Pa. He has written a number of books on education, philosophy, and religion, e.g., *The Mind of St. Paul . . . ,* New York, 1929. WW 27

HOLMES, DANIEL HENRY (July 16, 1851–Dec. 14, 1908), was born in New York City. Reared near Covington, Ky., and educated in France, he came to Cincinnati, where he studied law and was admitted to the bar in 1872. In 1883 he married Rachel Gaff of Cincinnati, and the following year left on an extensive tour of Europe. Under the pen name Daniel Henry, Jun., he published his first book, *Under a Fool's Cap,* in London. Though it was a distinguished volume of graceful lyrics based upon old nursery rhymes, it would probably have remained little known but for its discovery and republication by Thomas Bird Mosher around the turn of the century. Following his marriage his life appears to have been spent in shuttling back and forth between Europe and the Ohio Valley. He died in Hot Springs, Va., and was buried in Cincinnati.

Under a Fool's Cap: Songs, London, 1884.
Hempen Homespun Songs, Cincinnati, 1906.
A Pedlar's Pack, New York, 1906.

HOLMES, HARRY NICHOLLS (July 10, 1879–), chemist and educator, born in Lawrence County, Pa., was on the Oberlin College faculty, 1914–45, and after his retirement continued to live in Oberlin. He has written many scientific articles, chemistry textbooks, and *Fifty Years of Industrial Aluminum,* Oberlin, 1937, WW 30

HOLMES, CAPTAIN HOWARD. Pseud. See T. C. Harbaugh.

HOLMES, JAMES TAYLOR (Nov. 25, 1837–Feb. 17, 1916), lawyer, was born at Indian Shortcreek, Harrison County. He attended the county schools and was graduated from Franklin College in 1859. He served in the Civil War with the 52nd O.V.I. After the war he read law in Columbus, was admitted to the bar in 1867, and afterward practiced in Columbus, where he spent the remainder of his life.

52nd O.V.I. Then and Now, Columbus, 1898.

Richmond Revisited by a Federal; 1865–1905, Columbus, 1905.

HOLMES, MARGARET. Pseud. See Margaret Holmes E. Bates.

HOLMES, WILLIAM HENRY (Dec. 1, 1846–April 20, 1933), was born near Cadiz, Harrison County. He became interested in drawing while still a schoolboy and decided to make art his lifework. After spending one term at Willoughby Collegiate Institute, he graduated from McNeely Normal School, Hopedale, in 1870. He then went to Washington, D. C., where an official of the Smithsonian Institution observed him sketching a mounted bird. The unusual artistic skill shown in his work led to his being engaged as an artist. His connection with the Smithsonian lasted sixty years, during which period his major positions were as an artist with the U. S. Geological Survey, 1872–75, head curator of the Department of Anthropology at the National Museum, 1897–1920, chief of the U. S. Bureau of American Ethnology, 1902–10, and director of the National Gallery of Art, 1920–24. He also did field work in the Far West and represented the United States in scientific conferences in Europe and South America. He wrote a great many articles, reports, and technical monographs.

H. B. McConnell

Archaeological Studies among the Ancient Cities of New Mexico, 2 parts, Chicago, 1895–97.

HOLMGREN, VIRGINIA CUNNINGHAM. See Virginia Cunningham.

HOLMQUIST, AGNES. See Sigrid Arne.

HOLZWORTH, JOHN MICHAEL (May 28, 1888–), lawyer and explorer, was born in Cleveland, Cuyahoga County. He graduated from Columbia University in 1910, studied law at New York University, and was admitted to the bar in 1912. He practiced law in New York City and led expeditions to the Northwest and Alaska for the U. S. Biological Survey. He has written a number of books, e.g., *The Wild Grizzlies of Alaska . . . ,* New York, 1930. WW 30

HONLINE, MOSES ALFRED (May 19, 1873–June 13, 1927), religious educator, was born in Hillsboro, Highland County. He attended Otterbein College, 1897–98, and Ohio State University, 1898–1902. He held various executive positions in the United Brethren Church, the Y.M.C.A., and various Sunday school associations. He published several books relative to religious education, including *An Outline of New Testament History,* Pasadena, Calif., [1929]. WWW 1

HOOD, EDMUND LYMAN (Aug. 18, 1858–Aug. 14, 1931), clergyman and educator, was born in Ravenna, Portage County. He graduated from the University of Minnesota in 1880, Yale Divinity School in 1885, and New York University (Ph.D.) in 1899. He was superintendent of missions and schools of the Congregational Church in the Southwest, 1886–94, president and professor of church history at Atlanta Theological Seminary, 1905–19, a pastor in River Edge, N. J., 1919–24, and professor on the faculties of Honolulu Theological Seminary and the University of Hawaii, 1924–31. He wrote a number of books on religion and education, e.g., *The National Council of Congregational Churches of the United States,* Boston, [1901]. WWW 1

HOOKER, ISABELLA BEECHER (Feb. 22, 1822–Jan. 25, 1907), daughter of Lyman Beecher (q.v.), was born in Litchfield, Conn. She accompanied her father to Cincinnati in 1832, attended the school there founded by her sister Catherine (q.v.), but left after the death of her mother in 1835 to live with her sister Mary in Hartford, Conn. She married John Hooker, a lawyer, in 1841. She wrote and lectured on behalf of women's suffrage but was often at odds with the leaders of the movement, as she was with several of her brothers and sisters. She wrote a book defending the morality and domestic happiness of women reformers: *Womanhood: Its Sanctities and Fidelities,* Boston, 1874.

HOOPER, HENRY (Jan., 1830–Jan. 12, 1916), lawyer, was born in London, England. After coming to America, he studied at Cincinnati Law College and was admitted to the Ohio bar in 1863. He was assistant U. S. attorney in Cincinnati for over 25 years. He lived in Paris, France, for a number of years after his retirement. The first of the titles below was published under the pen name Ignio; the second, under Ducdame.

Morca, the Blind Page. A Tragedy in Five Acts, Cincinnati, 1855.

Wash Bolton, M.D.; Or, the Life of an Orator . . . , London, 1872.

The Lost Model. A Romance, Philadelphia, 1874.

HOOPER, OSMAN CASTLE (April 10, 1858–May 11, 1941), journalist and educator, was born near Alexandria, Licking County. He graduated from Denison University in 1879 and began newspaper work the following year as telegraph editor of the Columbus *Dispatch.* In subsequent years he served in the editorial departments of that paper, the Columbus *News,* and the Cincinnati *Enquirer.* He conducted a column in the *Dispatch,* a feature of which was a daily bit of verse. He was professor of journalism at Ohio State University, 1918–32. In 1928 he founded the Ohio Journalism Hall of Fame. He published several books, e.g., *History of Ohio Journalism 1793–1933,* Columbus, 1933. WWW 1

HOORMAN, FERDINAND (Feb. 9, 1892–March 31, 1932), Roman Catholic priest, was born in St. Mary's, Auglaize County. He studied at St. Joseph's College, Collegeville, Ind., and at St. Charles' Seminary, Carthagena, Mercer County, and was ordained to the priesthood in 1921. He was assistant editor of the *Precious Blood Messenger,* published in Carthagena, 1921–25, and was chaplain of Notre Dame Convent, Milwaukee, Wis., 1927–32. He published *Rivals on the Ridge,* New York, [1930].

HOOTMAN, GEORGE WARREN (July 29, 1861–Feb. 12, 1941), educator, was born near Hicksville, Defiance County. He attended Newville Academy, Ind., Defiance County Normal School, and Valparaiso University. He served on the faculty of Eureka College, Eureka, Ill. He died in Minneapolis, Minn. He wrote *Short Sketches for Children and Young People,* Minneapolis, 1934.

HOOVEN, HERBERT NELSON (Jan. 31, 1898–), born in Hazelton, Pa., taught in several universities, including Ohio University, 1932–35. After his retirement he lived in Coolville, Athens County. He has published several books, e.g., a volume of poems: *The Laughing One,* Athens, 1937. WW 28

HOOVER, DAVID (April 14, 1781–Sept. 12, 1866), born in Randolph County, N. C., spent about six years of his boyhood in Ohio before his parents moved to Indiana, where he spent the remainder of his life. He was a farmer and also was active in Democratic politics. He wrote *Memoirs . . . ,* Richmond, Ind., 1857.

HOOVER, GUY ISRAEL (Nov. 12, 1872–Feb. 10, 1943), clergyman and educator, was born in Croton, Licking County. He graduated from Hiram College in 1899 and was ordained to the Disciples of Christ ministry in the same year. After serving various pastorates in Ohio and other states, he was a member of the Butler University faculty, 1925–40. He died in Indianapolis. His writings include *The Disciples of Christ and Their Educational Work in Indiana,* [Indianapolis, 1916]. RLA 2

HOOVER, SIMON ROBERT (Sept. 25, 1867–June 28, 1936), clergyman and educator, was born in Bedford County, Pa. He graduated from Baldwin University in 1889. He taught in Cleveland high schools, 1896–1929. He was also an ordained minister in the Congregational Church. His death occurred in Cleveland. He wrote *A Son of the Nile,* Boston, 1927. WWW 1

HOPE, BOB (May 29, 1903–), comedian, born in Elthan, Kent, England, grew up in Cleveland, where his mother brought her family of six children after her husband died in 1907. He attended Cleveland schools, pursued a short-lived boxing career under the ring name of "Packy East," and sold automobiles. When he entered vaudeville, he dropped his baptismal name, Leslie Townes, in favor of Bob. His first important stage success came in *Roberta* in 1933. He made his first radio broadcast in 1935 and immediately became a national favorite. In his first moving picture, *The Big Broadcast of 1938,* he sang "Thanks for the Memory," which has since been his theme song, though with ever-varying lyrics. His unique blend of farce and audacious, rapid-fire wit has made him the best-known American comedian. He is especially beloved by servicemen for his willingness to appear, in war and in peace, at remote bases. He has written five books, including an account of his wartime tours: *I Never Left Home,* New York, [1944]. CB 41

HOPKINS, ARTHUR MELANCTHON (Oct. 4, 1878–March 22, 1950), theatrical producer, was born in Cleveland, Cuyahoga County. He attended Western Reserve Academy, Hudson. He began as a producer in New York City in 1912 and produced many successful plays, including *Anna Christie, What Price Glory?* and *The Petrified Forest.* He also produced numerous radio dramas and wrote several books about the theater, including *How's Your Second Act?* New York, 1918. WWW 2

HOPKINS, CHARLES EDWIN (Dec. 19, 1886–May 21, 1946), was born in Cincinnati, Hamilton County, where he graduated from Walnut Hills High School and the Y.M.C.A. Law School. He was an insurance man in Cincinnati for 35 years. He was interested in local history and wrote *Ohio, the Beautiful and Historic . . . ,* Boston, [1931].

HOPKINS, FLORENCE B. (Mrs. Ernest A.) (July 7, 1887–), born in California, Pa., has lived in Cleveland and Lakewood since 1915. She attended Cleveland College, Western Reserve University. She has published poems in various periodicals and a collection: *Along My Way,* Cleveland, [1940].

HOPKINS, LIVINGSTON (July 7, 1846–1927), artist, was born in Bellefontaine, Logan County. He attended school there and in Toledo until he was fourteen, when he went to work. After serving briefly with the 130th O.V.I., he became an artist on the Champaign, Ill., *Union.* He worked briefly on the staff of *Scribner's* and then as a free-lance comic artist. From 1870 to 1882 he was successful in New York; he sold sketches to many national magazines and illustrated books by Josh Billings, Petroleum Nasby, and others. His own book, *A Comic History,* was criticized when it appeared for its irreverence on the occasion of the national centennial celebration, but when reissued in a British edition it was well received. In 1883 Hopkins was invited to migrate to Australia to work for the Sydney *Bulletin.* After some hesitation, he accepted and spent the remainder of his life in that country. Though scarcely known in America or in his native state, he is still remembered in Australia as the greatest Down-Under cartoonist.

A Comic History of the United States . . . , New York, 1876.

HOPKINS, PAULINE BRADFORD MACKIE (July, 1874–May 21, 1956), born in Fairfield, Conn., grew up in Toledo and attended the schools of that city. She later lived in New York City. She published plays, articles, and novels under her maiden name, e.g., *Mademoiselle De Berny . . . ,* Boston, 1897.

HOPKINS, WILLIAM ROWLAND (July 26, 1869–), lawyer, born in Johnstown, Pa., graduated from Western Reserve University in 1896. He served on the Cleveland City Council, 1897–99, and was admitted to the bar in 1899. He was active in the construction of the Cleveland Short Line Railway. He was city manager of Cleveland, 1924–30.

The Street Railway Problem in Cleveland . . . , New York, 1896.

HOPLEY, JOHN EDWARD (Aug. 25, 1850–July 10, 1927), lawyer and journalist, was born in Elkton, Ky. In 1856 his parents moved to Bucyrus. He was admitted to the Ohio bar in 1875. He founded and edited the Bucyrus *Evening Telegrapher* and also edited the Bucyrus *Journal.* He served as consul in Southampton, England, and in Montevideo, Uruguay. He wrote *History of Crawford County, Ohio, and Representative Citizens,* Chicago, [1912]. WWW 1

HOPWOOD, AVERY (May 28, 1882–July 1, 1928), dramatist, was born in Cleveland, Cuyahoga County. He graduated from the University of Michigan in 1905, went to New York as correspondent for the Cleveland *Leader,* and in 1906 collaborated with Channing Pollock in writing *Clothes,* which was produced successfully. He collaborated with Mary Roberts Rinehart in writing *The Bat* (1920), and he also collaborated with Wilson Collison (q.v.) on plays like *Getting Gertie's Garter* (1921). Author of a great many highly profitable, though now forgotten, plays, Hopwood gave up writing in 1925. He drowned three years later while swimming at Juan-les-Pins on the French Riviera. DAB 9

HORCHOW, REUBEN (Aug. 9, 1895–Oct. 12, 1958), lawyer, was born in Portsmouth, Scioto County. After graduating from Yale University in 1916, he served in the artillery during World War I. He graduated from the University of Cincinnati Law School in 1926 and afterward practiced law and was engaged in personnel work. He served in the army, 1942–49, and was retired as a colonel. He wrote articles, pamphlets, and three books, e.g., *Careers for Young Americans in the Army and After,* [Washington, D. C., 1950].

HORN, WILLIAM (May 7, 1839–April 27, 1917), bishop of the Evangelical Church, was born in Oberfishbach, Prussia. When he was sixteen, his family migrated to Wisconsin. He learned English in a country school, taught school for several terms in Brown County, Wis., and became a preacher in northern Wisconsin. In 1871 he came to Cleveland as editor of the publications of his church. He edited magazines and Sunday school books, and in 1879 was appointed editor of the weekly paper, *Christliche Botschafter.* He was made bishop in 1891 and served until 1915. He translated a number of works from German, and his brief autobiography was published posthumously for members of his family.

Der Goldne Wegweiser . . . , Cleveland, 1881.

Leben und Wirken von Bischof Joh. Jakob Escher . . . , Cleveland, [1907].

Wegeblüten Gepflücht auf Langer Pilgerreise, Cleveland, 1907.

Autobiography of Bishop William Horn . . . , [Cleveland], 1920.

HORNBACK, FLORENCE MARY (June 22, 1892–), lawyer and educator, was born in Cincinnati, Hamilton County. She graduated from McDonald College of Law, Cincinnati, in 1921 and practiced in Cincinnati. She did graduate work in several universities and graduated from New York University (Ph.D.) in 1941. She taught at Xavier University for a time and is now a resident of Cincinnati. She has written numerous magazine articles and several devotional books for juvenile readers, e.g., *John and Joan and Their Guardian Angels,* Paterson, N. J., [1937]. WW 28

HORR, ALFRED REUEL (July 14, 1875–Nov. 3, 1958), banker, was born in Wellington, Lorain County. He graduated from Cornell University in 1895, was admitted to the bar in 1897, and practiced for two years in Cleveland. He was afterward an official in several Cleveland banks and trust companies. He died in Fort Lauderdale, Fla. His writings include *Embarrassing Dollars and Hints to Their Holders,* New York, 1935. WWW 3

HORSTMANN, IGNATIUS FREDERICK (Dec. 16, 1840–May 13, 1908), Roman Catholic priest, was born in Philadelphia, Pa. Ordained to the priesthood in 1865, he served Catholic schools and churches in Philadelphia until 1892, when he was made bishop of Cleveland. The remainder of his life was spent in Ohio.

The History of the Holy Catholic Bible . . . , Philadelphia, [1875].

HORTON, JOSHUA H. (c.1835–July 29, 1907), was born in Ohio, probably in Franklin County. During the Civil War he served in the 11th O.V.I. and the 94th O.V.I. He was captured late in 1862 but was paroled soon afterward. In Feb., 1863, he was discharged for disability. After the war he was a printer in Piqua, Dayton, and Tippecanoe City. He collaborated with Solomon Teverbaugh (1834–Feb. 6, 1884), a captain in the 11th O.V.I., in writing the regimental history below.

A History of the Eleventh Regiment . . . , Dayton, 1866.

HORTON, SAMUEL DANA (Jan. 16, 1844–Feb. 23, 1895), lawyer, was born in Pomeroy, Meigs County, the son of Valentine Baxter Horton, who served three terms in Congress. He attended Pomeroy Academy and the classical school of E. S. Brooks in Cincinnati before entering Harvard College, where he graduated in law in 1868. After two years of travel and study in Europe, he returned to Ohio and was admitted to the bar in Columbus in 1871. He presided over the meeting on Jan. 24, 1872, which founded the Cincinnati Bar Association. He practiced in Cincinnati and Pomeroy. Convinced that his father had been a political martyr to sound finance when he opposed the issuance of paper money in Congress in 1862, he devoted most of his life to the cause of international finance. Fellow bimetallists ranked him as the most learned and one of the ablest champions of their cause. His death occurred in Washington, D. C. Besides the titles below, he published a number of papers, letters, and articles.

Proportional Representation, [Philadelphia, 1873].

The Interest of the United States in the Silver Question, London, 1881.

The Position of Law in the Doctrine of Money, and Other Papers, London, 1882.

The Internationality of the Silver Question, New York, 1885.

Silver: An Issue of International Politics, Cincinnati, 1886.

The Silver Pound and England's Monetary Policy Since the Restoration, Together with the History of the Guinea, London, 1887.

Silver in Europe, New York, 1890.

HORTON, THOMAS CORWIN (Aug. 3, 1848–Feb. 27, 1932), clergyman, was born in Cincinnati, Hamilton County. He served as a Presbyterian evangelist and was ordained to the ministry in 1884. He served as pastor and as a Y.M.C.A. secretary in various cities; from 1915 to 1924 he was associate pastor of the Church of the Open Door, Los Angeles. He wrote several books on religious themes, including *Personal and Practical Christian Work,* Los Angeles, [1922]. WWW 1

HORTON, WALTER MARSHALL (April 7, 1895–), theologian, born in Somerville, Mass., has been on the faculty of Oberlin Graduate School of Theology since 1926. He has written a number of books on theological and religious themes, e.g., *Theism and the Modern Mood,* New York, 1930. WW 30

HOSEA, LUCY KLINCK RICE (Nov. 8, 1852–Sept. 30, 1921), was born in Hamilton, N. Y. In 1876 she became the second wife of Robert Hosea (q.v.) of Cincinnati. Her novel was published anonymously.

Eastward; Or, a Buddhist Lover. A Novel, Boston, [1890].

HOSEA, ROBERT (Feb. 15, 1811–Feb. 20, 1906), merchant, was born in Boston, Mass. In 1816 his father moved to Ross County, where he prospered buying produce and shipping it to the East. In 1826 his father moved to Cincinnati to open a wholesale grocery supply house. After a successful trading expedition to the South in 1835, Robert was able to invest in a steamboat. He built and commanded a series of steamboats that were active in the river trade. His son, Lewis Montgomery Hosea (Dec. 16, 1842–Jan. 26, 1924), served throughout the Civil War, and afterward delivered several significant historical papers that were published as pamphlets.

Glimpses of Europe; Or, Notes Drawn at Sight. By a Merchant, Cincinnati, 1859.

HOSFORD, FRANCES JULIETTE (Oct. 3, 1853–May 14, 1937), educator, was born in Ohio. She graduated from Lake Erie Seminary in 1872. After teaching school in Elyria and Painesville, she became a tutor in the preparatory department, Oberlin College in 1888, and she served at Oberlin in various capacities until her retirement in 1920. She wrote *Father Shipherd's Magna Charta; A Century of Coeducation in Oberlin College,* Boston, 1937, WO 1

HOSMER, FREDERICK LUCIAN (Oct. 16, 1840–June 7, 1929), Unitarian clergyman, born in Framingham, Mass., was pastor of the Church of the Unity, Cleveland, 1878–92. He composed a number of hymns that are still widely used, and with William C. Gannett he published three series of *The Thought of God in Hymns and Poems,* Boston, 1885, 1894, 1918.

HOSMER, HEZEKIAH LORD (Dec. 10, 1814–Oct. 31, 1893), journalist, lawyer, and judge, was born in Hudson, N. Y. In 1816 he came to Cleveland, where he studied law in the office of a relative, John W. Allen, and was admitted to the bar in 1835. He practiced for a short while, then moved on to the Maumee Valley and joined his brother, Stephen T. Hosmer, a pioneer printer in that region. He edited successively the Perrysburg *Journal* and the Maumee *Express;* in 1847 he bought an interest in and became editor of the Toledo *Blade.* In 1850 he and his brother became sole proprietors of the *Blade,* which had become a daily in 1848. He was a fluent and graphic writer, and his editorials attracted state-wide attention. In May, 1853, he sold his interest in the *Blade* and resumed the practice of law, but he continued to write. In 1860 his *Adela, the Octoroon* was published in Columbus. Dion Boucicault's greatest success, *The Octoroon,* a problem play about slavery which appeared in 1861, was drawn from Hosmer's novel. He had actively supported the candidacy of Abraham Lincoln, and following the inauguration he appeared in Washington seeking the position of Congressional Librarian. He was unsuccessful in getting the appointment, but his fellow townsman, James M. Ashley, was chairman of the House committee on territories, and Hosmer was appointed secretary of that committee, an appointment that proved to be the turning point in his career. When the Territory of Montana was organized in 1864, the influential Ashley—he had been one of the founders of the Republican Party in Ohio—had another Toledoan, Alfred Peck Edgerton, appointed governor of the new territory, and Hosmer became chief justice of the territorial supreme court on June 30, 1864. He arrived in the Territory in Oct., 1864, to find the people quite content with the effectiveness of their vigilantes and miners' courts. In the absence of a criminal or civil code, guided solely by a sketchy organic law which established no rules of procedure, Judge Hosmer opened court the first Monday of Dec., 1864, at Virginia City in the dining room of the Planters House, which added not a whit to the popularity of the new court, for dining hours depended upon its adjournment. At the close of the first sitting a citizen rose and addressed the court: "We are glad the Government has sent you here. We have some civil matters to attend to, but you had better let us take charge of the criminal affairs." The frontier community was far from content with ponderous legal procedure, and soon Hosmer was engaged in a wrangle with the legislature which culminated in a resolution calling upon him to resign. Hosmer served his full term. He made a trip to New York in the autumn of 1865 and while there delivered an address on Montana. It was a splendid circumstantial account of the Territory, its resources, its booming development, and its people, and was published in New York in 1866. After Hosmer's term as chief justice expired in 1869, he became postmaster at Virginia City, serving until 1872, when he moved to San Francisco. In 1887 he became one of that considerable number of Ohioans to espouse the cause of Delia Bacon (q.v.) when he published *Bacon and Shakespeare in the Sonnets,* in which he exploited the Baconian cipher theory. His death occurred in San Francisco. Besides the titles below, he published some separate addresses and a Toledo directory.

Ernest J. Wessen

Early History of the Maumee Valley, Toledo, 1858.

Adela, the Octoroon, Columbus, 1860.

Bacon and Shakespeare in the Sonnets, San Francisco, 1887.

HOSMER, JAMES KENDALL (Jan. 29, 1834–May 11, 1927), was born in Northfield, Mass. He graduated from Harvard University in 1855 and the Divinity School in 1859. He was professor of rhetoric and English literature at Antioch College, 1866–72, and later was a teacher and librarian in several other states. He wrote two novels, several biographies, and a number of distinguished historical works. Some recollections of Antioch College are found in *The Last Leaf . . .* , New York, 1912. WWW 1

HOSMER, JOHN ALLEN (1851–1907), was born in Toledo, Lucas County, the son of Hezekiah Lord Hosmer (q.v.). He accompanied his father on a trip from Montana Territory to New York City in 1865. Two years later *A Trip to the States, by Way of the Yellowstone and Missouri* was published in Virginia City. The book is frequently attributed to the elder Hosmer; however, the single surviving copy shows the author to have been J. Allen Hosmer. He died in California.

A Trip to the States, by Way of the Yellowstone and Missouri, with a Table of Distances, Virginia City, Montana Territory, 1867.

HOSTERMAN, ARTHUR DAVID (April 12, 1860–Feb. 6, 1939), born in Strattonville, Pa., was brought to Springfield as a boy. He attended Springfield schools and Wittenberg College. He afterward lived in Springfield, where he was president of Hosterman Publishing Company. He also operated a large fruit farm in Clark County.

Health, Wealth, and Wisdom . . . , Springfield, [1882].

Life and Times of James Abram Garfield . . . , Springfield, 1882.

HOTCHKISS, WILLIS RAY (Oct. 11, 1873–June 25, 1948), missionary-teacher, was born in Doylestown, Wayne County, but grew up in Cleveland, where his parents moved when he was small. After attending Oberlin Academy and Friends' Bible Institute, Cleveland, he went to Africa as a missionary in 1895. He founded Friends' Africa Industrial Mission in 1900 and Lumbwa Industrial Mission in 1905. He lectured in the United States for the National Holiness Missionary Society and wrote two books on his African experiences, e.g., *Then and Now in Kenya Colony; Forty Adventurous Years in East Africa,* New York, [1937]. WW 11

HOTT, JAMES WILLIAM (Nov. 15, 1844–Jan. 9, 1902), clergyman, was born in Winchester, Va. He was ordained to the ministry of the United Brethren Church and moved to Dayton in 1873, when he was named treasurer of the Missionary Society. He edited the *Religious Telescope,* 1877–89. In 1889 he was made bishop and sent to the Far West, but after his retirement in 1898 he returned to Dayton, where he spent the last four years of his life.

Journeyings in the Old World . . . , Dayton, 1884.

Sacred Hours with Young Christians, Dayton, 1892.

HOUCK, FREDERICK ALFONS (April 15, 1866–Oct. 19, 1954), clergyman, was born in Tiffin, Seneca County. He studied at Canisius College and at seminaries in Valkenberg, Holland, and Baltimore, Md. He was ordained to the Roman Catholic priesthood in 1900. He was pastor of St. Ann's Church, Toledo, 1912–51. His death occurred in Toledo. He wrote a number of books on religious themes, e.g., *Godward . . .* , St. Louis, Mo., 1927. OBB

HOUCK, GEORGE FRANCIS (July 9, 1847–March 26, 1916), clergyman, was born in Tiffin, Seneca County. After studying at Heidelberg College, Mount St. Mary's Seminary in Cincinnati, and St. Mary's Seminary in Cleveland, he was ordained to the Roman Catholic priesthood in 1875. He was pastor of St. Joseph's Church, 1875–77, and was then appointed secretary to Bishop Gilmour with the duties of the chancellorship added.

The Church in Northern Ohio and in the Diocese of Cleveland, from 1817 to September, 1887, New York, 1887.

Memoirs of and Labors of Amadeus Rappe . . . , Cleveland, [1888].

A History of Catholicity in Northern Ohio . . . , (with Michael W. Carr), 2 vols., Cleveland, 1903.

HOUF, HORACE THOMAS (1889–July 7, 1959), educator, born in Fulton, Mo., was professor of philosophy at Ohio University from 1935 until his death. His books include *Real Living and God's Help,* [Rio Grande, 1925]. DAS 3

HOUGH, FRANKLIN BENJAMIN (July 22, 1822–June 11, 1885), born in Martinsdale, N. Y., lived in Ohio about four years. He was principal of Gustavus Academy, 1844–46, and a student at Western Reserve Medical College, 1846–48. He later practiced medicine in New York State. A prolific writer with many interests, he wrote books, pamphlets, and reports on forestry, conservation, history, education, law, biography, and other subjects.

HOUGH, LYNN HAROLD (Sept. 10, 1877–), clergyman and educator, was born in Cadiz, Harrison County. He graduated from Scio College in 1898 and Drew Theological Seminary in 1905. He served as pastor of various Methodist churches, taught at Garrett Biblical Institute, 1914–19, and Drew Seminary, 1930–47. He has published many books, including sermons, addresses, religious books, and poems, e.g., *Flying over London and Other Verses,* New York, [1919]. WW 30

HOUK, ELIZA PHILLIPS THRUSTON (Oct. 23, 1833–Aug. 31, 1914), was born in Dayton, Montgomery County. She graduated from Cooper Female Seminary, Dayton, in 1849; in 1856 she married George W. Houk, lawyer and congressman. Besides the titles below, she published articles in Dayton newspapers and wrote several plays that were not published. She also patented a rural mailbox shaped like a cornucopia.

Puritan. A Poem in Seven Cantos, Cincinnati, 1868.

The Lamarks; Or, Marriageable Women, Cincinnati, 1889.

Louisa Varena . . . , [Dayton, 1905].

A Tribute to General Gates Phillips Thruston, [Dayton, 1914].

HOUSE, ABIGAIL (Nov. 8, 1790–Feb. 10, 1861), was born in Bloomfield, Conn. In 1812 she married Simeon Fish, and five years later they migrated to Chardon. Soon after their arrival her husband died, and the following year she married E. N. House. She spent the remainder of her life in Lenox, Ashtabula County. Her life story was published as required by the terms of her will.

Memoirs of the Religious Experience and Life of Abigail House . . . , Jefferson, 1861.

HOUSE, ERWIN (Feb. 17, 1824–May 20, 1875), clergyman and editor, was born in Worthington, Franklin County. His parents later moved to Lockland, where he was converted to Methodism. In 1846 he graduated from Woodward College, Cincinnati, and three years later was licensed to preach. He served for many years as an editor of the *Ladies' Repository* and the *Western Christian Advocate.* He published sermons and a Sunday school handbook. The volume cited below is a collection of narratives illustrative of Scriptural texts.

Scripture Cabinet . . . , Cincinnati, 1863.

HOUSTON, WILLIAM (Nov. 8, 1867–July 17, 1927), clergyman, was born in Urbana, Champaign County. He graduated from University of Wooster in 1890 and Allegheny Theological Seminary in 1893. After serving several Presbyterian pastorates, he became pastor at Ohio State University in 1910 and remained at that post until his death. He wrote *The Church and the University . . . ,* Columbus, 1926.

HOUSUM, ROBERT (Aug. 22, 1886–), was born in Cleveland, Cuyahoga County. After attending Bolton School and University School in Cleveland, he graduated from Yale University in 1898. He worked on the Cleveland *Leader* and the *News* and has written a number of plays, some of which were published a considerable time after their first production, e.g., a farce written in 1914: *Sylvia Runs Away . . . ,* New York, 1920. WWO

HOWARD, ALICE WOODBURY (Mrs. Rossiter), born in Rockford, Ill., lived in Cleveland from 1921 to 1930 while teaching at the Cleveland Museum of Art. She now lives in Bayside, N. Y. She has published several books for children, e.g., *Ching-Li and the Dragons,* New York, 1931.

HOWARD, CAPTAIN CHARLES. Pseud. See T. C. Harbaugh.

HOWARD, JAMES QUAY (Jan. 26, 1836–Nov. 15, 1912), was born in Newark, Licking County. He attended Ohio Wesleyan University and Marietta College and also studied law in the office of Samuel Galloway, Columbus attorney and early friend of Abraham Lincoln. After Lincoln's nomination in 1860, William Dean Howells (q.v.) was engaged to write a campaign biography of the candidate. Howells rebelled at the suggestion that he go to Springfield, Ill., to interview the little-known candidate, and Howard went in his stead. After the appearance of Howells' biography, a substantial clothbound volume that became one of the better-known documents of the 1860 campaign, the publishers saw a need for a cheap paper-bound campaign life, and Howard was employed to write it. It was completed too late for distribution in the campaign and remained unknown until a New York book dealer, the late Charles P. Everitt, discovered a remainder in 1901. However, perhaps because of the book but probably through the efforts of his mentor, Galloway, Howard was appointed U. S. consul at St. Johns, New Brunswick, in 1861 and served until 1867. He again capitalized upon a political campaign when in 1876 he wrote a campaign life of Rutherford B. Hayes, and in the following year he was appointed to a position in the New York Customs House, where he served until 1883. From time to time he did some editorial writing and contributed a number of articles to magazines. He was employed by the Library of Congress in 1897.

The Life of Abraham Lincoln . . ., Columbus, 1860.

The Life, Public Services and Select Speeches of Rutherford B. Hayes, Cincinnati, 1876.

History of the Louisiana Purchase, Chicago, 1902.

HOWARD, JOHN GORDON (Dec. 3, 1899–), clergyman and educator, was born in Tokyo, Japan, the son of missionary parents. A graduate of Otterbein College in 1922 and United Theological Seminary, Dayton, in 1925, he has been active in young people's work in the United Brethren Church. In 1945 he accepted the presidency of Otterbein College, a position he resigned in 1957 when appointed bishop. His books include *When Youth Worship*, St. Louis, Mo., [1940]. WW 30

HOWARD, JOHN HARRIS (Oct. 25, 1861–Feb. 19, 1950), was born in Monroe Township, Ashtabula County. After working as a printer in the office of the Ashtabula *News*, he went to New York City, where he worked on the Brooklyn *Eagle* and other newspapers. In 1890 because of poor health, he moved to Benzie County, Mich., where he operated a fruit farm. He died at Frankfort, Mich. He published *A History of Herring Lake*, Boston, [1929], and a book of verse: *Mint o' the Muse, by the Bard of Benzie*, Boston, [1929].

HOWARD, KATHERINE LANE (1858–July 5, 1929), was born in New York City, where she attended Drew Seminary. She lived in Cincinnati for a number of years and died in that city. Successful as an illustrator for books and magazines, she also published plays and poetry, e.g., *Poems*, Boston, 1914.

HOWBERT, ABRAHAM R. (June 2, 1825–Nov. 19, 1895), clergyman, was born in Roanoke County, Va. After graduating from Gettysburg Seminary in 1846, he came to Ohio, where he was licensed by the East Ohio Lutheran Synod. He served a number of Lutheran churches in Ohio; at the time of his retirement in 1892, he was serving a pastorate in Colorado. He spent the last three years of his life in Bellefontaine. During the Civil War he was chaplain of the 84th O.V.I. for five months in 1862 and afterward was a confidential agent of Governor Tod, assigned to report on the condition of Ohio regiments and on the need for chaplain service. He performed the same service for Governor Brough and was also an agent of the Sanitary Commission. Besides writing the title below, he compiled a worship manual.

Reminiscences of the War, [Springfield, 1888].

HOWE, ANDREW JACKSON (April 14, 1825–Jan. 16, 1892), physician and educator, was born in Paxton, Mass. He graduated from Harvard University in 1853 and Wooster Medical Institute in 1855. Having been invited to lecture in the College of Eclectic Medicine and Surgery in Cincinnati, he settled in that city in 1857. He was appointed to the chair of surgery in 1861 and served until his death. He not only achieved national distinction as a surgeon, but also was a member of the American Association for the Advancement of Science and the Cincinnati Society of Natural History. His first textbook, *Fractures and Dislocations* (1870), was followed by several others which achieved wide acceptance. A work designed for children and a selection of his papers, arranged by his wife, Georgiana L. Howe, were published posthumously. His death occurred in Cincinnati.

Miscellaneous Papers . . ., Cincinnati, 1894.

Conversations on Animal Life . . ., Cincinnati, 1897.

HOWE, EBER D. (June 9, 1798– ?), was born in Clifton Park, N. Y., the son of a doctor from Connecticut. He can be considered a one-man history of the Yankee drift westward into Ohio's Western Reserve. Indeed, he is so completely representative of his time, he blends so admirably into the general background, that his own outlines have been largely blurred and obscured. This, in a mild way, is a pity, for he deserves better, and there is yet pleasure in what he wrote. In 1811 his family moved to the Niagara District of Upper Canada, "under the reign of the old imbecile tyrant," George III. He was living there when the War of 1812 broke out, though he shortly escaped across the river to New York State, and, in May, 1814, he enlisted in the New York Volunteers, Batavia, Colonel Swift commanding. He was a cook for regimental and staff officers and, as such, saw rather than participated in the bloody inconclusiveness of Lundy's Lane. At that, he came away with an abiding distaste for wars and their consequences which he kept the rest of his life. He was discharged in 1815, a seventeen-year-old veteran in an indifferent world, equipped with six years of schooling, and a formidable knowledge of Webster's *Speller*, which had been his principal text through each of these years. Somewhere he had read that Ben Franklin had found himself in similar circumstances and had then proceeded to expand the education he picked up in a printing shop into greatness. Howe decided to try his hand at printing. His first stop was the Buffalo *Gazette,* then run by Smith and Hezekiah Salisbury. Preparing himself for the encounter, Howe set up a bold jingling with the two shillings he had in his pocket, stuck a cigar in his mouth (an act he later regarded as one of the silliest of his life), and asked for a job as an apprentice. The *Gazette* then had a circulation of 1,000 which required a two-day run on the old hand press. As Howe's salary climbed from $40 a year to $50, $60, and, finally $80, he was loaned out by the Salisburys to set type for other papers up and down the Lake Erie shore, notably the Erie *Gazette,* where he composed the first issue for Ziba Willes. In April, 1818, he found Buffalo too limiting. Taking a horse, saddle, bridle, and $25, he moved to Cleveland, a crossroads town of 200, which, if not the wilderness, was at least the jumping-off place. But it looked like an economic heaven to Howe and many another transplanted Yankee like him. For, really, Cleveland was only a neighborhood in a larger community of nearly 60,000—the Western Reserve, stretching from the Pennsylvania line to Sandusky. It was overwhelmingly, almost absolutely, New England in background, taste, outlook, and attitude. Howe felt at home at once and saw prosperity beckoning. There were only two newspapers in the whole Reserve: the Cleveland *Register,* limping along under the ministrations of the sickly Andrew Logan, and the Warren *Trump of Fame,* Thomas D. Webb, Prop. Howe issued some proposals for a new organ, the Cleveland *Herald,* which aroused absolutely no interest. Nothing daunted, he rode to Erie and there persuaded Willes that larger horizons were to be found in Cleveland. Willes agreed to bring his type and presses to Cleveland at the end of his first year in Erie. So it happened that the *Herald* was born, on Oct. 19, 1819, without a single subscriber. The first issue contained an obituary of Oliver Hazard Perry and a virulent attack on slavery—but, and here lies one of the quirks of Howe's Yankee conscience, it was soon printing advertisements for runaways. Writing his *Autobiography* at the age of eighty, Howe admits and regrets this inconsistency, but nothing he says and nothing he did in his later career offers much evidence that he would have acted differently had he again been forced to choose between principle and poverty. By 1822, the *Herald* had achieved some degree of stability and was well into the career which was to make it one of the most important of all sources of Western Reserve history. And Howe was restless. He moved to Painesville to establish the Painesville *Telegraph,* which first appeared on July 16, 1822, with five advertisements and 150 subscribers. Painesville, like Cleveland, was one of the little islands of people clustered throughout the Reserve. At the time, according to Howe, its principal commerce was based on corn whisky—always "blue ruin" to him—and maple sugar secured in trade from the Western Indians. It shortly afterward became the economic hub of Mormonism, when the Saints settled at nearby Kirtland. Howe joined most of the Gentiles in resentment of the strangers and was moved to write his first book, entitled in the 1840 edition *History of Mormonism; Or, a Faithful Account of That Singular Imposition and Delusion with Sketches of the Characters of Its Proprietors to Which Are Added Inquiries into the Probability That the Historical Part of the Golden Bible Was Written by One Solomon Spaulding, and by Him Intended to Have Been Published as a Romance.* The title pretty well sums up the book and its attitude. In it Howe displays a gift for blackening character by reporting contemporary bias which would look well in some current publications. Consider: "All who became intimate with them [the Smith family] unite in representing the general character of old Joseph and his wife, the parents of the pretended Prophet, as lazy, indolent, ignorant, and superstitious . . ." Or: "Joseph Smith, Jun., was well skilled in legerdemain, and thus the use of divining rods, which afforded him great facilities in translating . . ." And so on. Years later, in his *Autobiography,* Howe hints at the real reason for the popular hatred which he voiced. The Mormons moved into local politics, banking, and trade. In all these activities they proceeded with a monopolistic single-mindedness which could mean only trouble for the community Howe represented. When the Saints threatened to control elections, when they boasted that their bank would swallow all others, and, especially when they bought heavily and refused to pay as the depression of the mid-1830s deepened, then the Gentiles closed in, and Howe swung as big a club as any man. Howe gave over control of the *Telegraph* to his brother, Asahel, in Jan., 1835, after which it passed through the hands of many owners, and is today published as part of a small chain extending through northeastern

Ohio. Howe himself devoted his energies to commercial printing and the manufacture of woolens. In 1878 he wrote a short sketch of his life which concludes with a thirteen-point creed defending his conversion to spiritualism. The last of these is: "I do not promise to believe tomorrow exactly as I believe today, and I do not believe today exactly what I believed yesterday; for I expected to make, as I have made, some honest progress within twenty-four hours." Which is not a bad credo for a man of eighty, and it serves fairly to identify Eber D. Howe.

Lee Templeton

Mormonism Unvailed . . ., Painesville, 1834.

Autobiography and Recollections of a Pioneer Printer, Painesville, 1878.

HOWE, FREDERIC CLEMSON (Nov. 21, 1867–Aug. 3, 1940), lawyer, was born in Meadville, Pa. He graduated from Allegheny College in 1889 and Johns Hopkins University (Ph.D.) in 1922. He was admitted to the bar in 1894 and practiced in Cleveland until 1909. While in Cleveland, he was a member of City Council, 1901–03, and taught at Cleveland College of Law. During the 1930s he was associated with the Department of Agriculture. He wrote a number of books on social and political questions and his autobiography: *The Confessions of a Reformer,* New York, 1925. WWW 1

HOWE, GEORGE FREDERICK (Jan. 1, 1901–), educator, was born in Burlington, Vt. He graduated from the University of Vermont in 1922 and Harvard University (Ph.D.) in 1930. A member of the history faculty, University of Cincinnati, 1926–45, he is now a historian with the Department of Defense. He has written several textbooks, and *Chester A. Arthur . . .*, New York, 1934. DAS 3

HOWE, HENRY (Oct. 11, 1816–Oct. 14, 1893), historian, publisher, and bookseller, was born in New Haven, Conn., the son of a distinguished publisher, Hezekiah Howe, whose bookshop was a popular gathering place of the literati of New England. Among them were Benjamin Silliman, whose *American Journal of Science* was printed by the elder Howe, and Noah Webster, to whom young Henry carried proof sheets of the first edition of his great dictionary. Yale professors, eminent lawyers, and learned theologians frequented the shop. "The bookstore was a great education spot for me," wrote Henry Howe years later. His literary career was shaped by what he called a "life-directing incident" some time in 1838, when there came into his father's bookstore a copy of *Historical Collections of Connecticut* by a fellow townsman, John W. Barber, who had traveled from village to village, making pencil sketches and collecting material for the book. "It came upon the people like a work of magic," wrote Howe; "few had ever seen pictures of places with which they were acquainted. But here was a book that showed the very houses in which they had been born, the schoolhouses where they had been taught, the churches where they had worshipped. . . . Although born in an atmosphere of books, this impressed me more than any book I had seen. I felt that I would like of all things to dedicate my life to travelling and making such books for what Lincoln calls 'the plain people.' " During the next two years he was associated with his uncle, a stockbroker in Wall Street, "an uncongenial spot, where I felt that Tophet was not afar." In 1840 he completed arrangements with John W. Barber to help in producing a *Historical Collections* for New York. Barber was to travel by public conveyance to the larger cities, while Howe went afoot from village to village. In 1842 they began on New Jersey. Then came Virginia in 1843, a project that Howe undertook alone because of Barber's abolitionist sentiments; Howe covered the entire state, walking as much as fifty miles in a single day. This work was completed in the spring of 1845. When Howe canvassed a town for historical facts or drew a crowd around his sketching table in a public square, he displayed a previous work as a sample and solicited subscriptions for the one under preparation. This method made each work an assured success before the manuscript was placed in the hands of a printer. Yet in these transactions there were none of the sharp practices that typified some county histories of later years; no subscriber was permitted to pay his way into the book, and none was omitted because of his failure to subscribe. After completing the work on Virginia, Howe was ready for his most notable project—that on Ohio. Aged thirty, he was a veteran observer and chronicler. "Ohio," he wrote, "the young and rising state next attracted me, and proved a mine of ungathered history; all one had to do was to travel and to pick it up. Cincinnati was my first point, where I arrived in January, 1846. It was then the most important city of the West, the center of the highest refinement and cultivation, especially noted for its public spirit and its many people of mark. My first point after leaving Cincinnati was Marietta. I went there to begin at the beginning and was for several days the guest of Dr. Hildreth." Howe was singularly fortunate in making friends. A list of their names is a roster of men, the great and the near great, whose vigor at that time was making Ohio great. He was introduced to Judge Burnet by Henry Clay. Others encountered who became his lifelong friends were Caleb Atwater, Thomas Ewing, Thomas Corwin, Ephraim Squier, George Hoadly, S. S. Cox, Alphonso Taft, John Sherman, and Rutherford B. Hayes. Astride his white horse "Pomp," purchased after making his first hundred miles on foot, he made his way to the most remote corners of the state, seeking chroniclers of local events or old people who could tell him of incidents of pioneer life. Disarmingly genial, he never records difficulty in securing information. Austere John Sherman talked to him as freely as did the lonely farmer in the "black swamp" country. He devoted more than a year to gathering his materials—a figure of universal interest, astride "Pomp" carrying his pencils and papers in saddlebags, or sitting in a town square sketching a courthouse or main street. In Feb. 1847, he returned to New Haven to prepare the work for publication. It appeared the following September, a volume of 581 pages with the imprint, Cincinnati: Derby, Bradley & Co., 1847. Later printings with some revisions and additions followed in 1848, 1849, 1850, 1851, 1854, 1857, 1858, and 1875. The names of various printers appear on the title pages of these editions. With the *Collections* out of the way, Howe married Frances A. Tuttle of New Haven and settled in Cincinnati. Here he built up a prosperous business, compiling, publishing, and distributing through canvassers works of travel and history. In 1856 he began a work, planned for several volumes, which he expected to be the most important of his life—a history of the United States following the plan of his state histories. Into this venture went five years of labor, all of his savings, and considerable borrowed money. The first volume appeared almost simultaneously with the fall of Fort Sumter. The venture was a financial failure, and Howe's business was wiped out. During his remaining years in Cincinnati he managed to struggle along by republishing some of his earlier books and by compiling *Times of the Rebellion in the West.* In 1877 he gave up the struggle and returned with his family to New Haven. While he was still in Cincinnati and after he had returned to the East, many friends urged him to revise and bring up to date his *Historical Collections of Ohio.* The idea was attractive, but the urge was lacking. Finally, in the summer of 1885, he realized that it was now or never as his seventieth birthday was not far off. When his decision became known in Ohio, letters of encouragement came to him from all parts of the state. President Hayes invited him to his Fremont home, where in October he spent two weeks planning his second tour. Again he covered the state, this time by rail instead of horse and equipped with a camera instead of sketching-pencils. He finished his field work in March, 1887. Two years were required to put the accumulated material into shape for printing. The first volume of the appropriately named "Centennial Edition" appeared in 1889. Though it was favorably received, sales were disappointingly small. Receipts did not meet his financial obligations, much less provide the funds to continue. But friends everywhere rallied in support of a bill to authorize the purchase by the state of 1,200 copies for free distribution. The $12,000 thus provided enabled him to proceed, and in 1891 after six years of work, the book was completed in three quarto volumes instead of the projected two. Usually, however, the second and third volumes were bound together; the three separate volumes, which are now rare, were apparently reserved for original subscribers. Howe's financial difficulties, however, were not resolved. New sales were poor. Free distribution of 1,200 copies by the state, though it had tided him over earlier difficulties, eventually hurt further sales, as everywhere a repetition of free distribution was hoped for. After making every effort to raise money and mortgaging all his resources, he was still $14,000 in debt. So, at the age of 75, Henry Howe set out to sell his book personally in the larger cities; but again sales were disappointing. His death in Columbus brought his struggles to an end. A petition, joined in by hundreds, including five men who had served as governor of Ohio, resulted in legislative action to purchase the copyright and plates for $20,000. The widow was thus enabled to save her home and to clear a substantial portion of her husband's debts. The remainder was in time met by his son, Frank. And so this famous work became a state publication. Successive legislatures authorized printings of from 4,000 to 17,000 two-volume sets for distribution to schools, libraries, and historical societies. Legislators also gave them to individuals as a kind of patronage. The last edition was in 1908, by which time a saturation point apparently had been reached. The commonness of the book and its poor bindings, which were soon ruined, resulted in a loss of prestige. Yet for many of those who received it, the work was the first introduction to the history of their state and to events of note in their own county. Even today, it is a fascinating book for the general reader and a valuable source-book for the historian. Ohio owes more to Henry Howe than to any other man for gathering and preserving its varied and rich local history.

Carl Vitz

Historical Collections of the State of New York . . ., (with John W. Barber), New York, 1841.
Historical Collections of the State of New Jersey . . ., (with John W. Barber), New York, 1844.
Memoirs of the Most Eminent American Mechanics . . ., New York, 1844.
Historical Collections of Virginia . . ., Charleston, S. C., 1845.
Historical Collections of Ohio . . ., Cincinnati, 1847.
Historical Collections of the Great West . . ., 2 vols. in 1, Cincinnati, 1851.
The Travels and Adventures of Celebrated Travelers in the Principal Countries of the Globe . . ., Cincinnati, 1854.
Life and Death on the Ocean: A Collection of Extraordinary Adventures . . ., Cincinnati, 1855.
Adventures and Achievements of Americans . . ., Cincinnati, 1859.
Our Whole Country . . ., (with John W. Barber), 2 vols., Cincinnati, 1861.
The Loyal West in the Times of the Rebellion . . ., (with John W. Barber), Cincinnati, 1865.
The Times of the Rebellion in the West . . ., Cincinnati, 1867.
Odds and Ends, Containing Queer Happenings to Men and Things of Our Time . . ., (Pseud., Dr. Alate Wideawake), Cincinnati, 1868.
Over the World . . ., Philadelphia, 1883.
Historical Collections of Ohio . . ., 3 vols., Columbus, 1889–91.

HOWE, HERBERT ALONZO (Nov. 22, 1858–Nov. 2, 1926), astronomer, born in Brockport, N. Y., graduated from Chicago University in 1875 and in November of that year came to Cincinnati, where he worked at the Cincinnati Observatory until 1880. A breakdown in health induced him to move to Denver, Colo., where he distinguished himself in the field of astronomy. Most of his publications were technical, but he published one popular work: *A Study of the Sky,* Meadville, Pa., 1896.

HOWELL, JOSEPH MORTON (March 17, 1863–Dec. 27, 1937), physician, was born in Uniopolis, Auglaize County. In 1896 he began practicing medicine in Dayton. In 1922 President Harding named him the first United States minister to Egypt. The literary result of his diplomatic service was a volume that the British banned from Egyptian bookstores: *Egypt's Past, Present, and Future,* Dayton, [1929]. WWW 1

HOWELLS, WILLIAM COOPER (1807–Aug. 29, 1894), father of William Dean Howells and Annie T. Fréchette (qq.v.), was born in Hay, Wales, but was brought to America when he was a year old. His father, a converted Quaker, lived for brief periods in Massachusetts, New York, and Virginia before coming to Ohio in 1813. William grew up in Steubenville and on a farm in Harrison County. He learned the printing trade in Wheeling, Va., and there married Mary Dean in 1831. He apparently resented the privations of his boyhood imposed on him by his father's impractical nature. Despite his ambition, however, he was even more mobile than his father. He worked as a printer for brief periods in St. Clairsville, Mount Pleasant, Chillicothe, Cincinnati, and Martinsville (Martin's Ferry). In 1834 while working on the *Scioto Gazette* in Chillicothe, he was converted to the Swedenborgian faith. His numerous moves were partly due to his extreme abolitionist views. He remained in Hamilton, 1840–49, then spent a year and a half in Dayton, in 1851 attempted to start a paper mill near Xenia, went to Columbus in 1851, and in 1852 moved to Ashtabula and thence to Jefferson. With the coming of the Civil War, his views on slavery won him belated respect, and in 1864 he was elected to the state senate. In 1874 his son, William Dean, procured for him a post as consul at Quebec; he was later transferred to Toronto and resigned in 1883. Besides the posthumous volume listed below, he published a map of Ohio in 1843 and at least two lectures in pamphlet form.

Recollections of Life in Ohio, from 1813 to 1840, Cincinnati, 1895.

HOWELLS, WILLIAM DEAN (March 1, 1837–May 11, 1920), was born in Martin's Ferry, Belmont County. Martin's Ferry looks across the wide river to the West Virginia hills. Now a coal and steel town, it began as a trading station when the pioneer Zane family established a ferry service there. When Ebenezer Martin bought the ferry, sending Ohio hogs, sheep, and cattle across the river to Eastern markets, the settlement took his name. He was still steering his blunt boat across the river when William Dean Howells was born there in 1837. The only literary influence in the raw little river town was the child's father, William Cooper Howells (q.v.). An idealist with a love of printer's ink and political dispute, he had also the restless optimism of a frontiersman. He was a Quaker of Welsh descent; Howells' mother was Irish and Pennsylvania German. Though there were ten to provide for at the family table, the elder Howells followed the precarious trade of frontier journalism, crusading for abolition and the Free Soil Party. At Martin's Ferry he established a Free Soil magazine, which promptly failed. More lasting was the small brick house he built with his own ink-stained hands, and in that house his second son, William Dean, was born. In these years the tide of settlement was moving west, and the Howells family moved with it. In 1840 they settled in Hamilton, a town in the Miami Valley, twenty miles above Cincinnati. The journey by boat was young Howells' first clear memory, and he recalled in Hamilton frequent visits from his uncles, who were seasoned Ohio River boatmen. Friends of the elder Howells lent him money to buy a Whig newspaper, which he published for the next eight years. So Hamilton was the scene of William Dean Howells' boyhood, and he remembered it with vividness and affection all his life. The town of Hamilton had begun as a frontier fort, a link in the chain of strongholds Anthony Wayne used in his campaign of 1793–94. After the Indian wars it became a center of trade and settlement, and when the first segment of the Miami and Erie Canal was opened in 1827 the town began to grow. The busy life of the wharf basin, the political torchlight parades through the streets, the wooded islands in the Miami River, all remained fresh in Howells' memory when he wrote *A Boy's Town* many years later. Here he received his scanty schooling, which ended when he was twelve. More important than the schoolroom was his work in his father's print shop and the books on his father's shelves. In the richest of his reminiscent essays, "The Country Printer"—from *Impressions and Experiences* (1896)—he wrote: "The printing office was mainly my school." Like another sunburned Western boy, in another river town, he learned more from the pressroom than the classroom. Years later Howells and Mark Twain compared their experience as printer boys in the frontier West. After nine years in Hamilton the Howells family moved to Dayton, where for about two years the elder Howells published a daily newspaper. Young Howells delivered papers at four a.m. and often was setting type at midnight. When the paper failed, the family went to live in a log cabin on the Little Miami River in Greene County, where the ex-editor tried to convert a gristmill to the manufacture of paper. That experiment failed, but forty years later it provided material for a cheerful and charming book, *My Year in a Log Cabin.* The family next moved to northern Ohio, where they established newspapers at Ashtabula and Jefferson. From his later position of distance and achievement, Howells recalled his semifrontier boyhood with a warmth he did not feel in his growing years. He disliked the coarseness of rustic life and longed for genteel society and refinement. His instincts and interests pointed not to the frontier West but toward New England with its colonial past and its love of learning. He was an undersized youth, with more taste for poetry than for possum-hunting. Earnest, ambitious, intellectually curious, he felt more at home with older people than with companions of his own years. His strongest feelings were his "literary passions"—a love of Goldsmith, Cervantes, Irving, Chaucer, Shakespeare, Heine. He read avidly the books on his father's shelves and laboriously studied Latin, German, and Spanish. In German he was helped by a bookbinder, on whom he drew years later for the character of Lindau in *A Hazard of New Fortunes.* In 1856, aged nineteen, Howells went to the Ohio capital to write political correspondence for a few country papers. After a brief interval in Cincinnati as a reporter on the Cincinnati *Gazette,* he was back in Columbus writing for the *Ohio State Journal.* This looked like the beginning of a career, but Howells was not a newspaperman at heart. He was earnestly writing poems, a few of which were published in the newly established *Atlantic Monthly.* In 1860 he became joint-author with his roommate, John J. Piatt (q.v.), of a slender volume of poems. In that year he made a pilgrimage to New England and was generously received by Lowell, Holmes, and Hawthorne. When he returned to Ohio, his hopes were centered in Boston. The *Ohio State Journal* was a vigorous newspaper on the side of the young and growing Republican Party. When Abraham Lincoln was nominated for the Presidency, the *Journal's* young editorial writer was commissioned to write a life of Lincoln. Howells assumed the task without much interest. He sent a friend, James Quay Howard (q.v.), to Springfield to gather information on the prairie lawyer (years later he confessed: "I missed the greatest chance of my life.") and he quickly wrote *The Life of Abraham Lincoln* (1860), a rather perfunctory book. Yet it caused a turning point in Howells' life. After Lincoln's election the Ohio Republicans recommended Howells for a consular post. President Lincoln named him U. S. consul at Venice. So the Ohio youth embarked for an ancient and splendid city. Four happy and growing years Howells spent in Italy. In 1862, while on vacation in Paris, he married Eleanor Mead of Brattleboro, Vt., whom he had previously met in Columbus. Consular duties were light, and Howells found time to read, to study languages, to travel, and to write his pleasant observations in *Venetian Life* (1866) and *Italian Journeys* (1867). When he returned to the United States in 1865, he was a cultured and cosmopolitan man. After a brief association with the *Nation,* he was appointed in 1866 assistant editor of the *Atlantic Monthly.* Five years later he became editor-in-chief, a post he held for ten years. Through reading Tolstoy and Balzac, Howells had become convinced that fiction should portray not remote and romantic experience but real and familiar life. That conviction soon began to shape his own writing. His first narrative, *Their Wedding Journey* (1872), is a quiet record of a wedding trip on the St. Lawrence. *A Chance Acquaintance* (1873) uses the same background but presents a personal problem and a sustained theme. The theme is of social adjustment—a simple youth abruptly thrust into sophisticated society. This was Howells' own experience, and it provided, in many variations, the situations for many of his novels. In this first example of the theme, Howells' protagonist is an American girl, innocent and naive, whose father (like the elder Howells) was a Free Soil editor in the Middle West. Howells rooted his realism in personal memory and reflection. Further use of his own experience appears in *A Foregone Conclusion* (1875), *The Lady of the Aroostook* (1879), and *A Fearful Responsibility* (1881); all employ a Venetian background and draw comparisons between American and Italian character. In 1881 Howells resigned from the *Atlantic.* Now he began a series of novels concerned with ethical problems. *A Modern Instance* (1882) shows a shrewd and unscrupulous young journalist becoming alienated from his idealistic wife; it is the first American novel to use divorce as a significant theme. *The Rise of Silas Lapham* (1885) is a solid and impressive study of a self-made man who grows in character while failing in business. This novel, using Howells' knowledge of Boston society and his understanding of rural character, has achieved a permanent place in American fiction. *Indian Summer* (1886) is a deft study of a middle-aged widow in a romantic dilemma; its scene is Italy. *April Hopes* (1888) is a story of young love in New England, where a Puritan conscience with its ironclad code "makes no allowance for human nature." In 1886 Howells moved to New York and became a member of the editorial staff of *Harper's Magazine.* The metropolis, with its extremes of wealth and poverty, made him aware of economic problems. Events in the late 1880s forced his attention to industrial strife. The New York traction strike, the Haymarket Riots in Chicago, and his reading of Tolstoy and Henry George turned Howells to socialism and brought new themes into his novels. *Annie Kilburn* (1889) contrasts the "haves" and "have nots" in an industrial community. *A Hazard of New Fortunes* (1890) pictures a cross-section of New York society in a crisis brought on by a strike of streetcar workers. *A Traveler from Altruria* (1894) describes a Utopian republic founded on principles of altruism. *Through the Eye of the Needle* (1907) shows the Utopian republic as a society without money and therefore without waste, greed, or crime. Later novels in Howells' older style include *The Landlord at Lion's Head* (1897), with its robust characterization of the young New Englander Jeff Durgin, and *The Kentons* (1902), a story of an Ohio family who go to Europe. Of Ohio, his home for the first 24 years of his life, Howells wrote nothing until he had moved from New England to New York. His first Ohio scene appears in *A Hazard of New Fortunes;* though this is a New York novel, it describes the natural gas boom in northwestern Ohio and the mushroom growth of the town of Moffitt (Findlay) to account for the fortune of the character Dryfoos. The next year saw publication of *A Boy's Town,* his record of boyhood years in Hamilton. In 1893 appeared *My Year in a Log Cabin. The Coast of Bohemia* (1893) contains a brief but vivid picture of an Ohio county fair, and in *The Kentons* the opening Ohio scene soon gives way to New York and Europe. In 1897 appeared *Stories of Ohio,* a book for children. *New Leaf Mills* (1913) is based on the experience recalled in *My Year in a Log Cabin. The Leatherwood God* (1916) is a tale of religious fanaticism in the back country near Martin's Ferry in the 1820s.

Howells was the most productive and versatile writer of his time. His work includes short stories, poems, novels, dramas, travelogues, volumes of criticism and autobiography. For the last thirty years of his life he was the dominant figure in American letters. He gave valuable counsel and encouragement to such iconoclastic young realists as Crane, Garland, Norris, and Herrick. He received many honors and was chosen the first president of the American Academy of Arts and Letters. Howells' literary convictions are summed up in *Criticism and Fiction* (1891). He stressed the importance of common experience and the truthful rendering of motives and feelings. "Such beauty and such grandeur as we have is common beauty, common grandeur. . . . These conditions invite the artist to the study and appreciation of the common. . . . The arts must become democratic, and then we shall have the expression of America in art." He believed that art must serve morality and that it should provide an evaluation of character and experience. By the time of Howells' death, realism was firmly established in American fiction. Since then many novelists have gone further in portrayal of real experience, of economic strife, of physical passions, of psychological conflicts. Howells was a "reticent realist," restrained by the conventions of his time and by his own propriety and discretion. But he marked out the path that twentieth-century fiction has followed. The bibliography below includes only books. A complete list of his writings can be found in *A Bibliography of William Dean Howells,* compiled by William M. Gibson and George Arms, New York, 1948.

Walter Havighurst

Lives and Speeches of Abraham Lincoln and Hannibal Hamlin, (with John L. Hayes), Columbus, 1860.

Poems of Two Friends, (with John James Piatt), Columbus, 1860.

Venetian Life, London, 1866.

Italian Journeys, New York, 1867.

No Love Lost, a Romance of Travel, New York, 1869.

Suburban Sketches, Boston, 1871.

Their Wedding Journey, Boston, 1872.

A Chance Acquaintance, Boston, 1873.

Poems, Boston, 1873.

A Foregone Conclusion, Boston, 1875.

A Day's Pleasure, Boston, 1876.

The Parlor Car. Farce, Boston, 1876.

Sketch of the Life and Character of Rutherford B. Hayes . . . , New York, 1876.

A Counterfeit Presentment. Comedy, Boston, 1877.

Out of the Question. A Comedy, Boston, 1877.

The Lady of the Aroostook, Boston, 1879.

The Undiscovered Country, Boston, 1880.

Doctor Breen's Practice. A Novel, Boston, 1881.

A Fearful Responsibility and Other Stories, Boston, 1881.

A Modern Instance. A Novel, Boston, 1882.

The Sleeping Car. A Farce, Boston, 1883.

A Woman's Reason. A Novel, Boston, 1883.

A Little Girl among the Old Masters, Boston, 1884.

Niagara Revisited, Chicago, 1884.

The Register. Farce, Boston, 1884.

Three Villages, Boston, 1884.

The Elevator. Farce, Boston, 1885.

The Rise of Silas Lapham, Boston, 1885.

The Garroters. Farce, New York, 1886.

Indian Summer, Boston, 1886.

Tuscan Cities, Boston, 1886.

The Minister's Charge; Or, the Apprenticeship of Lemuel Barker, Boston, 1887.

Modern Italian Poets, Essays and Versions, New York, 1887.

April Hopes, New York, 1888.

A Sea Change; Or, Love's Stowaway . . . , Boston, 1888.

Annie Kilburn. A Novel, New York, 1889.

The Mouse-trap and Other Farces, New York, 1889.

A Boy's Town . . . , New York, 1890.

A Hazard of New Fortunes. A Novel, New York, 1890.

The Shadow of a Dream. A Story, New York, 1890.

Criticism and Fiction, New York, 1891.

The Albany Depot. Farce, New York, 1892.

An Imperative Duty. A Novel, New York, 1892.

A Letter of Introduction. Farce, New York, 1892.

A Little Swiss Sojourn, New York, 1892.

The Quality of Mercy. A Novel, New York, 1892.

Christmas Every Day and Other Stories Told for Children, New York, 1893.

The Coast of Bohemia. A Novel, New York, 1893.

Evening Dress. Farce, New York, 1893.

My Year in a Log Cabin, New York, 1893.

The Unexpected Guests. A Farce, New York, 1893.

The World of Chance. A Novel, New York, 1893.

A Likely Story. Farce, New York, 1894.

A Traveler from Altruria. Romance, New York, 1894.

My Literary Passions, New York, 1895.

Stops of Various Quills, New York, 1895.

The Day of Their Wedding. A Novel, New York, 1896.
Impressions and Experiences, New York, 1896.
A Parting and a Meeting. Story, New York, 1896.
The Landlord at Lion's Head. A Novel, New York, 1897.
An Open-eyed Conspiracy; An Idyl of Saratoga, New York, 1897.
A Previous Engagement. Comedy, New York, 1897.
Stories of Ohio, New York, 1897.
The Story of a Play. A Novel, New York, 1898.
Ragged Lady. A Novel, New York, 1899.
Their Silver Wedding Journey, 2 vols., New York, 1899.
Bride Roses. A Scene, Boston, 1900.
An Indian Giver. A Comedy, Boston, 1900.
Literary Friends and Acquaintance . . . , New York, 1900.
Room Forty-five. A Farce, Boston, 1900.
The Smoking Car. A Farce, Boston, 1900.
Heroines of Fiction, 2 vols., New York, 1901.
A Pair of Patient Lovers, New York, 1901.
The Flight of Pony Baker: A Boy's Town Story, New York, 1902.
The Kentons. A Novel, New York, 1902.
Literature and Life. Studies, New York, 1902.
Letters Home, New York, 1903.
Questionable Shapes, New York, 1903.
The Son of Royal Langbrith. A Novel, New York, 1904.
Miss Bellard's Inspiration. A Novel, New York, 1905.
Certain Delightful English Towns . . . , New York, 1906.
London Films, New York, 1906.
Between the Dark and the Daylight. Romances, New York, 1907.
The Mulberries in Pay's Garden, Cincinnati, [1907].
Through the Eye of the Needle. A Romance, New York, 1907.
Fennel and Rue. A Novel, New York, 1908.
Roman Holidays and Others, New York, 1908.
The Mother and the Father. Dramatic Passages, New York, 1909.
Seven English Cities, New York, 1909.
Imaginary Interviews, New York, 1910.
My Mark Twain. Reminiscences and Criticisms, New York, 1910.
Parting Friends. A Farce, New York, 1911.
Familiar Spanish Travels, New York, 1913.
New Leaf Mills. A Chronicle, New York, 1913.
The Seen and Unseen at Stratford-on-Avon, New York, 1914.
The Daughter of the Storage and Other Things in Prose and Verse, New York, [1916].
The Leatherwood God, New York, 1916.
Years of My Youth, New York, [1916].
The Vacation of the Kelwyns . . . , New York, [1920].
Eighty Years and After, [New York], 1921.
Mrs. Farrell, New York, [1921].

HOWENSTEIN, EMILY GUILLON FULLER. See Emily G. Fuller.

HOWENSTINE, E. JAY, JR. (Aug. 12, 1914–), economist, was born in Stanford, Ky., but his family moved to northern Ohio the year after his birth. He graduated from Elyria High School in 1932, Miami University in 1934, and Ohio State University (Ph.D.) in 1942. After teaching for two years at Park College, Mo., he joined the U. S. Bureau of Agricultural Economics in 1944. He now lives in Geneva, Switzerland. His writings include *The Economics of Demobilization,* [Washington, D. C., 1944].

HOWER, FRANK LESLIE (Feb. 17, 1903–), was born in Rawson, Hancock County, and attended the schools of that community. He joined the navy at the age of seventeen. Now retired, he lives in Los Angeles. He has published considerable fiction, some of it under the pen name Jack Rawson, e.g., *Brass Buttons,* Philadelphia, [1941].

HOWISON, GEORGE HOLMES (Nov. 29, 1834–Dec. 31, 1916), educator, born in Montgomery County, Md., was educated in Ohio, graduating from Marietta College in 1852 and Lane Seminary in 1855. He spent several years teaching in secondary schools of Ohio and Massachusetts before going to Washington University, St. Louis, where his interests centered on philosophy. He also taught at Harvard University, the University of California, and other schools. His most important work was *The Limits of Evolution . . . ,* New York, 1901. WWW 1

HOWLAND, CHARLES ROSCOE (Feb. 16, 1871–Sept. 21, 1946), army officer, was born in Jefferson, Ashtabula County. He attended Oberlin College for one year and graduated from the U. S. Military Academy in 1895. After retiring from the army as a brigadier general in 1935, he lived in Cleveland. His major literary work was *A Military History of the World War,* Fort Leavenworth, Kan., 1923. WWW 2

HOYT, ELIZABETH ORPHA (Dec. 7, 1834–?), was born in Athens, Athens County. She attended Ohio University and taught mathematics in Worthington Female Seminary, 1851–53. In 1854 she married John Wesley Hoyt (q.v.). They moved to Wisconsin in 1857. According to Coggeshall, she wrote "several little books for children," but only one such title has been discovered.

Little George and His Hatchet, Madison, [Wis.], 1858.

The Horticultural Embellishment of Schoolhouse Grounds, Madison, Wis., 1860.

HOYT, JAMES HUMPHREY (Nov. 10, 1852–March 21, 1917), lawyer, younger brother of Wayland Hoyt (q.v.), was born in Cleveland, Cuyahoga County. He graduated from Brown University in 1874, studied law at Harvard University, and afterward practiced in Cleveland. His only publication was a posthumous collection, privately printed: *Selections from the Speeches and Papers of James Humphrey Hoyt,* Cleveland, 1922. WWW 1

HOYT, JAMES MADISON (Jan. 16, 1815–April 21, 1895), father of James Humphrey Hoyt, Wayland Hoyt, and Lydia Hoyt Painter (qq.v.), was born in Utica, N. Y., and graduated from Hamilton College in 1834. He studied law in Utica and then in the Cleveland firm of Andrews and Foot. He was admitted to partnership in 1837 but retired from practice in 1853 to devote his time to real estate. He was a prominent citizen of Cleveland and was an active member of the Baptist Church, serving for over twenty years as president of the Ohio Baptist State Convention. His one book is an account of a European tour made in 1871 in the company of his son, Wayland Hoyt.

Glances on the Wing at Foreign Lands, Cleveland, 1872.

HOYT, JOHN WESLEY (Oct. 21, 1831–May 23, 1912), educator, was born in Franklin County. After graduating from Ohio Wesleyan University in 1849, he attended Cincinnati Law School and Ohio Medical College. He was professor of chemistry and medical jurisprudence at the Eclectic Institute, 1853–56. In 1857 he went to Wisconsin, where he published the *Wisconsin Farmer and Northeastern Cultivator* until 1867 and became a prominent figure in the agricultural and educational circles of that state. He is said to have been instrumental in reorganizing Wisconsin State University and in obtaining large additions to the endowment funds. He was one of the founders of the Republican Party, and President Hayes appointed him governor of Wyoming Territory, in which capacity he served from 1878 until 1882. The condition of his health forced him to move to California. In 1887 he had a bill before Congress for a National University to be endowed by the government, and in this same year he returned to Wyoming as the president of the State University, where he served until 1890. Besides the titles below, some of his speeches and educational reports were published.

Resources of Wisconsin, [Madison, Wis.?], 1860.

Studies in Civil Service . . . , New York, [1884].

Distinctive Feature of the Proposed University of the United States . . . , [Washington, D. C. 1887].

HOYT, WAYLAND (Feb. 18, 1838–Sept. 28, 1910), clergyman, was born in Cleveland, Cuyahoga County. He graduated from Brown University in 1860 and Rochester Theological Seminary in 1863. Ordained to the Baptist ministry in 1863, he served churches in Massachusetts, Ohio, New York, Pennsylvania, and Minnesota. He also taught for a time at Temple University. His death occurred in Salem, Mass.

Saturday Afternoon . . . , Philadelphia, [1889].

Walks and Talks with Charles H. Spurgeon, Philadelphia, [1892].

For Shine and Shade; Short Essays in Practical Religion, Philadelphia, [1899].

Helps Upward, Boston, [1899].

Home Ideals, Philadelphia, 1904.

The Teaching of Jesus Concerning His Own Person, New York [1907].

Some of the Reasons Why I Cannot Accept the Results of the Destructive Criticism of the Old Testament, Philadelphia, [1908].

HOYT, WILBUR FRANKLIN (March 13, 1864–June 25, 1930), educator, was born in Reedsville, Meigs County. He graduated from Ohio Wesleyan University in 1895. He taught science in several Midwestern colleges and from 1910 until his death was professor of physical science at Nebraska State Teachers College, Peru, Neb. Besides several chemistry textbooks and manuals, he wrote a "philosophy of science," *Science and Life . . . ,* [Peru, Neb.], 1927. WWW 1

HUBBARD, FRANK McKINNEY (Kin) (Sept. 1, 1868–Dec. 26, 1930), though commonly thought of as a Hoosier since his work was based on Indiana, where he lived and worked for nearly forty years, was born in Bellefontaine, Logan County. His parents, Thomas and Sarah Jane (Miller) Hubbard, and most of their six children, of whom Kin was the youngest, appear to have been "characters" with amiable eccentricities. Kin went no further in school than the seventh grade and then dropped out. Various jobs followed, including four years as a post office clerk and a brief stay in an art school in Detroit, where he had gone to develop his not inconsiderable drawing talent. Next came three years as a staff artist on the Indianapolis *News* and then more brief and unimportant jobs in one place after another. All this time Hubbard was stage-struck and fond of loud clothes—but shy and backward with girls. In 1899, at the age of 31, he went back to Indianapolis, where he was to spend the rest of his life. The time and the place were congenial to him. Indiana's finest crop of literary figures was in bloom: Booth Tarkington, Charles Major, George Ade, George Barr McCutcheon, James Whitcomb Riley, and Meredith Nicholson all became his friends. Among the newspapermen he associated with were several destined to national prominence: Kent Cooper, Roy Howard, Mark Thistlethwaite, Lowell Mellett, and Claude G. Bowers. Hubbard's work on the *News* consisted for the first three years of funny sketches and caricatures of celebrities at political and other gatherings. In 1904 he started drawing a rustic character, whom he named Abe Martin, with a humorous comment or two beneath the sketch. In time the character became the chinless loafer of subsequent fame, in a column-wide drawing; and the comments, always two unrelated short sentences, became the best-known part of the work. It was as a commentator on human nature and the passing scene, a homespun cracker-barrel philosopher, that Hubbard came into his own. Success, when it arrived, came in full measure, and he soon could afford to take a wife. He married Josephine Jackson in 1905; they had a son and a daughter who reached maturity and two boys who died in infancy. In the year of his marriage he brought out some of his work in book form, as he continued to do profitably until his death. Representative titles include *Abe Martin, of Brown County, Indiana,* Indianapolis, [1907]; *Abe Martin on Things in General,* Indianapolis, [1925]; *Abe Martin, Hoss Sense and Nonsense,* Indianapolis, [1926]; and *Abe Martin's Town Pump,* Indianapolis, [1930]. Around 1910 his work began to be syndicated, and in time some 200 papers all over the country were using it. He became moderately wealthy. His eccentricities were endless—and usually appealing: on a world cruise he kept his watch always on Indianapolis time, and historical backgrounds and native customs failed to interest him; he refused to tell his age; he enjoyed disagreeing with what other people said; he was bored by routine and would not cut his bond coupons. His stock character, Abe Martin, and Abe's various friends who appeared now and then were all supposed to live in Brown County, Indiana, a rugged, wooded section, perhaps the most backward and certainly the most inaccessible part of the state. Here the State of Indiana established the Brown County State Park two years after Hubbard's death, in part as a memorial to him and to the characters he had created. A few years later, his name was added to the Ohio Journalism Hall of Fame. Hubbard died of a heart attack. His funeral services were carried on a radio network, perhaps the first time this had been done. Americans are prone to pay their newspaper humorists well while they are alive and forget them after they are dead. Kin Hubbard, however, eccentric in this as in many other respects, was both well rewarded during his lifetime and then republished in newspapers for years after his death. His humor is still relished by many and is still being syndicated. Typical of his humor are the following specimens:

I got a letter from Rushville sayin' thet there wuz a Uncle Tom's Cabin troupe up ther last week an' th' dogs were good but they had poor support.

Elgin Tyler is the oddest feller. He'll take a drink o' liquor an' mebby he wunt take another for ten or fifteen minutes.

Newt Plum's son-in-law says he never saved a blamed cent until after his wife had quarreled with ever' dressmaker in town.

Th' weddin' last evenin' o' Miss Princess Bud an' Mr. Mingo Bain wuz th' most successful o' th' season, excellin' all former efforts by two pickle dishes.

Th' husband that has time t' git his breakfast downtown is liable t' be late for supper.

Nothin' upsets a woman like somebuddy gittin' married she didn't even know had a beau.

It's no disgrace t' be poor, but it might as well be.

Mr. Lemmie Peters got B-plus in salad makin' at th' state pharmacy board examination recently.

When you once git started it takes an awful strong will power t' keep from runnin' th' scale on a roastin' ear without stoppin'.

A feller with long whiskers hates t' carry a baby.

While goin' after fishin' worms in a field where his wife wuz plowin' Tipton Bud found a Indian dart.

If a woman's lips are thin an' droop at th' corners it's a sign her husband belongs t' all th' lodges he kin git into.

Walter Rumsey Marvin

HUBBARD, LUCIUS LEE (Aug. 7, 1849–Aug. 3, 1933), was born in Cincinnati, Hamilton County. After graduating from Harvard Law School in 1875, he was admitted to the Massachusetts bar. He later earned a doctorate at the University of Bonn in 1886. In 1893 he became state geologist of Michigan and served in that capacity until 1899. He was a notable bibliophile and wrote numerous papers on bibliographical matters. He became regent of the University of Michigan in 1911.

Summer Vacations at Moosehead Lake and Vicinity . . . , Boston, 1879.

Woods and Lakes of Maine: A Trip from Moosehead Lake to New Brunswick in a Birch Bark Canoe . . . , Boston, 1884.

The University of Michigan—Its Origin, Growth, and Principles of Government, Ann Arbor, 1923.

HUBBARD-KERNAN, WILL (1845–Jan. 28, 1905), journalist, was born in Bellefontaine, Logan County, the son of James Kernan. His mother was the sister of William and Thomas Hubbard, well-known Ohio newspapermen; the latter was the father of Frank McKinney "Kin" Hubbard (q.v.). He attended local schools and graduated from the University of Michigan in 1868. Will became an itinerant newspaperman whose meanderings took him from New York to the Dakotas and from Minneapolis to Okolona, Miss. His death occurred in Memphis, Tenn. Perhaps the author of the florid biographical foreword to *The Flaming Meteor* has his tongue in his cheek when he wrote: "After Edgar Allan Poe, the most brilliant poetic genius this country has produced, comes Will Hubbard-Kernan."

The Flaming Meteor. Poetical Works, Chicago, 1892.

HUBBART, HENRY CLYDE (April 14, 1882–), educator, born in Carthage, Mo., was a member of the Ohio Wesleyan University history department, 1917–52; since his retirement he has continued to live in Delaware. He wrote *Ohio Wesleyan's First Hundred Years,* Delaware, [1943]. WW 30

HUBBELL, GEORGE ALLEN (Aug. 15, 1862–Sept. 28, 1943), educator, was born in Springfield, Clark County. He taught school, 1881–85 and 1887–88, to finance his education at Antioch College, where he graduated in 1890; he earned his Ph.D. at Columbia University. He served on the Antioch College faculty, 1893–98, and also taught at other colleges, and was president of Lincoln Memorial University, Tenn., 1910–22. He died in Asheville, N. C., and is buried in Knoxville, Tenn. He published textbooks and a biography: *Horace Mann, Educator, Patriot and Reformer* . . . , Philadephia, 1910. WW 13

HUBERICH, CHARLES HENRY (Feb. 18, 1877–June 18, 1945), educator and lawyer, was born in Toledo, Lucas County. He graduated from the University of Texas in 1897, was admitted to the bar in 1898, and afterward studied at Yale University and in German universities. He taught at the University of Texas, Stanford University, and the University of Wisconsin. He has written professional articles and legal works, and *The Political and Legislative History of Liberia* . . . , 2 vols., New York, 1947. WWW 2

HUBERT, PHILIP GENGEMBRE (Jan. 9, 1852–Jan. 3, 1925), journalist, was born in Cincinnati, Hamilton County. He was educated in private schools in Boston and Paris and afterward was on the staff of the New York *Evening Post* and later on the New York *Herald.*

Liberty and a Living . . . , New York, 1889.

Inventors, New York, 1893.

The Stage as a Career, New York, 1900.

The Merchants' National Bank of the City of New York; A History . . . , New York, 1903.

HUDDILSTON, JOHN HOMER (Feb. 9, 1869–July 26, 1956), educator, was born in Cleveland, Cuyahoga County. He graduated from Baldwin University in 1890 and was an instructor there from 1890 to 1892. He did graduate work at Harvard University and in European universities, taking his Ph.D. at the University of Munich in 1897. He taught Greek, archaeology, and art history at the University of Maine from 1899 until his retirement in 1942. Besides the titles below, he published a textbook in New Testament Greek.

Greek Tragedy in the Light of Vase Paintings, New York, 1898.

Lessons from Greek Pottery . . . , New York, 1902.

HUDSON, JAMES FAIRCHILD (May 12, 1846–May 2, 1915), journalist, was born in Oberlin, Lorain County. After graduating from Oberlin College in 1867, he worked on a number of newspapers, including the Toledo *Blade,* the Youngstown *Register,* and the Pittsburgh *Commercial-Gazette.*

The Railways and the Republic, New York, 1886.

A Silver Symposium: Being an Analysis of the Money Issue . . . , Pittsburgh, Pa., 1896.

HUDSON, JAY WILLIAM (March 12, 1874–May 11, 1958), educator and lecturer, was born in Cleveland, Cuyahoga County. After studying at Hiram College and Oberlin College, he graduated from the University of California in 1905 and Harvard University (Ph.D.) in 1908. After serving in several universities, he joined the University of Missouri philosophy faculty, where he taught from 1908 until his retirement in 1944. He published novels and books on religion and education, e.g., *The College and New America,* New York, 1920. WWW 3

HUDSON, THOMSON JAY (Feb. 22, 1834–May 26, 1903), author and lecturer, was born in Windham, Portage County. He grew up on his father's farm, attended the local academy, and received private tutoring. Although his father intended him for the ministry, he preferred law and was admitted to the bar in 1857, then practiced for three years in Mansfield. From 1860 to 1886 he was a journalist in Michigan and Washington, D. C. He was employed by the U. S. Patent Office in 1880 and was chief examiner, 1886–93. His growing interest in psychical phenomena led to the publication of his first book, which was widely read. During the last ten years of his life he lectured and wrote on his theories of suggestion and autosuggestion.

The Law of Psychic Phenomena . . . , Chicago, 1894.

A Scientific Demonstration of the Future Life, Chicago, 1895.

The Divine Pedigree of Man . . . , Chicago, 1899.

The Law of Mental Medicine . . . , Chicago, 1903.

The Evolution of the Soul, and Other Essays, Chicago, 1904.

HUEBNER, FRANCIS CHRISTIAN (Dec. 11, 1869–April 12, 1954), lawyer, was born in Gnadenhutton, Tuscarawas County. After graduating from George Washington University, he was admitted to the Ohio bar in 1896. He was an official in the Post Office Department, Washington, D. C., 1897–1906, and practiced law in Fresno, Calif., 1907–46. He died in California.

The Moravian Missions in Ohio, Washington, D. C., 1898.

Charles Killbuck; An Indian's Story of the Border Wars of the American Revolution, Washington, D. C., 1902.

HUFFMAN, JASPER ABRAHAM (Feb. 28, 1880–), clergyman, born in Elkhart County, Ind., lived in Ohio from 1900 to 1922. He was ordained to the ministry of the Mennonite Brethren in Christ in 1904, graduated from Bonebrake Seminary in 1909, served a church in Dayton, and taught at Bluffton College and Witmarsum Seminary. He later taught at Marion College and Taylor University. He now lives at Winona Lake, Ind. He has written a number of books on religious themes, e.g., *Job a World Example,* New Carlisle, [1914]. WW 28

HUGENTABLER, ROBERT CAMPBELL (Aug. 14, 1862–March 29, 1936), educator, was born in Cincinnati, Hamilton County; but while he was a child, his parents moved to Miamitown, and he spent the remander of his life in that community. He taught country schools around Miamitown and owned a large apiary. He published a collection of poems: *The Resurrection and Other Poems,* Cincinnati, 1913.

HUGGINS, WILLIAM LLOYD (May 14, 1865–May 24, 1941), lawyer, was born on a farm in Highland County. In 1885 he went to Kansas, where he taught school and attended the Normal School of Emporia. While superintendent of schools, Lyons County, Kan., he read law, and he was admitted to the bar in 1897. He practiced in Emporia and also served as presiding judge of the Kansas Court of Industrial Relations, 1920–23. He wrote *Labor and Democracy,* New York, 1922. WWW 1

HUGHES, ADELLA PRENTISS (Mrs. Felix H.) (Nov. 29, 1869–Aug. 23, 1950), was born in Cleveland, Cuyahoga County. She attended Rockwell School in Cleveland and graduated from Vassar College in 1890. She was active in Cleveland musical endeavors for more than fifty years, was a founder of the Cleveland Symphony and its manager for fifteen years, and was instrumental in the building of Severance Hall. An account of her varied endeavors is found in her autobiography: *Music Is My Life,* Cleveland, [1947]. WWW 3

HUGHES, JASPER SEATON (May 9, 1843–May 17, 1926), clergyman, was born in Wilmington, Clinton County. After attending Hiram College and Butler University, he was ordained to the ministry of the Disciples of Christ Church. His Ohio pastorates were Hamilton and Yellow Springs; he also served churches in Indiana, New York, and Michigan. He died in Holland, Mich.

Mystery of the Golden Cloth . . . , Chicago, 1895.

The Seer of Patmos . . . , Indianapolis, 1899.

The Revelation, [Holland, Mich., 1910].

Christianity . . . , Grand Rapids, Mich., 1915.

The King's Trumpet . . . , Holland, Mich., [1921].

HUGHES, RUPERT (Jan. 31, 1872–Sept. 9, 1956), dramatist, novelist, biographer, and musicologist, lived in Missouri, Iowa, Connecticut, New York, and California. His Ohio connection is his attendance at Western Reserve Academy and Western Reserve University, where he earned an A.B. degree in 1892 and an M.A. in 1894. His preparatory school experiences furnished material for two popular novels about a group of athletically minded boys: *The Lakerim Athletic Club,* New York, 1897, and *The Dozen from Lakerim,* New York, 1899.

HUGHES, THOMAS J. (Nov. 19, 1865–Aug. 5, 1934), lawyer, was born in Delaware, Delaware County. He attended Greenville public schools and Ohio Wesleyan University, after which he read law in Greenville. He practiced in the West for a short time, but returned to Greenville, where he practiced until his death. Under the pen name Thomas Jayhews, he wrote a novel: *His Better Self . . . ,* Akron, [1910]. He also wrote on economic and political issues, e.g., *Economic Equity,* Dayton, 1931.

HUGHES, THOMAS LLOYD (Sept. 6, 1806–1896), was born in Denbyshire, Wales. He came to America in 1840 and settled in Oak Hill, Jackson County, where he lived until his death at the age of ninety. He was cashier and secretary of Jefferson Furnace. He wrote a column in the *Standard-Journal* for a number of years, published poems in Welsh, and wrote a life of Christ in Welsh.

Yr Emmanuel . . . , Utica, N. Y., 1882.

HULBERT, ARCHER BUTLER (Jan. 26, 1873–Dec. 24, 1933), educator, born in Bennington, Vt., graduated from Marietta College in 1895, was vice-principal of Putnam Military Academy, Zanesville, 1895–97, and was professor of history at Marietta, 1904–18. A prolific writer, especially on transportation history, he published more than a hundred books, e.g., *The Ohio River; A Course of Empire,* New York, 1906. DAB 21

HULL, ALEXANDER (Sept. 15, 1887–March 4, 1953), musician and educator, was born in Columbus, Franklin County. After graduating from Muskingum College in 1906, he taught voice in Zanesville for a year and afterward served as chairman of the music department, Pacific College, Oreg., 1908–35. He was a composer and also wrote short stories and a novel: *Shep of the Painted Hills,* New York, 1930. WWW 3

HULTMAN, HELEN JOAN (March 1, 1891–), educator, was born in Dayton, Montgomery County. She graduated from Denison University in 1912, taught in West Virginia for a few years, and in 1919 began teaching English at Stivers High School, Dayton. Her present home is Dayton. She has written a number of murder mysteries, most of them with an Ohio background, e.g., *Murder on Route 40,* New York, [1940].

HUMBLE, HENRY WILBUR (April 30, 1883–Jan. 11, 1941), educator, was born in Cincinnati, Hamilton County. He graduated from the University of Kansas in 1905 and the University of Cincinnati Law School in 1908. He afterward taught law at the University of Kansas and Brookings Law School. At the time of his death he was teaching English and history at the College of the City of New York. Besides legal works, he published poetry, e.g., *Lines on Literati and Other Poems,* New York, 1928. BDCP

HUMPHREY, WILLIAM DEPUE (April 14, 1900–), educator, was born in Sharpsburg, Pa., and is a graduate of Lafayette College. He taught in Findlay High School for a number of years and is now director of the evening school, Ohio Northern University. He has written *A Brief History of Gas and Oil in Findlay . . . ,* [Findlay, 1940].

HUMPHREYS, EVAN WILLIAMS (1816–1884), clergyman, was born in Wales and came to the United States in 1842. After attending Granville College and Meadville Theological Seminary, he was ordained to the ministry of the Christian Church. He preached in Clermont and Greene Counties. His death occurred in Yellow Springs. His only book contains biographies of 975 ministers.

Memoirs of Deceased Christian Ministers . . . , Dayton, 1880.

HUMPHREYS, MARY GAY (d.Oct. 10, 1915), was born in Ripley, Brown County. She traveled extensively in the Orient and served eight months in Philippine hospitals during the insurrection. In addition to the titles listed below, she edited several biographical books about the West. The first title was published under the pen name Elinor Gay, and the last two titles were published under the pen name Henry Somerville.

Skillful Susy, (with E. W. Boardman), New York, 1885.
Catherine Schuyler, New York, 1897.
Jack Racer, New York, 1901.
Racer of Illinois, New York, 1902.

HUMPHRIES, ADELAIDE MORRIS (Oct. 31, 1899–), was born in Columbus, Franklin County, lived in Cleveland for a number of years, and now lives in West Palm Beach, Fla. She has written numerous short stories for national magazines and more than twenty romantic novels, many of them serialized in magazines or newspapers. Her novels include *Inconstant Star,* New York, 1940. WWAW 1

HUMPHRIES, JACK. Pseud. See Jonathan F. Kelley.

HUNDLEY, WILL M. (c. 1860– ?), was born in Indiana near the Mississenewa Reservation, where his father was a teacher for some time. In 1877 he moved to Newtown, Hamilton County. He wrote an account of his experiences among the Indians: *Squawtown; My Boyhood among the Last Miami Indians,* Caldwell, Idaho, 1939.

HUNSINGER, CLARENCE S. (May 1, 1892–), was born in Flat Rock, Seneca County, the town in which he still lives. He founded the Rural-Urban Co-ordination Council, which attracted national attention, has supervised or advised community projects in many towns, and has lectured and published magazine articles. He has published two books on the subject of his major interest, e.g., *Accomplishing Rural Community Work,* [Flat Rock, 1938].

HUNT, EDWARD THOMAS EYRE (Aug. 1, 1885–March 5, 1953), born in Bellwood, Neb., lived on a farm near Springfield for several years before his death. After serving with the American Red Cross in Europe during World War I, he was a member of numerous governmental commissions and boards and was chief of the State Department Division of Protective Services from 1947 until his death. He published books on war relief, social and economic questions, and a panoramic historical novel: *Greathouse,* New York, [1937]. WWW 3

HUNT, GEORGE DILLWYN (March 13, 1819–Dec. 22, 1908), educator, was born in Brownsville, Pa. In 1830 his parents moved to a farm near Salem, Columbiana County, and he lived in and around Salem for the rest of his life. After attending Western Reserve College, he taught school and is said to have boasted that he taught sixty terms of school, but no two in the same place. One of his last public acts was to offer a silver tea set to the lady of his church (Baptist) who wrote the best essay on the subject "How to Prepare Sunday Dinner without Breaking the Sabbath." The prize was won by the pastor's wife. George D. Hunt died one week after moving to the home of a nephew in Elkrun Township, Columbiana County. The Preface of his novel *Albert Merton* states that incidents in the story have their "counterparts in western Pennsylvania and Ohio." This is borne out by the opinion of a local resident that Auntie Watson in the book was a local Salem woman known for her industry and skill. According to Hunt, she "could lay out a corpse or get up a wedding dinner" with equal dispatch.

Marion and Ella Thea Cox

Modern Pedagogy; A Poem, Salem, 1878.
Albert Merton, the Farm Hand . . . , Salem, 1893.
History of Salem and the Immediate Vicinity . . . , Salem, 1898.
The Pioneers of Columbiana County . . . , [n.p.], 1902.
Sophia Sidwell, an Heiress . . . , Salem, 1904.

HUNT, GEORGE MADDEN (Feb. 19, 1843–March 8, 1919), educator, was born near Wilmington, Clinton County. In 1861 he began teaching in the schools of Preble and Butler Counties, and in 1864 he moved to Iowa. He returned to Ohio to live for two brief periods, but the rest of his life was spent in the West. In 1884 he took his family from Sterling, Kan., to the Texas Panhandle. He died in Lubbock, Texas. A collection of his writings and some selections from other authors was published posthumously: *Early Days upon the Plains of Texas. Together with Poems, Prose and Selections,* Lubbock, Texas, [1920].

HUNT, HARRISON. Pseud. See W. Todhunter Ballard.

HUNT, HARRISON RANDALL (March 7, 1889–), educator, was born in Conneaut, Ashtabula County. A graduate of Allegheny College in 1912 and Harvard University (Ph.D.) in 1916, he taught zoology at the University of Mississippi, 1918–23, and Michigan State University, 1923–54. He has published articles and books on zoology and genetics, e.g., *Some Biological Aspects of War,* New York, [1930]. AMS 10

HUNT, JEDEDIAH (Dec. 28, 1815–May 9, 1860), was born in Candor, N. Y. He came to Ohio around 1840 and was a merchant in Chilo, Clermont County. He contributed to *Graham's* and other magazines.

The Cottage Maid: A Tale in Rhyme, Cincinnati, 1847.

An Adventure on a Frozen Lake: A Tale of the Canadian Rebellion of 1837–38, Cincinnati, 1853.

HUNT, SAMUEL FURMAN (Oct. 22, 1844–Jan. 12, 1907), lawyer and judge, was born in Springdale, Hamilton County. He graduated from Miami University in 1864 and Cincinnati Law School in 1867, was judge advocate general of Ohio in 1871, and served on the bench of the superior court, Cincinnati, 1878–90. Several of his speeches were published during his lifetime, and after his death his family published *Orations and Historical Addresses . . . ,* Cincinnati, 1908. WWW 1

HUNT, VIRGINIA LLOYD (March 27, 1888–), widow of Edward T. E. Hunt (q.v.), was born in Bayonne, N. J., and graduated from Columbia University. She has lived in Ohio for more than twenty years and now lives in the Simon Kenton house, Clark County, which she has restored. She has written *How to Live in the Tropics,* New York, [1942].

HUNT, WILLIAM ELLIS (Feb. 24, 1833–July 14, 1919), clergyman, was born in Pedricktown, N. J. After graduating from Jefferson College, Canonsburg, Pa., and Western Theological Seminary, Pittsburgh, he came to Coshocton as a Presbyterian minister in 1856. He spent the remainder of his life in that community.

Historical Collections of Coshocton County . . . , Cincinnati, 1876.

HUNTER, CORA WORK (Jan. 26, 1880–Jan. 14, 1951), was born in Hillsboro, Highland County. She attended Hillsboro schools, University of Wooster, and the University of Chicago. She taught English and German in Hillsboro for a time, and in 1907 she married Rutherford H. Hunter, a physicist, who taught at Cornell College, Iowa, 1907–11, and Wooster, 1911–18. She died in Pittsburgh, Pa. Mrs. Hunter published poems in many journals and for three years conducted a poetry column in the Wooster *Daily Record.* She also published a child's story in verse: *The Little Strawman,* Chicago, [1914].

HUNTER, DARD (Nov. 29, 1883–), was born in Steubenville, Jefferson County, where his father, William Henry Hunter (q.v.), was part-owner and editor of the *Gazette.* The elder Hunter moved to Chillicothe in 1900 to take charge of the *Daily News Advertiser,* with which members of the Hunter family were to be associated for many years. Dard Hunter studied at Ohio State University and is a graduate of Graphische Lehr und Versuchs-Anstalt. He also studied at Kunstgewerbe Schule in Vienna and at Royal Technical College in London. He married Helen Edith Cornell in 1908 while he was art director at Elbert Hubbard's Roycroft Shops in East Aurora, N. Y. Mrs. Hunter died March 2, 1951. In 1913 he settled with his family on a farm in New York State. In 1919 he returned to Chillicothe to live and ply his various bookish arts, which are the most diverse in the history of publishing. He has the distinction of being the first man in history to make a modern book in its entirety by his own efforts. His contributions to the art and science of papermaking are inestimable. For many years he has been connected with the world's greatest museum of paper, which bears his name. The Dard Hunter Paper Museum is housed in the two-million-dollar Charles Hayden Memorial Library, facing Memorial Drive at Massachusetts Institute of Technology in Cambridge. He disclaims any literary ability, but one has only to peruse his autobiography, *Before Life Began 1883–1923,* the story of the first forty years of his life, published in 1941 by the Rowfant Club of Cleveland, to discount his own modest estimate of his literary qualifications. Probably the two earliest works from his pen were articles entitled, "The Lost Art of Making Books" and "Ancient Papermaking" published by Alfred Fowler in *The Miscellany,* Kansas City, 1915. Students and bibliophiles the world around have perused and admired the magnificent handmade books of this master craftsman of Chillicothe. He made the type from which his books are printed by the same process used by the early type founders, cutting the punches by hand, striking them into bars of copper, which formed the matrices, and then casting these matrices by use of the hand mold. The first font of type has been presented to the Smithsonian Institution along with other devices and equipment used in the making of his first books. Each of his ten handmade masterpieces, eight from the Mountain House Press on the subject of papermaking and two (of which he is not the author) from his press at Marlborough-on-the-Hudson on the subject of etching, is the undying symbol of the ideal which has nurtured Hunter throughout his career. Over more than three decades he has produced but eight of his own completely handmade books, bearing witness to the diligence and animation with which he goes about his work and the wisdom he reveals in keeping them constantly in demand by publishing them only in extremely limited editions. There is a physical scarcity of samples of ancient papers and other specimens with which his books are profusely adorned, making them indispensable to students of papermaking and attractive to museums and collectors of rare books. Many times these rare volumes have been referred to as museum pieces, but they are contributions to art and literature. Hunter once owned and operated paper mills at Marlborough-on-the-Hudson and at Limerock, Conn.; and all of his Mountain House books as well as *Before Life Began* have been printed on handmade paper. Very few bookmen are aware that Dard Hunter was once Art Director at the Roycroft Shops in East Aurora, N. Y., where he was somewhat of a mystery to his fellow workers, according to Felix Shay in his *Elbert Hubbard of East Aurora.* Here Hunter actually started his career in the bookmaking arts, no doubt learning a great deal about them through trial and error. He designed many books for the Roycrofters from 1903 to 1910, and collectors who cannot afford the more expensive handmade books may buy for a song in secondhand bookshops specimens of Dard Hunter's early handiwork, immature though it may be. He has stated many times that he would like everyone to forget his Roycroft activities, but many of them are not such bad book-designing jobs for a neophyte art director. He has almost a complete collection of them, and my guess is that he would not part with them at any price. He also designed many bookplates, title pages, and head and tail pieces as a Roycroft catalog dated "1905 & 6" designed almost entirely by Hunter will attest. Some who know the work of his East Aurora days claim that the first book he designed for Hubbard was *Rip Van Winkle,* published in 1905, but he also designed *The Man of Sorrows* by Elbert Hubbard, which was published as early as 1904. To get a genuine perspective on the literary and scientific work to which Dard Hunter has devoted his entire career and has driven himself almost to total blindness, one need only examine a few of the eight impressive handmade Mountain House books, paragons of the art of bookmaking. Luckily for those who appreciate the epitome of the arts and crafts of bookmaking, let it be known that his *Papermaking by Hand in America* (1950) is printed from a font of type cut as cast by hand by his son, Dard, Jr., who will in days to come carry on for the edification of posterity the work of his illustrious father.

Lloyd E. Siberell

HUNTER, GEORGE (Dec. 20, 1835– ?), was born in Clermont County. In the spring of 1852 he accompanied his family across the plains to Oregon. He saw a great deal of service in the Klickatat and Yakima Country, took part in the Battle of Walla Walla in 1855, served with General Howard in the Nez Percés war, and provided an authentic account of his adventurous career in his autobiography.

Reminiscences of an Old Timer. A Recital of Actual Events, Incidents, Trials . . . of a Pioneer, Hunter, Miner and Scout of the Pacific Northwest . . . , San Francisco, 1887.

HUNTER, JANE EDNA (Dec. 13, 1882–), was born in Pendleton, S. C., the daughter of a tenant farmer and former slave. She worked in a Charleston hospital, attended Hampton Institute, and became a trained nurse. The large migration of Negroes to northern cities between 1910 and 1920 induced her to settle in Cleveland, where she founded the Phyllis Wheatley Association, a training school and refuge for Negro girls. The story of her endeavors to assist members of her race is found in *A Nickel and a Prayer,* [Nashville, Tenn., 1940].

HUNTER, ROBBINS (Sept. 23, 1880–May 3, 1954), lawyer, was born in Newark, Licking County. After graduating from Denison University and Ohio State University, he began law practice in Newark with his father, Samuel M. Hunter. He was probate judge of Licking County, 1910–21. He wrote a book of recollections, centered largely around his father: *The Judge Rode a Sorrel Horse,* New York, 1950.

HUNTER, WILLIAM HENRY (May, 1852–June, 1906), journalist, father of Dard Hunter (q.v.), was born in Cadiz, Harrison County. He edited the Cadiz *Sentinel,* 1874–75, the Steubenville *Gazette,* 1875–1900, and the Chillicothe *News-Advertiser,* 1900–06. Interested in state and local history, he wrote several articles in addition to the titles below.

Scotch Achievement, Steubenville, 1895.
Scotch-Irish Influence on American Journalism, Nashville, Tenn., 1896.
The Pathfinders of Jefferson County . . . , 2 vols., Columbus, 1898–99.

HUNTINGTON, WEBSTER PERIT (Feb. 20, 1865–Feb. 12, 1946), journalist, was born in Columbus, Franklin County, son of Peletiah W. Huntington, founder of Huntington National Bank. From 1880 to 1891 he lived in Keene, N. H., where he edited the Cheshire *Republican* and the *Evening Tribune.* After a year in Washington, D. C., as a news correspondent, he returned to Columbus, where he held editorial positions on the *Evening Dispatch,* the *Post,* and the *Press Post.*

The Three Spirits and Other Poems, Columbus, 1891.
The Signor, New York, [1898].
A Verse Book, Columbus, 1904.
The Perry Victory Memorial . . . , Akron, 1917.

HUNTLEY, FLORENCE CHANCE (1860–Feb. 1, 1912), was born in Alliance, Stark County. She wrote for various newspapers in Minneapolis, St. Paul, Washington, D. C., and Iowa City, and edited several texts on spiritualism, psychology, and religion.

The Dream Child, Boston, 1895.
Harmonics of Evolution . . . , Chicago, [1897].
The Gay Gnani of Gingalee . . . , Chicago, 1908.

HURST, FANNIE (Oct. 18, 1889–   ), was born in Hamilton, Butler County, in the home of her grandparents. Her parents were residents of St. Louis, Mo., but her mother wanted her child to be born in her own childhood home. Taken back to St. Louis a few weeks after her birth, Fannie Hurst is a native Ohioan but has not been a resident of the state. She graduated from Washington University, St. Louis, in 1909 and the following year did graduate work at Columbia University. One of America's most popular writers of fiction, she first found success in the short story. Her first novel, *Star Dust,* appeared in 1921 when she was established as a contributor to national magazines. Although she is an Ohioan only in the most tenuous sense, some of her fiction has an Ohio setting, e.g., *Back Street,* New York, 1931. ANT

HURST, SAMUEL H. (Sept. 22, 1831–July 28, 1908), was born in Union Township, Ross County. After teaching school for several terms, he attended Ohio Wesleyan University, where he graduated in 1854. He then taught school in Jackson while reading law and was admitted to the bar in 1858. He enlisted in the 73rd O.V.I., rose to the rank of colonel, and commanded the regiment during Sherman's march through Georgia. After the war he operated a fruit farm in Ross County, seved as internal revenue collector, 1869–75, and held a variety of other posts in Chillicothe.

Journal-History of the Seventy-third Ohio Volunteer Infantry, Chillicothe, 1866.

HUSCHART, FRANK M. (July 24, 1855–Feb. 3, 1938), businessman, was born in Lawrenceburg, Ind. In 1870 he came to Cincinnati. Beginning as an office boy for a packing company, he rose to general manager; in 1885 he joined a machinery company in Chicago as a partner. After his retirement in 1905 he lived in Cincinnati, where he was active in charitable and civic endeavors. He wrote an account of a round-the-world trip: *Doing Over . . . ,* Cincinnati, 1907.

HUSTON, PAUL GRISWOLD (June 22, 1873–April 19, 1960), was born in Cincinnati, Hamilton County. After attending Princeton University, he served for a time in the U. S. Bureau of Forestry and also taught in several schools, the last of which was Bolles School, Jacksonville, Fla. He retired in 1952. He died in Bay Pines, Fla. He wrote a book about his boyhood home: *Around an Old Homestead; A Book of Memories,* Cincinnati, [1906].

HUTCHINGS, CHESLEY MARTIN (Jan. 2, 1890–   ), educator, born in Durham, N. C., has been a member of the romance languages faculty, University of Cincinnati, since 1926. He has published a volume of poems: *Mezzotints,* New York, 1936, under the pen name Martin Chesley. His wife, Sabra Palmer Hutchings (May 17, 1890–July 6, 1949) and her brother, Jude Palmer, collaborated with him in writing *Oroondale,* Montpelier, Vt., 1944. DAS 3

HUTCHINGS, SABRA PALMER. See Chesley M. Hutchings.

HUTCHINS, FRANK WADE (March 20, 1858–Feb. 3, 1951), was born in Youngstown, Mahoning County. He attended Hiram College, studied law in his father's office, and practiced for a time in Ohio. His wife, Louise Cortelle Jones Hutchins (March 9, 1868–Nov. 22, 1950), was born in Kinsman, Trumbull County, and was educated at Lake Erie College. They lived in Chicago, Philadelphia, and Washington, D. C.; both died in Angola, Ind. They collaborated in writing a syndicated newspaper feature, magazine articles, and books, e.g., *Houseboating on a Colonial Waterway,* Boston, 1910, and *Thomas Jefferson,* New York, 1946.

HUTCHINS, LOUISE CORTELLE JONES. See Frank W. Hutchins.

HUTCHINS, WILLIAM JAMES (July 5, 1871–Feb. 20, 1958), Presbyterian clergyman and educator, father of Robert M. Hutchins, attended Oberlin Seminary, 1893–95, and was on the faculty of Oberlin Graduate School of Theology, 1907–20. His writings include *The Religious Experience of Israel,* New York, 1919.

HUTCHINSON, FRANK HUBBARD (Dec. 28, 1894–Dec. 25, 1934), composer and author, was born in Columbus, Franklin County. He attended North High School, and graduated from Williams College in 1917. After service in the artillery during World War I, he served for a time as music critic of the Columbus *Dispatch.* He studied at the Cleveland Institute of Music and later lived in Europe for several years. He was on the staff of the New York *Times* from 1931 until his death. Besides two travel books, he published a novel: *Chanting Wheels,* New York, 1922.

HUTCHINSON, VERONICA S. (Jan. 13, 1895–Sept. 5, 1961), was born in Cleveland, Cuyahoga County, and spent her life there. After taking library training at Carnegie Library School, she was children's librarian at Cleveland Public Library and for more than 25 years she was in charge of Halle's bookshop. She edited some anthologies for children and also published children's books, e.g., *The Circus Comes to Town,* New York, [1932].

HUTCHISON, HAZEL COLLISTER, educator, was born in Cleveland, Cuyahoga County. She graduated from Western Reserve University and studied at the Sorbonne and now teaches in the Cleveland schools. She has published poetry in various national magazines and has brought out a collection, *Toward Daybreak,* New York, [1950].

HYDE, SOLON (Nov. 12, 1838–Feb. 13, 1920), was born in Rushville, Fairfield County. Serving as a hospital steward during the Civil War, he was captured at Chickamauga on Sept. 20, 1863, and was imprisoned nearly eighteen months in several Confederate prisons. His temperately written book abounds in thrilling descriptions of his experiences. His death occurred in Los Angeles.

A Captive of War, New York, 1900.

HYSLOP, JAMES HERVEY (Aug. 18, 1854–June 17, 1920), educator, was born on a farm near Xenia, Greene County. He graduated from University of Wooster in 1877, taught in county schools and in McCorkle College, Sago. He studied in Germany in 1884 and earned his doctorate from Johns Hopkins University in 1887. He taught at Lake Forest University, Smith College, Bucknell University, and Columbia University. In 1902 he retired from teaching because of tuberculosis. He published several textbooks in logic, ethics, and psychology during the 1890s. After his retirement he became increasingly interested in spiritualism and published several books on psychic phenomena, e.g., *Borderland of Psychical Research,* Boston, 1906. He also published *Poems, Original and Translations,* Boston, 1915. DAB 9

I

IDELSOHN, ABRAHAM ZEBI (July 14, 1882–July 14, 1938), musician, was born in Phoelixburg, Latvia, where he studied music and served as a cantor. After spending seventeen years in Jerusalem studying Jewish music, he came to the United States in 1922. He lectured at Hebrew Union College, 1924–33, suffered a paralytic stroke in 1933, and left Cincinnati in 1935. He died in Johannesburg, South Africa, where he spent the last ten months of his life. Internationally recognized as an authority on Jewish music, he wrote and edited musicological works and also wrote *The Ceremonies of Judaism,* Cincinnati, 1929.

IGNIO. Pseud. See Henry Hooper.

IMHOFF, ALEXANDER JESSE (July 8, 1823–Aug. 10, 1901), clergyman, was born in Westmoreland County, Pa. He graduated from Wittenberg College in 1851 and the Seminary in 1852 and was ordained to the Lutheran ministry in 1853. He served pastorates in several Ohio communities; his longest service was at Urbana, 1867–73, 1876–89. He died at Findlay.

The Life of Reverend Morris Officer, A.M., Dayton, 1876.

INGALLS, FAY (July 12, 1882–   ), lawyer, was born in Cincinnati, Hamilton County. He graduated from Harvard College in 1904 and the Law School in 1907. After practicing law, 1907–22, he became president of Virginia Hot Springs Association. He has made his home in Hot Springs and has written a book about the community: *The Valley Road,* Cleveland, [1949]. WW 30

INGHAM, MARY BIGELOW (March 10, 1832–1924), was born in Mansfield, Richland County. After attending Norwalk Seminary and Baldwin Institute, she became a teacher in Cleveland at the age of eighteen. She also taught for a time at Ohio Wesleyan University before marrying Rev. William A. Ingham in 1866. They settled in Cleveland, where she was very active in the causes of women's suffrage and temperance. She wrote articles and travel letters for the Cleveland *Leader* and other periodicals. She was also active in Cleveland civic affairs and in missionary activities of the Methodist Church. Her last years were spent in Los Angeles.

First Methodist Episcopal Church of Cleveland . . . , (with L. D. Mix), Cleveland, 1884.

Women of Cleveland and Their Work, Cleveland, 1893.

INK, EVANGELINE (Dec. 19, 1883–Oct. 19, 1923), was born in Republic, Seneca County. She died in Tiffin. She published a number of short stories for children. Also, under her first name, Evangeline, she published a book on the dangers of tuberculosis and on the folly of compelling patients to go to sanitariums: *The New Acadians,* Chicago, 1904.

INSKIP, JOHN SWANEL (Aug. 10, 1816–March 7, 1884), clergyman, born in England, brought to America in 1821, was converted to Methodism when he was sixteen years old. In 1845 he was transferred from Philadelphia to Ninth Street Church, Cincinnati. He also served churches in Dayton, Urbana, Springfield, and Troy. He opposed the separation of men and women within the church, and for his liberalism he was rebuked by the Ohio Conference. He wrote an able defense, *Methodism Explained and Defended,* Cincinnati, 1851. The General Conference reversed the Ohio decision in 1852, and he was transferred to New York. His last years were devoted largely to evangelism.

IRELAND, THOMAS SAXTON (Dec. 16, 1895–   ), lawyer, was born in Cleveland, Cuyahoga County. He graduated from Princeton University in 1918 and Boston University Law School in 1923. He has practiced in New York City and Cleveland and has served as a news commentator on Cleveland and Akron radio stations. He has written several books on current issues, e.g., *The Great Lakes—St. Lawrence Deep Waterway to the Sea,* New York, [1934]. WW 30

IRWIN, DEMARIS (1851–1933), was born in Deersville, Harrison County. She died in the same community. Though blind, she wrote a number of poems, some of which were published in the collection listed below.

Flowers of the Wildwood . . . , Uhrichsville, 1875.

IRWIN, WILLIAM H. H. (1841–1879), lawyer, born in Greenfield, Highland County, collaborated with Samuel D. Crothers (q.v.) in writing a pamphlet history of Greenfield.

Centennial Historical Sketches of Greenfield, Ohio, and Vicinity, (with S. D. Crothers), Greenfield, 1876.

ISAACS, NATHAN (July 10, 1886–Dec. 18, 1941), lawyer and educator, was born in Cincinnati, Hamilton County. He graduated from the University of Cincinnati in 1907 and the law school in 1910. After being admitted to the Ohio bar in 1910, he served on the law faculties of Harvard University, University of Pittsburgh, Columbia University, University of Rochester, and Yale University. He served as editor of a number of important reference books. His writings include *The Law in Business Problems,* New York, 1921. WWW 1

ISHAM, ASA BRAINERD (July 12, 1844–Feb. 20, 1912), physician and educator, was born in Jackson County. He attended Marietta College, 1857–59. He worked on Michigan newspapers, served in the 7th Michigan Cavalry, and was wounded and captured in the spring of 1864. He graduated from the Medical College of Ohio in 1869. He taught at the Cincinnati College of Medicine and Surgery, 1876–80. Though his writings on the Civil War are not unimportant, he will long be remembered in medical circles as the editor of the classic *Sphygmography and Cardiography* by his father-in-law, Alonzo T. Keyt (q.v.). His manuscript autobiography was revised and published in 1957 by his grandson, Dr. A. Chapman Isham.

Through the Wilderness to Richmond . . . , Cincinnati, 1884.

Care of Prisoners of War, North and South . . . , Cincinnati, 1887.

Prisoners of War and Military Prisons . . . , Cincinnati, 1890.

An Historical Sketch of the Seventh Regiment Michigan Volunteer Cavalry . . . , New York, [1893].

ISHAM, MARY KEYT (Aug. 20, 1871–Sept. 28, 1947), neurologist, daughter of Asa B. Isham (q.v.), was born in Cincinnati, Hamilton County. She graduated from Wellesley College in 1894 and Laura Memorial Medical College in 1903. She practiced in Cincinnati, 1904–09, and Columbus, 1909–15, before moving to New York City. She published technical articles in medical journals, articles on psychology in the New York *Times,* and *Cosmos Unlimited,* New York, 1928. WWW 2

ISLER, ARNOLD HENRY (1849–Feb. 23, 1894), was born in Switzerland but was brought to the United States when he was five. Though only twelve years old when the Civil War began, he enlisted in the 23rd O.V.I. and served as a private from June, 1861, to Oct., 1862. In the 1870s he dealt in real estate and insurance in Columbus. He died in Cincinnati.

Wild Thoughts in Rhyme, Columbus, 1873.

ISRAEL, EDWARD L. (Aug. 30, 1896–Oct. 19, 1941), rabbi, was born in Cincinnati, Hamilton County, and graduated from the University of Cincinnati in 1917 and Hebrew Union College in 1919. He served congregations in Illinois, Indiana, and Maryland, and was active in many organizations. A number of his radio broadcasts were reprinted in *The Message of Israel Broadcasts,* Baltimore, 1939. WWW 1

J

JACKSON, EVA E. (Aug. 17, 1858–Dec. 27, 1956), was born in Eaton Township, Lorain County. She married Charles H. Jackson of Cleveland; she died in that city at the age of 98. She wrote a book for young readers: *Stories for the Twilight . . . ,* Chicago, 1912.

JACKSON, JESSE J., was born in Columbus, Franklin County. He graduated from Columbus East High School, attended Ohio State University, and worked as a postal clerk and as a probation officer in Columbus. He left Columbus in 1945 and now lives in New York City. He has written at least three novels centered on racial conflict, e.g., *Anchor Man,* New York, [1947].

JACKSON, THOMAS WRIGHT (Aug. 21, 1869–April 25, 1925), physician, was born in Akron, Summit County. He attended Akron public schools and graduated from Jefferson Medical College in 1892. He practiced in Akron and Philadelphia, was an army surgeon during the Spanish-American War, and served in the Bureau of Health, Philippine Islands. He died in Lake City, Fla. He wrote a book on tropical medicine and *Plague; Its Cause and the Manner of Its Extension . . . ,* [Philadelphia, 1916]. WW 8

JACOBS, ANNE MARGUERITE (1889–), was born in Cincinnati, Hamilton County. For more than forty years she was employed on the technical data staff of Wright Field. Now Mrs. Anne J. Heron, she lives in Dayton. She wrote a book on aeronautics: *Knights of the Wing,* New York, [1928].

JACOBS, FREDERICK BURKHAM (Jan. 5, 1880–Jan. 20, 1942), was born in South Hingham, Mass. After attending school in Quincy, Mass., he became a machinist and toolmaker. He joined the staff of Penton

Publishing Co., Cleveland, in 1917 and was editor of *Abrasive Industry,* 1920–32. He published short stories, technical articles, and *Industrial Turmoil, a Story of New England,* Kansas City, Mo., [1927].

JAGGAR, THOMAS AUGUSTUS June 2, 1839–Dec. 13, 1912), clergyman, was born in New York City. He was educated in city schools and by private tutors. Ordained to the Episcopal priesthood in 1863, he served as rector of various churches, 1863–1875. He served as bishop of southern Ohio, 1875–1905. He died in Cannes, France. Besides the title below, a number of his sermons and pastoral letters were published.

Personality of Truth, New York, 1900.

JAGGAR, THOMAS AUGUSTUS, JR. (Jan. 24, 1871–Jan. 17, 1953), geologist, son of Bishop Thomas A. Jaggar (q.v.), was born in Philadelphia, Pa. He grew up in Cincinnati, where his father moved in 1875. He graduated from Harvard University (A.B., 1893; Ph.D., 1897), taught at Harvard and Massachusetts Institute of Technology, and was a geologist with the U. S. Geological Survey. He died in Honolulu, Hawaii. Besides technical books, he published a volume of essays and lectures: *Union through the Ages,* [Honolulu?, 1948?]. WWW 3

JAMES, ALICE ARCHER SEWALL (1870–Sept. 20, 1955), daughter of Frank Sewall (q.v.), was born in Glendale, Hamilton County. She attended Urbana University. She married John H. James, an Urbana attorney, and spent most of her life in that community. Her paintings were exhibited in numerous galleries, and her illustrations and poems appeared in *Century, Harper's Monthly,* and other national magazines. She died in Columbus, where she had moved a short time before.

An Ode to Girlhood and Other Poems, New York, 1899.
The Ballad of the Prince, New York, 1900.
The Torch, a Pageant . . . , [Urbana, 1922].
The Morning Moon, Philadelphia, [1941].

JAMES, FLEMING (Jan. 11, 1874–Sept. 11, 1959), theologian, was born in Gambier, Knox County. He graduated from the University of Pennsylvania in 1895 and completed his doctorate there in 1899. After graduating from Philadelphia Divinity School in 1901, he was ordained deacon in the Episcopal Church and priest the following year. He served churches in various cities and taught at Berkeley Divinity School and the University of the South. His death occurred in Hamden, Conn. His writings include *Personalities of the Old Testament,* New York, 1939. WW 27

JAMES, FRANCIS BACON (June 10, 1864–May 21, 1924), lawyer, was born in Cincinnati, Hamilton County. He graduated from Cincinnati Law School in 1886 and was admitted to the bar in the same year. He served on the University of Cincinnati faculty, 1895–1912. He died in Washington, D. C., where he had practiced for several years. He published several legal works and *Advertising, and Other Addresses,* Cincinnati, 1907. WWW 1

JAMES, FRANKLIN. Pseud. See Robert F. Godley.

JAMES, HERMAN GERLACH (Jan. 2, 1887–), educator, was born in Philadelphia, Pa. He served as president of Ohio University, 1935–43. Besides numerous textbooks in government, he has published studies of South America, e.g., *Brazil after a Century of Independence,* New York, 1925. WW 30

JAMES, JOHN HOUGH (1800–1881), lawyer, banker, and railroad builder, born in Virginia, was brought to Cincinnati in 1813. After graduating from Cincinnati College in 1821, he was admitted to the bar. In 1826 he settled in Urbana, where he spent the remainder of his life. He was a founder of Urbana University, president of the Urbana Bank, and the town's most distinguished citizen. He wrote articles for magazines and newspapers, but, although he considered a literary career while a young man, the pamphlet below is his only recorded publication. He kept a diary for sixty years, however, which furnished much of the information for a book about his career: *Buckeye Titan* by William E. and Ophia D. Smith (1953).

May Colored Persons Vote in Ohio . . . , Columbus, 1860.

JAMISON, ALCINOUS BERTON (Sept. 1, 1851–Nov. 15, 1938), physician, was born near Wooster, Wayne County. After attending the University of Michigan, he graduated from Fort Wayne College of Medicine in 1878. He practiced briefly in Indiana and Michigan and in 1885 went to New York City, where he practiced for 53 years. He published several medical books and others, e.g., *The Making of a Super-race,* New York, 1926.

JANES, GEORGE MILTON (April 18, 1869–Dec. 24, 1936), educator, was born in Utica, N. Y. He graduated from Dartmouth College in 1901 and Johns Hopkins University (Ph.D.) in 1913. He served on the Kenyon College economics faculty, 1925–34, and after his retirement he lived in Oberlin. Besides books on labor unions and economics, he published *The Pilgrim Spirit, and Other Essays,* Pittsfield, Mass., 1904. WWW 1

JANIS, ELSIE (March 16, 1889–Feb. 28, 1956), comedienne, was born Elsie Janis Bierbower in Columbus, Franklin County. Her debut is said to have been made at the age of two when she imitated Anna Held in a church program. When she was five, she played in *East Lynne* in Columbus. She appeared with stock companies in Columbus until she was fourteen, when her mother took her to New York. She starred in vaudeville and in many plays and revues. During World War I she was the first woman entertainer permitted to visit troops in France and acquired the nickname "Sweetheart of the A.E.F." Her wartime experiences are recounted in *The Big Show,* New York, 1919. When her mother, who had accompanied her on all of her tours, died in 1930, Miss Janis retired from the stage, although she later made a few movie appearances. Best known as an impersonator and a singer, she composed a number of songs, wrote some fiction and poetry, and published several books of reminiscences, e.g., *So Far, So Good!* New York, 1932. WWW 3

JANNEY, RUSSELL DIXON (April 14, 1883–), theatrical producer, was born in Wilmington, Clinton County, where his father, Reynold Janney, was principal of the high school. The family moved to Chillicothe soon after Russell's birth, and in 1894 they moved to Keene, N. H. As Keene was a stopover for road shows between Montreal and Boston, Janney became familiar with the theater. He graduated from Yale University in 1906, wrote several vaudeville acts, and later became a magazine writer and press agent in London. He was for a time press agent for Theda Bara. He wrote or produced a great variety of dramas, the most famous being *The Vagabond King,* which he wrote with Rudolph Friml. At the age of 63, he wrote his first novel: *The Miracle of the Bells,* New York, 1946. The book was a best-seller and was the basis for a successful motion picture. WW 28

JARNAGIN, DOROTHY GREVE (June 1, 1884–), was born in Cincinnati, Hamilton County, but has spent most of her life in the South, where her parents moved in 1888. She graduated from the University of Tennessee in 1905. She was married to Professor Milton P. Jarnagin of the University of Georgia faculty; after his death she married Judge Samuel J. McAllester of Chattanooga, Tenn., who is also deceased. She is now a resident of Athens, Ga. She has published two books for girls, e.g., *Mardee Gray's Choice,* Boston, 1923. WWNAA 7

JASZI, OSCAR (Oszkar) (March 2, 1875–Feb. 13, 1957), educator, born in Hungary, came to the United States in 1925, and from that year until his retirement in 1942 was a member of the Oberlin College faculty. After retiring he continued to live in Oberlin. He wrote numerous articles and books on politics and foreign affairs, e.g., *The Dissolution of the Hapsburg Monarchy,* Chicago, [1929]. WWW 3

JAYHEWS, THOMAS. Pseud. See Thomas J. Hughes.

JEFFERSON, CHARLES EDWARD (Aug. 29, 1860–Sept. 12, 1937), clergyman, was born in Cambridge, Guernsey County. He graduated from Ohio Wesleyan University in 1882 and was superintendent of schools in Worthington, 1882–84. While studying law in Boston, he decided to become a minister and entered Boston University. Ordained to the Congregational ministry in 1887, he preached first in Chelsea, Mass., and afterward in the Broadway Tabernacle Church, New York City, from 1898 until his death. A liberal theologian and an advocate of internationalism and pacifism, he published many books, most of them collections of sermons and lectures. They include *Christianity and International Peace . . . ,* New York, [1915], and several books directed to his fellow ministers, e.g., *The Minister as Prophet,* New York, [1905]. DAB 22

JEFFREYS, RAYMOND JOHN (Jan. 23, 1896–), lecturer and writer, was born in Columbiana, Columbiana County. He entered Mount Union College in 1915, interrupted his college course to serve as a flying officer in France, and graduated from Mount Union in 1920. He operated a chain of newspapers in Columbiana County for a time, traveled as a news correspondent, and was in business in Cleveland. He also owned the Jeffreys Lecture Bureau and was executive secretary of Capitol College of Oratory and Music, Columbus. He now lives in Raleigh, N. C. He has published several books, e.g., *God Is My Landlord,* Chicago, [1947].

JEFFREYS, U. M. GRANT (May 20, 1864–Nov. 6, 1956), was born in Preston County, W. Va., but his parents moved to Seaman, Adams County, when he was a small child, and he grew up in that community. He taught country schools, served in the Spanish-American War, and was in the real-estate business in Monmouth, Ill., where he spent the greater part of his life. He died in Veterans' Hospital, Dayton. He wrote *The Story of the Man of the Ages,* Boston, [1929].

JEFFRIES, JAMES GRAYDON (1901–Aug. 4, 1936), was born in Sedalia, Madison County. He died in Brazil, Ind. Though crippled and blind, he wrote poems which were published in periodicals and in several collections, e.g., *Last Poems,* North Montpelier, Vt., 1937.

JEFFRIES, JOHN PARSONS (July 19, 1815–Aug. 13, 1888), lawyer, was born in Huntington County, Pa. He settled in Wooster in 1836, read law, and was admitted to the Ohio bar in 1842. For 25 years before publishing the book listed below, he collected materials regarding the early inhabitants of America.

The Natural History of the Human Races . . . , New York, 1869.

JENKINS, CHARLES FRANCIS (Aug. 22, 1867–June 6, 1934), inventor, was born near Dayton, Montgomery County. He graduated from Fountain City, Ind., High School and attended Earlham College. He was granted more than 400 patents on inventions in radio, photography, television, and motion pictures.

Picture Ribbons: An Exposition of the Methods and Apparatus Employed . . . , Washington, D. C., [1897].

Animated Pictures: An Exposition of the Historical Development of Chronophotography . . . , Washington, D. C., 1898.

Motion Pictures in Teaching, Washington, D. C., [1916].

Vision by Radio, Radio Photographs, Radio Photograms, [Washington, D. C., 1925].

Radiomovies, Radiovision, Television, [Washington, D. C., 1929].

The Boyhood of an Inventor, Washington, D. C., 1931.

JENKINS, EDWARD L. (Jan. 15, 1866–Dec. 28, 1908), actor, was born in Sharonville, Hamilton County, but throughout most of his career he considered Dayton his home, and he is buried in that city. After joining a minstrel show at the age of fourteen, he traveled with an *Uncle Tom's Cabin* troupe and with various stock companies. He died in Chicago. He wrote plays that were acted by companies with which he traveled, and he also wrote poems for periodicals, many of which were collected in *Home Made Rhymes,* Chicago, [1905].

JENKINS, HERMON DUTILH (Jan. 14, 1842–Oct. 31, 1918), clergyman, was born in Columbus, Franklin County. He graduated from Hamilton College in 1864 and Union Theological Seminary in 1867. Ordained to the Presbyterian ministry in 1868, he served as a pastor in Illinois, Iowa, and Missouri. He also contributed to numerous religious periodicals. His writings include *Christ's Boys and Girls,* Chicago, 1904.

JENKINS, OLIVER PEEBLES (Nov. 3, 1850–Jan. 9, 1935), educator, was born in Bantam, Clermont County. After graduating from Moores Hill College in 1869, he taught in high schools in several states, 1870-76, at Moores Hill, 1876–82, at Indiana State Normal School, 1883–86, and at DePauw University, 1886–91. He earned his Ph.D. at Indiana University in 1889 and taught at Stanford University, 1891–1916. After retiring he lived in California until his death. Besides textbooks in physiology, he wrote books on nature study, e.g., *Interesting Neighbors,* Philadelphia, [1922]. WWW 1

JENKINS, TIMOTHY. Pseud. See E. Burke Fisher.

JENKINSON, ISAAC (April 29, 1825–Oct. 25, 1911), lawyer and journalist, was born in Piqua, Miami County. He was admitted to the Indiana bar in 1850 and settled in Fort Wayne to practice. He edited the Fort Wayne *Gazette,* 1863–69, served as U. S. consul at Glasgow, 1869–74, and edited the Richmond *Palladium,* 1875–96. A speech on the policy of the peace party was published in 1863; otherwise, his only writing in book form was *Aaron Burr, His Personal and Political Relations with Thomas Jefferson and Alexander Hamilton,* Richmond, Ind., 1902. WWW 1

JENNEY, MARY PERRY (Dec., 1845–Dec. 18, 1928), was born in Columbus, Franklin County, but spent most of her life in Cincinnati. She was educated at Mount Auburn

Seminary, and in 1871 she married Herbert Jenney, an attorney. A collection of stories originally written for her grandchildren was posthumously published: *The Little Pioneers,* Cincinnati, 1928.

JENNINGS, ISAAC (Nov. 7, 1789–March 14, 1874), physician, was born on a farm near Fairfield, Conn. He studied medicine in Fairfield and at Yale University, where he graduated in 1828. In 1839 he moved to Oberlin, and except for a brief residence in Cleveland in the 1850s he spent the remainder of his life in that community. Before leaving Connecticut he had concluded that most medicines were worthless, and he began prescribing harmless pills and drops. His unorthodox view involved him in many controversies and diminished his practice to some extent. He was a trustee of Oberlin College, 1839–55.

Defense and Appeal of Isaac Jennings . . . , Oberlin, 1847.

Medical Reform: A Treatise on Man's Physical Being and Disorders . . . , Oberlin, 1847.

The Philosophy of Human Life . . . , Cleveland, 1852.

The Tree of Life; Or, Human Degeneracy: Its Nature and Remedy, New York, 1867.

JENNINGS, OTTO EMERY (Oct. 3, 1877–), biologist, was born in Olena, Huron County. He graduated from Ohio State University in 1903, and the University of Pittsburgh (Ph.D.) in 1911. He was on the staff of Carnegie Museum, Pittsburgh, 1904-50, and during most of that period was also on the faculty of the University of Pittsburgh. He wrote many scientific articles, several books on botany, and *A Series of Eight Radio Talks on Trees and Flowers of Spring,* [Pittsburgh], 1929. WW 30

JERMAIN, FRANCES DELAVAN PAGE (1829–Aug. 21, 1905), librarian, was born in Ann Arbor, Mich., the daughter of a Presbyterian clergyman. She grew up in Michigan and graduated from the state university. After her marriage to Sylvanus P. Jermain, she lived in Chillicothe; upon her husband's death in 1871 she took her six small children to Toledo. She was appointed reference librarian in 1879 and served as head librarian, 1884-1903. She published many articles in the Toledo *Blade,* and in 1880, wrote a cookbook. A posthumous memorial edition of a work by her was published: *In the Path of the Alphabet . . . ,* Fort Wayne, Ind., 1906.

JEWELL, LOUISE POND (April 17, 1867–Dec. 26, 1943), educator, was born in Oberlin, Lorain County. She graduated from Oberlin College in 1890 and taught for a number of years in New York secondary schools. She published articles and short stories in magazines and a novel: *The Great Adventure,* New York, [1911]. WWW 2

JEWETT, ISAAC APPLETON (Oct. 17, 1808–Jan. 14, 1853), lawyer, was born in Burlington, Vt. After graduating from Harvard in 1830, he read law. He practiced in Cincinnati and New Orleans. His death occurred in Keene, N. H. In 1833 he wrote a prize essay, published in the *Western Monthly Magazine,* "Themes for Western Fiction," in which he called for truthful treatment of frontier materials.

A Brief History and Defence of the Drama, [Cincinnati?, 1832?].

Passages in Foreign Travel, 2 vols., Boston, 1838.

Memorial of Samuel Appleton . . . , Boston, 1850.

JEWETT, JOHN BROWN (June 24, 1865–Jan. 24, 1938), was born in Newtown, Hamilton County. A lifelong recluse, he contributed many delightful poems and sketches to Ohio magazines and newspapers. In his *Tales of the Miami Country* he preserved entrancing bits of the folklore of the neighborhood in which he was born and spent his entire life: "Fiddler's Green," "Dr. Tetterhorn's Vision," and "McCullough's Station."

Tales of the Miami Country, Cincinnati, 1898.

JEWETT, SUSAN W. (fl.1840–71), born in Massachusetts, was the wife of a prominent Cincinnati engraver. Between the years 1840 and 1857 she contributed prose and poetry to Cincinnati newspapers and conducted a short-lived monthly juvenile magazine, the *Youth's Visitor. The Corner Cupboard,* published anonymously, is a collection of her poems and sketches.

The Parent's Gift: Consisting of a Series of Poems and Essays . . . , New York, 1843.

The Old Corner Cupboard . . . , Cincinnati, 1856.

From Fourteen to Fourscore, New York, 1871.

JOHNSON, DAVIS BEN (Dec. 30, 1880–Jan. 8, 1952), lawyer, was born near Matamora, Fulton County. He attended Fayette Normal School and taught school for about twelve years. After attending Chattanooga Law School, he was admitted to the bar in 1916. He practiced in Wauseon, held many local offices, served as county prosecuting attorney and in the Ohio Senate. He wrote verse as a pastime and published a collection: *Hodge-Podge,* [Wauseon, 1939].

JOHNSON, EDITH CHERRY (1879–), journalist, was born in New Lexington, Perry County. She grew up in Corning and Columbus, where she attended Miss Phelps' School for Girls and Ohio State University. In 1903 she moved with her family to Oklahoma, and in 1908 she became society editor of the *Daily Oklahoman.* Her columns were syndicated nationally. She now lives in Oklahoma City. Her writings include *Illusions and Disillusions, Touching upon Topics in Everyday Life,* Oklahoma City, 1920. WWAW 1

JOHNSON, EDWARD WOODWARD (Oct. 27, 1876–June 15, 1954), lawyer, was born in West Jefferson, Madison County. He graduated from Ohio Northern University in 1898 and the law school in 1903. He practiced in London and West Jefferson. He also owned a cotton plantation in Arkansas, which was the locale of his book, *The Shack by the River,* Boston, [1938].

JOHNSON, FRANKLIN (Nov. 2, 1836–Oct. 7, 1916), clergyman and educator, was born in Franklin, Warren County. He grew up in Oregon, where his parents migrated in 1845. After graduating from Colgate Theological Seminary in 1861, he was ordained to the Baptist ministry. He served pastorates in several states, and from 1892 until his retirement in 1908 he was on the faculty of the University of Chicago. Besides the titles below, he translated a number of works and published several Sunday school texts.

True Womanhood . . . , Cambridge, Mass., 1882.

The New Psychic Studies in Their Relation to Christian Thought, New York, 1887.

The Quotations of the New Testament from the Old . . . , Philadelphia, 1896.

The Home Missionaries, Chicago, 1899.

Have We the Likeness of Christ?, Chicago, 1902.

The Christian's Relation to Evolution . . . , Chicago, [1904].

JOHNSON, HAMMEL. Pseud. See Mamie L. Hammel and Mabel H. Faison.

JOHNSON, HOMER URI (May 20, 1830–Nov. 23, 1901), clergyman and educator, was born in Braceville, Trumbull County, the son of settlers from Connecticut. He became a lecturer and Methodist preacher, but he was best known as principal of academies in western New York, Pennsylvania, and northeastern Ohio. He wrote considerable poetry and some rather more effective prose. *The Great Co-Partnership* was published under the pen name Obed. During the 1880s he undertook a systematic investigation of the Underground Railroad and contributed a number of articles on the subject to *Arthur's Home Magazine* between 1883 and 1889. A projected two-volume collection of short stories on this subject never got beyond the first volume, *From Dixie to Canada.*

Concert Exercises in Geography . . . , Cleveland, 1860.

Seventeen-Seventy-six, and Other Poems, Cleveland, 1877.

The Great Co-Partnership, and Other Papers, Cleveland, 1879.

From Dixie to Canada; Romances and Realities of the Underground Railroad, Orwell, 1894.

Western Reserve Centennial Souvenir, Cleveland, 1896.

JOHNSON, JOHN ALEXANDER (Feb. 24, 1849–July 22, 1929), was born in Lynchburg, Va. He graduated from Hughes High School, Cincinnati, 1866. Though continuing to conduct a planing mill in Cincinnati, he moved to Covington, Ky., in 1883. He published *Three Visions; And Other Poems,* Cincinnati, [1912].

JOHNSON, SOLOMON (March 2, 1850–Sept. 17, 1918), lawyer and educator, was born in Fulton County. He attended Normal School at Bryan, served as school examiner of Williams County, and graduated from Ann Arbor Law School in 1880. In 1910 he made a world tour, which became the subject of his book, *Notes on Travels, Including a Trip around the World by Way of Australia,* Columbus, 1914.

JOHNSON, TOM LOFTIN (July 18, 1854–April 10, 1911), mayor of Cleveland, 1901–09, was born in Blue Spring, Ky. His father's service in the Confederate Army forced Tom to go to work at an early age. While employed by the Louisville Street Railroad, controlled by DuPonts, he invented the first fare-box; and from that time on, he rose rapidly with DuPont backing. He was associated with profitable steel mills and traction companies. Converted to the views of Henry George after reading *Progress and Poverty,* he represented political liberalism at its best during two terms in Congress, 1890–94, and during his mayoralty.

He was assisted by Elizabeth J. Hauser of Girard in writing his only book: *My Story,* New York, 1911. DAB 10

JOHNSON, WENDELL F. (July 28, 1893–), social worker, was born in Toledo, Lucas County. He served as executive director of the Child and Family Agency in Toledo, 1925–59. He now lives in California. He has published a number of magazine articles and a pamphlet: *Toledo's Nonpartisan Movement,* Toledo, 1922.

JOHNSON, WILLIAM EUGENE (March, 25, 1862–Feb. 2, 1945), temperance advocate, born in Coventry, N. Y., lived in Westerville, c.1914–22. Active in the prohibition movement, he was publicity director of the Anti-Saloon League; and for his activities in promoting enforcement of the 18th Amendment, he was nicknamed in the press "Pussyfoot" Johnson. He wrote many articles, brochures, and books against liquor, e.g., *The Federal Government and the Liquor Traffic,* Westerville, [1911]. OBB

JOHNSON, WILLIAM HANNIBAL (March 26, 1860–Jan. 4, 1934), educator and journalist, was born in Monroe County. He graduated from Denison University in 1885 and was professor of Latin there from 1894 to 1919. From 1920 until his death he was chief editorial writer for the Columbus *Evening Dispatch.* He published a pamphlet, *The War and World Opinion,* Granville, 1916. WWW 1

JOHNSON, WILLIAM SAVAGE (Aug. 26, 1877–Dec. 15, 1942), educator, was born in Portsmouth, Scioto County. Educated at Yale University, he taught English at various universities, his last position being at the University of Kansas. Besides professional articles, he published *Thomas Carlyle; A Study of His Literary Apprenticeship, 1814–1831,* New Haven, [Conn.], 1911. WWNAA 7

JOHNSTON, ARTHUR E. (Dec. 25, 1895–), was born in Elenora, Pa., but grew up in Youngstown and still lives in that city. He served in the Sixth Division in World War I, after which he worked in Youngstown as an engine rebuilder. He has written a novel, *'Tain't Me, It's Democracy Speakin',* Boston, [1948].

JOHNSTON, BERT (Aug. 19, 1898–Jan. 18, 1952), born in Montreal, Canada, came to the United States in 1924 and about 1930 settled in Cincinnati, where he was advertising director for the Kroger Company. In 1944 he opened his own agency, and in 1946 he founded a motion-picture production company to make industrial and commercial films. He published a book on advertising and labor-management relations: *One Nation for Sale,* Cincinnati, [1943].

JOHNSTON, HOWARD AGNEW (June 29, 1860–April 15, 1936), clergyman, was born in Greene County. After graduating from the University of Cincinnati in 1882 and Wayne Seminary in 1885, he was ordained to the Presbyterian ministry. He served churches in Ohio, Iowa, Illinois, New York, Colorado, Connecticut, and Wisconsin.

Studies in God's Methods of Training Workers, New York, 1900.
Bible Criticism and the Average Man, New York, [1902].
Studies for Personal Workers, New York, 1903.
Scientific Faith, Chicago, 1904.
The Beatitudes of Christ; A Study of the Way of the Blessed Life, Chicago, 1905.
The Famine and the Bread, New York, 1908.
Victorious Manhood, New York, [1909].
Enlisting for Christ and the Church, New York, 1919.
Scientific Christian Thinking for Young People, New York, [1922].
The Son of Nicodemus . . . , New York, [1925].
We Can Surely Believe: A Christian Answer to Current Atheism, New York, [1928].

JOHNSTON, JOHN (March 25, 1775–Feb. 18, 1861), was born near Ballyshannon, Ireland. He came to Perry County, Pa., with his parents in 1785. While at Carlisle, Pa., fired by the tales related by survivors of St. Clair's ill-fated expedition, he set out for Ohio. He served with the quartermaster's department of Wayne's army and wintered in Kentucky in 1795. Returning to Philadelphia, he was for several years employed in the War Department as a clerk. He was commissioned in 1806 and served as Indian agent at Piqua, where he gave great satisfaction both to the government and to the tribes under his charge. He was removed for political reasons by President Jackson in 1829. In 1841 he was appointed to negotiate a treaty of cession and removal with the Wyandots, the last of the native Ohio tribes. In carrying out this difficult task, he won the commendation of the government and the Indians. His *Account of the Present State of the Indian Tribes Inhabiting Ohio* appeared in the *Transactions* of the American Antiquarian Society for 1819. His valuable *Recollec-*

tions of the Last Sixty Years was published serially in Volume II of the Cincinnati *Miscellany* in 1846 and was republished in the edition below. He died in Washington, D. C.

Recollections of Sixty Years Indian Agent for U. S. Government at Piqua, Ohio, from 1806 to 1853, [Dayton], 1915.

JOHNSTON, JOHN BLACK (March 13, 1802–Oct. 24, 1882), clergyman, was born near Clarksburgh, Pa., but was reared in Hopedale. After graduating from Franklin College in 1829, he was ordained as a Presbyterian minister and served churches in Northwood and St. Clairsville. He died in the latter community.

Signs of the Times, 1858.
Psalmody, 1868.
The Prayer Meeting, 1870.

JOHNSTON, JOHN BLACK (Oct. 3, 1868–Nov. 19, 1939), educator, was born in Belle Center, Logan County. After graduating from the University of Michigan (A.B., 1893; Ph.D., 1899), he taught at the University of West Virginia, 1899–1907, and the University of Minnesota, 1907–37. He published many professional articles on neurology and education and books on education, e.g., *The Liberal College in a Changing Society,* New York, [1930]. WWW 2

JOHNSTON, JULIA HARIETTE (Jan. 21, 1849–March 6, 1919), was born in Salineville, Columbiana County. She attended high school in Peoria, Ill. She wrote for a number of Presbyterian magazines and also composed many hymns.

The School of the Master, and Other Religious Verses, New York, [1880].
Life of Adoniram Judson, Chicago, 1887.
Bright Threads, New York, [1897].
Indian and Spanish Neighbours, New York, [1905].
Who-Was-It? Stories, Boston, 1912.
Fifty Missionary Heroes Every Boy and Girl Should Know, New York, [1913].

JOHNSTON, NATHAN ROBINSON (Oct. 8, 1820–March 21, 1904), clergyman, was born in Hopedale, Harrison County. He graduated from Franklin College in 1843 and studied at Theological Seminary, Cincinnati. He was actively opposed to slavery and edited the *Free Press* at New Concord, 1848–49. Ordained in the Reformed Presbyterian Church, he served pastorates in Vermont and Minnesota, worked among freed Negroes at Beaufort, S. C., and in 1875 went to Oakland, Calif., as a missionary to the Chinese.

Looking Back from the Sunset Land; Or, People Worth Knowing, Oakland, Calif., 1898.

JOHNSTON, WILLIAM (April 1, 1804–1887), lawyer, born in Shippensburg, Pa., was brought to Jefferson County in 1808. Largely self-educated, he read law in Steubenville and later practiced in Carrollton. In 1839 he moved to Cincinnati, where he practiced law, served as U. S. Surveyor-General, 1841–45, and as judge of the superior court. He moved to Washington, D. C., in 1861 to practice law. A powerful orator, he delivered several addresses that were later published in pamphlet form.

Arguments to Courts and Juries, 1846–1874, Cincinnati, 1887.

JOHNSTON, WILLIAM ALEXANDER (May 30, 1864–Oct. 16, 1946), was born on a farm near Oil City, Pa. He attended public school in Greensburg, Pa., until he was fifteen, when he began working for the Pennsylvania Railroad. In 1890 he entered the employ of Ohio C. Barber as an engineer. He laid out the town of Barberton and designed numerous buildings. He was active in real estate around Akron and laid out a number of subdivisions and industrial centers. He wrote a recollection of his boyhood: *My Own Main Street,* Cincinnati, [1921].

JONES, ADOLPHUS EBERHARDT (1819–July 25, 1889), physician, born in Greensboro, Pa., studied at Cincinnati College in 1837, and graduated from Jefferson Medical College in 1841. He moved to Ohio in 1846 and afterward practiced in Fulton and Walnut Hills. During the Civil War he was military governor of the Cincinnati District, 1861–63, and after 1863 was Provost Marshal of the First District. In 1888 he was appointed Surgeon General of Ohio. He delivered several historical addresses that were published as pamphlets.

Extracts from the History of Cincinnati and the Territory of Ohio . . . , Cincinnati, 1879.

JONES, ALICE DANNER (April 12, 1854–March 22, 1926), daughter of John Danner (q.v.), was born in Canton, Stark County. She graduated from Denison University and taught there for a time. She later founded an academy for young ladies in Canton and also was a lyceum bureau lecturer. She died in Canton. She published *A McKinley Romance,* Akron, [1901], and a posthumous collection of her verse was published: *Poems,* [Canton], 1927.

JONES, CHARLES A. (c.1815–July 4, 1851), lawyer, was born in Philadelphia, Pa. His parents moved to Cincinnati when he was a child. He wrote for several newspapers and magazines before being admitted to the bar. In 1839 a series of satirical lyrics entitled "Aristophanaea" appeared in the Cincinnati *Gazette,* which attracted a great deal of attention. Jones's authorship was not known, even to the editor of the *Gazette.* He also wrote a series of poems for the same newspaper under the pen name Dick Tinto. He practiced law in New Orleans for several years, but returned to Cincinnati in 1851 because of failing health. He died in Mill Creek Township, Hamilton County. William D. Gallagher (q.v.) praised him for his use of Western subjects, but deplored the haste and carelessness of his habits of composition.

The Outlaw, and Other Poems, Cincinnati, 1835.

JONES, DAVID (1815–1896), a Quaker, was long a resident of West Milton, Miami County. In addition to his versified account of the murder of Levi Falknor, he assisted in writing *History of Miami County, Ohio* (1880).

The Death of Levi Falknor, a Poem, Dayton, [1836?].

JONES, GENEVIEVE ESTELLE. See Howard E. Jones.

JONES, HOWARD E. (Aug. 24, 1853–Dec. 12, 1945), physician, was born in Cleveland, Cuyahoga County, the son of Dr. Nelson E. Jones (q.v.). He graduated from Hobart College in 1875 and the Medical College of Ohio in 1876. He began to practice medicine with his father in 1878 in Circleville and spent the remainder of his life in that community, practicing medicine and serving as president of a Circleville utility company. Author of several pamphlets on historical subjects, he is primarily remembered for his connection with the monumental *Nests and Eggs,* which has been described as the most beautiful book ever published in the United States. Partly because he long outlived the rest of his family, he is generally credited with the major part of the work; and because he was reticent regarding the project, exact details of the production are difficult to ascertain. The idea for such a work probably originated with Nelson E. Jones, who spent more than $30,000 over the years in preparing it. The work was a co-operative effort of the Jones family. In 1877 Robert Clarke of Cincinnati agreed to publish such a work; and Adolph K. Krebs, Cincinnati lithographer, taught Genevieve Estelle Jones (1847–79) and her friend Eliza Shulze to draw on stone. When Genevieve died of typhoid fever Aug. 17, 1879, her mother, Virginia Smith Jones (1827–1906), took over the task of coloring the plates. Other artists who worked on the plates were Nellie Jacobs of Circleville, Josephine Klippart of Columbus, and Kate Gephart of Circleville. The work was issued in parts to be sold by subscription, but there were never more than twenty subscribers for the separate parts. Part I was completed in 1879, and Part XXIII in 1886. About 95 copies were produced. In accordance with a promise to the subscribers, most of the lithographic stones were destroyed. The texts accompanying most of the 68 plates were written by Howard Jones, but a few at least were written by his father, who also did much of the field work. The work is highly prized, not only for its rarity but also for the minute detail with which the eggs and nests were drawn. Nine uncolored sets are known to have been destroyed by fire.

Illustrations of the Nests and Eggs of Birds of Ohio, with Text, 2 vols., Circleville, 1886.

JONES, ICHABOD GIBSON (d.1857), physician and educator, was born in Unity, Maine. He received his medical education at the University of New York and came to Worthington in 1831. He became widely known for his teachings in eclectic medicine. He incorporated into the book below an unfinished work by Thomas Vaughan Morrow (April 14, 1804–July 16, 1850), organizer of Cincinnati Eclectic Medical College.

The American Eclectic Practice of Medicine, (with William Sherwood), 2 vols., Cincinnati, 1853–54.

JONES, IGNATIUS. Pseud. See Gorham A. Worth.

JONES, IRA LAFAYETTE (May 18, 1866–), was born in Jackson, Jackson County, where he attended public schools. After graduating from National Normal University, Lebanon, in 1886, he studied law in Chicago. Admitted to the bar in 1892, he practiced in Chicago until 1902 and afterward was in the publishing business in Washington, D. C. His novel *The*

Richer—The Poorer has its setting in southern Ohio.

Jones' Non-partisan Financial Catechism, [Chicago, 1896].

Beoni, the Sphinx; A Novel, [n.p., 1898].

The Richer—The Poorer, Chicago, 1902.

JONES, JOHN PETER (Sept. 4, 1847–Oct. 3, 1916), Congregational missionary to India, born in Wales, lived in Ohio in the late 1860s and early 1870s. While working in mines around Youngstown, he preached to Welsh miners. With money saved from his wages, he attended Western Reserve College and Andover Seminary. From 1878 to 1914 he was a missionary in India. He died in Hartford, Conn., and is buried in Oberlin. He wrote religious textbooks in Tamil for use in the Indian schools and several books on the mission effort, e.g., *India, Its Life and Thought,* New York, 1908. DAB 10

JONES, JOHN WILLIAM (Jan. 25, 1860–Sept. 28, 1930), educator, was born on a farm near Mineral Springs, Adams County. He taught in country schools before going to National Normal University, Lebanon, where he graduated in 1885. He was superintendent of schools in Manchester, 1885–95, and in 1895 became superintendent of the Ohio State School for the Deaf. He wrote textbooks for deaf children, a book on eugenics, and *The Education of Robert, a Deaf Boy,* Columbus, 1925.

JONES, JOSHUA HENRY, JR. (1876–1953), was born in Orangeburg, S. C., son of Bishop Joshua Jones, who was president of Wilberforce University. He attended Central High School, Columbus, and graduated from Brown University. He worked on the Providence, R. I., *Journal* and the Boston *Transcript* and was a librarian in the Boston Public Library. He wrote a novel and two volumes of poetry, e.g., *The Heart of the World,* Boston, 1919.

JONES, MABEL CRONISE (June 18, 1860–1920), was born in Tiffin, Seneca County. She attended Lake Erie College, Painesville. After marrying Thomas M. Jones, she lived in Harrisburg, Pa. She contributed to many newspapers in Ohio and Pennsylvania. Her publications include a book of verse: *Gettysburg,* Syracuse, N. Y., 1902. WWW 1

JONES, NELSON EDWARDS (Sept. 20, 1821–Dec. 15, 1901), physician, was born in Ross County. After graduating from Cleveland Medical College in 1846, he practiced in Cleveland for two years and in Iowa for four years. In 1853 he began practice in Circleville, where he passed the remainder of his life. An ardent sportsman and lover of nature, he began in 1877 to collect birds' nests and eggs; and he undoubtedly conceived the great *Nests and Eggs,* usually credited to his son, Howard E. Jones (q.v.).

The Squirrel Hunters of Ohio; Or, Glimpses of Pioneer Life, Cincinnati, 1898.

JONES, MRS. RICHARD. See Mabel Wagnalls.

JONES, ROBERT RALSTON (July 16, 1850–Oct. 19, 1930), engineer, was born in Bridgetown, N. J. As a civilian engineer with the U. S. Engineer Corps, he was stationed in Cincinnati, 1892–1930, and supervised construction of more than fifty locks and dams on the Ohio River. He wrote a book about the Ohio River and *Fort Washington at Cincinnati . . . ,* [Cincinnati?], 1902.

JONES, SAMUEL MILTON (Aug. 8, 1846–July 12, 1904), inventor, manufacturer, mayor of Toledo, 1897–1904, was born in Carnarvonshire, Wales. Little events in the broad retrospect of history have a way of producing impact on individuals in far-off places. When the victorious Roman legions overran Wales and built a little stone church in Bedd Gelert, it would have been hard to predict that this would be the big house which was first to impress "Golden Rule" Samuel M. Jones. Ty Mawr (translated "big house") witnessed the birth of the man who was to become Toledo's 29th mayor. When he was four years old, his family migrated to the United States and located in the vicinity of Rome, N. Y. His ability to make money was demonstrated early in his first venture in the Pennsylvania oil fields, where he was working by 1865. He moved from there to Lima in 1885 during the Ohio-Indiana oil boom. His invention of the "sucker rod" pioneered the facility for extracting oil from the earth. It was then that he organized the company that ultimately became the S. M. Jones Company of Toledo, and established a manufacturing arm in the Texas oil fields. His social concepts were rare, indeed, for the era in which he lived: municipal housing to replace slums and tenements, civil service for police and fire employees. He did not limit his concepts of social justice to governmental affairs, but he carried them on in his own private business by instituting profit-sharing and planned recreation for his employees. He made certain that his workers were able to obtain a good fifteen-cent lunch. He was a strong advocate of a single-tax system. He lived in the aura of equality and brotherhood. Here is a man whose schooling was limited to thirty months and yet who authored several articles and two books: a two-volume work entitled *Letters of Love and Labor* and another dealing with his concept of social philosophy, *The New Right.* First nominated the candidate for mayor as a compromise by the Republican Convention of 1896 and elected as a Republican that year, he was refused renomination by his party for a second term because of his strongly advocated reforms. Here was a man who seemed to lose all elements in his community. He lost his party. He was suspect by business. The clergy was in outright denunciation of his policy which made Toledo a haven of those who behaved, regardless of what they might have done elsewhere. When certain ministers urged him to drive out the ladies of the street, he replied: "Where to?" and then in turn suggested that each of the complainants take in one of these unfortunates and attempt to rehabilitate her, setting an example by which she might live. Whether this was a tongue-in-cheek suggestion will never be known, but it was never acted upon. He initiated the Independent Movement that made a strong imprint on Toledo political life for thirty or more years. He won overwhelmingly without any party support in 1899, 1901, and 1903. Only death kept him from a continuation of one of the most sensational political careers of his times. He gave unstintedly of his time to the public good. He donated all of his salary to the poor, encouraged his own employees to organize, marched in Labor Day parades at the head of his employees, read incessantly both poetry and prose. Burns, Emerson, Whitman, and Tolstoy were high on his list of preferences. The drive for greatness may have gained impetus from the big stone house in Wales, but the constant tribute to his parents made apparent the impact of their philosophy as he said: "I rest secure in the comforting belief, that they all earned their living and observed the divine injunction, 'In the sweat of thy face shalt thou eat bread'." One of his supporters summed up his life as follows: "Dreamer, idealist, poetic temperament and prophetic instinct and insight. His advocacy of strange doctrines has compelled men to think, yet he never sought to compel men." Yet, with all his dreams and his ideals, he retained the qualities of individual leadership and the ability to communicate with other individuals. He was never able to pass on to others the strength of communication that he, himself, possessed. This, no doubt, accounted for his inability to organize in a formal way the men and women dedicated to his philosophy. However, he made lasting impact as a man who was able to live, both in public life and in business, by the Golden Rule to such an extent that it became synonymous with his name.

Michael V. DiSalle

The New Right: A Plea for Fair Play through a More Just Social Order, New York, 1899.

Letters of Labor and Love . . . , 2 vols., Toledo, 1900–01.

JONES, THOMAS DAVID (Dec. 12, 1811–Feb. 27, 1881), sculptor, was born in Oneida County, N. Y. He came to Ohio with his parents, who settled in Licking County in 1837. For several years he worked on the Ohio canals as a stonecutter. He became a marblecutter in Cincinnati in 1841 and while so engaged began to execute portrait busts in wood, stone, and marble. In 1842 he opened a studio in Cincinnati and became a full-fledged sculptor. Among the notable men who sat for him were Zachary Taylor, Henry Clay, Thomas Corwin, Salmon P. Chase, and William Henry Harrison. In 1860 he was commissioned by a group of Columbus men to go to Springfield, Ill., to execute a bust of the Republican candidate. During the months that followed, his studio became a favorite hide-out for the harassed Lincoln. Jones was never reimbursed for his expenses or paid for the bust—a matter which became an open scandal in Ohio art circles. When the famous Cincinnati actor James E. Murdoch (q.v.) mentioned Jones to Lincoln, the latter exclaimed, "Oh! my man of mud!" The appellation clung to Jones for some years, and the episode was lampooned by John P. Frankenstein (q.v.) in his *American Art.* The bust which Jones had modeled in clay was finally cast in bronze and was bought by the State of Ohio in 1871 and placed in the capitol. It is Jones's best-known work. Jones contributed an account of his experiences with Lincoln to the Sacramento, Calif., *Weekly Union,* Nov. 4, 1873; it was reprinted in 1934. His last years were spent in abject poverty. He died in Columbus.

Sketch of the Life and Labors of Thomas D. Jones . . . , Columbus, 1871.

Memories of Lincoln . . . , New York, 1934.

JONES, VIRGINIA SMITH. See Howard E. Jones.

JONES, WILLIAM CAREY (1814–1867), journalist and lawyer, was born in Maine. He was brought to Chillicothe at the age of two. He learned the printing trade and before his twentieth birthday started a weekly in Chillicothe, the *Buckeye.* William Cooper Howells (q.v.), who first met him at this time, described him as unusually precocious. In May, 1836, Jones was in Iowa helping issue that state's first newspaper, the Dubuque *Visitor.* He returned to Chillicothe in the fall of 1836, where among other activities he studied law. In partnership with Seneca W. Ely he published the *Scioto Gazette* from Nov. 1, 1839, to Dec. 17, 1840. He went to New Orleans, was admitted to the Louisiana bar, and in 1844 became co-publisher of the New Orleans *Commercial Review.* He became a brother-in-law of John C. Frémont in 1847, when he married Eliza Benton, the eldest daughter of Senator Thomas Hart Benton of Missouri. After settling in California in 1849, he achieved fame as a lawyer and became a recognized expert on California land titles.

Land Titles in California, Washington, D. C., 1850.

Colonel Benton and His Contemporaries, [Washington, D. C., 1858].

Letters of William Carey Jones, in Review of Attorney General Black's Report to the President of the United States, on the Subject of Land Titles in California, San Francisco, 1860.

The "Pueblo Question" Solved . . . , San Francisco, 1860.

JONES, WILLIAM POWELL (Oct. 30, 1901–), educator, was born in Cochran, Ga. He graduated from Emory University in 1921 and Harvard University (Ph.D.) in 1927. Since 1930 he has been on the faculty of Western Reserve University, since 1954 as chairman of the English department. He has written professional articles, a textbook, and several books, e.g., *Thomas Gray, Scholar . . . ,* New York, 1937. WW 30

JONES, WILLIS KNAPP (Nov. 27, 1895–), educator, born in Matteawan, N. Y., has been a member of the romance languages department, Miami University, since 1923. Besides a number of Spanish textbooks and translations, he has published a novel about boarding school life: *The Hammon Twins,* New York, 1926. WW 28

JORDAN, DULCINA MASON (Mrs. James J.) (July 21, 1833–April 25, 1895), born in Marathon, N. Y., grew up in Indiana and spent most of her life in that state. She was, however, associate editor of the Cincinnati *Saturday Night* for three years. A poem on the Tyler-Davidson fountain, Cincinnati, is to be found in her one volume of verse: *Rosemary Leaves,* Cincinnati, 1873.

JORDAN, PHILIP DILLON (Nov. 7, 1903–), educator, born in Burlington, Iowa, was in the history department, Miami University, 1935–45. He wrote *Ohio Comes of Age,* vol. 5 in the *History of Ohio,* edited by Carl F. Wittke, Columbus, 1943, and several other books on history, politics, and folklore, e.g., *Singin' Yankees,* Minneapolis, Minn., 1946. WW 30

JOSEPH, HELEN HAIMON (Mrs. Ernest A.) (Aug. 28, 1888–), born in Atlanta, Ga., was brought to Cleveland when she was about twelve and has spent her life in that city. Interested in puppetry, she founded a puppet theater, devised puppetry kits, and wrote several books about marionettes and plays for puppet theaters, e.g., *Little Mr. Clown; The Adventures of a Marionette,* New York, [1932].

JOSEPH, JESSE MONTEFIORE (Nov. 24, 1884–), advertising executive, born in Baltimore, Md., came to Cincinnati in 1908 as advertising manager of Kline's. He later established his own advertising agency which he conducted until his retirement in 1955. He has published a story of a Jewish immigrant family in America: *Heritage,* Cincinnati, 1935. WWMW 49

JOSS, CATHERINE (Oct. 18, 1818–March 10, 1907), was born in Philadelphia, Pa. In 1829 her parents moved to Payne Township, Holmes County, where her father operated a tavern and store. On August 15, 1839, she married John Joss, who died in 1855. She later moved to Tuscarawas County and died at New Philadelphia. Although her autobiography devotes considerable space to the intemperance and unreliability of her late husband, it is also an interesting account of the Amish on the frontier.

Autobiography of Catherine Joss . . . , Cleveland, 1891.

JOYNER, FRED BUNYAN (April 16, 1895–), educator, born in Ethelsville, Ala., has been a member of the history department, Miami University, since 1922. He has written professional articles and a book: *David Ames Wells, Champion of Free Trade,* Cedar Rapids, Iowa, [1939]. WW 30

JUDKINS, CLYDE HOLLINGSWORTH. See Lavina A. J. Burtoft.

JUDSON, EDWARD CARROLL ZANE (Ned Buntline) (March 20, 1823–July 16, 1886), prolific author of dime novels, made a short stay in Ohio. In 1844 he published two issues of *Ned Buntline's Magazine* at Cincinnati. With $1,000 invested by Lucius A. Hine (q.v.), he then established the *Western Literary Journal and Monthly Magazine.* Although Judson appealed to Westerners' regional pride and urged them to support a Western journal, it survived only six issues (November, 1844–April, 1845). Judson went south, and Hine was left with a considerable burden of debts.

JUDSON, PHOEBE NEWTON GOODELL (Oct. 25, 1831–Jan. 16, 1926), was born in Vermilion, Erie County, the daughter of a pioneer minister of the region, J. W. Goodell. In 1849 she married Reverend Holden Allen Judson, also of a pioneer family. Her parents went to the Willamette Valley during the 1846 migration, and the young couple followed them in 1853. Judson established a store in Thurston County, Washington Territory, which he sold in 1861, when he moved to Lynden on Bellingham Bay, a village he served as the first mayor. Mrs. Judson contributed poetry to local newspapers. Also, shortly before her death, she wrote a book highly esteemed by those interested in the early history of the State of Washington: *A Pioneer's Search for an Ideal Home . . . ,* Bellingham, Wash., 1925.

JUERGENS, ARTHUR R. (Dec. 9, 1863–May 12, 1952), educator, was born in Buffalo, N. Y., but spent most of his adult life in Cincinnati and Springfield. He was music supervisor in the Springfield schools, 1892–1920, and lived in that city after his retirement. He published a volume of verse: *"Among the Wildflowers,"* [Springfield, 1937].

JUETTNER, OTTO (Feb. 3, 1865–Aug. 23, 1922), physician, was born near Breslau, Germany. He came to America in 1881, graduated from St. Xavier's College in 1885, and earned his M.D. at the Medical College of Ohio, Cincinnati, in 1888. While practicing in Cincinnati, he wrote several medical books and studies in the history of medicine, including a valuable historical account of the medical profession in Cincinnati: *Daniel Drake and His Followers,* Cincinnati, [1909]. WWW 1

JUNKIN, GEORGE (Nov. 1, 1790–May 20, 1868), Presbyterian clergyman and educator, born in Pennsylvania, spent three years in Ohio, 1841–43, as president of Miami University. His vigorous opposition to abolitionism created considerable controversy and led to his resignation. He stated his views in a pamphlet, *The Integrity of Our National Union, vs. Abolitionism . . . ,* Cincinnati, 1843.

K

KAIL, MARY E. (1827–Jan. 28, 1890), was born in Washington, D. C., but spent most of her life in Leesville, Carroll County. She wrote a number of patriotic poems and emotional lyrics. The collection of her verse was apparently financed by Mrs. Leland Stanford, to whom the volume is dedicated.

Crown Our Heroes, and Other Poems, Washington, D. C., 1887.

KAISER, RAMONA (Aug. 9, 1909–), was born in Indian Hill Village, Hamilton County. She was active in civic and literary organizations and lectured on Indians. She also wrote plays, poems, short stories. In 1954 she married Judson M. Bradley and has since lived in Arlington, Calif. She became interested in local history and wrote numerous feature stories for newspapers and a pamphlet on early Hamilton County: *Glimpses into the Past . . . ,* Madeira, 1940.

KALISCH, ISIDOR (Nov. 15, 1816–May 11, 1886), rabbi, born in Prussia, emigrated to America in 1849 and served pastorates in Cleveland, 1850–56, and Cincinnati, 1856–57. A leader in reform Judaism, he published while in Cleveland one of his most important works: *Wegweiser für Rationelle Forschungen in den Biblischen Schriften . . . ,* Cleveland, 1853.

KANTONEN, TAITO ALMAR (April 24, 1900–), Lutheran clergyman and educator, was born in Karstula, Finland; his parents came to the United States when he was four. In 1932 he became professor of systematic theology at Hamma Divinity School, Springfield, where he is still teaching. He has written numerous articles for religious publications and a number of books, e.g., *The Message of the Church to the World of Today,* Minneapolis, [1941]. WW 30

KARA GIORG. Pseud. See Gustav Brühl.

KARGER, ALFRED GUS (July 17, 1901–), was born in Washington, D. C., the son of Gus J. Karger, Washington correspondent for the Cincinnati *Times-Star.* He has lived in Ohio since 1920. He was a radio editorial commentator on WLW, Cincinnati, 1935–39. He was also an executive in a Cincinnati printing company, 1920–55. He served in World War II. He has published one book: *Thinking American,* New York, [1941].

KARN, ESTHER NELSON (Aug. 21, 1880–c.1935), was born near New Philadelphia, Tuscarawas County, but spent most of her life in Indiana. She was reared in De Kalb County, Ind., graduated from Hicksville, Ind., High School, attended De Silva School of Oratory in Fort Wayne, Ind., and afterward lived in that city, where her husband, S. A. Karn, was a music dealer.

"Snowflakes," Philadelphia, 1900.
Wild Roses, [Fort Wayne, 1915].
Lure of the Wilds, Boston, [1925].

KARR, ELIZABETH PLATT (? – ?), was born in Geneva, N. Y. Most of her life was spent in North Bend, Hamilton County. In 1879 she married Gen. Charles W. Karr, a prominent member of the Cincinnati bar and at one time adjutant general of Ohio.

The American Horsewoman, Boston, 1884.

KASER, MARGARET KATHARINE (Jan. 5, 1895–), was born in Middletown, Butler County. A graduate of the University of Cincinnati and Cincinnati Conservatory of Music, she taught music in Middletown, 1914–26, and later taught remedial English and mathematics in Cincinnati, 1944–54. In 1931 she married Edwin L. Ryan, president of Middletown Hydraulic Company, and since his death in 1954 she has served as president of the company. Under her maiden name, she published a collection of verse: *Silver Strings; Poems,* [New York, 1940].

KATES, PHILIP (1883–April 11, 1935), lawyer, was born in Cincinnati, Hamilton County. He attended St. Xavier's Academy and Cincinnati Law School, was admitted to the bar, and afterward practiced in Tulsa, Okla. He wrote *The Two Swords; A Study of the Union of Church and State,* Washington, D. C., 1928.

KATTERHENRY, EDWIN A. (Dec. 16, 1900–), clergyman, was born in St. Marys, Auglaize County. He was for a number of years pastor of Salem Church, Cincinnati, and now lives in Harvard, Neb. His writings include *God and I,* Cleveland, 1931.

KATZENBERGER, FRANCES ISABELLE (July 6, 1861–1938), was born near Pikeville, Darke County. She attended National Normal University, Lebanon, 1892–95, and traveled in Germany, 1901–03. Her home was in Greenville.

Westward Ho!, Dayton, 1895.
He Would Have Me Be Brave. A Story Taken from Life, Dayton, 1895.
The Three Verdicts, Cincinnati, 1898.

KAUFFMAN, CATHERINE (1859–May 21, 1948), was born in Springfield, Clark County, the daughter of a Methodist clergyman. She was interested in oil painting and wood carving. Her last years were spent in California; she died in Los Angeles.

As Nature Prompts. A Novelette, Cleveland, 1891.

KAUFMANN, PETER (Oct. 3, 1800–1869?), printer and publisher, was born in Maifield, Prussia, and came to America in 1820. He was a tobacconist in Philadelphia, and also studied for the ministry. He met Robert Owen in 1825 and settled in the Economy community in 1826. In 1827 he was the leader of a group that established Teutonia, an unsuccessful co-operative in Columbiana County. In 1828 he settled in Canton. After 1831, he edited and later owned the *Vaterlandsfreund.* He also edited *Deutsche in Ohio und Ohio Staatzeitung,* 1861–69, and published almanacs and textbooks. He was active in promoting the education of German children. The second title below was published simultaneously in German. He corresponded with Ralph Waldo Emerson, to whom he sent a copy of *The Temple of Truth.*

Betrachtung über den Menschen, Philadelphia, 1823.
A Treatise on American Popular Education, Canton, 1839.
The Temple of Truth . . . , Cincinnati, 1858.

KAY, GERTRUDE ALICE (July 8, 1884–Dec. 7, 1939), author and illustrator, was born in Alliance, Stark County, where she lived throughout her life. She was an illustrator for several magazines and also wrote and illustrated a number of books for children, e.g., *When the Sand-Man Comes,* New York, 1916. WWW 1

KEAN, MARTHA. Pseud. See Frances R. G. Gundry.

KEDAR, OBED, was the pseudonymous author of two pamphlets opposing the Civil War and the policies of Lincoln. According to Samuel Medary, he was a Quaker about sixty years old. The first work describes a vision in which an angel appeared to the author in Missouri and described the horrors of the war if it were continued. The second is largely concerned with the benefits of slavery.

A Vision: The Cause and Progress of the Present War, and its Final Termination . . . , Columbus, 1862.

Visions Concerning the Present War, Its Cause, Progress and Final Termination. Columbus, 1863.

KEELER, CLYDE EDGAR (April 11, 1900–), educator, was born in Marion, Marion County. He graduated from Denison University in 1923 and Harvard University (Ph.D.) in 1925. He has served on the faculties of various universities and since 1945 has been professor of biology at Georgia State College for Women. He has published many technical articles, several books on genetics and eugenics, two readers in the Cuna Indian language, and a book of poems: *Annotated Rhymes,* Cambridge, Mass., 1937. AMS 9

KEELER, HARRIET LOUISE (1846–Feb. 12, 1921), educator, was born in South Kortright, N. Y. At the age of fourteen she began teaching in Cherry Valley, N. Y. After graduating from Oberlin College in 1870, she entered the Cleveland public school system, where she was employed as a teacher (and, for eight months, as superintendent of schools) until her retirement in 1912. She was active in the women's suffrage movement. Besides nature books she published English textbooks. Her death occurred in Clifton Springs, N. Y., and she is buried in Oberlin.

The Wild Flowers of Early Spring . . . , [Cleveland], 1894.

Our Native Trees and How to Identify Them . . . , New York, 1900.

Our Northern Shrubs and How to Identify Them . . . , New York, 1903.

Our Garden Flowers . . . , New York, 1910.

The Life of Adelia A. Field Johnston . . . , [Cleveland, 1912].

Our Early Wild Flowers . . . , New York, 1916.

The Wayside Flowers of Summer . . . , New York, 1917.

Our Northern Autumn . . . , New York, 1920.

KEELER, LUCY ELLIOTT (Sept. 27, 1864–1930), was born in Fremont, Sandusky County. She attended Wells College, 1882–85, wrote for various magazines, and was on the staff of *Youth's Companion,* 1896–1911. She wrote a number of articles on local history and also published *If I Were a Girl Again,* New York, [1904]. OBB

KEELER, RALPH OLMSTEAD (Aug. 29, 1840–Dec. 17, 1873), journalist, was born on a farm in Wood County. When he was eight years old, he was sent to live with an uncle in Buffalo, N. Y., but he ran away and worked as a cabin boy on lake steamers and as a minstrel show performer. He studied at St. Vincent's College, Cape Girardeau, Mo., 1856–57, lived for a time in Toledo, attended Kenyon College, 1858–61, worked in the Toledo Post Office, studied for two years at University of Heidelberg, Germany, and closed this period of wandering in San Francisco, where he became Eastern correspondent of the *Alta California.* William Dean Howells (q.v.) took an interest in him, procured a position for him reading proof on the *Atlantic Monthly,* and published a number of his articles. Late in 1873 he was sent to Cuba by the New York *Tribune,* and on the return voyage he fell, or was thrown, from the ship. In a brief memorial Howells suggested that he was murdered by a Spanish officer who had confided in him without knowing that he was a reporter. He is the first in a succession of young writers whom Howells befriended with mingled benevolence and disapproval.

Gloverson and His Silent Partners, Boston, 1869.

Vagabond Adventures, Boston, 1870.

KEEN, SAMUEL ASHTON (May 12, 1842–1896), clergyman, was born in Delaware, Delaware County. After serving in the 83rd O.V.I., 1861–64, he enrolled at Ohio Wesleyan University, where he was graduated in 1868. He was a Methodist pastor in several communities and also traveled as an evangelist.

Faith Papers, Chicago, [1888].

Praise Papers: A Spiritual Autobiography, Chicago, [1894].

KEEP, JOHN (April 20, 1781–Feb. 11, 1870), clergyman, was born in Long Meadow, Mass. After graduating from Yale in 1802, he served Congregational churches in Massachusetts and Homer, N. Y., until 1834, when he came to Cleveland and organized a church. He was a trustee of Oberlin College and also served as financial agent. After serving churches in Wooster, Mansfield, and elsewhere, he settled in Oberlin in 1850. His death occurred in that community.

Narrative of the Origin and Progress of the Congregational Church in Homer . . . , [New York, 1833].

KEESY, WILLIAM ALLEN (c.1843–April 15, 1910), clergyman, was born in Richmond Township, Huron County. He served as a private in the 55th O.V.I. from Oct., 1861, until Dec., 1862, when he was discharged for disability. He later served in the 64th O.V.I. from Sept., 1864, to April, 1865. In 1869 he became a minister of the United Brethren Church and served pastorates in Richland, Seneca, and Huron Counties. He died in Tiffin.

War as Viewed from the Ranks . . . , Norwalk, [1898].

KEEVER, EDWARD W. (Oct. 9, 1889–), journalist, was born in Springboro, Warren County. He attended the George School, Bucks County, Pa., and Miami University, from which he graduated in 1912. He served in World War I and afterward was in advertising work in Dayton and worked on Dayton newspapers. Now retired, he lives in Dayton. His only book is a novel for boys: *Shorty in the Tank Corps,* New York, [1929].

KEIFER, JOSEPH WARREN (Jan. 30, 1836–April 22, 1932), lawyer, soldier, and legislator, was born on a farm near Springfield, Clark County. He attended local schools and spent one year at Antioch College. He read law and took an active part in politics, making fifty campaign speeches for Frémont, although he was not yet old enough to vote. Following that campaign he resumed the study of law and was admitted to the bar in 1858. At this time he became active in the organization of a local volunteer militia company. On April 27, 1861, he was commissioned a major in the 3rd O.V.I. Following a distinguished military career he was mustered out June 27, 1865, with the brevet rank of major general. He served in the 45th–48th and the 59th–61st Congresses and was Speaker of the House in the 47th Congress. He was a most active public speaker, and many of his speeches were published in public documents and in the publications of various organizations. His death occurred in Springfield.

Official Reports of J. Warren Keifer . . . , Springfield, 1866.

Ohio's Contribution, Sacrifice and Service in the War, Springfield, 1878.

A Forgotten Battle: Sailor's Creek, April 6, 1865, Cincinnati, 1888.

Slavery and Four Years of War, New York, 1900.

The Military History of Ohio, from the War of 1812, Including the Civil and Spanish American Wars, Columbus, 1903.

Did William Shaksper Write Shakespeare?, [Springfield, 1904].

Battle of Rich Mountain, Cincinnati, 1911.

KEIL, FREDERICK WILLIAM (Sept. 17, 1830–Aug. 15, 1909), was born in Ross Township, Butler County. He served in the 35th O.V.I. from Aug., 1861, to Aug., 1864. He died in Fort Wayne, Ind.

Thirty-Fifth Ohio . . . , Fort Wayne, Ind., 1894.

KELLAR, HARRY (July 11, 1849–March 10, 1922), magician, was born in Erie, Pa. He was reared in Painesville, where he graduated from high school in 1866. The following year he became manager of a famous team of spirit mediums, the Davenport Brothers. He became a performer in 1871 and toured the world as a magician. After 1884 he was a familiar figure on the American stage and enjoyed great popularity.

Kellar's Aids in Arithmetical Calculations, and Professional Tours around the World, [Philadelphia, 1885].

A Magician's Tour Up and Down and Round About the Earth. Being the Life and Adventures of the American Nostradamus, Harry Kellar, Chicago, 1886.

Kellar's Variety Entertainments; Being a Collection of Original Laughable Skits on Conjuring, Physiognomy, Juggling, Performing Feats, Wax Works, Panoramas, Phrenology . . . , Chicago, [1901].

KELLER, ALBERT GALLOWAY (April 10, 1874–Oct. 31, 1956), educator, was born in Springfield, Clark County. A graduate of Yale University (A.B., 1896; Ph.D., 1899), he spent his entire teaching career on the faculty of that institution, 1900–42. His works include *Through War to Peace,* New York, 1918. WWW 3

KELLERMAN, WILLIAM ASHBROOK (May 1, 1850–March 8, 1908), educator, was born in Ashville, Pickaway County. From 1891 until his death he was professor of botany at Ohio State University. He wrote a number of technical articles and botany textbooks.

Ohio Forest Trees . . . , Columbus, [1895].
Spring Flora of Ohio . . . , Columbus, 1895.

KELLEY, EDGAR STILLMAN (April 14, 1857–Nov. 12, 1944), composer, was born in Sparta, Wis. He studied music in Chicago and Germany, was music critic on the San Francisco *Examiner,* and lived in Germany, 1902–10. From 1910 until his death he served on the faculty of Western College for Women, Oxford. Besides his musical compositions, he wrote numerous essays on musical topics and *Chopin the Composer . . . ,* New York, 1913. WW 24

KELLEY, FRANCIS BEVERLY (July 15, 1905–), was born in St. Marys, Auglaize County. He graduated from Ohio Wesleyan University in 1928 and afterward wrote radio and press publicity for the Ringling Brothers Circus. His books about circus life include *Circus Holiday,* New York, [1942].

KELLEY, IRAD (1791–Jan. 21, 1875), born in Connecticut, came to Cleveland in 1812. He was postmaster, 1819–29, and afterward engaged in the insurance business and in various other enterprises. He died in New York City while en route to Rio de Janeiro to spend the winter. The volume below, which is probably the first book of original poetry published in Cleveland, was anonymous. The attribution to Kelley is based on a contemporary inscription on the title page; the book is also sometimes credited to James W. Ward (q.v.).

Yorick and Other Poems, Cleveland, 1838.

KELLEY, JONATHAN F. (Aug. 14, 1817–July 21, 1855), journalist, was born in Philadelphia, Pa. It is not known how much time Kelley spent in Ohio, but he was in Chillicothe in 1837 and the town served as the locale for several of his sketches. He also served in an editorial capacity on the *Great West* and other Cincinnati newspapers. An itinerant writer, he was better known by his pen names Falconbridge, Jack Humphries, and Stampede.

The Memoirs of Falconbridge, Philadelphia, 1856.

KELLEY, SAMUEL WALTER (Sept. 15, 1855–April 20, 1929), surgeon, was born in Adamsville, Muskingum County. He earned his M.D. from Western Reserve University Medical School in 1884, and also studied in London hospitals. He practiced in Cleveland. Besides medical works he wrote several books of general interest, e.g., *The Witchery o' the Moon, and Other Poems,* [Cleveland, 1919]. WWW 1

KELLOGG, CHARLOTTE (March 24, 1864–March 2, 1946), was born in Madison, Lake County. She graduated from Madison High School and from Lake Erie College for Women. She wrote several books, e.g., *Women of Belgium . . . ,* New York, 1917.

KELLOGG, ELIZABETH ROCKEY (April 10, 1870–), was born in Cincinnati, Hamilton County. She attended Wellesley College, was librarian of the Cincinnati Art Museum, 1909–29, and is still a resident of Cincinnati. She has published poems and plays, articles and pamphlets on art, and a brief biography: *Memories of Joseph Henry Gest . . . ,* Cincinnati, 1937.

KELLOGG, MINER KILBOURNE (Aug. 22, 1814–1889), artist, was born at Manlius Square, N. Y. He apparently received his basic training in art at the New Harmony, Ind., community under Charles Alexandre Lesueur. He began painting in Cincinnati in 1840 and later spent many years in Paris and Florence, where he became distinguished as a painter of national types, such as the Greek, the Jew, and the Moor. In Constantinople he painted a portrait of Raschid Pasha, prime vizier of the Sultan of Turkey. With him in Europe was his wife (Celia Logan Connelley, q.v.), from whom he was later divorced. He spent the last years of his life in Cleveland, and his death occurred in that city.

Justice to Hiram Powers . . . , [Cincinnati], 1848.
Mr. Miner K. Kellogg to His Friends, Paris, 1858.
Researches into the History of a Painting by Raphael of Urbino, Entitled "La Belle Jardiniere" . . . , London, 1860.
Documents Relating to a Picture by Leonardo Da Vinci, Entitled "Herodias," London, 1864.
Fine Arts in the United States . . . , Washington, 1870.

KELLOR, FRANCES ALICE (Oct. 20, 1873–Jan. 4, 1952), lawyer, was born in Columbus, Franklin County. After earning her law degree from Cornell University in 1897, she practiced for several years and also worked in the interests of women's suffrage. She became chief investigator for the Bureau of Industries and Immigration in New York in 1910. Besides textbooks and lectures, she published *Immigration and the Future,* New York, [1920]. WWW 3

KELLY, AMY (May 5, 1877–), educator, was born in Port Clinton, Ottawa County. She attended Lake Erie College for Women, graduated from Oberlin College in 1900, and did graduate work at Wellesley College. She taught English at Lake Erie College, 1900–05, at Wellesley College, 1907–21 and 1932–43, and at Bryn Mawr School for Girls, 1921–32. Now retired, she lives in Miami, Fla. She has written *Eleanor of Aquitaine and the Four Kings,* Cambridge, Mass., 1950.

KELLY, FRED CHARTERS (Jan. 27, 1882–May 23, 1959), journalist, was born in Xenia, Greene County. At the age of fourteen he was Xenia correspondent for Cleveland, Dayton, and Cincinnati newspapers. He attended the University of Michigan, 1900–02, after which he worked on the Cleveland *Plain Dealer* for several years. In 1910 he moved to Washington, D. C., where he conducted a newspaper column, first titled "Statesmen, Real and Near" and later "Kelly Opines," which was widely syndicated. While lecturing and doing freelance writing, he owned a 600-acre farm at Peninsula, Summit County. He was an ardent advocate of conservation and planted nearly 200,000 pine trees on his farm; he was equally ardent as a foe of billboards and conducted a long crusade against signs along the highways. In 1948 he moved to Kensington, Md. Besides numerous articles in national magazines, he wrote books on the stock market and other subjects and several biographies, including one of the Wright Brothers and one of the Indiana humorist, George Ade: *George Ade, Warm-hearted Satirist,* Indianapolis, [1947]. WWW 3

KELLY, MELVILLE CLYDE (Aug. 4, 1883–April 29, 1935), journalist and legislator, was born in Bloomfield, Muskingum County. He graduated from Muskingum College. He published several newspapers in Braddock, Pa.; served in the Pennsylvania House of Representatives, 1910–13; and served in the U. S. Congress, 1913–15 and 1917–35. His books include *Machine Made Legislation,* [Pittsburgh, 1912]. WWW 1

KELLY, SAMUEL JEWETT (July 17, 1866–Oct. 23, 1948), journalist, was born in Michigan of Cleveland parents, who returned to that city a few weeks after his birth. He attended Brooks Military Academy, Cleveland, and Kenyon Academy. In 1883 he joined the staff of the Cleveland *Herald;* and at various times in his later life he wrote for the *Press,* the *Plain Dealer,* the *Leader,* and the *News.* Historical feature stories were his special forte. He wrote *History of Saint Paul's Protestant Episcopal Church in the City of East Cleveland . . . ,* [East Cleveland], 1945.

KELLY, THOMAS RAYMOND (1893–Jan. 17, 1941), educator, was born near Chillicothe, Ross County. In 1903 his family moved to Wilmington, and he graduated from Wilmington College in 1913. After teaching for two years at Pickering College, Canada, he entered Hartford Theological Seminary, from which he graduated in 1919, his studies having been interrupted by service with German prisoners of war in England. After teaching at Wilmington College, 1919–21, he returned to Hartford Seminary to study philosophy and received his Ph.D. in 1924. He was in charge of a Quaker center, Berlin, Germany, 1924–25, and afterward taught at Earlham College, 1925–35, the University of Hawaii, 1935–36, and Haverford College, 1936–41. Besides a work on the philosophy of Emile Meyerson, he wrote essays for *The Friend,* a Quaker journal, which later were included in *A Testament of Devotion,* New York, [1941].

KELSO, ISAAC (? – ?), is listed in the 1853 Cincinnati directory as a publisher residing in Covington, Ky. Few details on his life are available. The reviewer in *Genius of the West* (Aug., 1855) refers to him as a Cincinnati author and to his book *Light, More Light* (sequel to *Danger in the Dark*) as "a weapon against Catholicism, disguised as a story. We do not apprehend that the 'danger in the dark' was very thoroughly exposed by the first book, and we think 'more light' will be needed than is given in the second one, before much good will be accomplished by Mr. Kelso's labors as a writer of romances. These books are spices to meet the popular taste, which Know-Nothingism has excited. They may have a run and put money in the author's pocket, but they will never enlighten or improve those who read them."

Danger in the Dark: A Tale of Intrigue and Priestcraft, Cincinnati, 1855.

Light, More Light; Or, Danger in the Dark . . . , Cincinnati, 1855 .

The Stars and Bars: Or, the Reign of Terror in Missouri, Boston, 1863.

Ringgold; Or, the Soldier Boy of the Wilderness . . . , Boston, 1865.

KEMP, HARRY HIBBARD (Dec. 15, 1883–Aug. 8, 1960), was born in Youngstown, Mahoning County. He went to sea at the age of seventeen and later traveled over the United States as a tramp. In 1919 he settled in Provincetown, Mass., where he was a friend of Eugene O'Neill and where he spent the remainder of his life. He published a variety of books, including several volumes of poetry, e.g., *The Passing God; Song for Lovers,* New York, 1919, and several novels, e.g., *More Miles . . . ,* New York, [1926]. WW 30

KEMPER, ANDREW CARR (1832–Aug. 15, 1905), physician, was born in Cincinnati, Hamilton County. After graduating from Miami Medical College and studying in Europe, he practiced in Cincinnati. During the Civil War he served on the staff of General Halleck and as assistant adjutant general. He died in Dayton.

The Night after the Battle . . . , Cincinnati, [1883].

The Obsequies of Orpheus . . . , Cincinnati, 1887.

KEMPER, FREDERICK AUGUSTUS (1799–1851), educator and clergyman, was born in Cincinnati, Hamilton County, the son of a Presbyterian minister. He taught in Walnut Hills and at Kemper Academy, Preble County. No record of his pastorates has been found.

Consolations of the Afflicted, Cincinnati, 1831.

KENDALL, CAROL SEEGER (Sept. 13, 1917–), was born in Bucyrus, Crawford County. She graduated from Ohio University in 1939. Wife of a professor of English at Ohio University, Paul M. Kendall, she has published a mystery novel: *The Black Seven,* New York, [1946].

KENDALL, EZRA FREMONT (Feb. 15, 1861–Jan. 23, 1910), vaudeville comedian, born in Allegheny County, N. Y., lived in Cleveland for several years before his death and is buried in that city. He published several humorous books, e.g., *Spots of Wit and Humor . . . ,* Cleveland, 1899.

KENLY, JULIE WOODBRIDGE TERRY CLOSSON (March 26, 1869–Jan. 8, 1943), was born in Cleveland, Cuyahoga County. She married Gen. William L. Kenly July 3, 1893. At the time of her death she lived in Washington, D. C. Her most successful works were nature books for children, e.g., *The Astonishing Ant,* New York, 1931. WWW 2

KENNAN, GEORGE (Feb. 16, 1845–May 10, 1924), journalist, was born in Norwalk, Huron County. He learned telegraphy in his boyhood. Before he was 21, he was en route to Siberia, employed as explorer and telegraphic engineer. He and his associates combed the country seeking the most favorable route for a trans-Siberian telegraph line. Upon the conclusion of this adventure Kennan wrote an account of his experiences: *Tent Life in Siberia,* a book which attracted widespread attention. Both in England and in the United States he became a popular lecturer on the Russian Orient. In 1885 he again went to Siberia, this time accompanied by the artist George A. Frost. He spent a year interviewing Russians in exile, and through his book *Siberia and the Exile System,* the stark horrors of that system were first exposed to the world outside the bounds of Russia. He served as correspondent in Cuba during the Spanish-American War and in Japan during the Russo-Japanese War. In 1902 he was sent to Martinique by the *Outlook* to study the volcano Mount Pelée. In addition to his books he wrote innumerable magazine articles.

Tent Life in Siberia . . . , New York, 1870.

Siberia and the Exile System, New York, 1891.

Campaigning in Cuba, New York, 1899.

Folk Tales of Napoleon, New York, 1902.

The Tragedy of Pelée . . . , New York, 1902.

A Russian Comedy of Errors . . . , New York, 1915.

The Chicago & Alton Case . . . , New York, [1916].

Misrepresentation in Railroad Affairs, New York, [1916].

E. H. Harriman's Far Eastern Plans, New York, [1917].

The Salton Sea . . . , New York, 1917.

E. H. Harriman, a Biography, 2 vols., New York, 1922.

KENNEDY, CHARLES E. (May 17, 1856–June 12, 1929), journalist, was born in West Farmington, Trumbull County. After attending Western Reserve Seminary, he came to Cleveland at the age of eighteen to become a reporter under his brother, James H. Kennedy (q.v.), city editor of the *Leader.* He later worked on the Cleveland *Herald,* the St. Louis *Post-Dispatch,* and the *Plain Dealer.* During his later years he was in the advertising business. His death occurred in Cleveland. He wrote *Fifty Years in Cleveland by One Who Lived the Bulk of Them in Newspaper Row . . .* , Cleveland, [1925].

KENNEDY, JAMES HENRY (HARRISON) (Jan. 17, 1849–Jan. 22, 1934), journalist, was born in Farmington, Trumbull County. After studying at Western Reserve Seminary, he worked on several Cleveland newspapers (the *Leader,* the *Herald,* and the *Sunday Voice*), 1872–89. He was editor of the *Magazine of Western History,* and moved to New York City when the headquarters of the magazine moved there. He was historian of the Ohio Society of New York and compiled its history. In 1915 he changed his middle name from Henry to Harrison. He died in Pasadena, Calif., where he had spent the last ten years of his life.

Early Days of Mormonism, Palmyra, Kirtland, and Nauvoo, New York, 1888.
The Bench and Bar of Cleveland, (with Wilson M. Day), Cleveland, 1889.
A History of the City of Cleveland . . . , Cleveland, 1896.
History of the Ohio Society of New York, 1885–1905 . . . , New York, 1906.
Surprise Island, the Pirate of the Sycamore Tree, New York, [1915].

KENNEDY, ROSE. Pseud. See Metta V. F. Victor.

KENNEDY, SARAH LEHR (Nov. 19, 1874–), was born in Ada, Hardin County. She graduated from Ohio Northern University in 1893. With her husband, Edward B. Kennedy, she spent several years in missionary work in China. She now lives in Ada. She has written a biography of her father, the founder of Ohio Northern: *H. S. Lehr and His School . . .* , Ada, 1938.

KENNEDY, WILLIAM SLOANE (June 3, 1822–July 30, 1861), clergyman, was born in Muncy, Pa. He graduated from Western Reserve College in 1846 and two years later was licensed to preach in the Congregational Church. He served in Brecksville, Sandusky, and Cincinnati. His *Life of Christ* was published in an enlarged edition in New York in 1860. His *Plan of Union* is a valuable general history of the Western Reserve, with biographical sketches of early missionaries and considerable general and statistical information. His death occurred in Cincinnati.

Messianic Prophecy and the Life of Christ, Hudson, 1852.
The Plan of Union; Or a History of the Presbyterian and Congregational Churches of the Western Reserve, Hudson, 1856.

KENNEDY, WILLIAM SLOANE (Sept. 26, 1850–1929), son of William S. Kennedy (q.v.) was born in Brecksville, Cuyahoga County, where his father was a Congregational minister. He attended Miami University, Yale University, and Harvard University. He later lived in West Yarmouth, Mass. Besides the titles below, he compiled several anthologies of poetry.

Henry W. Longfellow . . . , Cambridge, Mass., 1882.
John Greenleaf Whittier . . . , Boston, 1882.
Oliver Wendell Holmes . . . , Boston, 1883.
Wonders and Curiosities of the Railway . . . , Chicago, 1884.
The Poet as a Craftsman, Philadelphia, 1886.
John Greenleaf Whittier, the Poet of Freedom, New York, 1892.
Reminiscences of Walt Whitman . . . , London, 1896.
In Portia's Garden, Boston, 1897.
The Real John Burroughs . . . , New York, 1924.
The Fight of a Book for the World . . . , West Yarmouth, Mass., 1926.
Italy in Chains . . . , West Yarmouth, Mass., 1927.

KENT, MARVIN (Sept. 21, 1816–Dec. 10, 1908), was born in Ravenna, Portage County. He was educated at Tallmadge and Claridon Academies. At the age of 22 he became a partner in his father's store at Kent, and within a few years he was identified with the establishment of a flour mill, an extensive window-glass factory, and other local industries. In 1850 he conceived and projected the construction of the Atlantic and Great Western Railroad, designed to connect the Erie with the Ohio and Mississippi Railroad. Though presented as an address at a reunion of old employees of the road, his *History of the A.&G.W.R.R.* is a most important, unadorned, factual statement of the inception, projection, and construction of the railroad and an indispensable source on this subject.

History of the A.&G.W.R.R., Kent, [1899].

KENT, WILLIS. Pseud. See Wilson Collison.

KEPHART, CYRUS JEFFRIES (Feb. 23, 1852–July 22, 1932), bishop of the United Brethren Church, was pastor of First U. B. Church, Dayton, 1908–13. He published several books on religious subjects, e.g., *The Life of Jesus for Children . . .* , Dayton, 1894.

KEPHART, ISAIAH LAFAYETTE (Dec. 10, 1832–Oct. 28, 1908), clergyman and editor, was born in Clearfield County, Pa. He attended Otterbein College, was ordained as a United Brethren minister in 1863, and served through the remainder of the Civil War as a chaplain. After two years in Pennsylvania, he went to Iowa for his health; he operated a farm, taught school, and served as president of Westfield College, Westfield, Ill., 1885–89. In 1889 he came to Dayton as editor of the *Religious Telescope,* a position that he held until his death.

Biography of Jacob Smith Kessler . . . , Dayton, 1867.

The Tobacco Question, Dayton, 1882.

The Holy Spirit in the Devout Life, Dayton, [1904].

KEPLER, WILLIAM M. (Dec. 17, 1841–Nov. 24, 1909), educator, was born in Cuyahoga County. He served as a private in the 4th O.V.I. from June, 1861, to June, 1864. After the Civil War he lived in Berea; he was secretary of the Northern Ohio Conference of the Methodist Church and also taught at Baldwin University. His death occurred in Oberlin.

History of the Three Months' and Three Years' Service . . . of the Fourth Regiment . . . , Cleveland, 1886.

KERCHEVAL, ALBERT FARMER (March 10, 1829–Jan. 24, 1893), was born in Preble County. He went to California in 1849 and spent the remainder of his life in that state, living in Placerville, Sacramento, and Los Angeles. He died in Los Angeles.

Dolores; And Other Poems, San Francisco, 1883.

KERNAHAN, ARTHUR EARL (Nov. 3, 1888–Sept. 16, 1944), evangelist, was born in Mellette, S. Dak., but spent the last years of his life in Cleveland. Besides a number of sermons and pamphlets, he published several books on evangelism, e.g., *Adventures in Visitation Evangelism,* New York, [1928]. WWW 2

KERNAN, WILL HUBBARD. See Will Hubbard-Kernan.

KERR, ALVA MARTIN (Feb. 23, 1875–Nov. 1, 1928), editor and clergyman, was born on a farm near Troy, Miami County. He became a pastor of the Christian Church in 1896 and served rural churches in Ohio and Indiana. He edited the *Herald of Gospel Liberty,* Dayton, 1919–28, and wrote *Thinking Through; Facts and Principles to Clarify the Controversial Thinking in the Church,* New York, 1926. WWNAA 3

KERR, ALVAH MILTON (July 22, 1858–Sept. 26, 1924), editor, was born in Athens, Athens County, but was reared in Wisconsin. From 1876 to 1888 he was a railway telegraph operator and train dispatcher. After 1888 he was engaged in editorial work for several magazines.

Trean: Or, the Mormon's Daughter. A Romantic Story of Life among the Latter-Day Saints, Chicago, 1889.

An Honest Lawyer, a Novel, Chicago, 1892.

Young Heroes of Wire and Rail, Boston, 1903.

Two Young Inventors; The Story of a Flying Boat . . . , Boston, 1904.

The Diamond Key and How the Railway Heroes Won It . . . , Boston, 1907.

KERR, JAMES (Dec. 23, 1805–April 19, 1855), clergyman, was born in Kirk Collom, Scotland. He came to America in 1832, was ordained as a Presbyterian minister in Virginia, and in 1839 became pastor of the First Presbyterian Church, Cadiz, where he served until his death.

A Treatise on the Mode of Baptism . . . , Steubenville, 1844.

KERR, JOHN GLASGOW (Nov. 30, 1824–Aug. 10, 1901), medical missionary, was born in Adams County. After attending Denison University from 1840 to 1842, he studied with Kentucky doctors, attended Transylvania University and Jefferson Medical College, and received his M.D. in 1847. While practicing in southwestern Ohio, he heard a report by a Chinese on the suffering in his country. Kerr determined immediately to go to China as a Presbyterian missionary. He arrived in May, 1854. The remainder of his life was devoted to service in Kwangchow (Canton) as a practicing physician and as head of the hospital of the Medical Missionary Society. His writings included numerous medical works in Chinese. His last years were concentrated on the establishment of a hospital for the insane.

The Chinese Question Analyzed . . . , San Francisco, 1877.

Medical Missions, Philadelphia, 1895.

KERR, MINNIE MARKHAM (Aug. 23, 1879–Oct. 15, 1951), was born in Frankfort, Ky. The wife of John S. Kerr, she lived in Cleveland for many years and was a frequent contributor to Ted Robinson's columns in the *Plain Dealer.* She moved to Versailles, Ky., in 1948, and she died in that community. She published *The American Highway, and Other Poems,* Philadelphia, [1949].

KERR, MYRA WEHRLY (April 15, 1885–), now Mrs. David Mead, was born in Eaton, Preble County. She now lives in Dayton. An active clubwoman, she has written plays and sketches for presentation by various groups and also has written numerous newspaper articles. She published *Scrap-Basket Tid-Bits,* Greenfield, Ind., 1938.

KERR, WINFIELD SCOTT (June 23, 1852–Sept. 11, 1917), lawyer and legislator, was born in Monroe, Richland County. He attended Mansfield schools, graduated from the University of Michigan in 1879, and was admitted to the bar in the same year. He practiced in Mansfield and served in the Ohio Senate, 1888–92, and in the U. S. House of Representatives, 1895–1901. He died in Mansfield. Executor for the estate of John Sherman (q.v.), he published *John Sherman, His Life and Public Services,* 2 vols., Boston, 1908. WW 4

KERSHNER, GLENN ROBERT (July 20, 1884–), was born in Findlay, Hancock County. After attending Findlay College, he began a varied career that has included playing in the Detroit symphony orchestra, working as a cartoonist, and making numerous commercial and adventure films. His residence is now Honolulu, Hawaii. He has visited the South Pacific several times and published *Brown Barriers; A South Sea Story,* Hollywood, Calif., 1939.

KESTER, PAUL (Nov. 2, 1870–June 20, 1933), was born in Delaware, Delaware County, the younger brother of Vaughan Kester (q.v.). He was educated by tutors at Mount Vernon and Cleveland. His mother was a cousin of William Dean Howells (q.v.), who advised and encouraged both Paul and his brother in their literary careers. His first play was *The Countess Roudine,* produced in 1892 with Mrs. Fiske in the title role. Most of his plays were adaptations of novels or of plays by European writers. Many of them were not published in book form. His biggest successes were *Sweet Nell of Old Drury* (1900) and *When Knighthood Was in Flower* (1901). The general spirit of his dramas is romantic and extravagant, very different from the theories of his famous cousin, but Howells praised his novel about a Negro in the South, *His Own Country,* as one of "the three or four American novels which will merit remembrance."

Tales of the Real Gypsy, New York, 1897.
His Own Country, Indianapolis, [1917].
Conservative Democracy . . . , Indianapolis, [1919].
Diana Dauntless, a Romance of the Eighteenth Century, Philadelphia, 1929.

KESTER, VAUGHAN (Sept. 12, 1869–July 4, 1911), was born in New Brunswick, N. J. Brought to Ohio in his infancy, he was educated in the public schools of Mt. Vernon and by private tutors. In his youth he traveled extensively in the South and West and lived for some years on a ranch in Colorado. In the early 1890s he joined his brother Paul Kester (q.v.) in New York City and later became a member of the staff of the *Cosmopolitan.* Stimulated by the success of several short stories he had written for magazines, and encouraged and aided by his cousin William Dean Howells (q.v.), he wrote his first novel, *The Manager of the B & A,* New York, 1901. His most popular novel, *The Prodigal Judge,* Indianapolis, 1911, published but a short time before his death, was a best-seller, and his *The Just and the Unjust,* Indianapolis, 1912, was high on the list of best-sellers the following year. His other books include *The Fortunes of the Landrays,* Indianapolis, 1905; *John O' Jamestown,* Indianapolis, 1907; and *The Hand of the Mighty and Other Stories,* Indianapolis, [1913]. DAB 10

KETCHAM, BRYAN ELLSWORTH (March 17, 1898–), was born in Pleasant Plain, Warren County. After graduating from Miami University in 1925, he taught in Ohio schools, was a map draftsman in Hamilton County court house, and worked as a draftsman in Cincinnati. He has lectured on covered bridges and published a book: *Covered Bridges on the Byways of Indiana,* [Lockland?, 1949].

KETCHAM, WILMOT A. (Feb. 23, 1860–Dec. 16, 1928), was born in Toledo, Lucas County, and spent his life in that city. He wrote for several Toledo newspapers, was active in Boy Scout activities, and engaged in the insurance business. From boyhood he hunted and fished near Lake Erie. He was an authority on French-Canadians and Indians of the Great Lakes country and published *The Dance at Joe Chevalier, and Other Poems,* Toledo, [1904].

KETCHUM, ALTON HARRINGTON (Oct. 8, 1904–), advertising executive, was born in Cleveland, Cuyahoga County, and lived there until his graduation from Western Reserve University in 1926. He was with the United Press, 1926–27, went into advertising in 1927, and has been an official of McCann-Erickson, Inc., since 1934. He has also served on several commissions and agencies dealing with international relations. He has written several books, e.g., an account of a round-the-world trip: *Follow the Sun,* New York, 1930. WW 30

KEYES, CHARLES M. (Oct. 28, 1840–March 1, 1902), was born in Peoria, Ill. He served in the 123rd O.V.I. and the 16th O.V.I. from Aug., 1862, to June, 1865. After the Civil War he lived in Sandusky, where he served as a government gauger, as postmaster, 1880–87, and as county auditor. He later was steward of the Epileptic Hospital at Gallipolis.

The Military History of the 123rd Regiment . . . , Sandusky, 1874.

KEYES, JAMES (March 24, 1801–June 28, 1883), was born in Albemarle County, Va., but in 1811 his father moved to Scioto County. James learned carpentry, studied at Ohio University, made several trips on flatboats to New Orleans, and afterward operated a ferry on Scioto Brush Creek. His later life was spent in Portsmouth. Most of the biographical sketches making up his book were first published in the Portsmouth *Republican* and the Ironton *Register.*

Pioneers of Scioto County . . . , Portsmouth, 1880.

KEYSER, CASSIUS JACKSON (May 15, 1862–May 8, 1947), mathematician, was born in Rawson, Hancock County. He graduated from Normal University in 1883, taught in the public schools for several years, and earned his Ph.D. at Columbia University in 1901. He was on the Columbia faculty from 1897 until his retirement in 1927. He published a number of books on mathematics and philosophy, e.g., *Humanism and Science,* New York, 1931. WWW 2

KEYSER, LEANDER SYLVESTER (May 13, 1856–Oct. 18, 1937), clergyman and educator, was born in Tuscarawas County. He attended Wittenberg Seminary and was ordained to the Lutheran ministry in 1879. After serving various churches in Ohio and Indiana, he served on the faculty of Wittenberg College, 1911–32. His death occurred in Springfield.

The Only Way Out, New York, [1888].
Bird-dom, Boston, [1891].
In Bird Land, Chicago, 1894.
News from the Birds, New York, 1898.
John Westoff—Lutheran . . . , New York, 1900.
Babby Redstart, and Other Bird Stories, Topeka, Kan., 1901.
Birds of the Rockies . . . , Chicago, 1902.
Our Bird Comrades, Chicago, [1907].
The Rational Test . . . , Philadelphia, 1908.
A System of Christian Ethics, Philadelphia, 1913.
A System of Christian Evidence, Springfield, 1913.
Election and Conversion . . . , Burlington, Iowa, 1914.
A System of Natural Theism, Burlington, Iowa, 1917.
A System of General Ethics, Burlington, Iowa, 1918.
Contending for the Faith . . . , New York, [1920].
Man's First Disobedience . . . , New York, 1924.
The Doctrines of Modernism . . . , Chicago, [1925].
The Conflict of Fundamentalism and Modernism, Burlington, Iowa, 1926.
A Manual of Christian Ethics, Burlington, Iowa, 1926.
The Problem of Origins . . . , New York, 1926.
A Handbook of Christian Psychology, Burlington, Iowa, 1928.
The Philosophy of Christianity, Burlington, Iowa, 1928.
A Reasonable Faith . . . , Burlington, Iowa, 1933.

KEYT, ALONZO THRASHER (Jan. 10, 1827–Nov. 9, 1885), physician, was born in Higginsport, Brown County. He attended Parker's Academy, Felicity, studied medicine with Dr. William Johnston of Moscow, and received his M.D. from the Medical College of Ohio in 1848. In 1850 he moved to Cincinnati, where he remained until the end of his days. In 1873 his attention was attracted to the consideration of the graphic method in the portrayal of the movements of the circulation, as a result of which he devised a combined cardiograph and sphygmograph. His principal writings are included in the volume listed below.

Sphygmography and Cardiography, New York, 1887.

KIENER, MOTHER MARY ALOYSI (Oct. 25, 1882–), was born in Cuyahoga County. She attended Cleveland parochial schools and in 1901 became a member of the Congregation of the Sisters of Notre Dame. She studied at the University of Notre Dame, South Bend, Ind., (A.B., 1922;

Ph.D., 1930). She taught in Notre Dame High School, 1911–17, and was professor of English at Notre Dame College, Cleveland, 1917–47, where she is now in residence. She has written a number of devotional books and a biography: *John Henry Newman . . .* , Boston, 1933.

KILBOURN, JOHN (Aug. 7, 1787–March 12, 1831), author of Ohio's first best-seller, was born in Berlin, Conn. After graduating from the University of Vermont, he came to Worthington in 1810, where he was employed by his uncle, James Kilbourne, as principal of Worthington Academy. In 1815 he moved to Columbus and attempted to establish a newspaper, the *Columbian Gazette,* in opposition to former associates in Worthington, who were then publishing the *Western Intelligencer.* After only two numbers of the *Gazette* were issued, he sold the equipment and engaged in bookselling and publishing. His *Ohio Gazetteer* first published in July, 1816, filled a real need in the Eastern states. Following the War of 1812 thousands of families were deterred from emigrating to Ohio only by the lack of dependable information. These people had very definite ideas as to the kind of land they wanted, but were uncertain of where it could be found in the vast Ohio country. Returning soldiers had brought back yarns which were quite as conflicting as the bewildering claims of competing land speculators, and the slanted articles in newspapers were offset by bitter letters from misguided relatives and former neighbors. Not only was information vague as to the quality of land and the agricultural possibilities in different sections of the state, but no two local authorities agreed as to the systems of survey or the purchase requirements in the various districts. Grotesque blunders in the works of such distinguished geographers as Jedidiah Morse and Nathaniel Dwight added to the confusion: Chillicothe was placed on the Great Miami instead of the Scioto River, Kaskaskia and Mackinaw were located on the Wabash River, and thriving settlements were indicated where there were in fact only Indian reservations closed to white settlers. Drawing upon his own experiences, soliciting descriptive letters from reliable citizens in each county, and interviewing members of the legislature, Kilbourn painstakingly collected the material for his *Gazetteer.* Obviously a thorough and honest work, the very appearance of this sturdy little book of 166 pages from a press in frontier Ohio was reassuring. Inscriptions in surviving copies indicate that it was distributed from Vermont to Virginia. It caught on instantly, and in four months a second edition was forthcoming. The little frontier press—subject to the usual difficulty of obtaining enough paper to meet ordinary needs—was unable to supply the demand for the book. Two editions were published in 1817, one printed in Albany, N. Y., and the other in Baltimore, Md. Within two years after its first appearance, Kilbourn disclosed that over 6,000 copies had been sold, and the *Gazetteer* was far from finished. Edition followed edition, each revised and brought up to date. In the later 1820s it became the *vade mecum* of thousands of settlers and land speculators. Kilbourn reported that between 1826 and 1830 over 14,000 copies were sold. An ardent advocate of internal improvements, he began on June 21, 1828, to publish the weekly *Civil Engineer and Herald of Internal Improvement,* which he issued for twenty weeks. Extra numbers were printed, and these were bound and sold separately as *Public Documents Concerning the Ohio Canals.* He died in Columbus, leaving a wife and three small children.

Ernest J. Wessen

A Compendious System of Universal Geography . . . , Zanesville, 1813.

Columbian Geography; Or, a Description of the United States of America, Chillicothe, 1815.

The Ohio Gazetteer; Or, Topographical Dictionary . . . , Columbus, 1816.

The Ohio Manual . . . , Columbus, 1826.

Public Documents Concerning the Ohio Canals . . . , Columbus, 1828.

A Geography of the State of Ohio . . . , Columbus, 1830.

KILE, ORVILLE MERTON (Feb. 17, 1886–), agricultural economist, was born in New Vienna, Clinton County. He graduated from Ohio State University in 1912. He has held a number of educational and editorial positions related to agriculture; he was Washington representative of Sears Roebuck, 1933–48, and was active in organizing the farm bloc in Congress. His present address is Washington, D. C. He has published articles and books on agriculture, e.g., *The New Agriculture,* New York, 1932. WW 26

KILLITS, JOHN MILTON (Oct. 7, 1858–Sept. 13, 1938), lawyer and judge, was born in Lithopolis, Fairfield County. He graduated from Williams College in 1880 and completed his legal training at Columbia University in 1885. He was admitted to the bar in 1887 and began practice in Bryan. He later served as judge of the court of common pleas and of the U. S. district court. His home was in Toledo. He edited and wrote portions of *Toledo and Lucas County*, 3 vols., Chicago, 1923. WWW 1

KIMBALL, HEBER CHASE (June 14, 1801–June 22, 1868), Mormon leader, born in Sheldon, Vt., was converted to the teachings of Joseph Smith in 1832 while living in Mendon, N. Y. The next year he moved to the settlement of Latter-day Saints at Kirtland and except for missionary expeditions lived there until their removal in 1838. After Smith's death he was one of Brigham Young's chief counselors and remained a leader in the Mormon community until his death. He published *Journal of Heber C. Kimball . . .* , Nauvoo, Ill., 1840.

KIMBEL, HARRY MILTON (March 3, 1877–Aug. 20, 1956), clergyman, was born in North Lawrence, Stark County. He attended Canton public schools and graduated from Northwestern University in 1900. After living in Madison, Wis., for four years, he returned to Canton, where he founded and operated Charles Street Mission. In 1916 he established the Pilgrims' Mission. He was employed in Canton in the office of the county auditor for many years. He wrote a number of articles and pamphlets on religious themes and social questions, e.g., an account of his experiences as director of public safety in Canton: *Canton's Night*, [Canton], 1934.

KIMBERLY, ROBERT L. (July 3, 1836–June 15, 1913) was born in Connecticut. He enlisted in the 41st O.V.I. on Sept. 19, 1861, as a second lieutenant; when discharged on Sept. 5, 1865, he was colonel of the 191st O.V.I. A printer, he worked after the war in Cleveland and Toledo and in other states. He died in Dayton, Ky. The book below was a collaboration with Ephraim S. Holloway (q.v.).

The Forty-first Ohio Veteran Volunteer Infantry . . . , Cleveland, 1897.

KIMSEY, MRS. HOMER LEE. See Merl B. Cole.

KINCHELOE, SAMUEL CLARENCE (Nov. 20, 1890–), educator, was born near Georgetown, Brown County. He graduated from Drake University in 1916 and the University of Chicago (Ph.D.) in 1919. He taught sociology of religion at the University of Chicago, 1928–56. His special scholarly concern—the relationship of church and community life—is reflected in his books, e.g., *The American City and Its Church*, New York, [1938]. WW 30

KING, AGNES B. (? – ?), was born in Cleveland, Cuyahoga County, and was educated in that city. In 1913, after teaching school in Cleveland, she married William A. King. Following her husband's death, she lived in Ironton. Her last address in Ohioana files is West Palm Beach, Fla. She wrote a column for the Catholic *Columbian* and a book, *Duncan Davidson*, Philadelphia, [1928]. CWW 7

KING, FAYE (May 29, 1902–), born in Milford, Ky., lived in Dayton, 1918–48. Now Mrs. William C. Barnes, she lives in Marathon, Fla. She has written juvenile stories and has published a book for children: *Judy and the Golden Horse*, Caldwell, Idaho, 1947.

KING, HENRY CHURCHILL (Sept. 18, 1858–Feb. 27, 1934), educator, was born in Hillsdale, Mich. He graduated from Oberlin College in 1879 and Oberlin Seminary in 1882, joined the Oberlin faculty in 1884, and from 1902 until his retirement in 1927 was president of the college. A popular lecturer on religion and philosophy, he published many of his addresses as well as numerous books, e.g., *Fundamental Questions*, New York, 1917. WWW 1

KING, JOHN (Jan. 1, 1813–June 19, 1893), physician, born in New York City, came to Cincinnati in 1848 as secretary of the first national convention of Reform Medical Practitioners. In 1851, after a brief residence in Memphis, Tenn., he returned to the city to become professor of obstetrics in the Eclectic Medical Institute. Cincinnati was his home until his death. He sympathized with abolition and with the cause of labor and opposed any attempt to restrict medical practice. Some of his discoveries of therapeutic uses of American plants were important contributions to *materia medica*. His medical books were highly popular, and most of them passed through several editions.

The American Eclectic Dispensatory, Cincinnati, 1852.

The American Eclectic Obstetrics, Cincinnati, 1855.

The American Family Physician . . . , Cincinnati, 1857.

Women: Their Diseases and Treatment, Cincinnati, 1858.

The Microscopist's Companion . . . , Cincinnati, 1859.

Medical Chart, for the Use of All Persons Afflicted with Chronic Disease, Whether Males or Females, Cincinnati, 1863.

Urological Dictionary . . . , Cincinnati, 1878.

The Coming Freeman, or Justice and Equality to All, Cincinnati, 1886.

KING, MARGARET RIVES (July 1, 1819–May 1, 1898), was born in Virginia. In 1843 she married Rufus King (q.v.), Cincinnati lawyer and civic leader. Her death occurred in Cincinnati.

Memoirs of the Life of Mrs. Sarah Peter, 2 vols., Cincinnati, 1889.

A Memento of Ancestors and Ancestral Homes . . . , Cincinnati, 1890.

Old Cashmere Shawls, Cincinnati, 1892.

KING, RUFUS (May 30, 1817–March 25, 1891), lawyer, was born in Chillicothe, Ross County, the grandson of Governor Thomas Worthington. After attending Kenyon College, he graduated from Harvard College in 1839 and Harvard Law School in 1841. He was admitted to the Ohio bar in 1841 and practiced in Cincinnati. He rose to distinction in his profession and devoted much of his time, energy, and fortune to the promotion of science, history, and art in Cincinnati. According to W. H. Venable (q.v.), there was scarcely a literary institution in the Queen City that was not aided by his counsel and liberality. He was a frequent contributor to the *Evening Chronicle,* edited by his uncle, E. D. Mansfield (q.v.). He was dean of Cincinnati Law School, 1875–80, and lectured there until his death.

Ohio, First Fruits of the Ordinance of 1787, Boston, 1888.

KING, THOROLD. Pseud. See Charles Gatchell.

KING, WILLIAM FLETCHER (Dec. 20, 1830–Oct. 23, 1921), educator, was born near Zanesville, Muskingum County. He graduated from Ohio Wesleyan University in 1857. He joined the faculty of Cornell College, Mount Vernon, Iowa, in 1862, was named president in 1863, and served until 1908. After his retirement he continued to live in Mount Vernon. He published an autobiographical volume: *Reminiscences,* New York, [1915]. WWW 1

KINGSBURY, ELIZABETH (1865–1922), educator, was a graduate of Bucknell University and taught for many years in the schools of Defiance.

Tale of an Amateur Adventuress . . . , Cincinnati, 1898.

KINGSBURY, SARA R. (1876–Oct. 17, 1948), was born in Ohio, but was educated in Indianapolis public schools, graduated from Butler University in 1899, and died in Indianapolis. She published several novels and plays, e.g., *The Atonement,* Boston, [1905], and *Our Christ Liveth . . .* , New York, [1930]. IATB

KINGSLEY, CALVIN (Sept. 8, 1812–April 6, 1870), clergyman, born in Annsville, N. Y., served in northwestern Pennsylvania as a Methodist minister. When made bishop in 1864, he settled in Cleveland. He died in Beirut while on a trip around the world. A travel book was published posthumously: *Round the World . . .* , 2 vols., Cincinnati, 1871.

KINGSLEY, FLORENCE MORSE (July 14, 1859–Oct. 26, 1937), was born in Medina, Medina County. She attended Wellesley College, but married Charles R. Kingsley in 1882 before the completion of her studies. Though the mother of five children, this remarkable woman found time to produce over thirty books which were issued over the imprints of the country's leading publishers, as well as a great number of short stories and in her later years the scenarios of several motion pictures.

Titus, a Comrade of the Cross, Chicago, 1894.

Stephen, a Soldier of the Cross, Philadelphia, 1896.

Paul, a Herald of the Cross, Philadelphia, 1897.

Prisoners of the Sea . . . , Philadelphia, 1897.

The Cross Triumphant, Philadelphia, 1899.

The Transfiguration of Miss Philura, New York, 1901.

The Needle's Eye, New York, 1902.

Wings and Fetters . . . , Philadelphia, 1902.

Under the Stars, Philadelphia, 1903.

Kindly Light, Philadelphia, [1904].

The Singular Miss Smith, New York, 1904.

Tor, a Street Boy of Jerusalem, Philadelphia, [1904].

An Unrecorded Miracle, Philadelphia, [1904].

The Resurrection of Miss Cynthia, New York, 1905.

The Intellectual Miss Lamb, New York, 1906.

Balm in Gilead, New York, 1907.

The Princess and the Ploughman, New York, 1907.

Those Queer Browns, New York, 1907.

Truthful Jane, New York, 1907.

And So They Were Married, New York, 1908.

The Glass House, New York, 1909.

The Star of Love, New York, 1909.

Those Brewster Children, New York, 1910.

Francesca, Boston, [1911].

The Return of Caroline, New York, 1911.
To the Highest Bidder, New York, 1911.
Miss Philura's Wedding Gown, New York, 1912.
Wilhelmina Changes Her Mind, Boston, [1912].
Hurrying Fate and Geraldine, New York, [1913].
Veronica, New York, 1913.
The Heart of Philura, New York, 1914.
Meditations for Life and Power, Holyoke, Mass., 1916.
An Alabaster Box, (with Mary E. Wilkins Freeman), New York, 1917.
Neighbors, New York, 1917.
The Life of Henry Fowle Durant . . . , New York, [1924].

KINMONT, ALEXANDER (Jan. 5, 1799–Sept. 16, 1838), educator, was born in Angusshire, Scotland, and was educated in Edinburgh. His arm was torn off in an accident in a cotton factory, and he turned to schoolteaching. In 1823 he came to America and taught in Bedford, Pa., where he was converted to Swedenborgianism. Three years later, he came to Cincinnati and established Kinmont's Academy of Classics and Mathematics. One of the school mottoes was "Learn to do by doing." He was a stanch advocate of the classics and of freedom from discipline. He also served as pastor of the Second Swedenborgian Society, Cincinnati. The book below was published by subscription to aid his family after his death.

Twelve Lectures on the Natural History of Man . . . , Cincinnati, 1839.

KINNEY, BRUCE (Dec. 12, 1865–Oct. 15, 1936), clergyman, was born in East Townsend, Huron County. After graduating from Denison University in 1892, he entered the Baptist ministry. Besides serving as pastor of several churches he held various posts in the home missions department of the Baptist Church. His writings include *Mormonism; The Islam of America,* New York, [1912]. WWW 1

KINNEY, COATES (Nov. 24, 1826–Jan. 25, 1904), lawyer and journalist, was born in Penn Yan, N. Y. Memories of his early boyhood in the beautiful Finger Lakes region are reflected in many of his poems. In 1840 his parents moved to Ohio, where he spent the remainder of his life. He completed one term at Antioch College, read law under Thomas Corwin and Judge William Lawrence, and was admitted to the bar in 1856. He practiced for a short time, but he was drawn from the law by his greater interest in poetry and journalism. Before the Civil War, in which he served as a paymaster and was breveted lieutenant colonel, he edited the Xenia *News;* after the war he edited the Xenia *Torchlight* and was owner and editor of the Springfield *Globe Republic.* He also contributed to the Cincinnati *Times* and the *Ohio State Journal.* He served in the state senate, 1882–83. In 1888 he wrote the "Ohio Centennial Ode," but his most famous poem, "Rain on the Roof," was written much earlier—in 1849 when he was 23. Its sentimentality and easy lyrical flow made it widely popular, and it was often reprinted.

Keeuka and Other Poems, [Columbus, 1855].
Lyrics of the Ideal and the Real, [Xenia?, 1887].
Mists of Fire; A Trilogy and Some Ecologs, Chicago, 1899.

KINNEY, MURIEL (1865–), educator, was born in Upper Sandusky, Wyandot County. After graduating from Flora Stone Mather College in 1900, she taught English in the schools of Cleveland and Toledo. During the 1930s she lived in Woodbury, Conn. She published at least three books of verse, e.g., *Rainbow Gold, and Other Poems,* Boston, 1915. BDCP

KINNISON, CHARLES SHADRACH (Aug. 3, 1889–), was born in Jackson, Jackson County. He graduated from Ohio State University in 1911. After working in the U. S. Bureau of Standards, 1912–15, he was an advertising manager in Detroit until his retirement in 1953. For some time he published a poem a day in the Detroit *Times,* which was also syndicated in other newspapers. He also contributed poems to other periodicals and collected some of them in a volume, *'Round Home,* New York, [1927]. WWNAA 3

KINSEY, SAMUEL (May 26, 1832–June 8, 1883), farmer and clergyman, was born in Miami County. He established nurseries in Montgomery County in 1852 and also in Indiana. He was minister of a German Baptist Church, 1870–83, and edited the *Vindicator,* 1870–82. The volume listed below contains hymns, poems, and essays on religious subjects.

The Pious Companion . . . , Dayton, 1865.

KINSMAN, FREDERICK JOSEPH (Sept. 27, 1868–July, 1944), clergyman, was born in Warren, Trumbull County. Graduated from Keble College, Oxford University, in 1894 and ordained an Episcopal priest in 1896, he taught in various schools and served a pastorate in Massachusetts until 1908, when he was consecrated bishop of Delaware. He resigned in 1919 to enter the Roman Catholic Church. His death occurred in Lewiston, Maine. He published a number of books on religious themes, e.g., *Americanism and Catholicism,* New York, 1924. WWW 3

KIPLINGER, WILLARD MONROE (Jan. 8, 1891–), journalist, was born in Bellefontaine, Logan County. He graduated from Ohio State University in 1912 and was a reporter in Columbus, 1912–16. His newsletters from Washington, D. C., published since 1923, have achieved a reputation for reliability and accuracy both as reports and as forecasts. His books include *Washington Is like That,* New York, [1942]. WW 30

KIRCHER, RALF CHARLES (May 22, 1907–), advertising executive, was born in Pittsburgh, Pa. In 1929, after graduating from Ohio University, he entered the advertising business in Dayton, where he has headed his own agency since 1942. He has published humorous items in Dayton newspapers and in national magazines, some of them under the name of Fagin Fogg, and some humorous books, e.g., *Wrap It as a Gift,* New York, [1947].

KIRK, GRAYSON LOUIS (Oct. 12, 1903–), educator, was born on a farm near Jeffersonville, Fayette County. He graduated from Miami University in 1924 and the University of Wisconsin (Ph.D.) in 1930. He served on the Wisconsin faculty, 1929–40, and at Columbia University since 1940. He became provost of Columbia University in 1949, acting president in 1950, and president in 1953. He has published articles and books on international relations, e.g., *Philippines Independence: Motives, Problems, and Prospects,* New York, 1936. WW 30

KIRKPATRICK, CYNTHIA COLE (April 21, 1811–Dec. 27, 1888), was born at Penn Yan, N. Y., but was brought to Belpre Township, Washington County, in 1812. In 1833 she married Alexander Kirkpatrick and took up her residence in Rockland, where she spent the remainder of her life. Of her ten children five sons served in the Federal forces during the Civil War. Her *Poems for the Times* is perhaps the best of the known examples of the work of Ohio's serio-comic poets. Certainly she was the equal of Michigan's vaunted "sweet singer," Julia Moore. She interviewed President Lincoln in Dec., 1864, from her account of which meeting the following stanza is typical:

"I have been wounded, and therefore
cannot work,
I want a position as a clerk."
He says, "That position you shall have,
For your life for your country you
gave."

Nearly one half of the poems in her little volume are addressed to Lincoln or against his political adversaries.

Poems for the Times, Cincinnati, 1882.

KIRKPATRICK, GEORGE ROSS (Feb. 24, 1867–March 17, 1937), political lecturer, was born in West Lafayette, Coshocton County. After graduating from Albion College in 1893, he taught history at colleges in Kansas and Wisconsin and lectured on temperance. In 1903 he joined the Socialist Party and devoted himself to lecturing, teaching, and running for various offices as a Socialist. He died in San Gabriel, Calif. His opposition to World War I led several times to his being attacked by hostile mobs. His best-known work, translated into several languages, was *War—What For?* West Lafayette, [1910]. NC 27

KIRTLAND, LUCIAN SWIFT (Oct. 13, 1881–), journalist, was born in Poland, Mahoning County. He graduated from Yale University in 1903. During World War I he was a correspondent with the Russian army, and he later served in various parts of the world as a foreign correspondent. His present residence is Bronxville, N. Y. He wrote several books about the Far East, e.g., *Finding the Worth While in the Orient,* New York, [1926]. WW 27

KISER, SAMUEL ELLSWORTH (1862–Jan. 30, 1942), journalist, was born in Shippensburg, Pa. He was educated in Pennsylvania and Ohio schools. After coming to Cleveland in the early 1880s, he was active in journalistic work there: first as a reporter and then as managing editor of the Cleveland *Press,* and from 1896 to 1899 as a feature writer for the *Leader.* From 1900 to 1914 he was in Chicago, and from 1917 to 1919 he was editor of the Dayton *Daily News.*

"Budd Wilkins at the Show," and Other Verses . . . , Cleveland, 1898.

Georgie, Boston, 1900.

Love Sonnets of an Office Boy, Chicago, 1902.

Ballads of the Busy Days, Chicago, 1903.

Soul Sonnets of a Stenographer, Chicago, 1903.

Charles the Chauffeur, New York, [1905].

Thrills of a Bell Boy, Chicago, 1906.

The Whole Glad Year, Chicago, [1911].
Father, Chicago, [1912].
Mother, Chicago, [1912].
My Boy, Chicago, [1912].
The Land of Little Care, Chicago, 1913.
Glorious Day; Poems of Inspiration, New York, [1926].
It Is to Laugh; A Book of Jokes, New York, [1927].

KITCHELL, JOSEPH GRAY (April 25, 1862–June 1, 1947), was born in Cincinnati, Hamilton County. An active photographer, he invented in 1915 a subchromatic method of reproducing pictures. He wrote feature stories for many magazines and newspapers and a book: *The Earl of Hell,* New York, [1924]. WWW 2

KITCHEN, KARL KINGSLEY (March 2, 1885–June 21, 1935), journalist, was born in Cleveland, Cuyahoga County. From 1908 to 1933 he was a reporter and columnist for the New York *Evening World* and the New York *Sun.* His books include *The Night Side of Europe as Seen by a Broadwayite Abroad,* Cleveland, 1914. AATB

KITTREDGE, DANIEL WRIGHT (Sept. 2, 1879–Jan. 21, 1958), journalist, was born in Cincinnati, Hamilton County. After graduating from Harvard University in 1902, he worked on various newspapers, most of them in Philadelphia. He wrote at least two books, e.g., *A Mind Adrift,* Seattle, [1920].

KITTREDGE, ELIZABETH. See Margaret E. K. Wakeland.

KLAUPRECHT, EMIL (1815–1896), born in Germany, came to Paducah, Ky., in 1832 and in 1837 settled in Cincinnati. A lithographer by trade, he turned to journalism in 1843, when he founded *Fliegende Blatter,* the first illustrated German paper published in America. He edited *Republikaner* for about ten years and was on the staff of the Cincinnati *Volksblatt,* 1856–64. He was American consul at Stuttgart, 1864–69, and remained in that city after his removal by President Grant.

Cincinnati, oder, Geheimnisse des Westens, 3 vols. in 1, Cincinnati, 1854–55.
Deutsche Chronik in der Geschichte des Ohio-Thales und Seiner Haupstadt Cincinati in's Besondere . . . , Cincinnati, [1864].

KLEEMAN, RITA SULZBACHER HALLE (May 23, 1887–), was born in Chillicothe, Ross County. She graduated from Wellesley College in 1907. She married Louis J. Halle in 1907 and as Rita S. Halle published stories and articles in national magazines and a book on choosing a college. In 1934 she married Arthur S. Kleeman. Her later books include *Gracious Lady; The Life of Sara Delano Roosevelt,* New York, 1935. WW 30

KLEMM, LOUIS RICHARD (Dec. 8, 1845–1916), educator and banker, born in Düsseldorf, Germany, came to the United States in 1866. He served as assistant superintendent of schools, Cleveland, 1870–80, as principal of German Normal School, Cincinnati, 1880–84, and as superintendent of schools, Hamilton, 1884–87. He afterward lived in Washington, D. C., where he worked for the government as a specialist in foreign education, 1889–1910. From 1910 until his death he was president of the Society for Savings, Washington, D. C. Besides the titles below, he published papers on educational topics and German textbooks; he also compiled a collection of German poems.

Chips from a Teacher's Workshop . . . , Boston, 1888.
European Schools . . . , New York, 1889.
Public Education in Germany and in the United States, Boston, [1911].

KLINE, MAGDALENA (April 2, 1838–July 14, 1921), was born in Baden, Germany. Her parents brought her to Bucyrus in 1851, and in 1855 she moved to Van Wert, where she spent the remainder of her life. She was leader of the Society of the Faithful, a group of spiritualists in Van Wert, and she frequently lectured on spiritualism. The book listed below is a collection of her lectures and articles.

The Everlasting Gospel, Boston, 1882.

KLIPPART, JOHN HANCOCK (July 26, 1823–Oct. 24, 1878), was born near Canton, Stark County. He attended district schools until his ninth year. He worked in a wool carding factory and a drugstore in Canton, was a merchant in Massillon, 1840–47, and was postmaster of Osnaburg, 1847–50. He worked on the *Democratic Transcript* in Canton and was editor of the *American Liberal* in Cleveland. He then joined the editorial staff of the *Ohio Farmer,* where he remained until Dec., 1856, when he became corresponding secretary of the Ohio State Board of Agriculture, a position he held until his death. Possessed of a broad range of interests, a deep-seated understanding of the farmer's problems, and an imagination which often led to their solutions, Klippart enriched his annual reports of the board with authoritative, comprehensive essays on natural history and agricultural subjects. The 21 volumes of those reports are today prized as authoritative sources on the subjects covered. Editions in German were printed which encouraged emigration to western Ohio. In 1873 he was appointed one of three Commissioners of Fisheries. His first report of that commission is a volume which is today sought after by discriminating collectors of books on fishing. He also published a translation of Voltaire's *Zadig*. His death occurred in Columbus.

The Wheat Plant . . . , Cincinnati, 1860.
Theory and Practice of Land Drainage . . . , Cincinnati, 1861.

KNAGGS, NELSON S. (March 31, 1907–), born in Hagerstown, Md., an executive of Hilton Davis Chemical Co., has lived in Cincinnati for more than 25 years. He has published a history of the uses of natural waxes: *Adventures in Man's First Plastic . . .* , New York, 1947.

KNAUSS, WILLIAM H. (March 10, 1839–Jan. 18, 1917), was born in New Jersey. Before coming to Columbus in 1892, he was active in real estate and contracting in Missouri and Utah. His practice of presenting American flags to schools and other groups received considerable publicity. He died in Columbus. He wrote *The Story of Camp Chase . . .* , Nashville, Tenn., 1906.

KNEBEL, AARON G. (Sept. 15, 1874–April 22, 1938), Y.M.C.A. worker for 44 years, was born in Mankato, Minn., and grew up in Waco, Texas. At the time of his death he was general secretary of the Cleveland Y.M.C.A. He published an autobiography, *Four Decades with Men and Boys,* New York, 1936.

KNEPPER, MAMIE C. (Mrs. Russell M.) (May 26, 1884–), was born in Ironton, Lawrence County, but has lived for a number of years in Columbus. She has published poems in various newspapers and magazines and in 1944 published a collection: *Life Is a Mirror,* Columbus, [1944]. BDCP

KNIGHT, CHARLES LANDON (June 18, 1867–Sept. 26, 1933), journalist, was born in Milledgeville, Ga. He graduated from Columbia University in 1889, and after working on several newspapers and magazines, he became editor of the Akron *Beacon-Journal* in 1904 and remained with that newspaper until his death. He wrote *The Real Jefferson Davis,* Battle Creek, Mich., 1904. OBB

KNIGHT, GEORGE WELLS (June 25, 1858–Feb. 10, 1932), educator, was born in Ann Arbor, Mich. He graduated from the University of Michigan (A.B., 1878; Ph.D., 1884). After teaching history for a year at the University of Michigan, he became professor of history and English literature at Ohio State University in 1885. He was on the University staff until 1920 and was managing editor of the *Ohio Archaeological and Historical Quarterly,* 1887–89. He wrote a number of reports and contributed many articles on educational problems to professional journals. His death occurred in Columbus.

The Government of the People of the State of Ohio, Philadelphia, 1895.

KNIGHT, RUTH ADAMS (Mrs. Dickson Jay Hartwell) (Oct. 5, 1898–), was born in Defiance, Defiance County. She attended the University of Toledo and in 1918 began working on the Toledo *Times,* where she became dramatic and literary editor. In 1930 she moved to New York, and she now lives in Connecticut. She has written numerous radio scripts and several books, including a novel, *Women Must Weep,* [Boston, 1941]. WWAW 1

KNIGHT, THOMAS ARTHUR (Feb. 24, 1876–June 17, 1946), was born in Toronto, Ontario, Canada, but grew up in Cleveland, where his parents moved in 1877. He was on the staff of the Cleveland *Leader* and later was in the real-estate business in Cleveland and Brecksville. For many years he was active in the Early Settlers Association of the Western Reserve. He wrote several books and articles on historical subjects and as a young man published *The Country Estates of Cleveland Men . . .* , [Cleveland], 1903.

KNITTLE, RHEA MANSFIELD (June 4, 1883–Nov. 16, 1955), was born in Cleveland, Cuyahoga County. She spent most of her life in Ashland and West Salem. Besides numerous articles on antiques and pioneer life, she published an authoritative work, *Early American Glass,* New York, [1927]. WO 2

KNOBLE, CLIFF (1892–), was born in Lafayette, Allen County. After attending Ohio Northern University, he moved to Detroit, Mich. He wrote *His Own People,* Chicago, [1940].

KNOPF, CARL SUMNER (Sept. 20, 1889–June 23, 1942), clergyman and educator, was born in Columbus, Franklin County.

He graduated from the University of Southern California in 1913 and Yale Divinity School in 1915. He taught in California schools, was secretary of the Methodist Church in that state, and served on the University of Southern California faculty, 1922–41. In 1941 he was appointed president of Willamette University, Salem, Oreg. He wrote many articles and several religious textbooks and also published a series of lectures: *The Student Faces Life . . .*, Philadelphia, [1932]. WWW 2

KNORTZ, KARL (Aug. 28, 1841–1918), educator and journalist, was born in Garbenheim, Germany. After coming to the United States in 1863, he taught school in several cities, including Cincinnati. From May, 1873, to Feb., 1874, he edited *Der Deutsche Pionier*. His attempt to make the journal primarily a literary one failed, and he moved to Indianapolis, Ind., where he edited a newspaper. He later was a journalist in New York and a teacher in Evansville, Ind. He translated the verse of Longfellow, Whitman, and other poets into German and wrote extensively on the Indian, American history, and literature, e.g., *Geschichte der Nordamerikanischen Literatur*, Berlin, 1891.

KNOWLES, WILLIAM (1806–April 28, 1889), was born in England, but came to America as a boy and settled in Homer, where he spent the remainder of his life. He supported his large family by making brooms and also was sexton of the Homer Presbyterian church. Many of his poems first appeared in the Toledo *Blade*. The most attention was attracted by "Betsy and I Are One," but "When My Ship Comes Home" was also very popular.

Poems, Indianapolis, 1881.

KNOWLTON, DONALD SNOW (Nov. 22, 1892–), public relations executive, was born in Cleveland, Cuyahoga County. He graduated from Western Reserve University in 1914, was on the public relations staff of Union Trust Company, and is now a partner in Hill and Knowlton. He has published stories and articles in the *Atlantic Monthly*, *Harper's* and other national magazines and has also written *These Bankers*, New York, 1925, and a privately printed book recalling memories of his boyhood in Cleveland: *Brick House Stories*, Cleveland, 1936.

KNOWLTON, WILLIAM AUGUSTUS (May 16, 1838–Nov. 10, 1933), physician, was born in North Royalton, Cuyahoga County. After attending Twinsburg Academy and University of Wooster, he studied medicine with a Berea doctor. He practiced in Brecksville and Cleveland. His wife, Fannie Snow Knowlton, who died in 1926, was widely known as a composer. He died at the age of 95 in Cuyahoga Falls. His writings were compiled by Marion Wilcox and Bernice B. Knowlton: *Life, Letters and Speeches . . .*, 2 vols., Cleveland, 1938.

KOCH, FELIX JOHN (Jan. 15, 1882–Dec. 27, 1933), writer and photographer, was born in Cincinnati, Hamilton County. In 1904 he graduated from the University of Cincinnati. He published many feature stories illustrated by his own photographs and a number of travel books, e.g., *A Little Journey to Northern Wilds*, Chicago, [1908]. WWW 1

KOCH, KATHARINE ISABEL (Jan. 7, 1898–), educator, was born in Greenville, Darke County. She has taught in Indiana public schools since 1915. She graduated from the University of Chicago in 1937. She has written stories for children's magazines, a series of English textbooks, and a book for children: *Katie Meets Buffalo Bill*, New York, [1947]. WWAW 1

KOHLER, JULILLY HOUSE (Oct. 18, 1908–), was born in Cincinnati, Hamilton County. She graduated from Wellesley College in 1930, married John Michael Kohler in 1933, and has since lived in Kohler, Wis. She has written a number of books for children, e.g., *Farmer Collins*, Chicago, [1947]. WWAW 1

KOHLER, KAUFMANN (May 10, 1943–Jan. 28, 1926), rabbi, was born in Bavaria. A leader of reform Judaism in America, he had a distinguished career as rabbi and scholar in Detroit, Chicago, and New York before coming to Cincinnati in 1903 as president of Hebrew Union College. On his retirement in 1921, he returned to New York, where he spent the remainder of his life. An industrious scholar and a prolific writer, he wrote many books and articles. One of the most important (first published in German in 1910) is *Jewish Theology Systematically and Historically Considered*, New York, 1918. DAB 10

KOHR, HERBERT O. (Aug. 24, 1875–), was born in Winfield, Tuscarawas County. In 1896 at Fort Logan, Colo., he enlisted in the army; he was discharged in 1902 after serving in the Philippines and China. Soon after his discharge, while working as a construction foreman in Iowa, he lost his right arm and was blinded by a premature dynamite explosion. He now lives in Mount Vernon. He has written two books about his army experiences, e.g., *Around the World with Uncle Sam; Or, Six Years in the United States Army,* Akron, 1907.

KOLBE, PARKE REXFORD (April 23, 1881–Feb. 28, 1942), educator, was born in Akron, Summit County. He graduated from Buchtel College in 1901 and the University of Heidelberg (Ph.D.) in 1912. He was associated with Buchtel College as professor and president, 1905–25, and afterward served at other universities. Besides compiling a history of the University of Akron, he wrote on educational subjects, e.g., *Urban Influences on Higher Education in England and the United States,* [New York, 1928]. WWW 2

KONOPAK, FARONA (Sept. 2, 1895–), born in Philadelphia, Pa., lived in Toledo from 1929 until 1948, when her husband, Lothar T. Konopak, retired from business and moved to New Mexico. She has published many poems in magazines and newspapers and one collection: *Adobe in Sunlight,* New York, [1935].

KORNFELD, JOSEPH SAUL (Feb. 12, 1876–June 22, 1943), rabbi, was born in Austria-Hungary, but was brought to the United States when a child. After graduating from Hebrew Union College in 1898, he served as a rabbi in Arkansas and Canada. He was rabbi of B'nai Israel Temple, Columbus, 1907–21. He wrote *Judaism and International Peace,* [Cincinnati, 193- ?]. WW 14

KRAMER, STELLA (1870–July 5, 1936), historian, was born in Cincinnati, Hamilton County. She graduated from the University of Cincinnati (A.B. and M.A.) and Columbia University (Ph.D.). Her academic specialty was English craft guilds. She also studied at Oxford and the Sorbonne. She published an analysis of higher education and the elective system: *A Path to Understanding,* New York, 1933.

KRAPP, GEORGE PHILIP (Sept. 1, 1872–April 21, 1934), eminent pioneer authority on the English language in America, was born in Cincinnati, Hamilton County, and lived in southern Ohio until his graduation from Wittenberg College, Springfield, in 1894. The rest of his life, except for two years (1908–10) teaching English at the University of Cincinnati, was spent in Eastern universities, first as a graduate student at Johns Hopkins and during most of his life as a teacher at Columbia University. Professor Krapp was a graduate student at Johns Hopkins from 1894 to 1897, and went from there immediately to Columbia University, where he was a member of the English department for the rest of his life, except for the two years at the University of Cincinnati. He earned his Ph.D. degree from Johns Hopkins in 1899 and published his thesis in 1900 under the title *The Legend of St. Patrick's Purgatory: Its Later Literary History.* Although he is best known for his work on the American language, Professor Krapp was devoted to the study of early English texts. His first piece of extensive scholarly research was in this field, resulting in the publication in 1906 of his edition of *Andreas and the Fates of the Apostles.* He planned a complete edition of extant Anglo-Saxon poetical texts and near the end of his life finished three volumes of it: *The Junius Manuscript* (1931), *The Vercelli Book* (1932), and *The Paris Psalter and the Meters of Boethius* (1932). Professor Krapp's interest in the English language, shown in his early scholarly work in Anglo-Saxon, led him into the study of the history of the English language with the publication in 1909 of *Modern English: Its Growth and Present Use.* The application of early English texts to the study of prose style led him to write *The Rise of English Literary Prose* (1915). After these general books applying his great scholarship to practical application, Professor Krapp's publications fall into three main categories: textbooks, popularizations, and scholarly books in the field of linguistics. His two best textbooks, both based on considerable research, were both published in 1927: *A Comprehensive Guide to Good English* and *The Knowledge of English.* In the field of popularizations, he wrote a number of children's books with such inviting titles as *In Oldest England* (1912), *Tales of True Knights* (1921), *The Kitchen Porch* (1923), and *America, the Great Adventure* (1924). His translation of Chaucer's great poem, *Troilus and Criseyde,* was a Literary Guild selection in 1932. The pioneer scholarly exploration of the English language in America, however, remains Professor Krapp's greatest contribution. His first book in this field, *The Pronunciation of Standard English in America* (1919), precedes by several years the earliest edition of the work of another Ohio pioneer in the field, John S. Kenyon. His point of view, now almost universally accepted, was startling in 1919: "Pronunciation changes day by day, and dictionaries soon become antiquated. The intelligent person is one who makes his own dictionary as he goes along." A much more comprehensive work, and the one Professor Krapp will be remembered for, is the two-volume *The English Language in America* (1925). In view of the many publications of linguistic geographers and the interest shown by the monumental *Dictionary of American English,* Krapp's book is a pioneer work that set the pace for later studies. His treatment, he made plain in his preface, was not that of a special plea "for a distinctive American language," yet the scholarly approach to what was then a new subject—the pronunciation, history, vocabulary, proper names, style, dictionaries, inflection, and syntax of American English—was done with an authority that is still widely respected. He believed that "historical study brings American English into a closer relation to the central tradition of the English language than is commonly supposed to exist by those who have not looked at English in America from the historical and comparative angle." He would have been surprised but not shocked to see the tremendous strides made since 1925 in the field of the American language, in which he was a worthy pioneer.

W. Powell Jones

KREHBIEL, HENRY EDWARD (March 10, 1854–March 20, 1923), music critic, was born in Ann Arbor, Mich. He attended Cincinnati schools and studied law there, 1872–74, when he became music critic of the Cincinnati *Gazette.* In 1880 he accepted a position on the New York *Tribune,* which he held until his death. A prolific writer, especially on operatic subjects, he also compiled song collections. Several editions were published of his *How to Listen to Music . . .*, New York, 1896.

KRINGLE, KARAN. Pseud. See Emma S. Booth.

KROCK, GEORGE L. (March 27, 1908–Aug. 4, 1955), clergyman, was born in Cleveland, Cuyahoga County. After being ordained to the priesthood of the Catholic Church in 1939, he served churches in Akron and other cities. He wrote a book about China and the Catholic missionary effort there: *Stop Killing Dragons . . .*, [New York, 1947].

KROHN, WILLIAM OTTERBEIN (March 23, 1868–July 17, 1927), educator and physician, was born in Galion, Crawford County. He graduated from Western College, Toledo, Iowa, in 1887 and Yale University (Ph.D.) in 1889. After teaching at Western Reserve University and the University of Illinois, he studied medicine at Northwestern University, receiving his M.D. in 1905. He published numerous textbooks in psychology and hygiene and a travel book: *In Borneo Jungles among the Dyak Headhunters,* Indianapolis, [1927]. WWW 1

KRONENBERGER, LOUIS (Dec. 9, 1904–), novelist and drama critic, was born in Cincinnati, Hamilton County. He attended the University of Cincinnati, 1921–24, leaving without a degree to go to New York City, where he worked on the *Times.* He held editorial positions with Boni & Liveright, 1926–33, and Alfred A. Knopf, 1933–35. After five years on the staff of *Fortune,* he became drama critic for *Time,* a position he still holds. He has edited a number of anthologies and editions of eighteenth-century writers. He has also written novels, an analysis of contemporary society (*Company Manners*), and an account of social life in eighteenth-century England: *Kings & Desperate Men,* New York, 1942. TCA

KROUT, JOHN ALLEN (Oct. 3, 1896–), educator, was born in Tiffin, Seneca County. After attending Heidelberg College for three years, 1914–17, he graduated from the University of Michigan in 1918 and Columbia University (Ph.D.) in 1925. Since 1922 he has been on the Columbia faculty, as a member of the history department, as dean of the graduate school, and as vice-president. He has written several history textbooks and *The Origins of Prohibition,* New York, 1925. WW 30

KRUMBINE, MILES HENRY (Nov. 15, 1891–), clergyman, born in Schaefferstown, Pa., was ordained to the Lutheran ministry in 1914 and served as pastor of First Church, Dayton, 1918–26. In 1929 he became a Congregationalist and was pastor of Plymouth Church, Shaker Heights, 1929–52. He now lives in Hawaii. He has published a number of sermons and books on religious themes, e.g., *Ways of Believing,* New York, 1931. WW 27

KRUMM, HAZEL SHINN (Oct. 1, 1893–), was born in St. Louis, Mo., but grew up in Colorado. She lived in Cleveland, 1920–24, and since 1924 has lived in Columbus. She has written stories and poems for children and has published a collection of verse: *The Years like Foxes,* Columbus, 1942.

KUECHLER, OTTO (Nov. 17, 1873–Sept. 15, 1943), editor, born in Cincinnati, Hamilton County, spent most of his life in Columbus, where he was editor of *Hunter,*

Trader, Trapper magazine. He compiled a collection of stories about coon hunting, *Cooning With Cooners,* and wrote *Practical Fur Ranching,* Columbus, 1927. WWNAA 7

KUHLMAN, JOHN HENRY (Dec. 26, 1865–Oct. 15, 1946), clergyman, was born in Woodville, Sandusky County. He graduated from Capital University in 1886 and the seminary in 1889. Ordained to the Lutheran ministry, he served pastorates in Columbus, Newton Falls, Middletown, Springfield, and Loudonville. He wrote many pageants and pantomimes for use in Sunday schools and a book of poems, *Stars and Angels,* [Loudonville], 1923. RLA 2

KUHNS, WILLIAM T. (Nov. 11, 1866–May 5, 1954), was born in Bellefontaine, Logan County, but grew up in Canton, where his father, a Lutheran minister, moved in 1869. He operated a lumber business in Baltimore, Md., and in 1917 established a brokerage firm in Canton. He retired in 1940. He published *Memories of Old Canton and My Personal Recollections of William McKinley,* [Canton, 1937].

KUNNECKE, FRANCIS JOSEPH (Nov. 18, 1885–), clergyman and educator, born in Baltimore, Md., has lived in Ohio since 1898. He graduated from the University of Dayton in 1906, taught in the University of Dayton High School, 1906–09, studied at the University of Fribourg, Switzerland, 1909–13, and was ordained to the Roman Catholic priesthood in 1913. He taught at the University of Dayton, 1913–33, Elder High School, Cincinnati, 1934–36, and Our Lady of Cincinnati College since 1936. He has written *The Way Out and the Way Beyond,* [Dayton, 1932].

KUNZ, JOSEF LAURENZ (April 1, 1890–), lawyer, born in Vienna, Austria, came to America in 1932 and since 1934 has been professor of international law at the University of Toledo. He has written numerous legal articles in various languages, legal works, and *Wilson und Clemenceau,* Vienna, 1919. WW 30

KURTZ, DANIEL WEBSTER (Oct. 9, 1879–Nov. 22, 1949), clergyman, was born in Hartville, Stark County. He graduated from Mount Union College in 1903 and Yale Divinity School in 1908. He was a minister of the Church of the Brethren, 1904–14, and was ordained bishop in 1914. He served as president of McPherson College, 1914–27, and as president of Bethany Biblical Seminary, 1932–37. He afterward served as pastor of a church in LaVerne, Calif. He wrote a number of books on religious subjects, e.g., *Nineteen Centuries of the Christian Church,* Elgin, Ill., [1914]. WW 25

KYLE, LUCIE CLAIRE MILES (Nov. 13, 1912–), was born in Kentucky. She attended school and business college in Madison, Ind. She has done secretarial work but is now retired. Married to Forrest Kyle of Dayton, she has lived in that city since 1937. Her poems have appeared in the Dayton *Herald* and other periodicals, and she has published two collections, e.g., *Timber,* Philadelphia, [1949].

KYLE, MELVIN GROVE (May 7, 1858–May 25, 1933), Presbyterian clergyman and archaeologist, was born near Cadiz, Harrison County. He graduated from Muskingum College in 1881 and Allegheny Theological Seminary in 1885. He taught at Xenia Theological Seminary and was its president from 1922 to 1930. His explorations in the Near East and the relation of archaeology to the Old Testament are the subject matter of his books, e.g., *Moses and the Monuments . . . ,* Oberlin, 1920. WWW 1

KYRK, HAZEL (Nov. 19, 1886–Aug. 5, 1957), educator, was born near Delaware, Delaware County. A graduate of the University of Chicago (Ph.B., 1910; Ph.D., 1920), she served on several governmental agencies and taught at various schools, including Oberlin College, 1914–21, and the University of Chicago, 1925–57. She wrote numerous articles and books, e.g., *Economic Problems of the Family,* New York, 1933. WWW 3

L

LACEY, MARGARET ETHEL (1872–Dec. 16, 1948), educator, was born in Cincinnati, Hamilton County. After graduating from Hughes High School in Cincinnati, she attended New York University (A.B., 1911; Ph.D., 1916). She taught in the New York City schools, was a school principal, and was a member of the Board of Examiners. She died in Plattsburg, N. Y. She published a volume of poems: *Songs and Sonnets,* New York, [1940].

LACEY, THOMAS JAMES (1870–Feb. 5, 1944), clergyman, was born in Cincinnati, Hamilton County. He graduated from New York University and Seabury Divinity School, served a church in Alameda, Calif., 1897–1903, and in 1903 became rector of the Church of the Redeemer, Brooklyn, N. Y. His death occurred in Brooklyn. He published sermons and several books on religious groups, e.g., *Beginning at Jerusalem . . . ,* New York, [1909]. WWC 1

LACROIX, JOHN POWER (Feb. 20, 1833–Sept. 22, 1879), clergyman and educator, was born near Haverhill, Scioto County. After graduating from Ohio Wesleyan University in 1857, he taught for two years in New Orleans, preached in Methodist churches, 1860–63, and in 1863 joined the Ohio Wesleyan faculty. He wrote for a number of church papers and translated several works from German.

Outlines of Christian Ethics, New York, 1879.

LADD, GEORGE TRUMBULL (Jan. 19, 1842–Aug. 8, 1921), clergyman and educator, was born in Painesville, Lake County. After graduating from Western Reserve University in 1864, he preached in Ohio and Wisconsin, but it was in the fields of psychology and philosophy that he was to gain enduring fame. After teaching philosophy for a year at Bowdoin College, he went to Yale University in 1880, where he remained for over forty years, while he also lectured on philosophy at other institutions in the United States and in the Far East. He was a prolific writer in a number of fields, and several of his textbooks were translated and adopted in Japan, Russia, and India.

Principles of Church Policy . . . , New York, 1882.
The Doctrine of Sacred Scripture . . . , 2 vols., New York, 1883.
What Is the Bible? . . . , New York, 1888.
Philosophy of Mind . . . , New York, 1895.
Philosophy of Knowledge . . . , New York, 1897.
Essays of the Higher Education, New York, 1899.
A Theory of Reality . . . , New York, 1899.
Philosophy of Conduct . . . , New York, 1902.
The Philosophy of Religion . . . , New York, 1905.
The Doctrine of the Virtues as Applied to Business Life . . . , Tokyo, 1907.
America and Japan, New York, 1908.
In Korea with Marquis Ito . . . , New York, 1908.
Knowledge, Life and Reality . . . , New York, 1909.
Rare Days in Japan, New York, 1910.
What Can I Know? . . . , New York, 1914.
What May I Hope? . . . , New York, 1915.
What Ought I to Do? . . . , New York, 1915.
What Should I Believe? . . . , New York, 1915.
Secret of Personality, New York, 1918.
Intimate Glimpses of Life in India . . . , Boston, [1919].

LAIRD, HELENE REED (July 13, 1905–), born in New York City, lived in Cleveland from 1906 to 1945. Before her marriage to a University of Nevada professor, Charlton G. Laird, she was an editor for the World Publishing Company. She has published a number of stories for girls, e.g., *Nancy Keeps House,* Cleveland, [1947].

LAMAR, ASHTON. Pseud. See Harry L. Saylor.

LAMBORN, LEVI LESLIE (Oct. 10, 1829–June 14, 1910), physician, born in Chester County, Pa., of Quaker parents, was brought to Salem, Columbiana County, when he was eight years old. After reading medicine with a Damascus physician, he graduated from Western Reserve College in 1849. He practiced medicine in Mount Union for fifteen years and in Alliance for three before retiring to devote himself to real estate, banking, and publishing the Alliance *Ledger.* In the 1870s he imported carnations and raised them as a hobby. In the election of 1876 he ran for Congress against William McKinley; his practice of presenting a boutonniere to McKinley whenever they met was, according to Alliance tradition, the origin of the future President's preference for that flower.

Carnation Culture . . . , Alliance, 1887.

LAMME, BENJAMIN GARVER (Jan. 12, 1864–July 8, 1924), electrical engineer, was born in Clark County. As chief engineer for Westinghouse, he pioneered many advances in the field of electricity. His autobiography was published posthumously: *Benjamin Garver Lamme, Electrical Engineer,* New York, 1926. DAB 10

LA MONTE, JOHN LIFE (Oct. 10, 1902–Oct. 2, 1949), educator, was born in Columbus, Franklin County. He graduated from Ohio State University in 1922 and Harvard University (Ph.D.) in 1924. He taught at several universities, including the University of Cincinnati, 1931–40, and the University of Pennsylvania, 1940–49. A specialist in medieval history, he published a number of articles and books in the field, e.g., *The World of the Middle Ages . . .*, New York, [1949]. WWW 3

LA MOORE, PARKER (1897–Nov. 12, 1954), journalist, was born in Jamestown, N. Dak. After serving in World War I, he worked on newspapers in North Dakota and Oklahoma. He was associate editor of the Akron *Times-Press*, 1932–34, and afterward was editor of the Columbus bureau of Scripps-Howard Ohio newspapers. He died in Washington, D. C. He wrote a biography: *"Pat" Hurley, the Story of an American*, New York, 1932.

LAMOTT, JOHN HENRY (May 4, 1888–Feb. 15, 1960), clergyman, was born in Cincinnati, Hamilton County. He studied at Mt. St. Mary's-of-the-West, Norwood; American College, Rome, Italy; and Louvain, Belgium. After being ordained to the Roman Catholic priesthood in 1912, he taught at Mt. St. Mary's, and from 1923 until his death in Miami, Fla., he was pastor of Guardian Angels Church, Cincinnati. He wrote *History of the Archdiocese of Cincinnati, 1821–1921*, New York, 1921.

LAMPRECHT, STERLING POWER (Jan. 8, 1890–), educator, was born in Cleveland, Cuyahoga County. He graduated from Williams College in 1911, Union Theological Seminary in 1915, and Columbia University (Ph.D.) in 1918. He taught philosophy at Columbia University, University of Illinois, and Amherst College until his retirement in 1956. He now lives in Peacham, Vt. He has edited philosophical works, written numerous professional articles, and published several books, e.g., *Our Religious Traditions*, Cambridge, [Mass.], 1950. WW 29

LAMPSON, EDWARD CHESTER (Oct. 3, 1876–Nov. 10, 1957), journalist, was born in Hartsgrove, Ashtabula County. For 62 years he worked on the Jefferson *Gazette*, serving much of that time as editor. His numerous pamphlets include *A Real Cuyahoga Pioneer . . .*, [Jefferson, 1927].

LAMPTON, WILLIAM JAMES (1851–May 30, 1917), journalist, was born at Union Furnace, Lawrence County. He was educated in Kentucky schools and later attended Ohio Wesleyan University and Marietta College. He edited his own newspaper, the *Weekly Review*, at Ashland, Ky., 1877–78. Later he became a reporter on the Cincinnati *Times* and the Steubenville *Herald*. He also worked on the *Evening Star*, Washington, D. C., and the Louisville, Ky., *Courier Journal*. For a time he was part-owner and editor of the *Merchant Traveller* in Cincinnati. While he was with the Washington *Star* in 1890, he wrote his first "yawp" or *vers libre*. It was promptly rejected by the editor of the *Star*, and he sent it to Charles A. Dana, who published it in the New York *Sun* without editing, and Lampton had the satisfaction of seeing it copied in newspapers from coast to coast. He became known as a contributor of satirical verse on current topics to the New York daily newspapers, and many of his articles and poems appeared in popular magazines. The date of his first book, *Mrs. Brown's Opinions*, is usually given as 1886; however, it was mentioned as a successful book in the Cincinnati *Graphic* of June 3, 1885. He died in New York City.

Mrs. Brown's Opinions, [Cincinnati?, 1885?].

Yawps, and Other Things, Philadelphia, [1900].

The Confessions of a Husband . . ., New York, [1903].

The Trolley Car and the Lady . . ., Boston, 1908.

Tame Animals I Have Known, with Apologies to Such Wild Animals as May Feel Aggrieved by Comparison . . ., New York, 1912.

LAMSON, PEGGY FRIEDLANDER (Feb. 19, 1912–), was born in Cincinnati, Hamilton County, and lived there until 1933, when she married Roy Lamson, now a professor of English at Massachusetts Institute of Technology. She now lives in Cambridge, Mass. She has written several plays for the theater and television, articles and feature stories for magazines and newspapers, and a novel about a New England college: *The Charmed Circle*, Philadelphia, [1950].

LANDIS, FREDERICK (Aug. 18, 1872–Nov. 15, 1934), lawyer, editor, and congressman, was born in Seven Mile, Butler County, but resided throughout his adult life in Indiana. After graduating in law from the University of Michigan in 1895, he practiced in Indiana; he also served in the 58th and 59th Congresses. His writings include *The Angel of Lonesome Hill: A Story of a President*, [New York, 1910]. WWW 1

LANDIS, JOSIAH PENNABECKER (Oct. 27, 1843–Oct. 17, 1937), clergyman and educator, was born in Brickerville, Pa. After graduating from Otterbein University in 1869, he spent two years at Wayne Theological Seminary and was ordained to the United Brethren ministry in 1871. He served in several Ohio churches and was a member of the faculty of Bonebrake Theological Seminary, Dayton, from 1877 until his death; he served as president, 1909–21. He wrote *The Holy Trinity,* Dayton, 1902.

LANDSBERGER, FRANZ (June 4, 1883–), educator, born in Kattowitz, Germany, came to Cincinnati in 1939, a refugee from Nazi Germany. He was educated in European universities and was a professor and museum director in Germany until 1939. He was research professor and lecturer at Hebrew Union College and curator of the Jewish Museum there, 1948–58. He is now retired and lives in Cincinnati. Since coming to Ohio he has written *A History of Jewish Art,* Cincinnati, 1946. DAS 3

LANE, ETTA FREEMAN (Aug. 23, 1868–Nov. 11, 1945), educator, was born near Lilly Chapel, Madison County. She attended Ohio Northern University, after which she taught school for eight years. In 1895, after her marriage to Dr. L. S. Lane, she settled in Plain City. She was an active temperance worker and wrote *The Brownies' Banquet or Carnival . . . ,* [Plain City?, 1909].

LANE, LUMAN (Oct. 30, 1796–April 17, 1879), was born in Killingworth, Conn. He settled in Twinsburg in 1820. His volume of local history, written in collaboration with Ethan Alling (q.v.), provides a superlative account of pioneer life in the Western Reserve.

Locust Grove Cemetery. Twinsburgh, from 1817, by Ethan Alling, and from 1820, by Luman Lane, Akron, 1861.

LANE, SAMUEL ALANSON (June 29, 1815–June 16, 1905), was born in Suffield, Conn. His father, who trained him as a carriage-painter, died when Samuel was thirteen. Shortly after that, Sam got a job as a clerk in a store in South Lee, Mass. Then for a time he was a book salesman for Goodrich's *History,* traveling in South Carolina and Georgia. By 1834 he was learning something of writing, editing, and printing as a clerk and assistant editor of the *Southern Spy.* Lane was restless and we find him working his way to Mobile and New Orleans, but he found nothing to hold his interest. He fared no better in Louisville or Cincinnati. He then determined to visit "New Connecticut," as the Western Reserve in Ohio was called in those days. He had a friend named Squire Artemus W. Stocking, who lived in the village of Aurora, Portage County. After a short stay there, Lane decided to try his luck in Akron. Akron in 1835 was a bustling community on the Ohio Canal. It was just ten years old. Lane made silhouettes, painted scenery, and "variously served as hotel clerk, bartender, house-painter and school-teacher." In Sept., 1837, he started a small semi-monthly paper called the Akron *Buzzard.* The object of the paper was to expose the "blacklegism and other crookedness" then so prevalent in Akron and neighboring villages along the Canal. Sam was threatened and beaten, and had one nearly fatal encounter. In the spring of 1839, owing to fears of personal violence "to myself naturally indulged in by my young wife and the desire of my brother that I should join him in business, the *Buzzard* was discontinued." In 1843 he became a temperance lecturer, and within a year had started a temperance paper called the *Cascade Roarer.* This lasted about two years. In 1850 Lane joined the cavalcade of Akronites across the continent to California in search of gold. Chapter 55 of his *History* deals with this episode. The forty-page account is a classic in itself, replete with adventure and detail of the many difficulties encountered on such a trip. He saw "buffaloes by the million," had fever, experienced storms and pestilence. He gives a graphic account of crossing the Sierra Nevadas, and his picture of life in California in those days is a real contribution. In Sept., 1852, he sailed for home via Panama. Back in Akron Lane entered politics, serving in minor offices until 1856, when the Republican Party was organized and he was elected sheriff. He was re-elected in 1858 for four years. When he retired in 1861, Governor William Dennison offered him the post as probate judge but he declined. Lane then acquired a one-third interest in the *Beacon,* which burned in 1872, and he lost everything. In 1875 "after nearly fifteen years of the very hardest work of my life," he retired, but not for long because he was re-elected sheriff in 1878; and in 1881–83 he served a term as mayor. He died in Akron at the age of 89.

William D. Overman

Fifty Years and Over of Akron and Summit County, Akron, 1892.

LANG, WILLIAM (Dec. 14, 1815–Jan. 21, 1893), lawyer and judge, was born in

Sipperfield, Germany. In 1833 his family settled in Tiffin, where he later read law and was admitted to the bar in 1842. He practiced in Tiffin and held a variety of city and county posts. He was judge of probate court, 1850–55.

History of Seneca County . . ., Springfield, 1880.

LANGENWALTER, JACOB HERMANN (Jan. 12, 1877–), clergyman and educator, was born in Halstead, Kan. He graduated from Baldwin-Wallace College in 1904 and Oberlin Seminary in 1910, was ordained to the ministry of the Mennonite Church in 1902, and served as dean of Bluffton Seminary, 1914–19. He is now living in North Newton, Kan. His writings include *Christ's Headship of the Church According to Anabaptist Leaders, Whose Followers Became Mennonites,* [Berne, Ind., 1917]. RLA 2

LANGLOIS, MARINA HOLMES. See Thomas H. Langlois.

LANGLOIS, THOMAS HUXLEY (Feb. 19, 1898–), scientist, born in Detroit, Mich., has lived in Ohio since 1930. He was chief of fish management and propagation for the State Division of Conservation and Natural Resources, 1930–46; and since 1936 he has been on the zoology faculty of Ohio State University. Since 1954 he has been director of the Institute of Hydrobiology at Put-in-Bay. His wife, Marina Holmes Langlois (Aug. 17, 1895–), born in Bristol, Conn., has collaborated with him in writing many articles and books, e.g., *South Bass Island and Islanders,* [Columbus], 1948. AMS 9

LANGSTON, JOHN MERCER (Dec. 14, 1829–Nov. 15, 1897), lawyer and educator, was born in Louisa County, Va. His mother was Lucy Langston, the favorite slave of Ralph Quarles, by whom she bore three sons. Both parents died in 1834. Quarles made liberal provisions in his will for his three sons. Langston came to live with his father's old friend, William D. Gooch, in Chillicothe. After spending two years in a private school in Cincinnati, he graduated from Oberlin in 1849 and the theological department in 1854. He read law under Philomon Bliss of Elyria and was admitted to the bar in Sept., 1854. He was elected clerk of Brownhelm Township in 1855, the first Negro to be chosen to an elective office in the United States. In 1869 he became professor of law at Howard University, where he also served as dean, 1869–76. He was U. S. minister and consul general in Haiti from 1877 to 1885. He became president of Virginia Normal and Collegiate Institute at Petersburg, Va., in 1885. In 1888 he was the Republican nominee for Congress, and following a contest he was seated by the House in 1890. An unsuccessful candidate for re-election, he retired to his home in Washington, D. C. He was the author of numerous articles on a wide range of subjects in addition to a volume of his speeches, *Freedom and Citizenship,* and his dramatic autobiography, *From the Virginia Plantation to the National Capital.* His death occurred in Washington, D. C

Freedom and Citizenship . . ., Washington, D. C., 1883.

From the Virginia Plantation to the National Capital, or the First and Only Negro Representative in Congress from the Old Dominion, Hartford, Conn., 1894.

LANING, JAY FORD (May 15, 1853–Sept. 1, 1941), was born in New London, Huron County. He attended Baldwin University, read law, and in 1875 was admitted to the bar. He practiced in Norwalk until 1885, when he entered the publishing business. He thereafter wrote a number of legal works and textbooks, covering such subjects as arithmetic, shorthand, and history. He served in the Ohio senate and in the 60th Congress.

Coin's Financial School Exposed and Closed . . ., Norwalk, [1895].

LANKENAU, FRANCIS JAMES (April 26, 1868–July 15, 1939), clergyman, born in Fort Wayne, Ind., served Lutheran churches in New Orleans, 1891–1908, and was president of Luther College, 1902–08. From 1908 until his death he was a pastor in Napoleon. He published books on mission work and other religious topics, sermons, and *Occasional Addresses,* St. Louis, Mo., 1941. WWC 1

LANMAN, CHARLES (June 14, 1819–March 4, 1895), artist, explorer, and writer, born in Monroe, Mich., lived in Cincinnati while editing the Cincinnati *Chronicle,* 1846–47. A gifted man of varied talents, he published numerous magazine articles and books, e.g., *A Summer in the Wilderness . . .*, New York, 1847.

LAPHAM, INCREASE ALLEN (March 7, 1811–Sept. 14, 1875), was born in Palmyra, N. Y., and spent most of his mature life in Wisconsin. He was, however, in Portsmouth, 1830–33, working on the canal. His report on canals won him a position as secretary of the state Canal Commission, and he spent the next two years in Columbus. Though offered a position on the Ohio Geological Survey, he went to Milwaukee in 1836. He published a number of distinguished scientific works, e.g., *A Geographical and Topographical Description of Wisconsin . . .* , Milwaukee, 1844.

LAPIUS, S. Q. Pseud. See James B. Naylor.

LARKIN, BARBARA WEBB. See Barbara Webb.

LARKIN, STILLMAN CARTER (March 9, 1808–Jan., 1898), was born in Meigs County and spent his life on the family farm homestead. Ten years after his death his niece, Emeline Larkin Bicknell (q.v.), revised and published his county history, *The Pioneer History of Meigs County,* Columbus, 1908.

LARRABEE, WILLIAM CLARK (Dec. 23, 1802–May 5, 1859), Methodist clergyman and educator, born and reared in Maine, edited the *Ladies' Repository* in Cincinnati in 1852. He resigned when elected superintendent of public instruction in Indiana. A collection of his essays from the *Repository* was published: *Rosabower: A Collection of Essays and Miscellanies,* Cincinnati, 1855.

LARSEN, ELLOUISE BAKER (July 14, 1877–), was born in Dennis Port, Cape Cod, Mass., but has lived for many years in Lima. She has written short stories and lectured widely, is best known for her definitive *American Historical Views of Staffordshire China,* [New York, 1939]. WW 30

LARSON, ALICE, was born in Toledo, Lucas County. She attended the schools of Toledo and Oakland, Calif. In 1940 she was living in San Francisco. She published a book of poems: *Fog Horn and Gull Cry,* [San Francisco, 1936]. BDCP

LASHER, GEORGE WILLIAM (June 24, 1831–Feb. 22, 1920), clergyman, was born in Duanesburg, N. Y. He graduated from Colgate University in 1857 and Hamilton Theological Seminary in 1859. Ordained to the Baptist ministry in 1859, he served churches in New England and New York State before coming to Cincinnati in 1876, where he edited the *Journal and Messenger.* He died in Cincinnati.

Indebtedness of the World to Baptists for the Maintenance of a Pure Gospel, Cincinnati, 1891.

Story of Diaz, Cincinnati, 1894.

Theology for Plain People, Cincinnati, 1906.

LATCHAW, JOHN ROLAND HARRIS (Sept. 7, 1851–April 8, 1928), clergyman and educator, born in Venango County, Pa., was ordained to the ministry of the Christian Church in 1878. He graduated from Hillsdale College in 1881. He was president of Findlay College, 1884–93, was pastor of a Baptist church, Zanesville, 1893–95, and was president of Defiance College, 1896–1902, during which period he was also pastor of the Defiance Christian Assembly. He published and edited the *Truth Seeker,* compiled textbooks, and wrote *The Bride Unveiled; Or, the Book of Revelation Made Plain,* Muskegon, Mich., [1915].

LATHBURY, CLARENCE (Jan. 21, 1854–Nov. 10, 1939), clergyman, was born in Manchester, N. Y. After attending Lodi Academy and Oberlin College, he was ordained a Methodist minister in 1887. In 1891, after graduating from the New Church Theological School, Cambridge, Mass., he became a minister of the Church of the New Jerusalem. He served churches in Massachusetts and New York, and was at the Church of the Holy City, Cleveland, 1917–32.

God Winning Us, New York, [1898].

A Little Lower Than the Angels, New York, [1901].

The Code of Joy, Germantown, Pa., 1902.

The Being with the Upturned Face, New York, 1903.

The Balanced Life, New York, 1905.

The Great Morning, Minneapolis, 1911.

LATHROP, LORIN ANDREWS (1858–Jan. 19, 1929), diplomat, was born in Gambier, Knox County. After working as a newspaperman in San Francisco, he was appointed U. S. consul at Bristol, England; he later served in Cardiff, Wales, and Nassau, Bahama Islands. Under the pen name Kenyon Gambier, he published stories and novels, e.g., *The Girl on the Hilltop,* New York, [1920]. He published numerous articles in British newspapers under the pen name Andrew Loring and also used that name for *The Rhymers' Lexicon,* New York, [1905].

LATOURETTE, KENNETH SCOTT (Aug. 9, 1884–), Baptist clergyman and educator, born in Oregon, served on the faculty of Denison University, 1916–21, and resigned to join the faculty of Yale University. He has written a number of books on Asia and the missionary efforts there, e.g., *The Development of China,* Boston, 1917. WW 30

LATTA, SAMUEL ARMINIUS (April 8, 1804–Oct. 28, 1852), physician and clergyman, was born in Muskingum County. He studied medicine, was licensed, and practiced for three years, during which time he read theology. He became a local preacher in the Methodist Church and for several years practiced both professions. He gave up church work in 1840 and moved to Cincinnati, where he devoted his entire time to the practice of medicine. There his fight against homeopathy won for him a national reputation. After his death the Cincinnati Medical Society held a public memorial meeting for this remarkably versatile man.

Chain of Sacred Wonders, Cincinnati, 1849.
The Cholera in Cincinnati: Or, a Connected View of the Controversy between the Homeopathists and the Methodist Expositor . . . , Cincinnati, 1850.

LAUGHLIN, JAMES LAURENCE (April 2, 1850–Nov. 28, 1933), educator, was born in Deerfield, Portage County. He attended Mount Union College for a time before transferring to Harvard University (A.B., 1873; Ph.D., 1876). He taught political economy at Harvard, 1878–88, Cornell University, 1890–92, and the University of Chicago, 1892–1916. After his retirement he lived in Jaffrey, N. H. He wrote several influential studies of money and credit and numerous textbooks and monographs not listed below.

The History of Bimetallism in the United States, New York, 1886.
Facts about Money . . . , Chicago, [1895].
The Principles of Money, New York, 1903.
Reciprocity, (with H. Parker Willis), New York, [1903].
Industrial America; Berlin Lectures of 1906, New York, 1906.
Latter-day Problems, New York, 1909.
Suggestions for Banking Reform, Chicago, [1911].
Credit of the Nations; A Study of the European War, New York, 1918.
Money and Prices, New York, 1919.
A National Reserve Association and the Movement of Cotton in the South, Chicago, [191-?].
Banking Progress, New York, 1920.
A New Exposition of Money, Credit and Prices, 2 vols., Chicago, [1931].
The Federal Reserve Act, Its Origin and Problems, New York, 1933.

LAWALL, IRENE. See Irene L. Dornblaser.

LAWRANCE, HAROLD GAINES (May 21, 1882–), educator, was born in Toledo, Lucas County. He graduated from Oberlin College and did graduate work at the University of Minnesota. He has taught at several universities, including Stetson University, Winona College, and the University of Tennessee. He now lives in Knoxville, Tenn. He has worked on the Toledo *Blade,* the Cleveland *Leader,* and other newspapers, has written numerous newspaper articles and stories for young people, and a biography of his father: *Marion Lawrence; A Memorial Biography* . . . , New York, [1925]. WWNAA 3

LAWRANCE, URIAH MARION (Oct. 2, 1850–May 1, 1924), Sunday school worker, was born in Winchester, Adams County. In 1854 the family moved to Yellow Springs, where the father operated the Antioch College bookstore. Uriah attended the local schools and spent one year at Antioch. After twenty years as a salesman, he became secretary of the Ohio Sunday School Association in 1889 and devoted the rest of his life to promoting Sunday school activities. His best-known work, *How to Conduct a Sunday-School,* first published in 1905, was translated into a dozen languages. He published several other manuals and books, e.g., *My Message to Sunday School Workers,* New York, [1924]. DAB 11

LAWRANCE, WILLIAM IRVIN (March 3, 1853–Oct., 1935), clergyman, was born in Winchester, Adams County. After graduating from Antioch College in 1880 and from Harvard Divinity School in 1885, he became a Unitarian clergyman and served churches in several states. He also taught at Pacific Unitarian School for the Ministry. His writings include *The Social Emphasis in Religious Education,* Boston, [1918]. WWW 1

LAWRANCE, WILLIAM VICARS (Nov. 8, 1834–Jan. 5, 1905), lawyer, was born in Greene County. He grew up on a farm, attended school in Cedarville, studied at Antioch College from 1856 to 1858, and read law in Xenia. He was admitted to the Ohio bar in 1860. In 1861 he enlisted in the 12th O.V.I. and later transferred to the cavalry. He practiced law in Waverly, 1865–68, and afterward in Chillicothe, where he spent the remainder of his life.

Ellina, the Bride of Montross, Cambridge, [Mass.], 1873.
The Story of Judeth . . . , Cambridge, [Mass.], 1889.
Defeated but Victor Still, New York, [1898].
The Loves of Laos in Sonnets Sung, [Cincinnati, 1898].
Under Which Master . . . , New York, [1901].

LAWRENCE, ALBERT. Pseud. See Alberta E. I. C. Lawrence.

LAWRENCE, ALBERTA ELIZA INEZ CHAMBERLAIN (1875–), was born in Cleveland, Cuyahoga County. She was literary editor of the Pasadena *Star-News* and also published numerous book reviews. She edited *Who's Who among North American Authors,* 7 vols., 1921–39. Under the pen name Albert Lawrence, she also published a novel: *The Travels of Phoebe Ann,* Boston, 1908. WWNAA 7

LAWRENCE, EDA HAHNE (July 11, 1883–April 1, 1932), was born in Newark, Licking County. She spent much of her life in Cleveland and died in that city. Her poems appeared in various periodicals, and she published a collection: *The Truth about Fiction, and Collected Verse,* Cleveland, 1923.

LAWRENCE, IDA ECKERT (1864–), was born near Mansfield, Richland County. She attended high school in Topeka, Kan., and around 1900 was living in Toledo. She afterward lived in Los Angeles.

Day Dreams, Cincinnati, 1900.
Aubrey Messages, Evidence of Life, Memory, Affection after the Change Called Death . . . , Los Angeles, 1928.

LAWRENCE, JAMES (1792–Sept. 28, 1880), lived for a number of years in Cleveland. No details concerning his life are available. The book below, a collection of essays on spiritualism, was said to have been "written under angel influence."

Angel Voice from the Spirit World . . . , Cleveland, 1874.

LAWRENCE, JAMES COOPER (Feb. 10, 1890–Aug. 14, 1932), educator and businessman, was born in Columbus, Franklin County. From 1912 to 1927 he was an executive in various rubber and chemical companies. In 1928 he became assistant to the president of the University of Minnesota. His writings include *The World's Struggle with Rubber, 1905-1931,* New York, 1934. WWW 1

LAWRENCE, JEROME K. (July 14, 1915–), was born Jerome Lawrence Schwartz in Cleveland, Cuyahoga County. He graduated from Ohio State University in 1937 and after four years of writing for radio began free-lance writing with Robert E. Lee (q.v.). They have created many notable radio and television programs. Since 1951 they have done more writing for the stage, and their play based on the Scopes trial, *Inherit the Wind* (1955), won several awards. Lawrence has edited a collection of radio scripts and published a book for children: *Oscar, the Ostrich,* New York, 1940. WW 30

LAWRENCE, JOHN (Dec. 3, 1824–Aug. 7, 1889), clergyman and lawyer, was born in Wayne County. A United Brethren clergyman, he served churches in Sandusky and Michigan and edited the *Religious Telescope,* 1852–64, published in Dayton. After the Civil War he was judge of a freedman's court in Nashville, Tenn., for a time and later practiced law in that city. He died in Nashville.

Plain Thoughts on Secret Societies, Dayton, 1852.
The Slavery Question . . . , Dayton, 1854.
The History of the Church of the United Brethren in Christ, 2 vols., Dayton, 1860–61.

LAWRENCE, LOU (March 20, 1854–Nov. 24, 1932), was born in Amsterdam, Jefferson County. She taught in country schools of Belmont County and afterward operated an antique shop at her home in Barnesville. She wrote *The Confessions of an Old Maid,* [New York, 1904].

LAWRENCE, ROBERT. Pseud. See Robert L. Beum.

LAWRENCE, WILLIAM (June 26, 1819–May 8, 1898), lawyer and legislator, was born in Mount Pleasant, Jefferson County. He graduated from Franklin College in 1838 and Cincinnati Law School in 1840. He served in Congress, 1865–71 and 1873–77, and was comptroller of the treasury, 1880–85. He prepared an elaborate brief on impeachment that was used by Ben. F. Butler in his opening argument in the trial of President Andrew Johnson. An ardent advocate of protective tariff, he also prepared a ten-volume memorial to Congress advocating tariffs on wool. Several of his addresses were also published. He died in Kenton.

Brief Sketch of the Life and Public Serv-

ices of John Sherman . . . , [Cincinnati], 1888.

LAWYER, JAMES PATTERSON (Oct. 26, 1875–), was born in Guernsey County. He was land appraiser for the Osage Indian tribe in Oklahoma until his retirement in 1945. He now lives in Phoenix, Ariz. He has written *History of Ohio, from the Glacial Period to the Present Time,* Columbus, 1904.

LAYLANDER, ORANGE JUDD (March 11, 1858– ?), was born in Nashville, Holmes County. He was a school superintendent in Iowa, 1882–1900, an employee of Ginn and Company, 1900–06, and was engaged in business in Chicago, 1906–31. His most recent address in Ohioana files is Burt Lake, Mich. He published a collection of stories and poems: *Whittlings,* Cedar Rapids, Iowa, 1928.

LEACH, WILLIAM HERMAN (Dec. 19, 1888–), Presbyterian clergyman, born in Shinglehouse, Pa., has lived since 1924 in Lakewood, and has edited *Church Management,* published in Cleveland. He has written numerous pamphlets on practical problems of the church and also a number of entertainments for church presentation, e.g., *The Barbarian . . . ,* Franklin, 1924. WW 30

LEAHY, RICHARD P. (1867–June 6, 1940), was born near Tiffin, Seneca County. After graduating from Heidelberg College in 1889, he was in the real-estate business in Chicago; he later lived in Mobile, Ala., and Havana, Cuba. At the time of his death he was a resident of Bay City, Mich. He published two collections of verse, e.g., *Father Damien and Other Poems,* New York, [1938].

LEAVITT, HUMPHREY HOWE (June 18, 1796–March 15, 1873), congressman and judge, was born in Suffield, Conn., but grew up near Warren, where his father moved in 1800. He taught school, clerked in a store, and read law. Admitted to the bar in 1816, he practiced in Cadiz and Steubenville. He served two terms in Congress, 1830–34. In 1834 President Jackson appointed him federal district judge, and he served on the bench for nearly forty years. His most famous decision was his refusal of a writ of habeas corpus to Clement L. Vallandigham (q.v.) in 1863. This decision and some speeches were published during his lifetime. His autobiography, which he had written for his family, was published posthumously. In 1871 he resigned from the bench and moved to Springfield, where he spent his last two years.

Autobiography of the Hon. Humphrey Howe Leavitt . . . , New York, 1893.

LEAVITT, JOHN McDOWELL (May 10, 1824–Dec. 12, 1909), clergyman and educator, was born in Steubenville, Jefferson County. After graduating from Jefferson College in 1841, he studied law. He practiced a short time in Cincinnati and then attended the seminary at Gambier. He was ordained to the Episcopal priesthood in 1848. He taught at Kenyon College and Ohio University and was president of Lehigh University and St. John's College, Md. He founded and edited the *International Review.* His death occurred in Annapolis, Md. Of the titles below, *Visions of Solyma* was published anonymously, *Americans in Rome* appeared under the pen name Ray Aster, and *Alicia* appeared under the pen name Alexis.

Faith: A Poem in Three Parts, Cincinnati, 1856.

Afranius, and the Indumean . . . , New York, 1869.

The American Cardinal. A Novel, New York, 1871.

Hymns to Our King, New York, [1872].

New World Tragedies from Old World Life . . . , New York, 1876.

Visions of Solyma, Bethlehem, Pa., [1879].

Faith, the Periods and Other Poems, New York, [1884].

Kings of Capital and Knights of Labor, New York, 1885.

Americans in Rome; Or, Paul Errington and His Struggle. A Novel, New York, 1886.

Paul Errington and Our Scarlet Prince . . . , New York, [1894].

Visions of Solyma and Other Poems, New York, 1895.

Alicia; A Tale of the American Navy, 1898.

Reasons for Faith and Christianity . . . , New York, 1900.

Our Flag, Our Rose, Our Country, New York, 1908.

LEBERMAN, JOHN J. (Nov. 29, 1848–May 30, 1921), clergyman, born in Lebanon County, Pa., lived in Ohio 46 years. He was pastor of Paradise Evangelical and Reformed Church, Louisville, Stark County, 1873–1900, and afterward preached at churches in Beaver Creek, Lancaster, Akron, and Braddock, Pa. His last years were spent at Sugar Grove, Fairfield County.

A Popular Treatise on Baptism . . . , Dayton, 1886.

LECKLIDER, JOHN T. (July 18, 1840–Jan. 2, 1929), lawyer, was born on a farm near Dayton, Montgomery County. After reading law, he was admitted to the bar and practiced in Dayton. He published *Poems,* Boston, [1913].

LECKLITER, GRACE D., educator, was born in Worthington, Franklin County. A graduate of Ohio State University, she taught history and civics for a number of years in the Columbus schools. She now lives in Columbus. She has published a book of poems: *Spring Is Tomorrow,* Los Angeles, [1944].

LEDBETTER, ELEANOR EDWARDS (May 6, 1870–July 19, 1954), librarian, born in Holley, N. Y., lived in Cleveland for nearly fifty years. After 29 years' service with the Cleveland Public Library, she retired in 1935 as head of the Broadway Branch Library and continued to live in Cleveland until her death. She wrote several books on Americanization and on European groups in Cleveland, e.g., *The Slovaks of Cleveland . . . ,* [Cleveland, 1918].

LEE, ALFRED EMORY (Feb. 17, 1838–Aug. 31, 1905), lawyer and journalist, was born in Barnesville, Belmont County. He graduated from Ohio Wesleyan University in 1859. He served in the 82nd O.V.I., Nov., 1861–July, 1865. After the war he practiced law in Delaware, and in 1876 he was appointed private secretary to Governor Rutherford B. Hayes, who, as President, appointed him consul general at Frankfort am Main. In 1881 he became chief editorial writer of the *Ohio State Journal,* and in 1883 he was associated for a few months with the Toledo *Daily Telegram.* His *History of the City of Columbus* is one of the most informative and dependable of all Ohio local histories.

What Was Grant?, Columbus, 1885.
The Battle of Gettysburg, Columbus, 1888.
European Days and Ways, Philadelphia, 1890.
History of the City of Columbus . . . , 2 vols., New York, 1892.
Silver and Gold . . . , Columbus, 1893.

LEE, BENJAMIN FRANKLIN (Sept. 18, 1841–March 12, 1926), clergyman and educator, was born in Gouldtown, N. J. He graduated from Wilberforce University in 1872, taught there, 1873–76, and served as president, 1876–84. He edited the *Christian Recorder,* 1884–92, and served as bishop of the African Methodist Episcopal Church, 1892–1924.

Wesley the Worker, New York, 1880.

LEE, CHARLES C. Pseud. See Martha E. P. Rose.

LEE, ELLA DOLBEAR (July 4, 1866–June 15, 1954), was born in Marysville, Union County. After graduating from Marysville High School, she studied art at Tufts College and the New England Conservatory. She worked as an illustrator for books and magazines. In 1904 she married Charles C. Lee; she lived for a number of years in Philadelphia, but returned to Ohio before her death. Under the pen name Jean Finley she wrote a series of children's books in the 1920s known as the Blue Domers series; and under her own name she published another series, "Jean Mary's Adventures," e.g., *Jean Mary in Virginia,* New York, [1931].

LEE, GEORGE HYDE (1848–April 1, 1920), physician, was born in Mantua, Portage County. He graduated from Western Reserve College in 1868, was a journalist in Philadelphia and other cities, 1868–74, and graduated from Homeopathic Medical College, Cleveland, 1876. He practiced medicine in Washington, D. C., and wrote fiction as an avocation. His death occurred in Miami, Fla.

Kith and Kin, Washington, D. C., 1900.
What Was His Duty?, Washington, D. C., 1900.

LEE, GERTRUDE. See Gertrude L. Chandler-Tucker.

LEE, JAMES (Sept. 26, 1905–), journalist, was born in Mount Vernon, Knox County. A graduate of Georgetown University, Washington, D. C., he worked on the Los Angeles *Examiner* for a number of years and is now associate editor of *U. S. News and World Report* and lives in Washington, D. C. His writings include a book on the naval air transport service: *Operation Lifeline . . . ,* Chicago, [1947].

LEE, MARY CHAPPELL (Mrs. Frank) (July 7, 1849–May 5, 1932), educator, was born in Kingston, N. Y. She taught in the public schools of New York City, in various schools in Ohio and Kansas, and in a mission school among mountain whites in Grand View, Tenn. After her retirement she returned to Ohio and lived in Westerville. Besides the titles below, she published stories in *Youth's Companion* and other magazines.

The Losing Side, a Poem, and Why He Didn't Insure, a Dialogue, Columbus, 1888.

Knives and Forks; Or, Dwellers in Meridien, Boston, [1890].
Garret Grain; Or, the House Blessed, Boston, [1894].
Redmond of the Seventh; Or, the Boys of Ninety, Boston, [1897].
Professor Pin, Boston, [1899].
Mart Conner, Boston, 1900.
Little Boom No. I, Boston, 1902.
The Making of Major, Elgin, Ill., [1913].
The Double D's, Boston, [1914].

LEE, ROBERT EDWIN (Oct. 15, 1918–), was born in Elyria, Lorain County. He attended Ohio Wesleyan University, 1935–37. He has teamed with Jerome K. Lawrence (q.v.) to write numerous outstanding radio and television programs, musical comedies, and plays, notably *Inherit the Wind* (1955). He has also published *Television: The Revolution,* New York, [1944]. WW 30

LEET, LEWIS DON (July 1, 1901–), seismologist, was born in Alliance, Stark County. He graduated from Denison University in 1923 and Harvard University (Ph.D.) in 1930. He has been a member of the Harvard faculty since 1931. He has published a number of textbooks and technical studies and *Causes of Catastrophe; Earthquakes, Volcanoes, Tidal Waves, and Hurricanes,* New York, [1948]. WW 30

LEGGETT, MORTIMER DORMER (April 19, 1821–Jan. 6, 1896), educator and lawyer, was born on a farm near Ithaca, N. Y. When he was fifteen, his parents moved to Geauga County. He attended Kirtland Teachers School and Western Reserve College and was admitted to the bar in 1844. He practiced law and served as superintendent of schools in Akron, Warren, and Zanesville. During the Civil War he was colonel of the 78th O.V.I. After serving as Commissioner of Patents, 1871–74, he practiced in Cleveland, specializing in patent law. He also organized the Brush Electric Company. Besides the book below, he delivered some addresses that were published as separate pamphlets.

A Dream of a Modest Prophet, Philadelphia, 1890.

LEGLER, MARY FERGUSON (Dec. 31, 1886–), was born in Newark, Licking County. She attended Granville public schools and graduated from Denison University in 1906. Since her marriage to Ellis P. Legler, she has lived in Dayton. She has published a volume of poems: *Until the Day Break,* Los Angeles, 1939. BDCP

LEHMANN, HENRY G. (Dec. 27, 1842–Dec. 18, 1929), was born in Fort Wayne, Ind., but in 1845 his father settled in Delphos, Van Wert County. He served with the 32nd O.V.I. in the Civil War, afterward was associated with various stores in Convoy and Van Wert, and operated a farm. He opened his own dry goods store in 1888. He died in Van Wert. He wrote a book of Civil War memories: *Reminiscences of a Soldier . . . ,* Van Wert, [n.d.].

LEIGH, AMY ELIZABETH. Pseud. See Caroline H. W. Foster.

LEIGHTON, JOSEPH ALEXANDER (Dec. 2, 1870–May 19, 1954), clergyman and educator, was born in Orangeville, Ontario, Canada. He graduated from Trinity College, Toronto, in 1891, Cornell University (Ph.D.) in 1894, and Episcopal Theological Seminary, Cambridge, Mass., in 1896. He taught philosophy and served as chaplain at Hobart College, 1897–1910, and was professor of philosophy at Ohio State University, 1910–41. His home was in Worthington. He wrote several textbooks, more than a hundred articles, and several books on religion, education, and other subjects, e.g., *Social Philosophies in Conflict . . . ,* New York, 1937. WW 26

LEIGHTON, MARGARET CARVER (Dec. 20, 1896–), was born in Oberlin, Lorain County, where her father was a member of the college faculty. He accepted a position at Harvard, however, and she grew up in Massachusetts. After the death of her husband in 1935, she moved to California and began writing children's books, most of them on historical subjects, e.g., *The Secret of the Old House,* Philadelphia, [1941]. WW 30

LEISERSON, WILLIAM MORRIS (April 15, 1883–Feb., 1957), educator, born in Estonia, lived in Ohio about twelve years, while serving on the faculties of the University of Toledo, 1915–18, and Antioch College, 1925–34. After leaving Antioch he served on various government agencies and bureaus in Washington. He published several studies of economic and social problems, e.g., *Adjusting Immigrant and Industry,* New York, 1924. WW 29

LELAND, SAMUEL PHELPS (March 4, 1837–1910?), was born in Massachusetts but was brought by his parents to Huntsburg, Geauga County, at an early age. He studied at Hiram College, read law, and was admitted to the bar. He practiced law, lectured, and wrote for newspapers in various cities. He lived in Georgia, Tennessee, Illinois, Florida, and other states.

Geology vs. the Bible, Cleveland, 1860.
Poems, Chicago, 1866.
Peculiar People, Cleveland, 1891.
World Making; A Scientific Explanation of the Birth, Growth and Death of Worlds, Chicago, 1895.

LENDER, CHARLES FRANKLIN (March 21, 1886–), was born in St. Louis, Mo. A graduate of Ohio State University, he was in Y.M.C.A. work in Columbus and also was superintendent of relief and supervisor of old-age pensions there. He now lives in Los Angeles. He has written several historical narratives for young readers, e.g., *Down the Ohio with Clark,* New York, [1937].

LENDERMAN was apparently the pseudonym of a Cincinnati doctor who used a combination of lurid melodrama and humor to attack spiritualism and medical practices that he disapproved.

Lenderman's Adventures among the Spiritualists and Free-Lovers . . . , Cincinnati, 1857.
Lenderman's Thousand Characters and Ten Thousand Practical Facts . . . , Cincinnati, 1859.
Ourselves, Doctored and Undoctored, Looked at through Humor's Spectacles . . . , Cincinnati, 1860.

LENSKI, GERHARD EMMANUEL (July 24, 1890–), clergyman, son of Richard C. H. Lenski (q.v.), was born in Trenton, Butler County. He graduated from Capital University in 1910 and the seminary in 1914. Ordained to the ministry of the Evangelical Lutheran Church, he served a pastorate in Butler, Pa., 1914–18, and was pastor of Grace Lutheran Church, Washington, D. C., 1920–52. He was on the faculty of Pacific Lutheran Seminary, 1952–56, and now lives in Washington, D. C. He has written several books on devotional themes, e.g., *When God Gave Easter,* Minneapolis, 1941. WW 27

LENSKI, LOIS (Oct. 14, 1893–), was born in Springfield, Clark County. When she was five years old, her family moved to Anna, Shelby County. She was the fourth of five children of Rev. Richard C. H. Lenski (q.v.), a Lutheran minister, and it was a family joke that the Lenskis raised the population of Anna to 207. It may have been in that little town, where everybody must have known what everyone else was doing, that she developed her innate, keen sense of people—how they live, what they do, what their aspirations and problems are. Certainly her pleasure in and knowledge of that neighborly life, as well as of the ebullient ways of a large family, are reflected in her *Skipping Village* and *A Little Girl of 1900,* both of which were based on her childhood. As has so often happened, there emerged from this Midwestern small town a cosmopolitan in the making. In 1911 the family moved to Columbus, where Miss Lenski graduated in 1915 from Ohio State University College of Education. She never taught school; instead, despite her father's opposition, she went to New York City, studied for four years at the Art Students' League (working part time), thence to London to study for a year at the Westminster School of Art. It was in London that she made her first book illustrations, and back home again in New York she quickly found similar commissions. In 1927 she illustrated her first story, *Skipping Village,* soon followed by half a dozen picture books, a form in which she still works with understanding and skill—and so began her career as author-illustrator. In 1927, also, she had her first one-man show of paintings in New York. In 1921 Miss Lenski married Arthur S. Covey, the mural painter, and when their son Stephen was very young she wrote and illustrated picture books sparked by his needs and interests. Thus, because at one point Stephen was so preoccupied with automobiles, was born the famous Mr. Small, who first appeared unobtrusively in 1934 in *The Little Auto.* Since then he has delighted the children of three decades and of more than half a dozen countries in such roles as fireman, cowboy, farmer, and aviator, in books which are small miracles of interest, directness, and simplicity. In 1936 Miss Lenski, who has said that she hated history in school, published *Phebe Fairchild, Her Book,* the first of a group of historical stories for older children, and this seeming paradox is revelatory of her approach to writing. Like all her work, this story of a Connecticut child of the 1830s was rooted in personal experience. The Coveys had moved to a 1790 farmhouse near Torrington, Conn., and, as she wrote in *The Horn Book* (Dec., 1937): "When I decided to tell the story of our house, to fill it with people and describe the life they might have lived one hundred years ago, as soon as I looked at History from the human standpoint, it became absorbing and fascinating and very much alive." It is this intense interest in "the human standpoint," in the ordinary yet significant details of everyday lives—a century ago or today—that accounts for much of the vitality of Lois Lenski's books. One feels it in the regional stories which she began to write (turning necessity into an asset), when, in 1941, ill-health forced her to spend her winters in the South. There, with the instinct of the born storyteller, she recognized a new area of material and produced in 1943 *Bayou Suzette,* a story of Louisiana. Since then she has written more than a score of books about America, ranging from the hills of San Francisco to the cranberry bogs of Cape Cod. These stories are based on firsthand knowledge of the people and their background; several of them have been written at the urgent request of children. When the children of Blytheville, Ark., wrote to her asking her to tell *their* story, Miss Lenski went to Arkansas, picked cotton with them, and wrote *Cotton in My Sack.* In 1946 Miss Lenski received the much-coveted annual Newbery Medal for *Strawberry Girl,* a story of Florida crackers in the early 1900s. Unlike some regional writers, Lois Lenski is more interested in people than in landscape. She is deeply concerned with the way their lives and problems have been shaped by their environment. For all her sympathy and understanding, she is also uncompromisingly realistic; she is not afraid to portray the harsh details of poverty *(Judy's Journey),* the reckless extravagance of the new-rich *(Boomtown Boy),* or the shiftlessness of a poor-white family *(Strawberry Girl).* Like her style, her approach is forthright almost to the point of bluntness. Realism, forthrightness—these are qualities which children value more than we often realize. Combine them with good storytelling and it is no wonder that many children of America, country *and* city, have given Lois Lenski their allegiance.

Ellen Lewis Buell

LENSKI, RICHARD CHARLES HENRY (Sept. 14, 1864–Aug. 14, 1936), clergyman and educator, father of Lois and Gerhard E. Lenski (qq.v.), was born in Greifenberg, Prussia. He graduated from Capital University in 1885 and the seminary in 1887. Ordained to the Lutheran ministry, he served several Ohio churches, 1887–1911; he then served on the faculty of Capital University, 1916–28, and retired as dean emeritus. He published a number of sermons and books on religious subjects, e.g., *The Interpretation of St. John's Gospel,* Columbus, 1931. WWW 1

LENZ, ELLIS CHRISTIAN (March 26, 1896–), was born in Hartville, Stark County. After graduating from high school in Canton in 1916, he studied art in Chicago and Cleveland. He worked as a commercial artist from 1919 until 1942, when he became historian of the Cleveland ordnance district. He has written and illustrated an extensive history of firearms: *Muzzle Flashes . . . ,* Huntington, W. Va., 1944.

LEONARD, ADNA BRADWAY (Aug. 2, 1837–April 21, 1916), clergyman, father of Bishop Adna W. Leonard and Lena Leonard Fisher (qq.v), was born in Berlin Township, Mahoning County. After graduating from Mount Union College, he was ordained to the Methodist ministry in 1860 and served various churches in Ohio and elsewhere. He was corresponding secretary of the Missionary Society and Board of Foreign Missions, 1888–1912. He died in Brooklyn, N. Y., and is buried in Springfield. The year before his death he published his autobiography: *The Stone of Help . . . ,* New York, [1915]. WWW 1

LEONARD, ADNA WRIGHT (Nov. 2, 1874–May 3, 1943), clergyman, was born in Cincinnati, Hamilton County. He was ordained to the Methodist ministry in Rome, Italy, in 1901. He served pastorates in Italy and in Ohio and other states until his election as bishop in 1916. He was killed while touring army camps when the airplane in which he was traveling crashed in Iceland. His books include *Ancient Fires on Modern Altars,* New York, [1931]. WWW 2

LEONARD, DELAVAN LEVANT (July 20, 1834–Jan. 26, 1917), clergyman, was born in Pendleton, N. Y. After graduating from Hamilton College in 1859 and Union Theological Seminary in 1863, he was ordained to the ministry of the Congregational Church. He was superintendent of home missions in the Far West, 1863–81, came to Ohio as a pastor in Bellevue in 1888, and was chairman of the Ohio Church and Ministerial Supply Bureau, 1899–1906. His home was in Oberlin. He wrote for a number of religious magazines and newspapers.

A Hundred Years of Missions . . . , 1895.

1796–1896. A Century of Congregationalism in Ohio, Oberlin, 1896.

The Story of Oberlin; The Institution, the Community, the Idea, the Movement, Boston, [1898].

Missionary Annals of the Nineteenth Century. A History, a Book of Reference,

and an Interesting Story Combined . . . , Cleveland, [1899].
The History of Carleton College . . . , Chicago, [1904].

LEONARD, HENRY (Feb. 14, 1812–Dec. 7, 1889), merchant, was born in Basil, Fairfield County. After clerking in a Lancaster store for a few months, he opened his own store in Basil at the age of sixteen. As his business prospered, he was able to devote more and more of his time to the Reformed Church. From 1856 to 1887 he was financial agent of Heidelberg College and traveled far and wide in search of funds. He referred to himself as the "fisherman" and published a series of sketches in the *Western Messenger,* Dayton, which were published in book form the year of his retirement.

The Fisherman's Allegories, Dayton, 1887.

LEONARD, LEWIS ALEXANDER (July 10, 1845–Nov. 12, 1926), lawyer and journalist, was born in Poplar Island, Md. He practiced law for a time in Maryland, then moved to Lafayette, Ind., and then to Cincinnati, where he entered newspaper work. He was editor of the old Cincinnati *Star* when it was consolidated with the *Times* in 1880 and continued as editor of the *Times-Star* until 1882 and as managing editor, 1882–84. He later was associated with newspapers in Detroit, Philadelphia, and New York City. Upon retiring he returned to Cincinnati. He took an active interest in the public library of Cincinnati. He was editor-in-chief and wrote large portions of the last title in the list below.

Tales I've Heard Told, New York, 1898.
Life of Charles Carroll of Carrollton, New York, 1918.
Life of Alphonso Taft, New York, [1920].
Greater Cincinnati and Its People; A History, 4 vols., New York, 1927.

LEONARD, WILLIAM ANDREW (July 15, 1848–Sept. 21, 1930), clergyman, born in Southport, Conn., spent the last 41 years of his life in Ohio. After serving Episcopal churches in Brooklyn, N. Y., and Washington, D. C., he was consecrated bishop of Ohio in 1889. He lived in Cleveland and spent most of his summers in Gambier, where he did much to strengthen Kenyon College and Bexley Seminary. Besides the titles below, several of his addresses and sermons were published. He died in Gambier.

Via Sacra . . . , New York, 1875.
A Brief History of the Christian Church, New York, 1883.
A Faithful Life, New York, [1888].
The Story of the Prayer Book, New York, 1898.
Stephen Banks Leonard . . . , [Cleveland], 1909.

LEONHART, RUDOLPH (1832– ?), educator, born in Munich, Germany, was a teacher in Canton in the 1880s. He later taught in Tacoma, Wash. He wrote several novels, e.g., *The Treasure of Montezuma,* Canton, 1888.

LEROY, MARION. See Minnie W. B. Miller.

LESLIE, SARABETH. Pseud. See Sarah E. S. Leslie.

LESLIE, SARAH ELIZABETH SATTERTHWAITE (Aug. 6, 1864–Feb. 1, 1958), born in Adrian, Mich., and reared in central New York State, lived in Toledo from 1894 until her death at the age of 93. She published poems in various periodicals and anthologies. Under the pen name Sarabeth Leslie, she published several books, including a book of verse for children: *Morningshore Children,* New York, [1936], and a book of recollections of World War I: *Morningshore Joins the 37th,* New York, [1947]. BDCP

LeSOURD, LEONARD EARLE (May 20, 1919–), was born in Columbus, Franklin County, where his father was then a Methodist clergyman. He graduated from Ohio Wesleyan University in 1941. He now lives in Newton, Mass. While he was undergoing pilots' training during World War II, his letters to his parents were published under the title *Sky-Bent . . . ,* [Boston, 1943].

LESQUEREUX, CHARLES LEO (Nov. 18, 1806–Oct. 25, 1889), was born in Fleurier, Switzerland. He married a beautiful young baroness of the court of Saxe-Weimar. He began the study of mosses, peat bogs, glaciation, and other scientific subjects, and was elected to membership in the Society of Natural History at Neuchâtel; but the Sonderbund War caused him and his friend Arnold Guyot to follow Louis Agassiz to America. He worked for a time on a classification of the plants collected on Agassiz' 1848 expedition to Lake Superior, became Asa Gray's curator, and then came to Columbus to collaborate with William S. Sullivant (q.v.) in preparing their important *Musci Boreali-Americani.* Lesquereux died in Columbus in 1889, sixteen years after the death of Sullivant, and in this interval he established himself as America's foremost paleobotanist. Professor W. G. Farlow of

Harvard has written, "Although, by a fortunate chance, Lesquereux was able almost immediately on his arrival in America to turn to good account the knowledge of mosses acquired while he was in Europe, and although he was recognized in later years as, after Sullivant, the leading bryologist of America, it is chiefly to his knowledge of fossil plants that his high position among American scientific men is due. In the field of vegetable paleontology he unquestionably stood at the head in America. . . . The vast unexplored treasures of plants buried in the coal measures were very imperfectly known when Lesquereux arrived in America. He gradually began the study of those forms which were at hand, and as the different States developed their geological surveys materials accumulated in vast quantities, and Lesquereux was soon recognized as the one best fitted to prepare reports on the fossil plants. . . . In the opinion of experts his most important contribution to paleontology was 'Description of the Coal Flora of the Carboniferous Formation in Pennsylvania' in the *Second Geological Survey* of that state." Lesquereux reported also on fossil plants for the geological surveys of Kentucky (1857) and later of Illinois and Arkansas. In his report for Indiana (1884) he published his "Principles of Palaeozoic Botany," which Farlow said "might well be called an educational treatise." We cannot elaborate here Lesquereux's important theories of the origins of coal, prairies, clay, and petroleum, or his beliefs on the ages, character, interrelationships, and geographic plant distribution of various formations of different epochs of the geological calendar. His publications were numerous, and, while he wrote on conditions of climate and other ecological factors of various epochs, his work was fundamentally taxonomic. His *Contributions to the Fossil Floras of the Western Territories* in three parts, concerned with the Cretaceous and Tertiary flora, together with numerous less important writings, and a posthumous publication, *Flora of the Dakota Group,* emerged from his employment by the United States Geological and Geographical Survey of the Territories. Lesquereux's actual investigations, however, covered materials from New England to California and from Alabama north, and his paleobotanic studies embraced the whole of North America, parts of Europe, and even Australia and Asia. In 1864 he became an elected member of the National Academy of Sciences, and before his death he was a member or correspondent of more than twenty scientific societies of Europe and America. Charles Darwin and Asa Gray on different occasions honored Lesquereux, finding in his work important evidence bearing on theories of geographic plant distribution and evolution. Lesquereux's collections today are mainly at Harvard University and the National Museum. He was a jeweler and watchmaker by trade, and like Sullivant he regarded botany as his avocation. But, as Professor George Sarton of Harvard reiterated only a few years ago, Lesquereux "was perhaps the equal" as a scientist of his close friend Agassiz and "became eventually the leading palaeobotanist of the New World."

Andrew D. Rodgers, III

LEVERING, JOSEPH MORTIMER (Feb. 20, 1849–April 4, 1908), Moravian bishop, was pastor of a Moravian congregation at Uhrichsville, 1875–76. Author of many articles relative to the history of his church, he also published *A History of Bethlehem, Pennsylvania* . . . , Bethlehem, 1903.

LEVERING, ROBERT WOODROW (Oct. 3, 1914–), lawyer and congressman, was born in Fredericktown, Knox County. He graduated from Denison University in 1936 and George Washington University Law School in 1946. He practiced law in Mount Vernon and in 1958 was elected a member of the 86th Congress. He served in the army during World War II and has written an eyewitness account of the Philippine campaign: *Horror Trek; A True Story of Bataan* . . . , Dayton, 1948.

LEVI, HARRY (Aug. 7, 1875–June 13, 1944), rabbi, was born in Cincinnati, Hamilton County. He graduated from the University of Cincinnati in 1897 and Hebrew Union College in the same year. He served as a rabbi in Wheeling, W. Va., and Boston, Mass. He retired in 1939. Besides the title below, he published two collections of sermons and a number of articles in periodicals and books.

Jewish Characters in Fiction, Philadelphia, 1899.

LEVIN, DAN (March 7, 1914–), born in Simferopol, Russia, lived in Cleveland from 1921 to 1941. He attended Western Reserve University, worked as a reporter and social case worker in Cleveland, and was one of the founders of *Crossroad* and edited several issues. He served with the Marine Corps in World War II and afterward was with the press section of the United Nations. He has published a novel about a young Cleveland boy serving with the Marines: *Mask of Glory,* New York, 1949.

LEVINGER, ELMA EHRLICH (Oct. 6, 1887–), wife of Rabbi Lee J. Levinger (q.v.), was born in Chicago and moved to Columbus in 1925, where her husband was on the Ohio State University faculty, 1925–42. She published a number of stories for children, religious textbooks, and novels, e.g., *Grapes of Canaan,* Boston, [1931]. WW 30

LEVINGER, LEE JOSEPH (March 4, 1890–), rabbi, born in Burke, Idaho, lived in Columbus, 1925-42. He was director of B'nai B'rith, Hillel Foundation, Ohio State University, 1925-35, and director of the research bureau at Hillel Foundation, 1935–42. He now lives in Los Altos, Calif. His writings include *A Jewish Chaplain in France,* New York, 1921. WW 26

LEWIS, ALFRED HENRY (c.1858–Dec. 23, 1914), was born in Cleveland, Cuyahoga County, the son of a carpenter. He was admitted to the Ohio bar and practiced two or three years in Cleveland courts. For a few years in the early 1880s he was a wandering cowboy. Around 1885 he settled in Kansas City, Mo., where his parents were living, married Alice Ewing of Richland, Ohio, and began again to practice law. In 1890 an imaginary interview with an old cattleman was the turning point in his fortunes. The interview was published in the Kansas City *Times,* where his brother was city editor, and was copied in papers all over the country. After three years as head of the Washington bureau of the Chicago *Times,* he joined the Hearst organization and wrote for the *Cosmopolitan* and other Hearst magazines. He was a very prolific writer, and during his last years, which he spent in New York City, he turned out a great many books on politics, crime, and history. In his periodical writing he sometimes used the pen name Dan Quin. Of all his work, however, only the six Wolfville books seem memorable or even readable.

Wolfville, New York, [1897].
Sandburrs, New York, [1900].
Richard Croker, New York, 1901.
Wolfville Days, New York, [1902].
Wolfville Nights, New York, [1902].
The Black Lion Inn, New York, 1903.
The Boss, and How He Came to Rule New York, New York, 1903.
Peggy O'Neal, Philadelphia, [1903].
The President; A Novel, New York, 1904.
The Sunset Trail, New York, 1905.
Confessions of a Detective, New York, 1906.
The Story of Paul Jones, an Historical Romance, New York, [1906].
The Throwback; A Romance of the Southwest, New York, [1906].
When Men Grew Tall; Or, the Story of Andrew Jackson, New York, 1907.
An American Patrician; Or, the Story of Aaron Burr, New York, 1908.
Wolfville Folks, New York, 1908.
The Apaches of New York, New York, [1912].
Faro Nell and Her Friends . . . , New York, [1913].
Nation-Famous New York Murders . . . , New York, [1914].

LEWIS, BETTILU PORTERFIELD (Aug. 15, 1919–), born in Dallas, Texas, was brought to Ohio when a baby. After graduating from Duke University in 1941, she was in radio and advertising work in New Orleans, 1943–44, and has since lived in Canton and Cincinnati. Her short stories have appeared in national magazines, and she has published a volume of poems under her maiden name: *The Pleasure Is Mine,* Durham, N. C., 1940.

LEWIS, CHARLES BERTRAND (Feb. 15, 1842–Aug. 21, 1924), was born in Liverpool, Medina County, but spent most of his life in Michigan. As a boy he learned the printing trade in Pontiac and Lansing, Mich. A steamboat accident led to his writing "How It Feels to Be Blown Up," his first humorous writing and the beginning of his career as a humorist. In 1869 he joined the staff of the Detroit *Free Press,* and in 1891 he went to New York, where he conducted a daily column in the New York *World.* He published many ephemeral dime novels and plays. His books were published under the pen name M. Quad.

Goaks and Tears . . . , Boston, 1875.
"Quad's Odds" . . . , Detroit, 1875.
Brother Gardner's Lime-Kiln Club . . . , Chicago, 1882.
Sawed-off Sketches . . . , New York, 1884.
Field, Fort and Fleet . . . , Detroit, 1885.
Under Five Lakes . . . , New York, 1886.
Mr. and Mrs. Bowser and Their Varied Experiences, New York, [1899].
The Life and Troubles of Mr. Bowser . . . , Chicago, 1902.
The Humorous Mr. Bowser, New York, 1911.

LEWIS, ERVIN EUGENE (July 20, 1882–), educator, born in Orwell, N. Y., was on the Ohio State University education faculty, 1926–52. He is now living in Mount Dora, Fla. He has published a number of professional articles, textbooks, and *A Primer of the New Deal . . . ,* Columbus, 1933. WW 27

LEWIS, FRANKLIN ALLAN (Jan. 18, 1904–March 12, 1958), journalist, born in Lafayette, Ind., was a sports writer for the Cleveland *Press* from 1931 until his death at Lincoln, Ariz. He published *The Cleveland Indians,* New York, [1949]. WW 30

LEWIS, GEORGE W. (April, 1837–June 27, 1900), was born in Batavia, N. Y. He served in the 124th O.V.I., Aug., 1862–July, 1865. He died in Medina.

The Campaigns of the 124th Regiment . . . , Akron, 1874.

LEWIS, HIRAM WHEELER (March 11, 1843–Feb. 4, 1912), was born near Warren, Trumbull County. After attending Hiram College and Williston Seminary, Mass., he served with the 124th O.V.I., 1863–65. In 1869 he moved to Mississippi to operate a plantation owned by his father; he edited a newspaper there and served in the state legislature. In 1876 he moved to Wichita, Kan., where he operated a bank and other businesses and was active in the prohibition movement. He died in Chicago. His son, Frederick W. Lewis, edited his autobiography: *Hiram Wheeler Lewis, a Partial Autobiography . . . ,* Albion, N. Y., [1941].

LEWIS, ROBERT ELLSWORTH (Sept. 29, 1869–), born in Berkshire, Vt., was general secretary of the Y.M.C.A. in Ohio, 1909–29, during which period he lived in Cleveland. A former Y.M.C.A. worker in China, he wrote numerous articles on the Orient and several books, including *The Educational Conquest of the Far East,* New York, [1903]. WW 30

LEWIS, TRACY HAMMOND (Nov. 30, 1890–Nov. 7, 1951), was born in Richfield, Summit County. After graduating from Yale University in 1912, he worked on the New York *Times* and the *Morning Telegraph.* He served in the army on the Mexican border, and after World War I he joined an advertising firm. He wrote *Along the Rio Grande,* New York, 1916. WW 15

LEWISOHN, LUDWIG (May 30, 1882–Dec. 31, 1955), born in Berlin, Germany, but reared in Charleston, S. C., from the age of seven, taught German language and literature at Ohio State University, 1911–19. Considerable controversy arose because of his opposition to World War I, and he resigned to become dramatic critic of the *Nation.* From 1948 until his death in Miami, Fla., he was on the faculty of Brandeis University. Perhaps his most significant work was a life of Goethe, published in 1949; but he also published considerable provocative criticism, e.g., *Expression in America,* New York, 1932, and several novels, e.g., *The Island Within,* New York, 1928. WWW 3

LHAMON, WILLIAM JEFFERSON (Sept. 16, 1855–Oct. 21, 1955), clergyman and educator, was born in Gambier, Knox County. He attended Kenyon College for a time and graduated from Butler University in 1879. Ordained to the ministry of the Disciples of Christ Church, he served a church in Lima and also held pastorates in other states. He was on the faculty of Drury College, Springfield, Mo., and was head of Missouri Bible College, Columbia, Mo. He died in Columbia at the age of 100. Besides the titles below, he wrote leaflets on religious topics.

Studies in Acts . . . , St. Louis, 1897.

Missionary Fields and Forces of the Disciples of Christ, Cleveland, [1898].

Heroes of Modern Missions, Chicago, [1899].

The Character Christ, Fact or Fiction, New York, [1914].

LICHLITER, McILYAR HAMILTON (Aug. 23, 1877–), clergyman, was born in Butler, Pa. After graduating from Ohio Wesleyan University in 1900, he became a Methodist clergyman and served Methodist churches until 1919, when he became a Congregationalist. After five years at Central Church, Newton, Mass., he served the First Congregational Church, Columbus, 1924–42. He now lives in Akron. He has published sermons and a volume of lectures: *The Healing of Souls,* New York, [1931]. WW 26

LIEBHARDT, LOUISE (d. Nov., 1958), was born in Portsmouth, Scioto County, but spent much of her life in California. She attended the University of California and later edited a poetry column in the San Marino *Tribune.* She published a book of verse: *Love's a Thistle,* New York, 1941.

LIEBMAN, JOSHUA LOTH (April 7, 1907–June 9, 1948), rabbi, was born in Hamilton, Butler County. He attended public schools in Hamilton and Cincinnati, graduated from the University of Cincinnati in 1926 and Hebrew Union College in 1930, and served as rabbi of congregations in Lafayette, Ind., and Chicago. In 1939 he became rabbi of Temple Israel, Boston, Mass., and also preached on a national radio network. He achieved the best-seller list with a book uniting psychology and religion: *Peace of Mind,* New York, [1946]. CB 48

LIGHTNER, ADNA H. (July 14, 1849–June 21, 1939), was born in Athens, Athens County, the daughter of Frank and Amelia Cornell. After attending the local academy she was married, at the age of sixteen, to Dr. Samuel B. Lightner, who during the

Civil War had been commissioned surgeon major of the 8th Pennsylvania Cavalry. When mustered out, the doctor had settled briefly at Guysville, Athens County, to practice medicine; after several years spent in New Vienna, Clinton County, and Cincinnati, he brought his wife to Sabina, Clinton County, where the couple established a permanent home. When Mrs. Lightner died in 1939, she had been a resident of Sabina for 67 years. She was a Quaker and a charter member of Sabina Friends Church, established in 1877, when a persuasive revival meeting was held by Esther and Nathan Frame (q.v.). It was Quaker reticence, perhaps, which deterred her from speaking of herself as a writer. Certainly in the early days, the acquaintances who knew her as a busy mother occupied with home, church, and clubs were seldom aware of the novels and stories she had published. Yet, after discovering her ability to write, she made a typical contribution to a popular literary movement of the last century, when a remarkable number of women added the cultivation of home-grown fiction to their customary household duties. As a group, they had found a garden of domestic sentiment, where their readers were legion and their critics were in accord with Nathaniel Hawthorne, who called them a "d---d mob of scribbling women." Mrs. Lightner's first full-length novel, *Shadow and Sunshine,* was published at Cincinnati in 1884. It was later taken over by George P. Munro, rival of Beadle & Adams in the dime novel market, who reprinted it in his "Library of American Authors." Under the characteristic double title *Shadow and Sunshine; Or, Goldie Ransom's Triumph,* it had a large and steady sale, but only such a wordsmith as Harlan P. Halsey, who turned out two "Old Sleuth" paperbacks a month, could get much financial encouragement from Mr. Munro. Mrs. Lightner's second novel, *A Wayside Violet,* appeared in 1885. Both of these novels, together with the earlier two-part story *Fletcher Haven's Housekeeper,* were first printed in the pages of the *Masonic Review.* Her third novel, which she considered her best, was published only as a magazine serial. Entitled "Creta," it was a Civil War story with its setting in Georgia. The great bulk of Mrs. Lightner's writing was in the form of the short story. Her debut was made April, 1876, when "Who Was to Blame?" appeared in *Godey's Lady's Book.* It was followed by other stories for that magazine, together with frequent contributions to the *Ohio Farmer,* the Cincinnati *Post,* the *Masonic Review,* and almost all of the Sunday school papers of her time: *Penn Weekly, Classmate, Sunday School Advocate, Front Rank, Young Folks, Junior Christian Endeavor World,* and many others. Her stories for adults mingled sentiment and piety with a romantic determination to find rich, young husbands for her troubled heroines. The children's stories, to be found in the Sunday school papers, were an irresistible temptation to furtive reading during the progress of the Sunday morning sermon. Charming anecdotes and adventures, they often involved horses and dogs because Mrs. Lightner liked best to write about them. Although she recorded something of the manners and customs of village life in the late nineteenth century, her plots and characters were almost entirely imaginary. Only the Civil War incidents in "Creta" and a short story about her husband and his dog, "The Doctor's Assistant," were based upon fact. The plots, she said, "just came"; an idea would possess her, sometimes in the middle of the night, and the story would seem to write itself. She complained to her two children that her characters did not do at all what she had intended: they seemed to have a life of their own. She had something to say about this in a paper called "Inspirational Writing," read in 1891 before the Woman's Press Club of Cincinnati, an organization she helped establish. Her name passed through several mutations. In the Cornell family Bible, it was recorded Harriett Adine, but she called herself Ada, and her friends called her Addie. In her old age—still writing an occasional story, keenly interested in politics, and firmly established as the local authority on major league baseball—she was known to her fellow townsmen as Auntie Lightner. She signed her earliest children's stories Aunt Addie, but in all of her other writings she used the name with which she won her modest fame, Adna H. Lightner.

Gerald D. McDonald

Fletcher Haven's Housekeeper, [Cincinnati], 1883.

Shadow and Sunshine . . . , Cincinnati, 1884.

A Wayside Violet, Cincinnati, 1885.

LIGHTNER, HARRIETT ADINE CORNELL. See Adna H. Lightner.

LILIENTHAL, MAX (Oct. 16, 1815–April 5, 1882), rabbi, was born in Munich, Germany. After studying at the University of Munich, he spent five years in Russia investigating the education of Jewish children there. He came to New York City in 1845 and to Cincinnati in 1855. He was rabbi of Bene Israel congregation in Cincinnati and was a founder of Hebrew Union College. About two-thirds of the last volume below consists of his letters and essays.

Freiheit, Frühling und Liebe, Cincinnati, 1857.

Synopsis of the History of the Israelites . . . , Cincinnati, 1857.

Max Lilienthal; American Rabbi: Life and Writings, (David Philipson, ed.), New York, 1915.

LINCOLN, JAMES FINNEY (May 14, 1883–), industrialist, was born in Painesville, Lake County. He studied at Ohio State University, 1902–07. In 1907 he joined the Lincoln Electric Company in Cleveland and served as its president, 1928–54. He has published a number of pamphlets on politics, society, and the incentive plan in his company, e.g., *Intelligent Selfishness and Manufacturing,* Cleveland, [1942]. WW 30

LINCOLN, VICTORIA (Oct. 23, 1904–), born in Fall River, Mass., lived in Ohio, 1942–47, while her husband, Victor Lowe, whom she had married in 1934, served on the Ohio State University philosophy faculty. While an Ohio resident, she published a book containing three short novels: *The Wind at My Back,* New York, [1946]. WW 30

LINDEN, CHARLOTTE E. (Sept. 22, 1859–April 13, 1919), was born in London, Ontario, Canada, but lived in Clark County from 1868 until her death. She was grand lecturer of the Grand United Order of Odd Fellows of Ohio and was president of the Phyllis Wheatley Cultural Club in Springfield. She published *Autobiography and Poems,* Springfield, [1907].

LINDERMAN, FRANK BIRD (Sept. 25, 1869–May 12, 1938), was born in Cleveland, Cuyahoga County, and attended public schools in Lorain and Elyria. His mature life was spent in Montana, where he was a journalist and an insurance executive. He wrote stories of Western life, e.g., *Lige Mounts: Free Trapper,* New York, 1922. WWW 1

LINDLEY, HARLOW (May 31, 1875–Aug. 20, 1959), historian, born in Sylvania, Ind., became librarian of the Hayes Memorial Library and Museum in 1928. He was curator of history, Ohio Historical Society, 1929–34, and secretary, editor, and librarian of the Society, 1934–46. Most of his major works deal with Indiana history, but he planned and compiled the last volume of Wittke's *History of Ohio: Ohio in the Twentieth Century,* Columbus, 1942. He also wrote numerous articles and pamphlets on Ohio, e.g., *The Story of Ohio as Told by a Museum Exhibit,* [Columbus, 1932]. WW 27

LINDLEY, JACOB (June 13, 1774–Jan. 29, 1857), clergyman and educator, was born in Washington County, Pa. In 1800 he graduated from the College of New Jersey (Princeton) and was licensed to preach by his home presbytery. In 1803 he was pastor of the Presbyterian Church at Waterford. In 1805 he was appointed a trustee of the still-unfounded Ohio University, which was to be supported by a grant of two townships in Athens County. In 1808 he was named preceptor of the institution, and it opened its doors to three students; for four years he was the entire faculty. He taught at Ohio University and preached at the local Presbyterian church until 1826. After a brief pastorate at Walnut Hills, near Cincinnati, he left Ohio and spent the remainder of his life in the South and in Pennsylvania. In his old age, at the urging of his daughters, he published a book notable for the importance it attaches to the education of children below the age of three. He died in Connellsville, Pa.

Infant Philosophy, Containing an Analysis of the Faculties of the Mind, as Discovered in Their Development, with Directions for the Management and Training of Each in Its Earliest Stages, Uniontown, Pa., 1846.

LINDSTROM, ECHEL GEORGE (Feb. 24, 1879–), born in Sweden, was reared in Oil City, Pa., where he learned the printing trade. He first came to Cleveland in 1904 to work for the *Plain Dealer.* He lived in Jamestown, N. Y., 1906–16, and then returned to Cleveland, where he founded a printing house. He has been active in Masonic activities and has edited various fraternal publications. He has also written a history of Lakewood, stories about the Pennsylvania oil country, and a historical novel about the discovery of oil at Titusville: *Out of the Sand,* Cleveland, [1943].

LINHAM, HELEN LOOMIS (Sept. 21, 1887–), was born in Mansfield, Richland County, and still lives in that community. She is now married to Harry Roepke of Mansfield. She has written more than 3,000 poems, which have appeared in various periodicals and anthologies. She has also published three collections of poetry, e.g., *I Hear Earth Sing,* Dallas, Texas, [1936]. BDCP

LIPPARD, GEORGE (April 10, 1822–Feb. 9, 1854), novelist and biographer, lived in Cleveland, 1851–53, while serving as editor of a temperance paper. His books combine the sensational and the moralistic, e.g., *The Midnight Queen . . . ,* New York, [1853].

LISLE, WILLIAM McINTIRE (1842–Oct. 25, 1910), clergyman, was born in New Haven, Huron County. After graduating from Denison University in 1864 and Rochester Theological Seminary in 1867, he was ordained as a Baptist minister. In 1868 he arrived in Siam as a missionary, but ill health forced him to return to America after two years. He served churches in New England from 1870 to 1890, traveled as an evangelist, and spent his last years in West Newton, Mass. Besides the book listed below, he wrote a number of articles on religious subjects.

The Evolution of Spiritual Man, Boston, 1894.

LITCHFIELD, PAUL WEEKS (July 26, 1875–March 19, 1959), born in Boston, Mass., came to Akron in 1900. He was president of Goodyear Tire and Rubber Co., 1926–40, and chairman of the board, 1940–58. He published *The Industrial Republic . . . ,* Akron, 1919. OBB

LITTELL, SQUIER (Dec. 9, 1803–July 4, 1886), ophthalmologist, born in Burlington, N. J., and a resident of Philadelphia during most of his adult life, spent his boyhood in Ohio. After the death of his parents, he was adopted by his uncle, Squier Littell, of Butler County, and attended school near Lebanon. Author of many medical articles, he also published a pioneering book on eye-diseases: *A Manual of the Diseases of the Eye,* Philadelphia, 1837.

LIVELY, JAMES MADISON (Oct. 29, 1852– ?), was born in Jackson County. He attended public schools until he was seventeen, when he began teaching. After teaching school for ten years, he became a journalist and afterward worked as manager of steel-wire mills and coke ovens in various Midwestern states. He published *Science of Mind; Or, Individual and Communal Knowledge,* [Portland, Oreg.], 1933.

LIVERMORE, ABIEL ABBOT (Oct. 30, 1811–Oct. 30, 1892), clergyman, was born in Wilton, N. H. After graduating from Harvard and Cambridge Divinity School, he was ordained a Congregational pastor in 1836. He had published some sermons and lectures and a prize-winning essay entitled "The War with Mexico Reviewed" before coming to Cincinnati, May 26, 1850, to become a Unitarian pastor there. While he was in Cincinnati, he became widely known through the publication of his *Discourses,* Boston, 1854. He left Cincinnati in July, 1856, to become editor of the New York *Christian Inquirer.* Though his stay in Ohio was brief, he was one of a number of literary figures who presided over the troubled affairs of the Unitarian Church of Cincinnati and helped make the literary history of Ohio.

LIVERMORE, ELIZABETH DORCAS ABBOT (d. Sept. 13, 1879), was born in Windham, N. H. In 1838 she married her cousin, Abiel Abbot Livermore (q.v.). They lived in Cincinnati while he occupied a Unitarian pulpit, 1850–56. In Cincinnati, Mrs. Livermore found herself in a congenial circle of literary-minded friends and began at once to contribute poetry to Midwestern periodicals. She also published a book, *Zoë; Or, the Quadroon's Triumph,* 2 vols., Cincinnati, 1855. She enjoyed considerable popularity, but today is forgotten by all except the literary historians. In February, 1856, she started a weekly, the *Independent Highway,* which was discontinued the following September when her husband became editor of the *Christian Inquirer* and they moved to New York City.

LIVINGSTON, MIRIAM DRAKE (May 4, 1863– ?) was born in Delaware, Delaware County. She worked for a number of years as a teacher and as a parole officer at the Girls' Industrial School in Delaware. After her retirement in 1937, she lived in Cincinnati. She published a book of verse: *Beacon Lights,* New York, [1938].

LLOYD, CURTIS GATES (July 17, 1859–Nov. 11, 1926), botanist, was born in Florence, Ky., but spent his mature life in Cincinnati as a manufacturing pharmacist. With his brother, John Uri Lloyd (q.v.), he founded the Lloyd Library, containing volumes on pharmacy and botany, and the Lloyd Museum, a collection of dried fungi. He traveled throughout the world collecting and studying specimens of fungi. His opposition to botanists' practice of naming new species for themselves made him some enemies in the scientific world, but when he died in Cincinnati his reputation as a mycologist was world-wide. Besides technical articles, he published *Mycological Writings,* 7 vols., Cincinnati, [1898–1929]. WWW 1

LLOYD, JOHN URI (April 19, 1849–April 9, 1936), born in North Bloomfield, N. Y., grew up in Florence, Ky., a village a few miles south of Cincinnati. In 1863 he came to Cincinnati as an apprentice to a drug firm. At the age of 22, he became laboratory manager for a manufacturing drug concern. Later he became a partner and, with his brothers, took over the firm in 1885 and operated it successfully until his death. A man of great industry and ability, his work and interest extended to many fields. He was a skilled research worker in the chemical field, a botanist, and a prodigious writer. He served as professor of chemistry at the Cincinnati College of Pharmacy and later was president of the Eclectic Medical Institute. The Lloyd Library in Cincinnati, considered to be the outstanding collection in the field of plant chemistry, was established and endowed by Mr. Lloyd. His principal interest was pharmacy and drugs, and his scientific writings are largely in that field. His first work, *The Chemistry of Medicine,* was published by the author in 1881. His contributions to various journals from that time must, a biographer says, reach 5,000. Many of his contributions were read at the Literary Club of Cincinnati, of which he was a faithful member. Mr. Lloyd's first attempt at imaginative literature was a strange book that would probably be classed today as science fiction. The book, *Etidorhpa* (Aphrodite, spelled backward), was first published privately in 1895. Later editions (there were eighteen or more) were published commercially. Most of Lloyd's literary contributions were dialect tales of the Kentucky hills. One of these, *Stringtown on the Pike,* reached best-seller proportions. In order that his hill dialect might be correct, Lloyd prepared an extensive glossary which was checked by a friend who lived in the area. Other Kentucky tales were *The Red Head, Warwick of the Knobs,* and *Scroggins.* During his 71 years' residence in Cincinnati, John Uri Lloyd made many friends. His gentleness, his generosity, and the many-sidedness of his career were the subject of editorials in the Cincinnati newspapers when he died in Van Nuys, Calif., where he was visiting his daughter. "He was," said the *Times-Star,* "a kind of landmark in Cincinnati culture."

Ernest I. Miller

Etidorhpa; Or, the End of the Earth . . . , Cincinnati, 1895.

The Right Side of the Car, Boston, 1897.

Stringtown on the Pike . . . , New York, 1900.

Warwick of the Knobs . . . , New York, 1901.

Red Head, New York, 1903.

Scroggins, New York, 1904.

Life and Medical Discoveries of Samuel Thomson . . . , Cincinnati, [1909].

Felix Moses, the Beloved Jew of Stringtown on the Pike . . . , Cincinnati [1930].

Our Willie: A Folklore Story of the Gunpowder Creek and Hills, Boone County, Kentucky, Cincinnati, [1934].

LLOYD, SOPHIA WEBSTER (May 24, 1820–Aug. 17, 1903), mother of John Uri and Curtis G. Lloyd (qq.v.), was born in New Rochelle, N. Y. On Sept. 6, 1847, she married Nelson Marvin Lloyd, a schoolteacher and surveyor. They came west in 1853, when her husband was employed to survey a railroad in northern Kentucky. When the railway company went bankrupt, the Lloyds remained in Kentucky and established a school. In the last twenty years of her life, she lived in Norwood with her son John. She published poetry and stories in various periodicals, most of them religious papers. John Uri Lloyd published the volume of poems listed below.

Poems of Mrs. Sophia Webster Lloyd, Cincinnati, 1887.

LOBAN, ETHEL HARRIS (Oct. 27, 1892–), was born in Toledo, Lucas County, where she lived until she was twenty except for two years in Van Wert. In 1909 she married Dr. Joy Maxwell Loban. She now lives in California. She has published fiction in magazines and has written several mystery novels, e.g., *Signed in Yellow,* New York, 1930.

LOCKE, DAVID ROSS (Sept. 20, 1833–Feb. 15, 1888), journalist, political satirist, and originator of the "Rev. Petroleum V. Nasby" of Civil War fame, was born in Vestal, Broome County, N. Y., the sixth child and youngest son of Nathaniel Reed and Hester (Ross) Locke. His grandfather, John Locke, was a member of the Boston Tea Party and served as a minuteman in the Revolutionary War, and his father was a soldier in the War of 1812. David's formal education ended when he was ten, and he then began newspaper work as an apprentice to the publisher of the Cortland, N. Y., *Democrat* for a period of seven years. Thereafter he was always associated in some way with newspaper work. About 1850, at the age of seventeen, he began a two-year period of wandering about the country, North and South, as a journeyman printer. His travels in the South confirmed the strong antislavery sentiments he had received from his father. Very little is now known of the newspapers on which he worked during his period of wandering. He never talked much about where he had been during his travels. For a time he was at Pittsburgh and became a reporter and later assistant editor of the Pittsburgh *Chronicle*. There, he made the acquaintance of young James G. Robinson, and in 1852 they formed a partnership. During a strike among printers on the Pittsburgh daily papers, Robinson and Locke started on a western trip. They reached Plymouth, Richland County, and were induced by the citizens there to revive the *Advertiser,* which they did, with practically no funds whatever, in 1853. About two years later, the partners sold the Plymouth *Advertiser,* and, with Roeliff Brinkerhoff, they purchased the Mansfield *Herald,* which the three operated for a time. Early in 1856, Locke left the *Herald* and on March 20, 1856, purchased controlling interest in the Bucyrus *Journal.* Daniel Wheeler Locke, David's brother, joined him in Bucyrus as a partner for a few months, and then on April 21, 1857, his former partner, James G. Robinson, again became his associate. They brought the first cylinder press to Bucyrus, and each week Locke published a series of stories about Bucyrus and vicinity that had a wide appeal. While still at Plymouth, David Ross Locke had been married to Martha H. Bodine in March, 1855; they had three sons: Robinson, who was to follow his father as a journalist, Edmund, and Charles. About Nov. 13, 1861, Locke left the Bucyrus *Journal* with the intention of raising a company of volunteers for the war, but was persuaded by Governor William Dennison to continue with his newspaper work. A month later he acquired the *Hancock Jeffersonian* in Findlay, which he edited until Feb. 10, 1865. It was in the columns of the *Jeffersonian* that the famous "Nasby Letters" gained national popularity and attracted the attention of President Abraham Lincoln, who became one of Locke's most unreserved admirers. Lincoln invited Locke to Washington and offered him a place in the government, but Locke turned it down. He was later to refuse President Grant's offer of a foreign mission. Locke's influence upon the Civil War was characterized by George S. Boutwell, Secretary of the Treasury under President Grant, who, after the war was over, was credited with saying that "the North had won the war by three forces, 'The Army, the Navy, and the Nasby Papers.' " Chief Justice Salmon P. Chase was also credited with saying substantially the same thing—that the Nasby letters were "the fourth force in the reduction of the rebellion." Undoubtedly, the letters of Petroleum V. Nasby had a profound effect in solidifying Northern opinion against the South. The quaintly humorous yet bitingly satirical writings of the "Rev. Petroleum Vesuvius Nasby" were read by everyone and were a favorite with President Lincoln. Nasby was supposed to be a backwoods preacher, a Democrat who wanted to be a postmaster, a Copperhead, and was portrayed as a corrupt, cowardly man, a drunkard, and a liar, barely literate. In October, 1865, Locke took editorial charge of the Toledo *Blade,* and it was during his management of this newspaper that he reached the high point of his career. Within a few years he owned a controlling interest in the *Blade.* In addition to the daily, he began a weekly family edition, subtitled "Nasby's Paper," and boosted it to a national reputation with a circulation of 200,000. In 1871, while still maintaining his connection with the *Blade,* Locke moved to New York City to become managing editor of the New York *Evening Mail* and a member of the advertising agency of Bates & Locke. Later, he returned to Toledo and continued his Nasby letters until a few months before his death. The last Nasby letter from his pen was dated. Dec. 26, 1887. David Ross Locke had versatile talents and was a man of unusual achievements. For several seasons he shared the popularity of Mark Twain and Josh Billings (Henry W. Shaw, q.v.) on the lecture circuits. He was author and producer of at least one successful play in New York, *The Widow Bedott* (1879), and he was the author of verse, hymns, pamphlets, and books, including novels. Several of the books below were republished under variant titles. He and the noted cartoonist Thomas Nast, who illustrated several of his books and who created the visual image of Petroleum V. Nasby, became close friends and found they held similar views on the current political scene. Locke liked to sing, was a leader in his church choir, and frequently was heard singing old-fashioned hymns while at work in his office. When Locke returned to Toledo from New York, he took an energetic part in the social and economic life of the community, serving as alderman from the third district, 1886–1887, as a director of the Northern National Bank of Toledo, and as president of the Toledo Art Association. When he died, he left, it was said, an estate valued at nearly a million dollars.

Watt P. Marchman

The Nasby Papers . . . , Indianapolis, 1864.
Divers Views, Opinions, and Prophecies of Yoors Trooly Petroleum V. Nasby . . . , Cincinnati, 1866.
Nasby's Life of Andy Jonsun, New York, 1866.
Ekkoes from Kentucky . . . , Boston, 1868.
The Impendin Crisis uv the Dimocracy, Toledo, 1868.
The Struggles (Social, Financial and Political) of Petroleum V. Nasby . . . , Boston, 1872.
The Moral History of America's Life-Struggle, Boston, [1874].
Inflation at the Cross Roads . . . , New York, 1875.
The Morals of Abou Ben Adhem; Or, Eastern Fruit on Western Dishes . . . , Boston, 1875.
Nasby on Inflation, Philadelphia, [1876].
A Paper City, Boston, 1879.
The Democratic John Bunyan, Being Eleven Dreams by Rev. Petroleum V. Nasby, Toledo, 1880.
The Diary of an Office-Seeker . . . , Toledo, 1881.
Hannah Jane, Boston, 1882.
Nasby in Exile . . . , Toledo, 1882.
The Demagogue, a Political Novel, Boston, 1891.
The Nasby Letters, Toledo, 1893.

LOCKE, JOHN (Feb. 19, 1792–July 10, 1856), educator, was born in Lempster, N. H. In his infancy his family moved to Oxford County, Maine, where his father established the town of Locke Mills. He attended Silliman's lectures at Yale in 1815, and studied medicine and botany in New England. He engraved the 200 or more illustrations which appear in his *Outlines of Botany,* published in 1819. He experienced difficulties with his family over religious matters and, feeling that New England was dominated by religious intolerance, he went to Lexington, Ky., in 1821. The following year, he established the Cincinnati Female Academy, which he conducted until 1835. He then became professor of chemistry and pharmacy at the Medical College of Ohio, a chair which he held until that institution became a political pawn in 1850, when he was removed. After an unsuccessful attempt to establish a seminary for young ladies at Lebanon, he returned to Cincinnati in 1855. His scientific activities were many and varied. His contributions to the first geological survey of Ohio were outstanding. In conjunction with David D. Owen he surveyed the mineral lands of the northwest. At the request of the United States Coast Survey he devised his so-called electromagnetic chronograph, for which he received an award of $10,000 from the government. This was but one of his many important inventions in scientific apparatus. Besides his botany textbook, he published a grammar in 1827 and a geography text in 1828; he also published scientific articles and lectures.

LOCKE, WALTER (March 16, 1875–Oct. 23, 1957), journalist, was born in St. Marys, W. Va., but grew up in Nebraska, where his family moved in 1884. After working on the *Nebraska State Journal,* he joined the staff of the Dayton *Daily News* in 1927. He conducted a regular column in that newspaper and also published several books, e.g., *Whistling Post,* [Yellow Springs, 1934]. WWW 3

LOCKWOOD, LAUFA M. (March 9, 1896–), was born in Francisco, Ind., where she now resides. Her first husband, Frank Helsey, was killed in a mine explosion in 1926. In 1932 she married Will Lockwood of Ohio, and for thirteen years they lived in Chillicothe, where she worked in the county recorder's office. She has written numerous poems and articles and has published two collections of poetry, e.g., *The Way the Winter Came,* Columbus, [1949].

LOEB, CHARLES HAROLD (April 2, 1905–), born in Baton Rouge, La., was educated in the public schools of New Orleans and at Howard University. In 1926 he became a newspaperman, and since 1933 he has been on the staff of the Cleveland *Call and Post,* of which he is now managing editor. During World War II he was a correspondent for the Combined Negro Press. He has published a history of the Future Outlook League, a Cleveland organization dedicated to equal opportunities for Negroes: *The Future Is Yours . . .* , Cleveland, [1947].

LOGAN, BELLE V. (July 23, 1864–May 17, 1957), was born in Mount Pleasant, Iowa, but spent much of her life in Ohio. With her parents she came to Lebanon in 1882, where she married William Logan, Jr. After 1891 her husband edited the *Horse Review* in Chicago and New York City. Mrs. Logan lived in Ohio again from 1906 until her death and at various times taught music in Cincinnati, Dayton, and Lebanon. Besides the novel below, she wrote two piano textbooks.

Her Shattered Idol, Chicago, 1895.

LOGAN, CORNELIUS AMBROSE (Aug. 24, 1832–Jan. 30, 1899), physician and diplomat, the son of Cornelius Ambrosius Logan (q.v.), was born in Deerfield, Mass. In 1840 the family moved to Cincinnati, where he attended school. He completed his education at Auburn Academy and for a time was superintendent of St. John's Hospital, Cincinnati. In 1857 he went to Kansas. Though his medical career was marked by no outstanding scientific attainments, he did much to stabilize the practice of medicine on the frontier. He was envoy extraordinary and minister plenipotentiary to Chile, 1873–77, and minister resident to the Central American States, 1877–82. As literary executor of his cousin, Gen. John A. Logan, he published the latter's *The Volunteer Soldier in America* in 1887, for which he wrote a biographical memoir. His death occurred in California.

An Essay on the Remote and Proximate Causes of Miasmatic Fever, Leavenworth, [Kan.], 1861.

Report on the Sanitary Relations of the State of Kansas, Lawrence, [Kan.], 1866.

Physics of the Infectious Diseases . . . , Chicago, 1878.

LOGAN, CORNELIUS AMBROSIUS (May 4, 1806–Feb. 22, 1853), actor and producer, was born in Baltimore, Md. Little is really known about his youth, but according to standard biographical compilations he was a very busy boy. It is recorded that he began to study for the priesthood at St. Mary's College; made several trips to sea as a sailor and supercargo; spent three years with Paul Allen on the Baltimore *Morning Chronicle;* unsuccessfully attempted to start a newspaper in New York with William Leggett; and began his stage career in Philadelphia at the age of nineteen. It seems likely that he did attend St. Mary's, for William T. Coggeshall (q.v.), who was acquainted with Logan, rated him as a classical scholar of substantial attainments. Perhaps he worked as a boy for Paul Allen, whose connection with the *Morning Chronicle* extended from 1818 to 1824. Any association with William Leggett must have occurred after that gentleman's resignation from the navy in 1826. Logan is known to have appeared on the stage of the Tivoli Garden in Philadelphia in 1825, and the following year he was introduced to New York audiences as "a new actor from Philadelphia." He became very well known as a comedian, though in his later years he frequently appeared in tragic roles. According to Ludlow, "Mr. Logan's histrionic ability, unquestionably, was in the line of comedy. He may have had an innate tragic ability, but his face prevented him from showing it to advantage; it was unchangeably comic." He is said to have contributed many satirical articles to newspapers; and Coggeshall avers that his poem "The Mississippi" was copied by the *Edinburgh Review,* "prefaced by a handsome tribute to the author." He wrote many successful plays, few of which were published. In 1840 he settled down with his brood of gifted children in Cincinnati, where he resided until his death. His three daughters were: Eliza, who—despite physical handicaps—became very popular in the theaters of the Midwest; Olive; and Celia (Mrs. James F. Connelley) (qq.v.). His son, Cornelius Ambrose Logan (q.v.), became well known as a physician and diplomat. Perhaps no man contributed more to the development of the theater in Cincinnati than Logan. He arrived in the city at a time when editors, fearful of incurring the wrath of local ministers who had made the theater their favorite target, dared publish little more than a line or two concerning even the more noteworthy stage productions. The fine new National Theater had become the roost of local hoodlums, and the haunt of a few visitors seeking such titillation as might be afforded by a glimpse of the sins of the Queen City. Logan became manager of the National in 1841, but never gave up acting. During December of that year he appeared in *The School for Scandal, Charles II, Wild Oats,* and *Soldier's Daughter.* His temperate and learned reply to a blast from the pulpit of Lyman Beecher (q.v.) was widely copied, and was an important factor in discouraging further attacks from local pulpits. In 1846 he became half-owner and manager of the Athenaeum in Cincinnati, but later returned to the National. His managerial duties do not appear to have interfered with occasional tours. He frequently appeared in St. Louis, and as far south as New Orleans. His play *Cincinnati in 1949* was first performed at the National Theater on Feb. 17, 1849. Rewritten, it was presented in New York under the title of *Chloroform, or New York a Hundred Years Hence.* He thus found his popularity had not waned during an absence of years, for the play ran for eight successive nights, a remarkable performance for those days. His final appearance was at the National Theater during the holidays of 1852–53. He died of apoplexy on a steamboat near Wheeling, Va.

Ernest J. Wessen

The People's Lawyer, New York, [1855?].
Yankee Land. A Comedy in Two Acts, Boston, [1856?].
The Vermont Wool Dealer, New York, [185- ?].

LOGAN, INDIANA WASHINGTON. See Kelion F. Peddicord.

LOGAN, OLIVE (April 22, 1838–April 27, 1909), actress, was born in Elmira, N. Y. The daughter of Cornelius Ambrosius Logan (q.v.), she came to Cincinnati when the family settled there in 1840. She attended the Wesleyan Female Seminary. As the daughter of the prominent actor, dramatist, and manager—affectionately known in Cincinnati as "Old Logan"—and the sister of the plain and rotund but gifted leading lady Eliza Logan, she became interested in the stage at a very early date. She made her debut in Philadelphia at the Arch Street Theatre, Aug. 19, 1854. In fourteen years, she built a reputation as an actress which has endured to the present. She retired from the stage in 1868 and toured the country lecturing on women's rights, a field in which she appears to have enjoyed considerable success. In 1857 she married Henry A. Debille, from whom she was divorced in 1865. In 1871 she married the writer William Wirt Sikes, who died in 1883. She then married her secretary, James O'Neill, who was twenty years her junior. She dropped out of sight and little was heard of her until Lady Cook (before her marriage, Tennessee Claflin; see Tennessee C. C. Cook) discovered her living in abject poverty. Lady Cook supplied her with funds and provided for her care in London. Olive Logan became demented and, without the knowledge of her benefactress, was committed to the asylum at Banstead, where she died. The first and second titles below were published under the pen name Chroniqueuse.

Chateau Frissac; Or, Home Scenes in France, New York, 1860.
Photographs of Paris Life . . . , London, 1860.
Olive Logan's Christmas Story, Somebody's Stocking . . . , New York, [1867].
Olive Logan's New Christmas Story, John Morris's Money . . . , New York, 1867.
Apropos of Women and Theatres . . . , New York, 1869.
The Good Mr. Bagglethorpe, New York, 1869.
Before the Footlights and behind the Scenes . . . , Philadelphia, 1870.
The Mimic World . . . , Philadelphia, 1871.
Get Thee behind Me Satan! . . . , New York, 1872.
They Met by Chance . . . , New York, [1873].
The American Abroad, [n.p., 1882].

LOMAX, BLISS. Pseud. See Harry S. Drago.

LONG, FANNY F. (Feb. 5, 1859–Nov. 24, 1935), was born in Jackson, Jackson County. In the 1870s she began publishing poems in *Leslie's Sunday Magazine, Arthur's Magazine,* and religious periodicals. She died in Charleston, W. Va.

Ben Abbott, a Temperance Story, Cincinnati, 1896.

LONG, JEAN COMEANS (April 8, 1904–), was born in Osman, Ill., but has lived in Ohio since 1906. She completed nurse's training at Grant's Hospital, Columbus, and was a public health nurse in Middletown, 1925–30. She has lived in Columbus since her marriage to James M. Long in 1936 and has contributed poems and feature articles to the Columbus *Dispatch.* She has also published a collection of poems: *Earth Woman,* Columbus, [1941].

LONG, JULIUS W. (June 19, 1907–July 22, 1955), lawyer, was born in Bellefontaine, Logan County. After graduating from Ohio State University in 1931, he studied law, was admitted to the bar in 1939, and practiced in Bellefontaine. He wrote a number of detective stories, e.g., *Keep the Coffins Coming,* New York, [1941].

LONG, LINDLEY GRANT (July 17, 1868–Dec. 25, 1949), lawyer, was born in Quaker City, Noble County. He attended Ohio Normal University, Ohio Wesleyan University, and the University of Michigan Law School. After being admitted to the bar, he practiced in Dayton and other cities. He died in Lima. He published *Poems,* Dayton, 1911.

LONG, MASON (Sept. 10, 1842–Nov. 5, 1904), was born in Luray, Licking County. Left an orphan at the age of ten, he was reared in Medina County by a German farmer. After serving in the Civil War, he moved to Fort Wayne, Ind., in 1863. For fifteen years he was a drunkard and a professional gambler. After being converted to the Baptist Church, he became a professional reformer and lecturer. He died in Fort Wayne.

The Life of Mason Long, the Converted Gambler . . ., Chicago, 1878.
Fallen Women, Fort Wayne, 1880.
Save the Girls, Fort Wayne, 1883.

LONG, SIMON PETER (Oct. 7, 1860–Jan. 3, 1929), clergyman and educator, was born in Ashland County. After graduating from Capital University in 1883, he studied theology and was ordained to the Lutheran ministry in 1886. He served churches in Loudonville, Massillon, Columbus, and Mansfield, and also was president of Lima College and of Chicago Lutheran Bible School. He published sermons and books on religious topics, e.g., *Prophetic Pearls,* Columbus, 1913. WWW 1

LONGLEY, ALCANDER (1832–April 17, 1918), reformer, was born in Oxford, Butler County. At an early age he adopted Fourier's ideas and became a lifelong communitarian. About 1854 he joined the Cincinnati publishing firm headed by his brother Elias Longley (q.v.), which was engaged in publishing phonetic literature. He published the *Phalansterian Record* at Cincinnati, 1857–59. In 1868 he began the publication of *The Communist* in St. Louis; in 1885 he changed the name to *The Altruist* and continued to publish it until a few months before his death, which occurred in Chicago.

Communism: The Right Way and the Best Way for All to Live, St. Louis, 1880.

LONGLEY, ELIAS (Aug., 1823–1899), publisher, was born in Oxford, Butler County. He was the eldest of the five sons of Abner Longley, a Universalist minister who became an ardent Fourierist. He graduated from Woodward College and, after studying briefly for the ministry, became a newspaper reporter. In 1847 with his brother Cyrenius as junior partner, he established the firm of Longley & Brother in Cincinnati, a publishing house specializing in works designed to promote writing and printing reform. On Jan. 1, 1848, they began publishing the phonetic magazine *Tip of de Timz,* which during the twelve years of its existence was variously known as the *Phonetic Magazine,* the *Fonetic Advocat,* and finally as *Type of the Times.* In November, 1848, he founded and served as the first director of the American Phonetic Society. This organization, dedicated to promoting spelling reform, soon boasted a membership extending from Maine to Louisiana. The demand for its publications grew apace. The other brothers, Servetus, Septimus, and Alcander (q.v.), joined the firm. Phonetic editions of such works as Pope's *Essay on Man,* Gay's *Fables,* Johnson's *Rasselas,* and Goldsmith's *Vicar of Wakefield,* almanacs, a large number of phonetic textbooks, and many religious works poured from their presses and met with large sales all over the country. It began to look as if phonetic spelling were well on the way to national acceptance when the guns at Fort Sumter sounded the doom for this and many similar reforms. The firm was dissolved in 1862, and Elias turned to shorthand reporting—a field in which he achieved a national reputation. He was sent to report the speeches of Beecher and William Lloyd Garrison on the occasion of the rehoisting of the flag at Fort Sumter. He frequently revised and reissued his shorthand (or "phonography") manual, and he also wrote typewriting manuals. He served several years as a court reporter and spent his later life in Pasadena, Calif.

Ernest J. Wessen

Phonetic Spelling Familiarly Explained . . ., Cincinnati, 1849.
Romanic Reading Explained to Phonetic Readers, Cincinnati, 1849.
The Teacher's Guide to Phonetic Reading, Cincinnati, 1849.
Furst Fönetic Redur, Sinsinati, 1850.
American Manual of Phonography, Cincinnati, 1853.
Student's Pocket Medical Lexicon, Philadelphia, 1879.

LONGSWORTH, BASIL NELSON (May 14, 1828–Oct. 8, 1893), was born on a farm in Harrison County. In 1853 he made the overland trip to Oregon, where he appears to have served as an itinerant minister and schoolteacher. He was an observant traveler and kept a well-written, detailed diary of his trip across the plains, which was published by his family in 1927 and is a valuable contribution to the literature of the Overland Trail: *The Diary of Basil Nelson Longsworth . . .*, Denver, Colorado, 1927.

LONGWORTH, NICHOLAS (Jan. 16, 1782–Feb. 10, 1863), capitalist and horticulturist, was born in Newark, N. J. His boyhood was spent in comparative poverty because the property of his father, a Loyalist, was confiscated during the Revolution. He came to Cincinnati in 1803 and read law in the office of Judge Jacob Burnet (q.v.). Since he often accepted land in return for his legal services, the rapid rise of real-estate values in Cincinnati soon made him wealthy. In 1828, after considerable experimentation, he succeeded in producing excellent wine from Catawba and Isabella grapes. His success laid the foundation for the flourishing wine industry of Cincinnati. He also cultivated strawberries and black raspberries. Not an author in the usual sense of the word, he wrote numerous horticultural articles in addition to the title listed below. He also aided artists and writers and was, until his death, a principal figure in the cultural life of his adopted city.

A Letter from N. Longworth to the Members of the Cincinnati Horticultural Society, on the Cultivation of the Grape, and Manufacture of Wine, Also on the Character and Habits of the Strawberry Plant . . . , Cincinnati, 1846.

LONGWORTH, NICHOLAS (June 16, 1844–Jan. 18, 1890), lawyer and judge, was born in Cincinnati, Hamilton County. The grandson of Nicholas Longworth (q.v.), who had founded the family fortune, and the brother of Marie Longworth Storer (q.v.), he was the father of Nicholas Longworth, Speaker of the U. S. House of Representatives, and Mme. Clara L. de Chambrun (q.v.). He graduated from Harvard University in 1866, read law in Cincinnati, and was admitted to the bar in 1869. He served as judge of common pleas court, 1876–81, and on the state supreme court, 1881–83. Besides the two short novels below, he published a translation of Sophocles' *Electra.*

The Marquis and the Moon . . . , Cincinnati, 1889.

Silas Jackson's Wrongs, Cincinnati, 1889.

LOOKER, O. N. Pseud. See Nathan D. Urner.

LOOMIS, ELIAS (Aug. 7, 1811–Aug. 15, 1889), scientist and educator, born in Willington, Conn., was on the faculty of Western Reserve College in Hudson, 1837–44. He was later on the faculty of Princeton University, 1844–60, and of Yale University, 1860–89. He wrote a family history and a great many textbooks, which were widely used and which made him moderately wealthy. He also published many scientific papers and *The Recent Progress of Astronomy, Especially in the United States,* New York, 1850.

LOOMIS, ELISHA SCOTT (Sept. 18, 1852–Dec. 11, 1940), educator, was born in Wadsworth Township, Medina County. After graduating from Baldwin University in 1880, he taught in district schools until 1885, when he joined the mathematics faculty of his alma mater. He later taught at West High School, Cleveland, 1895–1923. He published several mathematics textbooks and genealogical pamphlets and *Life and Appreciation of Dr. Aaron Schuyler . . .* , [Berea, 1936].

LOOMIS, WALTER HARRISON (Jan. 16, 1874–), physician, born in Tunkhannock, Pa., graduated from the Cleveland Homeopathic Medical School in 1904. He practiced in Cleveland and operated the Eddy Road Hospital and later the East Cleveland Hospital. He published *The Health Hunter,* Cleveland, 1931.

LORD, JOHN KING (Oct. 21, 1848–June 26, 1926), educator, was born in Cincinnati, Hamilton County. His entire teaching career (1869–1916) was spent at his alma mater, Dartmouth College. He edited several Latin texts and wrote *A History of the Town of Hanover, N. H.,* [Hanover], 1928. WWW 1

LORD, LOUIS ELEAZER (July 14, 1875–Jan. 24, 1957), educator, was born in Ravenna, Portage County. He graduated from Oberlin College in 1897 and from Yale University (Ph.D.) in 1908. He was a member of the Oberlin faculty, 1898–1941, and of the Scripps College faculty, 1944–49. He published articles, textbooks, translations, and a series of lectures: *Thucydides and the World War . . .* , Cambridge, Mass., 1945. WWW 3

LORD, WILLIS (Sept. 15, 1809–Oct. 28, 1888), Presbyterian clergyman and educator, born in Bridgeport, Conn., was pastor of Broadway Presbyterian Church, Cincinnati, and a professor at Lane Seminary, 1850–54. He was again in Ohio when he served as president of University of Wooster, 1870–74. He also served briefly, 1877–78, as pastor of the First Presbyterian Church, Columbus, but resigned to live in Colorado for his health. Among his publications was *Christian Theology for the People,* New York, 1875.

LORENZ, CARL (March 31, 1858–April 30, 1924), journalist, born in Stuttgart, Germany, came to America in 1881. He was a school principal in Portsmouth, 1883–87, after which he moved to Cleveland. He was Sunday editor of *Waechter und Anzeiger.* Although he is said to have written fiction and poetry, his only book appears to have been a biography: *Tom L. Johnson, Mayor of Cleveland,* New York, 1911.

LORENZ, DANIEL EDWARD (May 24, 1862–Feb. 27, 1941), clergyman, was born in Canal Fulton, Stark County. He graduated from Otterbein College in 1884, from Union Theological Seminary in 1889, and from Columbia University (Ph.D.) in 1891. Ordained to the Presbyterian ministry in 1889, he served as a pastor in New York City for many years. He wrote at least two travel books, e.g., *The Mediterranean Traveller . . . ,* New York, [1905]. WW 8

LORENZ, EDMUND SIMON (July 13, 1854–July 10, 1942), clergyman, composer, and publisher, was born in North Lawrence, Stark County. He graduated from high school in Toledo in 1870 and afterward taught German in the Toledo public schools. He graduated from Otterbein College in 1880 and from Yale Divinity School in 1883, was a pastor in Dayton, 1884–87, served as president of Lebanon College, Pa., 1887–90, and founded a music publishing house in Dayton in 1890. He edited a number of hymn books, wrote articles on church music, hymns, and *The Singing Church; The Hymns It Wrote and Sang,* Nashville, [Tenn., 1938].

LORING, ANDREW. Pseud. See Lorin A. Lathrop.

LORING, JOHN ALDEN (March 6, 1871–May 8, 1947), naturalist, was born in Cleveland, Cuyahoga County. He served as field naturalist for the U. S. Biological Survey, 1892–97, for the U. S. National Museum, and for the Smithsonian-Roosevelt expedition to Africa, 1909–10. He wrote many articles and stories on animals for various magazines. Theodore Roosevelt wrote an introduction to his collection, *African Adventure Stories,* New York, 1914. WWW 2

LORING, PETER. Pseud. See Samuel Shellabarger.

LORRAIN, ALFRED M. (c.1787– ?), clergyman, was born in Maryland. During his infancy his family moved to Petersburg, Va. He went to sea as a cabin boy and had worked his way up to the rank of second mate when he received word from home, in 1812, that a volunteer regiment was forming at Petersburg to join the forces of Gen. William Henry Harrison on the northwestern frontier. He served through the siege of Fort Meigs, following which he returned to Virginia. Joining his brother in New Orleans in 1822, he took an active part in the affairs of the Methodist Church and was licensed to preach there by Bishop McKendree in 1823. He moved to Xenia in the same year, and from 1824 to 1861 he traveled on virtually all of the circuits in Ohio. He contributed frequently to the *Ladies' Repository* and edited the *Western Pilot,* 1854–55. Besides the title below, he published two volumes of "sea sermons."

The Helm, the Sword, and the Cross. A Life Narrative, Cincinnati, 1862.

LORRAINE, LOUIS, Pseud. See Louis P. Smith.

LOSE, GEORGE WILLIAM (Sept. 28, 1852–May 20, 1927), clergyman, was born in Pleasant Unity, Pa. After graduating from Capital University in 1871 and from the seminary in 1874, he was ordained to the Lutheran ministry and served as pastor of churches in Cridersville, Amanda, and Massillon. He also edited the *Lutheran Child's Paper* and *The Little Missionary* and was an assistant editor of the *Lutheran Standard.* Besides the titles below, he wrote other Sunday school stories that have not been located.

Esther and Other Poems, Columbus, 1883.
The Lives of the Twelve Apostles, Columbus, 1888.
Aunt Esther, Columbus, 1894.
Lutheran Foreign Missions, Columbus, [1897].
From Darkness to Light, Columbus, 1898.
The Melnore Parish, Columbus, 1899.
Around the Christmas Hearth, Columbus, 1900.
Promises Fulfilled. A Story . . . , [n.p., 1900?].
Dorothy, Chicago, 1903.
Peace on Earth, Columbus, 1905.
Christmas Eve at Eddington Place, Columbus, 1906.
Ralph the Orphan, Chicago, 1906.
Babette, or the Table Prayer, Columbus, 1907.
Theodore; Or, the Washerwoman's Son, Columbus, 1907.
Bread upon the Waters, Columbus, 1908.
Zaunie, the Basket Maker's Boy, Columbus, 1908.
Promises Fulfilled, Chicago, 1909.
The Secret of Happiness, Columbus, 1909.

LOTH, MORITZ (Dec. 29, 1832–Feb. 18, 1913), merchant, was born in Milotiz,

Austria, where he received his elementary education. He emigrated to the United States in 1852 and in 1859 arrived in Cincinnati, where he began a wholesale notions business and within ten years was regarded as one of the ablest businessmen in the city. He was an early leader in Reform Judaism and a communal worker of great enthusiasm. He wrote a number of articles for local publications under the pen name of Milotiz. His death occurred in Cincinnati.

Our Prospects; A Tale of Real Life, Cincinnati, 1870.
"The Forgiving Kiss" . . . , New York, 1874.
Pearls from the Bible, Cincinnati, 1894.
On a Higher Plane, Cincinnati, [1899].
Sunbeams, Cincinnati, [1899].

LOUCKS, MICHAEL May 28, 1850– ?), clergyman, was born in Fairfield County. He graduated from Heidelberg College in 1871 and was ordained to the ministry of the Reformed Church in 1873. He served churches in Akron, Somerset, and Dayton. He was on the staff of the publishing house of his church in Dayton, 1882–94, and edited the *Christian World.* His last known address (1896) was Dayton.

The Key to the Tree of Christianity, Dayton, 1892.

LOUTTIT, GEORGE WILLIAM (June 30, 1868–May 30, 1937), lawyer, was born in Dayton, Montgomery County, but grew up in Fort Wayne, Ind., where his family moved while he was a small boy. After graduating from the University of Michigan law school in 1890, he practiced in Fort Wayne. He died in Everett, Wash. He published several novels, e.g., *The Gentleman from Jay,* New York, [1903]. IATB

LOVE, JEANETTE F., educator, born near Gallipolis, Gallia County, taught school for several years. She lived in Columbus in 1941. She wrote *The Fall and Rise of Cushan, and Other Poems,* Columbus, 1911.

LOVE, JOHN WILLIS (Dec. 18, 1892–Sept. 21, 1958), journalist, was born in Shelby, Richland County. He graduated from Oberlin College in 1914, worked on the Cleveland *Plain-Dealer,* 1916–30, and after 1931 wrote a column in the Cleveland *Press.* He published a number of articles on business and economics and a history of the Elwell Parker Electric Company: *Lengthened Shadows . . . ,* Cleveland, 1943. WWMW 54

LOVE, JULIAN PRICE (June 10, 1894–), clergyman and educator, was born in Lexington, Ky. He graduated from Miami University in 1915, from Lane Seminary in 1918, and from the University of Cincinnati (Ph.D.) in 1930. He was pastor of a Presbyterian church in Dayton, 1918–21, and a member of the Lane Seminary faculty, 1921–31. In 1931 he joined the faculty of Louisville Presbyterian Seminary. His writings include *How to Read the Bible,* New York, 1940. WW 30

LOVEJOY. Pseud. See Samuel L. Gillespie.

LOVEMAN, ROBERT (April 11, 1864–July 10, 1923), was born in Cleveland, Cuyahoga County. In his early childhood his family moved to Dalton, Ga., where he attended the public schools. He became widely known for his verse, which frequently appeared in leading periodicals. His poem "April Rain" appeared in *Harper's Magazine,* May, 1901. In his letter of acceptance Hayden Carruth wrote: "We literally stopped the presses in order to get your little poem in the current issue of the magazine, but we will be willing to stop our presses any time you send us another like it."

A health unto the happy!
  A fig for him who frets!
It isn't raining rain to me,
  It's raining violets.

The poem was destined for immortality. Read and quoted often, it has been set to nearly forty melodies. Loveman died at his home in Georgia.

Poems, Tuscaloosa, Ala., 1889.
Poems, Philadelphia, 1897.
A Book of Verses, Philadelphia, 1900.
The Gates of Silence with Interludes of Song, New York, 1903.
Songs from a Georgia Garden and Echoes from the Gates of Silence, Philadelphia, 1904.
The Blushful South and Hippocrene; Being Songs, Philadelphia, 1909.
Sonnets of the Strife, with Songs, Boston, [1917].
Verses, [Binghamton, N. Y., 192?].

LOWE, JOHN WILLIAMSON (Nov. 15, 1809–Sept. 10, 1861), lawyer, was born in New Brunswick, N. J. He came to Batavia in 1833 as a printer, studied law under Judge Fishback, and was admitted to the bar in 1836. He practiced in Batavia from 1836 to 1854, except for one year's service in the Mexican War. He practiced law again in Dayton, 1854–55, and in Xenia, 1855–61. He was elected colonel of the 12th O.V.I., and was killed in the battle of Carnifex Ferry.

Poems, [Dayton?, 1862?].

LOWRIE, DONALD ALEXANDER (Jan. 29, 1889–), was born in Chatham, Medina County. A graduate of the College of Wooster, he has also studied in European universities and lived abroad for many years. He was an executive secretary for UNICEF, but is now retired and lives in New York City. He has published several translations and some original works, e.g., a biography, *Masaryk: Nation-Builder,* New York, 1930.

LOWRY, HOWARD FOSTER (July 26, 1901–), educator, was born in Portsmouth, Scioto County. He graduated from the College of Wooster in 1923 and from Yale University (Ph.D.) in 1931. Except for intervals of teaching and graduate study in various universities, he has been on the Wooster faculty since 1923 and has been president of the college since 1944. He has published essays, an anthology, several books on Matthew Arnold, and *The Mind's Adventure,* Philadelphia, [1950]. WW 30

LOWRY, ROBERT (March 28, 1919–), was born in Cincinnati, Hamilton County. He attended public schools there and spent a few months at the University of Cincinnati. In 1938 he bought a press and began issuing the *Little Man* magazine, in which many of his early stories appeared. He served in Europe during World War II and used his experiences as the basis for his first full-length novel: *Casualty,* [New York, 1946]. WW 30

LOWRY, ROBERT EATON (Nov. 2, 1846–April 17, 1917), lawyer, was born near Delaware, Delaware County. After graduating from Miami University in 1871, he taught school in Butler, Preble, and Montgomery Counties. He was county surveyor, Preble County, 1885–90, read law and was admitted to the bar in 1893, and afterward practiced in Eaton. He wrote *History of Preble County . . . ,* Indianapolis, 1915.

LOY, MATTHIAS (March 17, 1828–Jan. 26, 1915), clergyman and educator, was born in Cumberland County, Pa. In 1847 he came to Circleville and soon afterward began studying at the Lutheran Theological Seminary, Columbus. He was pastor of a church in Delaware, 1849–65, and served on the faculty of Capital University, 1865–1902. He was president of the university, 1881–90. Besides the titles below, he published sermons and hymns.

The Doctrine of Justification, Columbus, 1869.

Story of My Life, Columbus, 1905.

LOYSON, EMILIE JANE BUTTERFIELD (1833– ?), sister of Consul W. Butterfield (q.v.), was born in Oswego, N. Y., but grew up in Ohio. She began publishing poetry at the age of sixteen. In 1851 she married Captain E. R. Meriman; he died in 1867, and the following year she married Père Charles Hyacinthe Loyson, an apostate Catholic priest. She accompanied him as he lectured throughout the United States and Europe, advocating reform of the Catholic Church. She wrote an account of a visit to the Near East: *To Jerusalem through the Lands of Islam . . . ,* Chicago, 1905.

LUCAS, ANNA M., was born in Cincinnati, Hamilton County. She attended Cincinnati parochial schools, the University of Cincinnati, and Cincinnati Conservatory of Music. She has written stories and plays for Catholic magazines and at least six novels, e.g., *The Pendulum,* Belleville, Ill., [1936].

LUCAS, ELIZA SYMMES (Feb. 5, 1866–Jan. 3, 1957), was born near Vinton, Gallia County. She taught school for several years before and after graduating from Rio Grande College in 1901. For thirty years, until her retirement in 1949, she was state secretary of the G.A.R. in Ohio. She published a collection of poems: *Toast and Tea,* Columbus, [1919].

LUCCOCK, GEORGE NAPHTALI (March 31, 1857–Feb. 23, 1943), clergyman, was born in Kimbolton, Guernsey County. After graduating from University of Wooster in 1878, he was ordained to the Presbyterian ministry. He served churches in Iowa, Indiana, Washington, D. C., and Illinois, 1881–1917, and was pastor of the College Church at Wooster, 1917–27. He wrote many articles for religious periodicals and *The Home God Meant,* Philadelphia, 1922.

LUCCOCK, NAPHTALI (Sept. 28, 1853–April 1, 1916), clergyman, was born in Kimbolton, Guernsey County. He graduated from Ohio Wesleyan University in 1874 and from Western University of Pennsylvania (Ph.D.) in 1886. He was pastor of Methodist churches in Pennsylvania and Missouri and edited the *American Illustrated Methodist Magazine.* He was elected bishop in 1912. He wrote a history of Methodism and *The Royalty of Jesus,* Cincinnati, [1905]. WWW 1

LUCKIESH, MATTHEW (Sept. 14, 1889–), electrical engineer, born in Maquoketa, Iowa, has lived in Cleveland since

1910. He has been a research director with Nela Laboratories and with General Electric. He has written numerous books and articles on light and other aspects of physics, e.g., *Color and Colors,* New York, 1938. WW 30

LUDEY, CHARLES ADDISON (July 7, 1874–), lawyer and oilman, was born in Bellaire, Belmont County, but grew up in Beallsville and Woodsfield, Monroe County. After practicing law in Marietta for fifteen years, he moved to Oklahoma in 1910 to enter the oil business. His busy life is recounted in his autobiography, *Decision Reserved,* Philadelphia, 1941.

LUDLOW, ARTHUR CLYDE (June 4, 1861–April 16, 1927), clergyman, was born in Chardon, Geauga County. He graduated from Western Reserve University in 1887 and was ordained to the Presbyterian ministry in the same year. He was pastor of Miles Park Church, Cleveland, 1886–1923.

History of Cleveland Presbyterianism . . . , Cleveland, 1896.

The Old Stone Church . . . , Cleveland, 1920.

Centennial History of Western Reserve University, Cleveland, 1926.

LUDWIG, CHARLES (Sept. 15, 1881–), journalist, was born in Cincinnati, Hamilton County. He began as a copy boy on the *Times-Star* in 1894 and served on that newspaper until his retirement in 1953. He published a volume of reminiscences of the Miami and Erie Canal: *Playmates of the Towpath,* Cincinnati, 1929.

LUEDY, ARTHUR ERNEST (Jan. 17, 1894–), horticulturist, born in Cleveland, Cuyahoga County, and his wife, Mildred Van Devourt Luedy (Dec. 29, 1897–), born in Camp Run, Pa., are residents of Bedford. They have written articles in horticultural magazines, and one book: *The Christmas Rose,* Bedford, [1948].

LUEDY, MILDRED VAN DEVOURT. See Arthur E. Luedy.

LUETKEMEYER, MATHILDE JUNGE (Nov. 1, 1871–April 10, 1941), was born in Oskaloosa, Iowa, but spent much of her life in Cleveland. She graduated from Western Reserve University in 1902. Her husband, Edmund H. Luetkemeyer, was in business in Cleveland. Her poems appeared in various periodicals, and she published at least two collections, e.g., *Sheaves of Soul and Song,* Newport, Ky., [1931].

LUMMIS, CHARLES FLETCHER (March 1, 1859–Nov. 25, 1928), born in Lynn, Mass., edited the *Scioto Gazette,* Chillicothe, 1882–84. In Sept., 1884, he set out to walk to Los Angeles; he arrived in Feb., 1885, after numerous hardships and spent the remainder of his life in the Southwest. A prolific writer he wrote history, poetry, essays, and stories about his adopted region. One of the best of his many books was *The Land of Poco Tiempo,* New York, 1893.

LUNDY, BENJAMIN (Jan. 4, 1789–Aug. 22, 1839), abolitionist, born in Hardwick, N. J., of Quaker parents, came to Wheeling, Va., in 1808 and worked as a saddler. After several years he moved to Mount Pleasant and later to St. Clairsville, where in 1815 he organized the Union Humane Society, one of the first antislavery societies. He also contributed articles to *The Philanthropist,* published by Charles Osborn in Mount Pleasant. After two years in St. Louis, Mo., (1819–21), he returned to Ohio and established *The Genius of Universal Emancipation* in Mount Pleasant. This antislavery paper he soon moved to Greenville, Tenn., and later published in Baltimore, Md., and Washington, D. C. A pioneer abolitionist, Lundy is usually credited with converting William Lloyd Garrison to the cause of abolition. He published numerous pamphlets, the most influential of which was an anonymous argument against the annexation of Texas: *The War in Texas . . . ,* Philadelphia, 1836.

LUPTON, DILWORTH (Sept. 15, 1883–), clergyman, was born in Cincinnati, Hamilton County. He graduated from Sheffield Scientific School in 1905 and from Meadville School of Theology in 1916. After serving a church in Louisville, Ky., 1916–19, he was pastor of the First Unitarian Church, Cleveland, 1919–42. He conducted a column in the Cleveland *Press,* 1942–47. He now lives in Clearwater, Fla. He has published *Religion Says You Can,* Boston, [1938]. WW 27

LUTE is an unidentified author of Wyandot County. Her work discloses that she was a poor and pious lady who wrote poor and pious poetry. According to the late John D. Sears of Upper Sandusky, " 'Lute's Poems' are the unassisted work of a young lady who was brought up in Wyandot County, whose intellectual training was the work of our common and other schools, and whose heart here received the education of love, hope and disappointment which finds full expression in the volume before us."

Poems by Lute . . . , Dayton, 1858.

LUTHER, CLAIR FRANKLIN (Oct. 3, 1866–Sept. 11, 1938), clergyman, was born in Burton, Geauga County. He graduated from Painesville High School, attended Western Reserve University, 1885–87, graduated from Amherst College in 1889 and from Yale Divinity School in 1892, and was ordained to the Congregational ministry in 1892. He served as pastor of various New England churches, 1892–1937. His death occurred in Amherst, Mass. An authority on American coins and furniture, he published numerous articles and a book: *The Hadley Chest,* Hartford, Conn., 1935.

LUTZ, HARLEY LEIST (July 30, 1882–), educator, was born near Chillicothe, Ross County. He graduated from Oberlin College in 1907 and from Harvard University (Ph.D.) in 1914. He was on the Oberlin faculty, 1909–23, and also taught at Stanford University, 1923–28, and Princeton University, 1928–47. He now lives in Princeton, N. J. Besides economics textbooks and professional articles, he has written a book under the sponsorship of the National Association of Manufacturers: *Bring Government Back Home! . . .* , New York, 1950. WW 26

LUTZ, HARRY ELMER (Sept. 18, 1860–Dec. 12, 1950), lawyer and banker, was born in Circleville, Pickaway County. After graduating from Wittenberg College (A.B., 1879; M.A., 1881), he traveled in Europe and the Near East. He then read law in his father's office in Circleville and was admitted to the Ohio bar in 1883. He also owned and edited the Circleville *Union Herald* and served as postmaster of that community. In 1890 he moved to the State of Washington, where he organized the Bank of Clallam County, of which he was president for 29 years. He died in Los Angeles.

A Student's Views Abroad, Cincinnati, 1888.

LUTZ, RALPH HASWELL (May 18, 1886–), educator, son of Harry E. Lutz (q.v.), was born in Circleville, Pickaway County. He graduated from Stanford University in 1906 and from the University of Washington Law School in 1907. He also studied in Germany (Ph.D., Heidelberg, 1910). He has taught in the history departments of the University of Washington and of Stanford University, and has been professor emeritus at the latter institution since 1952. He has edited or written numerous historical studies, e.g., *The German Revolution,* Stanford University, 1922. WW 30

LUXON, NORVAL NEIL (May 16, 1899–), educator, was born in New London, Huron County. He graduated from Ohio State University in 1923 and from University of California (Ph.D.) in 1940. He was on the Ohio State journalism faculty, 1928–53, and is now dean of the School of Journalism, University of North Carolina. He has written numerous magazine articles, a journalism textbook, and the history of a magazine: *Niles Weekly Register . . .* , Baton Rouge, [La.], 1947. WW 30

LYBARGER, DONALD FISHER (Dec. 19, 1896–), born in Harrisburg, Pa., was admitted to the Ohio bar in 1923 and practiced in Cleveland until 1928. He has served as recorder of Cuyahoga County, 1933–50, and as common pleas judge since 1950. He has written books of family history and *The Origin of the Western Reserve,* [Cleveland, 1934]. WW 30

LYBARGER, EDWIN LEWIS (Sept. 29, 1840–June 27, 1924), merchant, was born in Wayne County. He served as a captain in the 43rd O.V.I., and after the war he settled at Spring Mountain, Coshocton County. He served in the state legislature, was a successful merchant in Warsaw, and was prominent in business circles in Coshocton. He published *Leaves from My Diary. Being the Transcript of the Daily Record I Kept during Sherman's March to the Sea and to the End of the War,* Warsaw, [1910].

LYBARGER, LEE FRANCIS (May 15, 1865–), lawyer, was born in Milwood, Knox County. He attended University of Wooster and Buchtel College, 1888–93, taught in Neff College of Oratory, Philadelphia, 1893–98, and was admitted to the Pennsylvania bar in 1900. He practiced in Mifflinburg, Pa., and was also a popular lyceum and Chautauqua speaker. He published several books and pamphlets on economics, e.g., *The Tariff—What It Is, How It Works, Whom It Benefits . . .* , Greenville, Pa., 1909. WWNAA 7

LYDENBERG, HARRY MILLER (Nov. 18, 1874–April 16, 1960), librarian, was born in Dayton, Montgomery County, the son of Wesley Braxton and Marianna Miller Lydenberg. As a boy he carried newspapers on a route in Dayton, and in the winter of 1888–89 he worked as a page in the Dayton Public Library, prefiguring at an early age his lifelong devotion to the care and dissemination of the printed word. After graduating from Dayton Central High School in 1892, he went to Harvard. There he completed four years' work in three and received his A.B. in 1897. While in Cambridge he worked in the Harvard College Library to help pay his student expenses. Before receiving his college degree he came to the Lenox Library, New York City, in 1896 as a cataloguer. Although the Lenox Library had been consolidated with the Astor Library and the Tilden Trust in 1895 to form the New York Public Library, the collections of the Lenox Library were still kept together in the old building on Fifth Avenue between 70th and 71st Streets, where they remained until the headquarters building of the New York Public Library was completed and opened in 1911. Mr. Lydenberg remained on the staff of the New York Public Library until 1941. He was in charge of manuscripts from 1896 to 1899, and was assistant to the director, Dr. John Shaw Billings (q.v.), from 1899 to 1908. For two decades, 1908–1927, he was chief reference librarian. Following Dr. Billings' death in 1913, Mr. Lydenberg's principal work and achievement was the building up of the great reference collection of the New York Public Library. In the nineteenth century, the Astor Library had become the finest reference collection in the United States. When the special collections of the Lenox Library were added to this, there was a great incentive to maintain the New York Public Library as one of the great reference libraries of the world. Mr. Lydenberg's work in this field was outstanding. In 1927 he became the library's assistant director, and in 1934, upon the retirement of Edwin Anderson, he became director—a position he held until 1941. During his directorship he was chief not only of the great reference library at 42nd Street, but also of the more than fifty branches of the circulation department. During these years of economic depression, Mr. Lydenberg sought to make the Library serve its teeming public to the fullest possible extent. In 1941–43 he was director-librarian of the *Biblioteca Benjamin Franklin* in Mexico City, an institution sponsored by Nelson Rockefeller for the improvement of relations between the United States and Latin America. From 1943 to 1946 he was director of the Board of International Relations of the American Library Association, with headquarters at the Library of Congress. In 1946 he visited Germany as a member of the American Library Mission. In 1947 he retired from active library work. Mr. Lydenberg is author of the standard *History of the New York Public Library,* a work of 643 pages published by the Library in 1923. The following year saw the publication of his monograph on Dr. John Shaw Billings, the inspiring chief under whom he worked during his early years in New York. Lydenberg and John Archer, chief of the library's printing shop and bindery, collaborated in the preparation of *The Care and Repair of Books* (1931), a standard work which has been reprinted several times. Mr. Lydenberg translated from the French of André Blum two works on subjects in which he was deeply interested: *On the Origin of Paper* (1934) and *The Origins of Printing and Engraving* (1940). During his directorship he devoted much careful attention to the voluminous annual reports of the New York Public Library. Between 1909 and 1942 he wrote more than 110 articles which were contributed to books and periodicals. These are largely devoted to various aspects of the public library movement, to the preservation of books, newspapers and other records, to important men in the library world, and to several special scholarly subjects. Mr. Lydenberg was president of the New York Library Club, the American Library Association, and the Bibliographical Society of America. He was secretary-treasurer of the American Council of Learned Societies, 1937–41, and a member of the Council's joint committee on materials of research. In 1949 he received the A.L.A.'s Joseph W. Lippincott Award for outstanding library work. In 1943 a 573-page *festschrift* was published: *Bookmen's Holiday: Notes and Studies Written and Gathered in Tribute to Harry Miller Lydenberg.* In his early years Mr. Lydenberg was much interested in rowing—on the Charles, Harlem, and North Rivers. He was an enthusiastic gardener during the many years he lived in Scarsdale.

George L. McKay

LYLE, WILLIAM W. (Feb. 20, 1826–Feb. 20, 1876), clergyman, was born in Pennsylvania. He was a chaplain with the 11th O.V.I., Jan., 1862–June, 1864. His death occurred in Licking County.

Lights and Shadows of Army Life . . . , Cincinnati, 1865.

LYMAN, EUGENE WILLIAM (April 4, 1872–March 15, 1948), theologian, born in Cummington, Mass., was on the faculty of Oberlin Theological Seminary, 1913–18, before joining the faculty of Union Theological Seminary, where he served 1918–40. He wrote while at Oberlin *The Experience of God in Modern Life,* New York, 1918. RLA 2

LYON, JESSICA. Pseud. See Cateau de Leeuw.

LYONS, JOHN FREDERICK (Sept. 12, 1878–), librarian, was born near Chandlersville, Muskingum County. He graduated from University of Wooster in 1901 and from McCormick Theological Seminary in 1904. After serving as a Presbyterian clergyman in Oregon, 1907–12, he joined the McCormick faculty as librarian and instructor in bibliography. He retired in 1949 and now lives in Chicago. He has written articles and *Centennial Sketch of the History of the Presbytery of Chicago,* Chicago, 1947. WW 27

LYTLE, JAMES ROBERT (April 9, 1841–Sept. 21, 1924), lawyer, was born in Fairfield County. During the last year of the Civil War, he served with the 159th O.V.I. He enrolled in Ohio Wesleyan University, read law during vacations, graduated in 1868, and was admitted to the bar in 1869. He practiced in Delaware. He edited and wrote portions of *20th Century History of Delaware County, Ohio . . . ,* [Chicago, 1908].

LYTLE, JOHN HORACE (Oct. 17, 1884–), advertising executive, was born in Dayton, Montgomery County. He organized J. Horace Lytle Company and was its president, 1919–45. Widely known as a hunting expert and as a judge of field trials, he was gun dog editor of *Field and Stream* for more than twenty years. He has written a number of books, both fiction and nonfiction, about hunting and dogs, e.g., *Sandy Oorang and Other Stories of Dogs and the Wilderness,* New York, 1922. WW 26

LYTLE, KATHERINE WILLIAMS (July 14, 1894–), was born in Churchill, Trumbull County. She attended Youngstown schools. Her last address in Ohioana files was Canton. She has published a volume of verse: *Words,* Boston, [1947].

LYTLE, WILLIAM HAINES (Nov. 2, 1826–Sept. 20, 1863), was born in Cincinnati, Hamilton County. During the Mexican War he served in the 2nd Ohio Infantry as a captain. He later served in the Ohio legislature. A major general during the Civil War, he was wounded at Carnifex Ferry and was killed at Chickamauga, Sept. 20, 1863. His best-known poem, "Antony and Cleopatra," first appeared in a Cincinnati newspaper, July 29, 1858. It had been sent to the editors by the Cincinnati poet, William W. Fosdick, with the comment "We predict a popularity and perpetuity for it unsurpassed by any Western production." The prediction was remarkably accurate, for after nearly a century of declamation, the popular lines beginning "I'm dying, Egypt, dying!" are still widely remembered as Lytle's, although the line itself is a direct quotation from Shakespeare (*Antony and Cleopatra IV, xv, 18*).

Poems of William Haines Lytle, (W. H. Venable, ed.), Cincinnati, 1894.

LYTTLE, CHARLES HAROLD (July 16, 1884–), clergyman and educator, was born in Cleveland, Cuyahoga County. He graduated from Western Reserve University in 1907 and from Meadville Theological Seminary in 1910. He served Unitarian churches in Brooklyn, N. Y., taught in Illinois and at Meadville Seminary, and was on the faculty of the University of Chicago, 1943–49. His writings include *The Pentecost of American Unitarianism . . . ,* Boston, [1920]. WW 30

LYTTLETON, KAY. Pseud. See Mary A. Amsbary.

M

MABIE, LOUISE KENNEDY (d. Nov. 10, 1957), was born in Cleveland, Cuyahoga County. She attended Horace Mann School, New York City, and was tutored at home. Married to Webster B. Mabie, she lived in California after 1923. Her death occurred in Los Angeles. She wrote short stories for *Saturday Evening Post* and other national magazines and published at least two novels, e.g., *The Wings of Pride,* New York, 1913. WWW 3

McADAM, DUNLAP JAMISON (Aug. 2, 1843–Feb. 15, 1925), educator and consulting engineer, was born in Moorefield, Harrison County. He left his studies at Ohio University to enlist in the 126th O.V.I., and after the war he attended Washington and Jefferson College. After serving as superintendent of schools in Carrollton (1870–72), he began a long tenure (1872–1914) as professor of mathematics at Washington and Jefferson. His writings include *Einstein's Relativity; A Criticism,* Boston, [1922]. WWW 1

McADAMS, FRANCIS MARION (Oct. 13, 1838–Nov. 6, 1886), was born in Union Township, Champaign County. He grew up on a farm, taught in district schools, and served as a sergeant in the 113th O.V.I., Aug., 1862–July, 1865. After the war he operated stores in Mutual and Mingo. In 1881 he settled in Richwood, and he died in that community.

Every-day Soldier Life, or a History of the One Hundred and Thirteenth Ohio Volunteer Infantry, Columbus, 1884.

McALISTER, MICHAEL (Feb. 1, 1809–Aug. 6, 1886), was born in County Down, Ireland. After coming to the United States in 1842, he lived for ten years near Marietta and in 1852 moved to Columbus. Between 1860 and 1882, he wrote for various newspapers under the name Thomas Addis. His only book is a nationalistic account of English persecution of the Irish.

An Authentic History of Ireland and Its People, [Columbus], 1880.

McALLESTER, MRS. SAMUEL J. See Dorothy G. Jarnagin.

McALLISTER, ANNA SHANNON (Mrs. Earl S.) (March 11, 1888–), was born in Cincinnati, Hamilton County, but has spent most of her life in Columbus, where she now resides. She graduated from Columbus School for Girls in 1905 and Ohio State University in 1909. She has written several biographies of women, e.g., *Ellen Ewing, Wife of General Sherman,* New York, 1936. WO 2

McALLISTER, FREDERICK BORMAN (Feb. 8, 1888–), clergyman, was born in Exeter, Pa. He graduated from Bucknell University in 1911 and Colgate-Rochester Divinity School in 1914 and was ordained to the ministry of the Baptist Church in the same year. After serving pastorates in other states, he served a Baptist church in Youngstown, 1931–42, and became pastor of Ninth Street Baptist Church, Cincinnati, in 1942. He is now living in that city. He has written *Frank Answers to Youth Questions,* New York, [1935]. WW 27

McALLISTER, HUGH. Pseud. See James A. Braden.

MACARTNEY, CLARENCE EDWARD NOBLE (Sept. 18, 1879–Feb. 19, 1957), clergyman, was born in Northwood, Logan County. His father, Dr. John Longfellow Macartney, was pastor of First Miami Reformed Presbyterian Church of Northwood and professor of natural sciences in Geneva Hall. Less than a year after Clarence's birth, the school was moved to Beaver Falls, Pa., where it became Geneva College. Here he spent his boyhood years. On the Geneva campus the Macartneys built a home which they called Ferncliffe. In later years it became the center for many a family reunion, and here Clarence returned after serious illness forced the relinquishing of his Pittsburgh pastorate, to suffer constant pain and yet to work on with his pen in perfect peace until the call came to join the Church Triumphant. At Ferncliffe he spent most of his youth, and in Geneva College he received a part of his collegiate training, going on to Denver University, Pomona College, and the University of Wisconsin, where he majored in history and earned his bachelor's degree in 1901. Then after a year's experience in newspaper work he moved on to Princeton, matriculating both in the university and the theological seminary. At the former he earned the master of arts degree in 1904, and at the latter the degree of bachelor of divinity in 1905. He did not seek a graduate fellowship or go abroad for further study, as friends urged him to do, but plunged at once into the work of the pastorate. However, his education went on throughout life, and by rigid self-discipline he became a master in several widely separated fields, and several institutions recognized his scholarship by conferring on him honorary doctorates. Nor did he choose an easy field. Soon after graduation from Princeton Seminary he accepted a call to the First Presbyterian Church, Paterson, N. J., not for what it offered but for what it needed. Paterson, a densely populated and highly industrialized area, with much grinding poverty and much seething discontent among its mill people, was enough to appall any beginner in the ministry. Indeed, Macartney seemed to be welcomed to the city with several bombing outrages, which were charged to organized groups of anarchists. But there he was ordained and installed by the Presbytery of Jersey City in the autumn of 1905, and there he labored for nine fruitful years. He became known as a strong preacher of the Christian faith, drawing thoughtful people from beyond the limits of his parish and his city. In 1914 he accepted a call to the Arch Street Church of Philadelphia. There he quickly made his pulpit a trumpeting tower for evangelical Christianity. There he continued with growing power and widening influence until summoned to Pittsburgh late in 1927. He left Arch Street, as he had left Paterson, with its membership almost doubled. During the turmoil of World War I he held the rudder steady, speaking always in accents of ardent but sober patriotism, yet never allowing men to forget that their enlistment was in a higher service, one more vital to the country's welfare than even the promotion of the war effort. During the early 1920s the fundamentalist-modernist controversy arose in the Presbyterian ranks. Macartney's convictions and his Covenanter antecedents made him a natural leader of the conservative party. He was, therefore, unanimously elected moderator of the General Assembly at the age of 45. He filled the office with distinction. In a difficult Assembly he was acclaimed by both parties for his absolute fairness. But with the two most aggressive fundamentalist leaders, J. Gresham Machen and Oswald T. Allis, both his classmates at Princeton, he could not see eye to eye. He had no sympathy with their vitriolic attacks on the motives of those who opposed them. He would have nothing to do with the formation of a schismatic "Orthodox Presbyterian Church." The atmosphere in Philadelphia continued tense with strife, and he probably welcomed an escape to Pittsburgh, where at that time there seemed to be more of brotherly love. Years later when a young friend asked why he had not gone into the Orthodox Church, he answered thoughtfully, "They spoke the truth, but not in love." The great downtown First Church of Pittsburgh had long been among the most active and influential in the entire denomination. Here for 26 years he preached twice each Sunday and once or twice on weekdays to congregations which crowded the building. With the help of a considerable staff, he carried on a tireless and effective pastoral ministry. Generally for two summer months he was found traveling; he traveled with a purpose, for on these journeys much of the material for his books was gathered. Most of his many books were written during his Pittsburgh ministry. The first threatening break in his robust health came in the late 1940s, and twice he underwent major surgery. In 1953 he was compelled to relinquish the work to which he had devoted 48 crowded years. He must stand high on any list of Ohio-born authors, both for the quantity and for the quality of his literary output. Almost sixty volumes of sermons, theological, and polemical works, and studies in American history flowed from his facile pen. Representative works include *The Parables of the Old Testament,* New York, [1916]; *Lincoln and His Generals,* Philadelphia, [1925]; *Paul the Man . . . ,* New York, [1928]; *Parallel Lives of the Old and New Testament,* New York, [1930]; *Right Here in Pittsburgh,* Pittsburgh, [1937]; and *Men Who Missed It . . . ,* Philadelphia, 1940.

E. B. Welsh

MACAULEY, CHARLES RAYMOND (March 29, 1871–Nov. 24, 1934), cartoonist and author, was born in Canton, Stark County. After winning a fifty-dollar prize offered by the Cleveland *Press* for the best cartoon, he began drawing political cartoons for Cleveland newspapers. In 1894 he moved to New York City, where he was a cartoonist for various newspapers. He won the Pulitzer Prize for cartooning in 1929. He wrote and illustrated *Fantasma Land,* Indianapolis, [1904]. WWW 1

McBRIDE, JAMES (Nov. 2, 1788–Oct. 3, 1859), was born near Greencastle, Pa. At the age of eighteen he came to Hamilton, where he spent the remainder of his life. According to Henry Howe, he made enough money on trading expeditions to New Orleans during the War of 1812 to devote himself to local history and archaeology. He served at various times as county sheriff, mayor of Hamilton, and clerk of county courts. He was a convert to Symmes' theory of concentric spheres and wrote a book describing it. He accumulated a library of 5,000 volumes, most of them related to Western history. His *Notes on Hamilton* was written in 1831, though not published until 1898.

Naval Biography . . . , Cincinnati, 1815.

Symmes Theory of Concentric Spheres; Demonstrating That the Earth Is Hollow, Habitable Within and Widely Open at the Poles, Cincinnati, 1826.

A Sketch of the Life and Character of John Reily, Dec'd, Hamilton, 1850.

Pioneer Biography. Sketches of the Lives of Some of the Early Settlers of Butler County, Ohio, 2 vols., Cincinnati, 1869–71.

Notes on Hamilton . . . , Hamilton, 1898.

McBRIDE, ROBERT W. (Jan. 25, 1842–May 15, 1926), lawyer, was born in Richland County. He attended the public schools of Mansfield and of Iowa, where his family moved in 1857. While he was living with relatives in Ohio in 1863, Governor David Tod organzed the 7th Independent Company of Ohio Voluntary Cavalry, which was to consist of one man from each county and was intended to serve as bodyguard to President Lincoln. McBride enlisted in the organization and became first corporal and company clerk. After the war he attended Kirkwood Academy in Iowa, was admitted to the bar in 1867, and practiced law in Iowa until 1890, when he moved to Indianapolis. He served as justice of the Indiana Supreme Court, 1890–93. In 1908 the survivors of "Lincoln's Body Guard" met in Columbus to form a permanent organization. McBride was elected secretary, and the following year published the history of the organization: *Lincoln's Body Guard, the Union Light Guard, the Seventh Independent Company of Ohio Volunteer Cavalry 1863–65,* [Indianapolis, 1908]. In 1926 he rewrote and expanded the work and issued it under the title *Personal Recollections of Abraham Lincoln . . . ,* Indianapolis, [1926]. He practiced law in Indianapolis until his death.

McCABE, LIDA ROSE (March 3, 1865–Dec. 9, 1938), journalist, was born in Columbus, Franklin County. After attending Columbus schools, she studied at the Sorbonne and Columbia University. She began contributing to the Cincinnati *Commercial Gazette* when she was eighteen. She was a correspondent for the New York *Tribune,* the *Herald,* the *Times,* the *Sun,* and the *Press.* She was the first woman correspondent to go to the Klondike. She also wrote for *Lippincott's* and other magazines.

Don't You Remember?, Boston, 1884.

The American Girl at College, New York, 1893.

Ardent Adrienne, the Life of Madame de La Fayette, New York, 1930.

McCABE, LORENZO DOW (Jan. 17, 1817–July 19, 1897), educator, was born in Marietta, Washington County. Orphaned at the age of six, he attended Marietta schools and worked in a store to earn his keep. He attended Ohio University and graduated in 1843. In 1845 he joined the faculty of Ohio Wesleyan University as professor of mathematics; in 1860 he was made professor of philosophy and remained on the faculty until his death. Twice during interregnums he served as acting president.

Light on the Pathway of Holiness, Cincinnati, 1872.

The Foreknowledge of God . . . , Cincinnati, 1878.

Divine Nescience of Contingencies, New York, 1882.

McCALEB, WALTER FLAVIUS (Oct. 17, 1873–), born in Benton City, Texas, and now a resident of Austin, spent ten years in Cleveland as organizer and manager of the Cooperative National Bank. He has organized labor banks in various cities. He has written 26 books, e.g. *Ring: A Frontier Dog,* New York, 1921, and *Theodore Roosevelt,* New York, 1931, but is best known as an authority on the life of Aaron Burr. He wrote *The Aaron Burr Conspiracy . . . ,* New York, 1903. WW 30

McCANDLISH, EDWARD GERSTELL (1887–Dec. 6, 1946), born in Piedmont, W. Va., lived in Van Wert in the 1930s. A reporter and an artist on the Washington *Post,* the Detroit *Free Press,* and other papers, he also designed children's toys and wrote and illustrated children's books. He died in North Brookfield, Mass. His children's books include *The Bunny Tot's Rainy Day Book,* New York, [1928].

McCANN, SISTER MARY AGNES (April 24, 1851–Oct. 12, 1931), was born in Cincinnati, Hamilton County. She attended Mt. St. Vincent Academy, Ohio Mechanics Institute, and Mt. St. Mary Seminary. After joining the Sisters of Charity in 1867, she served as treasurer of her community in Cincinnati for sixteen years and afterward taught in schools in Cincinnati, Springfield, and Bay City, Mich. She published several historical and biographical works concerning the Sisters of Charity, e.g., *The History of Mother Seton's Daughters . . . ,* New York, 1917.

McCARTY, IDA HELEN DOUTHETT (June 19, 1876–), was born on a farm near Orbiston, Hocking County. She attended public school at Nelsonville, and after graduating from high school at Athens in 1893 she began teaching school. She attended Ohio University while teaching at the Athens Children's Home. Since her marriage to Marshall B. McCarty in 1900, she has lived in Pennville, Ind. Her verse and prose have appeared in many periodicals, and she has published one book: *Mariam'ne of the Cedars,* New York, 1911. IATB

McCAUGHEY, MARETTA ROBISON (Aug. 13, 1852–Jan. 7, 1907), was born in Findlay, Hancock County. She taught in the Findlay schools for eight years before marrying George B. McCaughey in 1878. In 1887 they moved to Frankfort, Ind., where she spent the remainder of her life. Her poems appeared in numerous periodicals; and a collection was published by her family after her death from tuberculosis: *When Lilacs Bloom, and Other Poems . . .* , Cincinnati, [1909]. IATB

McCAULEY, WILLIAM FLETCHER (Dec. 6, 1858–March 13, 1915), clergyman, was born near West Salem, Wayne County. He graduated from Lebanon University in 1883 and Lane Theological Seminary in 1886. Ordained to the Presbyterian ministry in 1886, he served as pastor of churches in Dayton, Toledo, and Cincinnati. In 1911 he became a pastor in McKeesport, Pa.

Next Steps, Chicago, 1897.
The Bible in Story, Cincinnati, 1902.
The Bible in the Public Schools, [Cincinnati?, 1907?].

MACCHETTA, BLANCHE ROOSEVELT TUCKER (1853–Sept. 15, 1898), was born in Sandusky, Erie County. After studying singing in Italy, she made her debut at Covent Garden, London. She married Signor Macchetta, later Marquis d'Alligri. In 1877 she retired from the stage to devote herself to literature, but two years later she resumed her career, singing in *H.M.S. Pinafore* in England and the United States. She created a libretto from Longfellow's *Masque of Pandora* which was presented in Boston in 1882 with music by Alfred Cellier. She retired permanently in 1882 and afterward lived in London, where she served as correspondent for several periodicals.

The Home Life of Henry W. Longfellow . . . , New York, 1882.
Marked "In Haste." A Story of To-day . . . , New York, 1883.
Stage-struck . . . , New York, 1884.
Life and Reminiscences of Gustave Doré . . . , New York, 1885.
The Copper Queen . . . , [London], 1886.
Verdi . . . , London, 1887.
Victorien Sardou . . . , London, 1892.

McCLAIN, NAOMI STEVENS (Sept. 19, 1906–), was born in Bellefontaine, Logan County, where she attended local schools. She has published a collection of verse, illustrated by herself: *Thoughts along the Trail,* [Bellefontaine, 1944].

McCLELLAND, STEWART WINING (March 10, 1891–), clergyman and educator, was born in Austinburg, Ashtabula County. He graduated from Denison University in 1912 and McCormick Theological Seminary in 1915. After being ordained to the Presbyterian ministry, he served churches in Ohio and Michigan; he was president of Lincoln Memorial University, 1932–47. He lectured widely on Abraham Lincoln and also published a number of pamphlets, e.g., *Lincoln and Common Sense . . .* , [Los Angeles, 1946].

McCLINTICK, WILLIAM TRIMBLE (1819–Oct. 28, 1903), lawyer, was born in Chillicothe, Ross County. He practiced throughout his life in Chillicothe and became one of Ohio's distinguished attorneys. He wrote a number of articles for the Ohio State Archaeological and Historical Society and *Verses Written during a Busy Lawyer's Life,* Chillicothe, 1902.

McCLOSKEY, ROBERT (Sept. 15, 1914–), artist and writer, was born in Hamilton, Butler County. After studying art in Boston and at the National Academy of Design, New York City, he was awarded the coveted Prix de Rome in 1939. He served in the army in World War II and now spends his winters in New York State and his summers on an island off Cape Rosier, Maine. He has twice received the Caldecott Medal for his books for children, which he illustrates himself, e.g., *Make Way for Ducklings,* New York, 1941.

McCLUNG, DAVID WADDLE (Dec. 18, 1831–Aug. 18, 1916), was born on a farm in Seneca County. He attended district schools, taught school, and graduated from Miami University in 1854. He was superintendent of schools in Hamilton, edited the Hamilton *Intelligencer,* and read law. From April, 1861, to Nov., 1865, he served in the 3rd O.V.I. After the Civil War he was president of Hamilton Second National Bank for two years and held various posts in Cincinnati—assistant postmaster, surveyor of the port, and internal revenue collector. He died in Cincinnati and is buried in Hamilton.

The Centennial Anniversary of the City of Hamilton . . . , Hamilton, 1892.
Money Talks. Some of the Things It Says When It Speaks, Cincinnati, 1894.

McCLURE, DAVID (Nov. 18, 1748–June 25, 1820), missionary, born in Newport, R. I., visited the Indians around the forks of the Muskingum in 1772 and wrote a valuable account of this visit: *Diary of David McClure,* New York, 1899.

McCLURE, MARJORIE BARKLEY (Mrs. Franklin E.) (March 15, 1882–), was born in Newark, N. J. She graduated from Detroit Seminary in 1901, lived in Akron and Cleveland from 1910 to 1940, and now lives in Westport, Conn. She has published several novels, e.g., *Many Waters,* New York, 1926. WW 21

McCLURE, ROBERT EMERSON (June 12, 1896–), journalist, was born in Columbus, Franklin County. He attended Oberlin College for a time and graduated from Yale University in 1918. He published the Youngstown *Telegram* and later the Santa Monica *Evening Outlook.* He now lives in Los Angeles. He has published several novels, e.g., *A Fable for Wives . . .*, New York, 1932. WW 26

McCLURE, SAMUEL GRANT, JR. (March 7, 1900–July 25, 1922), was born in Columbus, Franklin County, but grew up in Youngstown, where his family moved in 1906. He graduated from Taft School in 1918 and spent one year in Sheffield School before transferring to Yale. He drowned in Lake Erie in a boating accident. After his death his family published privately a collection of his poems, prose pieces, and letters: *The Portfolio of Samuel G. McClure, Jr.*, Youngstown, 1922.

McCOMBS, RALPH L. F. (Oct. 5, 1897–), was born in Columbus, Franklin County. After graduating from Ohio State University in 1919, he taught school, worked on the Columbus *Citizen,* was public relations director for the Philadelphia Orchestra, 1942–46, and has held other public relations posts. He is now public relations counsel for Columbus Gallery of Fine Arts. He prepared the program books for the Philadelphia Orchestra for eight years and also published a mystery novel which has Music Hall, Cincinnati, as its setting: *Clue in Two Flats,* New York, 1940.

McCONN, CHARLES MAXWELL (July 22, 1881–April 15, 1953), educator, was born in Ironton, Lawrence County. He graduated from the University of Minnesota in 1903 and afterward served in various capacities on the faculties of the University of Illinois, Lehigh University, and New York University. His numerous articles and books under the pen name Max McConn include *Mollie's Substitute Husband,* New York, 1920, and several books on higher education, e.g., *College or Kindergarten?,* New York, 1928. WWW 3

McCONN, MAX. Pseud. See Charles M. McConn.

McCONNAUGHEY, JAMES PARKER (April 25, 1908–), was born in Dayton, Montgomery County. His wife, Susanne Rike McConnaughey, published her first novel, *Point Venus,* in 1951. They are now co-publishers of the Kettering *News.* He has published fiction in national magazines and several novels since the appearance of his first: *Village Chronicle,* New York, [1936].

McCONNAUGHEY, SUSANNE RIKE. See McConnaughey, James P.

McCONNELL, CHARLES MELVIN (Jan. 16, 1886–Sept. 7, 1957), clergyman, born in Indianapolis, Ind., graduated from Ohio Wesleyan University in 1907. After his ordination as a Methodist minister, he served several churches in Ohio, 1907–21. He was afterward on the faculty of the School of Theology, Boston University. He died in Deering, N. H. A specialist in problems of rural churches, he wrote several studies of the subject, e.g., *The Rural Billion,* New York, [1931]. WWW 3

McCONNELL, FRANCIS JOHN (Aug. 18, 1871–Aug. 18, 1953), clergyman, was born in Trinway, Muskingum County, the son of a Methodist preacher. The boy made outstanding scholastic records; he graduated from Ohio Wesleyan University in 1894 and Boston University School of Theology in 1897. His Ph.D. came from Boston two years later. Behind these bare details lies the fact that McConnell was regarded as the favorite pupil of personalist philosopher Borden P. Bowne, and would have found ready acceptance in the teaching profession. Indeed, in later years he did some classroom instruction at Columbia, Drew, Garrett, Scarritt, and Yale. He delivered the Lyman Beecher lectures at Yale, the Barrows lectures in India, and the Tipple lectures at Drew. He served as president of the Religious Education Association and of the Federal Council of Churches. After fifteen years as pastor of churches in Massachusetts and New York, he was president of DePauw University, 1909–14, a post from which he was elected to the episcopacy in the Methodist Church. In the development of his thought, two periods are clearly marked. During his early ministry his writings disclose a controlling theological and philosophical bent. The books of this period carry revealing titles: *The Diviner Immanence* (1906), *Christmas Sermons* (1909), *Religious Certainty* (1910), *Christian Focus* (1911), *The Increase of Faith* (1912), *Personal Christianity* (1914), *The Essentials of Methodism* (1916), and *Understanding the Scriptures* (1917). Then the theme changed. Not that the heavenly interest was absent from the later writings, but the landscape brought the earth into the foreground with the heavens arching always above. A predominant social interest came into view. In

1912 McConnell accepted the presidency of the infant Methodist Federation for Social Service and remained its head for more than 25 years. He was deeply involved in the Interchurch World Movement as a member of its committee on social action and played a prominent part in securing more humane working conditions, especially in the steel industry. Naturally his writings reflect these social convictions and activities. His later books suggest the change: *Democratic Christianity* (1919), *Public Opinion and Theology* (1920), *The Preacher and the People* (1922), *Is God Limited?* (1924), *The Christ-like God* (1927), *The Christian Ideal and Social Control* (1933), *Christianity and Coercion* (1933), and *Evangelicals, Revolutionists and Idealists* (1942). These with three biographical volumes—*Bishop Edward Gayer Andrews* (1909), *Borden Parker Bowne* (1929), and *John Wesley* (1939)—make a large and significant output for any one man. In these writings his strong ethical sense appears vividly; he insists on applying the highest concepts of moral responsibility to God as well as to men. Intellectually he has been counted one of America's ablest exponents of Christian truth and life. He had an inquiring, penetrating, gripping mind which seized and held an immense amount of both concrete fact and abstract truth. Add that this ample store was at instant command, and you have the picture of one equipped not only for the pulpit but also for the platform which is wide open for heckling or debate. He lent his name as officer or sponsor to a great variety of organizations with positive social objectives, some regarded with suspicion by conservatives. Opponents called him a radical, but one shrewd judge remarked that the men who followed McConnell very frequently went further than he himself did. His background of philosophy, his breadth of interests, his saving sense of humor kept his feet on the ground when lesser men were swept away by the currents of fads and panaceas. He had great charity for the weak and wide tolerance for the radical, coupled with considerable impatience for whatever savored of reaction. He could not quite see how any intelligent and open-minded man should not be marching in the front line instead of holding the fort. To him the engine in a car was far more interesting than the brakes. In other words, he was unmistakably a progressive. An author's books, however numerous and sincere, contain only a fraction of the real man, and his public functions cannot tell the whole story of his spirit and life. This man, with his fresh approach to many problems, his independent and original mind, his marvelous memory, was most loved and admired as a loyal friend, a kindly and thoughtful helper. Some of his little letters of sympathy and comfort and appreciation were doubtless as eloquent as anything in his books, and his personal appearance at moments of need often seemed like the visits of angels. He inspired in countless followers a crusading spirit. His writing and speaking and his personal influence all had one dominant theme:

> Live pure, speak true, right wrong, follow the King—
> Else, wherefore born?

Herbert Welch

MacCONNELL, SARAH ASTON WARDER (July 26, 1869–July 17, 1953), editor and novelist, was born in Springfield, Clark County, the descendant of a pioneer family. She lived in New York City, where she was well known in literary circles. She died in Catskill, N. Y. Her novels include *Why, Theodora!,* Boston, [1915].

McCONOHAY, AUGUSTUS PAYSON (July 31, 1838–Aug. 28, 1928), was born in Wooster, Wayne County, where he attended public schools. A peripatetic watchmaker, he went to California in 1861. He later located in Nevada City and remained there until the town was destroyed by fire in 1864, when he returned to Ohio and settled in Van Wert. He wrote a salty account of life in frontier Nevada City during all the excitement which followed the discovery of the nearby Comstock Lode: *Incidents As I Remember Them Closing 1865,* Van Wert, 1927.

McCOOK, HENRY CHRISTOPHER (July 3, 1837–Oct. 31, 1911), clergyman and naturalist, was born in New Lisbon, Columbiana County, the eldest son in the family of "Fighting McCooks," distinguished soldiers and sailors during the Civil War. Henry graduated from Jefferson College, Canonsburg, Pa., in 1859, studied theology, and was ordained to the Presbyterian ministry in 1861. He served as lieutenant and later as chaplain of the 41st Illinois Volunteers. After the war he served in city mission work in St. Louis, Mo., until 1870, when he was called to the Tabernacle Church, Philadelphia, where he remained until 1902. A prolific writer and an ardent amateur naturalist, he published poetry, fiction, technical articles, popular books on insects, sermons, and addresses.

The Natural History of the Agricultural Ant of Texas . . . , [Philadelphia], 1879.

The Honey Ants of the Garden of the Gods . . . , Philadelphia, 1882.

Tenants of an Old Farm . . ., New York, 1885.
The Women Friends of Jesus . . ., New York, 1886.
American Spiders and Their Spinningwork . . ., 3 vols., [Philadelphia], 1889–93.
Old Farm Fairies . . ., Philadelphia, 1895.
The Latimers . . ., Philadelphia, 1898.
The Martial Graves of Our Fallen Heroes in Santiago de Cuba, Philadelphia, 1899.
The Gospel in Nature, Philadelphia, 1902.
The Senator; A Threnody, Philadelphia, [1905].
Nature's Craftsmen . . ., New York, 1907.
Ant Communities and How They Are Governed . . ., New York, 1909.
Prisca of Patmos . . ., Philadelphia, 1911.
Quaker Ben . . ., Philadelphia, [1911].

McCOOK, JOHN JAMES (Feb. 2, 1843–Jan. 9, 1927), educator and clergyman and a member of the famed "Fighting McCooks" family, was born in New Lisbon, Columbiana County. He was reading law in Steubenville when the Civil War began. He served with McClellan's forces until 1863, when he entered Trinity College, Conn. He graduated from Berkeley Divinity School in 1866 and was ordained an Episcopal priest in 1867. He served a church in East Hartford, Conn., 1868–1927, and taught languages at Trinity College, 1883–1927. He lectured and wrote numerous magazine articles on social problems.

Pat and the Council, New York, 1870.

McCORD, CAREY PRATT (Sept. 25, 1886–), physician, born in Bibb County, Ala., lived in Ohio from 1920 to 1935 while serving on the University of Cincinnati medical faculty. He has written books on industrial hygiene and *A Blind Hog's Acorns; Vignettes of the Maladies of Workers,* New York, [1945]. WW 30

McCORMICK, ALEXANDER STEARNS (May 22, 1876–), Akron physician, was born in Montreal Canada. He was secretary of Summit County Medical Society, 1913–18 and 1921–42. Elected historian in 1942, he compiled material relating to the society and published it in *The History of Medicine in Summit County, Ohio,* New York, 1946. He has also published a number of medical articles and papers and composed many marches and songs.

McCORMICK, ANNE O'HARE (1882–May 29, 1954), journalist, was born in Wakefield, Yorkshire, England, but spent her girlhood in Columbus, where she graduated from St. Mary of the Springs Academy in 1898. Her journalistic career began in Cleveland, where she was associate editor of the *Catholic Universe Bulletin,* on which her mother, Teresa Beatrice O'Hare (q.v.), was once woman's page editor. After her marriage to Frank Joseph McCormick (q.v.), Dayton engineer and importer, she accompanied him on his trips abroad and sent back feature stories to the New York *Times.* In 1921 she was accepted as a free-lance correspondent of the *Times* and in 1926 became a member of its editorial staff. In 1937 she was awarded the Pulitzer Prize for foreign correspondence. A skillful interviewer and a tireless traveler, she was perhaps America's greatest woman journalist. Her books include *The Hammer and the Scythe . . .*, New York, 1928.

McCORMICK, FRANK JOSEPH (Dec. 7, 1871–Oct. 29, 1954), husband of Anne O'Hare McCormick (q.v.), was born in Dayton, Montgomery County, where his father operated a wholesale plumbing supply company. He was associated with his father's firm for a time and also was an importer and was engaged in the real-estate business. He published a volume of short stories: *Four-in-Hand . . .*, [Dayton, 1906].

MacCRACKEN, HENRY MITCHELL (Sept. 28, 1840–Dec. 24, 1918), clergyman and educator, was born in Oxford, Butler County. After graduating from Miami University in 1857, he taught school for a time in Cedarville and South Charleston. He studied theology at Xenia Seminary and Princeton and was ordained to the Presbyterian ministry in 1863. He was pastor of Westminster Church, Columbus, 1863–67, and of First Presbyterian Church, Toledo, 1868–81. He was chancellor of Western University of Pennsylvania, 1881–84, vice-chancellor of New York University, 1884–91, and chancellor, 1891–1910. While at N.Y.U. he originated the Hall of Fame. Several of his addresses were published. He was active in the American Institute of Christian Philosophy and published a series of lectures outlining its history: *A Propaganda of Philosophy . . .*, New York 1914. DAB 11

MacCRACKEN, HENRY NOBLE (Nov. 19, 1880–), educator, son of Henry Mitchell MacCracken (q.v.), was born in Toledo, Lucas County. He graduated from New York University in 1900 and Harvard University (Ph.D.) in 1907. After teaching English in several colleges, he became president of Vassar College in 1915 and served until 1946. He now lives in Poughkeepsie,

N. Y. He has edited several editions of Shakespeare, published textbooks and public addresses, and written a delightful account of his thirty years at Vassar, which is partly autobiographical but more importantly a discussion of higher education for women and of the history and problems of Vassar: *The Hickory Limb,* New York, 1950. WW 26

McCREA, MARGARETHE. Pseud. See Jessie M. Heiner.

McCULLOCH, ROSCOE CONKLING (Nov. 27, 1880–), lawyer and legislator, was born in Millersburg, Holmes County. After studying law at Ohio State University and Western Reserve University, he was admitted to the Ohio bar in 1903 and afterward practiced in Canton and Columbus. He served in Congress, 1915–21, and briefly in the Senate, 1929–30, when appointed to succeed Theodore E. Burton. He published *The Truth Will Keep Us Free. Who Defeated Ratification of the League of Nations?* [Bexley?, 1944]. WW 30

McCUSKEY, DOROTHY (Nov. 12, 1906–), educator, was born in West Lafayette, Coshocton County. She graduated from the College of Wooster in 1929 and Yale University (Ph.D.) in 1936. She has taught in several institutions, including Rio Grande College and Bowling Green University, and is now on the faculty of Western Michigan University. She has written *Bronson Alcott, Teacher,* New York, 1940. WWAW 1

McDERMONT, CLARKE (1823–April 7, 1881), physician, born in County Antrim, Ireland, came to the United States in 1840. After teaching school in Lexington, Ky., he studied medicine in New York City, Scotland, and Ireland. In 1852 he began practice in Dayton. He served in the Civil War as a surgeon, and after the war he was appointed surgeon general of Ohio. For criticizing the standards of Ohio medical training and practice, he was censured by the state medical society in 1867. He was surgeon-in-chief at the National Soldiers' Home, Dayton, 1867–74. Besides the title below, he wrote a report on inebriate asylums, which was printed in *Transactions* of the American Medical Society and as a separate work.

A History of the First Presbyterian Church of Dayton . . . , Dayton, 1880.

MacDILL, DAVID (Aug. 10, 1826–1903), clergyman and educator, was born in Morning Sun, Preble County. He graduated from Centre College, Ky., in 1849 and was ordained by the Chillicothe Presbytery in 1853. He served churches in Cherry Fork, 1853–76, and Henderson, Ill., 1877–84. In 1884 he became professor of apologetics and homiletics at Xenia Theological Seminary.

The Life and Character of Hon. Robert Morrison, Cincinnati, 1864.

Secret Societies . . . , Pittsburgh, Pa., 1867.

Mosaic Authorship of the Pentateuch . . . , Dayton, 1896.

Modern Pre-millennialism Discussed, Xenia, 1897.

Common Sense and Logic Applied to Darwinism and Teleology, Xenia, 1899.

McDONALD, GERALD DOAN (June 5, 1905–), librarian, was born in Wilmington, Clinton County. He graduated from Wilmington College in 1927. Since 1930 he has been on the staff of the New York Public Library. He has written articles, reviews, and a book: *Educational Motion Pictures and Libraries,* Chicago, 1942. WWLS 3

McDONALD, JOHN (Jan. 28, 1775–Sept. 11, 1853), was born in Northumberland County, Pa. In 1780 his family crossed the Ohio River—then considered the extreme Western frontier—and settled in the Mingo bottom. Here the boy developed into a highly skilled woodsman, acquired a thorough knowledge of the habits and tactics of hostile Indians, and somehow managed to become a proficient surveyor. Of this period in his life McDonald wrote: "I am unable to describe the life, the terror, tumult and confusion of an Indian alarm. Although I have, when young, repeatedly ran clinging to my mother's gown from our cabin to a place of more safety—the confusion and distressing scene of a family in flight, their cabins in flames, their all destroyed, the thousand restless cares and tender sorrows, to which they were incessantly exposed, language fails in describing." This is one of the few personal disclosures which he permitted to creep into his unpretentious *Biographical Sketches of General Nathaniel Massie, General Duncan McArthur, Captain William Wells, and General Simon Kenton; Who Were Early Settlers in the Western Country.* The title is an almost complete misnomer; for the book is an account of the adventures of his subjects on the Western frontier, with the narrator's participation in many of the episodes obscured by a reticence that amounts to a major fault. He wrote with authority on Simon Kenton's forays against the Indians, for as a boy in his teens he had accompanied Kenton. He could describe in minute detail the meager fare of Massie's "starvation tour," for he had shared it, just as he and his brother-in-law, Duncan McArthur, had shared the perils of a number of Massie's surveys in the Scioto and Little Miami regions. Too, he had gone through the War of 1812 with McArthur. When he wrote about William Wells, he was writing about a comrade-in-arms, a fellow member of Kibby's rangers, an organization of fearless scouts and spies who contributed in no small degree to the success of Anthony Wayne. He began writing his sketches for the *Western Christian Advocate* in 1834; only four of the more important ones were included in his book. The first of a series of six sketches on the Wetzel brothers was published in the same periodical on March 29, 1839. McDonald settled on Poplar Ridge, Ross County, in 1802. He was elected several times as justice of the peace and was advanced through the grades to the rank of colonel in the Ohio militia. After the War of 1812 he served two terms in the state senate.

Ernest J. Wessen

Biographical Sketches of General Nathaniel Massie, General Duncan McArthur, Captain William Wells, and General Simon Kenton; Who Were Early Settlers in the Western Country, Cincinnati, 1838.

McDONALD, STELLA BREYFOGLE, was born in Louisville, Ky. She attended Mills College. After marrying Morton McDonald in 1896, she lived in Columbus. Her address in 1950 was Oakland, Calif. She wrote *Clear Shining after Rain, and Other Stories,* New York, 1907.

MacDONALD, SUSANNE KUMLER RIKE (March 3, 1869–), was born in Dayton, Montgomery County, where she lived until 1900. In that year she and her husband, Dr. Everett A. MacDonald, moved to California, where she has lived ever since. Under the pen name Anne MacFarland, she has published three volumes of memoirs since 1955. She also published a book of verse: *The Silver Cord,* [Beverly Hills, Calif., 1933].

McDOUGAL, JOHN (1777–1821), born in Virginia, settled in Chillicothe in 1796. He served as clerk of the Territorial Court and also was a merchant in Chillicothe. His book, which he published at his own expense, probably won him few friends among the local lawyers because he said that he wrote it to protect people against shyster lawyers and land sharks. It was republished at least twice.

The Farmer's Assistant; Or, Every Man His Own Lawyer, Chillicothe, 1813.

McDOWELL, WILLIAM FRASER (Feb. 4, 1858–April 26, 1937), clergyman, was born in Millersburg, Holmes County. He graduated from Ohio Wesleyan University in 1879 and Boston University in 1882. After being ordained to the Methodist ministry in 1882, he served churches in Lodi, Oberlin, and Tiffin, was chancellor of the University of Denver, 1890–99, and was secretary of the Board of Education, Methodist Episcopal Church, 1899–1904. He was elected bishop in 1904 and served in Chicago, 1904–16, and Washington, D. C., 1916–32. He died in Washington, D. C. He published several books on religious themes, e.g., *In All His Offices,* New York, [1937]. WWW 1

McELEVEY, EVA L. (March 28, 1883–), born in Burlington, Iowa, has lived in Youngstown since her marriage to Paul H. McElevey in 1919. After graduating from Wellesley College in 1905, she taught school in Manchester, Iowa, until her marriage. She has written for children's magazines and has published a book of verse for children: *Dad and I,* New York, 1930.

McELROY, JOHN (Aug. 25, 1846–Oct. 12, 1929), journalist, was born in Greenup, Ky., and spent a brief but crucial portion of his life in Ohio. After learning the printing trade in St. Louis, he enlisted in the 16th Illinois Cavalry and served until Jan. 3, 1864, when he was captured by Confederate troops. He wrote a book about his prison stay: *Andersonville: A Story of Rebel Military Prisons . . . ,* Toledo, 1879. It was reprinted in 1957 as *This Was Andersonville.* After the war he came to Ohio to learn pharmacy in a drugstore in Ottawa. He married Elsie Pomeroy, daughter of the owner. He was in Chicago on the staff of the *Inter-Ocean,* 1868–74. From 1874 to 1884 he edited the Toledo *Blade.* He then joined the *National Tribune* in Washington, D. C., where he spent the remainder of his life. He wrote a number of biographies and other books, including nine humorous Civil War stories about an imaginary soldier, Si Klegg, which were first published in the *National Tribune.*

McELWAINE, ETHYL (Oct. 23, 1881–), was born in Grove City, Franklin County. She taught school in Washington Court House and other communities and is now living in Steubenville. Her poems have appeared in various newspapers and magazines, and she has published a collection: *Sunset Gold,* [Washington Court House], 1938.

MacELWANE, JAMES BERNARD (Sept. 28, 1883–Feb. 15, 1956), clergyman and educator, was born near Port Clinton, Ottawa County. He graduated from St. Louis University in 1910 and the University of California (Ph.D.) in 1923. He was ordained a Roman Catholic priest in 1918 and except for two years at the University of California (1923–25) was on the faculty of St. Louis University, 1912–56. An internationally recognized geophysicist, he wrote textbooks, numerous technical articles on seismology, and *When the Earth Quakes,* Milwaukee, [1947]. WWW 3

McENIRY, E. C. (April 11, 1891–), Catholic priest, was born in County Tipperary, Ireland. He came to New York City in 1910, was educated in that city, and was ordained to the priesthood in 1921. He became a teacher at Aquinas High School, Columbus, in 1922 and chaplain of Mt. Carmel Hospital in 1925. He is now chaplain of St. Mary's Hospital, Philadelphia. He has translated devotional works from Spanish, edited the *Meditations* of St. Thomas Aquinas, and written a pamphlet honoring Father Albert O'Brien: *Hero Priest of the Ohio Penitentiary Fire . . . ,* [Somerset, 1934].

MacFARLAND, ANNE, Pseud. See Susanne K. R. MacDonald.

McFARLAND, JEANNETTE (Oct. 30, 1887–), educator, was born in Cambridge, Guernsey County. She attended Muskingum College and was an English teacher at Cambridge High School for a number of years. She now lives in Cambridge. She has published several books, including a collection of travel letters and a book of verse: *The Guernsey Hills and Other Sketches,* Cambridge, 1930.

McFARLAND, ROBERT WHITE (June 16, 1825–Oct. 23, 1910), educator, was born near Urbana, Champaign County. After completing the district school at the age of fourteen, he alternately taught country schools and attended college until 1847, when he graduated from Ohio Wesleyan University. He taught at Greenfield Seminary, 1848–51, was superintendent of schools in Chillicothe, 1851–53, and taught at Madison College, 1853–56. He taught at Miami University, 1856–73, and Ohio State University, 1873–85. After serving three years as president of Miami University, 1885–88, he worked as a mining engineer. Perhaps his best-known accomplishment was computing the eccentricity of the earth's orbit and the longitude of its perihelion. He published many scientific articles and a number of textbooks on Virgil, mathematics, and astronomy. The pamphlet below recounts the service of the 86th O.V.I., in which he was lieutenant colonel.

The Surrender of Cumberland Gap, September 9, 1863, Columbus, 1898.

McGAFFEY, ERNEST (Aug. 30, 1861– ?), journalist and lawyer, was born in London, Madison County. In 1881 he went to Chicago, where he practiced law, wrote for the *Inter-Ocean* and other newspapers, and was secretary to Mayor Carter Harrison. His last known address was Los Angeles.

Poems of Gun and Rod, New York, 1892.
Poems, New York, 1895.
A California Idyl, San Francisco, [1899].
Poems of the Town, Boston, 1901.
Sonnets to a Wife, St. Louis, Mo., 1901.
Cosmos, Wausau, Wis., [1903].
Outdoors; A Book of the Woods, Fields and Marshlands, New York, 1907.
Ballades and Idyls, Los Angeles, 1931.
War, [Los Angeles, 1937].
Ballades, [Los Angeles, 1938].

MacGAHAN, JANUARIUS ALOYSIUS (June 12, 1844–June 9, 1878), foreign correspondent, was born on a small farm near New Lexington, Perry County. When he was seven, his father died, but he worked on the farm and attended local schools until he was sixteen. After working in St. Louis as a bookkeeper for two years, he resolved to go to Europe to study international law. After living for several years in London, Brussels, and Paris, he was preparing to return home when the Franco-Prussian War broke out. Here he found his true vocation. Partly through the influence of his cousin, General Philip Sheridan, he was made correspondent for the New York *Herald.* His dispatches describing the retreat of General Bourbaki and other events aroused widespread attention. After the war he covered news events in various parts of Europe. He was a favorite of the Russian czar's household. He developed a love for Russia and married a Russian girl. He covered the Russian campaign against Khiva, riding across central Asia to join the expedition, though forbidden to do so by the Russian government. He also reported the Carlist war in Spain, the voyage of the *Pandora* to the Arctic, and Turkish atrocities in Bulgaria. The last reports did much to win British sympathy for the Bulgarian cause and led to his being revered in Bulgaria as "the Liberator." Six years after his death from typhus in Constantinople, the Ohio Assembly arranged that his body be returned on a U. S. cruiser. His grave in New Lexington is still visited periodically by Bulgarian patriots and diplomats.

Campaigning on the Oxus, and the Fall of Khiva, New York, 1874.
The Turkish Atrocities in Bulgaria, London, 1876.
Under the Northern Lights, London, 1876.

McGAUGHY, JAMES RALPH (Sept. 4, 1888–June 21, 1954), educator, was born in Chesterville, Morrow County. He graduated from Park College in 1912 and Columbia University (Ph.D.) in 1924. He was a school superintendent in Ohio, a teacher at Ohio Wesleyan University, 1907–20, and a member of the education faculty, Columbia University, 1921–41. He lived in Chesterville after his retirement. He wrote numerous articles on educational problems, textbooks, and *An Evaluation of the Elementary School* . . . , Indianapolis, [1937]. WWW 3

McGAVRAN, SAMUEL B. (Nov. 25, 1847–1922), physician, was born near Conotton, Harrison County. He attended country schools until he was fourteen, spent two years at New Hagerstown Academy, taught school for five years, studied at Scio College, and in 1872 graduated from Cleveland Medical College. He practiced at Bowerston, 1874–82, and in 1882 moved to Cadiz, where he spent the remainder of his life.

A Brief History of Harrison County, Ohio, Cadiz, 1894.

M'GAW, JAMES FRANKLIN (1823–1872), was born in Chambersburg, Pa. When he was ten years old, his family settled in Massillon, where the boy attended local schools. For a time he taught at a country school seven miles south of Wooster, and during this period he wrote the new much-sought-after Brown narrative. In 1854 he moved to Washington, Richland County, and appears to have spent much of his time during the next few years in interviewing surviving pioneers and gathering material for his *Philip Seymour.* His first publication in Mansfield, *The Impressed Seaman,* was purely fictional and could have been drawn from any one of a dozen books then available in the vicinity. Nor was *Philip Seymour,* which followed, an entirely original work. M'Gaw's publisher, General Roeliff Brinkerhoff (q.v.), acquired the files of the Mansfield paper, the *Richland Jeffersonian,* in 1855. In the issues of March 28 and April 4, 1840, had appeared a story entitled "The Battle" by an anonymous author. This was an acceptable account of the Copus massacre in the autumn of 1812, and it was upon this framework that M'Gaw draped in fictional form the result of his several years of research. The book provides the most authentic source on one of the most colorful episodes in the frontier history of north central Ohio. During the Civil War M'Gaw taught school at Butler, Ind. He died at Tyner City, Ind.

A Thrilling Narrative of Samuel Brown's Horrible Sufferings and Miraculous Escape, Uhrichsville, 1852.
The Impressed Seaman; Life on Board a British Man-of-war, Mansfield, 1857.
Philip Seymour, or Pioneer Life in Richland County . . . , Mansfield, 1858.

McGEHEAN, THOMAS (April 10, 1835– ?), was born in Clermont County. Although he published an autobiography, information concerning his life is somewhat meager. He says that he grew up in Hamilton, where he learned the shoemaker's trade, dealt in horses and real estate, and served one term as marshal. He also says that he lived in Dayton, Covington, Ky., and Cincinnati. His book is largely devoted to an account of the murder of Thomas S. Myers in Hamilton, for which he was tried three times, and to lurid attacks on those he considered his enemies. Clement L. Vallandigham (q.v.), one of his defense attorneys, was accidentally shot at Lebanon while demonstrating to a colleague that Myers might have killed himself accidentally.

A History of the Life and Trials of Thomas McGehean . . . , Cincinnati, 1874.

McGIFFERT, ARTHUR CUSHMAN (March 4, 1861–Feb. 25, 1933), church historian, born in Sauquoit, N. Y., graduated from Western Reserve University in 1882; and after studying at Union Theological Seminary and in Germany, he was ordained a Presbyterian minister in Cleveland. He was on the faculty of Lane Seminary, Cincinnati, 1888–93, before accepting an appointment at Union Seminary, where he remained until 1927. A prolific scholar, he produced numerous historical and biographical works. He was induced to join the Congregational Church by a wave of controversy in Presbyterian governing bodies after the publication of *A History of Christianity in the Apostolic Age,* New York, 1897.

McGIFFERT, ARTHUR CUSHMAN, JR. (Nov. 27, 1892–), clergyman and educator, was born in Cincinnati, Hamilton County, the son of Arthur C. McGiffert (q.v.). He graduated from Harvard University in 1913 and Union Theological Seminary in 1917. He served as a Congregational pastor in Lowell, Mass., 1920–26, was on the faculty of Chicago Theological Seminary, 1926–39, was president of Pacific School of Religion, 1939–45, and president of Chicago Seminary since 1946. He has published *Jonathan Edwards,* New York, 1932. WW 30

McGIFFERT, JOSEPH NELSON (Dec. 8, 1829–June 20, 1896), clergyman, was born in New York City. After graduating from Auburn Seminary in 1853, he was ordained to the Presbyterian ministry and served churches in Hillsdale, N. Y., and Sauquoit, N. Y., 1853–66. He was installed pastor of First Presbyterian Church, Ashtabula, in 1866 and served there for the last thirty years of his life. He held various offices in the Cleveland Presbytery and the Synod of Ohio.

History of the Presbyterian Church of Ashtabula . . . , Ashtabula, 1876.

McGILL, MARY ROBSON (1870–March 1, 1926), was born in Nelsonville, Athens County, but spent much of her life in Columbus. She contributed poems, feature stories, and news stories to a variety of newspapers in Columbus and elsewhere. A collection of her writings was published: *You and Your Friends,* Columbus, [1906].

McGINNIS, FREDERICK ALPHONSO (Feb. 13, 1887–), educator, was born in West Mansfield, Logan County. He graduated from the University of Chicago in 1922 and the University of Cincinnati (Ed.D.) in 1940. He has served on the Wilberforce University faculty as professor of English, as dean, vice president, and registrar since 1922. Besides articles on education, he has published *A History and an Interpretation of Wilberforce University,* Wilberforce, 1941. WWMW 49

McGINNIS, RALPH JOCELYN (Nov. 13, 1894–), journalist, was born in Kingston, Ross County. He served in the French army, 1915–18, and in the A.E.F., 1918–19. He graduated from Miami University in 1921, was an Associated Press correspondent, 1921–28, headed the journalism department, Miami University, 1928–44, and since 1945 has edited the *Farm Quarterly* in Cincinnati. He has published *History of Oxford, Ohio . . . ,* Oxford, 1930. WW 30

MacGOWAN, ALICE (Dec. 10, 1858–March 10, 1947), sister of Grace MacGowan Cooke (q.v.), was born in Perrysburg, Lucas County. She was educated in Chattanooga, Tenn., where her father moved after becoming editor of the Chattanooga *Times.* She accompanied her sister to Upton Sinclair's Helicon Hall in New Jersey and from there to Carmel-by-the-Sea, Calif., where she spent the remainder of her life. She collaborated with her sister on several books and wrote several alone, including a novel of the Civil War: *The Sword in the Mountains,* New York, 1910. WW 21

McGRANE, REGINALD CHARLES (July 28, 1889–), educator, was born in Cincinnati, Hamilton County. He graduated from the University of Cincinnati in 1912 and the University of Chicago (Ph.D.) in 1915. He has been a member of the history department, University of Cincinnati, since 1915. Besides textbooks and historical articles, he has published *William Allen; A Study in Western Democracy,* [Columbus, 1925]. WW 30

McGREW, THOMAS FLETCHER (April 16, 1817–Nov. 4, 1903), banker, was born in Steubenville, Jefferson County. In 1865 he became cashier of Mad River National Bank, Springfield, and later was made president. He is buried in Springfield.

Letters from Europe, Cincinnati, 1885.
Mohammed and the Mohammedan Religion, Cincinnati, 1892.
A Study in Buddhism, Cincinnati, 1894.

McGROARTY, WILLIAM BUCKNER (Nov. 29, 1858–Nov. 9, 1950), was born in Cincinnati, Hamilton County. He spent a part of his boyhood in Georgetown, Brown County, and lived in Cincinnati again, 1880–91. In 1891 he moved to Virginia, where he spent the remainder of his life. He published numerous historical and genealogical papers and a book: *The Old Presbyterian Meeting House at Alexandria, Virginia . . . ,* Richmond, Va., 1940.

McGUFFEY, ALEXANDER HAMILTON. See William H. McGuffey.

McGUFFEY, WILLIAM HOLMES (Sept. 23, 1800–May 4, 1873), educator, was born in Washington County, Pa., but was reared on a farm near Youngstown, where his family moved in 1802. "William H. McGuffey was little more than McGuffey's Readers," a noted educator and historian of the Middle West wrote in 1898. His fame rests upon eleven elementary schoolbooks which bear the name McGuffey, and of which, it is estimated, more than 120,000,000 copies have been published since 1836. He was also a professor in three colleges, president of two universities, a popular speaker, and a minister in the Presbyterian Church. Of the eleven McGuffey schoolbooks, William compiled or supervised the compilation of the first four Readers, which were published by Truman & Smith of Cincinnati in 1836 and 1837. Some controversy exists over the amount of assistance he received from others. His chief collaborator was his younger brother, Alexander Hamilton McGuffey (1816–June 4, 1896), a teacher at Woodward College and later a lawyer. Alexander helped make the selections for the first four Readers. The *Primer,* published in 1837, is generally credited to William, but one writer who knew the family says that Mrs. McGuffey was the author. Alexander compiled the *Eclectic Progressive Spelling Book,* published probably in 1837, and *McGuffey's Rhetorical Guide or Fifth Reader* (1844). The *Sixth Reader* (1857), the *High School Reader* (1857), the *Eclectic Speaker* (1858), and the *Juvenile Speaker* (1860) were compiled by other editors employed by the publisher. William attended Washington College in Pennsylvania, and in March, 1826, he was elected professor of Latin, Greek, and Hebrew and ex-officio librarian at Miami University. In 1833 he was named professor of mental philosophy and philology. He spent ten years at Miami, the last five of them in open conflict with the administration of the university. In 1836 he was named to the presidency of Cincinnati College and became party to an effort to expropriate Miami's endowment for the Cincinnati institution. When that failed in the legislature, Cincinnati College withered, and McGuffey resigned in 1839 to accept the presidency of Ohio University at Athens. In 1843 he resigned from Ohio University and returned to Cincinnati, where he taught at Woodward College for two years. He was then named professor of philosophy at the University of Virginia, a position he retained until his death. McGuffey was twice married, first to Harriet Spinning of Dayton, who died in 1850 after bearing five children, and second to Laura Howard of Charlottesville, Va., who bore him a daughter. Early in his career at Miami, McGuffey developed an interest in elementary education and in teaching in the "common schools." He participated in the meetings of the Western Literary Institute and College of Professional Teachers, and was a speaker at teachers' conventions throughout the state. He was an associate of Calvin E. Stowe and Samuel Lewis in the common school movement and campaigned throughout Ohio with Lewis, superintendent of common schools, in an effort to develop the public school system. The Readers were a further contribution to the movement. They introduced a combination method of teaching spelling and reading, prescribed drills on the syllable for teaching enunciation, and used pictures to illustrate meaning. The Readers met with immediate success in the Middle West and the South. Within a year after the *Fourth Reader* was printed, Truman & Smith announced that they had published a quarter of a million of the McGuffey series, including the Primer and the Speller. In Sept., 1838, the publishers and McGuffey were sued by the publishers of Samuel F. Worcester of Massachusetts for having "pirated" several of Worcester's books and republished them. An injunction was granted against McGuffey's publishers, and a settlement was made out of court. Truman & Smith immediately revised the Readers, eliminating the challenged materials. During the nineteenth century the series was revised a number of times.

James H. Rodabaugh

McGUIRE, PAT. Pseud. See Charles R. Vaughan.

MACHETANZ, FREDERICK (Feb. 20, 1908–), artist, was born in Kenton, Hardin County. After graduating from Ohio State University in 1930, he studied art in Chicago. In 1935 he went to Alaska to visit an uncle and remained for two years. He has since returned periodically to Alaska and has lectured widely on his life there. He has written and illustrated a number of books, e.g., *On Arctic Ice,* New York, [1940].

McILVAINE, CHARLES PETTIT (Jan. 18, 1799–March 13, 1873), clergyman, born in Burlington, N. J., studied at the College of New Jersey (Princeton) and was ordained an Episcopal priest in 1823. His early career won him wide attention in Washington, D. C., and Brooklyn, N. Y., because of his effective evangelical preaching. Consecrated bishop of Ohio in 1832, he settled at Gambier the following year. His efforts did much to foster the growth of Kenyon College. In 1846 he moved to Clifton, which was thereafter his home and where he now is buried. He often traveled in England and on the Continent. Because of his cordial relations with the British, President Lincoln asked him to visit England in 1861 when diplomatic relations were under strain. He died in Florence, Italy, and before his body was returned to Ohio it was taken to England, where a funeral service was held in Westminster Abbey. He published numerous pamphlets, sermons, and charges to the clergy besides the listed titles.

Rev. Mr. M'Ilvaine in Answer to the Rev. Henry U. Onderdonk, Philadelphia, 1827.
The Evidences of Christianity . . . , New York, 1832.
Oxford Divinity . . . , Philadelphia, 1841.
The Sinner's Justification before God . . . , New York, 1850.
The Temple of God; Or, the Holy Catholic Church . . . , Philadelphia, 1860.
The Christian's Duty in the Present Crisis, [Cincinnati, 1861].
Righteousness by Faith . . . , Philadelphia, 1862.
The Work of Preaching Christ, Boston, 1871.

McINTOSH, BURR WILLIAM (1862–April 28, 1942), journalist and actor, was born in Wellsville, Columbiana County. After attending Lafayette College and Princeton University, he became a reporter on the Philadelphia *News* in 1884. In 1885 he made his stage debut and appeared in numerous plays. He was a correspondent in Cuba in 1898 and started the *Burr McIntosh Monthly* in 1902. During World War I he was an entertainer in France and Germany. His death occurred in New York City.

Summer Folks. Observations, Philadelphia, [1887].
The Little I Saw of Cuba, London, [1899].

McINTYRE, OSCAR ODD (Feb. 18, 1884–Feb. 14, 1938), journalist, was born in Plattsburg, Mo. His mother died when he was three, and two years later he was sent to live with his paternal grandmother in Gallipolis, Gallia County, the town that he later considered home. After attending Gallipolis Academy, he worked as a reporter on the Gallipolis *Daily Sun* and on the *Journal.* His father sent him to a Cincinnati business college, but he returned to journalism and worked on the East Liverpool *Morning Tribune,* 1904–05, the Dayton *Herald,* 1906, and the Cincinnati *Post,* 1907–11. Ray Long, for whom he had worked on the *Post,* persuaded him to move to New York in 1911. After several false starts he began free-lance writing in 1912, writing a column about New York and mailing it to newspapers to serve his various public relations clients. The column, "New York Day by Day," proved popular and was soon syndicated nationally. He also wrote for *Cosmopolitan,* edited by Ray Long, and other magazines. The image of a small-town boy in the metropolis and the blend of rustic innocence and urban sophistication proved irresistible to millions of readers. He published four collections of his columns and magazine pieces, e.g., *The Big Town . . . ,* New York, 1935. DAB 22

McKAY, GEORGE LESLIE (Oct. 12, 1895–), was born in Columbus Grove, Putnam County, but lived in Toledo, 1900–16. He attended the College of Wooster, 1914–16, served in World War I, graduated from the University of Chicago in 1920, and studied at the Library School of the New York Public Library. After teaching in Perrysburg for a year and serving with the American Red Cross in Paris for a year, he became curator of the Grolier Club, New York City, in 1923, and in 1944 he was made librarian. He has published numerous articles, catalogues, bibliographies, and other works, e.g., *Early American Currency . . . ,* New York, 1944. WWE 6

McKAY, LUCINDA E. (Sept. 7, 1840–Nov. 29, 1922), was born in Chester Township, Clinton County. A member of the Baptist church, she published several books of a religious nature, e.g., *The Book Sealed with Seven Seals and the Sounding of the Seven Angels . . . ,* Cincinnati, [1914].

McKAY, MARTHA NICHOLSON (1843–March 4, 1934), was born in Warren County. She married Horace McKay and thereafter lived in Indianapolis, Ind. She was active in civic affairs and the women's suffrage movement.

Literary Clubs of Indiana, Indianapolis, 1894.
When the Tide Turned in the Civil War, Indianapolis, 1929.

McKEE, PHILIP JUDSON (c.1892–March 29, 1957), advertising executive, was born in Dayton, Montgomery County. He worked in advertising and public relations counseling, and at the time of his death was head of his own firm. Sherwood Anderson wrote a preface for his novel, *Big Town,* New York, [1931].

McKELL, DAVID McCANDLESS (Dec. 4, 1881–), was born in Chillicothe, Ross County. He graduated from the U. S. Military Academy in 1904 and served in the U. S. Army until 1922. In 1922 he graduated from San Francisco Law School. He has been president of the Chillicothe Telephone Company since 1938. Actively interested in Ross County history, he has been president of the county historical society since 1947 and has published several historical articles and pamphlets, e.g., *Ross County's Little Known Indian Years, 1752-1774,* Chillicothe, 1942.

McKELVEY, A. T. (March 23, 1844– ?), was born in Belfast, Ireland, but was brought at the age of five to Wheeling, Va. He worked as a telegrapher and also operated a fruit farm in Belmont County. He was elected to the Ohio Assembly in 1887. He compiled *Centennial History of Belmont County* . . . , Chicago, 1903.

McKENNEY, RUTH (Nov. 18, 1911–), was born in Mishawaka, Ind., but her family moved to Cleveland when she was six. She grew up in that city and graduated from Shaw High School in 1928. While attending Ohio State University, she wrote for the *Lantern,* and in 1930 she was a reporter on the Columbus *Dispatch.* She also worked on the Akron *Beacon-Journal,* 1932–33, and on the New York *Post,* 1934–36. Active in left-wing reform movements of the 1930s, she was on the staff of *New Masses.* A series of stories in *The New Yorker* became her most successful book, *My Sister Eileen,* New York, [1938]. It was later highly popular as a play, a motion picture, and, retitled *Wonderful Town,* a musical comedy. She has lived abroad much of the time since 1947. The book that she once said she preferred to all her others is a study of labor conditions in Akron during the depression: *Industrial Valley,* New York, [1939].

McKEOWN, MATTHEW C. (1832–March 11, 1908), miner and grocer, was born in Ireland in 1832 and accompanied his parents to Wheeling, Va., in 1855. Three years later he went to Australia and New Zealand, where he spent ten years as a miner, an experience recounted in his only book. Upon his return in 1868 he settled in Barnesville, where he operated a grocery store until his death.

Some Memories of a Miner's Life . . . , Barnesville, 1893.

MACKIE, PAULINE BRADFORD. See Pauline B. M. Hopkins.

McKINLEY, CHARLES FREDERICK (Aug. 24, 1913–), educator, was born in Mansfield, Richland County. He graduated from Kenyon College and Trinity College, Dublin (Ph.D.). He has taught at Kenyon College, the State University of Iowa, and Queen Aliyah College, Iraq. He is now on the faculty of Hiram College. He has written *A Voyage to the British Isles* . . . , Mt. Vernon, 1940, and a novel: *Harriet,* New York, 1946.

McKINLEY, WILLIAM (Jan. 29, 1843–Sept. 14, 1901), 25th President of the United States, was born in Niles, Trumbull County. He was educated at Poland and Allegheny College, Pa. After serving in the Civil War with the 23rd O.V.I., he read law and in 1867 began practice in Canton, which was his residence thereafter. He took an active part in state politics and early in his career attracted the attention of Mark Hanna (q.v.) and other party leaders. He served in Congress, 1877–83 and 1885–91, and was governor, 1892–96. Elected to the Presidency in 1896 after a front porch campaign, conducted from his home in Canton, he was most successful in his relations with Congress. Generally conservative in his views, he was identified in the public mind with the protective tariff. On Sept. 6, 1901, he was shot in Buffalo, N. Y. He died eight days later and is buried in Canton. Besides the collections of speeches listed below, many of his addresses were issued separately as political pamphlets.

Speeches and Addresses . . . , New York, 1893.

Life and Speeches . . . , New York, 1896.

McKinley's Masterpieces . . . , Boston, 1896.

McKinley's Speeches in October . . . , Canton, [1896].

McKinley's Speeches in September, Canton, [1896].

The Tariff in the Days of Henry Clay, and Since . . . , New York, 1896.

Speeches and Addresses . . . , New York, 1900.

McKINNEY, ARTHUR LAYTON (Sept. 16, 1819–Feb. 20, 1901), clergyman and lawyer, was born in Clark County but was reared in Greene County. In 1843 he was ordained a minister of the Christian Church and preached in western Indiana. In 1853, after graduating from Wabash College, he was made principal of Antioch College preparatory school. In 1857 he organized the Christian Church at Troy. He served in the Civil War as chaplain of the 71st O.V.I. After the war he was elected to several offices in Miami County, and in 1879 he was admitted to the bar and began practice in Troy.

Memoir of Elder Isaac N. Walter, Cincinnati, 1858.

Positive Theology . . . , Cincinnati, 1860.

McKINNEY, FRANK LOUIS (Oct. 3, 1887–May 31, 1951), executive, was born in St. Louis, Mo. After working on the St. Louis *Globe-Democrat,* the Cincinnati *American,* and other newspapers, he joined the Ohio State Telephone Company in 1914. He was general commercial superintendent when the company was purchased by Ohio Bell Telephone Co. in 1921. He then served as secretary-treasurer of the Ohio Independent Telephone Association, 1921–44. After his retirement he lived in Pomona, Calif. He wrote *Our Looney Liberals,* Columbus, [1934].

McKINNEY, THOMAS EMERY (April 26, 1864–April 12, 1930), educator, was born in Hebron, W. Va. After graduating from Marietta College in 1887, he served on the faculty, 1890–1906, and later taught at Wesleyan University, Conn., 1906–08, and the University of South Dakota, 1908–28. He died in Marietta. His writings include *Essays and Addresses,* [Chicago, 1924]. WWW 1

MACKLEY, JOHN H. (Oct. 13, 1847–July 29, 1918), was born in Oak Hill, Jackson County. He served as a drummer in the first two years of the Civil War and as an infantryman from 1863 until the end of the war. He worked for a number of years on the Jackson *Standard,* owned by his father, and afterward was Columbus correspondent for the Cincinnati *Tribune* and was on the staff of the Cleveland *Plain Dealer.* He died in Cleveland.

Idle Rhymings. Collection of Thoughts Jotted Down in Leisure Moments, Jackson, 1885.

McKNIGHT, GEORGE HARLEY (April 24, 1871–Aug. 15, 1951), educator, was born in Sterling Valley, N. Y. After graduating from Cornell University (A.B., 1892; Ph.D., 1896), he studied in Europe for two years. He was a member of the English faculty, Ohio State University, 1899–1941. After his retirement he continued to live in Columbus. He published numerous professional articles and an important study of language: *English Words and Their Backgrounds,* New York, 1923. WW 23

McLAIN, JOHN SCUDDER (May 26, 1853–Nov. 17, 1931), journalist, was born in Brown County. After graduating from Wabash College in 1877, he edited newspapers in Kansas and Minnesota. He wrote *Alaska and the Klondike,* New York, 1905. WWW 1

McLANDBURGH, FLORENCE (April 22, 1850– ?), was born in Chillicothe, Ross County. In 1863 her family moved to Chicago, which remained her home thereafter, although she traveled widely. She published short stories in various periodicals.

The Automaton Ear, and Other Sketches, Chicago, 1876.

McLANE, WILLIAM WARD (Nov. 13, 1846–June 4, 1931), pastor of Second Presbyterian Church, Steubenville, 1878–83, wrote several books on religious themes, e.g., *The Cross in the Light of To-day,* Philadelphia, 1883.

McLAREN, WILLIAM EDWARD (Dec. 13, 1831–Feb. 19, 1905), Episcopal bishop of Illinois, was rector of Trinity Church, Cleveland, 1872–75. His writings include *The Holy Priest,* Milwaukee, 1899.

McLAUGHLIN, EDWARD (Jan. 9, 1798–Nov. 15, 1861), printer, was born near Stamford, Conn. Following an eventful career in the navy, he appears to have settled in Cincinnati around 1830. Edward D. Mansfield (q.v.) refers to him as a printer who settled in Cincinnati between 1828 and 1835. By 1841 he must have been well entrenched among the Cincinnati literati, for in that year he published his single volume of verse, which was dedicated to Nicholas Longworth and which contained poems inscribed to Peyton S. Symmes, Bellamy Storer, and Jacob Burnet. Yet he was soon forgotten, for by 1860 the well-posted William T. Coggeshall found it necessary to rely upon the preface of McLaughlin's book for biographical data. However, it is probable that he returned to the East, for his book was reissued in New York in 1850 as *The Coral Gift.*

The Lovers of the Deep: In Four Cantos; to Which Is Added a Variety of Miscellaneous Poems, Cincinnati, 1841.

McLAUGHLIN, GEORGE (c.1831–Oct. 11, 1893), brother of Mary Louise McLaughlin (q.v.), was born in Cincinnati, Hamilton County. He was employed as an accountant by various Cincinnati firms. He took his own life at the age of 62.

Art Work of Cincinnati, Chicago, 1893.

McLAUGHLIN, MARY LOUISE (Sept. 29, 1847–Jan. 16, 1939), artist, sister of George McLaughlin (q.v.), was born in Cincinnati, Hamilton County. In 1877 she began experimenting with pottery and produced the first decorative underglaze work done in the city. She organized the Pottery Club and built a kiln at her home in Mt. Auburn. She was also interested in wood carving, metalwork, and tapestry and won numerous medals for her work in these fields. After living as a recluse for almost twenty years, she died in Cincinnati. Besides technical manuals on art, she wrote *An Epitome of History from Pre-historic Times to the End of the Great War,* Boston, 1923. WWW 1

McLEAN, ARCHIBALD (Sept. 6, 1849–Dec. 15, 1920), clergyman, was born on a farm near Summerside, Prince Edward Island, Canada. He became a carriage maker, but in 1871, desiring to enter the ministry, he enrolled in Bethany College, W. Va. After graduating in 1874, he was ordained and became pastor of the Christian Church, Mount Healthy, where he remained until 1885. After 1885, he devoted as much of his time as possible to foreign missions. In 1888 he began to publish the *Missionary Intelligencer* in Cincinnati. He was president of the Ecumenical Missionary Society, 1900–19. Besides the titles below, he published tracts and sermons, most of them related to the missionary effort of his church.

A Circuit of the Globe; A Series of Letters of Travel . . . , St. Louis, Mo., 1897.

Where the Book Speaks . . . , New York, [1907].

Alexander Campbell as a Preacher . . . , New York, [1908].

Epoch Makers of Modern Missions, New York, [1912].

The Primacy of the Missionary, and Other Addresses, St. Louis, Mo., 1920.

The History of the Foreign Christian Missionary Society, New York, 1921.

MacLEAN, JOHN PATTERSON (March 12, 1848–Aug. 12, 1939), clergyman, was born in Franklin, Warren County. After studying at Normal University and St. Lawrence Seminary, he became a Universalist minister and preached in Ohio and other states until 1906. He later returned to the ministry in 1921, when he began preaching in Greenville. Besides the titles below, he wrote several studies of the MacLean family history, portions of Smithsonian Institution reports, and numerous articles. He died in Greenville and is buried in Franklin.

A Manual of the Antiquity of Man, New York, 1875.

Mastodon, Mammoth, and Man, Cincinnati, 1878.

The Mound Builders . . . , Cincinnati, 1879.

Jewish Nature Worship . . . , Cincinnati, 1882.

An Historical, Archaeological and Geological Examination of Fingal's Cave . . . , Cincinnati, 1890.

A Critical Examination of the Evidences Adduced to Establish the Theory of the Norse Discovery of America, Chicago, 1892.

An Historical Account of the Settlements of Scotch Highlanders in America Prior to the Peace of 1873 . . . , Cleveland, 1900.

The Archaeological Collection of the Western Reserve Historical Society, Cleveland, 1901.

A Sketch of the Life and Labors of Richard McNemar, Franklin, 1905.

Shakers of Ohio . . . , Columbus, 1907.

Flora MacDonald in America . . . , Lumberton, N. C., 1909.

An Epitome of the Superstitions of the Highlanders . . . , Franklin, 1917.

History of the Island of Mull . . . , Greenville, 1923.

McLEISH, JOHN LEWIN (Feb. 17, 1871–Feb. 2, 1928), physician, was born in Chicago. At the age of ten he came to Cincinnati, where he was educated in the public schools. He graduated from Princeton University in 1894 and the Medical College of Ohio in 1897. He practiced in Cincinnati, where he also was director of *Americanization Activities,* published in Cincinnati. During World War I he was managing editor of *American Home News,* published in London, England.

Iturbide, a Soldier of Mexico . . . , New York, [1898].

Highlights of the Mexican Revolution, Aurora, Mo., 1919.

The Americanization Problem in Cincinnati, Cincinnati, [1921].

McLEOD, CORNELIUS DONALD. See Xavier Donald MacLeod.

M'LEOD, DONALD (1779–July 22, 1879), was born in Inverness, Scotland, and attended the University of Aberdeen. He served in the British navy and also in the army, including service at the Battle of Waterloo. He settled in Prescott, Ontario, Canada, and participated in the rebellion of 1837, after which he fled to Cleveland. He was later pardoned by Queen Victoria. He died in Cleveland at the age of 100.

A Brief Review of the Settlement of Upper Canada . . . , Cleveland, 1841.

History of Wiskonsan . . . , Buffalo, 1846.

Donald McLeod's Gloomy Memories in the Highlands of Scotland . . . , Toronto, 1857.

MacLEOD, XAVIER DONALD (Nov. 17, 1821–July 20, 1865), clergyman, was born in New York City, the son of Alexander McLeod, a leader in the Reformed Presbyterian Church. A convert to the Episcopal Church in 1845, he was converted to Catholicism in 1852, became a priest, and altered his original name from Cornelius to Xavier. In the last few years of his life he was professor of rhetoric at Mount St. Mary's College. He was killed near Cincinnati in a railway accident. He published novels, biographies, and poetry. One of his novels was *Our Lady of Litanies,* Cincinnati, 1861.

McLUKE, LUKE. Pseud. See James S. Hastings.

McMAHON, AMOS PHILIP (Aug. 14, 1890–June 21, 1947), educator, was born in Warren, Trumbull County. He graduated from Harvard University (A.B., 1913; Ph.D., 1916), and from 1917 until his death was in the fine arts department of New York University. He published several books on art, e.g., *The Meaning of Art,* New York, [1930]. WWW 2

McMAHON, WILLIAM (Feb. 9, 1847– ?), clergyman, born in County Wicklow, Ireland, was brought to the United States when he was four years old. His parents lived in Cleveland until 1866 and then moved to Olmsted Falls. After graduating from St. Louis College in 1869 and from St. Mary's Seminary in 1872, he was ordained a Roman Catholic priest. He served three years at Elmore near Toledo and then became pastor of St. Bridget's Church, Cleveland. The book below is an account of a round-the-world trip which was a gift from the St. Bridget's congregation to commemorate the silver jubilee of his ordination.

A Journey with the Sun around the World, [Cleveland, 1900].

McMANUS, SILAS BETTES (Sept. 17, 1845–April 15, 1917), physician, was born in Rootstown, Portage County, but spent most of his life in Indiana. He graduated from Medical College, Fort Wayne. Throughout his career he contributed poems to various periodicals.

For What Would You Take Me; And Nine or Ten Other Rhymes, LaGrange, Ind., [1894].

Rural Rhymes, Cincinnati, [1898].

MacMANUS, THEODORE FRANCIS (1873–Sept. 12, 1940), advertising man, born in Buffalo, N. Y., lived for a number of years in Toledo. At the age of nineteen he was managing editor of the Toledo *Commercial.* He opened an advertising agency in Toledo, but later moved to Detroit, where he held contracts with various automobile companies. He died in Sudbury, Ontario, Canada. He published *The Sword-Arm of Business,* New York, [1927], and considerable poetry, including at least one collection: *A Book of Verse,* Detroit, 1922.

MacMASTER, HOMER EUGENE (Aug. 6, 1881–May 18, 1942), was born in Monroe County and also lived in Belmont County. A graduate of the College of Wooster, he was active in Boy Scout and Y.M.C.A. work. He died in San Marino, Calif. He collected Lincolniana as an avocation and published a volume of poetry: *Abraham Lincoln Looks across the Mall,* Boston, [1932].

MacMILLAN, GEORGE WHITFIELD (Aug. 19, 1827–May 6, 1918), clergyman, was born in York County, Pa. After graduating from Princeton Theological Seminary in 1857, he served several Presbyterian churches before becoming president of Richmond College, Jefferson County. He died in Richmond. He wrote *The Creation and Development of the Universe,* Steubenville, 1902.

McMILLAN, HOMER (Dec. 20, 1873–Feb. 8, 1958), clergyman, was born near Cedarville, Greene County. He graduated from Cedarville College in 1897 and from New Brunswick, N. J., Theological Seminary in 1900. After serving churches in New Jersey, California, and Georgia, he was general secretary of the Executive Committee of Home Missions, Presbyterian Church in the U.S., 1906–48. He wrote several books on religious themes, e.g., *Other Men Labored,* Richmond, Va., [1937]. WWW 3

MacMILLAN, MARION THAYER (Aug. 27, 1865–Sept. 20, 1949), was born in Cincinnati, Hamilton County. Her husband, Wade MacMillan, was on the medical faculty of the University of Cincinnati. After his death she lived in Oxford. She lectured widely on the influence of reflections in the water on primitive art and published a book on the subject: *Reflections: The Story of Water Pictures,* New York, [1936].

MacMILLAN, MARY LOUISE (1870–July 16, 1936), was born in Venice, Erie County. She attended high school in Hamilton and Wells College, afterward making her home in Cincinnati. She wrote a number of one-act plays popular with amateur theater groups, published poems in various magazines and a collection: *The Little Golden Fountain, and Other Verses,* Cincinnati, 1916. WO 2

McMILLEN, WHEELER (Jan. 27, 1893–), farm magazine editor, was born near Ada, Hardin County. After attending Ohio Northern University briefly, he became a reporter on the Cincinnati *Post* in 1912. He published the Covington *Republican,* 1914–18, operated a farm in Hardin County, 1918–22, was on the editorial staff of the *Country Home,* 1922–39, and edited the *Farm Journal,* 1939–55. His books about farming include *The Farming Fever,* New York, 1924. WW 30

MacMURRAY, CLAIRE (Feb. 12, 1899–), born in Huntington, Ind., has been a columnist on the Cleveland *Plain Dealer* for a number of years. Her column provided much of the material for her first book: *And Beat Him When He Sneezes,* New York, 1941. WWAW 1

McMURRAY, WILLIAM JAMES (Oct. 17, 1849–Sept. 8, 1931), journalist, was born in Newport, Ky. In 1859 his mother moved to Ohio, and he grew up in St. Marys and Wapakoneta. In 1880, after working for thirteen years in a store, he helped found the *Auglaize Republican,* a newspaper that he published for many years. He edited *The History of Auglaize County . . . ,* Indianapolis, 1923.

McNAMARA, JAMES R. (Feb. 6, 1877–Jan. 12, 1951), was born in Howland Township, Trumbull County. He lectured widely and published poems in various periodicals. He died in Niles, where he had lived for more than thirty years. He published six collections of verse, e.g., *Poems of Beautiful Sentiment,* Niles, [1928].

McNEAL, THOMAS ALLEN (Oct. 14, 1853–Aug. 7, 1942), journalist, was born in Marion County. He attended Oberlin and Hillsdale Colleges. After farming and teaching school, he settled in Medicine Lodge, Kan., in 1879. He was an editor of the Medicine Lodge *Cresset,* 1879–84, established the Kansas *Breeze* in 1894 and later consolidated it with the North Topeka *Mail* as the *Farmer's Mail and Breeze,* which he edited, and was associate editor of the Topeka *Daily Capital.*

Tom McNeal's Fables . . . , Topeka, Kan., 1900.

When Kansas Was Young, New York, 1922.

McNEMAR, RICHARD (Nov. 20, 1770–Sept. 15, 1839), Shaker leader, was born in Tuscarora, Pa. At the age of sixteen he began teaching school in Stone Valley, Pa. In 1789 he made his first trip to Kentucky, and during the next eight years he taught in Pennsylvania and Kentucky. In 1797 he was licensed to preach by the Presbytery in Caneridge, Ky. He became pastor of Turtle Creek church northwest of Cincinnati and soon built it into one of the largest Presbyterian churches in Ohio. In 1802 the Presbytery of Cincinnati charged him with heresy but permitted him to continue preaching. The following year he withdrew from the Synod and became one of the group known as Schismatics. In 1805 he was converted to Shakerism by three missionaries from the East, and most of his congregation followed his example. A man of enormous energy, he assisted in the founding of Union Village in 1812 and other societies, preached to the Indians, and made numerous trips to the Eastern Shaker communities and to those in Ohio, Kentucky, and Indiana. He wrote many hymns, songs, and poems. Owner of a printing press, he published innumerable leaflets, pamphlets, and broadsides—many of them extracts from his own writings. He was frequently threatened with mob violence and legal action, but his greatest disappointment came from within his own community. Freegift Wells of Watervliet, N. Y., who was appointed leader of Union Village in 1836, was instrumental in having McNemar expelled from the community in 1839 with only his clothes and his printing press. He was reinstated but died shortly thereafter. He sometimes used the pen name Eleazar Wright. The listing below is a highly abbreviated record of his enormous output.

The Kentucky Revival; Or a Short History of the Late Extraordinary Outpouring of the Spirit of God in the Western States of America . . . , Cincinnati, 1807.

"Shakerism Detected" Examined and Refuted in Five Propositions, Lebanon, 1811.

The Other Side of the Question . . . , (with others), Cincinnati, 1819.

A Concise Answer to the General Inquiry Who or What Are the Shakers, Union Village, 1823.

A Review of the Most Important Events Relating to the Rise and Progress of the United Society of Believers in the West . . . , Union Village, 1831.

A Series of Lectures on Orthodoxy and Heterodoxy . . . , Dayton, 1832.

McNICOL, HUGH S. (Aug. 6, 1866–Sept. 8, 1887), was born in Hillsboro, Highland County. Little is known of his life, but he is said to have been an invalid who died of tuberculosis shortly after the publication of his little book of verse.

The Rustic Poet and Other Poems, [Hillsboro, 1886].

McNULTY, JOHN (Nov. 1, 1895–July 29, 1956), journalist, born in Lawrenceville, Mass., lived in Columbus about eight years while working as reporter, dramatic critic, and columnist. Primarily remembered for his reporting of the New York scene for *The New Yorker,* he appears somewhat out of place in a collection of Ohio writers; but he has become a minor legend in the history of Columbus journalism. He is remembered, for example, for a telegram he sent to his editor while covering an out-of-town assignment: "Have been invited to join Marietta lodge of Elks. Please send birth certificate and more expense money." His books, collections of his *New Yorker* pieces, include *Third Avenue,* Boston, 1946.

MacPHERSON, GEORGIA HARTER, was born in Springfield, Clark County. A graduate of Wittenberg College, she has taught English and French there since 1921. Her poems have appeared in numerous anthologies and magazines, and she has published several collections, e.g., *Then Comes Song,* Dallas, Texas, [1939].

McPHERSON, LOGAN GRANT (Aug. 11, 1863–March 23, 1925), economist, was born in Circleville, Pickaway County. He was employed by various railroads as a statistician and traffic expert, and in 1910 he organized the Bureau of Railway Economics. Besides technical books, articles, and lectures, he published several popular discussions of economics, e.g., *How the World Makes Its Living,* New York, 1916. DAB 12

McPHERSON, LYDIA STARR (1827–1903), was born in Warnock, Belmont County. Her parents moved to Licking County when she was three and to Iowa when she was twelve. She taught school in Iowa and at 21 married D. Hunter, who died leaving her with five children to rear. In 1874 she moved to the Southwest after marrying Granville McPherson, editor of the *Oklahoma Star.* She published newspapers in several Texas towns.

Reullura, a Book of Poems, Buffalo, 1892.

MacQUEARY, THOMAS HOWARD (May 27, 1861–July, 1931), clergyman, was born in Virginia. He served as rector of the Episcopal Church in Canton, 1885–91, and while there he published his first book: *The Evolution of Man and Christianity,* New York, 1890. Because he appeared in this book to deny the virgin birth of Christ, he was tried for heresy in 1891 and was suspended from the ministry. He later became a Universalist clergyman in Minneapolis.

McRAE, MILTON ALEXANDER (June 13, 1858–Oct. 11, 1930), newspaper publisher, born in Detroit, was in Cincinnati from 1882 to 1887 as business manager of the *Post.* His success in raising its circulation from 6,000 to 200,000 led to his rapid rise in the Scripps-McRae newspaper chain and in the United Press Association. He retired in 1907 and spent the remainder of his life in Detroit, where he wrote his autobiography: *Forty Years in Newspaperdom . . . ,* New York, [1924]. DAB 12

McVEY, FRANK LeROND (Nov. 10, 1869–Jan. 4, 1953), educator, was born in Wilmington, Clinton County. He graduated from Ohio Wesleyan University in 1893 and Yale University (Ph.D.) in 1895. He taught economics at the University of Minnesota, 1896–1907, and was the first chairman of the Minnesota Tax Commission, 1907–09. He was president of the University of North Dakota, 1909–17, and the State University of Kentucky, 1917–40. Besides the titles below, he published textbooks and a number of addresses and papers.

The Populist Movement, New York, 1896.

The Government of Minnesota, Its History and Administration, New York, 1901.

The Taxation of Mineral Properties, Columbus, [1908?].

Railroad Transportation; Some Phases of Its History, Operation and Regulation, Minneapolis, 1910.

The Making of a Town, Chicago, 1913.

The Financial History of Great Britain, 1914–1918, New York, 1918.

McVEY, WILLIAM ESTUS (Dec. 13, 1885–Aug. 10, 1958), educator and congressman, was born at Lee's Creek, Clinton County. A graduate of Ohio University and the University of Chicago, he taught in Harvey, Ill., 1919–47. He also served in the 82nd-85th Congresses. His writings include *Know Your Vitamins,* Chicago, 1947. WWW 3

MacVEY, WILLIAM PITT (March 25, 1873–), clergyman and educator, was born in Toledo, Lucas County. He graduated from Des Moines College in 1892 and Drew Seminary in 1896. After serving as a Methodist clergyman in several cities, he became president of Hedding College in 1907. He published *The Genius of Methodism . . .* , Cincinnati, [1903]. WW 6

McVICKER, DAPHNE ALLOWAY (March 14, 1895–), was born in Cambridge, Guernsey County, but lived in Columbus, where her parents moved when she was a year old. She graduated from Ohio State University in 1916. Her husband, Vinton E. McVicker, was editor of the Scripps-Howard Bureau in Columbus. She now lives in New York City. She has published short stories and other fiction in national magazines, but her most successful work was an account of her twenty-year-long attempt to find a housemaid who would relieve her of household duties and give her time to write: *The Queen Was in the Kitchen,* New York, [1941].

MADDUX, BERTON J. (Aug. 4, 1871–Feb. 28, 1952), educator, was born in Cedar Point, Hamilton County. He attended Cincinnati schools, National Normal University, and Antioch College. He began teaching in Hamilton County schools in 1890 and afterward served as a teacher and principal in Springfield and other communities. The romantic novel below has its setting in Cincinnati and vicinity.

The Veil Withdrawn; A Novel, New York, 1900.

MADDY, HOMER BASIL (Jan. 16, 1886–), was born in Cadmus, Gallia County. When he was eleven, his family moved to Lawrence County. He attended Rio Grande College and Bliss College, Columbus, and taught in Lawrence County schools for a number of years before moving to Huntington, W. Va., in 1913. He was employed by a hardware company in Huntington for thirty years until his retirement in 1958. He is the author of several books of verse, e.g., *Ballads of Mountain and Prairie,* Shelbyville, Ind., [1941].

MADISON, HAROLD LESTER (Sept. 23, 1878–), naturalist, born in Warwick, R. I., lived in Cleveland, 1921–39, while on the staff of the Museum of Natural History. He now lives in Providence, R. I. While in Ohio he wrote several books on Ohio nature study, e.g., *Wild Flowers of Ohio,* Cleveland, [1938]. WW 24

MAGEE, JAMES H. (June 23, 1839– ?), was born in Madison County, Ill. His mother was a former slave. Despite a sketchy education he taught school for some years. In 1865 he became pastor of a Baptist church in Toronto, Canada, and continued his education while holding this position. In 1871 he came to Cincinnati as pastor of the Union Baptist Church. He is listed in the Cincinnati directory through 1876, but there is no record of him thereafter. While in Cincinnati he wrote his autobiography: *The Night of Affliction and Morning of Recovery. An Autobiography,* Cincinnati, 1873.

MAGEVNEY, HUGH LEGARE (Nov. 15, 1845–May 2, 1908), clergyman, born in Jackson, Mich., was ordained in the Jesuit order in Cincinnati in 1875. Widely known for conducting missions and retreats, he was stationed at various times in Marysville, Russia, Springfield, and Cincinnati. He published *A Legacy of Lectures and Verses,* Cincinnati, [1906].

MAGINNIS, SISTER MARY JOSEPHINE (July 4, 1872–), educator, was born in Zanesville, Muskingum County. A member of the Ursuline Sisterhood, she is a graduate of Notre Dame University and Fordham University. She served as directress of the Ursuline Academy, Cincinnati, and as assistant superior of the Ursuline Community, Brown County. She is now living in the Ursuline Convent, St. Martin, Brown County. She has published articles and poems in various periodicals and a book on convent life: *Peace Grows in My Garden,* New York, [1944].

MAGINNIS, SISTER MONICA (Nov. 27, 1870–Feb. 27, 1958), educator, was born in Zanesville, Muskingum County. She graduated from Catholic University of America in 1917 and Notre Dame University (Ph.D.) in 1926; she also studied in Spanish universities, 1933–36. A teacher in the School of Ursulines, St. Martin, Brown County, she wrote several books, including an account of her years in Spain: *And Then the Storm,* New York, 1937. CWW 10

MAGOON, ELIAS LYMAN (Oct. 20, 1810–Nov. 25, 1886), clergyman, born in Lebanon, N. H., was a Baptist pastor in Cincinnati, 1845–49. He later served churches in New York City, Albany, and Philadelphia, and was also popular as a lecturer. His books include *The Eloquence of the Colonial and Revolutionary Times . . .* , Cincinnati, 1847.

MAGOUN, F. ALEXANDER (March 4, 1896–), educator, was born in Oberlin, Lorain County, but was reared in New England. He served on the staff of Massachusetts Institute of Technology, his alma mater, 1920–50, and now lives in Jaffrey Center, N. H. His books include *The Frigate Constitution and Other Historic Ships*, Salem, Mass., 1928. WW 30

MAHAN, ASA (Nov. 9, 1799–April 4, 1889), Congregational clergyman and first president of Oberlin College, was born in Vernon, N. Y. Reared in an atmosphere of rigorous Calvinism, he passed through an intense period of inner doubt and self-examination in his seventeenth year which led to his acceptance of the concept of complete moral freedom. He graduated from Hamilton College in 1824 and Andover Seminary in 1827. Called to Sixth Presbyterian Church, Cincinnati, in 1831, he also served as a trustee of Lane Seminary and vigorously opposed the ruling that forbade discussion of the slavery question. When he was chosen president of Oberlin in 1835, eighty Lane students, led by Theodore Weld (q.v.), followed him, with the result that a theological department was established to accommodate them. Mahan's administration established the humane liberalism that characterized the subsequent policies of the college. Women were granted degrees from the first, and no student was denied admission because of his race. In 1850 Mahan resigned to accept the presidency of Cleveland University, which failed. He later preached in Michigan, was president of Adrian College, 1860–71, and after 1871 lived in England, where he was a popular preacher. He died in Eastbourne, England.

Scripture Doctrine of Christian Perfection . . . , Boston, 1839.
Doctrine of the Will, New York, 1845.
A System of Intellectual Philosophy, New York, 1845.
The True Believer . . . , New York, 1847.
The Science of Moral Philosophy, Oberlin, 1848.
Election and the Influence of the Holy Spirit, Boston, 1851.
Modern Mysteries Explained and Exposed . . . , Boston, 1855.
The Science of Logic . . . , New York, 1857.
Science of Natural Theology, Boston, 1867.
The Baptism of the Holy Ghost, New York, 1870.
Theism and Anti-theism in Their Relations to Science, Cleveland, 1872.
The Phenomena of Spiritualism Scientifically Explained and Exposed, London, 1875.
A Critical History of the Late American War . . . , New York, 1877.
Out of Darkness into Light . . . , London, 1877.
Autobiography, Intellectual, Moral, and Spiritual, London, 1882.
A System of Mental Philosophy, Chicago, 1882.
A Critical History of Philosophy, 2 vols., New York, 1883.

MAKIN, JOHN J. (June 30, 1898–), engineer, was born in Owensville, Clermont County. He served with the army in France during World War I and with the merchant marine in World War II. A graduate of Ohio Mechanics Institute, he has worked as an engineer and has also dealt in real estate. He now lives in Cincinnati. Under the pen name Neptune Rex, he has written a book about a man who served in both wars: *The Affairs of Judge Black,* New York, 1946.

MALDCLEWITH, RONSBY. Pseud. See Byron C. Smith.

MALINE, WILLIAM A. (Sept. 1, 1852–Dec. 30, 1933), lawyer, was born in Canton, Stark County. He attended public schools. In 1875 he moved to Youngstown, where he spent the remainder of his life. He was admitted to the bar in 1877, served two terms as city solicitor, and was a founder of the City Trust and Savings Company.

The Nineteenth Century and Other Poems, Cleveland, 1898.

MALLON, GUY WARD (April 28, 1864–Dec. 23, 1933), lawyer and banker, was born in Cincinnati, Hamilton County. He graduated from Yale in 1885 and Cincinnati Law School in 1888. He practiced law in Cincinnati, was president of Cincinnati Trust Company, took an active part in civic affairs, and was a founder of Consumers' League. He published a manual on election laws and several works on economic subjects, e.g., *Bankers vs Consumers,* New York, [1933]. WW 4

MALLORY, HENRY (Feb. 27, 1822–Dec. 21, 1904), physician, was born in Botetourt County, Va. In 1835 his father moved to a farm in Fayette County and the following year to Indiana. Henry graduated from Medical College, Cincinnati, in 1849 and practiced in Hamilton until 1861. He served for a time with the 4th Kentucky Volunteer Cavalry until discharged for disability. After farming briefly in Tennessee, he returned to Hamilton to practice medicine and passed the remainder of his life in that community.

Gems of Thought and Character Sketches . . . , Hamilton, 1895.

MALLORY, HERBERT SAMUEL (June 8, 1872–Dec. 30, 1927), educator, was born in Akron, Summit County. After attending Akron High School, Rutgers Academy, and Buchtel College, he graduated from Western Reserve University in 1899 and Yale University (Ph.D.) in 1904. He taught at several schools and colleges, the last of which was the University of Michigan, 1918–27. He was killed in an automobile accident at Ypsilanti, Mich. His writings include a novel, *Tempered Steel; A Romance,* New York, [1909].

MALONE, J. WALTER (Aug. 11, 1857–Dec. 30, 1935), clergyman and educator, was born in Clermont County. He graduated from Chickering Institute, Cincinnati, in 1877. He founded First Friends Church, Cleveland, served as its pastor for 25 years, organized four other churches in Cleveland and vicinity, and also founded Cleveland Bible Institute and served as its president.
The Gospel in Jonah, Cleveland, [1900].

MANAK, ROBERTA (Nov. 6, 1874–June 17, 1950), was born in Cleveland, Cuyahoga County. After graduating from Cleveland Normal School, she taught in the city schools for eight years. In 1904 she married Frank Manak, a lawyer and banker. She published a collection of poems: *Garden Episodes in Verse,* [Cleveland, 1937].

MANATT, JAMES IRVING (Feb. 17, 1845–Feb. 13, 1915), educator, was born near Millersburg, Holmes County, but was reared and educated in Iowa. He graduated from Iowa College in 1869 and Yale University (Ph.D.) in 1873. He taught at Denison University, 1874–76, and Marietta College, 1877–84. He was chancellor of the University of Nebraska, 1884–89, but was more effective as a teacher than as an administrator. After serving as consul at Athens, Greece, he joined the faculty of Brown University, where he served until his death.
The Mycenaean Age, (with Chrestos Tsountas), New York, [1897].
Aegean Days, London, 1913.

MANCHESTER, RAYMOND EARL (March 6, 1884–), educator, born in Battle Creek, Mich., was professor of mathematics and dean of men at Kent State University, 1920–54. After his retirement he continued to live in Kent and served two terms as mayor of the town. He has published numerous textbooks and several books of poetry for children, e.g., *In and Out the Garden Gate,* Menasha, Wis., [1929]. WWMW 6

MANDERSON, CHARLES FREDERICK (Feb. 9, 1837–Sept. 28, 1911), lawyer, was born in Philadelphia. In 1856 he came to Canton, where he read law and twice served as city solicitor. He served in the 19th O.V.I. and was retired because of wounds in Sept., 1864, with the brevet rank of brigadier general. After the war he practiced law in Canton and served as district attorney. In 1869 he moved to Nebraska and served two terms in the U. S. Senate. He wrote a romance of Civil War times which was derived largely from his own experience and observation: *The Twin Seven-Shooters,* New York, [1902]. DAB 12

MANN, HORACE (May 4, 1796–Aug. 2, 1859), educator, born in Franklin, Mass., served as president of Antioch College, 1852–59. In 1857 the college was sold for its debts, Mann putting up most of the money to redeem it. Despite his herculean efforts to keep it operating, debts mounted and in 1859 it was sold again. On the Antioch campus a monument bears a sentence from his baccalaureate address at the 1859 Commencement: "Be ashamed to die until you have won some victory for humanity." A few weeks later he was dead. He published many educational reports, speeches, textbooks, and articles. Many of his writings are found in volumes II and III of his works, edited by his wife, (Boston, 1867–68).

MANN, JACOB (Aug. 26, 1888–Oct. 23, 1940), rabbi and educator, was born in Przemsyl, Galicia. He studied at the University of London and was ordained as a rabbi in England. He came to the United States in 1920 and was professor of history at Hebrew Union College, 1922–40. He published several studies of Jewish religion and history, e.g., *The Bible as Read and Preached in the Old Synagogue . . . ,* Cincinnati, 1940.

MANN, MARY TYLER PEABODY (Nov. 16, 1806–Feb. 11, 1887), born in Cambridge, Mass., lived in Ohio from 1852 to 1859, while her husband, Horace Mann (q.v.), was president of Antioch College. During her Ohio stay she published a cookbook: *Christianity in the Kitchen . . . ,* Boston, 1858. She later wrote a life of her husband and edited his writings.

MANN, WILLIAM D'ALTON (Sept. 27, 1839–May 17, 1920), journalist, was born in Sandusky, Erie County. At the outbreak of the Civil War he was living in Grand Rapids, Mich., where he joined the 1st

Michigan Cavalry as a captain. He rose to the rank of colonel of the 7th Michigan Cavalry, and after the war he went to Alabama, where he was proprietor of the Mobile *Register* for several years. He pioneered in the manufacture of cotton-seed oil and was an unsuccessful candidate for election to Congress. Some profitable inventions enabled him to settle in New York in the 1870s. He achieved a noisome notoriety as editor of *Town Topics,* of which he acquired control in 1891. Hated and feared by his enemies and not much loved or trusted by his few friends, he became a most controversial figure, but both he and *Town Topics* seemed to thrive on controversy. His enemies charged that he favored those who lent him money and never tried to get it back, but none doubted his influence. He filled his columns with spiteful venom directed toward those who crossed him, and he never hesitated to devote space to building up the social prestige of his favorites. That *Town Topics* was an effective blackmailing device was the least of the charges aired in public prints, and under constant attack he gradually lost his influence. He founded *Smart Set* in 1900. He died in Morristown, N. J.

The Raiders . . . , London, 1876.

Fads and Fancies of Representative Americans at the Beginning of the Twentieth Century, Being a Portrayal of Their Tastes, Diversions and Achievements, New York, 1905.

The Currency Question . . . , New York, 1907.

MANNERS, WILLIAM (April 3, 1907–), was born William Rosenberg in Butler, Pa. While he was a baby his parents moved to Zanesville, where his father served as a rabbi. He graduated from Zanesville High School and studied for a time at the University of Cincinnati and Hebrew Union College. After abandoning the idea of becoming a rabbi, he went to New York City, where he was an editor for Hillman Publications. He now lives in Florida. He has written several books, e.g., an account of his father, Rabbi Harris Rosenberg: *Father and the Angels,* New York, 1947.

MANNHEIMER, LOUISE HERSCHMANN (Sept. 3, 1844–Dec. 17, 1920), was born in Bohemia. In 1866 her parents brought her to New York City, and three years later she married Sigmund Mannheimer. In 1884, after living in St. Louis, Mo., and Rochester, N. Y., they came to Cincinnati. Mrs. Mannheimer founded the Free Industrial School for Boys and was active in other Cincinnati charities. She moved to New York City in 1917 and died in that city. Her husband (May 16, 1835–Dec. 18, 1909) was born in Kemel, Germany. After teaching in Germany and in France, he came to Baltimore, Md., in 1865. He served on the faculty of Hebrew Union College, 1884–1909. Poems by both of the Mannheimers were collected and published posthumously by their daughters. The first title below was written by Mrs. Mannheimer.

How Joe Learned to Darn Stockings, Cincinnati, 1897.

Poems in German and English, New York, 1921.

MANNHEIMER, SIGMUND. See Louise H. Mannheimer.

MANSFIELD, EDWARD DEERING (Aug. 17, 1801–Oct. 27, 1880), was born at New Haven, Conn. His father, Jared Mansfield (q.v.), brought his family to Marietta in 1803, moving on two years later to the then frontier village of Cincinnati. Here they remained until the outbreak of the War of 1812, when the father was assigned to duty at West Point, and young Edward was bundled off to school in New Haven. He entered the U. S. Military Academy in 1815, graduating at the age of eighteen. The young warrior now entered Princeton, and graduated at the top of his class (in science) in 1822. After a family conference it was decided that the embryo scientist should be a lawyer and, accordingly, he entered the famous law school of Judge Gould at Litchfield, Conn. At this time Litchfield was not only the intersection of two great highways—the high road from New York to Boston and the most popular route from Hartford to the West—but it was also the seat of several popular schools, which were attended by the sons and daughters of many of New England's most distinguished families. It was at Sarah Pierce's school that he heard Harriet Beecher read and there that he met his wife, the gifted Mary Peck. Across the street from his boardinghouse was the home of Lyman Beecher, where he was a frequent guest. At one time or another the best scholars of New England tarried in Litchfield, and, with entree to the best families, young Mansfield seems to have met most of them. He began his career as a publicist in Litchfield by contributing articles to the stuffy Litchfield *Republican* in 1824. A number of his new friends and acquaintances were to play important roles in the cultural development of Cincinnati. Litchfield was a profoundly influential environment for the young man who, upon being admitted to the Connecticut bar in

1825, immediately turned his footsteps in the direction of the Queen City of the West. He arrived late in the spring of 1825, where he was met by Dr. Daniel Drake (q.v.), who had married his cousin. At the Drakes' home he found a kindred soul in the doctor's younger brother, Benjamin (q.v.), another lawyer with literary aspirations. Once settled in Cincinnati he went through the motions of establishing a law practice, and but little more, his one case in court being a dismal failure. Between the theater and many parties he and Ben Drake were busy young men during the winter of 1825–26, and there was a living to be made. Back in 1815 Dr. Drake had published his *Natural and Statistical View, or Picture of Cincinnati and the Miami Country.* Issued in an unusually large edition it had enjoyed a good sale, but it was long since obsolete, and there was a substantial demand for a similar work designed to encourage emigration to the Cincinnati area. So it was that Ben Drake and Mansfield began a toilsome house-to-house census of the city in the spring of 1826. The result, *Cincinnati in 1826,* was published in 1827. A sensible and well-written account of Cincinnati and the fertile country surrounding it, the book was a success. Besides a large local sale the English traveler, W. Bullock, bought hundreds of copies, which he took to London and bound in as an appendix to his *Sketch of a Journey through the Western States of North America,* published in London late in 1827. Within a year the pair were sharing the editorial chair of the weekly newspaper Cincinnati *Chronicle and Literary Gazette,* but Mansfield's health declined to the extent that he was forced to return to New England, where he remained for several years. In the autumn of 1832 he came back to Cincinnati to find that an incredible change in the cultural life of that city had taken place. Within a scant two years, between 1830 and 1832, there had arrived in Cincinnati a brilliant coterie of youngsters who were to make literary history. Among the newcomers were the Beecher sisters, James H. Perkins, Frederick William Thomas, Caroline Lee Hentz, C. E. Stowe, the young lawyers Salmon P. Chase and Timothy Walker, to say nothing of the scholarly Ormsby MacKnight Mitchel (qq.v.). He was welcomed into the newly formed Semi-colon Club, where he found a number of old friends from Connecticut, while he in turn welcomed Mitchel into his dingy law office on Third Street. Mitchel had been his father's favorite student and for a short time his assistant at West Point. Referring to this partnership in a profession for which neither man had much aptitude, Mansfield has tried to provide us a bit of the atmosphere of their office. To this end he writes of himself hunched over his desk writing his *Political Grammar,* while Mitchel sat in one corner occasionally reading aloud snatches from Quintilian. It is a misleading picture. Although their office may not have been crowded with clients, it must have been a rather hectic place. On his return Mansfield had rejoined Ben Drake on the editorial staff of the *Chronicle.* During his absence in the East the Western Literary Institute and College of Professional Teachers had been organized and dedicated to the creation of a system of free schools. This was a subject close to the hearts of both partners, and shortly they were deeply immersed in the affairs of that active organization. By 1834 Mansfield and Daniel Drake were laying their plans to promote the construction of a railroad from Cincinnati to the Carolina tidal waters. Harper's published his *Political Grammar* in 1834. It was favorably received and ran into many editions. With the merger of the *Chronicle* and the Cincinnati *Mirror* he was relieved for a time of his editorial duties. But in 1835 he accepted the professorship of constitutional law and history in Cincinnati College. The following year Dr. Drake and others re-established the *Chronicle* with Mansfield as editor. The paper became a daily in 1839 and was finally bought by his old friend, Nathan Guilford, in 1850, and merged with the *Atlas,* Mansfield continuing as editor until 1852. He was the founding editor of the *Railroad Record,* which he conducted until 1872, holding at the same time the office of Commissioner of Statistics for Ohio, an office to which he was appointed by Governor Salmon P. Chase in 1868. Though he wrote many books and pamphlets, the writing of these was but incidental to his career as a journalist. His books which will live longest are his *Daniel Drake* (1855) and his *Personal Memories* (1879). The former is recognized as a basic source on the life of the "Nestor of the Ohio Valley," while the latter is a frank and entertaining account of early days in Cincinnati, abounding in historical facts of permanent value. Many of his addresses and lectures were published as separate pamphlets. He died at his home, "Yamoyden," near Morrow.

Ernest J. Wessen

Cincinnati in 1826, (with Benjamin Drake), Cincinnati, 1827.

The Political Grammar of the United States . . . , New York, 1834.

Railroad from the Banks of the Ohio River

to the Tidewaters of the Carolinas and Georgia, Cincinnati, 1835.
Eulogy on the Life and Character of William Henry Harrison, Cincinnati, 1841.
The Legal Rights, Liabilities and Duties of Women . . . , Salem, [Mass.], 1845.
The Life of General Winfield Scott, New York, 1846.
The Mexican War: A History . . . , New York, 1850.
American Education, Its Principles and Elements . . . , New York, 1851.
Ohio and Mississippi Railroad . . . , Cincinnati, 1852.
On the Railway Connections of Philadelphia, with the Central West, Letters . . . , New York, 1853.
Memoirs of the Life and Services of Daniel Drake, M.D. . . . , Cincinnati, 1855.
Exposition of the Natural Position of Mackinaw City, and the Climate, Soil, and Commercial Elements of the Surrounding Country, Cincinnati, 1857.
The Issues and Duties of the Day, Cincinnati, 1864.
Articles on the Tariff, Cincinnati, 1865.
Popular and Authentic Lives of Ulysses S. Grant, and Schuyler Colfax, Cincinnati, 1868.
A Letter in Regard to Tariff on Iron and Labor, Cincinnati, 1869.
Personal Memories, Social, Political and Literary with Sketches of Many Noted People, 1803–1843, Cincinnati, 1879.

MANSFIELD, IRA FRANKLIN (June 27, 1842–June 8, 1919), coal operator, was born in Poland, Mahoning County. He graduated from Poland College in 1861, enlisted in the 105th O.V.I., and served throughout the Civil War. In 1865 he bought cannel coal mines in Beaver County, Pa., which he operated thereafter. He wrote several works on the history, the plants, and the insects of Beaver County, e.g., *Historical Collections. Little Beaver River Valley . . . ,* Beaver Falls, Pa., 1911.

MANSFIELD, JARED (May 23, 1759–Feb. 3, 1830), mathematician and surveyor, father of Edward D. Mansfield (q.v.), was born in New Haven, Conn. Thomas Jefferson appointed him surveyor of Ohio and the Northwest Territory in 1803. During his service he lived in Marietta, 1803–05, and Cincinnati, 1805–12. He published several scientific articles and *Essays, Mathematical and Physical . . . ,* New Haven, [1802], which has been called the first book of original research in mathematics by a native American.

MANYPENNY, GEORGE WASHINGTON (Nov. 29, 1808–1893), born in Uniontown, Pa., came to Washington, Guernsey County, in 1826 to edit the Washington *Republican,* owned by David Robb. He later lived in St. Clairsville and Zanesville. He was Commissioner of Indian Affairs in Washington, D. C., 1853–57, and he served as General Manager of Public Works in Ohio, 1861–73. He also was chairman of the Sioux Commission in 1876 and the Ute Commission in 1880.

Our Indian Wards, Cincinnati, 1880.

MAPLE, JOSEPH COWGILL (Nov. 18, 1833–1917), clergyman, was born in Guernsey County. He served as a Baptist minister in Missouri, Kentucky, and Iowa. He wrote a biography, *Life and Writings of Rev. William Pope Yeaman, S.T.D.,* Columbia, Mo., 1906.

MARCH, ANNE. Pseud. See Constance F. Woolson.

MARCUS, JACOB RADER (March 5, 1896–), rabbi and historian, was born in Connellsville, Pa. He graduated from the University of Cincinnati in 1917 and Hebrew Union College in 1920. He also studied in German and American universities. On the faculty of Hebrew Union College since 1920, he has published a number of books on Jewish history, e.g., *The Rise and Destiny of the German Jew,* Cincinnati, 1934. WW 30

MARFIELD, DWIGHT STEELE (Dec. 11, 1868–Nov. 4, 1955), clergyman and lawyer, was born in Circleville, Pickaway County. After graduating from General Theological Seminary, New York City, in 1891, he studied at Oxford. He was rector of Episcopal churches in Dayton, 1892–95, and Cincinnati, 1895–98. He then resigned from the ministry to enter Cincinnati Law School, where he was graduated in 1901. He practiced in Cincinnati until 1924, when he moved to New York City. Around 1929 he began writing mystery stories, e.g., *The Mandarin's Sapphire,* New York, 1938.

MARGOLIS, MAX LEOPOLD (Oct. 15, 1866–April 2, 1932), rabbi, born in Russia, came to the United States in 1889 and was on the faculty of Hebrew Union College, 1892–97 and 1905–07. He was a widely esteemed Biblical scholar and translator; he also published *A History of the Jewish People,* Philadelphia, 1927. DAB 12

MARGOLIS, SILVIA (Mrs. Oscar) (July 5, 1900–), born in Poland, has lived in Dayton since 1910. She has attended Ohio State University and the University of Dayton. She published collections of poetry in 1958 and 1959. Her first book, according to the publisher's foreword, consisted of "poems of psychic origin": *Letters to Jesus by a Jewess,* Dayton, [1925].

MARGRAT, MAE E., was born in Henry County. She graduated from Defiance College. In 1944 her address was Utica. She published a book of verse: *Voices of Yesterday,* Mount Vernon, [1941].

MARIO, QUEENA (Aug. 21, 1896–May 28, 1951), operatic soprano, was born in Akron, Summit County. After her debut with the San Carlo Opera Company in 1918, she sang with various companies and was with the Metropolitan Opera Company, 1922–39. She also taught singing in New York City and in Bethel, Conn. She published several mystery novels, e.g., *Death Drops Delilah,* New York, 1944. WWW 3

MARK, MARY LOUISE (Jan. 6, 1878–), sociologist, was born in Scioto County. She graduated from Ohio State University in 1903, served on several state and Federal agencies until 1913, and was on the Ohio State faculty from 1914 until she retired in 1943. Since her retirement she has lived in Westerville. She has published several sociological studies, including *Negroes in Columbus,* Columbus, 1928. WW 30

MARKHAM, WILLIAM COLFAX (Sept. 10, 1868–), was born in Bolivar, Tuscarawas County. He attended Baldwin University, 1883–86, and in 1891 graduated from Baker University, Baldwin, Kan. He owned the Baldwin *Ledger* for a time and later served as executive secretary of the American Association of State Highway Officials. He now lives in North Hollywood, Calif. He has published a book of verse: *Along the Highway of Life,* Washington, D. C., [1934].

MARLETT, MELBA BALMAT (Sept. 9, 1909–), educator, was born in Alliance, Stark County, but now lives in Berkeley, Mich. She graduated from the University of Michigan in 1929, taught English in Detroit schools, 1930–41, and married Norval Marlett in 1937. She has written numerous mystery novels, e.g., *Death Has a Thousand Doors,* New York, 1941. WWAW 1

MARLETTO, CHARLOTTE LOUISE (Feb. 14, 1911–), was born in Dayton, Montgomery County. She graduated from Steele High School in Dayton, became a registered nurse, graduated from Los Angeles State College, and is now a clinical psychologist with the American Institute of Family Relations in Los Angeles. Her poems have appeared in various periodicals, and she has published a collection: *Jewel of Our Longing,* West Los Angeles, [1948].

MARQUIS, SAMUEL SIMPSON (June 8, 1866–June 21, 1948), clergyman, was born in Sharon, Noble County. After graduating from Allegheny College and Harvard Divinity School, he served Episcopal churches in Massachusetts and Michigan, and from 1915 to 1921 headed the sociological department of the Ford Motor Company. He wrote *Henry Ford; An Interpretation,* Boston, 1923. WWW 2

MARSH, ROSWELL (1793–Aug. 17, 1875), lawyer, was born in Queechy, Vt. He came to Steubenville in 1821, was admitted to the bar in 1823, and was elected to the legislature in 1840. He was a member of a commission to investigate claims for losses sustained in Missouri during the Civil War. His death occurred in Steubenville.

Biography, the Life of Charles Hammond of Cincinnati, Ohio, Steubenville, [1863].

Important Correspondence . . . , [n.p., 1865?].

Defence of Edwin M. Stanton, Steubenville, 1873.

MARSHALL, CARRINGTON TANNER (June 17, 1869–June 28, 1958), lawyer, was born in Zanesville, Muskingum County. He graduated from Cincinnati Law School in 1892, practiced in Zanesville, 1892–1920, served as chief justice of the state supreme court, 1921–32, and afterward practiced in Columbus. He published several books, e.g., *A History of the Courts and Lawyers of Ohio,* 4 vols., New York, 1934. WWW 3

MARSHALL, ROBERT KOSSUTH (Oct. 31, 1901–), educator, was born in Mt. Airy, N. C. After graduating from Guilford College in 1925, he worked in a bank for four years before becoming a teacher. He has been a member of the English department, Ohio Wesleyan University, since 1939. He has written at least two novels on the hill country of his native state, e.g., *Little Squire Jim,* New York, [1949].

MARSHALL, THOMAS BRAINARD (Dec. 10, 1837–Jan. 28, 1916), was born in Casstown, Miami County. After graduating from Miami University in 1862, he served in the

Civil War. He wrote a regimental history: *History of the Eighty-third Ohio Volunteer Infantry . . .* , Cincinnati, 1912.

MARSTEN, FRANCIS EDWARD (Sept. 12, 1855–Aug. 22, 1915), clergyman, was born in Jersey City, N. J. After graduating from Amherst College in 1874 and studying at Andover Theological Seminary, he was ordained to the Presbyterian ministry in 1878. He was a pastor in Boston, Mass., 1878–82, and Columbus, 1883–98. He afterward was an editor of the New York *Evangelist* and the *Saturday Literary Review*. His death occurred in Boston, Mass.

"After Eighty Years" . . . , Columbus, 1886.
The Freedom of Christ and Other Lectures, Boston, [1891].
Songs of Life, Boston, [1891].
The Mask of Christian Science; A History of the Rise and Growth of the System . . . , New York, [1909].

MARSTON, CLARENCE DEAN (Feb. 26, 1881–), clergyman, born in Bangor, Calif., served Methodist churches in Ohio, was superintendent of the Steubenville District, 1930–36, and was head of the Methodist Children's Home, Berea, 1939–52. He now spends his summers in Lakeside and his winters in Avon Park, Fla. He has published a devotional book: *Life Is for That,* Winona Lake, Ind., [1940].

MARTIN, CHALMERS (Sept. 7, 1859–Feb. 28, 1934), clergyman and educator, was born in Ashland, Ky. He graduated from Princeton University in 1879 and Princeton Theological Seminary in 1882. Ordained to the Presbyterian ministry in 1883, he was a missionary in Siam for three years and served churches in New Jersey and New York. He served on the faculty of the College of Wooster, 1903–29. His death occurred in Wooster.

Apostolic and Modern Missions . . . , New York, 1898.

MARTIN, CHARLES ALFRED (Oct. 4, 1874–), clergyman, was born in Cleveland, Cuyahoga County. After graduating from John Carroll University and St. Mary's Seminary, Cleveland, he was ordained to the Roman Catholic priesthood in 1900. He has served churches in Sandusky, Youngstown, and Cleveland. His writings include *Catholic Religion . . .* , Cleveland, 1910. CWW 8

MARTIN, HARRY EDWIN (1887–), educator, was born in Sardis, Monroe County. He attended Gnadenhutton High School and in 1911 graduated from Scio College. He taught English and history at Mount Union College, 1912–20. He was later with Retail Trade Publications, Lakewood, and still lives in that city. He has published *The Tents of Grace, a Tragedy; And Four Short Stories,* Cincinnati, [1910]. OBB

MARTIN, JOHN BARTLOW (Aug. 4, 1915–), was born in Hamilton, Butler County, the son of an industrial contractor. He attended high school in Indianapolis, Ind., and graduated from DePauw University in 1937. After a year on the Indianapolis *Times,* he moved to Chicago, which is still his home, and began free-lance writing. He has published provocative articles in national magazines, and in recent years has written significant sociological analyses of crime in America. His first book was a regional study: *Call It North Country; The Story of Upper Michigan,* New York, 1944. CB 44

MARTIN, LAWRENCE AUGUSTINE (Jan. 14, 1865–), educator, was born in Fayette County. He was an educator in Missouri and wrote both verse and prose for magazines and newspapers. For several years he edited the *Teachers' Review,* published in Chillicothe, Mo.

Hallowe'en and Other Poems, Chillicothe, Mo., [1893].
Huxter Puck, and Other Poems, Chillicothe, Mo., 1895.

MARTIN, RENWICK HARPER (Sept. 14, 1872–Oct. 23, 1958), clergyman, was born in Sugartree, Highland County. He graduated from Geneva College, Beaver Falls, Pa., in 1895 and the Reformed Presbyterian Theological Seminary, Pittsburgh, in 1899. He was pastor in Beaver Falls, 1899–1916, president of Geneva College, 1916–20, and afterward held various administrative offices in the Reformed Presbyterian Church. He wrote *The Day; A Manual on the Christian Sabbath,* Pittsburgh, Pa., 1933. WW 27

MARTIN, SYLVESTER MITCHELL (Aug. 16, 1857–Sept. 27, 1937), evangelist, was born in Antioch, Monroe County. He began teaching school when he was fifteen and taught until he was thirty, when he turned to the ministry. After being ordained a minister of the Christian Church in 1885, he began preaching and conducted nearly 300 revivals. His experiences are recounted in *Thirty Years on the Firing Line, Shots from the Battery of Truth Which Have Been Somewhat Effective against the Entrenchments of Sin . . .* , Cincinnati, [1920]. WWW 1

MARTIN, VICTORIA CLAFLIN WOODHULL (Sept. 23, 1838–June 9, 1927), was born in Homer, Licking County. Her parents are said to have left Homer under suspicion of arson, and her girlhood was spent in various Ohio towns. Much of the time the family toured the state giving clairvoyant exhibitions and peddling an elixir of life. In 1853 Victoria married Dr. Canning Woodhull, from whom she was divorced in 1864. She may have married Colonel James H. Blood in 1866; their union, at any rate, was dissolved ten years later. In the late 1860s she and her sister, Tennessee C. C. Cook (q.v.), attracted the attention of the elder Cornelius Vanderbilt, largely no doubt through their claims to be spiritualistic mediums; and with his backing they opened a brokerage house in 1868. In 1870 they founded *Woodhull and Claflin's Weekly,* where they advocated free love and women's rights. Their most notorious action was accusing Henry Ward Beecher (q.v.) of intimacy with Mrs. Tilton; they were tried on charges of obscenity but were acquitted. Victoria in the same year was nominated for the Presidency by the Equal Rights Party. In 1877, soon after the death of Commodore Vanderbilt, the sisters left for England, which was their home thereafter. Whether the Vanderbilt family subsidized their trip to avoid litigation over the Commodore's will is a matter of dispute. In 1883 Victoria married John Biddulph Martin, a wealthy banker. She continued to lecture and write on women's rights, but as she grew older she turned her attention from free love to eugenics. Brilliant and energetic, she and her sister may have furthered the cause of women's rights to some extent; moreover, their antics undoubtedly contributed to the gaiety of nations.

Origin, Tendencies and Principles of Government . . . , New York, 1871.
A New Constitution for the United States of the World Proposed . . . , New York, 1872.
The Argument for Women's Electorial Rights . . . , London, 1887.
A Fragmentary Record of Public Work Done in America, 1871–1877, London, 1887.
Stirpiculture; Or, the Scientific Propagation of the Human Race, London, 1888.
The Alchemy of Maternity, [Cheltenham, 1889].
The Garden of Eden . . . , London, 1890.
The Human Body the Temple of God . . . , (with T. C. Cook), London, 1890.
Humanitarian Government, London, 1890.
The Rapid Multiplication of the Unfit, New York, 1891.
Paradise Found, London, [18- ?].

MARTIN, WILLIAM FRANK (Sept. 22, 1873–), clergyman, born in Lane, Kan., has lived in Ohio since 1904. A graduate of Baker University and Boston University, he was a pastor in the Ohio Conference of the Methodist Church and served pastorates in various Ohio towns. Since his retirement he has lived in Lakeside. He has published a play and a collection of verse: *Love and Life, and Other Poems,* Boston, [1920].

MARTIN, WILLIAM T. (April 6, 1788–Feb. 19, 1866), was born in Bedford County, Pa., and came to Columbus with his family in 1814. He was a carpenter and joiner, a merchant, and a teacher. He lived in Montgomery Township, where he held various offices. He was justice of the peace, 1820–48. He wrote "A Brief History of Columbus," which appeared in the *Columbus Business Directory,* 1843–44. His history of Franklin County is an interesting and informative work; it contains the earliest account of the captivity of Jeremiah Armstrong, who was ransomed after years as a Wyandot captive and became a hotel keeper in Columbus.

History of Franklin County . . . , Columbus, 1858.

MARTZOLFF, CLEMENT LUTHER (Nov. 25, 1869–Aug. 5, 1922), educator, was born in Perry County. He taught history at Ohio University for many years. He published numerous textbooks, a collection of poems by Ohio poets, and several studies of Ohio history, e.g., *History of Perry County, Ohio,* New Lexington, 1902. OBB

MASON, BERNARD STERLING (June 2, 1896–April 12, 1953), born in Warren, Mich., graduated from the University of Michigan in 1920 and Ohio State University (Ph.D.) in 1931. He was a Boy Scout executive in Toledo, 1920–21, and Columbus, 1921–24, an instructor on the Ohio State University faculty, 1924–33, and after 1933 a free-lance writer living in Cincinnati. He published a number of magazine articles and books on sports, camping, and woodcraft, e.g., *Jud Goes Camping,* New York, [1941]. WWW 3

MASON, CARL H. (Nov. 11, 1879–March, 1960), journalist, was born in Hamilton, Butler County. He attended Miami University for three years. In 1918 he joined Hearst Magazines and served in various administrative and editorial capacities; after retiring, he lived in Ramsey, N. J. He wrote several vaudeville acts and a number of short stories; several plays, some of them adaptations of novels;

and a historical novel about Napoleon: *The Clash of Steel,* New York, 1901.

MASON, EDWARD CAMPBELL (Nov. 17, 1864–March 31, 1937), lawyer, was born in Ravenna, Portage County. He graduated from Harvard University in 1888 and Harvard Law School in 1892. He practiced in Buffalo, N. Y., and Boston, Mass. His last residence was Winchester, Mass.

The Veto Power: Its Origin, Development and Function in the Government of the United States . . . , Boston, 1890.

MASON, FRANK HOLCOMB (April 24, 1840–June 21, 1916), journalist and diplomat, was born in Niles, Trumbull County. He attended Hiram College but did not graduate. He served in the Civil War, first with the 42nd O.V.I. and later with the 12th Cavalry. He was on the staff of the Cleveland *Leader* until 1880, when he joined the diplomatic service. He was stationed at various European consulates, 1880–1914.

The Twelfth Ohio Cavalry . . . , Cleveland, 1871.

The 42nd Ohio Infantry . . . , Cleveland, 1876.

The Life and Public Services of James A. Garfield . . . , London, 1881.

MASSEE, JASPER CORTENUS (Nov. 22, 1871–), clergyman, was born in Marshallville, Ga. Ordained to the Baptist ministry in 1893, he served churches in Mansfield and Dayton as well as in the South. He now lives in Atlanta, Ga. He has published sermons and books on religious themes, e.g., *Christ and Human Personality,* New York, [1941]. OBB

MASSIE, DAVID MEADE (Feb. 26, 1859–Sept. 3, 1927), lawyer, was born in Chillicothe, Ross County. He graduated from Princeton University in 1880 and Cincinnati Law School in 1882. He practiced law in Chillicothe and was active in banking and public utilities.

Nathaniel Massie, a Pioneer of Ohio. A Sketch of His Life . . . , Cincinnati, 1896.

MASTERS, MRS. JACK. See Catherine Young.

MASTON, DARIUS EARL (Sept. 30, 1875–Oct. 1, 1939), born in Blooming Grove, Coshocton County. He worked as a ticket agent for the Pennsylvania Railroad until an injury caused his retirement. He contributed verse and stories to various newspapers and magazines. A volume of verses recalling his childhood days was published: *Old Buckeye Days in Verse,* Boston, [1915].

MATHER, AMASA STONE (Aug. 20, 1884–Feb. 9, 1920), was born in Cleveland, Cuyahoga County, son of Samuel and Flora Stone Mather. He attended University School, Cleveland, and graduated from Yale University in 1907. After his graduation he made a round-the-world trip, which included several months of big game hunting in Africa. On his return he called on President Theodore Roosevelt, who asked his advice on African big game. In 1909 he entered his father's business. At the time of his death he was active in Cleveland commercial and civic activities. His African trip is described in a privately published work: *Extracts from the Letters, Diary and Notebooks* . . . , 2 vols., Cleveland, 1910.

MATHER, FREDERICK GREGORY (Aug. 11, 1844–Aug. 31, 1925), was born in Cleveland, Cuyahoga County. After graduating from Dartmouth College in 1867, he studied law in Cleveland for a time but never practiced. He worked on various newspapers in New York State. At the time of his death he lived in Stamford, Conn. He published *The Refugees of 1776 from Long Island to Connecticut,* Albany, N. Y., 1913. WWW 1

MATHERS, WILLIAM (? – ?), was born in Ireland, reared in Baltimore, Md., and came to Ohio just before the organization of the state. In his *Recollections,* William Cooper Howells (q.v.) recalled him ruefully: "He was ultra democratic in his views, and ascribed all the woes men suffered to aristocracy. . . . His notions of society were communistic, and he was very severe on corporations and banks. I thought he had money enough to pay for printing his book, which I found to be a mistake when he got it done."

The Rise, Progress and Downfall of Aristocracy . . . , Wheeling, 1831.

MATHEWS, ALFRED (Sept. 15, 1852–Oct. 15, 1904), journalist and historian, was born in Painesville, Lake County. He worked for a short time for the Painesville *Telegraph* and then joined the editorial staff of the Cleveland *Leader.* He was a free-lance writer and contributed many historical articles to the New York *Times* and other publications. He was associated with several concerns engaged in publishing county histories and wrote several himself and edited many others. He moved to Philadelphia in 1883. His last book, *Ohio and Her Western Reserve,* based on the untenable theory that Ohio was indebted to the Puritans for its moral and material progress, was received with bitter castigation at the hands of competent Ohio critics. His death occurred in Philadelphia.

History of Washington County, Ohio, [Cleveland], 1880.

History of Cass County, Michigan . . . , Chicago, 1882.

Histories of the Counties of Lehigh and Carbon, in the Commonwealth of Pennsylvania, (with Austin N. Hungerford), Philadelphia, 1884.

History of Wayne, Pike and Monroe Counties, Pennsylvania, Philadelphia, 1886.

Ohio and Her Western Reserve . . . , New York, 1902.

MATHEWS, ALFRED E. (June 24, 1831–Oct. 30, 1874), artist, was born in Bristol, England, but his parents came to Ohio when he was two years old. He learned to set type in the office of the *Ohio Democrat,* published in New Philadelphia, but became a painter rather than a printer. In his mid-twenties, he toured New England, painting outdoor scenes and collecting specimens. When the Civil War broke out, he was teaching school in Tuscaloosa County, Ala., and made his way back to Ohio on foot. He served throughout the war with the 31st O.V.I. He became a skillful draftsman and topographer. His *Pencil Sketches of Montana,* one of the earliest pictorial records of that region, is one of the most sought-after items of Western Americana today. The last eight years of his life were spent in Colorado.

Interesting Narrative; Being a Journal of the Flight of Alfred E. Mathews . . . , [n.p.], 1861.

Pencil Sketches of Colorado . . . , [New York], 1866.

Pencil Sketches of Montana, New York, 1868.

Gems of Rocky Mountain Scenery . . . , New York, 1869.

MATSON, CLARENCE HENRY (April 6, 1872–Oct. 17, 1943), was born in Kirtland, Geauga County. He was a journalist in Salina, Kan., 1891–97, Topeka, 1898–1907, and Los Angeles, 1908–12. He was secretary and traffic manager of Los Angeles harbor, 1912–20, and in 1920 he was employed by the Los Angeles Chamber of Commerce to develop foreign trade and shipping. His account of Los Angeles harbor was published posthumously: *Building a World Gateway . . . ,* Los Angeles, [1945]. WWW 2

MATSON, HENRY (June 23, 1829–May 21, 1901), clergyman, was born in Ellsworth, Mahoning County. After graduating from Oberlin Theological Seminary in 1861, he served several churches in Massachusetts and Ohio. He became librarian of Oberlin College in 1874 and served in that capacity until 1887. His death occurred in Oberlin.

References for Literary Workers . . . , Chicago, 1892.

Knowledge and Culture, Chicago, [1895].

MATSON, NEHEMIAH (July 19, 1816–Oct. 3, 1883), was born on a farm near Jacobsburg, Belmont County. He attended Franklin College and in 1836 went to Bureau County, Ill., with his parents and was engaged in farming. A surveyor and map maker, he produced the first map of Bureau County. He later lived in Princeton, Ill., where he was a businessman and a student of local history. He was a diligent writer on historical themes; however, he essayed one novel, *Raconter,* and a travel book, *Beyond the Atlantic,* an account of his observations during a visit to Europe in 1868. He left in his will a substantial fund for the establishment of a library at Princeton.

Map of Bureau County, Illinois, with Sketches of Its Early Settlement, Chicago, 1867.

Beyond the Atlantic . . . , Princeton, 1870.

French and Indians of Illinois River, Princeton, 1870.

Reminiscences of Bureau County . . . , Princeton, 1872.

Memories of Shaubena . . . , Chicago, 1878.

Pioneers of Illinois . . . , Chicago, 1882.

Raconter: Four Romantic Stories . . . , Chicago, 1882.

MATTHEWS, CHARLES GRANT (Sept. 1, 1869–Aug. 5, 1925), librarian, was born in Athens County. After graduating from Ohio University in 1893, he spent a year in Vancouver, Wash., as a high school principal. He joined the Ohio University library staff in 1896, became head librarian in 1905, and served in that capacity until his death. His poems appeared in the *Atlantic Monthly* and other national magazines, and he published a collection: *The Ohio Hills . . . ,* [Boston, 1924].

MATTHEWS, ESSIE COLLINS (April 24, 1858–March 26, 1932), was born in Barnesville, Belmont County, the daughter of Judge J. H. Collins. She married an Episcopal clergyman and lived in Maitland, Fla., where her death occurred. She was a skilled photographer and used her own photographs to illustrate a series of sketches of Negroes she had known: *Aunt Phebe,*

Uncle Tom and Others . . ., Columbus, 1915.

MATTHEWS, MOTHER EVA LEE (Feb. 9, 1862–July 6, 1928), was born in Cincinnati, Hamilton County, the daughter of Supreme Court Justice Stanley Matthews (q.v.). In 1891 she went with her brother Paul to work in a Nebraska mission. In 1896, having returned to Cincinnati, she and Beatrice Henderson began the Community of the Transfiguration under the auspices of the Episcopal Church, and in 1898 they were clothed as novices. The Episcopal convent and school were later moved to Glendale, and she served as mother superior until her death. A collection of her talks to children was published posthumously: *Transfigured Tales . . .*, Boston, [1930]. WO 2

MATTHEWS, STANLEY (July 21, 1824–March 22, 1889), Supreme Court justice, was born in Cincinnati, Hamilton County. He attended Woodward College, where his father was president, graduated from Kenyon College in 1840, read law in Cincinnati, and practiced in Tennessee for two years. After returning to Cincinnati, he filled several posts for brief periods, serving as judge of common pleas court, as a state senator, and as U. S. attorney for the southern district. In the Civil War he served in the 23rd O.V.I. and 51st O.V.I. until 1863, when he was elected to the superior court of Cincinnati. In 1877 he was elected to the U. S. Senate to fill the uncompleted term of John Sherman. When President Hayes nominated him for a Supreme Court vacancy, the Senate refused to confirm the appointment; when President Garfield named him to the Court four years later, he was approved by one vote. He served on the Supreme Court from 1881 until his death. Besides the title below, many of his addresses were published as separate pamphlets.

Orations before the Army of the Cumberland, Columbus, 1875.

MATTHEWS, THOMAS JOHNSTON (Jan. 26, 1788–Nov. 10, 1852), educator, father of Stanley Matthews (q.v.), was born in Leesburg, Va., of a Quaker family. He first came to Cincinnati in 1818, taught mathematics at Transylvania University, 1823–32, was president of Woodward College, Cincinnati, 1832–35, and was an officer of the Ohio Life Insurance and Trust Company, 1835–45. His last seven years were spent at Miami University, where he was professor of mathematics and astronomy. His only known publication was a refutation of the theory of John Cleves Symmes (q.v.).

A Lecture on Symmes' Theory of Concentric Spheres . . ., Cincinnati, 1824.

MATTHEWS, THOMAS STANLEY (Jan. 16, 1901–), journalist, was born in Cincinnati, Hamilton County. He graduated from Princeton University in 1922 and New College, Oxford University, in 1924. He was on the staff of *New Republic,* 1925–28, and *Time,* 1928–53. He now lives in England. He has published several books, both fiction and nonfiction, since his first novel, which was based on the Snyder-Gray trial: *To the Gallows I Must Go,* New York, 1931. WW 30

MATTOX, ABSOLOM H. (1843– ?), was born in Springfield, Clark County. He served in the 17th O.V.I., 1862–65, and after the war lived in Cincinnati, where he was employed by the Cincinnati Gaslight Company. In 1895 he moved to New York City. Besides writing the book listed below, he compiled *The Athens Home Coming Reunion . . .*, (1904?).

A History of the Cincinnati Society . . ., Cincinnati, 1880.

MAURER, DAVID W. (April 12, 1906–), educator, was born in Wellston, Jackson County, but grew up in New Philadelphia. A graduate of Ohio State University (A.B., M.A., Ph.D.), he has been for several years a member of the English department, University of Louisville. He has made a special study of language, especially the jargon of crime, and has published numerous articles, both technical and popular, and a book: *The Big Con; The Story of the Confidence Man and the Confidence Game,* Indianapolis, [1940].

MAXWELL, JAMES A. (April 7, 1912–), was born in Cincinnati, Hamilton County. He served with the Counter-Intelligence Corps in North Africa during World War II and is now a free-lance writer living in Cincinnati. He has published stories and articles in *The New Yorker* and other national magazines. He has published a collection of thirteen stories with their setting in Tripoli: *I Never Saw an Arab like Him,* Boston, 1948.

MAXWELL, SIDNEY DENISE (Dec. 23, 1831–Nov. 13, 1913), was born in Centerville, Montgomery County. He read law in Dayton and at the outbreak of the Civil War was a war correspondent for the Cincinnati *Commercial.* In 1864 he enlisted in the 131st O.V.I. and rose to the rank of colonel. After the war he engaged in journalism and insurance, and he was superintendent of the Cincinnati Chamber of Commerce, 1871–91, in which capacity he was very active in civic affairs. He published lectures and reports related to Cincinnati business and commerce.

The Suburbs of Cincinnati . . . , Cincinnati, 1870.

MAXWELL, WILLIAM (c.1755–1809), editor of the first book published in the Northwest Territory, was born in New York or New Jersey. Details concerning his early life are meager. Sometime between 1788 and 1792 he came west, settling first in Lexington, Ky., where he established a printing office. In 1792 he moved to Cincinnati and set up his press in a log cabin at the corner of Front and Sycamore Streets. Here with the assistance of his wife, Nancy, on Nov. 9, 1793, he published the first issue of *The Centinel of the North-Western Territory.* In 1796, after being appointed postmaster of Cincinnati, he sold the paper to Edmund Freeman, who renamed it *Freeman's Journal* and around 1800 moved it to Chillicothe. Before selling his press, William Maxwell published the Maxwell Code, a compilation entitled *Laws of the Territory of the United States, Northwest of the Ohio.* In 1799 he moved to a log cabin on the Little Miami River in Greene County. He served in the First General Assembly of Ohio in 1803 and was both an associate judge and sheriff of Greene County. He was buried on his farm in what is now Beaver Creek Township.

MAY, MAX BENJAMIN (July 21, 1866–Oct. 2, 1929), lawyer and judge, was born in Cincinnati, Hamilton County. After graduating from the University of Cincinnati in 1888, he studied at Harvard Law School and began practice in Cincinnati in 1890. He served as judge of common pleas court, 1913–19. His writings include *Isaac Mayer Wise, the Founder of American Judaism . . . ,* New York, 1916. **WWW 1**

MAYER, ALBERT IGNATIUS (1906–), was born in Cincinnati, Hamilton County. He graduated from Hughes High School in 1924 and the University of Cincinnati, where he played varsity football, in 1928. He was in the insurance business in Cincinnati in the 1930s and later lived in Florida for some time. He has written several books, e.g., a story of Germany in the tenth century: *Defense of the Castle,* New York, 1937.

MAYER, NATHAN (Dec. 25, 1838–July 10, 1912), physician, was born in Bavaria. In 1849 his parents brought him to Cincinnati. After graduating from Ohio Medical College, he studied in Paris. In 1861 he returned to the United States and served as a surgeon in the 14th Connecticut Volunteers. After the Civil War he practiced in Hartford, Conn., and his death occurred in that city. He wrote a number of poems in addition to the novels below.

The Fatal Secret . . . , Cincinnati, 1858.
Differences . . . , Cincinnati, 1867.
A Point of Honor . . . , Hartford, [1884].

MAYO, AMORY DWIGHT (Jan. 31, 1823–April 8, 1907), Unitarian clergyman and educator, born in Warwick, Mass., lived in Ohio for two brief periods: while pastor of Independent Christian Church, Cleveland, 1854–56, and the Church of the Redeemer, Cincinnati, 1863–72. He was deeply interested in public education, especially in the South, and many of his lectures on the subject were published. He was a strong advocate of Bible-reading in public schools. His views are expressed in *Religion in the Public Schools. Three Lectures . . . ,* Cincinnati, 1869.

MAYO, CASWELL A. (July 5, 1862–Jan. 13, 1928), born in Columbus, Miss., edited the *American Druggist* and other pharmaceutical publications. From 1920 until his death, he lived in Cincinnati, where he was dean of Queen City College of Pharmacy. He wrote a history of the Lloyd Library: *Lloyd Library and Its Makers . . . ,* Cincinnati, 1928.

MAYO-SMITH, RICHMOND (Feb. 9, 1854–Nov. 11, 1901), educator, was born in Troy, Miami County. After attending Dayton public schools, he graduated from Amherst College in 1875. He studied for two years in Europe, and in 1877 he joined the faculty of Columbia University, where he taught until his death.

The Influence of Immigration on the United States of America, Rome, 1888.
Emigration and Immigration . . . , New York, 1890.
Science of Statistics . . . , 2 vols., New York, 1895–99.

MEAD, MRS. DAVID. See Myra W. Kerr.

MEAD, EDWARD SHERWOOD (Jan. 25, 1874–Aug. 21, 1956), educator, was born in Medina, Medina County. He graduated from DePauw University in 1896 and the University of Chicago (Ph.D.) in 1899. He began teaching finance at the Wharton School of Finance and Commerce in 1907. He wrote numerous professional articles, textbooks, and some books on economics for the general reader, e.g., *The Careful Investor,* Philadelphia, 1914. WW 26

MEAD, GEORGE HERBERT (Feb. 27, 1863–April 26, 1931), educator, born in South Hadley, Mass., was brought to Oberlin in 1870, when his father was named professor of homiletics at Oberlin Seminary. He graduated from Oberlin College in 1883 and later studied at Harvard and in Germany. He taught philosophy at the University of Michigan, 1891–94, and at the University of Chicago, 1894–1931. He both contributed to and borrowed from the instrumentalist philosophy of his colleague at Chicago, John Dewey. Four volumes of his lectures and manuscripts, published posthumously, include *The Philosophy of the Present,* Chicago, 1932. DAB 21

MEAD, GEORGE WHITEFIELD (1865–Dec. 18, 1946), clergyman and educator, was born in Norwalk, Huron County. He graduated from Oberlin College in 1891 and was ordained to the Presbyterian ministry in 1894. He served various pastorates in the East and later was on the faculty of Berea College, Ky., 1917–19, and of Tusculum College, Tenn., 1929–38. He died in Asheville, N. C.

Modern Methods in Church Work; The Gospel Renaissance, New York, 1897.
Modern Methods in Sunday-school Work; The New Evangelism, New York, 1903.
The Great Menace: Americanism or Bolshevism?, New York, 1920.

MEALAND, RICHARD (c.1905–Feb. 19, 1958), was born in Greenfield, Mass. In 1914 his parents moved to Toledo, where he attended public schools. He worked as a reporter on the Toledo *Blade,* the Cleveland *News,* and several New York newspapers. He published short stories in various national magazines, was on the editorial staff of *Pictorial Review,* and was story editor for Paramount Pictures, 1939–46, and London representative of Paramount, 1951–56. He published considerable fiction, including a novel about a literary agent: *Let Me Do the Talking,* New York, 1947.

MEALS, GERTRUDE WHITTIER (Oct. 23, 1873–Aug. 18, 1943), was born in Pittsburgh, but lived in Cleveland for forty years. As Gertrude Whittier, she published *The Good Ship Mayflower,* [Cleveland, 1933].

MEANS, STEWARD (Aug. 4, 1852–March 11, 1940), clergyman, was born in Steubenville, Jefferson County. He studied at Kenyon College, 1869–72, and Union Theological Seminary, 1872–75. After his ordination as an Episcopal priest in 1876, he served churches in New Jersey, Ohio, New York, and Connecticut. His writings include *Saint Paul and the Ante-Nicene Church . . . ,* London, 1903. WWW 2

MEARS, ALICE MONKS (Aug. 21, 1911–), was born in West Chester, Pa. After graduating from Oberlin College in 1934, she lived in Hudson until 1948. Her poems have appeared in many magazines, and she has published a collection: *Brief Enterprise,* New York, 1945.

MEARS, DAVID OTIS (Feb. 22, 1842–April 29, 1915), clergyman, born in Essex, Mass., lived in Cleveland, 1893–95, while pastor of Calvary Presbyterian Church. He was one of the organizers of the Anti-Saloon League of Ohio and its first president. He published numerous addresses and sermons and several books, e.g., *Life of Edward Norris Kirk, D.D.,* Boston, 1877.

MEEK, BASIL (April 20, 1829–April 16, 1922), lawyer, was born in New Castle, Ind. After reading law, he was admitted to the Indiana bar in 1862. Two years later, he moved to Fremont, where he practiced law and served as clerk of courts. He was postmaster of Fremont, 1886–91. He wrote historical articles for various periodicals and *Twentieth Century History of Sandusky County . . . ,* Chicago, 1909.

MEEKER, EZRA (Dec. 29, 1830–Dec. 3, 1928), was born near Huntsville, Butler County. In 1837 his family moved to Indiana. He was married in 1851, and the following October the young couple set out for Iowa in an ox-drawn wagon. The next spring, with his wife and infant child, he joined a wagon-train for Oregon, and reached Portland on Oct. 1, 1852. After exploring the country north of the Columbia, he settled on the site of Puyallup, where he built the first cabin; he remained in this region for over fifty years as a farmer and hop-grower. An enthusiastic student of the history of the Pacific Northwest, he resolved when he was 75 to devote the rest of his days to the commemorative marking of the Oregon Trail. Starting out Jan. 29, 1906, with an ox-drawn replica of the covered wagon in which he had traveled to Oregon, he followed as much of the trail as was still open, identifying landmarks with painted inscriptions, and urging citizens of neighboring communities to set up more permanent memorials. In 1910 he repeated the performance, and in 1915 he covered a considerable part of the trail in an automobile. All of these trips were extended to tours of the East, where his picturesque outfit drew large crowds and resulted in his selling many copies of his books and thousands of souvenirs. He was a prolific writer, and if it be true that his works are poorly organized and he was careless as to dates and incidents, it is equally true that they continue to grow in esteem as indispensable sources on the settlement of the Pacific Northwest. His *The Ox-Team, or the Old Oregon Trail* is an exciting account of what befell him on his long, wild journey with an ox-team—a superb bull-whacker's tale. His *Ventures and Adventures* was revised and republished in 1916 as *The Busy Life of Eighty-Five Years of Ezra Meeker. . . .*

Ernest J. Wessen

Washington Territory West of the Cascade Mountains . . . , Olympia, 1870.
Hop Culture in the United States, Puyallup, [1883].
Pioneer Reminiscences of Puget Sound . . . , Seattle, 1905.
The Ox-Team; Or, the Old Oregon Trail, 1852–1906 . . . , Omaha, [1906].
Ventures and Adventures of Ezra Meeker; Or, Sixty Years of Frontier Life . . . , Seattle, [1908].
Story of the Lost Trail to Oregon, [Seattle, 1915].
Seventy Years of Progress in Washington, Seattle, 1921.
Kate Mulhall, a Romance of the Oregon Trail, New York, [1926].
Uncle Ezra's Short Stories for Children, Tacoma, [n.d.].
Uncle Ezra's Pioneer Short Stories for Children, to Point a Moral or Teach a Lesson, San Francisco, [n.d.].

MEEKER, JOTHAM (Nov. 8, 1804–Jan. 12, 1855), missionary and printer, was born in Hamilton County. He learned the printing trade in Cincinnati, but in the summer of 1825 he resolved to become a missionary. By the following November, he had joined the mission on the St. Joseph River in Michigan Territory. Here he became a school teacher to the Indians, devoting much of his time to learning their language. At Sault Ste. Marie, in Nov., 1832, he began his experiments in devising for the Indian languages an orthography which might be written or printed with the ordinary characters of our alphabet. In October of 1833, he was transferred to the Shawnee Mission near the present Kansas City, Kan., where he put his new system to the test. The following March he did the first printing in what is now Kansas when he produced a leaflet containing the text of a hymn in Shawnee. In all he printed some 65 works in English and in ten Indian languages, including a Shawnee newspaper, using his orthographic system. He published hymnbooks and translations of the Bible. In 1837 he moved to a mission of his own among the Ottawa near the present city of Ottawa, Kan. There he devoted the rest of his life to the temporal and spiritual welfare of his Indians.

MEEKER, NATHAN COOK (July 12, 1817–Sept. 29, 1879), was born in Euclid, Cuyahoga County. In 1835 a pedestrian journey took him to New Orleans, where he found employment on a local newspaper. Returning to Ohio after two years, he entered Oberlin College, from which he graduated in 1840. Shortly after graduation he visited relatives at his ancestral home in Newark, N. J., and remained to teach school in nearby Orange and in eastern Pennsylvania. It was during this sojourn that he met N. P. Willis, who accepted several of his poems and articles for the New York *Evening Post;* Meeker soon became a frequent contributor of special articles to various New York newspapers. He returned to Euclid in 1844. It was the heyday of religious and social cultism. Emerson wrote Carlyle: "We are all a little wild here with numberless projects of social reform; not a reading man but has a draft of a new community in his waistcoat pocket." Meeker returned home to find Fourier's teachings quite the vogue among Ohio intellectuals, with phalansteries springing up all over the state. In 1846 he joined the Trumbull Phalanx, located in Trumbull County. Irresponsible leadership was the most potent cause of the failure of the Fourieristic communities. Writing from intimate experience with such leaders, Horace Greeley said: "They are sure to jump into any new movement as if they had been born expressly to superintend and direct it, though they are morally certain to ruin whatever they lay their hands on." The Trumbull Phalanx was no exception. The first error of its leaders was a fatal one. They had located their community in ague-ridden bottom lands. An abandoned flourmill was renovated, and a tannery and wooden-bowl factory were built, but before these factories had gotten into production the community began to disintegrate because of its unhealthful location. Though he emerged nearly destitute, it was to prove an invaluable experience for young Meeker. In company with his brothers he opened a store in Euclid which seems to have been fairly prosperous. But in 1850 the Campbellites built a college at Hiram—then a crossroads so remote that the carpenters had to travel eight miles to get a pound of nails—and Meeker accepted the invitation of the college authorities to open a store there. In 1851 his first book appeared: *The Adventures of Captain Armstrong,* a tale concerned with the establishment of a communistic Utopia by castaways upon a South Pacific Island. At Euclid and then at Hiram, he continued to contribute articles to New York newspapers, many of them dealing with agricultural subjects. Nearly ruined by the financial panic of 1857, Meeker moved to Union County, Ill. It was a most logical move for a man of his inclinations, seeking to recoup his fortunes, for Union County was showing great promise of a wonderful horticultural development. He opened a store near Dongola and wrote articles for the Cleveland *Plain Dealer* and the New York *Tribune.* Shortly after the outbreak of the Civil War, an article he had written on Southern political leaders caught the eye of Horace Greeley, and Meeker was employed on the staff of the *Tribune.* During the war he was assigned to General Grant's headquarters as war correspondent. Solon Robinson, nationally known agricultural editor of the *Tribune,* was generally credited with being responsible for the broad circulation and national influence of the weekly edition. When Robinson retired in 1868, Meeker took over his editorial chair. His articles were well received and soon he was known across the country. In 1869 he toured the West, and out of this trip grew his plan to organize an agricultural colony there. With the support of Horace Greeley and the *Tribune,* his settlement got under way in December of 1869. His lessons had been learned by bitter experience. This time the community would not be located in miasmic swamps, private ownership of property would be recognized and private enterprise encouraged, cooperative principles would be applied in general, leaving the details to be worked out by the members. Upon these solid foundation stones, Greeley, Colo., was built. In 1878 William Alfred Hinds reported: "Today this village and community are the most prosperous in Colorado. Here 4,000 people have found happy homes." The sorry plight of the White River Utes in western Colorado had captured Meeker's interest and aroused his sympathy, with the result that he had arrived at some original ideas as to the proper management of Indians on reservations. In 1878 he became Indian agent at the White River reservation and promptly tried to sell his plans to the Utes. So repugnant to them was the suggestion that they support themselves by laboring in their fields that, on Sept. 29, 1879, they rose and massacred Meeker and all of the white male employees of the agency.

Ernest J. Wessen

The Adventures of Captain Armstrong, New York, 1851.

Life in the West; Or, Stories of the Mississippi Valley, New York, 1868.

MEES, ARTHUR (Feb. 13, 1850–April 26, 1923), composer, was born in Columbus, Franklin County. He was organist for the first Cincinnati May Festival in 1873 and in later years was chorusmaster and organist. He taught music, conducted choral and orchestral groups in various cities, and published a piano textbook and *Choirs and Choral Music,* New York, 1901. OCM

MEES, THEOPHILUS MARTIN KONRAD (July 13, 1848–July 25, 1923), clergyman and educator, father of Arthur Mees (q.v.), was born in Columbus, Franklin County. After graduating from St. Louis Theological Seminary in 1872 and studying two years in Germany, he was ordained to the Lutheran ministry. He taught at Capital University, was president of Teachers' Seminary, Woodville, 1888–1903, and rejoined the Capital faculty in 1903. He was editor of the *Journal of Pedagogy* and of the *Theological Magazine.*

Dogmengeschichtlicher Beitrag zur Entwickelung der Lehre von der Gnadenwahl Innerhalb der Lutherischen Kirche von 1522 bis 1580, Columbus, [1892?].

MEIGS, RETURN JONATHAN (Dec. 17, 1740–Jan. 28, 1823), born in Middletown, Conn., served as a major in Arnold's expedition against Quebec. His diary kept during the expedition was first published in the *American Remembrancer* in 1776, was republished in *Massachusetts Historical Collections* in 1814, and was privately published in the edition listed below. Appointed one of the surveyors for the Ohio Company, Meigs landed at the mouth of the Muskingum. A code of rules drawn up by him was adopted by the colonists. He frequently served as a mediator with the Indians and died while negotiating between Tennessee and the Cherokee nation.

Journal of the Expedition against Quebec . . ., New York, 1864.

MEIGS, RETURN JONATHAN (Nov. 17, 1764–March 29, 1824), son of the elder Return J. Meigs (q.v.), was born in Middletown, Conn. After graduating from Yale in 1785, he read law, and in 1788 he came to Marietta with the Ohio Company. He was appointed judge in 1798 and, when Ohio was admitted to the Union, he was made chief justice of the state supreme court. He also served in the U. S. Senate, 1808–10, and as governor, 1810–14. He resigned as governor to accept an appointment as postmaster general. After resigning in June, 1823, he lived in Marietta until his death the following year. The title below, which was written to encourage emigration, is attributed by some authorities, including Peter G. Thomson, to Nahum Ward (q.v.), but the preponderance of evidence favors Meigs's authorship.

A Brief Sketch of the State of Ohio . . ., Glasgow, 1822.

MELHORN, NATHAN RAYMOND (Dec. 23, 1871–Feb. 18, 1952), clergyman, was born in Ada, Hardin County. He studied at Ohio Northern University and taught school in Ohio for two years before entering Lutheran Theological Seminary, Philadelphia. Ordained to the Lutheran ministry in 1897, he served churches in eastern Pennsylvania until 1922. He was managing editor of *The Lutheran*, 1920–28, and was editor, 1928–45. He wrote widely for religious periodicals and under the pen name Raymond Etan published *The Diary of a Deacon*, Philadelphia, [1925].

MELINE, JAMES FLORANT (1813–Aug. 14, 1873), was born in the fort at Sackett's Harbor, N. Y., the son of a French officer in the U. S. Army. He graduated from St. Mary's College, Emmittsburg, Md. After coming to Cincinnati in 1832, he taught in St. Xavier's College, served as assistant editor of the *Catholic Telegraph*, and studied law in the office of William Greene (q.v.). He was admitted to the bar in 1835 and left at once for France, where he lived for several years and mastered the French, German, Italian, and Spanish languages. In 1838 he returned to Cincinnati, where he practiced law and for several years was a banker. He was the French consul in that city for a short time before the Civil War. During the war he served on the staff of General John Pope. Subsequently, he was chief of the bureau of civil affairs in the 3rd Military District with headquarters in Georgia, where he also served as correspondent of the New York *Tribune*. His later years were devoted to literature. He was a frequent contributor to the Cincinnati *Commercial*, the *Nation*, the *Catholic World*, and many other newspapers and magazines. His most distinguished work was his brilliant and learned dissection of Froude's literary method: *Mary, Queen of Scots, and Her Latest English Historian*. He died in Brooklyn, N. Y.

Two Thousand Miles on Horseback . . ., New York, 1867.

Commercial Travelling, Cambridge, Mass., 1869.

Life of Sextus the Fifth, New York, 1871.

Mary, Queen of Scots, and Her Latest English Historian . . ., New York, 1872.

MELISH, JOHN HOWARD (Oct. 12, 1874–), clergyman, was born in Milford, Clermont County. He studied at the University of Cincinnati, 1892–95, and graduated from Harvard University in 1896 and Episcopal Theological Seminary, Cambridge, in 1898. Ordained an Episcopal priest, he was assistant pastor of Christ Church, Cincinnati, 1900–04, and rector of Holy Trinity Church, Brooklyn, N. Y., 1904–49. He was removed from the latter post for refusing to oppose his son's alleged radical activities. His writings include a biography: *Franklin Spencer Spalding, Man and Bishop*, New York, 1917. WW 27

MELLON, EVELYN EMIG (May 29, 1895–), was born in Washington, D. C. A graduate of George Washington University, she worked on *Vanity Fair* and the *American Weekly*. Since her marriage in 1927 to DeForest Mellon, a Cleveland attorney, she has lived in Cleveland. She has published numerous articles on child development in parents' magazines, written a number of plays, some of which have been published separately, and has also published *Two Prize Plays and Four Others . . .*, Boston, [1929].

MELOY, WILLIAM T. (Oct. 4, 1838–Feb. 20, 1904), clergyman, was born in Taylorstown, Pa. After being ordained to the Presbyterian ministry in 1864, he came to Cadiz, where he served as a pastor until 1886, when he moved to Chicago. The setting of his novel *Lucille Vernon* is the town of Cadiz.

Lucille Vernon; Or, the Church at Lansington, Pittsburgh, 1881.

Wanderings in Europe, Chicago, 1892.

MENDENHALL, GEORGE (May 5, 1814–June 4, 1874), physician, born in Sharon, Pa., first studied medicine in Salem, Columbiana County. After graduating from the University of Pennsylvania in 1835, he settled in Cleveland, and in 1844 he moved to Cincinnati. He was one of the organizers of Miami Medical College in 1852 and served on its faculty. In 1870 he was president of the American Medical Association.

The Medical Student's Vade Mecum, Philadelphia, 1852.

MENDENHALL, JAMES WILLIAM (Nov. 1, 1844–June 18, 1892), clergyman, was born in Ohio. After graduating from Ohio Wesleyan University, he became a Methodist minister. He also served as editor of the *Methodist Review.* His death occurred in Colorado Springs, Colo.

Echoes from Palestine, Cincinnati, 1883.

Plato and Paul . . . , Cincinnati, 1886.

MENDENHALL, THOMAS CORWIN (Oct. 4, 1841–March 22, 1924), educator, was born near Hanoverton, Columbiana County. After attending district schools and Southwest Normal School, Lebanon, he taught in several high schools. In physics and mathematics, his lifelong specialties, he was largely self-educated. He was named the first professor of physics and mechanics at Ohio Agricultural and Mechanical College (Ohio State University), and served at that post 1873–78 and 1881–84; he taught in the intervening three years at Imperial University, Tokyo, Japan. He afterward was president of Rose Polytechnic Institute, Terre Haute, Ind., 1886–89, superintendent of the U. S. Coast and Geodetic Survey, 1889–94, and president of Worcester Polytechnic Institute, Worcester, Mass., 1894–1901. He lived in Europe, 1901–12, and then made his residence in Ravenna, Portage County, until his death. Besides the book listed below, he edited three volumes of the *History of the Ohio State University* (1920–26) and published a great many scientific papers and addresses.

A Century of Electricity, Boston, 1887.

MENKE, FRANK GRANT (Oct. 10, 1885–May 13, 1954), sports writer, was born in Cleveland, Cuyahoga County. A resident of Fairfield, Conn., he wrote for *Collier's* and other periodicals; edited *The Encyclopedia of Sports* (1944); assisted in the writing of several athletes' autobiographies; and wrote popular books on various sports, e.g., *The Story of Churchill Downs and the Kentucky Derby,* [New York], 1940.

MENTOR. Pseud. See Nathan D. Urner.

MERCER, JAMES KAZERTA (April 1, 1850– ?), journalist, was born in Bainbridge, Ross County, and attended the schools of that community. He spent sixteen years in newspaper work on the Pacific coast, worked in the document room of the U. S. Senate, and settled in Columbus in 1884.

Representative Men of Ohio 1896–97, (with C. N. Vallandigham), Columbus, 1896.

Representative Men of Ohio, 1904–1908 . . . , Columbus, [1908].

Ohio Legislative History . . . , 6 vols., Columbus, 1914–26.

MERCER, LEWIS PYLE (June 27, 1847–July 6, 1906), educator and clergyman, born in Chester County, Pa., came to East Rockport in 1868 to teach school. While there he began preaching in the Swedenborgian church. After successful pastorates in Detroit and Chicago, he returned to Ohio in 1901 as a pastor in Cincinnati; a year before his death, he was chosen president of Urbana University. He published numerous sermons, addresses, and books on Swedenborgian doctrine, e.g., *Swedenborg's Doctrine of Correspondence . . . ,* Chicago, 1889.

MEREDITH, L. P. (March 18, 1841– ?), dentist, was born in Xenia, Greene County. He learned dentistry from his father and practiced in Cincinnati. He also studied medicine and graduated from Ohio Medical College in 1871. He published lectures and pamphlets on dentistry as well as the volumes listed.

The Teeth and How to Save Them, Philadelphia, 1871.

Every-day Errors of Speech, Philadelphia, 1882.

MERRICK, FREDERICK (Jan. 29, 1810–March 5, 1894), clergyman and educator, was born in Wilbraham, Mass. Converted to Methodism in 1829, he resolved to become a minister and studied at Wesleyan University, Middletown, Conn. He was principal of Amenia Seminary, N. Y., 1834–38, and was then elected professor of natural science at Ohio University. He joined the Ohio Conference on trial in 1841 and was ordained an elder in 1843. Ohio Methodists were planning to found a college at Delaware, and as one of the financial agents Merrick did much to establish the school. In 1845, the year after it opened, he joined the faculty, where he served for the remainder of his life. He was president of the school, 1860–73. His only published book was a series of lectures. He died at Delaware, venerated as one of the founders of Ohio Wesleyan University.

Formalism in Religion, Cincinnati, 1865.

MERRILL, CATHARINE (Jan. 24, 1824–May 30, 1900), educator, was born in Corydon, Ind., and spent most of her life in that state, but in the late 1850s she taught in a Cleveland girls' school for a time. A posthumous collection of her writings was published: *The Man Shakespeare, and Other Essays,* Indianapolis, [1902]. IATB

MERRILL, STEPHEN MASON (Sept. 16, 1825–Nov. 12, 1905), clergyman, was born near Mt. Pleasant, Jefferson County, and was reared in Clermont County. He became a Methodist minister in the Ohio Conference in 1846. He was editor of the *Western Christian Advocate,* 1868–72, and was consecrated a bishop of the Methodist Church in 1872. He was an outstanding authority on ecclesiastical law. His death occurred in Keyport, N. J.

Christian Baptism; Its Subjects and Mode, Cincinnati, 1876.
The New Testament Idea of Hell, New York, 1878.
Second Coming of Christ Considered . . . , Cincinnati, 1879.
Doctrinal Aspects of Christian Experience, Cincinnati, [1882].
A Digest of Methodist Law . . . , New York [1885].
Outline Thoughts on Prohibition . . . , Cincinnati, 1886.
Sunday Paper, (with Theodore E. Schmauk), New York, 1889.
Organic Union of American Methodism, [Cincinnati], 1892.
Mary of Nazareth and Her Family . . . , Cincinnati, 1895.
Crisis of This World . . . , Cincinnati, 1896.
Atonement; A Brief Study, New York, [1901].
Sanctification: Right Views and Other Views, New York, [1901].
Discourses on Miracles, New York, [1902].

MERSHON, RALPH SMITH (Feb. 13, 1830–March 26, 1914), jeweler, was born near Trenton, N. J. He came to Zanesville in 1850 and spent the remainder of his life in that city. Owner of a jewelry store, he also invented a regulator for watches and various other mechanical devices. Most of his poems, which were privately published in 1911, were memorials of local events.

Saul of Tarsus: A Dramatic Poem, [Zanesville, 1889].
Poems, Zanesville, 1911.

MERTON, HOLMES WHITTIER (April 5, 1860–Jan. 18, 1948), lecturer and educator, was born in Lebanon, Warren County. After being educated by private tutors, he became a lecturer in 1880 and delivered many lectures on the "mental and physical life of man." He also served on the faculty of Pace Institute. He died in Stamford, Conn. His *Heliocentric Astrology* was published under the pen name Yarmo Vedra.

Descriptive Mentality, Boston, [1893].
Life and Healing, Boston, 1894.
Heliocentric Astrology; Or, Essentials of Astronomy and Solar Mentality . . . , Philadelphia, [1899].
Social Harmonism; Human Rights under Functional Government, New York, [1914].
How to Choose the Right Vocation . . . , New York, 1917.

MERZ, CHARLES (Feb. 23, 1893–), journalist, was born in Sandusky, Erie County, the son of Charles Hope Merz (q.v.). After graduating from Yale University in 1915, he joined the staff of *Harper's Weekly.* He served in the army during World War I, and afterward worked on the New York *World* until 1931. He then shifted to the New York *Times,* becoming its editor-in-chief in 1938. He has published several books, e.g., *The Dry Decade,* New York, 1931. WW 30

MERZ, CHARLES HOPE (Nov. 7, 1861–Oct. 14, 1947), physician, was born in Oxford, Butler County, the son of Karl Merz (q.v.). After graduating from Western Reserve College of Medicine in 1885, he began practicing in Sandusky. He was a prolific writer on the subject of Masonry, edited a number of Masonic magazines, and wrote *"The House of Solomon" of Francis Bacon . . . ,* Sandusky, 1916.

MERZ, KARL (Sept. 19, 1836–Jan. 30, 1890), musician and educator, was born in Bensheim, Hesse, the son of an accomplished musician whose training enabled Karl to become a church organist at the age of eleven. After teaching school for several years, he came to America in 1854 and taught music in various schools for girls until 1861, when he joined the faculty of Oxford Female College. He remained in Oxford until 1882, when he became director of the department of music and arts at University of Wooster. He was a regular contributor to *Brainard's Musical World,* published in Cleveland, and became editor of that publication in 1873. The magazine enjoyed a national circulation, and Merz's writings were widely read by musicians. Many of these articles, along with other essays and lectures, were collected by his son, Charles Hope Merz (q.v.), and published posthumously in a volume entitled *Music and Culture.* Among other works were several instruction books and a well known textbook: *The Elements of Harmony and Musical Composition* (1881). He died in Wooster.

Musical Hints for the Million, Cleveland, 1875.

Music and Culture, Cleveland, 1890.

METZ, WALTER C. (Feb. 1, 1879–June 18, 1936), banker, was born in Newark, Licking County. After graduating from Ohio State University in 1906, he went to work for the Newark Trust Company and became president of that bank in 1916. Besides the title below, he wrote a number of articles for magazines.

Prehistoric Remains in Licking County, Newark, [1899?].

MEYER, FULGENCE (May 30, 1876–Nov. 14, 1938), Catholic priest, born in Remich, Luxemburg, lived for 29 years in Cincinnati, where he was rector of St. Francis Preparatory School. He published numerous sermons and devotional books, e.g., *Back to God . . . ,* Cincinnati, 1928.

MEYER, HUGO RICHARD (April 1, 1866–June 15, 1923), was born in Cincinnati, Hamilton County. He graduated from Harvard University in 1892. He lived for a number of years in Australia, and his death occurred in Melbourne. He published several studies of state and municipal ownership, e.g., *The British State Telegraphs . . . ,* New York, 1907. WW 11

MICHAEL, BERTHA INWOOD (Dec. 16, 1876–   ) was born in Van Wert County. After teaching in district schools, she married O. A. Michael, a farmer. She lived in Scott for a number of years and is now a resident of Bryan. She has published *Home Poems and Summer Memories,* Boston, [1923].

MICHAEL, WILLIAM HENRY (July 14, 1845–May 16, 1916), journalist and diplomat, was born in Marysville, Union County. He served with Iowa troops in the Civil War until he was wounded at Shiloh, after which he joined the navy. His varied career included newspaper work in Iowa and Nebraska, the practice of law, a head clerkship in the Department of State, and a post as U. S. consul general in Calcutta.

Better Dead Than Houseless, Tariff in Story, Philadelphia, 1888.

History of the Department of State . . . , Washington, D. C., 1901.

The Declaration of Independence . . . , Washington, D. C., 1904.

MICHELFELDER, SYLVESTER CLARENCE (Oct. 27, 1889–Sept. 30, 1951), clergyman, was born in New Washington, Crawford County. After graduating from Capital Seminary in 1914, he was pastor of Lutheran churches in Willard, 1914–21, Pittsburgh, Pa., 1921–31, and Toledo, 1931–45. At the time of his death he was executive secretary of the Lutheran World Federation, Geneva, Switzerland. He published a book on marriage: *So You Are Thinking!,* Columbus, [1946]. WWW 3

MICHIE, PETER SMITH (March 24, 1839–Feb. 16, 1901), army officer, born in County Forfar, Scotland, grew up in Cincinnati, where his family settled in 1843. An 1863 graduate of U. S. Military Academy, he served brilliantly with the engineers during the last years of the Civil War and received the brevet rank of brigadier general. From 1867 until his death, he was on the faculty of the U. S. Military Academy. Besides the two works listed below, he wrote a number of technical works on military and scientific subjects, several of them intended for use as textbooks at West Point.

The Life and Letters of Emory Upton . . . , New York, 1885.

General McClellan, New York, 1901.

MIDDLING, THEOPHILUS. Pseud. See Denton J. Snider.

MIELZINER, MOSES (Aug. 12, 1828–Feb. 18, 1903), rabbi, born and educated in Prussia, came to America in 1865 and to Cincinnati in 1879. He was on the faculty of Hebrew Union College, 1879–1903. After the death of Isaac M. Wise (q.v.) in 1900, he served as president of Hebrew Union College until his death. Besides the works below, he published numerous articles on the Jewish religion and a number of sermons and addresses.

The Jewish Law of Marriage and Divorce . . . , Cincinnati, 1884.

Introduction to the Talmud . . . , Cincinnati, 1894.

MIESSE, JONATHAN (Feb. 15, 1817–1885), physician, was born in Reading, Pa. He began to practice medicine in Chillicothe in 1838 and practiced there for the remainder of his life.

A Journey to Egypt and Palestine, in the Year 1855, Chillicothe, 1859.

MILES, ROBERT PARKER HARRISON (July 11, 1866–Dec. 28, 1940), was born in Burnley, Lancashire, England, but made his home in Lakewood during his later years. An ordained Presbyterian minister, he held pastorates in New Jersey and New York, but was more active as a journalist and lecturer. He published *Three Men and a Woman. A Story of Life in New York,* New York, 1901. WWW 1

MILEY, JOHN (1813–1895), clergyman and educator, was born in Ohio. He was ordained to the Methodist ministry and after serving a number of churches became professor of systematic theology at Drew Seminary in 1873.

Treatise on Class Meetings, Cincinnati, 1851.

The Atonement in Christ . . . , New York, 1879.

Systematic Theology . . . , 2 vols., New York, 1892–94.

MILLER, ADAM (1810–July 29, 1901), clergyman and physician, was born in Maryland, but when he was four his parents, who were Mennonites, brought him to western Ohio. Converted to Methodism, he went to Knox County in 1830 and was licensed to preach. He was a circuit rider in Virginia, Indiana, and Ohio. In 1834 he met Wilhelm Nast (q.v.), who was to become the founder of German Methodism. Miller's advice was one of the influences that led Nast to become a Methodist preacher. After preaching in Cincinnati, Lebanon, and elsewhere, his health broke and he studied medicine. He became a homeopathic physician in Chicago, the city where he died at the age of 92. Besides the titles below, he published a speller and other textbooks.

Origin and Progress of the German Missions in the Methodist Episcopal Church . . . , Cincinnati, 1843.

Letters on Homeopathy, Cincinnati, 1849.

Experience of German Methodist Preachers, Cincinnati, 1859.

Plain Talk to the Sick . . . , Chicago, 1879.

A New System of Muscular Flexion and Hygienic Treatment . . . , Chicago, 1890.

The Hammer and the Nail . . . , Chicago, 1893.

Mind, Matter and Motion . . . , Chicago, 1896.

Footprints through Nature to the Supernatural, Chicago, 1899.

MILLER, CHARLES CHRISTIAN (Nov. 26, 1856–May 31, 1927), educator, was born in Baltimore, Fairfield County. He began teaching in rural schools at the age of sixteen and in 1883 graduated from Ohio State University. He served as teacher and as superintendent in a number of Ohio schools, held several posts in the Ohio State Department of Education, and was president of Lima College, 1905–08. He edited the historical portions of two county histories: *History of Allen County* . . . , Chicago, 1906, and *History of Fairfield County* . . . , Chicago, [1912]. OBB

MILLER, CHARLES GRANT (1866–Oct. 13, 1928), journalist, was born in Salem Township, Champaign County. He was for some time secretary to Donn Piatt (q.v.) and was also correspondent for the Cleveland *Leader,* the *Christian Science Monitor,* and other papers. Much of the memoir of Piatt was prepared by Ella Kirby Piatt (q.v.), but the book was published under Miller's name. The second work below, which argues that pro-British propaganda has falsified American history, was republished in 1928 as *The Poisoned Loving Cup.*

Donn Piatt: His Work and His Ways, Cincinnati, 1893.

Treason to American Tradition . . . , [n.p., 1921?].

MILLER, C. LOCKE (July 12, 1884–Sept. 19, 1954), educator, was born in Hartford, Trumbull County. After graduating from Hiram College in 1905, he studied at Harvard Law School and at Ott School of Oratory, Chicago. He taught in Trumbull County schools and at Central State Normal School, Lock Haven, Pa. Living in Youngstown in the later part of his life, he ran unsuccessfully for Congress seven times. He lectured widely, wrote radio plays, published numerous poems in the Youngstown *Telegram,* and a collection of verse: *Battle Song for Slaves and Other Lyrics and Satires,* New York, [1941].

MILLER, DAYTON CLARENCE (March 13, 1866–Feb. 22, 1941), educator, was born in Strongsville, Cuyahoga County, and graduated from Baldwin University in 1886. After teaching for one year at his alma mater, he joined the staff of Case Institute of Technology in 1890 and remained on that faculty throughout his career. Besides a physics textbook and a number of technical studies, he published a revised version of the Lowell Institute lectures that he had delivered in 1914: *The Science of Musical Sounds,* New York, 1916. WWW 1

MILLER, ELIZABETH KUMLER (Feb. 1, 1835–Oct. 23, 1905), was born near Millville, Butler County. She graduated from Otterbein College in 1858. Her poems appeared in various periodicals, and in a collection: *Poems,* Dayton, 1905.

MILLER, ELLEN BELL ROBERTSON (Aug. 27, 1859–Aug. 11, 1937), was born in New London, Huron County. She died in Warrensville. She wrote articles and stories on nature and *Butterfly and Moth Book . . .* , New York, 1912.

MILLER, ETHEL HULL (March 7, 1889–), was born in Hartford, Trumbull County. She attended Hiram College, 1907–09, and in 1908 married Myron Messenger Miller, who assisted her with some of her writings until his death in 1953. Now Mrs. David Duff, she lives in Poland, Mahoning County. She has written considerable juvenile fiction, e.g., *White-Saddle,* Greenville, Pa., [1934]. WW 26

MILLER, H. C. (May 18, 1841–Feb. 15, 1920), was born at Rockyhill, Jackson County. He was a second lieutenant in the First Ohio Heavy Artillery from July, 1863, to June, 1865. He died at Jackson.

First Ohio Heavy Artillery History . . . , [Jackson, 1899].

MILLER, HARRIET MANN (June 25, 1831–Dec. 25, 1918), born in Albany, N. Y., was brought to Ohio when she was eleven and lived here until around 1849. Relatively late in life she began writing articles and books about birds and animals, using the pen name Olive Thorne Miller, e.g., *Little Brothers of the Air,* Boston, [1892].

MILLER, HENRY RUSSEL (May 12, 1880–Dec. 16, 1955), lawyer, was born in Sidney, Shelby County. He graduated from Westminster College, New Wilmington, Pa., in 1899; read law and was admitted to the Pennsylvania bar in 1903; and afterward practiced in Pittsburgh. He wrote a number of books, including a history of the First Division (1920) and *The Ambition of Mark Truitt,* Indianapolis, [1913]. WWW 3

MILLER, MRS. HERMAN A. See Dorothy E. Reid.

MILLER, IRVING JOHN ARMITAGE (Oct. 14, 1866–), journalist, was born in Ohio. Except that he was a journalist and lived for many years in Marshalltown, Iowa, no details concerning his life have been discovered.

Fireside Poems, Marshalltown, Iowa, 1887.

Twilight Thoughts; A Poetic Reverie on Man, Chicago, 1912.

Today and Yesterday, Lyrics for Young and Old, Chicago, 1916.

MILLER, JAMES ALEXANDER (April 28, 1864–May 27, 1942), clergyman and educator, was born in Greenwood, N. Y. He graduated from New York University (A.B., 1888; Ph.D., 1891). Ordained to the Presbyterian ministry in 1891, he served several churches in New York State until 1919, when he came to Ohio. He was on the faculty of Ohio University, 1919–23, and was pastor of the Presbyterian church at Huntsville, 1923–41.

The History of the Presbytery of Steuben . . . , Angelica, N. Y., 1897.

MILLER, JAMES RUSSELL (March 20, 1840–July 2, 1912), clergyman, born in Harshaville, Pa., spent a part of his boyhood in Calcutta, Ohio, where his family moved when he was about fourteen. A Presbyterian clergyman, he was a prolific writer during his ministerial career and published many articles, sermons, and devotional books, e.g., *The Joy of Service,* New York, [1898].

MILLER, JOHN G. (? – ?), was a Columbus lawyer who established the *Ohio Confederate* at Columbus in 1836. For a while it was a Democratic and States' Rights paper, but in 1840 it fell into line behind William Henry Harrison for President. His *The Great Convention* is an account of the Ohio convention held at Columbus in February of 1840. In literary quality, it rises far above the usual campaign document and constitutes a valuable contribution to the history of American politics. He was rewarded with the appointment as postmaster at Columbus in 1841 and served until 1845, when he returned to the practice of law. He was practicing in Columbus in 1857.

The Great Convention . . . , Columbus, [1840].

MILLER, JOHN HENDERSON (May 11, 1845–April 19, 1923), clergyman, was born in Mansfield, Richland County. After graduating from Wittenberg College in 1868 and Princeton Theological Seminary in 1871, he was ordained as a Presbyterian minister and served pastorates in Kansas and Missouri, where he was also active in Masonic activities. His writings include *Where the Rainbow Touches the Ground,* New York, 1906. WWW 1

MILLER, LEO FRANCIS (March 23, 1885–), clergyman and educator, was born in Canton, Stark County. He graduated from the Pontifical College Josephinum, Worthington, in 1907 and from the Pontifical Gregorian University, Rome, in 1913. He has been on the faculty of the Pontifical College Josephinum since 1915 and has served as dean since 1945. He has written many articles and several books, e.g., *A History of Philosophy,* New York, [1927]. CWW 11

MILLER, LOUISE KLEIN (Aug. 7, 1854–Oct. 24, 1943), educator and landscape architect, was born near Centerville, Montgomery County. After graduating from Cook County Normal School, Chicago, Ill., in 1893, she taught in the schools of various states. In 1904 she became curator of school gardens in Cleveland. Her writings include *As I See It,* Portland, Maine, 1941. WWW 2

MILLER, MARION MILLS (Feb. 27, 1864–Nov. 25, 1949), was born in Eaton, Preble County. After graduating from Princeton University in 1886, he taught English there for five years and later was secretary of various political reform organizations. He lived in New York City for some time and then moved to Lexington, Ky., where he founded the Maxwelton Publishing Company. The last title below is a dramatization of the Oscar Wilde novel.

Parnassus by Rail, New York, 1891.
Practical Suggestions for Mother and Housewife, New York, [1910].
American Debate; A History of Political and Economic Controversy in the United States . . ., 2 vols., New York, 1916.
The Return of Odysseus; A Greek Choric Play in Two Continuous Acts . . ., Boston, 1917.
The Picture of Dorian Gray . . ., New York, 1931.

MILLER, MINNIE WILLIS BAINES (Jan. 8, 1845– ?), was born in Lebanon, N. H. She attended the public schools of Springfield and graduated from Wittenberg College. Most of her life was spent in Ohio. At the age of fourteen she published her first sketch in *Waverly Magazine.* Some of her magazine writing was published under the pen name Marion Leroy. In 1882 she edited the *Book of Good Behavior.* She also wrote stories and poems for various papers and magazines and lectured on temperance and women's suffrage.

The Silent Land. A Study, Cincinnati, 1890.
His Cousin, the Doctor. A Story. Cincinnati, 1891.
The Pilgrims' Vision, Cincinnati, 1892.
Mrs. Cherry's Sister; Or, Christian Science at Fairfax, Cincinnati, 1900.

MILLER, NOLAN (May 4, 1912–), educator, was born in Kalida, Putnam County. When he was eleven, his parents moved to Detroit, Mich., where he later attended Wayne University. He taught in a Detroit high school and at Wayne before returning to Ohio to teach English at Antioch College. He is now chairman of the department of literature and editor of the *Antioch Review* and *New Campus Writing.* He has published several novels, e.g., *A Moth of Time . . .*, New York, [1946]. ANT

MILLER, OLIVE THORNE. Pseud. See Harriet M. Miller.

MILLER, ROBERT J. (Feb. 1, 1853–March 9, 1934), clergyman, born in Hanover, Pa., spent a part of his boyhood in New Concord. After graduating from Muskingum College in 1873, he became a Presbyterian clergyman and served churches in Ohio and other states. He wrote a biography of John K. Montgomery, longtime president of Muskingum College: *A Christian Educator,* Pittsburgh, 1932.

MILLER, SADIE MATHERS (Nov. 21, 1867–), was born in Cambridge, Guernsey County. She attended Scio College. Her last known address is Los Angeles. Her poems appeared in magazines, anthologies, and a collection: *Moonlight and Memories,* Tucson, Ariz., 1930. BDCP.

MILLER, SAMUEL ALMOND (Aug. 28, 1837–Dec. 18, 1897), lawyer, was born in Coolville, Athens County. Admitted to the bar in Cincinnati in April, 1860, he built up an extensive and lucrative practice, during which he found time to annotate and prepare for the press the statutes and laws of Ohio, a work which covered some 3,600 pages. He was deeply engrossed in geology and paleontology, fields in which he gained wide recognition for a number of original discoveries. He was one of the founders of the Cincinnati Society of Natural History, and in Jan., 1874, he began publication of the *Cincinnati Quarterly Journal of Science.* He wrote a number of monographs on scientific subjects. Lavishly illustrated with original cuts, his *North American Geology and Palaeontology* was privately printed in an unfortunately small edition, and few copies of this important book are known. He died in Cincinnati.

The American Palaeozoic Fossils: A Catalogue of the Genera and Species . . . , Cincinnati, 1877.

North American Geology and Palaeontology for the Use of Amateurs, Students, and Scientists, Cincinnati, 1889.

MILLER, SAMUEL SMITH (May 16, 1827–April 6, 1916), was born on a farm in Bethel Township, Clark County. He attended Wittenberg College, taught school for a time, but during the greater part of his life operated a farm near Springfield.

Early Settlers and Early Times on Donnell's Creek . . . , [n.p.], 1887.

MILLER, THURMAN (Dusty) (Dec. 28, 1881–), journalist and lecturer, was born on a farm in Marshall Township, Highland County. He graduated from Wilmington College in 1907, taught school for five years, and edited the Wilmington *Daily News-Journal* until 1924. After 1924 he continued to write a daily column for the paper. In 1922 he began public speaking and was nationally popular as a lecturer and after-dinner speaker. Besides booklets and articles, he has published a book of sketches of his uncle, an attorney, William H. Miller: *Uncle Bill,* [Wilmington, 1943]. WW 22

MILLIGAN, ROBERT (July 25, 1814–March 20, 1875), born in County Tyrone, Ireland, grew up near Youngstown, where his parents settled around 1818. Converted to the Disciples of Christ Church and ordained a minister in 1844, he taught in several colleges. During the last few years of his life he published a number of religious books, e.g., *Reason and Revelation,* Cincinnati, 1868.

MILLS, CLARENCE ALONZO (Dec. 9, 1891–), physician and educator, born in Miami, Ind., graduated from the University of South Dakota in 1917 and did graduate work at the University of Cincinnati (Ph.D., 1920; M.D., 1922). He has taught at the University of Cincinnati Medical School since 1919, except for the years 1922–28, when he taught at Union Medical College, Peking, China. He has written several books on the relation of climate to health, e.g., *Living with the Weather,* Cincinnati, [1934]. WW 30

MILLS, JOB SMITH (Feb. 28, 1848–Sept. 16, 1909), clergyman, was born in Plymouth, Richland County. After graduating from Illinois Wesleyan University, he served as pastor of Otterbein University, 1874–80 and 1885–87, and taught at Western College, Iowa, 1887–93. After being elected bishop of the United Brethren church in 1893, he traveled widely in connection with mission work.

Mission Work in West Africa, Dayton, 1898.

Holiness, Dayton, 1902.

MILLS, LEWIS ESTE (Aug. 13, 1836–April 10, 1878), lawyer, was born in Morristown, N. J. After graduating from Yale University in 1856, he came to Cincinnati, where he read law in the office of his elder brother. He was admitted to the bar in 1858. During the Civil War, he was an aide on the staff of General R. B. Potter, Ninth Army Corps. Besides the titles below, he gave a speech on General John Pope's Virginia campaign of 1862 which was published as a pamphlet in 1870. He died in Florence, Italy.

Glimpses of Southern France and Spain, Cincinnati, 1867.

MILLS, RUTH. See Ruth M. H. Teague.

MILLS, WILLIAM (Sept. 1, 1811–Nov. 25, 1864), physician, was born near Knoxville, Jefferson County. He graduated from Franklin College in 1844 and also studied at Jefferson Medical College, Philadelphia. He practiced in New Athens from 1846 until his death.

Marrow of Practical Medicine . . . , St. Clairsville, 1848.

MILLS, WILLIAM CORLESS (Jan. 2, 1860–Jan. 17, 1928), museum director, was born at Pyrmont, Montgomery County. After graduating from Ohio State University in 1898, he became curator and librarian of the Ohio Archaeological and Historical Society. He was active in exploring mounds and village sites in Ohio, wrote many articles derived from his activities, and compiled *Archaeological Atlas of Ohio . . . ,* Columbus, 1914. WWW 1

MILLS, WILLIAM STOWELL (Nov. 14, 1850–Nov. 4, 1929), educator, was born in Reynoldsburg, Franklin County, but lived for a number of years in Lake County. He taught school in Ohio and later was a school principal in Brooklyn, N. Y., for 28 years. Besides the title below, he published an address, some poetry, and a work on genealogy.

The Story of the Western Reserve of Connecticut, New York, [1900].

MILNER, DUNCAN CHAMBERS (March 10, 1841–March 18, 1928), clergyman, was born in Mt. Pleasant, Jefferson County. He served in the Civil War with the 98th O.V.I., and afterward attended Washington and Jefferson College and Union Theological Seminary. Ordained to the Presbyterian ministry in 1868, he served pastorates in Kansas and Illinois. He wrote *Lincoln and Liquor,* New York, 1920. WWW 1

MILOTIZ. Pseud. See Moritz Loth.

MINER, JOHN THOMAS (Jack) (April 10, 1863–Nov. 3, 1944), naturalist, was born in Cuyahoga County and spent his boyhood there. In 1904 he established a bird sanctuary in Ontario, Canada. He wrote a syndicated column on conservation and nature, lectured widely, and published several books on the subject, e.g., *Jack Miner on Current Topics,* Toronto, [1929]. WW 16

MINER, LUELLA (Oct. 30, 1861–Dec., 1935), missionary-teacher, was born in Oberlin, Lorain County. She graduated from Oberlin College in 1884. In 1887 she went as a missionary to China, and during her long service there she taught in various schools and colleges. Her writings include *China's Book of Martyrs . . . ,* Cincinnati, [1903]. WWW 1

MINNICH, HARVEY C. (March 10, 1861–May 12, 1952), educator, was born in Union, Montgomery County. He graduated from Ohio Northern University in 1886 and served as superintendent of schools in Hutchinson, Kan. (1889–92), Hillsboro (1892–1902), and Middletown (1902–03). He was dean of the Miami University School of Education, 1903–29. He wrote *William Holmes McGuffey and His Readers,* New York, [1936]. WWW 3

MINNIG, SAMUEL R. (Jan. 21, 1847–Aug. 2, 1935), journalist, was born in Berne, Switzerland. He came to New Philadelphia, Tuscarawas County, in 1869, and in 1872 purchased *Der Beobachter,* a weekly German paper, which he published for forty years. He died in Dover, Tuscarawas County.

Erzähltes und Erleftes . . . , New Philadelphia, 1894.

MINOR, THOMAS CHALMERS (July 6, 1846–Feb. 18, 1912), physician, was born in Cincinnati, Hamilton County. After graduating from Ohio Medical College in 1867, he practiced in Cincinnati and held various municipal offices. He contributed many articles to professional journals and wrote a number of medical treatises, of which his *Notes on the Epidemiology of Ohio* is the best known. This work includes a valuable study of the history of the state and the topography, geology, population, hydrography, and climatology of the various counties. He is known to have written many poems and several opera librettos, none of which appears to have been published in book form. His novel *Her Ladyship* was published anonymously.

Notes on the Epidemiology of Ohio, [Cincinnati, 1877].

Her Ladyship, a Novel, Cincinnati, 1880.

Athothis, a Satire of Modern Medicine, Cincinnati, 1887.

MINTURN, JOSEPH ALLEN (June 20, 1861–April 3, 1943), lawyer, was born in Athens County. From the age of fifteen he was a resident of Indiana. In 1880 he graduated from Pennsylvania Military College. He then studied law and was admitted to the Indiana bar. He was widely known as a specialist in patent law.

The Inventor's Friend . . . , Indianapolis, [1893].

Price-Regulations under Patents, Indianapolis, [1916].

The Puritans; An Historical Poem . . . , Noblesville, Ind., 1917.

The American Spirit, Indianapolis, [1921].

Brown County Ballads . . . , [Indianapolis, 1928].

Frances Slocum of Miami Lodge . . . , Indianapolis, [1928].

Historical and Other Poems, Indianapolis, [1939].

MIRZA, YOUEL BENJAMIN (Dec. 23, 1888–Sept. 29, 1947), was born in Persia and came to America when he was fifteen years old. He studied at Ohio Wesleyan University, 1906–08, and later earned a Ph.D. in history at Johns Hopkins University. A member of the Society of Friends, he taught history at Earlham College, Richmond, Ind., until 1925, when he was employed by Elder & Johnston, Dayton, and placed in charge of the rug department. His writings include *When I Was a Boy in Persia,* Boston, [1920]. WWW 2

MITCHEL, FREDERICK AUGUSTUS (Dec. 4, 1839–Aug. 19, 1918), journalist, son of Ormsby MacKnight Mitchel (q.v.), was born in Cincinnati, Hamilton County. After graduating from Brown University in 1860, he served in the Civil War until August 17, 1863. He was later a staff editor of the

American Press Association, and lived in East Orange, N. J. Besides his books, he wrote a number of short stories.

Ormsby MacKnight Mitchel, Astronomer and General; A Biographical Narrative, Boston, 1887.

The Twenty Million Ransom, a Story of the Future, New York, 1890.

Chattanooga, a Romance of the American Civil War, New York, [1891].

Chickamauga, a Romance of the American Civil War, New York, [1892].

Sweet Revenge, a Romance of the Civil War, New York, 1897.

MITCHEL, ORMSBY MacKNIGHT (July 28, 1809–Oct. 30, 1862), astronomer, soldier, and undoubtedly one of the finest salesmen America has ever known, was born at what is now Morganfield, Union County, Ky. About three or four years later, his father, a surveyor, died, and in 1816, the widow brought her family to Lebanon, Warren County, to live with a married daughter. Here, until he was twelve, Mitchel received his early schooling from a brother, whose instruction included Latin, Greek, and arithmetic. At twelve he was apprenticed to a storekeeper. A false charge of lying caused Mitchel to run away and join a train of Conestoga wagons as a "waggoner boy." He next obtained employment as a clerk in a new store in Xenia. Learning that he could obtain a free education at the U. S. Military Academy, Mitchel applied to the Hon. William MacLean, U. S. Representative from Piqua, for an appointment. He was ordered to West Point for the entrance examination. He walked to Sandusky and from there worked his way to Buffalo on a lake boat and then along the Erie Canal and down the Hudson to the Point, where he arrived July 1, 1825, in time to take the examination. Despite his relatively meager education, Mitchel did well at West Point. He graduated in 1829, fifteenth in a class of 46, thirteen places below Robert E. Lee. He did so well in mathematics that he remained at the Point two more years as assistant professor of the subject. While at West Point, Mitchel engaged in two activities common to all soldiers—he grumbled about the food and he fell in love. His lady was a young widow of Cornwall-on-the-Hudson, Louisa Clark Trask. Besides courting and teaching, Mitchel managed to study law. In the summer of 1831, Mitchel was employed in the survey of the Philadelphia and Norristown Railroad. Upon its completion he undertook the survey of the Pennsylvania and Ohio Railroad, which he completed in November of 1831. Overcoming the objections of her parents, Mitchel married Louisa Trask on Sept. 10 of that same year. Shortly afterward he was assigned to Fort Marion, St. Augustine, Fla. There he served until July 30, 1832, when he resigned his commission in the Army. In October of 1832, Mitchel arrived in Cincinnati, planning to make it his permanent residence. His coming coincided with an outburst of intellectual activity following Mrs. Trollope's departure. Major artists were Joseph Dorfeuille and Hiram Powers. Nearly the entire Beecher clan was at Lane Seminary and at the center of Cincinnati's cultural activities. Daniel Drake was still the "spark plug" of Cincinnati's intellectual advance. Mitchel was quickly accepted into the inner circle and soon became a member of the Semi-Colon Club, formed probably in 1832, a literary society that antedated the present Literary Club by nearly twenty years. It was a way of life in which Mitchel took an active part and one which led directly to the Cincinnati Observatory. By the end of 1832, Mitchel had formed a law partnership with young Edward D. Mansfield (q.v.). Their office was on Third Street between Main and Walnut Streets, in what was then the heart of the business district. The young men were not particularly interested in the practice of law and were perfectly willing to devote themselves to more congenial tasks. Mansfield, in his *Autobiography,* tells of how he and Mitchel spent their time at the office. While Mansfield worked on his *Political Grammar,* Mitchel sat in his corner reading Quintilian on oratory and translating portions of it aloud to Mansfield. The result of this was that Mitchel published, in 1833, a translation of Quintilian "digested and prepared for the use of the American people." Inevitably, then, in 1834, Mitchel became a teacher and Mansfield became a professional writer. Before dissolving the partnership, however, both Mansfield and Mitchel joined Lyman Beecher's church, the Second Presbyterian. Also, perhaps as an indication that he had not quite made up his mind what to do, Mitchel became one of the incorporators of the Cincinnati Law Library. Nevertheless, according to Charles Cist (q.v.), Mitchel in 1834 opened his school—The Institute of Science and Languages—assisted by John A. Wilstack. This is far more tenable than the idea that the school opened in 1836, which would mean that Mitchel was without a job for two years. The 1836 date originated in the fact that the school first appears in the Cincinnati directory for that year, but the 1834 directory was published before the school opened, and there was no directory in 1835. In 1836 the Cincinnati College curriculum was revised by Daniel Drake and William McGuffey. Courses in the liberal arts and sciences were added to the curricula of law and medicine. Mitchel was appointed a professor of mathematics and astronomy, a position he held until the demise of the college. He is credited with teaching one of the first collegiate courses in civil engineering while at Cincinnati College. Apparently he could not get along on the salary the college paid him, for on May 3, 1837, he was engaged for $1,000 to survey the route of the newly formed Little Miami Railroad from Xenia to Cincinnati. On Aug. 24 at Dennison's Tavern, the railroad accepted Mitchel's route as far as Springfield and appointed him chief engineer at $2,500 a year. In addition—also while teaching—Mitchel sold 800 shares of the railroad's stock. In spite of the panic, the report of his survey was published in that same year, in Cincinnati. However, in May, 1838, he resigned as chief engineer, apparently because he was unable to work with his colleagues. As has been stated, Mitchel continued to teach while working for the Little Miami Railroad. Beginning in 1837 he took an active part in the Western Literary Institute and College of Professional Teachers. This was an association of professional teachers from all over the old Northwest and the border states. It met once a year each October, in Cincinnati for a grand convention and get-together. Like present-day teachers, the members of the Institute could generate a good deal of enthusiasm over lectures and discussions on such subjects as "Should the Art of Conversation Be Taught in the Schools?" or "How to Use the Blackboard." Such persons as Catherine Beecher, Archbishop John B. Purcell, the Rev. Alexander Campbell, Daniel Drake, William McGuffey, Milo G. Williams, B. P. Aydelott, and Albert Picket were among the active members. Strangely, Mitchel's name never appears on the list of members of the Institute although he took a most active part in its activities and served on many committees. In 1837 he talked on "The Importance of Civil Engineering as a Branch of Collegiate Education." In 1839 he was elected as Director from Ohio. A direct outgrowth of the Western Literary Institute was the organization, in 1840, of the Cincinnati Society for Promotion of Useful Knowledge. Its purpose was the promotion of adult education. It was divided into fourteen sections, each dealing with some phase of knowledge. Mitchel took a leading part in its organization and was head of the section on exact and mixed science. His lectures were well received by the public. During 1841 Mitchel continued to teach at Cincinnati College and to lecture for the Society for the Promotion of Useful Knowledge. He was also a member of the Board of Visitors to West Point Academy. This was probably Mitchel's last year of quiet, unexciting living, for with 1842 the fulfillment of his promise in life began. On Jan. 6, 1842, he was in Columbus attending a military convention that the Cincinnati *Gazette* darkly called a disguised Locofoco convention. Four days later, in command of ten men of the City Guard, he helped put down a riot that followed the suspension of the Miami Exporting Company and the Cincinnati Bank. During the winter Mitchel undertook, for the Society for the Promotion of Useful Knowledge, a series of three lectures on astronomy to be given in the ballroom of Mrs. Trollope's Bazaar. The course was announced as "a grand and noble crusade against the stars." The subject was "The Stability of the Solar System." With his ability to restate abstruse thoughts in simple language, intensified by enthusiasm and illustrated with transparencies of the heavens, Mitchel's lectures became an instant success. The people of Cincinnati were given an intimate glimpse into affairs closed to the vast majority of mankind. By popular demand, Mitchel was forced to redeliver his last lecture before an audience of nearly 2,000 in the largest available hall—the Wesley Chapel. At the end of his lecture he announced that he would devote the next five years of his life to erecting an astronomical observatory in Cincinnati: "I will go to the people and by the anvil of the blacksmith, by the workbench of the carpenter, and thus onward to the rich parlor of the wealthy, I will plead the cause of science. . . . I shall visit personally one thousand of our citizens and be refused by each and every one before I will yield and resign the effort. I am determined to show the autocrat of all the Russias that an obscure individual, in the wilderness city in a republican country, can raise here more money by voluntary gift in behalf of science than his majesty can raise in the same way throughout his whole dominions." On May 23, 1842, a public meeting was held in the hall of Cincinnati College to organize the Cincinnati Astronomical Society. Subscriptions of $6,500 at the rate of $25 a share were announced. Each share allowed two members of the family at a time to use the facilities of the Observatory. People from all walks of life subscribed to the stock—it was a genuine popular movement. Ten days later Mitchel was ordered to Europe to obtain a lens and to visit observatories to gain experience in their design and operation. He first visited several officials in Washington, but found them uninterested in the venture or skeptical of its success. After a tedious voyage of two months he reached England, where Sir George Airy of the Greenwich Observatory instructed him in the art of astronomical observation. Mitchel was primarily interested in finding a lens, however, and, unable to find one in England, he went on to France and then to Germany. In Munich he found an objective for a refracting telescope twelve inches in diameter. The price was $9,000. He returned to Cincinnati in October, and the Astronomical Society agreed to the purchase of the lens if Mitchel would raise the money. By the second week of November, he had personally raised $2,000. The first payment on the lens was then made. During 1843 Mitchel concentrated on obtaining an observatory. With the aid of Judge Jacob Burnet, he persuaded Nicholas Longworth (q.v.) to donate land on Mount Adams as a site for the observatory. Longworth stipulated that unless the building was completed promptly the land should revert to him. Mitchel also devoted himself to persuading John Quincy Adams to lay the cornerstone. On Nov. 9, 1843, in a pouring rain, Adams delivered an oration and laid the cornerstone before an audience of several thousand. The next day he gave his speech again for those citizens who had missed it the day before. For Mitchel, while it was all very gratifying, the work on the observatory was just beginning. During the next year, he personally supervised its construction—hiring the workmen, constructing brick and lime kilns, and raising the necessary funds to pay for everything. By Dec., 1844, the building was completed at a cost of $2,000, six months before Longworth's deadline. On Jan. 23, 1845, the telescope arrived, and within two months it was assembled and in place. On April 14, Mitchel took his first look through the Cincinnati Great Equatorial Refracting Telescope. If he ever had a happiest moment in his life, this was most certainly it. However, he had to face the fact that he was without a paying job, because on Jan. 19, 1844, the Cincinnati College was destroyed by fire, and with it went Mitchel's livelihood. Since the income from sightseers to the observatory was not enough for his support, he was granted permission to give a series of lectures in the East. Beginning in Boston, he was an immediate success. In New York he received a standing ovation. The income from lecture tours kept both the observatory and Mitchel going for years. When the observatory was completed and he was assured of an income, he could devote his time to astronomy. In July, 1846, he published the first number of the *Sidereal Messenger,* the first popular magazine on astronomy in America. In October he was joined by Henry Twitchell, a sailor from New Hampshire, who rendered him invaluable service for the next fifteen years. Mrs. Mitchel also assisted him. For the next decade he devoted himself to the unexciting, but important, job of remeasuring the multiple stars south of the equator as listed by Friedrich Von Struve in 1827. Also in this period, he found time to act as adjutant general of Ohio, 1847–48. In 1848 he perfected a magnetic clock and received an honorary M.A. from Harvard. The year 1848 also saw the demise of the *Sidereal Messenger.* During the winter of 1848–49, in order to increase his income, he surveyed the route of the Ohio and Mississippi Railroad and acted as chief engineer. In August he reported on a newly invented declination apparatus before the American Association for the Advancement of Science. Financial problems of the observatory remained difficult during the 1850s. Twice Mitchel proposed schemes to liquidate the observatory or refinance it, but to no avail. Consequently, in 1860, he accepted a position as head of the Dudley Observatory in Albany, N. Y., which he had helped to design. With the coming of the Civil War he was quick to offer his services. On Aug. 9, 1861, Lincoln appointed him a brigadier general of volunteers, and he was made commander of the Department of the Ohio. Later, when his command was united with the Department of the Cumberland, he served under General Don Carlos Buell. In April, 1862, he made his famous dash from Shelbyville, Tenn., to Huntsville, Ala., for which he was promoted to major general. However, his relationship with Buell grew increasingly difficult, and on Sept. 17 of that year he was ordered to command the Department of the South with headquarters at Hilton Head, S. C. Before he could organize his command, he died of yellow fever at Beaufort, S. C. Mitchel published nine books during his lifetime. In addition to reports of railroad surveys, he wrote a textbook on algebra, a translation of Quintilian, and a number of books on astronomy. These latter works are based on his very popular lectures. His *The*

Planetary and Stellar World was republished several times in England and America, as was the posthumous *The Astronomy of the Bible.* Most of his writings, however, appeared in periodicals such as his own *Sidereal Messenger* and in the annual reports of various organizations. Because of his ability to restate abstruse thoughts in simple language, his books on astronomy are easy to read and to understand. As a popularizer of a difficult scientific subject, he was most successful. His more technical works, while commensurably more difficult for a layman, are still lucidly and simply written. Upon his death Mitchel left a widow and five children. He had been honored with an M.A. from Harvard and an LL.D. from Washington College and had been made a Fellow of the Royal Astronomical Society, London. Somehow or other, Mitchel never quite rated as a genius. He was a good teacher, but by no means a William H. McGuffey. He was a good engineer but no Roebling or Dodge. He was a good astronomer but certainly no Galileo. His reputation in this field today is that of solid but unspectacular work. He was a good general, perhaps better than Buell, but he was no Grant or Lee. He is pre-eminent, however, as the man who, singlehanded, sold enough stock to a city of people fresh from the frontier and all its crude hardheadedness to build the first astronomical observatory in the Western Hemisphere.

Yeatman Anderson, III

Survey of the Little Miami Railroad . . . , Cincinnati, 1837.

A Course of Six Lectures on Astronomy . . . , New York, 1848.

The Planetary and Stellar Worlds . . . , New York, 1848.

Popular Astronomy. A Concise Elementary Treatise . . . , New York, 1860.

The Astronomy of the Bible . . . , New York, 1863.

MITCHELL, CHARLES ANDERSON (Jan. 18, 1864–July 13, 1948), clergyman and educator, was born in Springfield, Clark County. He graduated from Bellevue College in 1892 and Princeton Theological Seminary in 1896. He was ordained to the Presbyterian ministry in 1896, served on the Bellevue College faculty, with some interruptions during which he was doing advanced study, 1893–1902, and was on the faculty of Presbyterian Theological Seminary at Omaha, Neb., 1902–37. He wrote *The Model Prayer and Other New Testament Studies . . .* , Boston, 1918. WW 21

MITCHELL, DANIEL HOLMES (c.1883–May 9, 1909), was born in Cincinnati, Hamilton County. He died in Arizona at the age of 27. An elaborate book describing Arizona was published posthumously: *God's Country,* Cincinnati, 1910.

MITCHELL, MILDRED WILLEY (Jan. 9, 1898–), born in Freeville, N. Y., graduated from Oberlin College in 1918 and lived in Ohio for more than twenty years before moving to California. She now lives in San Jose. She has published a volume of verse: *Obbligato,* Boston, [1941].

MITCHELL, STEWART (Nov. 25, 1892–Nov. 3, 1957), was born in Cincinnati, Hamilton County. He graduated from Harvard University (A.B. 1915; Ph.D., 1933). He was managing editor of the *Dial,* 1919–20, and of the *New England Quarterly,* 1928–37. He was editor of Massachusetts Historical Society, 1929–39, and in 1947 he became its director. He published *Poems,* New York, 1921, and a biography: *Horatio Seymour of New York,* Cambridge, Mass., 1938. WWW 3

MITCHELL, THOMAS DUCHE (1791–May 13, 1865), physician, born in Philadelphia, was on the faculty of the Medical College of Ohio from 1831 to 1837. Author of a *materia medica* and numerous medical books and lectures, he published a pamphlet while in Ohio: *Hints on the Connexion of Labour with Study . . .* , Cincinnati, 1832.

MLAKAR, FRANK (May 15, 1913–), was born in Cleveland, Cuyahoga County, of Slovenian parents. He attended Collinwood High School, lived in New York for a time, and served as a medical sergeant in World War II. He married an Australian girl and has divided his time between New York and Melbourne. In his first novel, he recounts the sufferings of a Slovenian immigrant who comes to Cuyahoga City (Cleveland): *He, the Father,* New York, [1950].

MOERLEIN, GEORGE (June 8, 1852–Aug. 31, 1891), brewer, was born in Cincinnati, Hamilton County. He graduated from high school in 1869, after which he studied brewing in Bavaria, and in 1872 he joined his father's brewery. His book, which is an account of a trip around the world with two friends in 1881, was published simultaneously in German.

A Trip around the World, Cincinnati, [1886].

MOFFAT, JAMES CLEMENT (May 30, 1811–June 7, 1890), Presbyterian minister and educator, was professor of Latin and esthetics at Miami University from 1841 to 1852. In 1853 he joined the Princeton faculty. Besides lectures and sermons published during his stay in Ohio he published *A Rhyme of the North Country* in 1847. His best-known poetic effort, *Alwyn: A Romance of Study,* [New York, 1875], traces the spiritual struggles of its main character.

MOFFAT, JAMES DAVID (March 15, 1846–March 15, 1916), clergyman and educator, was born in New Lisbon, Columbiana County. He graduated from Washington and Jefferson College, Washington, Pa., in 1869 and was licensed to preach in 1871. He became co-pastor with his father of a Presbyterian church in Wheeling, W. Va., in 1872 and three years later succeeded his father as pastor. He was named president of his alma mater in 1881 and served until 1914.

Historical Sketch of Washington and Jefferson College, Washington, Pa., 1890.

MOLEY, RAYMOND (Sept. 27, 1886–), educator and journalist, was born in Berea, Cuyahoga County. He graduated from Baldwin-Wallace College in 1906, was superintendent of schools at Olmsted Falls, 1906–10, taught in Cleveland West High School, 1912–14, and Western Reserve University, 1916–19. He received his Ph.D. from Columbia University in 1918. He was director of the Cleveland Foundation, 1919–23. He served on the Columbia University faculty, 1923–54, and has been a contributing editor to *Newsweek* since 1937. Appointed an assistant secretary of state in 1933, he was one of the original advisers to President Roosevelt, popularly known as the Brain Trust. His best-known book is his account of his rapid disillusionment with most of the policies of the early New Deal: *After Seven Years,* New York, 1939. WW 30

MONA, VIVA. Pseud. See Peter F. Reed.

MONETTE, JOHN WESLEY (April 3, 1803–March 1, 1851), physician, was born near Chillicothe, Ross County. After attending Chillicothe schools, he graduated from Kentucky Medical College in 1822. In the late 1830s, he moved to Washington, Miss., where he became active in local and state politics. The discerning bookman, J. Christian Bay, has declared his *History of the Discovery and Settlement of the Valley of the Mississippi* to be "the best general descriptive history of American culture and progress in the middle west."

Observations on the Epidemic Yellow Fever of Natchez, and of the South-west, Louisville, Ky., 1842.

History of the Discovery and Settlement of the Valley of the Mississippi . . . , 2 vols., New York, 1846.

MONFORT, FRANCIS CASSATT (Sept. 1, 1844–Sept. 30, 1928), clergyman, was born in Greensburg, Ind. After graduating from Wabash College in 1864, he studied at McCormick Theological Seminary and Lane Seminary and was ordained to the Presbyterian ministry in 1870. His father, Joseph Glass Monfort (q.v.), began editing the *Presbyter* in Cincinnati in 1855; and in 1869 he changed its name to the *Herald and Presbyter.* Francis served at Fourth Presbyterian Church, Cincinnati, 1869–73, resigned to assume the editorship of the *Herald and Presbyter,* and was pastor of First Church, Cincinnati, 1879–88, while continuing his editorial duties. He published sermons in addition to the titles below.

Socialism and City Evangelization, Cincinnati, 1887.

The Law of Appeals, 1893.

Ecclesiastical Discipline, 1900.

Applied Theology, Cincinnati, [1904].

MONFORT, JOSEPH GLASS (Dec. 9, 1810–Feb. 1, 1906), clergyman and publisher, was born in Warren County. He graduated from Miami University in 1834 and was licensed to preach by the Presbyterian church in 1837. He served various pastorates and edited *Presbyterian of the West,* which he renamed the *Presbyter* and later the *Herald and Presbyter.* He settled in Cincinnati and established a publishing house, Monfort & Co., which published the magazine.

First Presbyterian Church in Walnut Hills, 1819–1888 . . . , Cincinnati, 1888.

MONNETTE, ORRA EUGENE (April 12, 1873–Feb. 23, 1936), banker and lawyer, was born near Bucyrus, Crawford County. After attending Ohio Wesleyan University, he read law and practiced in Bucyrus, Toledo, and Los Angeles. He also founded a bank in Los Angeles. Besides genealogical and historical works, his writings include a book of poems: *Red Shining Star,* [Los Angeles, 1927]. WWW 1

MONROE, JAMES (July 18, 1821–July 6, 1898), educator and legislator, was born in Plainfield, Conn., of Quaker parents. At the age of fourteen he was teaching school. He was persuaded by William Lloyd Garrison to lecture against slavery. He graduated from Oberlin College in 1846 and the seminary in 1849, and served on the faculty, 1849–62. He was a member of the state assembly, 1855–60, and the state senate, 1860–62, was U. S. consul at Rio de Janeiro, 1863–69, and served in the U. S. House of Representatives, 1871–81. From 1883 to 1896 he was again on the Oberlin faculty. Besides the title below, several of his speeches in Congress were published.

Oberlin Thursday Lectures, Addresses and Essays, Oberlin, 1897.

MONTEITH, JOHN (Jan. 31, 1833–May 4, 1918), clergyman and educator, was born in Elyria, Lorain County. After graduating from Yale University in 1856, he was ordained to the Congregational ministry. He served a church in Cleveland and others in Connecticut, Michigan, and Missouri. After retiring from the ministry because of ill health, he was in educational work in Missouri and California and later conducted a private school for girls in South Orange, N. J. Besides the novel below, he published a number of textbooks in natural history and geography.

Parson Brooks . . . , St. Louis, Mo., 1884.

MONTGOMERY, HELEN BARRETT (July 31, 1861–Oct. 18, 1934), minister and lecturer, was born in Kingsville, Ashtabula County. She graduated from Wellesley College in 1884 and was licensed as a Baptist minister in 1892. She was president of the American Baptist Foreign Missions Society, 1913–24. She lectured on foreign missions, also the subject of her books, e.g., *The Bible and Missions,* West Medford, Mass., [1920]. WWW 1

MONTGOMERY, MARCUS WHITMAN (June 21, 1839–Feb. 6, 1894), clergyman, born in Prattsburg, N. Y., and reared in Indiana, spent about six years in business in Cleveland in the 1870s. He afterward attended Yale Theological Seminary and became a Congregational minister in Fort Scott, Kan. Among other books he wrote a work intended to discourage Scandinavian converts to the Mormon faith; *Mormon Delusion* . . . , Boston, [1890].

MONTGOMERY, RENA WINTER (Oct. 24, 1900–), was born in Zanesville, Muskingum County. She was privately educated, specializing in languages. She now lives at Nashport. Her poems have appeared in many periodicals, and she has published a collection: *Windblown,* Columbus, [1942].

MONTGOMERY, RICHMOND AMES (July 16, 1870–July 16, 1950), Presbyterian clergyman and educator, born in Hendricks County, Ind., served in Ohio at three different times: as a pastor in Edgerton, 1896–98, and Xenia, 1904–09, and as president of Lane Seminary, 1926–32. He wrote *Reality in Religion* . . . , New York, [1941]. WWW 3

MONTGOMERY, THOMAS (June 16, 1837–July 13, 1907), was born in Lynchburg, Highland County, and spent his life in that community. He served in the 48th O.V.I. as a captain, Oct., 1861–Jan., 1865. With John Bering (q.v.), also of Lynchburg, a major in the 48th, he wrote the regimental history listed below.

History of the Forty-eighth Ohio Veteran Volunteer Infantry . . . , Hillsboro, 1880.

MOODY, GRANVILLE (Jan. 2, 1812–June 4, 1887), clergyman, born in Portland, Maine, grew up in Baltimore, Md., where his parents moved when he was four years old. In 1831 he came to Norwich, Muskingum County, where his elder brother was a merchant. Here he was converted to Methodism, and in 1833 he was licensed to preach. After serving on the Miami Circuit and in various pastorates, he was appointed to a church in Cincinnati in 1860. In 1861, after receiving the sanction of his congregation, he accepted command of the 74th O.V.I. He served with distinction until 1863, when he resigned because of illness and returned to the ministry. He retired in 1882. His autobiography was edited by Sylvester Weeks.

A Life's Retrospect . . . , Cincinnati, 1890.

MOODY, HELEN WATTERSON (May 17, 1860–Dec. 14, 1928), journalist, was born in Cleveland, Cuyahoga County. After graduating from University of Wooster in 1883, she worked in Cleveland on the *Leader* and the *Sun.* She then taught at Wooster for four years. In 1889 she joined the staff of the New York *Evening Sun.* In 1891 she married Winfield S. Moody, a journalist.

The Unquiet Sex, New York, 1898.

A Child's Letters to Her Husband, New York, 1903.

MOODY, MINNIE HITE (June 23, 1900–), was born in Granville, Licking County, where, in her childhood, she lived in the home of her maternal grandfather, George Washington Evans, whose great-grandfather, a gentleman from Wales, had settled in the hills to the north of the village site even before the determined little band of New

England pioneers set out from Granville, Mass., in 1805 to make the long journey by covered wagon into the Ohio country. Mrs. Moody's memories cling to her old Ohio home, and in the years of her maturity she has returned frequently to Granville for summer "vacations," during which she has worked strenuously at her writing. One of her novels, *Towers with Ivy* (1937), has its setting in this little college town. In due time she graduated from Granville High School, but her heart was not in formal education, and shortly after graduation she was married during World War I to Lt. Wilkie Osgood Moody, who had been a student at Denison University in Granville prior to war service. Mrs. Moody's marriage and the birth of two daughters—Elizabeth, born in 1919 at Newark, and Mary Louise, born at Altoona, Pa., in 1921—interfered with but did not stop her writing. This urge to express herself was too deeply implanted, too much a part of her very life, to be easily thwarted. As a matter of fact, her creative writing started almost as soon as she could write at all. She says: "I cannot remember when writing or planning something I wanted to write was not part of my consciousness." While still of school age she began sending her stories to magazine editors. She won prizes and kept on writing. She wrote for the "Children's Page" in magazines like *St. Nicholas* and *Little Folks*. After her marriage, in moments of leisure at the camps where her husband was stationed, she wrote for confession magazines. Eventually she settled with her family in Atlanta, Ga., where Mr. Moody became coach and athletic director in the Atlanta city schools and where they have lived ever since. Perhaps some explanation of Mrs. Moody's success as a writer may be found in her advice to ambitious young novelists, "*Never* pay any attention to interfering factors or forces," and in her comment on her own writing habits: "I work all day every day—and when I am not writing I am thinking about what I am going to write next." As a novelist, Mrs. Moody has published *Once Again in Chicago* (1933), the Indian summer romance of Henry and Mattie, who renew at the Century of Progress Exposition a love begun forty years before at the World's Fair; *Death Is a Little Man* (1936), the story of Eenie Weaver and her patient, courageous, and often noble struggle to overcome and surmount the difficulties of living with a worthless husband in "The Bottom," a Negro section of Atlanta; *Towers with Ivy* (1937), an atmospheric tale of an Ohio college town, the college a composite of several Ohio colleges, and the town, Granville; *Old Home Week* (1938), an unpretentious account of a typically American celebration in Prairieville, involving the extraordinary experiences of an ordinary American family; and *Long Meadows* (1941), Mrs. Moody's most ambitious book, an elaborate historical-genealogical novel, based on the records and legends of her own ancestors, telling effectively in the experiences of the Heydts the history of the American experience from pioneer days to the close of the Civil War. In gathering the material which furnished the background for this story, Mrs. Moody consulted historical documents, old letters, diaries, and journals; ransacked old courthouses in Virginia, Kentucky, Ohio, and other states; and traveled thousands of miles in locating places and scenes. She went over Boone's Wilderness Road and through Cumberland Gap exactly forty-two times! "My children," she says, "insist they have been reared in cemeteries and the dusty crypts of courthouses, where I was researching in genealogy, and in the ruins of tumbling forts." In book reviews for the Atlanta *Journal* and other papers and magazines, Mrs. Moody has shown judgment and taste in evaluating the work of others. Her poems, clear, simple, and homey, have appeared in various periodicals. She conducted a column in the *Journal* from 1938 to 1942. Minnie Hite Moody lives at Mistletoe Hill, Dunwoody, Ga., where amid the wild woodlands she cultivates her love of birds and trees and flowers and works at her chosen task of writing.

J. L. King

MOON, CARL (Oct. 5, 1879–June 24, 1948), artist and writer, was born in Wilmington, Clinton County. After 1904 he lived in the Southwest and in California, where he photographed, painted, and wrote about Indians. Besides illustrating books by his wife, Grace Moon, he wrote a number of books, e.g., *The Flaming Arrow*, New York, 1927. WWW 2

MOON, HENRY LEE (July 20, 1901–), was born in Pendleton, S. C. He attended Cleveland public schools and graduated from Ohio State University in 1924. After working on the Cleveland *Herald*, 1925–26, he became director of publicity at Tuskegee Institute. He is now director of public relations for the N.A.A.C.P. in New York City. He has written *Balance of Power: The Negro Vote*, New York, 1948.

MOONEY, JAMES DAVID (Feb. 18, 1884–Sept. 21, 1957), industrialist, was born in

Cleveland, Cuyahoga County. After studying engineering at New York University and Case Institute of Technology, he was with General Motors, rising to a vice presidency, and with Willys-Overland Motors, Toledo, from which he retired in 1949 as president and chairman of the board. He served in the army in World War I and in the navy in World War II. His home after his retirement was Oyster Bay, N. Y. His writings on business and economic subjects include *The New Capitalism,* New York, 1934. WWW 3

MOORE, AMBROSE B. (Nov. 4, 1861–Dec. 16, 1933), clergyman, was born in Holmes County. A clergyman in the Disciples of Christ Church, he served pastorates in Alliance, Findlay, Toledo, and Ashtabula. He also lived in Macon, Ga., and St. Louis, Mo., for a number of years. He died in Alliance. Besides the pamphlet below, he edited a book of Bible readings.

How to Use the Sword, Mansfield, 1895.

MOORE, DAVID HASTINGS (Sept. 4, 1838–Nov. 23, 1915), clergyman, was born in Athens County. He graduated from Ohio University in 1860 and was ordained to the Methodist ministry in the same year. He served with the 125th O.V.I. during the Civil War and afterward held pastorates in Columbus and Cincinnati. He was president of Cincinnati Wesleyan College, 1875–80, and Colorado Seminary, 1888–89. He was elected bishop in 1900. He wrote *John Morgan Walden, Thirty-fifth Bishop of the Methodist Episcopal Church . . . ,* New York, [1915]. WWW 1

MOORE, DAVID WILLIAM (1895–May 9, 1954), born in Highland County, lived in Cincinnati until 1935, while engaged in the advertising business. He also wrote fiction for a number of national magazines. In 1935 he moved to Bradenton, Fla., where he died of a heart attack in 1954. He published several books for boys, e.g., *Scoot McKay,* Philadelphia, [1939].

MOORE, EDWARD CALDWELL (Sept. 1, 1857–March 26, 1943), clergyman and educator, born in West Chester, Pa., younger brother of George F. Moore (q.v.), spent a part of his boyhood in Columbus and graduated from Marietta College in 1877. A member of the Harvard University faculty, he published addresses, textbooks, and several books on religious themes, e.g., *The Nature of Religion,* New York, 1936. WWW 2

MOORE, EDWARD E. (March 12, 1866–Oct. 23, 1940), journalist, was born on a farm in Lawrence County. He attended district schools and National Normal University, Lebanon. After teaching in Ohio schools for five years, he and his brother Elbert established the College Corner *Chronicle.* After publishing the newspaper from 1890 to 1898, they moved to Connersville, Ind. Approximately the last thirty years of his life were spent in Los Angeles. He published three books, e.g., *A Century of Indiana,* New York, [1910]. IATB

MOORE, ERNEST CARROLL (July 20, 1871–Jan. 23, 1955), educator, was born in Youngstown, Mahoning County. He graduated from Ohio Normal University in 1892 and the University of Chicago (Ph.D.) in 1898. He served in the education department of several universities, his longest tenure being at the University of California at Los Angeles, 1919–41. He was provost and vice president, 1927–36. He wrote many articles and books on education, e.g., *Fifty Years of American Education . . . ,* Boston, [1917]. WWW 3

MOORE, GEORGE FOOT (Oct. 15, 1851–May 16, 1931), clergyman and educator, born in West Chester, Pa., elder brother of Edward C. Moore (q.v.), graduated from Yale University in 1872 and Union Theological Seminary in 1877. He was ordained to the Presbyterian ministry in Columbus in 1878 and served as a minister in Zanesville, 1878–83. He afterward served on the faculty of Andover Theological Seminary, 1883–1901, and Harvard University, 1902–28. An authority on Judaism and on Greek philosophy, he published a number of significant works, e.g., *History of Religions,* 2 vols., New York, 1913–19. DAB 13

MOORE, JARED SPARKS (Sept. 29, 1879–April 10, 1951), educator, born in Cambridge, Mass., was a member of the philosophy department, Western Reserve University, 1907–50. He published a psychology textbook and a philosophical treatise: *Rifts in the Universe . . . ,* New Haven, 1927. WWW 3

MOORE, OLIN HARRIS (1885–), educator, born in Mt. Airy, N. C., was professor of romance languages at Ohio State University, 1920–55, and since his retirement has continued to live in Columbus. He has written a number of French textbooks and other works, e.g., *The Young King, Henry Plantagenet . . . ,* Columbus, [1925]. WW 30

MOORE, OPHA (Aug. 18, 1867–), was born in Parkersburg, W. Va. His father, a

United Brethren minister, served various churches in Ohio. He entered Otterbein College in 1883 and attended for three years. He was a reporter on the Columbus *Times,* worked for the Columbus Buggy Company, and held administrative posts under four Republican governors. He wrote numerous articles for magazines and newspapers and *History of Franklin County, Ohio,* 3 vols., Topeka, [Kan.], 1930.

MOORE, ROBERT BRADEN (Sept. 13, 1835–May 17, 1906), clergyman, born in Westmoreland County, Pa., was ordained to the Presbyterian ministry in 1860 after graduating from Western Theological Seminary. He served churches in Tiffin, 1867–72, and Upper Sandusky, 1873–76, and afterward was a missionary and an evangelist. He died in Vineland, N. J.

History of Huron Presbytery . . . , Philadelphia, 1892.

MOORE, THOMAS EMMETT (March 1, 1861–March 30, 1950), journalist, was born in Piketon, Pike County. After attending the public schools of Jackson, he read law and was admitted to the bar in 1881. He practiced for several years and then became managing editor of the Jackson *Sun* and later of the Jackson *Herald* and the Wellston *Daily Sentinel.* On these small papers his editorial work attracted wide attention. Writing in the Washington *Post,* Willard Holcomb said: "Once in a while one runs across a country editor with a highly original streak. Such a man is Thomas Emmett Moore. The fame of this editor's papers is due to his personality. He talks with a drawl that rivals Mark Twain's. Whether this is an indication or a concomitant of humor, may be a matter of conjecture, but certainly Mr. Moore shows in his work plenty of humor." He was on the Dayton *Journal,* 1912–20, and was chief editorial writer with the Cincinnati *Enquirer,* 1920–45. He died in Cincinnati. He published at least three novels, e.g., *The Haunted King,* Boston, 1910.

MOORE, WILLIAM THOMAS (Aug. 27, 1832–Sept. 7, 1926), clergyman, was born in Henry County, Ky. A leader in the Disciples of Christ Church, he served as a pastor in Cincinnati, 1867–78, and later served as a missionary in England and as an educator in Missouri. After his retirement in 1909, he lived in Florida. He edited two collections of sermons and wrote a history of the Disciples of Christ and a number of other books, e.g., *The Life of Timothy Coop* . . . , Cincinnati, [1889].

MOOREHEAD, WARREN KING (March 10, 1866–Jan. 5, 1939), archaeologist, son of William G. Moorehead (q.v.), was born in Siena, Italy. He attended Denison University and also spent four years studying the Ohio mounds. He later taught for 31 years at Phillips Academy, Exeter, Mass., and also conducted expeditions to various parts of the United States. A prolific writer on the Indian, prehistoric man, and archaeology, he wrote his first book on an Ohio subject: *Fort Ancient* . . . , Cincinnati, 1890.

MOOREHEAD, WILLIAM GALLOGLY (March 19, 1836–March 1, 1914), clergyman and educator, was born in Rix Mills, Muskingum County. After graduating from Muskingum College in 1858, he studied at Allegheny and Xenia Seminaries and was licensed to preach in 1861. He served as a Presbyterian missionary in Italy, 1862–69, and was pastor of First Church, Xenia, 1870–75. He began teaching at Xenia Seminary in 1873, became president in 1899, and remained a member of the faculty until his death.

Studies in the Mosaic Institutions, Pittsburgh, Pa., 1896.

Studies in the Four Gospels, Philadelphia, 1900.

Outline Studies in the New Testament . . . , New York, [1905].

Studies in the Book of Revelation, Pittsburgh, Pa., [1908].

MOOS, HERMAN (1836–Jan. 28, 1894), journalist and lawyer, was born in Hechingen, Germany. In 1839 his parents came to the United States and settled in Knoxville, Tenn. He was raised in Knoxville and became a merchant in business with his father. After the Civil War he came to Cincinnati, where he bought an interest in the *American Israelite,* which he edited for several years, and also published the *Literary Eclectic.* He founded several successful businesses and eventually drifted into the practice of law. At the time of his death he was generally recognized as one of the most distinguished members of the Cincinnati bar.

Mortara; Or, the Pope and His Inquisitors. A Drama . . . , Cincinnati, 1860.

Hannah; Or, a Glimpse of Paradise. A Tale . . . , Cincinnati, [1868].

MORE, ENOCH ANSON (April 11, 1854–June 2, 1932), brother of James B. More (q.v.), was born in Dayton, Montgomery County. He attended Dayton public schools, but spent much of his life in Colorado. His death occurred in Denver.

Let It Burn, St. Paul, [1892].
Out of the Past, Boston, 1895.
A Captain of Men, Boston, 1905.
A Vision of Empire, Boston, [1915].

MORE, JAMES BROOKES (March 29, 1859–June 9, 1942), publisher and poet, was born in Dayton, Montgomery County. He was the younger brother of Enoch A. More (q.v.). He lived in Massachusetts. He wrote *Sweet Maggie McGee–Red Cross Nurse. Ovid's Metamorphoses–I,* Boston, 1923. WWW 2

MORE, LOUIS TRENCHARD (April 9, 1870–Jan. 16, 1944), educator, born in St. Louis, Mo., brother of Paul Elmer More, was on the faculty of University of Cincinnati, 1900–40, serving as dean of the Graduate School, 1916–40. He published several books on science and scientists, e.g., *Isaac Newton, a Biography,* New York, 1934. WWW 2

MOREHEAD, LAVINIA MURDOCH ESPY (1818–July 15, 1900), was born in Columbus, Franklin County. She married Henry T. Morehead of Kentucky and afterward lived in that state.

Christmas Is Coming, and Other Poems . . . , Philadelphia, 1871.
Autumn Leaves Gathered for a Few Friends, New York, [1883].
A Few Incidents in the Life of Professor James P. Espy, by His Niece, Cincinnati, 1888.

MORGAN, ANNE EUGENIA FELICIA (Oct. 3, 1845–Dec. 23, 1909), educator, was born in Oberlin, Lorain County, the daughter of an Oberlin College professor. After graduating from Oberlin in 1866, she studied philosophy in Germany for two years. She taught briefly at Oberlin and at Vassar College and was on the faculty of Wellesley College, 1878–1900. At the time of her death, she was living in Saratoga, Calif.

The White Lady, 1886.
Philosophical Studies in Literature, Cambridge, [Mass.], 1889.

MORGAN, ARTHUR ERNEST (June 20, 1878–), civil engineer and educator, was born in Cincinnati, Hamilton County. After working as an engineer on various Federal, state, and private projects, he became president of Antioch College in 1920. He introduced the work-study plan and did much to revitalize the academic life of the school. He was director of T.V.A., 1933–38. He has published a number of pamphlets and books, including an autobiographical volume: *My World,* Yellow Springs, 1927, and a biography: *Edward Bellamy,* New York, 1944. WW 30

MORGAN, FLORENCE HOWER (Mrs. Edmund N.) (July 25, 1853–Jan. 11, 1941), was born in Burbank, Wayne County. Besides the book listed below, she compiled a book of poems: *Verses Written in Paris by Various Members of a Group of "Intellectuals,"* Cleveland, 1901. She died in Cleveland at the home of a daughter.

Though the Gods and the Years Relent . . . , New York, [1894].

MORGAN, LIBBIE S. CROWELL (July 24, 1840–Dec. 19, 1886), was born in Bloomfield Township, Trumbull County, where she spent her girlhood. She lived a few years in Cleveland but spent most of her adult life in Corning, Iowa. A collection of her verse was published posthumously.

Poems, Cincinnati, 1888.

MORGAN, LUCY GRISCOM (April 4, 1877–), born in Woodbury, N. J., has lived in Ohio since 1915. A graduate of the University of Pennsylvania, she taught for three years at Wellesley College and for six years at Antioch College. She married Arthur E. Morgan (q.v.) on July 6, 1911. Besides an account of Glen Helen and one of Antioch College, she has written *Finding His World; The Story of Arthur E. Morgan,* Yellow Springs, 1927.

MORGAN, THOMAS B. (1886–), journalist, was born in Tiltonsville, Jefferson County, and grew up in Steubenville. He attended the University of Pittsburgh and worked on several Pittsburgh newspapers. For eighteen years he was Associated Press correspondent in Rome and the Vatican. He has written several books on the Catholic Church and an account of his own experiences: *A Reporter at the Papal Court . . . ,* New York, 1937.

MORGAN, VIOLET (Nov. 15, 1898–), educator and historian, was born in Hillsboro, Highland County. She graduated from Wilmington College and has taught in schools near Hillsboro, including Samantha and Mowrystown. She has spoken before many groups on the folklore of southern Ohio and has written numerous feature stories for various newspapers on the same subject. She has also written a historical novel, *Squaw Winter,* and *Folklore of Highland County,* Greenfield, 1946.

MORGAN, WILLIAM YOAST (April 6, 1866–Feb. 17, 1932), journalist, was born in Cincinnati, Hamilton County, but spent the greater part of his life in Kansas, where he owned and edited the Hutchinson *News and Herald.* His books, which were originally written as letters for his newspaper, include *A Journey of a Jayhawker,* Topeka, 1905. WWW 1

MORGENSTERN, JULIAN (March 18, 1881–), rabbi and educator, born in St. Francisville, Ill., graduated from the University of Cincinnati in 1901 and Hebrew Union College in 1902. He began teaching at Hebrew Union College in 1907, became president in 1922, and retired in 1947. He wrote a number of studies of Jewish history and religion, e.g., *A Jewish Interpretation of the Book of Genesis,* Cincinnati, 1919. WW 26

MORIARTY, HELEN LOUISE (c.1872–Nov. 11, 1928), was born in Madison County, but spent most of her life in Columbus. A graduate of St. Joseph's Academy, she wrote for *American Magazine* and *Rosary Magazine* and was on the staff of the *Catholic Columbian.*

Idle Rhymes, Cincinnati, 1895.
The Hill People . . . , St. Louis, Mo., 1925.

MORRILL, BELLE CHAPMAN (Dec. 15, 1882–), librarian, was born in Amesbury, Mass. A graduate of Mount Holyoke College and Hartford Seminary, she was librarian in Girard, Trumbull County, 1929–43. She now lives in Rochester, N. Y. Her poems and short stories have appeared in various religious periodicals, and she has published several collections of verse, e.g., *Blue Platter,* Rochester, N. Y., 1945.

MORRILL, LILY LOGAN (1877–March 23, 1944), born in Richmond, Va., lived in Cincinnati after her marriage in 1905 to Albert H. Morrill, lawyer and chain-store executive. She published at least three books on the South and the Civil War, e.g., *Virginia's War,* Philadelphia, [1935].

MORRILL, MILO TRUE (May 13, 1865–June 22, 1921), clergyman, was born in North Washington, Iowa. After graduating from Carleton College in 1894, he was ordained to the ministry of the Christian Church. He served churches in New England until 1906, when he was appointed Secretary of Foreign Missions; from this time he edited the *Christian Missionary* in Dayton. He began lecturing on missions at Defiance College in 1908 and joined the regular faculty in 1919. His death occurred at Defiance. He wrote *A History of the Christian Denomination . . . ,* Dayton, 1912. OBB

MORRIS, ALVIN MARION (Dec. 11, 1861–Jan. 9, 1940), clergyman, was born near New Vienna, Clinton County. He was a minister in the Church of Christ for fifty years. In his later life he was a resident of Long Beach, Calif., but he died in Kansas City, Mo., where he was conducting a Bible study course. His writings include *The Prophecies Unveiled . . . ,* Winfield, Kan., 1914.

MORRIS, CHARLES EUGENE (May 21, 1884–), journalist, was born in Wapakoneta, Auglaize County. He worked on newspapers in Wapakoneta, Toledo, Springfield, Columbus, and other Ohio cities. Since 1956 he has been assistant editor of *St. Louis Medicine.* From 1916 to 1920 he was secretary to Governor Cox, and out of this experience published *Progressive Democracy of James M. Cox,* Indianapolis, 1920.

MORRIS, CLARA (March 17, 1848–Nov. 20, 1925), actress, was born in Toronto, Ontario, Canada. Although some sources give Cleveland as her birthplace, she apparently was born in Canada but grew up in Cleveland. Her mother, wife of a French-Canadian cab driver, discovered that he had married her bigamously and fled to Cleveland. Here Clara began acting in 1862 as an extra at the Cleveland Academy of Music. In 1869 she played at Wood's Theatre, Cincinnati, and the next year she was playing in New York. In 1874 she married Frederick C. Harriott. In the last quarter of the nineteenth century, she was probably the best-known American actress. After her retirement from the stage, she lived in Riverdale, N. Y.; and in her old age when in need of funds she turned to writing for a livelihood.

Little "Jim Crow," and Other Stories of Children, New York, 1899.
A Silent Singer, New York, 1899.
Life on the Stage; My Personal Experience and Recollections, New York, 1901.
A Pasteboard Crown . . . , New York, 1902.
Stage Confidences . . . , Boston, [1902].
Left in Charge, New York, [1904].
The Trouble Woman, New York, 1904.
The Life of a Star, New York, 1906.
The New "East Lynne" . . . An Entirely New and Original Novel, [New York, 1908].

MORRIS, EDWARD DAFYDD (Oct. 31, 1825–Nov. 21, 1915), clergyman and educator, was born in Utica, N. Y. He graduated from Yale University in 1849 and Auburn Theological Seminary in 1852. Ordained to the Presbyterian ministry, he served churches in Auburn, 1852–55, and Columbus, 1855–67, and taught at Lane Seminary, Cincinnati, 1867–97. After his retirement he lived in Columbus. Besides the titles below, he published theology textbooks, sermons, and readings from the Bible.

Outlines of Christian Doctrine, Cincinnati, 1880.

Ecclesiology . . . , New York, 1885.

Is There Salvation after Death? . . . , New York, [1887].

A Calm Review of the Inaugural Address of Prof. Charles A. Briggs, New York, [1891].

Thirty Years in Lane . . . , [Cincinnati, 1896].

The Theology of the Westminster Symbols . . . , Columbus, 1900.

A Book of Remembrance. The Presbyterian Church, New School . . . , Columbus, 1905.

MORRIS, JOSEPH A. (June 23, 1804–Sept. 6, 1899), was born in Burlington County, N. J. In 1837 he settled on a farm in Richland County. A Quaker, he traveled to hospitals during the Civil War, through the South after the war, and among the Indians of the West. A small volume of extracts from his journals and letters was published at Cardington in 1881; the enlarged version, prepared by his nephew Joseph Morris, was published posthumously in accordance with the terms of his will.

Reminiscences of Joseph Morris . . . , Mt. Gilead, 1899.

MORRIS, MARIAN. Pseud. See Verna W. Hiatt.

MORRIS, THOMAS ASBURY (April 28, 1794–Sept. 2, 1874), clergyman, was born near Charleston, Va. In 1814, the year after his conversion to Methodism, he became a minister and preached in the Ohio conference. In 1834 he was made editor of the *Western Christian Advocate,* published in Cincinnati, and in 1836 he was elected bishop. He died in Springfield.

Miscellany: Consisting of Essays, Biographical Sketches, and Notes of Travel, Cincinnati, 1852.

Sketches of Western Methodism, Cincinnati, 1852.

MORRISON, CHARLES CLAYTON (Dec. 4, 1874–), clergyman and editor, was born in Harrison, Hamilton County. He graduated from Drake University in 1898. A minister in the Disciples of Christ Church, he served pastorates in several Midwestern states. He edited *Christian Century,* 1908–47. He has published a number of books on religious subjects, e.g., *The Meaning of Baptism,* Chicago, [1914]. WW 29

MORRISON, MARION (June 2, 1821–Dec. 1, 1889), clergyman and educator, was born in Adams County. He graduated from Miami University in 1846, was licensed to preach by the Chillicothe Presbytery in 1849, and served as pastor in Tranquility for six years. He became a teacher of mathematics at Monmouth College, Ill., in 1856 and served there until 1862. From Aug., 1863, to Aug., 1864, he was chaplain of the 9th Illinois Volunteer Regiment. After the Civil War he served Presbyterian parishes throughout the Middle West. His last church was at Starkville, Miss., where his health broke down and he retired from the active ministry.

A History of the Ninth Regiment of the Illinois Volunteers, Monmouth, Ill., 1864.

MORROW, ELIZABETH REEVE CUTTER (May 29, 1873–Jan. 23, 1955), was born in Cleveland, Cuyahoga County. She graduated from Smith College in 1896. In 1903 she married Dwight W. Morrow, later U. S. ambassador to Mexico. She published a number of books, including a volume of poems: *Quatrains for My Daughter,* New York, 1931, and a volume of letters from occupied France: *"All Gaul Is Divided . . . ,"* New York, 1941. WWW 3

MORROW, JOSIAH (Aug. 26, 1838–Dec. 28, 1928), lawyer, was born on a farm near Foster, Warren County. After graduating from Miami University in 1859, he studied law at the University of Michigan. He practiced in Lebanon. A student of local history, he published biographical and historical articles in addition to the titles below.

History of Warren County, Chicago, 1882.

Life and Speeches of Thomas Corwin . . . , Cincinnati, 1896.

A Brief History of Lebanon . . . , Lebanon, 1902.

History of the Sycamore Associate Reformed Church . . . , [Cincinnati, 1930?].

MORROW, MARCO (July 18, 1869–Feb. 28, 1959), journalist, was born in Foster, Warren County. He was a reporter on the Springfield *Republic-Times,* 1890–94, and also edited *Womankind,* published in Springfield, 1895–99. Afterward he was assistant publisher of Capper Publications, Topeka, Kan., until his retirement in 1944. He died in Topeka. His writings include *Things to Tell the Merchant,* Lawrence, Kan., 1914. WWMW 49

MORSE, FLORENCE V. (Nov. 10, 1888–), was born in Van Wert, Van Wert County. In 1906 she graduated from the Castle School, N. Y. She lived in Van Wert until 1913, when she married Rev. Herman Morse, a Presbyterian clergyman, and she is now living once again in her native community. She has written numerous stories and magazine articles and a mystery novel: *Black Eagles Are Flying,* New York, 1943.

MORSE, RICHARD. Pseud. See Fred Eastman.

MORSE, ROBERT (Dec. 25, 1906–), was born in Toledo, Lucas County. After graduating from Princeton University in 1928, he studied painting in France. His last known address was New York City. He has published a volume of poems: *The Two Persephones,* [New York, 1942].

MORTIMER, PETER. Pseud. See Dorothy J. Roberts.

MORTON, LENA BEATRICE (June 15, 1901–), educator, born in Kentucky, was educated in Cincinnati, where her parents moved in 1917. She graduated from the University of Cincinnati in 1922 and taught in the Cincinnati schools, 1923–48. She received her Ph.D. degree at Western Reserve University in 1947, taught for two years at Langston University, Okla., and in 1950 joined the faculty of Lane College, Jackson, Tenn. She has published a number of articles, a book on her public school teaching, and *Negro Poetry in America,* Boston, 1925.

MOSELEY, EDWIN LINCOLN (March 29, 1865–June 6, 1948), educator, was born in Hawaii of missionary parents. He graduated from the University of Michigan in 1885. After teaching at Sandusky High School, 1889–1914, he joined the faculty of Bowling Green State Normal School and taught there until his retirement in 1936. He died in Bowling Green. He was best known in the scientific world for his work on long-range weather forecasting. He also published many articles, several textbooks and technical studies, and some works for general readers, e.g., a book for children: *Our Wild Animals,* New York, [1927]. AMS 8

MOSES, JASPER TURNEY (1880–1921), clergyman, was born in Richwood, Union County. A graduate of Butler University, he was ordained to the ministry in the Disciples of Christ Church and served as a missionary to Mexico. He died in Mexico City. He wrote a book about Mexico: *To-day in the Land of Tomorrow . . . ,* Indianapolis, [1907].

MOSES, WILLIAM JOHN BARR (June 27, 1874–June 17, 1946), journalist, born in Terrace, Minn., worked on newspapers in Minnesota, Wisconsin, and Tennessee before coming to Springfield, where he edited the *Daily News,* 1931–46. Author of poems, articles, and short stories in magazines, he also published a novel: *Dreaming River,* New York, [1909].

MOSHER, WILLIAM EUGENE (Nov. 26, 1877–June 1, 1945), educator, born in Syracuse, N. Y., was on the Oberlin College faculty, 1904–18, in the German department. He was later professor of political science at Syracuse University. He wrote German and social studies textbooks and *The Promise of the Christ-Age in Recent Literature,* New York, 1912. WWW 2

MOVIUS, ANNE MURRY (Jan. 14, 1874–April 18, 1957), was born in Cincinnati, Hamilton County. She attended public schools and private seminaries in Cincinnati, Rochester, N. Y., and St. Paul, Minn. In 1901 she settled in Bowbells, N. Dak., and in 1912 moved to Lidgerwood, N. Dak., where she spent the remainder of her life. She wrote pageants and plays for children and many poems, which were collected in two books, e.g., *Lights and Shadows,* [Ridgewood, N. J., 1936]. BDCP

MOWERY, WILLIAM BYRON (Aug. 15, 1899–April 2, 1957), was born in Adelphia, Ross County. He graduated from the University of Illinois in 1921. He wrote for various motion-picture companies, 1923–29, and after 1929 was a free-lance writer. He published stories in many magazines and also wrote a number of adventure novels, e.g., *Heart of the North,* New York, 1930. WWW 3

MOZANS, J. H. Pseud. See John A. Zahm.

MUENSCHER, JOSEPH (Dec. 21, 1798–Feb., 1884), clergyman, was born in Providence, R. I. A graduate of Brown University in 1821, he was ordained to the priesthood of the Episcopal Church in 1825. In 1833 he came to Ohio, where he was a professor at Gambier Seminary until 1841 and rector of St. Paul's Church, Mount Vernon, until 1855. His eyesight having failed, he could not fill a parish any longer, and he lived in Mount Vernon until his death.

Manual of Biblical Interpretation, Gambier, 1865.

The Book of Proverbs . . . , Gambier, 1866.

MULHANE, LAWRENCE WILLIAM (Feb. 21, 1856–May 2, 1925), Catholic priest, born in Berlin, Mass., was pastor of St. Vincent de Paul's Church, Mount Vernon, 1885–1925.

Leprosy and the Charity of the Church, Chicago, [1896].

Memorial of Major-General William Stark Rosecrans . . . , [Columbus, 1898].

MUNHALL, LEANDER WHITCOMB (June 7, 1843–Jan. 7, 1934), evangelist, was born in Zanesville, Muskingum County. He served throughout the Civil War with the 79th Indiana Volunteer Infantry, and in 1874 he became a Methodist evangelist. He lived in Germantown, Pa. His writings include *Breakers! Methodism Adrift,* New York, [1913]. WWW 1

MUNK, JOSEPH AMASA (Nov. 9, 1847–Dec. 4, 1927), physician, was born in Columbiana County and graduated from Eclectic Medical College of Ohio in 1869. After practicing in Ohio, Missouri, and Kansas, he settled in Los Angeles. During an excursion through Arizona with the G.A.R. in the 1880s, he became interested in the literature of the state. He began collecting Arizona materials in 1884, and by 1908 had acquired over 16,000 volumes, which he presented to the Southwest Museum. Besides a bibliography of Arizona literature and other writings related to his avocation, he published a book of personal essays: *Arizona Sketches,* New York, [1905]. WWW 1

MUNN, GLENN GAYWAINE (Feb. 17, 1890–   ), financial analyst, was born in Toledo, Lucas County. He graduated from the University of Michigan in 1914, taught in several universities for brief periods, and joined Paine, Webber, Jackson, & Curtis, New York City, in 1928. He has published several books on banking and finance, e.g., *Meeting the Bear Market . . . ,* New York, 1930. WW 30

MUNN, HIRAM H. (Sept. 25, 1838– ?), lawyer, was born near Cleveland, Cuyahoga County. He practiced law in Cleveland, but no other biographical details have been found.

History of the Declension of the Great Republic of the United States . . . , Cleveland, 1875.

MUNRO, THOMAS (Feb. 15, 1897–   ), born in Omaha, Neb., has been professor of art at Western Reserve University since 1931. He has written a number of books on aesthetics and the fine arts, e.g., *The Arts and Their Interrelations,* New York, 1949. WW 30

MURCH, JAMES DE FOREST (Oct. 23, 1892–   ), clergyman, was born in New Vienna, Clinton County. After graduating from Ohio University in 1915, he was ordained to the ministry of the Disciples of Christ Church. He was a pastor in Pittsburgh, 1915–16, assistant editor of the *Christian Standard,* 1916–18, editor of the *Lookout,* 1918–25, a professor at Cincinnati Bible Seminary, 1925–37, and a member of the editorial staff of the Standard Publishing Company, 1934–45. He has published hymns and pamphlets and several devotional books, e.g., *Studies in Christian Living,* Cincinnati, [1937]. WW 30

MURDOCH, JAMES EDWARD (Jan. 25, 1811–May 19, 1893), actor, was born in Philadelphia. He made his debut on the stage in Philadelphia in 1829. In the 1840s and 1850s he was probably the best-known American actor. In 1857 he settled on a farm near Lebanon, where he planted vineyards under the direction of experts brought from the Rhine Valley. During the Civil War he served as a nurse in Federal hospitals, gave readings for the benefit of the U. S. Sanitary Commission, and was a volunteer aide on the staff of General William S. Rosecrans. After the war he became professor of elocution at the Cincinnati College of Music. In 1865 he edited an anthology, *Patriotism and Poetry and Prose,* which contained articles about Abraham Lincoln and some of Lincoln's favorite poems.

Orthophony, or Vocal Culture in Elocution . . . , (with William Russell), Boston, 1845.

The Stage, or Recollections of Actors and Acting . . . , Philadelphia, 1880.

A Plea for the Spoken Language, Cincinnati, [1883].
Analytic Elocution . . . , Cincinnati, [1884].

MURPHY, DAVID ASBURY (April 3, 1842–Sept. 21, 1917), journalist, was born on a farm near Shamrock, Adams County. After serving in the Civil War, he worked on a number of newspapers in southwestern Ohio. He contributed numerous poems to newspapers and magazines, some of which were published in a book: *Pensive Pansies,* [Cincinnati, 1901].

MURRAY, CHARLES BURLEIGH (June 10, 1837–March 5, 1918), was born in Brandon, Vt., the son of Orson Murray (q.v.). He was educated in the school maintained by his father. He was a merchant in Cincinnati, 1862–72, and established the Cincinnati *Commercial Review* in 1872, which he consolidated with the Cincinnati *Price Current* and published under that name until 1912. He was recognized as an authority on the pork-packing industry. He wrote an autobiographical volume: *Life Notes . . . ,* Cincinnati, 1915. WWW 1

MURRAY, JAMES ORMSBEE (Nov. 27, 1827–March 27, 1899), clergyman and educator, born in Camden, S. C., lived in Springfield, Clark County, from his eighth to his nineteenth year. His father had emancipated his slaves and moved to Ohio. Murray lived in Springfield until 1848, when he entered Brown University. He later served as pastor of Congregational churches in the East and on the faculty of Princeton. He published sermons and other books, including a biography: *Francis Wayland,* Boston, 1891.

MURRAY, LOIS LOVINA ABBOTT (March 3, 1826– ?), was born in Licking County. In the late 1840s she accompanied her family to Indiana; in 1860 she moved with her husband, Samuel Murray, to Kansas. In 1878 she returned to Goshen, Ind.

Incidents of Frontier Life . . . , Goshen, Ind., 1880.

MURRAY, ORSON (Sept. 23, 1806–June 14, 1885), clergyman and reformer, was born in Orwell, Vt. He was educated at Castleton and Shoreham Academies. An aggressive reformer, he crusaded under a score of banners, ranging from dietetic reform to women's rights. Moncure Daniel Conway described him as "a sort of John Brown whose Harper's Ferry was orthodoxy." He was licensed as a Baptist preacher, and in 1835 he began publishing the *Vermont Telegraph,* the Baptist paper for the state. Becoming a Fourierite, he moved to Ohio in 1844 and established a community and school, Fruit Hills, near Foster, Warren County. At the same time he re-established the *Regenerator,* which he had published for a few months in New York City. Though the country's most brilliant reformers are known to have visited Murray at Fruit Hill, nothing seems to have been recorded concerning the community. After writing his own funeral sermon, entitled "Death-bed Thoughts," Murray died at Fruit Hills.

The Struggle of the Hour . . . , Fosters Crossings, 1861.

MUSSEY, REUBEN DIMOND (June 23, 1780–June 21, 1866), physician, born in Pelham, N. H., practiced medicine in Salem, Mass., and taught at Dartmouth College, Bowdoin College, and a medical college in Fairfield, N. Y., until 1838, when he was called to the Medical College of Ohio as professor of surgery. He served until 1852, when he resigned to take a similar position at Miami Medical College. He retired in 1857 and lived the remainder of his life in Boston, Mass. He published several lectures and pamphlets on temperance and medical subjects.

The Trials and Rewards of the Medical Profession, Cincinnati, 1853.
Health: Its Friends and Its Foes, Boston, 1862.

MYERS, ALLEN O. (Dec. 24, 1848– ?), was born in Circleville, Pickaway County. An incorrigible boy, he was placed in the Ohio Reform School by his mother. He was released from the school in 1867 and returned to Circleville, where he was apprenticed to a printer. In 1872 he became Columbus correspondent for the Cleveland *Leader.* He served as clerk of the Constitutional Convention in 1873, where he represented the Cincinnati *Enquirer* as well as the *Leader.* He toured Europe as a correspondent for the *Enquirer* in 1874. In company with others he established the Columbus *Daily Democrat* in 1878 and was its managing editor for some time. In 1883 he was elected to the Assembly to represent Franklin County. His career as a legislator has been compared to a rocket, but he left a number of enduring legislative monuments to mark his passage, and chief among them was prison reform. He harbored many bitter memories of his experiences in the reform school, and he fostered a number of laws to humanize the prison system of Ohio. His honesty of purpose and his unrelenting aggressive attacks against demagogues and grafters made him feared as a legislator and a journalist. His erratic disposition made hosts of enemies, and his *Bosses and Boodle in Ohio Politics* added not a whit to his popularity. In 1898 he bought a farm in Franklin County, where he was still living in 1907.

Bosses and Boodle in Ohio Politics . . . , Cincinnati, 1895.

The American Manual . . . , Columbus, 1900.

Alfalfa, "the Grass" in Ohio . . . , Columbus, 1907.

MYERS, BURTON DORR (March 30, 1870–Feb. 28, 1951), physician and educator, was born in Attica, Seneca County. He graduated from Buchtel College in 1893 and University of Leipzig (M.D.) in 1902. From 1903 until his retirement in 1940 he was on the faculty of the University of Indiana medical school. He wrote numerous medical articles and reviews and the second volume of *History of Indiana University*, [Bloomington, 1940]. WWW 3

MYERS, GARRY CLEVELAND (July 15, 1884–), educator, born in Sylvan, Pa., was in the education department of Western Reserve University, 1920–40. He wrote textbooks and technical studies in psychology and education and some books for the general reader, e.g., *Marriage and Parenthood,* Cleveland, [1941]. WW 28

MYERS, JAY ARTHUR (Nov. 25, 1888–), physician, was born in Croton, Licking County. He graduated from Ohio University in 1912, Cornell University (Ph.D.) in 1914, and the University of Minnesota (M.D.) in 1920. A specialist in diseases of the chest, he has been on the faculty of the University of Minnesota medical school since 1914. He has written a number of medical articles and books, e.g., *Man's Greatest Victory over Tuberculosis,* Springfield, Ill., [1940]. WW 30

MYERS, JOSEPH SIMMONS (Feb. 3, 1867–Oct. 17, 1953), journalist and educator, was born in Columbus, Franklin County. After graduating from Ohio State University in 1887, he worked for a year on the Columbus *Times* and for two years on the Cleveland *Leader.* He worked on various Pittsburgh newspapers, 1889–1914, and then served on the journalism faculty, Ohio State University, 1914–34. After retiring, he wrote a column for the Middletown *Journal* for a number of years. He died in Middletown. His writings include numerous articles, a portion of the official history of Ohio State University, and *The Genius of Horace Greeley,* Columbus, 1929. WWW 3

MYERS, PHILIP VAN NESS (Aug. 10, 1846–Sept. 20, 1937), educator, was born in Tribes' Hill, N. Y. He was president of Farmers' College, Cincinnati, from 1879 until 1890, when he joined the history faculty of the University of Cincinnati. He wrote textbooks in ancient history which were widely used.

Remains of Lost Empires . . . , New York, 1875.

History as Past Ethics . . . , Boston, [1913].

MYERS, PHINEAS BARTON (1888–), born in Brooklyn, N. Y., has lived in Ohio since 1916. He is now a resident of Dayton. He has published several books, including a mystery novel, a book on hypnosis, and two books on Lincoln, e.g., *Eighty-five Years after Lincoln . . .* , Dayton, 1950.

N

NASBY, REV. PETROLEUM V. Pseud. See David R. Locke.

NASH, ARTHUR (June 26, 1870–Oct. 30, 1927), was born in Tipton County, Ind. After attending a seminary in Battle Creek, Mich., he was ordained in 1894 as a minister of the Seventh Day Adventist Church. Dismissed from an Adventist school in Detroit for unorthodoxy, he wandered around the country as a hobo. After marrying Maud L. Southwell of Cleveland in 1899, he returned to the ministry as a Disciples of Christ minister at Bluffton. In 1902 he was asked to resign his pulpit because of a controversy over a funeral sermon praising a non-believer. He sold men's clothing until 1909, when he opened his own manufacturing plant in Columbus. In 1913 he moved his business to Cincinnati and built it into the largest direct-sale clothing firm in the country. He became convinced that the golden rule was basic to business success and therefore lowered prices of his clothing and raised his workers' wages. He lectured widely on the golden rule to service clubs and other organizations. He died in Cincinnati.

Philosophy of Satanology, [Bluffton?], 1900.

The Golden Rule in Business, New York, [1923].

NASH, HENRY SYLVESTER (Dec. 23, 1854–Nov. 6, 1912), clergyman and educator, was born in Newark, Licking County. He graduated from Harvard University in 1878 and Episcopal Theological Seminary, Cambridge, in 1881. The following year he was ordained to the Episcopal priesthood, and in 1884 he joined the faculty of Episcopal Theological Seminary, where he served until his death.

Genesis of the Social Conscience . . . , New York, 1897.

Ethics and Revelation, New York, 1899.

The History of the Higher Criticism of the New Testament . . . , New York, 1900.

The Atoning Life, New York, 1908.

Prayers and Meditations, New York, 1915.

NASH, JAY BRYAN (Oct. 17, 1886–), educator, was born in New Baltimore, Stark County. He graduated from Oberlin College in 1911 and New York University (Ph.D.) in 1929. After fifteen years in physical education work in California, he joined the N.Y.U. faculty in 1926 and served there until his retirement in 1953. He has published textbooks and books about physical education and athletics, e.g., *Spectatoritis,* New York, [1932]. WW 30

NASH, PHILIP CURTIS (Aug. 28, 1890–May 6, 1947), educator, born in Hingham, Mass., was dean of Antioch College, 1921–29, and president of the University of Toledo, 1933–47. He published a book calling for international cooperation: *An Adventure in World Order,* Boston, 1944. WWW 2

NASH, SIMEON (Sept. 21, 1804–Jan. 18, 1879), lawyer and judge, born in South Hadley, Mass., came to Gallipolis in 1832 to read law with Samuel F. Vinton. After being admitted to the Ohio bar in 1833, he practiced in Gallipolis for the rest of his life. He served in the Ohio Senate, 1839–43; in the constitutional convention of 1850; and as a judge of common pleas court, 1851–61. His book on the civil code passed through five editions and was used by lawyers throughout the state. It was remarkable in at least one respect—Nash had opposed the civil code when it was adopted in 1851 and had favored the continuation of the common law.

Pleading and Practice under the Civil Code, Cincinnati, 1856.

Morality and the State, Columbus, 1859.

Crime and the Family, Cincinnati, 1876.

NASMYTH, GEORGE WILLIAM (July 9, 1882–Sept. 20, 1920), sociologist, was born in Cleveland, Cuyahoga County. He was educated at Cornell University, earning a Ph.D. in 1909, and at German universities. He was active in the international student movement and was a press representative at the Paris Peace Conference. His writings include *Social Progress and the Darwinian Theory . . . ,* New York, 1916. WWW 1

NAST, WILHELM (June 15, 1807–May 16, 1899), founder of German Methodism, was born in Stuttgart, Germany, and graduated from the University of Tübingen. Though born into a Lutheran family and attracted to the ministry, he was troubled by religious uncertainty. In 1828 he came to America. After serving as a tutor in a Methodist home and as librarian and teacher of German at the U. S. Military Academy, he came to Ohio. During a winter spent on a farm in Gallia County, he met Adam Miller (q.v.). He joined the faculty of Kenyon College to teach German and Hebrew. A Methodist shoemaker took him to Methodist services, where he was converted and decided to enter the ministry. In 1835 he was appointed missionary to the German settlers of Cincinnati. James Gamble, an Irish soapmaker, encouraged him and supported his efforts. Nast traveled widely and preached in many German settlements. In 1838 he established a church in Cincinnati, and in 1839 he founded *Der Christliche Apologete,* which he edited for over fifty years. He was one of the founders of German Wallace College in Berea and served as its president, 1864–93.

Das Leben und Wirken des Johannes Wesley . . . , Cincinnati, 1852.

Was Ist und Will der Methodismus, Cincinnati, 1855.

Christological Meditations, Cincinnati, 1858.

Philosophie des Erlösungsplanes, Cincinnati, 1859.

A Commentary on the Gospels of Matthew and Mark . . . , Cincinnati, [1864].

Christologische Betrachtungen, Cincinnati, 1866.

The Gospel Records . . . , Cincinnati, 1866.

Theologische Betrachtungen, Cincinnati, 1867.

Das Christentum und Seine Gegensätze, Cincinnati, 1883.

NAVE, ORVILLE JAMES (April 30, 1841–June 24, 1917), army chaplain, was born at Galion, Crawford County, and graduated from Ohio Wesleyan University in 1870. After his retirement as an army chaplain, he lived in Los Angeles. His writings include *Bible Symbols . . .* , Lincoln, Neb., [1910]. WWW 1

NAYLOR, CHARLES WESLEY (Jan., 1874–), clergyman, was born in Athens County. He attended Ohio Northern University, 1890–91 and 1897–98. A clergyman, he served churches in Ohio and Indiana. His last address in Ohioana files is Anderson, Ind. His books include *God's Will and How to Know It,* [Anderson, Ind., 1925]. WWNAA 7

NAYLOR, JAMES BALL (Oct. 4, 1860–April 1, 1945), physician, was born in Penn Township, Morgan County. His father was killed in the Civil War. He attended district schools and spent one year in Stockport and a few months at Marietta Academy. He financed his medical education by teaching in country schools around Malta and by farmwork and clerking. After graduating from Starling Medical College in 1886, he practiced in Malta until his retirement in 1934; he was district health commissioner in Morgan County, 1920–34. For eight years he wrote a column for the Marion *Star,* and he also contributed to Columbus newspapers. His first book of verse, *Current Coins,* was published under the pen name S. Q. Lapius. His first book to catch the attention of the public was the semiautobiographical novel *Ralph Marlowe.*

Current Coins Picked up at a Country Railway Station, Columbus, 1893.
Under Mad Anthony's Banner, Columbus, 1899.
Rambling Reminiscences, [n.p., 1900?].
Ralph Marlowe . . . , Akron, 1901.
The Sign of the Prophet . . . , Akron, 1901.
In the Days of St. Clair . . . , Akron, 1902.
The Cabin in the Big Woods, Akron, 1904.
The Kentuckian . . . , Boston, 1905.
Old Home Week, Boston, [1906].
Witch Crow and Barney Bylow, New York, [1906].
The Little Green Goblin, Akron, [1907].
The Scalawags, New York, 1907.
Songs from the Heart of Things . . . , Columbus, 1907.
The Misadventures of Marjory, Boston, 1908.
Old Morgan County, McConnelsville, 1921.
A Book of Buckeye Verse . . . , Chicago, 1927.
Vagrant Verse, McConnelsville, 1935.

NEAD, PETER (Jan. 7, 1796–March 16, 1877), clergyman, was born in Hagerstown, Md. He farmed and operated a tavern in Virginia until around 1846, when he settled near Trotwood, Montgomery County. Originally a Lutheran, he became a Methodist and later a Baptist. He was pastor of a German Baptist church for a number of years. He helped found the magazine *The Vindicator* and contributed numerous articles to it.

Das Ursprüngliche Christenthum . . . , Harrisburg, 1836.

NEAR, MRS. MYRON F. See Jessie Glasier.

NEEDELS, EMMA EVERETT (July 21, 1875–March 15, 1937), was born in Columbus Grove, Putnam County. She attended Ohio Wesleyan University and after her marriage to George W. Needels lived in Detroit, Mich. She published a volume of verse: *Dear Heart,* [Detroit, 1927].

NEEF, FRANCIS JOSEPH NICHOLAS (Dec. 6, 1770–April 6, 1854), educator, taught briefly in Cincinnati and Steubenville after the failure of Robert Owen's New Harmony experiment in 1828. After serving in Napoleon's army, Neef had taught under Pestalozzi in Switzerland, and he later established a Pestalozzian school in Philadelphia. He wrote a pioneer discussion of pedagogy: *Sketch of a Plan and Method of Education . . .* , Philadelphia, 1808.

NEENAH. Pseud. See Francis J. Finn.

NEFF, CORNELIUS (1825–July 2, 1896), was born in Cincinnati, Hamilton County. He served in the 54th O.V.I. from March, 1864, to Aug. 15, 1865. His verses were inspired by the deaths of his comrades or by engagements in which his regiment participated. He died in Cleveland.

Neal Neff's New National Poems . . . , Cincinnati, 1866.

NEFF, ELIZABETH CLIFFORD (Aug. 24, 1851–March 21, 1933), was born in Paris, Ill., of Ohio parents. Shortly after her birth the family returned to Gambier. She later lived in Cleveland and in 1901 moved to Canton. She died in Lake Township, Stark County. Besides the title below, she wrote a book on genealogy and one on heraldry.

An Anglican Study in Christian Symbolism, Cleveland, 1898.

NEFF, ELIZABETH HYER (d.Aug. 1, 1942), was born in Greenfield, Highland County.

She graduated from Greenfield High School in 1873, and in 1875 she married William B. Neff (q.v.), who later served as common pleas judge in Cuyahoga County. She lived in Cleveland, where she was active in the Writers' Club. Her short stories appeared in numerous magazines, and she also published at least two books, e.g., *Altars to Mammon,* New York, 1908. WW 6

NEFF, EMERY EDWARD (March 23, 1892–), educator, was born in Delaware, Delaware County. He graduated from Barnesville High School in 1909, Ohio Wesleyan University in 1913, and Columbia University (Ph.D.) in 1924. He was a member of the Columbia English department, 1916–53, and since 1954 has been in the department of comparative literature. He has published numerous professional articles and several significant books, e.g., *Carlyle,* New York, [1932]. WW 28

NEFF, PETER (April 13, 1827–May 11, 1903), was born in Cincinnati, Hamilton County. He graduated from Kenyon College in 1849 and Bexley Seminary in 1854. After serving churches in Yellow Springs and Xenia, he retired from the ministry in 1866 because of chronic throat trouble. Experiments made with a Kenyon professor, Hamilton L. Smith, in 1854 had enabled Neff to perfect a process for taking colodion positives on thin iron sheets covered with black. Neff's melanotype (a name he invented) received the bronze medal of the American Institute in New York in 1856. Such japanned metal plates for photography later became known as ferrotypes and tintypes. Neff's interest in the oil fields of western Pennsylvania led to his leasing land in Coshocton County, where he discovered oil in 1865. His *Prospectus* compares this field with those of Venango County, Pa., and reports on the flow of the four Neff wells then producing. This publication with its accompanying map was presented to the legislature, and it activated a geological survey of the state. In 1866 Neff found that a lampblack could be obtained from the natural gas in this area, and soon he was producing it in great quantities for sale in the United States and Europe. His "Diamond Black" was awarded the diploma and medal of the International Exhibition at Philadelphia in 1876. The lampblack was used in making choice lithograph ink. For a number of years Peter Neff lived in Gambier in a house that is one of the best existing examples of domestic Gothic. A continuing benefactor of Kenyon College, he constantly enlivened the village life by his feuds with the college authorities. As he was not loath to rush into print, many newspapers of the period carry his frequent contributions. *Gambier Chimes* is an amusing pamphlet written in protest against the installation of Cambridge chimes at the college. His crotchety account enumerates the aggregate weight of the bells as 6,161 pounds, the number of daily strokes as 1,116, and the distance of his own house from the "cruel, inhuman torture" as 700 feet. He finally purchased an apparatus for switching off these bells during the night, the title to which he ceremoniously presented to the vestry when he left Gambier in 1888. He moved to Cleveland, where he spent his last years happily as librarian of the Western Reserve Historical Society. His death occurred in Cleveland.

Wyman W. Parker

Prospectus of the Neff Petroleum Company . . . , Gambier, 1866.

Gambier Chimes, Columbus, 1880.

NEFF, WILLIAM B. (April 30, 1851–Nov. 6, 1922), lawyer and judge, was born in Winchester, Preble County. He attended Ohio Wesleyan University, read law in Van Wert, and graduated from Cincinnati Law School in 1876. He began practice in Cleveland in 1876, was elected prosecuting attorney in 1890, and was five times elected to the common pleas bench. He wrote *Bench and Bar of Northern Ohio . . . ,* Cleveland, 1921.

NEIBLING, C. C. (c.1822–Aug. 2, 1886), was born in Lancaster, Fairfield County. In 1848 he moved to Circleville to teach in a boys' school, and the remainder of his life was spent in that community. He served as county clerk of courts in the 1850s, was a member of the Circleville city council, 1872–76, and was city engineer, 1876–84. His pamphlet describing the pursuit of Morgan's raiders is a humorous but accurate account of that event, published under the pen name C. C. Enn.

The Bloody First, or Twelve Days with the First Pickaway Throwing "Paw-Paws" at John Morgan, Circleville, 1863.

NEIDIG, WILLIAM JONATHAN (April 2, 1870–Feb. 7, 1955), was born in Western, Iowa. After teaching English at Stanford University, 1901–04, and the University of Wisconsin, 1905–11, he became a free-lance writer. In 1934 he settled in Napoleon, Henry County, where he spent the remainder of his life. His articles and stories appeared in national magazines, and he published several books, e.g., a book of poems: *The First Wardens,* New York, 1905. WW 24

NEIKIRK, MABEL E. (Sept. 28, 1891–Aug. 19, 1948), was born in Tiffin, Seneca County. She attended Heidelberg College. She died in El Paso, Texas, where she resided during the latter part of her life. She published several books for children, e.g., *Oscar—The Trained Seal,* New York, [1940].

NELAN, CHARLES (April 10, 1859–Dec. 6, 1904), artist, was born in Akron, Summit County. He attended Buchtel College and studied at the National Academy of Design, New York City. He became a cartoonist on the Cleveland *Press* in 1888 and later worked for syndicates and for the New York *Herald* and the Philadelphia *North American.*

Cartoons of Our War with Spain, New York, [1898].

NELSON, ANNETTE FITCH. See Annette Fitch Brewer.

NELSON, HELEN LATHROP (1877–), was born in Cincinnati, Hamilton County. A graduate of Smith College, she has been active in Cincinnati civic affairs and as executive secretary of Cincinnati Woman's Club. She has published stories and plays, e.g., *Wanted: A Quiet Old-fashioned Christmas,* Franklin, 1932.

NELSON, HENRY ADDISON (Oct. 31, 1820–Dec. 31, 1906), Presbyterian clergyman, born in Amherst, Mass., served on the faculty of Lane Theological Seminary, Cincinnati, 1868–74. His last years were spent in Wooster. He wrote a book for children: *Seeing Jesus,* Philadephia, [1869].

NELSON, RICHARD (July 9, 1822–April 4, 1900), educator, was born in County Down, Ireland, and was educated at Belfast Institute. After teaching school in Liverpool, he came to the United States in 1849. He lived for a brief time in Philadelphia, and in Barnesville before becoming a teacher in the schools of Wheeling, Va. In 1856 he established Nelson's Business College in Cincinnati. A branch was established in Springfield in 1882 under the management of his son, Richard J. Nelson. Both father and son wrote textbooks.

Suburban Homes for Business Men, on the Line of the Marietta Railroad. A Description of the Northeastern Suburbs . . . , Cincinnati, [1874].

NELSON, ROBERTA BERESFORD (Aug. 17, 1864–June 5, 1910), was born in Chillicothe, Ross County. She also lived in Hillsboro, Highland County. She published stories for children in *St. Nicholas* and other magazines.

Once upon a Time; Stories, Franklin, 1895.

NEPTUNE REX. Pseud. See John J. Makin.

NESBIT, WILBUR D. (Sept. 16, 1871–Aug. 20, 1927), was born in Xenia, Greene County, and was reared and educated in nearby Cedarville, where he began his newspaper career in the office of the Cedarville *Herald* in 1887. After two years on the *Herald* he went to Indiana, where he served on the editorial and advertising staffs of several newspapers. In 1896 he became a feature writer on the Baltimore *American;* his column in that paper, written under the nom de plume of Josh Wink, received recognition as one of the best bits of feature writing in the country. He joined the staff of the Chicago *Tribune* in 1899, and for a number of years conducted the famous column "A Line o' Type or Two." His next move was to the Chicago *Evening Post.* He then became director of the copy staff at the Mahin Advertising Company of Chicago. Not long afterward he acquired control of the company and changed its name to the Rankin Advertising Agency. He was vice president of this company at the time of his death. His best-known poem, "Your Flag and My Flag," is to be found in many anthologies. His collaborations with the well-known cartoonist Clare A. Briggs were notably effective. This remarkably versatile literary figure not only was one of the most popular toastmasters and after-dinner speakers of his day but also won a fame as a librettist which was solidly established by his co-authorship of the very successful musical comedy *The Girl of My Dreams.* He published at least 35 books, e.g., *The Trail to Boyland and Other Poems,* Indianapolis, [1904], *After-Dinner Speeches and How to Make Them,* Chicago, 1927, and *Sermons in Song; Poems of Homely Philosophy,* Chicago, 1929.

NETTLETON, ALVRED BAYARD (Nov. 14, 1838–Aug. 10, 1911), journalist and businessman, was born in Berlin, Delaware County. He graduated from Oberlin College in 1863. He served in the Civil War and was one of the youngest officers to win a brigadier general's star, a brevet rank accorded him at the time of his discharge, March 13, 1865. After the war he studied law, and in 1866 he bought a half interest in the Sandusky *Register,* which he edited for two and a half years. Jay Cooke met him on a visit to Gibraltar, his island home near Sandusky, and from then on Nettleton aided the banker in formulating and propagating his financial views. Possessed of the ability to express himself clearly and convincingly, he was well fitted for the post. He published the Chicago *Advance,* 1868–69. He was closely associated with Jay Cooke in the projection and construction of the Northern Pacific Railroad, 1870–75, and became perhaps the most important factor in the rehabilitation of that enterprise following its crash. He was managing editor of the influential Philadelphia *Inquirer,* 1875–76, and was the founding editor and proprietor of the Minneapolis *Daily Tribune,* 1880–85. From 1890 to 1893 he was assistant secretary of the U. S. Treasury. He retired from business in 1909.

How the Day Was Saved: A Sketch . . . , Philadelphia, 1874.
Trusts or Competition? . . . , Chicago, 1900.

NEUBECK, MARY COOK (Oct. 22, 1865–Nov. 24, 1947), was born in Cambridge, Guernsey County, and lived in Marietta. She published an account of the life of Barbara Cook Becker: *Twelfth Child in Wheels of Time,* Philadelphia, [1942].

NEUMARK, DAVID (Aug. 3, 1866–Dec. 15, 1924), educator, was born near Lwow, Poland. He earned his doctorate at the University of Berlin in 1906 and came to America the following year to join the Hebrew Union College faculty. From 1919 until his death he edited *Journal of Jewish Lore and Philosophy.* His books include *The Philosophy of the Bible,* Cincinnati, 1918. DAB 13

NEVE, JUERGEN LUDWIG (June 7, 1865–Aug. 12, 1943), Lutheran theologian, was born in Schleswig, Germany. From 1909 until his death he lived in Springfield, where he was professor of symbolics in Hamma Divinity School. His numerous books include *Introduction to Lutheran Symbolics . . . ,* Columbus, 1917. WWW 2

NEVIN, EDWIN HENRY (May 9, 1814–June 2, 1889), clergyman and educator, born in Shippensburg, Pa., served Ohio churches in Portsmouth, Poland, Mount Vernon, and Cleveland in the late 1830s and 1840s. He was also president of Franklin College, New Athens, 1840–44. His writings on religious subjects include *Warning against Popery,* Cleveland, 1851.

NEVIN, ROBERT PEEBLES (July 31, 1820–June 28, 1908), journalist, father of the composer Ethelbert Nevin, spent a few years of his boyhood in Chillicothe and attended the academy there. He lived most of his life in Pittsburgh, where he was active in the drug business, oil refining, and journalism. He published a collection of verse: *The "Beautiful River" and Other Poems,* Pittsburgh, Pa., [1899].

NEVIN, WILLIAM CHANNING (Jan. 1, 1844– ?), son of Edwin H. Nevin (q.v.), was born in New Athens, Harrison County, where his father was president of Franklin College. Though born in Ohio, he was educated in Massachusetts and spent his adult life in Philadelphia, where he practiced law and worked for various newspapers. Besides the title below, he wrote considerable fiction. His name does not appear in Philadelphia city directories after 1897.

History of All Religions, Philadelphia, 1871.

NEWBERRY, ARTHUR ST. JOHN (Dec. 17, 1853–Nov. 30, 1912), lawyer, was born in Cleveland, Cuyahoga County. A graduate of Harvard Law School, he practiced law in Cleveland and also organized the Sandusky Cement Co. with his brothers. With the assistance of his younger brother, William Belknap Newberry (1867–1930), he wrote two books on fishing that were published privately in small editions for his family and friends, e.g., *Caught on the Fly . . . ,* Cleveland, 1908.

NEWBERRY, WILLIAM BELKNAP. See Arthur St. John Newberry.

NEWBORN, ISI MANDELL (Rip) (July 16, 1906–), journalist, born in New York City, has lived in Ohio since he was two years old. He graduated from Miami University in 1929, and in 1930 began writing for the Cleveland *Press* sports department. He has published two books on horse racing, e.g., *If You're Going to Play the Races . . . ,* Cleveland, [1949].

NEWBROUGH, JOHN BALLOU (June 5, 1828–April 22, 1891), religious leader, was born near Springfield, Clark County. After graduating from dental college in Cincinnati in 1849, he went to the California gold fields and two years later to Australia. He returned to Cincinnati, 1857–59, and then practiced dentistry for a time in Philadelphia and New York. He was interested in spiritualism and automatic writing. With a number of orphans from Pearl River,

N. Y., and several followers, whom he called "faithists," he founded Shalam, a communistic community, in New Mexico. He was inspired by "angel embassadors" to compose the "Bible" for his followers. The book appeared in several editions.

Oahspe, a New Bible . . . , New York, 1882.

NEWCOMB, ALAN HARRISON (Feb. 28, 1921–), was born in Cleveland, Cuyahoga County. After graduating from Ohio Wesleyan University in 1942, he joined the Air Force and served as a pilot until the end of the war. Since 1946 he has been in radio and television work in North Carolina and now lives in Charlotte. He has written an account of his life in a German prison camp: *Vacation with Pay,* Haverhill, Mass., [1947].

NEWCOMB, ROBERT THOMAS (Sept. 11, 1914–Nov. 11, 1944), elder brother of Alan H. Newcomb (q.v.), was born in Delaware, Delaware County. He lived in Delaware and Cleveland. After graduating from Ohio Wesleyan University in 1936, he traveled and lectured in the United States and the West Indies. In 1939 he joined the U. S. Air Corps. While stationed at Wright Field, he was killed in an automobile accident at London, Madison County. He published a historical novel with its setting the time of Christ: *Janissa,* Haverhill, Mass., [1943].

NEWELL, WILLIAM REED (May 22, 1868–April 1, 1956), clergyman, was born in Savannah, Ashland County. He graduated from University of Wooster in 1891, studied at Princeton Theological Seminary, and in 1897 became an evangelist and interdenominational Bible class teacher. He published several scriptural commentaries and a book of verse: *Messages . . .* , Philadelphia, 1930. WW 26

NEWFANG, OSCAR (Jan. 24, 1875–Feb. 14, 1943), was born in Columbus, Franklin County. He attended Capital University, 1890–93, and afterward was an official of various New York City banks and a firm of woolen manufacturers. He published several books on political and economic questions, e.g., *Capitalism and Communism: A Reconciliation,* New York, 1932. WWW 2

NEWHALL, ROBERT DE SAUSSURE (c.1882–May 22, 1961), journalist, was born in Cincinnati, Hamilton County. After graduating from Princeton University, he attended Oxford University, England. He was a reporter for the Cincinnati *Post* and served as sports editor of the Cincinnati *Commercial Tribune,* 1913–30. After the *Commercial* discontinued publication, he was a sports announcer on a Cincinnati radio station for six years. He died in Sarasota, Fla., where he had spent his last years. He published a book made up of dialogues with a Cincinnati newsboy: *The Discourses of Jimmy,* Cincinnati, 1908.

NEWMAN, EDWARD MANUAL (March 16, 1872–April 16, 1953), traveler and lecturer, was born in Cleveland, Cuyahoga County. He attended Western Reserve University, 1889–93. He was associated for some time with Burton Holmes, and was with Theodore Roosevelt in Africa in 1908. Altogether, he made eight trips around the world, wrote nine books, and produced 158 travelogues. He also lectured throughout the United States. His books include *Seeing Paris,* New York, 1931. WWW 3

NEWMAN, GERTRUDE A. (Dec. 6, 1885–), was born in Cleveland, Cuyahoga County. She spent a part of her girlhood in New London, Huron County, and later attended the Cleveland School of Art. She designed a rag doll, Delicia, and wrote two books for children about this doll, e.g., *Delicia and Adolphus . . .* , Chicago, [1938].

NEWMAN, JOSEPH S. (Dec. 6, 1891–Nov. 10, 1960), president of Newman-Stern Company, was born in New London, Huron County, but spent most of his life in Cleveland. He attended Case Institute of Technology, wrote for several Cleveland newspapers, and wrote a science column for *St. Nicholas* magazine in 1916. He invented several toys and operated a large sporting goods store in Cleveland. He published several volumes of humorous poetry, e.g., *Poems for Penguins and Other Lyrical Lapses,* New York, [1941].

NEWSOM, WILLIAM MONYPENY (July 7, 1887–Feb. 1, 1942), stockbroker, was born in Columbus, Franklin County. After graduating from Yale University in 1909, he was an official in the Breakwater Company and in various brokerage houses. He contributed numerous articles to outdoor magazines and also wrote *Whitetailed Deer,* New York, 1926. WWW 2

NEWSOME MARY EFFIE LEE (Jan. 19, 1885–), librarian, born in Philadelphia, has lived in Wilberforce since 1896. She attended Wilberforce University, 1901–04, and Oberlin College, 1904–05. She is now librarian of the elementary school at Central State College. She has written one-act plays, magazine articles, and poems. Many of her poems have appeared in the Xenia *Gazette*. She has also published a collection of verse for children: *Gladiola Garden . . .* , Washington, D. C., 1940.

NEWTON, BENJAMIN GWERNYDD (1865–), clergyman, was born in Putnam County. Details on his career have not been discovered. Besides a volume of sermons, he published *The Ideal Mother . . .* , New York, 1904.

NEWTON, FRANCES HALLEY (Jan. 13, 1871–), was born in Xenia, Greene County, attended Xenia Seminary and Antioch College, but left Ohio in 1892 to live in Tennessee. She graduated from the University of Tennessee in 1896 and now lives in Ooltewah, Tenn. She has published a collection of poems: *Fernseed,* Philadelphia, [1948].

NEWTON, JOSEPH H. (Jan. 10, 1836–Nov. 4, 1922), was born in Smithfield, Jefferson County, but grew up in Holmes County, where his father moved when he was two years old. He learned the printing business in the office of the Holmes County *Farmer,* which his father published. He edited the paper, 1856–59, served as deputy auditor and county auditor for a number of years, and engaged in railroads and mining. In 1877 with J. A. Caldwell he began publishing county histories for Pennsylvania, West Virginia, and Ohio. In 1880 he became editor of the Newark *Advocate,* which he edited for over thirty years.

History of Venango County, Pennsylvania . . . , Columbus, 1879.

NICHOLAS, EDWARD (Nov. 26, 1906–), was born in Columbus, Franklin County, and lived in that city until he was thirteen, when his family moved to New Mexico. He graduated from Princeton University in 1929 and did graduate work in history at Harvard University and Trinity College, Cambridge University. He has maintained a part-time residence in Columbus while living near Roslyn, N. M. His experimental use of a biographical approach to history received widespread praise from critics when he published *The Hours and the Ages . . .* , New York, [1949]. He sketched American history from the Revolution to the Civil War, using both minor and major figures as symbolic of that history.

NICHOLS, CLIFTON MELVIN (1830–Feb. 9, 1903), journalist, born in Bolton, Mass., came to Ohio in 1848. From 1854 until his death he lived in Springfield, where he edited the *Nonpareil* and other newspapers. He also worked on the *Daily News* for many years.

Life of Abraham Lincoln . . . , New York, 1896.

A Summer Campaign in the Shenandoah Valley . . . , Springfield, 1899.

NICHOLS, GEORGE WARD (June 21, 1831–Sept. 15, 1885), born in Mt. Desert, Maine, and educated in Boston, came to Cincinnati after the Civil War. He married Maria Longworth in 1868 and spent the rest of his life in Cincinnati. He helped found the School of Design and wrote widely on art education. He was also president of the Harmonic Society, and a series of concerts that he organized led to the formation of the May Festival Association, which he also headed. He was also a founder of the College of Music. His efforts in behalf of the arts left a permanent impression on the cultural life of Cincinnati. His diary, kept while he served as aide to General Sherman, was the basis for *The Story of the Great March,* which sold very widely. *The Sanctuary,* a novel based on the same material, was not so well received.

The Story of the Great March . . . , New York, 1865.

The Sanctuary: A Story of the Civil War, New York, 1866.

Art Education Applied to Industry, New York, 1877.

Pottery; How It Is Made . . . , New York, 1878.

NICHOLS, MARY SARGEANT NEAL GOVE. See Thomas L. Nichols.

NICHOLS, REBECCA S. REED (Aug., 1820–1903), was born in Greenwich, N. J. She moved with her father, a physician, to Louisville, Ky., in 1836 and married Willard Nichols in 1837. In 1840 they went to St. Louis, where they edited a daily newspaper for a year; they then moved to Cincinnati, where she spent her most active years as a writer. She did her best work for Cincinnati newspapers, writing under the pen name Kate Cleveland. Her attempt to establish a literary journal, *The Guest,* was ill-advised, and only a few numbers appeared; however, there can be no doubt about her popularity. The Cincinnati *Commercial* entered into an arrangement by which she was paid a liberal price for an original poem to be delivered each week, and in 1851 her *Songs of the Heart and of the Hearthstone* was published in an imposing volume under the patronage of Nicholas Longworth.

Bernice: Or, the Curse of Minna, and Other Poems, Cincinnati, 1844.
Songs of the Heart and of the Hearthstone, Cincinnati, 1851.

NICHOLS, ROBERT M. (Jan. 25, 1890–July 19, 1953), editor and writer, was born in Wapakoneta, Auglaize County. For thirteen years he edited *Field and Stream,* and his books on hunting and field sports include *The Shotgunner,* New York, [1949].

NICHOLS, THOMAS LOW (1815–1901), reformer, born in Orford, N. H., published *Nichols Monthly* at Cincinnati, 1855–57. In it he and his wife, Mary Sargeant Neal Gove Nichols (Aug. 10, 1810–May 30, 1884), advocated spiritualism, vegetarianism, hydrotherapy, free love, and other reforms. In 1856–57 they conducted a water-cure establishment at Yellow Springs. In 1857 both were converted to Catholicism; when the Civil War broke out, they left the country and spent the rest of their lives in England and France. Ardent reformers, both lectured widely and wrote a great deal. They collaborated on *Marriage: Its History, Character, and Results . . . ,* Cincinnati, [1854].

NICHOLS, WILLIAM THEOPHILUS (March 31, 1863–Jan. 26, 1931), journalist, was born in Cincinnati, Hamilton County. After graduating from Yale University in 1884, he worked on the editorial staff of various newspapers in the East. He published short stories in national magazines and several books, e.g., *The Safety First Club,* Philadelphia, 1916. WWW 1

NICOLA, MILTON GEORGE (May 20, 1892–), clergyman, was born in Ravenna, Portage County. He graduated from Kenyon College and Bexley Seminary and served as rector of Episcopal churches in Coshocton, Mansfield, and Capitola-by-the-Sea, Calif. He now lives in Titusville, Pa. Under the pseudonym Clerinic, he was a frequent contributor to Ted Robinson's "Philosopher of Folly" column in the Cleveland *Plain Dealer.* He has also published novels, including one about World War I: *Tinkling Cymbals,* Chicago, [1934].

NICOLAY, JOHN GEORGE (Feb. 26, 1832–Sept. 26, 1901), private secretary to Abraham Lincoln and co-author of a ten-volume biography, was born in Bavaria. His father brought him to America in 1838. He spent part of his boyhood in Cincinnati and attended school there before his father moved farther west.

NIDA, STELLA HUMPHREY (Dec. 18, 1875–), was born in Richfield, Summit County. In 1902 she married William L. Nida (q.v.), who served as superintendent of schools in several Ohio cities. They later lived in River Forest, Ill., and San Diego, Calif. She has published many stories and plays in magazines, collaborated with her husband on several textbooks, and written books for children, e.g., *Letters of Polly, the Pioneer . . . ,* New York, 1916.

NIDA, WILLIAM LEWIS (1874–Aug. 14, 1936), educator, was born in Gallipolis, Gallia County. He attended Ohio Wesleyan University and Ohio State University. He taught in Gallipolis schools and later in River Forest, Ill., and San Diego, Calif. He wrote numerous textbooks for elementary schools, some in collaboration with his wife, Stella H. Nida (q.v.), and *Story of the World War, for Young People,* Oak Park, Ill., [1917]. WWNAA 3

NIESS, SISTER MARY VERA (May, 1902–), was born in Toledo, Lucas County. She graduated from Notre Dame College, Cleveland, in 1928 and the University of California (Ph.D.) in 1941, and is now mother superior of Notre Dame Convent, Cleveland. She has published textbooks and other works, e.g., *The Story of a Little Girl . . . ,* New York, [1935].

NILES, HENRY THAYER (1829–Jan. 13, 1901), lawyer, born in West Fairlee, Vt., graduated from Dartmouth College, and after two years' travel in Europe came to Urbana, where he taught Latin and Greek in Urbana College. He read law while in Urbana, was admitted to the bar, and practiced there and in Toledo. The second book listed below is a long poem on Buddhism and Christianity.

Railroad Transportation; Its Regulation by State and National Authority, Urbana, 1881.
The Dawn and the Day; Or, the Buddha and the Christ, [Toledo], 1894.

NINDE, EDWARD SUMMERFIELD (Jan. 1, 1866–Aug. 15, 1935), clergyman, was born in Cincinnati, Hamilton County. After his ordination to the Methodist ministry in 1891, he served various churches in Michigan, Rhode Island, and Pennsylvania.

Besides two books about hymns, he wrote a biography: *George Whitefield, Prophet-Preacher,* New York, [1924]. WWW 1

NIPGEN, ALVIN PROBASCO (Dec. 23, 1871–Jan. 30, 1936), lawyer, was born in Chillicothe, Ross County. He graduated from Yale University in 1894 and the University of Cincinnati Law School in 1896. He practiced law in Cincinnati, 1896–98, served for a few months in the 1st Regiment, Ohio Volunteer Cavalry, in 1898, and practiced law and engaged in mining in Montana, 1900–07. He retired in 1907. In 1917 he returned to Chillicothe, where he spent the remainder of his life.

In Ye Goode Olde Colony Dayes, New York, 1894.

The Moon Is Her Mirror; A Libretto in Three Acts, Butte, Mont., [1902].

NIXON, ANNA (c.1881–May 20, 1940), journalist, was born in Zoar, Tuscarawas County. After working as a reporter for the Cleveland *Press* in the 1920s, she returned to Zoar to spend the remainder of her life. Using the pen name Lucy Walling, she and Lucie Schneider, also an employee of the *Press,* wrote a novel which was serialized as *For Love of Eve* and published in book form as *Eve's Temptation,* New York, [1934].

NIXON, OLIVER WOODSON (Oct. 25, 1825–1906), physician and journalist, was born in Guilford County, N. C., but was reared in Indiana, where his father moved in 1830. He graduated from Farmers' College, Cincinnati, in 1848, taught for a time in Harveysburg, made a trip to California and Oregon in 1850, and graduated from Jefferson Medical College, Philadelphia, in 1855. He practiced for a time in Wilmington, and during the Civil War he served in the 39th O.V.I. and on the medical staff of the Army of Missouri. After the war he served two terms as Hamilton County treasurer. In 1870 he founded the Cincinnati *Chronicle,* later merged with the *Times.* In 1878 he and his brother purchased the *Inter-Ocean,* and thereafter he lived in Chicago. He sold his interest in the newspaper and retired in 1896. His book was probably the most influential in creating the legend of Marcus Whitman's ride from Oregon to persuade government officials not to relinquish the territory to Great Britain.

How Marcus Whitman Saved Oregon . . . , Chicago, 1895.

NOBLE, CYRUS W. (Sept. 14, 1871–May 29, 1945), physician, was born on a farm near North Fairfield, Huron County. After graduating from Eclectic Medical College, Cincinnati, in 1897, he practiced in Hoytville, Wood County, until 1910, when he moved to Toledo. He published *Memories,* [Toledo, 1922].

NOFFSINGER, JOHN SAMUEL (Dec. 21, 1886–   ), educator, was born in Dayton, Montgomery County. He graduated from Mt. Morris College, Ill., in 1913 and Columbia University (Ph.D.) in 1925. He has taught in Dayton and other cities, was superintendent of schools in the Philippine Islands, was president of Mt. Morris College, 1915–18, was director of the National Home Study Council, and has served on various other educational councils and agencies. Since 1952 he has been executive director of International Voluntary Services and has resided in Washington, D. C. His writings include *Correspondence School, Lyceums, Chautauquas,* New York, 1926. WW 27

NOLAN, PRESTON MEREDITH (Jan. 14, 1875–Jan. 9, 1931), was born in Uhrichsville, Tuscarawas County. He established his own firm of appraisers with headquarters in Chicago. He published several books, including a volume of verse and *Business First,* Chicago, [1928]. WWW 1

NOLEN, ELEANOR WEAKLEY (June 19, 1905–March 12, 1942), librarian, was born in Cincinnati, Hamilton County. After graduating from the School of Library Science, Western Reserve University, she worked in libraries in Cleveland, Philadelphia, and Cincinnati. She wrote numerous articles on children's literature and several books for children, e.g., an account of a trip to Cincinnati in 1840: *The Cowhide Trunk,* New York, [1941].

NORDHOFF, CHARLES (Aug. 31, 1830–July 14, 1901), journalist, born in Prussia, was brought to Cincinnati in 1835. He attended school there and at thirteen was apprenticed to a printer. A prolific writer in later life, he wrote several books about the sea, e.g., *Man-of-War Life . . . ,* New York, 1856, attacks on slavery, and a valuable account of communistic communities in America.

NORMAN, CARL ADOLPH (Jan. 12, 1879–   ), educator, was born in Borga, Finland. He graduated in engineering from the Royal Technical Institute, Stockholm, Sweden, in 1900. He came to the United States in 1902 and was on the engineering faculty of Ohio State University, 1917–50.

He now lives in St. Petersburg, Fla. He has published technical articles as well as articles on religion and economics and *A Galilean; Dramatic Poem in Six Acts,* [Columbus, 1929]. WW 27

NORRIS, EMORY (Dec. 30, 1909–), journalist, was born in Harrisburg, Franklin County. After graduating from Ohio State University in 1931, he taught school for three years in Bellville. After serving as an editor on the Federal Writers' Project, he became editor of the Grove City *Record* in 1938 and has since held that position except for service in the Air Force, 1943–47. He has published some poems under the pen name Alan Bodle and a collection under his own name: *Early Poems,* Grove City, [1941].

NORRIS, GEORGE WILLIAM (July 11, 1861–Sept. 2, 1944), Senator from Nebraska, 1913–43, was born on a farm in Sandusky County. He attended Baldwin University before moving to Indiana, where he studied law, and in 1885 to Nebraska, where he began his distinguished career of public service. His autobiography was published posthumously: *Fighting Liberal . . . ,* New York, 1945. WWW 2

NORTHROP, EVELYN (March 20, 1900–Feb. 10, 1939), educator, was born in New Paris, Preble County. After attending Preble County Normal School and Miami University, she taught in Ohio schools for a number of years. She published poems and plays, e.g., *A Merry Christmas, after All,* Dayton, [1934].

NORTHROP, STEPHEN ABBOTT (April 7, 1852–March 25, 1918), clergyman, was born in Granville, Licking County. After studying for three years at Denison University, he graduated from Colgate University in 1876 and Rochester Theological Seminary in 1877. He was ordained to the Baptist ministry in 1877 and served as pastor of churches in Michigan, Indiana, Missouri, California, and Kansas.

A Cloud of Witnesses . . . , Fort Wayne, Ind., [1894].

NORTON, ALICE MARY (Feb. 17, 1912–), librarian, was born and educated in Cleveland, Cuyahoga County. She served on the staff of the Cleveland Public Library, 1930-51. Using the pen name Andre Norton, she has written several historical novels, e.g., *Ralestone Luck,* New York, 1938. WWAW 1

NORTON, ANDRE. Pseud. See Alice M. Norton.

NORTON, ANTHONY BANNING (May 6, 1821–Dec. 31, 1893), was born in Mount Vernon, Knox County, the son of Daniel S. Norton, a slaveholding proprietor of extensive plantations in the Attakapas district of Louisiana, and one-time adventurous trader and mill operator, whose expeditions carried him into the upper Ohio valley region. Eventually finding himself involved in numerous promising business ventures centering around Mount Vernon, he settled there in 1817. Here he remained the rest of his days, though never relinquishing the idea of returning to his Louisiana plantations, which he continued to operate through an agent for nearly fifty years. In 1836, he took up the cause of Sam Houston, financing, equipping and sending to Texas a company of 67 men from Knox County and a second and somewhat larger company from Zanesville. Also, the presumption that he contributed heavily to the organization of similar companies from Washington, Pa., and Louisville, Ky., is not without some supporting evidence. Anthony B. Norton graduated from Kenyon College in 1840. He studied law at Washington, Pa., in the office of his father's old friends, John L. Gow and Thomas McGiffin, the latter an intimate friend and business associate of Henry Clay. Admitted to the bar at Portsmouth, he returned to Mount Vernon to practice his profession, in which he made little headway, for his ruling passion was politics—the politics of a congenital advocate of slavery and a burning disciple of Henry Clay. In 1844 he impulsively vowed not to cut his hair or shave his beard until Henry Clay became President of the United States, a resolution which rendered him a unique, and, in his old age, a most picturesque figure with his long flowing white hair and beard. Dissatisfied with the antislavery sentiments of the editor of their local organ, *The Day Book,* Mount Vernon Whigs forced him to discontinue publication in 1839 and advertised throughout Ohio for someone to come on and publish a paper. Under this call James Emmet Wilson, uncle of Woodrow Wilson, started the *Knox County Republican.* Even under the favorable auspices of the triumphant campaign of 1840, it was short-lived, folding up in the fall of 1841, and Wilson turned to preaching. Not until 1848 did the old line Whigs get their newspaper, when Norton established the weekly Mount Vernon *True Whig and Chippewa War Club.* He took over the editor's chair in

1852 and established and edited *Norton's Daily True Whig* in 1853. The support of both papers was largely derived from his own purse. His temperate editorials were a far cry from those of the early swashbuckling days of the *Chippewa War Club;* but as the antislavery firebrands fanned the flames of abolitionism in central Ohio, his position became increasingly difficult. In the fall of 1854 he was driven from the neighboring city of Mansfield by a mob of abolitionists. Toward the end of the following March he suspended his newspapers, and, announcing, "Ohio's going to Hell, and I'm going to Texas," he took off for more congenial surroundings in the Lone Star State. During a tour of Texas in 1851 he had met many of his father's old friends, including Sam Houston. Now, in 1855, he experienced no delay in getting established, and shortly his political career in Texas was in full swing. He established and edited *The Intelligencer* at Austin in November, 1856. He was elected to the Texas House of Representatives in 1857 and again in 1859, and during the recess of the first session of this legislature, Governor Sam Houston appointed him his adjutant general. With the intensification of the sectional struggle he again found himself in hot water, for he was a stanch Union man. On Jan. 24, 1860—with secession but a few days away—he appeared before the Texas legislature, and delivered a forthright speech in support of Governor Houston's stand against the South Carolina resolutions. And again, as late as April 8, 1861, smarting under the attacks of the editors of leading Texas newspapers that charged him with being an abolitionist, he appeared before the same body, and delivered a courageous speech in vindication of himself and in defense of the Union. It was a futile gesture, and, Texas having seceded from the Union, Norton seceded from Texas. He returned to the seclusion of his home in Mount Vernon, where he passed the time by writing his *History of Knox County*—an amusing yet valuable compilation—and in doing what he could to alleviate the condition of Texans in Ohio prison camps. After the end of the war he returned to Texas, where he refused two appointments proffered him by the Federal government. However, during the Provisional Government of Reconstruction, he accepted the post of judge in the rabidly pro-Southern district embracing Dallas and surrounding counties. Practically every lawyer in the district was bittery opposed to him, but came to respect him because of his just decisions. For a time he published *The Union Intelligencer* at Jefferson, until the press was destroyed by a mob and he had to take to the thickets of Van Zandt County for personal safety. President Grant appointed him postmaster of Dallas, an office which he held until 1879, when Hayes made him United States Marshal for North Texas. During his tenure of these offices he edited a weekly and daily newspaper, *Norton's Intelligencer.* In 1882 he was the Greenback Party's nominee for governor. He was again driven from Texas in 1888, but this time as "an invalid driven from his home in Texas by poison oak, to the banks of the Kokosing." On this occasion he wrote his *Reminiscences of the Log Cabin and Hard Cider Campaign.* At the back of this work he lists eight titles "by the same author." So far as is known, only one of these was ever published. He died at Dallas, Texas.

Ernest J. Wessen

Vindication of A. B. Norton, from the Attacks of His Enemies; Made in the Texas Legislature, April 8, 1861, [Austin, Texas, 1861].

A History of Knox County, Ohio, from 1779 to 1862 Inclusive . . . , Columbus, 1862.

The Great Revolution of 1840. Reminiscences of the Log Cabin and Hard Cider Campaign, Mount Vernon, 1888.

Tippecanoe Songs of the Log Cabin Boys and Girls of 1840, Mount Vernon, 1888.

NORTON, JESSIE (June 9, 1867–March 26, 1928), educator, was born in Cleveland, Cuyahoga County. She taught in Cleveland schools for 41 years. She composed rather melancholy poetry in order to encourage her pupils' interest in literature.

Sappho, a Classico-Historical Play for Girls, New York, 1894.

Hearts' Ease and Other Verses, Cleveland, 1898.

NORTON, WILLIAM HARMON (April 3, 1856–May 3, 1944), geologist, was born in Willoughby, Lake County. He graduated from Cornell College, Iowa, in 1875 and from 1875 until 1923 was a member of the faculty of his alma mater. He published a geology textbook, numerous technical reports and surveys, and *The Church and Social Action,* Chicago, [1936?]. WWW 2

NOTESTEIN, LUCY LILIAN (June 21, 1891–), educator and editor, sister of Wallace Notestein (q.v.), was born in Wooster, Wayne County. She graduated from the College of Wooster in 1911 and Radcliffe College in 1918. She taught English at the

University of Illinois, 1918–20, and Western Reserve University, 1920–23. She was associated with the Presbyterian Board of Missions, 1923–28, and was on the editorial staff of *Reader's Digest,* 1929–53. She now lives in Wooster. She completed a history of the college which had been begun by her father, Jonas O. Notestein, professor of Latin at the college for many years: *Wooster of the Middle West,* New Haven, [Conn.], 1937.

NOTESTEIN, WALLACE (Dec. 16, 1878–), educator brother of Lucy L. Notestein (q.v.), was born in Wooster, Wayne County, where his father was a professor of Latin. He graduated from University of Wooster in 1900. He served in the history departments of several universities and was Sterling professor of English history at Yale, 1928–47. He has published a number of books on English history, e.g., *English Folk; A Book of Characters,* New York, [1938]. WW 30

NOVOTNY, LOUISE MILLER (April 26, 1889–), born in Polk County, Iowa, moved to Cincinnati in 1925. She operated a private school of dramatics, 1925–38, and graduated from Cincinnati Bible Seminary in 1940. She now lives in Des Moines. She has published several books for use in Sunday schools and a play: *Jesus First . . . ,* [Butler, Ind., 1944].

NUGENT, ELLIOTT (Sept. 20, 1900–), was born in Dover, Tuscarawas County. His parents, who were on the Keith-Orpheum vaudeville circuit, took him on many of their tours, and he made his stage debut in Los Angeles at the age of four. After graduating from Dover High School in 1916, he entered Ohio State University. His three best-known stage comedies, *Kempy* (1922) and *The Poor Nut* (1925), which he wrote with his father, the late J. C. Nugent (q.v.), and *The Male Animal* (1940), done in collaboration with one of his oldest friends and admirers, all deal with aspects of life in Ohio. *Kempy,* in which Elliott played the title role in a performance rated by Heywood Broun one of the finest of that season, had as its setting Elliott's birthplace, Dover (called Calais in the play), and the other two comedies dealt with life in a university easily recognizable, in part, as his alma mater, Ohio State. *By Request* (1928), another hilarious comedy by the Nugents *fils et père,* told the story of a young Ohioan and his wife in New York's Greenwich Village. While still an undergraduate at Ohio State, young Nugent wrote a short story called "Larry Pyramids," which was bought by H. L. Mencken for the *Smart Set.* When *The Male Animal* played for a week in Baltimore in Dec., 1939, Mencken still remembered that story and said, "We expected to hear a lot more from its brilliant author." A lot more was heard from Elliott Nugent, but not in the form of magazine prose, for the theater was the medium nearest his heart, and most of his career since 1921 has been devoted to playwriting, as well as acting, directing, and producing, with occasional sojourns in Hollywood, where he became well known for his perceptive and intelligent writing, acting, and directing in many motion pictures. At the university Elliott had been a news editor of the Ohio State *Lantern* and associate editor and a chief contributor to the monthly *Sun-Dial,* and his stature as the most eminent alumnus of the university dramatic club, The Strollers, has not been challenged in the years that have followed. Elliott Nugent's sound knowledge of play construction is equaled by his skill in the writing of both comic and serious dialogue. To these natural abilities he brought another and unique talent, unsurpassed in American stage comedy—a quiet, persuasive, and often moving skill in the interpretation of such sensitive and complicated characters as the student, John Miller, in *The Poor Nut,* and the English professor, Tommy Turner, in *The Male Animal.* His basic literary gift informs his stage characterizations with a convincing authority. "No other actor," said the late playwright Philip Barry, "can bring such skill and sincerity to the presentation of a sensitive nature, a troubled spirit, or an embattled intellect." For nearly four decades his colleagues in the theater have been well aware that the Nugent touch at once lights up a play and deepens its significance.

James Thurber

NUGENT, JOHN CHARLES (April 6, 1868–April 21, 1947), actor, was born in Niles, Trumbull County. After making his first stage appearance at Somerset, he traveled with vaudeville troupes and repertory companies. He was especially popular as a monologist and wrote his own sketches. His last stage appearance was in Nov., 1946, after 47 years as a Broadway actor. He was author or co-author of many plays, e.g., a collaboration with his son, Elliott Nugent (q.v.): *The Poor Nut,* New York, 1925. He also wrote an autobiography: *It's a Great Life,* New York, 1940.

NYE, MARGARET FRETTER (Dec. 31, 1902–), was born in Cleveland, Cuyahoga County. Wife of a Cleveland attorney,

Walker H. Nye, she published weekly sketches in the Cleveland *News* and later collected them in an edition illustrated by herself: *Rabbits . . . and Other People,* New York, 1947.

NYE, NELSON CORAL (Sept. 28, 1907–), was born in Chicago, but grew up in Cleveland and Cincinnati. He studied at the Cincinnati Art Academy and other art schools and now lives in Arizona. He is a prolific writer of Western stories, e.g., *Gunfighter Breed,* New York, 1942, published under his own name. He has also published under various pen names: as Drake C. Denver, *Tinbadge,* New York, [1941], and as Clem Colt, *Hair-Trigger,* New York, [1940]. WWNAA 7

NYGAARD, NORMAN EUGENE (July 16, 1897–), clergyman, born in Minneapolis, Minn., was pastor of Presbyterian churches in Steubenville and Lisbon for approximately eight years. He is now pastor of First Presbyterian Church, Kimball, Neb. He has published devotional books, plays, sermons, and novels, e.g., *They Sought a Country,* New York, 1950.

O

OAK, VISHNU VITTHAL (Nov. 30, 1895–), educator, was born in Bombay, India. He graduated from St. Xavier College and from Clark University (Ph.D.) in 1937. He taught at Wilberforce University, 1927–30 and 1939–49, and is now on the faculty of Harris Teachers College, St. Louis, Mo. His writings include *The Negro Entrepreneur,* Yellow Springs, 1948. WWAE 13

OAKES (OCHS), GEORGE WASHINGTON (Oct. 27, 1861–Oct. 26, 1931), journalist, was born in Cincinnati, Hamilton County. The family moved to Tennessee in 1864, and he grew up in that state. He was associated with newspapers owned by his brother Adolph S. Ochs: the Chattanooga *Daily Times,* the Philadelphia *Ledger,* and the New York *Times.* In 1917, because of his indignation against Germany, he assumed Oakes as a family name. After his death William H. Schuyler edited *The Life and Letters of George Washington Ochs-Oakes . . . ,* [n.p., 1933]. DAB 13

OAKLEY, IMOGEN BRASHEAR (Oct. 14, 1854–Sept. 12, 1933), was born in Dover, Tuscarawas County. She graduated from Collegiate School, Pittsburgh, in 1871. She traveled extensively, and for a number of years she was chairman of the civil service department, General Federation of Women's Clubs. She died in Philadelphia. Her writings include *Six Historic Homesteads,* Philadelphia, 1935, and *Awake, America! And Other Verse,* Philadelphia, 1934.

OBED. Pseud. See Homer U. Johnson.

O'BRIEN, FREDERICK (June 16, 1869–Jan. 9, 1932), born in Baltimore, Md., became a reporter in Marion in 1894 after nearly ten years as a sailor and hobo. He worked as a reporter for the Marion *Mirror* and later for the *Star,* published by Warren G. Harding. This began his career as a newspaperman and traveler. After working on newspapers in various parts of the U. S. and Hawaii, he first achieved literary success in 1919 with an account of his stay in the Marquesas: *White Shadows in the South Seas,* New York, 1919. DAB 13

O'BRIEN, PATRICK (Feb. 20, 1844–June 22, 1930), clergyman and Irish nationalist, was born in County Wexford, Ireland. He was ordained to the Roman Catholic priesthood in Cleveland, July 21, 1872. He served parishes in Youngstown, Toledo, Cleveland, and Fremont. His only literary production, so far as is known, was a close imitation of Goldsmith's *Deserted Village.* The poem, which was written in 1874, is a militant plea for Irish independence.

The Emerald Isle: A Poem, Cleveland, 1890.

O'FERRALL, KIRK BASSETT (July 19, 1888–), clergyman, was born in Piqua, Miami County. He graduated from Kenyon College in 1909 and was ordained to the Episcopal priesthood in 1913. Between 1913 and 1930 he served churches in Dayton, Toledo, Lima, and Cleveland. In 1930 he became dean of St. Paul's Cathedral, Detroit, Mich. He now lives in California. He has published several travel books, e.g., *Summer Journeyings among the English Cathedrals,* Detroit, 1939. WW 26

OFFICER, MORRIS (July 21, 1823–Nov. 1, 1874), clergyman, was born near Millersburg, Holmes County. After graduating from Wittenberg College and Seminary, he was ordained a Lutheran minister in 1851. He served as a missionary in Africa, 1852–54 and 1860–61, and also established home missions in the United States. He later became a Congregationalist minister. He died in Topeka, Kan.

A Plea for a Lutheran Mission in Liberia, Springfield, 1855.

Western Africa a Mission Field . . . , Pittsburgh, 1856.

African Bible Pictures . . . , Philadelphia, 1859.

OGDEN, GEORGE CAMPBELL (March 10, 1841–Dec. 1, 1911), was born in Cincinnati, Hamilton County. Although he graduated from Miami University in 1863 and from Ohio Medical College in 1866, he did not practice medicine, but devoted himself to travel, painting, and literary pursuits. The posthumous collection of his verse, edited by Charles H. Fisk, was published by his sister, Laura O. Whaling: *Poems . . . ,* [Cincinnati, 1912].

OGDEN, GUSSIE DEBENATH (Jan. 31, 1862–April 9, 1945), was born in Alsace-Lorraine, but while still a child was brought to Cincinnati by her widowed mother. Married to a Cincinnati real-estate dealer, Frank M. Ogden, in 1889, she made her home in that city. She wrote several plays and considerable fiction, e.g., *Double Harness,* New York, [1930].

OGDEN, ROLLO (Jan. 19, 1856–Feb. 22, 1937), born at Sand Lake, N. Y., was a Presbyterian minister in Cleveland, 1880–81 and 1883–87. He abandoned the ministry for journalism and was later on the staff of the New York *Evening Post.* He wrote a volume for the American Men of Letters series: *William Hickling Prescott,* Boston, 1904.

OGDON, INA DULEY (April 3, 1872–), born in Rossville, Ill., but for many years a resident of West Toledo, wrote the words for a great many hymns, including "Brighten the Corner Where You Are." She also published stories, articles, and several volumes of verse, e.g., *A Keepsake from "The Old House,"* St. Louis, Mo., [1937]. WW 26

OGLESBY, WILLIAM DICKEY (1877–March 21, 1959), was born in Middletown, Butler County. A graduate of Yale University, he was president of the O. K. Paper Pail Manufacturing Company and vice president of the Oglesby–Barnitz Bank & Trust Company. His books for boys were published by the United Brethren publishing house.

Dick's Trip to Mexico in 1898, [n.p., 1898].

Dick's Journal of Camp Peerless, 1897–1898, [Dayton, n.d.].

Dick's Trip to California in 1894 . . . , [Dayton, n.d.].

O'HARA, JULIE CAROLINE (Dec. 15, 1868–Aug. 11, 1948), educator, was born in Cincinnati, Hamilton County, and spent her life in that city. She taught in Cincinnati schools and was a member of the Woman's Press Club. She has published many stories for children; a novel, *The Secret Shrine, a Romance,* London, [1934]; and a volume of poetry, *Attic Memories . . . ,* Cincinnati, 1934.

O'HARE, TERESA BEATRICE (? – ?), mother of Anne O'Hare McCormick (q.v.), was born in England. She lived in Columbus and Cleveland. Her last address in Ohioana files (1940) is Cleveland. She wrote poems and articles for a number of Catholic magazines.

Songs at Twilight, Columbus, 1898.

O. HENRY. Pseud. See William Sydney Porter.

OHLINGER, GUSTAVUS (July 15, 1877–), lawyer, was born in Washington, D. C. He graduated from the University of Michigan in 1899 and from the law school in 1902. He practiced law in Shanghai, China, 1903–05, and since 1905 has practiced in Toledo. He has published a legal textbook and *The German Conspiracy in American Education,* New York, [1919]. WWNAA 7

O'KANE, GERALD G. (May 8, 1902–), was born in Philadelphia, but was taken to Ireland as a child and lived there until 1922. He has lived in Akron since 1933. Now employed as a deputy in Summit County Probate Court, he has done considerable free-lance writing and has also supervised the indexing of the Akron *Beacon-Journal.* His poems have appeared in various periodicals, and he has written a novel about the Irish rebellion of 1916 and its aftermath: *St. Patrick Told the Shoemaker,* Philadelphia, [1948].

O'KANE, WALTER COLLINS (Nov. 10, 1877–), educator, was born in Columbus, Franklin County. After graduating from Ohio State University in 1897, he worked on various magazines until 1909, when he began graduate study. He taught entomology at the University of New Hampshire, was on the staff of New Hampshire Experimental Station, 1911–47, and since his retirement has continued to live in Durham, N. H. He has published articles, nature handbooks, and *Jim and Peggy at Apple-Top Farm,* New York, 1923. WW 26

OLCOTT, HENRY STEEL (Aug. 2, 1832–Feb. 17, 1907), theosophist, born in Orange, N. J., lived on a farm in northern Ohio, 1848–53. While there, he developed an interest in spiritualism that later led to his joining Mme. Elena Blavatsky in founding the Theosophical Society and in writing several books on spiritualism, e.g., *People from the Other World,* Hartford, Conn., 1875.

OLDHAM, SAMUEL (July 12, 1833–Dec. 31, 1911), was born in Cambridge, Guernsey County, but moved to Zanesville in 1849 and spent most of his life in that community. He worked on the Zanesville *Courier* and later became joint rate inspector for railroads serving Zanesville. He published *Poems and Historical Papers . . . ,* Zanesville, 1912.

OLDS, HELEN DIEHL (Mrs. Phelps) (April 29, 1895–), was born in Springfield, Clark County. After attending Wellesley College and the University of Texas, she completed her B.A. in 1921 at Wittenberg College. She has worked on several newspapers and for NBC radio programs. Besides numerous short stories published in magazines, she has written several novels for girls, e.g., *Joan of the Journal,* New York, 1930. WWAW 1

OLDS, JULIA GALLOWAY. See Julia Rebecca Galloway.

OLDS, ROBERT (May 30, 1916–), was born in Warren, Trumbull County. After graduating from Ohio Wesleyan University in 1938, he was with the United Press, 1938–41, served on the sports department of the Columbus *Citizen,* 1941–42, and joined the public relations staff of Curtiss-Wright Corporation, Columbus, in 1942. He is now a public relations counsel with the Ohio Education Association and edits the magazine *Trends.* He has published a book about a Navy bombing squadron: *Helldiver Squadron . . . ,* New York, 1944.

OLIN, JOHN MYERS (July 10, 1851–Dec. 7, 1924), lawyer, was born in Lexington, Richland County. A graduate of Williams College and the University of Wisconsin Law School, he practiced in Madison, Wis., and served on the law faculty of the University there. He wrote *Review of the Mooney Case . . . ,* [Madison?, 1920?]. WWW 1

OLIN, SAUL CHALMER (Oct. 12, 1903–), was born in Fairport Harbor, Lake County, but now lives in Lakewood. He has lectured on the history of the Great Lakes, worked on several newspapers, written advertising copy, and served with the War Manpower Commission during World War II. His writings include poetry, fiction, and a historical pamphlet: *The Story of Fairport . . . ,* [Fairport Harbor, 1946].

OLIVER, GEORGE FLETCHER (1853–Jan. 13, 1924), clergyman, was born in Uhrichsville, Tuscarawas County. A graduate of Mount Union College and Boston University, he was for many years pastor of First Friends Church, Cleveland. He wrote *A Trip through Bible Lands and Europe . . . ,* Champaign, Ill., 1915.

OLIVER, WADE WRIGHT (Aug. 30, 1890–), physician and educator, was born in Cincinnati, Hamilton County. He graduated from the University of Michigan in 1912 and from the University of Cincinnati Medical School in 1915. He was professor of bacteriology at Long Island College of Medicine, 1917–48, and since 1948 has been an official of the Rockefeller Foundation. He has published medical articles and a collection of poems: *Fantasia . . . ,* Portland, Maine, 1938. AMS 9

OLMSTEAD, MILLICENT (July 1, 1871–June 3, 1939), journalist, was born in Cleveland, Cuyahoga County. After studying at Miss Mittleberger's School for Girls, she studied in Europe. She worked on the Cleveland *Plain Dealer* and the Cleveland *Leader,* 1899–1905. She wrote for children's magazines and was in public relations work after 1908.

Daffy-Down-Dilly, [Cleveland], 1894.

The Land of Never Was . . . , Philadelphia, [1908].

The Land of Really True . . . , Philadelphia, [1909].

Harmony Wins. A Bright Little Girl Brings Music out of Discord, Boston, [1913].

OLSON, OSCAR THOMAS (1887–), clergyman, born in Chicago, became pastor of the Epworth-Euclid Methodist Church, Cleveland, in 1934. He has published various articles in religious magazines and a book of worship: *Some Values for Today,* New York, [1930]. WW 28

OLT, GEORGE RUSSELL (Nov. 10, 1895–June 28, 1958), educator, was born in Dayton, Montgomery County. He graduated from Lebanon University in 1916. He served on the faculty of Wilmington College, 1917–25, and after 1925 was professor of philosophy and psychology and dean of Anderson College, Anderson, Ind. His writings include *William Carey, Prophet to India,* Anderson, Ind., [1930]. WWW 3

OMWAKE, JOHN (Jan. 13, 1855–April 23, 1939), was born in Greencastle, Pa., but spent much of his life in Cincinnati. He was associated with several Cincinnati industries and was president of the U. S. Playing Card Co. and the U. S. Printing Co., 1906–32, and chairman of the board, 1932–39. He wrote a historical study which was privately published for his friends: *The Conestoga Six-Horse Bell Teams of Eastern Pennsylvania,* Cincinnati, 1930. WWW 1

OPPER, EMMA A. (1864–Feb. 13, 1946), artist, was born in Madison, Lake County, the sister of the pioneer comic-strip artist Frederick Burr Opper (q.v.). The family moved to New York City around 1884 but frequently returned to Madison for visits. Miss Opper moved to Monroe, Conn., in 1916; she died in Bridgeport, Conn. The second title below was written in collaboration with her brother.

Slate-and-Pencil People, New York, [1885].
Patchwork in Pictures and Print, New York, 1888.

OPPER, FREDERICK BURR (Jan. 2, 1857–Aug. 27, 1937), cartoonist, was born in Madison, Lake County, where he attended public school until he was fourteen. After a year working in the office of the Madison *Gazette,* he went to New York. He published cartoons in various comic magazines, joined Frank Leslie's staff in 1877, transferred to the humorous magazine *Puck* in 1881, and remained there until 1899. In that year he was employed by William Randolph Hearst and continued with the Hearst organization until 1932. F. Opper and Richard F. Outcault (q.v.) originated the comic strip. Opper's most famous strips were "Happy Hooligan," begun in 1899, "Alphonse and Gaston," "Our Antediluvian Ancestors," and "Maud the Mule." Numerous collections of his cartoons were published in addition to those listed. He also illustrated books by Mark Twain, Bill Nye, Finley Peter Dunne, and other humorists of the late nineteenth century.

Puck's Opper Book, New York, 1888.
This Funny World As Puck Sees It . . . , New York, [1890].
The Folks in Funnyville; Pictures and Verses, New York, 1900.
Willie and His Papa, and the Rest of the Family, New York, [1901].
Our Antediluvian Ancestors, London, 1903.
Happy Hooligan Home Again, New York, 1907.
Maud the Matchless, New York, 1907.

O.P.Q. Pseud. See Gorham Worth.

ORIANS, GEORGE HARRISON (April 19, 1900–), educator, was born in Marion, Marion County. He graduated from North-Central College, Ill., in 1922 and the University of Illinois (Ph.D.) in 1926, and has been in the English department of the University of Toledo since 1929. He has published professional articles, several textbooks, and *A Short History of American Literature . . . ,* New York, 1940. WW 30

ORR, CHARLES H. (Jan. 8, 1858–Feb. 17, 1927), librarian, was born in Xenia, Greene County, the son of John Orr (q.v.). He was librarian at Case Institute of Technology, Cleveland, for many years. He published a number of pamphlets, e.g., *Words,* Columbus, 1925.

ORR, GULIELMA DAY (Dec. 8, 1867–April 21, 1949), born in Allegheny, Pa., lived in Cincinnati approximately fifty years. She was active in the National League of American Penwomen, the Woman's Press Club, and the Daughters of the American Revolution. She wrote poems and short stories and *Sally in South Africa,* (with Henrietta Schiele), New York, [1929].

ORR, JOHN (Aug. 12, 1820–Dec. 30, 1883), was born in South Carolina. He was brought up in Princeton, Ind., where his family migrated because of their distaste for slavery. After teaching in Tennessee and Indiana, he came to Cedarville, where he served as principal of the public schools and as clerk of courts, 1863–81.

Some Thoughts on the Book of Revelation, Xenia, 1876.

ORR, MARY CASWELL (Dec. 21, 1912–), actress and writer, born in Brooklyn, N. Y., lived in Canton, 1926–41. She has appeared in numerous Broadway plays and on radio and television programs. Her short story "The Wisdom of Eve" was the basis for a successful motion picture, *All About Eve.* With Reginald Denham, her husband, she has written several plays, e.g., *Wallflower,* [New York, 1944]. WWAW 1

ORTH, SAMUEL PETER (Aug. 1, 1873–Feb. 26, 1922), educator, was born in Capac, Mich. He graduated from Oberlin College in 1896 and Columbia University (Ph.D.) in 1903. He taught political science at Buchtel College, 1897–1902, practiced law in Cleveland, 1903–12, and afterward taught political science at Cornell University. His writings include *The Boss and the Machine . . . ,* New Haven, Conn., 1918.

ORTLEPP, E. E. (April 23, 1867–Feb. 21, 1938), clergyman, born in Naumburg, Germany, came to America in 1888. The following year he came to Greenville as pastor of St. Paul's Lutheran Church, where he served, 1889–1901 and 1905–22. He wrote *The Story of Christ's Passion . . . ,* 3 vols., Burlington, Iowa, 1906–09.

OSBORN, CHARLES (Aug. 21, 1775–Dec. 29, 1850), clergyman and abolitionist, was born in North Carolina. As a Quaker minister, he preached and lived in various states. From 1817 to 1818 he published the *Philanthropist,* a pioneer abolitionist paper, in Mount Pleasant. He also lived in Ohio, 1827–30. In 1843 he was a leader in the formation of the Anti-Slavery Friends in Indiana. He published a testimony concerning this revolt in 1849. The Society of Friends published *Journal of That Faithful Servant of Christ, Charles Osborn . . . ,* Cincinnati, 1854.

OSBORN, HARTWELL (Aug. 17, 1840–Nov. 15, 1914), was born in Norwalk, Huron County. He served as a captain in the 55th O.V.I. during the Civil War. Afterward he was deputy collector of customs in Toledo, 1867–69, and was a manufacturer in Toledo, 1870–80. From 1880 until his death he was a railway commercial agent in the South and in Chicago. He died in Chicago. He wrote a history of his regiment: *Trials and Triumphs . . . ,* Chicago, 1904.

OSBORN, HENRY STAFFORD (Aug. 17, 1823–Feb. 2, 1894), clergyman and educator, was born in Philadelphia. He was ordained to the Presbyterian ministry in 1848 and served churches in Virginia and New Jersey. He became professor of chemistry and mining engineering at Lafayette College in 1866, and in 1870 accepted a professorship at Miami University. He taught there until 1873, when the school closed temporarily, and also served as pastor at Millville. Oxford remained his home until his death. Maps of the Holy Land that he published in Oxford were widely used in churches and Sunday schools. His books on mining and metallurgy were also widely known and went into several editions.

Little Pilgrims of the Holy Land, Philadelphia, 1857.

Palestine, Past and Present . . . , Philadelphia, 1859.

Plants of the Holy Land . . . , Philadelphia, 1860.

Metallurgy of Iron and Steel . . . , Philadelphia, 1869.

The New Descriptive Geography of Palestine, Oxford, 1877.

Ancient Egypt in the Light of Modern Discoveries . . . , Cincinnati, 1883.

A Practical Manual of Minerals, Mines, and Mining . . . , Philadelphia, 1888.

The Prospector's Field-Book and Guide . . . , Philadelphia, 1892.

OSBORN, HERBERT (March 19, 1856–Sept. 20, 1954), entomologist, born in Lafayette, Wis., was a member of the Ohio State University faculty, 1898–1933, and after his retirement continued to live in Columbus. A prolific author, he wrote many articles, texts, and books, including a short history of entomology written when he was 96 years old. His books include *Fragments of Entomological History, Including Some Personal Recollections of Men and Events,* Columbus, 1937. WWW 3

OSBORNE, GROVER PEASE (1848–June 6, 1932), clergyman, was born in Trumansburg, N. Y. He graduated from Kalamazoo College in 1871 and studied at Chicago Baptist Union Theological Seminary. Ordained to the Baptist ministry in 1875, he was a pastor in Toledo until 1887, when he became editor of the *Journal and Messenger,* published in Cincinnati. He died in Cincinnati.

Principles of Economics. The Satisfaction of Human Wants, Cincinnati, 1893.

OSBURN, MARY HUBBELL (Sept. 15, 1878–), musician, was born near Covden, Ill. She graduated from Fargo College, N. D., in 1903 and later studied music in New York and Paris. She came to Columbus in 1917 when her husband, Raymond C. Osburn, joined the Ohio State University faculty, and has been very active in the musical life of the city. She has composed songs and anthems, written numerous articles, and compiled a useful book: *Ohio Composers and Musical Authors,* [Columbus, 1942]. OCM

OSMUN, THOMAS EMBLY (Feb. 26, 1826–Oct. 26, 1902), elocutionist, was born in Montrose, Summit County. He studied at Oberlin College and in Europe. By sending his criticisms of actors' mispronunciations to newspapers, and by other means, he established himself as an arbiter of correct diction. All of his books were published under the pen name Alfred Ayres. Besides the titles below, he published a pronouncing manual, an elocution textbook, and several books on the misuse of words.

Acting and Actors . . . , New York, 1894.
The Mentor: A Little Book for the Guidance of Such Men and Boys As Would Appear to Advantage in the Society of Persons of a Better Sort, New York, 1894.

OSWALD, JOHN CLYDE (July 11, 1872–June 22, 1938), publisher, was born in Fort Recovery, Mercer County, where he began in the printing business in 1885. In 1894 he moved to New York City and edited *The American Printer,* 1897–1925. Besides technical works on printing, he wrote *Benjamin Franklin, Printer,* [New York], 1917. WWW 1

OTIS, CHARLES HERBERT (Jan. 25, 1886–   ), educator, born in Raymond, Neb., has served in the botany departments of several universities, including Western Reserve, 1916–27, and Bowling Green, 1930–55. After retiring in 1955 he continued to live in Bowling Green. He has published *Michigan Trees . . . ,* Ann Arbor, Mich., 1932.

OTIS, PHILO ADAMS (Nov. 24, 1846–Sept. 23, 1930), was born in Berlin Heights, Erie County, but spent most of his life in Chicago, where his parents moved in 1857. After graduating from Western Reserve College at Hudson in 1868, he joined his father's real-estate firm in Chicago. He was also active in the musical life of that city. He published a book of hymns, a church history, a history of the Chicago Symphony Orchestra, and a travel book: *Impressions of Europe, 1873–1874 . . . ,* Boston, [1922]. WWW 1

O'TOOLE, GEORGE BARRY (Dec. 11, 1886–March 26, 1944), clergyman and educator, was born in Toledo, Lucas County. He studied at St. John's University, Toledo, 1904–06, and at Urban University, Rome, Italy, 1906–12. Ordained to the Catholic priesthood in 1911, he was secretary to the bishop of Toledo, 1912–15, and a pastor in Bowling Green, 1915–17. He afterward taught philosophy, biology, and theology in various Catholic colleges and universities. He published *The Case against Evolution,* New York, 1925. RLA 2

OTT, EDWARD AMHERST (Nov. 27, 1867–May 19, 1952), educator, was born in Youngstown, Mahoning County. After studying at Hiram College, he graduated from Drake University in 1895. He served on the Drake faculty, 1891–1901. In 1932 he became advisor to a group of Cornell University students living in Llenroc Lodge on a co-operative basis. Besides the titles below, he published a public speaking textbook and a book on poultry-raising.

Sour Grapes; Or, Heredity and Marriage, Des Moines, [1896].
Philip Gerard, an Individual, Des Moines, [1899].
Hot Shots in the War on Poverty, Byron, N. Y., 1917.
Self Management Memos, Ithaca, N. Y., 1927.

OUTCAULT, RICHARD FELTON (Jan. 14, 1863–Sept. 25, 1928), artist, was born in Lancaster, Fairfield County. After studying at McMicken College, Cincinnati, he studied art in Paris. While doing technical drawings for journals in New York City, he contributed comic drawings to *Life* and *Judge.* In Nov., 1894, he was hired to do a colored drawing for the New York *World.* Soon afterward he created "Hogan's Alley" and "The Yellow Kid," and he thus shares with Frederick B. Opper (q.v.) the distinction of originating the modern comic strip. In 1896 the New York *Journal* hired him away from the *World* at a large salary; the *World* immediately hired another cartoonist to draw "The Yellow Kid." The resulting circulation war between the two papers led to their being known as "Yellow Kid" journals and, later, simply as "yellow" journals. Outcault later joined the New York *Herald* and in 1905 returned to the *Journal.* His most famous creation was "Buster Brown," a character that became a trademark for all sorts of products. He published several Buster Brown books, e.g., *Buster Brown Abroad,* New York, [1904]. DAB 14

OWEN, CAROLINE DALE. Pseud. See Caroline D. P. Snedeker.

OWEN, ELIZABETH THORNILEY (Feb. 27, 1871–   ), was born on a farm near

Marietta, Washington County. After her marriage to O. D. Owen in 1895, she lived in the West until 1910, when she returned to Ohio. She lived in Marietta and Beverly until 1955. She now lives in San Antonio, Texas. She has written pamphlets and articles on historical subjects, e.g., *Johnny-cake, etc., in the Ohio Country at the Muskingum . . .* , Beverly, [1932].

OWEN, WILLIAM MILLER (Jan. 10, 1832–Jan. 10, 1893), was born in Cincinnati, Hamilton County. He served in the Confederate army with the Washington Artillery of New Orleans. In 1890 he assisted Mrs. Jefferson Davis in the preparation of the military chapters of her *Memoirs* of her husband.

In Camp and Battle with the Washington Artillery of New Orleans. A Narrative of Events during the Late Civil War . . . , Boston, 1885.

OWENS, IRA S. (March 1, 1830–Feb. 19, 1913), farmer, was born in Xenia, Greene County, the son of a Methodist minister. He served Oct., 1861–July, 1865, in the 74th O.V.I. After the war he lived in Putnam County, Ind., for two years and then returned to a farm near Beavertown, Montgomery County, where he spent the remainder of his life. He revised his book about the war and republished it in 1884.

Greene County in the War . . . , Xenia, 1872.

P

PACIFICUS. Pseud. See Joshua R. Giddings.

PACK, ARTHUR NEWTON (Feb. 20, 1893–), was born in Cleveland, Cuyahoga County, the son of Charles Lathrop Pack (q.v.). He graduated from Williams College in 1914 and the Harvard School of Business Administration in 1915. His major interest has been forestry, and he has published several books on nature study and conservation, e.g., *Our Vanishing Forests,* New York, 1923. WW 30

PACK, CHARLES LATHROP (May 7, 1857–June 14, 1937), economist and founder of the Cleveland Trust Company, was born in Lexington, Mich. In 1870 his parents brought him to Cleveland, where he attended public schools and Brooks School. He also studied forestry in Germany. Although he traveled widely in Europe and the United States, Cleveland remained his home until 1900, when he moved to Lakewood, N. J. Besides books on forestry he wrote *All Honor to George Washington,* [Washington, D. C., 1930?]. WWW 1

PACKARD, JASPER (Feb. 1, 1832–Dec. 13, 1899), was born in Austintown, Mahoning County. In 1835 his parents moved to Indiana, where he grew up and distinguished himself as a Civil War soldier, congressman, and newspaper publisher. He died in Lafayette, Ind.

History of La Porte County, Indiana . . . , La Porte, 1876.

PACKARD, ROY DWIGHT (July 31, 1889–), was born in Cleveland, Cuyahoga County. He was employed by Standard Oil, 1904–54, and was Cleveland Division Manager, 1936–54. A student of Lincoln's career, he has written numerous articles, pamphlets, and books on Lincoln, e.g., *Lincoln and Franklin Roosevelt,* Cleveland, 1938.

PACKARD, SILAS SADLER (April 28, 1826–Oct. 27, 1898), educator, born in Cummington, Mass., was brought to Licking County when he was seven. He attended district schools and spent one term in Granville Academy. At sixteen he began teaching penmanship in Ohio and Kentucky schools; in 1848 while in Cincinnati he began teaching bookkeeping as well. This led to his lifework, the establishment of business colleges in New York and other cities. He published many textbooks in commercial education. Of most interest to Ohioans, however, is a description of pioneer life in Licking County, first read to the Ohio Society of New York and then published as a pamphlet: *My Recollections of Ohio . . .* , [New York?, 1890].

PADDOCK, BUCKLEY B. (Jan. 22, 1844–Jan. 9, 1922), was born in Cleveland, Cuyahoga County, but spent little of his life in Ohio. He spent his boyhood in the Northwest and at the age of sixteen enlisted in the Confederate army. After the Civil War he practiced law in Mississippi until 1873, when he moved to Fort Worth, Texas.

There he published the Fort Worth *Democrat* and engaged in banking and railroad building until his retirement in 1909. He prepared three historical works dealing with Texas, e.g., *History of Texas . . .*, 4 vols., Chicago, 1922. WWW 1

PAGE, HENRY FOLSOM (Feb. 2, 1821–Oct. 7, 1901), lawyer, was born in Circleville, Pickaway County. He was born Henry Page Folsom, but adopted his mother's family name because he did not like his father's side of the family. After graduating from Miami University and Harvard Law School, he began practicing in Circleville in 1845. He contributed many essays to professional journals. His work on Virginia Military District land titles is exhaustive and constitutes a valuable source for historians. At his death he left a part of his substantial estate for the establishment of a law school at Ohio State University.

The Law of Warrants, Entries, Surveys and Patents in the Virginia Military District in Ohio . . ., Columbus, 1850.
A View of the Law Relative to the Subject of Divorce, in Ohio, Indiana and Michigan, Columbus, 1850.

PAHLOW, GERTRUDE CURTIS BROWN (Jan. 12, 1881–Jan. 29, 1937), born in Reading, Mass., lived in Columbus from 1925 until her death. Her husband, Edwin William Pahlow (1878–1943), was professor of education at Ohio State University. She published a number of stories in national magazines and several novels, e.g., *The Bright Torch,* Philadelphia, [1933]. WWW 1

PAINE, BAYARD HENRY (April 27, 1872–April 19, 1955), lawyer and judge, was born near Painesville, Lake County. His family moved to Grand Island, Neb., where he attended school and later practiced law. He served as a district court judge, 1916–30, and on the Nebraska Supreme Court, 1931–49. He published an account of pioneer life in Nebraska: *Pioneers, Indians and Buffaloes,* Curtis, Neb., 1935. WWW 3

PAINTER, ELEANOR. See Eleanor P. Strong.

PAINTER, LYDIA ETHEL HOYT FARMER (July 19, 1842–March 8, 1909), was born in Cleveland, Cuyahoga County, the daughter of James Madison Hoyt (q.v.), a lawyer and a prominent Baptist layman. In 1864 she married Elihu J. Farmer (q.v.), and after his death in 1900 she married John Vickers Painter, Cleveland banker and socialite. She was active in musical and artistic activities in Cleveland and in the women's suffrage movement. A book on women's contributions to American life that she edited in 1893 bore an introduction by Julia Ward Howe. Her novels were religious in subject matter. *A Knight of Faith* was praised by William E. Gladstone. Of the last six books listed below, only *Memoirs* and *Under Egypt's Skies* were published under her own name; for the others she used the pen name G.E.X.

The Boys' Book of Famous Rulers, New York, [1886].
A Story Book of Science, Boston, [1886].
The Girls' Book of Famous Queens, New York, [1887].
The Life of La Fayette, the Knight of Liberty in Two Worlds and Two Centuries, New York, [1888].
A Knight of Faith, New York, [1889].
A Short History of the French Revolution, for Young People . . ., New York, [1889].
A Moral Inheritance, New York, 1890.
Aunt Belindy's Points of View, and a Modern Mrs. Malaprop . . ., New York, [1895].
The Doom of the Holy City. Christ and Caesar, New York, [1895].
The Chatelaine, Buffalo, N. Y., 1897.
The Rosary, [n.p., 1899].
The Memoirs of James and Meribah Farmer, [Cleveland, 1900].
My Athens & Songs to Her, [Wausau, Wis., 1903].
Italian Portraits in Engadine Frames, Wausau, Wis., [1904].
Under Egypt's Skies, [Wausau, Wis., 1910].

PALMER, EDWARD E. (June 24, 1871–), was born on a farm near West Salem, Wayne County. After attending district schools, he became a traveling salesman, handling a great variety of products. He invented a chipped glass name plate and engaged in several other enterprises. He has written an autobiography: *Forty Years of Hustling,* [Wooster, 1942].

PALMER, FRANCES LAKIN (Sept. 12, 1907–May 4, 1938), was born in Cleveland, Cuyahoga County. She graduated from Hathaway-Brown School in 1925 and Smith College in 1929. She was on the office staff of Oberlin Graduate School of Theology, 1935–37. A posthumous collection of her writings was privately published: *Poems and Prose . . .*, Cleveland, 1939.

PALMER, JOANNA (July 27, 1861–Jan. 26, 1953), was born in Cromwell, Iowa, but came to Bellefontaine while still a girl to live with an aunt. After her marriage to Dr. Harry E. Palmer, she lived in Dayton, where she was active in religious and social work. She published poetry and prose in religious periodicals and a pageant: *Gifts for Youth . . .* , New York, 1945.

PALMER, JOHN RANSOM (March 22, 1905–), physician, was born in Findlay, Hancock County. His family moved to Shreveport, La., where he attended high school. After graduating from Princeton University in 1928, he studied medicine. His last address in Ohioana files is New York City. Under the pen name Robert Goldsborough, he published a collection of poems: *Midstream—Midnight,* New York, 1938, and a book on European travel: *Where Every Prospect Pleases,* New York, 1939.

PALMER, WILLIAM FRANCIS (Oct. 11, 1862–Feb. 10, 1924), educator, was born in West Richfield, Summit County. After graduating from Baldwin University, Berea, in 1887, he did graduate work at the University of Michigan and Lake Forest College. In 1896 he began teaching Latin at West High School, Cleveland, where he served on the faculty until his death. He published *Ballads, Lyrics and Sonnets,* Cleveland, 1907.

PANCOAST, CHALMERS LOWELL (March 6, 1880–), journalist, was born on a farm near Bethesda, Belmont County. In 1887 his family moved to Newark, where he attended public schools. He worked on newspapers and magazines in various cities throughout the country and since his retirement has lived in Newark. He has published several books on newspapers, hotels, and masonry, e.g., *Cub,* New York, [1928].

PANSY. Pseud. See Isabella MacDonald Alden.

PARDEE, HELEN LANPHERE (Mrs. William E.) (Aug. 5, 1878–), born in Silver Creek, N. Y., has lived in Akron since 1903. A graduate of Fredonia State Teachers College, she taught in the schools of New York State and Akron. She was a member of the board of the Akron Public Library, 1927–45, and has been active in other civic affairs. She has published poetry and *A Story of the Akron Public Library, 1834–1942,* Akron, 1943.

PARGELLIS, STANLEY McCRORY (June 25, 1898–), librarian, was born in Toledo, Lucas County. He left Ohio in 1903 and attended public schools in Iowa, Idaho, and Texas. After graduating from the University of Nevada in 1918, he was a Rhodes scholar at Oxford. He taught history in several universities, completed his doctorate at Yale University in 1929, and has been librarian of Newberry Library, Chicago, since 1942. He has compiled several bibliographies and collections of documents, written numerous articles, and published a pamphlet: *Father Gabriel Richard,* Detroit, 1950. WW 30

PARK, CLYDE WILLIAM (June 30, 1880–), educator, was born in New Lexington, Perry County. He graduated from Ohio State University in 1907 and did graduate work at Harvard University. He served in the English department, University of Cincinnati, until his retirement in 1945. He has written several textbooks, radio scripts, articles, and a biography: *Ambassador to Industry; The Idea and Life of Herman Schneider,* Indianapolis, [1943].

PARK, SAMUEL (Nov. 21, 1810– ?), was born in Union Township, Licking County. In 1881 he was living in Marshall, Iowa. The pamphlet below contains an essay, "American Antiquities," which was also issued separately.

Notes on the Early History of Union Township, Licking County . . . , Terre Haute, 1870.

PARKER, CAROLINE HOLMES (Aug. 8, 1847–Feb. 22, 1926), educator, was born at Sugartree Ridge, Highland County. Her family moved to Hillsboro, where she graduated from Hillsboro Female College in 1868. After teaching school in Leesburg and other communities, she married John Milton Parker in 1872. Soon after the birth of her seventh child, her husband died, and she returned to teaching to support her family. Her last years were spent in Asheville, N. C.

Our Friends the Birds, Chicago, [1897].

PARKS, L. K. (Nov. 30, 1846–Jan. 8, 1925), lawyer, was born in Sheffield, Lorain County. After attending Hillsdale College and Oberlin College, he read law and was admitted to the bar in 1875. He practiced in Weston, Wood County, 1875–77, and afterward in Toledo. Around 1901 he moved to Los Angeles because of poor health.

With British and Braves, Story of the War of 1812, Cincinnati, [1898].

PARLETTE, RALPH ALBERT (Aug. 30, 1870–Nov. 19, 1930), was born near Delaware, Delaware County. After graduating from Ohio Northern University in 1891, he edited the Ada *University Herald* until 1897. He later edited the *Lyceum Magazine,* 1909–28. An inspirational lecturer, he traveled widely and also published numerous books and pamphlets on success, thrift, and happiness, e.g., *Pockets and Paradises,* Chicago, [1922]. WWW 1

PARRISH, ROB ROY McGREGOR (Jan. 15, 1846–March 11, 1924), was born in Noble County. His parents moved to Iowa in 1854. He was a harness maker in Independence, Oreg., 1863–90. In 1890 he moved to California. He took his own life at Schulavista, Calif. The book of poems below is his only known publication.

Echoes from the Valley, Portland, Oreg., 1884.

PARROTT, THOMAS MARC (Dec. 22, 1866–Feb. 6, 1960), educator, was born in Dayton, Montgomery County. He graduated from Princeton University in 1888 and the University of Leipzig (Ph.D.) in 1893. He was a member of the Princeton English faculty, 1896–1935, and after his retirement lived in Princeton. He edited a number of anthologies and other textbooks and also published a collection of essays: *Studies of a Booklover,* New York, 1904. WWW 3

PARRY, EMMA LOUISE (July 24, 1859–Jan. 18, 1940), educator, was born in Cincinnati, Hamilton County. She graduated from the University of Cincinnati in 1887 and also studied art in Europe. She served for many years on the staff of H. Thane Miller School, Cincinnati, and also lectured on art and archaeology.

Life among the Germans, Boston, [1887].
The Two Great Art Epochs, Chicago, 1914.

PARRY, WARD HUDSON (Sept. 20, 1894–Aug. 23, 1940), was born in Woodsfield, Monroe County. He graduated from Woodsfield High School in 1912 and Western Reserve University in 1916. He worked on the Akron *Times* and the Cleveland *Plain Dealer,* served in the ambulance service during World War I, was treasurer of the Franz Foundry and Machine Company, and in the early 1930s established a commercial photography business in Akron. He died at Daytona Beach, Fla. He wrote a novel which deals with the life of his father, Dr. John R. Parry of Woodsfield, and also with his own war experiences: *These Three,* Boston, [1929].

PARSON, DONALD (Jan. 10, 1882–), born in Washington, D. C., and now a resident of Brooklin, Maine, lived in Youngstown for fifteen years. He has published four books, including a collection of verse: *Glass Flowers,* Boston, 1936.

PARSONS, ALBERT ROSS (Sept. 16, 1847–June 14, 1933), pianist, was born in Sandusky, Erie County, but actually spent little of his life in Ohio. A gifted musician, he studied piano in New York and in Germany. While in Germany (1867–72), he knew Richard Wagner, and after returning to America he wrote and lectured on Wagner's work. He taught piano in New York City from 1872 until his death. Besides the titles below, he wrote songs and piano compositions, articles and books on piano technique, and a family history.

Parsifal; The Finding of Christ through Art . . . , New York, 1890.
New Light from the Great Pyramid . . . , New York, 1893.
The Road Map of the Stars . . . , New York, 1912.
Surf Lines That Mark Where Waves of Thought Formed Crest and Broke upon the Shore of a Wayfarer's Mind . . . , [New York, 1912].

PARSONS, JULIA STODDARD (1855–March 7, 1946), was born in Cleveland, Cuyahoga County, where her father, Richard C. Parsons (q.v.), edited the Cleveland *Herald.* She died at the age of 91 in Santa Barbara, Calif., where she had lived since 1907. Besides a book on nineteenth-century royalty, she published an autobiographical volume: *Scattered Memories,* Boston, [1938].

PARSONS, LAURA MATILDA STEPHENSON (Aug. 11, 1855–March 5, 1925), playwright, was born near Jefferson City, Mo. When she was five, her father died, and her mother moved to Chardon. In 1875 she married Wilder C. Parsons; their lives were spent in Chardon. Mrs. Parsons wrote a number of plays, most of them for performance in churches. She also composed songs to accompany the productions. She died in Chardon.

Colloquy of the Holidays . . . , Dansville, N. Y., 1889.
The District School at Blueberry Corners . . . , Dansville, N. Y., 1889.
Jerusha Dow's Family Album, Boston, 1894.
Living Pictures of the Civil War, Boston, 1894.
Scenes and Songs of Ye Olden Time . . . , Boston, 1894.

The Old Maids' Convention, Boston, 1899.
Aunt Jerusha's Quilting Party, Boston, 1901.
A Variety Contest . . . , Boston, 1901.
Scenes in the Union Depot, Boston, 1905.
The Rainbow . . . , Chardon, [1913].

PARSONS, RICHARD CHAPPELL (Oct. 10, 1826–Jan. 9, 1899), lawyer, congressman, and editor, was born in New London, Conn. In 1845 he came to Norwalk, where he read law, and in 1851 he was admitted to the bar in Cleveland. He held a variety of elective and appointive posts. He served in the Ohio Assembly, 1858–62, was collector of internal revenue in Cleveland, was marshal of the U. S. Supreme Court, 1866–72, and served one term in the House of Representatives, 1873–75. After being defeated for re-election, he resumed the practice of law and also edited the Cleveland *Herald,* 1877–80. Besides the collection below, some of his speeches were printed as pamphlets.
Selections from the Addresses and Writings . . . , Cleveland, 1892.

PARSONS, SAMUEL HOLDEN (May 14, 1737–Nov. 17, 1789), was born in Lyme, Conn. Beginning in 1762, he served in eighteen sessions of the Connecticut Assembly. He was commissioned a brigadier general in 1776 and was promoted to major general in 1780. In 1785 he was one of the commissioners named to treat with the Indians regarding lands in the territory northwest of the Ohio. As a result of their efforts the Indians ceded the tract of land upon which the city of Cincinnati now stands. On Oct. 23, 1787, he became the first judge in the territory of the United States northwest of the Ohio River. Washington nominated him as chief judge of the territory in 1789, an office which he held until his death. Not only was he one of the three directors of the Ohio Company, but he was also interested in the Western Reserve. In 1789 the State of Connecticut appointed him one of three commissioners to treat with the Wyandots and other tribes regarding their titles to the lands then called the Connecticut Western Reserve. With a view to making preliminary arrangements for the treaty he visited the Western Reserve in the fall of 1789, and while returning to his residence in Marietta he was drowned in the Big Beaver River. He wrote a description of mounds near Marietta, "Antiquities of Western States," which was published by the American Academy of Arts and Sciences in 1793. His writings were published in 1905 in the edition listed below.
Life and Letters . . . , (Charles Samuel Hall, ed.), Binghamton, N. Y., 1905.

PASCHALL, ALMA (March 29, 1878–), educator, was born in Clark County. She taught in the schools of Springfield, Akron, and Toledo. Now retired, she lives in Springfield. Besides poems published in many magazines and newspapers, she wrote in collaboration with Francis B. Pearson (q.v.) a story for children: *The Thrift Twins,* New York, 1933.

PATCHEN, KENNETH (Dec. 3, 1911–), one of the most respected of *avant-garde* writers, was born in Niles, Warren County. He was reared in Warren and attended high school there. He worked for a time in the steel mills, spent a year at Alexander Meikeljohn's Experimental College at the University of Wisconsin, and was a migratory worker in the early 1930s. He has lived in Connecticut and New York City and now lives in California. His writing, experimental in character, includes essays, novels, and surrealistic poems and plays. He probably received most praise for his satiric novel, *The Memoirs of a Shy Pornographer . . . ,* [New York, 1945]. He has published numerous books of poetry, e.g., *The Dark Kingdom . . . ,* New York, [1942], *The Selected Poems . . . ,* [Norfolk, Conn., 1946], and *Red Wine & Yellow Hair,* New York, [1949]. Some of his books have appeared in limited editions, for which he has painted an original water color to accompany each copy. TCA

PATERSON, ROBERT (Nov. 17, 1885–), journalist and lecturer, was born in Bellefontaine, Logan County. After attending Ohio State University he served on numerous newspapers in the Midwest and South and was an associate editor with McClure Newspaper Syndicate, 1922–26. He has lectured widely and has also published several books on American life, e.g., *Gas Buggy,* New York, 1933. WW 30

PATERSON, ROBERT GILDERSLEEVE (Sept. 18, 1882–), educator and public health specialist, was born in Columbus, Franklin County. He graduated from Ohio State University in 1905 and the University of Pennsylvania (Ph.D.) in 1909. He was executive secretary of the Ohio Public Health Association, 1911–46, and taught social administration at Ohio State University, 1925–47. After retiring, he settled in Tryon, N. C. He wrote numerous pamphlets and articles on public health and *Robert Harvey Reed, a Sanitary Pioneer in Ohio,* Columbus, [1935]. WW 30

PATTERSON, ANN VIRGINIA SHARPE (Sept., 1841–May 30, 1913), was born in Delaware, Delaware County. She graduated from Delaware Female Seminary. She contributed a number of children's stories to magazines under the pen name of Garry Gaines, which she also used for her first book. She lived for a number of years in Bellefontaine; then in 1892 she moved to Kokomo, Ind., where she spent the remainder of her life. Perhaps she is best remembered for her nation-wide birdhouse campaign among schoolchildren.

The American Girl of the Period: Her Ways and Views, Philadelphia, 1878.
Speeches, Prose, Rhyme and Jingle for the Trades' Carnival . . . , Springfield, 1889.
Supplement to Business Men's Jubilee, or Trades' Carnival . . . , Urbana, 1889.
Dickey Downy: The Autobiography of a Bird . . . , Philadelphia, [1899].
Lady of the Green Scarf: An Entertainment Exercise for Schools . . . , Chicago, [1910].

PATTERSON, ERNEST MINOR (July 17, 1879–), educator, was born in Cincinnati, Hamilton County. He graduated from Park College in 1902 and the University of Pennsylvania (Ph.D.) in 1912. He was on the faculty of the University of Pennsylvania, 1910–50. He published articles on economics, textbooks, and books related to business and economics, e.g., *The Economic Basis of Peace,* New York, [1939]. WW 30

PATTERSON, FREDERICK B. (June 22, 1892–), industrialist, was born in Dayton, Montgomery County. He attended Dayton schools and spent two years at a public school in England before beginning to work at National Cash Register, which was founded by his father. He worked in almost every department of the company before becoming president in 1921. He served in World War I and in the early 1920s was instrumental in raising money to found Wright Field. He now lives in Tucson, Ariz. He has written articles for business magazines and a book describing a hunting trip to British East Africa in 1927: *African Adventures,* New York, 1928. WW 26

PATTERSON, HARRIET-LOUISE HOLLAND (Nov. 21, 1903–), born in Chicago, graduated from Western Reserve University in 1926. She was associated with the Higbee Company, Cleveland, 1933–38. Ordained a minister in the Disciples of Christ Church, she was pastor of the Community Church, Chesterland, 1944–53. She is also an agent for tours of the Holy Land and a travel adviser. She has published several books on the Bible and travel, e.g., *Around the Mediterranean with My Bible,* Boston, [1941]. WWAW 1

PATTERSON, JAMES HOWARD (Feb. 8, 1867–April 13, 1949), educator, was born near Wellston, Jackson County. He attended country schools, studied at Morgan's Academy in Jackson, and attended Marietta College. After teaching in Jackson County, 1900–05, he went to West Virginia, where he taught school until his retirement in 1942. He published *Of Me I Sing; Or, Me and Education,* Nappanee, Ind., [1940].

PATTERSON, NELLIE (Oct. 22, 1878–Oct. 26, 1937), was born in Ross County. She lost her sight at the age of ten. In 1901 she graduated from Ohio State School for the Blind, Columbus. She afterward lived in Dayton. She later contracted arthritis, which left her a helpless invalid. Despite her infirmity she composed poetry, which was collected in *Poems,* Dayton, 1926.

PATTESON, SUSANNA LOUISE (Feb. 14, 1853–1922), was born in Zurich, Switzerland. She was educated in Zurich. After marrying G. Winston Patteson of Virginia in Cleveland on May 19, 1880, she lectured on nature and wrote many articles on nature for children's magazines. She was also a court reporter in Cleveland, 1898–1909. She wrote several books for children, e.g., *Letters from Pussycatville,* Philadelphia, [1903], and an account of her girlhood: *When I Was a Girl in Switzerland,* Boston, [1921].

PATTON, CARL SAFFORD (May 14, 1866–Oct. 16, 1939), clergyman, born in Greenville, Mich., lived in Ohio about ten years. A graduate of Oberlin College in 1888 and Andover Theological Seminary in 1892, he served Congregational churches in various states before coming to Columbus, where he was pastor of First Church, 1911–16. He died in Berkeley, Calif., while on the faculty of Pacific School of Religion. He wrote books on religion and the ministry and a book for children: *Two Minute Stories . . . ,* Chicago, 1930. WWW 1

PATTON, CLARA IRENE (July 1, 1877–), born in Owensboro, Ky., has lived in Cincinnati since 1900. She taught piano there for a number of years. She has published stories in the *Christian Herald,* the *Christian Standard,* and other church periodicals and has also published a short novel: *Miss Hadley's Finishing School,* Boston, [1930].

PAUL, JAMES (1757–July 9, 1841), was born in Pennsylvania, but grew up in Adams County. Robert Sherrard (1789–1874) interviewed Paul in 1826, and most of the pamphlet below consists of Paul's own description of his adventures.

A Narrative of the Wonderful Escape and Dreadful Sufferings of Colonel James Paul, after the Defeat of Colonel Crawford . . . , Cincinnati, 1869.

PAUL, NANNETTE BAKER (1866–April 10, 1928), lawyer, was born in Sunbury, Delaware County. After graduating from Washington, D. C., College of Law in 1900, she was admitted to the bar and practiced in Washington. She lectured on the Bible and other subjects and was active in the Susan B. Anthony Foundation. Besides legal works and books on parliamentary law, she published a biography of Susan B. Anthony: *The Great Woman Statesman . . . ,* New York, [1925]. WWW 1

PAULLIN, CHARLES OSCAR (c.1868–Sept. 1, 1944), naval historian, was born in Jamestown, Greene County. He studied at Antioch College, 1890–93, and earned his doctorate in history from the University of Chicago in 1904. He lectured on naval history at several universities and was on the research staff of Carnegie Institution, Washington, D. C., 1912–36. He wrote a number of articles and books on historical subjects, with special emphasis on the American navy. His books include a biography: *Commodore John Rodgers . . . ,* Cleveland, 1910. WWW 2

PAULY, KARL B. (May 8, 1900–), journalist, was born in Lebanon, Warren County. After graduating from Ohio State University in 1923, he was an Associated Press reporter for several years; in 1927 he joined the staff of the *Ohio State Journal.* He published *Bricker of Ohio, the Man and His Record,* New York, [1944].

PAVER, JOHN MILTON (July 14, 1839–Dec. 12, 1921), was born in Cincinnati, Hamilton County. He served in the 5th O.V.I. from April, 1861, to July, 1864. After the Civil War he lived in Cincinnati and Indianapolis, Ind. He died in Indianapolis. He wrote *What I Saw from 1861 to 1864 . . . ,* [Indianapolis, 1906?].

PAXSON, WILLIAM ALPHA (July 6, 1850–Jan. 16, 1933), lawyer and farmer, was born near Jamestown, Greene County. He attended Ohio Wesleyan University for two years, taught school, read law in Xenia, spent one year at Cincinnati Law College, and was admitted to the bar in 1874. He practiced law in Washington Court House, 1874–76, and in Jamestown from 1876 until his death. He also operated extensive farms. He wrote many poems on rural themes, but his only book was an autobiographical work: *A Buckeye Baron; A Rural Story of a Buckeye Boy,* Cincinnati, 1901.

PAYLER, ESTHER MILLER (Mrs. Louis) (July 22, 1896–), was born in Cincinnati, Hamilton County. She graduated from the University of Cincinnati in 1928 and taught in the public schools of Cincinnati and Germantown. She has published many stories for children in church papers and also a book: *Christ in Far Countries; Missionary Stories for Juniors,* Cincinnati, [1947].

PAYNE, CHARLES HENRY (Oct. 24, 1830–1899), born in Taunton, Mass., was president of Ohio Wesleyan University, 1875–88. His writings include *Daniel: The Uncompromising Young Man,* New York, [1872].

PAYNE, DANIEL ALEXANDER (Feb. 24, 1811–Nov. 29, 1893), educator, was born in Charleston, S. C. He came north to study at Gettysburg Seminary, 1835–37, joined the African Methodist Church in 1841, and after preaching in several cities was named bishop in 1852. In 1863 he purchased Wilberforce College, which had been established by the Methodists for the education of Negro children. The burden of debt under which he labored was increased in 1865 when the main building was destroyed by fire. He continued as president until 1876. He died in Xenia.

A Treatise on Domestic Education, Cincinnati, 1885.

Recollections of Seventy Years, Nashville, Tenn., 1888.

History of the African Methodist Episcopal Church, Nashville, Tenn., 1891.

PAYNE, PHILIP (Dec. 14, 1867–Jan. 27, 1927), lawyer, was born in Dayton, Montgomery County. After graduating from Cornell University in 1888, he read law and was admitted to the New York bar in 1890. In 1894 he was admitted to the Ohio bar. He later wrote for a number of newspapers and magazines. He died in Highland Park, Ill. He published several books, e.g., a novel: *The Mills of Man . . . ,* Chicago, 1903. WW 11

PEABODY, MRS. MARK. Pseud. See Metta V. F. Victor.

PEACOCK, THOMAS BROWER (April 16, 1852–March 1, 1919), was born in Cambridge, Guernsey County. He attended school in Zanesville, where his father edited the *Aurora.* He was for about ten years on the editorial staff of the Topeka, Kan., *Democrat.* He also lived in Texas. He patented a fire escape and several other inventions. Besides the volumes of poetry listed below, he wrote several plays.

Poems, Independence, Kan., 1872.
The Vendetta and Other Poems, Topeka, Kan., 1876.
The Rhyme of the Border War. A Historical Poem . . . , New York, 1880.
Poems of the Plains . . . , New York, 1888.
Columbian Ode, [Topeka, Kan., 1892].
Buffalo Bill; A Poem . . . , [Denver, Colo., 1913].

PEAKE, ELMORE ELLIOTT (March 25, 1871–), was born in Decatur, Brown County. After studying in local schools, he became a railroad telegrapher and was superintendent of telegraph for the Richmond and Danville Railroad in 1893. He began writing fiction in 1896. His last known address is LaGrange, Ill.

The Darlingtons, New York, 1900.
The Pride of Tellfair, New York, 1903.
The House of Hawley, New York, 1905.
The Little King of Angel's Landing, New York, 1906.

PEAKE, THOMAS DeWITT (March 19, 1843– ?), clergyman, was born in Princeton, Butler County. After attending Princeton schools and Hartsville Academy, he read law. He was a teacher for several years and then became a Methodist minister in Wisconsin. Besides the title below, he published lectures on religious subjects.

The Symbolism of Solomon's Temple, Cincinnati, 1896.

PEALE, NORMAN VINCENT (May 31, 1898–), clergyman, was born in Bowersville, Greene County. The son of a Methodist clergyman, he spent his boyhood in a number of Ohio towns. After graduating from Bellefontaine High School and Ohio Wesleyan University (1920), he was a reporter on the Findlay *Morning Republican* for a brief period. While reporting a Methodist conference, he was filled with enthusiasm for the ministry and worked his way through Boston University, graduating in 1924. After serving churches in Berkeley, R. I., (1922–24), Brooklyn, N. Y., (1927–30), and Syracuse, N. Y., (1930–32), he was called to Marble Collegiate Reformed Church, New York City. He established a religio-psychiatric clinic and built his church into a nationally known institution. His radio sermons, a syndicated column entitled "Confident Living," and a question-answer column in *Look* magazine have helped make him one of the best-known ministers of the century. His books, however, have done most to bring him public notice, especially *The Power of Positive Thinking,* published in 1952. Other titles include *The Art of Living,* New York, [1937], and *A Guide to Confident Living,* New York, [1948]. WW 30

PEARCE, LISTON HOUSTON (May 27, 1838–Feb. 24, 1924), clergyman, was born near Springfield, Clark County. He graduated from Northwestern University, served as a chaplain with the 132nd Illinois Infantry in the Civil War, and graduated from Garrett Biblical Institute in 1866. He afterward served Methodist churches in Michigan, Maryland, and New York. He wrote *Hilltop Views,* New York, [1922]. WWW 1

PEARL, MARY FRANCES (April 6, 1905–Jan. 16, 1948), born in Indianapolis, Ind., graduated from Oberlin Conservatory in 1920 and was a music supervisor in the Ohio public schools for ten years. After retiring because of illness, she lived in Mount Vernon. She published a collection of poems: *Runner in the Sand,* Mount Vernon, 1941.

PEARNE, THOMAS HALL (June 7, 1820–1901), clergyman and diplomat, was born in London, England. His parents came to America in 1825 and settled in central New York State. He became a Methodist minister in 1839, and in 1851 he was sent to Ohio as a missionary. He was American consul in Kingston, Jamaica, 1869–73. In 1873 he returned to Ohio and served churches in Dayton, Hillsboro, and Springfield.

Sixty-one Years of Itinerant Christian Life in Church and State, Cincinnati, 1899.

PEARSON, FRANCIS (FRANK) BAIL (Nov. 17, 1853–Sept. 26, 1938), educator, was born in Catawba, Clark County. He graduated from University of Wooster in 1885. He was principal of East High School, Columbus, 1897–1908, a member of the Ohio State University faculty, 1908–16, and state superintendent of public instruction, 1916–20. He wrote textbooks and articles on professional subjects and *Rev-*

eries of a Schoolmaster, New York, [1917]. WW 16

PEASE, ABRAHAM PER LEE (Sept. 11, 1847–June 26, 1926), physician, was born in Massillon, Stark County. After graduating from the medical department of University of Wooster in 1871, he practiced in Massillon from 1871 to 1904 except for three years (1872–75) in Pittsburgh. He traveled widely throughout the world and also was deeply interested in local history.

A Great Discovery in a Stone Quarry in Tuscarawas County . . . , [New Philadelphia, 1890].

Winter Wanderings . . . , New York, 1910.

PEASE, ELEANORE FAIRCHILD (c.1889–Nov. 29, 1958), was born in Elgin, Ill., and worked for David C. Cook Publishing Co. there before moving to Cleveland in 1923. She died in Sanford, Fla. She wrote a number of stories for young readers, e.g., *Brave Tales of Real Dogs,* Chicago, [1931].

PEASLEE, JOHN BRADLEY (Sept. 3, 1842–Jan. 4, 1912), educator, was born in Plaistow, N. H. After graduating from Dartmouth College in 1863, he came to Columbus and the following year moved to Cincinnati. He graduated in law from Cincinnati College in 1866. He was a school principal in Cincinnati, 1864–74, and was superintendent of Cincinnati public schools, 1874–86. He was clerk of Hamilton County Courts, 1888–95. He was an early advocate of conservation and forestry and the observance of Arbor Day.

Trees and Tree Planting . . . , Cincinnati, 1884.

Thoughts and Experiences in and out of School . . . , Cincinnati, 1900.

Occasional Verses and Sacred Songs, Cincinnati, [1905].

PEATTIE, MARGARET RHODES (Aug. 27, 1891–Oct. 16, 1946), born in Chicago, came to Columbus in 1920 when her husband, Roderick Peattie (q.v.), joined the Ohio State University faculty. She accompanied him on his exploring expeditions. Author of short stories in national magazines, she also wrote a novel about a New England village during World War II: *The Return,* New York, 1944.

PEATTIE, RODERICK (Aug. 1, 1891–June 18, 1955), geographer, was born in Omaha, Neb. He graduated from the University of Chicago in 1914 and Harvard University (Ph.D.) in 1920. He was on the Ohio State University faculty from 1920 until his death. A specialist in mountain geography and geopolitics, he wrote several textbooks, was editor of the American Mountains series, and wrote several volumes in that series. He also wrote an autobiography: *The Incurable Romantic,* New York, 1941. WWW 3

PECK, GEORGE WASHINGTON (Dec. 4, 1817–June 6, 1859), born in Rehoboth, Mass., lived in Ohio and Indiana in the late 1830s and early 1840s. For a time he edited the *Daily Sun* and the *Republican* in Cincinnati. He is best remembered today for a travel book: *Melbourne and the Chincha Islands; With Sketches of Lima, and a Voyage Round the World,* New York, 1854.

PECK, HARVEY WHITEFIELD (Oct. 30, 1879–), educator, was born in Warren, Trumbull County. He graduated from Oberlin College in 1905 and Yale University (Ph.D.) in 1913. He taught economics in several universities. He now lives in Winter Park, Fla. He published several books on economics, e.g., *Taxation and Welfare,* New York, 1925. WW 27

PECK, HIRAM DAVID (March 23, 1844–Oct. 11, 1914), lawyer and judge, born in Harrison County, Ky., graduated from Miami University in 1862 and completed his legal training at Harvard University in 1865. He practiced law in Cincinnati and was judge of the Superior Court, 1883–89. He published several legal handbooks. A collection of his writings was published posthumously: *Essays and Letters,* Cincinnati, 1915. WWW 1

PECK, JOHN WELD (Feb. 5, 1874–Aug. 10, 1937), lawyer and judge, was born in Wyoming, Hamilton County, and spent his boyhood in Mount Auburn. After attending Miami University for one year, he transferred to Harvard University, where he graduated in 1896. He graduated from Cincinnati Law School in 1898 and afterward practiced in Cincinnati. He served as U. S. District Court Judge, 1919–23. A collection of his writings was posthumously published: *John Weld Peck . . . ,* Cincinnati, 1938.

PECK, NELLE WRIGHT (Oct. 30, 1871–Oct. 26, 1931), daughter of a Cincinnati dentist, was born in Cincinnati, Hamilton County. After her death her husband, John Weld Peck (q.v.), published for the family her recollections of her girlhood in Switzerland: *Memories of a Childhood in Switzerland,* [Cincinnati, 1932].

PECK, WALTER EDWIN (Feb. 15, 1891–Jan. 15, 1954), educator, was born in Ashtabula, Ashtabula County. He attended the College of Wooster for two years and graduated from Hamilton College in 1913. After several years of college teaching, he earned a doctorate from Oxford University in 1922. He taught at Columbia University and Hunter College until 1929, when a scandal forced his resignation. For the last 25 years of his life he was one of the most picturesque figures on the New York Bowery. He wrote occasionally for the *Bowery News* to earn a little money. Tall and gaunt, he was known for his resonant voice as he recited Kipling's poems or lectured to sociology students visiting the Bowery. He had attracted international attention in 1925 by discovering two unpublished poems by Shelley and won critical acclaim for his book, *Shelley, His Life and Work . . .* , 2 vols., Boston, 1927. WW 16

PECKHAM, HARRY HOUSTON (Feb. 17, 1885–), educator, was born in Hiram, Portage County. After graduating from Hiram College in 1906, he did graduate work in English at several universities and afterward served on the faculties of North Carolina State College, Purdue University, and Ohio University. He wrote several textbooks and *Present-day American Poetry, and Other Essays,* Boston, [1917]. DAS 3

PEDDICORD, KELION FRANKLIN (Oct. 1, 1833–Aug. 28, 1903), was born on a farm near Barnesville, Belmont County. The family moved to Barnesville, where his father operated the Mansion House, and in 1846 they moved to Washington County. In 1850 Kelion began working on railroad construction in Virginia. He enlisted in the Confederate army in 1861, served under General Morgan, was captured and imprisoned until the end of the war. After the war he moved to Missouri, where he was a farmer, a hotel keeper, postmaster of Palmyra, and a banker. His sister, Indiana Washington Logan, edited a book which consists chiefly of a journal of his war experiences: *Kelion Franklin Peddicord of Quirk's Scouts, Morgan's Kentucky Cavalry . . .* , New York, 1908.

PEDEN, DON VINTON (July 4, 1888–Dec. 31, 1945), born in Huntington, Ind., came to Cleveland in 1916. He was president of Peden Equipment Co. and later edited two Masonic magazines, the *Bulletin* and the *Outlook.* He published a pamphlet of verse: *The "Son" of George Washington,* Cleveland, [1936].

PEEKE, GEORGE HEWSON (March 18, 1883–Dec. 26, 1915), clergyman, was born in Rotterdam, N. Y. He graduated from Rutgers University in 1857. After graduating from the Reformed Dutch Theological Seminary in 1860, he married Margaret Bloodgood (see below). After serving churches in Indiana, Iowa, New Jersey, and elsewhere, he arrived in Sandusky in 1883. He preached in Sandusky and Cleveland. He was also active in the prohibition movement. He died in Sandusky. He wrote *The Spiritual Body in Relation to the Divine Law of Life,* Boston, [1912].

PEEKE, HEWSON LINDSLEY (April 21, 1861–Feb. 17, 1942), lawyer, was born in South Bend, Ind., the son of George Hewson and Margaret Bloodgood Peeke (qq.v.). He graduated from Williams College in 1882, read law, and was admitted to the Ohio bar in 1885. He practiced in Sandusky, suported the prohibition movement, and frequently ran for office on the Prohibition ticket. In 1901 he established the Cornerstone Publishing Company to publish the Ohio State prohibition paper. Interested in local history, he was president of Firelands Historical Society for a number of years and wrote several books on historical subjects, e.g., *The Centennial History of Erie County, Ohio,* 2 vols., [Cleveland], 1925.

PEEKE, MARGARET BLOODGOOD (April 8, 1838–1908), was born in Mechanicsville, N. Y. She taught in the New York public schools, 1853–54, and in her own school in Irvington, N. J., 1855–59. In 1860 she married Rev. George H. Peeke (q.v.), a Presbyterian minister. She lived in various cities where her husband held pastorates, including Sandusky (1883–90) and Cleveland (1890–94). She also traveled widely, teaching Hermetic philosophy. Her largest following was in the Cleveland-Sandusky area. She spent her last years in Sandusky.

Born of Flame. A Rosicrucian Story, Philadelphia, 1892.

Zenia, the Vestal; Or, the Problem of Vibrations, Boston, 1893.

Numbers and Letters: Or, the Thirty-two Paths of Wisdom, New York, [1908].

PEERY, RUFUS BENTON (April 9, 1868–Oct. 25, 1934), born in Burke's Garden, Va., was a Lutheran minister in Wooster, 1924–31. He also served in Japan as a missionary, and as a result of this experience he wrote *The Gist of Japan,* Chicago, 1897.

PEET, STEPHEN DENISON (Dec. 2, 1831–May 24, 1914), clergyman and archaeologist, was born in Euclid, Cuyahoga County. He graduated from Beloit College in 1851 and Andover Seminary in 1854. Ordained a Congregationalist minister in 1855, he served various churches in the Midwest, including one at Ashtabula. He was fascinated by the mounds in Ohio and Wisconsin and was a founder of the Ohio Archaeological Association in 1875. In 1878 he founded the *American Antiquarian and Oriental Journal,* which he edited until his death. Although many of his speculations concerning the Mound Builders have been disproved, he was an important pioneer in arousing interest in archaeology. He died in Salem, Mass.

The Ashtabula Disaster, Chicago, 1877.
Emblematic Mounds and Animal Effigies, Chicago, 1890.
The Mound Builders; Their Works and Relics, Chicago, 1892.
The Cliff Dwellers and Pueblos, Chicago, 1899.
Ancient Monuments and Ruined Cities . . . , Chicago, 1904.
Myths and Symbols . . . , Chicago, 1905.

PEIRCE, PAUL SKEELS (Oct. 25, 1874–March 31, 1951), educator, born in Niagara County, N. Y., was professor of economics at Oberlin College, 1921–40. He published several technical works in the field of social studies and *The Freedmen's Bureau . . . ,* Iowa City, 1904. WWW 3

PEIRCE, THOMAS (1786–1850), was born in Chester County, Pa. Left fatherless at the age of five, he began working at an early age and learned the saddler's trade. When he was 24, he entered a Quaker boarding school at New Garden, Pa. After coming to Cincinnati three years later, he became a successful merchant and began writing poetry for local newspapers. As a director of the Circulating Library of Cincinnati, he was associated with the town's leading literary figures, Daniel and Benjamin Drake. In 1816 he published his earliest known volume of verse, a twelve-page carriers' address for the patrons of the *Western Spy.* Five years later he began to enliven the stuffy columns of the *Spy* with a series of witty, satirical odes, biting caricatures of Cincinnati's most prominent citizens and provocative exposures of local follies. In 1822 they were collected and published as *The Odes of Horace in Cincinnati,* Ohio's first noteworthy contribution to Western poetry. "Billy Moody," a series of 29 chapters recounting the travels of a Yankee schoolmaster in the West, was published in the *National Republican and Ohio Political Register* in 1823. These are believed to have been collected and published in a pamphlet, no copy of which is known to exist. *The Muse of Hesperia,* published anonymously in 1823, was awarded a prize offered by the Philomathic Society of Cincinnati College; but Peirce never claimed the prize or acknowledged the poem. In 1822 he gave up his business interests to study medicine. He graduated in 1827, but returned to commercial pursuits instead of practicing medicine. He died in Cincinnati.

A Present from the Carrier of the Western Spy, to Its Patrons . . . , [Cincinnati, 1816].
A Poetical Gift to the Patrons of "The Western Spy" . . . , Cincinnati, [1817].
The Odes of Horace in Cincinnati . . . , Cincinnati, 1822.
The Muse of Hesperia, a Poetic Reverie, Cincinnati, 1823.

PELHAM, RICHARD W. (1797–1873), was a member of the Shaker community in Warren County, and he helped found North Union, Groveland, and other communities. The pamphlet below was also published in Cincinnati, and he undoubtedly wrote others.

The Shaker's Answer to a Letter from an Inquirer, Union Village, 1868.

PELIKAN, JAROSLAV JAN, JR. (Dec. 17, 1923–), clergyman and educator, was born in Akron, Summit County, and lived there for a few years of his early childhood. He graduated from Concordia College, Fort Wayne, Ind., in 1942, Concordia Seminary, St. Louis, Mo., in 1946, and the University of Chicago (Ph.D.) in 1946. He has served on the faculties of Valparaiso University, 1946–49, Concordia Seminary, 1949–53, Federated Theological Faculty, University of Chicago, 1953–60. He is now teaching at Yale University. He has written numerous articles for religious periodicals, is now editing Luther's *Works,* and has published several books on religious themes, e.g., *From Luther to Kierkegaard . . . ,* St. Louis, Mo., [1950].

PEMBERTON, BENJAMIN ALDUS (1865–1922), was born on a farm near West Milton, Miami County, in a Quaker family. After attending West Milton High School and Earlham College, Ind., he taught school for a time. Because of ill health he spent much of his later life in Colorado and Arizona. During his years in the West, he wrote about his native county in a volume of poems: *Traditions of the Miami Valley . . . ,* Dayton, [1912].

PEMBERTON, LOVELL BEARSE (Nov. 25, 1866–), engineer, was born in Bethel, Clermont County. Few biographical details are available, but he was an architectural engineer and lived for many years in California.

Sappho and Other Songs, Los Angeles, 1895.

Prometheus Unbound. A Lyrical Drama, Franklin, 1896.

A Modern Pilgrimage to Palestine, Philadelphia, 1923.

The Dance at the Spring and Other Poems, Boston, 1929.

PENDLETON, EDMUND (1845–1910), was born in Cincinnati, Hamilton County. He was educated by private tutors. During the Civil War he served with the 4th New York heavy artillery. He was president of the Cincinnati Exposition of Arts and Industries, 1875–79, and was later president of the Cincinnati Musical Festivals.

A Conventional Bohemian, New York, 1886.

A Virginia Inheritance, a Novel, New York, 1888.

One Woman's Way, a Novel, New York, 1891.

A Complication in Hearts; A Novel, New York, 1893.

PENDLETON, GEORGE HUNT (July 19, 1825–Nov. 24, 1889), was born in Cincinnati, Hamilton County. After attending Cincinnati schools and studying under private tutors, he made a European tour, 1844–46. On his return he read law with Stephen Fales and was admitted to the Ohio bar in 1847. Serving in the U. S. House of Representatives, 1857–65, he was a leader of the peace Democrats. He opposed many of Lincoln's policies, and in 1864 he was candidate for vice-president on the National Democratic ticket. He served in the U. S. Senate, 1879–85, and as minister to Germany from 1885 until his death in Brussels, Belgium. Many of his speeches in Congress were published in pamphlet form. The collection of letters and speeches listed below was probably issued as a campaign document.

Hear George H. Pendleton, [Richmond, 1864?].

PENDLETON, JAMES MADISON (Nov. 20, 1811–March 4, 1891), born in Spotsylvania County, Va., was a Baptist minister in Hamilton, 1862–65. He published numerous articles and books on religious themes and an autobiography: *Reminiscences of a Long Life,* Louisville, Ky., 1891.

PENN, IRVINE GARLAND (Oct. 7, 1866–July 21, 1930), clergyman, born in Lynchburg, Va., lived in Cincinnati for many years while filling various positions in the Methodist Church. At the time of his death in Cincinnati, he was secretary of the board of education of his church.

The Afro-American Press and Its Editors, Springfield, Mass., 1891.

PENN, JULIUS AUGUSTUS (Feb. 19, 1865–May 13, 1934), army officer, was born in Mattoon, Ill., but after completing his army career, lived in Batavia, Clermont County. His only book was published for private circulation among members of his regiment: *A Narrative of the Campaign in Northern Luzon, P. I. . . . ,* [Batavia], 1933. WWW 1

PENNELL, ORRIN H. (1870–Dec. 26, 1938), clergyman, was born in Champion, Trumbull County. After graduating from Girard High School and West Farmington Seminary, he was a Methodist minister in various Ohio communities for nearly fifty years. The book listed below was reissued in 1904.

Religious Views of Abraham Lincoln, Alliance, [1899].

PENNELL, WILLIAM WESLEY (Feb. 2, 1853–Sept. 30, 1930), physician, was born in Benton, Holmes County. After graduating from Western Reserve University in 1882, he practiced medicine in Holmes and Knox Counties for forty years. He contributed numerous papers to professional journals and wrote at least three books, e.g., *The Buckeye Doctor . . . ,* New York, [1903].

PENNINGTON, BENJAMIN LINVILL (March 23, 1837–Jan. 15, 1907), was born in Gap, Pa. When he was two months old, his parents moved to Champaign County, where he grew up. In 1860 he went to Cleveland. After serving with the 150th O.V.I. he became a ship broker and later owned several Great Lakes ships. He retired from Lakes trade in 1883 and entered the hardware business. The collection of short stories listed below is his only known publication.

The Strange Case of Dr. Richard Kedgway and Other Matters, [Cleveland, n.d.].

PENNOCK, ANNA M. See Anna M. Pennock Bird.

PEPPER, CHARLES MELVILLE (Nov. 11, 1859–Nov. 4, 1930), journalist and government official, was born in Ohio, probably in

Morrow County. After graduating from University of Wooster in 1881, he worked on the Chicago *Tribune* and the New York *Herald,* 1886–1901. He was an official in the Department of Commerce, a foreign trade advisor to the State Department, and served on numerous commissions and agencies.

To-morrow in Cuba, New York, 1899.

Every-day Life in Washington, with Pen and Camera, New York, 1900.

Guatemala, the Country of the Future . . . , Washington, D. C., 1906.

Panama to Patagonia; The Isthmian Canal and the West Coast Countries of South America, Chicago, 1906.

Republica de Colombia . . . , Washington, D. C., 1908.

Life-Work of Louis Klopsch; Romance of a Modern Knight of Mercy, New York, [1910].

American Foreign Trade . . . , New York, 1919.

The Life and Times of Henry Gassaway Davis, 1823–1916, New York, 1920.

PEPPER, GEORGE WHITFIELD (July 11, 1833–Aug. 6, 1899), clergyman, was born in Ballinagarrick, Ireland. After studying at Royal Belfast Academical Institution, he came to America in 1854 and entered Bexley Seminary at Kenyon College. Admitted to the North Ohio Conference of the Methodist Episcopal Church in 1855, he filled several pulpits in Coshocton and Morrow Counties. In 1861, as the result of a war sermon delivered at Keene, he formed the nucleus of the 80th O.V.I. and assumed command of Company H. Following the Civil War he re-entered the ministry and served in numerous pastorates in northern Ohio until his appointment as U. S. Consul at Milan, Italy, in 1890. His book about Sherman's campaign is one of the best-written narratives contributed by Ohio writers to literature of the Civil War. He died in Cleveland.

Personal Recollections of Sherman's Campaigns, in Georgia and the Carolinas, Zanesville, 1866.

Under Three Flags; Or, the Story of My Life . . . , Cincinnati, 1899.

PERCIVAL, MILTON OSWIN (Feb. 26, 1883–), educator, was born in Ashland, Ashland County. He graduated from Harvard University (A.B., 1906; Ph.D., 1914) and served on the English faculty of Ohio State University, 1917–53. He published *William Blake's Circle of Destiny,* New York, 1938. DAS 3

PERKINS, EDNA BRUSH (March 25, 1880–Oct. 11, 1930), was born in Cleveland, Cuyahoga County. She attended Hathaway-Brown School and Western Reserve University. In 1903 she began an active career of social service by working at the Lend-a-Hand Mission, Cleveland. She married Roger G. Perkins in 1905. She was also active in the women's suffrage movement and was a founder of the Women's City Club of Cleveland. She was studying painting before her death in Cleveland and exhibited her paintings in several cities. She traveled widely and wrote two travel books, e.g., *A Red Carpet on the Sahara,* Boston, [1925].

PERKINS, GEORGE (April 1, 1844–Dec. 2, 1926), was born in Chillicothe, Ross County. He served as a private in the 149th O.V.I. from May to August, 1864. After the Civil War he was a clerk and a bookseller in Chillicothe, and his death occurred in that community. The first title below was published under the pen name George Dulac.

Before the Dawn; A Story of Paris and the Jacquerie, New York, 1888.

Pat McFree, the Irish Patentee. A Farce in One Act, Clyde, 1898.

A Summer in Maryland and Virginia; Or, Campaigning with the 149th Ohio Volunteer Infantry . . . , Chillicothe, [1911].

PERKINS, JACOB BISHOP (Dec. 20, 1854–Dec. 26, 1936), industrialist, was born in Warren, Trumbull County. He was educated in private schools in Cleveland and at Greylock Institute, Mass. His death occurred in Cleveland. He wrote a book of reminiscences of his experiences fox-hunting in England and in the Cleveland area: *J. B.'s Final Bulletin,* Cleveland, 1937.

PERKINS, JAMES HANDASYD (July 31, 1810–Dec. 14, 1849), author and editor, was born in Boston, Mass. He had the good fortune to attend the famous Round Hill School directed by George Bancroft and Joseph Cogswell. Such a stimulating atmosphere undoubtedly instilled a vision of society that a commercial career in Boston did not satisfy. After a short try at business, he struck out for the West, arriving in Cincinnati in 1832. There he studied law in the offices of Hon. Timothy Walker, who had been his mathematics instructor at Round Hill. He passed the bar in 1834 but discovered the practice of law intellectually depressing amid practical standards that were not morally consistent with his ideals. He found the society of the West most congenial and, now concentrating on creative writing, soon became a vital force in the literary life of the Queen City. His legal training later resulted in his making a selection under the advice of Judge Story from the decisions of Chief Justice Marshall: *The Writings of John Marshall . . . Upon the Federal Constitution,* Boston, 1839. Perkins now became active in all directions in an intellectual climate which he helped make exciting. Unhampered by an existing literary tradition, he wrote widely for all the literary organs. He contributed essays, poems, and stories to the successful *Western Monthly Magazine* (1833–36) edited by James Hall (q.v.). He became editor early in 1834 of the *Saturday Evening Chronicle,* which he purchased in 1835 to unite with the Cincinnati *Mirror,* published by William D. Gallagher and Thomas H. Shreve (qq.v.). For six months the three friends edited this paper jointly. In 1834, Perkins married Sarah H. Elliott, who had been living with her sister, Mrs. Samuel E. Foote. The Footes, well established in the city, enjoyed a society that Mrs. Trollope during her unhappy stay in Cincinnati never knew. Men such as Perkins contributed much to Cincinnati's early development from a frontier shipping post to a cultural metropolis. Perkins happily combined an Eastern education and observations from foreign travel with an active enthusiasm for the life and recent history of the West. His gentle humor and interest made him a desired member of the intellectual societies of the 1830s such as The Inquisition and the Semi-Colon Club, whose members included Gallagher, Channing, and Harriet Beecher Stowe. His addresses at the Mechanics Institute were noted for their humor and wide resources of information. He became an organizer and an important lecturer of the Western Literary Institute and College of Professional Teachers, a unique educational venture of this period. Later he joined with such leaders as Lyman Beecher, O. M. Mitchel, and C. E. Stowe to lecture before an auxiliary organization of great popularity, the Cincinnati Society for the Promotion of Useful Knowledge. He was likewise known as a generous patron of the Young Men's Mercantile Library. Perkins assisted Rev. Ephraim Peabody and later his own cousin, Rev. W. H. Channing, in editing that most important magazine of the time, the *Western Messenger.* This periodical, published by the Western Unitarian Association, was devoted to religion and literature. Published in Cincinnati and Louisville from 1835 to 1841, it was tinged with transcendentalism but was primarily interested in literature. The magazine first published Emerson's poetry and original contributions by John Keats which were supplied in manuscript by his brother George, who lived in Louisville. It became an early outlet for writings of those associated with the Concord group such as Margaret Fuller and Elizabeth Peabody. Containing the finest literature of the period, far outclassing other periodicals of the Ohio Valley, it was the forerunner and the harbinger of the world-famous transcendental *Dial.* Perkins himself contributed articles, poetry, and reviews of solid merit. Entering with zest into all the literary ventures of this new publishing center which was so congenial to literature and the arts, Perkins also placed several short stories in Gallagher's short-lived *Hesperian* (1837–39). Historical and critical articles published in the *North American Review* and the *New York Quarterly* in 1838 had been originally projected by Perkins as books, but procrastination was as much a part of his make-up as was his widely ranging interest. However, in Jan., 1838, he gave an address before the Ohio Historical Society of Columbus on "Subjects of Western History" which was so successful that he immediately projected a book which he did ultimately carry through to completion. This *Annals of the West* is his major published work and is a great source of historical data. It was enormously successful, going into two printings for each of two subsequent editions. Perkins, who wished recognition as a creative and critical writer, is known chiefly for this historical reference book of entertaining excerpts unimaginatively arranged in chronological order. His interest in history was continuous, and he was elected first president of the Cincinnati Historical Society, organized in 1844. At the time this society and the Ohio Historical Society were united in 1849, Perkins was made vice president and recording secretary. President Harrison was proudly claimed by Cincinnati and after his untimely death, Perkins was called upon to revise the campaign biography by C. S. Todd and B. Drake. The resulting popularly priced edition of *Sketches of the Civil and Military Services of William Henry Harrison* included two additional chapters by Perkins on the political campaign of 1840 and on Harrison's inauguration and brief administration of one month. In 1839 Perkins was chosen to head a Ministry-at-Large to distribute charity from the First Congregational Society and the American Unitarian Association. This office he administered so happily and humbly that his further efforts culminated in the establishment of a central Relief Union, a charitable intelligence office similar to the present-day Community Chest. This is perhaps his chief memorial, for he is ever known and remembered in Cincinnati for his charitable and educational work. In 1841 he was drafted to replace his cousin, Reverend William H. Channing (q.v.), as pastor of the Unitarian Society of Cincinnati. He was a truly successful preacher although never himself satisfied with his services. He remained as pastor under protest after 1847 until his tragic suicide in a fit of depression on Dec. 14, 1849. Perkins was a literary power behind the scenes in Cincinnati, but he never carried through the projects which ought to have brought him some wider measure of recognition. His forte apparently lay in his ministry, yet his aspirations were for a creative ideal that his powers could not attain.

Wyman W. Parker

Annals of the West . . . , Cincinnati, 1846.
The Memoir and Writings of James Handasyd Perkins, (William Henry Channing, ed.), Cincinnati, 1851.

PERKINS, SARAH MARIA CLINTON (April 23, 1824–Dec. 2, 1905) was born in Ostego, N. Y. After teaching in district schools for several years, she married Rev. Owen Perkins of Savoy, Mass. When his health failed, she replaced him in the pulpit and also lectured on temperance. In 1880, after his death, she moved to Cleveland, where she spent the remainder of her life. She published Sunday school stories for children and temperance stories.

Helen; Or, Will She Save Him?, New York, 1886.
Six of Them, Cleveland, 1898.
Pioneer Work. Seventy Years of Temperance Work . . . , [Cleveland, n.d.].

PERRIN, JOHN WILLIAM (March 19, 1861–July 14, 1924), educator, was born in Eugene, Ind. He graduated from Wabash College in 1889. He taught at Allegheny College, 1894–98, and Western Reserve University, 1898–1904. In 1905 he became librarian of Case Library. He died in Cleveland. His writings include articles and pamphlets on education; he also wrote *History of the Cleveland Sinking Fund of 1862,* Cleveland, 1913. WWW 1

PERRY, ELIZABETH WILLIAMS (March 5, 1823–June 24, 1914), was born in Cincinnati, Hamilton County, the daughter of Micajah Williams, Surveyor-General of the Northwest Territory. Wife of Aaron F. Perry, a Cincinnati attorney, she took an active part in the cultural life of the city and was one of the founders of the Women's Art Museum. Her book about flowers, begun when she was 78, was published posthumously by her daughters.

A Sketch of the Ohio Company, [n.p., 1900?].
Studies of a Plant Lover, Cincinnati, 1921.

PERRY, OLIVER HAZARD (April 12, 1817–Dec. 23, 1864), was born in Cleveland, Cuyahoga County. By the time he was nineteen years old, he had become an enthusiastic hunter of every species of game with which the wilds of Ohio and Michigan then abounded. Possessed of ample means, he enjoyed nothing so much as a protracted hunting expedition with his friends, and his solitary hunts often lasted several months. It was his practice to preserve careful and detailed accounts of his experiences on these expeditions, so that he and his friends might recall and enjoy in afterlife their thrilling adventures and pleasures. In 1899 his hunting diaries were published in a limited edition. Not only are they a valuable contribution to the literature of the period, but they also constitute the finest account of hunting in the Midwest during the first half of the nineteenth century. He was killed in a railroad accident in 1864.

Hunting Expeditions of Oliver Hazard Perry of Cleveland Verbatim from His Diaries . . . , Cleveland, 1899.

PERRY, ROBERT E. (May 12, 1881–), was born in Greenville, Darke County. He has coached high school plays in Bradford and Covington and has written a number of plays and pageants on historical subjects. He lives in Bradford, Darke County. He has also written *Treaty City, a Story of Old Green Ville,* Bradford, 1945.

PETER, WILLIAM WESLEY (Dec. 1, 1882–1958), was born in Elliston, Ottawa County. He graduated from Northwestern College, Naperville, Ill., in 1904 and Rush Medical College, University of Chicago, in 1910. He served as a health officer and edited medical magazines in China, 1915–26, and became medical director of the Navajo area in 1934. He published several books on health and medicine, e.g., *Mastodons, Microbes and Man,* New York, 1931. WW 21

PETERS, GEORGE NATHANIEL HENRY (Nov. 29, 1825–Oct. 7, 1909), clergyman, born in New Berlin, Pa., graduated from the theological department, Wittenberg College, in 1850. After being ordained to the ministry the following year, he served Lutheran churches in Woodbury, Xenia, and Plymouth. He retired from the ministry in 1858 because of ill health and settled in Springfield. In 1871 he moved to Nebraska and was one of the organizers of the Nebraska Synod. His book, which is based on a wide range of millennial writings, is esteemed today by some religious groups because of its emphasis on the imminent second coming of Christ.

The Theocratic Kingdom of Our Lord Jesus, the Christ, 3 vols., New York, 1884.

PETERS, WILLIAM E. (July 25, 1857–Nov. 15, 1952), was born in Somerville, Butler County, but spent much of his life in Athens. He graduated from National Normal University, Lebanon, taught school in Shelby County, and worked as a civil engineer for several railroads. In 1891 he was admitted to the Ohio bar. He wrote several technical works on law and on engineering and also published *Athens County and Where and How to Find,* Athens, 1942.

PETERSON, FLORENCE (Feb. 17, 1894–), educator, was born in Dayton, Montgomery County. After graduating from Ohio Wesleyan University in 1917, she became personnel manager of Selby Shoe Co., Portsmouth, 1917–28, served as director of Wisconsin Unemployment Relief, 1930–34, and in the U. S. Department of Labor, 1934–47. She taught at Bryn Mawr College, 1947–51, after which she joined the faculty of Rollins College. She has written numerous articles on labor, government bulletins, and one book: *American Labor Unions . . . ,* New York, [1945]. WW 30

PETTY, ORVILLE ANDERSON (Feb. 20, 1874–Aug. 12, 1942), clergyman, was born in Cadiz, Harrison County. He graduated from Muskingum College in 1898 and Pittsburgh Theological Seminary in 1901. He served churches in Colorado, Illinois, and Connecticut, and was president of Arnold College, 1929–30. He wrote several books on religious themes, e.g., *Common Sense and God . . . ,* New Haven, Conn., 1936. WWW 2

PHELAN, JOHN JOSEPH (Oct. 17, 1871–Jan. 25, 1944), clergyman, was born in Nantucket, Mass. After serving as pastor of Immanuel Baptist Church, New Bedford, Mass., 1902–12, he came to Toledo, where he spent the remainder of his life. He wrote a regular column in the *Homiletic-Expositor* for a number of years and also wrote several pamphlets on commercialized amusements and juvenile delinquency in Toledo, e.g., *Pool, Billiards and Bowling Alleys . . . ,* Toledo, [1919].

PHELPS, GEORGE H. (Sept. 24, 1854–April 2, 1941), lawyer, was born in Cattaraugus County, N. Y. In 1888 he came to Findlay, where he practiced law. Under his own name he published *Six Stories* [Detroit], 1916, and under the name Patrick Quinn Tangent, *The New Columbia . . . ,* Findlay, 1909.

PHILIPSON, DAVID (Aug. 9, 1862–June 29, 1949), rabbi and educator, was born in Warsaw, Ind. He came to Cincinnati in 1878 and graduated from the University of Cincinnati and Hebrew Union College in 1883. He served as rabbi of Har Sinai Congregation in Baltimore, Md., 1884–88, and spent the remainder of his life in Cincinnati. He was rabbi of B'ne Israel Congregation, 1888–1938, and joined the faculty of Hebrew Union College in 1891. He edited *The Selected Writings of Isaac M. Wise* (1900), *Reminiscences by Isaac M. Wise* (1901), and *Letters of Rebecca Gratz* (1929), and also contributed many articles to magazines.

The Jew in English Fiction, Cincinnati, 1889.

The Oldest Jewish Congegration in the West, Cincinnati, 1894.

Old European Jewries, Philadelphia, 1894.

A Holiday Sheaf, Cincinnati, 1898.

The Reform Movement in Judaism, New York, 1907.

The Jew in America, Cincinnati, 1909.

Max Lilienthal—American Rabbi, New York, 1915.

Centenary Papers and Others, New York, 1919.

History of the Hebrew Union College, [Cincinnati], 1925.

My Life as an American Jew; An Autobiography, Cincinnati, [1941].

Children's Harvest Service, New York, [n.d.].

Lectures, New York, [n.d.].

The Reform Movement in America, New York, [n.d.].

PHILLIPPI, JOSEPH MARTIN (March 2, 1869–Sept. 27, 1926), clergyman and editor, was born in London Mills, Ill., but lived for many years in Dayton. A minister of the United Brethren Church, he edited the *Religious Telescope,* and wrote *Shakerism . . . ,* Dayton, 1912. WWW 1

PHILLIPS, BENJAMIN F. (1802–1882), was born in Connecticut. In 1820 he came to Ashtabula County with two of his brothers. He worked as a saddler and harness maker, and was also a dairyman. His book of local history was "compiled from early records and verbal accounts of old residents."

Condensed History of New Lyme, Ashtabula County . . . , Jefferson, 1877.

PHILLIPS, DAVID GRAHAM (Oct. 31, 1867–Jan. 24, 1911), born in Madison, Ind., spent a little over two years in Cincinnati. After graduating from Princeton University in 1887, he secured a position on the *Times-Star* by the classic method of appearing at the office every day until the editor sent him out on a story. He was hired away from the *Times-Star* by the *Commercial Gazette.* In 1890 he went to New York and about a year later, under the pen name John Graham, published his first novel: *The Great God Success* . . . , New York, 1901. He is best remembered for his muckraking articles, "The Treason of the Senate," published in *Cosmopolitan* in 1906, and for his last novel: *Susan Lenox, Her Fall and Rise,* New York, 1917.

PHILLIPS, HAROLD COOKE (Nov. 26, 1892–), clergyman, was born in Jamaica, B.W.I. He came to the United States in 1912, graduated from Denison University in 1919, and was ordained to the Baptist ministry in 1922, after graduating from Union Theological Seminary. He was pastor of First Baptist Church, Cleveland, 1928–58. He has published sermons and several books on religious themes, e.g., *Life That Is Life Indeed,* New York, 1928. WW 30

PHILLIPS, JOHN HERBERT (Dec. 12, 1853–July 21, 1921), educator, was born in Covington, Ky., but was brought to Jackson at an early age. After graduating from Marietta College in 1880, he became a school teacher and was associated with various schools in Alabama. He published works on education and *Old Tales and Modern Ideals* . . . , New York, [1905]. WWW 1

PHILLIPS, PHILIP (Aug. 13, 1834–June 25, 1895), born in Cassadaga, N. Y., lived in Marion, 1860–62, and in Cincinnati, 1862–67. He wrote several books of sacred songs which sold very widely. A singing evangelist, he made a world tour in 1875, which he recorded in *Song Pilgrimage Around and Throughout the World* . . . , New York, 1880. He died in Delaware, where he had spent his last years.

PHILLIPS, WILBUR HARE (May 24, 1876–Sept. 12, 1939), journalist, born in Shenandoah, Iowa, was brought to Zanesville when he was three months old. He attended Zanesville public schools, worked on newspapers in Zanesville, Columbus, and Uhrichsville, and served in the Spanish-American War. He studied law, was admitted to the bar in 1908, and practiced for two years. In 1911 he became managing editor of the Oberlin *News,* and from 1922 until his death he owned the paper. He wrote a useful account of Oberlin: *Oberlin Colony, the Story of a Century,* Oberlin, 1933. OBB

PHISTERER, FREDERICK (Oct. 11, 1836–July 13, 1909), was born in Stuttgart, Germany, but lived in Ohio briefly in 1860 and again in the early 1870s, while he was engaged in business in Columbus. He served in the U. S. Army, 1855–60 and 1861–70. He wrote *New York in the War of the Rebellion* . . . , Albany, 1890.

PIATT, DONN (June 29, 1819–Nov. 12, 1891), was born in Cincinnati, Hamilton County. When he was eight years old, his family moved to Mac-o-cheek in Logan County. He attended district schools and the public schools of Urbana and Bellefontaine and also spent a short time at the Athenaeum (Xavier University). Under his father's urging he studied law, but after marrying Louise Kirby (see Louise K. Piatt) in 1847 he settled on the family estate at Mac-o-cheek. He served as judge of common pleas court, Hamilton County, 1852–53, and as secretary of the American legation, Paris, 1853–55. During the Civil War he was a captain in the 13th O.V.I. and rose to the rank of lieutenant colonel. In 1868 he went to Washington as correspondent for the Cincinnati *Commercial,* and in 1871 he founded the magazine *Capital.* In his nine years as an editor he aroused the ire of most political leaders of the day by his outspoken attacks on corruption. His violent disapproval of the electoral commission's resolution of the Hayes-Tilden election of 1876 led to his being indicted, but the charges were later dropped. He died at Mac-o-cheek, where he spent his last years. The concluding chapters of his biography of General Thomas were written by Henry Van Ness Boynton (q.v.). His iconoclastic opinions in *Memories of the Men Who Saved the Union,* particularly his low regard for Grant and Sherman, created a considerable stir.

Life in the Lobby. A Comedy in Five Acts, Washington, D. C., 1875.

An Infamous Record . . . , [n.p., 187- ?].
Memories of the Men Who Saved the Union, New York, 1887.
The Lone Grave of the Shenandoah, and Other Tales, Chicago, 1888.
General George H. Thomas, a Critical Biography, Cincinnati, 1893.
Poems and Plays, Cincinnati, 1893.
The Reverend Melancthon Poundex; A Novel, Chicago, 1893.
Sunday Meditations . . . , Cincinnati, 1893.

PIATT, JOHN JAMES (March 1, 1835–Feb. 16, 1917), was born at James' Mills (now Milton), Ind. Though one of the minor voices in nineteenth century American literature, he spoke in his own authentic tones and created a body of distinctive verse. He has variously been heralded as the poet of Ohio, the poet of the West, and the poet of the Ohio Valley. While such poems as "Western Pioneer," "Western Windows," and "Fire before Seed" might sustain the second title, it is the last of these designations that Piatt himself preferred, for Franklin County, Ohio, Shelby County, Ill., Louisville, Ky., and North Bend, Hamilton County—all places where he resided—were within the limits of what may be called the Ohio River Country. But to the state of Ohio itself he was attached not only by fifty years of residence, but also through the writing of odes for Ohio events such as the dedication of the Cincinnati Music Hall in 1877 and the centennial of the city of Cleveland. A number of his early poems, moreover—"The King's Tavern," "The Mower in Ohio," "The Lost Farm," "Apple-Gathering," "Grandfather Wright," and "Moore's Chimney"—all have reference to the Ohio scene, and these include some of his best pieces. Born in Indiana of Huguenot stock, Piatt, at the age of six, was brought by his parents to a farm near Franklinton, Franklin County. During school terms he lived with an uncle in Columbus, attending grammar classes at Capital University and working in off-hours as a printer's devil in the plant of the *Ohio State Journal,* a publication owned by his uncle. He spent over two years at Kenyon College, but when his roving father took up a new farm in Shelby County, Ill., John's services were badly needed and he lived there for a time. But already as a lad Piatt had become interested in poetry, especially that of Longfellow, and had delved into the more popular plays of Shakespeare. In the long winter hours on the Illinois farm, he penned a number of poems, including "Taking the Night Train," "Prairie Fires," and "The Forgotten Well." Some of these efforts came to the notice of George D. Prentice, editor of the Louisville *Journal.* On the strength of their merits Piatt was made the editor's secretary, and his verses began to appear in the poet's corner of the paper. In 1859 two events of importance occurred: "The Morning Street" was accepted by Lowell for the *Atlantic Monthly,* and Piatt made a trip to Columbus, renewed acquaintance with William Dean Howells (q.v.), and with him projected a volume of verses, printed in 1860 as *Poems of Two Friends.* In all, 49 of the pieces were Piatt's, and over half of these subsequently reappeared in later collections. In 1860 Lincoln's election led to a clerkship in the Department of the Treasury for Piatt, through the Secretary, Ohioan Salmon P. Chase. On the strength of these brighter financial prospects, Piatt married Sarah Morgan Bryan (see Sarah M. B. Piatt), a young lady from Kentucky who had contributed to Prentice's *Journal.* They established their first home in Georgetown, D. C., where until 1867 Piatt retained his connection with the Treasury Department. Shortly after their marriage, the two poets joined talents in *The Nests at Washington.* This volume included, among the more meritorious poems, "The Blackberry Farm," "My Nightmare," "The Bluebird's Burial," and "The Dark Street." In wartime Washington things were unsettled, but the Piatts entertained W. D. Howells and other visitors, and made friends with W. D. O'Connor, E. C. Stedman, and Walt Whitman. Failing in an effort to get transferred to the customs office in New York City in 1866, Piatt resigned his government post in the next year and established a home in North Bend. Immediately he made journalistic connections with the Cincinnati *Chronicle.* He transferred to the *Commercial* in 1869, and during the 1870s was a steady contributor to newspapers, even during his two terms as Librarian of Congress. In the decade after 1865 Piatt brought out three books of verse. *Sunshine and Firelight* (1866) reprinted much of the first two volumes but added a group of war poems, twelve in number. *Western Windows,* published the next year, with a New York imprint dated 1869, added a group of sonnets, "The Dear President," and reprints from his contributions to *Harper's. Landmarks* (1872) contained strictly new material, but all the poems after the first six were extremely brief. In the late 1870s Piatt was back in Cincinnati, where a postoffice position occupied most of his waking hours. In 1882, upon the inauguration of Chester A. Arthur as President, Piatt was made U. S. consul at Cork, Ireland, a post he maintained until 1893. In the decade of the 1880s Piatt wrote a book of essays, *Pencilled Fly-Leaves;* published *At the Holy Well* (1887); and rearranged earlier poems under such titles as *A Book of Gold and Other Sonnets* (1889) and *Idyls and Lyrics of the Ohio Valley* (1881, 1888). When the Democrats returned to power in 1893, Piatt came back to North Bend. Here, at 58, he continued his literary work as a regular contributor to the Cincinnati *Enquirer* and special reviewer for other journals. After 1892 Piatt added to his list only two volumes of verse: *Little New World Idyls* (1893) and *Odes in Ohio* (1897). As the creative impulse dimmed somewhat, Piatt kept his literary interests alert by editing several collections of poetry and performing editorial duties for *The Midland.* Late in his seventies, he suffered a carriage accident which invalided him to the end of his life. He died in Cincinnati. His wife, three sons, and a daughter survived him. Piatt is not a poet who sets the soul on fire. One does not go to him for general optimism, exuberance, or lines of high emotional pitch. Some of his verses are mere fanciful exercises. But there is a freshness in his better pieces which arises from personal experience and from memory—the kind of newness which only a Western poet could supply and which led to overly enthusiastic appraisals of his writings. Nevertheless, many of his lines are healthy, vital, and perceptive. In others there is an element of sadness not altogether dispelled by visions of spring or the upwelling of joy that comes from love, romance, and domesticity. Sometimes there is too much pathos of a variety reminiscent of the graveyard school. In the main, the sadness is personal and convincing. The world which he cherished, the rural world of the pioneer, was being destroyed by so-called progress, by the mushrooming of cities, by the foreclosing of mortgages, by the cutting down of trees, and by the crowding of the prairies. His tragedies, therefore, are those of the Civil War, the passing of old associations and the breakup of ways of life dear to him. Sometimes he is satisfied with merely recording the change, and then his lines seem placid. At other times there is a nostalgic sadness as he regards these changes, and this reaches the reader with force. His poetry, though it frequently lacks the fire of the participant, at least is marked by immediacy and truth. In the best of it, he tried not to substitute for reality the higher similitudes of the imagination. At times, as in "The Pioneer's Chimney," "The Mower in Ohio," and "Antaeus," he selected subjects worthy of his genius, and, while he may not have achieved greatness in the result, there is a full measure of worthiness. He wrote with the pulse of a way of life which had passed, and thus he avoided the artistic inconsequence which marked much of the unreal verse of his age. One wishes that he had supplied a whole volume on western phases. His reputation today might be greater than it is.

G. Harrison Orians

Poems of Two Friends, (with William Dean Howells), Columbus, 1860.

The Nests at Washington, and Other Poems, (with Sarah M. B. Piatt), New York, 1864.

Poems in Sunshine and Firelight, Cincinnati, 1866.

Western Windows and Other Poems, New York, 1869.

Landmarks and Other Poems, New York, 1872.

Poems of House and Home, Boston, 1879.

Pencilled Fly-Leaves: A Book of Essays . . . , Cincinnati, 1880.

Idyls and Lyrics of the Ohio Valley, Cincinnati, 1881.

The Children Out-of-Doors . . . , (with Sarah M. B. Piatt), Cincinnati, 1885.

At the Holy Well, with a Handful of New Verses, Cincinnati, 1887.

A Book of Gold, and Other Sonnets, London, 1889.

A Return to Paradise . . . , London, 1891.

Little New World Idyls, and Other Poems, New York, 1893.

Odes in Ohio, and Other Poems, Cincinnati, 1897.

How the Bishop Built His College in the Woods, Cincinnati, [1906].

PIATT, LOUISE KIRBY (Nov. 25, 1826–Oct., 1864), wife of Donn Piatt (q.v.), was born in Cincinnati, Hamilton County. In 1853 her husband took her to France for medical treatment. Her experiences in Paris, while he served as secretary of the American legation, furnished material for her book, an epistolary story.

Bell Smith Abroad, New York, 1855.

PIATT, SARAH MORGAN BRYAN (Aug. 11, 1836–Dec. 22, 1919), was born in Lexington, Ky. She graduated from Henry Female College, New Castle, Ky. Her poems published in the Louisville *Journal* attracted favorable attention. In 1861 she married John James Piatt (q.v.). They lived in Washington, D. C., until 1867, when they settled in North Bend. They lived in Ireland from 1882 to 1893 while John J. Piatt was serving as American consul, but they returned to North Bend after his retirement. Mrs. Piatt wrote the greater part of her poetry while living in Ireland, and her poems aroused great admiration in England, where some critics compared her with Mrs. Browning. She spent her last years in Caldwell, N. J., and her death occurred in that community.

A Woman's Poems, Boston, 1871.
A Voyage to the Fortunate Isles, Boston, 1874.
Poems in Company with Children, Boston, [1877].
That New World, and Other Poems, Boston, 1877.
Dramatic Persons and Moods, with Other New Poems, Boston, 1880.
An Irish Garland, Boston, 1885.
In Primrose Time . . . , Boston, 1886.
Mrs. Piatt's Select Poems . . . , Boston, 1886.
Child's-World Ballads . . . , Cincinnati, 1887.
The Witch in the Glass, Boston, 1889.
An Irish Wild-Flower . . . , New York, 1891.
An Enchanted Castle, and Other Poems . . . , New York, 1893.
Poems, 2 vols., London, 1894.
The Gift of Tears, Cincinnati, 1906.

PICARD, GEORGE HENRY (Aug. 3, 1850–Oct. 7, 1916), physician, was born in Berea, Cuyahoga County. After graduating from Baldwin University in 1869, he studied medicine in Cincinnati. After 1877 he practiced in New York City.

A Matter of Taste; A Novel, New York, 1884.
A Mission Flower; An American Novel, New York, 1885.
Old Boniface; A Novel, New York, 1886.
Madame Noël, New York, 1900.
The Bishop's Niece, Boston, 1905.

PICKET, ALBERT (April 15, 1771–Aug. 3, 1850), educator, spent his last 24 years in Cincinnati and did much to establish that city as a publishing center and also to advance the cause of public education in Ohio. From the publication of his first textbook, a speller, in 1804, he produced many grammars and readers that were widely used throughout the country. His son, John W. Picket, collaborated in the preparation of many of them. In Cincinnati, Picket operated a school for girls, served on the board of education, and around 1829 organized the teachers of the area into the Western Literary Institute and College of Professional Teachers. Not so well known as McGuffey, Ray, or Spencer, Picket was an important pioneer in educational writing.

PICKET, JOSEPH W. (Jan. 28, 1832–Nov. 14, 1879), missionary, was born in Andover, Ashtabula County. He graduated from Allegheny College in 1855 and Yale University in 1858. His was a long and colorful career as a missionary in the West. He entered the field at Cheyenne, Wyo., in 1878. After serving in the mining camps in the Black Hills of Dakota, he went to Leadville, Colo. His journal covering this experience is full of accurate descriptions, most important to the historian of the West. He died in the wreck of a stagecoach near Leadville.

Memoirs of Joseph W. Picket . . . , Burlington, Iowa, 1880.

PIERCE, EDWARD LILLIE (March 29, 1829–Sept. 5, 1897), born in Stoughton, Mass., came to Cincinnati in 1852 and read law for a time in the office of Salmon P. Chase. He later served as Chase's secretary in Washington. His most notable publication in later life was a four-volume life and letters of Charles Sumner, Boston, 1877–93.

PIERCE, ERNEST P. (c.1879–Feb. 23, 1959), was born in Lorain, Lorain County. He was a manufacturer in Cleveland. He died in Southgate, Calif., and is buried in Elyria. With Clara McClean, he published a collection of mystical poems: *Infiniverse,* New York, [1940].

PIERCE, SILAS CASS (Jan. 1, 1851–May 16, 1933), clergyman and educator, was born in Morgan County. A graduate of National Normal University, Lebanon, he was superintendent of schools in Straightsville and Shawnee. He was also a Disciples of Christ minister and served numerous Ohio pastorates. He died in North Eaton. Besides the title below, he published a grammar textbook.

Materialism against Itself . . . , Cincinnati, 1884.

PIERCE, SQUIER LITTELL (March 6, 1832– ?), lawyer, was born in Butler County. He was admitted to the bar in 1852 and moved to Wasioja, Minn., in 1856. He later practiced in St. Paul and Dodge Center, Minn.

Di, a Story, Philadelphia, 1891.
Stolen Steps, a Story, Philadelphia, 1892.

PIERCY, CAROLINE BEHLEN (Dec. 31, 1886–April 2, 1955), was born in Cleveland, Cuyahoga County, and spent her life in that city. She graduated from Lake Erie College and did graduate work in England and at Western Reserve University. Wife of a Shaker Heights physician, Dr. Harry Piercy, she published several books, including an account of the Shaker community at North Union and a story for children: *Rosamond; The Memoirs of a Rag Doll,* [Cleveland, 1941].

PIERO, ELDA MAE (May 9, 1883–), was born in Canton, Stark County, and still lives in that community. After graduating from Canton High School, she attended Wittenberg College for two years. She was employed at Wittenberg for a time, and for 21 years worked for the Canton Welfare Federation. She has published poems in numerous periodicals and anthologies, three collections of poetry, and a pageant: *The Temple of Praise . . . ,* Philadelphia, [1922]. BDCP

PIERSON, HAMILTON WILCOX (Sept. 22, 1817–Sept. 7, 1888), clergyman, born in Bergen, N. Y., was a Presbyterian minister and state librarian of Ohio, 1885–86. He published a biography of Jefferson and an interesting account of his own activities during the 1850s as agent of the American Bible Society: *In the Brush; Or, Old-Time Social, Political, and Religious Life in the Southwest,* New York, 1881.

PIKE, JAMES (July 13, 1834–186-?), soldier and scout, was born in Leesburg, Highland County. His father, Samuel Pike, edited various newspapers in the Middle West; he was an ardent Democrat, and his convictions nearly resulted in violence during the Civil War while he was editing a Hillsboro newspaper. James learned the printing trade and in 1858 went to Missouri as an itinerant printer. In search of adventure he decided to go to Kansas, but was persuaded instead to accompany a Colonel Johnson in driving horses to Texas. The horses, which he discovered later had been stolen, were safely driven to Texas, and Pike joined the Texas Rangers in 1859. When the Civil War began, he returned to Ohio and enlisted in the 4th Ohio Volunteer Cavalry. He served as a scout and spy in the Secret Service during the war and was afterward commissioned and stationed in the West. According to legend, he shot himself during an Indian raid when he beat his jammed rifle against a rock and exploded the cartridge. His stirring account of his adventures was published by J. R. Hawley of Cincinnati, but most of the edition was destroyed in a fire. The Texas portion of his narrative was edited by Carl L. Cannon and reprinted in 1932 by Princeton University Press.

The Scout and Ranger: Being the Personal Adventures of Corporal Pike, of the Fourth Ohio Cavalry . . . , Cincinnati, 1865.

PILCHER, ELIJAH HOMES (June 2, 1810–April 7, 1887), clergyman and educator, was born in Athens, Athens County. After attending Ohio University, he was ordained to the Methodist ministry and served churches in the United States and Canada. He was one of the founders of Albion College, Mich., where he served on the faculty, and was also a founder of the agricultural college at Lansing, Mich. He died in Brooklyn, N. Y.

History of Protestantism in Michigan, Detroit, 1878.

PINKERTON, LEWIS LETIG (Jan. 28, 1812–Jan. 28, 1875), clergyman, was born in Maryland but grew up in Pennsylvania and Virginia. He came to Ohio in 1831 and studied medicine in Trenton, Butler County. He practiced in Carthage, 1835–39. Having been converted to the Disciples of Christ Church in 1830, he was called to the ministry, gave up medicine, and moved to Kentucky, where he became a leader in his church. His writings were collected in *Life, Letters and Addresses of Dr. L. L. Pinkerton,* (John Schackleford, Jr., ed.), Cincinnati, 1876.

PINNEY, NELSON AUGUSTUS (Feb. 4, 1844–Nov. 19, 1920) was born in Windham, Portage County. He served in the 104th O.V.I., Aug., 1862–June, 1865. After the war he operated a farm near Windham and worked on bridge construction in northeastern Ohio. He died at Edinburg.

History of the 104th Regimental Ohio Volunteer Infantry . . . , Akron, 1886.

PIPP, WASHINGTON JEFFERSON VAN BUREN. Pseud. See Collin Ford.

PITBLADO, EDWY GUTHRIE (Dec. 29, 1871–Aug. 8, 1939), clergyman, was born in Dunfermline, Scotland. After graduating from Columbia University in 1896 and from Berkeley Divinity School in 1899, he was ordained to the priesthood of the Episcopal Church in 1900. He served as rector of churches in Salem and Toledo, 1902–08, and afterward served churches in various other states. With his brother, Charles Bruce Pitblado, he wrote *Nareen,* Toledo, [1908].

PITMAN, BENN (July 22, 1822–Dec. 28, 1910), educator, was born in Trowbridge, Wiltshire, England. He is said to have studied under the direction of the poet, George Crabbe. His brother, Isaac, had invented a system of phonography; Benn assisted him and, versatile genius that he was, engraved most of the plates that appeared in their textbooks. From 1843 until 1852 he lectured throughout Great Britain on the phonetic system of shorthand. He arrived in America in 1853. After stopping briefly in New York City and Washington, D. C., he made his way to Cincinnati, where he was assured of a warm welcome. At this time Cincinnati was the center of alphabetic reform; the American Phonetic Society had been organized there in 1848, and for several years it had served as American agent for Isaac Pitman's publications. Here Benn immediately founded the Phonographic Institute. He had planted his seed in fertile ground, for his first pupil was none other than the influential Alphonso Taft, then over forty years old. His first textbook, *The Reporter's Companion,* appeared in 1854, to be followed quickly by several others; all enjoyed large sales as a result of the growing popularity of the Pitman system. Perhaps his greatest distinction was in being selected as the official reporter of the state trials during and following the Civil War, including the trial of the assassins of Abraham Lincoln. The printed reports of those trials, which he edited and compiled, stand as enduring monuments to his professional ability. An especially profitable turn was his invention of a process for electroplating engravings in 1856. Benn Pitman had prospered, and he could well afford to devote most of his time to his avocations, which included wood carving, pottery making, china painting, and the making of stained glass windows. In 1873 he became associated with the Cincinnati Art Academy, where he taught artistic wood carving and lectured on art until 1892. Many public buildings and private homes in Cincinnati are decorated with superb examples of the work of his pupils. It was Pitman who started the pottery fad in 1875, which led directly to the famous Rookwood Pottery. He died in Cincinnati.

Ernest J. Wessen

The Reporter's Companion, Cincinnati, 1854.
Manual of Phonography, Cincinnati, [1855].
History of Shorthand, Cincinnati, 1856.
The Teacher, a Treatise on the Best Method of Imparting a Knowledge of Phonography, Cincinnati, [1856?].
A Plea for American Decorative Art, Cincinnati, 1895.
Sir Isaac Pitman; His Life and Labors . . . , [Cincinnati, 1902].
A Plea for Alphabetic Reform, [Cincinnati, 1905].
Solution of the Alphabetic Problem, [n.p., n.d.].

PITTENGER, WILLIAM (Jan. 31, 1840–April 24, 1904), clergyman, was born on a farm near New Somerset, Jefferson County. He attended local schools and qualified for a teaching certificate at the age of sixteen. He taught near Ravenna, and in other localities. While he was teaching, he gained some experience in writing through his association with Alexander Clark (q.v.), who was publishing the *School Visitor.* Following his enlistment in the 2nd O.V.I., April 17, 1861, his letters from the front began to appear in the Steubenville *Herald* and were widely read. A participant in the daring Andrews Railroad Raid—a thrilling episode which electrified the nation—Pittenger was captured but was soon exchanged. After his return to the North, he was sent to a sanitarium in Pennsylvania to regain his health. It was at this time that he wrote his simple, dramatic narrative, *Daring and Suffering.* His old friend, Clark, found a publisher for the book in Philadelphia. It appeared late in 1863 and enjoyed large sales. As new material became available, the book was rewritten; the final edition appeared in 1893, after all official documents had become available. Despite recriminations of other raiders after the war, Pittenger remained the best known participant in the Andrews Raid. He entered the Pittsburgh Conference of the Methodist Church in 1864 and remained in the active pastorate of that denomination until his death. He went to California in 1902, and died in that state at Fallbrook.

Daring and Suffering: A History of the Great Railroad Adventure, Philadelphia, 1863.
Oratory, Sacred and Secular . . . , Philadelphia, 1868.
How to Conduct a Public Meeting . . . , New York, 1878.
The Extempore Speaker, Philadelphia, 1882.
How to Become a Public Speaker, Philadelphia, 1887.
The Debater's Treasury, Philadelphia, 1891.

PIXLEY, FRANK (Nov. 21, 1867–Dec. 30, 1919), dramatist, was born in Richfield, Summit County. After attending Buchtel College, he graduated from Ohio State University in 1886 and then taught at

Buchtel College, 1887–90. He edited the Akron *Times* for a brief period and wrote for the Chicago *Times-Herald,* 1899–1902. He wrote a great many plays and musical comedies, e.g., *Apollo . . . ,* San Francisco, 1915. His most famous line was probably "Vas You Effer in Zinzinnati?" which appeared in *Prince of Pilsen,* produced in 1903. WWW 1

PLAGEMANN, WILLIAM WALTER JOSEPH (Bentz Plagemann) (July 27, 1913–), was born in Springfield, Clark County, and was educated in the public schools of Cleveland. While serving in the navy during World War II, he was stricken with infantile paralysis; he underwent treatment in various navy hospitals and at Warm Springs, Ga. His reputation has risen steadily since the publication of his first novel: *William Walter,* New York, [1941].

PLATT, CYRUS (Sept. 20, 1818–Jan. 18, 1899), jeweler, was born in Columbus, Franklin County. After learning watchmaking in New Jersey and Philadelphia, he worked for short periods in Columbus and Worthington before moving to Delaware, where he spent the remainder of his life. His wife, whose life and letters he published, was a native of Burlington, N. J.; she died Aug. 21, 1877.

St. Peter's Protestant Episcopal Church, Delaware, [n.p., 1880?].

Life and Letters of Mrs. Jeanette H. Platt, Philadelphia, 1882.

PLATT, GEORGE WASHINGTON (March 7, 1875–Dec. 20, 1951), lawyer, was born in Denver, Colo., but was brought to Cincinnati while still a child and spent his life in that city. After graduating from the Y.M.C.A. Night Law School, he was admitted to the Ohio bar and began practice in 1898. He was active in several movements for governmental economy and was president of a taxpayers' organization at the time of his death. He wrote *A History of the Republican Party,* Cincinnati, 1904.

PLATT, RUTHERFORD HAYES (Aug. 11, 1894–), was born in Columbus, Franklin County, and attended the schools of that city. An advertising executive in New York City, he has written books on how to choose a vocation, e.g., *You Can't Fail . . . ,* New York, 1929, and is also known for his writings and photography of plant-life, e.g., *This Green World,* New York, 1942.

PLIMPTON, FLORUS BEARDSLEY (Sept. 4, 1830–April 23, 1886), journalist, was born in Palmyra, Portage County. After studying for three years at Allegheny College, he began working in the office of the *Western Reserve Transcript* in Warren in the spring of 1851. In 1852 he edited a Whig campaign newspaper at Niles, Mich. He worked on the *Portage Whig,* Ravenna, the Elmira *Daily Republic,* and the Pittsburgh *Daily Dispatch,* 1854–60. In 1860 he moved to Cincinnati to work on the *Daily Commercial,* and he spent the remainder of his life in that city. Concerning his poetry, his colleague Murat Halstead (q.v.) wrote: "Boy and man, through the changes of forty years, he found poetry the finer, higher, truer expression of himself. . . . He touched the harp because it comforted him. There were things to say that could not otherwise be said; there were tones, rays of light, to trace through melodies unheard by, and illuminations invisible to, others–pathways into the infinite space that seemed to promise the divine achievement of the humanly unattainable." Although he is best known for his poetry, his first book has long since come to be recognized as a rarity in the field of Americana. He died in Cincinnati.

The Lost Child; Or, the Child Claimed by Two Mothers: A Narrative of the Loss and Discovery of Casper A. Partridge among the Menomonee Indians . . . , Cleveland, 1852.

Poems . . . , Cincinnati, 1886.

PLUM, WILLIAM RATTLE (March 24, 1845–April 28, 1927), was born in Massillon, Stark County. After graduating from high school in Cuyahoga Falls, he worked in telegraph offices in Atwater and Cleveland. He served in the Military Telegraph Corps during the Civil War, and during the last year of the war he was chief cipher operator on the staff of General George H. Thomas. After the war he studied law at Yale University, and in 1867 he was admitted to the bar in Chicago, Ill., where he practiced until his retirement in 1900.

The Military Telegraph during the Civil War . . . , 2 vols., Chicago, 1882.

The Sword and the Soul . . . , New York, 1917.

PLUMB, CHARLES SUMNER (April 21, 1860–March 4, 1939), educator, born in Westfield, Mass., taught for many years in the School of Agriculture, Ohio State University. Besides the books below, he wrote many articles, bulletins, and textbooks.

Indian Corn Culture, Chicago, 1895.

Little Sketches of Famous Beef Cattle, Columbus, 1904.

POCOCK, ARTHUR FRANKLIN (Feb. 18, 1919–), geologist, was born in Akron, Summit County. He graduated from the College of Wooster in 1941. His address in 1959 was Guatemala City, Guatemala. He has written an amusing account of his wartime service in Greenland while a member of the U. S. Coast Guard: *Red Flannels and Green Ice,* New York, [1949].

PODA, JOHN (July 19, 1907–), was born in Akron, Summit County. He worked in an Akron publishing plant and was active in union activities. He has served in the Ohio legislature, on the Akron council, and on the Summit County board of commissioners. He has published at least two collections of poetry, including a pamphlet of poems of social protest: *72 Poems,* Akron, 1939.

POESE, WILLIAM (May 23, 1908–), was born in Cleveland, Cuyahoga County. He graduated from Kenyon College in 1930, did graduate work at Western Reserve University, and began teaching in the Cleveland public schools in 1933. An avocational interest in jewels and gem cutting led him to write *Gem Stone Lore,* Colorado Springs, 1948.

POFFENBARGER, LIVIA NYE SIMPSON (March 1, 1862–Oct. 27, 1937), was born in Pomeroy, Meigs County, but spent much of her life in Point Pleasant, W. Va., where she owned and managed the *State Gazette.* She wrote a number of books and pamphlets on West Virginia history, e.g., *The Battle of Point Pleasant* . . . , Point Pleasant, W. Va., 1909. WWW 1

POINCE, ADAH DODD (April 8, 1867–June 21, 1955), was born in Berkeley County, W. Va. After her marriage to William Poince in 1892, she lived in Dayton. She lectured on history and politics and was active in the Presbyterian Church. She traveled widely and was a Chautauqua lecturer.

Venus McFarland, [n.p., 1900].

POLHAMUS, WILLIAM HENRY HARRISON (Aug. 5, 1842–May 22, 1919), lawyer, was born in New York State. He served in the Civil War, and was captured and imprisoned in Libby Prison. In 1887 he began the practice of law in Cleveland; he was also active in the G.A.R. He died in Lakewood. He published *Cedar Creek: A Poem,* Cleveland, 1901.

POLING, DANIEL ALFRED (Nov. 30, 1884–), clergyman, born in Portland, Oreg., began his preaching career in Canton, 1904–07. He also did graduate work at Ohio State University, 1907–09, and was candidate for governor of Ohio on the Prohibition ticket in 1912. A prolific writer of books and articles, he has also published several novels, e.g., *The Heretic,* New York, 1928. WW 30

POLLARD, EDWINA OBENAUER (Nov. 27, 1902–), was born in Dayton, Montgomery County. She graduated from Ypsilanti Teachers College, Mich., and from the University of Wisconsin. She now lives in Oxford, where her husband, Harry S. Obenauer, is professor of mathematics at Miami University. She writes a column for the Oxford *Press* and has written stories and poems for children and a book of verse: *The Winged Echo,* Prairie City, Ill., [1949].

POLLARD, JAMES EDWARD (Oct. 25, 1894–), journalist and educator, was born in Chambersburg, Pa. He was educated at Ohio State University (A.B., 1917; Ph.D., 1939), was on the staff of the *Ohio State Journal,* 1920–29, and has been on the journalism faculty, Ohio State University, since 1932. He has written numerous articles, journalism textbooks, a history of the university, and books on American journalism, e.g., *The Presidents and the Press,* New York, 1947. WW 30

POLLARD, JOHN ALBERT (Dec. 24, 1901–), educator, brother of James E. Pollard (q.v.), was born in Chambersburg, Pa. His parents moved to Toledo in 1905, and he grew up in that city. He graduated from Ohio State University in 1924 and from Yale University (Ph.D.) in 1937. He has taught at several schools, including Antioch College and the University of Toledo, and is now vice president of the Council for Financial Aid to Education. He has written a biography: *John Greenleaf Whittier, Friend of Man,* Boston, 1949. DAS 3

POLLOCK, ARLO D. (Sept. 18, 1908–), was born in Jennings Township, Van Wert County, and now lives in Delphos. He began operating a turkey ranch in the 1930s and is now president of Middle Point Banking Co. He has published articles in poultry magazines and one book: *After the Storm,* Delphos, 1937.

POLSKY, THOMAS (May 5, 1908–), was born in Akron, Summit County. He graduated from Harvard University in 1929 and worked on Akron newspapers in the 1930s.

His last address in Ohioana files is Asheville, N. C. He has written several mysteries, e.g., *Curtains for the Editor,* New York, [1939].

POND, FREDERICK EUGENE (April 8, 1856–Nov. 1, 1925), born in Packwaukee, Wis., edited the *Sportsmen's Review* in Cincinnati, 1897–1917. Under the pen name Will Wildwood, he edited books on field sports by various writers, compiled gun trial and field trial records, and wrote several books, e.g., *Hand-book for Young Sportsmen . . . ,* Milwaukee, 1876.

POND, MARIAM BUCKNER (Aug. 7, 1891–), was born in Leroy, Medina County. Her father, a minister, left Ohio when she was a girl, but in 1929 she settled in Hudson. After the death of her husband, Colonel Daniel H. Pond, she married an Australian rancher, Murdoch E. MacKenzie, and moved to Australia in 1956. She has written a novel about three sisters with psychic powers: *Time Is Kind; The Story of the Unfortunate Fox Family,* New York, 1947.

POOLE, WILLIAM FREDERICK (Dec. 24, 1821–March 1, 1894), librarian, born in Salem, Mass., served as librarian in the Cincinnati Public Library, 1871–73, after which he moved to Chicago, where he headed the public library and organized the Newberry Library. In 1848 he published the first version of an indispensable reference book, *Poole's Index to Periodical Literature.* He also published several significant monographs and articles on historical subjects.

POOLEY, J. H. (Nov. 17, 1839–Dec. 11, 1897), physician, born in Cambridgeshire, England, was brought to the United States when he was a child. He grew up in Dobbs Ferry, N. Y., and in 1860 graduated from the College of Physicians and Surgeons, N. Y. He was a surgeon in the Civil War for two years, practiced at Yonkers, N. Y., 1863–75, was on the faculty of Starling Medical College, 1875–83, and in 1883 helped found Toledo Medical College, where he taught until his death. He wrote many articles and at least one book on medicine and surgery. His death occurred in Toledo.

Memoir of Samuel D. Turney, M.D. . . . , Cincinnati, 1878.

PORTER, JAMES A. (1836–Jan. 13, 1897), was born in Bellefontaine, Logan County. After serving as a bugler and bandmaster in the Civil War, he taught music in Galion, Urbana, and Greenville. After retiring because of illness, he wrote the novel listed below.

A Prince of Anahuac. A Histori-Traditional Story . . . , Cincinnati, [1894].

PORTER, JERMAIN GILDERSLEEVE (Jan. 8, 1852–April 14, 1933), astronomer, born in Buffalo, N. Y., and educated at Hamilton College, came to Cincinnati in 1884 as director of the Observatory. He retired as active director in 1930. Though most of his publications are catalogues of stars and technical articles, he published one book for the general reader: *The Stars in Song and Legend,* Boston, 1901. DAB 15

PORTER, WILL (Jan. 22, 1833–1913), journalist and lawyer, was born in Hanging Rock, Lawrence County. He learned the printing trade at Ripley, worked for a while on the Cincinnati *Daily Times,* and studied law in his spare time. He was admitted to the Indiana bar in 1854. The following year he went to Iowa and entered the office of the *Iowa Statesman* at Fort Des Moines. He bought the *Statesman* in 1857 and changed its name to the *Iowa State Journal.* He sold out in 1860 and began practicing law. He was chief Iowa correspondent for the Chicago *Times* for over twenty years and also wrote special correspondence for New York newspapers.

Annals of Polk County, Iowa, and City of Des Moines, Des Moines, Iowa, 1898.

PORTER, WILLIAM SYDNEY (O. Henry) (Sept. 11, 1862–June 5, 1910), born in Greensboro, N. C., and later a resident of Texas and New York, can be classified only as an involuntary Ohioan. After working as a bank teller in Austin, Texas, 1891–94, he was summoned two years later to testify concerning a shortage of funds. If he had appeared, he would probably have been exonerated, but instead he fled to the Honduras. On returning because of the illness of his wife, he was arrested, tried, and sentenced to five years in prison. He was imprisoned in the Ohio Penitentiary, Columbus, from April 25, 1898, to July 24, 1901. He is included in this volume because he wrote at least twelve short stories during this period, because he was encouraged to write fiction by Dr. John M. Thomas of Columbus, and because he probably borrowed his famous pen name from the captain of the guards, Orrin Henry. It has also been suggested facetiously that his pen name was an acronym: OHio pENitentiaRY.

PORTER, WILLIAM TOWNSEND (Sept. 24, 1862–Feb. 16, 1949), physiologist, was born in Plymouth, Richland County. After graduating from St. Louis Medical College in 1885, he studied in Germany. He was on the Harvard medical faculty, 1893–1928. In addition to a textbook in physiology and a number of technical monographs, he wrote *Shock at the Front,* Boston, [1918]. WWW 2

PORTERFIELD, BETTILU. See Bettilu P. Lewis.

POSEGATE, MABEL (1885–April 28, 1950) was born in Cincinnati, Hamilton County, where she attended high school, business college, and the University of Cincinnati. In 1905 she married Charles S. Posegate. She was appointed poet laureate of Ohio in 1936 by the Poet Laureate League of Washington, D. C., and was active in state and national poetry societies. She died in Cincinnati. She published several collections of verse, e.g., *Once When Arcturus Shone,* Brattleboro, Vt., 1935. WWW 3

POST, CHARLES ASA (Oct. 28, 1848–May 2, 1943), banker, was born in East Cleveland, Cuyahoga County. He entered the banking business in 1869 and afterward served as an official of several Cleveland banks. In his later years he became interested in local history and published a book about Doans Corners and another about sleighing on Euclid Avenue: *Those Were the Days, When Hearts Were Kind and Sports Were Simple,* Cleveland, 1935.

POST, LOUIS FREELAND (Nov. 15, 1849–Jan. 10, 1928), reformer, born in Vienna, N. J., edited the Cleveland *Recorder,* 1896–97. He published a number of books, most of them on Henry George, whose single-tax theories he advocated, e.g., *The Single Tax . . . ,* Cedar Rapids, Iowa, 1899.

POTEAT, EDWIN McNEILL (Nov. 20, 1892–Dec. 17, 1955), clergyman, born in New Haven, Conn., was pastor of Euclid Avenue Baptist Church, Cleveland, 1937–43. He died in Raleigh, N. C. He wrote a number of books, both prose and poetry, e.g., *Jesus and the Liberal Mind,* Philadelphia, [1934], and *Centurion, a Narrative Poem,* New York, 1939. WWW 3

POTTENGER, FRANCIS MARION (Sept. 27, 1869–), physician, was born in Ohio. He graduated from Otterbein College in 1892 and from Cincinnati College of Medicine and Surgery in 1894. He practiced at Norwood, 1894–95, and afterward at Monrovia and Los Angeles, Calif., specializing in diseases of the lungs and throat. He now lives in Pasadena, Calif. He has published a number of technical medical works, an autobiography (1952), and a book for the general reader: *Tuberculosis and How to Combat It; A Book for the Patient,* St. Louis, 1921. WW 29

POTTS, FRANK E. (Oct. 3, 1904–) was born in Dayton, Montgomery County. He attended the University of Dayton, worked for the Frigidaire Division of General Motors, and since 1955 has been employed by a Dayton advertising agency. His writings include a book for the juvenile reader: *The Contented Canary . . . ,* [Cincinnati], 1928.

POTTS, PIPSISSIWAY. Pseud. See Rosella Rice.

POTWIN, LEMUEL STOUGHTON (Feb. 4, 1832–Jan. 9, 1907), clergyman and educator, was born in East Windsor, Conn. After graduating from Yale University in 1854, he studied at the Theological Institute of Connecticut and was ordained as a Congregational minister. He taught school, served a church in Bridgewater, Conn., and spent six years in the publication department of The American Tract Society, Boston. He served on the Western Reserve faculty, 1871–1906. He wrote religious textbooks and many articles.

Here and There in the Greek New Testament, New York, 1898.

Selections from the Editorial Essays . . . , (Julia H. Potwin, ed.), Cleveland, 1907.

POUNDS, JESSIE HUNTER BROWN (Aug. 31, 1861–March 3, 1921), was born in Hiram, Portage County, and spent her girlhood in Cleveland. She was educated at Hiram College. She married John E. Pounds, who served as college pastor at Hiram. Some of her stories and pageants were published separately in pamphlet form, and some of her works appeared under her maiden name, Jessie Hunter Brown. She wrote more than 800 hymns, including "Beautiful Isle of Somewhere," which became popular after it was played at President McKinley's funeral.

Norman Macdonald, Cincinnati, 1887.

A Woman's Doing, Cincinnati, 1887.

Roderick Wayne, Cincinnati, 1889.

The Ironclad Pledge, a Story of Christian Endeavor, Cincinnati, 1890.

A Popular Idol . . . , Cincinnati, 1901.

The Young Man from Middlefield, St. Louis, 1901.

Rachel Sylvestre, a Story of the Pioneers, Cincinnati, [1904].

Pioneer Missionaries . . . , Indianapolis, [1907].

POWELL, DAWN (Nov. 28, 1897–), was born in Mount Gilead, Morrow County. Her mother died when she was a small child, and Dawn lived with her aunts in various Ohio towns. After her father's remarriage in 1909, she went to the home of an aunt in Shelby, where she attended school and worked on the *Daily Globe.* She graduated from Lake Erie College in 1918, served as a yeoman in the navy, and in 1920 married Joseph R. Gousha, an advertising man. A prolific writer, she has published many novels. She has used Ohio as the setting for *The Bride's House,* New York, 1929, and *Dance Night,* New York, 1930. Her most successful novel is, perhaps, *The Locusts Have No King,* New York, 1948. WWAW 1

POWELL, ELMER ELLSWORTH (Aug. 16, 1861–July 7, 1947), clergyman and educator, was born in Clayton, Ill. He graduated from the University of Michigan in 1885 and from the School of Theology, Boston University, in 1890. He taught at a Methodist school in Italy, 1890–96, and at Franklin and Marshall College, 1900–05. He was professor of philosophy at Miami University, 1905–22, and after his retirement he continued to live in Oxford. He wrote *Spinoza and Religion . . . ,* Chicago, 1906.

POWELL, JOHN WESLEY (March 24, 1834–Sept. 23, 1902), geologist, born in Mount Morris, N. Y., the son of an itinerant Methodist minister, spent a part of his boyhood in Jackson and later attended Oberlin College for a time. He published a number of papers, reports, and books on Indian languages and the physiography of the West.

POWELL, THOMAS EDWARD (Feb. 20, 1842–April 22, 1925), lawyer, was born in Delaware, Delaware County. He served in the Civil War from May, 1862, until his discharge as a sergeant in Aug., 1864. He then attended Ohio Wesleyan University, and was admitted to the Ohio bar in 1867. He practiced in Delaware and Columbus. He wrote *The Democratic Party of the State of Ohio . . . ,* 2 vols., [Columbus], 1913. WW 11

POWELL, THOMAS WATKINS (Sept. 7, 1797–Dec. 12, 1882), lawyer, was born in Glamorganshire, Wales. His father came to America in 1800, settling in Utica, N. Y. Thomas studied at an academy in Utica for two terms and began to read law; in 1819 he came to Canton, where he completed his law studies. He was admitted to the bar in 1820, practiced for ten years in Perrysburg, moved to Delaware in 1830, and practiced there for the rest of his life. In the 1830s he established in Delaware a resort hotel, the Mansion House, which became the first building of Ohio Wesleyan University. In addition to the title below, he published two legal works.

The History of the Ancient Britons and Their Descendants, Delaware, 1882.

POWELL, WARREN THOMSON (Nov. 28, 1884–Dec. 28, 1946), clergyman, was born in Delaware, Delaware County. After graduating from Ohio State University in 1907, he taught English for four years, and then attended Garrett Biblical Institute. Ordained to the Methodist ministry in 1917, he was active in young people's work in the Methodist Church and after 1929 was a student counselor at Boston University. His writings include *Recreational Leadership for Church and Community,* New York, [1923]. WWW 3

POWER, EFFIE LOUISE (Feb. 12, 1873–), librarian, born in Conneautville, Pa., attended high school in Cleveland, and was on the staff of the Cleveland Public Library, 1895–1903 and 1920–37. She also taught at City Normal School, Cleveland, 1903–08. She was librarian at the Pompano, Fla., Public Library, 1942–51, and has lived in Pompano since her retirement. She edited a number of book lists and story collections, and wrote several stories for children, e.g., *Osceola Buddy, a Florida Farm Mule,* New York, 1941. WW 27

POWERS, STEPHEN (July 21, 1840–April 2, 1904), journalist, was born in Waterford, Washington County. After graduating from the University of Michigan in 1861, he was a war correspondent for the Cincinnati *Commercial* and other periodicals. After the war he toured Europe as a correspondent, and in 1868 he walked from Port Royal, S. C., to San Francisco, Calif. His first book, *Muskingum Legends,* is patterned after Washington Irving's *Sketch Book.*

Muskingum Legends . . . , Philadelphia, 1871.

Afoot and Alone; A Walk from Sea to Sea by the Southern Route . . . , Hartford, Conn., 1872.

Tribes of California, Washington, D. C., 1877.

The American Merino: For Wool and for Mutton . . . , New York, 1887.

PRATHER, JOHN (July 30, 1843–May 29, 1921), was born in West Union, Adams County. When he was thirteen, his family moved to Manchester. His autobiography recounts his Civil War experiences, first as a sutler's clerk and later as a soldier in the 91st O.V.I. After the Civil War he was inspired by visions to preach, but he was never ordained. His occupation as the first rural mail carrier in Manchester led to a quarrel with the postmaster. The local Methodist minister supported Prather's opponent, and after a lengthy controversy Prather was expelled from his church. When he published his book, he was superintendent of the local Baptist Sunday School and a member of a Methodist church, in Kentucky.

Scenes and Incidents in the Life of an Expelled Member of the M.E. Church, Aberdeen, 1879.

PRATT, ANNA M. (July 23, 1844–July 23, 1928), educator, born in Massachusetts, was brought to Cleveland when she was six years old and spent the remainder of her life in that city. She taught for a number of years in the Cleveland schools and died in Cleveland at the age of 84.

Flower Folk . . . , New York, 1890.

Friends from my Garden . . . , New York, 1890.

Little Rhymes for Little People, Cleveland, 1896.

PRATT, CORNELIA ATWOOD (d. 1929), was born in Bryan, Williams County. After graduating from Vassar College, she worked on the New York *Critic* and the St. Paul *Globe.* She married William D. Comer of Seattle, Wash., in 1903 and afterward worked on the Seattle *Post-Intelligencer.*

A Book of Martyrs, New York, 1896.

The Daughter of a Stoic, New York, 1896.

The Preliminaries; And Other Stories, Boston, 1912.

PRATT, DWIGHT MALLORY (April 18, 1852–April 12, 1922), clergyman, was born in West Cornwall, Conn. He graduated from Amherst College in 1876 and Hartford Theological Seminary in 1880. He served as pastor of Walnut Hills Congregational Church, Cincinnati, 1900–14. He lived in Cleveland, 1919–22. He wrote *The Master's Method of Winning Men,* New York, [1922]. WWW 1

PRATT, PARLEY PARKER (April 12, 1807–May 13, 1857), born in Burlington, N. Y., settled in Ohio before he was 21 and for a time was associated with Sidney Rigdon (q.v.). In 1830 he joined the Church of Latter-day Saints and was a member of the Kirtland settlement, where he was ordained an apostle. He traveled widely as a missionary and published several Mormon pamphlets. His autobiography, edited by his son, was published in 1874 and reissued in 1938.

PRENTISS, HARRIET DOAN McREYNOLDS (Dec. 14, 1862–March 25, 1951), was born in Cleveland, Cuyahoga County. She was educated in Cleveland and in Michigan. She married Irvin R. Prentiss, brother of Adella P. Hughes (q.v.). Around 1920 she moved to Philadelphia; her death occurred in that city. She wrote books on New Thought and a collection of poems: *Golden Hours . . . ,* New York, [1940]. WWNAA 7

PRESBREY, FRANK SPENCER (May 22, 1855–Oct. 10, 1936), born in Buffalo, N. Y., lived in Ohio for four years while he published and edited the Youngstown *Daily News-Register,* 1881–85. He later moved to New York City, where he published a history of advertising and wrote a number of guidebooks for travelers, e.g., *To Far Away Vacation Lands,* [New York, 1895].

PRESCOTT, JAMES S. (Jan. 26, 1803–April 3, 1888), was born in Lancaster, Mass. At the age of sixteen he became a stonemason. About the same time he became a Baptist, and in 1825 he went to Oneida, N. Y., as a Baptist missionary. In 1826 he went to Cleveland, where he was hired to do masonry for the Shaker community in North Union Village. After living in the community for a short time, he joined the society and spent the remainder of his life at North Union, teaching school and serving as an elder.

The Social Evil, North Union, 1870.

PRESNELL, FRANK G. (June 24, 1906–), engineer, was born in Torreón, Mexico, where his father was working as a metallurgist. Educated at Antioch College and Ohio State University, he has worked as a designer and engineer for various concerns. He was a resident of Ohio for forty years, living most of that time in Chillicothe; he now lives in Los Angeles. He has written several mystery novels, e.g., *Send Another Coffin,* New York, 1939.

PRESTON, MARGARET JUNKIN (May 19, 1820–March 28, 1897), born in Milton, Pa., daughter of George Junkin (q.v.), lived in Oxford, 1841–44, while her father was president of Miami University. She published several volumes of prose and poetry, e.g., *Old Song and New,* Philadelphia, 1870.

PREYER, HUGO (Jan. 20, 1847– ?), journalist, was born in Prussia. He was publisher of *Ohio Staats Zeitung,* published in Canton, and the *Colorado Staats Zeitung.* He was active in reform organizations, and in 1878 was a candidate for lieutenant governor of Ohio on the Greenback ticket.

Ten Years' Practical Experience in Grape and Small Fruit Culture, Canton, 1875.

PRICE, EMERSON (April 2, 1902–), journalist, was born in Dublin, Franklin County, and attended public schools there. He has worked on the Akron *Times-Press* and the Cincinnati *Post* and is now book editor of the Cleveland *Press.* He has written for magazines under the pen name Hugh Hanley and has published a novel about the adventures of a boy in Scatterfield, an imaginary Ohio town near an industrial city: *Inn of That Journey,* Caldwell, Idaho, 1939.

PRICE, IRA MAURICE (April 29, 1856–Sept. 18, 1939), educator, was born near Newark, Licking County. He graduated from Denison University in 1879, Baptist Union Theological Seminary in 1882, and the University of Leipzig (Ph.D.) in 1887. After teaching in several institutions, he joined the faculty of the University of Chicago, where he served from 1892 to 1925. Besides the titles below, he wrote several textbooks and grammars.

The Monuments and the Old Testament . . . , Chicago, 1899.

The Drift of Biblical Research, Past and Present, Philadelphia, 1900.

The Ancestry of Our English Bible . . . , Philadelphia, 1907.

The Dramatic Story of the Old Testament History, New York, 1929.

PRICE, JUNIUS LUCIEN (Jan. 6, 1883–), was born in Kent, Portage County. He graduated from Western Reserve Academy in 1901 and Harvard University in 1907. He wrote reviews and editorials for the Boston *Transcript,* 1907–14, and for the Boston *Globe,* 1914–22. His books include an account of Amherst College during the administration of Alexander Meikle-John: *Prophets Unawares, the Romance of an Idea,* New York, [1924]. WW 30

PRICE, MERLE (Oct. 22, 1884–Jan. 22, 1960), was born in Millport, Meigs County. He worked for a number of years in the state welfare department and in the Ohio State Department of Commerce in Columbus. He died in Bellaire, Belmont County. He published a collection of poems: *The Heart Has Its Daybreak,* Emory University, Ga., 1950.

PRICE, WARWICK JAMES (Nov. 25, 1870–April 6, 1934), was born in Cleveland, Cuyahoga County. He graduated from Yale University in 1894, was a master of St. Paul's School for four years, and afterward lived in Philadelphia as a free-lance writer for magazines and newspapers. He published a collection of poems: *Nearest Things,* Philadelphia, [1919]. WWW 1

PRINCE, BENJAMIN F. (Dec. 12, 1840–Sept. 11, 1933), educator, was born in Westville, Champaign County. He graduated from Wittenberg College in 1865, joined the faculty the following year, and remained a member of the college staff until his death. Because of his professional training and his fine personal library, his history of Clark County is superior to most local histories: *A Standard History of Springfield and Clark County . . . ,* Chicago, 1922. WWW 1

PRINGLE, MARY POAGUE (Oct. 26, 1877–Dec. 10, 1957), librarian, was born in Springfield, Clark County. She served on the staff of Warder Public Library, Springfield, and was later with the St. Paul, Minn., Public Library and at the Library of the University of Hawaii. She died in Honolulu. With Clara A. Urann of Cleveland, she wrote *Yule-tide in Many Lands,* Boston, [1916].

PRUESER, SARA V. (April 11, 1869–Sept. 8, 1936), educator, was born in Defiance County. She graduated from Defiance High School and from Defiance College, after which she taught in the county and the city schools. She published poems in periodicals and anthologies and a book for young readers: *Our Dooryard Friends,* Chicago, 1915.

PRYOR, HELEN SLOMAN (March 7, 1901–), was born in Dayton, Montgomery County. Since 1940 she has been a member of various government boards and agencies. With her husband, William Clayton Pryor (q.v.), she has written a number of books for children, e.g., *The Cowboy Book . . . ,* New York, [1938]. WWAW 1

PRYOR, WILLIAM CLAYTON (July 15, 1894–March 30, 1949), journalist and government official, was born in Camden, Preble County. He worked on newspapers in Camden, Cincinnati, Springfield, and Columbus, and was an associate editor of the Ohio Farm Bureau. At the time of his death in Paris, France, he was head of the Education and Publication Service, U. S. Soil Conservation Service. He wrote a number of books for children, most of them in collaboration with his wife, Helen Sloman Pryor (q.v.). Their joint publications include *The Steamship Book . . .* , New York, [1934].

PULTE, JOSEPH HIPPOLYTE (Oct. 6, 1811–Feb. 25, 1884), homeopathic physician, was born in Westphalia. After coming to America in 1834, he was converted to homeopathy and practiced in Allentown, Pa., for six years. In 1840, en route to St. Louis, his original destination in America, he stopped at Cincinnati, decided to practice medicine there, and remained for the rest of his life. He lectured at Cleveland Homeopathic College and in 1872 founded Pulte Medical College in Cincinnati. He published numerous medical articles and some addresses. The *Domestic Physician* passed through many editions.

Organon Der Weltgeschichte, Cincinnati, 1846.
Homeopathic Domestic Physician . . . , Cincinnati, 1850.
Woman's Medical Guide . . . , Cincinnati, 1853.

PUMMILL, JAMES (Dec. 12, 1828–Feb. 1, 1912), journalist, was born in Cincinnati, Hamilton County. He learned the printing trade in Cincinnati and wrote essays and poems for the *Ladies' Repository* and the *Knickerbocker Magazine.* He was for a time editor of the Aurora, Ind., *Commercial,* but returned to Ohio. He was associated with various Cincinnati periodicals and with the Methodist Book Concern. His last years were spent at his home, Russet Cottage, near Cincinnati.

Fruits of Leisure, Circleville, 1846.
Fugitive Poems, Cincinnati, 1852.
Russet Leaves, Philadelphia, 1870.

PURCELL, JOHN BAPTIST (Feb. 26, 1800–July 4, 1883), clergyman, was born in Mallow, Ireland. In 1818 he came to Baltimore, Md., where he taught for two years before entering Mount Saint Mary's College; after studying there and in Paris, he was ordained to the Roman Catholic priesthood in 1826. After teaching at Mount Saint Mary's for a few years, he was appointed bishop of Cincinnati, and in 1850 he was named archbishop. No one did more to strengthen the Roman Catholic Church in Ohio. He built schools, convents, and churches and replied with a minimum of antagonism to attacks on his church. In the Mexican War, and especially in the Civil War, he insisted that the primary duty of Catholics was to support the nation. In 1836 he participated in a public debate with Alexander Campbell (q.v.), a record of which was published in 1837. His brilliant leadership came to a tragic end in the late 1870s. From the beginning of his service in Cincinnati, immigrants had entrusted their money to him; he had invested this money in property which could not be immediately liquidated, and the fund was unable to meet its obligations. In 1879 Archbishop Purcell retired to the Ursuline convent in Brown County, where he spent the last years of his life. Besides the pamphlet listed below, he wrote many articles and pastoral letters. Some of his sermons were also published.

Jesus Christ and the Resurrection, Baltimore, 1874.

PURINTON, DANIEL BOARDMAN (Feb. 15, 1850–Nov. 27, 1933), educator, born in Preston County, Va., served as president of Denison University, 1890–1901. His writings include *Christian Theism . . .* , New York, 1889.

PURVIANCE, LEVI (Sept. 7, 1790–April 9, 1873), clergyman, was born in Iredell County, N. C. He spent his boyhood in Tennessee and Kentucky, and also lived for a time in Indiana. In 1823 he was ordained to the ministry of the Christian Church; he preached in Miami, Warren, Darke, and Preble Counties. He spent ten years in Morristown, Ill., 1852–62. On returning to Ohio, he continued to preach until his death. Besides the title below, he wrote numerous articles for religious periodicals.

The Biography of Elder David Purviance . . . , Dayton, 1848.

PÜTERSCHEIN, HERMANN. Pseud. See William A. Dwiggins.

PUTNAM, ALBIGENCE WALDO (March 11, 1799–Jan. 20, 1869), great-grandson of Israel Putnam, was born in Marietta, Washington County. He studied law and practiced in Mississippi until 1836, when he settled in Nashville, Tenn., where he spent the remainder of his life. He wrote a number of articles on Tennessee history and was president of the state historical society.

History of Middle Tennessee; Or, Life and Times of Gen. James Robertson, Nashville, Tenn., 1859.

PUTNAM, J. WESLEY. Pseud. See Harry S. Drago.

PUTNAM, RUFUS (April 9, 1738–May 4, 1824), organizer of the Ohio Company, was born in Sutton, Mass. He served both in the French and Indian War and in the American Revolution. With a party of settlers, on April 7, 1788, he founded Marietta. He served as a judge of the Northwest Territory, as a brigadier general in action against the Indians, as a commissioner in negotiating Indian treaties, as U. S. surveyor-general, and as a delegate to the state constitutional convention of 1802. Not primarily a literary man, he left journals and correspondence that were published long after his death.

Journal of Gen. Rufus Putnam Kept in Northern New York . . . , Albany, N. Y., 1886.

The Memoirs of Rufus Putnam . . . , (Rowena Buell, ed.), Boston, 1903.

PYE, ERNEST (Oct. 6, 1881–July 14, 1959), educator, born in Faribault, Minn., graduated from Oberlin College in 1909 and from the Seminary in 1911. He maintained legal residence in Ohio while teaching in Turkey, 1911–25, and in Greece, 1925–32. He later lived in Winter Park, Fla. He wrote *The Biography of a Mind: Bosworth of Oberlin . . . ,* New York, [1948].

Q

QUAD, M. Pseud. See Charles B. Lewis.

QUICK, JOHN HERBERT (Oct. 23, 1861–May 10, 1925), born in Grundy County, Iowa, lived in Springfield from 1909 to 1916, while editing *Farm and Fireside.* Author of many articles and several novels, the best of which have their setting in early Iowa, he also published an autobiography: *One Man's Life . . . ,* Indianapolis, [1925]. DAB 15

QUIGLEY, MARTIN JOSEPH (May 6, 1890–), publisher, was born in Cleveland, Cuyahoga County. He attended Niagara University and Catholic University of America, worked as a reporter, 1910–13, and since 1916 has been president of Quigley Publishing Co., which issues periodicals related to motion pictures and television. He has published *Decency in Motion Pictures,* New York, 1937. WW 30

QUIN, DAN. Pseud. See Alfred Henry Lewis.

QUINAN, JOHN RUSSELL (Aug. 7, 1822–Nov. 11, 1890), physician and historian, born in Lancaster, Pa., lived in Cincinnati during his early years and attended Woodward College in that city. He also attended Marietta College. He practiced medicine in Baltimore, Md., and produced an important volume of medical history: *Medical Annals of Baltimore from 1608 to 1880 . . . ,* Baltimore, 1884.

QUINBY, GEORGE WASHINGTON (Dec. 20, 1810–Jan. 10, 1884), clergyman, was born in Westbrook, Maine. He began preaching in 1835 and was pastor of several Universalist churches in Maine before coming to Cincinnati, where he was editor of the *Star of the West* for several years and of the *Gospel Banner* from 1864 until 1884. He died in Augusta, Maine.

Marriage and Duties of the Marriage Relation . . . , Cincinnati, 1852.

The Salvation of Christ, Cincinnati, 1852.

Brief Exposition and Defence of Universalism, Cincinnati, 1854.

The Gallows, the Prison, and the Poorhouse . . . , Cincinnati, 1860.

Heaven Our Home, Cincinnati, 1860.

QUINN, DANIEL (Sept. 21, 1861–March 3, 1918), clergyman and educator, was born in Yellow Springs, Greene County. After graduating from Mt. St. Mary's College in 1883, he was ordained to the Roman Catholic priesthood. He studied and taught in Athens, Greece, for several years and received his doctorate from the University of Athens in 1893. He taught at Catholic University, 1893–98, and Antioch College, 1906–10. He published a report on Greek education in 1898 and *Helladian Vistas,* Yellow Springs, 1908. WWW 1

QUINN, JOHN (April 24, 1870–July 28, 1924), lawyer, was born in Tiffin, Seneca County. After graduating from Georgetown

University in 1893 and Harvard University in 1895, he practiced law in New York City until his death. He was widely known in the United States and Europe as a collector of rare books and modern art. He conducted a widespread correspondence with writers and artists, and when his letters, which are now in the New York Public Library, are released, they will undoubtedly provide much useful information on artistic and literary movements of his day. He was the compiler and partial author of *The Irish Home-Rule Convention . . .*, New York, 1917. WWW 1

R

RADDATZ, WILLIAM JOSEPH (Feb. 25, 1880–July 29, 1940), was born in Cleveland, Cuyahoga County. He graduated from John Carroll University in 1901. President of a printing company, he was active in Cleveland civic affairs. He collected Shakespearean materials as an avocation and published three books on Shakespeare, e.g., *Shakespeare Wrote Shakespeare,* Cleveland, [1921].

RAFF, GEORGE WERTZ (March 25, 1825–April 14, 1888), lawyer, judge, and banker, was born in Tuscarawas County. Self-educated, he was clerk of the supreme court of Stark County, 1848–50, and judge of the probate court, 1852–55. In 1887 he founded the Central Savings Bank of Canton. His publications were compiled for laymen, among whom they were found useful and enjoyed a good sale. He died in Canton.

Guide to Executors and Administrators in Ohio . . ., Cleveland, 1859.
A Manual of Pensions, Bounty and Pay . . ., Cincinnati, 1862.

RAIMOND, C. E. Pseud. See Elizabeth Robins.

RAINS, MARIE CURTIS (July 7, 1884–May 13, 1953), born in Maysville, Ky., taught for a number of years in Bond Hill Kindergarten, Cincinnati. She published two popular books for children, e.g., *Lazy Liza Lizard,* Philadelphia, [1938].

RAINS, PAUL BOYD (Jan. 22, 1895–   ), clergyman, was born in Cincinnati, Hamilton County. A graduate of Transylvania University and College of Bible, Lexington, Ky., he was ordained to the ministry of the Disciples of Christ Church in 1921. He served pastorates in several states, was a chaplain in World War II, and was director of Christian education for the Metropolitan Church Federation, St. Louis, Mo. He now lives in High Ridge, Mo. He has written many articles and pamphlets and a biography: *Francis Marion Rains,* St. Louis, Mo., 1922.

RALPH, PHILIP LEE (July 10, 1905–   ), educator, born in Antigo, Wis., has lived in Ohio since 1945, when he joined the history department of Lake Erie College for Women. He has published a study of the seventeenth-century English gentleman: *Sir Humphrey Mildmay . . .*, New Brunswick, [Conn.], 1947. DAS 3

RALSTON, CHESTER FAIRMAN (May 21, 1870–April 5, 1955), clergyman, was born in Fairview (now Jewett), Harrison County. After graduating from Oberlin College in 1892 and the Seminary in 1894, he served as a Baptist minister for 25 years in New York State and in Monroeville and Warren. He later was in the insurance business in Oberlin. He wrote *Light in the Shadows of the Valley,* Boston, [1909].

RAMSAY, JANET (April 15, 1889–Jan. 27, 1940), musician, was born in Cadiz, Harrison County, the daughter of a Presbyterian minister. She studied music in Europe and became a concert pianist and a writer on musical subjects. She died in New York City. She wrote poetry, short stories, and novels, e.g., *The Bright Threshold,* New York, 1927.

RAMSAY, WILLIAM W. (Sept. 11, 1835–April 29, 1909), clergyman, was born in Winchester, Adams County. As a Methodist minister he served several large urban churches. He was a friend of President McKinley, who is said to have called him "by far the greatest pulpit orator in America." In his later life he lectured and wrote widely on astronomy. He died in Detroit, Mich.

Sky Wonders, Boston, 1893.

RANDALL, DAVID AUSTIN (Jan. 14, 1813–June 27, 1884), clergyman, was born in

Colchester, Conn. He attended Canandaigua, N. Y., Academy. He was pastor of a Baptist church in Columbus, was corresponding secretary of the Ohio Baptist Convention, 1850–63, and chaplain of the Ohio Asylum for the Insane, 1854–56. He edited a temperance paper, the *Washingtonian,* for many years. He died in Columbus.

The Handwriting of God in Egypt, Sinai, and the Holy Land . . . , Columbus, 1862.

Ham-Mishkan, the Wonderful Tent . . . , Cincinnati, 1886.

RANDALL, EMILIUS OVIATT (Oct. 28, 1850–Dec. 18, 1919), lawyer, educator, and historian, was born in Richfield, Summit County. He graduated from Cornell University in 1874, read law, and was admitted to the Ohio bar in 1890. He was on the Ohio State University law faculty, 1893–1909, became official reporter of the Supreme Court of Ohio in 1895, and served as secretary of the Ohio Archaeological and Historical Society, 1894–1919. With Daniel J. Ryan (q.v.) he prepared a widely used five-volume history of Ohio (1912). He also published numerous historical studies, e.g., *The Serpent Mound, Adams County . . . ,* Columbus, [1905]. WWW 1

RANDALL, PAULINE BOLLARD (Nov. 19, 1852– ?), was born in Austinburg, Ashtabula County. She lived in Lockport, N. Y., and other communities where her husband, Charles W. Randall, served as superintendent of public schools. After his death she lived with a daughter in Columbus, Ga. Her published volumes of poetry include *While the Heart Is Young,* [Columbus, Ga., 1936].

RANKIN, JEREMIAH EAMES (Jan. 2, 1828–Nov. 28, 1904), clergyman, and president of Howard University, 1889–1903, spent the last year and a half of his life in Cleveland and died in that city. A Congregational minister, he published numerous sermons and several volumes of poems, some of them in Scots dialect, e.g., *The Auld Scotch Mither, and Other Poems . . . ,* Boston, 1873.

RANKIN, JOHN (Feb. 4, 1793–March 18, 1886), clergyman and abolitionist, was born in Jefferson County, Tenn. In 1814 he graduated from Washington College, Jonesboro, Tenn. While serving as pastor of two Presbyterian churches at Carlisle, Ky., he founded an antislavery society, and in 1822 moved to Ripley, where for 44 years he was a Presbyterian pastor. An active member of the antislavery movement, he was mobbed for his views many times. The letters which he addressed to his brother about 1824, dissuading him from slaveholding, were published and ran through many editions. His house in Ripley, overlooking the Ohio River, was a refuge for escaping slaves; it is now a museum. He is said to have told Mrs. Stowe the story of Eliza and her child which she used in *Uncle Tom's Cabin.* He founded the American Reform Book and Tract Society of Cincinnati, and in 1845 he founded the Free Presbyterian Church, which excluded slaveowners. Of his nine sons, seven served in the Union Army during the Civil War. He died in Ironton.

Letters on American Slavery, Addressed to Mr. Thomas Rankin, Merchant at Middlebrook, Augusta County, Va., Boston, 1833.

An Address to the Churches; In Relation to Slavery, Medina, 1836.

A Practical Work on the Covenant of Grace, Ripley, 1840.

A Short Memoir of Samuel Donnell, Esq., Cincinnati, 1854.

RANKIN, RICHARD G. (1821–June 17, 1889), son of John Rankin (q.v.), was born in Paris, Ky. He served as a captain in the 7th Ohio Cavalry, Aug., 1862–June, 1865. His death occurred in Ripley.

History of the Seventh Ohio Volunteer Cavalry, Ripley, 1881.

RANSOHOFF, JOSEPH (May 26, 1853–March 10, 1921), physician, was born in Cincinnati, Hamilton County. After graduating from the Medical College of Ohio in 1874, he studied in London. Internationally recognized as a surgeon, he practiced in Cincinnati and taught at the Medical College of Ohio. A posthumous collection of his writings was published: *Under the Northern Lights and Other Stories,* Cincinnati, 1921. WWW 1

RANSOM, JOHN CROWE (April 30, 1888–), born in Pulaski, Tenn., has been on the Kenyon College faculty since 1937 and has edited the *Kenyon Review* since 1939. A member of the faculty of Vanderbilt University from 1914 to 1937, he was a leader of the Fugitives, the Southern agrarians active at Vanderbilt in the mid-1920s. His poems have won him a reputation as one of the most distinguished of modern American poets. Even more influential, perhaps, as a critic, he supplied the name and many of the basic concepts of the dominant tendency in modern criticism in his volume *The New Criticism,* Norfolk, Conn., [1941]. TCA

RANSOM, REVERDY CASSIUS (Jan. 4, 1861–April 22, 1959), clergyman and bishop, was born in Flushing, Belmont County. He served in various ways as a lecturer, politician, and reformer; in 1903 he led a crusade against a policy syndicate in Chicago. He was the first Negro to serve on the Ohio Pardon and Parole Commission. He retired as bishop of the American Methodist Church in 1952. He died at his home near the Wilberforce campus. His writings include *The Negro; The Hope or the Despair of Christianity,* Boston, 1935.

RAPER, HOWARD RILEY (Oct. 7, 1886–), dentist, was born in Chillicothe, Ross County, the younger brother of John W. Raper (q.v.). After graduating from Indiana Dental College in 1906, he taught there until 1918, when he moved to Albuquerque, N. M. A pioneer in the use of X rays for examining the teeth, he published several technical books on dentistry and radiography and *Men against Pain; The Epic of Anesthesia,* New York, 1945. WW 28

RAPER, JOHN WOLFE (Jack) (Feb. 20, 1870–Dec. 12, 1950), journalist, was born in McArthur, Vinton County. After attending school in Chillicothe, he worked on various newspapers before joining the Cleveland *Press,* where he served for many years. His column, "Most Anything," was published under the pen name Josh Wise. After retiring in 1947, he lived in Albuquerque, N. M. He wrote plays and vaudeville sketches and published a book of sayings from his columns: *What This World Needs,* Cleveland, [1945]. WWO

RAPKING, AARON H. (April 15, 1886–), clergyman, was born near Sardis, Monroe County. After graduating from Baldwin Wallace College in 1912 and Garrett Biblical Institute in 1914, he served Methodist churches in Huntington and Haverhill and also taught at Buckhannon College, W. Va. He now lives near Lost Creek, W. Va. Since 1919 he has written a weekly message, published by the Methodist Board of Education, and he has also written a book: *Building the Kingdom of God in the Countryside,* New York, [1938].

RAPP, WILHELM (July 14, 1828–March 1, 1907), journalist, born in Germany, lived in Cincinnati, 1855–56, while editing the *Turner-Zeitung* and serving as president of the Turnerbund. As a speaker and writer, he was influential in encouraging German-Americans to oppose slavery and to support the Republican Party. He later edited *Der Wecker* in Baltimore and the *Illinois Staats-Zeitung* in Chicago. He published a collection of speeches and essays: *Erinnerungen Eines Deutsch-Amerikaners an das Alt Vaterland,* Chicago, 1890.

RAREY, JOHN SOLOMON (Dec. 6, 1827–Oct. 4, 1866), who Emerson said "turned a new leaf in civilization," was born in Groveport, Franklin County. His father, Adam Rarey, an innkeeper and a breeder of horses, gave young John encouragement and opportunity to develop his natural talent for handling colts. As a boy he earned a reputation as a horse-trainer, training his first unbroken colt at the age of twelve. Based on experience gained on his father's farm, Rarey doubted the current practice of "breaking" colts by the use of cruel methods. Gradually he evolved a new idea based on extreme kindness, the object being to convince the horse that man is his natural master and friend, then to establish confidence and finally obedience. By 1855 his ideas had crystallized into a definite system, which he then proved by experimentation with wild horses and mules in Texas. Rarey then started his career as a teacher of horsemanship, giving his first public demonstration at Columbus in 1856. To each of his pupils, under pledge of secrecy, he gave a 62-page book of instructions, *The Modern Art of Taming Wild Horses,* which he had copyrighted on Sept. 14, 1855, in an effort to protect his ideas. The title page is dated 1856. This book, presenting an entirely new system of training, completely revolutionized methods of "breaking" horses. Its humane methods are still basic. Immediately Rarey was charged with plagiarism—charges demonstrably false. But worse—over thirty piracies of the book appeared, even piracies of piracies, under various authors and misleading titles. They probably sold by the thousands. Rarey made a few attempts to stem the tide, but soon gave up. About this time R. A. Goodenough, a Toronto merchant, "saw that there was money to be made out of the Rarey system," and persuaded Rarey to form a partnership with him. After a successful visit to Canadian military authorities, Rarey and Goodenough arrived in England on Nov. 29, 1857, with excellent letters of introduction. But in Aug., 1858, Goodenough returned home, "not having been profitable to Rarey." Rarey's immediate success in England provoked some skepticism; occasional criticism appeared in the press. Finally a letter in the London *Morning Post* of March 2, 1858, challenged Rarey to tackle Cruiser, "a noble creature, but fiend incarnate," owned by Lord Dorchester. Rarey accepted the dramatic challenge. After an exhibition of tremendous courage, Cruiser was completely subdued within three hours. The victory was impressive; Rarey became "the great Lion of the London season," and gave no fewer than four command performances before Queen Victoria. Much of Rarey's success in England was due to the interest taken in him by Henry Hall Dixon. It was he who convinced the famous Messrs. Tattersall that general adoption of Rarey's system "would confer invaluable benefit on . . . the great horse interest," and it was he who organized the first subscription of 5,000 guineas, a class of pupils headed by the Queen and Prince Consort and made up almost entirely of members of the aristocracy. But again in an effort to protect his interests Rarey unwittingly ran into trouble. His pupils were pledged to secrecy, but when he arranged for his book to be copyrighted in England, his publisher issued a regular trade edition, whereupon Rarey immediately released his pupils from their pledges. This incident gave Dixon a chance to edit a new edition of *The Modern Art,* which was badly needed. The original was far from satisfactory. The London 1858 edition, as enlarged by Dixon, was competently illustrated, and clearly explained Rarey's principles. Later Rarey gave demonstrations throughout the British Isles, and then he toured France, Russia, Sweden, Norway, Turkey, Egypt, and Arabia. On May 16, 1860, he received from the Royal Society for the Prevention of Cruelty to Animals a gold medal "for the great services he had rendered to humanity." It is estimated that his European tour netted Rarey over $100,000. When Rarey returned to America in 1860, he was acclaimed as a national hero and was even suggested for the Presidency. In 1862 he rendered services to the Army of the Potomac. After a series of exhibitions in many American cities, Rarey suffered a stroke of paralysis in Dec., 1865. He died in Cleveland. Dixon described him as "of middle height, and well proportioned figure, wiry and active rather than muscular—his complexion effeminately fair . . . altogether his appearance and manners are eminently gentlemanly."

Robert W. Henderson

The Modern Art of Taming Wild Horses, Columbus, 1856.

RATHBORNE, ST. GEORGE HENRY (Dec. 26, 1854–Dec. 16, 1938), born in Covington, Ky., spent part of his boyhood in Cincinnati and attended the public schools of that city. A highly prolific writer of dime novels and books for boys, he turned out over 300 titles under various pen names: Aleck Forbes, Duke Duncan, Harrison Adams, Harry St. George, Marline Manly, Hugh Allen, Charles L. Wrenn, John M. Foster, Doctor Mark Merrick, and others.

RATTERMANN, HEINRICH ARMIN (Oct. 14, 1832–Jan. 6, 1923), self-educated historian and man of letters, was born near Osnabrück, Germany. He arrived in Cincinnati with his parents in 1846, and though he was forced to go to work as a common laborer he found something besides sheer drudgery in Cincinnati—he found opportunity to study the many books to which he had free access, and he made the most of it. Also, a gifted musician he found congenial and often influential friends. In 1850, the year in which his father died and the boy became the sole support of his mother and two younger children, he was one of the organizers of the famous German singing society, the Sangerbund; and in 1857 he became a charter member of the Männechor as well as the Orpheus in 1858. A skilled rhymer, he wrote much verse in German and English, work distinguished by the production of an occasional gem. Much of his verse was published under the pen name Hugo Reimmund. In 1858 he founded the German Mutual Fire Insurance Company of Cincinnati and Hamilton County, which became one of the most successful institutions of its kind in the United States. Though he never acquired great wealth, his income was quite adequate to support his large family in comfort and to permit him the avocations close to his heart. He acquired a notable library, engaged in historical research which often required him to make extensive trips, and became a prolific writer. Among the several librettos for operas performed in Cincinnati that he wrote were *The Poacher, Oberon, The Interrupted Sacrifice,* and *Die Fehme im Froschreiche* with music by a local composer. From 1874 until its suspension in 1887 he was editor of the monthly historical journal *Der Deutsche Pionier,* esteemed as an invaluable source for the history of the German element in the United States. In 1906 he began to publish a compilation of selections from his work. Only eleven of the projected eighteen volumes had been published when the work was discontinued because of the condition of his health. During the last years of his life he was both deaf and blind. He died in Cincinnati at the age of 91.

Ernest J. Wessen

Geschichte des Grossen Amerikanischen Westens . . . , Cincinnati, 1875.
General Johann Andreas Wagener . . . , Cincinnati, 1877.
Early Music in Cincinnati. An Essay . . . , Cincinnati, 1879.
Geschichte der Deutschen Gemeinde der Hoffnungsvollen Kirch, in Boone County, Kentucky, Cincinnati, 1880.
Andreas Gross . . . , Cincinnati, 1883.
Adolph Strauch . . . , Cincinnati, 1884.
Anna Ottendorfer . . . , Cincinnati, 1885.
Karl August Varnhagen von Ense . . . , Cincinnati, 1885.
Zur Feier der Goldenen Hochzeit von Gustav und Sophie Körner, Cincinnati, 1886.
Aktenmässige Geschichte der Temperens—Gesetzgebung im Staate Ohio, Cincinnati, 1889.
Der Anregende Einfluss der Deutschen auf die Entdeckung Neuen Welt . . . , Cincinnati, 1892.
Albrecht Dürer . . . , Cincinnati, 1896.
Gustav Körner . . . , Cincinnati, 1902.
Johann Bernhard Stallo . . . , Cincinnati, 1902.
Die Pseudo-Unabhängigkeits-Erklärung vom Mecklenburg County, N. C. . . . , Philadelphia, [1904?].
Nord-Amerikanische Vögel in Liedern . . . , Cincinnati, 1904.
Adolph Zipperlen . . . , Cincinnati, 1905.
Gesammelte Ausgewählte Werke, 11 vols., Cincinnati, 1906–12.
Letters of Heinrich Armin Rattermann to the German American Poet-Priest, John E. Rothensteiner, Joliet, 1938.

RAWSON, CLAYTON (1906–), was born in Elyria, Lorain County. In 1928 he graduated from Ohio State University, where he edited the *Sun Dial;* the following year he studied at Chicago Art Institute. In 1932 he moved to New York to work as an illustrator; he has also worked in an editorial capacity for various publishers. He lives in Mamaroneck, N. Y. He has written several mystery novels, some under his own name and some under the pen name Stuart Towne, e.g., *Death Out of Thin Air,* New York, [1941].

RAWSON, JACK. Pseud. See Frank L. Hower.

RAY, E. S. (July 16, 1865–Nov. 17, 1932), physician, was born in Byers, Jackson County. After attending National Normal University, Lebanon, he taught school in Madison and Jackson Counties to finance his medical education. He graduated from Jefferson Medical College, Philadelphia, and practiced in Hamden for forty years. He published many articles advocating temperance and a novel: *The Song of the Pines,* Boston, 1909.

RAY, JOSEPH (Nov. 25, 1807–April 17, 1856), physician and educator, was born in West Liberty, Va. Son of Quaker parents, he began teaching at the age of sixteen to finance his education. Between intervals of teaching he attended Ohio University, Franklin College, and Ohio Medical College in Cincinnati. He came to Cincinnati in 1829, practiced medicine there, 1832–34, and taught at Woodward High School, 1831–51, where he served as principal from 1851 until his death. He wrote several arithmetics and algebra textbooks that were very widely used. The titles below are pamphlets defending his texts against unfavorable reviewers.

Calumny Refuted . . . , [Cincinnati, 1855].
An Exposure of the Falsehood of "Justice," [Cincinnati, 1855].

RAYMOND, DANIEL (1786–1849?), born in New Haven, Conn., practiced law in Baltimore, where he produced the work for which he is chiefly remembered: *Thoughts on Political Economy,* Baltimore, 1820, an attempt to devise economic theories suited to the New World. Details concerning his later years are unavailable, but he apparently moved to Cincinnati around 1840.

RAYMOND, ROSSITER WORTHINGTON (April 27, 1840–Dec. 31, 1918), mining engineer and lawyer, was born in Cincinnati, Hamilton County, but he spent most of his boyhood in Brooklyn, N. Y., where his father was a school principal. After studying three years in Germany, he served in the army, 1861–64, and then became a consulting mining engineer. While U. S. commissioner of mining statistics, 1868–76, he issued annual reports. He studied law, was admitted to the bar in 1898, and was generally considered an expert on mining law. He was active in Plymouth Church and its Sunday school; when Henry Ward Beecher died in 1887, he was offered the pastorate but declined. He published numerous technical papers and other works, memorials to various associates, and many stories for children. His only novel, *Brave Hearts,* was published under the pen name Robertson Gray.

The Christmas Angel, New York, 1869.
The Children's Week, New York, 1871.

Mines and Mining of the Rocky Mountains, the Inland Basin, and the Pacific Slope, New York, 1871.
Mines, Mills, and Furnaces of the Pacific States and Territories . . . , New York, 1871.
Brave Hearts. An American Novel, New York, 1873.
Mining Industry of the Rocky Mountains . . . , New York, 1874.
The Man in the Moon, and Other People, New York, 1875.
Treasures from Fairy Land, (with Grace Greenwood [Sarah Jane Lippincott]), New York, [1879].
Camp and Cabin: Sketches of Life and Travel in the West, New York, 1880.
The Merry-Go-Round; Stories for Boys and Girls, New York, 1880.
Evolution of Animal Life, Boston, 1889.
Alfred Raymond . . . , [New York?, 1901?].
Peter Cooper, Boston, [1901].
The Feast of Lights . . . , [Norwood, Mass.], 1910.
Christus Consolator, and Other Poems, New York, [1916].

READ, MATTHEW CANFIELD (Aug. 21, 1823–1902), educator and lawyer, was born in Williamsfield, Ashtabula County. When he was twelve, his family moved to Mecca, Trumbull County. He attended district schools and Grand River Institute, showing from an early age an interest in botany and geology. After graduating from Western Reserve College in 1848, he taught school in Columbus and Gustavus and read law in Jefferson. He edited the *Family Visitor* at Hudson, 1851–53, practiced law in Summit County, and served as general relief agent in the Sanitary Commission during the Civil War. After the war he was a deputy internal revenue collector and an assistant geologist with the Geological Survey. He wrote a great many articles and reports on scientific subjects.

Archaeology of Ohio, Cleveland, [1888].

READ, OPIE POPE (Dec. 22, 1852–Nov. 2, 1939), author of many novels and humorous books, born in Nashville, Tenn., was in Cleveland from 1881 to 1883 while on the staff of the *Leader.* He was best known as the Arkansas Traveler.

READ, THOMAS BUCHANAN (March 12, 1822–May 11, 1872), artist and poet, was born in Chester County, Pa. Apprenticed to a tailor after his father died, he ran away and went to Pittsburgh and then to Cincinnati by flatboat in 1837. In Cincinnati he worked rolling cigars and painting signs. He was hired by Shobal Vail Clevenger to inscribe tombstones and through this association learned the rudiments of sculpture. He wrote verse for the *Times* and the *Chronicle* and for a time wandered through Ohio as an itinerant portrait painter. With the assistance of Nicholas Longworth, he established a studio in Cincinnati and attracted considerable notice through a painting of William Henry Harrison, but in 1841 he returned East and opened a studio in Boston. In 1846 he moved to Philadelphia, and though he lived in Europe and in Cincinnati for brief periods, Philadelphia remained his permanent residence for the remainder of his life. He frequently visited Cincinnati as the guest of his brother-in-law, Cyrus Garrett, a manufacturer of plows. His most famous work, "Sheridan's Ride," was written in Cincinnati on the afternoon of Oct. 31, 1864, and was delivered that evening in Pike's Opera House by James E. Murdoch (q.v.). He was a prolific poet, publishing at least twenty volumes, and his sentimental, melodramatic verse was highly admired during his lifetime.

REAM, LAURA (1828–1913), journalist, was born in Lebanon, Warren County. Her parents moved to Indianapolis, Ind., when she was a child, and she spent her life in that city. She was a correspondent for the Cincinnati *Daily Commercial.* The book listed below was apparently written as a piece of railroad promotional literature.

History of a Trip to the Great Saginaw Valley . . . , Indianapolis, 1871.

REAM, MICHAEL VALENTINE (Oct. 4, 1852–Feb. 17, 1935), lawyer and judge, was born in Shanesville, Tuscarawas County. After graduating from University of Wooster in 1877, he read law and was admitted to the bar in 1879. He practiced in New Philadelphia and served as judge of the probate court, 1902–06. Under the pen name Valmaer he wrote a satire, *Lawyer's Code of Ethics . . . ,* St. Louis, Mo., 1901.

REBER, GEORGE (1809–May 18, 1875), lawyer, was born in Lancaster, Fairfield County. He settled in Sandusky in 1838 and thereafter practiced law in that city. His *Therapeutae* is described in a county history as a "book of an infidel nature."

Therapeutae. St. John Never in Asia Minor . . . , [New York, 1872].
The Christ of Paul . . . , New York, 1876.

RECK, WALDO EMERSON (Dec. 28, 1903–), was born in Gettysburg, Darke County.

He graduated from Wittenberg College in 1926, was director of public relations and professor of journalism, Midland College, 1926–40, was director of public relations, Cornell University, 1940–48, and has been vice president of Wittenberg University since 1948. He has published *Public Relations . . .*, New York, 1946. WW 30

RECKLESS, WALTER CADE (Jan. 19, 1899–), sociologist, born in Philadelphia, Pa., has been on the faculty of Ohio State University since 1940. He has published sociology textbooks and *Vice in Chicago*, Chicago, [1933]. WW 30

REDHEAD, ALICE CRAIG (July 30, 1896–), was born in Napoleon, Henry County. She attended Western Reserve University. Her stories, poems, and articles have appeared in numerous periodicals, and she has published a long narrative poem: *The Last Battalion*, Cincinnati, 1944.

REDINGER, RUBY V. (April 3, 1915–), educator, was born in Cleveland, Cuyahoga County. She graduated from Fenn College in 1936 and Western Reserve University (Ph.D.) in 1940. She taught English and philosophy at Fenn College, 1941–51, and is now on the faculty of Baldwin-Wallace College. Besides articles and book reviews, she has written a novel with a college campus as its background: *The Golden Net*, New York, [1948].

REED, CHARLES ALFRED LEE (July 9, 1856–Aug. 28, 1928), physician and educator, born at Wolf Lake, Ind., spent the greater part of his life in Cincinnati. After graduating from Cincinnati College of Medicine and Surgery in 1874, he practiced in Cincinnati and taught at Cincinnati College of Medicine and Surgery, 1882–96, and the University of Cincinnati, 1902–17. Besides the sociological study and novel listed below, his writings include many articles in magazines and newspapers and several medical books.

Christian Science . . ., Cincinnati, 1898.
The First Estate, Boston, 1927.

REED, FANNIE KIMBALL (1870–1950), educator, was born in North Fairfield, Huron County. She studied music in France, Italy, and Germany, and afterward taught in the schools of Cleveland and Norwalk. She died in North Fairfield.

A Chopin Nocturne, and Other Sketches, Cleveland, 1900.

REED, HENRY (Nov. 25, 1809–Aug. 21, 1892), journalist, was born in Sharon, Conn. He worked on newspapers in Toledo and other Ohio communities. After serving on the *Ohio State Journal* and the Cincinnati *Commercial*, he and his brother Samuel R. Reed founded the Cincinnati *Penny Post*, a venture which proved unsuccessful. During the Civil War he lectured and wrote in favor of the toleration of slavery and secession. He was on the staff of the Cincinnati *Enquirer* for a number of years before retiring to San Francisco, Calif., where his death occurred.

The Secession of the Whole South an Existing Fact . . ., [Cincinnati, 1861].
For the People, the Public Debt: What to Do with It, Cincinnati, [1868].

REED, JAMES A. (Nov. 9, 1861–Sept. 8, 1944), U. S. Senator from Missouri, 1911–19, was born near Mansfield, Richland County. In 1864 his parents moved to Iowa, where he grew up. In 1887, after being admitted to the Iowa bar, he moved to Kansas City, Mo., where he practiced law. He published some addresses and *The Rape of Temperance*, New York, 1931. WWW 2

REED, LUELLA (Sept. 24, 1895–), was born in Indiana but has lived in Dayton since 1915. She has published a number of short stories and a novel: *Sari Bron*, Boston, [1945].

REED, ORVILLE SIBBITT (Oct. 17, 1843–Sept. 27, 1924), clergyman and educator, was born in New Philadelphia, Tuscarawas County. A graduate of McNeely Normal School, Hopedale, he was a schoolteacher and a Disciples of Christ minister in Pennsylvania, Indiana, and Colorado. He died in Pueblo, Colo. His writings include *Cartaphilus; Or, the Wandering Jew . . .*, Cincinnati, 1902.

REED, PETER FISHE (May 5, 1819–1887), was born in South Boston, Mass. Left an orphan at the age of nine, he became an itinerant house and sign painter. He arrived in Cincinnati about 1840 and apparently resided there a longer time than anywhere else. According to William H. Venable, he was a "man of weird and delicate fancy, almost a genius, but lacking in will-power and practical qualities—a painter, poet and romancer [who] wrote for the *Genius of the West* some impressive verses and several pieces of remarkable insight and subtlety." He wrote for the Cincinnati *Weekly Columbian* in 1846 and 1847 under the pen name Viva Mona. In the early 1850s he went to Vernon, Ind., where he farmed for several years; after losing his farm he moved on to Indianapolis. He returned to Cincinnati about 1864, went to Chicago in 1867, and then moved to Santa Barbara, Calif., and finally to Cedar Rapids, Iowa, where he spent the remainder of his life.

Incidents of the War; Or, the Romance and Realities of Soldier Life, [Indianapolis, 1862].

The Voices of the Wind, and Other Poems, Chicago, 1868.

Beyond the Snow: History of Trim's Adventures in Nordlichtschein, Chicago, 1873.

REED, SARAH ANN (March 16, 1838–Jan. 27, 1934), was born in Ashtabula, Ashtabula County. She was educated in Erie, Pa., and spent most of her life in that city, where she will be long remembered for her philanthropies. She published several books, e.g., *A Romance of Arlington House,* Boston, [1908].

REED, VERNER ZEVOLA (Oct. 13, 1863–April 21, 1919), was born in Richland County. He engaged in mining, oil, banking, and ranching in Colorado, Wyoming, and other states. He made an intensive study of American Indian myths and folklore. He wrote numerous articles for periodicals.

Lo-To-Kah, New York, 1897.

Tales of the Sunland, New York, 1897.

Adobeland Stories, Boston, 1899.

The Soul of Paris, and Other Essays, New York, 1913.

REEDER, ALBERT (Feb. 27, 1839–March 9, 1920), was born and spent his life in South Charleston, Clark County. He served as justice of the peace in that community for many years. He wrote *Sketches of South Charleston, Ohio . . . ,* [Columbus, 1910].

REEDER, MYRTLE L. (Dec. 12, 1891–), was born in Oskaloosa, Ill. She has lived in Ohio for the past thirty years. Now Mrs. Myrtle Troutt, she is active in Columbus and Ohio poetry societies and has also written a number of songs. Her poems have appeared in Columbus newspapers and other periodicals, and she has published a collection: *Hills of Clay,* Columbus, [1942].

REEDER, RUDOLPH REX (Jan. 5, 1859–Oct. 13, 1934), social worker, was born in Lebanon, Warren County. He graduated from Illinois State Normal University in 1895 and Columbia University (Ph.D.) in 1900. He became superintendent of N. Y. State Orphanage in 1900. He lectured on educational topics and published books and pamphlets on education, e.g., *Training Youth for the New Social Order,* Yellow Springs, 1933. WW 11

REEMELIN, CHARLES (Carl Gustav Rümelin) (May 19, 1814–Jan. 16, 1891), was born in the free city of Heilbronn, Württemberg, Germany, where he was reared in the lingering bitterness of his people against the despotic transfer of their old free city to the kingdom of Württemberg. Though his father was a prosperous wholesale grocer, the boy's home life was an unhappy one. He came to America in 1832, arriving at Cincinnati the following year. Here he was uncommonly prosperous in the grocery business; within four years after his arrival he had acquired the *Volksblatt,* and in 1843 he retired from the grocery business to his farm. He then began the study of law and in 1848 was admitted to the bar. In 1844 he was elected to the lower house of the General Assembly and in 1846 to the Senate. He was a member of the Constitutional Convention of 1850. Though a very active Democrat, his early boyhood experiences had made him too radical to become a leader in his party. He served his state with distinction in various appointive offices. Tiring of politics he retired again to his farm near Cincinnati, where he spent the rest of his days contributing enlightening articles to historical, agricultural, and other periodicals.

Marie Dickoré

The Vine-Dresser's Manual, an Illustrated Treatise on Vineyards and Wine-Making, New York, 1855.

Der Puritaner in China, Cincinnati, 1867.

The Wine-Maker's Manual, New York, 1868.

Treatise on Politics as a Science, Cincinnati, 1875.

A Critical Review of American Politics, Cincinnati, 1881.

Historical Sketch of Greene Township, Hamilton County . . . , Cincinnati, 1882.

Geschichtliche Skizze Eines Amerikanischen Township, Cincinnati, 1887.

Life of Charles Reemelin, in German: Carl Gustav Rümelin, from 1814–1892: Written by Himself, Cincinnati, 1892.

REESE, LLOYD W. (June 20, 1897–), educator, was born in Vaughnsville, Putnam County. A graduate of Ohio Northern University, he taught in Vaughnsville and Gomer, was a school superintendent in Fayette and Geauga Counties, and served in the Ohio Department of Education and the Veterans' Administration. He edited the *High School Teacher* for ten years and also wrote nearly a hundred radio plays. He is now an educational advisor in Saigon. His wife, Marie Reese (July 22, 1901–May 23, 1952), was born in Gomer, Allen County, and also graduated from Ohio Northern. They collaborated in writing *The Parade of the Presidents . . .* , Columbus, 1940.

REESE, MARIE. See Lloyd W. Reese.

REEVE, JAMES KNAPP (May 19, 1856–Oct. 25, 1933), publisher, was born in Hancock, N. Y. He established a publishing house at Franklin around 1892, and in partnership with Seymour S. Tibbals (q.v.) he founded *The Editor* there in 1895. Tibbals retired from the firm in 1900, and Reeve later moved the publication to Deposit, N. J. He was manager of the Outing Publishing Company, 1904–09, and afterward lived in Franklin for the rest of his life. Besides the titles below, he published several textbooks and manuals for writers. His daughter, Agnes Marie Reeve, conducted a writers' service in Franklin for a number of years and published a textbook on short-story writing.

Vawder's Understudy . . . , New York, 1896.

The Three Richard Whalens: A Story of Adventure, New York, 1897.

REEVE, SIDNEY ARMOR (March 27, 1866–June 12, 1941), engineer, was born in Dayton, Montgomery County. He graduated from Sheffield Scientific School in 1885. He was engaged in engineering, 1887–94, and taught at Worcester Polytechnic Institute, 1896–1906. He was a consulting mechanical engineer in New York City from 1908 until his retirement in 1931. He wrote a number of technical studies and other books, e.g., *The Natural Laws of Social Convulsion,* New York, [1933]. WWW 1

REEVES, MRS. AL. See Grace H. Sourek.

REEVES, ARTHUR MIDDLETON (Oct. 7, 1856–Feb. 25, 1891), was born in Cincinnati, Hamilton County. After the Civil War he attended the Friends Academy, Richmond, Ind. After traveling extensively in the United States and Europe, he learned the printer's trade and established the Richmond *Palladium.* After making a brilliant scholastic record, he graduated from Cornell University in 1878. He acquired an excellent knowledge of several languages, and especially directed his enthusiasm to Norse. He translated various sagas and stories from Old Norse. The preparation and publication of *The Finding of Wineland the Good* was his outstanding achievement.

The Finding of Wineland the Good; The History of the Icelandic Discovery of America . . . , London, 1890.

Jan, a Short Story, Chicago, 1892.

REGESTER, SEELEY. Pseud. See Metta V. F. Victor.

REICHERT, VICTOR EMANUEL (March 17, 1897–), rabbi, born in Brooklyn, N. Y., taught English at the University of Cincinnati, 1921–24, was ordained in 1926, and has since been at Rockdale Avenue Temple. Besides essays and books on the Jewish religion, he has published *The Tower of David, and Other Poems,* [Cincinnati, 1946]. WWMW 54

REID, ALEXANDER M. (April 20, 1827–March 24, 1918), clergyman, was born in Beaver County, Pa. He graduated from Jefferson College in 1849, traveled in Europe, and was licensed as a Presbyterian minister in 1857. In 1857 he became principal of a Female Seminary founded by Charles C. Beatty in Steubenville, and in 1866 he purchased the school. He supplied numerous Presbyterian churches in the vicinity of Steubenville, and a number of his sermons were printed.

Biographical Sketch of Mrs. Hetty Elizabeth Beatty, New York, 1883.

REID, DOROTHY E. (Jan. 12, 1900–), was born in Bucyrus, Crawford County. She graduated from Ohio State University in 1925. In 1933 she married Herman A. Miller, then a professor at Ohio State University. She has served as editor of *Current Events,* national school newspaper, since 1932, and has written numerous booklets used in schools. She now lives in Middletown, Conn. Her poems, which appeared in various national magazines, were collected in *Coach into Pumpkin,* New Haven, [Conn.], 1925.

REID, HIRAM ALVIN (1834–1906), journalist, was born in New Lisbon, Columbiana County. After working on newspapers in various cities, he died in Pasadena, Calif.

Wild Fire. A Few Eccentric Poems . . . , Cleveland, 1854.

REID, JAMES HALLECK (April 14, 1862–May 22, 1920), father of the screen star Wallace Reid, was born in Cedarville, Greene County, and spent his boyhood there and in Cincinnati, where his parents moved around 1872. He was a theatrical producer, an actor in plays and motion pictures, and a prolific playwright. He wrote a number of melodramas in the 1880s and 1890s which apparently were not published. One of his plays, *The Night before Christmas,* has its setting in Cedarville. He is said to have written more than 200 plays, e.g., *The Confession . . . ,* New York, 1921.

REID, THOMAS MAYNE (April 4, 1818–Oct. 22, 1883), prolific writer of novels, plays, and poetry, was born in Ballyroney, Ireland. He served in the Mexican War, and on leaving the army he lived with Donn Piatt (q.v.) at Mac-o-chee, 1848–49. While there, he wrote *The Rifle Rangers,* London, 1850.

REID, WHITELAW (Oct. 27, 1837–Dec. 15, 1912), journalist, was born near Xenia, Greene County. After attending Xenia Academy, he graduated from Miami University in 1856. He served for a year as superintendent of schools in South Charleston and edited the Xenia *News* for two years. In 1861 he was Columbus correspondent of the Cincinnati *Times,* reporting the sessions of the state legislature. As correspondent of the Cincinnati *Gazette,* he wrote under the pen name Agate and became nationally known for the keenness with which he reported both military and political events. After the Civil War he made two tours of the South, worked on his history of Ohio's participation in the war, and served briefly as city editor of the Cincinnati *Gazette.* In 1868 he joined the staff of the New York *Tribune,* became managing editor, and was generally recognized as Horace Greeley's second-in-command. After Greeley's death in 1872, he was chosen editor-in-chief. He built the *Tribune* into one of the most influential newspapers in the country. He was candidate for vice-president on the unsuccessful Republican ticket in 1892, and in 1905 he was appointed ambassador to the Court of St. James. He died in London. Numerous separate speeches were published in addition to the titles below.

After the War: A Southern Tour . . . , Cincinnati, 1866.
Ohio in the War . . . , 2 vols., Cincinnati, 1868.
Horace Greeley, New York, 1879.
Problems of Expansion, as Considered in Papers and Addresses, New York, 1900.
How the United States Faced Its Educational Problem, London, 1906.
The Rise of the United States, London, 1906.
London Commemorations . . . , London, 1909.
The Scot in America and the Ulster Scot . . . , London, 1912.
American and English Studies . . . , 2 vols., New York, 1913.

REIGHARD, FRANK H. (Oct. 8, 1867–), was born near Delta, Fulton County. He graduated from Fayette Normal School in 1887 and Ohio Northern University in 1892. He taught school, served several terms in the state legislature, and published a newspaper in Wauseon, where he now lives. He also wrote and edited *A Standard History of Fulton County . . . ,* 2 vols., Chicago, 1920.

REIMMUND, HUGO. Pseud. See Heinrich A. Rattermann.

REINI, GRACE. Pseud. See Grace M. R. Finlayson.

REISENDEN. Pseud. See William E. Hathaway.

REISER, OLIVER LESLIE (Nov. 15, 1895–), educator, was born in Columbus, Franklin County. A graduate of Ohio State University (A.B., 1921; Ph.D., 1924), he has taught philosophy at the University of Pittsburgh since 1926. He has published a number of articles and books, most of them treating the relationships between philosophy and science, e.g., *A New Earth and a New Humanity,* New York, 1942. WW 30

REMENYI, JOSEPH (Dec. 1, 1892–Sept. 25, 1956), educator, born in Pozsony, Hungary, came to America in 1914, and was on the faculty of Western Reserve University from 1929 until his death. He published many critical and literary essays in Hungarian and English, e.g., *Hungarian Literature,* [Washington, 1946?]. WWMW 49

REMPEL, RUTH FOGLE WOOSTER (Mrs. Dietrich G.), a lifelong resident of Summit County, is a graduate of Akron Law School, an artist, and a musician. Wife of an Akron toy manufacturer, she has published a book for children: *Deegie and the Fairy Princess,* Akron, 1949.

REMSBURG, JOHN ELEAZER (Jan. 7, 1848–Sept. 23, 1919), reformer, was born in Fremont, Sandusky County. Toward the end of the Civil War he served a few months in the army and then taught school for fifteen years. He became one of the more successful lecturers who capitalized on the vogue of iconoclastic ideas between 1880 and 1910. His books were of a most ephemeral character and were produced to sell to his enthusiastic audiences of "free thinkers." No doubt many have escaped cataloguers. He died in California.

Thomas Paine, the Apostle of Religious and Political Liberty, Boston, 1880.
The Image Breaker, [New York], 1882.
Paine and Wesley, Atchison, Kan., 1882.
False Claims of the Church, New York, [1883].
Bible Morals. Twenty Crimes and Vices Sanctioned by Scripture . . . , New York, [1885].
Sabbath Breaking, New York, [1885].
The Fathers of Our Republic . . . , Boston, 1887.
Abraham Lincoln: Was He a Christian?, New York, [1893].
Was Washington Christian?, New York, [1899].
The Decline of Faith, New York, [18- ?].
Protestant Intolerance, New York, [18- ?].
Jefferson an Unbeliever, New York, [1900?].
The Bible, New York, [1903].
Six Historic Americans . . . , New York, [1906].
Chicago Belle, New York, 1907.
The Christ, New York, 1909.
The Creed of Christ, [New York, 1910?].
Exempting the Churches, New York, 1916.
Piety and the Slave Trade, [New York, 191- ?].

RENICK, MARION LEWIS (1905–), was born in Springfield, Clark County. She graduated from Wittenberg College in 1926. She edited *My Weekly Reader,* 1945–51, and in 1951 joined the Ohio School of the Air as a script supervisor and broadcaster. She also teaches radio writing at Ohio State University. She has written at least twenty books for children, most of them related to athletics, e.g., *Tommy Carries the Ball,* New York, [1940], and *Champion Caddy,* New York, 1943.

RENICK, WILLIAM (Nov. 12, 1804–May 17, 1881), was born in Chillicothe, Ross County. His family were the founders of the beef-cattle industry in the United States. In 1804–05 his father, George, was the first to drive a herd of fat cattle over the Alleghenies to the Eastern market. In 1833 the Renicks organized a group of men in Ohio and Kentucky to buy from England the best of the improved cattle of that country. In 1853 William bought the first drove of cattle to be driven north from Texas. Although his *Memoirs* contains some fine articles on Ohio history, the book is especially valuable as a basic source on the history of the cattle trade in America.

Memoirs, Correspondence and Reminiscences . . . , Circleville, 1880.

RENNELSON, CLARA H. MORSE (Jan. 15, 1845– ?), was born in Norwalk, Huron County. After marrying Rev. W. H. Rennelson, she lived in Brooklyn, N. Y. No other biographical details have been discovered.

Social Heroism, Toronto, 1878.
Kinsman All. A Story for Youth and Age, Philadelphia, [1899].

RENNICK, SUSAN (July 14, 1845–Oct. 26, 1927), educator, was born in Liverpool, England, but her parents brought her to Cincinnati when she was four years old, and she spent her life in that city. She taught in the city schools for 55 years. She published a book of inspirational biographies: *Buckeye Boys Who Have Become Presidents,* Chicago, [1911].

RENNIE, YSABEL FISK (Mrs. Robert A.) (May 9, 1918–), born in Los Angeles, has lived in Columbus for about twelve years. Since moving to Ohio, she has written a novel about copper mining, *The Blue Chip;* earlier, she published a history of modern Argentina: *The Argentine Republic,* New York, 1945. WWAW 1

RENWOOD, BARRY. Pseud. See Marshall R. Hall.

RESTON, JAMES BARRETT (Nov. 3, 1909–), journalist, was born in Clydebank, Scotland. His family came to Dayton when he was a year old, but returned to Britain because of illness in the family. In 1920 they returned to Dayton, where he graduated from Oakwood High School in 1927. In his senior year he won the Ohio State high school golf championship. After graduating from the University of Illinois in 1932, he was sports editor of the Springfield *News,* 1932–33, publicity agent for Ohio State University Athletic Association, 1933–34, and publicity director for the Cincinnati Reds, 1934. In 1934 he joined the Associated Press and in 1939 the staff of the New York *Times.* In 1941 he joined the *Times* Washington Bureau and has served as its chief since 1953. He has been awarded Pulitzer Prizes for journalism in 1945 and in 1957. Four years (1937–41) in England furnished the background for his first book: *Prelude to Victory,* New York, 1942. WW 30

RETTIG, JOHN (Sept. 5, 1858–May 1, 1932), artist, was born in Cincinnati, Hamilton County. He attended Cincinnati schools and St. Joseph College. As a young man he painted the drop curtain for the opera house, then the largest curtain in use in the world. In 1886 he staged the first of the outdoor spectacles which made him known in his native city: *The Fall of Babylon.* He wrote and designed a number of other pageants, most of them sponsored by the Order of the Cincinnati. His wife, May Milligan Rettig, also an artist, helped compile data for the spectacles. In 1906 Rettig went to Holland, where he remained for several years and where his most successful paintings were produced. At the time of his death in Cincinnati, his pageant in honor of St. Anthony of Padua and St. Elizabeth of Hungary was in progress at Music Hall.

The Fall of Babylon . . . , [Cincinnati], 1887.

Rome under Nero . . . , Cincinnati, 1887.

"Rhodopis." A Spectacular Play . . . , [Cincinnati, 1888].

Moses; Or, the Bondage of Egypt . . . , Cincinnati, 1890.

The Sublime, Historical Bible Spectacle, the Fall of Nineveh . . . , [Buffalo], 1892.

REVERE, PAUL A. (Sept. 25, 1872–Nov. 23, 1951), was born in New Hampshire. A resident of Cleveland before and after the Spanish-American War, he served in the 10th O.V.I. from July, 1898, to March, 1899. He was a journalist after his military service, and at the time of his death in Gloucester, Mass., was an antique dealer.

Boys of '98. A History of the Tenth Regiment . . . , [Augusta, Ga.], 1899.

Cleveland in the War with Spain, Cleveland, 1900.

REX, NEPTUNE. Pseud. See John J. Makin.

REYNOLDS, BARBARA LEONARD (June 12, 1915–), was born in Milwaukee, Wis., but from 1943 to 1951 lived in Yellow Springs, where her husband, Earle L. Reynolds, was associated with Fels Institute. She now lives in Hawaii. She has published numerous magazine articles and a mystery novel laid in Glen Falls, an imaginary town near Dayton: *Alias for Death,* New York, [1950].

REYNOLDS, JEREMIAH N. (1799–1858), was born in Cumberland County, Pa. He escaped greatness and permanent fame only by a very narrow margin. He knew the leading American statesmen of his time, including the Presidents, and was an intimate of the one man besides Christopher Columbus who is recognized as the discoverer of a new continent. "He has written much, and well," said Edgar Allan Poe, who paid him a further compliment by using Reynolds' writing as a source for his own. His story of a legendary white whale, Mocha Dick, was undoubtedly known to Herman Melville. For years his name made news, and even his enemies conceded that he was the man most directly responsible for the great United States Exploring Expedition of 1838–42. He was a successful lecturer on the hollow earth theory of John Cleves Symmes (q.v.), on the desirability of exploration in the South Seas, and on the infallibility of the Whig Party. He was an adventurer, too, with a stirring but unverified record of melodramatic action within the Arctic Circle and in the territory of the Araucanian Indians. He accompanied his mother and stepfather, Job Jefferis, to Clinton County in 1808. He later wrote of himself, in his boyhood, as a "dweller in the western forests," where he was forced to be "self-relying." Attired in leather breeches and a linsey wamus, he worked his way through the subscription schools taught by Robert Way and then became a teacher himself. He attended Ohio University with Robert Way in 1819, and the following year taught school at the old Court House in Wilmington. He again entered Ohio University, but found it necessary to leave before his course of study was completed. He arranged to continue his studies, however, with Francis Glass (q.v.). In 1824 Reynolds became editor of the Wilmington *Spectator.* But a voice, which proclaimed "To All the World! I declare the earth is hollow and habitable within," lured him away from his newspaper. He joined Captain John Cleves Symmes as a lecturer, first in Ohio, then in Pittsburgh, Philadelphia, Baltimore, and other cities. In 1826, when the New York *Mirror* first published two articles by Reynolds on the "Symmes' Hole" theory, the editor took an unusual interest in the young author, who described himself as "a youth in years, a child in science." The writing was found to be "always interesting, and sometimes eloquent," and a great career was predicted for Reynolds in the exploration of new ideas. Even while lecturing on the theory, Reynolds found himself in disagreement with some of its aspects, and quite outgrew it as a greater concept began to form itself in his mind. As early as 1822 Symmes had petitioned Congress for an expedition to demonstrate his theory. Reynolds now began to urge that an expedition be sent to chart all of the lands that could be found in the South Seas and to make a scientific study of them. In June, 1828, he was appointed by the Secretary of the Navy to collect information for the use of such an expedition. Three months later he turned in his report, based on interviews with sea captains who had sailed the southern waters, together with an examination of their logbooks, charts, and journals. It was not published until 1835, when the exploring expedition was again under consideration by Congress. Meanwhile, the Secretary of the Navy completed preparations for an expedition to be made in 1829. It was canceled on the grounds of economy when Andrew Jackson took office in March of that year. But Reynolds' report was full of the most tantalizing entries about islands uncharted and uncertain. Since it was one of the most enticing invitations to exploration ever compiled, it is not surprising that its author was unwilling to give up the idea of sailing south of the Cape. He approached the captains he had interviewed for his report, and at length a private expedition was organized. Reynolds sailed as a scientist with Captain Nathaniel B. Palmer, who had already made the voyage by which he was later to be given honor as the true discoverer of the continent of Antarctica. On the voyage the ships engaged in sealing, but the rumored lands to the west were not found, and no opportunity came to sail for the pole. Explorations were made in Patagonia, Staten Land, the Shetlands, and in empty Antarctic seas. An outbreak of scurvy forced them back to Chile, where Reynolds and Captain Palmer made plans to sail for the North Pole. Desertions among the crew became so numerous at this news that Palmer left Reynolds in Chile and returned to the United States with his cargo. Reynolds, disappointed because his voyage had fallen short of expectations, devoted his restless energies to the exploration of Chile and the territories to the south. He was at Valparaiso in Oct., 1832, when the U. S. frigate *Potomac* entered the harbor. The *Potomac,* under Commodore John Downes, had sailed from New York Aug. 26, 1831, on a punitive expedition against the natives on the coast of Sumatra, and had then visited Java, China, and various Pacific islands. Reynolds was taken aboard as secretary to the Commodore, and spent the next year and a half with the frigate as it moved along the coast of South America. He was asked to write a history of the long voyage, which was published in 1835 as *Voyage of the United States Frigate Potomac.* The introduction and first chapter were published separately in 1834. The section on Peru was so highly considered in that country that it was translated into Spanish and published there. After his book was successfully launched, Reynolds again turned his efforts to a national exploring expedition. He had become a master of the literature of exploration, and his own voyages had given proof that too little was known about the waters in which America had a vital interest. The Ohio delegation to Congress gave its full support to the expedition, which was significant since it was popularly believed that only states along the coast would be benefited. Through their spokesman, Thomas L. Hamer, they also urged that Reynolds be given a suitable appointment in the enterprise. It was Reynolds' own speech, however, delivered from the rostrum of the House of Representatives, which led directly to the passage of an act authorizing the expedition. His many writings on the subject, first published by the newspaper press, were later collected into several volumes, while his Congressional speech, published as part of a 300-page book, was enthusiastically reviewed by Poe in the *Southern Literary Messenger.* A long delay, however, followed the official authorization, and the cool clarity of scientific exposition, notable in most of Reynolds' work, gave way to acid pamphleteering. When the exploring expedition, with its corps of scientists, sailed without him, something went out of his life which was never replaced. Friends rallied to his support, and Poe wrote of "his great and laudable exertions to get up the American South Polar expedition, from a personal participation in which he was most shamefully excluded." The New York *Times* said that "he has served his country and the cause of science and humanity nobly." Reynolds' position was further reinforced by the fact that Thomas ap Catesby Jones also ran into strong interference, and resigned his appointment as commander of the expedition. In 1839, while living at the Astor House in New York, Reynolds attracted large audiences with political lectures delivered at National Hall. In the following year he toured Connecticut, giving a series of campaign addresses. On May 1, 1841, he became a member of the law firm of Dutcher, Reynolds & Platt, with offices in Wall Street. He became a successful lawyer, his specialty being maritime law. He was in Ohio in 1843, where he lectured on the Indian problem. In 1848 he organized a stock company for mining in Mexico, and served as its president. But his health had failed, and he died in 1858. He was buried in New York. A full account of Reynolds' personal adventures during his absence from this country, 1829–34, never appeared. In 1835 he promised that the particulars of his voyage with Captain Palmer, as well as a narrative of his subsequent travels by land through Chile and the Araucanian and Indian territories, would be given to the public. Certain parts appeared in such periodicals as the *Knickerbocker,* New York *Mirror, Southern Literary Messenger,* and the *New Yorker* (1838–43). They carry the narrative of his adventures and explorations to the Shetlands, Staten Land, South America, and Mocha, where the white whale story was unfolded. "Mocha Dick" was first printed in the *Knickerbocker,* May, 1839, and reprinted at London in the following year as a part of "The Romancist and Novelists Library." Its first separate publication was in the form of a British penny dreadful. The complete manuscript of the journal was last heard of in Sept., 1843, when Reynolds wrote to the *Southern Literary Messenger* that all of his papers, long untouched, were still in his desk. His interests had changed, and he was now "wedded to the law." The letter accompanied a long piece called "Rough Notes of Rough Adventures," which appeared in the Dec., 1843, issue of the *Messenger.* It marked his last contribution to a literary periodical, although there are indications that newspapers of a later date carried some work from his pen. Since some of his earlier writings appeared under the pseudonyms of "Citizen" and "Citizen of the United States," it is possible that other works, unsigned or pseudonymous, will eventually be recognized. It is a striking thing about Reynolds that as each new fact about him is uncovered, his stature grows and his career takes on new interest.

Gerald D. McDonald

Remarks on a Review of Symmes' Theory . . . , Washington, D. C., 1827.

Explore the Southern Polar Regions . . . , Washington, D. C., 1828.

Voyage of the United States Frigate Potomac . . . , New York, 1835.

Pacific Ocean and South Seas . . . , [Washington, D. C., 1835].

Address on the Subject of a Surveying and Exploring Expedition to the Pacific Ocean . . . , New York, 1836.

Exploring Expedition. Correspondence between J. N. Reynolds and the Hon. Mahlon Dickerson . . . , [New York, 1838?].

Pacific and Indian Oceans . . . , New York, 1841.

Sketches of the Country on the Northern Route from Belleville Illinois to the City of New York . . . , Belleville, 1854.

Mocha Dick; Or, the White Whale of the Pacific . . . , London, [1870].

RHODES, CHARLES DUDLEY (Feb. 10, 1865–Jan. 24, 1948), army officer, brother of Daisy Rhodes Campbell (q.v.), was born in Delaware, Delaware County. He graduated from Columbian University in 1885 and the U. S. Military Academy in 1889. He served in the Army until his retirement as a major general in 1929. He saw action in Cuba and the Philippine Islands during the Spanish-American War and in France during World War I.

History of the Cavalry of the Army of the Potomac . . . , Kansas City, Mo., 1900.

Robert E. Lee, the West Pointer, [Richmond, 1932].

RHODES, DUDLEY WARD (Feb. 25, 1849–Aug. 3, 1925), clergyman, was born in Marietta, Washington County. He attended Marietta College for three years and was graduated from Cornell University in 1869 and Philadelphia Divinity School in 1873. He was rector of St. Paul's Episcopal Church, Cincinnati, 1874–76, helped found and served as first rector of Church of Our Saviour, Mount Auburn, served a church in St. Paul, Minn., 1896–1901, and returned to Church of Our Saviour, where he served until his retirement in 1908.

Creed and Greed, Eight Lectures, Cincinnati, 1879.

RHODES, HARRISON GARFIELD (June 3, 1871–Sept. 21, 1929), was born in Cleveland, Cuyahoga County. After attending Western Reserve University for one year, he transferred to Harvard University, where he graduated in 1892. He died in Hereford, England, where he had lived at intervals and worked as business agent of various American magazines. He wrote the stage version of *Ruggles of Red Gap,* a number of guide books, e.g., *In Vacation America,* New York, [1915], and considerable fiction, e.g., *High Life, and Other Stories,* New York, 1920. WWW 1

RHODES, JAMES FORD (May 1, 1848–Jan. 22, 1927), historian, was born in Cleveland, Cuyahoga County, a descendant of the New England families that pioneered in the Western Reserve. He was the second son of Daniel P. Rhodes and was reared in a comfortable bourgeois environment. He attended Cleveland public schools, studied briefly at the University of the City of New York and the University of Chicago, and climaxed his education with a year of study and travel in Europe. His early intellectual interests centered about history and philosophy, and for a time he dreamed of becoming a journalist or a literary man. Ultimately, however, he decided to join his father in the coal and iron business, and in 1874 he was made a partner in the firm of Rhodes & Company. Rhodes built a comfortable personal fortune within a decade, and in 1885 he retired from business to devote his energies to the historical profession. Beginning with a program of wide reading, he gave special attention to the masterpieces of historical literature in order to learn historiographical techniques. In 1885–86 he marked his professional apprenticeship by publishing several articles and reviews in the *Magazine of Western History,* and the next year he began research for his monumental *History of the United States from the Compromise of 1850.* With the publication and favorable reception of the first two volumes of this work in 1893, Rhodes emerged as an important historian. Five subsequent volumes (III, 1895; IV, 1899; V, 1904; VI and VII, 1906) served to enhance the author's fame. Over a decade later, he published two volumes dealing with contemporary history: *History of the United States from Hayes to McKinley* (1919) and *The McKinley and Roosevelt Administrations* (1922). The nine volumes were published as a unit in 1928. Of Rhodes' other published writings, the most noteworthy are *Historical Essays* (1909) and *The History of the Civil War* (1917). Rhodes' fame rests chiefly on his seven volumes devoted to the era 1850–77. To the formidable task of synthesizing two decades of sectional controversy, he brought great industry in research and remarkable skill in handling a vast bulk of data. He made extensive use of newspaper files and governmental documents, recognized the need for careful digestion of source materials, and displayed a forthright candor in the presentation of his ideas. Though his literary style was not brilliant, Rhodes marshaled his facts with clarity, coherence, and drama. The result was a sweeping epic of the rise and fall of the slave power and a classic depiction of the titanic dimensions of the great sectional crisis. Rhodes subordinated the complex aspects of American development to the central theme of the struggle over slavery, and his presentation reflected a moralistic, pro-Northern perspective. Admittedly a narrator rather than an analytical interpreter, Rhodes placed greatest stress upon political developments. But politics to him meant essentially a clash between rival leaders, and all too often he failed to penetrate to the broader environmental causes involved in political issues. Moreover, Rhodes' history was weakened by important and paradoxical omissions. Recognizing the importance of social and economic determinants, he nevertheless gave them scant consideration in his narratives. Similarly, appreciative of the significance of sectionalism in nineteenth-century America, he did not balance his comprehension of Northern conditions with a corresponding knowledge of Southern and Western development. Rhodes was sympathetic with the contemporary pattern of Republican and industrial predominance, and he allowed his personal viewpoint to dominate his presentation of American history. Although many of Rhodes' judgments have been revised and many of his omissions have been illuminated, his pioneering synthesis of the sectional controversy still stands as a major historiographical landmark. In the context of the age in which he wrote—with its limitations on perspective and accessible materials—he was a truly notable historian. Contemporary students still read his volumes with profit, and professional scholars still use his works as a point of departure for their researches. In 1891 Rhodes moved from Ohio to live in Massachusetts. He was elected to membership in the Massachusetts Historical Society in 1895, and was named president of the American Historical Association in 1898. He died at Brookline, Mass.

Roman J. Zorn

History of the United States from the Compromise of 1850, 7 vols., New York, 1893–1906.

Historical Essays, New York, 1909.

Lectures on the American Civil War . . . , New York, 1913.

History of the Civil War . . . , New York, 1917.

History of the United States from Hayes to McKinley, 1877–1896, New York, 1919.

Commemorative Tribute to Barrett Wendell, [New York], 1922.

The McKinley and Roosevelt Administrations, 1897–1909, New York, 1922.

Commemorative Tribute to William Roscoe Thayer, New York, 1924.

RICE, AUGUSTUS EPHRAIM (Nov. 26, 1847–March 15, 1909), banker, was born in Elmore, Ottawa County. He settled in Fremont in 1865 and began working as an errand boy at First National Bank. He was later first cashier of Fremont Savings Bank, and in 1888 he organized Croghan Bank, of which he was president until his death.

Small Talk about Business, Fremont, 1892.
Postal Savings Banks. Their Evil Effects upon the Country, [Fremont, 1898].
Practical Bank Advertising . . . , Fremont, 1900.

RICE, HARRY E. (Jan. 20, 1869–March 28, 1940), journalist, was born in South Vienna, Clark County. He worked on several Springfield newspapers and finally joined the Springfield *Democrat* in 1888. He later acquired ownership of this paper, which he sold to James M. Cox in 1905. In 1906 he bought the Xenia *Herald and Democrat-News.* He served as postmaster of Xenia from 1916 to 1924. Besides his journalistic writing, he published a fanciful novel: *Eve and the Evangelist; A Romance of A.D. 2108,* Boston, [1908].

RICE, HARVEY (June 11, 1800–Nov. 7, 1891), lawyer and journalist, was born in Conway, Mass. After graduating from Williams College in 1824, he came to Cleveland, where he opened a school and studied law. He was admitted to the bar and began practice in 1826. He served for a year as editor of the *Independent News-Letter,* which he bought in 1828 and which later became the Cleveland *Plain Dealer.* He served a term in the legislature and was clerk of the court of common pleas, Cleveland, 1833–34. In 1851 he was elected to the state senate. For years educational leaders had been advocating educational reform in Ohio; consulting with all concerned, Rice drafted the new school law, which was passed against stout opposition and which brought him state-wide recognition. He was a prolific contributor to magazines.

Mount Vernon, and Other Poems, Cleveland, 1858.
Letters from the Pacific Slope . . . , New York, 1870.
Nature and Culture, Boston, 1875.
Select Poems, Boston, 1878.
Incidents of Pioneer Life in the Early Settlement of the Connecticut Western Reserve, Cleveland, 1881.
Sketches of Western Life, Cleveland, 1887.
The Founder of the City of Cleveland and Other Sketches, Boston, 1892.

RICE, NATHAN LEWIS (Dec. 29, 1807–June 11, 1877), clergyman, born in Garrard County, Ky., was pastor of Central Presbyterian Church, Cincinnati, 1845–53. Author of numerous polemical works, he engaged in a four-day debate in Oct., 1845, with Jonathan Blanchard (q.v.) on the subject of slavery, a report of which was published in 1846. He also wrote *Phrenology Examined . . . ,* New York, 1849.

RICE, ROSELLA (Aug. 11, 1827–1888), was born in Perrysville, Ashland County. She wrote articles, stories, and poems for a variety of newspapers and magazines, including *Godey's Lady's Book* and *Home Magazine.* Some of her magazine fiction was published under the pen names Chatty Brooks and Pipsissiway Potts.

Mabel: Or, Heart Histories, Columbus, 1858.

RICE, WILLIAM HENRY (Sept. 8, 1840–Jan. 10, 1911), clergyman, born in Bethlehem, Pa., was minister of the Moravian church, Gnadenhutton, Tuscarawas County, 1897–1909. He returned to his native town in Pennsylvania before his death. He wrote *David Zeisberger and His Brown Brethren,* Bethlehem, Pa., 1897.

RICH, SISTER MARY PAULA (1863– ?), was born in Boston, Mass. After becoming a Roman Catholic nun, she taught in Hamilton County for more than thirty years. She wrote several devotional books, e.g., *The Virgin-Mother,* New York, 1934. CWW 7

RICHARD, JAMES WILLIAM (Feb. 14, 1843–March 7, 1909), Lutheran theologian, born near Winchester, Va., taught at Wittenberg College, 1885–88. He wrote a great many articles and reviews, a history of Lutheranism, and a biography: *Philip Melanchthon . . . ,* New York, 1898.

RICHARDS, CLARICE ESTERBROOK (1875–), was born in Dayton, Montgomery County. She attended Bradford Academy, Mass., and in 1900 married Jarvis Richards. They bought a ranch in eastern Colorado, and her life there furnished material for a book: *A Tenderfoot Bride; Tales from an Old Ranch,* New York, [1920].

RICHARDS, JAMES AUSTIN (March 27, 1878–), clergyman, born in Andover, Mass., was pastor of First Church, Oberlin, 1928–42. He now lives in Lakeland, Fla. He has published numerous articles and two devotional books, e.g., *The Sufficiency of Jesus,* New York, [1927]. WW 24

RICHARDS, JOHN THOMAS (Oct. 13, 1851–July 19, 1942), lawyer, born in Ironton, Lawrence County, was reared on a farm in Kane County, Ill. After being admitted to the Illinois bar, he practiced in Chicago. He wrote *Abraham Lincoln, the Lawyer-Statesman,* Boston, 1916. WWW 2

RICHARDS, JOSEPH HAVENS COWLES (Nov. 8, 1851–June 9, 1923), clergyman and educator, was born in Columbus, Franklin County. He was received into the Society of Jesus in 1872, was associated with various Catholic schools as teacher or administrator, including ten years as president of Georgetown College, 1888–98, and was also affiliated with Catholic organizations in California, Maryland, and New York. He wrote a biography of his father, Henry L. Richards: *A Loyal Life . . . ,* St. Louis, Mo., 1913. WWW 1

RICHARDSON, ALBERT DEAN (Oct. 6, 1833–Dec. 2, 1869), journalist, born in Franklin, Mass., worked on Cincinnati newspapers from 1853 until 1857. In 1857 he went to Kansas as a correspondent for the Cincinnati *Gazette;* here he met Horace Greeley and began a connection with the New York *Tribune* that continued until his death. As a *Tribune* correspondent during the Civil War, he was captured on May 3, 1863, and was held in Confederate prisons for eighteen months. An account of his imprisonment is found in *The Secret Service, the Field, the Dungeon, and the Escape . . . ,* Hartford, Conn., 1865. He wrote a campaign biography of Grant in 1868. Rumors of his engagement to marry Abby Sage McFarland reached the ears of her recently divorced husband, Daniel McFarland, a confirmed drunkard with paranoic tendencies. The enraged McFarland shot Richardson at his desk in the *Tribune* office on Nov. 25, 1869. He was married on his deathbed to Mrs. McFarland, who published his fugitive writings as *Garnered Sheaves . . . ,* Hartford, Conn., 1871.

RICHARDSON, ANNA STEESE SAUSSER (April 5, 1865–May 10, 1949), was born in Massillon, Stark County. After graduating from Philadelphia Normal School for Girls in 1885, she married William M. Richardson. Beginning in 1894 she worked for various Midwest newspapers, the McClure syndicate, the New York *World,* and *The Woman's Home Companion.* Her books, all directed to feminine readers, include *Adventures in Thrift,* Indianapolis, [1916]. WWW 2

RICHARDSON, JONATHAN M. See L. B. Welch.

RICHARDSON, JULIUS MILLER (Nov. 4, 1862–Dec. 27, 1948), lawyer and educator, was born in Sugar Creek Township, Tuscarawas County. Largely self-educated, he began teaching in the schools of his home county when he was eighteen. While teaching he read law and was admitted to the bar. He served as superintendent of schools in Mineral City and as principal of West North School, Canton. In 1908 he began the practice of law in New Philadelphia; he also lectured widely on political and religious subjects. He published four books, e.g., *God and Man . . . ,* [Mansfield, 1930], and *"Schoenbrunn," an Epic of the Romance and Tragedy of the First Village in Ohio,* New Philadelphia, 1931.

RICHARDSON, LEANDER PEASE (Feb. 28, 1856–Feb. 2, 1918), journalist, was born in Cincinnati, Hamilton County. At the age of sixteen he began writing for the Chicago *Inter-Ocean.* He edited the *Dramatic News,* 1891–96, and worked on the New York *Morning Telegraph,* the New York *Inquirer,* and other papers. Besides the novels listed below, he adapted French plays and operettas for American production and also wrote some original plays, e.g., *The Millionaire* (1891) and *Under The City Lamps* (1893). He was manager and publicity director for William A. Brady and other producers.

The Dark City . . . , Boston, 1886.
Lord Dunmersey . . . , New York, 1889.
The Prairie Detective, New York, 1889.

RICHARDSON, LYON NORMAN (July 20, 1898–), educator, was born in Andover, Ashtabula County. He graduated from Western Reserve University in 1921 and Columbia University (Ph.D.) in 1931. He was editor of the Kinsman *Journal,* 1917–22. He has been on the English faculty, Western Reserve University, since 1923, and since 1946 has been director of the university libraries. Besides numerous professional articles and textbooks, he has published *A History of Early American Magazines, 1741–1789,* New York, 1931. WW 30

RICHARDSON, ROBERT (Sept. 25, 1806–Oct. 22, 1876), physician, born in Pittsburgh, Pa., lived in Wellsburg and Carthage from 1829 until about 1836. Converted to the Disciples of Christ Church by Walter Scott (q.v.), formerly his teacher, he wrote many articles and books on devotional and theological themes. He later taught at Bethany College.

RICHARDSON, WILL S. (1864–), was born in Camp Chase, Franklin County. Except that he was a mail-order druggist in Marietta for many years, no biographical details are available. The book of poems listed below appears to have been his only publication.

To a Skeleton and Other Happy Thoughts, Buffalo, 1895.

RICHMOND, CECIL JANE (March 11, 1894–), was born in Dayton, Montgomery County. After graduating from Dayton Normal School, she taught in county schools. She has written for the Dayton *News,* the *Ohio State Journal,* and the Columbus *Dispatch.* As Betty Fairfax she wrote a column for teen-agers in the latter newspaper, 1954–57, and she also has written books on the same subject. In 1926 she was married to Claude J. Bartlett, who died in 1941; in 1949 she married James A. Groves. As Cecil Richmond Bartlett she published a campaign biography of Vic Donahey: *Honest Vic . . . ,* [Columbus, 1935]. She also published several plays before her marriage, e.g., *Special Plays for Special Days,* Franklin, 1920.

RICKENBACKER, EDWARD VERNON (Oct. 8, 1890–), aviator, was born in Columbus, Franklin County. Widely known as an auto racer, he went to France in June, 1917, as a member of General Pershing's motorcar staff, but soon was made commanding officer of the 94th Aero Pursuit Squadron. He became the best-known American air ace of the war, received the Congressional Medal, and described his experiences in *Fighting the Flying Circus,* New York, [1919]. Between the two world wars and since World War II, he has served as an executive of various aviation companies and air lines. His experiences in 1942, when he spent three weeks on a life raft in the Pacific after his plane was forced down at sea, are described in *Seven Came Through,* New York, 1934. WW 30

RICKERT, MARTHA EDITH (July 11, 1871–May 23, 1938), educator, was born in Canal Dover, Tuscarawas County. After graduating from Vassar College in 1891, she taught in Chicago high schools for five years and at Vassar College for two. She completed her Ph.D. at the University of Chicago in 1899. She abandoned teaching for writing until 1924, when she joined the English department of the University of Chicago, where she served until her death. During part of the period 1900–24, she lived in England; she published modernizations of medieval romances and other works, and several novels, e.g., *Folly,* London, 1906, and *The Reaper,* Boston, 1904. After her return to teaching she collaborated with John M. Manly on several textbooks, medieval books, and surveys of contemporary literature. An indefatigable worker, she contributed much to the field of medieval studies especially to Chaucer scholarship. DAB 22

RICKOFF, ANDREW JACKSON (Aug. 23, 1824–March 29, 1899), educator, born in Mercer County, N. J., graduated from Woodward College, Cincinnati. He served as superintendent of schools in Portsmouth, Cincinnati, and Cleveland shortly after the middle of the nineteenth century. He later moved West and died in San Francisco, Calif. Besides the title below, he published readers and arithmetic textbooks.

Past and Present of Our Common School Education . . . , Cleveland, 1877.

RIDDELL, JOHN LEONARD (Feb. 20, 1807–Oct. 7, 1865), physician, born in Leyden, Mass., spent four years in Ohio, 1832–36; he taught at Ohio Reformed Medical College, Worthington, and at Cincinnati Medical College. In 1836 he went to the Medical College of Louisiana, where he taught until his death. He published *A Synopsis of the Flora of the Western States,* Cincinnati, 1835.

RIDDLE, ALBERT GALLATIN (May 28, 1816–May 16, 1902), was born in Monson, Mass. As a year-old baby, he joined the trek of New England immigrants into Connecticut's Western Reserve when his Scotch- and Welsh-blooded parents carried him to Geauga County. When he was seven, his father died, and by the time he was twelve, as the fifth of eight children he went to work to help support the family as a farmer and carpenter. In 1835 he entered Western Reserve College at Hudson, and later went two years to an academy in Painesville. He read law under Seabury Ford and was admitted to practice in 1840. His already-apparent talent for debating and oratory was employed in favor of William Henry Harrison, for he was an antislavery Whig. Settling in Chardon, he was elected prosecuting attorney. He personally called the meeting in Chardon which resulted in formation of the Free-Soil Party in Ohio, and his continued activity in this direction made him one of the organizers of the emergent Republican Party. Caroline Avery became his wife in 1845. They had seven children. In 1850 Riddle moved to

Cleveland, and, though an active partisan of Fremont and later of Chase, he was restive in political activity, and even before his election to Congress in 1860 he wrote, "I found I was unfitted for politics. . . ." Riddle was active in Congress, especially in behalf of a bill to abolish slavery in the District of Columbia. When the Civil War broke out, he was one of a party of Congressmen who drove out to the Bull Run battlefield to see how the Cleveland Greys were making out. In the confusion of the debacle that followed, Riddle seems to have been calmer and more resolute than most, but on his return to Washington he wrote a descriptive letter to his wife which was highly critical of the conduct of some of the troops, especially the officers. Mrs. Riddle handed the letter over to the Cleveland papers. They published it—so edited as to distort his views, Riddle always maintained. The resulting storm of criticism, which represented Congressmen as joy-riders at the battle, practically riding down those who had borne the battle in their efforts to escape the field, ruined Riddle politically. In 1862 he did not run for re-election, but returned to law practice and literary activities, both more congenial than politics. A brief mission to Matanzas, Cuba, as consul charged with getting information on blockade running, closed the war period. He then settled to the practice of law in Washington. He was Law Officer of the District of Columbia from 1877 to 1889, and taught law at Howard University. Beginning about 1873 his literary activity began to take precedence even over law. Beginning with *Bart Ridgeley* (1873) and running up close to the turn of the century, six novels, several biographies, his memoirs, and a constant stream of newspaper articles and short stories (largely never collected) flowed from his pen. Some of his legal arguments and addresses were also printed. He had a national following, especially among those who knew the Western Reserve background, which he used freely. Riddle died in Washington, D. C., where he was buried in Rock Creek Cemetery.

Willis Thornton

Bart Ridgeley; A Story of Northern Ohio, Boston, 1873.

Law Students and Lawyers. The Philosophy of Political Parties and Other Subjects: Eight Lectures, Washington, D. C., 1873.

The Portrait; A Romance of the Cuyahoga Valley, Boston, 1874.

Alice Brand. A Romance of the Capital, New York, 1875.

The Life, Character and Public Services of Jas. A. Garfield, Philadelphia, 1880.

The House of Ross, and Other Tales, Boston, 1881.

The Hunter of the Shagreen. A Descriptive Poem, (Anon.), Cleveland, 1882.

Castle Gregory; A Story of the Western Reserve Woods in Olden Times, Cleveland, 1884.

Elmer Riddle; A Sketch of His Life, Cleveland, 1884.

Mark Loan; A Tale of the Western Reserve Pioneers, Cleveland, 1884.

Old Newbury and the Pioneers, [Cleveland, 1885].

The Life of Benjamin F. Wade, Cleveland, 1886.

The Tory's Daughter; A Romance of the North-west, 1812–1813, New York, 1888.

Ansel's Cave. A Story of Early Life in the Western Reserve, Cleveland, 1893.

Recollections of War Times, New York, 1895.

RIDER, WILLIAM HARPER (Feb. 3, 1853–Feb. 19, 1932), clergyman, was born in Martins Ferry, Belmont County. After graduating from Scio College, he was admitted on trial to the Pittsburgh Conference in 1872. He later attended Drew Seminary, graduating in 1882. During his 44 years in the Methodist ministry, he served churches in Ohio, Minnesota, California, New Hampshire, and Michigan. After retiring in 1916, he returned to Cleveland to live. He died in East Cleveland. While pastor of Euclid Avenue Methodist Church, he published the volume of verse listed below.

The Loom of Life, Cleveland, 1899.

RIES, WILLIAM FREDERICK (March 4, 1865–Jan. 29, 1944), was born near Norwalk, Huron County. His parents moved to Weston, Wood County, when he was fifteen. He graduated from Valparaiso University. In 1898 he moved to Toledo, where he operated a business college. He lectured widely on health and physical culture. A pamphlet, *Men and Mules,* is said to have sold two million copies. He also wrote *Perfect Health Based on Science and Experience,* Toledo, [1922].

RIFE, DAVID CECIL (Jan. 3, 1901–), geneticist, was born in Cedarville, Greene County. He graduated from Cedarville College in 1922 and Ohio State University (Ph.D.) in 1933 and was a member of the Ohio State faculty, 1930–57. He has written several articles on heredity and a book on the same subject: *Dice of Destiny . . . ,* Columbus, 1945. WWMW 49

RIGDON, SIDNEY (Feb. 19, 1793–July 4, 1876), born in Piny Fork, Pa., first came to Ohio in 1819 as a Baptist preacher in Warren. He returned to Pennsylvania for a time, but was back in Ohio in 1824 as a tanner. Increasingly attracted to the doctrines of Alexander Campbell, he preached in the Western Reserve for a time without any denominational commitment. In 1828 he was a Disciples of Christ preacher in Bainbridge and the next year in Mentor. In 1830 when four Mormon elders on their way to Missouri stopped at Mentor, Rigdon was converted by Parley P. Pratt (q.v.). In December he met Joseph Smith at Fayette, N. Y. He accompanied the prophet to Kirtland and was cashier of the bank Smith established there. After the failure of the bank, Rigdon and Smith fled to Missouri in Jan., 1838. After the death of Smith, Rigdon aspired to the leadership of the church; and he refused to follow Brigham Young to Utah. His last years were passed in Pennsylvania and Friendship, N. Y. A rumor circulated for many years to the effect that Sidney Rigdon compiled the *Book of Mormon* from a book by Solomon Spaulding (q.v.). Although this has been disproved, Rigdon probably did write *Lectures on Faith,* issued under the name of Joseph Smith.

RIGGS, STEPHEN RETURN (March 23, 1812–Aug. 24, 1883), missionary to the Indians, was born in Steubenville, Jefferson County. After studying in the Latin School at Ripley, he attended Jefferson College, Pa., and Western Theological Seminary. Licensed by the Chillicothe Presbytery in 1836, he went the next year to the upper Minnesota River, where he began his lifework as missionary and teacher among the Sioux. He wrote many articles on the Indians for magazines and newspapers and translated or wrote more than fifty books, including primers, dictionaries, grammars, hymns, and books of the Bible.

Tah-Koo Wah-Kan; Or, the Gospel among the Dakotas, Boston, [1869].

Mary and I. Forty Years with the Sioux, Chicago, [1880].

RIGHTMIRE, GEORGE WASHINGTON (Nov. 15, 1868–Dec. 23, 1952), educator, was born at Center Furnace, Lawrence County. He graduated from Ohio State University in 1895 and later studied law there while teaching in the Columbus public schools. He practiced in Columbus, 1904–19, was a member of the law faculty, 1902–25, and was president of the University, 1925–38. He compiled several legal books and also published *Democracy, What Is It?,* Columbus, 1944. WWW 3

RIHBANY, ABRAHAM MITRIE (Aug. 27, 1869–July 5, 1944), clergyman, was born in Lebanon, Syria. He came to the United States in 1891, studied at Ohio Wesleyan University for a year, and after preaching in Michigan was pastor of First Unitarian Church, Toledo, 1902–11. He published a number of books, including his autobiography: *A Far Journey,* Boston, 1914. WWW 2

RIKER, BEN H. (Jan. 19, 1889–   ), was born in St. Paris, Champaign County. He attended St. Paris schools and graduated from Ohio State University. He was for many years head of the book department, L. S. Ayres & Company, Indianapolis, and he still lives in that city. He has written a book about St. Paris in the late nineteenth century, when his father manufactured pony wagons there: *Pony Wagon Town . . . ,* Indianapolis, [1948].

RIKER, JOHN F. (Oct. 1, 1828–April 7, 1909), was born in Hamilton County but grew up in Champaign County, where his parents moved while he was a child. In 1852 he made the overland trip to California, the subject of his only book. He served in the Civil War and afterward lived in St. Paris, Champaign County.

Journal of a Trip to California . . . , [Urbana, 1856].

RILEY, JAMES (Oct. 27, 1777–March 15, 1840), was born in Middletown, Conn. He first went to sea at the age of twelve, and he was master of the brig *Commerce* when that vessel was wrecked on the coast of Africa in Aug., 1815. Riley and his crew were held as slaves by the Arabs and were forced to endure incredible hardships and cruelty. He was finally ransomed by William Wilshire, the British consul at Mogadore. Late in 1816 he turned up in New York with a manuscript narrative of his adventures, but William A. Mercien, the publisher to whom it was offered, rejected it as being too carelessly written. At the suggestion of Thurlow Weed, then associated with Mercien, Riley rewrote the book with the assistance of Anthony Bleecker, a schoolteacher. The book was reprinted in England and enjoyed a large sale in both countries. Riley made a trip to Ohio in 1818 and the following year became deputy surveyor charged with the survey of the "New Purchase" in the Maumee River valley. He brought his family to

Chillicothe in 1820 and the following year established them in a crude home on the St. Marys. Here in 1822 he laid out a town, which he named Wilshire in honor of his old friend. Because of the condition of his health he moved his family to New York in May of 1828 and returned to his profession of mariner. He died at sea. His son, James W. Riley (1817–1870), later brought his family to Ohio, where he published the *Sequel to Riley's Narrative.*

An Authentic Narrative of the Loss of the American Brig Commerce, Wrecked on the Western Coast of Africa . . . , New York, 1816.

Sequel to Riley's Narrative . . . , Columbus, 1851.

RIMANOCZY, RICHARD STANTON (March 28, 1902–), was born in Cincinnati, Hamilton County, and attended Miami University, 1921–25. After being associated with several Cleveland firms, he moved to New York in 1938 to become editorial director of the American Economics Foundation. He has published books and articles on economics and with Fred G. Clark (q.v.) *How to Be Popular Though Conservative,* New York, [1948]. WW 30

RINKLIFF, GEORGE LOUIS (Aug. 5, 1887–), was born near Bourneville, Ross County. He worked as a reporter, 1907–14, was secretary to the Springfield city manager, 1914–19, served as city manager of various cities, and was associate secretary of the Lutheran Layman's Movement, 1937–38. Now living in Springfield, he has written articles and fiction for magazines and a book: *Administering God's Gifts* Philadelphia, [1928].

RIPLEY, ROSWELL SABINE (March 14, 1823–March 29, 1887), army officer, was born in Worthington, Franklin County. He graduated from the U. S. Military Academy in 1843, served in the Mexican War and at various army posts, and resigned from the Army in 1853 to enter business in Charleston, S. C. He was an officer in the Confederate army during the Civil War, but his quarrels with General Beauregard and others kept him in South Carolina throughout most of the war, except for the Battle of Antietam, where he was wounded. He lived in England for a time after the war and later spent much of his time in New York City, where he died, although his legal residence remained Charleston. Besides the title below, which he wrote while on leave from the Army in 1848–49, he published a pamphlet on the fortification of Morris Island.

The War with Mexico, 2 vols., New York, 1849.

RISLEY, SAMUEL DOTY (Jan. 16, 1845–April 1, 1920), ophthalmologist, was born in Cincinnati, Hamilton County. He served in the Civil War, attended the State University of Iowa, 1865–68, studied medicine at the University of Pennsylvania, 1868–70, and practiced and taught in Philadelphia. His only book was written in collaboration with Roland G. Curtin: *A Medical Pilgrimage to the Republic of Panama . . . ,* [Philadelphia?], 1905. WWW 1

RITCHIE, ANDREW (Dec. 26, 1826–1897), clergyman, was born in Aberdeenshire, Scotland. He served a Presbyterian church in Greenfield and from 1865 until his death was secretary of the Western Tract Society. The second title below is a life of John Rankin of Ripley.

Life and Writings of . . . Samuel Crothers . . . , Cincinnati, 1857.

The Soldier, the Battle, and the Victory . . . , Cincinnati, [1876?].

RITCHIE, JAMES MONROE (July 28, 1829–Aug. 17, 1918), lawyer, was born in Dunfermline, Scotland. His family came to America in 1832, settling first in Ogdensburg, N. Y. James taught school in New York and Ohio, read law, and was admitted to the Ohio bar in 1857. He practiced for a short time in Lorain County but in 1858 began to practice in Toledo, where he lived until his death. Using S.E.E. as a pen name, he published numerous poems in Toledo newspapers. His son, also a lawyer, edited a posthumous collection: *Poetical Thoughts . . . ,* (Byron Foster Ritchie, ed.), Toledo, [1927].

RITTER, FREDERIC LOUIS (June 22, 1834–July 6, 1891), musician, born in Strasbourg, Alsace, came to Cincinnati in 1856 and remained until 1861. While there he founded the Cecilia Society and the Philharmonic Orchestra. He left Cincinnati for New York and afterward taught at Vassar College, 1867–91. He wrote a number of technical works on music and several histories, e.g., *Music in America,* New York, 1883.

RIVES, MARIE THOMPSON (Jan. 1, 1844–Aug. 7, 1924), daughter of Eliza J. and James H. Thompson (qq.v.), was born in Hillsboro, Highland County. She was the wife of Dr. Edward Rives. She collaborated with her mother and sister in the writing of *Hillsboro Crusade,* and also wrote a pamphlet: *Traveler's Notes,* Hillsboro, 1915.

ROACH, CORWIN CARLYLE (1904–), clergyman and educator, was born in Cleveland, Cuyahoga County. A graduate of Yale University in 1925 and Yale Divinity School in 1927, he is a priest of the Episcopal Church. In 1930 he joined the faculty of Bexley Divinity School, Kenyon College, where he has been dean since 1940. He has published *Preaching Values in the Bible,* Louisville, Ky., 1946. RLA 2

ROARK, WARREN C. (Feb. 2, 1902–), clergyman, was born in Kentucky but has lived in Ohio since his childhood. A graduate of Mount Union College in 1934 and Oberlin Graduate School of Theology in 1942, he has been a minister of the Church of God in Canton for many years. His writings include *Light on the Christian's Path,* Anderson, Ind., [1949].

ROBB, CHARLES (Jan. 5, 1826–Sept. 20, 1872), farmer, was born near New Richmond, Clermont County. He was an organizer of The Poets' Union of Clermont and Brown Counties; members brought their compositions to the meetings for criticism. He served in the Civil War as a commissary sergeant in the Kentucky Volunteer Infantry. He was active in Republican politics of his county and was a popular lecturer on agricultural topics. His collected poems were published posthumously by his niece, Mrs. M. L. Robb Hutchinson.

Pandora's Box: A Story of Heathen Mythology, Cincinnati, 1859.
Poems of Charles Robb, Chicago, [1910].

ROBBINS, ARCHIBALD (Nov. 19, 1792–Dec. 27, 1859), was born in Wethersfield, Conn. He came to Ohio around 1830, operated a store at Griffithsburg, and in 1840 established the first store at Solon. Having served as first mate of the famous brig *Commerce* under Captain James Riley (q.v.), Robbins published his account of the hardships of the shipwrecked crew of that vessel. Although it never achieved the popularity of Riley's narrative, his book went through six large editions in its first year. He died in Solon.

A Journal Comprising an Account of the Loss of the Brig Commerce . . . , Hartford, [Conn.], 1817.

ROBBINS, THOMAS (Aug. 11, 1777–Sept. 13, 1856), clergyman, born in Norfolk, Conn., was sent in 1803 as a missionary to the Western Reserve. After serving two years, he returned to Connecticut. He was keenly interested in antiquarian subjects and accumulated a valuable library of books and pamphlets. Several of his sermons were published. His diary, published in two volumes, 1886–87, covers his Ohio experiences.

ROBERTS, ANNA SMITH RICKEY (1827–Aug. 10, 1858), was born in Philadelphia, but lived in Ohio for a number of years. Her husband, Solomon W. Roberts, was chief of the Ohio and Pennsylvania Railroad. She contributed poems to the *Columbian and Great West.*

Forest Flowers of the West, Philadelphia, 1851.

ROBERTS, CHARLES HUMPHREY (Oct. 11, 1847–Nov. 30, 1911), lawyer, was born in Mt. Pleasant, Jefferson County. After teaching school and working as superintendent of construction for the Camden Iron Works, Philadelphia, he determined to become a lawyer. He graduated from the University of Michigan law school in 1878 and afterward practiced in Chicago. The novel listed below deals with Quakers in Ohio.

"Down the O-Hi-O," Chicago, 1891.

ROBERTS, CLARK (Aug. 13, 1805–Nov. 30, 1885), physician, was born in Vienna, Trumbull County. After graduating from the medical school of Illinois College in 1846, he practiced medicine in Illinois. During the Civil War he served with the 101st Illinois Volunteers. He died at Winchester, Ill.

A Theorem on Planetary Motion; Or, Sunshine and Shadow, St. Louis, Mo., 1881.

ROBERTS, DOROTHY JAMES (Sept. 5, 1903–), born in Elizabeth, W. Va., lived in Marietta, 1910–43, and now lives in Mamaroneck, N. Y. She attended Denison University and Marietta College, but completed her work at Barnard College in 1925; she also did graduate work at the University of Wisconsin. Under the pen name Peter Mortimer, she published a mystery story: *If a Body Kill a Body,* New York, 1946. She has also published short stories and several novels under her own name. An Ohio River town is the setting for a portion of *A Man of Malice Landing,* New York, 1943. WWAW 1

ROBERTS, WILLIAM CHARLES (Sept. 23, 1832–Nov. 27, 1903), clergyman, born near Aberystwyth, Wales, came to America in

1849. A Presbyterian minister, he served as pastor of First Church, Columbus, 1862–64, during which time he was one of the founders of University of Wooster. He wrote many articles, pamphlets, and books in Welsh and in English on religious topics.

ROBERTSON, CHARLES (July 13, 1799–March 24, 1884), physician, was born near Leesburg, Va. At the age of ten he learned the printing trade, and when his family moved to St. Clairsville in 1812 he was a printer on the *Repository.* At the age of twenty he was named postmaster of St. Clairsville, and in his leisure time he studied medicine with a local doctor. In 1823 he began practice in Barnesville; the following year he moved to Woodsfield, and in 1826 he settled in McConnelsville, where he practiced until his death.

History of Morgan County . . . , Chicago, 1886.

ROBERTSON, JOHN (1854–Nov. 5, 1926), physician, was born in Linloch, Scotland. His parents brought him to Toronto, Ontario, Canada, in 1858 and later settled in Michigan, where he spent his young manhood. In 1885 he began writing poetry and prose in support of prohibition and temperance. He practiced medicine in Cincinnati, and his death occurred in that city. He invented several pieces of medical apparatus.

The Confidential Friend, a Book for Women of All Ages and Conditions . . . , Cincinnati, 1890.

ROBINS, ELIZABETH (Aug. 6, 1862–May 9, 1952), actress, born in Louisville, Ky., spent a part of her girlhood in Zanesville, where she attended Putnam Female Seminary. When she was seventeen, her father took her to Colorado. She became an actress, toured with James O'Neill, and later settled in England, where she played Ibsen during the 1890s and numbered among her friends Oscar Wilde, Bernard Shaw, and Henry James. She published more than twenty books, including a novel, published under the pseudonym C. E. Raimond, that has its setting in Zanesville: *The Open Question; A Tale of Two Temperaments,* New York, 1899. The story of her busy life is told in an autobiography: *Both Sides of the Curtain,* London, [1940].

ROBINSON, BEN CARL (Jan. 12, 1890–), was born in Albany, Tuscarawas County, and has spent his entire life in his native county. He studied at the Chicago Art Institute, 1911–13, and has since written on fishing, hunting, and travel for many national magazines. He is at present living in Newcomerstown and is fishing editor of *Fur, Fish, Game* magazine. He has published three books on outdoor sports, e.g., *Muskellunge Fishing,* New York, 1925.

ROBINSON, CHALFANT (March 14, 1871–Dec. 31, 1946), historian and museum curator, was born in Cincinnati, Hamilton County. He graduated from the University of Cincinnati in 1893 and Yale University (Ph.D.) in 1902. After serving in the history departments of Mount Holyoke College, Smith College, and Yale, he became curator of medieval manuscripts at Princeton University in 1920. He wrote a number of monographs and books on historical subjects, e.g., *A History of Two Reciprocity Treaties . . . ,* [New Haven, 1904]. WWW 2

ROBINSON, DANIEL SOMMER (Oct. 19, 1888–), educator, born in North Salem, Ind., was professor of philosophy, Miami University, 1922–29. While at Miami he published *The God of the Liberal Christian . . . ,* New York, 1926. WW 30

ROBINSON, EDWARD STEVENS (April 18, 1893–Feb. 27, 1937), educator, was born in Lebanon, Warren County, and grew up in Norwood, Hamilton County. After graduating from the University of Cincinnati in 1916, he studied at the Carnegie Institute of Technology and University of Chicago (Ph.D., 1920). He served on the faculty of the University of Chicago, 1920–27, and Yale University, 1927–37. Recognized as one of the nation's leading pyschologists, he published important studies of memory and fatigue and also wrote a book relating law and psychology: *Law and the Lawyers,* New York, 1935. DAB 22

ROBINSON, EDWIN MEADE (Ted) (Nov. 1, 1878–Sept. 20, 1946), journalist, was born in Lima (Howe), Ind., the son of William Edwin and Alice Maude Drake Robinson. His father was a native of Connecticut and a direct descendant of John Robinson, minister of the Pilgrims. He taught his son to love books, bass fishing, and theological disputation. Ted was graduated from Howe School in 1894. He enrolled in Wabash College, where he became the popular student known as Ted Robinson. It was here that he developed a facility for graceful writing, and as the writer of the words of the college song he endeared himself to Wabash men. After receiving his A.B. in 1900, he spent a year as a teacher of English in Attica, Ind. He then joined the staff of the Indianapolis

Sentinel, remaining with this paper and the Indianapolis *Journal* until 1904. Ted Robinson was truly a product of the Indiana school of writing so important in that decade—Booth Tarkington, George Ade, and the others—a school that produced a realism that understood the good as well as the evil and whose style was always graceful without being precious. The Indiana writers wrote social novels that managed to be popular without being angry and historical novels with modest bosoms. They wrote them with an urbane simplicity in a style often flavored with the pleasant taste of *belles-lettres.* Ted went to the Cleveland *Leader* in 1904, and in 1908 he married Martha Coon. He joined the Cleveland *Plain Dealer* in 1910 as associate editor and columnist. His column, "Philosopher of Folly," achieved immediate success. With his almost daily poem he became one of the country's most effective writers of light verse—light in the sense of non-heavy, non-pompous, but not in the sense of trivial. Some of his lines touched the deepest sympathies that man possesses. Under his direction after 1922, the book section of the *Plain Dealer* became one of the country's best with a strong influence upon northern Ohio book buyers. Robinson lectured at Cleveland College on philology, 1926–42. He received an honorary Litt.D. degree from Wabash College in 1927. Although Ted was not a native Ohioan, he *found* himself in Cleveland and became such an integral part of the city that to countless Clevelanders Ted *was* Cleveland. He died in Provincetown, Mass., where he spent his summers and was greatly loved. His publications include *Mere Melodies,* Philadelphia, 1918, *Piping and Panning,* New York, 1920, *Enter Jerry,* New York, 1921, *The Curious History of a Nursery Rhyme,* Cleveland, 1932, and *Life, Love and the Weather,* Cleveland, 1945. During his later years his poems and his person seemed to have a whispering, almost friendly intimacy with Death that his friends found very gallant and inspiring. The poem published the very day his death was announced seemed a prophecy:

And this will happen, when the brawl
Of life at last forbears to maul
My tired bones and blood runs slow.
How good to murmur as I sprawl
At ease—and truly after all—
The Autumn comes—and I must go.

Milton G. Nicola

ROBINSON, ELMO ARNOLD (Jan. 1, 1887–), clergyman, was born in Portland, Maine. He was ordained as a Universalist minister in New York City in 1912 and preached for some time at Plain City and Woodstock. He was living in Palo Alto, Calif., when he published *The Universalist Church in Ohio,* [Akron?], 1923.

ROBINSON, GEORGE FOGLESONG (May 8, 1838–May 17, 1901), was born in Xenia, Greene County. He enlisted in the 74th O.V.I. in 1861, but was discharged for disability after seven months. He worked as a carpenter and operated a farm. He died in Xenia. He compiled a roster of Greene County Civil War soldiers and wrote *History of Greene County . . . ,* Chicago, 1902.

ROBINSON, GIL (1844–Aug. 17, 1928), circus owner, born in Buckaman, Va., spent much of his life in Cincinnati. He served in the Civil War and afterward operated a tent show founded by his father in 1824. He made at least one trip to Asia to obtain animals for the circus and traveled more than a million miles with the show. He was one of the founders of the United States Playing Card Company. He died in Cincinnati. He wrote his autobiography: *Old Wagon Show Days,* Cincinnati, [1925].

ROBINSON, HENRY MARTIN (1845–April, 1907), son of Rev. John Robinson (q.v.), was born in Ashland, Ashland County. He was a sutler's clerk during the Civil War, was engaged in business in Vicksburg, Miss., and was a fur trader in Canada.

The Great Fur Land . . . , New York, 1879.

ROBINSON, HOWARD (July 17, 1885–), educator, was born in Redwood Falls, Minn. He graduated from Hamline University in 1908, Union Theological Seminary in 1911, and Columbia University (Ph.D.) in 1916. After teaching in Canada and Minnesota, he came to Ohio in 1924 and has taught at Miami University, 1924–35, Ohio State University, 1935–37, and Oberlin College, 1937–50. He has published professional articles, textbooks, and other books, e.g., *Bayle, the Skeptic,* New York, 1931. WW 28

ROBINSON, JENNIE MAY (Aug. 2, 1882–Nov. 12, 1933), was born in Sidney, Shelby County. She lived for many years in Toledo and died in that city. She wrote *"The Comforter" . . . ,* [Toledo], 1928.

ROBINSON, JOHN (Jan. 27, 1814–June 15, 1888), clergyman, was born in Westmoreland County, Pa. At the age of seventeen he was apprenticed to a tin-plater at Cadiz, where he also joined the Presbyterian Church. He worked at his trade to pay for his education. After graduating from Franklin College in 1837, he attended Western Theological Seminary in Pennsylvania. In 1840 he was licensed to preach by the Steubenville Presbytery; he was ordained the following year. After serving multiple pastorates for three years, he was called to First Presbyterian Church, Ashland, where he served, 1844–84. He aided in the establishment of University of Wooster. Among his eight children was Henry M. Robinson (q.v.).

The Testimony and Practice of the Presbyterian Church in Reference to Slavery . . ., Cincinnati, 1852.

ROBINSON, JOHN BUNYAN (April 11, 1834–1912), educator, was born in Oceola, Crawford County. After graduating from Ohio Wesleyan University in 1860, he was principal of Mount Washington Seminary near Cincinnati. He afterward served as president of Willoughby College, of Fort Wayne College, of New Hampshire Seminary and Female College, and of Jennings Seminary.

Infidelity Answered . . ., Boston, 1875.
Emeline; Or, Home, Sweet Home, Boston, 1876.
The Serpent of Sugar Creek Colony, a Temperance Narrative of Pioneer Life in Ohio, Philadelphia, 1885.
The Epworth League . . ., Cincinnati, 1890.
The New Woman and Other Poems, Chicago, 1896.
Epic Ballads of the Land of Flowers, Deland, Fla., 1905.
Epic Ballads of "Uncle Sam," [Philadelphia, 1909?].
Bird or Feather Convention . . ., Rutherford, N. J., 1910.

ROBISON, W. SCOTT (March 6, 1835–Dec. 3, 1913), publisher, was born in Fultonville, N. Y. He operated a company in Cleveland which published directories and similar books.

History of the City of Cleveland . . ., Cleveland, 1887.

ROCKEFELLER, JOHN DAVISON (July 8, 1839–May 23, 1937), industrialist, born in Richford, N. Y., came to Cleveland in 1853. He attended Cleveland High School for two years and worked for a commission merchant for three and a half years. In 1859, with Maurice B. Clark, he founded a commission business which prospered during the Civil War. In 1863 he built his first oil refinery, and two years later he sold his commission business to devote all his time to oil. His skill in organizing the business, his ruthless struggle for control of oil refining and transportation, and the phenomenal growth of Standard Oil of Ohio after its incorporation in 1870 are all familiar pages in the history of American business. In 1883–84, with other executives of the company, he moved to New York and established headquarters there. In Cleveland he had lived simply and unostentatiously in a large house on Euclid Avenue and at a summer home at Forest Hills. He was superintendent of the Sunday school at Euclid Avenue Baptist Church for many years. He published an autobiographical volume: *Random Recollections of Men and Events,* New York, 1909. DAB 22

ROCKEFELLER, JOHN DAVISON, JR. (Jan. 29, 1874–May 12, 1960), capitalist and philanthropist, was born in Cleveland, Cuyahoga County, and lived there until 1884, when his father moved to New York. Although he entered his father's office in 1897 and engaged in business, most of his efforts were devoted to the administration of the Rockefeller charities. He published a number of separate addresses and a collection: *The Personal Relation in Industry,* New York, [1923]. CB 41

ROCKEL, WILLIAM MAHLON (July 18, 1855–March 23, 1931), lawyer and judge of the circuit court, was born near Tremont City, Clark County. He practiced law in Springfield and published a number of legal works, notably *Rockel's Complete Ohio Probate Practice,* and a county history: *20th Century History of Springfield and Clark County, Ohio . . .*, Chicago, 1908. OBB

ROCKEY, CARROLL JACOB (April 11, 1885–Aug. 15, 1961), clergyman, was born in Miamisburg, Montgomery County. After graduating from Wittenberg College in 1908 and Chicago Lutheran Theological Seminary in 1911, he served churches in the Middle West, 1911–57, and after retiring from the ministry he lived in Ferndale, Mich. He published three books treating religious themes, e.g., *Fishing for Fishers of Men,* Philadelphia, [1924].

ROCKWELL, ALPHONSO DAVID (May 18, 1840–April 12, 1933), physician, born in New Canaan, Conn., attended Kenyon College and lived for a time near Milan, where his father had bought a farm. He taught school and studied medicine here for a time. He served a brief enlistment in the 85th O.V.I., and after medical study in New York he joined the 6th Ohio Cavalry as a surgeon. A pioneer in the field of electro-therapeutics, he practiced in New York and published numerous technical works. He also published an autobiography: *Rambling Recollections . . .* , New York, 1920. DAB 16

ROCKWELL, VERA C. (Mrs. Leo L.), was born in Glenford, Perry County. She attended Denison University for a time and graduated from Bucknell University in 1911. She has taught Spanish in several schools, her longest tenure being at Bucknell, 1919–31. Her home is in Hamilton, N. Y. She has written *The New Pioneers,* Boston, [1940]. WWAW 1

ROCKWOOD, FLOZARI SUTTON-HEMINGWAY (Oct. 3, 1894–April 14, 1954), was born Florence Sutton-Hemingway in Yorkshire, England. She came to America in 1907, married Roy H. Rockwood in 1911, and was for several years a dancer in vaudeville, using Princess Flozari as her stage name. She lived in Mansfield, 1913–17, and in Cleveland after 1917. She conducted an entertainment service for a number of years and also founded Pegasus Studio, which published many magazines and pamphlets containing her own poems and those of others. She published a great many poems in magazines and newspapers and several pamphlet anthologies, e.g., *The Lost Rendezvous, and Other Prize-Winning Poems,* Cleveland, 1947.

RODABAUGH, JAMES HOWARD (Nov. 11, 1910–), historian, was born in Cincinnati, Hamilton County. He graduated from Miami University in 1932 and Ohio State University (Ph.D.) in 1937. After teaching at Denison University in 1938, he served as assistant director of the Ohio Historical Records Survey, 1938–40, as assistant director of research at Hayes Memorial Library, 1940–44, and since 1944 as a director of the Ohio State Archaeological and Historical Society. He is editor of the *Ohio Historical Quarterly.* He has written a number of significant articles on Ohio history, compiled a bibliography of Ohio archaeology, and published *Robert Hamilton Bishop,* Columbus, 1935. WWMW 54

RODEHEAVER, HOMER ALVAN (Oct. 4, 1880–Dec. 18, 1955), musician, was born in Union Furnace, Hocking County. He was musical director for Billy Sunday's evangelistic services, 1909–31, traveled with other evangelists, and organized his own company to publish hymns and gospel music. He wrote several books of recollections, e.g., *Twenty Years with Billy Sunday,* Nashville, [1936]. WWW 3

RODGERS, ANDREW DENNY, III (Jan. 19, 1900–), lawyer, was born in Columbus, Franklin County. He graduated from Ohio Wesleyan University in 1922 and Ohio State University law school in 1925. After his admission to the bar in 1926, he practiced in Columbus. He has published poetry, e.g., *Rocks before the Mansion,* [Los Angeles, 1940], and several biographies of American scientists, e.g., *Liberty Hyde Bailey . . .* , Princeton, [N. J.], 1949. WWMW 6

RODKEY, FREDERICK STANLEY (Jan. 31, 1896–), educator, born in Irving, Kan., taught history at Miami University, 1921–29. Since 1929 he has been on the faculty of the University of Illinois. His writings include *An Historical Approach to the World Problems of Today . . .* , Urbana, Ill., 1934. DAS 3

ROE, EDWARD REYNOLDS (1813–Nov. 6, 1893), physician, was born in Lebanon, Warren County, but spent much of his life in Illinois. He served in the 33rd Illinois Infantry from Aug., 1861, to July, 1863; he left the army as a lieutenant colonel. He afterward practiced medicine in Illinois.

The Gray and the Blue. A Story . . . , Chicago, 1884.
God Reigns . . . , Chicago, [1888].
Dr. Caldwell . . . , Chicago, 1889.
Joe; A Remarkable Case, Chicago, 1889.
Belteshazzar; A Romance of Babylon, Chicago, 1890.
The World against Her, Chicago, 1891.
Virginia Rose, Chicago, 1892.

ROE, GEORGE MORTIMER (Oct. 30, 1848–Aug. 20, 1916), journalist, born in Clyde, N. Y., came to Cincinnati in 1872. He worked on the *Gazette,* 1872–84, and on the *Enquirer,* 1884–86. In 1886 he became associate editor of the *Times-Star.* He died in Long Beach, Calif., where he had lived for about ten years.

Our Police . . . , Cincinnati, 1890.
Cincinnati: The Queen City of the West . . . , Cincinnati, 1895.
Pure Water; How to Quench the Thirst and How Not to Quench It . . . , College Corner, 1900.

ROEBEN, FREDERICK B. (Oct. 5, 1878–), born in Rastede, Germany, came to the United States in 1900. Soon afterward he settled in Cincinnati, where he worked as an engineer at Procter & Gamble Co. until his retirement in 1945. He now lives in Orlando, Fla. He published a book about his early life: *Lure of the Sea,* New York, [1950].

ROEPKE, MRS. HARRY. See Helen L. Linham.

ROGERS, GEORGE (May 5, 1805–July 6, 1842), clergyman, was born in London, England. Born an Episcopalian, he became a Methodist minister, and in 1830 while in Philadelphia he became a Universalist. He made his home in Cincinnati from the early 1830s until his death, but traveled widely in Ohio and other states preaching and lecturing. His autobiography was published anonymously after his death.

Memoranda of the Experience, Labors, and Travels of a Universalist Preacher . . . , Cincinnati, 1845.

ROGERS, JOSEPH MORGAN (April 9, 1861–May 16, 1922), journalist, was born in Decatur, Brown County, and graduated from Berea College in 1879. After one year in the Indian Service, he served on the editorial staffs of various newspapers; from 1890 on, he was with the Philadelphia *Inquirer.* He died at Germantown, Pa. His writings, historical and biographical in nature, include *The True Henry Clay,* Philadelphia, 1904. WWW 1

ROGERS, LEBBEUS HARDING (July 26, 1847–Dec. 16, 1932), was born in Cincinnati, Hamilton County, and attended the public schools of that city. While president of a business supply company, he lived in New York City. He died in Portland, Oreg. His novel *The Kite Trust* has a Cincinnati setting.

The Kite Trust . . . , New York, [1900].

ROGERS, MARGARET DOUGLAS (Sept. 8, 1870–June 8, 1925), was born in Cincinnati, Hamilton County. She attended Miss Nourse's School, Cincinnati, and also studied music in Philadelphia, where her family lived, 1887–92. While living in Philadelphia, she published a volume of poems under her maiden name. In 1893 she married William Cook Rogers, an official of the Piqua Handle and Manufacturing Company. She spent the remainder of her life in Piqua, where she was active in civic and cultural activities. Her plays were popular with college dramatic groups.

Poems, Philadelphia, 1892.
The Gift . . . , Piqua, 1913.
Echo and Narcissus . . . , [Piqua, 1924].
The Kiss of Aphrodite . . . , [Piqua, 1925].

ROGERS, PAUL PATRICK (Jan. 5, 1900–), educator, was born in Snohomish, Wash. He has been professor of Spanish at Oberlin College since 1929. He graduated from the University of Mississippi in 1921 and Cornell University (Ph.D.) in 1928. He has published professional articles, Spanish textbooks, and *Goldoni in Spain,* Oberlin, 1941.

ROGERS, SAMUEL (Nov. 6, 1789–1877), clergyman, was born in Charlotte County, Va. In 1793 his parents moved to Kentucky. Converted to the Christian Church during a revival, he became an itinerant preacher. He preached along the Ohio River from Cincinnati to Portsmouth, and around 1819 he moved to Clinton County. He later lived on a farm in Darke County. He preached in neighboring states and made several missionary trips to Missouri. His autobiography was edited by his son, Elder John Rogers.

Autobiography of Elder Samuel Rogers, Cincinnati, 1880.

ROGERS, VOLNEY (Dec. 1, 1846–Dec. 3, 1919), lawyer, was born in Rogers, Columbiana County. In 1870 he began the practice of law in Youngstown. A lover of nature, he founded Mill Creek Park, a project that is the subject of his book, *A Partial Description of Mill Creek Park . . . ,* [Youngstown, 1904].

ROGERS, WILLIAM ALLEN (May 23, 1854–Oct. 20, 1931), artist, was born in Springfield, Clark County. He began his artistic career by painting fancy scrolls on plows and machinery produced by a manufacturer of farm implements. At fourteen he was supplying cartoons to a group of Midwestern newspapers, thus becoming the first American cartoonist to be syndicated. He later became a distinguished illustrator and expressed the opinion that his best work was done in illustrating stories for young people, a view shared by many sentimental oldsters. As a boy, Booth Tarkington believed that the illustrator of *Toby Tyler* "must be a pretty fine man." However, it is the consensus of art historians' opinion that Rogers' claim to fame rests on his ability as a cartoonist. In 1873 he joined the staff of the New York *Daily Graphic.* In 1877 he began a long association with Harper's when he joined their art staff, which included such notable artists as Edwin A. Abbey, Howard Pyle, C. S. Reinhart, A. B. Frost, and Thomas Nast. When Nast broke with Harper's in 1880, Rogers succeeded him, but it was not until the turn of the century that he began to work almost exclusively on cartoons. His work appeared in *Harper's Weekly, Life, Puck,* and the New York *Herald.* His sensational World War I cartoons, collected in *America's Black and White Book,* brought him membership in the French Legion of Honor. After serving as director of the Illustrators' School for Disabled Soldiers, 1920–22, he joined the staff of the Washington *Post.* He died in Washington, D. C.

Ernest J. Wessen

Hints at Politics . . . , New York, 1899.
America's Black and White Book . . . , New York, [1917].
A World Worth While . . . , New York, 1922.
Danny's Partner, New York, 1923.
The Miracle Mine . . . , New York, [1925].
The Lost Caravan, New York, [1927].

ROLAND, CHARLES (Aug. 6, 1831–June 1, 1918), journalist, was born in Washington County. At the age of fourteen he learned the printing business in the office of the *Ohio Eagle,* Lancaster. He edited that newspaper, 1856–66, then acquired the Greenville *Democrat,* which he edited until 1899, when he turned the paper over to his sons. After his retirement, he traveled in Europe and later published his travel letters in book form.

Tour of Central Europe . . . , Greenville, [1900].

ROLLINGPIN, COMMODORE. Pseud. See John H. Carter.

ROLLINS, HORACE JUDSON (Oct. 2, 1845–Feb. 22, 1935), artist, was born in Miami County. He spent the greater part of his life on the family estate midway between Troy and Piqua. He studied painting at McMicken College and Cincinnati Art School and in New York City. He specialized in landscape painting, the chief subject of the first title below. *Yetta Ségal* prophesies the future blending of races into a "cosmopolite" single race.

Studio, Field and Gallery, New York, [?].
Yetta Ségal, New York, 1898.

ROMAN, FREDERICK WILLIAM (Nov. 19, 1876–April 9, 1948), educator, was born in Sidney, Shelby County. He graduated from National Normal University, Lebanon, in 1897, attended Yale University, and graduated from the University of Berlin (Ph.D.) in 1910. After teaching economics and sociology in several universities, he organized Associated Forums in 1926 and the Roman Forum in 1935. His books include *The New Education in Europe . . . ,* New York, 1930. WWW 2

ROMIG, EDNA DAVIS (Jan. 16, 1889–), educator, was born in Rarden, Scioto County. She graduated from DePauw University in 1911 and taught English there for the next two years. After the death of her husband, Albert Stanley Romig, in 1919, she joined the University of Colorado faculty and taught there until her retirement in 1955. She has published a number of volumes of verse and prose, e.g., *Marse Lee,* Philadelphia, [1930]. WW 30

ROOD, JOHN (Feb. 22, 1902–), writer and wood sculptor, was born in Athens County. He has been artist-in-residence at Ohio University and the University of Minnesota. He has published a novel: *This Is My Brother,* Chicago, 1936. WWNAA 3

ROOS, FRANK JOHN, JR. (Jan. 10, 1903–), artist and educator, was born in Chicago, Ill. He was on the faculty of Ohio State University, 1928–46, and since 1946 has taught at the University of Illinois. Besides studies of early American architecture, he has published *An Illustrated Handbook of Art History,* [New York, 1937]. WW 30

ROOT, EDWARD TALLMADGE (March 19, 1865–Oct. 7, 1948), clergyman, was born in Springfield, Clark County. After graduating from Yale University in 1887 and the Divinity School in 1890, he was ordained to the Presbyterian ministry. He was pastor of several churches in New England and was secretary of the Massachusetts Federation of Churches, 1904–30.

"The Profit of the Many," the Biblical Doctrine and Ethics of Wealth, Chicago, 1899.
The Redemption of Paradise Pond; Barbara; Stories of Rhode Island Life, Providence, R. I., 1908.
The Bible Economy of Plenty, New York, 1939.
A Christian Idea of Wealth . . . , Philadelphia, 1941.

ROOT, ERNEST ROB (June 23, 1862–April 19, 1953), was born in Medina, Medina County. After attending Oberlin College, he was an official of a Medina bank and was president of the A. I. Root Company, well-known manufacturers of beeswax. He wrote

Facts about Bees . . . , Medina, 1907. WWNAA 7

RORICK, ISABEL SCOTT (April 13, 1900–), was born in Toledo, Lucas County. She was educated in private schools in Toledo and at the Master's School, Dobbs Ferry, N. Y. The wife of a Toledo banker, she has published stories in national magazines. Sketches first published in a Junior League magazine resulted in two books, e.g., *Mr. and Mrs. Cugat, the Record of a Happy Marriage,* Boston, 1940. WW 28

RORIMER, JAMES JOSEPH (Sept. 7, 1905–), museum director, was born in Cleveland, Cuyahoga County. After graduating from Harvard University in 1927, he joined the staff of the Metropolitan Museum of Art in New York City, and from 1934 to 1955 was curator of medieval art. He has been director of the museum since 1955. During World War II he served with the Seventh Army as monuments officer and was responsible for discovering and restoring many art treasures, including the stained glass from Strasbourg cathedral. He has written several professional articles and books, and in collaboration with Gilbert Rabin wrote a book based on his wartime experience: *Survival: The Salvage and Protection of Art in War,* New York, [1950]. WW 30

ROSE, MARTHA EMILY PARMELEE (March 5, 1834–May 5, 1923), was born in Norton, Delaware County. In 1847 her family moved to Oberlin, and in 1855 she graduated from Oberlin College. She married William Grey Rose, later mayor of Cleveland. She was active in Cleveland civic affairs. Under the pen name Charles C. Lee, she wrote a story of Oberlin: *Character Building* (1906), and a series of articles about French trade schools that influenced the establishment of manual training classes in Cleveland. Under her own name she edited a history of the Western Reserve and wrote a travel book: *Travels in Europe and Northern Africa . . .* , Cleveland, 1901.

ROSE, WILLIAM GANSON (Oct. 29, 1878–Aug. 15, 1957), advertising executive, was born in Cleveland, Cuyahoga County. He graduated from Western Reserve University in 1901, was drama critic on the *Plain Dealer,* 1902–07, served as public relations counsel for several private and civic enterprises, and founded his own firm in 1918. He published a number of books, most of them on historical subjects, e.g., *Cleveland; The Making of a City,* Cleveland, [1950]. WW 29

ROSE, WILLIAM RUSSELL (Sept. 12, 1851–Feb. 16, 1927), journalist, born in Ithaca, N. Y., worked on the *Sunday Voice* and the *Press* in Cleveland before joining the *Plain Dealer* in 1896. He wrote editorials and a humorous column; a collection of his Sunday pieces was published: *Stories,* Cleveland, 1927.

ROSECRANS, SYLVESTER HORTON (Feb. 5, 1827–Oct. 21, 1878), clergyman, was born in Homer, Licking County. While a student at Kenyon College, he received a letter from his brother William, later to become famous as a Civil War general, describing his conversion to Catholicism. Sylvester followed his brother's example, transferred to St. John's College, Fordham, N. Y., studied in Rome, and was ordained to the priesthood in 1852. He served as a curate, rector, and teacher in Cincinnati until 1862, when he was named titular bishop and coadjutor. In 1867 he was transferred to St. Patrick's Church, Columbus, and the following year was made bishop. He established numerous schools and churches, built St. Joseph's cathedral, and did much to strengthen the church.

The Divinity of Christ . . . , Cincinnati, 1866.

ROSENBERG, WILLIAM. See William Manners.

ROSENBERGER, ELIZABETH DELP (1864–May 11, 1951), born in Mainland, Pa., lived in Miami County for 25 years. A graduate of Juniata College, she served on the faculties of Bridgewater College and Blue Ridge College. In 1893 she married Dr. A. S. Rosenberger, who died in 1913. In 1919 she married Rev. P. J. Blough and moved to Johnstown, Pa. She wrote articles for the *Gospel Messenger* and at least three books, e.g., *The Scarlet Line, and Other Bible Stories,* Elgin, Ill., 1903.

ROSENTHAL, MIRIAM (Oct. 7, 1901–), was born in Lebanon, Warren County. Formerly on the Dayton *Journal* and the Dayton *News,* she has been engaged in fund raising and public relations work in Dayton since 1932. She has written a pictorial history of the Dayton Fire Department for juvenile readers: *The Junior Fire Chief,* New York, [1934].

ROSS, ABEL HASTINGS (April 28, 1831–May 13, 1893), clergyman, born in Winchenden, Mass., attended Oberlin preparatory department and college, 1851–57. After his ordination as a Congregational minister, he served churches in Springfield, 1866–73, and Columbus, 1873–75. He was also lecturer on church polity at Oberlin Seminary, 1871–91. He published sermons, books, and pamphlets on church organization and articles on religious topics. He wrote *Manual of Congregationalism,* Oberlin, 1889.

ROSS, DENMAN WALDO (Jan. 10, 1853–Sept. 2, 1935), educator, was born in Cincinnati, Hamilton County, but was reared in New York City, attended Harvard University, and spent his life in Cambridge, Mass. He earned a doctorate in history at Harvard in 1880; but after the death of his father in 1884, he turned his attention to art. He lectured on design at Harvard and was a trustee of the Boston Museum for over forty years. He published several influential papers and books on esthetic theory, e.g., *A Theory of Pure Design . . . ,* Boston, 1907. DAB 21

ROSS, EDMUND GIBSON (Dec. 7, 1826–May 8, 1907), printer, journalist, U. S. Senator, was born in Ashland, Ashland County. After learning the printing business in Huron, he was an itinerant printer for a number of years. Strongly opposed to slavery, he led a party of colonists into Kansas in 1856. The next year he and his brother bought the *Kansas Tribune,* published in Topeka. In 1866, after serving with Kansas troops on the Missouri border, Ross was appointed to the U. S. Senate to complete the term of James H. Lane, who had committed suicide. Although he opposed virtually all of President Johnson's policies, he voted against conviction in the impeachment trial. His vote was regarded as the turning point of the trial, and he was assailed on all sides. He completed his term as an independent, and in 1872 he joined the Democratic Party. He published various newspapers in Kansas, 1871–82. In 1882 he went to New Mexico and worked as a printer. He served as governor of the Territory, 1885–89, and spent the remainder of his life in Albuquerque. Besides the titles below, he published magazine articles and some speeches.

History of the Impeachment of Andrew Johnson . . . , [Santa Fe, N. M.], 1896.

A Reminiscence of the Kansas Conflict, Albuquerque, N. M., [1898].

The Pilgrim and the Cavalier in Kansas, [Washington, D. C., 1917?].

ROSS, HARRY H. (Nov. 27, 1880–), was born in Fremont, Sandusky County. A graduate of Oberlin, he was on the Toledo *Blade* for several years. He is now living in Toledo. For about ten years he conducted tours of the Lake Erie islands, the subject of his book, *Enchanting Isles of Erie . . . ,* [Lakeside?, 1949].

ROSS, JAMES (April 15, 1867–Dec. 14, 1940), educator, attended Moore's Hill College, Ind., after which he taught in the public schools of Sandusky and Cleveland. He wrote a book on the public schools: *The Heart of Democracy . . . ,* Sandusky, [1930].

ROSS, OLIN JONES (1858–Jan. 16, 1941), lawyer, was born in Fayette County, Pa., but grew up in southern Illinois. He later settled in Hillsboro. He read law, was admitted to the bar in 1882, and began practice in Columbus in 1907. He was an outspoken freethinker, published pamphlets and lectured widely, and was also a prolific writer of letters to newspaper editors. In 1914 he founded the Rationalist Society in Columbus. He wrote a fanciful account of a train taken to Europe and its effect on civilization: *The Sky Blue . . . ,* Columbus, 1904.

ROSS, W. W. (Dec. 24, 1824–March 4, 1906), educator, was born in Medina County. He attended the schools of Seville. He began teaching at Twinsburg in 1840 and became superintendent of schools in Fremont in 1864.

The Wants of Ungraded Schools, Fremont, 1879.

Tariff Reform, Fremont, 1888.

ROSSITER, FREDERICK MAGEE (March 12, 1870–), physician, was born in Elmore, Ottawa County. He graduated from Battle Creek College in 1893 and Rush Medical College in 1896. He was on the staff of Battle Creek Sanitarium, 1897–1902, and in general practice, 1902–28. He was also a professor at the College of Medical Evangelists, Los Angeles, 1922–26. He published a number of medical books for general readers, some of them in collaboration with his wife, Mary Henry Rossiter, e.g., *The Story of a Living Temple . . . ,* Chicago, 1902. WW 26

ROTHENBURGER, WILLIAM FREDERICK (March 5, 1874–), clergyman, was born in Holgate, Henry County. He graduated from Ohio Normal University in 1898 and Hiram College in 1900. After being ordained a minister in the Disciples of Christ Church, he served various churches in the Midwest, including Ashtabula, 1900–

05, and Cleveland, 1908–18. He now lives in Indianapolis, Ind. He has published numerous religious articles and tracts, and *The Cross in Symbol, Spirit and Worship,* Boston, [1930]. WW 27

ROTSVALD, FRED C. Pseud. See Mildred W. Benson.

ROURKE, CONSTANCE MAYFIELD (Nov. 14, 1885–March 23, 1941), educator and writer, was born in Cleveland, Cuyahoga County. She graduated from Vassar College in 1907, studied abroad for three years, and taught English at Vassar, 1910–15. She wrote several biographies and a seminal analysis of American humor that profoundly affected the study of American literature and folklore: *American Humor; A Study of the National Character,* New York, [1931]. WWW 1

ROUSE, E. S. S. (Feb. 23, 1795–April 26, 1883), was born in Pittstown, N. Y. He served in the War of 1812 and emigrated to Muskingum County in 1818. He settled in Knox County in 1832, and in 1850 he moved to Mount Vernon, where he operated a woolen mill and edited the weekly *Home Visitor.* He died in Mount Vernon.

The Bugle Blast; Or, Spirit of the Conflict . . . , Philadelphia, 1864.

ROWE, EDNA B. (Sept. 13, 1890–Dec. 2, 1953), educator, was born in Dupont, Putnam County. A graduate of Columbia University, she taught at Bowling Green University and the University of Toledo and was president of a private elementary school in Toledo. She published articles on elementary education, textbooks, and *Bible Stories for Little Folk,* Cincinnati, [1926].

ROWE, EDWINA. Pseud. See Sara T. Drukker.

ROWE, FRANK HENRY (Nov. 1, 1892–), industrialist, was born in Coalton, Jackson County, and now lives in Portsmouth. Until his retirement in 1957, he served as safety director, personnel manager, and director of industrial relations in various steel plants in Scioto County. He has published magazine articles on the steel industry and a book: *History of the Iron and Steel Industry in Scioto County* . . . , Columbus, 1938.

ROWE, FREDERICK LOUIS (Dec. 27, 1866–May 12, 1947), editor, was born in Akron, Summit County. He edited the *Christian Leader,* 1896–1946, in Cincinnati and also operated his own publishing firm. His death occurred in Cincinnati. He wrote *Letters to an Orphan, from a Business Man to His Stenographer,* Cincinnati, [1911].

ROWELL, ADELAIDE CORINNE (Dec. 6, 1884–), librarian, was born in Cleveland, Cuyahoga County. In 1890 her family moved to Chattanooga, Tenn., where she was reared. After attending the local schools and the University of Tennessee, she was on the staff of the Chattanooga Public Library, 1915–46. She now lives at Lookout Mountain, Tenn. She wrote a number of one-act plays and a novel for juvenile readers: *Touchdown,* New York, 1942. WWAW 1

ROWLAND, JAMES (Oct. 24, 1814–Nov. 9, 1854), clergyman, was born in Windsor Locks, Conn. He attended Yale University for two years, studied medicine, and practiced for several years in New England before entering the ministry. He was pastor of the Presbyterian Church, Circleville, 1844–54. A number of his sermons were printed.

The Consecrated Way, Circleville, 1847.

ROWLEY, CHARLES E. (1843– ?), evangelist, was born in Red Lion, Warren County. A teacher of music and the composer of several hymns, he became a member of the evangelistic team of Rice and Rowley. He is believed to have spent his last years in Hardin County. He compiled song books and wrote an autobiography that contains interesting material concerning farm life in Ohio in the mid-nineteenth century: *Apples of Gold,* Findlay, 1925.

ROY, ANDREW (July 19, 1834–Oct. 19, 1914), was born in Lanarkshire, Scotland. After coming to America in 1850, he settled in Jackson County. He served in the Civil War, was captured at Gaines Hill, and was held in Libby Prison until exchanged in 1863. In 1874 he was appointed state mine inspector, a position he held until his death. He wrote a number of articles on mines and mining.

The Coal Mines . . . , Cleveland, 1876.

The Practical Miner's Companion . . . , Columbus, 1885.

Recollections of a Prisoner of War, Columbus, 1905.

A History of the Coal Miners of the United States . . . , 3rd ed., Columbus, [1907].

ROYCE, CHARLES C. (1845–1923), ethnologist, was born in Defiance, Defiance County. He published a number of papers in reports of the U. S. Bureau of American Ethnology and *Rambling Notes of a Rambling Tour through Egypt, Palestine and Europe,* [Washington, D. C., 1913].

ROYER, HOMER L. (Oct. 6, 1906–), educator, was born in Darke County. After graduating from Manchester College in 1929, he became a teacher in Ohio schools. He has been a school principal in Findlay, 1939–42, a teacher and principal in Dayton, 1942–50, and an assistant to the Dayton superintendent of schools since 1950. With Ollie E. Fink (q.v.) he published *Buckeye Tales,* Chicago, [1945].

ROYSE, NOBLE KIBBY (1841–1890), educator, was born in Newtown, Hamilton County. A graduate of Woodward High School, he was a principal in the Cincinnati school system for many years. Besides the titles below, he published textbooks and manuals.

Some Ancient Melodies and Other Experiments, Cincinnati, 1882.

A Study of Genius, Chicago, 1891.

RUBINOW, ISAAC MAX (April 19, 1875–Sept. 1, 1936), physician and social worker, was born in Grodno, Russia, and came to the United States in 1893. He graduated from Columbia University in 1895, New York University (M.D.) in 1898, and Columbia (Ph.D.) in 1914. He practiced medicine and was associated with various government bureaus and agencies. From 1929 until his death he was secretary of B'nai B'rith. He was a resident of Cincinnati during the latter part of his life. He published a number of books on insurance and social and political questions, e.g., *The Quest for Security,* New York, [1934]. WWW 1

RUDY, JACOB MARVIN (1865–May 6, 1930), clergyman, was born near Westminster, Allen County. A graduate of Ohio Northern University and the University of Chicago, he was ordained as a Disciples of Christ minister and served churches in Ada, Buffalo, N. Y., and Chicago. He was also popular as a lecturer. He wrote *Our Nation's Peril,* Chicago, 1918.

RUDY, STELLA M. (1888–Dec. 25, 1943), missionary, was born in Dayton, Montgomery County. A member of the Christian Church, she served as a missionary in China, 1914–28, and also edited a religious magazine, *Junior Boys and Girls.* She wrote a number of stories for children, which were published in at least three collections, e.g., *New Rainbow Missionary Stories,* Harrisburg, Pa., 1943.

RUESS, STELLA KNIGHT (July 9, 1879–), was born in Cincinnati, Hamilton County. She married Christopher Ruess in 1905. She studied at the University of Southern California. Her last address in Ohioana files is Los Angeles. She has published *Poems in Trees,* [Hollywood, Calif., 1930]. BDCP

RUETENIK, HERMAN JULIUS (Sept. 20, 1826–Feb. 22, 1914), clergyman and educator, was born in Demerthin, Germany. He came to America in 1848, taught school in Easton, Pa., and was ordained to the ministry of the Reformed Church in 1852. He came to Toledo as a missionary and also was a minister in Cleveland. He served on the faculty of Heidelberg College and later was president of Calvin College, Cleveland. Besides the titles below, he published German primers and grammars.

Aus der Indianer-Zeit . . . , Cleveland, [1881].

Berühmte Deutsche-Vorkämpfer für Fortschritt, Freiheit und Friede in Nord-Amerika . . . , Cleveland, 1888.

The Pioneers of the Reformed Church in the United States . . . , Cleveland, 1901.

RUGGLES, KENT P. (June 26, 1880–May 16, 1957), was born in Milan, Erie County. In 1906 he moved to Akron, where he was employed by the Ohio State Telephone Company and later by Goodyear Tire and Rubber Company. He wrote a book on salesmanship: *Fool-Things That Kill Business,* Cuyahoga Falls, [1922].

RULISON, NELSON SOMERVILLE (April 24, 1842–Sept. 1, 1897), Episcopal bishop, born in Carthage, N. Y., was pastor of St. Paul's Church, Cleveland, 1876–84, before being elected assistant bishop of central Pennsylvania. He published sermons and other religious writings, e.g., *History of St. Paul's Church . . . ,* Cleveland, 1877.

RÜMELIN, CARL GUSTAV. See Charles Reemelin.

RUNNING, CORINNE (Oct. 5, 1914–), was born in Van Wert, Van Wert County. She graduated from Michigan State Teachers College in 1936 and now lives in Seattle, Wash. She has been writing fiction since 1940. Her books include *Garden Shower,* New York, 1948. WWAW 1

RUNYAN, GEORGIE DRURY (July 20, 1844-June 25, 1920), was born in Aroostook County, Maine. In 1856 her family moved to Springfield, where she later married Dr. Frank C. Runyan, a dentist. She died in California and is buried in Springfield. She wrote for *Ladies' Home Journal* and other women's magazines. Her only published book is a sweeping survey of American history, apparently written to commemorate the fourth centennial of Columbus' discovery.

400 Years of America . . . , Springfield, 1892.

RUPP, ISRAEL DANIEL (July 10, 1803–May 31, 1878), historian, born in Cumberland County, Pa., came to Cincinnati in 1830 and was for a time the postmaster at Rupp's, Marion County. In 1832 he returned to Pennsylvania, where he published a number of books on early history of the state.

RUSK, ROGERS D. (Nov. 17, 1892–), educator, was born in Washington, D. C., but was reared in Morgan County and has continued to spend his summers there. After graduating from Ohio Wesleyan University in 1916, he taught for a year at Niles High School. He completed his doctorate at the University of Chicago in 1925. He has taught at North Central College, Ill., 1919–28, and Mount Holyoke, 1928–57. He has published numerous articles in scientific journals, several textbooks, and a history of physics: *Atoms, Men and Stars . . .* , New York, 1937. WW 28

RUSLER, WILLIAM (March 7, 1851–June 25, 1929), was born in Shawnee Township, Allen County. He attended township schools and Lima High School. After teaching school for a time, he operated a farm in Allen County until his retirement in 1910. He published *A Standard History of Allen County . . .* , 2 vols., Chicago, 1921.

RUSSELL, ADDISON PEALE (Sept. 8, 1826–June 24, 1912), was born in Wilmington, Clinton County. He apparently knew exactly what he wanted his life to be, and he shaped it accordingly. As he might plan a book, he blocked out the years, giving a preparatory period to journalism, a season to the ripening experience of public service, then moving on to the achievement of a contemplative life, so ordered that he might attain wisdom through reading and honor through writing. His parents, Charles and Mary MacNabb Russell, had come to Ohio from Virginia in 1815. He received his brief schooling in a local subscription school. His father owned a woolen mill where Addison worked until he was sixteen, when he was indentured as an apprentice in the printing office of the Zanesville *Gazette.* In 1845 he became editor of the Hillsborough *News,* and two years later joined the staff of the *Western Star* in Lebanon. Returning to Wilmington in 1852, he purchased a half-interest in the Clinton *Republican,* which he held until 1860. His association with strongly Republican newspapers brought him into politics and led to the second phase of his career, as a state official. In 1850 he was appointed clerk of the Ohio state senate. From 1855 to 1857 he served as a member of the Ohio general assembly, and from 1857 to 1861 he held the office of secretary of state. In the following year he was appointed financial agent of the State of Ohio, with offices at 25 William Street in the City of New York. Twice reappointed to this post, he remained in New York until 1868. In that year he returned to Wilmington, announced his retirement, and at once embarked upon a new career as a writer. One book had already come from his pen while he lived in New York: *Half Tints,* which he published at the age of 42. It was to be followed by a half-dozen volumes which were to inspire other writers to speak of him as the "Western Washington Irving" and the "Ralph Waldo Emerson of Ohio." His style, as revealed in *Half Tints,* was already urbane and polished: distinctive, yet clearly in the great tradition of the English essayists. Dr. Russell devoted almost half a century to reading. He regarded his writing seriously, but it was the incidental by-product of a long attachment to his library. In *A Club of One* he wrote of the lone member, "He read, he thought, and sometimes he recorded." In *Sub-Coelum* he says, "Life in literature was the life . . . most relished." Both of these statements may be taken as a personal confession. He was unusually shy about making more direct reference to himself, and when his writing called for the first person singular, he invented masquerades for himself as author, and omitted his name from the title page. In *Half Tints* he employed the pleasant fiction of a married man, living in a metropolitan hotel, who wrote a series of letters to a friend of his youth. In *A Club of One* he was the hypochondriac, "who might have been sociable," blessed with a wife who never interfered with his reading or attempted to cure his imagined ailments. His reputation was built on a series of books of a highly literary nature. With anecdotes and apt quotation, mainly from the standard authors of English and French literature, he sorted and selected his material, fashioning essays on character and conduct. In his day they served to prove (and it seemed important then) that a writer of taste and style could build an ivory tower in a small Ohio town, and produce books which seemed to emerge from a shady porch in Concord or from long afternoons in the British Museum. The books had a good press, and Houghton, Mifflin kept them in print for many years after their original publication. It was a rare occurrence when a reviewer took him to task, deplored his use of quotation, and claimed that his own contribution to his books was almost entirely restricted "to a copious use of conjunctions." Because he wrote so well, everyone may now wish that he had given more of himself and less of what "someone had said." This is emphasized by the fact that his book on Tom Corwin, Ohio governor and United States Senator, has come to be regarded as his best. Russell knew Corwin, and he was able to recall him in such a way that Corwin's character, wit, mental powers, and oratorical genius—the very man, himself—live in these delightful pages. Russell's imagination was also stirred by the old town of Lebanon, where Corwin lived, and the men with whom he associated. "Giants there were in those days in the little valley," he wrote. In his final book he put aside paste and scissors, to write without benefit of quotation. Describing a community not as it was but as he would have it, *Sub-Coelum* continues to be an unusual contribution to utopian literature. Remarkable for what it omits, Russell's version of the ideal society reveals nothing in the way of political readjustment, the revolutionary force of scientific invention, or the unfolding of a philosophical idea. It was, instead, based on an enlightened change in people's conduct: they had adopted the rule of common sense and had stopped doing the things that had long annoyed the author. A critic in the *Dial* observed that it was a society adjusted to people "with shaky nerves and east-wind susceptibilities." In his later years, Dr. Russell became Wilmington's grand old man of letters, the final source of authority on matters of historical and literary interest. Though kind and genial, he fulfilled this role with sufficient dignity to arouse feelings of awe in some of his townsmen. His manners were courtly and he held to many of the customs and habits of the past. After Wilmington's public library was opened, he spent much of his time in its reading room. Once, walking toward the library, nose in book, he stepped into the soft cement of a newly spread pavement. He looked at his feet, then turned his eyes to the sky. "When," he demanded, "are You going to get this world finished?" He had a wide circle of acquaintance among Ohio's literary men, and when he died, his friend W. H. Venable read a memorial tribute at his funeral.

Gerald D. McDonald

Half Tints . . ., New York, 1867.
Library Notes, New York, 1875.
Thomas Corwin, a Sketch, Cincinnati, 1881.
Characteristics. Sketches and Essays, Boston, 1884.
A Club of One . . ., Boston, 1887.
In a Club Corner . . ., Boston, 1890.
Sub-Coelum . . ., Boston, 1893.

RUSSELL, HOWARD HYDE (Oct. 21, 1855–June 30, 1946), lawyer and reformer, was born in Stillwater, Minn. He taught school and practiced law in Iowa, 1874–82, was a clergyman, 1885–93, and founded the Anti-Saloon League in Ohio in 1893. He lived in Westerville, and held various offices in the Anti-Saloon League.

A Lawyer's Examination of the Bible, Chicago, [1893].

RUST, HERMAN (Dec. 8, 1816–Aug. 8, 1905), clergyman and educator, was born in Bremen, Germany. After coming to the United States in 1841, he studied at Mercersburg College and Seminary until 1849, when he was licensed to preach by the Evangelical and Reformed Church. He served a church in Cincinnati, 1851–62, and was a member of the Heidelberg College faculty, 1862–1902. A selection of his theological writings was posthumously published by his son, John Benjamin Rust (q.v.): *A Memorial Volume . . .*, Tiffin, 1924.

RUST, JOHN BENJAMIN (Sept. 5, 1856–Sept. 8, 1938), clergyman and educator, was born in Cincinnati, Hamilton County. After graduating from Heidelberg College in 1877, he served as minister of several Evangelical and Reformed churches in Ohio; he was a member of the Heidelberg faculty, 1914–35. His writings include *Modernism and the Reformation,* New York, [1914]. OBB

RUST, ORTON J. (Aug. 14, 1882–Nov. 4, 1951), journalist, was born in Clark County. After graduating from National Normal University, Lebanon, he taught school for a time; he served for many years in the advertising department of the Springfield *Daily News.* He died in Springfield. He published poems and several pamphlets and books, e.g., *Roosevelt Takes Hold . . . ,* [Springfield, 1933].

RUST, RICHARD SUTTON (Sept. 12, 1815–Dec. 22, 1906), educator and clergyman, born in Ipswich, Mass., came to Ohio in 1859. He was president of Wilberforce University, 1859–63, and Wesleyan Female Seminary in Cincinnati, 1863–65. He was active in various societies and commissions organized to assist the Negro, and in 1866 he helped found the Freedmen's Aid Society of the Methodist Episcopal Church. He was corresponding secretary for more than twenty years and did much to provide educational facilities for the Negro in the South. Besides the title below, he edited *Freedom's Gifts* in 1840 and a tribute to Bishop Isaac W. Wiley in 1885. He died in Cincinnati.

The Freedmen's Aid Society of the Methodist Episcopal Church, Cincinnati, [1880].

RUTER, MARTIN (April 3, 1785–May 16, 1838), clergyman, was born in Charlton, Mass. He was a Methodist minister in New England until 1820, when he established the Western branch of the Methodist Book Concern at Cincinnati, which under his management became a potent factor in developing Cincinnati as a publishing center in the first half of the nineteenth century. After eight years in Cincinnati, he served as president of Augusta College, Ky., and later of Allegheny College. He died in Texas, where he was serving as a missionary. He published *The Martyrs, or a History of Persecution,* Cincinnati, 1831.

RUTLEDGE, GEORGE PERRY (May 16, 1869–June 20, 1947), clergyman, born in Blacksburg, Va., was pastor of Broad Street Church, Columbus, 1913–16, and edited the *Christian Standard* in Cincinnati, 1916–22. He published a number of sermons and books on religious questions, e.g., *Center-Shots at Rome; A Series of Lectures on Catholicism . . . ,* Cincinnati, [1914]. WWW 2

RYALL, LYDIA J. (1850–June 30, 1920), was born in Ashland, Ashland County. She published one book, *Sketches and Stories of the Lake Erie Islands,* Norwalk, 1913.

RYAN, DANIEL JOSEPH (Jan. 1, 1855–June 15, 1923), lawyer and historian, was born in Cincinnati, Hamilton County. After reading law he was admitted to the bar in 1877. He practiced law in Portsmouth, held several local offices, served two terms in the General Assembly, and was active in the Republican Party. In addition to the titles below, he published many articles on state history, collaborated with Emilius O. Randall (q.v.) on a five-volume history of Ohio, and compiled a most useful bibliography: *The Civil War Literature of Ohio . . . ,* Cleveland, 1911.

Arbitration between Capital and Labor . . . , Columbus, 1885.

A History of Ohio . . . , Columbus, 1888.

The Cuban Question in American Diplomacy, [Columbus?], 1897.

Masters of Men; A Retrospect in Presidential Politics, Columbus, 1915.

Ohio in Four Wars, a Military History, Columbus, 1917.

Historic Failures in Applied Socialism, Columbus, 1920.

Lincoln and Ohio, Columbus, 1924.

RYAN, DON (Sept. 14, 1889–   ), was born in Ryansville, Lawrence County. After graduating from Ironton High School, he studied for two years at West Virginia University. He worked on the Ironton *Register,* the Cincinnati *Enquirer,* and the *Ohio State Journal* before leaving Ohio for Los Angeles, where he has been a reporter, movie actor, and script writer. He has also written at least two books, e.g., *A Roman Holiday,* New York, 1930.

RYAN, MRS. EDWIN L. See Margaret K. Kaser.

RYAN, JAMES A. (July 1, 1874–Sept. 16, 1939), was born in Sandusky, Erie County. He attended Sandusky schools, learned the printing business, and was a printer in Sandusky, 1888–94. He was a reporter on the Sandusky *Register,* 1894–1900, was press agent for Cedar Point, managed theaters in several cities, and served as postmaster of Sandusky, 1914–23. Interested in local history, he was active in the Firelands Historical Society and wrote *The Town of Milan . . . ,* [Sandusky], 1928. OBB

RYAN, WALTER ANTHONY (April 30, 1878–Sept. 2, 1948), lawyer, was born in Cincinnati, Hamilton County. He graduated from the University of Cincinnati in 1898, was admitted to the Ohio bar, and practiced in Cincinnati until his retirement in 1946. He published a book on corporation law and a collection of poems: *Childhood Verse,* Cincinnati, 1903.

RYDER, ARTHUR WILLIAM (March 8, 1877–March 21, 1938), educator, was born in Oberlin, Lorain County. He graduated from Harvard University in 1897 and the University of Leipzig (Ph.D.) in 1901. He taught Sanskrit at Harvard, 1901–06, and the University of California, 1906–38. He published several translations during his lifetime; published posthumously was *Original Poems; Together with Translations from the Sanskrit,* Berkeley, Calif., 1939. WWW 1

RYDER, JAMES FITZALLEN (1826–June 2, 1904), photographer, born in New York City, came to Cleveland in 1850. He operated a photography studio on Superior Avenue for more than thirty years. He is said to have been the first American photographer to retouch negatives. He published a book of reminiscences: *Voigtländer and I in Pursuit of Shadow Catching . . . ,* Cleveland, 1902.

RYDER, MELVIN (Jan. 26, 1893–), publisher, was born in Cadiz Junction, Harrison County. He graduated from Ohio State University in 1915, served on the *Stars and Stripes,* was associated with the Kiplinger Washington Agency, 1921–24, and was afterward an executive of several advertising and publishing firms. Since 1940 he has been president of the Army Times Publishing Company. In his final year at Ohio State, he published *Rambles Round the Campus,* Boston, 1915. WW 30

RYDER, ROBERT OLIVER (March 9, 1875–March 16, 1936), journalist, was born in Oberlin, Lorain County. After graduating from Phillips Academy in 1894, he studied at Yale University and Williams College. He joined the staff of the *Ohio State Journal* in 1898 and served as editor, 1919–30. He died in Berkeley, Calif. He wrote *Young Lady across the Way . . . ,* Boston, [1913].

S

SAALFIELD, ADAH LOUISE SUTTON (June 8, 1860–Nov. 17, 1935), was born in Brooklyn, N. Y. She graduated from Hunter College and on Aug. 1, 1885, married Arthur J. Saalfield. In 1898, her husband took over the Werner Publishing Co., Akron, and expanded the children's book department; in 1900, the name of the firm was changed to the Saalfield Publishing Co. She lived in Akron from 1898 until her death. She published many articles, stories, and poems in various periodicals. She undoubtedly wrote or contributed to more of the publications of her husband's firm than those listed below. The first seven titles were published under her maiden name; the last two, under the pen name Louise A. Field.

Lingua Gemma. A Cycle of Gems . . . , New York, [1894].
Mr. Bunny, His Book, Akron, [1900].
Seeds of April's Sowing, Akron, 1902.
Sweeter Still Than This, Akron, [1905].
Teddy Bears, Akron, [1907].
A Little Maid in Toyland, Akron, 1908.
Mushroom Fairies, Akron, [1910].
Peter Rabbit and his Pa, Akron, 1916.
Peter Rabbit and his Ma, Akron, 1917.

SABINE, GEORGE HOLLAND (Dec. 9, 1880–), educator, was born in Dayton, Montgomery County. After graduating from Cornell University (A.B., 1903; Ph.D., 1906), he served on the philosophy faculty of several universities, including Ohio State, 1923–31; he also taught at Sage School of Philosophy, Cornell University, 1931–48, and since his retirement has lived in Ithaca, N. Y. His writings include *A History of Political Theory,* New York, [1937]. WW 26

SABINE, WALLACE CLEMENT WARE (June 31, 1868–Jan. 10, 1919), physicist, was born in Richwood, Union County. He graduated from Ohio State University in 1886. He began graduate study at Harvard University in 1886, was appointed an assistant in physics in 1889, and was a member of the Harvard faculty until his death. The deficiencies of the auditorium of Fogg Art Museum aroused his interest in architectural acoustics, the field in which he made his most significant contribution. He published a textbook and occasional technical papers. A posthumous collection was also published: *Collected Papers on Acoustics,* Cambridge, 1922. DAB 16

SAFFORD, JAMES MERRILL (Aug. 13, 1822–July 3, 1907), geologist and educator, was born in Muskingum County. He graduated from Ohio University in 1844. He taught at Cumberland University, Lebanon, Tenn., 1848–72, and at Vanderbilt University, 1875–1900. He was state geologist of Tennessee, 1854–60 and 1871–1900. With only a compass and a pocket level, he traversed the state on foot and on horseback to compile the first title listed below. He died in Dallas, Texas.

A Geological Reconnaissance of the State of Tennessee, Nashville, 1856.
Geology of Tennessee, Nashville, 1869.
Introduction to the Resources of Tennessee, (with J. B. Killebrew), Nashville, 1874.

SAFFORD, WILLIAM EDWIN (Dec. 14, 1859–Jan. 10, 1926), naval officer and scientist, was born in Chillicothe, Ross County, the son of William H. Safford (q.v.). He graduated from the U. S. Naval Academy in 1880; in the same year, after a chance meeting with Alexander Agassiz, he resolved to equip himself for scientific collecting on naval cruises. His life in the navy provided him with exceptional opportunities for observation in remote places, and he acquired an encyclopedic knowledge of the cultures of the peoples of the South Seas, as well as of ancient American cultures. The remarkable breadth of his interests is indicated by a bibliography of more than 100 scientific papers and lectures. He resigned from the navy in 1902 to become assistant botanist in the U. S. Department of Agriculture; in 1915 he was promoted to economic botanist, the position he held at the time of his death. The work that established his reputation as an ethnobotanist is virtually a handbook of the island of Guam and its history: *The Useful Plants of Guam . . . ,* Washington, 1905.

SAFFORD, WILLIAM HARRISON (Feb. 19, 1821–April 20, 1903), lawyer, was born in Parkersburg, Va., where he was educated at Asbury Academy and studied law. In 1848 he moved to Chillicothe, where he became a distinguished jurist. His two books on Harman Blennerhassett are indispensable sources on the subject of the so-called Burr conspiracy.

The Life of Harman Blennerhassett . . . , Chillicothe, 1850.
The Blennerhassett Papers . . . , Cincinnati, 1861.

SAGE, RUFUS B. (March 17, 1817–Dec. 23, 1893), was born in Upper Middletown (Cromwell), Conn. He learned the printing trade in the local printing office, and in 1837 he came to Marietta, where a married sister was living. Here he taught school and worked on the Marietta *Gazette.* He also worked briefly as a printer in Circleville and Columbus. In 1840 he published the *Harrisonian Straightout* in Columbus. In May, 1841, he started for the Oregon territory, and for the next three years he lived in the West as a free trapper and as a member of various groups. His wanderings took him from Fort Hall to New Mexico. In July, 1844, he was back in Columbus, where he published political newspapers supporting Henry Clay and opposing the annexation of Texas. After a brief period of editing the Chillicothe *Gazette,* 1844–45, he returned to Connecticut, where he passed the remainder of his life as a farmer. His book passed through several editions, some with altered titles. His only other time in Ohio was a visit in 1846–47 to sell the book.

Scenes in the Rocky Mountains . . . , Philadelphia, 1846.

ST. CLAIR, ARTHUR (March 23, 1736–Aug. 31, 1818), governor of the Northwest Territory, 1789–1820, was born in Thurso, Scotland. As an ensign in the British army, he served in Canada during the French and Indian War; after resigning from the army in 1762, he purchased a large tract of land in western Pennsylvania. During the Revolution he served with some distinction throughout Washington's New Jersey campaign, but his military record was sullied by his evacuation of Fort Ticonderoga in the summer of 1777. As governor of the Northwest Territory, he alienated many frontiersmen by his conservative views, his overbearing manner, and his opposition to statehood for Ohio; and he was finally removed by President Jefferson in 1802. While still territorial governor, he led an expedition against the Miami Indians; his force was surprised and defeated on Nov. 4, 1791. In 1812, while living in comparative poverty in Pennsylvania, he published a defense of his conduct: *A Narrative of the Manner in Which the Campaign against the Indians, in the Year One Thousand Seven Hundred and Ninety-one Was Conducted . . . ,* Philadelphia, 1812.

SALMANS, LEVI BRIMNER (March 19, 1855–Jan. 29, 1938), missionary, was born in Hocking County. He graduated from Asbury University in 1880 and Drew Theological Seminary in 1883. Ordained to the Methodist ministry in 1882, he was a missionary in Mexico from 1885 until his retirement in 1927. He was head of a Methodist boys' school, established a medical mission at Guanajuato, and founded Good Samaritan Hospital and a nurses' training school. He died in Pasadena, Calif. He published numerous books in both Spanish and English, e.g., *Christian Healing; Or, Mexican Evangelism . . .* , Guanajuato, Mexico, 1919. WW 11

SAMPSON, MARTIN WRIGHT (Sept. 7, 1866–Aug. 22, 1930), educator, was born in Cincinnati, Hamilton County. He graduated from the University of Cincinnati in 1888 and afterward studied in Munich. He taught English at the University of Iowa, 1889–91, Stanford University, 1892–93, Indiana University, 1893–1906, and Cornell University, 1908–30. He published a textbook on composition, edited several literary works, and wrote poems, plays, and a collection of stories originally intended for his own children: *The Good Giant,* Boston, 1928. DAB 16

SANDERS, JAMES HARVEY (Oct. 9, 1832–Dec. 22, 1899), agriculturist, was born in Union County and attended public schools there. In 1852 he moved to Iowa, where he began his career as a journalist. He edited the *Western Stock Journal,* the *National Livestock Journal,* the *Spirit of the Times,* and the *Breeders' Gazette.* He compiled several studbooks and a treatise on barn-building. He committed suicide in Memphis, Tenn.

Horse Breeding . . . , Chicago, 1885.

The Breeds of Live Stock, and the Principles of Heredity . . . , Chicago, 1887.

SANDERS, THOMAS JEFFERSON (Jan. 18, 1855–Dec. 26, 1946), educator, was born near Burbank, Wayne County. After graduating from Otterbein College in 1878, he was a school superintendent in Ohio and Indiana, 1878–91. He was president of Otterbein College, 1891–1901, and was professor of philosophy there, 1901–31. He wrote a number of articles on education and philosophy.

Philosophy of the Christian Religion, Dayton, 1890.

SANDERSON, EUGENE CLAREMONT (March 24, 1859–1940), clergyman, was born in Fayette County. He graduated from Drake University (A.B., 1883; B.D., 1893). Ordained to the ministry of the Disciples of Christ in 1883, he preached as an evangelist and as pastor of several churches in the Northwest. In 1895 he founded Eugene Bible University, Eugene, Oreg., and served as its president until 1929. He published *Bible and History Studies . . .* , Eugene, Oreg., 1912. WW 16

SANGER, MARGOT (Dec. 5, 1890–), was born in Toledo, Lucas County. She attended Toledo schools and Ferry Hall, Lake Forest, Ill. She has conducted children's radio programs in Toledo, Cleveland, and other cities, and has published a collection of stories: *Anne to Zonia,* New York, [1950].

SANTLEY, MARY McDERMOTT (Dec. 4, 1842–Dec. 19, 1921), educator, was born in Ontario, Richland County. After graduating from Baldwin University in 1865, she taught French at Conference Seminary, Maumee, until her marriage to W. R. Santley in 1868. She later taught art at Baldwin University, 1899–1902. She was active in the Methodist Church and in the temperance movement.

An Elect Lady, Cleveland, 1892.

Margery Rae, Cleveland, 1892.

Indian Romances, and Other Poems, Cleveland, 1911.

SANTMYER, HELEN HOOVEN (Nov. 25, 1895–), was born in Cincinnati, Hamilton County. She graduated from Wellesley College in 1918 and from Oxford University, England, in 1927. She worked on the editorial staff of *Scribner's Magazine,* taught English at Wellesley College and at Cedarville College, and is now in the reference department of the Dayton Public Library. She lives in Xenia. She has published fiction, poetry, and essays in various magazines, and has also published three novels, e.g., *Herbs and Apples,* Boston, 1925. WW 21

SARCHET, CYRUS PARKINSON BEATTY (Nov. 17, 1828–July 31, 1913), was born in Cambridge, Guernsey County, and was educated in the schools of that city. Though a successful farmer, he found time to write many articles on local history, which he contributed to local newspapers over a period of fifty years. He died in Cambridge. He also wrote a family history and *History of Guernsey County, Ohio,* 2 vols., Indianapolis, 1910.

SATTLER, ERIC ERICSON (Nov. 4, 1859–July 5, 1926), physician, was born in Cincinnati, Hamilton County. He graduated from Woodward High School in 1878 and from Miami Medical College in 1882; he also studied medicine in Europe. He was the first doctor to call attention to the nerve endings in the cornea. He died in Cincinnati.

A History of Tuberculosis . . . , Cincinnati, 1883.

SAUER, LOUIS WENDLIN (Aug. 13, 1885–), pediatrist, was born in Cincinnati, Hamilton County. He graduated from the University of Cincinnati in 1907 and from Rush Medical College in 1913. He practiced in Chicago and Evanston, Ill., specializing in pediatrics and immunology, and taught at Northwestern University. Besides medical articles, he has published a popular book on the care of children: *Nursery Guide for Mothers and Nurses,* St. Louis, 1923. WW 30

SAUER, McKINLEY HOBART (Mack) (June 28, 1896–Feb. 5, 1960), journalist, was born in Powellsville, Scioto County, and lived near Leesburg, Highland County. He owned and edited several newspapers, including the Leesburg *Citizen* and the New Vienna *Reporter,* and also operated a radio station in Hillsboro. He published poems and stories in various magazines, broadcast over a Middletown radio station, and was widely popular as a speaker. He published *The Editor Squeaks,* [Greenfield, 1941].

SAUNDERS, DAVID BALL (Aug. 29, 1907–Nov. 23, 1926), was born in Cincinnati, Hamilton County. He graduated from Walnut Hills High School in 1925 and was attending Marietta College when he died. A memorial edition of his verse was published: *Poems of David Ball Saunders,* Cincinnati, 1927.

SAVAGE, ANN PAYNE (Sept. 10, 1890–), was born in Sandusky, Erie County. She attended Sandusky schools. She has lived for much of her life in Flint, Mich., where her husband, Beryl M. Savage, is an engineer with General Motors. She has written several magazine articles and a novel: *Erie Kerrelly,* Philadelphia, 1944.

SAVAGE, THOMAS JEFFERSON (Jan. 15, 1852–Feb. 19, 1928), physician, was born in Fayette County. He practiced medicine in Bowersville, Greene County, for many years. Later he moved to Xenia, where he established a sanitarium and limited his practice to alcoholics. He wrote a book on alcoholism and *The Old Doctor's Vision, and Other Poems,* [Xenia, 1920].

SAWVEL, FRANKLYN B. (Oct. 3, 1850–Jan. 23, 1933), educator, was born in Germano, Harrison County. He graduated from Hopedale College in 1875 and afterward taught at Augusta Academy, Northeastern Ohio Normal College, and Thiel College. He published *Logan the Mingo,* Boston, [1921]. WW 11

SAWYER, FRANKLIN (July 13, 1825–Aug. 23, 1895), lawyer, was born on a farm in Auburn Township, Richland County (now a part of Crawford County). Admitted to the Ohio bar in 1847, he practiced in Norwalk until the outbreak of the Civil War. He joined the 8th O.V.I. as a captain in June, 1861; was wounded at Spottsylvania Court House on May 12, 1864; and was discharged as a lieutenant colonel on July 13, 1864. He resumed his law practice in Norwalk.

A Military History of the 8th Regiment . . . , (George A. Groot, ed.), Cleveland, 1881.

SAWYER, LEICESTER AMBROSE (July 28, 1807–Dec. 29, 1898), clergyman, born in Pinckney, N. Y., came to Columbus in 1840 to become president of Central College. Before leaving Ohio in 1850, he also served Presbyterian churches in Columbus and Monroeville. He later gave up the ministry to become a journalist. He translated portions of the Bible and wrote several books on theological questions, e.g., *Critical Exposition of Baptism . . . ,* Cincinnati, [1844].

SAXBY, HOWARD (1854–May 2, 1923), journalist, was born in Corydon, England, the son of an Anglican rector. After working as a reporter in London, he came to the United States in the late 1870s. In 1893 he established *Saxby's Magazine* in Cincinnati. He was popular as a humorous lecturer and after-dinner speaker. His death occurred in Cincinnati.

As through an Eye-glass, Cincinnati, 1892.
Wifely Worries and Other Poems . . . , Cincinnati, 1894.
Saxby's Scrapbook . . . , Cincinnati, 1897.
Dulcamara; Selections in Prose and Verse . . . , Cincinnati, [190- ?].

SAYLER, HARRY L. (Feb. 13, 1863–May 31, 1913), prolific writer of books for boys, was born in Montgomery County. His family moved to Shelbyville, Ind., in 1868. He graduated from Asbury University in 1885, edited the Wabash *Times* for a brief period, and in 1888 moved to Chicago. His books, which appeared in "The Airship Boys" series and similar series, were published under various pen names, including Ashton Lamar, Elliott Whitney, and Gordon Stuart. A typical title is *When Scout Meets Scout; Or, the Aeroplane Spy,* Chicago, [1912]. AATB

SAYLOR, LETTIE HOSKINS (Jan. 16, 1900–), born in Rockcastle County, Ky., has lived in Cincinnati since 1940. She has published poetry in various magazines and anthologies, and is the author of several novels about Kentucky, e.g., *Cradle Valley*, New York, 1946.

SAYRS, WILLIAM CHRISTOPHER (Nov. 18, 1861–Feb. 23, 1937), educator, was born in Sabina, Clinton County. He was educated at Wilmington College and Haverford College. He taught in Cincinnati high schools until 1923, and after his retirement he taught at Cincinnati Bible Seminary. He published a grammar textbook and a long religious poem: *The Temple Smith*, Cincinnati, 1935.

SCHAEFER, JACK WARNER (Nov. 19 1907–), was born in Cleveland, Cuyahoga County. He graduated from Oberlin College in 1929 and for a number of years served on the editorial staffs of various newspapers. He has written considerable fiction about the West. His best-known novel is *Shane*, Boston, 1949, the basis of a notable motion picture. WW 30

SCHAFF, DAVID SCHLEY (Oct. 17, 1852–March 2, 1941), Presbyterian clergyman and educator, was professor of church history at Lane Seminary, Cincinnati, 1897–1903. He published several books on religious themes, including a biography, *John Huss; His Life, Teachings and Death . . .*, New York, 1915. WWW 1

SCHAFF, MORRIS (Dec. 28, 1840–Oct. 19, 1929), army officer, was born in Kirkersville, Licking County. He graduated from the U. S. Military Academy in 1862 and served in the army until 1871. He wrote several books on the Civil War, e.g., *The Sunset of the Confederacy*, Boston, [1912], and a charming account of pioneer life in central Ohio: *Etna and Kirkersville*, Boston, 1905. WWW 1

SCHAUFFLER, GRACE LEAVITT (Nov. 25, 1894–), sister of Robert H. and Rachel C. Schauffler (qq.v.), was born in Cleveland, Cuyahoga County. A graduate of Oberlin College, she was a reporter for some years on the Oberlin *Times* and still lives in Oberlin. She has published several books for children, e.g., *Hi! Winkie*, New York, [1928].

SCHAUFFLER, RACHEL CAPEN (March 9, 1876–), educator, was born in Brünn (Brno), Austria (now Czechoslovakia), where her father, Henry Albert Schauffler, was serving as a Congregationalist missionary. The family was brought to Cleveland in 1881, when the Missionary Society called her father to work among the Bohemians of that city. Known as the "apostle to the Slavs," he established several churches and a training school for missionaries in Cleveland. Rachel grew up in Cleveland and graduated from Central High School. After graduating from Vassar College in 1897, she taught school in the East. She now lives in Meriden, Conn. She published *The Goodly Fellowship*, New York, 1912. WW 12

SCHAUFFLER, ROBERT HAVEN (April 8, 1879–1945), was born in Brünn (Brno), Austria (now Czechoslovakia), the son of Henry A. Schauffler and brother of Grace L. and Rachel C. Schauffler (qq.v.). His father came to Cleveland in 1881, and Robert's boyhood was spent in that city. He attended the music academy of Northwestern University and studied the cello under Bruno Steindel of the Chicago Symphony. After graduating from Princeton in 1902, he studied music in Germany and appeared in America and Europe as a professional cellist. He also achieved some success as a sculptor while residing in New York City. He wrote a number of books of travels, poetry, and familiar essays, but perhaps was best known for his biographies of composers, e.g., *Beethoven, the Man Who Freed Music*, 2 vols., New York, 1929. WW 27

SCHEIBE, FRED KARL (Dec. 2, 1911–), educator, born in Kiel, Germany, came to the United States in 1928. He was on the faculty of Western College for Women, Oxford, 1947–51, and of the University of Cincinnati, 1952–54. He is now on the faculty of Thiel College. His writings include a collection of poems: *Reflections*, [Oxford, 1948]. DAS 3

SCHENCK, EARL (May 13, 1889–), was born in Columbus, Franklin County. After graduating from Ohio State University in 1911, he was an actor in New York and Hollywood until an eye disorder forced his retirement. He went to Hawaii, where he wrote and produced plays. He also visited Fiji, New Zealand, Samoa, and other areas. After returning to the United States in 1938, he lectured on Polynesia. During World War II, he served as a consultant to the U. S. Navy. In 1958 he returned to Papeete, Tahiti, where he now lives with his wife and son. He has written three books on his experiences, e.g., *Come unto These Yellow Sands*, Indianapolis, [1940].

SCHENCK, LUCETTA (Aug. 12, 1855–Feb. 2, 1944) was born in Franklin, Warren County. She died in Chicago, Ill. Her book covers the church history of Franklin from 1796, and the history of the Franklin Presbyterian Church from 1817 to 1884.

The History of the Presbyterian Church of Franklin, Ohio, Lebanon, 1886.

SCHENCK, ROBERT CUMMING (Oct. 4, 1809–March 23, 1890), lawyer, congressman, and diplomat, was born in Franklin, Warren County, the son of William C. Schenck, the founder of the town. He graduated from Miami University in 1827, was admitted to the bar in 1833, and practiced in Dayton. He served in Congress from 1843 to 1851, when he was appointed minister to Brazil. He worked for the nomination of Lincoln and campaigned for him. In 1861 he was appointed brigadier general. He was wounded at Second Bull Run and resigned from the army on Dec. 3, 1863, with the rank of major general. He served again in Congress until 1870, when he was named ambassador to Great Britain, a post he filled until 1876. Afterward he returned to Washington, D. C., where he practiced law for the remainder of his life. In the summer of 1872, while he was visiting at an English country house in Somersetshire, his hostess asked him to write down some of the rules of the American game of poker. He was surprised and complimented several weeks later when he received copies of the rules that a fellow guest had printed on a private press. In 1880 he permitted his rules to be republished in America, with the result that he became recognized as an authority on the game and also received considerable criticism from American religious groups. Except for some of his speeches in the House of Representatives, *Draw* was his only publication.

Draw Rules for Playing Poker, [n.p., 1872].

SCHEVILL, FERDINAND (Nov. 12, 1868–Dec. 10, 1954), educator, was born in Cincinnati, Hamilton County, the elder brother of Rudolph Schevill (q.v.). He graduated from Yale University in 1889 and from the University of Freiberg, Germany, (Ph.D.) in 1892. He was on the history faculty of the University of Chicago, 1892–1937. Author of several popular textbooks on European history, he also wrote biographies, e.g., *Karl Bitter . . . ,* Chicago, [1917]. WWW 3

SCHEVILL, RUDOLPH (June 18, 1874–Feb. 17, 1946), educator, was born in Cincinnati, Hamilton County. He graduated from Yale University in 1896 and from the University of Munich (Ph.D.) in 1898. He taught languages at Bucknell University, Yale University, and the University of California. He edited an eighteen-volume edition of the works of Cervantes and wrote a biography: *Cervantes,* New York, 1919. WWW 2

SCHIFF, BESSIE IKE (Sept. 20, 1889–), educator, was born in St. Paris, Champaign County. She taught in the public schools of Shelby County and now lives in Sidney. A number of her poems have been printed in magazines and anthologies. Her stories for children include *The Traveling Gallery,* Chicago, 1936. WO 1

SCHILLING, JOHN L. (1842–May 8, 1911), was born in Harper's Ferry, Va. He came to Toledo in 1895 and was engaged in the insurance business in that city for the remainder of his life.

A Digression, Respectfully Dedicated to the Colored Citizens of the United States, Wheeling, [W. Va.], 1883.

Burst Asunder! . . . , [Bellaire], 1892.

The Three Emancipators . . . , [Bellaire, 1892].

The Story of John Brown's Raid . . . , Toledo, 1895.

SCHILLING, ROBERT WILSON (April 1, 1878–), physician, was born in Jewett, Harrison County. After graduating from Ohio State University in 1901, he attended the medical school and began practice in New Somerset in 1903. Except for service in the Medical Corps, 1917–19, he has since practiced in Jefferson County. Now a resident of Toronto, he has been county health officer since 1953. He has written two books of stories about the country around Toronto and Knoxville, e.g., *The Yellow Creek Stories,* [Toronto, 1947].

SCHLESINGER, ARTHUR MEIER (Feb. 27, 1888–), historian, was born in Xenia, Greene County, the son of Bernhard and Katherine Feuerle Schlesinger. His father, a German immigrant, who had few educational opportunities in Germany, served for thirty years as a member of the Xenia School Board and derived great satisfaction from the fact that all his children could enjoy the advantages of a university education in the land of his choice. His son Arthur received his undergraduate degree from Ohio State University in 1910, went on to Columbia for graduate study in history, and received his M.A. degree from that University in 1911 and his Ph.D. in 1917. In 1914, he married Elizabeth Bancroft of Columbus, and became the father of three children: a daughter who died in infancy, and two sons, Arthur Meier, Jr. (q.v.) and Thomas Bancroft. In 1912, Schlesinger returned to Columbus as a member of the department of American history of Ohio State University, to begin a teaching career which was to continue for 42 years. He remained in Columbus until 1919, when he left for Iowa to become the head of the department of history at the state university in Iowa City. During his five years there, he was unusually successful in building a strong department and in attracting a notable group of graduate students, some of whom made distinguished records as teachers and productive scholars in later years. In 1924, Schlesinger left the Middle West for a professorship at Harvard, where he taught until his retirement in 1954, and where he held the Francis Lee Higginson professorship after 1931. He also served at various times as visiting professor at the universities of London, Edinburgh, and Leyden. Although his major interests have always been in teaching, directing scholarly research, and publication, Schlesinger has served on a number of public commissions. In 1918 and 1919, as chairman of the Historical Commission of Ohio, he directed the collection of the source materials for World War I now on deposit in the Library of the Ohio Historical Society in Columbus; during World War II, he served on the committee on the records of war administration of the U. S. Government. As a member of several other Federal commissions, he has been concerned with a variety of problems, ranging from freedom of the press and the American Indian to the preparation of national historical publications. From 1948 to 1954, he was chairman of the United Labor Commission of Massachusetts. From 1924 to 1941, he was a member of the Social Science Research Council, and served as its chairman, 1930–1933. He has been a trustee of Radcliffe College since 1942, and at present is chairman of the committee of consultants for the preparation of a biographical dictionary of notable American women, sponsored by Radcliffe College. Needless to add, he has been active in many historical societies, serving as a member of their executive councils and editorial boards. In 1942, he was elected president of the American Historical Association, the highest honor which the historical guild can bestow upon one of its members. Schlesinger's major interest has always been in teaching, in stimulating and directing promising young scholars in their research, and in his own long list of scholarly publications. His doctoral dissertation at Columbia, *The Colonial Merchants and the American Revolution,* which won the Justin Winsor prize of the American Historical Association, was a brilliant, pioneering examination of the economic causes of the American Revolution. His *New Viewpoints in American History* (1922), a series of penetrating essays into neglected fields, led to a number of studies that broke new ground. In 1925, Schlesinger wrote the second volume of the Hockett and Schlesinger *Political and Social History of the United States,* long the leading college text in the field, which went through three revised editions. Schlesinger's special interest in American cultural and intellectual history, a field in which he is universally respected as an important pioneer, led to the publication by the Macmillan Company of the thirteen-volume *History of American Life,* under the joint-editorship of Schlesinger and the late Dixon Ryan Fox, with each volume written by a recognized expert in the field of social and cultural history. Schlesinger's own contribution, *The Rise of the City* (1933), stimulated much interest in the complex problems arising from the urbanization of our society, and was directly responsible for much research and publication by other scholars in this long neglected area. Other volumes which give further evidence of Schlesinger's wide range of interests are his history of American books on etiquette (1946), his *Paths to the Present* (1949), *The American As Reformer* (1950), and his excellent latest volume (published in 1957), *Prelude to Independence, the Newspaper War on Britain, 1746–76,* in which he returns to a study of the period in which he first won recognition among American historians. Schlesinger also has coauthored numerous volumes concerned with social and cultural history, American literature, and the social sciences. His contributions to the professional journals are too numerous to mention, although some, like his short essay "A Critical Period in American Religion, 1875–1900" in the *Proceedings of the Massachusetts Historical Society,* (June, 1932), merit special attention. Perhaps the fact that the many honors he has received include six honorary doctorates, and that fourteen books have been dedicated to him is the most impressive evidence of the lasting contribution Schlesinger has made to American historiography.

Carl Wittke

SCHLESINGER, ARTHUR MEIER, JR. (Oct. 15, 1917–), was born in Columbus, Franklin County, where his father, A. M. Schlesinger, Sr. (q.v.), was a member of the faculty of Ohio State University. The Schlesingers in American history join the Clarks in economics (John Bates Clark and his son, John Maurice) as one of the few father-son combinations to earn outstanding reputations in a single discipline. In due course, A. M. Schlesinger, Sr., joined the Harvard faculty; so, too, did the son. After graduating from Harvard with highest honors in 1938 (his senior thesis became his first book: *Orestes A. Brownson: A Pilgrim's Progress,* 1939), after enjoying three productive years as a member of the Society of Fellows of Harvard University (the Pulitzer Prize-winning *The Age of Jackson,* 1945, was written during this period), after serving with distinction in the Office of War Information and the Office of Strategic Services during the war, and free-lancing briefly after the war, Arthur M. Schlesinger, Jr., joined the Harvard faculty in 1947 as one of the youngest associate professors ever appointed by that institution. Now on leave as an adviser to President Kennedy, he is one of Harvard's best-known teachers and scholars. In a mere dozen years he has produced more than most men of letters do in a lifetime. *The Vital Center* (1949) is a vigorous statement of the anticommunist liberal position. *The General and the President* (1951), written with Richard Rovere, is a penetrating analysis of the fundamental issues raised by the MacArthur case. *A Guide to Politics* (1954), written in collaboration with Quincy Howe, is a lively survey of the American political scene. He is now hard at work on his major study, *The Age of Roosevelt.* The first volume, *The Crisis of the Old Order,* appeared in 1957; the second, *The Coming of the New Deal,* in 1959; and the third, *The Politics of Upheaval,* in 1960. The remaining volumes are eagerly awaited. Reviewers have acclaimed his work as "brilliant," "cogent," "significant," "rich," "pioneering," "exhaustive," "painstaking," etc. Bernard De Voto predicted that *The Age of Jackson* would "create a school," and surely the fresh, daring, and sharply drawn analogies between our past and our present have had a notable impact on the writing of American history. Like all great historians, he helps us rediscover the present in the past. In Gerald W. Johnson's words, Schlesinger has "the enormous merit of saying something." No one will put down the Roosevelt volumes, for example, without the feeling that he has gained new insight into the meaning and continuity of the American experience. Schlesinger has said of himself that he is primarily interested in the relationship between thought and action—in tracing the course ideas take as they travel from men of thought to men of action. One of the extraordinary facts about this energetic man is the combination of thought and action in his own life. He was a founder and long-time national vice-chairman of Americans for Democratic Action. He has actively participated in Democratic politics at the local, state, and national levels. I know personally, from his extraordinary help to me in the 1952 and 1956 Presidential campaigns, the depth of his thought and the vigor of his action. He is probably as well informed as any man about the functioning of American political institutions, and he may be found wherever and whenever the good fight for the free society calls. His weapons are ideas—made instruments of action by his remarkable control over the words which express them. The list of Schlesinger's articles on topics of current importance in national life is too long to catalogue here, but he has been a frequent contributor to such journals as *Fortune* and *Life* (his exposure of the American Communist Party for *Life* will long be remembered as a model of its kind). His short pieces are timely, keen, wise, and combative, for he is a fighting man. The writing, like the man, makes exceedingly good company. To know him is to value him as a warm, friendly, courageous, high-spirited person, who finds interest in everything and makes every occasion pleasurable—a delightful guest and, with his charming and talented wife and endearing family, a sparkling host. Arthur Schlesinger's reputation is already solidly established at the ripe young age of 43. As a reviewer said not long ago, his work is a "permanent enrichment" of American historical writing. Perhaps most important in a country in which many people "take" history as children "take" medicine, he has taught thousands of his countrymen to enjoy, with him, the rediscovery of our past as a means to understanding where we are and where we are going.

Adlai E. Stevenson

SCHMECKEBIER, LAWRENCE ELI (March 1, 1906–), born in Chicago Heights, Ill., was director of Cleveland Institute of Art, 1946–54. He has published several books on the fine arts, e.g., *Modern Mexican Art,* Minneapolis, [1939]. WW 30

SCHMITT, BERNADOTTE EVERLY (May 19, 1886–), educator, born in Strasburg, Va., was on the history staff of Western Reserve University, 1909–14. On the

University of Chicago faculty, 1914–46, he wrote a number of historical works, including one for which he received the Pulitzer Prize: *The Coming of the War . . .* , 2 vols., New York, 1930. WW 30

SCHMUTZ, GEORGE S. (July 22, 1846–Sept. 25, 1908), was born in Chester Township, Wayne County. He served as a private in the 102nd O.V.I., Aug., 1862–June, 1865. He was captured at Athens, Ga., in Sept., 1864, and was imprisoned for the remainder of the war. His death occurred in Wooster. He wrote *History of the 102nd Regiment . . .* , [Wooster], 1907.

SCHNEIDER, FREDERICK WILLIAM (Dec. 28, 1862–Dec. 18, 1941), clergyman and educator, was born in Boonville, Ind. He graduated from German Wallace College in 1886 and from Drew Theological Seminary in 1889. He lived in Ohio at various intervals: as a teacher at German Wallace College, 1886–94 and 1897–1909; as a Methodist pastor in Delaware, 1894–95; and as an official of the Methodist Board of Sunday Schools in Cincinnati, 1914–20. His writings include *System der Christlichen Lehre,* Cincinnati, [1908]. WWW 2

SCHNEIDER, HERBERT WALLACE (March 16, 1892–), educator, son of Frederick W. Schneider (q.v.), was born in Berea, Cuyahoga County. A graduate of Columbia University (A.B., 1915; Ph.D., 1917), he has taught philosophy and religion at his alma mater since 1918. He is editor of *The Journal of Philosophy* and has written significant studies of Fascism in Italy and of religion and philosophy in America, e.g., *The Puritan Mind,* New York, [1930]. WW 30

SCHNEIDER, HERMAN (Sept. 12, 1872–March 28, 1939), educator, born in Summit Hill, Pa., was on the University of Cincinnati faculty from 1903 until his death. As dean of the college of engineering and commerce, he introduced the co-operative system. He published a number of books and pamphlets on educational subjects, e.g., *Thirty Years of Educational Pioneering . . .* , [Cincinnati], 1935. WWW 1

SCHNEIDER, NORRIS FRANZ (June 20, 1898–), educator, was born in Lowell, Washington County. Since graduating from Ohio State University in 1921, he has taught English in the Zanesville schools. He has been a feature writer for the Zanesville *Sunday Times Signal* since 1944 and has published a number of books on Ohio history, e.g., *Y Bridge City; The Story of Zanesville and Muskingum County, Ohio,* Cleveland, [1950]. WWMW 6

SCHOCKMAN, CARL S. (Feb. 6, 1912–), was born in Coldwater, Mercer County, and still lives in that community, where he owns a tire service company. Around 1930 he and his brother made a "hobo" trip through the United States. Later, while recovering from an attack of tuberculosis, he wrote his memories of that trip: *We Turned Hobo . . .* , Columbus, [1937].

SCHODDE, GEORGE HENRY (April 15, 1854–Sept. 15, 1917), clergyman and educator, born in Allegheny, Pa., graduated from Capital University in 1872 and from the Seminary in 1874. He studied in Germany and graduated from the University of Leipzig (Ph.D.) in 1887. After serving as a Lutheran pastor at Canal Winchester for one year and at Martins Ferry for two, he joined the Capital faculty in 1880. Internationally known as a conservative Biblical scholar, he published many articles, a translation of the Book of Enoch, and *The Protestant Church in Germany . . .* , Philadelphia, [1901]. DAB 16

SCHOLAE, DR. Pseud. See James D. Gillilan.

SCHOLL, JOHN WILLIAM (Aug. 17, 1869 Sept. 2, 1952), educator, was born near Springfield, Clark County. He graduated from Valparaiso University in 1896 and from the University of Michigan (Ph.D.) in 1905, taught at Chattanooga Normal School, 1896–1900, and was a member of the German Department, University of Michigan, 1902–39. He lectured widely on patriotic themes during World War I. He published many poems in periodicals and also wrote a family history.

The Light-bearer of Liberty . . . , Boston, [1899].
Social Tragedies, and Other Poems, Boston, [1900].
Ode to the Russian People, Boston, [1907].
Hesper-Phosphor, and Other Poems, Ann Arbor, 1910.
Children of the Sun, Poems, Ann Arbor, 1916.
In Gaea's Garden, Ann Arbor, [1932].
The Rose Jar, Ann Arbor, [1936].
Strenae, Ann Arbor, 1942.
Yellow Dwarf and Haughty Rose, Ann Arbor, 1942.
Beads to Tell, Ann Arbor, 1943.
A Midwest Wife, Ann Arbor, 1943.

SCHOULER, WILLIAM (Dec. 31, 1814–Oct. 24, 1872), born in Scotland, was brought to America when he was two years old and spent most of his life in Massachusetts, where he had a distinguished career as an editor and a public servant. He was in Ohio for five years, as part-owner of the Cincinnati *Gazette,* 1853–56, and as editor of the *Ohio State Journal,* 1856–58. His major book was *A History of Massachusetts in the Civil War,* 2 vols., Boston, 1868–71.

SCHRAMM, WILBUR LANG (Aug. 5, 1907–), educator, was born in Marietta, Washington County. He graduated from Marietta College in 1928 and from the State University of Iowa (Ph.D.) in 1932. He has been on the faculties of three universities: Iowa, 1935–47; Illinois, 1947–55; and Stanford, 1955– . He founded the Iowa Writers Workshop in 1937 and has been active in communications research. He has published several books on mass communications and some fiction, e.g., *Windwagon Smith and Other Yarns,* New York, [1947]. WW 30

SCHUETTE, CONRAD HERMAN LOUIS (June 17, 1843–Aug. 11, 1926), clergyman, born in Hanover, Germany, was brought to the United States in his early boyhood. He graduated from Capital University in 1863 and the Lutheran Seminary in 1865. After serving as pastor of a church in Delaware, 1865–73, he was on the Capital faculty, 1873–95, and afterward served as president of the Evangelical Lutheran Synod, 1895–1925. He published several devotional books and *Wiggie: Or, Incidents and Accidents from the Earlier and Earliest Years of My Life . . . ,* Columbus, 1916. WWW 1

SCHUETTE, WALTER ERWIN (Nov. 14, 1867–Aug. 10, 1955), clergyman, son of Conrad H. L. Schuette (q.v.), was born in Delaware, Delaware County. After graduating from Capital University in 1885 and the Lutheran Seminary in 1888, he was ordained to the Lutheran ministry and served as a pastor in Michigan, Ohio, and West Virginia. He also edited the *Lutheran Standard* and other magazines.

Her Place Assigned. A Story . . . , Philadelphia, [1898].

The Best Possible Sunday School, Columbus, [1927?].

God Save the Home! . . . , Columbus, [1940].

SCHUH, LEWIS HERMAN (July 7, 1858–Sept. 29, 1936), clergyman, was born in Galion, Crawford County. He graduated from Capital University in 1860 and was ordained to the Lutheran ministry in 1883. He was on the Capital faculty, 1895–1900, and was president of the college, 1901–12. He also served as pastor of Lutheran churches in Canal Winchester, Grove City, and Toledo. He published sermons and books on religious and social themes, e.g., *How to Make Marriage a Success,* Columbus, 1904. WWC 1

SCHULKERS, ROBERT FRANC (July 21, 1890–), was born in Covington, Ky. While still in high school he began writing stories for boys; the first appeared in the Cincinnati *Enquirer* in 1904. In 1911 he joined the staff of the *Enquirer,* and in 1918 his "Seckatary Hawkins" stories became a regular feature of the Sunday juvenile page. The stories were syndicated in more than a hundred newspapers, reprinted in book form, and dramatized in radio broadcasts. He left the *Enquirer* staff in 1926, but returned to the paper in 1943 and is still employed there. The first of the series was *Adventures in Cuba . . . ,* Cincinnati, 1921; the last was *The Ghost of Lake Tapaho,* Cincinnati, 1932. Of the eleven books in the series, all were published under the pen name Seckatary Hawkins except for *Stormie the Dog Stealer* New York, 1925, which was published under his own name.

SCHULZE, EDWARD CHARLES (Dec. 17, 1887–), lawyer, was born in Uhrichsville, Tuscarawas County. After attending Marion Academy, he graduated from Scio College and from the University of Pittsburgh School of Law. A resident of East Cleveland, he has published a book of verse: *Pilot Lights,* New York, [1946].

SCHULZE, MILDRED ELEANOR (Nov. 14, 1907–), librarian, was born in Cincinnati, Hamilton County. She graduated from the University of Cincinnati in 1930 and from the University of Illinois Library School in 1943, and has served as librarian in Mariemont and Elmwood. She is now librarian at Bonham Public Library, Wyoming, Hamilton County. She has written a history of Elmwood: *Elm Tree Days,* [Lockland, 1946].

SCHUMANN, MARY KANENGEISER (Sept. 25, 1885–), was born in Youngstown, Mahoning County. She attended Youngstown schools and Columbia University. In 1905 she married Lloyd Schumann, from whom she was divorced in 1929. She taught at Youngstown College, 1932–34. After marrying Meredith Hayes in 1934, she lived in New York City and Pittsfield,

Mass.; she now lives in Bedford, N. Y. She began selling short stories and serial fiction to magazines in 1914. Her first novel in book form had a modern setting: *Strong Enchantments,* Philadelphia, 1933. She has also written several historical novels with an Ohio background, e.g., *Strife before Dawn,* New York, 1939.

SCHURZ, WILLIAM LYTLE (Nov. 25, 1886–), was born in South Lebanon, Warren County. He graduated from the University of California (B. Litt., 1911; Ph.D., 1915) and afterward taught at the University of Michigan, 1915–18. An expert on Latin America, he has served in various governmental agencies and bureaus and has been associated with the American Institute for Foreign Trade since 1946. He was on the staff of the New York *Herald-Tribune,* 1926–40, and has written a number of books on South America and the Philippine Islands, e.g., *The Manila Galleon . . . ,* New York, 1939. WW 30

SCHUYLER, AARON (Feb. 7, 1828–Feb. 1, 1913), born in Seneca County, N. Y., was professor of mathematics at Baldwin University, 1862–75, and president, 1873–85. He wrote a number of textbooks in mathematics, philosophy, and surveying. He also wrote *The Human Soul . . . ,* Cincinnati, 1859.

SCHWARTZ, JEROME LAWRENCE. See Jerome K. Lawrence.

SCHWARZWALDER, JOHN (June 21, 1917–), was born in Columbus, Franklin County. After graduating from Ohio State University in 1937, he studied voice in New York City. In 1941 he became a major in the Counter-Intelligence Corps. He is now general manager of the University of Minnesota television station. He has published an account of his wartime experiences: *We Caught Spies,* New York, [1946].

SCHWERTNER, THOMAS MARIA (1888–Feb. 17, 1933), clergyman, was born in Canton, Stark County. Educated at Canisius College and in Europe, he was ordained to the Roman Catholic priesthood in 1908. He taught at Immaculate Conception College, Washington, D. C., served several parishes in New York and Washington, and lectured widely in the United States and Great Britain. He wrote several books on religious themes, e.g., *St. Albert the Great,* New York, [1932]. CWW 1

SCHWIEBERT, ERNEST GEORGE (Oct. 17, 1895–), educator, was born in Deshler, Henry County. He graduated from Capital University in 1921 and from Cornell University (Ph.D.) in 1930. He has taught history in several universities and for a time after World War II was with the Office of Military Government for Bavaria. A specialist in the history of the Reformation, he has published several articles and books, notably *Luther and His Times . . . ,* St. Louis, [1950]. WWMW 49

SCOTT, DANIEL F. (Feb. 24, 1830–Jan. 17, 1912), was born in Salem, Columbiana County, but spent most of his life in Hillsboro, where he operated a grocery store and also was in the lumber business.

A History of the Early Settlement of Highland County, [Hillsboro], 1890.

SCOTT, FRANK JESUP (1828–June 13, 1919), architect and landscape gardener, was born in Columbia, S. C., the son of Jesup W. Scott (q.v.). Frank designed many buildings and estates in the Toledo area. In 1876 he built the Hotel Madison in Toledo and operated it for a time. He died in Nice, France, where he had spent the last ten years of his life.

The Art of Beautifying Suburban Home Grounds of Small Extent . . . , New York, 1870.

Suggestions Concerning a National Currency, [Toledo, 1873].

National Works, Toledo, 1878.

The Gospel of Bi-Metallism, [Toledo, 1893].

The Evolution of Suffrage . . . , [Toledo?, 1903].

Portraitures of Julius Caesar . . . , New York, 1903.

The Present Status of the Project for a Toledo University . . . , Toledo, 1903.

SCOTT, HENRY DICKERSON (Feb. 26, 1893–April 21, 1947), steel company executive, was born in Bridgeport, Belmont County. After graduating from Yale in 1914, he worked in various administrative posts in steel plants at Steubenville and Wheeling, W. Va. From 1943 until his death, he was chairman of Scott Lumber Co., Bridgeport. He published *Iron & Steel in Wheeling,* Toledo, 1929. WWW 2

SCOTT, HERVEY (Jan. 30, 1809–c.1896), dentist, was born near Old Town, Greene County. He attended Ohio Medical College, Cincinnati, and began to practice medicine in 1836. In 1839, one year after he settled in Lancaster, he turned to dentistry. He was a practicing dentist for nearly fifty years. In 1891 he moved to Toledo to live with a daughter. His interest in the pioneer past resulted in numerous newspaper sketches, as well as the volume listed below.

A Complete History of Fairfield County, Ohio, Columbus, 1877.

SCOTT, JESUP WAKEMAN (1798–Dec. 23, 1873), journalist, was born in Fairfield County, Conn. From 1818 to 1830 he lived in South Carolina, where he taught school and practiced law. In 1830 he moved to Florence, Huron County, and started a monthly paper, *Ohio and Michigan Register and Emigrant's Guide.* A strong belief in the potential growth of inland cities induced him to invest heavily in land along the Maumee. In 1833 he moved to Perrysburg and operated *The Miami of Lake Erie.* His land holdings so increased in value that he was able to retire to Bridgeport, Conn., where he built a home. In 1837, however, the panic forced him to sell his Bridgeport property and return to Ohio. For a few years in the 1840s he edited the Toledo *Blade.* He lived most of his remaining years in Toledo, dealing in real estate. With a few friends, he donated 150 acres for an "industrial university and phonetic college," which became the nucleus of the University of Toledo.

A Presentation of Causes Tending to Fix the Position of the Future Great City of the World in the Central Plain of North America . . . , Toledo, 1868.

SCOTT, JOHN (April 14, 1824–Sept. 23, 1903), lawyer, was born near Richmond, Jefferson County. He attended district schools, read law in Steubenville, and was admitted to the Ohio bar. After serving in the Mexican War, he taught school and edited the *Kentucky Whig.* In 1856 he moved to Nevada, Iowa, where he practiced law until 1898; the last five years of his life were spent in Des Moines. During the Civil War he commanded the 32nd Iowa Regiment, 1862–64. He is the probable author of *Encarnacion Prisoners,* which was published anonymously. Besides the titles below, he wrote a family history.

Encarnacion Prisoners . . . , Louisville, Ky., 1848.

Story of the Thirty-second Iowa Infantry Volunteers, Nevada, Iowa, 1896.

SCOTT, JOSEPH M. (Jan. 9, 1830–Dec. 18, 1919), farmer, was born and reared in Utica, Licking County. From 1852 to 1902 he lived on a large farm south of Alexandria. He served in the Civil War with the 76th O.V.I. The historical sketch listed below was published in the *Pioneer Society Pamphlets.*

Our Early Times. Historical Sketch of St. Alban's Township, Newark, 1873.

SCOTT, MILTON ROBINSON (Oct. 21, 1841–June 9, 1921), journalist, was born in Jacksontown, Licking County. He attended Marietta College and served three years in the 76th O.V.I. He was an early advocate of women's suffrage and published a paper in the late 1860s devoted to that cause. He also founded and edited the Newark *Banner.* He died in Newark.

Henry Elwood, a Theological Novel, Newark, 1892.

Prison Reform, and Other Topics, Newark, 1894.

Ernest Marble, the Labor Agitator, Newark, 1895.

Paul Vernon, Prisoner, Newark, 1900.

Essay on Truth, Newark, [1903].

Essay on Lincoln . . . , Newark, 1906.

A Few Thoughts on Crimes and Criminals, Newark, 1911.

SCOTT, ROBERT PITTIS (1852–July 26, 1918), inventor, was born in Cadiz, Harrison County, where his father operated a jewelry store. From boyhood Robert showed an interest in machines; he patented his first invention when he was eighteen, and during his lifetime he patented forty more, including an apple and peach parer, a cherry seeder, and a pea huller. In 1893 he became interested in motor-driven vehicles and invented what he called a "go-devil," a combination of the modern motorcycle and automobile, in which he used to ride through the streets of Cadiz. While attending the Paris Exposition of 1900, he bought a gasoline runabout and brought it to Cadiz. It was said to be the first automobile driven over the Alleghenies. In the hope of being the first to fly over the same mountains, he worked for some time on a model resembling the modern helicopter. He owned a large farm in Virginia and also bought the Williamsburg *Gazette.* His book on cycling contains one of the earliest discussions of pneumatic tires.

H. B. McConnell

Cycling Art, Energy, and Locomotion . . . , Philadelphia, 1889.

SCOTT, SAMUEL PARSONS (July 8, 1846–May 30, 1929), lawyer and student of Spanish history and law, was born in Hillsboro, Highland County. After graduating from Miami University in 1866, he studied law and afterward practiced in Leavenworth, Kan., and San Francisco. In 1875 he returned to Hillsboro to manage the family properties. The last 54 years of his life were largely devoted to research and writing on early Spanish history. He took the position that the Moorish control of Spain gave the country its most brilliant culture. In the latter part of his life, he devoted himself to translating Spanish legal codes. He died at Hillsboro.

Through Spain: A Narrative of Travel and Adventure . . . , Philadelphia, 1886.
History of the Moorish Empire in Europe, 3 vols., Philadelphia, 1904.

SCOTT, VIRGIL (Aug. 1, 1914–), educator, was born in Vancouver, Wash. When he was ten, his family came to Cleveland, where he attended public school. After attending Heidelberg College for three years, he transferred to Ohio State University, from which he graduated in 1936. He taught in Franklin High School, Warren County, for four years before returning to Ohio State, where he completed his doctorate in 1945. He taught for two years at the University of Minnesota and is now on the faculty of Michigan State University. He has published several novels. Considerable excitement and speculation were aroused in Franklin and Columbus when he published a fictional account of a young teacher's difficulties in a small Ohio town and at a midwestern university: *The Hickory Stick,* New York, 1948. ANT

SCOTT, WALTER (Oct. 31, 1796–April 23, 1861), founder with Alexander Campbell (q.v.) of the Disciples of Christ, was born in Dumfries, Scotland. He came to America in 1818 and to Pittsburgh the following year. In 1821, while teaching school and preaching in Pittsburgh, he met Alexander Campbell and wrote for *The Christian Baptist,* which Campbell founded in 1823. Scott came to Steubenville in 1826 and, in the following year, preached as an evangelist for the Mahoning Baptist Association; most of his numerous converts became members of the rapidly growing Disciples of Christ. Scott remained in Ohio until 1844, living in Canfield, Cincinnati, and Carthage. He returned to Pittsburgh in 1844, remained there until 1850, and spent the last eleven years of his life in Kentucky. To his power as an evangelist is due much of the rapid growth enjoyed by the Disciples of Christ denomination.

The Gospel Restored, Cincinnati, 1836.
A Review of Prof. Stowe's Pamphlet against All Millennial Arithmetic . . . , Cincinnati, 1843.
The Messiahship, Or the Great Demonstration, Cincinnati, 1859.

SCOTT, WILLIAM BERRYMAN (Feb. 12, 1858–March 29, 1947), educator, was born in Cincinnati, Hamilton County. He graduated from Princeton University in 1877 and served on the faculty, 1883–1930.

Preliminary Report upon the Princeton Scientific Expedition of 1882, (with W. F. Magie), Princeton, N. J., 1882.
A History of Land Mammals in the Western Hemisphere, New York, 1913.
The Theory of Evolution . . . , New York, 1917.
Physiography; The Science of the Abode of Man, New York, [1922].
Some Memories of a Palaeontologist, Princeton, 1939.

SCOTT, WILLIAM FORSE (Dec. 27, 1844–1933), lawyer, was born in Dayton, Montgomery County. He attended the schools of Dayton and Washington, D. C. He served in the 4th Iowa Cavalry throughout the Civil War. After the war he read law, was admitted to the bar, and after 1870 practiced in New York City.

The Story of a Cavalry Regiment. The Career of the Fourth Iowa Veteran Volunteers . . . , New York, 1893.
Philander P. Lane, Colonel of Volunteers in the Civil War, Eleventh Ohio Infantry, [New York?], 1920.

SCRANTON, STAFFORD S. (April 23, 1848–1918), lawyer, was born in Fort Recovery, Mercer County. He attended National Normal University, Lebanon, read law, was admitted to the bar, and afterward practiced in Celina. He wrote *History of Mercer County . . . ,* Chicago, 1907.

SCRIBNER, HARVEY (March 19, 1850–Jan. 21, 1913), lawyer, was born in Mt. Vernon, Knox County. In 1869 his parents moved to Toledo, where he studied law in his father's office and was admitted to the bar in 1871. He spent the remainder of his life in Toledo.

My Mysterious Clients, Cincinnati, 1900.
A Messenger from Santa Claus, and Other Christmas Stories, Toledo, [1904].
Memoirs of Lucas County and the City of Toledo . . . , Madison, Wis., 1910.

SCUDDER, JOHN MILTON (Sept. 8, 1829–Feb. 17, 1894), physician, was born in Harrison, Hamilton County. After working as a cabinetmaker and as a painter and operating a general store, he became interested in eclectic medicine and graduated from Eclectic Medical Institute, Cincinnati, in 1856. He taught at the institute from 1857 until his death and edited the *Eclectic Med-*

ical Journal, 1861–94. His leadership was largely responsible for the success of the institute and for the prestige of eclectic medicine in Cincinnati. His books, though largely intended for professional readers, were widely used and went through numerous editions.

A Practical Treatise on the Diseases of Women . . . , Cincinnati, 1857.
Materia Medica and Therapeutics, Cincinnati, 1860.
The Eclectic Practice of Medicine, Cincinnati, 1864.
Domestic Medicine: Or, Home Book of Health . . . , Cincinnati, 1865.
On the Use of Medicated Inhalations . . . , Cincinnati, 1866.
The Principles of Medicine, Cincinnati, 1867.
The Eclectic Practice in Diseases of Children, Cincinnati, 1869.
A Familiar Treatise on Medicine, Cincinnati, 1869.
Specific Medication and Specific Medicines, Cincinnati, 1870.
On the Reproductive Organs, and the Venereal, Cincinnati, 1874.
Specific Diagnosis . . . , Cincinnati, 1874.

SEAGRAVE, GORDON STIFLER (March 18, 1897–), surgeon, was born in Rangoon, Burma, the son of Baptist missionaries. In 1909 his family returned to America and settled in Granville, where he spent his boyhood and graduated from Denison University in 1917. In 1922, the year after his graduation from Johns Hopkins Medical School, he sailed for Burma, where he operated a Baptist hospital, trained nurses, and distributed tracts. During World War II, while serving under General Joseph W. Stilwell, he set up base hospitals and accompanied the army on the retreat from Burma. His family, who were evacuated in 1943, spent the war years in Granville. In 1950 Dr. Seagrave was accused of treason by a Burmese court and was sentenced to six years' imprisonment. After being cleared by a second trial, he returned to his hospital. He published several books on his Burmese life, including an autobiography, which was a best-seller: *Burma Surgeon,* New York, [1943]. WW 29

SEARCH, PRESTON WILLIS (April 10, 1853–Dec. 12, 1932), educator, was born in Marion, Marion County. He attended University of Wooster and Clark University and also did graduate work in Europe. He was a school principal and superintendent in various Ohio cities, 1874–88, and later held educational posts in Colorado and California. He died in Carmel-by-the-Sea, Calif. He wrote a number of articles and books on educational subjects, e.g., *An Ideal School . . .* , New York, 1901. WWW 1

SEARIGHT, FRANK THOMPSON (1875–Aug. 10, 1912), journalist, was born in East Liverpool, Columbiana County. He became a cub reporter on *The Daily Crisis* in 1890 and afterward worked on *The Evening Review.* After leaving East Liverpool, he worked on newspapers in Pittsburgh, Buffalo, New York City, Cleveland, Denver, and San Diego. He died in Los Angeles as a result of injuries suffered in an automobile accident. He wrote a number of magazine articles and an account of the San Francisco earthquake and fire: *The Doomed City . . .* , Chicago, [1906].

SEARL, FERNANDO CORTEZ (July 18, 1825–June 26, 1904), lawyer, was born on a farm in Vernon Township, Scioto County. After attending district schools, he began teaching at the age of sixteen. In 1859 he settled in Portsmouth, where he read law, was admitted to the bar in 1863, and served for a time as probate judge. He practiced law in Portsmouth and operated several farms in the surrounding area. A volume of his verse was published posthumously by his son, Clinton M. Searl: *Collected Poems of Fernando C. Searl,* Portsmouth, 1930.

SEARS, ANGELINE B. (Sept. 20, 1817–Dec. 15, 1848), was born in Cincinnati, Hamilton County. She was converted to Methodism in 1830, and in 1842 she married Rev. Clinton W. Sears. The book below, drawn from her letters and diary, was compiled by Melinda Hamline, wife of Leonidas Hamline (q.v.).

Memoirs of Mrs. Angeline B. Sears . . . , Cincinnati, 1851.

SEARS, EDMUND HAMILTON (April 6, 1810–Jan. 16, 1876), clergyman, was born in Sandisfield, Mass., and spent his entire life in that state except for a period in Toledo as a missionary of the American Unitarian Association, 1837–39. He wrote a number of popular hymns, including "It Came upon a Midnight Clear," and published several influential books on religious themes, e.g., *The Fourth Gospel, the Heart of Christ,* Boston, 1872.

SEARS, PAUL BIGELOW (Dec. 17, 1891–), educator, was born in Bucyrus, Crawford County. He graduated from Ohio Wesleyan University in 1913 and the University of Chicago (Ph.D.) in 1922. He has served on the faculties of the University of Nebraska, 1919–27, the University of Oklahoma, 1927–38, Oberlin College, 1938–50, and Yale University since 1950. Besides professional articles on conservation and ecology, he has published several books, e.g., *Deserts on the March,* Norman, Okla., 1935. WW 30

SEASONGOOD, MURRAY (Oct. 27, 1878–), lawyer, was born in Cincinnati, Hamilton County. He graduated from Harvard College in 1900 and from the law school in 1903, after which he practiced in Cincinnati. He was mayor of Cincinnati, 1926–30. He has published a number of legal texts and articles and several books on local government and the fight against corruption, e.g., *How Political Gangs Work . . . ,* New York, 1932. WW 30

SE CHEVERELL, JOHN HAMPTON (Feb. 6, 1841–June 16, 1910), physician, was born in Harpersfield Township, Ashtabula County. At an early age he began writing items for the *Forest City Gleaner.* He enlisted in the 29th O.V.I. in Aug., 1861, was captured at the battle of Winchester in 1862, was imprisoned briefly and paroled; in June, 1862, he was discharged for physical disability. A year later, he enlisted in the 2nd Ohio Heavy Artillery and served until June, 1865. He studied medicine and began practice in 1867; after 1877 he practiced in Jefferson, where he died. His regimental history is based on journals kept by members of the 29th O.V.I.

Journal History of the Twenty-ninth Ohio Veteran Volunteers . . . , Cleveland, 1883.

SECKATARY HAWKINS. Pseud. See Robert F. Schulkers.

SEDGWICK, ANNE DOUGLAS (March 28, 1873–July 19, 1935), novelist, born in Englewood, N. J., spent two years of her girlhood living with her grandmother in Ross County. She later studied art in Paris and, after her marriage in 1908 to Basil de Selincourt, she lived in England. She wrote considerable fiction, e.g., *Tante,* New York, 1911.

S.E.E. Pseud. See James M. Ritchie.

SEESHOLTZ, ANNA GROH (Jan. 24, 1883–), educator, born in Myerstown, Pa., lived much of her life in Ohio. She graduated from high school in Canton in 1900 and from Western Reserve University in 1904. She later studied in Germany and, in 1934, completed her doctorate at Columbia University. After teaching in Canton, 1904–12, she did educational work for the Y.W.C.A., the Home Missions Council, and the United Lutheran Church. On her retirement in 1945, she moved to Clearwater, Fla. She has published many articles and several books on religious themes, e.g., *Saint Elizabeth, Her Brother's Keeper,* New York, [1948].

SEGALE, SISTER BLANDINA (Jan. 23, 1850–Feb. 23, 1941), educator, was born in Cicagna, Italy. She was brought to Cincinnati as a child. A Roman Catholic nun, she taught in the parochial schools of Steubenville and served as a missionary in New Mexico, 1875–97. With her older sister, Sister Justina, she established Santa Maria Institute, a social center for Italian immigrants in Cincinnati. Her death occurred in Delhi Township, Hamilton County. She wrote a book concerning a Sister of Charity in the Southwest, based on her own letters to Sister Justina: *At the End of the Santa Fe Trail,* [Columbus, 1932].

SEIBERT, BENJAMIN ELLIS (Feb. 4, 1883–), lawyer, was born in Urbana, Champaign County. After teaching school he studied law and was admitted to the bar in 1907. He served two terms as city solicitor of Urbana and now lives in that community. He has written legal articles and a pamphlet: *A Rational View of Life,* Toledo, 1912.

SEID, RUTH (July 1, 1913–), was born in Brooklyn, N. Y., but grew up in Cleveland, where her parents moved while she was a child. She worked in Cleveland as a stenographer and later was employed on the Works Progress Administration Writers' Program. She was publicity director for the Cleveland Red Cross, 1941–46. She now lives on a farm near Novelty, Geauga County. She began writing in the 1930s and published several short stories in national magazines. She received the Harper award and widespread critical acclaim for her first novel, published under the pen name Jo Sinclair: *Wasteland,* New York, [1947]. WWAW 1

SEITZ, DON CARLOS (Oct. 4, 1862–Dec. 4, 1935), journalist, was born in Portage, Wood County. He worked on newspapers in Brooklyn and Albany, N. Y., before joining the New York *Recorder* in 1891. Soon afterward he was hired by Joseph Pulitzer, who made him business manager of the New York *World* in 1898, a post he held until 1923. A political and social liberal, he was wholeheartedly supported by Pulitzer and was encouraged to ignore pressure from advertisers and other outside agencies. A prolific writer, he published many magazine articles, some volumes of verse, e.g., *The Buccaneers . . .* , New York, 1912; travel books, e.g., *Elba and Elsewhere,* New York, 1910; and biographies, e.g., *Braxton Bragg, General of the Confederacy,* Columbia, S. C., 1924. DAB 21

SEITZ, ISAAC (Aug. 2, 1828–1890), lawyer and clergyman, was born in Bloom Township, Seneca County. He attended township schools and Heidelberg College, read law, and was admitted to the bar in 1854. He practiced law, except for service with the 164th O.V.I., until 1875, when he became minister of the Tiffin Baptist Church. His autobiography is largely devoted to his conversion.

The Christian Experience of Elder Isaac Seitz . . . , Toledo, 1879.

SELF, MARGARET CABELL (Feb. 12, 1902–), was born in Cincinnati, Hamilton County. She studied at The New York School of Applied Design for Women, 1917–19, and was a portrait painter, 1923–38. Since turning to literature, she has published a number of books on horsemanship and some children's stories, e.g., *Red Clay Country,* New York, 1936. WW 30

SELFRIDGE, SMITH. Pseud. See William C. Tichenor.

SELTZER, CHARLES ALDEN (Aug. 15, 1875–Feb. 9, 1942), was born in Janesville, Wis., but was brought to Columbus when he was still a baby. He grew up in Columbus and in New Mexico. After some experience as a cowboy, he settled in Cleveland. A carpenter and builder by trade, he served as building inspector under Mayor Tom Johnson. He wrote many stories of his Western experiences before publishing his first successful novel: *Two-Gun Man,* New York, 1911. He lived in North Olmsted and served as mayor of that community, 1926–32. His son, Louis B. Seltzer, is editor of the Cleveland *Press.* Highly popular as a writer of Western stories, he turned out an average of a book a year; his last appeared the year before his death: *So Long Sucker,* New York, 1941. WWW 1

SELWYN, EDGAR (Oct. 20, 1875–Feb. 13, 1944), actor, producer, and playwright, was born in Cincinnati, Hamilton County. He was an actor in *Secret Service* with William Gillette, was a founder of Metro-Goldwyn-Mayer, wrote a number of motion-picture scripts, and produced more than 175 plays. His plays include a comedy, produced in 1910 and later published: *The Country Boy,* New York, 1917. WWW 2

SEMPLE, DAISY (Jan. 25, 1879–Sept. 29, 1954), educator, was born in Pittsburgh, Pa., but was brought to Toledo as a child. She studied dancing in Toledo and in New York, and for many years she and her sister conducted dancing classes in Toledo. She also taught in the Toledo schools for 35 years. She wrote a book for children: *Tommy and Jane and the Birds,* Akron, [1929].

SESSIONS, FRANCIS CHARLES (Feb. 27, 1820–March 25, 1892), banker, was born in South Wilbraham, Mass., and came to Columbus in 1840. He worked as a clerk in a dry goods store, was engaged in the wool industry, 1856–69, and became president of the Commercial National Bank when it was organized in 1869. He held many benevolent and educational positions during his lifetime. He had a faculty for close and sharp observation of men and places and wrote of his travels in a lively, concise, and entertaining manner.

On the Wing through Europe. By a Business Man, Columbus, [1880].

From the Land of the Midnight Sun to Volga, New York, 1890.

From Yellowstone Park to Alaska, New York, 1890.

In Western Levant, New York, 1890.

SETHMAN, WILLIAM G. (Dec. 16, 1901–), was born in Cleveland, Cuyahoga County, and attended Cleveland public schools. After living in New York City for a number of years, he returned to live in Cleveland. He has written several books, e.g., *Sonnets,* [Detroit, Mich., 1924].

SEVERANCE, MARK SIBLEY (Oct. 28, 1846–Jan. 20, 1931), was born in Cleveland, Cuyahoga County. He graduated from Harvard University in 1869 and was an assistant librarian of Congress for three years. In 1875 he settled in Los Angeles, where he spent the remainder of his life. He was an executive of the Southern Pacific Railroad and was engaged in real estate and orange-growing.

Hammersmith: His Harvard Days, New York, 1878.

SEWALL, FRANK (Sept. 24, 1837–Dec. 7, 1915), clergyman and educator, born in Bath, Maine, was ordained in the Church of the New Jerusalem in 1863. The first 23 years of his ministry were spent in Ohio. He was pastor of Swedenborgian churches in Glendale, 1863–76, and Urbana, 1870–86. During his Urbana years he was also president of Urbana University. After leaving Ohio he spent two years in Glasgow, Scotland, and was pastor of a Washington, D. C., church from 1889 until his death. Besides the titles below, he published numerous magazine articles and addresses, a textbook, several translations, volumes of sermons, hymnals, and worship books.

Angelo, the Circus Boy, Philadelphia, 1879.

The New Ethics . . . , New York, 1881.

The New Metaphysics . . . , London, 1888.

Dante and Swedenborg, with Other Essays on the New Renaissance, London, 1893.

The Angel of the State; Or, the Kindergarten in the Education of the Citizen . . . , Boston, 1896.

Swedenborg and Modern Idealism . . . , London, 1902.

The Pulpit and Modern Thought . . . , Boston, [1905?].

Spirit as Object . . . , Philadelphia, 1910.

Swedenborg and the 'Sapientia Angelica.' London, 1910.

"The Only-Begotten" in Swedenborg's Cosmology and Theology, Philadelphia, [1914].

The Bright Gate and the Vision Beyond, [Philadelphia, 1915].

SEXTON, LYDIA CASAD (April, 1799–c.1892), was born in Sussex County, N. J. In 1814 she accompanied one of her brothers to Ohio. After a short stay in Cadiz she moved to Fairfield, where she was converted to the United Brethren faith. In 1843 she moved with her husband to Jasper County, Ind. She preached in United Brethren churches for many years, and in 1870 she served as chaplain of Kansas Penitentiary. She died in Seattle, Wash.

Autobiography of Lydia Sexton . . . , Dayton, 1882.

SEYMOUR, FLORA WARREN (1888–Dec. 9, 1946), lawyer, was born in Cleveland, Cuyahoga County. She graduated from George Washington University in 1906 and from Washington College of Law in 1915. She was a member of the Illinois bar and lived in Chicago. She wrote a number of books on historical subjects, most of them intended for children, e.g., *Daniel Boone, Pioneer,* New York, [1931]. WWW 2

SEYMOUR, THOMAS DAY (April 1, 1848–Dec. 31, 1907), educator, was born in Hudson, Summit County. In 1870 he graduated from Western Reserve College, where his father was professor of Greek and Latin. After two years' study in Europe, he taught Greek at Western Reserve, 1872–80; in 1880 he accepted a professorship at Yale University, where he taught for the rest of his life. Recognized internationally as a classical scholar, he published a number of Greek and Latin texts, a family history, and *Life in the Homeric Age,* New York, 1907. DAB 17

SHACKLETON, ELIZABETH FLEMING (Aug., 1871–May 27, 1936), wife of Robert Shackleton (q.v.), was born in Cleveland, Cuyahoga County, and was educated in Cleveland schools. She lived in New York City after 1895 and died in Fairfield, Conn. She collaborated with her husband on several books and also wrote *Touring through France,* Philadelphia, 1925. WWNAA 3

SHACKLETON, ROBERT (Dec. 26, 1860–Feb. 24, 1923), journalist, born in Mazomanie, Wis., was reared and educated in Cleveland. After studying law at the University of Michigan, he was admitted to the Ohio bar in 1861. In 1890 he married Elizabeth Fleming (see above) of Cleveland, and in 1895 they moved to New York City, where he held various editorial positions. He died in Hyères, France. In addition to his books, he wrote for numerous periodicals.

Toomey and Others, New York, 1900.

Many Waters; A Story of New York, New York, 1902.

The Great Adventurer, New York, 1904.

Adventures in Home-making, (with Elizabeth Shackleton), New York, 1910.

The Quest of the Colonial, (with Elizabeth Shackleton), New York, 1910.

Unvisited Places of Old Europe, Philadelphia, 1913.

The Charm of the Antique, (with Elizabeth Shackleton), New York, [1914].

Four on a Tour in England, (with Elizabeth Shackleton), New York, [1914].

The Book of Boston, Philadelphia, 1916.

The Story of Harper's Magazine, 1850–1917, New York, [1916].

The Book of New York, Philadelphia, 1917.

The Book of Philadelphia, Philadelphia, 1918.

The Book of Chicago, Philadelphia, 1920.

The Book of Washington, Philadelphia, 1922.

SHADE, WILLIAM HENRY TAYLOR (Jan. 16, 1864–April 20, 1945), journalist, was born in Centerville, Gallia County. For eight years he was a musician with Liberates' Band and Opera Company and also traveled with minstrel shows. He worked on the New York *Telegraph,* the Chicago *Inter-Ocean,* the Cincinnati *Tribune,* and other newspapers and also edited papers in Ohio and Iowa. He died in Resada, Calif. His volume of poems is dedicated to Charles H. Collins (q.v.) of Hillsboro.

Buckeyeland and Bohemia, Hillsboro, 1895.

SHAFER, BOYD CARLISLE (May 8, 1907–), historian, was born in Crestline, Crawford County. He graduated from Miami University in 1929 and the State University of Iowa (Ph.D.) in 1932. He served on the faculties of Stout Institute, 1932–42, and the University of Arkansas, 1947–53. Since 1953 he has been editor of the *American Historical Review.* He has written numerous historical articles and, in collaboration with his wife, Carol L. Shafer, a collection of letters on economic problems: *Life, Liberty, and the Pursuit of Bread,* New York, 1940. WW 30

SHAFER, CLAUDE (Jan. 7, 1878–), cartoonist, was born at Little Hocking, Washington County, but has lived in Cincinnati since 1885. Because of the death of his father, he attended school only until the age of ten. While working in Cincinnati, he attended the Art Academy at night, and around 1901 achieved his ambition of becoming a cartoonist. He worked on the *Enquirer,* the *Post,* and finally on the *Times-Star,* first as a sports cartoonist and later as an editorial cartoonist. His drawings have been reproduced and exhibited widely. A collection of them was published as *Claude Shafer's Cartoon Guide of Ohio,* New York, [1939].

SHAFER, ROBERT (Dec. 24, 1889–Jan. 6, 1956), educator, born in Hagerstown, Md., taught literature at the University of Cincinnati, 1923–55. He published several textbooks, including a widely used anthology of English literature. He took part in the controversy over the New Humanism in the early 1930s, associating himself with its proponents. His position is reflected in *Paul Elmer More and American Criticism,* New Haven, 1935. WWW 3

SHANKLAND, FRANK NORTH (June 28, 1880–March 14, 1958), was born in Willoughby, Lake County. He graduated from Western Reserve University in 1902. He worked for the American Clay Machinery Co. and for Andrews School and was Lake County Treasurer for four years. In 1931 he joined the staff of Saalfield Publishing Co., Akron, and wrote a series of nature books for young readers which sold more than a million copies, e.g., *Friends of the Forest, Observations of Wild Animal Life,* Akron, [1932].

SHANNON, MARY EULALIE FEE (Feb. 9, 1824–Dec. 26, 1855), was born in Flemingsburg, Ky. When she was a small child, her family moved to Clermont County. She contributed poems to Cincinnati periodicals. In 1854 she married John Shannon, editor of a newspaper in Auburn, Calif., and the last two years of her life were spent in that state. She lectured and gave readings from her poetry. Her poems were published under the pen name Eulalie.

Buds, Blossoms, and Leaves . . . , Cincinnati, 1854.

SHARKEY, DONALD C. (Aug. 31, 1912–), was born in Middletown, Butler County. After graduating from the University of Dayton in 1934, he was an associate editor in the firm of George A. Pflaum until 1949. He edited the *Young Catholic Messenger,* 1939–49. His books include *The Lost Prince,* New York, 1940. CWW 11

SHARP, KATHARINE DOORIS (1845–Sept. 19, 1935), was born in Glasmullagh, England. When her father died, her mother brought her family of eight children to Zanesville. In 1872 Katharine married Dr. Henry J. Sharp, a physician of London, and the remainder of her life was spent in that Madison County community. She was active in the women's suffrage movement, did considerable botanical research, and wrote numerous newspaper articles.

Eleanor's Courtship, and the Songs That Sang Themselves, Cincinnati, 1888.
The South Ward, Cincinnati, 1891.
The Doctor's Speaking Tube, and Other Poems, Boston, 1904.
Jocelyn West; A Tale of the Grand Canyon, New York, [1912].
Summer in a Bog, Cincinnati, [1913].

SHARP, ROBERT LEE (Dec. 28, 1824–Aug. 24, 1891), was born in Belmont County. In 1852 he crossed the plains to California, and his diary of the trip is an important addition to the literature of the overland trail. In 1863 he served in the Fairfield County Militia, a regiment which took an active part in pursuing and capturing the Morgan raiders. After the Civil War he opened a quarry in Fairfield County and shipped building stone throughout the Midwest. William Hale Sharp edited his diary.

Life and Diary of Robert Lee Sharp . . . , [n.p., n.d.].

SHARP, WILLIAM GRAVES (March 14, 1859–Nov. 17, 1922), ambassador to France, 1914–19, was born in Mount Gilead, Morrow County. He attended high school in Elyria and graduated from the University of Michigan law school in 1881. After practicing law for a short time, he founded the Lake Superior Iron and Chemical Company. He was a member of the House of Representatives, 1909–15. Though untrained in diplomacy, he served effectively as ambassador to France during the difficult war years. His memoirs, edited by Warrington Dawson, were published posthumously: *The War Memoirs of William Graves Sharp . . . ,* London, 1931. DAB 17

SHARPE, DORES ROBINSON (Jan. 23, 1886–), Baptist clergyman, born in New Brunswick, Canada, was executive secretary of the Cleveland Baptist Association, 1925–53. He has published books on religious themes and a biography: *Walter Rauschenbusch,* New York, 1942. WW 30

SHARPE, HOWARD GRANVILLE (Oct. 20, 1880–), born in Fort Griffin, Texas, spent his boyhood in Wooster, Wayne County, and attended school there. A graduate of Dartmouth College, he served in the Spanish-American War and World War I. He now lives in Los Angeles. He has written many short stories and several novels, e.g., a novel about the Philippines during World War II: *Crimson Philippine Jungle,* Los Angeles, [1943].

SHARTS, JOSEPH WILLIAM (Sept. 14, 1875–), lawyer, was born in Hamilton, Butler County. He graduated from Harvard University in 1897, served in the Spanish-American War, and was admitted to the bar in 1899. He practiced in Dayton, and several of his cases attracted wide attention. He was counsel for Eugene V. Debs at his trial in Cleveland in 1918 and for Bishop William M. Brown (q.v.) at his heresy trial, 1924–25. He edited the *Miami Valley Socialist* in the 1920s. Now retired from active practice, he lives in Dayton. He has written several novels, e.g., *Ezra Caine,* Chicago, 1901, and a volume of local history: *Biography of Dayton . . . ,* Dayton, 1922. WW 30

SHAW, ALBERT (July 23, 1857–June 25, 1947), editor, was born in Shandon, Butler County. He graduated from Iowa (Grinnell) College in 1879 and Johns Hopkins University (Ph.D.) in 1884. He was editor of the Minneapolis *Tribune,* 1883–90, and in 1891 established the *Review of Reviews* and served as its editor until 1937. Besides the titles below, he published numerous addresses and magazine articles in pamphlet form.

Icaria, a Chapter in the History of Communism, New York, 1884.

Cooperation in the Northwest, Baltimore, 1888.

Municipal Government in Continental Europe, New York, 1895.

Municipal Government in Great Britain, New York, 1895.

Life of Col. Geo. E. Waring, Jr., the Greatest Apostle of Cleanliness . . . , New York, 1899.

The Business Career in Its Public Relations, San Francisco, [1904].

The Outlook for the Average Man, New York, 1907.

Political Problems of American Development, New York, 1907.

A Cartoon History of Roosevelt's Career . . . , New York, [1910].

Abraham Lincoln . . . , New York, 1929.

International Bearings of American Policy, Baltimore, 1943.

SHAW, ARCHER H. (Jan. 6, 1876–), journalist, was born in North Ridgeville, Lorain County. After graduating from Oberlin College in 1897, he worked on newspapers in Lorain and Springfield, Mass. He was on the Cleveland *Plain Dealer,* 1902–41, serving most of that time as chief editorial writer. He has edited an encyclopedia of Lincolniana, but his major work is *The Plain Dealer; One Hundred Years in Cleveland,* New York, 1942.

SHAW, A. VERE (Nov. 20, 1887–), investment counsel, was born in Sidney, Shelby County. He graduated from Ohio State University in 1909 and Harvard Law School in 1913. He has been an investment counselor in Boston and New York City, and since 1930 he has operated his own firm in New York. He has written *The Case against Short Selling . . . ,* [New York, 1932]. WWCI 8

SHAW, AVERY ALBERT (Oct. 2, 1870–March 18, 1949), born in Nova Scotia, lived in Ohio while pastor of East End Baptist Church, Cleveland, 1911–14, and while president of Denison University,

1927–40. His writings include a group of religious talks to children: *Jack-in-the-Pulpit . . .* , Philadelphia, [1923]. WWW 2

SHAW, BEN ROY (1827?–1900), was born in Canada. He lived in Wooster for a number of years. No details concerning his life have been found.

Songs in the Night, Wooster, 1887.

SHAW, HENRY WHEELER (April 21, 1818–Oct. 14, 1885), humorist, born in Lanesboro, Mass., lived for about a year in Norwalk, where he worked as an auctioneer. As Josh Billings, he was famous for his "allminax," which were published from 1869 to 1880.

SHAW, WILLIAM WALTER (March 27, 1861–Aug. 15, 1951), was born on a farm near Coshocton, Coshocton County, and lived in that town for nearly fifty years before moving to California. He operated a printing business and a novelty advertising business. His poems, many of them relating to the experiences of a traveling salesman, were published in *Reveries of a Drummer . . .* , Los Angeles, [1926].

SHAWAN, JACOB ALBRIGHT (June 16, 1850–May 2, 1927), educator, was born at Wapakoneta, Auglaize County, and was educated at Oberlin College. He served as superintendent of schools in several Ohio cities, including Columbus (1889–1916). A trip to Europe resulted in his writing a travel book: *Recent Glimpses in Europe . . .* , [Columbus, 1902]. OBB

SHAWHAN, JAMES MARTIN (April 21, 1857–April 6, 1929), was born near Pittsburgh, Pa. His parents came to Ohio when he was a few months old; they lived on a farm in Roxbury for about a year and then settled in Lowell, Washington County. He was a barber in Marietta for many years. His poems appeared in various newspapers, and he also published a collection: *Unpolished Pebbles,* [Marietta?], 1902.

SHEATSLEY, CLARENCE VALENTINE (Nov. 25, 1873–Jan. 19, 1943), clergyman, was born in Paris, Stark County. He graduated from Capital University in 1895 and Capital Seminary in 1898. Following two years' study in Germany, he was ordained to the Lutheran ministry. After serving pastorates in Pennsylvania, he was on the faculty of Capital University, 1917–29. His writings include *History of the Evangelical Lutheran Joint Synod of Ohio . . .* , Columbus, 1919. WWW 2

SHEATSLEY, JACOB (June 20, 1859–Aug. 31, 1953), clergyman, was born in Paris, Stark County. After attending Capital University and Lutheran Theological Seminary, Columbus, he was ordained to the Lutheran ministry in 1887. He served churches in Canaan, Delaware, and Columbus, and edited the *Lutheran Standard* and other magazines. He published sermons and textbooks.

The Holy Service, Columbus, 1897.

Narratives on the Catechism, Columbus, 1901.

SHEEHAN, MURRAY (Dec. 15, 1887–), educator, was born in Hamilton, Butler County. He graduated from Miami University in 1908 and afterward studied at the Sorbonne. He taught at Miami University, the University of Wisconsin, and the University of Arkansas and became superintendent of students at the Royal Thai Legation, Washington, D. C., in 1930. He is now on the faculty of Chulalongkorn University, Bangkok, Siam. He wrote the texts for many Haldeman-Julius Little Blue Books and also published a satirical novel: *Half-Gods,* New York, 1927. WW 24

SHEEHAN, PERLEY POORE (June 11, 1875–Oct. 1, 1943), journalist, was born in Cincinnati, Hamilton County. After graduating from Union College in 1898, he was European correspondent for several newspapers and was Paris editor of the New York *Herald,* 1905–07. In 1908 he became an associate editor of Munsey publications. He wrote several novels, motion-picture scenarios, plays, and a book about the movies: *Hollywood as a World Center,* [Hollywood, 1924]. WW 16

SHEERIN, JAMES (May 6, 1865–Dec. 24, 1933), clergyman, born in Armadale, Scotland, was brought to the United States in 1870, and lived in Ohio for several intervals. After graduating from Kenyon College in 1892, he was ordained an Episcopal priest and served as rector of various churches, including Ashtabula, 1893–95, and Warren, 1909–11. After his retirement in 1930 he lived in Bucyrus, and his death occurred in that community. His writings include a biographical study: *Henry Codman Potter . . .* , New York, [1933]. WWW 1

SHELDON, RUTH LOUISE GIFFORD (Jan. 9, 1846–March 27, 1926), born in Fitchburg, N. Y., spent most of her life in Akron. She was married to Charles E. Sheldon, chairman of Whitman and Barnes Manufacturing Company.

Flexible Morals, New York, 1898.
Red, White & Blue Days, New York, 1898.
Scraps, Akron, 1898.
Dolly, a Daughter of New England, Akron, [1905].
Social Silhouettes, New York, [1907].
Robbing Peter to Pay Paul, Akron, 1908.

SHELLABARGER, SAMUEL (May 18, 1888–March 20, 1954), born in Washington, D. C., was headmaster of Columbus School for Girls, 1938–46. A graduate of Princeton University and Harvard University (Ph.D.), he taught English at Princeton, 1914–38, except for five years in Switzerland, 1923–28. He wrote mysteries and romances under the pen names John Esteven and Peter Loring, e.g., *Grief before Night,* Philadelphia, 1938, but he was most widely known for his highly popular historical novels, e.g., *Captain from Castile,* Boston, 1945. WWW 3

SHEPARD, ENOCH (Oct. 23, 1742–Sept. 17, 1821), was an early settler of Marietta, where he was a deacon of the First Presbyterian Church. His only known publication is the book listed below.

Thoughts on the Prophecies; Applicable to the Times, Marietta, 1812.

SHEPARDSON, DANIEL (Dec. 1, 1868–Nov. 25, 1905), clergyman, was born in Granville, Licking County. He attended Granville Academy, graduated from Denison University in 1888, and received his doctorate in Biblical literature from Yale University in 1891. He taught for a time in the American Institute of Sacred Literature. Despite the fact that he was paralyzed in 1893 and was forced to preach from a wheelchair, he traveled widely as an evangelist. He died in Honolulu, Hawaii. He wrote *Studies in the Epistles to the Hebrews,* Chicago, 1901.

SHEPARDSON, FRANCIS WAYLAND (Oct. 15, 1862–Aug. 9, 1937), educator, was born in Cheviot, Hamilton County. Son of a Baptist minister, he graduated from Denison University in 1882, Brown University in 1883, and Yale University (Ph.D.) in 1892. After finishing college he taught at the Young Ladies' Institute, Granville, where his father was principal, and he edited the Granville *Times,* 1887–90. Upon completion of his doctorate at Yale, he was called to the University of Chicago as the personal secretary of William Rainey Harper (q.v.), its president. He then became dean of the senior schools and from 1897 to 1917 held professorial rank in the field of American history. He later was an editorial writer for the Chicago *Tribune* and director of the Department of Registration and Education of the State of Illinois. He took an active part in the American fraternity movement, becoming general secretary of Beta Theta Pi in 1917 and serving as its historian and editor of its magazine, 1917–31. He became the first secretary of the National Interfraternity Conference in 1909 and also held several posts in Phi Beta Kappa. He demonstrated that Greek letter societies have a real place in American colleges. He wrote a family history; *The Beta Book . . . ,* Menasha, Wis., 1927, and many articles relating to the fraternity; and *Denison University, 1831–1931; A Centennial History,* Granville, 1931.

Karl W. Fischer

SHEPARDSON, GEORGE DEFREES (Nov. 20, 1864–May 26, 1926), electrical engineer, younger brother of Frances W. Shepardson (q.v.), was born in Cheviot, Hamilton County. He graduated from Denison University in 1885, did graduate work at Cornell University, and was on the engineering faculty, University of Minnesota, from 1891 until his death. Besides technical books and articles, he wrote *The Religion of an Electrical Engineer,* New York, [1926]. WWW 1

SHEPFER, HAROLD REED (Aug. 23, 1896–), clergyman, son of William H. Shepfer (q.v.), was born in Scio, Harrison County. He graduated from Thiel College in 1920 and Hamma Divinity School, Springfield, in 1929. After serving several churches in Pennsylvania, he retired from the ministry in 1958. He has written *When Death Speaks . . . ,* Burlington, Iowa, 1937. RLA 2

SHEPFER, WILLIAM HENRY (Oct. 22, 1870–Oct. 8, 1957), clergyman, was born in Ragersville, Tuscarawas County. After graduating from Chicago Theological Seminary, he was ordained to the Lutheran ministry in 1901. He served pastorates in Ohio, Indiana, and Pennsylvania. After retiring in 1931 he lived in Cuyahoga Falls until 1937 and in Defiance for the last twenty years of his life. He wrote *The Bible and Science; A Popular Apologetic,* Burlington, Iowa, 1938. RLA 2

SHEPHERD, ARTHUR (Feb. 19, 1880–), composer and pianist, born in Paris, Idaho, has lived in Cleveland since 1920. He served as assistant conductor of the Cleveland Orchestra and as professor of music at Western Reserve University. Best known as a composer, he has published one book: *The String Quartettes of Ludwig van Beethoven . . .* , [Cleveland], 1935. WW 30

SHEPHERD, WILLIAM GUNN (June 13, 1878–Nov. 4, 1933), journalist, was born in Springfield, Clark County. He was widely known as a correspondent for the United Press and as a writer for *Collier's Weekly* and other magazines. His experiences as a reporter are the basis of *Confessions of a War Correspondent,* New York, [1917]. WWW 1

SHERIDAN, PHILIP HENRY (March 6, 1831–Aug. 5, 1888), army officer, was born in Albany, N. Y.; but soon after his birth his father, an Irish immigrant, brought his family to Somerset, Perry County, where he worked on construction of canals and roads. After an education in district schools, the boy was appointed to the U. S. Military Academy in 1848 and graduated in 1853; his graduation was delayed one year because of a suspension for fighting with a cadet officer. He served along the Rio Grande and in the Northwest and was promoted to captain in 1861. After his appointment as colonel of the 2nd Michigan Cavalry in May, 1862, he rose rapidly in the army; his national prominence came after Grant placed him in full command of the cavalry of the Army of the Potomac in April, 1864. His victories in the wilderness in the late spring and his devastation of the Shenandoah Valley in the fall of 1864 made him one of the major architects of Northern victory. After the war he was a military governor in the South, commanded the Division of the Missouri, and in 1884 succeeded William T. Sherman (q.v.) as general-in-chief of the army. He wrote his memoirs during the last year of his life. His only other publications were official reports.

Personal Memoirs . . . , 2 vols., New York, 1888.

SHERIDAN, WILLIAM (1830–Dec. 16, 1913), clergyman, was pastor of a Baptist church in Toledo for thirty years.

A Consecrated Life; Or, the Biography of John Sheridan, [Toledo, 1898].

SHERLOCK, HERBERT ARMENT (March 7, 1899–), artist, was born in Canton, Stark County. After graduating from the Cleveland School of Art in 1921, he worked in an engraving plant, operated a studio, and since 1942 has been staff artist on the Canton *Repository*. He wrote and illustrated a history of firearms: *Black Powder Snapshots,* [Huntington, W. Va., 1946].

SHERMAN, CHRISTOPHER ELIAS (Dec. 28, 1869–May 6, 1940), civil engineer, was born in Columbus, Franklin County. After graduating from Ohio State University in 1894, he worked with several state surveys before joining the Ohio State University engineering faculty in 1896. He published several technical works and textbooks, and *A Journey to the Land of Kingdom Come, and Other Journeys in Prose and Verse,* Columbus, 1936. WWW 1

SHERMAN, FRANKLYN COLE (Dec. 23, 1873–May 3, 1942), clergyman, born in Chicago, lived in Ohio for approximately 25 years. He was rector of St. Paul's Episcopal Church, Akron, 1918–28, and of Grace Church, Cleveland, from 1928 until his death. He wrote *Religion Applied to Life . . .* , Cleveland, [1934].

SHERMAN, JOHN (May 10, 1823–Oct. 22, 1900), younger brother of William T. Sherman (q.v.), was born in Lancaster, Fairfield County. After attending school in Lancaster and Mount Vernon until he was fourteen, he worked on the canals. He later read law in Mansfield, 1840–44. He practiced in Mansfield and dealt in lumber and real estate until 1855, when his long public career began with his election to the House of Representatives. He served in the House, 1855–61, in the Senate, 1861–77 and 1881–97, was Secretary of the Treasury, 1877–81, and Secretary of State, 1897–98. He had hopes of the Presidency in the 1880s, but failed to win the Republican nomination. Conservative by temperament, especially on economic issues, he was willing to compromise—a willingness that helps account for his success in Ohio politics. Besides the titles below, many of his separate addresses were issued as pamphlets.

Selected Speeches and Reports . . . , New York, 1879.

John Sherman's Recollections . . . , 2 vols., Chicago, 1895.

SHERMAN, SYLVESTER MORRILL (Dec. 23, 1842–Dec. 27, 1930), physician, was born in Wheeling, Va., but grew up in Columbus. After graduating from high school, he taught school for several terms. He served in the 133rd O.V.I., May, 1864–Aug., 1864, as a first sergeant. He returned to teaching after the war. In 1875 he graduated from Eclectic Medical College, Cincinnati. He practiced in Garrett, Ind., 1875–

83, and in Columbus after 1883. His death occurred in Columbus.

History of the 133rd Regiment . . ., Columbus, 1896.

SHERMAN, WILLIAM TECUMSEH (Feb. 8, 1820–Feb. 14, 1891), army officer, was born in Lancaster, Fairfield County, the son of Charles R. Sherman, a judge of the state supreme court, who died suddenly in 1829, leaving eleven children. On the death of his father, William, or "Cump" as he was known in the family, was taken into the home of Thomas Ewing, who later procured for him an appointment to the U. S. Military Academy. After graduating in 1840 he served in the South and in the Mexican War. He married Ellen Boyle Ewing, his guardian's daughter, in 1850. In 1853 he resigned from the army, after which he spent eight restless years in various activities—as a banker in California, superintendent of a military academy in Louisiana, and president of a street railway company in St. Louis. He was appointed colonel in May, 1861, but his erratic behavior and his disdain for newspaper correspondents delayed full recognition of his abilities. He won the confidence of Grant, however, and the two generals functioned perfectly as a team. His Atlanta campaign and march to the sea made him second only to Grant among the Northern heroes after the war. He commanded the Division of Mississippi for a time after the war and succeeded Grant as general-in-chief in 1869. On retiring from the army in 1883, he lived in St. Louis for three years and spent the rest of his life in New York City. Besides the titles below, some of his separate speeches were issued as pamphlets.

General Sherman's Official Account of His Great March . . ., New York, 1865.
Memoirs . . ., 2 vols., New York, 1875.
The Sherman Letters . . ., (Rachel Sherman Thorndike, ed.), New York, 1894.
Home Letters . . ., (M. A. DeWolfe Howe, ed.), New York, 1909.
General W. T. Sherman as College President . . ., (Walter L. Fleming, ed.), Cleveland, 1912.

SHERRARD, ROBERT. See James Paul.

SHERWOOD, ISAAC RUTH (Aug. 13, 1835–Oct. 15, 1925), journalist, soldier, and congressman, was born in Stanford, N. Y. He studied at Antioch College, 1854–56, and afterward at the Ohio Law College, Poland. He married Katherine Margaret Brownlee (see below) of Poland, Sept. 1, 1859. While studying law, he published the *Williams County Gazette* in Bryan and wrote one of the few favorable reviews of Whitman's *Leaves of Grass*. He served in the Civil War with the 14th O.V.I. and the 111th, which he commanded during the last year of the war. He wrote for the Toledo *Commercial* and the Cleveland *Leader*, and edited the Toledo *Journal*, 1875–84, and the Canton *News-Democrat*, 1888–98. He served a total of nine terms in the U. S. Congress: 1873–75, 1906–20, and 1922–24. Several of his speeches and papers were published and an autobiography: *Memories of the War*, Toledo, 1923. DAB 17

SHERWOOD, KATHARINE MARGARET BROWNLEE (Sept. 24, 1841–Feb. 15, 1914), was born in Poland, Mahoning County. She attended Poland Union Seminary, and while still a student there she married Isaac R. Sherwood (q.v.) on Sept. 1, 1859. They went to live in Bryan, where he owned and edited the *Williams County Gazette*. When Lincoln issued his first call for volunteers, Isaac Sherwood enlisted as a private and served to the end of the war, rising to the rank of brigadier general. During his absence his wife assumed the management and editorship of the paper, thus beginning a long and brilliant career as author and journalist. For ten years she and her husband edited the Toledo *Journal*. She was women's editor of the *National Tribune*, the official publication of the Grand Army of the Republic. She contributed political satires to the New York *Sun* while it was under the management of Charles A. Dana. Traveling extensively in Europe, she earned her way by writing travel letters for the American Press Association. She felt that the greatest honor ever paid her was an invitation from a group of Southerners to commemorate the heroism of a Southern soldier. She wrote the poem for the unveiling of the statue of General Albert Sydney Johnston at New Orleans on April 6, 1887. General Sherwood was representing the Toledo district in Congress when she died in Washington, D. C. Secretary of State William Jennings Bryan delivered the funeral address.

Katherine Sherwood Roberts

Campfire, Memorial-Day, and Others, Chicago, 1885.
Dream of Ages, a Poem of Columbia, Washington, D. C., 1893.

SHERWOOD, ROBERT EDMUND (1864–March 9, 1946), publisher and bookseller, was born in St. Clairsville, Belmont County. At the age of eleven he ran away to join a circus, and he was a clown with Barnum

& Bailey for 28 years. He became interested in books and opened a bookstore in Michigan; he later owned other shops in the Midwest and New York. He compiled books of jokes and other collections and also wrote a book of verse: *Hold Everything!,* New York, [1929].

SHETRONE, HENRY CLYDE (Aug. 10, 1876–Nov. 24, 1954), archaeologist, was born in Millersport, Fairfield County. He attended Denison University, served in the Spanish-American War as a telegrapher, and worked on various newspapers before joining the staff of the Ohio State Museum in 1913. He was director of the museum from 1928 until his retirement in 1947. He wrote numerous articles on historical and archaeological subjects and an important survey of prehistoric cultures: *The Mound Builders . . . ,* New York, 1930.

SHIELDS, GEORGE OLIVER (Aug. 26, 1846–Nov. 11, 1925), conservationist, was born in Batavia, Clermont County. He enlisted in the Union Army in 1864 and was wounded at Resaca, Ga. He hunted and fished in all parts of North America and wrote articles about the outdoors for various periodicals. Many of his writings were signed Coquina. He founded the magazine *Recreation* in 1894 and organized the League of American Sportsmen in 1898. An ardent conservationist, he campaigned against the use of automatic shotguns and tried to encourage nature photography. He lectured widely on conservation. He also edited books on big game, dogs, and game fish. He died in New York City, where he had spent his last years in near-poverty.

Rustlings in the Rockies: Hunting and Fishing by Mountain and Stream, Chicago, 1883.
The Battle of the Big Hole . . . , Chicago, 1889.
Cruisings in the Cascades . . . , Chicago, 1889.
Camping and Camp Outfits. A Manual . . . , Chicago, 1890.
The Blanket Indians of the Northwest, New York, 1921.

SHIELDS, PAULINE RICE (Oct. 31, 1867–Sept. 20, 1955), was born in Cincinnati, Hamilton County. She was educated at Hillebrandt Classic School and the University of Cincinnati. She was for some time editor of the women's page, Cincinnati *Post,* also contributed poems to various magazines and newspapers, and published one collection: *Life's Windows,* Cincinnati, [1925]. WWNAA 3

SHIELS, WILLIAM EUGENE (Feb. 2, 1897–), educator, was born in Cincinnati, Hamilton County. He entered the Jesuit order in 1916, graduated from Gonzaga University in 1922, and earned his doctorate at the University of California in 1933. He has been professor of history at Xavier University, Cincinnati, since 1946. Besides history texts he has published a biography of a Jesuit priest: *Gonzalo De Tapio . . . ,* New York, 1934. WW 30

SHIMP, ELLIS HOWARD (Sept. 7, 1898–), was born in Buffalo, Guernsey County. He lived in Ohio until 1944, when he moved to Clairton, Pa. An employee of U. S. Steel since 1918, he has written poems as an avocation; they have been published in various periodicals and in a collection: *Remorse, and Other Poems,* [Cambridge], 1921.

SHINN, ASA (May 3, 1781–Feb. 11, 1853), born in New Jersey of Quaker parents, was converted to Methodism in 1798 and in 1803 was one of the organizers of the Hocking Circuit. He was transferred to Maryland in 1807 but was again in Ohio, 1829–33, serving in Cincinnati as president of the Ohio Conference of the newly organized Methodist Protestant Church. He published several pamphlets and two books on theology, e.g., *An Essay on the Plan of Salvation . . . ,* Baltimore, 1813.

SHINN, ROGER LINCOLN (Jan. 6, 1917–), educator, was born in Germantown, Montgomery County. He graduated from Heidelberg College in 1938 and Union Theological Seminary in 1941. In 1951, after service in Europe during World War II, he received his Ph.D. from Columbia University. He joined the Heidelberg philosophy faculty in 1948 and in 1954 began teaching at Vanderbilt University. Besides magazine articles and reviews on religious subjects, he has published *Beyond This Darkness,* New York, 1946.

SHINN, WILLIAM HENRY (March 19, 1867–Nov. 28, 1932), journalist and lawyer, was born in Northwest Township, Williams County. After attending district schools, he went to Montpelier, where he learned the printing business. He taught school and worked on newspapers in Ohio, Michigan, Kentucky, and Indiana. From 1897 to 1912 he worked for Northwestern Historical Society, publishers of county and local histories. In 1912 he returned to Williams County, bought the Montpelier *Enterprise,* which he published until 1916, served in the state legislature, 1916–18, and in 1918 began the practice of law.

Plain Duty; A Political Plan for the Campaign of 1900, La Grange, Ind., 1900.
The County of Williams . . . , Madison, Wis., 1905.

SHIVELL, PAUL (Sept. 25, 1874–), born in Indianapolis, Ind., was educated in Dayton and Springfield public schools and at Phillips Academy, Andover, Mass. He operated a farm at Pleasant Hill, Miami County, 1903–15, and afterward lectured widely and operated the Stillwater Press. He designed his own books and printed his poems on a hand press. He now lives in Dayton.

Poems and Fragments, [Springfield], 1896.
Ashes of Roses, [Dayton], 1898.
Stillwater Pastorals, Pleasant Hill, 1908.
Stillwater Pastorals and Other Poems, Boston, 1915.
By the Banks of the Stillwater, Dayton, 1919.
Selections from Published Poems, Dayton, 1944.

SHOCKEY, SAMUEL W. (April 25, 1858– ?), was born in Roundhead Township, Hardin County. According to his autobiography, he began an eventful career by running away from home at the age of nine to become a peddler. He was an evangelist for the Ohio Holiness Alliance and later traveled throughout the country as a phrenologist and palmist. He enlisted in the army in 1883 but deserted after about a year. A confirmed drunkard, he reformed in 1891 and apparently became a temperance lecturer.

Twenty-five Years Fighting Fate . . . , Boston, [1892].

SHOEMAKER, MICHAEL MYERS (June 26, 1853–Aug. 11, 1924), was born in Covington, Ky., the son of Robert M. Shoemaker, a railroad builder. He studied at Cornell University, 1870–72. He had business interests in Cincinnati and maintained a home in that city throughout his life, but he traveled throughout the world. He died in Paris, France. He published about a dozen travel books, e.g., *Winged Wheels in France,* New York, 1906. WWW 1

SHOLTIS, GEORGE E. (Aug. 4, 1921–), born in Freeland, Pa., has lived in Akron since 1943. A graduate of Pennsylvania State University, he is a process research engineer with Goodyear Tire and Rubber Company. He has published a book of humor: *Moronic Machinations,* Philadelphia, [1948].

SHOOK, CHESTER R. (June 23, 1884–), lawyer and judge, was born in Troy, Miami County, but his family moved to Cincinnati when he was two years old and he has spent his life in that city. He graduated from the University of Cincinnati Law School in 1906, practiced law in Cincinnati, and served as judge of common pleas court, 1927–33. The study of Lincoln's career was his long-time hobby, and he published a volume of essays on various aspects of Lincoln: *The Lincoln Story,* Cincinnati, [1950].

SHORT, JOHN THOMAS (May 1, 1850–Nov. 11, 1883), clergyman and educator, was born in Ohio, probably in Delaware County. After graduating from Ohio Wesleyan University in 1868, he attended Drew Theological Seminary and became a Methodist minister. He also studied at the University of Leipzig, where he earned a Ph.D. degree. In 1877 he joined the Ohio Wesleyan faculty, and two years later he became professor of history and philosophy at Ohio State University, where he was teaching at the time of his death.

The Last Gladiatorial Show, Cincinnati, 1872.
The North Americans of Antiquity . . . , New York, 1880.
Ohio; A Sketch of Industrial Progress, Columbus, 1882.

SHOTWELL, WALTER GASTON (Dec. 27, 1856–March 11, 1938), lawyer and judge, was born in Cadiz, Harrison County. After attending Franklin College, he graduated from Yale University in 1878. He read law in his father's office and was admitted to the bar in 1880. He served two terms as prosecuting attorney of Harrison County. He was elected judge of common pleas court in 1889 and served in that capacity until 1905, when he retired to devote his time to literary pursuits. He was an admirer of Washington Irving, whose influence is apparent in the book of sketches entitled *Driftwood,* New York, 1927. At the time of his death he left a completed manuscript of a biography of Irving. He also wrote *Life of Charles Sumner,* New York, [1910], and *The Civil War in America,* 2 vols., New York, 1923.

SHREVE, THOMAS HOPKINS (Dec. 17, 1808–Dec. 22, 1853), born in Alexandria, Va., came to Cincinnati in 1830. With William Davis Gallagher (q.v.), he published the Cincinnati *Mirror,* 1833–36; he also published five issues of the *Western Messenger* in 1835. For these and other periodicals he wrote essays, stories, and poems. In 1838 he moved to Louisville, Ky., where he engaged in a wholesale dry goods business and was assistant editor of the Louisville *Journal.* He wrote a novel: *Drayton, a Story of American Life,* New York, 1851.

SHRIBER, IONE SANDBERG (Mrs. Kenneth W.) (Sept. 28, 1911–), born in Emeigh, Pa., has lived in Akron since 1922. She attended Akron schools and has been active in civic activities in that city and in Florida, where she spends her winters. She has written a number of mystery novels, e.g., *Murder Well Done,* New York, [1941].

SHRINER, CHARLES ANTHONY (Oct. 14, 1853–March 26, 1945), journalist, was born in Cincinnati, Hamilton County. After graduating from Xavier University in 1872, he was a reporter on the New York *Herald* and later worked on various newspapers in Paterson, N. J. He edited a history of Paterson, wrote on birds of New Jersey, and published an autobiography: *Random Recollections . . . ,* Paterson, N. J., 1941. WWW 3

SHUEY, EDWIN LONGSTREET (Jan. 3, 1857–Sept. 27, 1924), was born in Cincinnati, Hamilton County. After his father, William J. Shuey (q.v.), moved to Dayton in 1865, he attended the public schools of that city. He graduated from Otterbein College in 1877, studied law, taught school at various academies, and in 1885 settled in Dayton to manage the bookstore of the United Brethren Publishing House. He was head of the welfare department, National Cash Register Company, 1897–1900, a position that led to his writing the book listed below, and was in the advertising and sales department of Lowe Brothers, Dayton, 1900–18. He also published papers and pamphlets related to Y.M.C.A. work and the United Brethren Church.

Factory People and Their Employees . . . , New York, [1900].

SHUEY, WILLIAM JOHN (Feb. 9, 1827–Feb. 21, 1920), clergyman, was born in Miamisburg, Montgomery County. A clergyman of the United Brethren Church, he served pastorates in Dayton and Cincinnati and was a missionary in Sierra-Leone, Africa, 1854–55. He was publishing agent of the United Brethren Publishing House, 1864–97, and business manager of Bonebrake Seminary, 1897–1901. He retired in 1901. He wrote pamphlets and many articles for the *Religious Telescope.* His only book, so far as is known, was a collaboration with Daniel K. Flickinger (q.v.).

Discourses on Doctrinal and Practical Subjects, Dayton, 1859.

SHULL, JAMES MARION (Jan. 23, 1872–Sept. 1, 1948), botanist and artist, was born in Clark County. He taught art at Antioch College, 1896–98, and in Ohio public schools and served as staff artist for the Department of Agriculture in Washington, D. C. He wrote and illustrated *Rainbow Fragments; A Garden Book of the Iris,* New York, 1931. WWW 2

SHULL, LENA MEARLE LARKIN (Sept. 22, 1883–Jan. 25, 1960), was born near South Charleston, Clark County. She attended Antioch College and took nurse's training in Kansas City, Mo., and Denver, Colo. In 1907 she married Charles A. Shull, who taught at the University of Chicago. After his retirement in 1944 they moved to Asheville, N. C. She organized the Poetry Council of North Carolina and belonged to many other literary organizations. Her poems appeared in various magazines, and she also published several collections, e.g., *Rainbow through the Web,* Emory University, Ga., [1944].

SHULL, SAMUEL PETER (Aug. 3, 1865–Feb. 8, 1949), educator, was born in Virden, Ill. The following year his parents, who had been Ohio residents, returned to Ohio. He served as a teacher and superintendent of schools in various Ohio counties and in Indiana, contributed poems and articles to several magazines, and in 1893 founded and edited *Ingleside Magazine.* He died in Greenfield.

Matrimonial Adaptation; Or, Phrenology, Applied to Home Life and the Domestic Relation . . . , Osborn, 1888.

SHULTZ, JOSEPH S. (March 13, 1863– ?), educator, was born in De Graff, Logan County. He taught for many years at Wilder College.

Observations in the North-west, Containing an Account of a Trip to Alaska . . . , Ada, 1892.

SHUTTER, MARION DANIEL (Aug. 4, 1853–Aug. 31, 1939), clergyman, was born in New Philadelphia, Tuscarawas County. He graduated from University of Wooster in 1876 and was ordained to the Baptist ministry in 1881. He served as a Baptist and Universalist minister in Minneapolis,

Minn., and also contributed to several historical studies of Minnesota.

Wit and Humor of the Bible. A Literary Study, Boston, 1893.
Applied Evolution, Boston, 1900.
Rev. James Harvey Tuttle, D.D.; A Memoir, Boston, 1905.
The Citizen and Political Socialism in Minneapolis, [Minneapolis, 1918].

SIBBERELL, LLOYD EMERSON (Sept. 18, 1905–), was born in Kingston, Ross County. He attended Kingston public schools and Chillicothe Business College. Since 1924 he has been with the Norfolk & Western Railroad, serving in Cincinnati, Winston-Salem, N. C., and Columbus. A rare-book collector, he has published many articles on books, writers, and publishing. He has a special interest in the Powys family and has compiled a bibliography of John Cowper Powys. His publications include a pamphlet: *Tecumseh . . . ,* Chillicothe, 1944. WWMW 6

SIBLEY, EDWARD CARROLL (Jan. 18, 1906–Jan. 6, 1949), was born in Toledo, Lucas County. He graduated from Harvard University in 1927 and then studied abroad. After several years in the investment business, he was a free-lance author and lecturer and lived in Beverly Hills, Calif. He served in the U. S. Army during World War II and afterward taught at Washington University, St. Louis. He has published several books, e.g., a collection of biographical sketches: *Barrie and His Contemporaries . . . ,* Webster Groves, Mo., 1936. WW 26

SIBLEY, WILLIAM GIDDINGS (Feb. 29, 1860–Jan. 30, 1935), journalist, was born in Racine, Meigs County. After graduating from Marietta College in 1881, he was a clerk in a general store at Racine until 1887. He then founded and edited the *Meigs County Tribune* until 1889, when he became state librarian of Ohio. He edited the Gallipolis *Tribune,* 1890–1920. He worked briefly on the Omaha *Bee* and the Chicago *Daily Journal of Commerce.* After retiring in 1924, he spent his last years in Gallipolis. His writings include *The French Five Hundred, and Other Papers,* Gallipolis, 1901. WWW 1

SIDDALL, JOHN MacALPINE (Oct. 8, 1874–July 16, 1923), journalist, was born in Oberlin, Lorain County. After graduating from Oberlin College in 1898, he worked on the Cleveland *Plain Dealer* until 1901. He was secretary of the public schools of Cleveland, 1902–04, and was on the editorial staff of the *American Magazine,* 1906–23. He wrote *Sid Says,* New York, 1917.

SIEBERT, WILBUR HENRY (Aug. 30, 1866–Sept. 4, 1961), educator and historian, was born in Columbus, Franklin County. He graduated from Ohio State University in 1888 and did graduate work at Harvard University and the University of Leipzig, 1888–91. He was a member of the history faculty of Ohio State University, 1898–1925; in 1925 he was named research professor of history. His major research interests were the Loyalists during the period of the Revolution and the Underground Railroad. On both subjects he published many articles and monographs in addition to the titles listed below. He also wrote several portions of *The History of the Ohio State University* (1938).

The Underground Railroad from Slavery to Freedom . . . , New York, 1898.
The Government of Ohio . . . , New York, 1904.
Loyalists in East Florida, 1774–1785, 2 vols., New Haven, Conn., 1929.
Vermont's Anti-slavery and Underground Record . . . , Columbus, 1937.

SIEDEL, FRANK (Sept. 5, 1914–), was born in Strongsville, Cuyahoga County. After graduating from Ohio State University in 1936, he worked as a radio writer in Pittsburgh and New York City. He returned to Ohio in 1941 to write educational radio programs, and in 1947 he began the popular series drawn from Ohio's past, *The Ohio Story,* which has won numerous awards. He has published two books based on the scripts from that program; the first of them was *The Ohio Story,* Cleveland, [1950].

SIEWERS, CHARLES G. See Sarah M. Siewers.

SIEWERS, SARAH M. (March 1, 1855–April 22, 1926), physician, was born in Cincinnati, Hamilton County. Her family moved to Kentucky when she was a child, and she grew up on a farm near Newport. While teaching in the Newport schools, she attended Eclectic Medical College, Cincinnati, and graduated in 1891. She practiced medicine and lectured in support of temperance and women's rights. She practiced in Massillon and died in that city. A posthumous collection of her verse was published: *Humanity, Wise and Otherwise,* [n.p., 1927]. The volume also contains a few poems and translations by her father, Charles G. Siewers (1815–1882).

SIGLER, PEARL NIXON (June 15, 1870–May 10, 1943), lawyer, was born in Columbus, Franklin County, but lived most of his life in Dayton, where he practiced law for more than forty years. He was active in church work, lectured on religious topics, and wrote *God Speaks Again in Palestine,* [Dayton, 1935].

SILL, EDWARD ROWLAND (April 29, 1841–Feb. 27, 1887), born in Windsor, Conn., moved with his family to Cleveland in 1852; within the same year he was sent to Cuyahoga Falls to live with relatives. He was educated at Phillips Exeter Academy (1855), Western Reserve Academy, Hudson, (1856), and Yale University, from which he graduated in 1861. In December of that year he sailed in the *Sierra Nevada* for California, where he landed in March. The manuscript account of his voyage is in the Yale University Library and has been published: *Around the Horn: A Journal, December 10, 1861 to March 25, 1862,* Stanley T. Williams and Barbara D. Simison, eds., New Haven, Conn., 1944. It resembles Dana's *Two Years before the Mast,* though it lacks the vigor and compelling interest of that work. Sill's first sojourn in California (1862–66) reveals him as a man trying to find himself; he was for a time a post-office clerk, a rancher, and a student of law and medicine. In 1866 he was back in Cuyahoga Falls for a brief visit. The following year he made another false start by attending, briefly, the Divinity School at Harvard. A few months in New York convinced him that journalism was not his forte. In Feb., 1867, he married his cousin, Elizabeth Newbury Sill of Cuyahoga Falls. In 1869 appeared *The Hermitage and Other Poems,* the only volume he published. (*The Venus of Milo and Other Poems,* 1883, was privately printed.) Such was the critical reception of *The Hermitage* that Sill vowed never again to venture into book publication. From 1868 to 1870 he taught high school in Cuyahoga Falls and briefly in Wadsworth. An offer in 1871 of a position in the high school of Oakland took him back to California; there he was to remain until 1882, save for a few months in Europe. Daniel Coit Gilman, president of the recently established University of California, offered Sill the chair of English in 1875. For eight years he lectured with marked success and developed himself intellectually. He continued to write verse, though he was chary of publishing it. Precisely what prompted Sill's resignation as professor of English is hard to say, but one gathers that he regarded the stress upon science and technology at the expense of the humanities as regrettable; moreover, he made himself unpopular by his advocacy of coeducation. Before leaving Berkeley, he established a correspondence with Thomas Bailey Aldrich, who had become editor of the *Atlantic Monthly* in 1881. Sill's last years were spent in Cuyahoga Falls. He published extensively in the *Atlantic,* sometimes under his own name and often under the pseudonym Arthur Hedbrook. In 1887 he underwent a minor operation in Cleveland, and died unexpectedly Feb. 27. His range as a poet is limited in form, subject, and mood. Some of his verses had, even in their own time, interest for only a few readers—his numerous "school" poems, for instance—but possess none for us today. A few scattered poems continue to command our respect: "Five Lives," "A Fool's Prayer," "Opportunity," and "Truth at Last." Various commentators have sensed in his work the doubts and reconsiderations of Clough; others have detected the influence of Tennyson, particularly in "Opportunity." In such pieces as "Every-Day Life," "Strange," "Two Views of It," and "Momentous Words," it is the *Satires of Circumstances* by Hardy which we recall. But he was not essentially a derivative poet, for he had his own idiom and his own music. If he looks back to some poets, he anticipates others. He is to be thought of as a minor poet, but his place as such seems secure. There is nothing meretricious in his work, nothing tawdry.

Charles Duffy

The Hermitage and Other Poems, New York, 1868.

The Venus of Milo and Other Poems, Berkeley, Calif., 1883.

Poems, Boston, [1887].

Hermione, and Other Poems, Boston, 1899.

Christmas in California, San Francisco, [189- ?].

The Prose of Edward Rowland Sill . . . , Boston, 1900.

SILVER, ABBA HILLEL (Jan. 28, 1893–), rabbi, born in Lithuania, graduated from the University of Cincinnati and Hebrew Union College in 1915. Since 1917 he has been rabbi of the Temple, Cleveland. He has published several books relative to Jewish history and religion as well as a collection of addresses: *Religion in a Changing World,* New York, 1930. WW 30

SILVER, DEBBIE HORWITZ (1855–March 26, 1932), was born in Sandusky, Erie County, but attended school in Cleveland and spent most of her life in that city. She published a collection of poems: *Scenario,* New York, 1925.

SILVER, JESSE FORREST (Aug. 8, 1872–), clergyman, was born in Canton, Stark County. He attended Mount Union College, 1891–94. After being ordained to the Free Methodist ministry in 1897, he served various churches in Pennsylvania and traveled as an evangelist. He published several books on religious topics, e.g., *The Lord's Return, Seen in History and in Scripture as Pre-millennial and Imminent,* New York, [1914]. WW 16

SIMKINS, JOSHUA DEAN (March 29, 1856– ?), educator, was born near Fallsburg, Licking County. He attended Martinsburg Academy and National Normal University. In 1880 he graduated from the law school of Iowa State University. He began teaching in Ohio in 1882 and also served as superintendent of schools in St. Marys and in Newark. He wrote *Early History of Auglaize County,* St. Marys, 1901.

SIMMONS, ALBERT DIXON (Nov. 11, 1891–), was born on Prince Edward Island, Canada. In 1924 he settled in Cleveland, where he was outdoor editor for the Cleveland *News* and wrote a regular column, "Outdoor News." He has published a book on game birds: *Wing Shots . . . ,* New York, [1936].

SIMPSON, HELEN V. (Dec. 12, 1915–), was born in Clarksburg, W. Va., but her parents moved to Ohio when she was three years old. She has lived in Mahoning and Trumbull Counties. She was living in Warren, where her husband was a member of the fire department, when she wrote her book, *One Son—Indivisible,* Boston, [1948].

SIMPSON, MARIAN BERRY (Mrs. Richard B.) (Nov. 16, 1893–), born in Milford, N. H., has lived in Cleveland since 1924. Author of stories and poems published in many periodicals, she has also published a volume of verse: *Granite Soil and Other Poems,* Portland, Maine, 1941.

SIMPSON, MATTHEW (June 21, 1811–June 18, 1884), clergyman, was born in Cadiz, Harrison County. His father having died when Matthew was a year old, he was instructed and assisted by his uncle, Matthew Simpson, a judge. He studied medicine with a Cadiz doctor and began to practice in 1833. The following year he determined to become a Methodist preacher and was licensed to preach on the St. Clairsville circuit. His power as an orator assured his swift rise in the church. He preached at Pittsburgh, 1835–37, taught at Allegheny College, 1837–39, and served as president of Indiana Asbury University, 1839–48. In 1848 he became editor of the *Western Christian Advocate,* and in 1852 he was elected bishop. During the Civil War he lectured widely in support of the Union, and Lincoln is said to have called him the greatest orator he ever heard. He was chosen to deliver the eulogy of Lincoln at the graveside service in Springfield, Ill. He lived in Pittsburgh, Evanston, Ill., and Philadelphia; but he traveled widely throughout the world and was admired as a powerful preacher. A volume of his sermons was published posthumously in 1885. He died in Philadelphia.

Funeral Address Delivered at the Burial of President Lincoln . . . , New York, 1865.
Hundred Years of Methodism, New York, 1876.
Cyclopedia of Methodism . . . , Philadelphia, 1878.
Lectures on Preaching . . . , New York, 1879.

SIMRALL, MARGARET MONFORT (Dec. 14, 1877–), was born in Cincinnati, Hamilton County. She attended Cincinnati public schools, Miss Nourse's private school, and Smith College. She was married to L. Bartow Simrall, now deceased, and since 1947 she has lived in Venice, Fla. She has published short stories and poems in various periodicals, and also a collection of verse: *I Touched Her Hand . . . ,* Philadelphia, [1936].

SIMS, JAMES (? – ?), was probably a schoolteacher in Cincinnati, but no details concerning his life have been discovered. His *Philosophical Essays* apparently was an indirect attack on the theory of John Cleves Symmes (q.v.).

Philosophical Essays, on the Conformation of Matter and the Earth, Cincinnati, 1823.
An Essay upon Planetary Motion, Cincinnati, 1824.

SIMS, NEWELL LeROY (Dec. 3, 1878–), educator, born near Fremont, Ind., was pastor of Grandview Heights Congregational Church, Columbus, 1914–15, and professor of sociology, Oberlin College, 1924–44. After his retirement he continued to live in Oberlin. He has published several sociology textbooks and *Ultimate Democracy and Its Making,* Chicago, 1917. WW 26

SINCLAIR, JO. Pseud. See Ruth Seid.

SINGING SYBIL. Pseud. See Metta V. F. Victor.

SIPLE, PAUL ALLMAN (Dec. 18, 1908–), explorer, was born in Montpelier, Williams County. Chosen from all the Boy Scouts in the nation, he accompanied Admiral Byrd to the Antarctic, 1928–30. He graduated from Allegheny College in 1930 and Clark University (Ph.D.) in 1939. He has made numerous expeditions to the Antarctic, and since 1946 has been a biogeographer with the Department of Defense. He has written technical reports and books for the general reader, the most popular of which was the account of his first expedition: *A Boy Scout with Byrd,* New York, 1931. WW 30

SISSON, HERBERT GAY (Sept. 1, 1894–March 29, 1949), was born in McArthur, Vinton County. He died in Dayton, where he was engaged in public relations work. He published *Poems of Progress,* Dayton, [1924].

SKINNER, ROBERT PEET (Feb. 24, 1866–), diplomat, was born in Massillon, Stark County, where he operated the *Evening Independent,* 1886–97. After entering the diplomatic service in 1897, he served as U. S. consul in various European cities. His last service was as ambassador to Turkey, 1933–36. His service as commissioner plenipotentiary to negotiate a treay between the United States and Ethiopia in 1903 resulted in his only book: *Abyssinia of Today . . . ,* New York, 1906. WW 30

SLATER, MARY WHITE (June 17, 1868–April 22, 1954), was born in Cincinnati, Hamilton County, where she attended public schools. After attending the University of Chicago and Columbia University, she lived in Ironton, where she was active in civic and cultural affairs. She published short stories and poems in national magazines and also two collections of verse, e.g., *The Child Book,* Philadelphia, 1940.

SLAUGHTER, GERTRUDE ELIZABETH TAYLOR (Nov. 29, 1870–), was born in Cambridge, Guernsey County. She graduated from Bryn Mawr College in 1893. Since 1896 she has lived in Madison, Wis., where her husband, Moses S. Slaughter, was professor of Latin at the state university until his death in 1923. She has published several books of travel and biography, e.g., a life of Frederic II: *The Amazing Frederic,* New York, 1937. WW 30

SLAUGHTER, LINDA WARFEL (Feb. 8, 1840–July 3, 1920), was born in Cadiz, Harrison County. After attending Oberlin College, she went to Kentucky as a home missionary of the Presbyterian Church. In Kentucky in 1868 she married Dr. B. Franklin Slaughter, an army officer, and accompanied him to Camp Hancock, Dakota Territory. She taught school in Dakota and also wrote for the Bismarck *Tribune.* She died in St. Cloud, Minn. Her first two books were written before her marriage. Many copies of *The New Northwest* were sent to Europe and the East to encourage emigration.

Early Efforts . . . , Philadelphia, 1868.
The Freedom of the South, Cincinnati, 1869.
The New Northwest . . . , [Bismarck, N. Dak.], 1874.

SLIVERS, ASH. Pseud. See Charles C. Burnett.

SLOAN, JANE HUNTER (Aug. 12, 1887–), born in Sioux City, Iowa, lived in Cleveland, 1911–50. She now lives in Los Altos, Calif. She has published poetry in various periodicals and anthologies and one collection: *Prairie Vagabond,* New York, [1939].

SLOAN, RICHARD ELIHU (June 22, 1857–Dec. 14, 1933), lawyer and judge, was born in Preble County. After reading law for a time in Hamilton, he went to Denver, Colo., where he was a reporter on the *Daily Rocky Mountain News.* Returning to Ohio, he entered Cincinnati Law School in 1882 and graduated in 1884. Admitted to the Arizona bar in 1885, he opened an office in Phoenix. He served as judge of the territorial supreme court, 1889–1909, and in 1909 by appointment of President Taft he became Arizona's last territorial governor. Besides editing a four-volume history of Arizona, published in 1930, he published an autobiographical volume: *Memories of an Arizona Judge,* Stanford University, Calif., 1932. DAB 17

SLOANE, WILLIAM MILLIGAN (Nov. 12, 1850–Sept. 11, 1928), educator, was born in Richmond, Jefferson County. When he was six years old, his father became pastor of a church in New York City. After graduating from Columbia College in 1868, he taught in a private school and in 1873 became secretary and research assistant to George Bancroft. He taught Latin at Princeton, 1877–83, and was Seth Low Professor of History at Columbia, 1896–1916. His most highly esteemed work was his four-volume *Napoleon Bonparte.* A number of his addresses were published as pamphlets.

Life and Works of James Renwick Sloane, New York, 1888.

The French War and the Revolution, New York, 1893.

The Life of James McCosh, New York, 1896.

Life of Napoleon Bonaparte, 4 vols., New York, 1896.

The French Revolution and Religious Reform . . . , New York, 1901.

Party Government in the United States of America, New York, 1914.

The Powers and Aims of Western Democracy, New York, 1919.

Greater France in Africa, New York, 1924.

SLOCUM, CHARLES ELIHU (Dec. 30, 1841–June 7, 1915), physician and historian, was born in Northville, N. Y. In 1871, two years after his graduation from the College of Physicians and Surgeons, Columbia, he began practice in Defiance. Although he contributed a number of articles to professional magazines and was on the Defiance College faculty, he will be remembered as the founder of the Charles Elihu Slocum Library, Ohio Wesleyan University, and as the author of several genealogical works. He also wrote a book on the Maumee River basin, which, though drawn largely from secondary sources, is extremely useful: *History of the Maumee River Basin . . . ,* Toledo, [1905]. WWW 1

SLOCUM, STEPHEN ELMER (June 5, 1875–), engineer, was born in Glenville, N. Y. He graduated from Union College in 1897 and Clark University (Ph.D.) in 1900 and taught at the University of Cincinnati, 1900–20, except for one year at the University of Illinois. In 1920 he moved to Philadelphia, where he worked as an engineering consultant. He now lives in Ardmore, Pa. He has published a number of technical works on mathematics and engineering and a historical novel about the Netherlands: *Beggars of the Sea,* New York, 1928. WW 28

SLOSSER, GAIUS JACKSON (June 2, 1887–), clergyman, was born near Hoytville, Wood County. He graduated from Ohio Wesleyan University in 1912, Boston University School of Theology in 1915, and King's College, University of London, (Ph.D.) in 1928. After serving several Methodist churches in Massachusetts, 1917–25, he was on the faculty of Western Theological Seminary, 1928–56. He published several books on religious themes, e.g., *Christian Unity, Its History and Challenge in All Communions, in All Lands,* New York, 1929. WW 30

SLUSSER, LEWIS. See John Danner.

SMALLEY, EUGENE VIRGIL (July 18, 1841–Dec. 30, 1899), journalist, was born in Randolph, Portage County, but spent part of his boyhood in western New York, where his mother returned after the death of her husband. In 1855 he returned to Ohio and was a teacher in Painesville and an itinerant printer until the outbreak of the Civil War. He enlisted in the 7th O.V.I. and wrote on the war for various newspapers until he was wounded at Port Republic. After the war he worked as a clerk in Washington, D. C., published the *Mahoning Register,* Youngstown, for a brief period, and served as correspondent for various newspapers. In 1882 he was engaged by Henry Villard to edit the history of the Northern Pacific Railroad, and for the rest of his life he was associated with the advertising department of that railroad. In 1884 he moved to St. Paul, Minn., where he lived until his death.

The Republican Manual . . . , New York, 1880.

History of the Northern Pacific Railroad, New York, 1883.

American Journalism. An Appendix to the Encyclopædia Britannica, Philadelphia, 1884.

A Brief History of the Republican Party . . . , New York, 1884.

SMARIUS, CORNELIUS FRANCIS (March 3, 1823–March 2, 1870), clergyman, born in Telburg, Holland, was a teacher in Cincinnati, 1843–49; during this period he published considerable poetry in various periodicals. Ordained to the priesthood of the Roman Catholic Church in 1849, he was subsequently a pastor in St. Louis, Mo., vice president of St. Louis University, and a missionary. He wrote *Points of Controversy . . . ,* New York, 1865.

SMART, CHARLES ALLEN (Nov. 30, 1904–), was born in Cleveland, Cuyahoga County. His father, George Smart (1863–1925), was the first editor of the Columbus *Citizen.* After graduating from Harvard University in 1926, Charles did editorial work for three years and taught at Choate School, Conn., 1932–34. He operated a farm at Oak Hill near Chillicothe, 1934–42, served in the navy during World War II, and in 1946 became writer-in-residence at Ohio University. He also lived in Mexico in the 1950s. He has published several novels, but his greatest popular success came from his non-fiction account of his farming experiences: *R.F.D.*, New York, [1938]. ANT

SMART, JAMES HENRY (June 30, 1841–Feb. 21, 1900), was born in Center Harbor, N. H. He was principal of the Intermediate School, Toledo, 1863–65, before moving on to Indiana. During his stay in Ohio he wrote a pioneer work on physical culture, a work that has escaped the attention of his biographers: *A Manual of Free Gymnastic and Dumbbell Exercises . . .*, Cincinnati, [1864].

SMEAD, WESLEY (Dec. 23, 1800–Jan. 6, 1871), physician and banker, was born in Westchester County, N. Y. After working for some years as a printer, he studied at Ohio Medical College and began practice in Cincinnati. He was president of the Citizens' Bank, Cincinnati, 1843–57. A philanthropist, he gave generously to charity, and in 1850 he founded the Widow's Home, Cincinnati.

Guide to Wealth: Or, the Pathway to Health, Peace, Competence, Cincinnati, 1856.

SMILEY, JEROME CONSTANT (1858–May 16, 1924), historian, was born in Miami County, but spent much of his life in Colorado. He served as curator of Colorado State Historical Society, 1910–20. After his retirement he returned to Ohio. He died in Springfield. He published historical sketches, a history of Colorado, and *History of Denver . . .*, Denver, 1901.

SMILEY, JIM. Pseud. See Raymond S. Spears.

SMITH, ABBIE NORA (1856– ?), was born in Monroeville, Huron County, and attended the schools of that community. Her later years were spent in California; she was living in Los Angeles in 1937.

Bobtail Dixie . . ., New York, [1900].

King Gobbler, Boston, [1906].

Dolly Days & Dolly Ways . . ., San Francisco, [1916].

SMITH, ARTHUR HARMS (Jan. 25, 1867–March 5, 1945), clergyman, was born in Wapakoneta, Auglaize County. In 1872 his family moved to Mansfield and in 1883 to Springfield, where he graduated from Wittenberg College in 1888 and Wittenberg Seminary in 1891. He was pastor of Fourth Lutheran Church, Springfield, 1904–08, and of Trinity Church, Ashland, until his retirement in 1941. He wrote *Preachers and Preaching,* Philadelphia, [1925]. OBB

SMITH, BYRON CALDWELL (Aug. 28, 1849–May 4, 1877), educator, was born in Island Creek, Jefferson County. After attending Illinois College at Jacksonville, 1863–68, he studied philology in German universities for six years. He was on the faculty of the University of Kansas, 1872–74. He died of tuberculosis in Boulder, Colo. The first posthumous volume listed below consisted of letters written to his parents from Europe. The second, letters to Kate Stephens, his fiancée, was edited and republished in 1930 as *The Love-Life of Byron Caldwell Smith.*

A Young Scholar's Letters . . ., (Day Otis Kellogg, ed.), New York, 1897.

The Professor's Love-Life, Letters by Ronsby Malclewith, New York, 1919.

SMITH, CHARLES H. (Nov. 23, 1837–Aug. 13, 1912), born in Taunton, Mass., came to Cleveland in 1856. He enlisted in the 7th O.V.I. as a private and rose to the rank of major. After the Civil War he studied law at Ohio State University and was admitted to the bar in 1871 but did not practice. He was in the grain business and later in banking. He wrote *The History of Fuller's Ohio Brigade, 1861–1865 . . .*, Cleveland, 1909.

SMITH, CHARLES HENRY (June 8, 1875–Oct. 18, 1948), banker and educator, was born in Woodford County, Ill. In 1913 he joined the faculty of Bluffton College; in 1920 he became president of Citizens National Bank, Bluffton. His books on the Mennonite Church include *The Story of the Mennonites,* Berne, Ind., [1914]. OBB

SMITH, CHARLES MITCHELL. See Gerard Fowke.

SMITH, CLAYTON CHANEY (May 5, 1845–Jan. 9, 1919), clergyman, was born near Warren, Trumbull County. He was educated at Hiram College and became a Disciples of Christ minister. He served churches in several states and was also secretary of the Board of Negro Evangelism of the American Christian Missionary Society.

Our Mission in Jamaica, Indianapolis, 1897.

The Life and Work of Jacob Kenoly, Cincinnati, [1912].

Negro Education and Evangelization, [Indianapolis, n.d.].

SMITH, DELAZON (1816–Nov. 18, 1860), born in Berlin, N. Y., was brought to Ohio as a child. Shortly after Oberlin College opened, he enrolled as a student. In 1836 he left the college in a huff and soon afterward published a scurrilous attack on the institution under the cover title *Oberlin Unmasked,* issued, he said, "as an exposé of the impositions he suffered at the institution." Friends of the college are said to have destroyed all the copies of the book they could locate. Smith studied law and was admitted to the bar. For a time he edited the *Western Empire* in Dayton. In 1846 he moved to Iowa, where he became a Methodist preacher, and in 1852 he emigrated to Oregon. He served a term in the territorial legislature and was a Senator in 1859. In the last year of his life he edited the *Oregon Democrat.* He died in Portland, Oreg.

A History of Oberlin, or New Lights of the West. Embracing the Conduct and Character of the Officers and Students of the Institution . . . , Cleveland, 1837.

SMITH, DON (Jan. 4, 1891–), realtor, was born in Van Wert, Van Wert County, where he attended public schools. He also studied at the College of Pharmacy, Ohio Northern University, and served in World War I. He has been a realtor in Van Wert for more than thirty years. Despite a serious eye condition which impedes his reading, he has written a biographical work that has been issued in four editions: *Peculiarities of the Presidents* . . . , [Van Wert, 1938].

SMITH, DONNAL VORE (Jan. 3, 1901–), educator, was born in Van Wert County. He graduated from Bowling Green University in 1924 and the University of Chicago (Ph.D.) in 1929. He taught in the Delta schools, 1924–26, was on the faculty of New York State Teachers College, Albany, 1929–43, and has been president of State Teachers College, Cortland, N. Y., since 1943. He has published several textbooks in social studies and *Chase and Civil War Politics,* Columbus, 1931. WW 30

SMITH, EDGAR FAHS (May 23, 1856–May 3, 1928), educator, born in York, Pa., was on the science faculty of Wittenberg College, 1883–88. He afterward taught at the University of Pennsylvania. He wrote a number of biographies of chemists and books about chemistry, e.g., *Chemistry in America* . . . , New York, 1914. WWW 1

SMITH, ELLA MAY DUNNING (March 12, 1860–Sept. 28, 1934), journalist, was born in Uhrichsville, Tuscarawas County. She was on the faculty of Phelps Collegiate School in Columbus, worked on the Columbus *Dispatch* for ten years, and for twenty years edited the music department of the *Ohio State Journal.* She composed songs and also wrote *Philip's Mother,* [Columbus, 1928]. OBB

SMITH, ERNEST ASHTON (July 4, 1868–Dec. 28, 1926), educator, was born in Fletcher, Miami County. He graduated from Ohio Wesleyan University in 1888 and Johns Hopkins University (Ph.D.) in 1900. He was on the faculty of Allegheny College, 1898–1910 and 1913–16, and from 1925 until his death he was president of State Normal School, La Crosse, Wis. His writings include *Allegheny—A Century of Education, 1815–1915,* Meadville, Pa., [1916]. WWW 1

SMITH, GEORGE BANCROFT (Nov. 16, 1867–Oct. 18, 1940), businessman, was born in Phillipsburg, Montgomery County. In 1880 his parents moved to Brookville, and in 1888 he came to Dayton to work in a store as a clerk and bookkeeper. He was later associated with a number of Dayton manufacturing concerns and was extremely active in civic affairs; from 1916 until his death he was financial representative of Charles F. Kettering. He published a book of poems: *Timothy and Red Clover,* Dayton, 1919. WWO

SMITH, GEORGE THOMAS (Oct. 16, 1843–Dec. 17, 1920), clergyman, was born in Cincinnati, Hamilton County. A graduate of Bethany College, W. Va., and a Disciples of Christ clergyman, he served as a missionary in Japan for a number of years. He died in Champaign, Ill.

Critique of Higher Criticism, Winfield, Kan,. 1900.

SMITH, MRS. GRANVILLE M. See Hildegarde Angell.

SMITH, HARIETTE KNIGHT (Oct. 28, 1855– ?), was born in Hudson, Summit County. After graduating from Young Woman's Institute, Auburn, N. Y., in 1877, she wrote for the Boston *Transcript,* the *Congregationalist, Outlook,* and other periodicals. She lived in Boston, Mass.

The History of the Lowell Institute, Boston, 1898.

SMITH, HENRY LADD (June 24, 1906–), educator, was born in Cleveland, Cuyahoga County. He graduated from Yale

University in 1929 and the University of Wisconsin (Ph.D.) in 1946. He worked on newspapers in Canton, Cleveland, and Tacoma, Wash., and taught journalism at several universities in the Midwest. He was on the University of Wisconsin faculty, 1947–54, and is now director of the School of Communications, University of Washington. He has published articles and three books, e.g., *The History of Commercial Aviation in the United States,* New York, 1942. WWMW 49

SMITH, HENRY PRESERVED (Oct. 23, 1847–Feb. 26, 1927), clergyman, was born in Troy, Miami County. He graduated from Amherst College in 1869 and Lane Seminary in 1872. He studied in Germany for three years in the 1870s and was professor of Old Testament at Lane Seminary, 1877–93. Conservative by nature, he avoided as long as possible the controversies over higher criticism of the Bible. When he defended Charles A. Briggs before the General Assembly of the Presbyterian Church, his views immediately aroused opposition. He was tried for heresy and suspended from the ministry in 1892. He left Cincinnati in 1893 and afterward taught at Amherst College, Meadville Theological School, and Union Seminary. His articles, reviews, and books assure him a place in the history of American theological scholarship.

Inspiration and Inerrancy . . . , Cincinnati, 1893.
The Bible and Islam . . . , New York, 1897.
A Critical and Exegetical Commentary on the Books of Samuel, New York, 1899.
Old Testament History, New York, 1903.
The Religion of Israel, an Historical Study, New York, 1914.
Essays in Biblical Interpretation, Boston, 1921.
The Heretic's Defense . . . , New York, 1926.

SMITH, JAMES B. (July 15, 1838–April 3, 1918), manufacturer, was born in St. Catharines, Ontario, Canada. After teaching school and working as a cooper in Michigan and Missouri, he settled in Van Wert in 1883 and was engaged in the cooperage and stave business there. His only publication was a collection of letters from a hunting camp in Louisiana: *Camp Marsh Letters* . . . , Van Wert, [n.d.].

SMITH, JAMES POWER (July 4, 1837–Aug. 6, 1923), clergyman, was born in New Athens, Harrison County. He graduated from Jefferson College, Pa., in 1856 and Union Theological Seminary, Va., in 1861. He joined the Confederate army as a captain and was an aide on the staff of General Jackson; after Jackson's death, he served on the staff of General Ewell. Ordained to the Presbyterian ministry in 1866, he served churches in Virginia, edited the *Central Presbyterian,* 1892–1909, and was president of the Presbyterian Board of Publication in Richmond. He died in Greensboro, N. C. Besides the title below, he wrote two papers on Jackson and one on Lee that were reprinted as pamphlets.

Brightside Idyls, [Richmond?], 1896.

SMITH, JEAN MOORE (April 29, 1905–), born in Sherrard, W. Va., has lived in Ohio since about 1936 while teaching in the schools of Mt. Lebanon and Painesville. Besides poems in various periodicals, she has published a short novel: *Miss Nancy's Christmas Carol,* New York, [1946].

SMITH, JENNIE (Aug. 18, 1842– ?), evangelist, was born in Vienna, Clark County; she also lived in Bellefontaine and Dayton. An invalid during the first forty years of her life, she was intensely interested in religion and spoke to Methodist groups while lying on a special couch. In 1882 she was cured by prayer and was able to walk for the first time. She was active in the temperance movement and traveled widely as an evangelist. Because she was sponsored by the Baltimore and Ohio Railroad, she was known as the Railroad Evangelist. In 1922 she called on President Harding, whom she had known in Marion. Her three autobiographical volumes deal chiefly with her early life and her religious experience.

Valley of Baca . . . , Cincinnati, 1876.
From Baca to Beulah . . . , Philadelphia, 1880.
Ramblings in Beulah Land . . . , 2 vols., Philadelphia, 1886–88.

SMITH, JOSEPH (July 15, 1796–Dec. 4, 1868), clergyman and educator, born in Greensburg, Pa., was a Presbyterian minister in St. Clairsville for a time and later was president of Franklin College until criticism of his conservative views regarding slavery led to his resignation. He became general agent of the Board of Missions in 1847. He wrote a history of his alma mater, Jefferson College, and a history of Presbyterianism in the West: *Old Redstone* . . . , Philadelphia, 1854.

SMITH, JOSEPH (Dec. 23, 1805–June 27, 1844), Mormon leader, born in Sharon, Vt., was a resident of Kirtland from 1831 to 1838. He founded the Church of Jesus

Christ of Latter-Day Saints on April 6, 1830. In November of the same year, after the conversion of Sidney Rigdon (q.v.), he established a settlement at Kirtland. Failure of the bank that he had founded led to his flight to Missouri seven years later. Besides the *Book of Mormon, A Book of Commandments,* and an autobiography, Smith published a collection of sermons and revelations: *Doctrine and Covenants of the Church of the Latter Day Saints . . . ,* Kirtland, 1835.

SMITH, JOSEPH (Nov. 6, 1832–Dec. 10, 1914), Mormon leader, son of the founder of the church, Joseph Smith (q.v.), was born in Kirtland, Lake County, and spent his early years there. He accompanied the Mormons to Missouri and Illinois, but after his father's murder his mother remained in Nauvoo. In 1860 he accepted the presidency of the Reorganized Church of Latter-Day Saints. He vigorously opposed polygamy and maintained that his father had never advocated it. Most of his writings were letters and tracts attacking the practice. His memoirs appeared in the *Saints' Herald* between Nov., 1934, and July, 1937, but do not seem to have been published in book form.

History of the Church, (with Heman C. Smith), 4 vols., 1900–03.
Plural Marriage in America . . . , Lamoni, Iowa, [1903].
One Wife or Many?, Lamoni, Iowa, [n.d.].
The Rejection of the Church, Lamoni, Iowa, [n.d.].
Who Then Can Be Saved?, [Plano, Ill., n.d.].

SMITH, JOSEPH PATTERSON (Aug. 7, 1856–Feb. 5, 1898), was born in West Union, Adams County. After learning the printing trade, he became a reporter, and in 1876, while traveling as a political correspondent of the Cincinnati *Commercial,* he met William McKinley, to whose political fortunes he afterward devoted himself. He edited newspapers in Lebanon, Batavia, West Union, Urbana, and Toledo. As editor of the Urbana *Daily Citizen* he was first to suggest McKinley's nomination for the governorship. In 1892, after his election, Governor McKinley appointed him state librarian. In 1893 he compiled *Speeches and Addresses of William McKinley.* He resigned as librarian in 1896 to work for his mentor's nomination for the Presidency. On March 29, 1897, President McKinley appointed him director of the Bureau of the American Republics. His health, however, which had never been robust, failed, and he died in Miami, Fla.

History of the Republican Party in Ohio and Memoirs of Its Representative Supporters, 2 vols., Chicago, 1898.

SMITH, JUDSON (June 28, 1837–June 29, 1906), clergyman, born in Middlefield, Mass., was a resident of Ohio for more than twenty years. He attended Oberlin College for a time before graduating from Amherst College in 1859. He graduated from Oberlin Seminary in 1863 and served the following year as a tutor in Latin and Greek, was on the faculty of the college and the seminary, 1866–84, and also lectured on modern history at Lake Erie Seminary, Painesville, 1879–84. He left Ohio to serve on the American Board of Commissioners for Foreign Missions, to whose endeavors he devoted the rest of his life.

Lectures in Church History . . . , Oberlin, 1881.
A History of the American Board Missions in Africa . . . , Boston, 1905.

SMITH, LOUIS P. (Sept. 14, 1867–July 31, 1943), lawyer, was born in Hamilton, Butler County, but spent much of his life in Toledo. Before becoming a lawyer he taught school for several years. At the time of his death in Toledo, he was a resident of the Lorraine Hotel, apparently the source of his pen name, Louis Lorraine, under which he published *The Rocky Road to Riches,* Boston, [1941].

SMITH, LUCY HAHN KING (Oct. 29, 1871–June 23, 1940), educator, was born in Chesnut Hill, Franklin County. After studying at New England Conservatory of Music, she married Alfred F. Smith. She taught music in the public schools of Kansas and at Central College for Women, Lexington. Mo. She died in Nashville, Tenn. She published a book of poems: *Cadences,* Cedar Rapids, Iowa, 1929. BDCP

SMITH, MARY PRUDENCE WELLS (July 23, 1840–Dec. 17, 1930), was born in Attica, N. Y. After graduating from the high school in Greenville, Mass., she taught there for three years. In 1864 she became the first woman to be employed in a Massachusetts bank. In 1875 she married Judge Fayette Smith of Cincinnati; he died in 1903, and a few years later she returned to Greenville, Mass. Some of her stories were published under the pen name P. Thorne.

Jolly Good Times; Or, Child-Life on a Farm, Boston, 1875.
Jolly Good Times at School . . . , Boston, 1877.
The Browns, Boston, 1884.

Miss Ellis's Mission, Boston, 1886.
Their Canoe Trip, Boston, 1889.
Jolly Good Times at Hackmatack, Boston, 1891.
More Good Times at Hackmatack, Boston, 1892.
Jolly Good Times Today, Boston, 1894.
A Jolly Good Summer, Boston, 1895.
The Young Puritans of Old Hadley, Boston, 1897.
The Young Puritans in King Philip's War, Boston, 1898.
What Women Have Done in Literature in the United States since 1649, Boston, 1899.
The Young Puritans in Captivity, Boston, 1899.
The Young and Old Puritans of Hatfield, Boston, 1900.
Four on a Farm, Boston, 1901.
The Boy Captive of Old Deerfield, Boston, 1904.
The Boy Captive in Canada, Boston, 1905.
Boys of the Border, Boston, 1907.
Boys and Girls of Seventy-Seven, Boston, [1909].
Two in a Bungalow, Boston, 1914.
Three in a Camp, Boston, 1916.
Five in a Ford, Boston, 1918.

SMITH, MILES WOODWARD (Nov. 23, 1889–), clergyman, was born in Cincinnati, Hamilton County. He graduated from William Jewell College, Liberty, Mo., and Newton Theological Institution in 1917. After preaching in Baptist churches in Missouri, Massachusetts, and Ohio, he entered the educational branch of the Baptist Church and edited Sunday school publications, 1930–50. He is now director and editor of the Department of Book Publication. He has published several books on religious themes, e.g., *On Whom the Spirit Came; A Study of the Acts of the Apostles,* Philadelphia, [1948]. Also, under the pen name S. M. Woodward, he has published popular fiction, e.g., *Shot in the Pulpit,* London, [1939]. WW 26

SMITH, OBERLIN (March 22, 1840–July 18, 1926), engineer, was born in Cincinnati, Hamilton County. He lived in Bridgeton, N. J., where he founded and operated Ferracute Machine Co. Besides technical books and articles, he published *The Material, Why Not Immortal?,* Boston, [1921]. WWW 1

SMITH, OPHIA D. (Feb. 19, 1891–), was born in Walnut Grove, Mo. She has lived in Oxford since 1926, when her husband, William E. Smith (q.v.), joined the Miami University history faculty. She has lectured on state and local history and has published numerous articles. She has also published a useful volume of local history: *Old Oxford Houses and the People Who Lived in Them,* Oxford, 1941.

SMITH, PERCY KENDALL (Nov. 6, 1875–), was born in Painesville, Lake County. He attended Painesville schools and Amherst College, was associated with several Painesville banks and business firms, and from 1907 until his retirement in 1928 was president of the Painesville Metallic Binding Co. He has published articles on local history in the Painesville *Telegraph* and a book: *Abstractions of an Introvert . . . ,* Painesville, [1945]. WWMW 49

SMITH, PETER (1753–Dec. 31, 1816), physician, was born in Wales. When he was a child, his parents came to the United States and settled in New Jersey. Although he chose to refer to himself as "Father Smith" or "the Indian Doctor," according to his grandson, General Joseph Warren Keifer (q.v.), he was a graduate of Princeton and a full-fledged doctor of medicine. After leaving New Jersey he lived for a short while in Georgia, and then made his way to the Ohio country and settled in Cincinnati about 1794. Ten years later he moved with his family to Donnel's Creek, Clark County, where he apparently served as a Baptist minister and as a physician. Referring to Smith's book, *The Indian Doctor's Dispensatory,* as the first materia medica published west of the Allegheny Mountains, John Uri Lloyd reprinted it in the *Lloyd Library Bulletin* in 1901. Of the original edition only a very few copies are known to exist, and it has long been a prime desideratum of collectors of early Midwestern books. Peter Smith died on his farm in Clark County.

The Indian Doctor's Dispensatory, Being Father Smith's Advice Respecting Diseases and Their Cure . . . , Cincinnati, 1813.

SMITH, PRESERVED (July 22, 1880–May 15, 1941), historian and educator, was born in Cincinnati, Hamilton County, the son of Henry Preserved Smith (q.v.). He graduated from Amherst College in 1901 and Columbia University (Ph.D.) in 1907. He served on the faculties of Williams College, 1904–06, Amherst College, 1907–14, Harvard University, 1919–20, and Cornell University, 1922–41. An authority in the field of Reformation history, he published a number of significant biographies and historical works, e.g., *The Age of the Reformation,* New York, 1920. WWW 1

SMITH, ROBERT PHILIP (April 7, 1863–Aug. 4, 1955), clergyman, was born in Groveport, Franklin County. After attending Ohio Normal University in 1889, he taught school to pay his expenses at Ohio Wesleyan University, where he graduated in 1895. After being ordained to the Methodist ministry, he served churches in Montana and was president of Kansas Wesleyan University, 1908–15. In 1915 he returned to Montana to become pastor of First Methodist Church, Bozeman. He published *Religious Optimism,* Boston, [1922]. WW 16

SMITH, SARAH LOUISA HICKMAN (June 30, 1811–Feb. 12, 1832), born in Detroit, Mich., lived in Cincinnati, 1829–31. While there, she contributed poems to the *Gazette.* Some of her verse was compiled in *Poems,* Providence, [R.I.], 1829.

SMITH, SOLOMON FRANKLIN (April 20, 1801–Feb. 14, 1869), comedian and theater manager, born in Norwich, N. Y., came to Cincinnati in 1818. After roaming about Ohio, Indiana, and Kentucky for a time, he joined Alexander Drake's theatrical company in Cincinnati and also studied law. He founded a Jacksonian newspaper, the *Independent Press and Freedom's Advocate,* in 1822, but he sold it the next year to travel as an actor and a manager. He left the stage in 1853 to practice law in St. Louis. He published several books of reminiscences, e.g., *The Theatrical Apprenticeship and Anecdotical Recollections of Sol Smith . . . ,* Philadelphia, 1846.

SMITH, VINCENT EDWARD (Aug. 20, 1915–), educator, was born in Lockland, Hamilton County. He attended Xavier University and earned his Ph.D. from Catholic University in 1947. Since 1950 he has been on the faculty of the University of Notre Dame. Besides several books on philosophy and physics, he has published a biography: *Julie, Exponent of Catholic Action,* [Reading, 1938]. CWW 11

SMITH, WALTER GEORGE (Nov. 24, 1854–April 4, 1924), lawyer and banker, was born in Logan County. He graduated from the University of Pennsylvania in 1873 and the law school in 1877. He practiced law in Philadelphia and also was manager of Beneficial Saving Fund.

Life and Letters of Thomas Kilby Smith, Brevet Major-General, United States Volunteers 1820–1887, New York, 1898.

"The Exponent of Democracy," [Philadelphia, 1918].

Fidelis of the Cross . . . , New York, 1926.

SMITH, WILLIAM ERNEST (April 30, 1892–), educator, born in Licking, Mo., has been on the history faculty, Miami University, since 1926 and has served as dean of the graduate school since 1950. He is married to Ophia D. Smith (q.v.). He has published several historical and biographical works, e.g., *The Francis Preston Blair Family in Politics,* New York, 1933. WW 30

SMITH, WILLIAM HENRY (Dec. 1, 1833–July 27, 1896), journalist, was born in Austerlitz, N. Y., but when he was two years old his parents moved to Homer, Licking County. There William Henry attended public school until he went to Green Mount Seminary near Richmond, Ind. While at the seminary in 1855, he contributed an article to the *Type of the Times,* a Cincinnati paper, and was asked to join its editorial staff. After leaving that paper Smith served as Columbus correspondent of the Cincinnati *Commercial* (1858–59), was one of the editors of the Cincinnati *Gazette* (1859–63), and editor of the *Odd-Fellows' Casket and Review* (1859–61). He became one of Ohio's most influential citizens, yet is one of the least known. One of the nation's leading newspapermen of the post-Civil War decades, Smith was also secretary of state of Ohio, a governor-maker, a president-maker, and a capable historian. In 1863 Smith began to push John Brough for the gubernatorial nomination on the Union ticket. He played a prominent role in Brough's election over Clement Vallandigham in 1864, and was named his private secretary. That summer Smith maneuvered the nomination of Rutherford B. Hayes for Congress, and Hayes won. Smith was elected Ohio's secretary of state the same year, and during his two terms there were two remarkable accomplishments: first, he won a position of power in the Republican Party in Ohio; second, he collected the personal papers and portraits of a number of Ohio's early governors, including the papers of Arthur St. Clair, first governor of the Northwest Territory. In Jan., 1867, Smith urged Hayes to run for governor and led the movement for his nomination. Soon after Hayes's election Smith resigned as secretary of state to join the staff of the Cincinnati *Chronicle* early in 1868. In Oct., 1869, he became general manager of the Western Associated Press, with offices in Chicago. In his new position Smith pressed Hayes to run for higher office, managed the campaign for his nomination for the Presidency in 1876, and was particularly effective in winning the support of Southern leaders for Hayes in the post-election contest. Smith was one of Hayes's closest advisers during his Presidency. Although Smith could have had almost any office he wanted, he accepted only the collectorship of the port of Chicago. He immediately undertook an investigation of the maladministration of the port under his predecessor, which resulted also in the disclosure of frauds in the New York customs house and the removal of Chester A. Arthur and A. B. Cornell as collector and naval officer respectively. The end of the Hayes Administration found Smith in a strong position in the newspaper world. He had made the Western Associated Press into an effective and financially successful organization, and in Jan., 1883, when that organization united with the New York Associated Press, he was named general manager of the combination. Soon after that he raised money to support the development of the linotype machine, and in 1885 he was one of the organizers and became treasurer and a director of the Mergenthaler Printing Company, which was established to manufacture the revolutionary typesetting machine. Smith retired from the management of the Associated Press in 1892, but became co-owner of the Indianapolis *News* in 1893. During the remaining few years before his death Smith wrote a history of slavery in this country. It was published posthumously in 1903 under the title *A Political History of Slavery.* His first notable work, produced at the request of the Ohio General Assembly, was *The St. Clair Papers. The Life and Public Services of Arthur St. Clair . . . with His Correspondence and Other Papers.* In 1885 he published a small volume, originally an address, on Charles Hammond (q.v.). In 1888, in an article entitled "Unpublished Washington Letters" in the *Magazine of American History,* XIX, 114-143, Smith disclosed the inaccuracies and alterations in Jared Sparks's edition of the writings of George Washington. In Dec., 1889, Smith appeared before the American Historical Association, of which he was a member, to give a paper on the "The Correspondence of the Pelham Family, and the Loss of Oswego to the British," which was published in the association's *Papers,* IV (1890). In his introduction to this paper Smith stressed the need to collect and preserve the manuscript records of the past. At the time of his death Smith was working on a life of Hayes, who had asked that Smith be his official biographer. Smith sorted and arranged many of the Hayes papers, but it remained for his son-in-law, Charles R. Williams, to write the biography.

James H. Rodabaugh

The St. Clair Papers. The Life and Public Services of Arthur St. Clair . . ., 2 vols., Cincinnati, 1882.

A Political History of Slavery . . ., 2 vols., New York, 1903.

SMUCKER, ISAAC (Dec. 14, 1807–Jan. 31, 1897), was born in Shenandoah County, Va. He came to Newark as a young man and spent his life in that community. Interested in local history, he was secretary of the Pioneer Association and delivered a number of papers that were printed as separate pamphlets. He also wrote for the *Western Monthly Magazine,* the *Ladies' Repository,* and other periodicals.

Our Pioneers . . ., Newark, 1872.

Mound Builders' Works Near Newark, Ohio, [n.p., 1881].

SMYSER, WILLIAM EMORY (Sept. 17, 1866–May 24, 1935), educator, born in Baltimore County, Md., joined the English Department, Ohio Wesleyan University, in 1900 and served on the faculty until his death. He was registrar, 1904–20, and dean, 1917–35. He published numerous articles on religious and literary subjects and *Tennyson,* New York, [1906]. WWW 1

SMYTHE, BRANDT GEORGE (Aug. 21, 1843–April 15, 1931), lawyer, was born in Newark, Licking County. After graduating from Union College in 1864, he read law and was admitted to the Ohio bar in 1866. He practiced in Newark for 65 years and at the time of his death was the oldest practicing lawyer in Ohio. His only book was published posthumously: *Early Recollections of Newark,* Newark, 1940.

SMYTHE, GEORGE FRANKLIN (Oct. 21, 1852–Aug. 25, 1934), clergyman and educator, was born in Toledo, Lucas County. He graduated from Western Reserve University in 1874, served Episcopal churches in Oberlin, Elyria, Toledo, and Mt. Vernon, and was on the faculty of Kenyon College, 1900–03 and 1915–20. His writings include *Kenyon College, Its First Century,* New Haven, [Conn.], 1924. WWW 1

SNEDEKER, CAROLINE DALE PARKE (March 23, 1870–Jan. 22, 1956), was born in New Harmony, Ind.; she was a descendant of Robert Dale Owen, founder of the community. She spent her later girlhood in Cincinnati, where she attended public schools and Miss Armstrong's School. After her marriage in 1903 to Rev. Charles H. Snedeker, dean of the Cincinnati Cathedral, they moved to Hempstead, Long Island. After her husband's death in 1927, she lived in Cincinnati and Long Island, but traveled widely. She wrote a number of books, most of them historical novels for young readers, e.g., *The Coward of Thermopylae,* New York, 1911, and *The Beckoning Road,* New York, 1929. Under the pen name Caroline Dale Owen, she wrote *Seth Way; A Romance of the New Harmony Community,* Boston, 1917. WWW 3

SNIDER, DENTON JAQUES (Jan. 9, 1841–Nov. 25, 1925), educator and lecturer, was born near Mount Gilead, Morrow County. He graduated from Oberlin College in 1862. In 1864 he became a teacher of Latin at the College of the Christian Brothers in St. Louis, Mo. Here he soon came under the influence of William Torrey Harris and Henry C. Brokmeyer, was converted to the philosophy of Hegel, and was an organizer of the St. Louis Philosophical Society. From 1867 to 1877 he taught in the St. Louis schools; he devoted the next three years to European travel. On his return he became a very popular lecturer and traveled throughout the country until 1897. Returning to St. Louis in 1897, he installed himself in a boardinghouse in the most squalid part of the city and devoted his declining years to writing. The greater part of his extensive bibliography was produced after his retirement from the lecture platform. These books he published himself under the imprint of Sigma Publishing Company and sold direct to members of the extensive following that he had acquired during his lecture tours. *Johnny Appleseed's Rhymes* and *Lincoln in the Black Hawk War* were published under the pen name Theophilus Middling.

Clarence; A Drama, St. Louis, 1872.
System of Shakespeare's Dramas, St. Louis, 1877.
Delphic Days, St. Louis, [1880].
A Walk in Hellas . . . , 2 vols., St. Louis, 1881–82.
Agamemnon's Daughter. A Poem, Boston, 1885.
An Epigrammatic Voyage, Boston, 1886.
Goethe's Faust . . . , Chicago, 1886.
The Freeburgers. A Novel, [St. Louis, 1889].
Psychology and the Psychosis, St. Louis, [1890].
The Shakespearean Drama . . . , St. Louis, [1890].
Homer in Chios . . . , St. Louis, [1891].
Homer's Iliad, St. Louis, [1891].
Commentary on the Literary Bible, St. Louis, 1892.
Dante's Inferno. A Commentary, St. Louis, 1892.
Dante's Purgatory and Paradise, St. Louis, [1892].
Prorsus Retrorsus, St. Louis, 1892.
Froebel's Mother Play Songs . . . , St. Louis, [1895].
Homer's Odyssey . . . , St. Louis, [1895].
Johnny Appleseed's Rhymes . . . , St. Louis, [1895].
World's Fair Studies, St. Louis, [1895].
The Will and Its World . . . , St. Louis, [1899].
The Life of Frederick Froebel . . . , Chicago, [1900].
The Psychology of Froebel's Play-Gifts, St. Louis, [1900].
Social Institutions in the Origin, Growth, and Interconnection . . . , St. Louis, [1901].
The State, Specially the American State, Psychologically Treated, St. Louis, [1902].
Ancient European Philosophy . . . , St. Louis, [1903].
Modern European Philosophy . . . , St. Louis, [1904].
Architecture as a Branch of Aesthetic, Psychologically Treated, St. Louis, [1905].
Feeling, Psychologically Treated . . . , St. Louis, [1905].
The American Ten Years' War, 1855–1865, St. Louis, [1906].
The Father of History; An Account of Herodotus, St. Louis, [1907].
A Tour in Europe, St. Louis, [1907].
Abraham Lincoln . . . , St. Louis, [1908].
European History, Chiefly Ancient . . . , St. Louis, [1908].
Cosmos and Diacosmos . . . , St. Louis, [1909].
Lincoln in the Black Hawk War . . . , St. Louis, [1910].
A Writer of Books in His Genesis . . . , St. Louis, [1910].
The Biocosmos . . . , St. Louis, [1911].
Lincoln and Ann Rutledge . . . , St. Louis, [1912].
Lincoln in the White House . . . , St. Louis, [1913?].
Music and the Fine Arts . . . , St. Louis, [1913].
Lincoln at Richmond . . . , St. Louis, [1914].
Goethe's Life-Poem . . . , St. Louis, [1915].
The House of Dreamery . . . , St. Louis, [1918].
The St. Louis Movement in Philosophy, Literature, Education, Psychology, with Chapters of Autobiography, St. Louis, 1920.
A Biography of Ralph Waldo Emerson . . . , St. Louis, 1921.
A Biographic Outline of Homer . . . , St. Louis, 1922.
A Biography of Dante Alighieri . . . , St. Louis, 1922.

A Biography of William Shakespeare . . . , St. Louis, 1922.
The Redemption of the Hamlets . . . , St. Louis, 1923.
The Shakesperiad . . . , St. Louis, 1923.
The Rise of Young Shakespeare . . . , St. Louis, 1925.

SNIDER, VAN A. (Oct. 27, 1869–Sept. 13, 1935), lawyer and judge, was born in Walnut Township, Fairfield County. He read law, was admitted to the Ohio bar in 1896, and served as probate judge of Fairfield County, 1921–29. A member of the Ohio National Guard, he was called into service during World War I. The American Legion sponsored his book, *Fairfield County in the World War,* Lancaster, [1926].

SNOW, ELIZA ROXEY (Jan. 21, 1804–Dec. 5, 1887), sister of Lorenzo Snow (q.v.), was born in Becket, Mass. Her family migrated to Mantua when she was little more than an infant in arms. As a young woman she contributed considerable verse to the local press. In April, 1835, she followed her mother and sister in joining the Mormon church, and she moved to Kirtland in December of that year. She gained prominence among the Mormons as a teacher and later as president of the Women's Relief Society. She was secretly married to Prophet Joseph Smith on June 29, 1842. In 1849 she became one of the wives of Smith's successor, Brigham Young. Many of the most popular Mormon hymns were from her pen.

Poems, Religious, Historical and Political, 2 vols., Liverpool and Salt Lake City, 1856–77.
Hymns and Songs, Salt Lake City, 1880.
Biography and Family Record of Lorenzo Snow, Salt Lake City, 1884.

SNOW, JANE ELLIOTT (June 14, 1837–Aug. 22, 1922), was born on a farm near Royalton, Fairfield County. She taught school in Parma and lived there until 1892, when she settled in Cleveland. She lectured frequently on women's rights and other subjects. She published a family history and *Bits of Verse,* [Cleveland], 1916.

SNOW, LORENZO (April 3, 1814–Oct. 10, 1901), Mormon leader, younger brother of Eliza Roxey Snow (q.v.), was born in Mantua, Portage County. He left Oberlin College in 1836 and joined his family in Kirtland, where they had been converted by the Mormons. He was baptized in June, 1836, and was an active missionary for several years. After the murder of Joseph Smith, he adhered to Brigham Young's faction and made the trek to Iowa, thence to Utah. After two years as a missionary in Europe, he was sent with fifty families to Brigham City in northern Utah, where he lived most of the remainder of his life. His practical sense and organizing ability were demonstrated in the successful co-operative he founded in Brigham City. He was imprisoned for a year, 1886–87, for polygamy. He served as president of the church during the last three years of his life.

The Only Way to Be Saved: An Explanation of the First Principles of the Doctrine of the Church of Jesus Christ of Latter-day Saints, Liverpool, 1855.

SNOW, ROYALL HENDERSON (Jan. 21, 1898–), born in Chicago, has been a member of the English faculty, Ohio State University, since 1928. Co-editor of two widely used anthologies and author of articles on various subjects, he has also published several collections of poetry, including *This Experimental Life,* New York, [1930]. DAS 3

SNOW, SAMUEL (? – ?), was a resident of Strongsville. Little is known of his life, but he had apparently lived in the community for some years before 1838, the year in which he joined the secret organization "Hunters and Rangers," formed to aid the insurrectionary movement in Canada. One of four Strongsville men captured by the British, Snow was first sentenced to be hanged but was afterward banished to Van Diemen's Land (Tasmania). Pardoned in 1845, he returned to Strongsville. His simple narrative is one of the best accounts of this little-known episode.

The Exile's Return: Or, Narrative of Samuel Snow Who Was Banished to Van Dieman's Land for Participating, in 1838, in the Patriot War in Upper Canada, Cleveland, 1846.

SOCKMAN, RALPH WASHINGTON (Oct. 1, 1889–), clergyman, was born in Mount Vernon, Knox County. He graduated from Ohio Wesleyan University in 1911, Union Theological Seminary in 1916, and Columbia University (Ph.D.) in 1917. He was minister of Christ Church, New York City, 1917–61, has lectured widely, and has preached on a national radio program for 33 years. He has published several books on religious themes, e.g., *Life for Tomorrow,* New York, 1939. WW 30

SOHN, RUTH SOUTHARD (Mrs. Frank E.) (Oct. 17, 1907–), born in Atco,

N. J., has lived in Toledo since 1937. Under her maiden name, she has published a novel: *No Sad Songs for Me,* New York, 1944.

SOLA. Pseud. See Olive S. L. Anderson.

SOMERVILLE, HENRY. Pseud. See Mary G. Humphreys.

SOPER, EDMUND DAVISON (July 18, 1876–Oct. 24, 1961), clergyman and educator, born in Tokyo, served on the Ohio Wesleyan University faculty, 1910–14, and returned as president, 1928–38, after teaching at Northwestern University and Duke University. On leaving Ohio Wesleyan, he joined the faculty of Garrett Biblical Institute, Evanston, Ill., where he lived thereafter. He wrote textbooks on comparative religions and a book on the World Conference on Faith and Order, held in 1927: *Lausanne: The Will to Understand . . . ,* New York, 1928. WW 27

SOUREK, GRACE HAGGERTY (Nov. 28, 1886–), was born in Oxford, Mass. She attended the University of Akron, taught in the public schools of New England and Ohio, and in 1913 married Joseph F. Sourek, an Akron lawyer, now deceased. Now Mrs. Al Reeves, she lives in Akron and St. Petersburg, Fla. She has written a novel about pioneer life in northwestern Ohio: *Wildflower,* New York, 1928.

SOUTHARD, RUTH. See Ruth S. Sohn.

SOUTHWORTH, GEORGE CHAMPLIN SHEPARD (Dec. 13, 1842–Feb. 19, 1918), educator, was born in West Springfield, Mass. A graduate of Yale University in 1863 and Harvard Law School in 1865, he taught at Bexley Seminary, Kenyon College, 1881–89. After traveling in Europe for the next eight years, he returned to Glendale, Hamilton County, where he spent the remainder of his life. He wrote a family history in addition to the listed titles. The posthumous collection of his writings was edited by his son, George S. Southworth.

Six Lectures Introductory to the Study of English Literature, Cambridge, [Mass.], 1887.

Essays and Poems . . . , [Indianapolis?, 1929?].

SOUTHWORTH, JAMES GRANVILLE (Oct. 18, 1896–), educator, born in Monroe, Mich., has lived in Ohio since 1931. He has taught English at Heidelberg College, 1931–34, and the University of Toledo since 1934. He has written several books on modern English and American literature, e.g., *Sowing the Spring; Studies in British Poets from Hopkins to MacNeice,* Oxford, 1940. WW 30

SOWERS, DELLA (d.Jan. 13, 1950), was born in Allensville, Vinton County. A resident of McArthur, she served two terms as justice of peace and was advertising agent for the McArthur *Democrat-Enquirer* and the Wellston *Daily Sentinel.* She also conducted a poetry column in the *Enquirer.* She died in McArthur as the result of injuries suffered in an automobile accident in Sept., 1948. Her poems appeared in numerous anthologies and periodicals, and she published a collection: *Maple Dawn,* Columbus, [1948]. BDCP

SPAHR, CHARLES BARZILLAI (July 20, 1860–Aug. 30, 1904), journalist, was born in Columbus, Franklin County, the son of a Methodist minister. After attending Columbus public schools, he graduated from Amherst College in 1881, taught in a Columbus high school for a short time, and studied at the University of Leipzig and Columbia University, where he received his Ph.D. in 1886. He was on the editorial staff of *Christian Union (Outlook)* until 1904. His editorials and articles on sociological and economic questions represented a consistently liberal viewpoint and nearly always were written in support of a minority opinion or group. In 1904 he became owner and editor of *Current Literature,* but while on a tour of Europe for the sake of his health, he disappeared on Aug. 30, 1904, from the ship on which he was traveling from Ostend to Dover. His body was recovered Sept. 21.

An Essay on the Present Distribution of Wealth . . . , New York, [1896].

America's Working People, New York, 1900.

SPANGLER, HELEN KING (May 27, 1840–March 11, 1884), was born in Newark, Licking County. Except for the fact that she died in Coshocton, no other details have been discovered. The action of her only novel takes place in England.

The Physician's Wife. A Novel, Philadelphia, 1875.

SPANGLER, MARY A. (Dec. 9, 1846–1907), born near Berne, Switzerland, was brought to America when she was five years old. She grew up in Upper Sandusky, graduated from Northwestern College in Illinois, and taught in Greensburg, Summit County. After her marriage to George H. Spangler of Canton in 1878, she lived in Canton, where she was active in the temperance movement and civic affairs. Her one book is a discussion of women's rights and duties.

Domestic Economy, New York, 1893.

SPANTON, ALBERT I. (Nov. 28, 1872–Aug. 31, 1955), educator, born in Sunderland, England, came to the United States in 1885. He graduated from Buchtel College in 1899, was assistant principal of Buchtel Academy, 1900–04, taught English at Buchtel College, 1905–43, and served as dean, 1914–38. He published articles in various periodicals and a history of Buchtel: *Fifty Years of Buchtel . . .* , Akron, 1922. OBB

SPARKES, BOYDEN (Jan. 6, 1890–May 18, 1954), was born in Cincinnati, Hamilton County. He entered journalism in 1907, when he began working on the Cincinnati *Commercial;* he worked on various newspapers until 1924, after which he devoted himself to magazine writing. He died in Wilson, N. C. He wrote several books, e.g., *Hetty Green, a Woman Who Loved Money,* New York, 1930. WWW 3

SPARKS, EDWIN ERLE (July 16, 1860–June 15, 1924), educator, was born on a farm near Newark, Licking County. After spending a year at Ohio Wesleyan University, he transferred to Ohio State University, where he graduated in 1884. He was a school principal in Portsmouth and Martins Ferry, 1885–90, taught at Pennsylvania State College, 1890–96, and the University of Chicago, 1896–1908, and served as president of Pennsylvania State College, 1908–20. Perhaps his most important contribution to education was his encouragement of extension courses. He was also popular as a lecturer and wrote several textbooks.

The Expansion of the American People . . . , Chicago, 1900.

The Men Who Made the Nation . . . , New York, 1901.

The Beginnings of Chicago, [Chicago, 1903].

Plain Talks on American History . . . , Chicago, 1904.

National Development, 1877–1885, New York, 1907.

SPARROW, WILLIAM (March 12, 1801–Jan. 17, 1874), clergyman, and educator, born in Charlestown, Mass., lived eighteen years in Ohio. In 1822 he came to Huron County, where his father had moved earlier. He taught in Worthington and in Cincinnati College, where Bishop Philander Chase (q.v.) was president. In 1824 he accepted a professorship, but the following year he was persuaded by Bishop Chase that he should assist in founding a seminary. He became principal of the school when it was opened on the Bishop's farm near Worthington and was vice president when it was moved to Gambier as Kenyon College. Sparrow was ordained an Episcopal priest in 1826; the next year he married a sister-in-law of Bishop Chase. He remained at Kenyon for ten years after the resignation of Bishop Chase, but his low-church views made his situation increasingly uncomfortable, and in 1841 he resigned to accept a professorship in Alexandria, Va., where he served until his death. Besides the pamphlet listed below, a number of his sermons and letters were published.

A Reply to the Charges and Accusations of the Rt. Rev. Philander Chase, D.D., Gambier, 1832.

SPAULDING, SOLOMON (1761–Oct. 20, 1816), clergyman, born in Ashford, Conn., after preaching in the East, came to New Salem (Conneaut) in 1809 and operated an iron foundry there for about four years. While in Ohio he wrote a romance about ancient inhabitants of America: *The Manuscript Found.* He was unable to find a publisher for his manuscript, but when Mormons arrived in northeastern Ohio twenty years later, their detractors, notably Eber D. Howe (q.v.), maintained that Spaulding's novel had somehow furnished the historical framework for the *Book of Mormon.* The belief was widely held until 1884, when James H. Fairchild (q.v.), president of Oberlin College, discovered the manuscript and found little resemblance to the *Book of Mormon.*

SPAYTHE, JACOB A. (Oct. 8, 1869–Sept. 23, 1934), was born in Guernsey County. He attended Findlay public schools, taught in Findlay, and worked in the office of the Findlay city auditor for fifteen years. He later worked for Firestone Rubber Company. His death occurred in Fort Myers, Fla. He wrote *History of Hancock County . . .* , Toledo, 1903.

SPEARS, JOHN RANDOLPH (April 21, 1850–Jan. 25, 1936), journalist, was born in Van Wert, Van Wert County. He worked on a country newspaper as a young boy, entered the U.S. Naval Academy in 1866, but resigned in 1869 to return to journalism. After working on several papers in upstate New York, he joined the editorial staff of the New York *Sun*. He traveled extensively for the *Sun*, visiting Greenland, Patagonia, Mexico, and remote sections of the United States. He wrote many stories and articles for magazines.

Illustrated Sketches of Death Valley . . ., Chicago, 1892.
The Gold Diggings of Cape Horn . . ., New York, 1895.
The Port of Missing Ships, and Other Stories of the Sea, New York, 1897.
The History of Our Navy . . ., 5 vols., New York, 1897–99.
Our Navy in the War with Spain, New York, 1898.
The Fugitive; A Tale of Adventure . . ., New York, 1899.
The American Slave Trade . . ., New York, 1900.
Anthony Wayne . . ., Philadelphia, 1903.
A History of the Mississippi Valley . . ., New York, 1903.
David G. Farragut, Philadelphia, [1905].
Captain Nathaniel Brown Palmer, New York, 1907.
The Story of the New England Whalers, New York, 1908.
The Story of the American Merchant Marine, New York, 1910.
Master Mariners, New York, [1912].
Buying for the Long Pull, New York, 1922.
Biography of John Bloomfield Jervis, C.E., New York, 1933.

SPEARS, RAYMOND SMILEY (Aug. 2, 1876–Jan. 26, 1950), was born in Bellevue, Huron County, where he attended public schools. He worked on the New York *Sun*, 1896–1900, and afterward was a prolific writer on outdoor life. He also wrote a number of scenarios for motion pictures. Some of his work appeared under the pen name Jim Smiley. He died in Inglewood, Calif. He wrote a number of books, e.g., *A Trip on the Great Lakes . . .*, Columbus, [1913]. WWW 3

SPEARY, NELLIE BEST (Jan. 29, 1872–June 8, 1943), was born in Marietta, Washington County. In 1899 she married C. Frederick Speary, an oil field operator. She was active in civic affairs of Marietta and wrote a book, sponsored by the Marietta Music Club: *Music and Life in Marietta . . .*, Marietta, 1939.

SPECTACLES. Pseud. See John H. A. Bone.

SPENCER, ABBIE KELLEY (June 11, 1859–May 4, 1908), was born in Hartford, Trumbull County. She taught school, and her husband, Charles F. Spencer, was a teacher in various communities, including Chesterfield, Kipton, and Oberlin. She died in Cleveland.

"Considerations." A Novel, New York, 1894.

SPENCER, CHARLES EDGAR (1856–1916), was born in Somerset, Perry County. Except that he was living in Somerset in the 1870s, no details on his life have been found.

Rue, Thyme, and Myrtle, a Collection of Poems and Songs, Philadelphia, 1876.
The Viking, Guy, Legend of the Moxahala, and Other Poems, Philadelphia, 1878.

SPENCER, EDNA EARLE COLE (Sept. 14, 1881–), was born in Barnesville, Belmont County. She attended Mount Union College and Hartford School of Religious Education and was director of the Children's Division, New Jersey State Council of Religious Education. In 1917 she married John D. Spencer, who died in 1949; in 1955 she married Rev. E. Graham Wilson and now lives in Bronxville, N. Y. An active Sunday school worker, she has dramatized Bible stories for children, and published them as *The Good Samaritan and Other Biblical Stories . . .*, [New York, 1915].

SPENCER, OLIVER M. (Sept., 1781–May, 1838), born in Mendham, N. J., was captured by Indians when he was eleven and lived with them for more than two years. In 1803 he became a clerk in the Miami Exporting Company, Cincinnati, and by 1815 he was president of the company. In 1815 he was ordained as a Methodist minister. His business prospered and he was active in humanitarian projects in southwestern Ohio. His account of his captivity first appeared in the *Western Christian Advocate* in 1834.

Indian Captivity, a True Narrative . . ., Washington, Pa., 1835.

SPENCER, PLATT ROGERS (Nov. 7, 1800–May 16, 1864), originator of Spencerian penmanship, was born in Dutchess County, N. Y. In 1810 the family moved to Jefferson, which remained his home for the rest of his life. Fascinated by handwriting from an early age, he practiced writing on every available material—sand, leather, and snow. He clerked in a store, did bookkeeping, and taught a country school. By 1820 he had developed the characteristic semi-angular, intricate calligraphy that was to become so familiar to schoolchildren of the nineteenth century. He traveled to academies and business colleges expounding his system. Addicted to alcohol in his early manhood, he became a total abstainer in 1832 and devoted much of his time after that to the cause of temperance and to abolition. He was treasurer of Ashtabula County for twelve years, was intensely interested in its early history, and served as the first secretary of the county historical society. His system of handwriting was contained in innumerable copybooks and textbooks, the first of which was issued in 1848. He died at Geneva.

SPENGLER, JOSEPH JOHN (Nov. 19, 1902–), educator, was born in Piqua, Miami County. He graduated from Ohio State University (A.B., 1926; Ph.D., 1930) and has been on the economics faculty of Duke University since 1932. He has written professional articles, textbooks in economics, and several studies of population, e.g., *France Faces Depopulation,* Durham, N. C., 1938. WW 30

SPERRY, PAUL (Jan. 11, 1879–Sept. 3, 1954), clergyman, was born in Ashtabula, Ashtabula County. A graduate of George Washington University in 1902 and New Church Theological School, Cambridge, Mass., in 1905, he was pastor of Swedenborgian churches in New England, 1905–15, and of the Church of the Holy City, Washington, D. C., 1915–42. He died in Maine. His writings include *Words of Life; Practical Meditations on Sacred Subjects,* [Philadelphia, 192- ?]. WW 27

SPIVEY, THOMAS SAWYER (Feb. 27, 1856–Nov. 7, 1938), manufacturer, born in Gallatin, Ill., graduated from Cumberland Presbyterian College in 1879 and settled in Cincinnati the same year; he remained there for ten years and afterward lived in various cities. Inventor of a fireproof safe, he was able to retire in 1897 and devote himself to travel and writing. Although his home was Shawneetown, Ill., at the time of his death, he died in Cincinnati, where he was undergoing medical treatment. He wrote a number of articles and books, e.g., *Dr. Paul McKim,* New York, 1908. WWW 1

SPLAN, JOHN (May 6, 1849–May 11, 1918), horseman, spent much of his life in Cleveland, Cuyahoga County. Known as "the artist of the sulky," he traveled throughout the United States and Europe as a driver and as an owner of many famous trotting horses. He died in Lexington, Ky., and is buried in Cleveland.

Life with the Trotters . . . , Chicago, 1889.

SPOFFORD, AINSWORTH RAND (Sept. 12, 1825–Aug. 11, 1908), librarian, born in Gilmanton, N. H., lived in Cincinnati from 1844 to 1861. While working in Mrs. Elizabeth Truman's bookstore, he imported a wide selection of the writings of the New England transcendental writers. In 1859 he became associate editor of the Cincinnati *Commercial,* and in 1861, while in Washington, D. C., to report the Battle of Bull Run, he was appointed chief assistant to the Librarian of Congress. In 1864 President Lincoln named him chief librarian, a post he filled with distinction until 1897. Besides the titles below, he edited a number of elaborate anthologies and wrote many articles, pamphlets, and historical papers.

The Higher Law Tried by Reason and Authority . . . , New York, 1851.

The Copyright System of the United States . . . , [Washington, D. C., 1892].

The New Library Building, [Washington, D. C., 1895].

A Book for All Readers . . . , New York, 1900.

SPOONER, LYSANDER (Jan. 19, 1808–May 14, 1887), lawyer, born in Athol, Mass., spent about six years in northwestern Ohio in the late 1830s and early 1840s. An inveterate controversialist, he published many pamphlets, including several opposing slavery, e.g., *The Unconstitutionality of Slavery,* Boston, 1845.

SPRAGUE, MARSHALL (March 14, 1909–), was born in Newark, Licking County. After graduating from Princeton University in 1930, he worked as a reporter in Tientsin, China, and in Paris. He later lived for a time in New York City, West Virginia, and most recently Colorado Springs, Colo. He has published articles in many national magazines. A serious illness led to his writing a humorous and philosophical book: *The Business of Getting Well,* New York, [1943].

SPRAGUE, MARY APLIN (Feb. 17, 1849–Jan. 23, 1939), educator, was born in Newark, Licking County. A graduate of Sanford's Female Seminary, Cleveland, she taught in Newark High School. She published articles and fiction in national periodicals.

An Earnest Trifler, Boston, 1880.

SPRAGUE, ROSEMARY (June 29, 1923–), born in New York City, has lived in Ohio since she was a small child. She graduated from Bryn Mawr College in 1941 and Western Reserve University (Ph.D.) in 1950. Now Mrs. Edward G. Whittington Bush, she lives in Cleveland and is a lecturer at Fenn College. She has published several novels, most of them historical stories for young readers, e.g., *Northward to Albion,* New York, [1947].

SPRAGUE, WILLIAM CYRUS (Feb. 25, 1860–Nov. 29, 1922), lawyer and publisher, was born in Malta, Morgan County. After graduating from Denison University in 1881 and Cincinnati Law School in 1883, he practiced in Ohio, Michigan, and Minnesota for nineteen years. He then settled in Chicago, where he conducted a publishing firm and a correspondence school. In addition to compiling several legal texts, he edited professional periodicals and, for a time, the *American Boy.* He compiled the first three volumes below and wrote the others.

Eloquence and Repartee in the American Congress, Detroit, 1895.
Flashes of Wit from Bench and Bar, Detroit, 1895.
Sprague's Speeches . . . , Detroit, 1898.
Three Boys in the Mountains, New York, 1902.
Napoleon Bonaparte; A History Written for Boys, New York, 1903.
The Boy Courier of Napoleon . . . , Boston, 1904.
Felice Constant . . . , New York, 1904.
The Boy Pathfinder . . . , Boston, [1905].
Davy Crockett, New York, 1915.

SPRECHER, SAMUEL (Dec. 28, 1810–Jan. 10, 1906), clergyman and educator, was born in Washington County, Md. After graduating from Gettysburg Theological Seminary in 1836, he served Lutheran churches in Pennsylvania, Maryland, and Virginia until 1849, when he was called to the presidency of Wittenberg College. He served as president, 1849–74, and as a member of the faculty, 1874–84. He published a number of theological articles, and some of his addresses and sermons were published in pamphlet form. He died at the home of a daughter in San Diego, Calif.

The Groundwork of a System of Evangelical Lutheran Theology, Philadelphia, 1879.

SPRENG, SAMUEL PETER (Feb. 11, 1853–April 19, 1946), clergyman, was born in Wayne County. After attending Northwestern College, Naperville, Ill., 1872–75, he was ordained as a minister of the Evangelical Association. He was pastor of several Ohio churches, 1875–83, was presiding elder of the Columbus District, 1883–86, edited the *Evangelical Messenger,* Cleveland, 1887–1907, and served as bishop, 1907–30.

Rays of Light on the Highway to Success, Cleveland, 1885.
The Life and Labors of John Seybert, First Bishop of the Evangelical Association, Cleveland, 1888.
The Most Popular Book in the World, Cleveland, 1903.
The Sinner and His Saviour; The Way of Salvation Made Plain, Cleveland, [1906].

SPRIGLE, RAY (Aug. 14, 1886–Dec. 22, 1957), journalist, was born in Akron, Summit County. After studying for a year at Ohio State University, he became a reporter on the Ohio *Sun* in 1906. He also worked on Ohio newspapers in Akron and Canton before joining the Pittsburgh *Post* in 1916. He was awarded a Pulitzer Prize in 1938. He published short stories in various magazines and wrote one book: *In the Land of Jim Crow,* New York, 1949. WWW 3

SPRINGER, WALTER GLEN (July 5, 1892–), journalist, was born in Cambridge, Guernsey County. After graduating from Marietta College in 1917, he worked on newspapers in Marietta, Wooster, and Cleveland. He also worked in the public relations division of the Columbia Broadcasting System. He now lives in Phoenix, Ariz. He has published a book of poems: *The Hudson and Its Moods,* New York, 1929.

SPROAT, AMASA DELANO (Jan. 28, 1802–Nov. 28, 1885), druggist, was born in Stockbridge, Vt. He lived on his father's farm until he was sixteen, and then walked to Ohio to clerk in a drugstore operated by two uncles. In 1829 he began his own business, which he conducted until 1881, when he turned it over to his sons. An advocate of an elaborate universal alphabet, he published *Child's Letter Book* in 1834 in addition to the titles below.

A System of Breviscripture, Chillicothe 1846.
An Endeavor towards a Universal Alphabet, Chillicothe, 1857.
Monalpha, 1870.

SQUIER, EPHRAIM GEORGE (June 17, 1821–April 17, 1888), was born in Bethlehem, N. Y. His residence in Ohio was brief, but it was in Chillicothe that his first scientific aspiration took form. Self-educated, he taught school in his youth and became a qualified civil engineer, but in 1841 he turned to literary work and became a special writer for Albany newspapers. He became the leading writer for the *New York State Mechanic,* a periodical dedicated to prison reform. In 1844 he established the *Journal* at Hartford, Conn., with "Henry Clay, one first, one last and only choice" as its slogan, and was credited with swinging that state to Clay. He left Hartford in 1845 to become editor of the *Scioto Gazette* at Chillicothe. Here in association with Edwin Hamilton Davis (q.v.), who had been studying the Indian mounds of Ohio for over fifteen years, he began compiling *Ancient Monuments of the Mississippi Valley,* destined to be the first publication issued by the Smithsonian Institution in 1848. In addition to Davis a number of archaeologists contributed to the book. Among others, Charles Whittlesey (q.v.) contributed about twenty plans and many field notes. Squier's contribution was largely editorial, yet the honors fell to him, and publication of the book was the turning point in his career. He was appointed clerk of the Ohio assembly in 1846, but in 1848 he bowed out of the Ohio scene and returned to New York. He served as *chargé d'affaires* in Central America, 1849–50. He became chief editor of the publishing house of Frank Leslie in 1860. His wife divorced him in 1873 and married Leslie a year later, at which time Squier suffered a mental breakdown. He was eventually confined in an insane asylum, where he died in 1888. A prolific writer, he published many articles and books, most of them dealing with Central and South America.

SQUIER, LEE WELLING (July 28, 1859– ?), was born in Fredericktown, Knox County. He served in the U. S. Consular Service in Japan, 1881–87. After his return he lived for a year in Steubenville, where he worked as an insurance agent. He became an executive in a number of fraternal insurance companies and was an actuarial authority on such organizations. He was also president of the Conowingo Marble and Minerals Company. He lived in Germantown, Pa. His writings include *A Lamb to the Slaughter; An American Girl's Experience in the Orient* . . . , Greensburg, Pa., [1901]. WW 14

SQUIRES, EDITH LOMBARD (1884–June 2, 1939), was born in New York City. She was trained as a concert pianist, but after her marriage she gave up her musical career. She lived in Zanesville until 1924, when she moved to Richmond, Ind., where she spent the rest of her life. She wrote several plays and radio scripts and also published at least two volumes of poetry, e.g., *Luminous Dust,* Dallas, Texas, [1939].

STABLER, ALVIN K. (April 5, 1869–June 29, 1916), educator, was born in Bethany, Butler County. In 1905 he moved to Arizona, where he was superintendent of Phoenix Union High School for a number of years. He published a volume of poems: *Arizona Sunshine,* [Phoenix, Ariz., 1915].

STABLETON, JOHN KAY (Jan. 14, 1858–Sept. 16, 1939), educator, was born in Manchester, Adams County. After graduating from Ohio Wesleyan University in 1882, he was a teacher and school superintendent in Nebraska and Illinois.

Diary of a Western Schoolmaster, Chicago, [1900].

Your Problems and Mine in the Guidance of Youth, Bloomington, Ill., [1922].

STACK, HARRY VAN, born in Sessalong, Transvaal, South Africa, has lived in Sandusky since 1943 and since 1945 has been a feature writer and columnist for the Sandusky *Register.* For about twenty years before coming to Sandusky, he was lecturer and guide aboard the English-Australian convict ship *Success,* which toured U. S. ports in the interest of prison reform. He has written several books about Africa, e.g., *Echoes of Sessalong* . . . , Cleveland, 1943.

STAFFORD, EDWARD RUSSELL (April 8, 1874–Dec. 2, 1950), clergyman, born in Estill County, Ky., was brought to Ohio while a baby and spent his life in the state. After attending Wellston schools, he graduated from Ohio Northern University in 1894. Ordained to the Methodist ministry, he served churches in Beaver, Columbus, Marietta, Cincinnati, Hamilton, and several other Ohio communities. He was superintendent of the Zanesville District, 1928–34. After his retirement in 1946, he lived in Cincinnati. He wrote *Shop Talks* . . . , Cincinnati, [1910]. RLA 2

STAGG, ABRAHAM (June 12, 1830– ?), was born in Franklin County. He attended Otterbein College and taught penmanship there for a time; he later graduated from Ohio Wesleyan University.

Biographical Sketches of the Fifty-sixth Ohio Senate . . . , Columbus, 1864.

Biographical Sketches of the Fifty-sixth Ohio House . . . , Columbus, 1865.

STAIR, GRACE (Sept. 27, 1873–April 13, 1947), was born in Fremont, Sandusky County. After her marriage to Edward Douglas Stair, Detroit newspaper publisher, she lived in Detroit, Mich., where she was active in charitable and civic activities. She died in Palm Beach, Fla. She wrote fiction for various magazines and published historical novels, e.g., *A Lady of France,* New York, 1930. WWNAA 6

STALLO, JOHANN BERNHARD (March 16, 1823–Jan. 6, 1900), scientist, lawyer, and diplomat, was born in Sierhausen, Germany. In 1839 he came to Cincinnati, where an uncle was already living. He taught in a Catholic school and studied at St. Xavier's College. Serving as a professor of chemistry and physics at St. John's College, Fordham, N. Y., 1844–47, he devoted his spare hours to the study of philosophy. Returning to Cincinnati, he read law and was admitted to the bar in 1849. While practicing successfully, he studied philosophy and science and often lectured on scientific, religious, and educational topics. In 1885 President Cleveland appointed him minister to Italy, and on the completion of his service four years later he settled in Florence, where he spent the remainder of his life.

General Principles of the Philosophy of Nature . . ., Boston, 1848.
Alexander von Humboldt . . ., Cincinnati, 1859.
Concepts and Theories of Modern Physics, New York, 1882.
Reden, Abhanlungen und Briefe, New York, 1893.

STAMPEDE. Pseud. See Jonathan F. Kelley.

STANLEY, JOHN (Oct. 1, 1845–Jan. 10, 1907), was born on a farm in Athens County. In 1863 he enlisted in the O.V.I., and after the war he farmed until 1885, when he moved to Chillicothe, where he was city marshal, claims agent for the Baltimore & Ohio Railroad, and game warden. With the assistance of Burton E. Stevenson (q.v.), then a young police reporter, he wrote *Twelve Years of Crimes and Criminals . . .*, Columbus, 1903.

STANLEY, LYSANDER MALMSBERRY (April 26, 1846–April 6, 1923), was born of Quaker parents near Damascus, Mahoning County. He read law and passed the bar examination but never practiced. Instead, he was a newspaperman all of his life. He worked on papers in Salem and Sebring, and from 1901 until his death he wrote for the Alliance *Review*. Many of his poems appeared in his column in that paper, "Pa and Ma." They dealt with local persons and events and were read eagerly in the local area. His "Fun at Dasmascus" recalls the fun he had as a boy during maple sugar making. His poem "The Automobile" records the first sight of a "contraption, made to imitate a surrey" in Damascus village. Many of his poems deal with local events during Civil War days; others reflect his love for the countryside.

Marion and Ella Thea Cox

Poems, Alliance, 1900.

STANLEY-BROWN, KATHERINE OLIVER (April 30, 1892–), was born in Philadelphia, Pa. She graduated from Vassar College in 1915, married Rudolph Stanley-Brown, grandson of President Garfield, in 1922, and settled in Cleveland, where her husband was a practicing architect until 1934. She now lives in Washington, D. C. She has written stories and articles on travel and architecture and several books, e.g., a history of American architecture written for young readers: *The Young Architects*, New York, 1929. RC 27

STANTON, ROBERT LIVINGSTON (March 28, 1810–May 23, 1885), clergyman, born in Griswold, Conn., graduated from Lane Seminary in 1836 and served Presbyterian churches in Mississippi and Louisiana, 1839–51. He was president of Oakland College in Mississippi, 1851–54. He was pastor of a Chillicothe church, 1855–62, a professor in Danville seminary, 1862–66, and president of Miami University, 1866–71. He later was an editor of the *Herald and Presbyter*, published in Cincinnati. Besides the titles below, some of his sermons were printed in pamphlet form.

The Church and the Rebellion . . ., New York, 1864.
Vindication of the General Assembly of the Presbyterian Church (O.S.), of 1866, from the Aspersions of Rev. William Brown, D.D., [Cincinnati?, 1876?].

STARBUCK, JOHN CLIFFORD (Dec. 25, 1864–Feb. 6, 1951), was born in Deserted Camp near Wilmington, Clinton County. He attended Wilmington College and lived in Ohio for 38 years before moving to Massachusetts. Throughout his life he was interested in psychic phenomena and pneumatherapy or spiritual healing. He published a number of pamphlets and a book of poems and essays: *The Problem of Life & How to Solve It*, Boston, 1932.

STARK, J. CARROLL (1830–1908), clergyman, was born in Stow, Summit County. A graduate of Hiram College and a Disciples of Christ minister, he traveled widely as an evangelist and also served pastorates in Ohio and at least seven other states. He died in Tennessee. His writings include *The King and His Kingdom . . .*, Hamilton, Ill., 1902.

STARLING, WILLIAM (Jan. 25, 1839–Dec. 10, 1900), engineer, was born in Columbus, Franklin County. He studied engineering at New York University, served in the Civil War, managed a Mississippi plantation until 1882, and was an engineer on the Levee Board, 1882–98. He died in Greenville, Miss. He wrote magazine articles and reports on the Mississippi.

The Floods of the Mississippi River . . . , New York, 1897.

STATES, FANNIE M. (Oct. 14, 1866–June 25, 1949), educator, was born on a farm near Norwalk, Huron County. She taught for 35 years in the schools of Norwalk, and her death occurred in that community. She wrote *Myrtle's Choice, the Story of a Girl Missionary,* Rock Island, Ill., [1932].

STEARNS, LUCY PEASE (c.1839–July 7, 1896), was born in Berea, Cuyahoga County. She attended Oberlin Preparatory School and in 1861 graduated from Oberlin College, where her father served on the faculty. After her marriage to Charles W. Stearns, she lived in Berea and Cleveland, but she died in Oberlin.

Children's Stories for Grown Folks, Cleveland, 1895.

STEARNS, THEODORE (June 10, 1880–Nov. 2, 1935), composer, son of Lucy P. Stearns (q.v.), was born in Berea, Cuyahoga County. He studied at Oberlin College and at Wurzbach, Bavaria. He played viola in the Cleveland Philharmonic Orchestra, edited *Étude,* 1899–1900, and was music critic for several newspapers. From 1932 until his death he was chairman of the music department, University of California. He wrote *The Story of Music,* New York, 1931. WWW 1

STEARNS, WALLACE NELSON (Aug. 26, 1866–Feb. 3, 1934), educator, was born in Chagrin Falls, Cuyahoga County. He graduated from Canfield Normal College, 1886, Ohio Wesleyan University, 1891, and Boston University (Ph.D.), 1899. He served on the faculties of several colleges and universities; from 1923 until his death he was professor of Biblical literature, Illinois Women's College.

An Analysis of United States History . . . , Madison, 1886.

A Manual of Patrology . . . , New York, 1899.

A Manual on Hebrew Private Life for Popular Use, New York, [1910].

A Working Basis, and Other Essays, Boston, [1914].

What Three College Men Did, [Fargo?, N. Dak., n.d.].

STEELE, MARY DAVIES (1843–Feb. 25, 1897), was born in Dayton, Montgomery County, the daughter of Robert W. Steele (q.v.). Though a semi-invalid throughout her life and confined to her bed in her last years, she took an active part in Dayton club life and civic affairs. She published articles and poems in various periodicals, including the *Atlantic Monthly.*

A Happy Life, Dayton, 1895.

Early Dayton . . . , (with Robert W. Steele), Dayton, 1896.

STEELE, ROBERT WILBUR (July 3, 1819–Sept. 24, 1891), was born in Dayton, Montgomery County. He read law but never practiced because of ill health. He was an active civic leader, served for thirty years on the Dayton Board of Education, and was one of the founders of the Dayton Library Association. He was deeply interested in local history and collected notes and other materials on which his daughter, Mary D. Steele (q.v.), based *Early Dayton,* in which he is named coauthor.

Historical Sketch of the Public Schools of Dayton . . . , [Dayton, 1876].

Early Dayton . . . , (with Mary Steele), Dayton, 1896.

STEEN, MOSES DUNCAN ALEXANDER (April 24, 1841–June 22, 1924), clergyman, was born at Blue Creek, Adams County. After graduating from Miami University in 1866, he was licensed as a Presbyterian minister and was ordained in 1870. He served churches in Ohio, Pennsylvania, Kentucky, Illinois, Colorado, Washington, and California. Besides the title below, he wrote family histories and religious tracts. He died in Worthington.

Scriptural Sanctification . . . , Alamosa, Calif., 1885.

STEEP, THOMAS (April 3, 1880–Sept. 3, 1944), journalist, was born in Cincinnati, Hamilton County. As a correspondent for various newspapers and syndicates, he traveled widely in the United States, Asia, and Europe. He published a collection of sketches of Chinese life: *Chinese Fantastics,* New York, [1925]. WWW 2

STEER, HARRIET (Aug. 20, 1795–Aug. 1, 1883), was born in Doe Run, Pa., but grew up on a farm near Zanesville. After teaching school in Mount Pleasant, she married Samuel Steer, and they moved to Cincinnati in 1833. After her husband died in 1838, she kept a boardinghouse. She was active in Cincinnati charities. The book below contains some of her letters and an account of her life by her daughter, Sarah R. Steer, who prepared it for publication.

Through Grace to Glory. Memory Sketches from the Life of Harriet Steer, Concord, N. H., 1887.

STEINER, EDWARD ALFRED (Nov. 1, 1866–June 30, 1956), clergyman and educator, was born in what is now Czechoslovakia. After graduating from Oberlin Seminary in 1891, he was ordained to the ministry in the Congregational Church. He served churches in Springfield, 1896–99, and Sandusky, 1899–1903. He then joined the faculty of Grinnell College, where he served as professor of applied Christianity until 1941. After his retirement he lived in Claremont, Calif. He published a number of books, including an autobiographical volume: *From Alien to Citizen* . . . , New York, [1914]. WWW 3

STEINER, JESSE FREDERICK (Feb. 25, 1880–), educator, was born in St. Paris, Champaign County. A graduate of Heidelberg College in 1901 and the University of Chicago (Ph.D.) in 1915, he taught at North Japan College, Sendai, 1905–12, and at several American universities, including the University of Washington, 1931–48. He now lives in Seattle. He has written several books on sociological questions, e.g., *Americans at Play* . . . , New York, 1933. DAS 2

STELLHORN, FREDERICK WILLIAM (Oct. 2, 1841–March 17, 1919), clergyman and educator, was born in Hanover, Germany. After graduating from Concordia College in 1862, he was ordained to the Lutheran ministry and served churches in Missouri and Indiana. He taught at Northwestern University, 1869–74, and at Concordia College, 1874–81. In 1881 he joined the faculty of Capital University, where he taught theology and German, was president from 1894 to 1900, and afterward was dean of the seminary. He also edited *Lutherische Kirchenzeitung* and *Theologische Zeitblaetter.* He wrote other Biblical commentaries besides those listed below.

Worum Handelt Es Sich Eighentlich in dem Geganwärtigen Lehrstreit über die Gnadenwahl? . . . , Columbus, 1881.

Books of the New Testament, Columbus, 1891.

Der Schriftbeweis des Lutherischen Katechismus . . . , Columbus, 1912.

The Epistle of St. Paul to the Romans . . . , Columbus, 1918.

STEPHENS, DAVID STUBERT (May 12, 1847–Sept. 1, 1921), clergyman and educator, was born in Springfield, Clark County. After graduating from Adrian College in 1868, he studied in Scotland and was ordained to the Methodist ministry. He joined the Adrian philosophy faculty in 1874 and served as president of the college, 1881–88. He edited the *Methodist Recorder,* 1888–96, and in 1896 became chancellor of Kansas City University.

Wesley and Episcopacy, 1892.

STEPHENS, JOHN VANT (Sept. 16, 1857–March 3, 1946), clergyman, was born near St. Louis, Mo. A Presbyterian minister, he was on the faculty of Lane Theological Seminary, Cincinnati, 1910–32. He published many books and pamphlets on religious and historical subjects and also an autobiography: *Fourscore* . . . , Cincinnati, 1938. WWW 2

STEPHENS, MRS. PETER J. See Henrietta Henkle.

STEPHENSON, GENEVA (June 3, 1901–), was born in Portsmouth, Scioto County. After graduating from Ohio State University in 1925, she taught at Marietta College and Ohio State. She wrote radio scripts and served as program director of the Ohio School of the Air. She now lives in Columbus. She described life in eighteenth-century England in her first novel, *Spring Journey,* New York, 1939. ANT

STEPHENSON, HENRY THEW (April 22, 1870–Dec. 29, 1957), educator, younger brother of Nathaniel W. Stephenson (q.v.), was born in Cincinnati, Hamilton County. After graduating from Ohio State University in 1894, he joined the English department, Indiana University, as an instructor; in 1919 he became chairman of the department. He died in Florida.

Patroon Van Volkenburg . . . , Indianapolis, [1900].

The Fickle Wheel; A Tale . . . , Indianapolis, [1901].

Shakespeare's London, New York, 1905.

The Elizabethan People, New York, 1910.

A Handbook of Shakespeare, New York, 1914.

The Study of Shakespeare, New York, 1915.

Christie Bell of Goldenrod Valley . . . , Indianapolis, 1918.

The Ettrick Shepherd: A Biography, [Bloomington, Ind., 1922].

STEPHENSON, NATHANIEL WRIGHT (July 10, 1867–Jan. 17, 1935), journalist and educator, was born in Cincinnati, Hamilton County. He worked on the *Cincinnati Daily Tribune,* 1892–1900, and graduated from Indiana University in 1896. He taught history at the College of Charleston, 1902–23, was a visiting professor at Yale University and Columbia University, and taught at Scripps College from 1927 until his death in Claremont, Calif. He wrote several textbooks in American history; novels, e.g., *The Beautiful Mrs. Moulton,* New York, 1902; and a number of distinguished historical studies, e.g., *Abraham Lincoln and the Union . . . ,* New Haven, 1918. DAB 21

STERN, HERMAN ISIDORE (April 22, 1854–July 3, 1926), clergyman, was born in Galion, Crawford County. He spent a few years of his childhood in Ohio and later was pastor of a German Reformed church in Cincinnati for a short time. He attended the schools of Louisville, Ky., and a seminary at Sheboygan, Wis. As a minister of the German Reformed Church and later the Presbyterian Church, he served in Indiana and California. Around the turn of the century he published local color stories about Indiana in national magazines. In 1905 he moved to Berkeley, Calif., which remained his home for the remainder of his life. A fervent Socialist, he attempted to unite his political ideals with his Christian beliefs.

Evelyn Gray; Or, the Victims of Our Western Turks . . . , New York, 1890.

The Gods of Our Fathers . . . , New York, 1898.

A Socialist Catechism, Berkeley, Calif., 1912.

STERNBERGER, ESTELLE MILLER (1886–), was born in Cincinnati, Hamilton County. She attended the University of Cincinnati, 1907–11, and the Community School of Jewish Philanthropy, 1907–14. She was executive secretary of the National Council of Jewish Women, 1920–32, and edited *The Jewish Woman,* 1921–32, and *The Woman's Review,* 1932–40. She published *The Supreme Cause; A Practical Book about Peace,* New York, 1936. WW 30

STEVENS, GEORGE E. (July 2, 1842–Nov. 30, 1917), was born in Cincinnati, Hamilton County. He operated a bookstore there and was associated with the Methodist Book Concern. He died in Granville, where he spent his later years.

The City of Cincinnati . . . , Cincinnati, 1869.

STEVENS, GEORGE WASHINGTON (Jan. 16, 1866–Oct. 29, 1926), journalist and museum director, was born in Utica, N. Y., where he attended public schools and Utica Academy. In 1889 he came to Ohio, where he was a reporter on the Springfield *Republican-Times* for a few months; he then went to Toledo, where he worked on the Toledo *Bee* and the Toledo *Times* and spent five years in the advertising business. In 1903 he became the first director of the Toledo Museum of Art. The museum flourished under his direction and enjoyed a reputation as one of the best American art museums among cities of comparable size.

The King and the Harper, Together with Other Poems, Toledo, 1900.

Things, Toledo, 1903.

STEVENS, ISAAC NEWTON (Nov. 1, 1858–Feb. 11, 1920), lawyer, was born in Newark, Licking County. After reading law in Burlington, Iowa, he began practice in Denver, Colo., in 1880. He held various political offices in Colorado and also had business interests in Philadelphia. He died in Overbrook, Pa. He published at least three books, e.g., *An American Suffragette; A Novel,* New York, 1911. WWW 1

STEVENS, NINA DE GARME SPALDING (Jan. 29, 1876–March 12, 1959), born in Port Huron, Mich., was married June 12, 1902, to George Washington Stevens (q.v.). She served as assistant director of the Toledo Museum of Art, 1905–39. Her last years were spent in Paris, France. She wrote a life of her husband: *A Man and a Dream . . . ,* [Hollywood, Calif., 1941?].

STEVENS, VINCENT SAMUEL (March 20, 1872–), born in Chicago, was secretary of the Akron Chamber of Commerce, 1908–37, and also was director of the Akron Art Institute. He now divides his time between Akron and Clearwater, Fla. He has written three novels, e.g., *What Doth It Profit a Man?,* Philadelphia, [1944].

STEVENSON, BURTON EGBERT (Nov. 9, 1872–), anthologist, author, librarian, was born in Chillicothe, Ross County, with an overwhelming ambition, even as a child, to write and patient persistence to match it. There was no inheritance of means or literary talent in his family of building tradesmen. At seven he sold newspapers on the streets after school, then inevitably found his way to the pressroom as a printer's devil. With old type and cast-off fragments, he fashioned a makeshift press and set up a little print shop; at twelve he began publication of a monthly titled *The Boys' Own,* which he continued until he graduated from high school at seventeen. A kindly Presbyterian minister, Dr. Biggs, and Mr. David Meade Massie (q.v.), impressed by Stevenson's obvious merit, secured for him a scholarship at Princeton University, which covered his tuition. There, for three years, he absorbed learning and wrote poetry, supporting himself first by typesetting and later as a correspondent for the old United Press and the New York *Tribune* among others. Scanning *Cap and Gown* undergraduate poets of that era, Franklin P. Adams discovered 22 subsequent literary lights (including Stevenson) with this trait: "Every poem written by these young collegiates was formally rhymed. Proving nothing, except possibly that there is no better training for a writer of anything than the composition of rigorous verse." But a better "finishing school" awaited Stevenson in Chillicothe on his return home for summer vacation at the end of his third year. George H. Tyler, editor of the Chillicothe *Leader,* offered him a reporting berth on that paper. Forgetting Princeton and formal education, Stevenson accepted the post, later moving to city editor spots on the Chillicothe *Daily News* and the Chillicothe *Advertiser.* Here he was exposed to that extraordinary "school of experience" which had sharpened styles and polished authors for almost a century (among others. William Carey Jones, Otway Curry, E. G. Squier, Charles F. Lummis, John and Henry Holcomb Bennett). A highly articulate woman, Elizabeth Butler, became his wife in 1895 and devoted her life to his career. Together they assumed the task of developing the City Library in Chillicothe when Stevenson was named Librarian in 1899, a position he held until 1957, becoming Librarian Emeritus in that year. The stimulating company of books and some new-found leisure provided the ideal atmosphere in which to write. Although he had published a small volume of verse in his collegiate days, Stevenson turned now to the historical novel because he believed that its informality offered a refreshing approach to the human side of history. *At Odds with the Regent, a Story of the Cellamare Conspiracy,* published in 1901, dealt with French history; its immediate successor pictured Washington's role in Braddock's Defeat and was titled *A Soldier of Virginia* (1901). As personal admiration for the writing of Tolstoy and Sienkiewicz had swayed him to the historical novel, affection for the past masters of detective fiction now carried him into that field. "The pleasure to be had from a good one [detective story]," he wrote, "is of a unique and satisfying kind. The reader is invited to take part in a mathematical demonstration, in which the symbols are men and women, with just enough of the background of life to give them reality. The problem to be solved is one of human conduct, and the solution is reached when one has found X, the unknown quantity—usually the criminal." Stevenson's *The Holladay Case* (1903), quickly followed by *The Marathon Mystery* (1904), put him on the high road to eminence in the field. He considers *The Mystery of the Boule Cabinet* (1912) as his best, with some justification; now a classic in the field, it was an immediate success in book form and as a melodrama coauthored by the distinguished actress, Eleanor Robson (Mrs. August Belmont), and Harriet Ford. Translations have appeared in most of the European languages, including the Scandinavian, in Braille, and even in Latin. Stevenson's restless talent roved the field. He wrote books for boys (the first: *Tommy Remington's Battle,* 1902), some of which were based on his recollections of railroad reporting (like *The Young Section Hand,* 1905, and its successors), and children's textbooks (*A Child's Guide to Biography, American,* 1909). Like most librarians, Stevenson was assailed with requests of teachers and schoolchildren for "suitable poems" and the elusive source of too-familiar quotations. With characteristic method he and Mrs. Stevenson began compiling these to meet the need. *Days and Deeds: A Book of Verse* appeared in 1906 and *Days and Deeds: Prose* in 1907. Contrary to the spirit of his time, he thought that literature of the past, including poetry, should be approached through that of the present. After compiling *Favorite Poems in English* (1911), he hazarded the pitfalls of contemporary poetry and the myriad problems of source and attribution to prove his thesis by editing *The Home Book of Verse,* first published in 1912. Trips abroad, as a respite from such editorial tension, became the order of the day. Never neglecting an opportunity, he used them as material for two travel books: *The Spell of Holland* (1911) and *The Charm of Ireland* (1914). World War I brought Camp Sherman to Chillicothe's outskirts and a problem for librarian Stevenson: officers and men wanted to borrow books. On his own initiative, he opened a state-wide campaign for book donations, set up an organizational headquarters in the basement of the Chillicothe Library, was appointed camp librarian by Major General Glenn, and began supplying the need in such an orderly fashion that the Executive Committee of the American Library Association, after a visit there, sent other camp librarians for preliminary training. In the fall of 1917 he went to Washington, D. C., to head the national campaign for books, and in Jan., 1918, was appointed European Director of the A.L.A.'s Library War Service. Accompanied by his wife, he left for Paris, where he set up headquarters and supervised the distribution of some two million books and over six million magazines to the men of the armed forces. General Pershing, in a personal letter, which now hangs on the wall of his study, expressed the nation's thanks for this outstanding service to the A.E.F. At war's end, Stevenson converted the Paris headquarters into The American Library, first of its kind designed to provide accurate information about this country for Europeans. In 1925 he returned to serve for five years as its director, but came home disillusioned with the prospects of ever interesting Europe in America. Life in France had made him a gourmet, developed his appreciation of music, art, and gothic architecture, and, of course, provided grist for more novels. Phenomenal diligence, coupled with the natural seclusion of his home atop Carlisle Hill in Chillicothe, enabled him to undertake the exhausting task of preparing *The Home Book of Quotations,* first published in 1934. Variations were tracked through countless volumes and many languages to their remote sources, verified and reduced to thousands of paper slips, sorted, checked, and rechecked before printing. Not content, he produced three similar compendiums: *The Home Book of Proverbs, Maxims and Familiar Phrases* (1948), *The Home Book of Bible Quotations* (1948), and *The Standard Book of Shakespeare Quotations* (1953). Since then he has published a dramatization of his earlier novel *A King in Babylon* (1955), written *A Garland of Gold* (1959), and begun preparation of a long-promised autobiography. He was elected a member of the National Institute of Arts and Letters in 1928 and of the famous Century Club of New York in 1930. The Ohioana Library Association recognized his significant contribution to American literature by conferring on him its Career Medal in 1949, and Marietta College added a "Litt.D. (honorary)" in 1955 to demark the scholarly status he had attained beyond the realm of formal education. Sight of fifteen feet of Stevenson's books on the shelves of his living room invariably prompts the visitor to utter the "infinite-capacity-for-taking-pains" phrase. A more appropriate earlier one from Cicero (and *The Home Book of Quotations*) is at hand: "Genius is fostered by industry." Stevenson's own favorite is Emerson's dictum: "The high prize of life, the crowning fortune of a man, is to be born with a bias to some pursuit which finds him in employment and happiness."

Eugene D. Rigney

STEVENSON, LOUIS LACY (Nov. 28, 1879–Feb. 7, 1953), journalist, was born in Kenton, Hardin County. He worked on the Kenton *News-Republican,* 1896–1903, and in 1904 became city editor of the Traverse City, Mich., *Record.* He was on the staff of the Detroit *News,* 1910–52; in 1921 he was made city editor, and in 1923 he was made New York correspondent. His column, "The Seven Million," was a regular feature of the *News* and was syndicated in other newspapers. He wrote *Big Game,* New York, [1924].

STEVENSON, RICHARD TAYLOR (Sept. 24, 1853–Aug. 19, 1919), clergyman and educator, was born in Taylorsville, Ky. He graduated from Ohio Wesleyan University in 1873, was ordained to the Methodist ministry and served churches in several Ohio communities, and in 1893 became professor of history at Ohio Wesleyan. He died in Delaware.

One Hundred Years of Methodism in Ohio, Cincinnati, 1898.

The Growth of the Nation, 1809 to 1837 . . . , Philadelphia, [1905].

The Missionary Interpretation of History, Cincinnati, [1905].

John Calvin . . . , Cincinnati, [1907].

Missions versus Militarism, Cincinnati, [1916].

STEVENSON, THOMAS M. (Feb. 19, 1828–Jan. 27, 1898), educator and clergyman, was born in Norwich, Muskingum County. After graduating from Muskingum College, he was superintendent of schools in Dresden and McConnelsville and also served as a Presbyterian minister. He was chaplain of the 78th O.V.I., 1861–65. He died in Dresden, Muskingum County.

History of the 78th Regiment . . . , Zanesville, 1865.

STEWARD, ANN (Aug. 29, 1898–   ), was born in Cincinnati, Hamilton County. She studied at the University of Cincinnati and the University of Michigan, acted and wrote for the Theatre Workshop, Cincinnati, and did social work for several years. In 1935 she moved to a farm in northern Kentucky.

Her dramatic writings include a play for children: *Cupid's Choice* . . . , Dayton, [1929]. She has also written novels, the first of which was *Let the Earth Speak,* New York, 1940. ANT

STEWARD, SAMUEL M. (July 23, 1909–), was born in Woodsfield, Monroe County. He attended Ohio State University (A.B., 1931; Ph.D., 1934), and has served on the faculties of several universities, the last being De Paul University, Chicago, 1947–56. He is now a free-lance artist and writer living in Chicago. While a student at Ohio State, he published a volume of short stories: *Pan and the Firebird,* New York, 1930; he has also published numerous articles and a novel: *Angels on the Bough,* Caldwell, Idaho, 1936.

STEWARD, THEOPHILUS GOULD (April 17, 1843–Jan. 11, 1924), clergyman and educator, was born in Gouldtown, N. J. Ordained in the African Methodist Episcopal Church, he served several pastorates in the East. In 1891 he was appointed chaplain of the 25th U. S. Infantry. While he was in the Philippines, 1899–1902, his wife lived at Wilberforce; after he retired from the army in 1907, he joined the Wilberforce University faculty as instructor in history and languages.

Memoirs of Mrs. Rebecca Steward . . . , Philadelphia, 1877.

Genesis Reread . . . , Philadelphia, 1885.

A Charleston Love Story . . . , New York, [1899].

How the Black St. Domingo Legion Saved the Patriot Army in the Siege of Savannah . . . , Washington, D. C., 1899.

The Colored Regulars in the United States Army . . . , Philadelphia, 1904.

The Haitian Revolution . . . , New York, [1914].

STEWART, ANNA BIRD (Sept. 28, 1880–), educator and lecturer, was born in Cincinnati, Hamilton County. After graduating from the University of Cincinnati in 1903, she taught English in Paducah, Ky., H. Thane Miller School for Girls, Cincinnati, and Saint Mary's College, Ind. She was in advertising work in New York City, 1910–30. She has traveled extensively in England and France and has lectured to schools and library groups throughout the United States. She has published many plays, stories, and poems for adults and for young readers, e.g., a volume of poetry: *The Birds Began to Sing,* New York, 1930. WW 28

STEWART, CHARLES DAVID (March 18, 1868–), was born in Zanesville, Muskingum County, the son of Andrew and Sarah (Emery) Stewart. Five years after his birth, the family followed the Baltimore and Ohio Railroad roundhouse, in which the father worked, to Newark and Springfield and then to Garrett, Ind. But malaria and homesickness drove the boy back to his grandparents in Zanesville for the greater part of his boyhood. He left school early and tried his hand at various jobs over the country, working as drug clerk, steamboat deck hand, blacksmith's helper, cowboy, and dime museum attraction billed as "The man who talks backward." A period of newspaper work awakened his desire to write and also revealed his lack of knowledge. He studied literature, languages, and history while he learned the art of wood engraving in Milwaukee. When photo-engraving was introduced, he became a pioneer in the field. In 1915–16 he was executive secretary to the governor of Wisconsin. From 1890 to the present, 67 or more of his contributions have been published in *Century Magazine* and the *Atlantic Monthly.* In later years nature subjects attracted him, and his book *Fellow Creatures* (1935) has been compared to the work of John Burroughs and John Muir. His novels include *The Fugitive Blacksmith* (1905), *Partners of Providence* (1907), *The Wrong Woman* (1912), *Finerty of the Sand House* (1913), *Buck* (1919), and *Valley Waters* (1922), a story with Zanesville as its setting. The latter book prompted William Lyon Phelps to say that Zanesville should give Stewart "the freedom of the city and erect a monument to him while he is yet alive." *Essays on the Spot* appeared in 1910 and *Prussianizing Wisconsin* in 1919. He considers *Some Textual Difficulties in Shakespeare* (1914) as the one of his books most assured of permanence. Since 1907 he has lived in Hartford, Wis.

Norris F. Schneider

STEWART, DONALD OGDEN (Nov. 30, 1894–), was born in Columbus, Franklin County. He graduated from Phillips Exeter School and Yale University (1916). He served in the navy during World War I. Throughout most of the 1920s he lived abroad, chiefly in Paris and Vienna. He made his first appearance as an actor in 1928 in Philip Barry's *Holiday;* in 1931 he also appeared in his own play, *Rebound.* In the 1930s he was identified with many liberal causes, especially in anti-Fascist organizations. He was president of the League of American Writers, 1937–41. A resident of

California, he has been a writer for a number of outstanding motion pictures. He is still best known perhaps for his first book, *A Parody Outline of History* . . . , New York, 1921. WW 30

STEWART, ELIZA DANIEL (April 25, 1816–Aug. 6, 1908), temperance worker, was born in Piketon, Pike County. After teaching school for a number of years, she was married in 1848 to Hiram Stewart, who died within a few months. Throughout her life she was an active worker for temperance, lecturing and writing against liquor and taking an active part in organizing the W.C.T.U. in Ohio. She also worked for women's rights and in 1869 helped organize the first women's suffrage organization in Springfield, where she lived for many years. Her last five years were passed in Hicksville. During the Civil War she visited many hospitals, and grateful soldiers called her "Mother Stewart," the name with which she signed her two books.

Memories of the Crusade; A Thrilling Account of the Great Uprising of the Women of Ohio in 1873, against the Liquor Crime, Columbus, 1888.

The Crusader in Great Britain . . . , Springfield, 1893.

STEWART, GEORGE BLACK (Feb. 28, 1854–June 23, 1932), clergyman, was born in Columbus, Franklin County. He graduated from Princeton University in 1876 and after graduating from Auburn Seminary was ordained to the Presbyterian ministry. He served churches in Auburn, N. Y., and Harrisburg, Pa., 1878–99, and was president of Auburn Seminary, 1899–1926. He wrote several books on religious themes, e.g., *A Study of the Life of Jesus* . . . , Boston, [1907]. WWW 1

STEWART, GIDEON TABOR (Aug. 7, 1824–June 10, 1909), lawyer and journalist, born in Johnstown, N. Y., attended Oberlin College, and was admitted to the Ohio bar in 1846. He was auditor of Huron County, 1850–56; edited the Dubuque, Iowa, *Times,* 1861–65, and afterward was associated with newspapers in Norwalk and Toledo. A perennial candidate for public office, he was an ardent advocate of prohibition and published several speeches as pamphlets; he also wrote *Famed in American History. The Lives of John Adams and John Quincy Adams* . . . , [Norwalk?, 1906].

STEWART, JANE AGNES (April 16, 1860–Feb. 2, 1944), was born in Boston, Mass., but lived for many years in Toledo. She wrote a number of books on women's suffrage and temperance and two autobiographical volumes, the first of which was *I Have Recalled, a Pen-Panorama of a Life,* Toledo, 1938. WWW 2

STEWART, NIXON B. (Sept. 7, 1840–March 1, 1915), clergyman, was born in Cambridge, Guernsey County. He served in the 52nd O.V.I. during the Civil War, was later active in the G.A.R., and was regimental secretary for many years. A minister in the East Ohio Conference of the Methodist Church, he died in Scio.

Dan McCook's Regiment, 52nd O.V.I. . . . , [Clayville], 1900.

STEWART, ROBERT (Jan. 31, 1839–Oct. 23, 1915), clergyman, was born in Sidney, Shelby County. After graduating from Jefferson College in 1859 and Allegheny Seminary in 1865, he was ordained to the ministry of the Presbyterian Church. He served churches in Ohio and New York, 1866–72, and taught at Newburg Seminary, N. Y., 1872–78. Except for an interval of eight years (1892–1900), which he spent in the United States, he served for the remainder of his life as a missionary and teacher in India. Besides the titles below, he wrote two family histories and translated a number of works into Urdu. He died at Sialkot, Punjab.

Filled with the Spirit, 1896.

Life and Work in India . . . , Philadelphia, 1896.

Apostolic and Indian Missions Compared, 1903.

Hinduism Historically Considered, [n.d.].

STEWART, THOMAS MILTON (May 13, 1866–Dec. 10, 1945), occulist and neurologist, was born in Cincinnati, Hamilton County. He graduated from Pulte Medical College, Cincinnati, in 1887 and also studied abroad. While practicing in Cincinnati, he also lectured on comparative mythology and wrote several books, including *Symbolic Teaching* . . . , Cincinnati, 1914. WWW 2

STEWART, WILLIAM MORRIS (Aug. 9, 1829–April 23, 1909), lawyer and Senator, born in Galen, N. Y., spent much of his childhood in Trumbull County. He attended Farmington Academy for three years. In 1850 he went to California, where he was fairly successful as a miner. After reading law, however, he found a far more profitable field in Nevada. He was counsel for several mining companies and amassed a considerable fortune. He served as Senator from Nevada, 1864–75 and 1887–1905. His chief relation to literary history is the fact that in 1868 he invited Mark Twain to become his personal secretary. The relationship lasted less than a week, and each man seems to have cherished a lively animosity toward the other for the rest of his life. Stewart published many of his Senate speeches and legal arguments. George R. Brown edited his *Reminiscences* . . . , New York, 1908. DAB 18

STIBITZ, GEORGE (March 1, 1856–March 11, 1944), clergyman, was born in Schuylkill County, Pa. From 1907 to 1934 he was on the faculty of Central Theological Seminary of the Reformed Church, Dayton. His writings include *Messianic Prophecy* . . . , Cleveland, 1923. WWW 2

STICKELL, MRS. CHARLES B. See Dorothy P. Albaugh.

STILES, HENRY REED (March 10, 1832–Jan. 7, 1909), physician and historian, born in New York City, edited the Toledo *Blade* in 1856. He later practiced medicine and devoted himself to genealogy and local history in New England and New York. He edited or wrote a great many works, e.g., *Bundling; Its Origin, Progress and Decline in America,* Albany, [N. Y.], 1869.

STILLE, SAMUEL HARDEN (Aug. 19, 1896–), was born in Warner, Washington County. When he was seven, his family moved to a farm near Lower Salem, where he now operates a craft center, "Arlendale." He began lecturing at the age of sixteen, was later a member of the Speakers' Bureau of the Republican Party, and lectured throughout the United States. He has also written for the Cincinnati *Enquirer,* the Zanesville *Times Signal,* and other newspapers. He has published poems, books, and articles on Americanism, and a book of sketches of persons and events in Ohio history: *Ohio Builds a Nation* . . . , Chicago, [1939].

STILWELL, WILLIAM T. (c.1840– ?), was born in Ohio. He was living in Logan County in 1872, when he married Nancy Catherine Whitely, sister of William Whitely, manufacturer of reapers. Stilwell became general manager of the Whitely plant in Springfield. In the early 1890s he was a broker in Baltimore, Md.

Public Benefactors of the 19th Century, Springfield, 1887.

STIMSON, RODNEY METCALF (Oct. 26, 1822–Feb. 15, 1913), was born in Milford, N. H. After graduating from Marietta College in 1847, he taught in country schools and read law. He was admitted to the bar in 1849, published the Ironton *Register,* 1850–62, served in the Ohio senate, 1869–73, was director of the state library, 1877–79, and was librarian of Marietta College, 1881–92.

The Marietta Reading Club . . . , Marietta, 1894.

STIPP, JOSEPH ASBURY (Nov. 7, 1845–Dec. 1, 1907), dentist, was born in Ohio, probably in Shelby County. He served in the 154th O.V.I. from May to Sept., 1864, and in the 8th Ohio Volunteer Cavalry from March to July, 1865. After the Civil War he was a dentist in Toledo; his death occurred in that city.

The History of the 154th Ohio Volunteer Infantry, Toledo, 1896.

STIVERS, EMMONS BUCHANAN (May 6, 1857–Jan. 11, 1931), educator and lawyer, was born in Fincastle, Brown County. In 1876 he became a teacher, and in 1883 he was appointed superintendent of schools in West Union. During his residence there, he published a newspaper, *The Index,* and studied law. In 1888 he was admitted to the bar, and in 1890 he settled on a farm in Brown County. He served in the state assembly. Besides writting two history textbooks, he collaborated with Nelson W. Evans (q.v.) in writing a history of Adams County.

A History of Adams County . . . , (with Nelson W. Evans), West Union, 1900.

STOCKELL, WILLIAM (1788– ?), was born in Malton, England. He ran away from home in 1803 and served in the British and French navies and also shipped on whaling vessels. He claimed to have deserted the English and to have served under Perry at the Battle of Lake Erie. He settled in Cincinnati in 1823.

The Eventful Narrative of Captain William Stockwell . . . , (Edwin A. Atlee, ed.), Cincinnati, 1840.

STOCKHAM, ALICE BUNKER (Nov. 8, 1833–Dec. 3, 1912), was born in Cardington, Morrow County. She attended Olivet College and Eclectic Medical College, Cincinnati, where she graduated in 1854. She practiced in Indiana and Illinois and later established the Stockham Publishing Company to publish her own works and other books. She was an active worker for women's suffrage and social reform. In 1900 she established a school of philosophy at Williams Bay, Wis. She later lived at Alhambra, Calif.

Tokology, a Book of Maternity, Chicago, 1883.
Koradine Letters; A Girl's Own Book . . . , (with Lida Hood Talbot), Chicago, 1893.
Karezza; Ethics of Marriage, Chicago, 1896.
Tolstoi; A Man of Peace, Chicago, [1900].
The Lover's World; A Wheel of Life, Chicago, [1903].

STOCKING, AMER MILLS (Sept. 26, 1858–March 31, 1943), clergyman, was born near North Madison, Geauga County. He graduated from National Normal University, Lebanon, in 1884 and taught school for several years. After becoming a clergyman in 1885, he served as pastor of several Methodist churches in Illinois. He published poetical paraphrases of Biblical stories and a "metrical epic": *The Saukie Indians and Their Great Chiefs Black Hawk and Keokuk,* Rock Island, Ill., 1926.

STOLL, ELMER EDGAR (Feb. 11, 1874–May 24, 1959), educator, was born in Orrville, Wayne County. He graduated from University of Wooster in 1893 and Harvard University (Ph.D.) in 1895 and afterward studied in Germany. He taught English at Western Reserve University, 1906–12, and the University of Minnesota, 1914–42. Though specializing in Shakespeare, he published a number of influential articles and books on varied literary subjects, e.g., *From Shakespeare to Joyce . . . ,* New York, 1944. WW 30

STONE, JAMES KENT (Nov. 10, 1840–Oct. 14, 1921), clergyman, born in Boston, lived in Gambier for five years, 1863–68. While teaching Latin at Kenyon College, he studied theology and became an Episcopal clergyman. Named president of the college in 1867, he resigned the following year because his high-church leanings were incompatible with local conditions. In 1869 after the death of his wife, he became a Roman Catholic, and in 1872 he was ordained to the priesthood. Numerous editions were printed of his volume written after his conversion: *The Invitation Heeded . . . ,* London, 1870.

STONE, JULIUS FREDERICK (June 1, 1855–July 25, 1947), was born near Devil's Lake, Mich. He was in the coal business in Columbus, 1885–1903, and afterward was an official of the Seagrave Co., manufacturers of fire engines. He died in Santa Monica, Calif., at the age of 92. An active explorer of the Grand Canyon and other regions, he wrote a book about his explorations along the Colorado River: *Canyon Country; The Romance of a Drop of Water and a Grain of Sand,* New York, 1932. WWW 2

STONE, MARY AMELIA BOOMER (June 19, 1823– ?), was born in Sutton, Mass. She married Andros B. Stone of Charlton, Mass., and in 1858 they settled in Cleveland. The subject of her first book was her brother, who was killed in the Civil War.

Memoir of George Boardman Boomer . . . , Boston, 1864.
Development of Painting in the 16th Century . . . , Chicago, 1885.
A Summer in Scandinavia, New York, [1885].

STOOKESBURY, SINA ETHEL (March 27, 1879–Dec. 13, 1951), was born in Fairfield, Columbiana County. Her lifetime was spent in Columbiana and Carroll Counties. She was a piano teacher for a number of years. She published two volumes of poetry, e.g., *Given Gold,* [Akron, 1913].

STORER, BELLAMY (Aug. 28, 1847–Nov. 12, 1922), lawyer, congressman, and diplomat, was born in Cincinnati, Hamilton County, the son of a distinguished lawyer and judge bearing the same name. He graduated from Harvard College in 1867 and the law school of Cincinnati College in 1869. He practiced law in Cincinnati and served two terms in Congress, 1891–95. In 1886 he married Maria Longworth Nichols, widow of George Ward Nichols (q.v.). He and his wife were converted to Catholicism in 1896. An active supporter of William McKinley, he was made minister to Belgium in 1897 and later served in Spain, 1899–1902, and Austria-Hungary, 1902–06. The evidence indicates that President Theodore Roosevelt removed him from the latter post after realizing the impropriety of a Presidential hint that Archbishop Ireland be made a cardinal. Storer presented his side of the controversy in *Letter . . . to the President and the Members of His Cabinet . . . ,* [Cincinnati?, 1906]. DAB 18

STORER, ELROY TEMPLIN (Aug. 16, 1884–Aug. 17, 1955), physician, was born in Seaman, Adams County. He graduated from Miami University in 1907 and the medical school of the University of Cincinnati in 1911. After practicing for five years at Rockford, he settled in Middletown, where he practiced for the remainder of his life and took an active part in civic affairs. He published a collection of verse: *They Made the News,* Philadelphia, 1943.

STORER, MARIA LONGWORTH NICHOLS (March 20, 1849–April 30, 1932), was born in Cincinnati, Hamilton County, the daughter of Joseph and Annie Reeves Longworth. In 1868 she married George Ward Nichols (q.v.), president of Cincinnati College of Music. Interested in all phases of Cincinnati's cultural life, she founded Rookwood Potteries in 1880. Her husband died in 1895, and the following year she married Bellamy Storer (q.v.). She died in Paris, France, where she had lived for some time with her niece, the Countess de Chambrun (q.v.). Mrs. Storer published a number of novels, e.g., *Probation,* St. Louis, Mo., 1916.

STORMS, ALBERT BOYNTON (April 1, 1860–July 1, 1933), Methodist clergyman and educator, born in Lima, Mich., was president of Baldwin-Wallace College, 1918–1933. His writings include *The Master Secret,* Cincinnati, [1913]. WWW 1

STOTT, ROSCOE GILMORE (Oct. 29, 1880–Jan. 12, 1957), born in Franklin, Ind., was on the faculty of the Ohio School of the Air, 1930–33, and lived in Cincinnati until about 1945. A popular lecturer and a prolific writer, he has published many books, e.g., a book of poems: *The Man Sings,* Cincinnati, [1914]; a book on Americanization: *The Smiths Discover America . . .* , Chicago, [1920]; and a religious novel: *Doorway to Dawn,* Grand Rapids, Mich., 1940. WWW 3

STOUGH, HENRY WELLINGTON (Aug. 15, 1870–Oct. 27, 1939), clergyman and evangelist, was born in Pulaski, Williams County. After studying at Oberlin College, Moody Bible Institute, and Chicago Theological Seminary, he was ordained to the Congregational ministry in 1896. In 1901 he began conducting evangelistic services and lecturing. His books include *Across the Dead Line of Amusements,* New York, [1912]. WWW 1

STOVER, ROSS HARRISON (Nov. 30, 1888–), clergyman, was born in Mechanicsburg, Champaign County; when he was five, his family moved to Springfield, where he attended public school and graduated from Wittenberg College in 1912. After being ordained in 1915 he served a pastorate in Wapakoneta. In 1919 he became pastor of Messiah Lutheran Church in Philadelphia. His writings include *What Do We Know about Life after Death? . . .* , Grand Rapids, Mich., [1941]. RLA 2

STOWE, ANSEL ROY MONROE (Aug. 30, 1882–July 16, 1952), educator, born in Walkerton, Ind., graduated from Harvard University in 1905 and Columbia University (Ph.D.) in 1909. He served as president of the University of Toledo, 1914–25. He published several studies of higher education, e.g., *Modernizing the College,* New York, 1926. WWW 3

STOWE, CALVIN ELLIS (April 26, 1802–Aug. 22, 1886), educator, born in Natick, Mass., was on the faculty of Lane Seminary, Cincinnati, 1833–50. A graduate of Bowdoin College and Andover Seminary, he was versed in several languages. In 1834, his wife, Eliza Tyler Stowe, died; and on Jan. 6, 1836, he married Harriet Beecher, daughter of Lyman Beecher, the president of the seminary (qq.v.). In 1850 he accepted a call to Bowdoin College, where he remained two years. He taught at Andover Seminary, 1852–64, after which he and his wife lived in Hartford. He is generally believed to have encouraged her writing and occasionally to have suggested themes and characters. Calvin Stowe's chief service to the State of Ohio was in the field of public education. He assisted in founding the College of Teachers in Cincinnati in 1833. In 1836 he went abroad to purchase books for Lane Seminary and to investigate the public school systems of Europe. His report, published in 1837, was distributed to every school district in Ohio and did much to encourage the establishment of common schools.

Introduction to the Criticism and Interpretation of the Bible, Cincinnati, 1835.

Report on Elementary Education in Europe . . . , Columbus, 1837.

A Letter to R. D. Mussey, M.D., on the Utter Groundlessness of All the Millennial Arithmetic, Cincinnati, 1843.

Origin and History of the Books of the Bible . . . , Hartford, Conn., 1867.

STOWE, HARRIET ELIZABETH BEECHER (June 14, 1811–July 1, 1896), was born in Litchfield, Conn. Over a hundred years ago, "a little bit of a woman . . . about as thin and dry as a pinch of snuff" sat on the back steps of her Brunswick, Maine, home in order to escape the noise of her six boisterous children and began to scribble away in the hope of selling a few scenes of life in Ohio. She needed enough money to buy a silk dress to wear on the Sabbath like other Bowdoin College faculty wives. The scratches of her quill pen were kindling a little fire that was destined to flare into a holocaust that would envelop the nation. To Harriet Beecher Stowe, as her pen raced on, recollections of Ohio brought little happiness. Her eighteen years in Cincinnati had ended in disillusionment and tragedy. Her father, America's greatest preacher, Lyman Beecher (q.v.), had dreamed of bringing New England's light and learning to the "benighted West" when he made his "hegira" in 1832 with his large family from Litchfield, Conn., in order to guide and direct the newly established Lane Seminary in the Queen City of the West. But during his incumbency the Presbyterian Synod was rent by differences over dogma. Only by scouring the woods of Ohio and the neighboring states had the dynamic orator been able to secure enough students to keep the little institution in Walnut Hills operating. The most distinguished of its professors, America's authority on Biblical exegesis, Calvin Stowe (q.v.), could earn only a thousand dollars a year from his teaching. Western Female Seminary, the school for young ladies so hopefully established by the already famous Catherine Beecher (q.v.) with the help of her sister Harriet, had passed into other management and been forced to close its doors. Catherine had gone off lecturing on education, merely lending the use of her name to the school where she had hoped her younger sister might be able to earn her salt. The younger sister had seen opportunity beckoning in another direction. Her best friend, Eliza Tyler Stowe, had died leaving a widower who needed secretarial help with his Biblical studies. Harriet had become his amanuensis. Shortly thereafter her marriage to the learned Professor Stowe had ended her association with Western Female Seminary. However, it had not solved her financial problems. The swift coming of six children had but added to them. Harriet had been self-supporting from the age of fourteen when she had gone to Hartford as both teacher and pupil in the first of the many schools her sister Catherine established. There she had acquired facility with pen and brush. That facility had stood her in good stead as the wife of an indigent, though famous, professor. Judge Hall's *Western Monthly Magazine* had continued to print, as it had before her marriage, the "sketches" she wrote, and admiring, or pitying, friends had bought the pictures she painted. But it was only a mite that she had been able to add to the family income. Cincinnati's early literary society, the oddly named Semi-Colon Club, had welcomed into its midst the Beechers and the Stowes, but the great financial crisis of 1837 had ended its activities. Its suspension had left the newcomers from Connecticut longing for the culture of the East and resentful of the "fleshpots" of the West. They had resented, too, the pigs that wandered freely about Porkopolis, as meat-packing Cincinnati came to be called. They also had resented the violence so foreign to the life they had known in the prim villages of Connecticut, violence that had flared again and again in the Western metropolis. Savage mobs had wrecked the shop where James Birney printed his *Philanthropist* and had thrown his presses into the river. It should be noted that Cincinnati, though safeguarded from slavery by the Ordinance of 1787, was nevertheless the gateway to the South and dependent upon that area for much of its financial prosperity. Its people saw little to be gained by tolerating the antislavery agitators. In the early spring of 1850, immediately upon learning of her husband's appointment to Bowdoin, Harriet Stowe had fled from cholera-infested Cincinnati to the salubrious climate of Maine. There as she sat on her back steps in Brunswick, she called to mind stories she had heard in Ohio of pursuit and capture, or escape, of fugitive slaves. She remembered how she and Calvin had had the privacy of their own home invaded by slave hunters who had learned of a runaway employed by the Stowes. She recalled how, in the dead of night, under threat of Federal punishment, Calvin had driven the slave girl far out Montgomery Pike and successfully hidden her in the home of John Van Zandt. She remembered the story John Rankin (q.v.) had told on her visit to Ripley, as he pointed across the Ohio and both of them heard from the Kentucky shore the baying of bloodhounds thwarted in their pursuit by the swirling waters of the river. Harriet recalled with horror the frightfulness of the previous summer in Cincinnati when death in the form of cholera stalked the streets and visited almost every home. She could hear the drivers of the wagons collecting the corpses calling, "Bring out your dead." She lived again the agonizing hours when she watched over her stricken baby boy and could only pray that the death agony would soon be over. She had fled the dread place and hoped longingly for Calvin's safe arrival in Maine at the close of the school year in time to rejoice in the arrival of her seventh child. Meanwhile she wrote like the driving of Jehu—furiously. The fury of a zealot impelled her pen. God wrote the words, she repeatedly said. Harriet had shown years before in 1836 her capacity for being inspired by the wrath of God. She had gone to Cincinnati firmly convinced that public affairs were matters that should be left in the hands of men. Women, following St. Paul's injunction, should not only keep silent in the churches but also should refrain from discussing the political questions of the day even in the privacy of their family circles. The sentiment for the abolition of slavery had been winning converts in the North ever since the New England slave traders had had their business cut off by the prohibition of the importing of slaves after 1808. Harriet had remained aloof from discussions of the subject. William Lloyd Garrison's *Liberator* had not won the support of any of the Beechers. However, when the young bloods of Cincinnati led the mob into Birney's print shop and destroyed his presses, Harriet abandoned her conservative ideas on the position of women. She wrote letters, under the pseudonym of "Franklin," to the editor of the Cincinnati *Journal*. Lane Seminary had tried to keep the Stowes in Cincinnati by offering Calvin half as much again as Bowdoin offered. Calvin was willing, but Harriet was convinced that her pen could bring in enough to justify the removal of the family to New England. The *Geography* that she had written in narrative style was now in its fifth edition, thanks to the use of her well-known sister Catherine's name on the title page. An article called "Uncle Lot," first presented at a meeting of the Semi-Colon Club, had subsequently brought her first prize and fifty dollars in a contest sponsored by Hall's *Western Monthly Magazine*. "Uncle Lot," in which John Erskine said "the heroic flame already burns," had been followed by other sketches of New England life. In 1843 she had succeeded in selling a collection of these stories to Harper's under the title *The Mayflower*. For some years she had been writing sermons and moral advice for newspapers, particularly for Dr. Gamaliel Bailey's *National Era*. So it was that as a regular contributor she had discussed with Dr. Bailey the publication of stories based upon her personal contacts with slavery during her years in the West. The idea for a series of stories dealing with slavery had come to her in a "vision" during church service not long after she went to Maine. Faith in supernatural manifestations was commonplace in the Stowe household. Scriptural authority was the basis of Calvin Stowe's personal conviction of his own psychic powers. Her brother, Henry Ward Beecher (q.v.), had encouraged her in believing she was divinely appointed to reveal the iniquity of slavery. One Sabbath morning at church as Harriet relaxed from her weekday cares of cooking, washing, ironing, scrubbing, and teaching her few private pupils, she heard little the preacher said. She was thinking out a proposed sermonette to be entitled "Earthly Care a Heavenly Discipline." She recalled the slaves as she had seen them at work when she was visiting in Kentucky. Suddenly she saw a "vision," a vision of an aged Negro slave being beaten to death. This Negro became "Uncle Tom" and his story began to develop in the mind of the author. In the days that followed, one picture crowded upon another in the dreaming eyes of the artist-author. She wrote feverishly during every spare moment. Her sketches of slavery in action were eagerly accepted by *National Era*. Dr. Bailey agreed to pay $300 for "three or four sketches." The "three or four" stretched into forty, but the compensation remained unchanged. Carried away by enthusiasm for her subject the usually money-conscious Harriet disregarded the differential between literary effort and financial reward. She felt herself inspired like John on Patmos. She must write what she had seen and heard while she lived in Ohio. God willed that by her pen she should awaken her countrymen to the dreadful cancer that was destroying the nation. The weekly installments of her story rarely failed to reach the publisher on time. In Feb., 1852, Calvin Stowe, as his wife's legal guardian, went to Boston and signed a contract for the publication of her "sketches" which John P. Jewett agreed to bring out in two volumes under the title *Uncle Tom's Cabin*. Another Boston firm, Phillips and Sampson, had earlier refused to consider printing the novel when Catherine Beecher brought it to them. Fear of losing their Southern trade caused them to decline the book that was to bring great riches to those who printed it and reprinted it through the years that followed. John P. Jewett, although influenced to publish it because of his wife's enthusiasm when she read the installments in *National Era,* had so little faith in the success of the book that he tried to persuade Calvin Stowe to pay half the cost of publication. The impecunious Stowe pushed away what would have meant eventually a vast fortune, insisting instead upon a 10 per cent royalty on sales. Harriet, on learning of the signing of the contract, said with delight, "I hope it will make enough so I may have a silk dress." Three thousand copies were sold the day of publication, March 20,

1852. The remaining two thousand vanished the second day. Twenty thousand copies sold in three weeks. Three power presses ran 24 hours a day, but the publisher had to apologize continually for being "thousands of copies behind orders." In eight weeks the book had made literary history in America—a hundred thousand copies had been sold. By the end of the year Jewett announced he had disposed of 305,000 copies. Harriet herself was no mean press agent. She sent complimentary copies to leading literary and political figures in America and England. Well-couched personal letters accompanied her gifts to Sumner, Longfellow, Whittier, Kingsley, Dickens, and Victoria's Prince Consort. An enterprising, if not ethical, young American sent a copy to an English publisher with a request for a recompense of five pounds sterling. That publisher's unauthorized edition proved so profitable that English printers began to rival one another in bringing out both de luxe and inexpensive copies. England's greatest illustrators, including the famous Cruikshank, vied with one another for the privilege of drawing sketches of little Eva and Uncle Tom. A British "railway edition" brought its publisher the sale of 150,000 copies before Christmas of 1852. Only one of the many publishers of *Uncle Tom's Cabin* in England felt any twinges of conscience about making a fortune from the unauthorized printing of the book. That one sent Harriet a donation of 500 pounds. Later when Harriet renewed her copyright she managed to secure recognition of her rights abroad. Printings in various countries of Europe in 1852 brought the total sales to 2,500,000 copies. Pirated translations were made into French, Russian, Swedish, Finnish, Dutch, German, Spanish, Portuguese, and Italian. Word came to Harriet of the appearance of editions in Hungarian, Wallachian, Armenian, Hindu, and Javanese. Rival publishers carried on controversies regarding the correctness of their translations. Tauchnitz brought out an authorized version in German with an introduction by Mrs. Stowe. In America Jewett found it profitable to publish a German edition for the vast numbers of German immigrants who were flooding the country after the futile struggles for freedom in the *Vaterland* in 1848. For the 100,000 who came from Wales into the coal fields of Pennsylvania and Ohio, Robert Everett brought out a Welsh translation without asking the author's permission. Mrs. Stowe realized she had no copyright protection abroad, but she felt she was entitled to royalties on Everett's Welsh edition printed in America. She brought suit against the publisher, but the courts held against her on the grounds that a translation was an original work. The 10 per cent royalty to which Calvin Stowe had agreed brought a handsome revenue to the Stowes from the fabulous number of sales of the one-dollar edition and the dollar-and-a-half de luxe copies. Harriet could afford more than a Sunday-best dress. She needed more, too, for she was deluged with invitations to the most distinguished dwellings in America, aristocratic country homes and town houses in England, and famous literary salons in Paris. In 1952 on the occasion of the hundredth anniversary of the publication of *Uncle Tom's Cabin* a statement appeared in *Publisher's Weekly* that, although no exact figures can be ascertained, the sale of the book at home and abroad has far exceeded that of any other book save the Bible. Before the year 1852 had ended, the New York *Independent* was proclaiming that it had secured the services of Mrs. Harriet Beecher Stowe as a weekly contributor of stories, essays, poems, and sketches to its columns. Harriet had become America's first woman columnist. Every word indited by her pen sold at top-level prices. In quick succession came a series of books. Through her long life she continued to be a contributor to the religious journal *Christian Union.* Her old timidity and conformity to the accepted custom for a wife to be represented in business matters by her husband vanished with the success of *Uncle Tom's Cabin.* Harriet negotiated all contracts, even those for reconstruction of a home in Andover, Mass., where Calvin Stowe had found wider scope for his teaching. Harriet's famous brother, Henry Ward Beecher, thundered from his pulpit against the theater. Nevertheless the nation's most famous actors and actresses were thrilled to have a chance to appear in one or another of the many dramatic versions of *Uncle Tom's Cabin* which soon were playing in every city in the country. But this tremendous theatrical success of the story brought no royalties. Song writers poured forth hundreds of pathetic ditties about the story in the lachrymose fashion of the day. Popular artists at home and abroad vied with one another in painting Eliza's perilous journey across the ice or Uncle Tom reading to little Eva. Every art gallery had at least one "Tom" picture. The reading of *Uncle Tom's Cabin* brought about great interest in the Scriptures. Paris bookstalls were swamped with calls for the Bible, "la Bible véritable de l'Oncle Tom." Men and women who had strayed from orthodoxy sought, like Heinrich Heine, to understand how

Sacred Writ had so transformed and ennobled the life of an almost illiterate slave. Alfred de Musset was so touched by the tale that he influenced cynical French literary critics to weep with him and George Sand over the tender passages. Less than a year after the publication of *Uncle Tom's Cabin,* 500,000 British women who had read the book signed "An Affectionate and Christian Address of Many Thousands of Women of Great Britain and Ireland to their Sisters, the Women of The United States of America." The Queen's closest friend, the Duchess of Sutherland, had secured as co-sponsors of the "Address" the wives of the most prominent men in England. Names such as Palmerston, Tennyson, and Dickens led the list of signers. The 26 folio volumes of signatures were sent to the most widely known woman in the world, Harriet Beecher Stowe. At the invitation of her Scottish admirers Harriet went to Glasgow and from there made a triumphal tour of the British Isles, France, and Italy, a tour that had repercussions on both sides of the Atlantic. Queen Victoria and her Prince Consort had wept over the pages of the lavender-bound volume Harriet had sent them. Without doubt the Queen would have received the famous tourist had diplomatic complications not prevented. On Harriet's next tour an apparently casual meeting at a railway station was contrived. The British Government was keenly aware that it was the slave labor of the South that furnished the raw cotton that was enriching the mill owners of Lancashire. The British Cabinet and Parliament realized that cordial relations with America depended on the delicate balance of power between proslavery and antislavery forces in the Congress of the United States. Therefore, the royal couple might weep over the plight of Eliza and her child teetering on the ice floes in the Ohio River; they might even acknowledge with a nod the presence of Calvin and Harriet Stowe; but they must not by any overt act seem to give recognition to a woman whose inflammatory words were threatening the peace of a sister nation. In writing *Uncle Tom* Mrs. Stowe undoubtedly meant to give a true picture of slavery in action, showing both the kindly parental attitude of some masters and mistresses and the inhuman cruelty of those who regarded the slaves as chattels. She contrasted Uncle Tom's humility with George Harris' determination to rebel against the institution that embittered his life. She made her most despicable character, the slave driver Simon Legree, a man from Vermont, not from the South. A prim New England spinster is the one who brings out Topsy's perverseness. The angel of the book is a little Southern girl. Unquestionably Mrs. Stowe had strong convictions on the subject of slavery. Her experiences in Cincinnati had filled her with indignation against the institution. She saw a chance to picture a phase of American life new to fiction and at the same time call attention to the iniquity of holding human beings in bondage. Her Connecticut Yankee acumen joined with her New England conscience in producing the book. Its phenomenal success transformed her into the "crusader in crinoline" known to history. In *Uncle Tom's Cabin* the abolitionists found a weapon far more powerful than all the tracts put out by Birney and Garrison. This tale of sale "down the river" with its disregard of family ties touched the hearts of the American people as perfervid oratory never had. It awakened the nation's conscience to a determination to destroy the canker in the land of the free. Men and women, boys and girls (Harriet brought out a shortened version for children) swore to die if necessary to break the chains of slavery. Sumner and Seward and Lincoln raised their voices against the evil. Henry Ward Beecher thundered in his pulpit as did many another divine. But far more effective than all of these was the novel wept over by millions of Americans in the quiet of their homes. The Great Emancipator himself greeted Harriet as the "little lady who made this big war." In the South Mrs. Stowe herself symbolized the wickedness of the North in attacking the fundamental right of private property guaranteed by the Constitution. No words were too bitter to apply to the woman who was inflaming the world against the proprietors of the great plantations in Georgia, Alabama, Mississippi, Tennessee, and the Carolinas. In less than ten years after the publication of *Uncle Tom* thousands of men were dying "to make men free." The government warred against the secession of the Southern States; but the men who defended that government with their lives fought to break the chains that bound a lovable slave and to still the baying of hounds pursuing a devoted wife fleeing to the land of freedom. The simple, direct telling of the tale made it understandable to the semiliterate as well as to the erudite. The power of the tale to sway men's minds and direct their actions lay in Mrs. Stowe's ability to portray in words the pictures she saw in her mind's eye. Since 1852 millions of readers have thrilled to this tale of "Life among the Lowly," the subtitle Calvin Stowe gave the book. The crusade inspired by the lady who succeeded in draping over her crinoline the most expensive of silks goes on in this country as the children and grandchildren and great-grandchildren of former slaves struggle with ever-increasing success for complete integration into the broad stream of American life. Today few Americans read the book. Negro children may perchance attend a school called the Harriet Beecher Stowe School, but scarcely one of them reads the story that played such an important role in the history of the race. Those who do read the book delight in its vivid pictures, but the stirring appeal of *Uncle Tom's Cabin* has gone with the days of long ago that it portrays. Slavery in America is no more. In the lands behind the Iron Curtain the book unfortunately is playing a part in the Cold War. *Uncle Tom's Cabin* is being used as a weapon against the United States. Since the end of World War II new translations of the novel have appeared in Russia, Poland, and Bulgaria. In the Middle East an Arabic version made its appearance in 1954, advertised as a picture of the life of the Negro in America. The subtitle *Life among the Lowly* has been made to have a definite appeal to a class-conscious proletariat. In lands where the lowly know little of American life of today, designing dictators can present the pathetic story of Uncle Tom with powerful effect upon those who still remember the sting of the knout of Czarist days in Holy Russia.

Alma M. Bevis

The Mayflower: Or, Sketches of Scenes and Characters among the Descendants of the Pilgrims, New York, 1843.
Uncle Tom's Cabin; Or, Life among the Lowly, Boston, 1852.
A Key to Uncle Tom's Cabin . . . , Boston, 1853.
Uncle Sam's Emancipation . . . , Philadelphia, 1853.
Sunny Memories of Foreign Lands, 2 vols., Boston, 1854.
The Christian Slave. A Drama Founded on a Portion of Uncle Tom's Cabin . . . , Boston, 1855.
Geography for My Children, Boston, 1855.
The Two Altars; Or, Two Pictures in One, [New York, 1855].
Dred; A Tale of the Great Dismal Swamp, 2 vols., Boston, 1856.
The Minister's Wooing, New York, 1859.
Agnes of Sorrento, Boston, 1862.
The Pearl of Orr's Island . . . , Boston, 1862.
Little Foxes, Boston, 1866.
House and Home Papers, Boston, 1867.
Queer Little People, Boston, 1867.
Religious Poems, Boston, 1867.
The Chimney-Corner, Boston, 1868.
Men of Our Times . . . , Hartford, Conn., 1868.
Oldtown Folks, Boston, 1869.
Lady Byron Vindicated . . . , Boston, 1870.
My Wife and I . . . , New York, 1871.
Pink and White Tyranny. A Society Novel, Boston, 1871.
Palmetto-Leaves, Boston, 1873.
Women in Sacred History . . . , New York, 1874.
We and Our Neighbors . . . , New York, [1875].
Betty's Bright Idea . . . , New York, 1876.
Footsteps of the Master . . . , New York, 1877.
Poganuc People . . . , New York, [1878].
A Dog's Mission . . . , New York, 1881.

STRAIN, FRANCES BRUCE (1892–), educator, born in Milwaukee, Wis., lived in Ohio for about ten years. She was a lecturer on sex education for the Cleveland Community Chest, 1929–30, and director of sex education for the Cincinnati Social Hygiene Society, 1930–38. She has written a number of books on love and marriage, e.g., *Love at the Threshold* . . . , New York, 1939. WW 30

STRAIN, RODNEY (Feb. 14, 1841–1910), was born in London, Madison County, the son of a doctor. After serving in the Civil War, he moved to Logansport, Ind., in 1866. He operated a drugstore, 1866–85, and was a funeral director, 1885–1910. He served as trustee, elder, and clerk of session at First Presbyterian Church.

History of the First Presbyterian Church of Logansport . . . , Logansport, 1898.

STRANATHAN, MAY (Dec. 12, 1865–July 29, 1952), was born near Cumberland, Guernsey County, and spent most of her life in that community. She was a reporter for the Pittsburgh *Dispatch* for about ten years and for the Honolulu *Advertiser* for two. She published a short novel with an Ohio background: *The Huff Case,* Boston, [1912].

STRATTON, CLARENCE (Sept. 17, 1880–Sept. 13, 1951), educator, born in Philadelphia, Pa., was director of English in the Cleveland high schools, 1921–46. After his retirement he continued to live in Cleveland. He died at Boothbay Harbor, Maine. He published a number of English textbooks and several adventure novels, e.g., *Swords and Statues* . . . , Philadelphia, [1937]. WWW 3

STRATTON, JENNIE M. (? – ?), was born near Salem, Columbiana County. She came to Cleveland in 1879 and was active as a mission worker, temperance advocate, and writer of juvenile stories.

Kitty's Jewels, Cleveland, 1890.
Cecil's Crown, Cleveland, 1891.

STRAUCH, ADOLPHUS (Aug. 30, 1822–April 25, 1883), was born in Eikersdorf, Silesia. He was trained at Botanical Gardens, London, and after coming to Cincinnati he landscaped several large estates; but his major work was at Spring Grove Cemetery, where he became superintendent in 1860.

Spring Grove Cemetery: Its History and Improvements . . . , Cincinnati, 1869.

STRAUSS, JOSEPH BAERMANN (Jan. 9, 1870–May 16, 1938), engineer, was born in Cincinnati, Hamilton County, the son of a portrait painter. He graduated from the University of Cincinnati in 1892 with a degree in engineering. He was associated with various Chicago engineering firms. Widely known for designing the Golden Gate Bridge, San Francisco, he also originated improvements in bascule bridges. He died in Los Angeles. Besides writing a technical work on bascule bridges, he contributed poems and essays to various periodicals; a collection of his writings was published: *By-Products of Idle Hours,* [Chicago, 1921]. DAB 22

STRAUSS, MOSES (Nov. 9, 1872–July 14, 1938), journalist, born in Keokuk, Iowa, was educated in Cincinnati. He worked on several Cincinnati newspapers and was managing editor, Cincinnati *Times-Star,* 1923–37. His writings include a pamphlet, *What's the News?,* [New York], 1928. WWW 1

STREATOR, MARTIN LYMAN (Nov. 12, 1843–July 22, 1926), clergyman, was born in Pennsylvania. He lived in Cleveland for a number of years, serving as a minister of the Christian Church. His death occurred in Cleveland.

The Anglo-American Alliance in Prophecy . . . , New Haven, Conn., 1900.

STREET, ELWOOD VICKERS (Nov. 23, 1890–), social worker, was born in Cleveland, Cuyahoga County. He worked on the Cleveland *Leader,* 1907–13, and graduated from Western Reserve University in 1912. He has served as director of community funds and welfare in various American cities. He has published several textbooks in social work and *Sympathy and System in Giving,* Chicago, 1921. WW 30

STREETER, JOHN WILLIAM (Sept. 17, 1841–June 4, 1905), physician, was born in Austinburg, Ashtabula County, the son of a Congregational clergyman. In 1851 the family moved to Henrietta, N. Y., but four years later they returned to Ohio when the father accepted a professorship at Otterbein University. After teaching school in western Indiana for four years, John served with the First Michigan Light Artillery, 1862–65. He studied medicine at the University of Michigan and Hahnemann Medical College, Chicago, 1865–68. He was a founder of Chicago Homeopathic College in 1877, served on the staffs of several hospitals in Chicago, and in 1888 established Streeter Hospital. He died at his summer home in Lake Forest, Ill. He published two novels: *Doctor Tom,* New York, 1904, and *The Fat of the Land . . . ,* New York, 1904.

STRICKLAND, WILLIAM PETER (Aug. 17, 1809–July 15, 1884), clergyman, born in Pittsburgh, graduated from Ohio University and afterward was an itinerant Methodist minister in Ohio for several years. He later was an agent of the American Bible Society. From 1856 until his death he lived in New York City, where he preached and did editorial work. He was a prolific writer of books on religious and historical subjects, e.g., *The Genius and Mission of Methodism,* Boston, 1851.

STROHM, ISAAC (Dec. 11, 1810– ?), born in Pennsylvania, came to Ohio in 1835. He lived in Butler County and in Bath Township, Greene County. He was employed in the U. S. Treasury Department, 1850–55, and for a few months was confidential clerk of Thomas Corwin (q.v.). He wrote a memoir of Corwin to accompany the edition of his speeches.

Speeches of Thomas Corwin . . . , Dayton, 1859.

STRONG, ANNA LOUISE (Nov. 8, 1885–), journalist, born in Friend, Neb., lived in Ohio for a few years during her childhood. She graduated from Oberlin College in 1905. As a representative of various newspapers and press associations, she visited Russia several times; in 1930 she founded the Moscow *Daily News,* an English-language newspaper. She now lives in Peiping, China. She has written a number of books, e.g., *Spain in Arms,* New York, [1937]. WW 24

STRONG, AUGUSTUS HOPKINS (Aug. 3, 1836–Nov. 29, 1921), clergyman, born in Rochester, N. Y., was pastor of First Baptist Church, Cleveland, 1865–72, where John D. Rockefeller (q.v.) was one of his congregation. Later, while Strong was working for a Baptist university in New York, he introduced Rockefeller to William Rainey Harper (q.v.) and thus indirectly assisted the founding of the University of Chicago. He published several influential theological works and some books for general readers, e.g., *The Great Poets and Their Theology,* Philadelphia, 1897.

STRONG, ELEANOR PAINTER (Sept. 12, 1891–Nov. 3, 1947), singer, born in Walkerville, Iowa, lived in Cleveland from 1931 until her death. Between 1913 and 1931 she sang in numerous operas and operettas in Europe and America. Victor Herbert is said to have written *Princess Pat* for her. She retired after her marriage to Major Charles H. Strong, and after her retirement she was active in Cleveland musical organizations. Under her maiden name she published a historical novel based on the life of Robert Schumann: *Spring Symphony,* Toronto, [1941].

STRONG, GEORGE AUGUSTUS (1832–March 6, 1912), clergyman, was born in Norwich, Conn. After graduating from Kenyon College, he worked in a bank for a time. He was prominent in literary circles of Cincinnati and was known throughout Ohio as a humorous poet. He attended Virginia Theological Seminary and was ordained as an Episcopal priest. After serving churches in Pennsylvania and Ohio, he was on the Kenyon College faculty, 1868–79. He became rector of Christ Church, New Bedford, Mass., after leaving Kenyon and remained there until retiring from the ministry in 1888. His parody of Longfellow's *Hiawatha,* which also satirizes hydropathy, was published under the pen name Marc Antony Henderson, Jr. In the second edition (1856), it was renamed *The Song of Milkenwatha.*

The Song of Milgenwater: Translated from the Original Feejee, Cincinnati, 1856.
Songs of the Pacific . . . , San Francisco, 1889.

STRONG, JOSIAH (Jan. 19, 1847–April 28, 1916), clergyman, was born in Naperville, Ill. In 1852 his parents moved to Hudson, where he graduated from Western Reserve College in 1869. After studying at Lane Seminary, he became a Congregational minister in Wyoming in 1871. He served as chaplain at Western Reserve, 1873–76, was a pastor in Sandusky, 1876–81, was secretary of home mission work in Ohio, Kentucky, and Virginia, 1881–84, and in 1884 became pastor of a church in Cincinnati. His book *Our Country,* which demanded that the church concern itself with social problems, made him nationally famous, and he was in great demand as a lecturer. He served as secretary of the American Evangelical Alliance, but when it proved too conservative he formed the League for Social Service. He lectured on social issues throughout the United States and Europe. An important pioneer in the Social Gospel movement, he was also a zealous supporter of American expansionism; and he is remembered today chiefly for his views on Anglo-Saxon superiority and manifest destiny.

Our Country: Its Possible Future and Its Present Crisis, New York, 1885.
The New Era . . . , New York, [1893].
The Twentieth Century City, New York, [1898].
Expansion under New World Conditions, New York, [1900].
Religious Movements for Social Betterment, New York, [1900].
The Times and Young Men, New York, [1901].
The Next Great Awakening, New York, 1902.
The Challenge of the City, New York, [1907].
My Religion in Everyday Life, New York, 1910.
Our World, 2 vols., New York, 1913–15.

STRONG, SIDNEY DIX (Jan. 25, 1860–Dec. 30, 1938), clergyman, was born in Seville, Medina County. He graduated from Oberlin College in 1881 and from the seminary in 1884. He later served as a pastor in Ohio, Illinois, Washington, and Australia, 1887–1922. He was an associate editor of *Unity* and correspondent for the Melbourne *Age.* Besides the titles below, he published sermons and edited several anthologies.

The Child in the Midst . . . , Chicago, [1896].
Talks to Boys and Girls . . . , Chicago, 1902.
The Cradle Child; Or, an Epic of the Life of God . . . , Seattle, [1912].

STUART, GORDON. Pseud. See Harry L. Sayler.

STUART, GRAHAM HENRY (Jan. 27, 1887–), educator, was born in Cleveland, Cuyahoga County. He graduated from Western Reserve University in 1908 and the University of Wisconsin (Ph.D.) in 1918. He was professor of political science, Stanford University, 1924–52. He wrote a number of books on diplomacy and foreign policy, e.g., *American Diplomatic and Consular Practice,* New York, [1936]. WW 30

STUCKENBERG, JOHN HENRY WILBRANDT (Jan. 6, 1835–May 28, 1903), clergyman and educator, was born in Hanover, Germany, but was brought to America when he was four years old. He grew up in Pittsburgh and Cincinnati and graduated from Wittenberg College in 1857. After studying theology there for an additional year, he was ordained to the Lutheran ministry. He served churches in Davenport, Iowa, and Pittsburgh, and in Europe. He was on the faculty of Wittenberg College, teaching theology and sociology, 1873–80. He made numerous trips to Germany, his longest stay being fourteen years as pastor of the American Church in Berlin, 1880–94. A pioneer in the idea of a Social Gospel, he also specialized in international law and the need for peace among nations. His social thinking is summed up in his statement, "The church must be the embodiment of the social principles and practices of the New Testament." A prolific writer, he produced many articles and books, including the first biography of Immanuel Kant in English: *The Life of Immanuel Kant,* London, 1882. His most significant work was *Sociology, the Science of Human Society,* 2 vols., New York, 1903.

STUDER, JACOB HENRY (Feb. 26, 1840–1904), publisher, was born in Columbus, Franklin County. After attending Columbus schools, he became a printer. In 1872 he founded the Board of Trade in Columbus. In 1878 he began publishing in Columbus several ornithological works drawn from the texts of established ornithologists. He later moved to New York City, where he published books under the aegis of the so-called Natural Science Association of America, of which he was president.

Columbus, Ohio; Its History, Resources and Progress, [Columbus, 1873].

Studer's Popular Ornithology . . . , Columbus, 1878.

The Birds of North America . . . , New York, 1888.

STUHLDREHER, HARRY A. (Oct. 14, 1901–), was born in Massillon, Stark County. He graduated in 1925 from the University of Notre Dame, where he was one of Knute Rockne's famed "four horsemen." After serving as football coach at Villanova College, 1925–36, and the University of Wisconsin, 1936–50, he took a position with U. S. Steel Corporation. He wrote a biography of his college coach: *Knute Rockne, Man Builder,* Philadelphia, [1931]. WW 28

STURGEON, MRS. CLIFFORD B. (Sept. 28, 1907–Feb. 21, 1954), was born in Newark, Licking County. After graduating from Ohio State University in 1929, she did publicity work in Hollywood, Calif., and was an assistant librarian in Newark. She was also treasurer of a ceramic tile company in Huntington Beach, Calif. Under her maiden name, Molly E. Corne, she wrote several mystery novels, e.g., *Death at the Manor,* New York, [1938].

STURTEVANT, JULIAN MONSON (July 26, 1805–Feb. 11, 1886), educator, born in Warren, Conn., lived in Tallmadge, 1816–22, where he attended an academy. After graduating from Yale University, he was on the faculty of Illinois College, Jacksonville, 1831–85, serving as president, 1844–76. He published addresses, occasionally contributed articles to religious periodicals, and wrote two books. Ten years after his death, his son edited his autobiography: *Julian M. Sturtevant. An Autobiography,* New York, [1896].

SULLIVAN, OSCAR MATTHIAS (Jan. 2, 1881–Feb. 16, 1955), lawyer, was born in Canal Fulton, Stark County. He graduated from Ohio State University in 1905, worked on the *Ohio State Journal* and taught school for a number of years, and graduated from Minnesota College of Law in 1923. He practiced law and served on various government agencies until his retirement in 1951. He wrote two books on the rehabilitation of disabled persons and a biographical novel about James J. Hill: *The Empire-Builder . . . ,* New York, [1928]. WWW 3

SULLIVANT, JOSEPH (Dec. 3, 1809–June 23, 1882), brother of William S. Sullivant (q.v.), was born in Franklinton, Franklin County. He attended Ohio University and Centre College, Ky. He was one of the founders of the Historical and Philosophical Society of Ohio and for half a century took an active interest in all of the scientific and literary enterprises of Columbus. Besides the title below, he published a family history and a catalogue of shells and fossils.

Historical Sketch Relating to the Original Boundaries and Early Times of Franklin County . . . , Columbus, 1871.

SULLIVANT, WILLIAM STARLING (Jan. 15, 1803–April 30, 1873), was born in the small, rough wilderness town of Franklinton in the Virginia Military District on the west bend of the Scioto River near its junction with the Olentangy, a region otherwise known as the "Forks of the Scioto." Six years earlier, Lucas Sullivant, William's father and the town's proprietor, had founded Franklinton, and tradition has it that William was the first white child born there. A physician was summoned from Cincinnati to attend Sarah Starling Sullivant, his mother, and his birth took place in the town's first brick home. In 1803, at the first state legislature in Chillicothe, the county of Franklin was created and Franklinton was made the county seat. One of Lucas' larger ambitions for his town was thereby realized, and during the following years a jail, church, school, courthouse, and other log buildings, together with roads and bridges, were constructed, most of them by him. Another ambition was realized only in part. Four centrally located lots were dedicated, at least for a time, "for public Buildings only, that is, for a State house or Courthouse and as Commons." The home of William's birth was built near there. But a state house was never built because in 1812 "the permanent seat" of Ohio's government was established by the legislature on "lands, situated on the east bank of the Scioto River, opposite Franklinton." Lucas, with the aid of his newly acquired wealth, joined with Lyne Starling, his brother-in-law, and other members of a syndicate of landowners on the High Bank opposite Franklinton; and a new town, soon called Columbus, became the site of the new state capital. After many years the county seat was transferred to Columbus, which absorbed Franklinton. William's father had been born in Mecklenburg County, Va., but while a young man he had migrated to Washington, Ky., where in the midst of quite an aristocratic community he followed several occupations, chiefly that of surveyor. His lifelong friend and father-in-law, Colonel William Starling, also migrated with his family from Virginia to a plantation near Harrodsburg, Ky.; and to the care of his grandfather, William at the age of eight or nine was sent for his lower school education. William probably attended for about six years a celebrated private academy maintained by the prominent educator Samuel Wilson in Jessamine County, where sons of some of the best families of Kentucky received their early education. During the summer of 1818 he may also have attended Transylvania University, and the following year he completed at Ohio University his preparation for Yale College, where he registered as a student in Nov., 1819. His journey from Franklinton to New Haven was made by horseback, and only one classmate resided west of the Allegheny Mountains. His courses for the most part were classical rather than scientific, and although he planned to take graduate study, he was called home the year of his graduation by the death of his father. He and his two brothers, Michael and Joseph, divided their father's large estate, and for years he was absorbed in his own interests in stage coach, canal, and turnpike companies, banks, grain and lumber mills, stone quarries, real estate, and farms. In 1824 he married Jane Marshall, daughter of Alexander Keith Marshall of Kentucky, niece of Chief Justice John Marshall; but within a year, delicate in health and still in her teens, she died soon after the birth of their child. Until 1834 he remained a widower and then married Eliza Griscom Wheeler of New York. At this time he built his beautiful home on "Sullivant Hill" west of Franklinton and began to retire from business to devote more time to studying the sciences: ornithology, conchology, and, pre-eminently, botany. About 1838 he established a scientific correspondence with America's leading botanists, John Torrey and Asa Gray, and the science of botany which theretofore had been a delightful pastime became a sincere avocation. He and Mrs. Sullivant studied the flowering plants of Ohio, and by 1840 he published *A Catalogue of Plants in the Vicinity of Columbus* and in 1842 an "Account of Three Undescribed Plants of Central Ohio." Seven years later, he completed for T. G. Lea his *Catalogue of Plants Collected in the Vicinity of Cincinnati.* A saxifragaceous genus and species, *Sullivantia Sullivantii,* was named by Asa Gray in honor of Mr. and Mrs. Sullivant's discovery of the plant in Highland County in 1840. When in 1850 Mrs. Sullivant died of cholera, a wreath of this plant in flower was carved in marble on her tombstone. He later married his wife's niece, Caroline Sutton, who bore him several children. Unlike Eliza, she was never his co-worker in botany. During 1839–40 Sullivant attempted to study fungi and lichens and cryptogamia other than the mosses; but, while grasses and sedges were also objects of interest, he soon made mosses and hepatics his specialties. Writing of his total work on mosses, Gray told Charles Darwin in 1877 that Sullivant had done "for muscology in this country more than one man is likely ever to do again."

Before the Ohio Academy of Science in 1911, Dr. T. C. Mendenhall characterized Sullivant as having become "the foremost authority as a bryologist in this country, without a superior anywhere in the world." Gray regarded Sullivan's exsiccate sets, *Musci Alleghanienses* (1845), as laying "the foundation for the study of North American Muscology" in America. To Gray's famous *Manual of the Botany of the Northern United States,* Sullivant contributed the work on mosses and hepatics. Sullivant prepared the musci for the botanical work of the United States Exploring Expedition in the South Pacific Islands under Commander Wilkes (1838–42). Other important American exploring expeditions chose him for systematic determinations of their moss and hepatic materials: for example, Commodore Perry's expedition to the China Seas and Japan; Charles Wright's collections on the North Pacific Exploring Expedition under Captain Rodgers; Lt. Whipple's explorations and surveys near the 35th parallel to determine a railroad route from the Mississippi River to the Pacific Ocean; and the similar explorations in California and Oregon under Lieutenants Williamson and Abbott. Collections of many individual explorers—Wright, Parry, Fendler, Lindheimer, Spruce, and others—reached Sullivant; and he was able to determine the moss species of many interesting floral regions: Cuba, northern South America, and a multitude of other localities in the Western Hemisphere. State geological surveys sent collections: for instance, M. A. Curtis from the North Carolina survey and D. D. Owen and C. C. Parry from their survey in Wisconsin, Iowa, Minnesota, and Nebraska. Sullivant's work was recognized abroad. Abundant exchanges of plant specimens with leading bryologists and botanists there enhanced the value and extent of his herbarium, all or most of which he bequeathed to Harvard University. This constitutes today an important part of the Farlow Herbarium of cryptogamic botany there. He was honored by memberships in Phi Beta Kappa (1823), the Academy of Natural Sciences of Philadelphia (1884), the American Academy of Arts and Sciences (1845), the American Philosophical Society (1862), the National Academy of Sciences (1872), and other scientific societies. Sullivan's greatest work, *Icones Muscorum* (1864), was illustrated by 129 copperplates and was received "as a work of art as well as of science" and "the most exquisite of all illustrated bryological works." His *Supplement to the Icones Muscorum* (1874) and his *Manual of the Mosses of North America* (1895) were published posthumously, the former completed by Leo Lesquereux (q.v.) and the latter published under the names of Lesquereux and Thomas P. James.

Andrew D. Rodgers, III

SUMMERBELL, NICHOLAS (March 8, 1816–Jan. 4, 1889), clergyman, was born in Westchester, N. Y. After working as a tailor in New York City, he studied for the ministry and was ordained in the Christian Church in 1839. In 1850 he moved to Cincinnati, where he served as pastor of the First Christian Church. He was later a pastor in Dayton and served in other pulpits in the area. He edited the autobiography of Elder Matthew Gardner (q.v.) and is said to have written a large number of religious tracts, copies of which have not been found. He died in Yellow Springs.

Discussion on the Trinity . . . , Cincinnati, 1855.

Some Notes of the Life and Some of the Writings of Nicholas Summerbell, Dayton, 1900.

SUMNER, CLARENCE WESLEY (May 2, 1885–Nov. 21, 1952), librarian, born in Noblesville, Ind., was librarian, Youngstown Public Library, 1926–45, and after his retirement lived at Perrysburg. He published several books on education and children, e.g., *The Birthright of Babyhood,* New York, 1936. WW 27

SUPER, CHARLES WILLIAM (Sept. 12, 1842–Oct. 9, 1939), educator, was born in Pottsville, Pa. He graduated from Dickinson College in 1866 and studied at Tübingen, Germany. From 1872 to 1878 he was professor of languages at Cincinnati Wesleyan College. After a year of reading law, he went to Ohio University as professor of Greek and German. In 1883 he was appointed president, and he served until 1901. In addition to his books, he wrote numerous articles and monographs.

A History of the German Language, Columbus, 1893.

Wisdom and Will in Education, Harrisburg, Pa., 1902.

A Liberal Education . . . , Syracuse, N. Y., 1907.

German Idealism and Prussian Militarism, New York, 1916.

Pan-Prussianism, Its Methods and Its Fruits, New York, 1918.

A Study of a Rural Community, Oberlin, 1922.

A Pioneer College and Its Background [Dickinson], Salem, Mass., 1923.

A Pioneer College and Its Background [Ohio University], Salem, Mass., 1924.
Salt and Potatoes, Salem, Mass., 1927.

SUPLEE, THOMAS DANLY (April 17, 1846–May 2, 1928), Episcopal priest, born in Philadelphia, Pa., was headmaster of Harcourt School, Gambier, 1882–85. He published a collection of poems and a biography: *The Life of Theodorick Bland Pryor . . . ,* San Francisco, 1879.

SUTTON, ADAH LOUISE. See Adah L. S. Saalfield.

SUTTON, JOSEPH JACKSON (June 17, 1842–Dec. 30, 1922), was born in Lawrence County, where he attended the common schools. He served four months in the 87th O.V.I. and later served in the 2nd West Virginia Cavalry, March, 1863–June, 1865. After the Civil War he was in the lumber business in Portsmouth, West Virginia, and North Carolina. He died in Dayton.

History of the Second Regiment West Virginia Volunteers . . . , Portsmouth, 1892.

SWANDER, JOHN I. (May 3, 1833–Jan. 9, 1925), clergyman and educator, born in Hope, N. J., graduated from Heidelberg Seminary in 1859 and afterward served churches in Dayton, Chillicothe, Lancaster, Springfield, and Fremont. He was on the Heidelberg faculty, 1888–1904. Besides the books listed below, several of which are in verse, he published a family history and many sermons and addresses.

The Substantial Philosophy . . . , New York, [1886].
The Reformed Church. A Sketch of Its History . . . , Dayton, [1889].
The Invisible World . . . , Dayton, 1891.
The Evolution of Religion, Philadelphia, 1906.
The Divinity of Our Lord . . . , Cleveland, 1907.
The Mercersburg Theology . . . , Philadelphia, 1909.
Autobiography . . . , Philadelphia, 1911.
Romance in Religion, Tiffin, 1915.
Dr. Swander's Farewell Address, Tiffin, 1916.
The Catholic Church, Tiffin, 1917.
The Christian Life Triumphant in All Saints . . . , Tiffin, 1918.
The Great Apostasy, Tiffin, 1918.
The Blindness and the Blunders of Modern Infidelity, Tiffin, 1919.
The Evolution of a Farmer Boy . . . , Tiffin, 1919.

SWARTWOUT, ANNIE FERN CAMPBELL (June 5, 1888–), was born in Darke County. She is a niece of Annie Oakley and traveled with her for many years. When her aunt died, she wrote a syndicated news story about her. Much later, she published a book about her famous relative: *Missie, an Historical Biography of Annie Oakley,* Blanchester, 1947.

SWARTZ, JOEL (Aug. 18, 1827–1914), clergyman, born in Shenandoah County, Va., graduated from Capital Seminary in 1854. He held Lutheran pastorates in Ohio and was on the Wittenberg College faculty, 1865–68. He published several volumes of poetry, e.g., *Dreamings of the Waking Heart, with Other Poems,* Harrisburg, Pa., 1877.

SWEET, WILLIAM WARREN (Feb. 15, 1881–Jan. 3, 1958), educator, born in Baldwin, Kans., graduated from Ohio Wesleyan University in 1902 and later served on the faculty, 1911–13. An authority on religious movements in America, he served on the University of Chicago faculty, 1927–46, and published numerous articles and several books, e.g., *Circuit-Rider Days in Indiana,* Indianapolis, 1916. WWW 3

SWIFT, EDGAR JAMES (July 24, 1860–Aug. 30, 1932), educator, was born in Ravenna, Portage County. He graduated from Amherst College in 1886, studied in Europe, and obtained his Ph.D. degree from Clark University in 1903. He was in the psychology department of Washington University, 1903–32. His writings include psychology textbooks, articles, and *Mind in the Making . . . ,* New York, 1908. WWW 1

SWIGART, FRANK (1840–1912), was born in Ohio but spent his life in Indiana, where his parents moved when he was two years old. He served in the Civil War with the 46th Indiana Volunteers and later wrote the history of his regiment. He also wrote *Mary Lawson,* Boston, [1909]. IATB

SWIGGETT, HOWARD (Nov. 17, 1892–March 7, 1957), businessman and writer, was born in Ripley, Brown County. He graduated from Yale University in 1914 and served on the Italian front in World War I. He left business in 1940 to join the British Supply Mission. Besides adventure novels and historical works, he wrote three novels about big business, the last of which was published posthumously: *The Durable Fire,* Boston, 1957.

SWINEFORD, ALFRED P. (Sept. 14, 1836–1909), journalist, was born in Ashland, Ashland County. At the age of fifteen he was an apprentice printer on the Ashland *Union,* and in 1853 he went to Fond du Lac, Wis. He worked on various newspapers in Wisconsin, Minnesota, and Michigan. He served as governor of Alaska, 1885–89. His death occurred in Alaska.

Swineford's History of the Lake Superior Iron District . . . , Marquette, 1871.
Alaska—Its History, Climate and Natural Resources, Chicago, [1898].

SWING, ALBERT TEMPLE (Jan. 18, 1849–Sept. 21, 1925), theologian, father of Raymond Gram Swing (q.v.), was born in Bethel, Clermont County. He graduated from Oberlin College in 1874 and Yale Divinity School in 1877 and was ordained to the Congregational ministry in 1878. After serving several pastorates, he was on the faculty of Oberlin Seminary, 1893–1916. He wrote several biographies and historical works relative to church history, e.g., *Outline of the Doctrinal Development of the Western Church* . . . , Oberlin, 1904. WWW 1

SWING, DAVID (Aug. 23, 1830–Oct. 3, 1894), clergyman, was born in Cincinnati, Hamilton County, the son of a river pilot who died of cholera in 1832. His mother married James Hageman, a blacksmith, and David grew up on a farm near Williamsburg, Clermont County. He graduated from Miami University in 1852 and taught Latin and Greek and served as principal of the preparatory department, 1853–66. While at Miami he had studied theology and had supplied nearby Presbyterian churches. In 1866 he accepted a call to Chicago. His sermons were widely reprinted and attracted numerous readers. In 1874 Francis L. Patton, a theological professor, accused him of heresy before the Chicago Presbytery. Although the case, which attracted national attention, ended in the verdict "not proved," he resigned his pulpit in 1875. In the same year the nondenominational Central Church was established, and here he preached to large crowds until his death. His sermons were published separately and in several collections. He was also in great demand as a public speaker, and several addresses were published separately in pamphlet form.

Motives of Life, Chicago, 1879.
Club Essays, Chicago, 1881.
Address to the New Generation . . . , Rockford, Ill., [1888].
Art, Music and Nature . . . , Chicago, 1893.
Old Picture of Life, 2 vols., Chicago, 1894.
Thoughts That Will Live . . . , Chicago, 1895.
Truths Leaf by Leaf . . . , Chicago, 1905.
The Message of David Swing to His Generation; Addresses and Papers . . . , Chicago, [1913].

SWING, RAYMOND GRAM (March 25, 1887–), news analyst, son of Albert Temple Swing (q.v.), was born in Cortland, N. Y., where his father served as a Congregational minister for one year. He spent much of his boyhood in Oberlin and was educated at Oberlin College. He began newspaper work in Cleveland and later served as Berlin and London correspondent of several American newspapers. In the 1930s he became a well-known news commentator over leading broadcasting systems and also contributed many articles to American and English magazines. He now lives in Jamaica, B. W. I. His writings include *Forerunners of American Fascism,* [New York, 1935]. WW 29

SWINGLE, EMMA FRANCES (Dec. 20, 1865–March 15, 1916), was born on a farm near Cannelville, Muskingum County. She worked as a railway telegrapher. Her death occurred in Cleveland, and she is buried in Zanesville.

Muskingum Melodies, Columbus, 1897.

SWISHER, JAMES (June 6, 1849–May 7, 1924), was born near Cable, Champaign County. He was reared on the family farm and was educated in country schools. When he was thirteen, he ran away to Columbus and enlisted in the 66th O.V.I.; his father discovered him and took him home. The following year he enlisted under the name of James Jackson; he served throughout the war and rose to a first lieutenancy. After the war he entered Ohio Wesleyan University. After teaching in a country school for one term, he went to Mexico, where his uncle held a mining concession. When the concession was not renewed, Swisher walked 1,500 miles to Stockton, Calif. He worked for three years in Carson City, Nev., as a sawmill hand, after which he was appointed a government surveyor, working in Texas and Utah. His adventures up to 1880 are covered fully in his only book. After returning to Champaign County in December of 1878, he again taught school and served as a surveyor and as city engineer of Urbana.

How I Know; Or, Sixteen Years' Eventful Experience . . . , Cincinnati, 1880.

SWOYER, GROVER ELMER (July 28, 1886–), clergyman, was born in Ashville, Pickaway County. After graduating from Wittenberg College in 1913 and Chicago Theological Seminary in 1917, he served Lutheran churches in various Ohio and Pennsylvania cities until his retirement in 1958. He has published *The Saving Presence,* Grand Rapids, Mich., [1940]. RLA 2

SYLVESTER, JANET HART. See Janet Hart Diebold.

SYMMES, AMERICUS (Nov. 2, 1811–1897), son of John Cleves Symmes (q.v.), was born in Bellefontaine, Mo. He lived for some years near Hamilton, but spent most of his life as a farmer and iron founder in Louisville, Ky. His book supports his father's theory of a hollow earth with openings at the poles.

The Symmes Theory of Concentric Spheres, Demonstrating That the Earth Is Hollow, Habitable Within, and Widely Open about the Poles, Louisville, Ky., 1879.

SYMMES, JOHN CLEVES (Nov. 5, 1780–May 28, 1829), nephew of Judge John C. Symmes of Cincinnati, was born in Sussex County, N. J. He served in the War of 1812 and sometime before 1818 conceived the idea which was an overriding obsession throughout the rest of his life. It was announced in the first broadside listed below, which began "I declare the earth is hollow, and habitable within, containing a number of solid concentrick spheres, one within the other, and that it is open at the poles 12 or 16 degrees. . . ." He lectured on his theory, published other proclamations besides those listed below, and petitioned Congress in 1822 and 1823 and the Ohio General Assembly in 1824, suggesting an expedition to investigate his claims. Although his monomania made Symmes a target of satire in Cincinnati and elsewhere, he was taken seriously by James McBride, Jeremiah N. Reynolds, and Americus Symmes (qq.v.), all of whom wrote on the Symmes hypothesis. Captain Symmes died in Hamilton and was buried in Ludlow Park there beneath a monument bearing a hollow globe.

To All the World! . . . , [St. Louis, Mo., 1818].

Arctic Memoir, Cincinnati, 1819.

T

TACKENBERG, CHARLES WILLIAM (Feb. 1, 1877–Aug. 9, 1948), educator, was born in Cincinnati, Hamilton County, and spent his life in that city. He taught in Cincinnati schools, 1894–1938. He wrote poems, some of which were collected in *Children of Phantasy,* and also wrote plays for performance by students.

Children of Phantasy, Cincinnati, 1899.

Bound for the Devil, [Cincinnati?, 1925].

TAEUSCH, CARL FREDERICK (Jan. 20, 1889–), educator, was born in Wapakoneta, Auglaize County. After attending University of Wooster for two years, he taught school in California, 1909–11, before completing his undergraduate training at Princeton University in 1914. He completed his doctorate at Harvard University in 1920. He taught philosophy and ethics at several universities, including Harvard, 1927–35, and served in the U.S. Department of Agriculture, 1935–45. Besides professional articles and reviews, he has published *Professional and Business Ethics,* New York, 1926. WW 30

TAFEL, GUSTAV (Oct. 13, 1830–Nov. 12, 1908), lawyer, was born in Munich, Bavaria. He came to Cincinnati in 1847, and the next year he was one of the founders of the *Turnverein,* the first German gymnastic association in the United States. He learned the printing trade in the office of the Cincinnati *Gazette,* and in 1855 he became city editor of the *Volksblatt.* After studying law with Judge Stallo, he was admitted to the bar in 1858. During the Civil War he served in the 9th O.V.I. and the 106th O.V.I. He helped compile the volume below and wrote its introduction. After the war he practiced law in Cincinnati and took an active part in local politics. He served as mayor of the city, 1897–99.

"Die Neuner." Eine Schilderung der Kriegsjahre des 9ten Regiments Ohio Vol. Infanterie vom 17, April, 1861, bis 7, Juni, 1864. Mit Einer Einleitung von Oberst Gustav Tafel. Cincinnati, 1897.

TAFT, CHARLES PHELPS (Sept. 20, 1897–), son of William Howard Taft and Helen Herron Taft (qq.v.), was born in Cincinnati, Hamilton County. He graduated from Yale University in 1918 and from the Yale Law School in 1921. Since his admission to the Ohio bar in 1922, he has practiced in

Cincinnati and has been active in the civic affairs of that city, serving on the council and as mayor. He has written several books on political matters, e.g., *You and I—and Roosevelt,* New York, [1936]. WW 30

TAFT, HELEN HERRON (1861–May 22, 1943), wife of William Howard Taft and mother of Robert A. and Charles P. Taft (qq.v.), was born in Cincinnati, Hamilton County. She married William H. Taft, then a young Cincinnati lawyer, on June 19, 1886. She died in Washington, D. C., at the age of 82. Her four years as mistress of the White House are described in her *Recollections of Full Years,* New York, 1914.

TAFT, HENRY WATERS (May 27, 1859–Aug. 11, 1945), lawyer, brother of Horace D. and William H. Taft (qq.v.), was born in Cincinnati, Hamilton County. After graduating from Yale University in 1880, he studied law and was admitted to the bar in 1882; he practiced in New York City. He published several books, e.g., *Japan and America . . . ,* New York, 1932. WWW 2

TAFT, HORACE DUTTON (Dec. 28, 1861–Jan. 28, 1943), lawyer and educator, brother of William H. and Henry W. Taft (qq.v.), was born in Cincinnati, Hamilton County. After graduating from Yale University in 1883, he studied at Cincinnati Law School and was admitted to the bar in 1885. He spent three years as a tutor at Yale and founded Taft School, Watertown, Conn., where he served as headmaster until his retirement in 1936. He died in Watertown. He wrote his autobiography: *Memories and Opinions,* New York, 1942. WWW 2

TAFT, ROBERT ALPHONSO (Sept. 8, 1889–July 31, 1953), U. S. Senator, was born in Cincinnati, Hamilton County, the elder brother of Charles P. Taft (q.v.). He graduated from Yale University in 1910 and from Harvard Law School in 1913. After being admitted to the Ohio bar in 1913, he practiced in Cincinnati and took an increasingly active interest in politics. He served in the Ohio House, 1921–26, in the Ohio Senate, 1931–32, and in the U. S. Senate, 1939–53. Regarded as the spokesman for conservative, though flexible, elements of his party, he was known to millions as "Mr. Republican." He published *A Republican Program; Speeches and Broadcasts,* [Cleveland], 1939. WWW 3

TAFT, WILLIAM HOWARD (Sept. 15, 1857–March 8, 1930), 27th President of the United States and Chief Justice of the U. S. Supreme Court, was born in Cincinnati, Hamilton County, the son of Judge Alphonso Taft. After attending Woodward High School, he graduated from Yale University in 1878 and from Cincinnati Law School in 1880. He practiced in Cincinnati and began at once to take an active part in Republican politics. He served on the Ohio superior court, 1887–90, was solicitor general of the United States, 1890–92, and judge of the Federal circuit court, 1892–1900; he was appointed president of the Philippine Commission in 1900, and served as governor-general of the Philippines, 1901–04. He was Theodore Roosevelt's Secretary of War, 1904–09. His election to the Presidency and his later break with Roosevelt are well known. After leaving the White House, he taught at Yale Law School, 1913–21, and served as Chief Justice of the Supreme Court, 1921–30. Of a reflective and judicial turn of mind, he unquestionably was happier on the bench than in the political arena. Many of his addresses, Presidential messages, and legal opinions were published; his other books consist chiefly of revised lectures, e.g., *Four Aspects of Civic Duty,* New York, 1906. DAB 18

TAIT, JOHN ROBINSON (Jan. 14, 1834–July 29, 1909), artist, was born in Cincinnati, Hamilton County. After graduating from Bethany College in 1852, he went to Europe, where he remained three years, devoting himself to literature and painting. He seems to have abandoned the pen in favor of the brush following the appearance of his first books in 1859. He lived in Düsseldorf until 1871, studying under August Weber and Andreas Achenbach. He later studied in Munich. Upon his return to the United States he lived in Baltimore. He designed the Art Hall at the second Cincinnati exposition. His paintings were displayed in various cities of the United States. He died in Baltimore, Md.

Dolce Far Niente, Philadelphia, 1859.

European Life, Legend and Landscape, Philadelphia, 1859.

TALBERT, ERNEST LYNN (Aug. 19, 1879–   ), educator, was born in West Elkton, Preble County. He graduated from Butler College and from the University of Chicago (Ph.D.) in 1909. He was a member of the University of Cincinnati philosophy faculty, 1914–44, and since his retirement has continued to reside in Cincinnati. Among his publications is *Opportunities in School and Industry for Children of the Stockyard District,* Chicago, 1912. DAS 2

TALLANT, EDITH (May 9, 1881–June 21, 1957), was born in Columbus, Franklin County. She graduated from Vassar College in 1905 and was, until her retirement in 1941, an English teacher in South High School, Columbus. She wrote three books of juvenile fiction, e.g., *Danny and Prue,* New York, [1938].

TAMAS, ISTVAN (Aug. 8, 1907–), journalist, was born in Pécsvárad, Hungary. He came to the United States in 1938 and to Cleveland in 1943. He studied at the Sorbonne in Paris and was a journalist and an author in Budapest before coming to the United States. He is now foreign news and book editor of a Hungarian newspaper, *Szabadság* (Liberty), published in Cleveland. His writings include *The Adventures of John Háry, Hungarian Hussar,* (Gwen Harrison, trans.), Budapest, [1939].

TANEYHILL, RICHARD N. (1822–Nov. 29, 1898), lawyer, was born in Maryland and came with his parents to Barnesville, Belmont County, in 1832. After reading law he practiced in Barnesville and made the study of local history and archaeology his avocation. Many articles which he contributed to the Barnesville *Enterprise* under the pen name R. King Bennett were collected and published as *History of Barnesville, Ohio. The Leatherwood God,* his account of the religious imposter, Joseph C. Dylks, first appeared in Number Seven of the *Ohio Valley Historical Series* and was later published as a book by Robert Clarke (q.v.). In the *Nation,* it was declared to be "one of the most extraordinary narratives of religious fanaticism we have ever met with," it was dealt with at length in a favorable review in the London *Saturday Review,* and William Dean Howells used the book as the basis for his novel of the same name. Taneyhill died in Barnesville.

The Leatherwood God. An Account of the Appearance and Pretensions of Joseph C. Dylks in Eastern Ohio in 1828, Cincinnati, 1870.

History of Barnesville, Ohio, Barnesville, [1899].

TANGENT, PATRICK QUINN. Pseud. See George H. Phelps.

TANNEHILL, IVAN RAY (March 13, 1890–May 2, 1959), meteorologist, was born in McConnelsville, Morgan County. He graduated from Denison University in 1912. He served in the U. S. Weather Bureau, 1914–54, and was chief of the bureau when he retired. He wrote many articles and government pamphlets and a book, *Hurricanes: Their Nature and History . . . ,* Princeton, [N. J.], 1938.

TARSHISH, JACOB (Dec. 8, 1892–), rabbi, was born in Lithuania but was brought to the United States while he was still a small child. He graduated from the University of Cincinnati in 1914 and from Hebrew Union College in 1915. He has served as rabbi of congregations in several cities, including Columbus, 1922–33. He now lives in White Plains, N. Y. He has lectured widely and for some years conducted a radio program on which he was known as The Lamplighter. His writings include *Judaism and Socialism,* [Cincinnati, 193-?]. WW 28

TATE, JANE BEVERLIN (Jan. 11, 1922–), was born in Lima, Allen County. She spent part of her girlhood in Roanoke, Va., and graduated from Harcum Junior College, Pa. During World War II, she worked in the military intelligence division of the War Department. She now lives in Washington, D. C. Her poems have appeared in many periodicals, and she has published at least three collections, e.g., *These Are for You,* Portland, Maine, [1949].

TAYLOR, ALTA (March 25, 1885–Sept. 4, 1954), was born in Windham, Portage County. She worked for many years on the editorial staff of Saalfield Publishing Company, Akron. In 1940 she married James A. Braden (q.v.). She wrote or edited a number of books for children, some of them published under the pen name Althea L. Clinton, e.g., *Billy Whiskers in Mischief,* Akron, [1926].

TAYLOR, ARCHIBALD ALEXANDER EDWARD (Aug. 27, 1834–April 23, 1903), clergyman and educator, was born in Springfield, Clark County. He attended school in Cincinnati and studied seven years at Princeton, graduating from the Theological Seminary in 1857. After being licensed by the Presbytery of Cincinnati, he served pastorates in Kentucky, Iowa, the District of Columbia, and Cincinnati until 1873, when he became president of University of Wooster. During his ten-year administration, he made notable contributions to the development of that institution. From 1888 to 1891 he edited *Mid-continent,* a Presbyterian weekly. From 1892 to 1899 he was pastor of Westminster Presbyterian Church in Columbus and thereafter lived in that city until his death.

Our Fallen Leader . . . , Philadelphia, 1865.

Claudia Procula and Other Verses, Columbus, 1899.

TAYLOR, BENJAMIN FRANKLIN (July 19, 1819–Feb. 24, 1887), journalist and poet, born in Lowville, N. Y., spent the last six years of his life in Cleveland. A prolific writer, he published many popular poems on rural themes, which were collected in his *Complete Poetical Works . . .* , Chicago, 1886, and also published a great deal of prose, including a novel: *Theophilus Trent . . .* , Chicago, 1887.

TAYLOR, CHARLES BOARDMAN (Feb. 6, 1846–Aug. 21, 1928), clergyman, was born in Ellsworth, Mahoning County. He served in the 86th O.V.I. for three months in 1862 and in the First Heavy Artillery, 1862–65. After the war he attended Marietta College and Lane Seminary; after graduating from the seminary in 1870, he was ordained to the Presbyterian ministry. He taught school in Illinois for six years, after which he served churches in southern Ohio for fifty years. He contributed to a number of newspapers. He died in McArthur.

Early History and War Record of Wilkesville and Salem, Cincinnati, 1874.

The Presbytery of Athens, Logan, [1914?].

TAYLOR, EDWARD LIVINGSTONE (March 20, 1839–May 29, 1910), lawyer, was born in Columbus, Franklin County. He graduated from Miami University in 1860, read law, and was admitted to the bar in 1862. He practiced in Columbus until his retirement in 1908. Descendant of a pioneer family, he was deeply interested in the early history of Ohio and wrote a number of articles for the *Ohio State Archaeological and Historical Quarterly.* A few months before his death, he published a collection of his historical essays: *Ohio Indians and Other Writings,* Columbus, 1909. **WWW 1**

TAYLOR, FREDERICK WILLIAM (Jan. 11, 1853–April 28, 1903), clergyman, was born in Toledo, Lucas County. He graduated from Western Reserve College in 1873 and General Theological Seminary, New York City, in 1876. Ordained to the Episcopal priesthood in 1877, he served churches in Danville and Springfield, Ill., and was named bishop in 1901. He died in Wisconsin. He wrote several historical and religious articles for periodicals.

The Confession of Our Christian Faith . . . , New York, 1883.

TAYLOR, GEORGE LANSING (Feb. 13, 1835–July 26, 1903), clergyman, was born in Skaneateles, N. Y. When he was twelve, his parents brought him to Ohio, where he spent his formative years. After attending Ohio Wesleyan University for two years, he transferred to Columbia University, from which he graduated in 1861; the following year he was ordained as a Methodist clergyman. He published many sermons and addresses in pamphlet form, but is best remembered in Ohio for his centennial poem, "The Northwest." He died in Brooklyn, N. Y.

Elijah, the Reformer, a Ballad-epic and Other Sacred and Religious Poems, New York, 1885.

Ulysses S. Grant: Conqueror, Patriot, Hero; An Elegy and Other Poems, New York, 1885.

What Shall We Do with the Sunday-school?, New York, 1886.

The Progress of Learning, a Poem . . . , New York, [1887].

The New Africa; Its Discovery and Destiny, New York, 1888.

Asters and Golden-rod, and Other Poems, New York, [1904].

TAYLOR, JAMES WICKES (Nov. 6, 1819–April 28, 1893), lawyer and journalist, was born in Eddytown, N. Y. After graduating from Hamilton College in 1838, he read law with his father; after being admitted to the bar, he moved to Cincinnati in 1842. In 1844 he began practice with Salmon P. Chase (q.v.). He established the Cincinnati *Morning Signal,* but the paper expired within a year and he turned to free-lance writing for local papers. In 1847 he published his first book, *The Victim of Intrigue,* a novel written to vindicate the reputation of Ohio's first Senator, John Smith, who had been unjustly implicated in the Burr conspiracy. In 1850 Taylor became editor of the Sandusky *Daily Mirror,* and while holding this position he had ample time to use scissors and paste pot to produce his *History of Ohio.* Judiciously and thoroughly edited, it became a popular school text. He was state librarian from 1854 until 1856, when he joined the exodus of Ohio lawyers to the Minnesota Territory, where he opened a law office in St. Paul. When Salmon P. Chase became Secretary of the Treasury in 1861, Taylor was appointed a special agent of the Treasury. President Grant made him U. S. Consul at Winnipeg, Manitoba, in 1870—a post that he held until his death.

The Victim of Intrigue—A Tale of Burr's Conspiracy, Cincinnati, 1847.

History of the State of Ohio. First Period, 1650–1787, Sandusky, 1854.

A Manual of the Ohio School System . . . , Cincinnati, 1857.

The Railroad System of Minnesota . . . , St. Paul, 1859.
Northwest British America and Its Relations to the State of Minnesota, St. Paul, 1860.
The October Election. How Can a Democrat Most Effectually Support the Government and the Union by His Vote?, St. Paul, 1861.
Alleghania: A Geographical and Statistical Memoir . . . , St. Paul, 1862.
The Sioux War; What Shall We Do with It? The Sioux Indians; What Shall We Do with Them? . . . , St. Paul, 1862.
Mineral Resources of the United States, (with John R. Browne), Washington, 1867.
Forest and Fruit Culture in Manitoba, Winnipeg, 1882.
"A Choice Nook of Memory." The Diary of a Cincinnati Law Clerk, 1842–1844, (James T. Dunn, ed.), Columbus, 1950.

TAYLOR, JOB (Jan. 2, 1876–Jan. 17, 1936), manufacturer, born in Dudley, England, spent much of his early life in Lima. After attending Lima College, University of Wooster, and Harvard University, he joined the staff of the American Steam Board Company at Lima. He was later an executive of the United Box Board Company. He was associated with several other companies before retiring in 1926. He died in Roanoke Rapids, Va., and is buried in Lima. He wrote an account of labor conflicts in the Pennsylvania coal mines: *Broken Links,* Boston, 1908.

TAYLOR, JOSEPH RUSSELL (July 10, 1868–March 30, 1933), educator, was born in Circleville, Pickaway County. After graduating from Ohio State University in 1887, he taught drawing and English there from 1889 until his death. He published several books, e.g., *Our Dancing Days,* Boston, 1922. WWW 1

TAYLOR, KATHERINE KELLEY (Oct. 29, 1889–), was born in Cleveland, Cuyahoga County, the daughter of Dr. Samuel W. Kelley (q.v.). She graduated from Bryn Mawr College in 1910 and married William R. Taylor, a Cleveland architect, in 1911. She has published a volume of poetry: *The Sea Gull's Daughter and Other Poems,* Cleveland, [1937].

TAYLOR, LANDON (1812–1885), clergyman, born in New York State, came with his parents to Scioto County in 1835. He did farm work, taught school, and was a clerk at Franklin Furnace before becoming a Methodist preacher. He preached in southern Ohio until 1845, and then went to Iowa, where he preached in various communities until 1883, when he returned to Scioto County to live with a son at Wheelersburg. The volume listed below is autobiographical.
The Battlefield Reviewed . . . , Chicago, 1881.

TAYLOR, MARSHALL WILLIAM (July 1, 1846–Sept. 11, 1887), clergyman, born in Lexington, Ky., the son of slave parents, was made pastor of Union Methodist Episcopal Church, Cincinnati, in 1887; he had previously served as presiding elder of the Ohio District of his church, 1878–83. He published several books, e.g., a biography: *The Life, Travels, Labors, and Helpers of Mrs. Amanda Smith . . . ,* Cincinnati, 1886.

TAYLOR, MARY ABIGAIL MELLOTT (Feb. 3, 1847– ?), educator, was born near Beallsville, Monroe County. Except that she taught in the public schools, no other biographical facts have been discovered. She wrote *The Historic Meaning of Prophecy,* Cincinnati, 1910.

TAYLOR, PETER HILLSMAN (1917–), was born in Trenton, Tenn. After graduating from Kenyon College in 1940 and serving in the army during World War II, he taught at various universities before joining the Kenyon English faculty in 1952. Since 1957 he has been on the faculty of Ohio State University. Generally regarded as one of the most skillful young writers, especially in the field of the short story, he has published four collections in book form, the first being *A Long Fourth and Other Stories,* New York, [1948], TCA

TAYLOR, ROBERT EMMETT (July 3, 1889–Sept. 3, 1956), educator, born in Piper City, Ill., was on the faculty of the University of Cincinnati, 1923–54. Author of several accounting textbooks, he also wrote a biography of a fifteenth-century Franciscan friar: *No Royal Road, Luca Pacioli and his Times,* Chapel Hill, [N. C.], 1942.

TAYLOR, ROBERT STEWART (May 2, 1838–Jan. 28, 1918), was born in Ross County. Admitted to the Indiana bar in 1860, he practiced in Fort Wayne, Ind. In 1881, President Garfield appointed him to the Mississippi River Commission. He became known as an authority on the river, and many of his addresses on the subject were published separately. A posthumous collection of his writings was published: *Mississippi River Improvement; Collected Speeches and Magazine Articles,* [n.p., 1921?].

TAYLOR, STELLA WEILER (Jan. 28, 1869–April 1, 1953), was born in Hamilton, Butler County. She wrote a column for the Hamilton *Journal-News,* 1931–48. A selection of her columns was published: *Rosemary; A Series of Lavender Scented Memories of Other Days in Hamilton,* Hamilton, 1940.

TAYLOR, WILLIAM ALEXANDER (April 25, 1837–Aug. 7, 1912), journalist, was born in Perry County. From 1865 to 1910, he worked on various Ohio newspapers; his longest tenure was 25 years with the Cincinnati *Enquirer. Ohio Statesman and Annals of Progress* was a collaboration with his son, Aubrey C. Taylor, (Jan. 28, 1875–Nov. 26, 1898).

Eighteen Presidents and Contemporaneous Rulers, Pittsburgh, 1876.
Tariff Lessons . . . , Columbus, 1878.
The Peril of the Republic, Columbus, 1886.
Ohio Statesmen and Annals of Progress . . . , Columbus, 1889.
Roses and Rue, Buffalo, 1895.
Intermere, Columbus, 1901.
Ohio in Congress from 1803 to 1901 . . . , Columbus, 1901.
The Book of Ohio, Toledo, 1902.
Evolution of the Statesman, Columbus, 1905.
Centennial History of Columbus and Franklin County, Ohio, 2 vols., Chicago, 1909.

TEAGUE, RUTH MILLS (May 5, 1896–), born in North Manchester, Ind., grew up in Columbus and also lived in Toledo. She graduated from Ohio State University in 1918. She now lives in Annandale, N. J., and is a regular contributor to the *Ladies' Home Journal.* Under her maiden name she has published a mystery story: *Leading Lady,* [New York, 1936].

TEAL, ANGELINE GRUEY (Aug. 28, 1842–Sept. 3, 1913), was born on a farm in southern Ohio; when she was three years old, her parents moved to Noble County, Ind., and she spent her life in that state. On Jan. 1, 1866, she married Dr. Norman Teal of Kendallville, Ind., the community in which she lived thereafter. She published stories and poems in various periodicals.

John Thorne's Folks . . . , Boston, 1884.
Muriel Howe, New York, 1892.
The Rose of Love, New York, 1893.
The Speaker of the House, Chicago, [1894].

TEETOR, HENRY B. (? – ?), lawyer, began practice in Cincinnati after the Civil War. He was the first mayor of the Cincinnati suburb Wyoming in 1874, and also served as U. S. Gauger.

The Past and Present of Mill Creek Valley . . . , Cincinnati, 1882.
Sketch of the Life and Times of Col. Israel Ludlow . . . , Cincinnati, 1885.

TELLO, MANLY (1842–April 4, 1905), journalist and lawyer, was born in Porto Santo, Madeira Islands, where his parents, whose home was Brooklyn, N. Y., were visiting. He served in the Confederate Army from 1861 to 1863, when he was captured and imprisoned in the North. He came to Cleveland in 1877, edited the *Catholic Universe,* 1877–93, and practiced law, 1893–1905. Thirty-one years after his death, his daughter published a collection of his writings for private circulation: *Once upon a Time; Verses and Stories for Children,* [Pittsburgh, Pa.], 1936.

TENNEY, LUMAN HARRIS (Oct. 1, 1841–Feb. 10, 1880), was born in North Amherst, Lorain County. He entered Oberlin College in 1859 but left school in September, 1861, to enlist in the Second Ohio Cavalry. After the war he worked on the construction of the Northern Pacific Railroad, taught school, and established a colony of farmers at Glyndon, Minn. His war diary was published posthumously by the family: *War Diary of Luman Harris Tenney, 1861–1865,* Cleveland, 1914.

TERRY, MARSHALL ORLANDO (June 21, 1848–Oct. 11, 1933), physician, born in Watervliet Center, N. Y., was brought to Plymouth in 1850 and later lived in Ashtabula. He graduated from Homeopathic Hospital College, Cleveland, in 1872, and practiced there for a short time before moving to Utica, N. Y., where he practiced for many years. He died in California and is buried in Ashtabula. He served in the Spanish-American War. During World War I, he published a collection of his articles on military medicine: *The Soldier's Medical Friend . . . ,* Norwood, Mass., 1917. DAB 18

TERRY, THEODORE BRAINARD (Jan. 2, 1843–Jan. 1, 1916), agriculturist and writer, was born in Lafayette, N. Y., but was educated at Painesville Academy and Western Reserve College. In 1870 he bought a rundown farm at Hudson and operated it successfully. He lectured widely at farmers' institutes and was associate editor of *Practical Farmer.*

The A B C of Potato Culture . . . , Medina, 1885.

How to Grow Strawberries . . . , Medina, 1890.

Our Farming; Or, How We Have Made a Run-down Farm Bring Forth Both Profit and Pleasure . . . , Philadelphia, 1893.

How to Keep Well and Live Long, Philadelphia, [1909].

What I Do, See and Hear, with Health Hints . . . , Philadelphia, [n.d.].

TEVERBAUGH, SOLOMON. See Joshua H. Horton.

THATCHER, OLIVER JOSEPH (Nov. 10, 1857–Aug. 19, 1937), historian, was born in the Beech Grove neighborhood near Wilmington, Clinton County. His Quaker parents, Joseph and Deborah Hadley Thatcher, died before he was five, and he was taken into the home of an elder sister. He was a studious child with a real hunger for books. Many years later he wrote: "You can have no idea of the booklessness of my youth. The Bible, McGuffey's readers, which were used in school, Kidd's *Elocution,* one poor Little Rollo book, Peter Parley's *History,* a heart-rending novel called *Ida May,* and the experiences of a woman who served the North as a spy in the war '61–'65—and a few dime novels—are all the books that I can recall before I started to college. I was crazy for books to read, but I could not get them. I read and re-read every one that I had. It was considered wicked to read novels, and they used to whip me when they found me behind the woodpile or down in the orchard with one of the old dime novels, or with the well-worn copy of *Ida May.* I wept and wailed more over that worthless book than I did over the whippings it occasioned." He attended a country school and advanced in it with such speed that he became its teacher when no older than some of his students. Later he attended Wilmington College—pitching hay in summer, tutoring in winter—and was graduated in 1878. He taught school for the next three years in Wilmington and Xenia. After a year's private study, he entered Union Theological Seminary in 1882 and, on his graduation in 1885, was awarded a traveling fellowship. He spent the three following years in Europe at the universities of Berlin, Marburg, and Geneva and at the School of Classical Studies in Athens. Upon his return to this country, he became professor of church history at United Presbyterian Theological Seminary. His first book, *The Patience of Hope,* was published in 1889. It was compiled as a tribute to Joseph H. Wright, the man who had inspired him to embark upon post-graduate studies. Wright had been pastor of the First United Presbyterian Church of Xenia from 1880 until his death in 1889, and the two men had become friends while Thatcher was principal of schools at the Ohio Soldiers' and Sailors' Orphans' Home. In 1892, Thatcher joined the University of Chicago as a member of its first faculty and remained there as associate professor of medieval history until 1906. His vacations were spent in European travel and study. In 1894, he received his Ph.D. from the University of Chicago, and published *A Sketch of the History of the Apostolic Church,* dedicated to his great teacher at the University of Berlin, Adolf Harnack. It was as a historian and not as a theologian that he approached his subject, and he punctured some popular eccelesiastical theories in the process. During the next decade he turned to the history of Europe in the Middle Ages. Most of his books of this period were designed primarily as textbooks, but Dr. Thatcher was a pioneer in the revolt against slavish devotion to them. He believed the use of a single text to be "a misfortune and a calamity," and presented the subject so that teacher and student would turn to the wider sources of historical literature. His original contributions to scholarship were presented as special articles, most of them in German periodicals, and in his *Studies Concerning Adrian IV,* the result of a sabbatical year spent in study at the Vatican Library. Thatcher was also something of an athlete: during his years in Europe he became a skilled mountain climber, and he is still remembered in the old Beech Grove neighborhood as the first pitcher in Clinton County to throw a curve ball. At Chicago he worked closely with Coach Stagg in the development of the University's football team. Robert Morss Lovett in *All Our Years* wrote of him as a "picturesque academic figure . . . on the field every afternoon in the season as a volunteer coach, and tutoring the members of the team in the evening to keep them eligible to play." A man of extraordinarily wide interests, he feared submersion in one period of world history. He left the University after fourteen years and returned to Wilmington, where he intended to become a farmer. During the next ten years, however, he was frequently in the classrooms of Wilmington College, where he lectured on European history. His services were donated to his alma mater. In 1908 he bought a controlling interest in the Clinton *Republican,* and he edited that Wilmington newspaper until 1911. He was elected to the Ohio General Assembly in 1912 and again in 1914. It was during these years that he served as chairman of the Ohio State School Survey Commission. The commission was instructed to make a study of the state's schools, to determine the degree of efficiency with which they were conducted, and to make recommendations for the improvement of the public school system. Its *Report to the Governor of Ohio,* published in Columbus in 1914, became the basis of the new law governing Ohio schools. At the end of his second term in the state legislature, Dr. Thatcher moved to California, where he became a fruit grower. He died in San Bernardino. The manuscript of his final work, a group of essays on social life of the Middle Ages, was completed in that year, but disappeared at the time of his death.

Gerald D. McDonald

The Patience of Hope, New York, 1889.
A Sketch of the History of the Apostolic Church, Boston, 1894.
Studies Concerning Adrian IV, Chicago, 1903.

THAYER, FRANK (Aug. 18, 1890–), educator, was born in Conneaut, Ashtabula County. After graduating from Oberlin College in 1912, he read law in Jefferson and worked on the Conneaut *News-Herald.* He began teaching in 1916 and joined the University of Wisconsin journalism faculty in 1936. His writings have dealt with journalism, especially its relation to the law. His books include *Newspaper Management,* [New York, 1926]. WW 30

THAYER, GEORGE AUGUSTINE (Dec. 6, 1839–Oct. 4, 1925), clergyman, born in Randolph, Mass., was pastor of First Congregational Church, Cincinnati, 1882–1916, and after his retirement continued to live in Cincinnati. He published many addresses and papers on the Civil War and *The First Congregational Church . . . ,* Cincinnati, [1917]. WWW 1

THIRKFIELD, WILBUR PATTERSON (Sept. 25, 1854–Nov. 7, 1936), clergyman, was born in Franklin, Warren County. He graduated from Ohio Wesleyan University in 1876 and from Boston University in 1881. He was president of Gammon Theological Seminary, Atlanta, Ga., 1883–1900, was general secretary of the Freedmen's Aid Society, 1900–06, and was president of Howard University, 1906–12. He was elected a Methodist bishop in 1912 and retired in 1928. He died in Brooklyn, N. Y. He compiled worship books and a hymnal and wrote several books on religion, e.g., *The Personality and Message of the Preacher,* New York, [1914]. WWW 1

THOBURN, ISABELLA (March 29, 1840–Sept. 1, 1901), educator, was born near St. Clairsville, Belmont County. She attended public schools, Wheeling Female Seminary, and the Cincinnati Academy of Design. She taught in various Ohio communities, and was active in relief work during the Civil War. In 1869, at the urging of her brother, James M. Thoburn (q.v.), she went to Lucknow, India, where she devoted the rest of her life to the education of women. During her longest furlough in the United States (1886–91), she was active in organizing the Methodist deaconess movement. She died in Lucknow of Asiatic cholera. She wrote numerous articles. Her only book is a biography of one of her teachers and closest friends.

Phoebe Rowe, Cincinnati, 1899.

THOBURN, JAMES MILLS (March 7, 1836–Nov. 28, 1922), clergyman, was born in St. Clairsville, Belmont County. He graduated from Allegheny College in 1857 and became a Methodist minister the following year. In 1859 he was sent as a missionary to India, where he was later joined by his sister Isabella (q.v.). In 1888 he was elected missionary bishop for India, and he performed the duties of that office until he retired in 1908. He was a prolific writer of articles for periodicals.

My Missionary Apprenticeship, New York, 1884.
India and Malaysia, Cincinnati, 1892.
The Deaconess and Her Vocation, Cincinnati, 1893.
Christless Nations . . . , New York, 1895.
Light in the East . . . , Chicago, 1898.
The Church of the Pentecost, Cincinnati, 1901.
Life of Isabella Thoburn, Cincinnati, [1903].
The Christian Conquest of India, New York, 1906.
India and Southern Asia, Cincinnati, 1907.

THOBURN, JOSEPH BRADFIELD (Aug. 8, 1866–March 2, 1941), was born in Bellaire, Belmont County, but was taken to Kansas when his family emigrated there in 1871. He was a printer, journalist, and historian. He wrote *A History of Oklahoma,* (with Isaac M. Holcomb), San Francisco, 1908. WWW 1

THOMAS, CHARLES CYRUS (Feb. 19, 1909–), educator, was born in Kingston, Ross County. He attended Chillicothe Normal School, taught in Ohio schools, and graduated from Kent State University in 1939. He is now a teacher in Los Angeles. He published a volume of poems while he was a student at Kent: *A Black Lark Caroling,* Dallas, Texas, [1936].

THOMAS, DANIEL DRIVER (Jan. 2, 1859–Dec. 1, 1931), educator and clergyman, was born on a farm near Williamstown, Hardin County. He graduated from Ohio Northern University, and his only book was published while he was a student there. He taught in Ohio schools for thirty years and at Mt. Morris College, Ill. He also served as a minister of the Church of the Brethren in Ohio and Arizona. He died in Allen County.

Poems of Adelphia, Ada, 1897.

THOMAS, EBENEZER SMITH (June 19, 1775–Oct. 22, 1845), journalist, was born in Cambridge, Mass. After learning the printing trade in Worcester, Mass., under his uncle, Isaiah Thomas, he was a bookseller in Charleston, S. C. He edited the *City Gazette* there, 1810–16, and afterward lived for some years in Baltimore, Md. In 1829 he brought his family to Cincinnati, where he spent the remainder of his life. His eight children included Frederick W., Lewis F., Martha M., and Mary E. Thomas (qq.v.). In Cincinnati, he edited the Cincinnati *Daily Advertiser* until 1835 and the *Evening Post* until 1839. His two books were written in Cincinnati.

Reminiscences of the Last Sixty-five Years . . . , 2 vols., Hartford, 1840.

Reminiscences of South Carolina, Hartford, 1840.

THOMAS, EDITH MATILDA (Aug. 12, 1854–Sept. 13, 1925), was born in Chatham, Medina County. During the years when George Sterling, Lloyd Mifflin, and William Vaughan Moody were crowding their lines close upon the heels of classical myth, she flashed upward in the poetical heavens to her zenith. From 1885 to 1920 hers was a name to reckon with in American verse, but as the mythological and legendary materials declined in popularity, her reputation diminished with them. Neglected at length by the critics and crowded out of modern anthologies by the press of new material, the poetry of this able Keatsian poet is now rarely called to the attention of students. Yet at the turn of the century, reputable literary authorities hailed her work enthusiastically. Howells described her as one possessing a "fame in which she need envy no others of our time." E. C. Stedman, poet and critic, declared in 1900 that "her place is secure among the truest living poets of our English tongue." Emerson Venable announced in his *Poets of Ohio* (1909) that her poems had rarely been equaled by any writer of her sex on either side of the Atlantic. Fred Lewis Pattee in 1919 reprinted four of her poems and gave her high praise: "The leader of the feminine poets of the later period unquestionably is Edith M. Thomas." Her *A New Year's Masque* (1885) he referred to as "one of the significant first volumes" published by women in the thirteen years following 1875, and rated her as a "distinctive poet of the era—the third generation of poets in America." As late as 1923 Robert U. Johnson declared in his memoirs that Edith Thomas was one of the three or four best living poets. Unfortunately, time has failed to substantiate the appraisals made so confidently by Johnson and his contemporaries. Today, even among the minor voices, she is frequently overshadowed by some of her erstwhile rivals to fame—Ina Coolbrith, Louise Guiney, Lizette W. Reese. Edith M. Thomas lived for her first seven years in the Ohio towns of Chatham, Kenton, and Bowling Green. Upon the death of her father in 1861, she and her sister were taken by their mother to Geneva, where Edith, reveling in the beauty of her surroundings, acquired that love of nature that later prompted so much of her verse. Subsequently, in classes at the Geneva Normal Institute, she discovered the world of Greek classics—the complex hierarchy of Greek gods and the riot of Greek legends. Upon these sources her early poems drew so heavily that the abundant allusions plus the Greek restraint and the finish of her work led Pattee to pronounce the author "more Greek than American." After a brief turn at teaching and at typesetting, she spent most of the 1870s in transferring the observations of field and stream to poetic pages. This early work she marketed in the papers of Geneva and Cleveland and in other out-of-town repositories for amateur pieces. But the encouragement of a favorite uncle, James Thomas; the interest of a hostess in New York (after 1881), Mrs. Botta; and the ministrations of Helen Hunt Jackson, who recognized her powers, resulted in serious consideration of Miss Thomas' scrapbook, and a welcome to the columns of the new *Century Magazine.* After four years of varied periodical activity came the publication of *A New*

Year's Masque (1885), which scored an immediate success and led to a collection of nature essays, *The Round Year* (1886). *Lyrics and Sonnets* (1887) and *The Inverted Torch* (1890) followed, and after such triumphs *Scribner's,* the *Atlantic Monthly, Harper's,* the *Nation,* the *Critic,* and the *Independent* readily accepted her contributions. Upon the death of her mother in 1887, Edith Thomas moved permanently to New York, where she not only met prominent literary men, but also found adequate critical and creative inspiration for further work. She did etymological research for the *Century Dictionary* and assumed editorial duties for *Harper's Magazine,* to which and like assignments she devoted herself, as well as to her poetry, until her death in 1925. During her later years, the lyrical impulse came ever more rarely to her. But at the close of her career she could look back upon forty years of verse writing, during which time she had held her literary materials up to the high standards of classic craftsmanship. Edith Thomas had displayed from the beginning an intimate acquaintance with nature: she had lingered with affection over the beauty of wayside shrubs, the pageantry of sunsets, the drowsiness of mid-August days, the whistling woods—writing, as she herself expressed it, "out of the depths of her womanly consciousness and experience." What she wrote of H. H. Jackson was equally applicable to her own efforts:

Thou didst love Nature and her very mood:
Beneath thine eye the frail flower of the wood
Uplifted not in vain its fleeting sign,
And on the hearth the mast-tree's blaze benign,
With all its sylvan lore was understood!

Jessie B. Rittenhouse edited a selection of her poems shortly after her death, and this volume, with its attendant life, has been the chief source of what reputation she enjoys today.

G. Harrison Orians

A New Year's Masque, and Other Poems, Boston, 1885.
The Round Year, Boston, 1886.
Lyrics and Sonnets, Boston, 1887.
Children of Autumn . . . , New York, 1888.
Children of Spring . . . , New York, 1888.
Children of Summer . . . , New York, 1888.
Children of Winter . . . , New York, 1888.
Babes of the Nations . . . , New York, 1889.
Heaven and Earth; An Antiphon, New York, 1889.
The Inverted Torch, Boston, 1890.
Fair Shadow Land, Boston, 1893.
In Sunshine Land, Boston, 1895.
In the Young World, Boston, 1896.
A Winter Swallow, with Other Verse, New York, 1896.
The Dancers, and Other Legends and Lyrics, Boston, 1903.
Cassia, and Other Verse, Boston, 1905.
Children of Christmas, and Others, Boston, 1907.
The Guest at the Gate, Boston, 1909.
The Flower from the Ashes, and Other Verse, Portland, Me., 1915.
The White Messenger, and Other War Poems, Boston, [1915].

THOMAS, ELEANOR (Aug. 1, 1898–), was born in Columbus, Franklin County. She graduated from Wells College in 1921. Now a resident of Boston, she has written a number of textbooks for the elementary grades, edited *My Weekly Reader,* and published several children's stories, e.g., *Mr. Totter and the Five Black Cats,* New York, 1942.

THOMAS, FREDERICK WILLIAM (Oct. 25, 1806–Aug. 27, 1866), son of Ebenezer S. Thomas (q.v.), was born in Providence, R. I., but grew up in Baltimore, Md., and Charleston, S. C. An accident in his early manhood left him lame. He read law and was admitted to the bar in 1828. By 1831 he was in Cincinnati, where his father was editor of the Cincinnati *Daily Advertiser.* Although he traveled widely in the 1830s, Cincinnati apparently was his residence throughout the decade. During this period, he wrote his long Byronic poem *The Emigrant* and three novels. In 1841 he was in Washington, D. C., as a clerk in the Treasury Department. Around 1850 he was in Cincinnati again for a brief period as a Methodist clergyman. He afterward worked on the Richmond *Enquirer* and other papers. He died in Washington, D. C. Despite his poems and fiction, which were fairly popular, he is usually remembered in literary history only for his correspondence with Edgar Allan Poe, which began in 1841 and continued until Poe's death in 1849.

The Emigrant, Or, Reflections While Descending the Ohio . . . , Cincinnati, 1833.
Clinton Bradshaw . . . , Philadelphia, 1835.
East and West. A Novel, Philadelphia, 1836.
Howard Pinckney. A Novel, 2 vols., Philadelphia, 1840.
The Beechen Tree: A Tale Told in Rhyme, New York, 1844.
Sketches of Character . . . , Louisville, Ky., 1849.

An Autobiography of William Russell, Baltimore, 1852.
John Randolph of Roanoke . . . , Philadelphia, 1853.

THOMAS, KATHARINE GARFORD (Mrs. James B.) (July 17, 1883–), was born in Elyria, Lorain County, and still lives in that community. She attended Taconic School for Girls, Lakeville, Conn., and Miss Baldwin's School, Bryn Mawr, Pa., and also studied music at Oberlin Conservatory and in New York City. She has been very active in the civic and cultural life of Elyria. She has published poetry in various periodicals and a collection, *Old Oak Trees,* and has also written a biography of her great-aunt, Katharine Moody Smith: *Auntie Kate, Her Journey through Ninety Years,* Columbus, 1949.

THOMAS, LEWIS FOULK (Nov. 3, 1808–May 26, 1868), lawyer, was born in Baltimore County, Md., son of Ebenezer S. Thomas (q.v.). In 1829 he came to Cincinnati, where he worked on the Cincinnati *Daily Advertiser* and the *Evening Post,* and also read law. When the *Evening Post* was suspended in 1839, he went to Louisville, Ky., where he edited the *Daily Herald* for a time. Early in 1840 he went to St. Louis, where, with the paintings of J. C. Wild before him, he went to work on the book for which he is chiefly remembered. Drawing upon newspaper files, reports, histories, and personal interviews with officers of the American Fur Company, he wrote the text of *The Valley of the Mississippi.* Around 1845 he moved to Washington, D. C., where he practiced law until his death.

Osceola, a Drama, Cincinnati, 1838.
The Valley of the Mississippi . . . , St. Louis, 1841.
Inda, a Legend of the Lakes; With Other Poems, St. Louis, 1842.
Rhymes of the Routs in Mexico . . . , Washington, D. C., 1847.
Cortez the Conqueror. A Tragedy . . . , Washington, D. C., 1857.

THOMAS, LEWIS FRANCIS (Nov. 1, 1886–Feb. 13, 1950), educator, was born in Pioneer, Williams County. A graduate of Denison University in 1910 and of the University of Chicago (Ph.D.) in 1925, he served on the faculty of Washington University, St. Louis, 1919–50. His writings include *The Geography of the Saint Louis Trade Territory,* [St. Louis], 1924. WWW 3

THOMAS, LOWELL JACKSON (April 6, 1892–), was born in Woodington, Darke County, and he remained an Ohioan until he was eight, when his father, a physician and a scholarly man, took him to Colorado. If he must be regarded as a world citizen, as of course he is, he was first a very young citizen of Ohio, and thus we Ohioans claim him as our own. In a rough and brawling Colorado mining town, he sharpened his sense of adventure which in later years was to carry him over all the earth. He also continued to acquire something of equal value. His father was a man devoted to literature and a man greatly moved by color and form. The poetry and prose of the great masters were familiar to him, and he could—and did—recite the classics from memory. When Lowell was a small child in Ohio, his father gently but firmly directed him into this same pursuit of literature. The boy continued to be schooled in the same manner in Colorado. He also learned voice control from his diligent parent. Thus Lowell learned early to express himself in spoken and written prose which carried dignity, power, and purpose. The resonant quality of his voice in later years was to charm millions of radio, television, and newsreel listeners. It was in Colorado that Lowell was first touched with printing ink. He became a printer's devil and later a reporter. During his life he has been reporter, editor, and associate editor for a dozen newspapers and other periodicals. He was to prove himself a student of large talents. He attended four universities, the first at Valparaiso in Indiana, where he tended a furnace, waited on tables, and worked in a laundry to cover a four-year course in two years. He gathered two more degrees at the University of Denver, and then set out for Chicago with the idea of studying law. In earning his way he became a Chicago newspaper reporter and a friend of several men who were on their way to greatness, including Carl Sandburg, Ben Hecht, and Harry Hansen. After a year in Chicago he set out for the West Coast to write a series of newspaper articles, and then headed for Alaska. He acquired a canoe, and, alone, shot Miles Canyon and White Horse Rapids and paddled down the Yukon. He continued northward to the edge of the Arctic Ocean, where he was adopted into a tribe of Indians. Among the few white men he met was a lonely miner who befriended him and gave him a set of magnificent photographs of Eskimos and caribou. With these he came back to the States and set himself up as a lecturer on Alaska with great financial success. He returned to Alaska the following summer with his own camera to enlarge his knowledge of the Far

North and his gallery of fine photographs. Shortly after America entered World War I, Lowell Thomas was married to Frances Ryan, and from this union one son, Lowell, Jr., was born. He has followed in his father's footsteps as explorer, adventurer, and writer, establishing in his own right a world-wide reputation. With America at war but a short time, Franklin K. Lane, then Secretary of the Interior, devised a plan to send Thomas to Europe with a roving commission to visit all fronts and report to the American people on what he saw and heard. This assignment led to one of his greatest adventures. While in Venice, he heard of General Allenby's appointment to command the Allied forces in the Near East. He obtained permission from the British War Office to join Allenby. While with Allenby's army he heard rumors of a British officer who had united the hostile Arab tribes in a fierce war against the Turks. His trail of adventure finally led him to the man, who was, of course, Lawrence of Arabia. Thus Thomas brought to the outside world for the first time the fantastic story of the man whose genius was responsible for organizing the Arab revolt against Turkey, which led to the defeat of the Turks and the triumphant entry of the Arabs into Damascus. It has been said of Thomas that he has visited more remote areas of the earth than any other living man, but between trips he has been busy with books and lectures making armchair adventurers of millions of Americans. A man with enormous energy—and with a voice that can charm the birds from the trees—he became, between the two great wars, a radio commentator. In the mid-1930s it is estimated that he spoke daily to some twenty million Americans over the radio. His reporting was—and continues to be—impersonal and wholly unbiased. Yet he has many hobbies besides travel. He once managed a baseball team, and he has been known to take friends on rattlesnake hunts. He loves horses and once acquired an outlaw horse which he gentled until it became the best performer in his stables. Thomas has not greatly slackened his pace after his long and distinguished career. He is still much sought after as a lecturer. He continues to write. He maintains offices in New York City, but lives at Hammersley Hill, Pawling, N. Y. More, however, than any other living man who writes and talks, his office and home are the earth on which he lives; and nowadays there is in Lowell Thomas' eyes the faraway look of a man who would like to make his next adventure to the moon or stars or some other new and challenging and hitherto unvisited place. Lowell Thomas is a remarkable man, perhaps the greatest writer-speaker-adventurer the Twentieth Century has had. A representative sampling of the nearly fifty books he has written includes *Beyond Khyber Pass,* New York, [1925]; *The Boy's Life of Colonel Lawrence,* New York, [1927]; *Raiders of the Deep,* New York, 1928; *Kabluk of the Eskimo,* Boston, 1932; *Men of Danger,* New York, 1936; and *These Men Shall Never Die,* Philadelphia, [1943].

Louis B. Seltzer

THOMAS, MARTHA McCANNON (Jan., 1818–Jan. 23, 1890), daughter of Ebenezer S. Thomas (q.v.), was born in Charleston, S. C., and in 1829 came to Cincinnati, where she lived for the rest of her life. She was the founding editor of the *Young People's Monthly* in 1858. From Dec. 22, 1863, to Jan. 2, 1864, she edited the *Ladies' Knapsack,* published by the Great Western Sanitary Fair, Cincinnati. Her most successful literary work was *Captain Phil,* several editions of which appeared within a few years of its first publication. She died in Cincinnati. The first title below was published anonymously.

Life's Lesson. A Tale, New York, 1854.

Captain Phil; A Boy's Experience in the Western Army during the War of the Rebellion, New York, 1884.

THOMAS, MARY ELIZA VON ERDEN (Dec. 8, 1814–Dec. 6, 1897), daughter of Ebenezer S. Thomas (q.v.), was born in Charleston, S. C., and accompanied her father to Cincinnati in 1829. She apparently adopted the name Mary Von Erden Thomas at an early age. She served as a nurse throughout the Civil War. She died in Washington, D. C.

Winning the Battle; Or, One Girl in Ten Thousand, Philadelphia, [1882].

THOMAS, NORMAN MATTOON (Nov. 20, 1884–), was born in Marion, Marion County, son of Rev. Welling E. Thomas and Emma Mattoon Thomas. One of his grandfathers was a minister; the other, a missionary. The boy grew up in an atmosphere of Calvinism which drew a sharp line between good and evil and placed them poles apart, with no hope of compromise between the Lord's bright hosts and the dark legions beyond the pale. This attitude shaped all of his future efforts. After a brilliant high school career and a year at Bucknell, he entered Princeton, from which he graduated in 1905 after significant exposure to Woodrow Wilson's thought and teaching. He spent the next six years working in settlement houses in the New York slums, where men take a strong stand on the evidences of life and faith, and studying in Union Theological Seminary, where another viewpoint was in vogue. They were years of turmoil as he attempted to reconcile the two; his ordination examination took an entire afternoon, and the doggedness with which the Presbytery probed the depths of his growing unorthodoxy was turned into front-page copy by the newspapers. For six years he was pastor of East Harlem Presbyterian Church —one of a group of churches and settlement houses comprising American Parish on the upper East Side. The years he spent among the poor there and the shock of World War I, which clashed with his principles of Christian pacifism, led him formally to adopt Socialism in 1917. The final break with his pastorate came when he supported Morris Hillquist, the Socialist candidate for mayor of New York. It was not an expedient time to assert any form of political independence. Thomas was subjected to the persecutions in vogue at the moment—shadowing by Justice Department agents, wire tapping, interrogation, attempted suppression of his writings by postmaster general Burleson, the rowdy brutalities of postwar red-baiting. The time at which he made his choice, however, was one of Thomas' strengths. "What I like about Norman," one of the old-line party members has said, "is that he came to us when everybody else was running away." Thomas spent the next decade in a fight for wider political expression. With Roger Baldwin, he founded the American Civil Liberties Union. He entered politics in 1924 as a candidate for governor of New York; he ran for mayor of New York City in 1925, for the state senate in 1926, for alderman in 1927, and for President of the United States in 1928, 1932, 1936, 1940, and 1944. Under his leadership, the Socialist Party has followed with textbook faithfulness the role of a militant third party: it has provided ideas while failing to elect candidates. For one striking example: by 1935, 22 of the 26 planks of the Socialist Party's 1932 platform had either been put into effect (though often modified), or were being considered as possible laws or treaties, or had been achieved by informal but effective measures (e.g., the cancellation of war debts). Thomas' position cannot be summed up in a word or classified with a label. He regards Marx as an extremely important social thinker—but that much even a conservative would have to admit. To him, Marxian theory, while basic, must be considered only in the light of recent advances in technology and social organization, and, especially, in terms of the dynamic psychology of Freud and his followers. In Thomas' own thought there seems to be as much of the forces that shaped Thorstein Veblen as of those that Marx and Engels unleashed. This has brought bitter criticism from the extreme left wing, but it undoubtedly has added to his effectiveness as a political leader. He shares experiences that many Americans have undergone, and he speaks a language that they recognize; no undeviating Marxist can hope to do these things. In speech and writing, Thomas is clear and convincing; he is given to sudden, unexpected flashes of metaphor which brilliantly illuminate a point. Some of his critics have protested that he appeals more to emotion and inspiration than to cold fact. This may be true, though few can best him in a showdown debate. After all, when we first hear the voice crying from the wilderness, it is not likely to stir us by quoting from *Statistical Abstracts.* A few of his more influential books include *The Conscientious Objector in America,* New York, 1923; *As I See It,* New York, 1932; *The Choice before Us . . . ,* New York, 1934; *After the New Deal, What?,* New York, 1936; *Socialism on the Defensive,* New York, 1938; *Russia—Democracy or Dictatorship?,* New York, 1939; and *We Have a Future,* Princeton, 1941. "It was my fortune," he wrote in 1951, "to be born in an era of hope." Let it stand as commentary on the life and accomplishments of this gentle, angry man who, without ever having a major party at his back, has influenced our political thought and action as much as any man living.

Lee Templeton

THOMAS, ROLLA L. (Aug. 17, 1857–Dec. 28, 1932), physician, was born in Harrison, Hamilton County. After graduating from Asbury University in 1878 and from Eclectic Medical College in 1880, he practiced in Harrison until 1887, when he moved to Cincinnati to join the faculty of Eclectic Medical College. He published *The Eclectic Practice of Medicine,* Cincinnati, 1906. WWW 1

THOMAS, RUTH (Oct. 29, 1907–), educator, was born in Cheshire, Gallia County. After graduating from Ohio University in 1928, she taught in Gallia County and now lives in Rio Grande. She has written articles for periodicals and has published a collection of poems: *Flint and Fireflies,* Boston, [1942].

THOMAS, THOMAS EBENEZER (Dec. 23, 1812–Feb. 3, 1875), clergyman and educator, was born in Chelmsford, England. In 1834 he graduated from Miami University, where he was an active abolitionist. After being ordained by the Cincinnati Presbytery, he served Presbyterian churches in Harrison and Hamilton. He was president of Hanover College, Ind., 1849–55, professor in the Theological Seminary, New Albany, Ind., 1854–57, pastor of the First Presbyterian Church, Dayton, 1858–71, and professor at Lane Theological Seminary, Cincinnati, 1871–75. He died in Cincinnati. His son, Alfred Addison Thomas (July 4, 1845–March 3, 1916), an attorney in Dayton, edited his letters, which are mostly concerned with the antislavery struggle: *Correspondence of Thomas Ebenezer Thomas . . . ,* [Dayton?], 1909.

THOMAS, THOMAS HEAD (Feb. 23, 1881–), was born in Dayton, Montgomery County. He graduated from Harvard University in 1903, lived in Italy for many years, and now lives in Wayne, Pa. He has written *French Portrait Engraving of the XVIIth and XVIIIth Centuries,* London, 1910. WW 26

THOMPSON, AARON BELFORD (April 5, 1873–Jan. 26, 1929), was born in Rossmoyne, Hamilton County. Around 1900 he moved to Indianapolis, where he spent the remainder of his life; there he was encouraged to write by James Whitcomb Riley, who wrote the preface for his *Harvest of Thoughts.* He gave public readings of his poetry, as did his two sisters, also born in Rossmoyne: Priscilla Jane Thompson (? – ?), author of *Gleanings of Quiet Hours,* Rossmoyne, 1907; and Clara Ann Thompson (1875?–1950?), author of *A Garland of Poems,* Boston, [1926].

Morning Songs, Rossmoyne, 1899.
Echoes of Spring, Rossmoyne, 1901.
Harvest of Thoughts, Indianapolis, 1907.

THOMPSON, ADELE EUGENIA (1849–April 1, 1929), was born in Mansfield, Richland County. She lived for a time in Cleveland but spent most of her life in Middlefield, Geauga County. She wrote for magazines and newspapers. Several of the titles below were published in the "Brave Hearts" series for young readers.

Beck's Fortune, Boston, 1899.
Betty Seldon, Patriot, Boston, 1901.
Brave Heart Elizabeth . . . , Boston, 1902.
A Lassie of the Isles, Boston, 1903.
Polly of the Pines . . . , Boston, [1906].
American Patty, a Story of 1812, Boston, [1909].
Nobody's Rose . . . , Boston, [1912].

THOMPSON, CLARA ANN. See Aaron B. Thompson.

THOMPSON, DAVID DeCAMP (April 29, 1852–Nov. 10, 1908), journalist, was born in Cincinnati, Hamilton County. He graduated from Ohio Wesleyan University in 1876, and from 1892 until his death he was on the editorial staff of the *Northwestern Christian Advocate.* He died in St. Louis, Mo.

Abraham Lincoln, the First American, Cincinnati, 1894.
John Wesley as a Social Reformer, New York, 1898.

THOMPSON, ELIZA JANE TRIMBLE (Aug. 24, 1816–Nov. 3, 1905), daughter of Gov. Allen Trimble (q.v.), was born in Hillsboro, Highland County. After attending Hillsboro schools and a private school in Cincinnati, she married James H. Thompson (q.v.) in 1837. On the evening of Dec. 23, 1873, a Boston lyceum lecturer, Dio Lewis, delivered a lecture at the Hillsboro Music Hall in which he advanced a plan for fighting the liquor traffic by uniting in prayer with and for the liquor sellers of the town. The movement was started in Hillsboro at once with Mrs. Thompson at its head. According to Frances E. Willard, this was the start of the famous Women's Crusade, from which developed the Woman's Christian Temperance Union. In writing her account of the crusade, Mrs. Thompson was assisted by her two daughters, Mrs. Mary M. T. Tuttle and Mrs. Marie T. Rives (qq.v.).

Hillsboro Crusade Sketches and Family Records, Cincinnati, 1896.

THOMPSON, GEORGE (Aug. 12, 1817–Feb. 4, 1893), clergyman, was born in Madison, N. J. In 1832 his parents migrated to Jersey, Licking County. In 1835 George entered Oberlin College, where he came under the influence of the abolitionist Theodore Weld (q.v.). In 1841, in Quincy, Ill., he was arrested and sentenced to twelve years in prison for helping some slaves escape. While in prison he composed poems to hymn meters, which he later published in *The Prison Bard.* Pardoned after serving five years, he lectured against slavery and studied theology at Oberlin. In 1848 he went to Sierra Leone, Africa, with a band of missionaries. In 1856 he returned to Oberlin, bringing two African boys to be educated there. He next served as a missionary in northern Michigan, where he organized several Congregational churches. In 1879 he returned to Oberlin so that his children could attend the college.

Prison Life and Reflections . . . , Oberlin, 1847.
The Prison Bard: Or, Poems on Various Subjects . . . , Hartford, 1848.
Thompson in Africa . . . , New York, 1852.
The Palm Land; Or, West Africa, Illustrated . . . , Cincinnati, 1859.
Africa in a Nutshell for the Million . . . , Oberlin, 1881.

THOMPSON, GEORGE W. (May 14, 1806–Feb. 24, 1888), lawyer and judge, was born in St. Clairsville, Belmont County, but spent most of his life in Virginia and West Virginia. He practiced law in Virginia in the 1840s and was elected to the House of Representatives in 1851, but resigned from Congress to serve as judge of the circuit court, 1851–60. Because of his opposition to secession, he retired from public life in 1860. He died near Wheeling, W. Va. Most of his books appeared anonymously.

Biographical Sketch of Hon. Linn Boyd . . . , Washington, 1852.
The Living Forces of the Universe . . . , Philadelphia, 1866.
Deus-Semper . . . , Philadelphia, 1869.
The Administration of Good and Evil, 1870.
Nos, Victuri, Salutamus, Wheeling, 1884.
The Song of Eighty, Wheeling, 1886.

THOMPSON, HENRY ADAMS (March 23, 1837–July 8, 1920), clergyman and educator, was born in Stormstown, Pa. He graduated from Jefferson College in 1858 and was licensed to preach by the United Brethren Church two years later. He taught at Otterbein College, 1862–67, was superintendent of schools in Troy, 1862–71, and was president of Otterbein, 1872–86. He afterward served in various editorial capacities in the United Brethren Publishing House, Dayton.

Our Bishops . . . , Chicago, 1889.
Biography of Jonathan Weaver, D.D. . . . , Dayton, 1901.
Bible Study and Devotion . . . , Dayton, [1904].
Women of the Bible . . . , Dayton, [1914].

THOMPSON, HUGH HOGUE (Oct. 13, 1819–April 29, 1899), clergyman, was born near Loydsville, Belmont County. After serving pastorates in Pennsylvania, he retired to spend the remainder of his life in Urbana. Besides the book below, he wrote a family history.

A History of Sidney Presbytery, 1879.

THOMPSON, JAMES HENRY (Sept. 27, 1812–Aug. 6, 1900), lawyer and judge, was born near Harrodsburg, Ky. After teaching school while reading law, he was admitted to the Kentucky bar in 1831. In 1837 he married Eliza J. Trimble, daughter of Allen Trimble (qq.v.). He was admitted to the Ohio bar in 1838, practiced in Cincinnati until 1842, and after 1842 lived and practiced in Hillsboro. In 1881 he was named judge of the district court. Besides the title below, some of his speeches were published separately in pamphlet form.

The History of the County of Highland . . . , Hillsboro, 1878.

THOMPSON, PRISCILLA JANE. See Aaron B. Thompson.

THOMPSON, RUTH LOCKWOOD (July 5, 1905–), was born in Cleveland, Cuyahoga County. She graduated from Hathaway-Brown School, Cleveland, 1923, and from Smith College, 1927. Since 1940 she has lived in Putney, Vt. She has contributed poems to magazines under the pen name Ruth T. Grandin and has published a collection of verse under her own name: *In and Out of Time,* New Orleans, [1929].

THOMPSON, WARREN SIMPSON (April 29, 1887–), educator, born in Weeping Water, Neb., joined the sociology department of Miami University in 1922 and still lives in Oxford. A specialist in population problems, he has published a number of articles, monographs, and books on the subject, e.g., *Danger Spots in World Population,* New York, 1929. WW 27

THOMPSON, WILLIAM TAPPAN (Aug. 31, 1812–March 24, 1882), humorist, was born in Ravenna, Portage County. When he was eleven, his mother died and he was taken to Philadelphia. His father died soon afterward, and he went to work for the *Daily Chronicle.* In 1830 he was made assistant to James D. Westcott, secretary of the Florida Territory, and while serving there he read law. In 1835 he was associated with Augustus Baldwin Longstreet, author of *Georgia Scenes,* in publishing the *States Rights Sentinel.* The *Family Companion and Ladies' Mirror,* which he published in the early 1840s, contained humorous sketches written by him under the pen name Major Joseph Jones. These sketches, in various editions, were highly popular and are the basis of his reputation as a humorist. After several years in Baltimore, he began editing the Savannah *Morning News* in 1850 and continued with that paper until his death. A stalwart defender of slavery, he served as a Confederate volunteer in 1864. His political editorials were forceful and often bitter. Although he was a spokesman for the Deep South, the backwoods life portrayed in his sketches is thought by some to reflect his boyhood memories of the Western Reserve. The sketches in his posthumous volume, *John's Alive,* were edited by his daughter, Mrs. May A. Wade.

Chronicles of Pineville . . . , Philadelphia, [1843].
Major Jones's Courtship . . . , Madison, Ga., 1843.
Major Jones's Sketches of Travel . . . , Philadelphia, 1848.
The Slaveholder Abroad, Philadelphia, 1860.
John's Alive; Or, the Bride of a Ghost, and Other Sketches, Philadelphia, 1883.

THOMSON, EDWARD (Oct. 12, 1810–March 22, 1870), clergyman and educator, was born in Portsea, England. In 1818 he was brought to Wooster, where his father opened a drugstore. After studying medicine at Jefferson Medical College, Philadelphia, 1828–29, he began practice at Jeromeville, Wayne County. He was converted to Methodism in 1831 and was admitted to the Ohio Conference on trial in 1832. He served as pastor in Sandusky and Cincinnati and as principal of Norwalk Seminary, 1838–42. He was chosen the first president of Ohio Wesleyan University and served until 1860, when he became editor of the *Christian Advocate and Journal,* published in New York City. In 1864 he was elected bishop and soon afterward was sent to the Orient to tour Methodist missions. He died in Wheeling, W. Va.

Essays, Educational and Religious, (Edward D. Roe, ed.), Cincinnati, 1855.
Essays, Moral and Religious, Cincinnati, 1856.
Letters from Europe . . . , Cincinnati, 1856.
Sketches Biographical and Incidental, Cincinnati, 1857.
Our Oriental Missions . . . , 2 vols., Cincinnati, 1870.
Evidences of Revealed Religion, New York, 1872.
Christ as a Teacher, New York, 1883.
Selected Essays, Cincinnati, 1893.

THOMSON, PETER GIBSON (Dec. 16, 1851–July 10, 1931), manufacturer, was born in Cincinnati, Hamilton County. At the age of fourteen, he began working in the bookstore of Robert Clarke Co., and he later operated his own bookstore for six years. He entered the field of color printing, specializing in children's books and valentines. As he prospered, he devoted much of his time to the collection of books regarding the Northwest Territory—a project that culminated in the publication of his great bibliography. In 1892 he founded a factory for the manufacture of coated paper in Hamilton. By 1901 it was the largest such plant in the world with branches in several cities. His bibliography is undoubtedly the most useful single work for the study of Ohio literature.

A Bibliography of the State of Ohio . . . , Cincinnati, 1880.
Catalogue of Books Relating to the State of Ohio, the West and North-west, [Cincinnati, 1890].

THOMSON, WILLIAM McCLURE (Dec. 31, 1806–April 8, 1894), missionary, was born in Spring Dale, Hamilton County. He graduated from Miami University in 1828, studied at Princeton Seminary for two years, and was ordained as a Presbyterian minister in 1831. He served as a missionary in Palestine and Syria from 1833 to 1876, establishing schools and mission stations. In his travels through the Holy Land, Thomson studied closely the topography and archaeological evidence. His observations are embodied in *The Land and the Book . . . ,* a description of the region correlated with the Bible. The book sold very widely and was published in numerous editions.

The Land and the Book . . . , 2 vols., New York, 1859.

THORNBURY, DELMAR LEON (Aug. 15, 1881–), lawyer, was born in Beallsville, Monroe County. After graduating from the University of Nebraska in 1902, he taught school in Nebraska and California, 1902–13, and in 1913 began the practice of law. He published *California's Redwood Wonderland, Humboldt County,* [San Francisco, 1923]. WW 17

THORNDIKE, ASHLEY HORACE (Dec. 26, 1871–April 17, 1933), educator, born in Houlton, Maine, served on the English faculty of Western Reserve University, 1898–1902. He taught at Columbia University from 1906 until his death. He wrote a number of textbooks and literary studies, the most influential of which probably was *Tragedy,* Boston, 1908. WWW 1

THORNDIKE, LYNN (July 24, 1882–), educator, born in Lynn, Mass., was a master at University School, Cleveland, and was on the history faculty, Western Reserve University, 1909–24. He afterward taught at Columbia University and still lives in New York City. He has published numerous history textbooks and *A History of Magic and Experimental Science . . .* , 8 vols., New York, 1923–58. WW 27

THORNE, CHARLES EMBREE (Oct. 4, 1846–Feb. 29, 1936), agriculturist, was born in Greene County. He attended Michigan Agricultural College and Antioch College. He served as farm manager at Ohio State University, 1877–81, as associate editor of *Farm and Fireside,* 1882–88, and as conservation chief at the Ohio Agricultural Experiment Station in Wooster.

The Complete Poultry Book, Springfield, [1882].

The Handy Horse Book . . . , Springfield, 1883.

Farm Manures, New York, 1913.

The Maintenance of Soil Fertility, New York, 1930.

THORNE, P. Pseud. See Mary P. W. Smith.

THORNTON, EDWIN WILLIAM (Aug. 20, 1863–Nov. 14, 1940), clergyman, was born near West Middleburg, Logan County. After being ordained a minister of the Disciples of Christ Church, he served pastorates in various cities and for 24 years was an editor at the Standard Publishing Company, Cincinnati. After retiring in 1934, he moved to Canton, where he spent the remainder of his life. He wrote many articles and pamphlets on Sunday school work and published a book for Sunday school teachers: *Common Sense; A Study of Mind and Method . . .* , Cincinnati, [1913]. WWW 3

THORNTON, GEORGE B. (March 1, 1881–), was born in Aberdeen, Brown County. After attending high school in Higginsport, he served in the Spanish-American War, attended Walden University, Tenn., and Tuskegee Institute, served in the army again, and was on the staff of Tuskegee Institute. In 1941 he came to Washington Court House. He now lives in Wilberforce. He has published several collections of verse, e.g., *Great Poems,* Wilberforce, 1946.

THORNTON, JESSY QUINN (Aug. 24, 1810–Feb. 5, 1888), lawyer, born near Point Pleasant, Va., grew up in Champaign County, where his parents moved while he was a child. After studying law in Virginia, he practiced in Missouri and Illinois. In 1846 he went to Oregon, where he was active in the establishment of the territorial government. His book was written in 1848, while he was in Washington, D. C., working for the establishment of Oregon as a territory: *Oregon and California in 1848 . . .* , 2 vols., New York, 1849.

THORNTON, WILLIS (March 10, 1900–), was born in Cleveland, Cuyahoga County. He attended public schools in Akron and graduated from Western Reserve University in 1921. He was a reporter on the Cleveland *Press* and the Washington *Daily News,* wrote syndicated feature stories for N.E.A., served in World War II, lectured on journalism at Western Reserve University, and in 1959 became director of the Western Reserve University Press. He has published several books on biographical and historical topics, e.g., *The Life of Alfred M. Landon,* New York, [1936].

THRUSTON, GATES PHILLIPS (June 11, 1835–Dec. 8, 1912), attorney, was born in Dayton, Montgomery County. He graduated from Miami University in 1855 and from Cincinnati Law School in 1859. He practiced in Dayton until the Civil War. He served throughout the war and was breveted brigadier general in 1865. From 1865 until his death he practiced law in Nashville, Tenn. Besides the titles below, he wrote many articles on historical subjects and a family history.

The Antiquities of Tennessee . . . , Cincinnati, 1890.

Personal Recollections of the Battle in the Rear at Stone's River . . . , Nashville, [1906?].

THUMA, HELEN DOAN (Aug. 12, 1881–), was born in Cincinnati, Hamilton County, and still lives in that city. She has published a volume of poems: *Golden Sunsets,* Cincinnati, 1933.

THURBER, JAMES GROVER (Dec. 8, 1894–Nov. 2, 1961), was born in Columbus, Franklin County. William Faulkner was once said to have listed the five most important U. S. authors of the twentieth century in this order: Thomas Wolfe, himself, John Dos Passos, Ernest Hemingway, and John Steinbeck. In any such list, however, the name of James Thurber most surely belongs. It might even be argued that when future critics of American literature appraise the work of U. S. authors of the period, say 1930 to 1960, they may well conclude that Thurber belongs among the top three. From the time he began writing successfully for *The New Yorker* in 1927,

Thurber in the next third of a century built a tremendous reputation as a humorist. That he is one, and an outstanding one, there is no doubt. That until his eyesight failed completely he was an artist, even if somewhat accidentally, is also true. But in time Thurber is most likely to be regarded as a serious writer. In his own view, Thurber so regards himself, and it dismays and annoys him somewhat that readers and critics have failed to discern the serious vein beneath the apparent humor. At 66 Thurber is tall, slim, and straight, with distinctive gray hair brushed straight back at the sides and with a tuft of black in front for contrast. He has a way of looking directly at you, although he can no longer see anything. He has a trick of putting his left hand to his chin in a ruminative fashion. But words tumble from his lips in a steady stream and he can talk effortlessly for hours with very little prompting. When people are introduced to him he invariably responds, "I'm glad to see you," or if it is someone he knows, it's "I'm glad to see you again." He is a chain-smoker, lighting his own cigarettes, pinching them out when they have served their purpose, and feeling unerringly for the ash tray in front of him. Socially, he drinks scotch and soda steadily, with no side effects. The biographical sketch of Thurber in Volume XXXI of *Who's Who in America* says of him "in journalistic work since 1920." Actually Thurber's strivings, as he himself reported in the chapter in *The Thurber Album* devoted to Robert O. ("Bob") Ryder, longtime editor and paragrapher of the *Ohio State Journal,* began as far back as his high school days. Certainly also he continued to develop this interest during his years on the Ohio State University campus, especially on campus publications. He toiled on *The Lantern,* the University newspaper, and *The Sun-Dial,* the campus humor magazine, which continued to brag four decades later that Thurber was its most distinguished former editor. Thurber himself on occasion has put the figure for his reportorial newspaper experience at seven to ten years. In 1920 he returned to Columbus from Paris, where he had been a code clerk in the U. S. embassy, to become a $25-a-week reporter on the Columbus *Dispatch.* For the next four years, as he tells it, he learned to be a journeyman reporter the hard way under hard-boiled Norman ("Gus") Kuehner, *Dispatch* city editor. Kuehner, no college man himself, scoffed at all college men on a newspaper staff, and Thurber was one of those who helped pay the price for this inferiority complex on Kuehner's part. With an incipient novel stirring in his bosom, Thurber returned to Paris in 1924–25. The novel apparently died aborning, and to keep body and soul together Thurber joined the staff of the Paris edition of the Chicago *Tribune* at $12 a week. The next year he went to New York City, where he caught on as a reporter with the *Evening Post.* After a series of rejection slips, he finally made a connection with *The New Yorker* in 1927, an association that was to remain unbroken for more than a third of a century. During those three decades, in fact, three men personified *The New Yorker:* Harold Ross, E. B. White, and Thurber. Thurber was the second of three sons of Charles L. and Mary Agnes Fisher Thurber. He attended Columbus East High School and Ohio State University. Both the city and the University have played a large part in his writings. So have the members of his family, especially his mother and his maternal grandfather. This is particularly true of his autobiographical writings. The real Thurber country, of course, is Columbus and central Ohio. In a message to the mayor of Columbus when it was recognized as an All-American city in 1959, Thurber wrote: "I have always waved banners and blown horns for Good Old Columbus Town, in America as well as abroad, and such readers as I have collected through the years are all aware of where I was born and brought up, and they know that half of my books could not have been written if it had not been for the city of my birth." Although he never completed the requirements for a degree, Ohio State University has been important in Thurber's life. He went there as a freshman in 1913, withdrew, re-entered, and left again in 1918. The campus and its people figured in *The Male Animal,* which he wrote in collaboration with Elliott Nugent (q.v.), and in some of his other writings. *The Thurber Album,* "a new collection of pieces about people," was dedicated to the late Herman A. Miller of the University English faculty. When he was putting the book together, Thurber said it was about people who had influenced his life. Three of its sixteen chapters were devoted to outstanding Ohio State English professors: Joseph Russell Taylor, William Lucius Graves, and Joseph Villiers Denney, Arts College dean and English department head. In April, 1960, Thurber returned to the campus to speak at the dedication of the new $2,250,000 Denney Hall. On that occasion he described the three men as having "meant so much to Ohio State, to all of us here, to me and my life, and to my work." He recalled also that "It was natural, it was inevitable," twenty years earlier, when he and Elliott Nugent began writing *The Male Animal,* that they "should pattern our Dean of English in the play, Dr. Damon, upon the length and light of Joe Denney." At the dedication he spoke also of the late Herman Miller as having "meant as much to me as any man who ever lived." For years the University had a rigid policy of requiring military drill of all freshmen and sophomores unless excused for physical disability or other necessity. The Arts College also had a biological science requirement. Because of his impaired vision, Thurber was in difficulty on both counts. In his botany course he was unable to see through a microscope, even with his "good" eye. Thurber has an incredible memory. He is one of very few persons gifted with actual total recall. This may have been sharpened by his blindness, but he had it long before he finally lost the use of what little sight remained in his "good" eye. In a recorded interview for *The Paris Review,* he dealt with this at some length and said he got his unusual power of memory from his mother. Not only can he dredge isolated and unrelated names, facts, and dates out of the past, but he can also recall entire conversations and even commencement addresses. The final loss of his little remaining eyesight compelled Thurber to change his methods. In the 1920s and 1930s he literally composed at the typewriter. When he and Nugent were collaborating on *The Male Animal,* Nugent would say they had all their characters in the living room, now what were they going to do with them. Thurber's reply was that he did not know and could not tell until he sat down at his typewriter, then he would find out. When he could no longer work at the typewriter, he switched to black copy pencil on yellow paper, scrawling about twenty words to a page. The final stage was to learn to compose in his head and then dictate to a secretary, revising by having the output read and reread to him. As with many writers, rewriting and revision are much more of a task for Thurber than the original writing. In the *Paris Review* interview he told how his still unpublished "The Train on Track Six" was completely rewritten fifteen times. He estimated there must have been nearly 240,000 words in all, yet the final version was not more than 20,000 words. He recalled having written only one piece quickly. On another occasion, when his wife criticized something he had written as "high school stuff," he told her to wait until the seventh draft when it would work out all right. He could not explain why the first draft or two of everything he wrote read as if it had been "turned out by a charwoman." Thurber credits E. B. White more than Harold Ross, editor of *The New Yorker,* with influencing his style of writing. After his years of newspaper writing, he says, it was White who really taught him about writing and especially how to clarify journalese. The author also says he never quite knows when he is not writing; he may find himself working at a party or at the dinner table, but it is more likely to be at the morning sessions with himself devoted to turning things over in his mind. He explans that he has to do this because of his eyes. Thurber is a stickler for details, with a real passion for accuracy in his writing, especially in factual pieces. When he was doing the piece about Ryder for *The Thurber Album,* he recalled seeing Ryder in his electric runabout but never at the wheel of the Cadillac that he drove in later years. He recalled Col. E. S. Wilson, Ryder's father-in-law, not as "a pumpkin pie man" as some insisted, but "mainly as a cherry pie man." He credits Ryder, a widely quoted newspaper humorist, with having been the one who first inspired him. For minor details, such as an earlier Ryder street address, Thurber relied upon Columbus newspapermen who had also known and worked for Ryder. On their word he accepted the fact that the editor always wore a black bow tie and, after his health failed, lived in a house on a hillside overlooking "Oakland Bay" in Berkeley, Calif. Thurber was most unhappy after publication when he learned that Ryder actually affected dark blue ties and, as anyone should have known, it was San Francisco Bay. In a letter of the time from Bermuda, he wrote: "The *New Yorker* under Ross didn't make that many mistakes in two years, and I hope it's only a passing letdown as a result of grief and a natural lack of concentration in the months following his death." This was not long after Ross died. His attention was called to the fact that the name of Joseph S. Myers, longtime journalism head at Ohio State, was spelled "Myers" and not "Meyers" as it appeared. In a postscript he protested, "I know how to spell Myers, but the *New Yorker* checkers found it spelled Meyers in some official Ohio State records, and changed it without telling me. They also wanted to spell "Chic" Harley's name Chick, but I prevented that. It appears as Chick in a standard sports source book, which also lists him as a fullback. I stopped that, too. . . ." Thurber feels strongly about many issues, including the recurring one of academic freedom. In 1951, for example, he objected to the adoption by Ohio State University trustees of a rule under which outside speakers had to be screened before they could come to the campus. "Such a gag rule," he remarked in a letter, "is likely to extend rather than to decrease in time. I wonder what they will do in the case of various men, like myself, who have spoken, without notes, to English and journalism classes." He noted that he had always been "a vehement anti-communist, a fact that could be proved in a few hours of research, but I have no doubt that, like almost all writers, I will one day be named as a Red." He felt positive that "a communist speaker could not possibly sway an Ohio State audience and that in refusing to let communists talk, the university deprives itself of a wonderful chance to heckle and confound such speakers. If we cannot be strong enough Americans to withstand such arguments, if we are in such danger of being politically debauched, then all we have in the Western Conference is the greatest football area in the world. . . ." An author or an artist may not have the best perspective of himself. Nevertheless, his opinions and impressions about his work and himself are sometimes valuable, often significant, and certainly interesting. For the preparation of this sketch, Thurber was asked seven specific questions, which he answered promptly. The questions and the replies follow:

Q. What aspects of your work do you now regard as most important?

A. I try to make as perceptive and helpful a comment on the human predicament as I can, in fables, fairy tales, stories, and essays. I am surprised that so few people see the figure of seriousness in the carpet of my humor and comedy. My favorite recent book is *Further Fables for Our Time,* which strives to say things sharply, but entertainingly, about men and women, Man and Woman, politicians and people. I am proud that it won the award given in 1957 by the Fund for the Republic of the Ford Foundation for the work in the entire field of imaginative literature that had done the most for the cause of liberty and justice. It was selected by a committee that included two professors, a poet, and a librarian, and represented the country at large.

Q. Do you think your drawings will hold interest as long as your writings?

A. I have no idea what things of mine, if any, will be remembered after I am dead, and I don't give it much thought. You can get any kind of opinion you want about the drawings. On the whole, my work, as writer and cartoonist, has been as well received in England as here, whatever that may indicate.

Q. What do you regard now as your best single work?

A. I let other people pick my best single work, and never speculate about it. *Further Fables for Our Time* is the best from a social consciousness viewpoint, I guess, but I should also include my original book, *Fables for Our Time.* I have often said, "My best book is the one I'm working on."

Q. Apart from what is in the *Album,* who had the greatest influence upon you in what might be called your formative years?

A. As Thornton Wilder has said, we are all influenced by other writers to begin with, but must throw off that influence as we mature. I had to throw off the influence of Henry James and Joseph Hergesheimer, and the tendency to write such a Jamesian sentence as this: "First of all, it occurred to me, there was one thing, to begin with, to do," and such a Hergesheimerism as this: "He remembered a girl in a boat, on a river, when it was summer, and afternoon."

Q. Would you say that any other living writer has influenced you, consciously or unconsciously?

A. When I went to *The New Yorker* in 1927, after ten years of newspaper writing, I learned a lot from E. B. White's fine clarity and pure declarative sentences. The way I write now, however, is absolutely my own, I think.

Q. What has been your most productive period, or would you say that you are still in it and see no immediate end to it?

A. I have published five books since 1955, and got the play on [*A Thurber Carnival*], written about twenty pieces, and am working now on two new fairy tales and a play. In my spare time I have written five thousand letters.

Q. Speculating, do you think you might have found some other outlet if *The New Yorker* had not been available to you?

A. I had written for *Harper's,* the *Sunday Times, World, Herald, Kansas City Star,* and *Vanity Fair,* and others, and had been offered editorial jobs on *Liberty* and on *Time* before going to *The New Yorker.*

As of 1960 a tally of Thurber's output showed 23 books and two plays. The plays were *The Male Animal* (1940), done in collaboration with actor Elliott Nugent, a fellow Ohioan, and *A Thurber Carnival.* Both plays were Broadway hits and *The Male Animal,* which had a Broadway revival in the early 1950s, was also made into a movie. The première of *Carnival,* appropriately, was in Columbus. It continued to undergo furious Thurber rewriting and revision until it reached New York some six weeks later. A current British film, *The Battle of the Sexes,* starring Peter Sellers, is based on the Thurber story "The Catbird Seat." Only one of the book-length works was the result of a collaboration. This was the humorous *Is Sex Necessary?* (1929), which was done with E. B. White. His other works, some of them collections of pieces which appeared originally in *The New Yorker,* include *The Owl in the Attic* (1931); *The Seal in the Bedroom* (1932); *My Life and Hard Times* (1933); *The Middle Aged Man on the Flying Trapeze* (1935); *Let Your Mind Alone* (1937); *The Last Flower* (1939); *Fables for Our Time* (1940); *The Secret Life of Walter Mitty* (1942); *My World—and Welcome to It* (1942); *Many Moons* (1943); *Men, Women and Dogs* (1943); *The Great Quillow* (1944); *The Thurber Carnival* (1945); *The White Deer* (1945); *The Beast in Me, and Other Animals* (1948); *The Thirteen Clocks* (1950); *The Thurber Album* (1952); *Thurber Country* (1953); *Thurber's Dogs* (1955); *Further Fables for Our Time* (1956); *The Wonderful O* (1957); *Alarms and Diversions* (1957); and *The Years with Ross* (1959). A number of the books, as noted, were autobiographical in nature. Among these were the familiar *My Life and Hard Times* and *The Thurber Album.* Even *The Years with Ross,* although mainly about his longtime *New Yorker* colleague, necessarily had much in it about Thurber. Before 1940, when his eyesight failed completely, Thurber illustrated several books by other authors. One of these, in 1938, was *How to Raise a Dog,* by J. R. Kinney. Another, a year later, was *Men Can Take It* by Elizabeth Hawes. Two others were *No Nice Girl Swears* by Alice Leone Moates, and *In a Word* by Margaret Ernst. He wrote four musical comedies for Scarlet Mask, a men's dramatic group on the Ohio State campus. In order, these were *O My! Omar; Many Moons; The Cat and the Riddle*; and *Tell Me Not.* Various Thurber pieces have been included in anthologies of one sort or another. *The Male Animal,* for example, was republished in a standard collection of ten plays. The well-known piece "The Night the Bed Fell" has appeared in countless anthologies, and "The Secret Life of Walter Mitty" is in at least thirty. "The Catbird Seat" and "University Days" have been reprinted many times. Apart from the world-wide acclaim for his work, various honors have come to Thurber, academic and otherwise. In 1953 he was awarded the Ohioana Sesquicentennial medal from the Ohioana Library Association. In 1957 his *Further Fables for Our Time,* as noted, won the award given by the Fund for the Republic. Kenyon College was the first to confer an honorary degree upon him; in 1950 it gave him a Litt. D. The next year Williams College followed with an L.H.D. In 1953 he was the recipient of a Litt. D. from Yale. It is not generally known that in 1951 he declined an honorary degree from Ohio State because of disagreement over the trustee "speakers' rule," which he regarded as a violation of academic freedom. As of 1960 James Thurber is full of years but still full of works, as his plans for the future attest. For 35 years he has made New York the center of his activity, but, cosmopolite though he is, he has remained at heart an Ohioan. He could not be present to receive the Ohioana Sesquicentennial medal, but his message was read for him. He said in part: "It is a great moment for an Ohio writer living far from home when he realizes that he has not been forgotten by the state he can't forget." Many of his books, he added, "prove that I am never very far away from Ohio in my thoughts, and that the clocks that strike in my dreams are often the clocks of Columbus." In passing, he paid tribute also to his mother, who died in 1955 at the age of 89, saying that "without her I never would have been able to write what I have managed to write." Whatever his ultimate stature, James Grover Thurber undoubtedly stands first among Ohio writers of the mid-twentieth century and certainly among America's top three or four of that period. At the time of his 55th birthday, in 1949, a writer in the New York *Times Sunday Magazine* called him "America's most subtle and gifted humorist." *Time* magazine the next year put it a little differently. It said that Thurber was "only every other inch a comic writer; in between, he is a psychologist as keen as any now writing in the U. S." E. B. White once said of him that "Thurber inhabits a world of his own." There is no question of his rank as the top American humorist of his time, but there are strong signs of a growing awareness of the underlying serious purpose of much of his writing. From what he has said publicly and privately, this is how he would want it.

James E. Pollard

Editor's Note: James Thurber died in New York City shortly after the above biographical sketch was set in type.

THURSTIN, WESLEY S. (June 11, 1838–July 23, 1910), lawyer, was born on a farm near Bowling Green, Wood County. He served throughout the Civil War in the 111th O.V.I. and later wrote the history of his regiment. A graduate of the University of Michigan Law School, he practiced in Toledo. His death occurred in that city.

History One Hundred and Eleventh Regiment O.V.I., Toledo, 1894.

THURSTON, HOWARD (July 20, 1869–April 13, 1936), magician, was born in Columbus, Franklin County. He was educated at Moody and Sankey School, Northfield, Mass. He performed as a magician from an early age and made several world tours with Harry Kellar (q.v.) and alone. He published books on card tricks, a mystery drama, *The Demon,* and an autobiography: *My Life of Magic,* Philadelphia, [1929]. WWW 1

THWING, CARRIE F. BUTLER (April 30, 1855–April 24, 1898), was born in Farmington, Maine. A graduate of Vassar College, she married Charles F. Thwing (q.v.) in 1879, and in 1890 she came with him to Cleveland. Her book was posthumously published.

Journal of a Tour in Europe, Cleveland, 1899.

THWING, CHARLES FRANKLIN (Nov. 9, 1853–Aug. 24, 1937), clergyman and university president, was born in New Sharon, Maine, a small village in southeastern Franklin County, the son of a tanner. He was descended through his mother from Stephen Hopkins, who came in the Mayflower, and through his father, Joseph Perkins Thwing, from Benjamin Thwing, who migrated from England to Massachusetts in 1635. Thwing's secondary education was secured at Phillips Andover Academy, from which he graduated at the age of eighteen and where he spent a postgraduate year before entering Harvard College in 1872. At the Academy he distinguished himself as a student, a debater, and a writer. In 1876 he was graduated from Harvard *cum laude,* ranking third in his class. Two years before, he had had the rare distinction of election to Phi Beta Kappa as a sophomore. He entered the Phillips Andover Theological Seminary in 1876, graduating in 1879. Upon graduation he was ordained a Congregational minister and began his career as pastor of the North Avenue Congregational Church of Cambridge, Mass., serving there until 1886. A second pastorate was then begun at the Plymouth Congregational Church of Minneapolis, Minn. This ended in 1890 with his acceptance of a repeated invitation to become president of Western Reserve University in Cleveland. On November 11, 1890, at the age of 37, he was inaugurated and he served in that position until his retirement in 1921. From a superficial point of view, Western Reserve was not an impressive institution. It had developed out of Western Reserve College for men, founded in 1826 in the village of Hudson, about 25 miles south of Cleveland. Its name was derived from that of the northeastern section of Ohio, which was the "Connecticut Western Reserve" and was settled to a considerable extent by former residents of that New England state. The old college was modeled on the New England colleges and drew largely on them for its teachers. In 1844 a medical school in Cleveland affiliated as the medical department of the college. In 1882 a wealthy Cleveland business man, Amasa Stone, offered to the trustees of the college a considerable endowment and a free site in Cleveland, on condition that the college be removed to Cleveland and that its name be changed to Adelbert College of Western Reserve University, in memory of Mr. Stone's son who had been drowned while a student at Yale. This offer was accepted by the trustees. The shift embittered the townspeople of Hudson, as well as many of the alumni of the Hudson days. A further source of conflict was the introduction of coeducation by President Carroll Cutler (1872–1886). In 1888 the "coeducation" was changed to "co-ordination" by the creation of the College for Women (now Flora Stone Mather College of Western Reserve University), with a separate campus and, eventually, with a separate faculty. Since both the move and the struggle over coeducation had left a trail of resentment on the part of some alumni, students, faculty, and the public, it is apparent that Dr. Thwing was not picking a bed of roses. At the time of his inauguration in 1890, the number of students was eighty in Adelbert College, 45 in the College for Women, and 121 in the Medical School—246 in all. The faculty numbered forty, and there were four buildings on the two campuses, in addition to the medical school in the downtown area. By 1921, when Dr. Thwing retired, the number of faculties had increased to eight by the addition of the Schools of Law, Dentistry, Pharmacy, Graduate Study, and Social Work, and the Department of Religious Education. The faculty had grown to 181, the student body to 2,118. The budget had risen from $100,-

000 to $700,000; the library, from 25,000 volumes to 150,000; the four buildings, to 22. Dr. Thwing survived his retirement by sixteen years, dying in Cleveland at the age of 83. He was married twice: in 1879 to Carrie F. Butler (see Carrie F. B. Thwing), who bore him two daughters and a son, of whom the latter survives; and in 1906 to Mary Gardiner Dunning (d.1931). President Thwing was an impressive figure, tall, solidly built, not inclined to stoutness. His normal aspect was serious but he smiled easily and laughed heartily. His very pronounced New England accent was worn down only slightly in fifty years of living in the Middle West. With his equipment of body and speech he could have been a forbidding figure, but he was not. Dr. Thwing was a very industrious man. Throughout much of his tenure he arrived at eight o'clock every morning at his office in the administration building, a room opening directly off the main entrance. His door was always open. If he was not to be seen, it was probably because he was concealed behind the large rolltop desk that presented its back to the door. Anyone from a freshman to a trustee could enter and be received with courtesy and friendliness. For a good part of his tenure, he knew every undergraduate by name. This was possible because he had developed a memory for names and faces while in the ministry; after each church service he had formed the habit, with Mrs. Thwing's help, of going over the names of all members of the congregation who had been present. In 1902 one freshman (the writer) took his mother in to meet Dr. Thwing. The next time they met was at the baccalaureate service, four years later, when the student was graduating. The father and mother of the young man were waiting at the back of the church for the appearance of their son. Dr. Thwing stopped on his way out of the church and said, "How do you do, Mrs. Gehlke." His mnemonic ability was assisted by his meeting all freshmen in sections of thirty or less in a required course in the Bible. In addition, he frequently led daily chapel in the two colleges, so that he remained in continuous contact with all undergraduates. Though a man of very serious aspect and great dignity, he could meet social situations with neatness, humor, and dispatch. One very hot summer afternoon Professor Bourland, who was noted among his colleagues for his quick-wittedness, was reading in his office. His shoeless feet were on his desk, his shirt was open to the third button, and he was smoking a black, odorous pipe. Someone knocked on the door. "Come in," he called. There stood the president with a very distinguished-looking man, who might have been a foreigner. With a perfectly straight face, Dr. Thwing asked, "Have you seen Professor Bourland?" "No," replied the astonished, but resourceful, Professor Bourland, "he was here, but he left about fifteen minutes ago." The President and the visitor withdrew. Some years after his retirement, Mrs. Thwing lured him into taking a hand at bridge, a totally new experience for most clergymen of his generation. After about three rounds had been played, Dr. Thwing threw his cards face up on the table and said, "My dear, if I must go to hell, I should prefer some other way!" When some student in his course in the Bible made an answer which did neither his intelligence nor his knowledge credit, Dr. Thwing would say very seriously, "Your answer is significant," and go on to the next student. Very few students, if any, failed this course. Undergraduates of Dr. Thwing's era remember the faculty receptions which occurred four or five times a year. A receiving line, headed by the president and consisting usually of four professors, each with his wife, constituted the one hurdle for the undergraduate antecedent to the tea and cookies. A popular sport among the students was noting the corruption of their surnames as they passed from a perfect pronunciation by Dr. Thwing through the eight repetitions following. At one of the teas Dr. Thwing, in conversation with a student, said, "Mr. Smith, you reek of tobacco." This was true. "Don't you like tobacco, Dr. Thwing?" "I do *not!* Beah is bittah, tobacco is bittah. I do not like bittah things. Therefore I do not like beah or tobacco!" This is a fairly accurate suggestion of both his style and his accent. The President's residence, across the street from the campus of the College for Women, was known to many of the students. He kept open house for faculty and students on Sunday afternoons. Dr. Thwing's recreation was writing. In addition to many articles he was the author of more than thirty books, of which 28 had titles including the words "education," "college," or "university." The title of his first published work was *American Colleges, Their Students and Work* (1878). It was published before his graduation from Andover Theological Seminary. In 1887 he and his wife issued a study on *The Family* (second edition, 1913). After his career as president of the university began, came *The College Woman* (1894). From 1900 to 1920, eighteen of the nineteen titles are in his favorite field. From 1920, the

year before he retired, to 1935, two years before his death, eight of the eleven titles fall in the general class of higher education. Dr. Thwing had among his friends many persons of distinction whom he characterized in brief appraisals in his two volumes *Guides, Philosophers and Friends. Studies of College Men* (1927) and *Friends of Men. A Second Series of Guides, Philosophers and Friends* (1933). His last published work was *The American College and University; A Human Fellowship* (1935). If Dr. Thwing's devotion to his career as university president could be summarized with the words "This one thing I do," certainly his published works are a further evidence of the unity of the man and the job throughout a period of 45 years, from 1890 to 1935. During his presidency Dr. Thwing received numerous honors. He was secretary of the Board of Trustees of the Carnegie Foundation for the Advancement of Teaching; he was an elector of the Hall of Fame; life senator and (1922–1928) president of the United Chapters of Phi Beta Kappa; member of the Society of Arts and Sciences, and of the American Academy of Arts and Sciences; and an honorary member of the Colonial Society of Massachusetts, as well as a member of a number of other local and national boards of trustees.

Charles E. Gehlke

American Colleges, Their Students and Work, New York, 1878.
The Reading of Books: Its Pleasures, Profits, and Perils, Boston, 1883.
The Family: An Historical and Social Study, (with Carrie F. Butler Thwing), Boston, 1887.
Within College Walls, New York, 1893.
The College Woman, New York, 1894.
The American College in American Life, New York, 1897.
Carrie F. Butler Thwing; An Appreciation by Friends . . . , Cleveland, 1899.
The Choice of a College for a Boy, New York, 1899.
College Administration, New York, 1900.
God in His World, Boston, 1900.
The Youth's Dream of Life, Boston, 1900.
If I Were a College Student, New York, 1902.
A Liberal Education and Liberal Faith . . . , New York, 1904.
A History of Higher Education in the United States since the Civil War, Boston, 1910.
Universities of the World, New York, 1911.
Letters from a Father to His Son Entering College, New York, 1912.
The Recovery of the Home, Philadelphia, 1912.
Letters from A Father to His Daughter Entering College, New York, 1913.
Notes on the History of the College for Women of Western Reserve University . . . , Cleveland, 1913.
The American College, What It Is, and What It May Become, New York, 1914.
Education According to Some Modern Masters, New York, 1916.
The Ministry; An Appeal to College Men, Boston, 1916.
The Training of Men for the World's Future, New York, 1916.
The College Gateway . . . , Boston, 1918.
The American Colleges and Universities in the Great War . . . , New York, 1920.
Human Australasia . . . , New York, 1926.
Guides, Philosophers and Friends . . . , New York, 1927.
The American and the German University . . . , New York, 1928.
Education and Religion . . . , New York, 1929.
American Society: Interpretations of Educational and Other Forces, New York, 1931.
Friends of Men . . . , New York, 1933.
The American College and University; A Human Fellowship, New York, 1935.

TIBBALS, SEYMOUR SELDEN (Feb. 9, 1869–Jan. 8, 1949), journalist, publisher, and playwright, was born in Cincinnati, Hamilton County. When he was nine, his father died, and his mother moved to Franklin, Warren County, where he spent the remainder of his life. He was for a time a partner in Eldridge Entertainment House. From 1889 until his death he also owned and edited the Franklin *Chronicle,* in which he regularly published a column, "The Rounder." He married Mary Eldridge in 1918. He published a number of plays for presentation by clubs and schools, e.g., *Christmas at Biddy Flinn's,* Franklin, 1931. WWW 3

TIBBLES, THOMAS HENRY (May 22, 1838–May 14, 1928), journalist, was born in Washington County. Numerous legends arose concerning his early life. He is said to have run away from home at the age of six and been taken to Missouri by a group of emigrants. He was with John Brown in Kansas in 1856. He attended Mount Union College for a time. During the Civil War he served as a guide on the plains, and after the war he was an itinerant Methodist preacher. In the 1870s he worked on various Nebraska newspapers. In 1879 he aroused national attention by defending a group of Poncas who had traveled from Oklahoma to join the Omahas. Tibbles found attorneys for the Poncas, and after they were freed he lectured widely on the Indian problem. In 1881 he married a girl of the Omaha tribe. He was active in the National Farmers' Alliance and the Populist movement and was a candidate for Vice-President on the People's Party ticket in 1904. He founded the *Independent* at Lincoln, Neb., in 1895, edited the *Investigator,* 1905–10, and wrote for the Omaha *World-Herald* from 1910 until his death. His book on the Poncas was published under the pen name Zylyff.

The Ponca Chiefs . . . , Boston, 1880.
Hidden Power. A Secret History of the Indian Rug . . . , New York, 1881.
The American Peasant. A Timely Allegory, Chicago, 1892.

TICHENOR, WILLIAM COLLETT (Sept. 3, 1868–July 28, 1947), lawyer, was born in Lebanon, Warren County. He practiced law and lived on a farm near Waynesville. Under the pen name Smith Selfridge, he published a pamphlet of poems and songs in 1939; he also published a legal study of farm contracts and *A Guide to Fort Ancient,* Lebanon, 1916.

TIFFANY, JOEL (1811–1893), lawyer, was born in Connecticut, but lived in northeastern Ohio for more than twenty years. He practiced law in Elyria, 1835–48, and later lived in Cleveland and Painesville. After leaving Ohio in the late 1850s, he lived in New York City, Albany, and Chicago. He lectured widely on spiritualism, temperance, and abolition. A debate with Isaac Errett (q.v.) was published as *Modern Spiritualism Compared with Christianity,* Warren, 1855. He also published several legal works.

A Treatise on the Unconstitutionality of American Slavery . . . , Cleveland, 1849.
Lectures on Spiritualism . . . , Cleveland, 1851.
A Treatise on Government . . . , Albany, N. Y., 1867.
Man and His Destiny . . . , Chicago, 1880.
The Astral World, Higher Occult Powers, Chicago, 1910.

TIFFANY, NINA MOORE (Sept. 2, 1852–Sept. 29, 1958), was born in Cincinnati, Hamilton County. In 1889 she married the eminent Minnesota attorney Francis Buchanan Tiffany, and after her marriage she lived in St. Paul, Minn. She died in St. Paul at the age of 106.

Pilgrims and Puritans . . . , Boston, 1888.
William Lloyd Garrison, Boston, 1888.
From Colony to Commonwealth . . . , Boston, 1891.
Samuel E. Sewall . . . , New York, 1898.
Harm Jan Huidekoper, (with Francis Tiffany and Francis Buchanan Tiffany), Cambridge, [Mass.], 1904.
Pathbreakers, Boston, 1949.

TILDES, OLGA ALICE (March 28, 1901–July 23, 1950), educator, was born in Cleveland, Cuyahoga County. She attended Cleveland Normal School, taught for more than twenty years in the Cleveland schools, and graduated from the University of Chicago in 1929. She died in Cleveland. She published a book on spiritualism: *The Art of Communion,* Boston, [1945].

TILLINGHAST, HENRY BUCKLEY (1835–July 26, 1894), was born in Vernon Heights, Erie County. In 1866 he moved to Toledo, where he operated the Toledo Saw Works. His death occurred in Toledo. The posthumous volume below was edited by Lamoille Till.

Biographical Selections from the Writings . . . , Toledo, 1897.

TINTO, DICK. Pseud. See Charles A. Jones.

TIPPETT, EDWIN JAMES, JR. (Nov. 20, 1892–), president of the Toledo Printing Company since 1911, was born in Toledo, Lucas County, and lived there until 1952, when he moved to Lambertville, Mich. He attended Toledo schools and was a student at the University of Toledo, 1912–13. He served in World War I and since 1921 has been editor and publisher of the Toledo *American Legion Press.* Besides magazine articles he has published a book on the experiences of an enlisted man in World War I: *Who Won the War?* . . . , [Toledo, 1920].

TIPPY, WORTH MARION (Nov. 8, 1866–Oct. 4, 1961), clergyman, born in Larwill, Ind., was pastor of several Methodist churches in Indiana and of Epworth Memorial Church, Cleveland, 1905–15. He spent his last years in Laurel, Miss. He published several books relating to the work of the church, e.g., *The Church and the Great War,* New York, [1918]. WW 26

TIPTON, THOMAS W. (Aug. 5, 1817–Nov. 26, 1899), lawyer, clergyman, and legislator, was born in Cadiz, Harrison County. He grew up on a farm, graduated from Madison College, Pa., read law, and was admitted to the Ohio bar in 1844. He served in the Ohio legislature and was employed by the U. S. Land Office, 1849–52. In 1853 he began the practice of law in McConnelsville, and three years later he was ordained to the Methodist ministry. Around 1859 he emigrated to Brownsville, Neb. He was chaplain of the 1st Nebraska Infantry, served in the U. S. Senate, 1867–75, and afterward practiced law. His recollections of his busy life were published by the Nebraska State Historical Society: *Forty Years of Nebraska . . .*, Lincoln, 1902.

TITTLE, ERNEST FREMONT (Oct. 21, 1885–Aug. 3, 1949), clergyman, was born in Springfield, Clark County. He graduated from Ohio Wesleyan University in 1906 and Drew Theological Seminary in 1908. As a pastor he served various churches in Ohio and Illinois. He delivered lectures at various universities and divinity schools; many of these lecture series were published in book form. He also published sermons and *The Religion of the Spirit . . .*, New York, [1928]. WWW 2

TITTLE, WALTER ERNEST (Oct. 9, 1883–), artist, was born in Springfield, Clark County. He attended Springfield schools and studied art in New York City under Robert Henri. He now lives in Connecticut. Widely known as an illustrator and portrait painter, he has published several books, including an account of his experiences in 1942–43 while President Roosevelt was sitting for his portrait: *Roosevelt as an Artist Saw Him*, New York, [1948]. WW 30

TITUS, HAROLD HOPPER (Feb. 23, 1896–), educator, was born in St. Martins, New Brunswick, Canada. After graduating from Acadia University in 1920, he came to the United States, where he graduated from Colgate-Rochester Divinity School in 1923 and the University of Chicago (Ph.D.) in 1926. He has been on the faculty of Denison University since 1928. Besides textbooks in philosophy and ethics, he has written *What Is a Mature Morality?*, New York, 1943. WW 30

TITUS, JOHN HENRY (Feb. 1, 1853–Oct. 20, 1947), was born in Jefferson, Ashtabula County. His personal history is filled with legends, most of which he apparently originated during his old age in New York City. He claimed to have worked as a tanner while a boy and to have written his first poems on scraps of bark while in the tannery. In his old age he claimed to have written more than 1,800 poems. In 1872, he said, he published "The Face on the Bar Room Floor" in the Ashtabula *Sentinel*—a claim rendered somewhat dubious by the fact that he first made it in 1929 when a defendant in a rent case in New York City and by the fact that a search of the *Sentinel* for 1872 does not reveal the poem. The poem in its familiar version was claimed earlier by an actor, Hugh Antoine D'Arcy. At any rate, Titus' verson was published with a note that it was the fifth canto of an epic, *The Ideal Love,* which has never appeared: *The Face on the Bar Room Floor . . .*, New York, [1933].

TITUS, MURRAY THURSTON (Nov. 5, 1885–), missionary, was born in Batavia, Clermont County. He graduated from Ohio Wesleyan University in 1908, studied for a year at the University of Chicago, and in 1910 went to India as a Methodist missionary. He served in India until 1951 and was professor of missions, Westminster Theological Seminary, Md., 1951–55. He has written articles and books on the mission field, e.g., *The Young Moslem Looks at Life,* New York, [1937]. WW 27

TODD, JOHN (Nov. 10, 1818–Jan. 31, 1894), clergyman, was born in West Hanover, Pa. His family emigrated to Ohio, and in 1835 he became one of the first students to enroll at Oberlin College. He completed his theological course in 1844 and was ordained as a Congregational minister in the same year. After serving as a pastor in Clarksfield for six years, he moved to Tabor, Iowa. An active abolitionist, he is said to have assisted John Brown. His recollections were published in the Tabor *Beacon* before their posthumous publication in book form: *Early Settlement and Growth of Western Iowa; Or, Reminiscences,* Des Moines, Iowa, 1906.

TODD, WALTER EDMOND CLYDE (Sept. 6, 1874–), ornithologist, was born in Smithfield, Jefferson County. He was employed by the U. S. Department of Agriculture, 1891–99, and was curator of ornithology, Carnegie Museum, Pittsburgh, 1899–1944. He now lives in Beaver, Pa. He has published numerous professional articles and *Birds of Western Pennsylvania . . .*, [Pittsburgh], 1940. WW 26

TOMLINSON, ATHELIA M. (Feb. 7, 1845–Jan. 24, 1915), was born and reared in Cincinnati, Hamilton County. Her father, Ebenezer Spencer, was editor of the Cincinnati *Times.* In 1869 she married Dr. Samuel B. Tomlinson. She died in Avondale.

The Summerland and Other Poems, Cincinnati, 1889.

TOMLINSON, WILLIAM WEST (Nov. 28, 1893–), educator, was born in Salem, Columbiana County. After graduating from

Swarthmore College in 1917, he served in the navy, was an executive of the Scott Paper Company for several years, and operated a firm of educational publicists. He has been a member of the administrative staff of Temple University since 1942. His writings include *The Flickering Torch; An Appraisal of What We Call Freedom,* New York, [1942]. WW 30

TOON, GLADYS E. (Sept. 3, 1893–), was born in Cleveland, Cuyahoga County. She lived in Ohio until 1930, when she married William H. Betty. She now lives in Lakeland, Fla. She has written articles and fiction for a variety of periodicals, and she has also published a collection of stories: *The Animal Story Book,* Akron, [1928].

TOPE, HILDRED (March 14, 1900–), educator, was born in Sherrodsville, Carroll County. She is married to J. Clayton Tope. She has taught in the Dellroy schools and is now teaching music in Carrollton. She has published numerous short stories and plays for boys and girls and a novel: *Whoa Ginger!,* New York, 1945.

TOPE, HOMER W. (May 28, 1859–June 4, 1936), clergyman and temperance advocate, was born in Dellroy, Carroll County. After graduating from Harlem Springs College, Carroll County, in 1885 and Mt. Airy Theological Seminary in 1888, he was ordained as a Lutheran minister. He served churches in Ohio and Illinois and was an official of the Anti-Saloon League. He published *Lecture on Gustavus Adolphus,* Albany, N. Y., 1903. WWW 1

TOPE, MELANCTHON (Jan. 28, 1858–April 28, 1945), phrenologist, was born in Leavittsville, Carroll County. After his marriage in 1883 to Permelia Gamble, he lived in Bowerston until his death; he taught school there and also edited the Bowerston *Patriot.* In 1895 he established a correspondence school in phrenology, and he also published the *Phrenological Era,* 1905–30. His writings include a family history, charts and pamphlets on phrenology, and *A Biography of William Holmes McGuffey . . . ,* Bowerston, 1929.

TOPPIN, ISABEL WHITEHOUSE, was born in Newport, Ky., but her family later moved to Cincinnati. In 1914 she married James Toppin, and they lived in Brooklyn, N. Y., while he was associated with the New York *Sun.* In 1919 they returned to Ohio and purchased the Genoa *Times,* and a year later they established a weekly, the *Sun,* in Toledo. Since her husband's death in 1949, she has edited and published the paper with the assistance of her son. She has been active in the temperance movement and in civic affairs. Her poems have appeared in numerous periodicals, and she has published two collections, the first being *Poems of Isabel Whitehouse Toppin,* Toledo, [1927]. WO 2

TORRENCE, FREDERIC RIDGELY (Nov. 27, 1875–Dec. 25, 1950), was born in Xenia, Greene County. He was educated at Miami University and Princeton University. On graduating from Princeton he settled in New York City, where he published his first book and where he worked for six years in the New York Public Library. In 1914 he married Olivia Howard Dunbar, also a writer. He later served on the editorial staffs of the *Cosmopolitan* and *New Republic.* Among his closest friends were William Vaughan Moody and Edwin Arlington Robinson. He was deeply interested in the theater, especially in plays about and for Negroes. He was a pioneer in this field; his *Plays for a Negro Theatre* was a harbinger of *Emperor Jones, Porgy,* and other plays of the Negro renaissance of the 1920s. He died in New York City. As a rule, a biographical sketch of a noteworthy man limits itself to recording his accomplishments. But with Ridgely Torrence, I feel it is not only permissible but imperative to speak of the man himself. Vis-à-vis with Ridgely Torrence, one knew oneself confronting a beautiful person rather than a handsome man. His courtesy, his culture, and his spiritual refinement made themselves immediately felt. He was tall and erect and rather loosely articulated. I remember his springing, youthful gait, with a slight "give" at the waist, as he would set out of an evening to walk from the MacDowell Colony to the village of Peterborough. When I first met Ridgely, he was growing gray, though in youth he must have been blond. His eyes, very wide-open, were of brightest azure. Those extraordinary eyes and the serenity of his manner gave me the title of a poem that, alas, never progressed beyond the title, since it indicated though it did not fully express what I had intended to convey: "Light-struck Apollo and the White Poppy." The white poppy was Olivia, Ridgeley's wife, who by her fragility, her pallor, her quivering sensitivity, and her dark unfathomable eyes suggested that delicate blossom at whose heart cluster the dark seeds of sleep. Whenever they were in a room together, Olivia's eyes sought her husband's face, as if she found no other object worthy of her regard. Although I saw the Torrences from time to time in New York, it was at the MacDowell Colony, on many successive visits, that I came into closest contact with them. The more discerning Colonists tried to sit at the same table with Ridgely, for his conversation—lively, urbane, graceful, informed—was a pleasure not to be missed. Though never pedantic, he was a scholar. Sensing this, I questioned him once about the hexameter. At once he launched upon a discourse, telling me that the only perfect hexameters were in Greek; for only the Greek language provided the quantities that gave this poetic measure its characteristic balance. "There are two pretty good ones in the King James Bible, though," and he quoted: "How art thou fallen from heaven, O Lucifer, son of the morning!" and "God has gone up with a shout, the Lord with the sound of a trumpet." "They are good," he said, "but not quite this," and he recited a verse from Homer, the only word of which I understood was Age mém nón. His voice rang through the room, and I caught the two spondees at the end of the line. Another time he was speculating about four lines occurring in Emerson's poem "Uriel":

Line in nature is not found;
Unit and universe are round;
In vain produced, all rays return;
Evil will bless and ice will burn.

He turned to me and said, "Ask your friend Einstein whether an American poet nearly a hundred years ago had not already intuited his theory of the bending of light." I wrote to the Professor, whose answer was almost as enigmatic as the verse: "It has not yet been decided whether the universe is finite or infinite." Another small incident shows his playful wit. I lamented one evening that I had lost several working hours because when I approached my studio a large snake, coiled and rearing a foot into the air, blocked my path. I threw unavailing stones, but was too timid to approach. The snake had enjoyed an unmolested sun bath for several hours. Ridgely looked at me with a twinkling smile. "I took you for too much of a woman not to welcome a conversation with a serpent." I have to tell only one other experience, heartbreaking yet inspiring. After Ridgely's death I visited Olivia. Never have I been witness to a grief so devoid of egoism. Slow tears fell one by one, as if squeezed from the almost sightless eyes. Without a handkerchief, she rubbed them away with her clenched knuckles. "Oh," she cried, "I want it shouted from the housetops, I want everyone to know what a great poet he was . . . what a great poet!" And in a hushed voice, "And to think . . ." it was a barely audible whisper, a whisper of wonderment, "to think he chose me!" Not a word of self-pity, though I learned afterward that since the failing of her eyesight she had been almost totally dependent on her husband for her daily needs. In her self-forgetfulness, she was like some ancient figure of tragedy. Strong, though stricken—this white poppy!

Jean Starr Untermeyer

The House of a Hundred Lights, Boston, 1900.
El Dorado. A Tragedy, New York, 1903.
Abelard and Heloise, New York, 1907.
Granny Maumee, the Rider of Dreams, Simon the Cyrenian; Plays for a Negro Theatre, New York, 1917.
Hesperides, New York, 1925.
The Story of Gio . . . , New York, 1935.
Common Sense, Play in One Act, New York, [1941].
Poems, New York, 1941.
The Story of John Hope, New York, 1948.

TOULMIN, HARRY AUBREY (Nov. 25, 1890–), lawyer, was born in Springfield, Clark County. After graduating from the University of Virginia in 1911 and Ohio State University Law School in 1913, he was admitted to the bar and, except for his service in both World Wars, has practiced in Dayton and Cincinnati. He has written several books, both technical and general, e.g., *Patents and the Public Interest,* New York, 1939. WW 30

TOURGEE, ALBION WINEGAR (May 2, 1838–May 21, 1906), jurist, author, and diplomat, was born in Williamsfield, Ashtabula County. He lived through the exciting years of the Civil War and post-Civil War period and became one of the sharpest if not soundest observers of the national scene. He is best known for a series of Reconstruction novels in which government policies in the South are arraigned. In political interpretations his faction follows in the tradition of Garland and Adams, though his suggestions for bettering social conditions depend not upon high consecration or Populist theory but upon education and the Christian Socialism of Washington Gladden and W. D. P. Bliss. He was educated in the Kingsville Academy and the University of Rochester. Tourgee taught for a short time in Wilson, N. Y., but he was just the right age on the outbreak of the War Between the States to volunteer for the 27th New York Regulars. He returned to civil life for a time after a serious wound in the first Battle of Bull Run (from which he never fully recovered), and during this period studied law in Painesville and Ashtabula. He re-entered the army with the 105th Ohio Volunteers. He was again wounded, taken prisoner, and languished in four different Confederate prisons. He finally resigned from the army in 1863 after being twice arrested for insubordination, though the occasions, when examined, contribute to an appreciation of his independence of character and of his radical sympathy. In 1864 he was admitted to the bar, practicing law in Painesville and Ashtabula until he moved to Greensboro, N. C., in 1865. Here he lived until 1879, working as pension agent, author, lecturer, businessman, editor, and, above all, judge. He became a powerful political figure as judge of the superior court, 1868–75. Returning to the North in 1881, he settled in Mayville, N. Y., where he produced the bulk of his fictional work, drawing freely on his earlier experiences for inspiration. From 1897 he was U. S. consul at Bordeaux, France. During his later years he was the author of legal works. Despite his time-consuming career of publicist and politician, Tourgee found time in the 22 years after 1874 to write sixteen stories which may be classified as novels or novelettes. These may be divided into four groups: (1) Civil War novels, (2) novels of entertainment, (3) historical novels sans propaganda, and (4) purpose novels. The most vivid of his stories were his Civil War pieces, in which he treated the American scene from 1850 to 1880, with emphasis upon sectionalism from the days of the Compromise of 1850 through Reconstruction. *Hot Plowshares* (1883) traced the rise of antislavery sentiment in the North and its development among Southern slaveholders, contrasting the motives and ideals of the two sections. Tourgee pictured the tremendous industrial growth of the Northern cities and attempted to interpret the regional differences leading up to the war, but the interpretation was inadequate and weak. *Figs and Thistles* (1879), partly autobiographical and dealing primarily with the war period in the North, was distinctive for its vivid battle scenes. Appearing long before Crane's *Red Badge of Courage,* it had the authority of Tourgee's actual battle experience. Included also was political and financial satire, directed principally against the Credit Mobilier. *The Story of a Thousand* (1896), a history of the 105th Ohio Volunteers, proved the autobiographical character of the war interpretation. *Toinette* (1874), published under the pen name Henry Churton, treated the caste and love problem of a Southerner and an octoroon and touched upon Southern views in the same period as *Figs and Thistles.* It was the first real Reconstruction novel. *A Fool's Errand* (1879), the best known of all Tourgee's novels, related the experiences of a Northern Republican in the South during the Reconstruction, his failures, and his gradual acquisition of tolerance. When the novel was published anonymously, it aroused a storm of public interest that sent it speedily into the best-seller list. Guesses at the identity of the author were numerous and included the names of Edmund Kirk and Harriet Beecher Stowe. Its writer was hailed as the Victor Hugo of America. Proclaiming that the Reconstruction Act had failed dismally, Tourgee sought for a solution that would bring happiness to a desolated region and relieve the tensions that had built up. The Ku Klux terror, further amplified in *The Invisible Empire* (1880), furnished true incidents in which Tourgee could blacken the Ku Kluxers and point to the paradox of liberated slaves called upon to exercise duties of citizenship without training or education. Although the novel has lost its first appeal, it has remained a small but significant contribution to American literature. *Bricks Without Straw* (1880) had a talismanic title that carried half its burden. Dealing with the same Reconstruction era, it told the same story of education as the two books which preceded it. At times in these books Tourgee took rather positive positions and was accused of prejudice and bias. But, though he concentrated on a straightforward message to the exclusion of the rampant corruption of the era, he was not particularly partisan in his views, and he did point to the failure of the governmental policies after 1868. The prose study *An Appeal to Caesar* (1884) was a restatement of his ideas about the Negro. Two short stories, "Tante Angelique" and "Zouri's Christmas," and two novelettes, *John Eax and Mamelon* (1882), completed Tourgee's interpretation of America from 1850 to 1880. The novels of entertainment followed Tourgee's most serious and more effective work. *Black Ice* (1885) was a story of the romantic vindication of a woman's character. *With Gauge and Swallow* (1889) presented a series of tales about a law firm. *An Outing with the Queen of Hearts* (1894) was an account of a summer holiday on an island in Lake Erie. *The Man Who Outlived Himself* (1898), a novelette, dealt with amnesia. Examples of Tourgee at his best and at his worst may be found in the historical novels devoid of propaganda. The most interesting novel in his whole repertoire was *Button's Inn* (1887), which combined a history of the rise of Mormonism with the story of a persistent ghost. *Out of the Sunset Sea* (1893) went back to the discovery of America for its setting, but failed to recapture the glamour of that age. The purpose novel *Murvale Eastman, Christian Socialist* (1889) attacked the problem of capital and labor as had novels by Aldrich, Hay, and Howells; but Tourgee raised the question of the economic duty of Christians. *Pactolus Prime* (1890) returned to special pleading for the Negro. Tourgee was at his best when he was writing realistically of events which he knew. As a creative writer, he was seriously limited by inadequate characterization, lack of imaginative variety in plot construction, and a proclivity toward indoctrination. On the other hand, his burning sincerity has never been questioned, his historical pictures are interesting if somewhat prejudiced, and his prose style combines accuracy, directness, and concreteness. As a writer he commanded respect for his straightforward manner and the philosophical wisdom of his observations. Finally, the range and intensity of his own experiences afforded him both vivid images and memorable incidents, and these combine to make at least a small portion of his work enduring.

Susannah R. West

Toinette. A Novel, New York, 1874.
Figs and Thistles: A Romance of the Western Reserve, New York, 1879.
A Fool's Errand by One of the Fools, New York, 1879.
Bricks without Straw, New York, 1880.
The Invisible Empire, New York, 1880.
A Royal Gentleman, New York, 1881.
John Eax and Mamelon: Or, the South without the Shadow, New York, [1882].
Hot Plowshares, New York, [1883].
An Appeal to Caesar, New York, 1884.
Black Ice, New York, 1885.
Button's Inn, Boston, 1887.
Letters to a King, Cincinnati, 1887.
The Veteran and His Pipe, Chicago, 1888.
Murvale Eastman, Christian Socialist, New York, 1889.
With Gauge and Swallow, Attorneys, Philadelphia, 1889.
Pactolus Prime, New York, [1890].
A Son of Old Harry, New York, 1891.
Out of the Sunset Sea, New York, 1893.
An Outing with the Queen of Hearts, New York, 1894.
Mortgage on the Hip Roof House, Cincinnati, 1896.
The Story of a Thousand, Buffalo, 1896.
The War of the Standards; Coin and Credit versus Coin without Credit, New York, 1896.
The Man Who Outlived Himself, New York, 1898.

TOWNE, ROBERT DUKE (Jan. 4, 1866–Feb. 24, 1952), journalist, was born in Warren, Trumbull County. He graduated from Lawrence University, Canton, N. Y., in 1888. He worked on various newspapers in the East and was editor of *Judge* in 1905. He published a series of rhymed stories for children, e.g., *The Teddy Bears in a Smashup . . . ,* Chicago, [1907]. WWW 3

TOWNE, STUART. Pseud. See Clayton Rawson.

TOWNSEND, EDWARD WATERMAN (Feb. 10, 1855–March 16, 1942), was born in Cleveland, Cuyahoga County, and attended public and private schools in that city. In 1875 he went to San Francisco, where he began writing for newspapers and magazines. In 1893 he moved to New York City and began writing stories of Bowery life which became widely popular. He settled in Montclair, N. J., in 1900 and served in Congress as a Representative from New Jersey, 1911–15.

Chimmie Fadden Explains; Major Max Expounds, [New York, 1895].
"Chimmie Fadden"; Major Max; And Other Stories, New York, [1895].
A Daughter of the Tenements, New York, [1895]
Near a Whole City Full, New York, 1897.
The Yellow Kid in McFadden's Flats, New York, 1897.
Days like These; A Novel, New York, 1901.
Chimmie Fadden and Mr. Paul, New York, 1902.
Fort Birkett; A Story of Mountain Adventure, New York, 1903.
Lees and Leaven; A New York Story of Today, New York, 1903.
A Summer in New York; A Love Story Told in Letters, New York, 1903.
"Sure"; New "Chimmie Fadden" Stories, New York, 1904.
Reuben Larkmead, a Story of Worldlings, New York, [1905].
Our Constitution; Why and How It Was Made—Who Made It and What It Is, New York, 1906.
Beaver Creek Farm, New York, 1907.
The Climbing Courvatels, New York, [1909].

TOWNSLEY, GARDNER H. (Oct. 11, 1898–), journalist, born in Vincennes, Ind., moved to Ohio in 1916. Editor of the *Western Star,* Lebanon, he has published a pamphlet about the town: *Historic Lebanon . . .*, [Lebanon, 1940].

TRACIE, THEODORE C. W. (1836?–Sept. 30, 1886), served in the Ohio Light Artillery from Aug. 6, 1862, to June 28, 1865. He apparently lived in California after the Civil War, but no other biographical information has been discovered. His book describes service in eastern Tennessee.

Annals of the Nineteenth Ohio Battery . . ., Cleveland, 1878.

TRACY, LENA HARVEY (Oct. 11, 1860–1941), was born at Hare Creek in northwestern Pennsylvania. After teaching in a country school for several terms, she attended Antioch College, where she graduated in 1893. She then became a deaconess of the Christian Church, Springfield, and in 1897 she was named the first welfare director of National Cash Register Company, Dayton. She moved to New York City in 1901, and her later life was spent in New Jersey. Her autobiography was posthumously published: *How My Heart Sang . . .*, New York, 1950.

TRACY, RUSSEL LORD (Dec. 10, 1860–May 17, 1945), banker, was born in Mansfield, Richland County. He studied at Oberlin College, 1877–80, and graduated from Carleton College in 1882. In 1884 he organized a loan and trust company in Salt Lake City, where he spent the remainder of his life. Under the pen name T. Shirby Hodge, he wrote *The White Man's Burden; A Satirical Forecast,* Boston, [1915], and he also published an autobiography: *Some Experiences of Russel Lord Tracy,* [Salt Lake City, 1941].

TRADDLES, MOSES. Pseud. See Clinton Collins.

TRAINA, LOUIS C. See Lewis Corey.

TRAUTMAN, MILTON BERNHARD (Sept. 7, 1899–   ), naturalist, was born in Columbus, Franklin County. He was a research assistant with the Ohio Division of Conservation, 1930–34, a research assistant in the University of Michigan Department of Zoology, 1935–40, and a research associate at Stone Laboratory, Ohio State University, 1940–55. He is now curator of the vertebrate collections, Ohio State Museum, Columbus. He has published many articles and books, most of them dealing with Ohio fauna, e.g., *The Birds of Buckeye Lake, Ohio,* Ann Arbor, [Mich.], 1940. AMS 9

TRAVER, AMOS JOHN (Sept. 1, 1889–   ), clergyman and educator, was born at Hartwick Seminary, N. Y. After his ordination to the Lutheran ministry in 1912, he served several pastorates and held various executive positions in the Lutheran Church. He served as professor of practical theology, Hamma Divinity School, Springfield, 1943–59. His books include *The Christ Who Is All,* Philadelphia, 1929. WW 30

TREAT, IDA (1889–   ), born in Joliet, Ill., was brought to Cleveland when she was eight years old. She attended Cleveland schools and Western Reserve University. After two years of graduate study at the Sorbonne, she taught Romance languages at Western Reserve, 1913–19. Until 1941 she lived in France, where she wrote for French and American magazines. She married André Bergeret, a French naval officer. She published an account of Brehat, an island off the coast of Brittany where she had a summer home: *The Anchored Heart . . .*, New York, [1941].

TREFFINGER, CAROLYN ELIZABETH (Oct. 24, 1891–   ), educator, was born on a farm near Seville, Medina County. She attended Wittenberg College and taught in Ohio schools; her last position before her retirement was in Wadsworth, where she was an elementary school principal. She now lives in Hastings, Neb. She has published at least three books for children, e.g., *Jimmy's Shoes,* Philadelphia, [1934].

TRESSLER, DONALD KITELEY (Nov. 7, 1894–   ), food chemist, was born in Cincinnati, Hamilton County. He graduated from the University of Michigan in 1913 and Cornell University (Ph.D.) in 1918. He has taught in several universities and done research for various governmental agencies and bureaus. He has published many professional articles and several technical books, and *The Wealth of the Sea,* New York, [1927]. WW 30

TRETTIEN, AUGUSTUS WILLIAM (Sept. 3, 1867–July 1, 1936), educator, born in Appleton, Wis., was professor of psychology, University of Toledo, 1915–32, and operated a psychological clinic in Toledo, 1932–36. He wrote several psychology textbooks and *Arthur Trent: Choosing a Career,* Boston, [1934]. WWW 1

TREUTHART, JAMES LOUIS (Feb. 6, 1838–April 15, 1915), was born in Zweisemmen, Switzerland, but came to Portsmouth with his parents around 1845. He served in the 104th O.V.I. and spent the remainder of his life in Portsmouth, where he was an examiner for the city schools. His long poem, employing epic conventions, surveys the history of the world with special emphasis on the Civil War and the Columbian Exposition.

The Milliad (One Thousand Verses): A Poem of Justice and of Liberty. An Epic of the Ages as Also of the United States, New York, 1894.

TRIMBLE, ALLEN (Nov. 24, 1783–Feb. 3, 1870), governor of Ohio, 1826–30, was born in Augusta County, Va. With his father he visited Ohio in 1801, 1802, and 1804; on their last trip they built a log cabin in Highland County, and after his father's death the next year, Allen brought the family there to live. He settled in Hillsboro around 1809 and served in the Ohio House, 1816–17, and in the Senate, 1817–25. After he retired from public life in 1830, he devoted most of his attention to agriculture and iron manufacturing. His autobiography was published by the family 39 years after his death: *Autobiography and Correspondence of Allen Trimble . . . ,* (Mary McArthur Thompson Tuttle and Henry Burton Thompson, eds.), [Columbus?], 1909.

TRIMBLE, JOSEPH M. (1807–May 6, 1891), clergyman, was born in Hillsborough, Ky., but grew up in Ohio, where his parents moved while he was a small child. After graduating from Ohio University in 1828, he became a Methodist minister. He also taught at Augusta College, Ky., for five years. He was an active supporter of Ohio Wesleyan University during its early years and served on its board of trustees for forty years. The work below, which was published anonymously, is an account of his grandmother.

Memoir of Mrs. Jane Trimble . . . , Cincinnati, 1861.

TROLLOPE, FRANCES MILTON (March 10, 1780–Oct. 6, 1863), born in Bristol, England, was perhaps the most controversial temporary resident of Ohio in the nineteenth century. Wife of an unsuccessful English lawyer, she was persuaded by her friend Frances Wright D'Arusmont (q.v.) that by coming to America she might recoup the family fortunes. After a brief, disillusioning stay at Frances Wright's settlement at Nashoba, Tenn., she came to Cincinnati in Feb., 1828. She remained in the city until March, 1830. On Third Street she constructed an elaborate bazaar, later known as "Trollope's Folly." An architectural monstrosity combining Moorish, Gothic, and Egyptian styles, the building was intended to raise the cultural level of the city and, also, the fortunes of the Trollope family. The project was an unqualified failure, and Mrs. Trollope began making notes for a description of American society with special attention to the Queen City. The resulting book was published on her return to England: *Domestic Manners of the Americans,* London, 1832. It was used by the Tories to illustrate the vulgarities of a democracy as they battled the Reform Bill. Although it outraged American readers, especially residents of Cincinnati, the book is a racy account of Jacksonian democracy in the United States. Mrs. Trollope, after the publication of this book, wrote a great many novels and travel books.

TROUTT, MYRTLE L. See Myrtle L. Reeder.

TRUE, HIRAM L. (June 4, 1845–Oct. 22, 1912), physician, was born in Athens, Athens County. After graduating from Weethee Medical College and Eclectic Medical Institute, Cincinnati, he practiced in McConnelsville until his death. The second book below was published under the pen name Don Allen.

The Resurrection of Jesus. An Agnostic's View, New York, [1893].

The Cause of the Glacial Period, Cincinnati, 1902.

TRUEBLOOD, BENJAMIN FRANKLIN (Nov. 25, 1847–Oct. 26, 1916), Quaker educator, born in Salem, Ind., was president of Wilmington College, 1874–79. Especially after 1890 he devoted himself to the cause of international peace. He edited the *Advocate of Peace,* 1892–1915, and published numerous articles and essays on pacifism and a book: *The Federation of the World,* Boston, 1899.

TUCKER, WILLIAM JEWETT (July 13, 1839–Sept. 29, 1926), clergyman and educator, born in Griswold, Conn., taught school in Columbus, 1861–63. He later was on the Andover Seminary faculty and was president of Dartmouth College, 1893–1909. He published a number of books, e.g., *The Making and the Unmaking of the Preacher,* Boston, 1898.

TUCKLEY, HENRY (d.Aug. 23, 1909), clergyman, born in England, was pastor of Methodist churches in Cincinnati and Springfield in the 1880s. He died in Springfield, Mass. He wrote several books, e.g., *Life's Golden Morning . . . ,* Cincinnati, 1886.

TULLY, JIM (June 3, 1888–June 22, 1947), was born in St. Marys, Auglaize County. With little formal education, this "literary bum" had wide, firsthand experience with various unattractive aspects of American life while he was still a boy. In the early years of the twentieth century he was on the road as a tramp, farm laborer, chainmaker, circus roustabout, prize fighter, reporter, and tree surgeon (Tully, characteristically, called it "tree fakir"). In the 1920s he was a successful hard-boiled novelist whose forte was crude and brutally realistic stories, drawn from his violent early life. Then, ironically, this specialist in low life became one of the most highly paid publicity agents and writers in Hollywood. Born in a log cabin, he received his only formal education in an orphanage, from five to eleven years of age. Placed on a farm when he was eleven, he ran away after eighteen months and spent several years on the road. During this time he read widely (Dostoevski, Carlyle, Balzac, Dumas, Twain, and Conrad) and dreamed of being a writer. He had his first work published while he was working as a chainmaker in Kent, when he had a poem on Keats printed in a newspaper column. Stimulated by Joseph Conrad's *Almayer's Folly,* he spent eight years writing a semiautobiographical first novel, *Emmett Lawler;* his first version was only one paragraph, but it was 100,000 words long. After Tully had disappointing reactions from Upton Sinclair (who returned his manuscript unread) and Harold Bell Wright ("He bawled hell out of me. He said I was no good."), a sympathetic Rupert Hughes helped him revise the 100,000-word paragraph into a crude but readable novel and told him with kindly overstatement, "You will be a very great writer." *Emmett Lawler* was published in 1922. His next two novels, *Beggars of Life* (1924), later dramatized by Maxwell Anderson as *Outside Looking In,* and *Jarnegan* (1925), made the "hobo author" a successful and famous name of the twenties. For more than a decade, the life he had experienced in prisons, the circus, the boxing ring, and as a tramp furnished him with material for such hastily written but vigorous books as *Shanty Irish* (1928), *Shadows of Men* (1930), and *Ladies in the Parlor* (1935). During this period Tully migrated to Hollywood and found a profitable welcome there for his special talents of frankness and glibness. His prolific writing on the characters and antics of the film colony was wide-ranging; he was, for a while, press agent for Charlie Chaplin and was having material published concurrently in such diverse magazines as *Vanity Fair, Scribner's, True Confessions, American Mercury, Pictorial Review,* and *Photoplay.* His life in Hollywood, although antithetical to his picaresque early days in Ohio, was, perhaps, just as unusual and legendary. He was blunt and aggressive and a hard drinker; his vivid and witty conversation was "a mixture of Billingsgate and Shakespeare, a poet pelting you with manure." He once defended a fight he had with John Gilbert. "I didn't hit him," he explained, "he was swinging away at me, and it looked to me as if he'd fan himself to death. So I just put him to sleep for his own protection." The one-time tramp made $80,000 a year, acquired a $100,000 estate, and was proud of owning "Hollywood's best library." His early promise was not fulfilled and his able journalistic talent, praised earlier by Mencken and Krutch, was used increasingly to produce motion-picture fan magazine articles and other lucrative trivia. However, Jim Tully, one of the most original and striking personalities of the American literary scene in the early twentieth century, made a vivid and worth-while contribution to the development of the hard-boiled novel of low life.

Paul H. Chapman

TUNISON, JOSEPH SALATHIEL (Nov. 9, 1849–April 21, 1916), journalist, was born near Bucyrus, Crawford County. After attending Denison University, he worked on the Cincinnati *Gazette,* 1874–83, the New York *Tribune,* 1884–96, the *Ohio State Journal,* 1901–03, and the Dayton *Journal,* 1903–07. During his last years, which were spent in East Liverpool, he was a free-lance writer.

The Cincinnati Riot: Its Causes and Results, Cincinnati, 1886.

Master Virgil . . . , Cincinnati, 1888.

The Sapphic Stanza, Granville, 1890.

The Graal Problem from Walter Map to Richard Wagner, Cincinnati, 1904.

Dramatic Traditions of the Dark Ages, Chicago, 1907.

TURNER, HARRIET MACKEY (Aug. 31, 1875–), educator, was born in Pike County, but grew up in Circleville, where her parents moved a few years after her birth. She graduated from Circleville High School in 1895 and afterward taught in the schools of Circleville and Lancaster until 1918. She wrote *Stories of Pioneer Days,* Boston, [1936].

TURNER, LIDA WILSON, was born in Cincinnati, Hamilton County. She attended Florida and North Carolina schools and graduated from Asheville College for Young Women. Her address in 1940 was Atlanta,

Ga. Her poems have appeared in various periodicals, and she has published a collection: *Flagstones and Flowers,* Oglethorpe University, Ga., [1934]. BDCP

TURNER, LUCY MAE (Nov. 13, 1884–), educator, was born in Zanesville, Muskingum County, the daughter of a former slave and the granddaughter of Nat Turner, leader of a slave rebellion in Virginia. She graduated from Zanesville High School in 1903, Wilberforce University in 1908, and Ohio State University in 1934. She taught in the public schools of East St. Louis, Ill., 1910–55, and in 1950 earned a law degree from St. Louis University. She now lives in East St. Louis. She has published at least three books, including a book of poems: *'Bout Cullud Folkses,* New York, [1938].

TURPIE, DAVID (July 8, 1829–April 21, 1909), lawyer, was born in Hamilton County. After graduating from Kenyon College in 1848, he moved to Logansport, Ind., where he was admitted to the bar. The remainder of his life was spent in Indiana, where he filled various judicial and legislative posts, including two terms in the U. S. Senate, 1887–99. He published several speeches and an autobiographical volume: *Sketches of My Own Times,* Indianapolis, [1903]. WWW 1

TUTTLE, EMMA ROOD (July 21, 1837–June 4, 1916), wife of Hudson Tuttle (q.v.), was born in Braceville, Trumbull County. She attended Hiram College. Throughout her life she lectured on spiritualism and gave dramatic readings. She assisted her husband in writing some of his books, wrote songs, and compiled a book of recitations and a textbook for Free Thought Sunday schools. She died in Berlin Heights.

Blossoms of Our Spring, Boston, 1864.
Gazelle . . . , Boston, 1866.
From Soul to Soul, New York, 1890.
Asphodel Blooms and Other Offerings, Chicago, 1901.

TUTTLE, HUDSON (Oct. 4, 1836–Dec. 14, 1911), spiritualist, was born in Berlin Heights, Erie County. After attending Homeopathic Medical College, Cleveland, he operated a farm near Berlin Heights, lectured on spiritualism, and conducted a publishing company. In 1857 he married Emma Rood (see above), then a resident of Cleveland, who also lectured on spiritualism and collaborated on some of his books. All of his books, he claimed, were written while he was in a "semi-trance."

Scenes in the Spirit World . . . , New York, 1855.
Arcana of Nature . . . , 2 vols., Boston, 1860.
The Origin and Antiquity of Physical Man Scientifically Considered . . . , Boston, 1866.
The Career of the God-Idea in History, Boston, [1869].
The Career of the Christ-Idea in History, Boston, [1870].
Arcana of Spiritualism . . . , Boston, 1871.
Stories for Children, Toledo, 1874.
The Cross and the Steeple: Their Origin and Signification, Toledo, 1875.
Career of Religious Ideas . . . , New York, 1878.
The Ethics of Spiritualism . . . , Chicago, 1878.
Clair, a Tale of Mormon Perfidy, Chicago, 1881.
Studies in the Out-lying Fields of Psychic Science, New York, [1889].
Religion of Man and Ethics of Science, New York, 1890.
Secrets of the Convent, Philadelphia, 1892.
Heresy, or Led to the Light, Chicago, 1895.
The Philosophy of Spirit, and the Spirit-World, Berlin Heights, 1896.
Mediumship and Its Laws . . . , Berlin Heights, 1900.
Evolution of the God and Christ Ideas, Berlin Heights, [1906].
A Golden Sheaf, Berlin Heights, [1907].
Stories from beyond the Borderland, Berlin Heights, [1909].

TUTTLE, JOSEPH FARRAND (March 12, 1818–June 8, 1901), born in Bloomfield, N. J., was brought to Ohio in 1832. He graduated from Marietta College in 1841 and Lane Seminary in 1844. He was a tutor at Marietta in 1843 and Presbyterian pastor in Delaware, 1845–47. He was a pastor in New Jersey until 1862, when he became president of Wabash College, Crawfordsville, Ind. He published many addresses and a book for young men: *The Way Lost and Found . . . ,* Philadelphia, 1870.

TUTTLE, MARGARETTA MUHLENBERG (Sept. 2, 1877–Feb. 15, 1958), was born in Cincinnati, Hamilton County, where her father was on the staff of the Cincinnati *Enquirer.* She graduated from the University of Cincinnati in 1900. She wrote articles and short stories for national magazines, motion-picture scripts, and novels. One of her novels was the basis of a film by Cecil B. DeMille: *His Worldly Goods . . . ,* Indianapolis, [1912].

TUTTLE, MARY McARTHUR THOMPSON (Nov. 5, 1849–Sept. 1, 1916), daughter of Eliza J. and James H. Thompson (qq.v.), was born in Hillsboro, Highland County. After graduating from Hillsboro College in 1868, she studied art at McMicken University, Cincinnati, and in Europe. She lectured on painting and also exhibited her own paintings. She collaborated with her mother and sister in writing *Hillsboro Crusade Sketches,* an account of the temperance struggle, and also wrote several books, e.g., a novel: *International Ties,* [Washington, D. C., 1915]. WWW 1

U

UDELL, CORNELIUS (Oct. 22, 1807–Feb. 14, 1879), brother of John Udell (q.v.), was born in New York State, but spent most of his adult life in Jefferson, where he worked as a carpenter. His book is the first local history published about Ashtabula County.

Condensed History of Jefferson . . . , Jefferson, 1878.

UDELL, JOHN (June 22, 1795– ?), was born in New York City. In 1810 his father settled on a farm in northern Pennsylvania, and in 1816 the family moved to Ashtabula County, where John married and became a farmer. An organizer of the Jefferson Baptist Church, he was sent to New York in 1833 to solicit funds for a building. After traveling more than 2,000 miles in the dead of winter, he returned to find his family deeply in debt, his father accused of heresy for reading Alexander Campbell's *Millennial Harbinger,* and himself suspected of appropriating money from the building fund. In 1842 he took his family to Missouri, where he became a salesman of religious books. In 1850 with his two sons he made his first overland trip to the California gold fields. After a second trip in 1852, he returned by sea in 1855. His first book, a factual account of his restless wanderings, records that he had traveled a total of 110,410 miles; but when that book was published, he had not taken his most eventful trip. In 1858 he started for California by way of the Santa Fe Trail, and his was the first large emigrant party to attempt Beale's new route to the Colorado River. The Mohave Massacre on Aug. 30, 1858, forced the party to return to Albuquerque, where they spent the winter. After reaching California the next year, Udell published his journal. It was republished in Jefferson in 1868. It appears that Udell spent his last years with relatives in Ashtabula County.

Incidents of Travel to California, across the Great Plains . . . , Jefferson, 1856.

Journal of John Udell, Kept during a Trip across the Plains . . . , Suisun City, Calif., 1859.

UHL, LEMON LEANDER (Feb. 24, 1848–Feb. 27, 1943), clergyman, was born in Pleasant Ridge, Holmes County. He graduated from Wittenberg College (A.B., 1871; B.D., 1872) and Johns Hopkins University (Ph.D., 1889). In 1873 he went to Guntur, India, as a missionary. He founded a high school there and also later taught at Madras University. He died in Gettysburg, Pa.

The Decay of Christianity, Madras, India, 1885.

Guntur Flora, Madras, India, 1930.

UHL, MIRIAM ALMA (Sept. 28, 1906–March 6, 1926), was born in Wisconsin, but spent most of her life in Cincinnati. She died at the age of nineteen, and after her death her mother, Anna M. Uhl, published a short novel about the Dark Ages: *To-day We Smile—To-morrow We Weep; A Melo-Tragedy,* Cincinnati, [1927].

UMBSTAETTER, HERMAN DANIEL (Feb. 26, 1851–Nov. 25, 1913), magazine publisher, was born in Parma, Cuyahoga County. He attended Cleveland schools and worked on newspapers in that city until 1872. After fourteen years in New York and Baltimore, he moved to Boston, where he founded *The Black Cat* in 1895. Stories he wrote for his magazine were published in several collections, e.g., *The Red-hot Dollar, and Other Stories from The Black Cat,* Boston, 1911. WWW 1

UNA. Pseud. See Mary A. M. Ford.

UNDERHILL, ABEL (d. Sept., 1887), physician, was born in the early 1800s near Poughkeepsie, N. Y. He studied medicine in New York City, became a hydrotherapist in 1845 and a spiritualist in 1848. He first came to Ohio to live in the Quaker settlement at Kendal (Massillon). He died in Akron.

The Arrest, Trial and Acquittal of Abby Warner, for Spirit Rapping . . . , Cleveland, 1852.

UNDERWOOD, CHARLOTTE WOOLLEY (March 5, 1914–), was born in Cincinnati, Hamilton County. She studied at Sarah Lawrence College and Columbia University. Now Mrs. Charles M. Underwood, she lives in Rockville Centre, N. Y. Under the pen name Joan Charles, she has published several novels, e.g., *Son and Stranger,* New York, [1945]. WWAW 1

UNDERWOOD, MATILDA JANE DOWNING (April 10, 1851–March 24, 1932), was born in Centre County, Pa. After her marriage to Zephaniah Underwood in 1871, she lived on a farm near Harveysburg. She was a minister of the Society of Friends. She wrote an Indian story based on legends learned from older members of her family: *Blue Belle of the Forest . . .* , [Wilmington, 1919].

UNTERMEYER, JEAN STARR (May 13, 1886–), born in Zanesville, Muskingum County, is more interesting as a poet than as a subject for a biographer; that is, unless the biographer should choose to seek to interpret the inner life of his subject on the basis of a careful analysis of the poems. Mrs. Untermeyer herself has given all the external facts that one needs to know. She received her education until just past fifteen from the Zanesville public schools and Putnam Seminary. She then attended Mrs. Alexander Kohut's School on West 58th Street for college preparatory work. She did special work at Columbia University, but left without a degree in order to marry Louis Untermeyer on Jan. 23, 1907. The only child from this marriage, a son, died in 1927 a month after his nineteenth birthday. Although separated from Untermeyer for some years, her marriage to him was not legally dissolved by divorce until 1951. Jean Starr Untermeyer's first artistic interest was music. Although she began the study of piano at six and her desire was to be a composer, it was as a lieder singer that she made her professional debut in Vienna in 1924 following 15 years of preparation. After two years in Europe she gave up this career in 1925. Her knowledge of German and music admirably fitted her to translate Oscar Bies's *Schubert the Man,* published in 1928. From 1940 to 1945, she worked on another translation from the German, Hermann Brock's *The Death of Virgil.* In addition to her musical interests, she was a voracious and, as she tells us, an undiscriminating reader "but not particularly of poetry." Although her first dedication to poetry came to her as a result of the prose essay "Dreamers and Doers," her active and adult interest stemmed from the ferment of the American renaissance in poetry that began about 1912. The leading poets of the period often gathered at the Untermeyer home for reading and discussion of their poems. Under this stimulus she began to write poems in secret, a secrecy which she maintained for three years until her husband found the poems and sent them to publishers. The best poems of her first four volumes—*Growing Pains* (1918), *Dreams Out of Darkness* (1921), *Steep Ascent* (1927), *Winged Chariot* (1936)—were republished as *Love and Need* (1940). Since 1940, she has published but one slim volume, *Later Poems* (1958). Mrs. Untermeyer has also been teacher and critic. In 1936–37, she was an active participant at the Summer Writers' Conference at Olivet College. In 1940 she accepted the chair of creative literature at Olivet; and from 1948 to 1951 she taught and lectured at the New School of Social Research, New York City. Occasionally she has reviewed books. As a reviewer she is clear, concise, perceptive, and objective. She is aware that "a poet must be shrewd . . . in the sense of being a keen discerner of values" ("Problem of Patchen," *Saturday Review of Literature,* March 22, 1947). It is as a poet, however, that Mrs. Untermeyer has done her most lasting work. In her short essay "A Page for Poets" (*Forum,* July, 1938), she has furnished us with some of the criteria by which, I think, she would wish to be judged. "Poetry," she tells us, "paradoxical as it may seem, is an affair of the most personal and, at the same time, the least personal implications. For any real poetry to be created there must be the utmost indriving concentration of all the poet's powers. But this intensification of attention has a strange result. . . . When I say 'utmost indriving concentration,' I do so in an effort to crystallize a repeated experience. . . . But, until the experience is truly felt and unerringly communicated, it is not poetry, however neatly it is confined in verse forms. . . . Poetry is not a limited mode of writing but rather a condition of living of which the writing is the 'testament.' . . . It begins in an awareness of eternal things—an awareness only heightened by the impact of the physical world, that has meaning in and beyond itself." That this has been her steady conviction is apparent from the fact that she has given a fuller statement of this idea in an early poem, "Reply":

Do you seek the true poem? Stop
your pruning and sieving,

The poem is less in the line than the living;
Less shaking the heart out of man than in giving.

The poem is the deed, though it go unrecorded.
The poem is the need, whether silent or worded;
And love is the seed, neither scattered nor hoarded.

Mrs. Untermeyer's poems cover a narrow range: love, religion, and nature, essentially, although a few poems deal with moral or ethical ideas. It is the love poems, however, which are the most interesting. Although they are deeply personal, they are at the same time universal, furnishing a commentary on Byron's statement that "love for a man is a thing apart, 'tis woman's whole existence." More specifically they are an articulate exposition of the antagonistic emotional reactions resulting from the biological differences in the sexes. Although lacking the concentration of many of her lyrics, "Eve before the Tree" is her fullest and least personal treatment of the subject. Caught in the communion of love, Eve

. . . saw beyond the borders of this world . . .
Clouds etched with recurring lightning smote my eyes;
Infinity stretched out beneath my feet;
Glories undreamed of in my calmer hours
Caught me and swept me into heaven itself,
Palpitant and rapturous through the night.
But Adam drank his cup of ecstacy
In one quick draught as a parched traveler would
So overeager for the offered joy.
So headlong, he could scarcely savor it.
And then completed but left unimpaired,
Unscathed by that all-too-smiling blast,
Turned sighing softly from my restless arms
And slept—and left me to my chafing dreams.

Eve eats the apple in order to learn what parts the lovers "in the hour of love . . . into aloof and separate mountain peaks," and feels that the rewards, the continuous searching for knowledge, more than compensated for expulsion from Eden and its attendant punishments. A variation on this theme, in this instance a highly personal episode, is "Spring"—a case of the temporarily wandering husband and his return to the mother-wife, and the more generalized but equally personal "Reply from the Citadel." Other poems—such as "Hors Beata," "Two of Us," "Possession," "Deliverance," "Anti-Erotic," "Rebirth," the dedication to *Steep Ascent,* "Brief Ballad of Lilith," and "Song of an Ordinary Woman"—are interesting to a woman because she can so intimately associate herself with the communicated experience, and to a man because he can learn of experiences which he cannot even share vicariously so foreign are they to him, but which he knows exist. Religion is the subject for many of Mrs. Untermeyer's poems, but it is not the religion of dogma or creed. It is the religion of self-dedication and constant becoming. Her best expression occurs in such poems as "Zanesville," "On Temples," "The Passionate Sword," "Old Man," and "Spent." Where her subject is Biblical or, one might say, impinges on the orthodox, she is less successful. That she detests hypocrisy of any sort is evident in "Church Sociable" or "Tolerance and Truth." She is close to nature, and some of her most evocative poems are those directly concerned with nature as a subject or as a source for her images. In poems like "High Tide," "Lake-Song," "Glimpse in Autumn," and "April Conceit" she reveals a strong influence of the "imagist" school. Prosodically, Mrs. Untermeyer shows the strong influence of poets like Emily Dickinson and Sara Teasdale, occasionally that of Amy Lowell and Edna Millay. In her most recent work her influences are different—Hopkins, Eliot, and others—and the change of influences is beneficial. Her "Meditations" have a new quality. At her best, her lyrics are straightforward, musical, reasonably concise, competent, and easily grasped. She approaches but never achieves a poem that asserts its immortality. Mrs. Untermeyer is a minor poet, but her work will be more valuable as a mirror of the temper of the American renaissance in poetry that began in 1912 and has not yet ended than as that of a major poet because of unique qualities. Although we are now in a different phase of the renaissance—a phase of a higher general competence than the earlier one, it is still too early positively to discern those of the mid-century who will equal or surpass the greater ones of that era. But even though a minor poet, Mrs. Untermeyer's work will continue to be valuable for the person who would understand a woman's attitude toward love. Her frank integrity never permits her to distort the truth.

James G. Southworth

UPDEGRAFF, DAVID BRAINARD (Aug. 23, 1830–May 23, 1894), Quaker evangelist, was born in Mount Pleasant, Jefferson County, where he attended public schools. After one year at Haverford College (1851), he entered business in Mount Pleasant. Soon after he started holding prayer meetings in his home in 1869, he was in demand as a preacher throughout the Midwest and East. Several of his views were disapproved by orthodox Quakers; he approved baptism, pastors, and congregational singing, and disapproved silent worship and the doctrine of the inner light. He edited the *Friend's Expositor,* 1887–93, and expressed his views there. The first two titles below are pamphlets defending his ideas on baptism; the third is a collection of addresses.

An Address to the Ohio Yearly Meeting on the Ordinances, Columbus, 1885.
The Ordinances: An Interview, Richmond, Ind., 1886.
Old Corn . . . , Boston, 1892.

UPHAM, ALFRED HORATIO (March 2, 1877–Feb. 17, 1945), educator, was born in Eaton, Preble County. He graduated from Miami University in 1897 and Columbia University (Ph.D.) in 1908. He was on the Miami faculty, 1897–1900, 1906–10, and 1913–20. He also taught at the Agricultural College of Utah, 1902–05, and Bryn Mawr College, 1910–13, was president of the University of Idaho, 1920–28, and served as president of Miami, 1928–45. Besides literature textbooks, he published *Old Miami, the Yale of the Early West,* Hamilton, 1909. WWW 2

UPTON, HARRIET TAYLOR (c.1861–Dec. 17, 1953), was born in Ravenna, Portage County. When she was six years old, her parents moved to Warren, where she lived most of her life. Wife of a Warren lawyer, George M. Upton, she was active in politics and public affairs. She was treasurer of the National Woman's Suffrage Association for fifteen years and also served as vice-chairman of the National Republican Executive Committee. For many years she was associated with the Ohio Department of Public Welfare. Early in the 1940s she moved to Pasadena, Calif., where she spent the remainder of her life. Besides the books below, she wrote articles and stories for children and in 1927 wrote her autobiography for private circulation.

Our Early Presidents: Their Wives and Children, Boston, [1891].
A Twentieth Century History of Trumbull County . . . , 2 vols., Chicago, 1909.
History of the Western Reserve . . . , (with Henry G. Cutler), 3 vols., Chicago, 1910.

UPTON, WILLIAM TREAT (Dec. 17, 1870–), educator, was born in Tallmadge, Summit County. After graduating from Oberlin College in 1896, he studied for two years in Vienna. He was on the faculty of Oberlin Conservatory of Music, 1898–1936, and was also widely known as an organist. He now lives in Harper's Ferry, W. Va. He wrote numerous biographical, critical, and technical articles on music and *Art Song in America . . . ,* Boston, [1930]. WW 25

URBAN, SEPTIMUS R. Pseud. See Nathan D. Urner.

URNER, MABEL HERBERT (June 28, 1881–March 1, 1957), journalist, was born in Cincinnati, Hamilton County. She was married to Lathrop Colgate Harper, but wrote under her maiden name. Her "Helen and Warren" column was syndicated in American, British, and Canadian newspapers for more than thirty years. She died in New York City. She published several books, e.g., *The Married Life of Helen and Warren,* Boston, [1925]. WWW 3

URNER, NATHAN DANE (Jan. 12, 1839–Feb. 19, 1893), journalist, was born in Cincinnati, Hamilton County. In 1862 he became a reporter on the New York *Tribune,* where he later served as city editor and as Horace Greeley's private secretary. His vivid description of a fire at Barnum's Museum in 1865 was reprinted throughout the country and was included by Barnum in his autobiography. A hack writer for Beadle and Street & Smith, Urner wrote novels and etiquette books, e.g., *Gold-dust Darrell . . . ,* New York, 1890, and *Never: A Hand-book for the Uninitiated and Inexperienced . . . ,* New York, 1883. Among his pen names were Septimus R. Urban, O. N. Looker, Mentor, and Burke Brentford.

UTTER, WILLIAM T. (Feb. 2, 1895–), educator, was born near Riverside, Calif. He graduated from Northwest Missouri Teachers College in 1921 and the University of Chicago (Ph.D.) in 1929. Descended from Ohio ancestors on both sides of his family, he returned to Ohio in 1924 to teach at Ohio State University; since 1929 he has been on the history faculty of Denison University. He has held various local offices in Granville and has written a history of the community (1956). He also wrote volume II of the *History of Ohio,* edited by Carl Wittke: *The Frontier State . . . ,* Columbus, 1942. WWMW 6

V

VAIL, HENRY HOBART (May 27, 1839–Sept. 2, 1925), publisher, born in Pomfret, Vt., came to Dayton in 1861. He taught school for a time, served with the 131st O.V.I. in 1864, and after the war joined the firm of Sargeant, Wilson, Hinkle, Cincinnati. He was made a partner in 1874 and remained with the firm, which changed its name several times before it was bought by American Book Company in 1890. In New York he was editor-in-chief, 1890–1907, and vice president, 1904–11. He supervised the new series of Ray arithmetics in 1877 and the new series of McGuffey readers in 1878. He published *A History of the McGuffey Readers,* Cleveland, 1910. WWW 1

VAIL, ISAAC NEWTON (1840–Jan. 26, 1912), geologist, was born in Barnesville, Belmont County. Around 1890 he went to California, where he died at Pasadena. Besides the titles below, he published a number of pamphlets and a magazine, *The Annular World* (1895–98). Most of his writings pertain to his theory of a concentric series of vapors once surrounding the earth, from which the earth was gradually formed.

The Waters above the Firmament, or the Earth's Annular System, Cleveland, [1885].

What Was It? Eden's Flaming Sword, Pasadena, Calif., 1896.

Alaska, Land of the Nugget. Why?, Pasadena, Calif., 1897.

The Deluge and Its Cause . . . , Chicago, 1905.

VAIL, THEODORE NEWTON (July 16, 1845–April 16, 1920), pioneer organizer of the Bell Telephone Company, was born near Minerva, Carroll County, but spent most of his life outside Ohio. He grew up in New Jersey and Iowa. In 1889 after retiring from the Bell Company, he settled in Vermont; but he was also active in several projects in Argentina, and he was president of American Telephone and Telegraph Company, 1907–19. A collection of his papers and addresses was published privately: *Views on Public Questions . . . ,* [New York?], 1917. DAB 19

VALLANDIGHAM, CLEMENT LAIRD (July 29, 1820–June 17, 1871), lawyer and leader of the Peace Democrats or Copperheads during the Civil War, was born in New Lisbon, Columbiana County. He attended New Lisbon Academy, founded by his father, and Jefferson College, Pa. After reading law he was admitted to the bar in 1842 and practiced in New Lisbon until 1847, when he moved to Dayton. Proud of his Virginia ancestry, he spoke for slavery and states' rights as early as 1840. While serving in the House of Representatives, 1857–63, he spoke vehemently in favor of compromise with the South. His antiwar speeches led to his arrest May 5, 1863, in Dayton. Lincoln banished him to the South, but he took up residence in Windsor, Canada, was Democratic candidate for Ohio governor in the bitter campaign of 1863, and received many delegations from the North. In 1864 he returned to Ohio, but was not arrested. He was a strong supporter of General McClellan in the Presidential campaign of 1864. He practiced law after the war. His last political act was to persuade the state Democratic convention of 1871 to abandon its former views and adjust to the new postwar situation. A brilliant fanatic, he won the admiration of some and the scorn of many. He shot himself accidentally while defending Thomas McGehan (q.v.) and demonstrating how the murder of which McGehan was accused had really occurred. Besides the collections below, many of his speeches were published separately.

The Record of Hon. C. L. Vallandigham on Abolition, the Union, and the Civil War . . . , Cincinnati, 1863.

Speeches, Arguments, Addresses, and Letters . . . , New York, 1864.

VALLANDIGHAM, JAMES LAIRD (1812–1904), older brother of Clement L. Vallandigham (q.v.), was born in New Lisbon, Columbiana County. He practiced law there with his brother for a time and later lived in Hanover, Licking County. He became a minister after the Civil War. He died in Lebanon, Warren County. His first memoir of his brother was a short work of 64 pages, but the second title below is a full-scale book of nearly 600 pages.

Biographical Memoir . . . , New York, 1864.

A Life of Clement L. Vallandigham . . . , Baltimore, 1872.

VALMAER. Pseud. See Michael V. Ream.

VANCE, J. WILSON (Dec. 20, 1845–Nov. 10, 1911), journalist, was born in Findlay, Hancock County. He served in the 21st O.V.I. from 1861 to March, 1866. He won the Congressional Medal of Honor at the Battle of Stone's River. After the Civil War he spent a year at Harvard Law School; he then became Washington correspondent for various newspapers. In 1904 he became editor of the *Square Deal.* He died in Chattanooga, Tenn.

Little Amy's Christmas, New York, 1880.
Princes' Favors . . . , New York, 1880.
God's War, New York, 1889.
Big John Baldwin . . . , New York, 1909.
Stone's River, the Turning Point of the Civil War, New York, 1914.

VANCE, MARGUERITE (Mrs. William L.) (Nov. 27, 1889–), born in Chicago, lived in Wilmington and Cleveland for 21 years. In Cleveland she worked in Higbee's book department. She left Cleveland in 1934 and moved to New York City, where she was children's book editor for E. P. Dutton & Co. Now retired, she lives in New York. She has written more than twenty books for young readers, e.g., *A Star for Hansi,* New York, 1936.

VANCE, ROWLAND BOYD (Sept. 8, 1919–), was born in Columbus, Franklin County. He graduated from East High School, Columbus, in 1936 and Yale University in 1940. After World War II, in which he served as a Marine, he studied at the American Academy of Dramatic Arts. He directed and acted in a number of plays and is now an associate director with Columbia Broadcasting System. During his Marine Corps training at Quantico, Va., he wrote *They Made Me a Leatherneck,* New York, [1943].

VANCE, VIRGINIA E. LOCKHART (July 21, 1834–March 25, 1929), was born in Adams County. She was educated in Parkersburg, Va., and later returned with her family to a farm near West Union. After her marriage in 1861 she moved to Kansas, where she lived until her death. Collections of her verse were privately printed and given to friends and relatives.

On the Parnassian Hills, [n.p., n.d.].

VAN CLEEF, EUGENE (Jan. 17, 1887–), educator, was born in Chicago. A graduate of the University of Chicago in 1908 and Clark University (Ph.D.) in 1926, he served on the Ohio State University geography faculty, 1921–57, and since his retirement has continued to live in Columbus. He has published numerous professional articles, several textbooks, and *The Story of the Weather,* New York, [1929]. WW 28

VAN DEMAN, ESTHER BOISE (Oct. 1, 1862–May 3, 1937), archaeologist, was born in South Salem, Ross County. She grew up in Kansas, where her family moved in the early 1870s. She graduated from the University of Michigan in 1891 and the University of Chicago (Ph.D.) in 1898. After teaching Latin and archaeology at several colleges, she joined the American School, Rome, in 1906 and remained there until her death. She published a number of articles on Roman architecture and *The Building of the Roman Aqueducts,* [Washington, D. C.], 1934. DAB 22

VAN FOSSAN, WILLIAM HARVEY (Nov. 4, 1855–July 23, 1948), educator, was born in Glasgow, Columbiana County. After graduating from Mount Union College in 1882, he was a school superintendent in Lisbon and East Palestine, president of New Lyme Institute, Ashtabula County, and was associated with Macmillan Company, 1907–35. He wrote historical articles and a book: *The Story of Ohio,* New York, 1937.

VAN HORNE, DAVID (Dec. 11, 1837–April 12, 1930), clergyman and educator, was born in Glen, N. Y. A graduate of Union College and New Brunswick Theological Seminary, he was ordained to the ministry of the Reformed (Dutch) Church in 1867. He served pastorates in Greenwich, N. Y., Dayton, and Philadelphia, Pa., until 1888, when he became president of Heidelberg Theological Seminary, Tiffin. After his retirement he lived in Dayton.

A History of the Reformed Church in Philadelphia . . . , Philadelphia, 1876.
The Mountain Boy of Wildhaus . . . , Philadelphia, 1884.
Tent and Saddle Life in the Holy Land, Philadelphia, 1885.
Religion and Revelation . . . , Dayton, 1892.
The Church and the Future Life, Cleveland, 1904.

VAN HORNE, THOMAS BUDD (July 6, 1821–April, 1895), clergyman, was born in Lebanon, Warren County. After graduating from Denison University in 1847, he served there as a tutor, studied at Newton Theological Institution, and was a school principal in the West. He was ordained to the Baptist ministry in 1853 and served a church in Arkansas until 1860. He returned to Ohio, became superintendent of schools in Franklin, and in 1862 entered the service as chaplain of the 13th O.V.I. He later served as post chaplain at national cemeteries in Chattanooga, Tenn., and Marietta, Ga., and at National Soldiers' Home, Dayton.

History of the Army of the Cumberland . . ., Cincinnati, 1875.

The Life of Major-General George H. Thomas, New York, 1882.

VAN KIRK, JAMES WILLIAM (Feb. 27, 1858– ?), clergyman, was born in Feed Springs, Jefferson County. After graduating from Mount Union College and Boston University School of Theology, he preached in the East Ohio Conference of the Methodist Church. He wrote *Brotherhood: The Call of the Century,* Youngstown, [1908].

VAN KIRK, WALTER WILLIAM (Nov. 11, 1891–July 6, 1956), clergyman, was born in Cleveland, Cuyahoga County. He graduated from Ohio Wesleyan University in 1917 and Boston University School of Theology in 1920. He served Methodist churches in New England, 1920–25, and was secretary of the Department of International Justice and Goodwill in the Federal Council of Churches, 1925–50. He published several books on religion and international peace, e.g., *Religion Renounces War,* New York, 1934. WWW 3

VAN NOSTRAND, MRS. JOHN. See Nell B. Dorr.

VAN TASSEL, CHARLES SUMNER (July 22, 1858–Oct. 15, 1942), journalist, was born in Milton Township, Wood County. His father was a teacher in the Indian Mission School on the Maumee River near Grand Rapids. He worked on a number of newspapers in Ohio: the Sandusky *Register,* the Columbus *Post,* the Toledo *Post,* and the Toledo *Bee.* After he retired from journalism to devote himself to historical research, he wrote several works, including a history of Bowling Green and *Story of the Maumee Valley, Toledo, and the Sandusky Region . . .*, 4 vols., Chicago, 1929.

VARNUM, JAMES MITCHELL (Dec. 17, 1748–Jan. 10, 1789), was born in Dracut, Mass. He was admitted to the bar in 1771, served with distinction in the Revolutionary War, and was a member of the Continental Congress. He was a director of the Ohio Company, and in 1787, despite his poor health, he accepted an appointment as United States judge for the Territory Northwest of the Ohio River. He arrived in Marietta June 5, 1788, and a month later delivered a Fourth of July oration that was published in Newport, R. I., making him the author of one of the first works written in Ohio. He died in Marietta.

VAUGHAN, CHARLES RAYMOND (Sept. 17, 1893–Oct. 12, 1947), clergyman, was born in Georgesville, Franklin County. A graduate of the University of Pittsburgh, he was a Methodist minister and later was affiliated with the Presbyterian church. He was also a journalist and radio broadcaster. After witnessing a teen-age street fight in Columbus, he founded Boy-Land Clubs to combat delinquency and also edited a magazine, *Boy-Land.* His writings on the subject include a book, published under the pen name Pat McGuire: *The Bread and Water of Affliction,* Pataskala, [1947].

VAUGHAN, DANIEL (c.1820–April 6, 1879), scientist, was born in County Clare, Ireland. He came to the United States about 1836 and conducted a school in Bourbon County, Ky. In 1850 he moved to Cincinnati, where he became a lecturer on chemistry in the Eclectic Medical Institute. Possessed of an excellent education and great mathematical ability, he was in demand as a lecturer on astronomy and natural phenomena at Midwestern educational institutions. He held the chair of chemistry at the Cincinnati College of Medicine and Surgery, 1860–72, and then dropped from sight. Only the attendants at the Cincinnati Public Library knew the slight, shawl-draped figure that haunted the library's reading rooms. In April, 1879, he was found prostrated by pulmonary hemorrhages and near starvation in a tenement room.

A New System of Vegetable Physiology, Cincinnati, 1848.

Destiny of the Solar System, Cincinnati, [1854].

Popular Physical Astronomy . . ., Cincinnati, 1858.

Vegetation Traced to Natural Causes, [n.p., 185-?].

VEDRA, YARMO. Pseud. See Holmes W. Merton.

VENABLE, EMERSON (Dec. 22, 1875–), educator, was born in Cincinnati, Hamilton County, the son of William H. Venable (q.v.). He graduated from the University of Cincinnati in 1898, served with the 1st Ohio Volunteer Cavalry during the Spanish-American War, and taught English at Walnut Hills High School, Cincinnati, 1900–34. He now lives in Santa Monica, Calif. He edited a collection of poetry by Ohioans in 1909 and his father's poems in 1925. He wrote *The Hamlet Problem and Its Solution,* Cincinnati, 1912. WW 29

VENABLE, WILLIAM HENRY (April 29, 1836–July 6, 1920), historian of literary culture in the Ohio Valley and a contributor to that culture as teacher, poet, novelist, essayist, and public speaker, was born in a log cabin near Waynesville, Warren County. A family background of Quakerism—he was a descendant of Quaker preacher William Venable, who settled near the Delaware River about 1680, and the son of pioneering Quaker parents—strongly influenced his character development and helped to shape his thinking. In 1843 the family moved to a farm about seven miles north of Lebanon, where Venable grew up in an environment that combined the hardships of near-pioneer life with the general enlightenment of a cultivated household. While he attended district school, his father encouraged him to read Plutarch, Shakespeare, *Don Quixote,* and Lewis and Clark's *Journal.* Many years later, in *A Buckeye Boyhood* (1911) he gave a vivid account of his intellectual and moral development, especially of the influence of Nature at a time when vast stretches of the Midwest were still unclaimed from the wilderness. Venable early decided to become, like his father, a teacher. When only seventeen he was teaching at Sugar Grove. Later, at the Southwestern State Normal School in Lebanon, he won distinction for versatile scholarship in language, literature, history, and science. After six years as student and teacher, he spent the year 1860 as principal of Jennings Academy in Vernon, Ind. It was the only year he ever spent outside Ohio. After his marriage in 1861 to Mary Ann Vater of Indianapolis, he moved with his young wife to Cincinnati, then the "Metropolis of the Midwest." Here he was to devote almost a quarter-century to the posts of teacher, principal, and eventually proprietor of a widely known college preparatory school, the Chickering Institute. Disposing of his school interest in 1886, Venable busied himself during the following three years in various literary ventures and in public speaking in Ohio and neighboring states. During the years from 1889 to 1900 he returned to teaching, to become head of the English Department at Hughes High School and then at Walnut Hills High School in Cincinnati, while still finding the time to publish a series of textbooks on English poetry. In 1900 he retired from teaching to devote the rest of his life to writing in a variety of fields. His death, following a long illness, occurred in his eighty-fifth year. He is buried in Spring Grove Cemetery at Cincinnati. As a child Venable loved to compose verses and in his teens frequently contributed to local newspapers. During his years at Chickering Institute, and especially in the period that followed, he found many opportunities for expression by pen and tongue. He was happy in the "Queen City of the West" and grateful for its cultural resources, which he celebrated in a "Civic Ode." Whether in verse or prose, Venable displayed intense interest in the history of his community, state, and nation and in the beauties of Nature. And he had an almost Wordsworthian conviction of the importance of natural beauty in the development of human character. His *School History of the United States* (1872) was for many years a standard textbook in the schools of Ohio and other states. A volume of essays entitled *Let Him First Be a Man* (1893) sets forth his ideal of teaching as the arousing of an intense desire for excellence, moral and intellectual. His popular romance *A Dream of Empire; Or, the House of Blennerhassett,* (1901) was a best-seller of its day. Benjamin Parker called it "The one great novel of the Burr-Blennerhassett episode and one of the strongest, most successfully constructed and captivating of modern historical romances." To most adult readers of his time, Venable was perhaps best known as a poet. His verses, edited and issued after his death in a complete edition (1925) by his son and literary executor, Emerson Venable (q.v.), reveal the scope of his interests as well as his poetic gifts. James Whitcomb Riley called him "The sweetest warbler of the whole enduring flock." Widely known in their time were his "Sage of the Oak," the pastoral "June on the Miami," the Floridian Sonnets, inspired by a holiday spent in the Southern state, and the elegiac sonnets in memory of his close friend and fellow poet Coates Kinney (q.v.). Probably nothing he ever wrote, however, won greater popularity than his ingenious "My Catbird." Venable's most notable achievement as a man of letters was his *Beginnings of Literary Culture in the Ohio Valley* (1891). This work of more than 500 pages is a valuable record of American cultural sources. It reflects the author's own pioneer family background, his erudition in Ohioana, his curiosity about literary origins, and his unflagging energy. He referred to the volume rather lightly as "a repository of accumulated notes," and it does indeed include data from various lectures and journalistic pieces. Yet it is an irreplaceable survey of the cultural beginnings of our early Western society in the period brought to a close by the Civil War. During his long, active career in Cincinnati, Venable wrote a great many essays and newspaper articles and delivered numerous public addresses on the art of teaching, on libraries and other literary institutions of the state, and on famous personages of Ohio. In recognition of his contributions to letters, he received several honorary degrees—Master of Arts from Asbury University in 1864, Doctor of Laws from Ohio University in 1886, and Doctor of Letters from the University of Cincinnati in 1917. His lifework revealed in happy coordination the gifts of the imaginative writer and the spirit of the devoted public servant. Among the authors of Ohio he should be listed as "Educator, Historian, Poet, Essayist, Novelist"—in that order. In his work the ultimate objective of the teacher was never far in the background. To him education was "the supreme science of life, and conduct its application." William Henry Venable was, until his last illness, a man intensely devoted to his calling as teacher and writer and to encouraging the arts of self-expression in others. His frail physique never deterred him from arduous tasks. During his later years his reputation had spread far from his suburban home in Cincinnati's Tusculum Heights, where he sought to keep as closely in touch with Nature as he had been in the boyhood cabin at Waynesville. His influence as a writer-educator in the Ohio Valley has been considerable. He took as an injunction upon himself a passage of his own: "Words are deeds. He who speaks well, or writes well, does service as practical as the sowing of grain, the steering of a ship, or the curing of a wound."

Joseph Sagmaster

The Teacher's Dream, New York, 1881.
Melodies of the Heart . . . , Cincinnati, 1885.
Footprints of the Pioneers in the Ohio Valley . . . , Cincinnati, 1888.
Beginnings of Literary Culture in the Ohio Valley . . . , Cincinnati, 1891.
John Hancock, Ph.D. A Memoir . . . , Cincinnati, 1892.
Let Him First Be a Man, and Other Essays . . . , Boston, 1893.
The Last Flight, Cincinnati, 1894.
Tales from Ohio History for Home and School, Norwalk, 1896.
A Dream of Empire; Or, the House of Blennerhassett, New York, 1901.
Tom Tad, New York, 1902.
Saga of the Oak, and Other Poems, New York, 1904.
Cincinnati, a Civic Ode . . . , [Cincinnati?, 1907?].
Floridian Sonnets, Boston, 1909.
A Buckeye Boyhood, Cincinnati, 1911.
June on the Miami; An Idyll, Cincinnati, 1912.
A Centennial History of Christ Church . . . , Cincinnati, 1918.
The Poems of William Henry Venable, (Emerson Venable, ed.), New York, 1925.

VENABLE, WILLIAM MAYO (Feb. 14, 1871–June 2, 1955), engineer, was born in Cincinnati, Hamilton County, the son of William H. Venable (q.v.). He graduated from the University of Cincinnati in 1892, served in the Spanish-American War, and worked in Cuba for a time after the war. He afterward was employed by various engineering firms and for four years lived in Pittsburgh, where he was recognized as a patent expert. Besides the title below, he published numerous scientific and technical papers and books.

The Second Regiment of United States Volunteer Engineers; A History, Cincinnati, [1899].

VER BECK, WILLIAM FRANCIS (June 1, 1858–July 13, 1933), was born in Belmont County. He attended Belmont County schools, but spent the greater part of his later life in Mansfield. Under the name Frank Ver Beck, he wrote and illustrated books about comic animals for children.

The Dumpies and the Arkansas Bear, (with Albert B. Paine), New York, 1898.
Acrobatic Animals, New York, 1899.
The Three Bears, New York, 1899.
Beasts and Birds, New York, 1900.
A Handbook of Golf for Bears, New York, 1900.
Book of Bears, Philadelphia, 1906.
The Little Lost Bear, London, 1915.
Short Little Tales from Bruintown, Philadelphia, 1915.
Ver Beck's Bears in Mother Gooseland, London, 1915.
Timothy Tuttle's Great Day, London, 1916.
The Donkey Child, New York, 1918.
The Elephant Child, New York, 1920.
The Little Bear Who Ran Away from Bruintown, Boston, 1923.
The Arkansas Bear Complete, (with Albert B. Paine), Philadelphia, 1925.
Little Black Sambo and the Baby Elephant, Philadelphia, 1925.
Little Black Sambo and the Monkey People, Philadelphia, 1929.

Little Black Sambo and the Crocodiles, Philadelphia, 1930.
Little Black Sambo in the Bears' Den, Philadelphia, 1930.

VERSTEEG, JOHN MARINUS (Sept. 9, 1888–), clergyman, born in Den Helder, Holland, came to America in 1900 and has lived in Ohio since 1932. He has served Methodist churches in Cincinnati, 1932–46, and Athens, 1951–57, was superintendent of the Lima District, 1946–51, and since 1957 has been director of libraries at Methodist Theological Seminary. He has written several books on religion and stewardship, e.g., *Perpetuating Pentecost,* Chicago, 1930. WW 30

VICKERS, LEONARD B. (1833–1892), was born in Akron, Summit County. He died in Pueblo, Colo. No further biographical details have been found, but the title pages of his books identify him as "Leonard B. Vickers, Angel of God."

The Loud Voice . . . , Portland, Oreg., 1864.
Civil Theology . . . , [Ada], 1873.

VICKERY, WILLIS (Nov. 26, 1857–Sept. 26, 1932), lawyer and judge, was born in Sandusky County. After graduating from Boston University Law School in 1884, he practiced in Sandusky, Erie, and Huron Counties, and after 1896 he practiced in Cleveland. He served as judge of common pleas court, 1908–18, and after 1918 as judge of the court of appeals. He collected a large Shakespeare library and lectured on Shakespeare's life and works. He was active in the Rowfant Club and was responsible for several fine editions published by that organization. He wrote *The Rowfant Bindery . . . ,* Cleveland, 1928. OBB

VICTOR, FRANCES FULLER (May 23, 1826–Nov. 14, 1902), elder sister of Metta Fuller Victor (q.v.), was born in Rome, N. Y. In 1839 her parents moved to Wooster, where both sisters wrote for various periodicals. Around 1851 they moved to New York, a fact which led many to compare them to Alice and Phoebe Cary (qq.v.). But Frances soon returned to Ohio to care for her parents, and in 1853 she married Jackson Baritt of Pontiac, Mich., and temporarily gave up thoughts of a literary career. No details are available concerning the next nine years. In 1862 she married Henry Clay Victor, a naval engineer and brother of Orville J. Victor (q.v.), Metta's husband. In 1863 her husband was ordered to San Francisco, and she accompanied him. After the Civil War they lived in Portland, Oreg. After her husband was killed in the wreck of the *Pacific* in 1875, she returned to California. For eleven years she worked for H. H. Bancroft (q.v.) doing research for his historical volumes and writing portions of several of them. In her old age she lived in near-poverty in Oregon. She died in Portland.

Poems of Sentiment and Imagination . . . , (with Metta Fuller), New York, 1851.
Fresh Leaves from Western Woods, (with Metta Fuller), Buffalo, 1852.
The River of the West . . . , Hartford, Conn., 1870.
All Over Oregon and Washington . . . , San Francisco, 1872.
The Women's War with Whisky . . . , Portland, Oreg., 1874.
Eleven Years in the Rocky Mountains . . . , Hartford, Conn., 1877.
The New Penelope and Other Stories and Poems, San Francisco, 1877.
Atlantis Arisen . . . , Philadelphia, 1891.
The Early Indian Wars of Oregon . . . , Salem., Oreg., 1894.

VICTOR, METTA VICTORIA FULLER (March 2, 1831–June 26, 1885), was born near Erie, Pa. In 1839 her parents moved to Wooster, where she attended the seminary and began writing for local papers when she was thirteen. While in her midteens she was writing for the New York *Home Journal* under the pen name Singing Sybil. With her sister Frances (q.v.) she went to New York, where they were known as "The Sisters of the West." In 1856 she married Orville J. Victor (q.v.) and became one of the most popular in his corps of Beadle writers. Her greatest success probably came with *Maum Guinea,* said to have been praised by Lincoln. In the bibliography below, which undoubtedly is incomplete, *The Senator's Son* was republished in 1855 as *Parke Madison;* the *Miss Slimmens* books were published under the pen name Mrs. Mark Peabody; and *The Dead Letter* and *The Figure Eight* appeared under the pen name Seeley Regester. She also compiled several cookbooks. Other pen names used in her writings for Beadle were Corinne Cushman, Eleanor Lee Edwards, and Rose Kennedy.

Last Days of Tul, Boston, 1846.
Poems of Sentiment and Imagination . . . , (with Frances Fuller), New York, 1851.
Fresh Leaves from Western Woods, (with Frances Fuller), Buffalo, 1852.
The Senator's Son . . . , Cleveland, 1853.
The Arctic Queen, Sandusky, 1856.
Mormon Wives . . . , New York, 1856.

Miss Slimmens' Window and Other Papers, New York, 1859.
Maum Guinea and Her Plantation "Children," New York, [1861].
The Two Hunters . . . , New York, [1866].
Who Was He? . . . , New York, [1866].
The Dead Letter . . . , New York, 1867.
Too True: A Story of To-day, New York, 1868.
The Figure Eight . . . , New York, [1869].
Passing the Portal . . . , New York, 1876.
Miss Slimmens' Boarding House . . . , New York, 1882.
Abijah Beanpole in New York . . . , New York, 1884.
Mrs. Rasher's Curtain Lectures . . . , New York, [1884].
The Brown Princess . . . , New York, 1888.
The Phantom Wife, New York, 1888.
Born to Betray . . . , New York, 1890.
Guilty or Not Guilty . . . , New York, 1890.
The Gay Captain, New York, 1891.
Who Owned the Jewels? . . . , New York, [1891].

VICTOR, ORVILLE JAMES (Oct. 23, 1827–March 14, 1910), editor, was born in Sandusky, Erie County. After graduating from Norwalk Academy in 1847, he read law, and from 1851 to 1856 he was associate editor of the Sandusky *Register.* After his marriage to Metta Fuller (see above) in 1856, he served as editor of various magazines, and in 1861 he became chief editor for Beadle publications. He is sometimes inaccurately credited with inventing the dime novel, but the first novel published by Beadle appeared in 1860, a year before he joined the staff. He did, however, do much to popularize this form of fiction. Although his name appeared on none of the paperbound Beadle novels, he advised and assisted the writers. His own writings, which were nonfiction, history and biography, can be fairly described as reasonably accurate but pedestrian. His *History of the Southern Rebellion* was first published in weekly parts.

The Life of Joseph Garibaldi . . . , New York, [1860].
The American Rebellion. Some Facts and Reflections for the Consideration of the English People . . . , London, [1861].
The History, Civil, Political and Military, of the Southern Rebellion . . . , 4 vols., New York, [1861–68?].
The Life and Exploits of John Paul Jones . . . , New York, [1861].
The Life of Maj.-Gen. Geo. B. McClellan . . . , New York, [1861].
Incidents and Anecdotes of the War . . . , New York, [1866].
Men of the Time: Being Biographies of Generals . . . , 3 vols., New York, 1862–63.
Pittsburg Landing . . . , New York, [1862].
History of American Conspiracies . . . , New York, [1863].
The Private and Public Life of Abraham Lincoln . . . , New York, [1864].
The Life and Times of Colonel Ethan Allen . . . , New York, [1876].
The Life and Times of Israel Putnam . . . , New York, [1876].

VICTOR, SARAH MARIA (May 5, 1827– ?), was born in Pickaway County. After the Civil War she settled in Cleveland. In 1876 she was convicted of murdering her brother by putting arsenic in a mince pie. In 1887 she published the story of her life, a book that mingles sensational incidents with moralizing and protestations of her innocence; it was edited by Harriet L. Adams (q.v.). She was pardoned in 1887, and she sold the book in the streets of Cleveland, hoping to convince the public that she was innocent of the crime for which she had been imprisoned.

The Life Story of Sarah M. Victor, for Sixty Years. Convicted of Murdering Her Brother . . . , Cleveland, 1887.

VIETZEN, RAYMOND CHARLES (Sept. 5, 1907–), was born near Elyria, Lorain County, and still lives in that county. He graduated from high school in Elyria and also studied at Oberlin College. While operating an automobile repair shop in Elyria, he has made a hobby of collecting Indian relics. He has conducted explorations in Ohio and Kentucky, and owns and operates the Indian Ridge Museum. He has published a number of articles and books on archaeological and historical subjects, e.g., *The Immortal Eries,* [Elyria], 1945.

VILLARD, HENRY (April 10, 1835–Nov. 12, 1900), journalist and financier, was born in Bavaria. He came to America in 1853 and made his way to Cincinnati, where he remained for a number of months. Returning to Cincinnati late in 1858, he was employed by the Cincinnati *Commercial,* and was sent to Kansas as a correspondent. He retained his connection with the *Commercial* through the Republican National Convention at Chicago in 1860. He published his memoirs in 1904 and earlier wrote *The Past and Present of the Pike's Peak Gold Regions* . . . , St. Louis, Mo., 1860.

VINCENT, BEATRICE MARY (Oct. 16, 1911–), was born in Maple Heights, Cuyahoga County. After graduating from Ursuline College for Women in 1934, she taught English in Maple Heights public schools. She was fashion director at the May Company, 1943–51, and since 1953 has been careers and beauty editor for the Cleveland *Press.* She has published *Make Mine Success,* New York, 1950. WWAW 1

VINCENT, BOYD (May 18, 1845–Jan. 14, 1935), clergyman, was born in Erie, Pa. He was consecrated coadjutor bishop of southern Ohio in 1889 and was bishop from 1904 until 1929. He lived in Cincinnati.

God and Prayer . . . , New York, 1897.
Recollections of the Diocese of Southern Ohio, Milwaukee, Wis., 1934.

VINCENT, CLARENCE AUGUSTUS (Dec. 17, 1859–March 31, 1943), clergyman, was born in Bainbridge, Ross County. After graduating from Oberlin College in 1884 and the Seminary in 1888, he was ordained a Congregational minister. He served a church in Sandusky, 1894–98, and also preached in other states before he retired from the ministry in 1941.

Acts of Modern Apostles, Boston, 1893.
Providence in America; Or, the Problems of Self-Government, Sandusky, [1898].
Night and the Stars, Chicago, 1906.

VINCENT, JOHN MARTIN (Oct. 11, 1857–Sept. 22, 1939), educator, was born in Elyria, Lorain County. He graduated from Oberlin College in 1883 and Johns Hopkins University (Ph.D.) in 1890. He served on the Johns Hopkins faculty, 1889–1925, and wrote a number of articles and textbooks on history and government.

Government in Switzerland, New York, 1900.
Historical Research . . . , New York, 1911.

VINCENT, THOMAS MacCURDY (Nov. 15, 1832–May 9, 1909), army officer, was born near Cadiz, Harrison County. After graduating from the U. S. Military Academy in 1853, he served in the army until 1896, when he retired as a brigadier general. During the Civil War he was in charge of the organization of volunteer forces. He died in Zanesville. He delivered addresses on Lincoln and Stanton and on the Battle of Bull Run that were published as pamphlets.

The Military Power of the United States during the War of the Rebellion, New York, 1881.

VOGT, PAUL LEROY (May 28, 1878–March 3, 1953), educator, was born in Upper Sandusky, Wyandot County. He graduated from Ohio Northern University in 1901 and the University of Pennsylvania (Ph.D.) in 1907. He was on the sociology faculty of Miami University, 1911–15, and of Ohio State University, 1915–17, and became superintendent of rural work in the Methodist Church in 1917. He published articles and books, e.g., *Church Cooperation in Community Life,* New York, [1921]. WW 13

VOKOUN, FRANK JOSEPH (March 20, 1900–), surgeon, was born in Cleveland, Cuyahoga County. He graduated from Western Reserve University (A.B., 1921; M.D., 1924) and in 1925 began practice in Cleveland. He served in World War II and now lives in Lakewood. Besides medical articles he has published a volume of poems, the title of which is taken from his summer home, Montauk Acres: *Montauk Melodies . . . ,* Cleveland, 1930. WWO

VOLLMER, PHILIP (Nov. 28, 1860–Dec. 10, 1929), clergyman and educator, born in Frankenthal, Germany, came to the United States in 1878. Ordained to the Presbyterian ministry in 1884, he taught in various seminaries and was on the faculty of Central Theological Seminary, Dayton, 1907–23. He published textbooks, study guides, and *John Calvin . . . ,* Philadelphia, [1909]. WWW 1

VOLZ, J. ALBERT (1896–), was born in Fort Recovery, Mercer County, and attended the schools of that community. After serving in the Third Divison during World War I, he was an assistant postmaster in Coldwater and still lives in that community. He has written a number of articles and booklets on Ohio history, e.g., *Rambles in Ohio,* Carthagena, 1935.

VON ENGELN, OSKAR (July 3, 1880–), educator, was born in Dayton, Montgomery County. A graduate of Cornell University (A.B., 1908; Ph.D., 1911), he taught geography and geology at his alma mater, 1907–49. Since his retirement he has continued to live in Ithaca, N. Y. Besides textbooks and laboratory manuals, he has written *At Cornell,* Ithaca, [1909]. WW 27

VON MARTELS, HEINRICH W. (Nov. 7, 1803–April 18, 1896), was born in Germany. He lived in Missouri, 1832–33, and on his return to Germany published the book listed below. In 1845 he went to

Texas and California, where he made and lost a fortune. He came to Cincinnati in 1850, edited the *Volksfreund,* and operated a farm in Clermont County.

Der Westliche Theil der Vereinigten Staaten von Nordamerika, Osnabrück, 1834.

VOORHEES, DANIEL WOLSEY (Sept. 26, 1827–April 10, 1897), was born in Liberty Township, Butler County, but was taken by his family to Indiana when he was two months old. He served as a Democrat in the House of Representatives and in the Senate. He was instrumental in the building of the Library of Congress. He won wide renown as an orator, and in addition to the title below, many of his speeches were published separately.

Forty Years of Oratory; Daniel Wolsey Voorhees Lectures, Addresses and Speeches . . . , Indianapolis, 1898.

VORN HOLZ, MIRANDA L. (April 22, 1823–Jan. 19, 1900), born in Kentucky, lived in Cincinnati after 1852. An active worker in the Methodist church, she served as an evangelist in Ohio and Kentucky and in the West. Her autobiography was edited and published by her daughter, Ida Vorn Holz Calkers.

The Old Paths, Cincinnati, 1898.

VOSS, ELIZABETH NIENABAR (March 24, 1862–Nov. 19, 1942), was born in Cincinnati, Hamilton County, and spent her entire life in tnat city. Her poems appeared in various periodicals, and she also published at least two collections of verse, e.g., *The Soul's Voice,* Boston, [1920]. AATB

W

WADDELL, CHARLES CAREY (March 3, 1868–June 11, 1930), journalist, was born in Chillicothe, Ross County. He graduated from Marietta College in 1889, was on the staff of the Chillicothe *News,* 1890–93, served as mayor of Chillicothe, 1893–97, owned and edited the *Daily News* until 1900, and after 1901 devoted himself to writing. Sometimes using the pen name Charles Carey, he published many stories and serials in magazines. His published books include *The Van Suyden Sapphires,* New York, 1905. WWW 1

WADDLE, ANGUS L. (March 16, 1826–Sept. 12, 1901), was born in Chillicothe, Ross County. He lived near Barrets Mills and was a weaver by trade. He died in Columbus.

Three Years with the Armies of the Ohio, and the Cumberland, Chillicothe, 1889.

WADE, DECIUS SPEAR (Jan. 23, 1835–Aug. 3, 1905), lawyer and judge, was born near Andover, Ashtabula County. His uncle was Benjamin Franklin Wade, Senator from Ohio, 1851–69, and leader of the Radical Republicans during and after the Civil War. Decius taught school while attending Kingsville Academy and also read law in his uncle's office at Jefferson. Admitted to the bar in 1857, he practiced in Jefferson and served as Ashtabula County probate judge, 1860–67. In 1871 he was appointed chief justice of Montana, a position he held until 1887. His decisions were significant in the shaping of mining and irrigation laws. Besides his judicial decisions, he wrote newspaper articles on Montana history and the novel listed below. In 1895 he returned to Ashtabula County, where he spent his last ten years.

Clare Lincoln. A Novel, Cambridge, Mass., 1876.

WADE, JANE. Pseud. See Nancy M. W. Woodrow.

WADSWORTH, LENORAH ARBEL (Nov. 23, 1890–April 3, 1953), born in Vincennes, Ind., was brought to Ohio while still a small child and spent her life in Norwood, Hamilton County. She published a volume of verse: *To Meet Your Need, Poems of Sunny Sanity,* [New York], 1946.

WAGENHAUSER, NITA (1903–), was born in Morehouse, Mo., but lived for a number of years in Henry County. She has written articles and fiction for Sunday school papers and religious magazines and has also published *Little Stories of Christ's Passion,* Paterson, N. J., 1941.

WAGER, CHARLES HENRY ADAMS (Dec. 20, 1869–July 1, 1939), educator, born in

Cohoes, N. Y., was professor of English at Kenyon College, 1897–1900, and at Oberlin College, 1900–35. After his retirement he continued to live in Oberlin. He published a collection of essays: *To Whom It May Concern,* Chicago, 1928. WWW 1

WAGGONER, CLARK (Sept. 6, 1820–July 2, 1903), journalist, was born in Milan Township, Huron County. From the age of thirteen he worked as an apprentice printer in Milan and Newark. After brief associations with various newspapers, he edited the Toledo *Blade,* 1856–65, and published the Toledo *Commercial,* 1866–76. Active in the Republican Party, he was a leader in Toledo civic affairs. He served as collector of internal revenue, 1877–82.

History of the City of Toledo and Lucas County . . . , New York, 1888.

A Plea for Equal Rights. The Railway: Its Uses and Its Abuses . . . , Toledo, 1894.

WAGNALLS, MABEL (April 20, 1872–March 22, 1946), was born in Atchison, Kan. Her father, Adam Wagnalls, was a partner in the publishing firm of Funk & Wagnalls and co-founder of the *Literary Digest.* She studied music in Europe and made her American debut as a pianist in 1891. She married Richard Jones. While living in Lithopolis, Fairfield County, her parents' native town, she corresponded with O. Henry (William S. Porter, q.v.); his letters to her were published in 1922. In 1925 she established a memorial library in Lithopolis in honor of her parents, and on her death she left the village $2,500,000. She died in New York City and is buried in Lithopolis. She wrote a number of piano compositions and books with musical backgrounds.

Miserere . . . , New York, 1892.

Stars of the Opera . . . , New York, 1898.

Selma the Soprano, New York, 1899.

The Palace of Danger . . . , New York, 1908.

The Rose-Bush of a Thousand Years, New York, 1918.

The Light in the Valley . . . , New York, 1925.

The Mad Song, New York, 1926.

The Immortal Sinner, New York, 1933.

WAITE, FREDERICK CLAYTON (May 24, 1870–March 30, 1956), educator, was born in Hudson, Summit County. He graduated from Western Reserve University in 1892 and from Harvard University (Ph.D.) in 1898. He was on the medical faculty of Western Reserve University, 1892–95 and 1901–40. He wrote numerous scientific articles and several historical studies of Western Reserve, e.g., *History of the School of Dentistry of Western Reserve University,* Cleveland, 1940. WWW 3

WAKELAND, MARGARET E. K. (Mrs. Edward W.) (Aug. 21, 1920–), born in Evanston, Ill., settled in Cincinnati in 1930. She now lives in Fort Worth, Texas. Under her maiden name, Elizabeth Kittredge, she has published a book of verse: *The Moon Shines at Sundown,* Boston, [1950].

WALBRIDGE, WILLIAM SPOONER (Sept. 19, 1854–Nov. 23, 1935), industrialist, born in Boston, Mass., was engaged in the furniture business in that city until 1898, when he came to Toledo to join the Owens Bottle Machine Co. A leader in the Toledo glass industry, he wrote the history of bottle manufacture in the United States: *American Bottles, Old & New . . . ,* Toledo, 1920. OBB

WALD, LILLIAN D. (March 10, 1867–Sept. 1, 1940), social worker, was born in Cincinnati, Hamilton County, but grew up in Rochester, N. Y., and spent her mature life in New York City. After attending the New York Hospital Training School for Nurses, 1889–91, she began the study of medicine. Asked to organize home-nursing courses among the immigrant families on the lower East Side of New York, she abandoned her medical studies and in 1893 established a nursing center on Jefferson Street. Two years later the Nurses' Settlement was moved to 265 Henry Street, where Miss Wald lived until her retirement in 1933. She was a pioneer in the field of public health nursing. She wrote two books about the Henry Street Settlement: *The House on Henry Street,* New York, 1915, and *Windows on Henry Street,* Boston, 1934. DAB 22

WALDEN, ROBERT L. (Nov. 11, 1868–), lawyer, was born in Wellington, Lorain County. While attending Baldwin University, 1892–95, he wrote for Cleveland newspapers. He worked on the Norwalk *Daily Chronicle,* 1896–99, and published the Wellington *Enterprise,* 1899–1902. After being admitted to the bar in 1904, he practiced in Wellington until his retirement in 1940. He has written many articles on local history and other subjects for the *Enterprise,* and has published a collection of poems: *Candles on the Stairs, and Other Poems,* New York, [1949].

WALDMAN, MILTON (Oct. 4, 1895–), journalist, was born in Cleveland, Cuyahoga County. He graduated from Yale University in 1917 and did graduate work at the Sorbonne, 1922–23. He became a reporter in 1917 and was associate editor of the London *Mercury,* 1924–27. For many years he has lived in England and Italy. He has published novels, biographies, and historical studies, e.g., *Joan of Arc,* New York, [1935]. WW 30

WALKE, HENRY (Dec. 24, 1808–March 8, 1896), naval officer, was born in Princess Anne County, Va., but lived in Chillicothe from 1811 until 1827, when he was appointed a midshipman in the navy. He retired as a rear admiral in 1871. During the first years of the Civil War, he commanded gunboats on the Mississippi; he later commanded the sloop *Sacramento* in the Atlantic, 1863–65. He was a skillful artist and illustrated his book on the Civil War period.

Naval Scenes and Reminiscences of the Civil War . . . , New York, 1877.

WALKER, ALEXANDER (Oct. 13, 1818–Jan. 24, 1893), journalist, born in Fredericksburg, Va., edited the Cincinnati *Enquirer,* 1855–57. He wrote *Jackson and New Orleans . . . ,* New York, 1856.

WALKER, CHARLES MANNING (Dec. 25, 1834–Jan. 25, 1920), journalist, was born in Athens, Athens County. He graduated from Ohio University and around 1855 moved to Indianapolis, where he taught in the Institute for the Blind and worked on several Indianapolis newspapers.

History of Athens County, Ohio . . . , 2 vols., Cincinnati, 1869.

Sketch of the Life, Character, and Public Services of Oliver P. Morton . . . , Indianapolis, 1878.

Hovey and Chase . . . , Indianapolis, 1888.

WALKER, JAMES BARR (July 29, 1805–March 6, 1887), clergyman, born in Philadelphia, came in the late 1820s to Ravenna, where he bought an interest in the *Western Courier* and read law. At Western Reserve College he came under the influence of Theodore D. Weld (q.v.), who inspired him to vigorous abolitionism. As an agent of the American Bible Society, he traveled throughout western Ohio and afterward conducted the *Ohio Observer,* an abolition paper, at Hudson. Ordained by the Presbytery of Portage, he served a church in Akron, 1837–39, and then moved to Cincinnati, where he conducted an abolitionist paper, *The Watchman of the Valley,* 1840–42. Here, he wrote *The Philosophy of the Plan of Salvation,* first published anonymously with an introduction by Calvin E. Stowe (q.v.). The book went through many editions in the United States and in Europe. He served churches in Mansfield, 1842–46 and 1850–57, and Sandusky, 1857–63. He later attempted to found a college at Benzonia, Mich., and after the failure of that project, taught and preached in Wheaton, Ill., until his death.

Philosophy of the Plan of Salvation . . . , New York, 1841.

God Revealed in the Process of Creation . . . , New York, 1855.

Philosophy of Skepticism and Ultraism . . . , New York, 1857.

The Philosophy of the Divine Operation in the Redemption of Man, London, 1862.

The Doctrine of the Holy Spirit . . . , Chicago, 1869.

The Living Questions of the Age . . . , Chicago, 1869.

Poetry of Reason and Conscience . . . , Chicago, 1871.

Experiences of Pioneer Life in the Early Settlements and Cities of the West, Chicago, 1881.

WALKER, MARY EDWARDS (Nov. 26, 1832–Feb. 21, 1919), physician, born in Oswego, N. Y., practiced medicine in Columbus for a short time after her graduation from Syracuse Medical College in 1855. During the summer of 1864, she was attached to the 52nd O.V.I. as a contract surgeon. A vehement advocate of women's rights, she wore men's clothes and lectured widely. She was also a believer in spiritualism. She wrote *Unmasked, or the Science of Immorality . . . ,* Philadelphia, 1878.

WALKER, ROLLIN HOUGH (Dec. 19, 1865–Aug. 4, 1955), clergyman and educator, was born in Columbus, Franklin County. He graduated from Ohio Wesleyan University in 1888 and Boston University School of Theology (B.D., 1892; Ph.D., 1908). A member of the Ohio Wesleyan faculty for many years, he wrote articles and several books on the Bible and other religious themes, e.g., *Jesus and Our Pressing Problems,* New York, [1935]. WWW 3

WALKER, THOMAS BARLOW (Feb. 1, 1840–July 28, 1928), was born in Xenia, Greene County. In 1855 his widowed mother moved to Berea, where he taught school and attended Baldwin University. In 1863 he married and settled in Minneapolis. Working as a surveyor he became familiar with the timberlands of northern

Minnesota. Lumbering and Minneapolis real-estate transactions made him wealthy. He devoted much of his time and fortune to the acquisition of paintings, jewelry, and other art objects. An extreme conservative, he opposed most reforms. Several of his public addresses were published in pamphlet form.

Free Silver Coinage, and the Inevitable Evils That Would Result from It, [Minneapolis, 1894?].

The Relation of the Tariff to the Public Welfare . . . , Minneapolis, 1916.

WALKER, TIMOTHY (Dec. 1, 1806–Jan. 15, 1856), lawyer and judge, was born in Wilmington, Mass. He graduated from Harvard College in 1826, taught school, and spent a year studying law at Harvard. In 1830 he came to Cincinnati, where he read law and was admitted to the bar. He became the law partner of Edward King and Salmon P. Chase. He contributed to Cincinnati periodicals and was an active member of the Semi-Colon Club. At the suggestion of Judge John C. Wright, he joined in establishing the Cincinnati Law School in 1833 and for a time was in charge of that institution. In 1842 he was named president judge of the Hamilton County common pleas court. The result of his teaching in the law school was the composition of his *Introduction to American Law.* He was a strong advocate of the codification of the laws of the state. He died in Cincinnati. A number of his public addresses were published as separate pamphlets.

The Dignity of the Law as a Profession, Cincinnati, 1837.

Introduction to American Law . . . , Philadelphia, 1837.

WALKER, WILLIAM (March 5, 1800–Feb. 13, 1874), was born in what is now Gibraltar, Mich., a member of the Wyandot tribe. He was educated at Philander Chase's academy in Worthington. Upon completing his education, he returned to the Upper Sandusky reservation, where he became a leader of the Wyandot nation, taught in the mission school, and, according to Henry Howe (q.v.), was the tribe's head chief. Walker left with his tribe for Kansas in 1843. Ten years later he was appointed provisional governor of the Nebraska Territory. He contributed many articles to newspapers and periodicals. His journals were published by the Nebraska State Historical Society. He died at Kansas City, Mo.

The Journals of William Walker . . . , Lincoln, Neb., 1899.

WALLACE, FRANCIS, was born in Bellaire, Belmont County. In 1923 he graduated from Notre Dame University, where he had worked as a sports reporter and publicity director. For twelve years he was a staff reporter for various New York newspapers, specializing in football, baseball, and boxing. Since then his residence has been Bellaire, but he has worked as a writer for several motion-picture studios and as a commentator on radio and television. He invented the Football Preview, which ran in the *Saturday Evening Post,* 1937–48, and in *Collier's,* 1949–56. He has written numerous short stories and articles and fifteen books, most of them on athletics, e.g., *Razzle-Dazzle,* New York, [1938].

WALLACE, FREDERICK STEPHEN (Oct. 12, 1838–Oct. 10, 1924), engineer, was born in Onondaga County, N. Y. When the Civil War began, he was living in Cincinnati. He enlisted in the 2nd O.V.I. in April, 1861, later served in the 52nd O.V.I., the 61st O.V.I., and the 82nd O.V.I., and was discharged as a major in July, 1865. He lived in Cincinnati for a time after the war, and then moved to Georgia and Tennessee; he died in Chattanooga. He wrote a regimental history: *The Sixty-first Ohio Volunteers . . . ,* Marysville, 1902.

WALLACE, FREDERICK T. (1819–March 24, 1895), was born in Waterbury, Vt. He was admitted to the bar in Massachusetts and served a term in the Massachusetts legislature before coming to Cleveland around 1853. In Cleveland he practiced law and dealt in real estate, served on the city council, and was a frequent contributor to the *Plain Dealer.* He is said to have written a number of pamphlets on Cleveland cemeteries and their occupants, but none has been located. His *Men and Events* is a compilation of anecdotes pertaining to his life in Cleveland.

The Cleveland Viaduct. Retrospective and Prophetic, Cleveland, 1879.

Men and Events of Half a Century, Cleveland, 1882.

Nuggets, or Secrets of Great Success, (with Sarah K. Bolton), Cleveland, 1892.

WALLING, LUCY. Pseud. See Anna Nixon.

WALLINGTON, NELLIE URNER (Feb. 13, 1847–Jan. 12, 1933), journalist, was born in Cincinnati, Hamilton County. She graduated from Woodward High School, Cincinnati, in 1864 and afterward worked on the Philadelphia *Commercial Times* and other magazines and newspapers. She died in Parkerford, Pa. Her writings include *Historic Churches of America,* New York, 1907. WW 9

WALLIS, LOUIS (1876–), was born in Columbus, Franklin County. He was an optician in Columbus and later lived in Chicago and California. He wrote *By the Waters of Babylon; A Story of Ancient Israel,* New York, 1931.

WALTER, EUGENE (Nov. 27, 1874–Sept. 26, 1941), playwright, was born in Cleveland, Cuyahoga County, where he attended public schools. He worked on newspapers in Cleveland, Cincinnati, and other cities and served as business manager of various theatrical companies. He wrote his first play in 1902 and had his first success in 1907 with *The Undertow.* Author or adaptor of a number of popular plays, he received most attention for his somewhat daring and melodramatic drama, *The Easiest Way . . . ,* [New York, 1908]. WWW 1

WALTERMIRE, BEECHER WESLEY (May 18, 1858–Dec. 31, 1932), lawyer, was born in Sedalia, Mo. After reading law in Kenton, he was admitted to the bar in 1882 and practiced in Findlay; he also served as mayor of that community. He later moved to Columbus.

The Adventures of a Skeleton. A Tale of Natural Gas, New York, [1890].

Buckeye Ballads, [Toledo], 1906.

WALTERS, RAYMOND (Aug. 25, 1885–), educator, born in Bethlehem, Pa., was president of the University of Cincinnati, 1932–55. He has published annual statistics on college and university enrollment since 1919. Author of numerous magazine articles, he has also published a family history and other books, e.g., *Stephen Foster: Youth's Golden Gleam . . . ,* Princeton, [N. J.], 1936. WW 30

WALTERS, ZELIA MARGARET (Feb. 3, 1875–), was born on a farm near Lodi, Medina County. She attended an Akron high school and Akron Normal School. She taught classes in children's storytelling at Chautauqua and elsewhere. She was married to Harry H. Walters, now deceased; she lives at present in Wallingford, Pa. She has written a number of religious books for children, e.g., *The Children's Crusade,* Elgin, Ill., [1928].

WALTON, FRANCIS. Pseud. See Alfred Hodder.

WALTON, GEORGE EDWARD (Dec. 25, 1839–July 9, 1917), physician, was born in Cincinnati, Hamilton County. In 1864 he graduated from Bellevue Hospital Medical College, New York, and in 1866 he began practice in Cincinnati. He also served on the faculty of Cincinnati Medical College. In 1890 he moved to Daytona, Fla. He died in Terre Haute, Ind., while visiting his son. He wrote a number of medical articles and pamphlets.

The Mineral Springs of the United States and Canada . . . , New York, 1873.

WALTON, JOSEPH (1817–1898), was born on a farm near Barnesville, Belmont County, and spent his entire life in that area. He was, as the titles of his books indicate, a member of the Society of Friends.

Brief Biographies of Some Members of the Society of Friends . . . , Philadelphia, [187-?].

Incidents and Reflections Containing Illustrations of Christian Truths, Philadelphia, 1888.

Incidents Illustrating the Doctrines and History of the Society of Friends, Philadelphia, 1897.

WALTZ, ELIZABETH CHERRY (Dec. 10, 1866–Sept. 19, 1903), journalist, was born in Columbus, Franklin County, and attended the schools of that city. Left a widow at an early age, she worked on the Cincinnati *Tribune,* 1895–97, and on the Springfield *Republic-Times,* 1897–98. In 1898 she married Frederick H. Waltz and settled in Louisville, Ky., where she was literary editor of the *Courier-Journal* until her death. She wrote a number of stories for *Century Magazine,* published in book form as *Pa Gladden; The Story of a Common Man,* New York, 1903, and a posthumously published novel attacking divorce: *The Ancient Landmark . . . ,* New York, 1905. WWW 1

WAMBAUGH, SARAH (March 6, 1882–Nov. 12, 1955), was born in Cincinnati, Hamilton County. After graduating from Radcliffe College in 1902, she spent three years on the staff of that institution as an assistant in history and government. In 1934 she was appointed by the League of Nations to help organize the Saar plebiscite; she later served the U. S. government and the United Nations in various advisory capacities. She died in Cambridge, Mass. She wrote magazine articles and books, e.g., *The Saar Plebiscite . . . ,* Cambridge, Mass., 1940. WWW 3

WANAMAKER, REUBEN MELVILLE (Aug. 2, 1866–June 18, 1924), lawyer and judge, was born in North Jackson, Mahoning County. After studying at Ohio Northern University, he read law in Lima for two years and was admitted to the Ohio bar in 1893. He began to practice in Akron and was elected prosecuting attorney in 1895. He won widespread attention for his vigorous action against the participants in the riots of 1900. He served as judge of common pleas court, 1906–12, and of the state supreme court, 1912–24. He took his own life in Columbus when under treatment for a nervous breakdown. He wrote a number of articles for the *Saturday Evening Post* and also published a book: *The Voice of Lincoln,* New York, 1918. DAB 19

WARD, ARTEMUS. Pseud. See Charles F. Browne.

WARD, DURBIN (Feb. 11, 1819–May 22, 1886), lawyer, born in Augusta, Ky., was brought up in Fayette County, Ind. He studied at Miami University for two years, read law with Thomas Corwin (q.v.), and became his partner in 1842. He held various state offices and was prominent in the affairs of the Democratic Party. He served in the Civil War with the 17th O.V.I. His speeches were edited and published posthumously by his widow, Elizabeth Probasco Ward.

Life, Speeches and Orations of Durbin Ward, of Ohio, Columbus, 1888.

WARD, GILBERT OAKLEY (Feb. 21, 1880–Feb. 24, 1944), librarian, born in New York City, lived in Cleveland from 1908 until his death. He was associated with the public school libraries, 1908–13, and with the Public Library, 1913–44. He published several articles and pamphlets on library work and also wrote poems, a number of which were published posthumously in *Sunset Freight,* Cleveland, 1944. WWW 2

WARD, JAMES E. D. (1838–Oct. 3, 1899), was born in New Jersey. He served as a private in the 12th O.V.I. from June, 1861, to July, 1864. He died in Montgomery County. His volume is the first history of an Ohio Civil War regiment to be published in book form.

Twelfth Ohio Volunteer Infantry, Ripley, 1864.

WARD, JAMES WARNER (June 5, 1816–June 28, 1897), was born in Newark, N. J. His father, a publisher and bookseller, died when the boy was four years old. Ward grew up in Boston and his early years in Ohio are quite obscure; it has been said that he opened a school in Columbus in 1834, but this seems an unlikely venture for an eighteen-year-old boy. The book *Yorick and Other Poems,* probably the first book of poems published in northern Ohio, appeared anonymously; it is sometimes attributed to Irad Kelley (q.v.). Ward studied medicine at the Medical College of Ohio, and in 1851 he joined the faculty of the Ohio Female College near Cincinnati. In 1854 he resigned to establish and edit the *Horticultural Review and Botanical Magazine* in association with John A. Warder (q.v.). He was employed by the Cincinnati publishing house of H. W. Derby & Co., 1855–59. In 1859 he moved to New York City. While in Ohio he contributed many scientific articles and poems to various periodicals. He served in the New York customs house, 1859–74, and as librarian of the Grosvenor Library, Buffalo, N. Y., 1874–96. He died in Buffalo.

Yorick and Other Poems, Cleveland, 1838.
Woman. A Poem, Cincinnati, 1852.
Home Made Verses . . . , Boston, 1857.
The Song of Higher-Water, New York, 1868.

WARD, MAY ALDEN (March 1, 1853–Jan. 15, 1918), was born in Mechanicsburg, Champaign County. She graduated from Ohio Wesleyan University in 1872 and the following year married Rev. William G. Ward (q.v.). She wrote articles on European literature for various periodicals and lectured on literary subjects. She lived in Cleveland for a number of years before moving to Franklin, Mass.

Dante, a Sketch of His Life and Works, Boston, 1887.
Petrarch, a Sketch of His Life and Works, Boston, 1891.
Old Colony Days, Boston, 1896.
Prophets of the Nineteenth Century . . . , Boston, 1900.
The Influence of Women's Clubs . . . , Philadelphia, [1906].

WARD, NAHUM (Oct. 23, 1785–April 6, 1860), was born in Shrewsbury, Mass. He came to Marietta in June, 1809, remained six weeks, and returned two years later to settle. He became the owner of large tracts of land in Washington, Meigs, and adjacent counties. The anonymous booklet listed below was drawn largely from the work of Thomas Hutchins and other travelers. Some authorities attribute it to Ward, although the best evidence favors the authorship of Return J. Meigs (q.v.). In any event, the book was issued in Scotland while Ward was there to promote the sale of his land. He was successful in his ventures and became an influential citizen of Marietta. The Unitarian Church in that community was built at his expense in 1855.

A Brief Sketch of the State of Ohio, One of the United States in North America . . ., Glasgow, 1822.

WARD, VIRGINIA LEE (d.Jan. 6, 1957), born in Lexington, Ky., lived in Norwood about thirty years. Active in civic affairs, she was executive secretary of the Norwood Service League, 1917–34. In 1934 she moved to Mt. Sterling, Ky., where her husband, Nelson E. Ward, operated a chain of theaters. Her poems appeared in various periodicals, and she published a novel: *The Welcome Stranger,* Philadelphia, [1943].

WARD, WILLIAM GODMAN (Nov. 5, 1848–Nov. 3, 1923), educator, was born in Sandusky, Erie County. He graduated from Ohio Wesleyan University in 1872 and Drew Theological Seminary in 1873, and also studied abroad. He taught history and political science at Baldwin University, 1887–90, and also served on the faculties of several other colleges.

The Poetry of Robert Browning, Boston, 1898.

Tennyson's Debt to Environment . . ., Boston, 1898.

WARDEN, LEWIS CHRISTOPHER (Aug. 26, 1913–), lawyer and judge, was born in St. Clairsville, Belmont County. After practicing law in Columbus and Gallipolis, where he also served as common pleas judge, he moved to Rochester, N. Y., where he joined the Lawyers Cooperative Publishing Company. His writings include *The Life of Blackstone,* Charlottesville, Va., 1938. WWMW 49

WARDEN, ROBERT BRUCE (Jan. 18, 1824–Dec. 3, 1888), lawyer, was born in Bardstown, Ky. He began reading law in Cincinnati in 1840 and was admitted to the bar in 1845. He became judge of the court of common pleas in Cincinnati in 1850, and reporter of the supreme court of Ohio in 1853. When but thirty years of age, he was appointed to the state supreme court, to fill the vacancy created by the resignation of chief justice John A. Corwin. While in Columbus he undertook the course of study at the Starling Medical School, where he later lectured on the forensic doctrines of insanity. He returned to Cincinnati during the Civil War and moved to Washington in 1873. Though for a time he advanced rapidly in his chosen profession, he was a man of more literary than legal ability. He died in Washington.

Ardvoirlich. Tragedy, Cincinnati, 1857.

A Familiar Forensic View of Man and Law, Columbus, 1860.

A Voter's Version of the Life and Character of Stephen Arnold Douglas, Columbus, 1860.

Law for All, Washington, D. C., 1873.

An Account of the Private Life and Public Services of Salmon Portland Chase, Cincinnati, 1874.

An Appeal by the Author of the "Best Abused Book of the Period," Washington, D. C., 1876.

An Essay on the Law of Art, Washington, D. C., 1878.

A Study of the Law, Washington, D. C., 1878.

Sketches of American Law, Washington, D. C., 1879.

Authors and Reviewers, Washington, D. C., 1880.

An Earnest Call, [Washington, D. C.], 1880.

A Book of Type and Types . . ., Washington, D. C., 1885.

Letters, [Washington, D. C.], 1885.

Aspects of Adjudication, Washington, D. C., 1886.

At or Near the Capital: Familiar Letters to a Young American from an American Who Is No Longer Young . . ., Washington, D. C., 1886.

WARDER, JOHN ASTON (Jan. 19, 1812–July 14, 1883), physician, and horticulturist, was born near Philadelphia, Pa. In 1830 his family moved to Springfield, Clark County. After graduating from Jefferson Medical College in 1836, he began practice in Cincinnati and took an active part in the scientific and medical life of the city. He was one of the founders of the Cincinnati Astronomical Society, the Western Academy of Natural Sciences, the Cincinnati Horticultural Society, the Ohio Medical College, and the Cincinnati Society of Natural History. Although he was an eminent physician, he did his most notable work in horticulture and forestry. In 1854 he conducted the *Horticultural Review and Botanical Magazine* with James W. Ward (q.v.). In 1855 he moved to a farm at North Bend. He contributed many articles to horticultural and agricultural periodicals. He was a member of the Ohio State Board of Agriculture, 1871–76, served as U. S. Commissioner to the World's Fair in Vienna in 1873, for which he prepared the American report on *Forests and Forestry,* and was president of the American Forestry Association, 1875–82. In scientific circles he is remembered for describing, in 1853, the *Catalpa speciosa,* which had not been recognized as a distinct species until that time. He was among the first to arouse public interest in the beautifying of public and private parks. He died at North Bend.

A Geological Reconnoisance [sic] of the Arkansas River, Cleveland, 1854.

Hedges and Evergreens . . . , New York, 1854.

American Pomology. Apples, New York, [1867].

An Essay on Timber Planting in Ohio, Columbus, 1880.

WARE, JOSEPH (June 20, 1841–Aug. 31, 1922), was born in Mechanicsburg, Champaign County, a town that his ancestors had helped to settle. A graduate of Adrian College, Mich., he operated a farm in Champaign County and wrote several books of verse, e.g., *Links of Gold,* Boston, 1914.

WARE, NATHANIEL A. (c.1780–1854), lived in Cincinnati for some years after 1840. Little is known of his life except that he became wealthy through land speculation in the South and West. His writings include *Harvey Belden . . . ,* Cincinnati, 1848.

WAREING, ERNEST CLYDE (May 29, 1872–Feb. 4, 1944), clergyman, was born in Volga, Ind. He graduated from Asbury University in 1898 and was ordained to the Methodist ministry in 1901. He lived in Cincinnati while editing the *Western Christian Advocate,* 1912–32. He wrote a number of books on religious subjects, e.g., *Critical Hours in a Preacher's Life,* New York, [1923]. WWW 2

WARFEL, LINDA. See Linda W. Slaughter.

WARING, ROGER L. (April 21, 1890–), architect, was born in Tecumseh, Mich. He lived in Cleveland, 1921–29, returned in 1942, and still lives there. His poems have appeared in various periodicals, and he has published a collection: *Places in the Heart, in Life, in Nature, in Fun,* New York, 1928.

WARNER, ADONIRAM JUDSON (Jan. 13, 1834–Aug. 3, 1910), born in Wales, N. Y., and reared in Wisconsin, settled in Marietta after the Civil War. He was active in oil, coal, and railroad enterprises and served three terms in Congress, 1879–85. Beginning in the 1870s he devoted more and more of his energy to the money question and wrote and spoke widely in favor of free silver. He was the first president of the Bimetallic League. He died in Marietta.

The Appreciation of Money . . . , Philadelphia, 1877.

The Problem of Resumption Re-examined . . . , [Marietta, 1878].

Our Debt Abroad. How It Has Grown, and How It Is Affected by the Appreciation of Gold, Washington, [D. C.], 1895.

Facts about Silver, Chicago, [1896].

WARNER, HENRY EDWARD (Jan. 17, 1876–April 11, 1941), journalist, was born in Elyria, Lorain County. He was on the staff of a number of newspapers and after 1910 worked on the Baltimore *Sun.* His writings include *Songs of the Craft,* Washington, D. C., [1929]. WWW 2

WARNER, HORACE EVERETT (Jan. 10, 1839–Oct. 29, 1930), lawyer, was born in Lake County. After graduating from Beloit College in 1867, he read law and practiced in Iowa. His writings include *The Cricket's Song, and Other Melodies,* Philadelphia, 1907. WWW 1

WARREN, FREDERICK MORRIS (June 9, 1859–Dec. 7, 1931), educator, born in Durham, Maine, was on the Western Reserve University faculty, 1881–83 and 1891–1901. Besides French textbooks and professional articles, he wrote *A History of the Novel Previous to the Seventeenth Century,* New York, 1895.

WARREN, JOSIAH (1798–April 14, 1874), reformer, was born in Boston, Mass. He settled in Cincinnati as an orchestra leader in 1820. There he displayed an exceptional inventive talent. In 1823 he was granted a patent for a lard-burning lamp and established a lamp factory, which proved to be a profitable venture. The returns from a series of inventions in the field of printing enabled him to indulge his radical theories of social reform. He joined Robert Owen in the experiment at New Harmony, Ind., but after two years returned to Cincinnati. In May, 1827, he established his "equity store," for which he is best remembered in Ohio. Founded on the principle that interchanges of goods and services should be based solely upon direct cost, his store gave and received labor-notes in transactions with its customers. In large measure the store served as an employment exchange, and it soon became one of the most popular mercantile establishments in the city. People referred to it as the "Time Store" because of the clock used by the proprietor to determine the time involved and the compensation due him for his services in waiting upon customers. At the end of two years he closed his store without profit or loss. The village of Equity, established by him in Tuscarawas County in

1830, was abandoned two years later because of the unhealthful conditions in its locality. The first number of his *Peaceful Revolutionist* appeared in January of 1833, but failed to survive the year. He founded the village of Utopia in Clermont County in 1847, a community that went on progressing in a quiet way for many years after he left Ohio. He returned to Boston in 1850, and the following year he founded the Village of Modern Times on Long Island. He died in Boston.

Ernest J. Wessen

Equitable Commerce . . . , Cincinnati, 1846.

Written Music Remodeled, and Invested with the Simplicity of an Exact Science . . . , Boston, 1860.

True Civilization an Immediate Necessity, and the Last Ground of Hope for Mankind . . . , Boston, 1863.

WARREN, MANLY (1829–June 9, 1864), was born in Marietta, Washington County. He served for a time as county recorder. The book below contains some poems by Harriet E. Warren.

Rhymes Written at Random, Marietta, 1852.

WARWICK, FRANK M. (Jack) (Jan. 15, 1861–Jan. 12, 1947), journalist, was born on a farm near Caledonia, Marion County. In 1884 he and Warren G. Harding founded the Marion *Star;* although Warwick sold his share of the business, he remained as editor until 1904, when he joined the Toledo *Blade.* He wrote editorials and a column of paragraphs for the *Blade* for many years. His autobiographical volume, bearing the same title as his column, is partly made up of material previously printed in the *Blade* and partly of fresh material: *All in a Lifetime,* [Toledo], 1938.

WASHBURNE, HARRY RICHARD (July 24, 1911–), journalist, was born in Middleport, Meigs County. A graduate of Ohio State University, he has worked for the International News Service, Washington, D. C., and for the Los Angeles *Herald & Express,* and other newspapers. He now lives in Los Angeles. He has published a book of verse: *Hooray For a Roué,* Boston, [1942].

WASHBURNE, HELUIZ CHANDLER (Mrs. Carleton W.) (Jan. 25, 1892–), was born in Cincinnati, Hamilton County. She worked as a commercial artist and as a fashion adviser and wrote a travel column in the Chicago *Daily News,* 1943–44. She published a travel book in the form of letters: *Letters to Channy . . .* , Chicago, [1932], and a number of books for children, e.g., *Little Elephant Catches Cold,* Chicago, 1937. WW 30

WASON, ROBERT ALEXANDER (April 6, 1874–May 11, 1955), was born in Toledo, Lucas County, but grew up in Indiana. He was a clerk in a general store; "roughed it" in the West, according to his own account; and served in the artillery for nine months during the Spanish-American War. He lived in Mountain Lakes, N. J. He wrote a number of short stories, vaudeville sketches, and novels, e.g., *And Then Came Jean . . .* , Boston, [1913]. WWW 3

WATERMAN, LUTHER DANA (Nov. 21, 1830–June 30, 1918), physician, born in Wheeling in western Virginia, lived in Ohio from 1832 to 1855. He attended Miami University, taught school, and studied medicine at the Medical College, Cincinnati. In 1855 he moved to Indiana, where he passed the remainder of his life. He was one of the founders of Indiana Medical College, taught there for many years, and was widely recognized as a leader in his profession. The volume of poetry listed below was republished in 1922.

Phantoms of Life . . . , New York, 1883.

WATERS, WILSON (Oct. 11, 1855–June 13, 1933), clergyman, was born in Marietta, Washington County. After graduating from Marietta College in 1876, he engaged in business in Marietta for ten years, studied for the ministry, and was ordained in the Protestant Episcopal Church in 1891. He served churches in Massachusetts, was librarian of the Lowell Historical Society, and was active in other libraries and associations devoted to local history. Besides the titles below, he published a family history.

The History of Saint Luke's Church, Marietta . . . , Marietta, 1884.

Paragraphs, Portraits and Pictures Supplementary to the History of Saint Luke's Church . . . , [Marietta?], 1911.

History of Chelmsford, Massachusetts, Lowell, 1917.

WATSON, AMELIA B. (Nov. 25, 1858–June 13, 1946), was born in Fairfield County, but spent most of her life in Delaware County. She graduated from Ohio Wesleyan University and studied at LaSalle Music Conservatory, Boston. Her poems appeared in various periodicals, and she published a collection: *Sonnets,* [Columbus, 1934].

WATSON, DAVID KEMPER (June 18, 1849–Sept. 28, 1918), lawyer, was born near London, Madison County. He graduated from Dickinson College in 1871 and Boston University Law School in 1873. From 1876 until his death he practiced in Columbus, and he died in that city. Besides the titles below, he published several legal books and a number of speeches.

History of American Coinage, New York, 1899.

The Constitution of the United States . . . , 2 vols., Chicago, 1910.

WATSON, EMILE E. (Feb. 7, 1885–Feb. 1, 1958), was born in Saline County, Mo., of Ohio-born parents. He graduated from William Jewell College, Mo., in 1908 and afterward came to Columbus to assist in establishing the workmen's compensation system. In 1920 he became an independent consulting actuary in Columbus. Besides discussions of workmen's compensation, he published several pamphlets opposing communism, e.g., *Is Civilization Gaining or Losing Ground?,* [Columbus?, 1948?].

WATSON, MARY DEVEREAUX (d. Feb. 19, 1914), born in Marblehead, Mass., spent much of her early life in Cleveland, where her father, General John H. Devereaux, was president of several railroads. She later lived in Englewood, N. J.

Betty Peach, [n.p., 1896].

From Kingdom to Colony, [n.p., 1899].

Up and Down the Sands of Gold, [n.p., 1901].

Lafitte of Louisiana, [n.p., 1902].

WATSON, SAMUEL NEWELL (Feb. 27, 1861–March 27, 1942), clergyman, born in Lyons, Iowa, was rector of Episcopal churches in Chillicothe, 1897–1903, and Akron, 1903–12. He was rector of the American Church in Paris, France, 1912–18. He wrote *Those Paris Years . . . ,* New York, [1936]. WWW 2

WATTS, MARY STANBERY (Nov. 4, 1868–May 21, 1958), was born on a farm in Delaware County. She attended Sacred Heart Convent, Cincinnati, 1881–84, and in 1891 married Miles Taylor Watts of Cincinnati. She lived in that city for the remainder of her life. She published short stories in various magazines and wrote some plays, e.g., *Three Short Plays,* New York, 1917, but she is remembered chiefly for the fourteen historical novels that she published between 1908 and 1924; the most successful of these was *Nathan Burke,* New York, 1910. It deals with the Scioto River country at the time of the Mexican War and is told with such verisimilitude that many readers accepted its story as literal truth. TCA

WAUGH, ALICE GRACE (Jan. 28, 1880–), was born in Fairfield County. After teaching in Ohio for seven years, she went to North Dakota, where she taught a one-room school and lived on a homestead claim. She now lives with a daughter in Peekskill, N. Y. She has published a volume of poems: *Travelogues and Tales,* Columbus, 1947.

WAY, WILLARD V. (Aug. 8, 1807–Aug. 25, 1875), lawyer, born in Otsego, N. Y., settled in Perrysburg, Lucas County, in 1834. In his will, he left money to build the Way Library in Perrysburg and set up a fund which is still being used to purchase books. His only publication was a discussion of the Ohio-Michigan boundary dispute.

The Facts and Historical Events of the Toledo War of 1835 . . . , Toledo, 1869.

WAYT, HUGH (1877–Nov. 30, 1955), clergyman, was born in Glen Easton, W. Va. A graduate of Bethany College, he was ordained to the ministry in the Disciples of Christ Church. He served churches in North Fairfield, Barnesville, Zanesville, Mount Vernon, and other Ohio towns. He lived in Mount Vernon for many years before his death, which occurred at Moundsville, Va. His writings include *The True Source of a Happy Life,* [St. Louis, Mo., 1909].

WEAVER, JAMES BAIRD (June 12, 1833–Feb. 6, 1912), lawyer and political leader, was born in Dayton, Montgomery County, but was an Ohioan only by birth. In 1835 his father moved to Cassopolis, Mich., and in 1843 to Iowa. James studied law in Cincinnati in 1855 and returned to Bloomfield, Iowa, to practice. He was active in the Republican Party, served in the Civil War, and spent eight years in Congress. He broke with his party on the currency question and was active in the Farmers' Alliance and in its successor, the People's Party. He was a candidate for the Presidency in 1892; the first title below was written as a campaign document.

A Call to Action . . . , Des Moines, 1892.

Past and Present of Jasper County, Iowa, 2 vols., Indianapolis, 1912.

WEAVER, JONATHAN (Feb. 23, 1824–Feb. 6, 1901), clergyman, was born in Carroll County. He grew up on a farm and was largely self-educated. After being ordained to the ministry of the United Brethren Church in 1847, he preached on the Ohio circuit and for eight years was an agent of Otterbein College. He was elected bishop in 1865 and was re-elected seven times.

Divine Providence . . . , Dayton, 1873.

The Doctrine of Universal Restoration . . ., Dayton, 1878.
Heaven; Or, That Better Country, Dayton, 1899.
Christian Theology . . ., Dayton, 1900.

WEBB, BARBARA (Aug. 11, 1898–), born in Los Angeles of Ohio-born parents, lived in Ohio for about thirty years. She attended Dayton public schools and later studied at Florida State College for Women, Madison College, and the University of Florida. She worked as a reporter on the Lorain *Times-Herald* and the Cleveland *Plain Dealer.* Her marriage to Monte Bourjaily, a newspaperman, ended in divorce in 1934; she later married Schuyler Larkin, from whom she was divorced in 1946. She is the mother of Vance Bourjaily (q.v.). She has published short stories and articles, a cookbook, and nine light novels, several of which were first published as newspaper serials. She has also published a book of children's stories: *Mother Goose Secrets . . .*, Boston, [1925].

WEBB, TESSA SWEAZY (Jan. 31, 1886–), was born near Logan, Hocking County. She graduated from Columbus Business College in 1912 and was on the staff of the Agricultural Extension, Ohio State University, 1918–54. She has been active in several poetry societies, edited a poetry column in the Columbus *Dispatch,* and originated the annual Ohio Poetry Day. She now lives in Columbus. Her poems have appeared in various periodicals, and she has published several collections, e.g., *Window by the Sea,* Columbus, [1942]. WW 30

WEBBER, AMOS RICHARD (Jan. 21, 1852–Feb. 25, 1948), lawyer and judge, was born in Hinckley, Medina County. He graduated from Baldwin University in 1876 and was admitted to the bar in the same year. He practiced in Elyria, served in the U. S. House of Representatives, 1903–07, and was judge of common pleas court, 1932–44. His writings include a history of Elyria and a biography of the founder of Baldwin University: *Life of John Baldwin, Sr. . . .*, [Cincinnati?, 1925]. WWW 2

WEBSTER, EDNA ROBB (June 29, 1896–), born in Marshalltown, Iowa, lived in Cleveland for 23 years. She has made expeditions to the Yucatan and has lectured on Mayan civilization. She has written feature stories for several newspaper syndicates and has also written novels, e.g., *Loretta, a Love Story,* New York, [1932]. Her daughter, Marjorie Ellen Webster (Aug. 23, 1919–), was born in Cleveland, Cuyahoga County, studied at Cleveland School of Art, and in 1946 was operating a commercial art studio in Hollywood, Calif. Mother and daughter collaborated on a volume of verse: *Double Reflections,* New York, [1947].

WEBSTER, MARJORIE ELLEN. See Edna R. Webster.

WEDEL, LOIS (July 19, 1906–), was born in Cleveland, Cuyahoga County. Following her graduation from Western Reserve University in 1928, she worked for an advertising agency. After becoming interested in writing and illustrating juvenile literature, she studed art. She has published a collection of stories about life in early Cleveland: *Pioneer Tales of a Great City,* Columbus, [1944].

WEED, CLARENCE MOORES (Oct. 5, 1864–July 20, 1947), naturalist and educator, was born in Toledo, Lucas County. He graduated from Michigan Agricultural College in 1883. After serving as entomologist and botanist at the Ohio Experiment Station, 1888–91, he was on the faculty of New Hampshire College of Agriculture and Mechanic Arts, 1891–1904. In 1904 he joined the faculty of the State Teachers College, Lowell, Mass., where he served as president, 1932–35. He died in Lowell. Besides the titles below, he published textbooks and articles.

Insects and Insecticides . . ., Hanover, N. H., 1891.
Fungi and Fungicides . . ., New York, 1894.
Ten New England Blossoms and Their Insect Visitors, New York, 1895.
Life Histories of American Insects, New York, 1897.
Stories of Insect Life, Boston, 1897.
Seed Travellers . . ., Boston, 1898.
Nature Biographies . . ., New York, 1901.
Birds in Their Relations to Man . . ., Philadelphia, 1903.
The Flower Beautiful, Boston, 1903.
Our Trees, How to Know Them . . ., Philadelphia, 1908.
Wild Flower Families . . ., Philadelphia, 1908.
Seeing Nature First, Philadelphia, 1913.
Butterflies Worth Knowing, New York, 1917.
Insect Ways, New York, 1930.

WEEKS, FRANK EDGAR (Jan. 20, 1857–Feb. 27, 1946), physician, was born in Henrietta Township, Lorain County. After attending Oberlin College, he graduated from the medical department of Western Reserve

University in 1883. He practiced for brief periods in Kipton and Vermilion and after 1886 practiced in Clarksfield. He published several genealogical works, a history of the Clarksfield schools, and *Pioneer History of Clarksfield,* Clarksfield, [1908].

WEEKS, JOSEPH DAME (Dec. 3, 1840–Dec. 26, 1896), journalist, born in Lowell, Mass., lived for about a year in Cincinnati. While in Cincinnati he published *History of the Knights of Pythias . . . ,* Cincinnati, 1871.

WEEKS, OLIVER DOUGLAS (Sept. 4, 1896–), educator, was born in Marion, Marion County. He graduated from Ohio Wesleyan University in 1918 and the University of Wisconsin (Ph.D.) in 1924. He has been a member of the department of government, University of Texas, since 1924. He has written numerous professional articles and several books on political questions, e.g., *Two Legislative Houses or One,* Dallas, 1938. WWAE 19

WEETHEE, JONATHAN PERKINS (1812–?), educator, was born in Dover Township, Athens County, where his parents had settled in 1798. After graduating from Ohio University in 1833, he studied medicine, was a Presbyterian minister in New England and Canada, and founded an academy at Amesville. In 1861 he organized Weethee College at Mt. Auburn near Millfield. His writings on mineral and clay deposits encouraged the development of the lower Hocking Valley.

The Coming Age, Its Nature and Proximity, Chicago, 1884.
The Eastern Question in Its Various Phases . . . , Columbus, 1887.
Sunday Creek Valley. Its Mineral Resources and Prospective Wealth, Athens, 1892.

WEIDENTHAL, LEO (April 23, 1878–), journalist, was born in Cleveland, Cuyahoga County, and has spent his entire life in that city. After working on the *Leader* and the *World,* he was City Hall reporter for the *Plain Dealer* for ten years. In 1917 he became editor of *The Jewish Independent.* He was active in the establishment of the Shakespearean Garden in 1916 and for several years has been president of the Cleveland Cultural Garden Federation. He wrote the story of the Shakespearean Garden: *From Dis's Waggon . . . ,* Cleveland, 1926.

WEINLAND, JOSEPH E. (June 23, 1871–Dec., 1936), clergyman, was born in Bethlehem, Pa. He served as pastor of Moravian churches in Gnadenhutton and Dover, Tuscarawas County. He was interested in local history, served as president of the county historical society, and wrote *The Romantic Story of Schoenbrunn . . . ,* Dover, 1928.

WEIR, HUGH COSGRO (May 18, 1884–March 16, 1934), was born in Virginia, Ill. He became a reporter on the Springfield *Sun* at the age of sixteen and later worked on the Dayton *Herald, Ohio State Journal,* and other papers. He was a free-lance magazine writer, 1908–16, and he also wrote more than 300 motion-picture scenarios. He opened an advertising agency in 1928 and at the time of his death was editorial director of Tower Magazines, Inc. He wrote several books, including a number in the Great American Industries series, e.g., *The Young Telephone Inventor . . . ,* Boston, [1917]. WW 17

WEIR, LEBERT HOWARD (Sept. 20, 1878–Nov. 13, 1949), was born near Scottsburg, Ind., and spent most of his life in that state. He lived in Cincinnati, 1904–10, while serving with Associated Charities and as probation officer of juvenile court. When he died in Indianapolis, he was a representative of National Recreation Association. He published a number of studies of recreation, e.g., *Europe at Play . . . ,* New York, 1937. IATB

WEIR, WILLIAM FIGLEY (Dec. 28, 1861–March 2, 1949), clergyman and educator, was born in Augusta, Carroll County. He graduated from Washington and Jefferson College in 1886 and Western Theological Seminary, Pittsburgh, in 1889. After being ordained to the Presbyterian ministry, he served Ohio churches in Mingo Junction, Toronto, Cambridge, Ashtabula, and Wooster. He was on the staff of the Board of Christian Education, 1916–31, and taught at Presbyterian College of Christian Education, Chicago, 1931–42. He published several books on religious themes, e.g., *Giving the Men a Chance,* Chicago [1931]. WWW 3

WEISENBERGER, FRANCIS PHELPS (Oct. 31, 1900–), educator, was born in Defiance, Defiance County. After attending Defiance College, he graduated from the University of Michigan (A.B., 1922; Ph.D., 1929). He has been a member of the Ohio State University faculty since 1924. He has written professional articles, a history of Ohio with E. H. Roseboom, biographical studies, and *The Passing of the Frontier* in the five-volume *History of the State of Ohio,* edited by Carl Wittke, Columbus, 1941. DAS 3

WEISMAN, RUSSELL (Feb. 7, 1890–Nov. 8, 1949), educator, was born near Van Wert, Van Wert County. He graduated from Adelbert College, Western Reserve University, in 1912. From 1919 until his death he was on the Western Reserve faculty in the department of economics and also was an editorial writer for the Cleveland *Plain Dealer.* He published *Key to Recovery,* Cleveland, [1938]. WWW 2

WEISS, LEAH (1877–Aug. 11, 1952), was born in Russia. Her husband, Alexander Weiss, was a rabbi in Cincinnati and other cities. Mrs. Weiss began a relief kitchen and food distribution center in Cincinnati in 1929 and operated it until three weeks before her death. She published a novel: *I Object,* Cincinnati, [1923].

WEIST, CARL SIRENO (Feb. 16, 1886–), clergyman, was born in Basil, Fairfield County. He graduated from Ohio Wesleyan University in 1911 and Andover Seminary in 1915. He was associate minister of the Congregational church, Gloucester, Mass., 1911–15, served with the Y.M.C.A. in Russia and as a chaplain with the A.E.F. in France, 1915–18, was minister of the Community Church, Mount Vernon, N. Y., 1919–53, and served Congregational churches in Lovell, Maine, 1953–57. Since retiring from the ministry, he has lived in Ridgeville, Conn. Besides several volumes of sermons, he has published poems in magazines and newspapers and a collection of poetry: *Wisteria, a Cluster of Clambering Halforisms,* [New York, 1921].

WELCH, ANTHONY CUMMINGS (April 26, 1859–July 25, 1930), clergyman, was born in Harrison County. He graduated from Scio College in 1879 and was ordained to the Methodist ministry in 1881. He served Ohio churches in Youngstown and Niles before moving to the West. He wrote *Character Photography . . . ,* New York, [1902]. WW 4

WELCH, HERBERT (Nov. 7, 1862–), clergyman and educator, was born in New York City. Ordained to the Methodist ministry in 1890, he served a number of churches before coming to Ohio as president of Ohio Wesleyan University, 1905–16. As a bishop, 1916–36, he served in the Orient. He now lives in New York City. He has published a book of biographical sketches of missionaries: *Men of the Outposts . . . ,* New York, [1937]. WW 26

WELCH, JOHN (Oct. 28, 1805–Aug 5, 1891), lawyer and judge, was born near Cadiz, Harrison County. After graduating from Franklin College in 1828, he operated a sawmill and gristmill at Rome until 1833. During this period he read law and was admitted to the bar in 1833. He practiced in Athens, served as prosecuting attorney, was a member of the state senate and of the 32nd Congress. He was judge of common pleas court, 1862–65, and of the state supreme court, 1865–78. In 1878 he resumed the practice of law in Athens. He had a mathematical turn of mind, and this interest is reflected in his only book. He died in Athens.

Mathematical Curiosities . . . , [Athens], 1883.

WELCH, L. B. (1822–April 18, 1890), physician, was born in Clinton County. In 1849 he settled in Wilmington, where he practiced until his death. He collected geological and archaeological specimens as an avocation. With Jonathan M. Richardson (July 19, 1826–June 5, 1905), born in Dayton, Montgomery County, a lumber dealer, who opened 56 Indian mounds at his own expense, Welch collaborated in writing the pamphlet below concerning a mound near Wilmington.

An Illustrated Description of Pre-historic Relics Found Near Wilmington, Ohio, Wilmington, 1879.

WELD, THEODORE DWIGHT (Nov. 23, 1803–Feb. 3, 1895), abolitionist, born in Hampton, Conn., entered Lane Seminary in 1833 but withdrew when the trustees suppressed the antislavery society he had organized. He led his rebels to Oberlin, where their enrollment necessitated the establishment of a theological department. Persuasive and zealous, Weld is credited with converting many prominent figures to abolitionism: Harriet and Henry Ward Beecher, Gamaliel Bailey, Arthur and Lewis Tappan, Charles B. Storrs, Beriah Green, and many others. All of his writings were published anonymously. One of the most influential was *The Bible against Slavery,* New York, 1837.

WELKER, MARTIN (April 25, 1819–March 15, 1902), lawyer, judge, and educator, was born in Knox County. After his admission to the bar in 1840, he practiced at Millersburg. He served as judge of the sixth judicial district, 1852–57, was lieutenant-governor, 1857–58, and served in the 188th O.V.I. from Feb. to Sept., 1865. He also served in the U. S. House of Representatives, 1865–71, and as U. S. judge for the northern district, 1873–89. During his service as a judge, he taught political science and international law at University of Wooster. His unpretentious little book is an excellent account of the life and customs on Ohio farms in the 1830s. He died in Wooster.

Farm Life in Central Ohio Sixty Years Ago, Wooster, 1892.

WELLMAN, WALTER (Nov. 3, 1858–Jan. 31, 1934), journalist and explorer, was born in Mentor, Lake County, but attended school in Michigan. When he was 21, he founded the evening Cincinnati *Post;* he was correspondent of the Chicago *Herald,* 1884–1911. A daring explorer, he made two attempts to reach the North Pole by air, and in 1910 he attempted to cross the Atlantic by airship. Most of his writings deal with his personal experiences, e.g., an account of his attempt to cross the Atlantic: *The Aerial Age . . . ,* New York, 1911. DAB 19

WELLS, AMOS RUSSELL (Dec. 23, 1862–March 6, 1933), born in Glens Falls, N. Y., graduated from Antioch College in 1883, and taught Greek and geology there, 1883–91. In 1891 he became editor of the *Christian Endeavor World,* published in Boston. A prolific writer, he published more than eighty books, most of them on religious topics, e.g., *Golden Rule Meditations,* Boston, 1893.

WELLS, A. WADE (March 7, 1883–Feb. 16, 1958), was born in Caldwell, Noble County. He grew up on a farm near Caldwell, attended Olive School, and graduated from Caldwell High School. He served in the U. S. Department of Justice, was general manager of Bradford's Detective Service in Washington, D. C., was superintendent of the Masonic Children's Home, Richmond, Va., and at the time of his death conducted a real-estate business in Newark, Licking County. Besides poems and historical articles published in newspapers, he wrote *Hail to the Jeep,* New York, [1946].

WELLS, BERTRAM WHITTIER (March 5, 1884–), educator, was born in Troy, Miami County. He graduated from Ohio State University in 1911 and the University of Chicago (Ph.D.) in 1917. He was a member of the University of North Carolina botany faculty, 1919–54. Besides many professional articles and monographs, he has published *The Natural Gardens of North Carolina . . . ,* Chapel Hill, [N. C.], 1932. AMS 9

WELLS, EDMUND (Feb. 14, 1846–July 7, 1938), was born in Lancaster, Fairfield County. At the age of sixteen he arrived in the Pike's Peak gold fields, where he spent two years. He later settled in Arizona. He died in San Diego, Calif., and is buried in Prescott, Ariz. Prospector, Indian fighter, packer, trapper, businessman, and judge of the superior court of Yavapai County, he was an integral part of his adopted state. His experiences are recounted in *Argonaut Tales, Stories of the Gold Seekers and the Indian Scouts of Early Arizona,* New York, [1927].

WELLS, SARAH FURNAS (Dec. 10, 1834–Aug. 20, 1912), was born in Newton Township, Miami County. She graduated from the Quaker Academy in 1856, attended Earlham College and Oberlin College, and studied medicine in Philadelphia. In 1873 while living in San Francisco she married Rufus Wells, a balloonist, with whom she traveled throughout the world. Her book is a record of their experiences. After her husband was injured in a balloon ascension, she practiced medicine in St. Louis, Mo., where she spent the remainder of her life.

Ten Years' Travel around the World . . . , West Milton, 1885.

WELSH, ALFRED HIX (Sept. 7, 1850–1889), educator, was born in Fostoria, Seneca County. After graduating from Baldwin University in 1872, he taught for three years at Buchtel College. He taught rhetoric at Columbus High School, 1876–85, and then joined the English faculty of Ohio State University. He was widely known for his series of textbooks on rhetoric, grammar, and mathematics. He died in Columbus.

The Conflict of Ages, Columbus, 1877.

The Development of English Literature and Language, 2 vols., Chicago, 1882.

Man and His Relations, Cincinnati, 1885.

WELSH, ISAAC (April 9, 1814–Nov. 29, 1875), was born in Washington Township, Belmont County. He was a farmer and an antislavery Whig who became prominent in the political affairs of his day. He served in the Ohio General Assembly and in the state senate. The so-called Welsh Resolutions of 1863, expressing the sentiment of the Ohio General Assembly on the war and pledging the support of the state to the Union and protesting against the sentiment of sympathy with secession, virtually became the keynote of the anti-Vallandigham campaign. He served as treasurer of Ohio from 1871 until his death.

Agricultural Survey of Belmont County, [St. Clairsville, 1869].

WELSHIMER, HELEN LOUISE (Feb. 17, 1901–Dec. 23, 1954), journalist, was born in Millersburg, Holmes County, the daughter of Pearl H. Welshimer (q.v.). She graduated from Hiram College in 1923. She worked as a reporter and feature writer on the Canton *Daily News* and the Akron *Beacon-Journal.* From 1929 to 1937 she wrote feature stories and serial novels for Newspaper Enterprise Association, and she also wrote for King Features. Among her books are a collection of poems: *Singing Drums,* New York, 1937, and a novel: *Love without Music,* New York, 1940. WWW 3

WELSHIMER, PEARL HOWARD (April 6, 1873–Aug. 16, 1957), clergyman, was born in York, Union County. He graduated from Ohio Northern University in 1894 and Hiram College in 1897. Ordained to the ministry of the Disciples of Christ Church, he served a church in Millersburg, 1897–1901, and First Christian Church, Canton, 1902–57. He published a volume of sermons, religious articles and tracts, and *Concerning the Disciples . . . ,* Cincinnati, 1935. WWW 3

WELTMER, SIDNEY ABRAM (July 7, 1858–Dec. 5, 1930), born in Wooster, Wayne County, was taken when he was seven years old to Missouri, where he spent the rest of his life. After preaching and teaching school, he founded Akinsville Normal School and served as its first president, 1885–89. He later founded the Weltmer Institute of Suggestive Therapeutics and experimented with hypnotism and autosuggestion. From 1901 to 1909 he published a magazine, *Weltmer's Magazine of Suggestive Therapeutics.* Some of his pamphlets might be classified as textbooks.

Regeneration; A Discussion of the Sex Question . . . , Nevada, Mo., 1898.
Suggestion Simplified, [Nevada, Mo., 1900].
The Real Man, Nevada, Mo., 1901.
Telepathy and Thought Transference, [Nevada, Mo.?, 1902].
Day Dreams, Nevada, Mo., 1916.
The Healing Hand . . . , Nevada, Mo., 1918.

WELTY, CORA GOTTSCHALK (July 31, 1876–July 2, 1951), was born in Berne, Ind. After graduating from Indiana State Teachers College, Terre Haute, she taught school for a time and then married B. F. Welty, a Lima attorney. She lived afterward in Lima. She wrote a work of fiction about the Amish: *The Masquerading of Margaret,* Boston, 1908.

WELTY, EDWIN ARTHUR (Dec. 5, 1853–Sept. 18, 1928), was born in Canal Dover, Tuscarawas County, but grew up in Missouri and spent most of his life there. At the age of eighteen he spent some time in the Rocky Mountains and was present during the attack on Major Thornburg's command. He settled in Oregon, Mo.; his death occurred in St. Joseph. He published poems in numerous periodicals.

Ballads of the Bivouac and the Border, Buffalo, [N. Y.], 1896.

WELTY, J. JEROME (1860–1934), lawyer, was born in Williamstown, Hancock County. He was educated at Ohio Normal University and Northwestern University. He was president of Florida State Normal College, 1896–97, a lawyer in Springfield, 1898–1918, and an attorney in the U. S. General Land Office, Washington, D. C., 1918–33. The collection of poems listed below was his only book.

Sunshine and Frost, Columbus, 1894.

WEMBRIDGE, ELEANOR HARRIS ROWLAND (1882–Feb. 19, 1944), born in Massachusetts, was referee of the girls' division of Cleveland Juvenile Court for a number of years. A graduate of Radcliffe College (A.B., 1903; A.M., 1904; Ph.D., 1905), she also taught psychology at Mount Holyoke College and Reed College. She wrote *The Right to Believe,* Boston, 1909. RC 27

WENDTE, CHARLES WILLIAM (June 11, 1844–Sept. 9, 1931), clergyman, born in Boston, Mass., was pastor of First Unitarian Church, Cincinnati, 1876–82. He afterward served churches in California and New England, and was recognized as a world leader among liberal religious groups. His numerous books include *What Do Unitarians Believe? . . . ,* Cincinnati, 1877, and an autobiography: *The Wider Fellowship . . . ,* Boston, 1927.

WERNER, HERMAN (Nov. 1, 1856–1944), was born in Württemberg, Germany, and served three years with the Royal Prussian Cavalry before coming to Akron in 1880. He enlisted in the U. S. Cavalry in that year and served until 1899. He saw service in all parts of the West and in the Spanish-American War. In 1899 he joined his brother Paul in The Werner Company, Akron, one of the largest book publishing companies in the country. An account of some of his Western adventures was published for members of the family in an edition of 100 copies: *On the Western Frontier with the United States Cavalry Fifty Years Ago,* [Akron, 1934].

WERTHNER, ELIZABETH HIPPARD. See William B. Werthner.

WERTHNER, WILLIAM B. (Jan. 27, 1855–Feb. 27, 1929), educator, was born in Dayton, Montgomery County. From 1874 until his retirement in 1925, he taught botany in Dayton high schools. He was also active in encouraging the planting of trees along Dayton streets. After his death his wife, Evangeline Hippard Werthner, a poet, completed the writing of his book: *Some American Trees,* New York, 1935.

WESELOH, HEINRICH (Nov. 1, 1852–Aug. 30, 1925), clergyman, was born in Osterwesede, Germany. After coming to the United States as a young man, he graduated from Concordia College in 1873 and Lutheran Seminary, St. Louis, Mo., in 1876. Soon after his ordination he came to Cleveland, where he was for many years pastor of Immanuel Evangelical Lutheran Church. He died in Cleveland. He wrote many articles in German and in English for periodicals.

Das Buch des Herrn und Seine Feinde, St. Louis, Mo., 1898.

Gottes Wort Eine Gotteskraft . . . , St. Louis, Mo., 1903.

Die Herrlichkeit Gottes in der Natur, St. Louis, Mo., 1906.

WESLEY, CHARLES HARRIS (Dec. 2, 1891–), educator, was born in Louisville, Ky. He graduated from Fisk University and took his doctorate at Harvard University. He has been president of Central State College since 1942. He has written a number of articles and books on the Negro in America, e.g., *The History of Alpha Phi Alpha; A Development in Negro College Life,* Washington, D. C., 1929. WW 30

WEST, DOROTHY. Pseud. See Mildred W. Benson.

WEST, JOHN DOUGLAS (Jan. 12, 1824–March 13, 1914), physician, was born in Akron, Summit County. In 1828 his father moved to a farm in Carroll County. John entered Franklin College in 1849, but was forced to abandon his studies two years later when his father died. While serving as principal of Neville Institute, he studied medicine with Dr. Benjamin Ogden of East Liverpool. In 1863 he began to practice in Dellroy, and in 1866 he moved to Hopedale, where he practiced and spent the remainder of his life.

Maidenhood and Motherhood. Ten Phases of a Woman's Life, Chicago, 1886.

WESTERFIELD, RAY BERT (Feb. 6, 1884–), educator, was born in Bradnor, Wood County. He graduated from Ohio Northern University in 1907 and Yale University (Ph.D.) in 1913. After serving as a high school principal in Bradnor and Paulding, 1905–10, he was a member of the Yale faculty, 1913–52. He published numerous textbooks, technical studies of economics, and *Our Silver Debacle,* New York, [1936]. WW 30

WESTERVELT, WILLIAM DRAKE (Dec. 26, 1849–March 9, 1939), clergyman, was born in Oberlin, Lorain County. After graduating from Oberlin College and Seminary (1871, 1874), he was ordained to the ministry of the Congregational Church. A missionary in Hawaii for many years, he wrote several books on the Hawaiian Islands, e.g., *Hawaiian Historical Legends,* New York, [1923]. WWNAA 3

WESTON, ASA MINOR (Sept. 24, 1836–1905), educator, was born in Cleveland, Cuyahoga County. He studied at Oberlin College for three years and graduated from Antioch College in 1857, a member of the first graduating class. He taught school in Clinton County, served in the 50th O.V.I., was a school principal in Vernon, Ind., for two years, and joined the Hiram College faculty in 1867. After teaching at Hiram for two years, he joined the faculty of Eureka College, Ill. He spent his last years in Indiana, farming and preaching in Disciples of Christ churches.

The Evolution of a Shadow . . . , Cincinnati, 1886.

WESTON, STEPHEN FRANCIS (March 10, 1855–March 7, 1935), educator, born in Madison, Maine, spent most of his life in Ohio. He graduated from Antioch College in 1879 and Columbia University (Ph.D.) in 1903. He was on the faculty of Western Reserve University, 1894–1900, and Antioch College, 1902–25. He edited a collection of peace orations and also published *Historical Sketch of the Intercollegiate Peace Association . . . ,* Yellow Springs, 1910. WWW 1

WESTWOOD, HORACE (1884–Dec. 24, 1956), clergyman, born in Yorkshire, England, came to Canada in 1901 and to the United States in 1905. Ordained to the ministry of the Methodist Church in 1906, he became a Unitarian in 1910 and was pastor of churches in Ohio, Canada, California, and South Carolina. He served a church in Youngstown for a time and was pastor of First Unitarian Church, Toledo, 1919–27. He died in Clearwater, Fla., where he had moved in 1950. While in Toledo he wrote a regular column for the *Blade.* His writings include *This Do and Live . . . ,* Boston, 1938.

WETMORE, CLAUDE HAZELTINE (1863–?), was born in Cuyahoga Falls, Summit County. He attended Western Reserve University and École Polytechnique, Lausanne. He traveled throughout the world. His last known address was St. Louis, Mo.

Sweepers of the Sea . . . , Indianapolis, [1900].
Fighting under the Southern Cross . . . , Chicago, [1901].
Incaland, a Story of Adventure in the Interior of Peru . . . , Boston, [1902].
In a Brazilian Jungle . . . , Boston, 1903.
Out of a Fleur-de-Lis . . . , Chicago, [1903].
The Battle against Bribery . . . , St. Louis, Mo., 1904.
Queen Magi's Little People, St. Louis, Mo., 1913.
Bedtime Stories, New York, 1914.
Queen Tiny's Little People, New York, 1914.
Capitol Removal, [Chicago, 1926].

WEYER, ANTHONY (Dec. 25, 1784–May 25, 1845), physician, was born in Baltimore, Md. He was living in St. Clairsville by 1809 and spent the remainder of his life in that community. His medical book, one of the earliest in the region, was printed by Horton J. Howard.

The Family Physician, Or Poor Man's Friend, and Married Lady's Companion . . . , St. Clairsville, 1831.

WHALLON, EDWARD PAYSON (March 30, 1849–June 3, 1939), clergyman and editor, was born in Putnamville, Ind., graduated from Hanover College in 1868 and from Union Theological Seminary in 1872. After serving as pastor of several Presbyterian churches, he edited successively *The Church at Work, The Herald and Presbyter,* and *The Presbyterian* in Cincinnati, where he also served as a supply pastor. His writings include *Pastoral Memories . . . ,* Cincinnati, 1907. WWW 1

WHARTON, FRANCIS (March 7, 1820–Feb. 21, 1889), lawyer, clergyman, and educator, born in Philadelphia, Pa., was professor of history and literature at Kenyon College, 1856–63. A practicing attorney in Philadelphia before coming to Ohio, he published several influential legal works. He also wrote two books on religious themes, the first of which was published while he lived in Ohio: *A Treatise on Theism . . . ,* Philadelphia, 1859.

WHEATON, JOHN MAYNARD (May 13, 1840–Jan. 28, 1887), physician, was born in Columbus, Franklin County. After graduating from Denison University in 1860, he studied medicine, served as an assistant surgeon in the 188th O.V.I., and after the war began practice in Columbus and also served on the faculty of Starling Medical College. From boyhood he was deeply interested in the out-of-doors and wildlife, and throughout his medical practice this interest was the basis of his avocation. He published a number of articles on ornithology and also prepared a "Catalogue of Birds of Ohio," which was published in the *Ohio Agricultural Report for 1860,* and a "Report on the Birds of Ohio," published in volume 4 of the *Report of the Geological Survey of Ohio, 1879.*

WHEELER, ADA M. (May 23, 1854–May 31, 1942), educator, was born in Mohawk, Coshocton County. A graduate of Lake Erie Seminary and Cincinnati Normal School, she began teaching in Cincinnati in 1871. In 1912 she was named principal of Windsor School, the first woman to be appointed to such a post in Cincinnati, and she served until her retirement in 1925. She wrote *Stories in Verse,* [Cincinnati, 1933].

WHEELER, EDWARD JEWITT (March 11, 1859–July 15, 1922), editor and publisher, was born in Cleveland, Cuyahoga County. He graduated from Ohio Wesleyan University in 1879. He was associated with Funk and Wagnalls, editing *Literary Digest* from 1895 to 1905 and afterward *Current Literature* (*Current Opinion*). He lived in New York City.

Stories in Rhyme for Holiday Time, New York, 1884.
Prohibition: The Principle, the Policy and the Party . . . , New York, 1889.

WHEELER, OLIN DUNBAR (May 1, 1852–Sept. 10, 1925), was born in Mansfield, Richland County. After attending Baldwin University, he spent several years in business and was a topographer with Major J. W. Powell's survey of the Columbia River, 1874–79. In 1892 he was placed in charge of advertising for the Northern Pacific Railway, and his booklets on the Northwest were sponsored by that company.

Indianland and Wonderland . . . , St. Paul, 1894.

Sketches of Wonderland . . . , St. Paul, 1895.
Yellowstone National Park . . . , St. Paul, 1901.
The Trail of Lewis and Clark . . . , 2 vols., New York, 1904.
Eastward through the Storied Northwest . . . , [St. Paul?, 1907].

WHEELER, WILLIAM WEBB (Feb. 15, 1845–June 7, 1925), merchant, was born in Ashtabula County, but spent much of his life in St. Joseph, Mo. He published a number of accounts of his travels, e.g., *Encircling the Globe,* [St. Joseph, Mo.], 1910. WWW 1

WHELAN, JAMES (Dec. 8, 1823–Feb. 18, 1878), clergyman, born in Kilkenny, Ireland, studied at the Dominican monastery, Somerset, and was ordained a priest there in 1846. He engaged in missionary work around Somerset, 1846–52, and served as president of St. Joseph's College, Perry County, 1852–54. As Bishop of Nashville, he was permitted in 1864 to cross the Confederate lines to visit Bishop Spalding at Louisville. Accusations of passing information to Northern troops led to his mental breakdown. He resigned his see in 1864. He died in Zanesville.

Catena Aurea . . . , St. Joseph's College, 1871.

WHERRY, ELWOOD MORRIS (March 26, 1843–Oct. 5, 1927), missionary, born in South Bend, Pa., served in India, 1867–1922. The last five years of his life were spent in Cincinnati. He translated books into Urdu, wrote books in that language, and published several books on religion and the mission field, e.g., *Zeinab, the Panjabi* . . . , New York, [1895].

WHINERY, VERNA. Pseud. See Verna W. Hiatt.

WHIPPLE, MARGARET. See Margaret W. Follet.

WHITACRE, DONALD DU MONT (June 29, 1920–), journalist, was born in Harveysburg, Warren County, and now lives in Clarksville. He attended Wilmington College, Pacific Oxford College, and Lincoln College. He writes a syndicated column, "Curious Facts," has published articles in numerous magazines, and has written *Little Known Facts about Ohio,* [Marietta, 1947].

WHITE, CHARLES BROWNE (April 13, 1870–March 20, 1945), was born in Newark, Licking County. After graduating from Denison University in 1893, he taught for one year at Tallequah Academy, Okla., and then returned to Granville to teach Latin at Doane Academy, 1894–1907. He retired from teaching in 1907 and managed farm properties inherited by his wife near Granville. He was active for many years in the Granville Historical Society. After his death selections of his writing were published: *The Philosopher of Mount Parnassus,* Granville, [1948].

WHITE, CHARLES EDWARD (Aug. 2, 1848–March 18, 1923), educator, was born in Wayne, Wood County, but spent most of his life in New York State, where his parents moved during his boyhood. After graduating from Cazenovia Seminary in 1867, he taught in several country schools. From 1887 until his death, he was principal of Franklin Public School in Syracuse, N. Y. He published several arithmetic textbooks. He also wrote many poems, collected in *Poems of School and Life,* [Syracuse, 1916]. His best-known poem was "A Teacher's Prayer."

WHITE, JOHN CAMPBELL (May 31, 1870–), clergyman and educator, was born in Wooster, Wayne County. He graduated from University of Wooster in 1890. He was general secretary of the Y.M.C.A., Calcutta, India, 1893–1903, was president of Wooster, 1915–19, and held various administrative offices in the United Presbyterian Church. He was pastor of First United Presbyterian Church, Mansfield, 1942–47, and now lives in Monroe. He wrote *Missions and Leadership* . . . , Wooster, 1915. WW 27

WHITE, JOHN W. (1814-Feb. 16, 1885), was born in Middlebury, Vt. He edited the Mount Vernon *True Whig* and worked on other newspapers. He died in Mount Vernon.

The Book of Chronicles! . . . , Mount Vernon, 1858.
George Seymour; Or, Disappointed Revenge. A Drama, Mount Vernon, 1858.

WHITE, JOHN WILLIAMS (March 5, 1849–May 9, 1917), educator, was born in Cincinnati, Hamilton County. After graduating from Ohio Wesleyan University in 1868, he studied in Germany and traveled in Greece. He received his Ph.D. in classical philology from Harvard in 1877, and was on the faculty, 1877–1909. He wrote many Greek textbooks and scholarly articles, and *The Verse of Greek Comedy,* London, 1912. DAB 20

WHITE, RALPH JEROME (Jan. 28, 1882–), clergyman, was born in Kent, Portage County. He graduated from Wittenberg College in 1907 and the Seminary in 1909. He served as a pastor in Ohio, 1909–16, as a missionary in British Guiana and Argentina, 1916–24, and as a pastor in Grand Rapids, Mich., 1924–54. He has written *Six Years in Hammock Land; An Historical Sketch of the Lutheran Church in British Guiana . . .*, Philadelphia, [1922]. RLA 2

WHITE, WILBERT WEBSTER (Jan. 16, 1863–Aug. 12, 1944), clergyman and educator, was born in Ashland, Ashland County. After graduating from University of Wooster in 1881 and Xenia Theological Seminary in 1885, he was ordained to the Presbyterian ministry. He served a church in Illinois, 1885–86, was on the Xenia Seminary faculty, 1890–95, taught at Moody Bible Institute, 1895–97, and was a missionary in India and England, 1897–1900. In 1900 he founded the Bible Seminary in New York City and served as its president until 1940. Besides the titles below, he published textbooks on memory training and a collection of Bible readings.

Inductive Studies in Twelve Minor Prophets, New York, 1894.
Thirty Studies in the Gospel by John, New York, [1896].
Thirty Studies in the Revelation, New York, 1897.
Availing Prayer, New York, 1899.
Old Testament Records . . ., New York, [1900].
Studies in Old Testament Characters . . ., New York, [1900].
Thirty Studies in the Gospel by Matthew, New York, 1903.
The Resurrection Body . . ., New York, [1923].

WHITE, WILLIAM WISNER (Nov. 27, 1866–Jan. 6, 1935), lawyer, was born in Ithaca, N. Y. He graduated from Princeton University in 1888, studied law, and afterward practiced in Cleveland. He published *Poems and Sketches*, [Cleveland, 1925]. RC 27

WHITEFORD, ROBERT NAYLOR (June 28, 1870–Jan. 6, 1959), educator, was born in Crawfordsville, Ind. A graduate of Wabash College (A.B., 1890; Ph.D., 1893), he was professor of English, University of Toledo, 1910–38. Besides literature textbooks, he wrote *Motives in English Fiction*, New York, 1918. WWW 3

WHITEHAIR, CHARLES WESLEY (Jan. 7, 1887–June 12, 1933), banker, born in Selma, Ind., graduated from DePauw University in 1909. He was a Y.M.C.A. worker and a correspondent in World War I. After the war he was engaged in banking and insurance in Cleveland and lived in Shaker Heights. He lectured on his war experiences and published several books, e.g., *Out There*, New York, 1918. WWW 1

WHITEHEAD, JOHN (Sept., 1819–1905), lawyer, was born in Jersey, Licking County, but after the death of his father he was reared in the home of an uncle in Newark, N. J. He was admitted to the New Jersey bar in 1840 and practiced in that state.

The Judicial and Civil History of New Jersey, [Boston], 1897.
The Passaic Valley of New Jersey . . ., 2 vols., New York, 1901.
Memorial Sketch of the Life of Compatriot William McKinley . . ., [New York, 1903].

WHITELEATHER, MELVIN KERR (June 15, 1903–), journalist, was born in Damascus, Mahoning County. After graduating from Ohio State University in 1925, he worked on various newspapers and was a foreign correspondent for the Associated Press and for the Philadelphia *Evening Bulletin*. He has published a book on foreign relations: *Main Street's New Neighbors*, Philadelphia, [1945]. WW 30

WHITLOCK, BRAND (March 4, 1869–May 24, 1934), writer, humanitarian, statesman of the progressive era, and courageous diplomat, was born in Urbana, Champaign County, the son of a Methodist minister, Elias D. Whitlock. During his boyhood he shared the drab existence of a Methodist preacher's household in rural Ohio towns where his father had a succession of ministries, relieved by summers spent in the more lively and urbane home of his grandfather, Joseph Carter Brand, who had been consul to Nuremberg and brought to Urbana facets of European culture. His formal schooling ended upon his leaving high school, but the rest of his life was a continuous process of self-education. He preferred newspaper work to college, serving as a reporter on the Toledo *Blade*, 1887–90, and on the Chicago *Herald*, 1891-93. A series of articles he wrote on John Peter Altgeld when the latter was running for governor in 1892 led to a post in the office of the secretary of state at Springfield, Ill., where he remained throughout Altgeld's administration. These were seminal years for Whitlock. His newspaper jobs trained him in concise, accurate reporting. In Springfield he imbibed Altgeld's radical humanitarianism and shared his travail in pardoning the men unjustly convicted of murder in the Haymarket riot. There began his lifelong friendship with Clarence Darrow (q.v.), who helped direct his literary tastes as well as his social thinking. He prepared himself for the law, wrote his first short story to be published, and married Ella Brainerd, of whom Newton Baker wrote, "She was half of his heart, half of his head, and more than half of his courage." After Altgeld's defeat Whitlock removed to Ohio, took the state bar exams, and hung out his shingle in Toledo in 1897. His vocation was the law but almost as important was his avocation of letters. From this time until he resigned from the ambassadorship to Belgium, his was a dual career. In his first novel, *The Thirteenth District* (1902), he individualized a political type he had observed during his Chicago and Springfield years. Without moral strictures and in a sense with sympathy, he traced the disintegration of the ambitious, personable, but morally flabby Jerome Garwood, Congressman from the thirteenth district. The style, the ethical tone, and the psychological twists are those of William Dean Howells, who was Whitlock's "first literary hero" and who encouraged the young writer. But the scenes and characters are Whitlock's own. There followed a number of short stories, mainly on political themes, later collected in *The Gold Brick* (1910) and *The Fall Guy* (1912), and two slighter novels, *Her Infinite Variety* (1904) and *The Happy Average* (1904). Because of his humanitarian sympathies for the poor and the outcast, he was attracted in his legal practice to the defense of criminals and to a study of criminal procedures and prison conditions. Out of this knowledge he penned *The Turn of the Balance* (1907), an important novel in the literature of exposure, shocking the public by its revelations of the barbarities practiced in American penitentiaries. Such an interest brought him to the notice of the great humanitarian mayor of Toledo, Samuel Milton ("Golden Rule") Jones (q.v.), and a friendship flourished when the two discovered a mutual enthusiasm for Tolstoy, Whitman, and Emerson. When the mayor died in office, Whitlock was urged to assume the leadership of the Jones movement. He vacillated, for he knew this would curtail, if not end, his leisure for writing, but he finally yielded to the importunings of Lincoln Steffens, Tom L. Johnson (q.v.), the hero of Cleveland's civic revival, and a group of Toledo Independents. First elected in 1905, Whitlock served as Toledo's mayor for eight years. No innovator, he took his reform ideas from Jones and Johnson, enthusiastically espousing the leading progressive principles of the day—home rule for cities, municipal ownership of utilities, the initiative and referendum, direct primary nonpartisan elections, and women's suffrage. He came to share the belief of civic reformers that the city was the hope of democracy, and that the failure of municipal institutions was caused not by too much democracy but by too little. His record in the mayor's office was one of efficient, humane service for the public good. By 1913 he was determined to retire from politics. He confided to his friends that the mayor's job had become the "veriest slavery" to him and that he longed to realize his dream of a literary career. Hypersensitive to criticism, he winced at enduring again the slander of a campaign and the heckling of do-gooders, forever abusing him for failing to stamp out the saloon. Also he needed to earn more money. Finally, he wished to satisfy the reverse side of his dual nature. Intellectually he was a democrat and friend of the common man, but emotionally he was an aristocrat, loving fine clothes and fine living, preferring the society of the rich and well born, from whom the nature of his reform battle had separated him. During his years as mayor he had not abandoned his literary interests. He found surcease from the political hurly-burly by closing himself in his study with his books and his pen. Most of his writing was nonfictional—essays on democracy, city government, municipal ownership of utilities, and pen sketches of leading Ohio reformers. The most distinguished is a pamphlet, *On the Enforcement of Law in Cities* (1910), a humane and graceful statement of his philosophy on civic morals, a challenge to the cant of the moral reformers. In the months immediately following his retirement, he wrote a charming volume of reminiscences, *Forty Years of It* (1914). It sparkles with vivid portraits of his family and friends and with bright, humorous anecdotes. While slighting many events in his own career, it is a fascinating record of his own intellectual growth and is sprinkled with sage observations distilled from his experiences. Whitlock did not long hold to his decision to renounce politics for literature; in Dec., 1913, he was sworn in as minister to Belgium. In that quiet diplomatic post he anticipated that he could play his dual role with reversed emphasis. Such hopes were smashed when Belgium was thrown into the vortex of World War I by the German invasion in Aug., 1914. Whitlock's next three years were consumed mainly in organizing and maintaining the relief of the Belgian people. It is no small tribute to his tact, patience, and administrative talent that the "revictualling" continued at a steady pace. His *Journal* gives a candid day-by-day account of the heavy labor this entailed, especially the task of smoothing the friction and jealousies which existed among the personalities involved. Later he published an account of these years; *Belgium: A Personal Narrative* (1919) spares personalities but otherwise is as accurate and straightforward as the *Journal.* "One of the few classics" of World War I—an encomium bestowed upon it by Allan Nevins—*Belgium* is more than a record of events; it is an indictment of military tyranny built not upon accounts of atrocities but upon the cumulative, grinding effect of armed despotism upon a once free people. With the signing of the Armistice, Whitlock returned to Brussels to spend what were perhaps the three most satisfying years of his life. He basked in the adulation and honors showered upon him, relished the court life and the intimacy with which the King and Queen favored him, and satisfied his craving for art objects and fine books. It was characteristic of him to take on the color of whatever environment he was in; he played the role of ambassador to perfection. Had there been no change in administration at home, he might have remained in the diplomatic service, but a year after Harding's election Whitlock was again a private citizen. By saving a part of his salary and reaping substantial royalties from his books, he had earned a competence sufficient to support himself and his wife in modest style. He could now devote himself exclusively to letters. Although it might have been expected that he would return to the United States, he chose to linger in Europe, never quite happy with the decision. Nevertheless, except for occasional brief visits to America he lived abroad until his death at Cannes, France. This last span of years was his most creative and yet the least satisfying, because he was continually piqued by his lack of popularity. His was a voice out of the past, drowned by the more strident tones of Sinclair Lewis, John Dos Passos, Ernest Hemingway, and others. Whitlock wrote two discerning novels about expatriate Americans: *Uprooted* (1926) and *Transplanted* (1927), drawing tellingly upon his European observations; then he returned to the theme of Midwestern politics in *Big Matt* (1928), though with less success than in *The Thirteenth District.* In 1931 he published two slender romances, *Narcissus* and *The Stranger on the Island,* and a tract against prohibition, *The Little Green Shutter,* which contains well-aimed thrusts at the American attitude toward drinking. If these, though good of their kind, are only of ephemeral interest, two others have "qualities of permanence"—to quote Nevins again—and deserve a better fate than their present neglect. One is Whitlock's finest novel, *J. Hardin & Son* (1923). The portraits of Joshua Hardin and his son, Paul, are of high artistry; the life of a drab Midwestern town, Macochee (Urbana), is portrayed with unvarnished truth; and certain scenes—a revival meeting, a local-option election—are reported with pungency and freshness. Though the style is again that of Howells, Whitlock shows that he is of a younger generation by his frank handling of sex. His other significant work was a biography: *Lafayette* (1929), the best life of that revolutionary French aristocrat in any language. This romantic titled figure, who kept his faith in constitutional democracy unimpaired, was a congenial subject for Whitlock. It stirred his interest in the past, which became more and more his solace. He left unfinished a novelized history of mid-nineteenth-century Ohio and notes for a life of Jefferson. Brand Whitlock falls short of greatness as a writer and statesman, but to say this is merely to concede his limitations so that his virtues and real contributions may not appear in a false light. His reputation at home has suffered partly from neglect but more particularly from the malevolence of former friends. He deserves to be restored to the esteem due him for his contributions to literature and politics. As a writer he left four or five titles which will have a permanent place on the shelves of American literature. An individualist in the best American tradition, he was a consistent foe with pen and voice of rigid dogma, hypocrisy, and cant. A humanitarian, he sought to alleviate suffering wherever he found it —among the criminal outcasts and forgotten poor of Toledo or among the starving Belgians. A major figure in the progressive era, he helped to regenerate the political and social morals of his city and state. The record of these contributions will outlive the slurs of his detractors and will shine through the mist of neglect that now shrouds Brand Whitlock.

Landon Warner

WHITLOCK, WILLIAM FRANCIS (Oct. 20, 1833–1909), clergyman and educator, was born on a farm near Dayton, Montgomery County. He taught school in Montgomery and Preble Counties, graduated from Ohio Wesleyan University in 1859, and afterward was associated with his alma mater as a professor and administrator for more than forty years. He wrote *The Story of the Book Concern,* New York, [1903?]. WWW 1

WHITMAN, ALBERY ALLSON (May 30, 1851–June 29, 1901), was born in Hart County, Ky., of slave parents. He worked at manual labor in northern Kentucky and southern Ohio, attended Wilberforce University at intervals, and taught school. In 1876 he was made pastor of a church in Springfield and also served as financial agent of Wilberforce. During this period he published a volume of poetry: *Not a Man, and Yet a Man,* Springfield, 1877. He later served as a pastor in various states. He published several volumes of poetry and was probably the major Negro poet before Paul Laurence Dunbar (q.v.).

WHITMAN, HOWARD (May 6, 1914–), journalist, was born in Cleveland, Cuyahoga County. After graduating from Western Reserve University in 1935, he was a correspondent in Europe for two years. He was moderator of the television program "Probe," 1957–58. He is the author of numerous magazine and newspaper articles on social problems, and *Let's Tell the Truth about Sex,* New York, [1948].

WHITMER, DAVID (Jan. 7, 1805–Jan. 25, 1888), born near Harrisburg, Pa., was one of the three witnesses who attested to Joseph Smith's translation of the golden plates into the *Book of Mormon.* He accompanied the Mormons to Kirtland, but was one of the first to migrate to Missouri. He was excommunicated in 1838 and continued to live in Ray County, Mo. In his old age he dictated a pamphlet describing the translation of the plates and other episodes in the early history of the Mormon Church: *An Address to All Believers in Christ . . . ,* Richmond, Mo., 1887.

WHITNEY, ELLIOTT. Pseud. See Harry L. Sayler.

WHITNEY, HELEN LOOS (April 21, 1894–), born in Iowa City, Iowa, has lived in Glendale, Hamilton County, since 1920. She graduated from the University of Iowa in 1915. Her husband, Nathaniel R. Whitney (q.v.), was an economist at Procter & Gamble. She has written a biographical memoir: *Isaac Althaus Loos,* Iowa City, 1947.

WHITNEY, LORENENZO HARPER (Sept. 12, 1834–1912), lawyer, was born in Berlin Heights, Erie County, but spent none of his adult life in Ohio. In 1852 he was a miner in California; later he studied law in Illinois and was admitted to the bar in 1858. He served in the Civil War with Illinois troops and after the war practiced law in Chicago. His projected history of the Civil War covers events only as far as June 10, 1861; no later volumes were issued.

The History of the War for the Preservation of the Federal Union . . . , Philadelphia, 1863.

Life and Teachings of Zoroaster . . . , [Chicago, 1905].

A Question of Miracles; Parallels in the Lives of Buddha and Jesus, Chicago, 1908.

WHITNEY, NATHANIEL RUGGLES (Sept. 6, 1882–), economist, born in Lykens, Pa., was professor of finance, University of Cincinnati, 1920–23, and an economist for Procter & Gamble Co., Cincinnati, 1923–52. He now lives in Glendale. He has published books on economics and banking and *The Sale of War Bonds in Iowa,* Iowa City, Iowa, 1923. WW 26

WHITTAKER, JAMES THOMAS (March 3, 1843–June 5, 1900), physician and educator, was born in Cincinnati, Hamilton County. He graduated from Miami University in 1863 and the Medical College of Ohio in 1867. He taught at the Medical College of Ohio and was pathologist at Good Samaritan Hospital. He also edited the *Cincinnati Clinic,* 1871–76, and wrote several important medical works. His pleasing style and versatility appeared to good advantage in his novel *Exiled for Lèse Majesté.* He died in Cincinnati.

Exiled for Lèse Majesté, Cincinnati, 1898.

WHITTERN, CHARLES S. (1858–Jan. 30, 1934), was born in Parma, Cuyahoga County. After teaching school in Parma for a time, he came to Cleveland in 1884 and became a deputy clerk in the courthouse. He filled various official posts in the court for more than thirty years. He published a small volume of verse: *The Little Red School-house and Other Poems,* Cleveland, 1902.

WHITTIER, GERTRUDE. See Gertrude W. Meals.

WHITTLESEY, CHARLES (Oct. 4, 1808–Oct. 18, 1886), was born in Southington, Conn. His family settled in Tallmadge, Summit County, in 1813. He graduated from the U.S. Military Academy in 1831. Resigning from the army at the close of the Black Hawk War, he opened a law office in Cleveland, and also became part-owner and co-editor of the *Whig and Herald.* He found himself when, in 1837, he was appointed assistant geologist of Ohio under William W. Mather. Here he was in association with a brilliant corps, which included such men as S. P. Hildreth, John Locke, and J. W. Foster, and here he acquired the broad knowledge upon which his reputation as a geologist was based. Financed by Joseph Sullivant (q.v.), a wealthy amateur archaeologist of Columbus, during the years 1839 and 1840 he made a survey of the works of the Mound Builders. About twenty of his plans and some of his notes were included in the great work of Ephraim G. Squier and Edwin H. Davis (qq.v.). In 1844 he was employed as geologist by a Detroit company to explore the copper regions of Michigan. He became head of a subcorps under the brilliant geologist, David Dale Owen, and was thus engaged in the U. S. Geological Survey of Wisconsin, Iowa, and Minnesota from 1847 till 1851. Subsequently he found his services as a mining engineer in that region in much demand. He served with distinction in the Civil War from April 17, 1861, until April, 1862, when bad health forced him to resign following the battle of Shiloh, where he was in command of the third brigade of General Lew Wallace's division. In 1867 he was one of the original organizers of the Western Reserve Historical Society. The spread of his interests ranged over a wide field of subjects—geology, agriculture, history, archaeology, and religion. He was a confirmed pamphleteer—disputatious, and, on the matter of archaeological attributions, inclined to be pontifical. In one of his many tracts he held the so-called Cincinnati tablet to be a fraud, a position he was forced to abandon in the light of evidence presented by the Cincinnati book-dealer Robert Clarke (q.v.). He produced nearly 200 tracts, a bibliography of which was compiled by C. C. Baldwin and published by the Western Reserve Historical Society in 1887. He died in Cleveland.

Ernest J. Wessen

A Discourse Relating to the Expedition of Lord Dunmore of Virginia against the Indian Towns upon the Scioto in 1774, Cleveland, 1842.

A Sketch of the Settlement and Progress of the Township of Tallmadge, Cleveland, 1842.

Bouquet's Expedition into the Muskingum Country Oct., 1764, [Cleveland, 1846].

Outline Sketch of the Geology of Ohio, [n.p., 1848].

Ancient Earthworks of Ohio, Washington, D. C., 1850.

Fugitive Essays, upon Interesting and Useful Subjects, Relating to the Early History of Ohio . . . , Hudson, 1852.

Ancient Mining on the Shores of Lake Superior, [Washington, D. C., 1863].

Mineral Resources of the Cordilleras of North America . . . , Cleveland, 1863.

Early History of Cleveland, Ohio . . . , Cleveland, 1867.

Contributions to the Geology of Ohio, Cleveland, 1869.

Inside View of the Geological Appointments, [Cleveland?, 1870].

History of the Coal and Iron Business from Cleveland As It Is, 1872, [Cleveland, 1872?].

Topographical and Historical Sketch of the State of Ohio, Philadelphia, 1872.

General Wallace's Division, Battle of Shiloh. Was It Tardy?, [Cleveland?, 1875?].

Battle of Shiloh Church, [Cleveland], 1882.

War Memoranda. Cheat River to the Tennessee, 1861–1862, Cleveland, 1884.

Theism and Atheism in Science, [Cincinnati, 1886].

WIBORG, FRANK BESTOW (April 30, 1855–May 12, 1930), was born in Cleveland, Cuyahoga County. After graduating from Chickering Institute, Cincinnati, in 1874, he organized a firm to manufacture printer's ink, Ault and Wiborg Co. At the time of his death he was president of the New York branch of the company. He wrote a history of printer's ink and *A Commercial Traveller in South America . . . ,* New York, 1905. WWW 1

WICKENDEN, ARTHUR CONSAUL (April 24, 1893–　　), clergyman and educator, was born in Toledo, Lucas County. He graduated from Denison University in 1915 and the University of Chicago (B.D., 1921; Ph.D., 1931). After being ordained to the ministry in the Baptist Church, he served several churches in the Middle West, 1921–27, and has been professor of religion, Miami University, since 1927. He has published several books on religious themes, e.g., *Youth Looks at Religion,* New York, 1939. WW 28

WICKES, THOMAS (Oct. 31, 1814–Nov. 10, 1870), clergyman, was born in Jamaica, Long Island, N. Y. He graduated from Yale University in 1834, was ordained to the ministry in 1839, and served as pastor of First Congregational Church, Marietta, 1840–69, before resigning because of ill health. He died in Orange, N. J. Besides the title below, he published at least one collection of sermons.

The Son of Man, Boston, [1868].

WICKEY, HARRY HERMAN (Oct. 14, 1892–), artist, was born in Stryker, Williams County. In 1915 he studied in New York under George Bellows and Robert Henri. His etchings are represented in most major museums and galleries in the United States. He has written an autobiography: *Thus Far, the Growth of an American Artist,* New York, [1941]. WW 30

WICKLINE, WILLIAM ALVIN (March 5, 1899–Feb. 5, 1942), educator, was born in Rio Grande, Gallia County. He graduated from Rio Grande College in 1922 and received a master's degree from Ohio State University in 1933. He was a teacher and superintendent in various Ohio schools for 21 years. He died at Oberlin. The year before his death, he published a little book of personal philosophy: *A Man-made God . . . ,* [Oberlin, 1941].

WICKS, KATHERINE GIBSON (Sept. 13, 1893–), born in Indianapolis, Ind., was on the educational staff of the Cleveland Museum of Art, 1916–46. Under her maiden name, Katherine Gibson, she has published considerable juvenile fiction, e.g., *The Golden Bird and Other Stories,* New York, 1927. WW 30

WIDEAWAKE, DR. ALATE. Pseud. See Henry Howe.

WIDNEY, JOSEPH POMEROY (Dec. 26, 1841–July 4, 1938), physician, was born in Miami County, where he attended public schools. In 1862 he moved to California. After serving two years in the Civil War, he studied medicine and around 1868 began practicing in Los Angeles, the city where he lived for the rest of his life. He was a founder of the University of California in 1880, became the first dean of its medical school in 1885, and served as president of the university, 1892–95. Most of his books were written after an automobile accident damaged his eyesight in 1929.

The Way of Life . . . Three Essays, Los Angeles, 1900.

Race Life of the Aryan Peoples, 2 vols., New York, 1907.

Ahasuerus; A Race Tragedy, Los Angeles, 1915.

The Faith That Has Come to Me, Los Angeles, [1932].

The Genesis and Evolution of Islam and Judaeo-Christianity, Los Angeles, [1932].

The Lure and the Land; An Idyl of the Pacific, Los Angeles, [1932].

Whither Away? The Problem of Death and the Hereafter, Los Angeles, [1934].

The Three Americas . . . , Los Angeles, [1935].

Race Life and Race Religions . . . , Los Angeles, [1936].

Civilizations and Their Diseases . . . , Los Angeles, [1937].

The Song of the Engle Men . . . , Los Angeles, [1937].

WIEAND, ALBERT CASSEL (Jan. 17, 1871–July 17, 1954), educator, was born in Wadsworth, Medina County. He graduated from the University of Chicago in 1901 and afterward studied in Germany. He founded Bethany Bible Seminary in 1905, served as president until 1932, and taught there until 1946. He published several books on religious themes, e.g., *The Prayer Life and Teachings of Jesus,* New York, [1932]. WWW 3

WIERWILLE, VICTOR PAUL (Dec. 31, 1916–), clergyman, was born in Shelby County and now lives in Van Wert. A graduate of Mission House College and Seminary, Plymouth, Wis., he has done graduate work in theology at Princeton Seminary and Burton Seminary. He served as pastor of the Evangelical and Reformed Church, Van Wert, 1944–57; he resigned in 1957 to devote all his time to writing and teaching a course in "Power for Abundant Living." He is the founder of the Way International and has lectured throughout the world. He has published many pamphlets and books, e.g., *Victory through Christ,* Van Wert, 1945.

WIGGINS, LIDA KECK (Jan. 5, 1874–July 2, 1946), was born in Batavia, Clermont County. She attended Cedarville schools. After her marriage to Forrest Wiggins of Springfield, she lived in that city and wrote society news for Springfield newspapers. She spent her last years in Beacon, N. Y. She wrote *Know Thy Neighbor; Or, Character Reading . . . ,* Naperville, Ill., [1909].

WIGHT, FRANCIS ASA (Feb. 16, 1854–Dec. 14, 1942), clergyman, was born in Andover, Ashtabula County. He attended Transylvania University, was ordained to the ministry of the Disciples of Christ Church, and served pastorates in Ohio, Pennsylvania, and California. He published numerous religious books, e.g., *Revelation—Christ's Return,* Harrisburg, Pa., [1931]. WWW 2

WIKE, MURLIE BURNS (Feb. 24, 1889–), was born near Yellow Springs, Greene County. In 1896 her parents moved to a farm outside Springfield, where she lived for many years. In 1943 she moved to Van Nuys, Calif., where she now lives. She has written numerous nature sketches for young readers, e.g., *Birds of a Feather Stories . . . ,* Chicago, [1925]. WWNAA 7

WILBUR, JAMES BENJAMIN (Nov. 11, 1856–April 28, 1929), banker, was born in Cleveland, Cuyahoga County. He lived in Colorado for a number of years as a banker and rancher. From 1891 until his retirement he was president of Royal Trust Co., Chicago. He later lived in Manchester, Vt. He wrote a biography: *Ira Allen, Founder of Vermont . . . ,* 2 vols., Boston, 1928. WWW 1

WILCOX, ALANSON (Feb. 23, 1832–June 15, 1924), clergyman, was born in Hinckley, Medina County. He was secretary of the Ohio Society of the Disciples of Christ, 1884–95, and also served as a Sunday school evangelist. He published an autobiography in 1912 and a useful history: *A History of the Disciples of Christ in Ohio,* Cincinnati, [1918].

WILCOX, FRANK NELSON (Oct. 3, 1887–), artist and educator, was born in Cleveland, Cuyahoga County. He attended Cleveland schools, graduated from the Cleveland School of Art in 1910, and afterward studied in Europe. He taught at the Cleveland School of Art for twenty years. Besides professional articles, he published *Ohio Indian Trails,* Cleveland, 1933.

WILCOX, PHINEAS BACON (Sept. 26, 1798–March 25, 1863), lawyer, was born in Middletown, Conn. After graduating from Yale University in 1821, he was admitted to the bar and practiced for forty years in Columbus, where he acquired a wide reputation as a specialist in land titles. He compiled a number of legal works. The book below was published anonymously.

A Few Thoughts by a Member of the Bar, Columbus, 1836.

WILDER, LUCY BEELER (May 15, 1889–), was born in Hamilton, Butler County. She attended Hamilton public schools, the University of Cincinnati, and the University of Chicago. In Chicago she married Dr. Russell M. Wilder in 1911. After World War I, in which her husband served as Chief of Gas Warfare, they settled in Rochester, Minn. In 1932 she established a bookstore in that community. With the co-operation of the Mayo brothers, she wrote a history of the Mayo Clinic which has been published in two subsequent editions: *The Mayo Clinic,* Minneapolis, 1936.

WILDER, MARGARET BUELL (April 4, 1904–), journalist, was born in Newark, Licking County. She graduated from Smith College in 1926. She has written a number of television shows, motion-picture scripts, and adaptations. Her first book, a series of letters written to a soldier by his wife, appeared first in the Dayton *Journal-Herald: Since You Went Away . . . ,* New York, [1943].

WILDER, THEODORE (Dec. 29, 1837–March 8, 1871), was born in Chester, Meigs County. He enlisted in the 7th O.V.I. in April, 1861, was wounded at Cedar Mountain, Va., Aug. 9, 1862, and was discharged in October of the same year. Company C, whose history he wrote, was composed chiefly of Oberlin students and faculty members.

The History of Company C, 7th Regiment, O.V.I., Oberlin, 1866.

WILDES, THOMAS F. (June 1, 1834–March 28, 1883), lawyer, was born in Racine, Canada. In 1839 his parents brought him to Ohio, and in 1861 he settled in Athens, where he edited the Athens *Messenger* until Aug., 1862, when he became lieutenant colonel of the 116th O.V.I. After being discharged from the army in Sept., 1865, he studied law, and after his graduation from Cincinnati Law School in 1866, he practiced in Athens.

Record of the One Hundred and Sixteenth Regiment . . . , Sandusky, 1884.

WILDMAN, EDWARD EMBREE (1874–May 5, 1956), educator, was born in Selma, Clark County. He taught in the public schools of Philadelphia and wrote articles and books on nature study, e.g., *Penn's Woods, 1682–1932,* Philadelphia, 1933.

WILDMAN, MARIAN WARNER (Oct. 14, 1876–), was born in Norwalk, Huron County. She graduated from Western Reserve University in 1898, and in 1914 she married Jesse A. Fenner of Cleveland. She published several books, e.g., *A Hill Prayer, and Other Poems,* Boston, 1904, and some under her married name, e.g., *Betty's Beautiful Nights,* New York, [1916]. WW 11

WILEY, FARIDA ANNA (May 23, 1887–), naturalist, was born in Sidney, Shelby County. She was a member of the Department of Education, American Museum of Natural History, 1921–55, and still conducts classes for adults there. She has edited several volumes in the Great American Naturalist series and has written a book on ferns: *Ferns of Northeastern United States . . . ,* [Easton, Pa., 1936].

WILEY, HUGH (Feb. 26, 1884–), was born in Zanesville, Muskingum County. He worked as a construction engineer in the United States, Canada, and Mexico, and served as a captain during World War I. He now lives in Berkeley, Calif. He has published fiction in the *Saturday Evening Post* and other national magazines and a number of popular novels, e.g., *Lady Luck,* New York, 1921. WW 25

WILHELM, DONALD GEORGE (Jan. 23, 1887–Feb. 25, 1945), lecturer, was born in Defiance, Defiance County. After graduating from Harvard University in 1912, he wrote articles and short stories for many national magazines and lectured widely. His books include *The Story of Iron and Steel,* New York, 1935. WWW 2

WILKIN, ROBERT NUGEN (May 4, 1886–), lawyer and judge, was born in New Philadelphia, Tuscarawas County. He graduated from the University of Virginia law school in 1908 and in the same year was admitted to the Ohio bar. He practiced in New Philadelphia and served as judge of the U. S. District Court, 1939–49. He has published legal articles and several books, e.g., *Eternal Lawyer, a Legal Biography of Cicero,* New York, 1947. WW 30

WILKINS, ERNEST HATCH (Sept. 14, 1880–), educator, born in Newton Centre, Mass., was president of Oberlin College, 1927–46. A specialist in Italian literature, he published textbooks, critical and historical studies, and a collection of essays: *Living in Crisis,* Boston, 1937. WW 30

WILLARD, FRANCES ELIZABETH CAROLINE (Sept. 28, 1839–Feb. 18, 1898), temperance advocate, born in Churchville, N. Y., spent a part of her girlhood in Oberlin, where her parents moved to attend Oberlin College. A prolific writer, she published many articles and books, including an autobiography: *Glimpses of Fifty Years . . . ,* Boston, 1889.

WILLARD, THEODORE ARTHUR (Dec. 10, 1862–Feb. 3, 1943), manufacturer, born in Castle Rock, Minn., lived in Cleveland. He invented the Willard storage battery and headed the Willard Storage Battery Company with headquarters in Cleveland. He wrote a number of books, e.g., a novel, *The Wizard of Zacna . . . ,* Boston, [1929]. WWW 2

WILLCOX, R. N. (July 20, 1831–Feb. 28, 1913), was born at Mystic River, Conn. In 1850 he went to California, and on his return in 1860 he traveled through the Midwest in search of a desirable location for farming. He finally settled near Bowling Green in 1870. He lived in other Ohio areas, and when his book was published he was living in Avery. His rambling account of his adventures contains digressions on spiritualism and other subjects, but also contains vivid descriptions of Gold Rush life.

Reminiscences. Of California Life. Being an Abridged Description of Scenes Which the Author Has Passed through in California and Other Lands . . . , [Avery], 1897.

WILLENBORG, LEE L. (July 22, 1878–Sept. 16, 1944), was born in Massillon, Stark County. He studied at the Cleveland School of Art and Drexel Institute. At the time of his death he was living in Massachusetts. He published *Prep Scraps,* Chicago, [1927]. WWNAA 7

WILLIAMS, ALBERT B. (April 4, 1847–Sept. 8, 1911), clergyman, was born in Holmes County. After graduating from Bethany College, he was ordained to the ministry of the Disciples of Christ Church in 1875 and served pastorates in Wadsworth and Mount Vernon. He resigned from the ministry in 1900 because of ill health. He prepared a county history, published posthumously: *Past and Present of Knox County,* 2 vols., Indianapolis, 1912.

WILLIAMS, ALBERT RHYS (Sept. 28, 1883–), was born in Greenwich, Huron County. He graduated from Marietta College in 1904 and Hartford Theological Seminary in 1907. He was minister and director of Maverick Church and Forum, Boston, 1907–

14. He was an assistant in the Commissariat for Foreign Affairs, Russia, 1917–18, and afterward made three extended visits in Russia to study the folk life and customs. He has published a number of books on Russia, e.g., *The Russian Land,* New York, 1927. WW 30

WILLIAMS, ALFRED (1829–Feb. 8, 1901), was born in Fairfield County. In 1856 he settled in Circleville, where he later edited the *Union-Herald.* He was appointed to a post in the State Department by President Hayes and remained in that position until his death.

The Inter-Oceanic Canal and the Monroe Doctrine . . . , New York, 1880.

WILLIAMS, ARTHUR BALDWIN (April 11, 1874–Aug. 18, 1951), naturalist, born in Montclair, N. J., lived in Cleveland for more than forty years. On the staff of the Cleveland Museum of Natural History, he wrote numerous articles, books on birds and geology of Cuyahoga County, and *The Native Forests of Cuyahoga County, Ohio,* Cleveland, 1949.

WILLIAMS, BEN AMES (March 7, 1889–Feb. 4, 1953), was born at the home of his maternal grandparents in Macon, Miss. Soon after his birth his parents returned to his father's home in Jackson. Here Ben Ames's father, Daniel Webster Williams (q.v.), became editor and owner of the Jackson *Standard Journal.* Ben Ames's roots were deep in Ohio. His paternal grandfather came direct from Wales to Oak Hill. His mother's people settled Ames Township, Athens County, soon after Marietta was settled. His father and mother met at Ohio University. When Ben was fourteen he went East to preparatory school and then to Dartmouth. After graduating from college he returned to Jackson for a short time to manage his father's newspaper, while the latter served in the Ohio senate. In 1910 he began his writing career as a reporter on the Boston *American.* He worked for the newspaper for four years, but he said, "Every night of those four years I was trying to write short stories." He achieved spectacular success as a short-story writer soon after he resigned from the newspaper. In 1917 the *Saturday Evening Post* published one of his stories, and for many years thereafter it published a great many Ben Ames stories. A number of his short stories were collected and published, by popular demand, in *Thrifty Stock* (1923) and *Fraternity Village* (1949). His first novel was published in 1919: *All the Brothers Were Valiant,* and he soon became one of the most popular novelists of his day, writing many best-sellers. He wrote some 35 novels before his untimely death. His writing ranged over a wide field: psychological studies (*Leave Her to Heaven,* 1944); sociological studies (*Time of Peace,* 1942); adventure stories (*The Silver Forest,* 1926); historical novels (*House Divided,* 1947); regional studies (*Owen Glen,* 1950). *House Divided* was the novel Williams said he had always wanted to write. It is a family story before and during the Civil War. He said it represented some fifteen years of preparatory thought and study, topped by 52 months of concentrated labor. The novel shows his remarkable ability to present two sides of an issue and be fair to each. *Owen Glen* is the novel his Ohio friends had always wanted him to write—the story of the Welsh in Ohio. The scene is his own county of Jackson and the book is the story of a boy, Owen Glen, growing to manhood in the local mining community. There are two central characters, Owen Glen and the local newspaper editor. Between the boy and the editor is a beautiful relationship which is based on the author's memory of his own father. All who knew Ben Ames were aware of his deep devotion to his mother and father, and in *Owen Glen* he memorializes this relationship. The author develops three themes in *Owen Glen:* the youth of the United States in the 1890s, the birth and growth of the United Miners' Union, and the story of the small American town of yesterday. He does this largely by using the editorials and personals that appeared in his father's newspaper. Ben Ames had talked often of wanting to write a good Ohio novel, and he succeeded in giving an excellent study of Jackson County in the latter part of the nineteenth century. Mr. Williams once said that he was no born writer, but one who succeeded by virtue of sheer energy, persistence, and hard work. He was a painstaking student of social history and traveled widely for the purpose of gaining insight into human nature in different locales. His books are crowded with details of everyday life but they are animated with action. His material is well organized; many of his descriptive passages are memorable, some of his characters are unusually well developed, and the reader is impressed by his quality of tolerance. Above all, Ben Ames Williams was a master raconteur, a skill which contributed no small part to his happy and successful writing career.

Florence R. Head

WILLIAMS, BERTYE YOUNG (Mrs. Karl H.) (Feb. 25, 1876–Feb. 15, 1951), was born in Hamersville, Brown County, but spent most of her life in Cincinnati. She was active in cultural activities in that city, and with Annette P. Cornell (q.v.) she founded *Talaria,* a poetry quarterly. Her poems appeared in numerous magazines, newspapers, and anthologies, and she published several collections, e.g., *House of Happiness,* New York, 1928. WWW 3

WILLIAMS, BERYL (Nov. 15, 1910–), was born in Columbus, Franklin County. After graduating from New Jersey College for Women in 1932, she did newspaper and editorial work until 1940; since then she has devoted herself to free-lance writing. She married Samuel Epstein in 1938 and now lives in Long Island, N. Y. As Beryl Williams she has written several nonfiction books, e.g., *Lillian Wald: Angel of Henry Street,* New York, [1948]. She and her husband have collaborated on many books for children, some published under their own names and some under various pen names: e.g., as Adam Allen, *Dollar a Share,* New York, [1943], and as Douglas Coe, *Road to Alaska,* [New York, 1943]. WWAW 1

WILLIAMS, BYRON (April 22, 1843–Feb. 15, 1915), was born near East Liberty, Clermont County. After attending Ohio Wesleyan University, he taught and served as school superintendent in Williamsburg and Milford. He lectured widely on historical and military subjects. In his later years he devoted himself to local history, and wrote articles and books, e.g., *History of Clermont and Brown Counties . . . ,* 2 vols., Milford, 1913.

WILLIAMS, CAROLINE LOUISE RANSOM (Feb. 24, 1872–Feb. 1, 1952), Egyptologist, was born in Toledo, Lucas County. After graduating from Mount Holyoke College in 1896, she taught at Lake Erie College, studied at the University of Berlin (1900–03), and completed her doctorate at the University of Chicago in 1905. She taught at Bryn Mawr College, 1905–10, and was a curator in the Metropolitan Museum of Art, New York City, 1910–16. After marrying Grant Williams, a Toledo realtor, in 1916, she lived in Toledo. Widely honored as an archaeologist, she wrote technical articles and monographs, many published under her maiden name, e.g., *The Stela of Menthuweser,* New York, 1913.

WILLIAMS, CHARLES DAVID (July 30, 1860–Feb. 14, 1923), clergyman, was born in Bellevue, Huron County. He graduated from Kenyon College in 1880 and was ordained deacon in the Episcopal Church in 1883 and priest in 1884. He served as rector of Fernbank and Riverside, 1884–89, and of Trinity Church, Steubenville, 1889–93, as dean of Trinity Cathedral, Cleveland, 1893–1906, and as bishop of Michigan, 1906–23. A liberal thinker, he believed that the church should take a stand on political and social issues. His views were expressed in several books, e.g., *The Christian Ministry and Social Problems,* New York, 1917. DAB 20

WILLIAMS, CHARLES LUTHER (June 8, 1851–Aug. 5, 1933), clergyman and educator, was born in Imlaystown, N. J. He graduated from Princeton University in 1878, became a Baptist minister, and taught English literature at Denison University, 1893–1921. He died in Granville. His writings include *The American Student and the Rhodes Scholarships . . . ,* Detroit, 1903. WWW 1

WILLIAMS, DANIEL JENKINS (Dec. 22, 1874–May 29, 1952), clergyman, was born in Genesee, Wis. He graduated from the University of Wisconsin in 1899, Union Theological Seminary in 1903, and Ohio State University (Ph.D.) in 1914. He served Presbyterian churches in Columbus, 1907–11 and 1923–33, and was also a pastor in Wisconsin, Iowa, and Florida. He wrote *One Hundred Years of Welsh Calvinistic Methodism in America,* Philadelphia, 1937. WWC 1

WILLIAMS, DANIEL WEBSTER (Oct. 31, 1862–July 8, 1932), journalist, father of Ben Ames Williams (q.v.), was born in Jackson County. He attended Ohio University and in 1887 married Sara Ames, a niece of General James Longstreet. He taught school for eight years and was editor of the Jackson *Standard-Journal* for forty years. He served as American consul at Cardiff, Wales, 1905–07.

A History of Jackson County, Ohio, Jackson, 1900.

WILLIAMS, EDWARD IRWIN FRANKLIN (June 22, 1886–), educator, was born in Wooster, Wayne County. He graduated from Heidelberg College in 1914 and Columbia University (Ph.D.) in 1941. He was a member of the education department, Heidelberg College, 1915–56, and also served as registrar, 1938–51. He wrote a history of Heidelberg College and a biography: *Horace Mann, Educational Statesman,* New York, 1937. WW 29

WILLIAMS, EDWARD THOMAS (Oct. 17, 1854–Jan. 27, 1944), clergyman, was born in Columbus, Franklin County. After graduating from Bethany College in 1875, he was ordained to the ministry of the Disciples of Christ Church. He served as pastor in various cities, 1875–87, and as a missionary in China, 1887–96; but later became a Unitarian. He was an official of the U. S. State Department in China, 1896–1918, and a member of the University of California faculty, 1918–27. He published a number of magazine articles and *China Yesterday and To-day,* New York, [1923]. WWW 2

WILLIAMS, EGERTON RYERSON (Feb. 1, 1873–Feb. 13, 1925), lawyer, was born in Toledo, Lucas County. He graduated from Yale University in 1894 and Albany Law School in 1896. Admitted to the New York bar in 1896, he practiced in Rochester until 1907, after which time he lived in Italy. He wrote several books on Italy, e.g., *Hill Towns of Italy,* Boston, 1903. WW 6

WILLIAMS, FRANKWOOD EARL (May 18, 1883–Sept. 24, 1936), neurologist, was born in Cardington, Morrow County. He graduated from the University of Wisconsin in 1907 and completed his medical studies at the University of Michigan in 1912. He was for many years associated with the National Committee for Mental Hygiene. He wrote articles, textbooks, and *Russia, Youth, and the Present-Day World . . . ,* New York, [1934]. WWW 1

WILLIAMS, GEORGE WASHINGTON (Oct. 16, 1849–Aug. 4, 1891), was born in Pennsylvania. After serving in the army during the Civil War and in the Mexican army, he came to Cincinnati in 1876 as pastor of the Union Baptist Church. He read law in the office of Alphonso Taft and was admitted to the Ohio bar. While preparing a Fourth of July oration, he became interested in the history of his race and spent the next six years compiling *History of the Negro Race in America from 1619 to 1880 . . . ,* New York, [1882]. In 1883 he moved to Boston, where he wrote a history of Negro troops in the Civil War. He died in Blackpool, England.

WILLIAMS, JOHN CLARK (May 6, 1877–Sept. 7, 1947), clergyman and educator, was born in Walnut Grove, Logan County. He graduated from Ohio State University in 1904. He was pastor of Methodist churches in Whitehouse, Arlington, Middletown, and Columbus, and was on the faculty of Kansas City University and was president of Westminster College, Tehuacana, Texas. He published *The Man of God . . .* ,Tehuacana, Texas, [1916]. WWW 2

WILLIAMS, JOHN FLETCHER (Sept. 25, 1834–April 28, 1895), librarian and historian, was born in Cincinnati, Hamilton County. In 1852 he graduated from Ohio Wesleyan University, and three years later he went to St. Paul, Minn., where he became a journalist. He was secretary and librarian of the Minnesota Historical Society, 1867–93. He contributed many articles to the *Collections* published by the Society, compiled a bibliography of Minnesota, and also wrote a family history. He died in Rochester, Minn.

The Early History of St. Paul . . . , [St. Paul], 1867.

History of the Newspaper Press of St. Paul . . . , [St. Paul, 1871].

A History of the City of St. Paul, and of the County of Ramsey, Minnesota, St. Paul, 1876.

A Tribute to the Memory of Rev. Harvey Shipp Widney . . . , St. Paul, 1888.

WILLIAMS, JOHN SHOEBRIDGE (1790–April 22, 1878), was born in Carteret County, N. C. In 1800 his widowed mother brought him to Belmont County, where he attended local schools, including one headed by Aquila M. Bolton (q.v.), and learned surveying from their landlord, the versatile Horton J. Howard. He taught school in Barnesville and in 1812 went to Pennsylvania, where he worked on the construction of roads and canals. He surveyed the right of way for the Chesapeake and Ohio Canal, but seems to have fallen into disfavor with his superiors because of his advocacy of the substitution of railroads for certain projected sections of the canal. In 1826 he returned to Ohio, where he surveyed and superintended construction on the National Road, the Maysville Pike, and other roads. Not only was Williams one of the first professional engineers in the Midwest to advocate construction of railroads, but in 1835 he was associated with Daniel Drake and Edward D. Mansfield (qq.v.) in promoting a railroad from Cincinnati to Charleston, S. C. Apparently competent and progressive, Williams gained neither fame nor fortune from his professional career. Little is known of his personal life. The rare glimpses caught through random references are not very revealing. He was the only Ohio buyer present at the auction of Thomas Jefferson's library in 1829 and bought several lots of books. In his otherwise technical *Report of the Engineer to the President of the Hanging Rock and Lawrence Furnace Railroad Company,* he inserted a historical account of the colorful, now all but forgotten Ohio River town of Hanging Rock—an incongruity that demonstrates his abiding interest in pioneer life in Ohio. It is as the founding editor of the *American Pioneer* that he will be remembered. The first number of this monthly periodical was published in Chillicothe in Jan., 1842, at a time when Williams was engaged in several engineering projects. On completing these engagements in October, he moved the editorial offices to Cincinnati, where he maintained his residence for a number of years. The statement "Devoted to the objects of the Logan Historical Society" on the title page has led bibliographers and historians to assume that the *American Pioneer* was the official publication of that body. However, statements in the text and on the wrappers make it evident that it was a private enterprise. Its quasi-official character probably brought contributions that would not otherwise have been received. S. P. Hildreth (q.v.), Lyman Draper, Felix Renick, Neville Craig, and Elisha Whittlesey (q.v.), were among those who contributed valuable articles and notes. Firsthand accounts of pioneer life, personal narratives, descriptions of Indian warfare, and biographical sketches of pioneers have served to make the work of unique value to students of the early history of the Ohio Valley. In closing the first volume, he announced the completion of all professional engagements and indicated that it was his intention to devote his entire time to editing volume two, stating on the verso of the back wrapper, "All that we possess is at stake upon the issue." Complaining of the sedentary life he was leading and his resultant poor health, he suspended publication with number 10 of volume II in Oct., 1843. In the final number he wrote, "Ten fine children have in times past sat around my table. Other kinds of wealth I never was adept at either collecting or keeping together." With this valedictory he abandoned his magazine and returned to engineering. He died in Viola, Iowa, at the home of a son.

Yeatman Anderson, III

Report of the Engineer to the Association for the Promotion of Internal Improvements in the State of Kentucky, [n.p., 1829].

Address to an Enterprising Public upon the Improvements of Roads, and the Introduction of Track Roads, (with John Hartman), Cincinnati, 1833.

Fulton, O. Citizens. Railroad Proceedings and Address of Fulton and Vicinity, to the People of Ohio, Cincinnati, 1835.

Report of the Engineer to the President of the Hanging Rock and Lawrence Furnace Railroad Company, Cincinnati, 1837.

A True History of the Massacre of Ninety-six Christian Indians at Gnaddenhutton . . . , New Philadelphia, 1841.

WILLIAMS, KENNETH POWERS (Aug. 25, 1887–Sept. 25, 1958), educator, was born in Urbana, Champaign County. He graduated from Indiana University in 1908, began teaching mathematics there in 1909, and earned his doctorate at Princeton University in 1913. He published several mathematics textbooks and technical scientific works; and he also wrote an excellent book on the Civil War: *Lincoln Finds a General . . . ,* New York, 1949. WWW 3

WILLIAMS, LEWIS JAMES (March 4, 1877–June 11, 1949), was born in Green Bay, Wis., and spent his boyhood in New York City, but passed most of his adult life in Toledo. He served on several Toledo newspapers and at the time of his death was manager of Smith & Biler, Toledo. His poems appeared in various periodicals, and he published at least two collections, e.g., *Down the Road with the Buckeye Poet,* Toledo, 1923.

WILLIAMS, NATHAN WINSLOW (Aug. 26, 1860–Dec. 29, 1924), lawyer, was born in Cleveland, Cuyahoga County. He studied at Baltimore City College, Johns Hopkins University, and Columbia Law School. Admitted to the Maryland bar in 1883, he practiced in Baltimore and spent the rest of his life in that city. Under the pen name Richard Dallas, he wrote *A Master Hand; The Story of a Crime,* New York, 1903. WWW 1

WILLIAMS, SAMUEL (1786–1859), born in Carlisle, Pa., arrived in Chillicothe in 1807. He moved to Cincinnati in 1815, when he became chief clerk of the Surveyor General's office, and resided there until his death. He seems to have started accumulating original historical source documents on his first arrival in Ohio, and in 1839 he organized the Western Methodist Historical Society in an unsuccessful attempt to find a safe repository for his large collection. In Sept., 1839, he submitted a memorial to the Methodist Conference in Cincinnati which resulted in starting the *Ladies' Repository,* a periodical destined to be the longest lived and most successful literary magazine published west of the Allegheny Mountains. Not only was he the founding father of this distinguished periodical, but he was also its managing editor and was largely responsible for its liberal editorial policy. Beginning in 1851 he contributed in fourteen installments, over a period of four years, his valuable series of personal memoirs entitled *Leaves from an Autobiography*. Therein he gave an account of his experiences in Pennsylvania, Virginia, and Ohio from 1790 to 1815. This work is probably the most valuable source on the early days of the Kanawha River country. His *Two Western Campaigns in the War of 1812–13* was published in the *Ohio Valley Historical Series,* Cincinnati, 1871. Peter Thomson in his *Bibliography* (1246) stated that the work was not published separately. However, Robert Clarke & Company published Williams' work in a pamphlet of 53 pages, bound in their familiar blue paper wrappers.

Two Western Campaigns in the War of 1812 . . . , Cincinnati, 1871.

WILLIAMS, SAMUEL WESLEY (1827–Feb. 14, 1928), clergyman and educator, was born in Chillicothe, Ross County. His father, Samuel Williams (q.v.), founded the *Ladies' Repository,* published in Cincinnati. After graduating from Ohio Wesleyan University in 1848, he taught at Ohio Wesleyan and at McKenohee College, Ill., and later served on the editorial staff of the Methodist Book Concern. He died at the age of 100 in Wyoming, Hamilton County. He wrote *Pictures of Early Methodism in Ohio,* Cincinnati, [1909].

WILLIAMS, STEPHEN RIGGS (Aug. 22, 1870–Feb. 24, 1954), educator, was born in Kalgan, North China. He graduated from Oberlin College in 1892, taught for two years in Lima, and graduated from Harvard University (Ph.D.) in 1898. He joined the Miami University faculty in 1900 and taught there until his retirement in 1940. Besides articles and monographs in the field of zoology, he published a book of local history: *The Saga of Paddy's Run,* Oxford, 1945. WW 21

WILLIAMS, STEPHEN WEST (March 27, 1790–July 6, 1855), physician and educator, was born in Deerfield, Mass. He read medicine under his father, practiced and taught medicine, and was a lecturer at Willoughby University, 1838–53. He wrote genealogical works, a textbook on medical jurisprudence, and *American Medical Biography . . .* , Greenfield, Mass., 1845.

WILLIAMS, SUSAN MARY (June 27, 1905–), educator, was born in Dayton, Montgomery County. A teacher in the Dayton public schools, she has written a story for young children: *Toby, the Little Lost Dog,* New York, 1942.

WILLIAMS, THOMAS JEFFERSON (Nov. 30, 1840–Feb. 3, 1907), born in Oneida County, N. Y., came to Jackson County in 1854. He worked at the iron furnaces in the summers and attended district schools in the winters. In 1861 he enrolled at Ohio University, but on the outbreak of war he enlisted in the 56th O.V.I. and served for four and a half years, rising to the rank of first lieutenant. After the war he was in the iron business in Jackson until 1887, and later served two terms as clerk of courts.

An Historical Sketch of the 56th Ohio Volunteer Infantry . . . , Columbus, 1899.

WILLIAMS, WALTER ROLLIN (March 10, 1884–), missionary, was born in Washington Township, Union County. He attended high school in Hardin County and graduated from Ohio Wesleyan University in 1907. He was recorded a minister of the Friends Church in 1908, served in various communities, and was a missionary in China, 1909–27. He was missionary superintendent of the Friends Church, 1943–54. He now lives in Damascus, Columbiana County. He has published three books on missionary work, e.g., *These Fifty Years with Ohio Friends in China . . .* , Damascus, [1940].

WILLIAMS, WHITING (March 11, 1878–), was born in Shelby, Richland County. After graduating from Oberlin College in 1899, he studied for a year in Germany and for another year at the University of Chicago. He was manager of the Bureau of University Travel, 1901–04, assistant to the president, Oberlin College, 1904–12, and executive secretary of Cleveland Welfare Federation, 1912–16. He now lives in Cleveland. He studied labor conditions in Europe and the United States and lectured and wrote on problems of labor and management, e.g., *Horny Hands and Hampered Elbows . . .* , New York, 1922. WW 28

WILLIAMS, WILLIAM ASBURY (May 30, 1854–May 6, 1938), clergyman, was born in Beallsville, Monroe County. He graduated from Franklin College in 1876 and Western Theological Seminary in 1880, and was ordained to the Presbyterian ministry in 1885. He taught at Franklin College, 1880–87, and served as president, 1887–1901. In 1902 he moved to Moundsville, W. Va., and in 1908 he moved to Philadelphia. After 1920 he lived in Camden, N. J. He wrote *The Evolution of Man Scientifically Disproved,* Camden, 1925.

WILLIAMS, WILLIAM GEORGE (Feb. 25, 1822–1902), clergyman and educator, son of Samuel Williams (q.v.), was born in Chillicothe, Ross County, but his parents moved to Cincinnati when he was seven years old, and he grew up in that city. After graduating from Woodward College in 1844, he became principal of the preparatory department, Ohio Wesleyan University, and in 1847 he was elected to the faculty to teach ancient languages. He became a Methodist minister in 1856 and was secretary of the Central Ohio Conference for many years. He published a grammar textbook in 1887 which was widely used, and he also wrote two books on religious themes, e.g., *Baptism . . . ,* Cincinnati, [1901]. WWW 1

WILLIAMSON, CHARLES W. (May 12, 1835–Dec. 31, 1919), educator, was born on a farm in Perry County. He taught school in order to finance his education at Heidelberg College and also studied law at Cleveland Union Law School. He served as superintendent of schools in Napoleon, New Bremen, and Wapakoneta, his longest tenure being in the latter community. He published *History of Western Ohio and Auglaize County . . . ,* Columbus, 1905.

WILLIAMSON, FIELD. Pseud. See Hope Field.

WILLIAMSON, HORACE GREELY (May 1, 1880–Dec. 30, 1943), was born in Cincinnati, Hamilton County. He attended Cincinnati public schools and the Curry School of Acting, Boston, Mass. He appeared on Chautauqua platforms, reading his own humorous poems and stories. He was for some time secretary of the Cincinnati Rotary Club and was director of advertising for the Baldwin Piano Co.

Old Hollyhocks, and Other Poems and Recitations, Cincinnati, 1900.
Things Worth While . . . , Cincinnati, [1906].

WILLIAMSON, ISAAC DOWD (April 4, 1807–Nov. 26, 1876), clergyman, was born in Pomfret, Vt. A Universalist minister, he began preaching in Albany, N. Y. He preached in several other cities before coming to Cincinnati, where he was pastor of Plum Street Church. His death occurred at Anderson's Ferry, five miles below Cincinnati. He edited several religious newspapers, including *The Star of the West.* Besides sermons and books defending the Universalist faith, he was an active worker in the Independent Order of Odd Fellows and wrote *The Philosophy of Odd Fellowship* and other works on the principles and ideals of that organization. In his writings he used his religious beliefs to defend fraternal groups.

An Argument for the Truth of Christianity, New York, 1836.
Exposition and Defense of Universalism, New York, 1840.
The Philosophy of Universalism . . . , Cincinnati, 1866.
An Examination of the Doctrine of Endless Punishment . . . , Cincinnati, 1867.
Rudiments of Theological and Moral Science, Cincinnati, 1870.

WILLIARD, GEORGE WASHINGTON (June 10, 1818–Sept. 17, 1900), clergyman and educator, was born in Frederick County, Md. He graduated from Marshall (Franklin and Marshall) College in 1838 and was ordained to the ministry of the Reformed Church in 1840. After serving churches in Columbus and Dayton, he was elected president of Heidelberg College in 1866 and served until 1890. He then taught at Ursinus College, but in 1895 he returned to Dayton, where he organized a church and lived until his death. Besides the titles below, he published a text on comparative religion and edited an anthology for family reading.

The History of Heidelberg College . . . , Cincinnati, 1879.
Life, Work and Character of Henry Leonard, Dayton, 1890.

WILLKIE, WENDELL LEWIS (Feb. 18, 1892–Oct. 8, 1944), unsuccessful candidate for the Presidency in 1940, born in Elwood, Ind., practiced law in Akron, 1919–29. He left Akron to become an attorney for the Commonwealth Southern Corporation; he became its president in 1933, and his struggle against the Tennessee Valley Authority first brought him national prominence. During and after the 1940 campaign, many of his speeches were published. His most important book was *One World,* New York, 1943. WWW 2

WILMORE, AUGUSTUS CLELAND (June 2, 1849–April 24, 1933), clergyman and educator, was born in Jackson, Jackson County. After studying at DePauw University, he taught school in Indiana, 1867–77. He was pastor of United Brethren churches in Indiana, 1877–1918. He died in Winchester, Ind. He wrote *History of the White River Conference of the Church of the Brethren . . .*, Indianapolis, 1925.

WILSHIRE, HENRY GAYLORD (June 7, 1861–Sept. 7, 1927), was born in Cincinnati, Hamilton County. He attended Woodward High School and Harvard University. He became a merchant in 1884, and in 1900 he became publisher of *Wilshire's Magazine,* which he continued publishing and editing under various titles until 1915. He appears to have established some sort of a record as an itinerant officeseeker, having been Socialist candidate for the House of Commons, from Manchester, England, in 1894, candidate for the Canadian Parliament in 1902, and candidate for Congress from New York in 1904. He died in New York City. His writings include *Socialism Inevitable,* New York, [1907].

WILSON, CALVIN DILL (July 12, 1857–April 28, 1946), clergyman, born in Baltimore, Md., was pastor of Presbyterian churches in Franklin, 1893–1903, and Glendale, 1903–32. After his retirement he continued to live in Glendale. He edited a book of Bible stories for children in 1896. He wrote other books for children, poetry, and religious discussions, e.g., *The Divine Religion of Humanity,* Philadelphia, 1902. WWW 2

WILSON, EARL (May 3, 1907–   ), journalist, was born in Rockford, Mercer County. He spent two years at Heidelberg College and graduated from Ohio State University in 1931. He became night-club editor and columnist for the New York *Post* in 1942 and has published several books, e.g., *Pikes Peek or Bust,* New York, 1946. He assisted in the writing of the autobiography of his fellow Ohioan, the animal trainer, Clyde Beatty, born in Bainbridge in 1905: *Jungle Performers,* New York, [1941]. WW 30

WILSON, EDWARD STANSBURY (Oct. 6, 1841–Dec. 18, 1919), journalist, was born in Newark, Licking County. He served in the Civil War, 1862–65, with the 91st O.V.I. He was owner and editor of the Ironton *Register,* 1865–99, U. S. marshall in Puerto Rico, 1900–05, and editor of the *Ohio State Journal,* 1905–19.

An Oriental Outing . . ., Cincinnati, 1894.
Keynotes of Education . . ., Cincinnati, 1898.
Political Development of Porto Rico, Columbus, 1905.
The Poetry of Eating . . ., Columbus, 1908.

WILSON, MRS. E. GRAHAM. See Edna E. C. Spencer.

WILSON, ELLA GRANT (Sept. 7, 1854–Dec. 16, 1939), florist, born in Jersey City, N. J., was brought to Cleveland when she was six years old. She operated a florist's shop and was widely known in Cleveland as a floral arranger, decorating homes for weddings and other occasions. She was garden editor of the *Plain Dealer,* 1918–24. She wrote *Famous Old Euclid Avenue of Cleveland . . .*, [Cleveland], 1932.

WILSON, ERASMUS (June 10, 1842–Jan. 14, 1922), journalist, was born in Belmont County. He served in the Civil War with the 98th O.V.I., and after the war he wrote for several newspapers in Pittsburgh, where he made his home until his death. The first book below is made up of articles that originally appeared in the Pittsburgh *Dispatch.*

Quiet Observations on the Ways of the World, New York, 1886.
Standard History of Pittsburgh . . ., (with Weston A. Goodspeed), Chicago, 1898.

WILSON, FRAZER ELLS (Sept. 10, 1871–July 17, 1958), merchant and historian, was born in Dallas (Ansonia), Darke County. He settled in Greenville in 1873 and spent his entire life there except for a few years in Dayton. He operated a dry goods store in Greenville, 1892–1937, and made history his avocation. In 1901 he helped to found the Greenville museum and served for some time as its curator. He wrote his first book on the occasion of the centennial of the Treaty of Greenville, and wrote another for the sesquicentennial. He died in Dayton.

The Treaty of Greenville . . ., Piqua, 1894.
The Peace of Mad Anthony, Greenville, [1909].
History of Darke County . . ., 2 vols., Milford, 1914.
Advancing the Ohio Frontier . . ., Blanchester, 1937.
Arthur St. Clair . . ., Richmond, [Va., 1944].
Around the Council Fire . . ., Greenville, 1945.
Fort Jefferson, the Frontier Post of the Upper Miami Valley . . ., [Greenville?, 1950].

WILSON, GILBERT LIVINGSTONE (1868–June 9, 1930), was born in Clifton, Clark

County. He graduated from Wittenberg College in 1896 and also attended Princeton Theological Seminary and the University of Minnesota. At the time of his death he lived in St. Paul, Minn. For the American Museum of Natural History, he conducted research among the Mandan Indians of North Dakota. His writings include *Myths of the Red Children . . .*, Boston, 1907.

WILSON, GROVE (Dec. 6, 1883–Oct. 11, 1954), journalist and editor, was born in Greenville, Darke County, and attended public schools there. He worked on newspapers in Minnesota, Maryland, and New York, and was on the editorial staff of *Popular Science Monthly* and other magazines. He wrote several novels, e.g., *Sport of the Gods . . .*, New York, 1926, and a biography of Jane Welsh Carlyle: *Temperamental Jane . . .*, New York, 1931. WWW 3

WILSON, HENRY H. (Jan. 1, 1854–June 28, 1941), lawyer, was born in Sandusky County and attended Bryan Academy before moving to Lincoln, Neb., where he practiced law and taught at the University of Nebraska. Charles T. Fairfield edited Wilson's *Occasional Addresses . . .*, Lincoln, Neb., 1929. WWW 1

WILSON, JOHN ALFRED (July 25, 1832–March 28, 1904), was born near Worthington, Franklin County. When he was seventeen, he moved with his father to a farm near Haskins, Wood County, and, except for his war service, he spent the rest of his life in that area. A member of the 21st O.V.I., he took part in the Andrews Raid, when 22 volunteers, a number of them from northwest Ohio, attempted to destroy the rail line between Marietta, Ga., and Chattanooga, Tenn. The raiders stole a Confederate locomotive; when it ran out of fuel, they were captured and imprisoned. Wilson later escaped from prison and made his way to Key West, Fla. He was discharged for disability in 1864 and after the war operated a store in Perrysburg; his death occurred in that community.

Adventures of Alf Wilson . . ., Toledo, 1880.

WILSON, JOHN BYERS (1857–June 29, 1929), physician, was born in Adams County. After graduating from Ohio Medical College, he practiced in Cincinnati for 45 years. As an avocation he wrote poetry, some in rustic dialect, which was collected in *Reminiscent Rhymes and Other Verse*, [Cincinnati, 1911].

WILSON, JOSEPH G. (June 23, 1874–Feb. 2, 1957), physician, was born in Guernsey County. After graduating from the University of Pennsylvania Medical School in 1898, he served in the Spanish-American War, after which he practiced medicine until 1906. In 1906 he joined the U. S. Public Health Service. After 1930 he specialized in psychiatric treatment of Federal prisoners. He wrote several books on prison problems, e.g., *Are Prisons Necessary?*, Philadelphia, [1950]. WWW 3

WILSON, JOSHUA LACY (Sept. 22, 1774–Aug. 14, 1846), clergyman, born in Bedford County, Va., grew up in Kentucky, where he was ordained to the Presbyterian ministry in 1804. In 1808 he was called to the First Presbyterian Church, Cincinnati, and preached there for the remainder of his life. A conservative Calvinist, he engaged in many controversies and led the prosecution of Lyman Beecher (q.v.) for heresy. He published sermons in addition to the pamphlets listed below.

Episcopal Methodism; Or, Dagonism Exhibited . . ., Cincinnati, 1811.

Four Propositions Sustained against the Claims of the American Home Missionary Society, New York, 1831.

The Faith Kept . . ., Cincinnati, 1835.

One Proposition Sustained against the New School, Cincinnati, 1835.

Plea . . . on the Trial of Dr. Beecher, for Dangerous Errors, Cincinnati, 1837.

Relations and Duties of Servants & Masters, Cincinnati, 1839.

WILSON, LAWRENCE (Sept. 2, 1842–June 22, 1922), was born in Southington, Trumbull County. He attended district schools and Calkin's Commercial College, Oberlin. He enlisted as a private in the 7th O.V.I. in June, 1861, rose to the rank of first sergeant, and after being wounded three times was discharged in July, 1864, for physical disability. After the war he worked in the U. S. Treasury Department and the Department of the Interior. He wrote a book that Ryan describes as one of the best Ohio regimental histories: *Itinerary of the Seventh Ohio Volunteer Infantry . . .*, New York, 1907.

WILSON, MILTON LEROY (Dec. 10, 1828–Dec. 1, 1909), journalist, was born in Thornville, Perry County. He published the *American Tribune* and other newspapers in Newark and a Swedenborgian Sunday

School paper, the *Monthly Voice.* In 1863 he published some early pieces by Mary H. Catherwood (q.v.), whose biography he later wrote: *Biography of Mary Hartwell Catherwood,* Newark, 1904.

WILSON, OBED JAY (Aug. 30, 1826–Aug. 31, 1914), publisher, was born in Bingham, Maine. He came to Cincinnati in 1846, taught school for a time, and read law. He became a book agent and later a partner in Sargent, Wilson, and Hinkle, publishers of the McGuffey Readers and other textbooks. After retiring in 1877 he traveled widely in Europe, Asia, and Africa.

A Visit to the Alhambra, Cincinnati, [n.d.].

WILSON, RACHEL MACK (c.1888–July 3, 1961), born in Illinois, lived in Cleveland from 1909 to 1935. Wife of Sidney Wilson, Cleveland industrialist, she published poems in the Cleveland *Plain Dealer* and in national periodicals. In 1932 she founded the Ohio Poetry Society. She died in Louisville, Ky., at the home of her son. Her collections of verse include *The Sacred Acre,* New York, 1928.

WILSON, ROBERT FORREST (Jan. 20, 1883–May 9, 1942), was born in Warren, Trumbull County. He served as a correspondent for newspapers in Cleveland and elsewhere. With Benedict Crowell (q.v.) he wrote a six-volume history of World War I. He also wrote a life of Harriet Beecher Stowe: *Crusader in Crinoline . . . ,* Philadelphia, [1941]. WWW 2

WILSON, SAMUEL RAMSEY (June 4, 1818–March 3, 1886), clergyman, was born in Cincinnati, Hamilton County. He graduated from Hanover College in 1836 and Princeton Theological Seminary in 1840. He preached at Presbyterian churches in Cincinnati and Louisville, Ky. Sympathetic to the Southern cause throughout the Civil War and during Reconstruction, he became spokesman for those who entertained similar views and defended his stand with great brilliance. A number of his sermons and addresses were published separately in pamphlet form.

Twelfth Street Graveyard and First Presbyterian Church, [Cincinnati, 1858].

WILSON, THOMAS (July 18, 1832–May 4, 1902), lawyer and archaeologist, born in New Brighton, Pa., was apprenticed to a carriage-maker in Salem, Columbiana County, for two years. Later, after reading law in Iowa, he practiced in Marietta for a short time. In Washington, D. C., he was the law partner of Thomas Corwin (q.v.). He was intensely interested in prehistoric man and served as curator of archaeology in the Smithsonian Institution, 1887–1902. He published a number of articles in the *Ohio Archaeological and Historical Quarterly* which were also issued in pamphlet form, e.g., *The Arkansas Traveller,* Columbus, 1900.

WILSON, WILLIAM (Dec. 25, 1803–Dec. 9, 1873), clergyman, was born in Donegal, Ireland. He came to the United States in 1823, graduated from Union College in 1827, and was licensed to preach by the Reformed Presbyterian Church in 1831. Around 1838 he was sent to Cincinnati as a domestic missionary, and he spent the rest of his life in that city.

Protest against the General Synod of the Reformed Presbyterian Church, Cincinnati, 1850.

WINCHESTER, MARIE MOON (May 31, 1897–), was born in Jeffersonville, Fayette County. After graduating from London High School, she attended Ward-Belmont College, Nashville, Tenn. She married James M. Winchester, and now lives in London, Madison County. Her poems have appeared in various periodicals and anthologies, and she has published a collection of verse: *Other Worlds Are Empty,* New York, [1941].

WINDSOR, ANTHONY H. (Sept. 18, 1837–July 14, 1912), clergyman, was born in New York. He served as a chaplain in the 91st O.V.I., April, 1864–June, 1865, and after the Civil War served churches in Ohio. His death occurred in Logan County.

History of the Ninety-first Regiment, O.V.I., Cincinnati, 1865.

WINE, MARY STONER (Aug. 11, 1885–May 1, 1959), was born near Ladoga, Ind. She graduated from Manchester College in 1910 and was married to Grover L. Wine. She moved to Ohio in 1940 and from 1946 until her death lived in Covington, Miami County. Author of many hymns and poems, she published two collections of verse, e.g., *Patchwork and Rhythm,* Elgin, Ill., [1949].

WING, CONWAY PHELPS (Feb. 12, 1809–May 7, 1889), clergyman, was born near Marietta, Washington County. He graduated from Hamilton College in 1828 and Auburn Seminary in 1831, was ordained to the Presbyterian ministry, and served various churches in western New York, Alabama, and Carlisle, Pa. Besides the titles below, he published several genealogical works.

History of the Presbyteries of Donegal and Carlisle, Carlisle, Pa., 1876.

A History of the First Presbyterian Church of Carlisle, Pa., Carlisle, Pa., 1877.

History of Cumberland County, Pennsylvania . . . , Philadelphia, 1879.

WING, JOSEPH ELWYN (Sept. 14, 1861–Sept. 10, 1915), agriculturist, was born in Hinsdale, N. Y. When he was six years old, his family settled on a small farm near Mechanicsburg. He worked on the farm and in 1889 took over its management. His success in raising alfalfa and sheep soon attracted widespread attention, and he lectured extensively on farming and contributed numerous articles to agricultural journals. His *Alfalfa Farming in America* (1909) was recognized as an authoritative book. He died in Marion. Besides three books on agriculture, he wrote *In Foreign Fields; Sketches of Travel in South America and Western Europe,* Chicago, 1913. DAB 20

WING, MARJORIE MEEKER (Nov. 5, 1893–), was born in Bradford, England, where her father, Claude Meeker, was serving as U. S. consul. She grew up in Columbus and graduated from Columbus School for Girls in 1911. She married Shirley T. Wing and published a collection of verse under her married name: *Color of Water,* New York, 1928. Now Mrs. Vivian Collins, she lives in St. Augustine, Fla.

WINGET, DeWITT HARRIS (Feb. 22, 1850–Feb. 5, 1933), was born in Marysville, Union County. Around 1859 his family moved to Kansas, and he grew up there. Under the name Dan Winget, he published a book about his friend William F. Cody: *Anecdotes of Buffalo Bill . . . ,* Clinton, Iowa, 1912.

WINK, JOSH. Pseud. See Wilbur D. Nesbit.

WINTER, NEVIN OTTO (June 14, 1869–Sept. 2, 1936), lawyer and journalist, was born in Benton, Holmes County. He graduated from Ohio Wesleyan University in 1891 and the law school of Ohio State University in 1897. After being admitted to the bar in 1897, he began practice in Toledo. He also traveled widely for several newspapers and a syndicate and lectured on foreign affairs. He died in Galion. He wrote a number of travel books, e.g., *Mexico and Her People of Today . . . ,* Boston, 1907. He also wrote *A History of Northwest Ohio . . . ,* 3 vols., Chicago, 1917. WWW 1

WINTERMUTE, MARTHA VAN DEMARK (Sept. 6, 1841–Jan. 1, 1918), was born in Berkshire, Delaware County. She graduated from Ohio Wesleyan University in 1861. After her marriage to Dr. Alfred Wintermute, she lived near Newark. She wrote and lectured for women's suffrage and temperance and has been described by a descendant as a "ladylike crusader." She contributed much verse to Ohio periodicals. Her death occurred at her home near Newark. Her only book was privately published.

Eleven Women and Thirteen Men, Newark, 1887.

WIRRIES, MARY MABEL (Jan. 14, 1894–), born in South Bend, Ind., lived in Wood County for a number of years. Her last address in Ohioana files is Phoenix, Ariz. She has published poetry: *Gay Witch April and Other Poems,* [Tucson, Ariz., 1936], and a number of novels for young readers, e.g., *Mary Rose at Boarding School,* Cincinnati, 1924. AATB

WISE, ISAAC MAYER (March 29, 1819–March 26, 1900), rabbi and founder of Reform Judaism, was born in Steingrub, Bohemia. His resolution, he wrote in his autobiographical *Meine Bücherei,* was "never to torture humanity with a book; if at all possible, [he] would never write one." This is, to say the least, a rather astonishing statement when one considers the many volumes, not to mention innumerable sermons, essays, book reviews, and editorials that poured from his pen. It was a pen as active as it professed to be reluctant. "I was forced to act contrary to my resolve," he declared. "I had to write . . . often without desire and against my conviction." Founder and editor of two weekly newspapers—the English language *Israelite* (still published today in Cincinnati as *The American Israelite*) and the German language *Die Deborah*—playwright, novelist, historian, pedagogue, theologian, liturgist, polemicist, Wise never permitted his literary diffidence to inhibit his literary energies. Perhaps even more remarkable is the fact that at least one of his productions, *Reminiscences,* deserves to be numbered among the literary classics of nineteenth-century American Jewry. For this spiritual heir of the French Revolution and its attendant, if hotly contested, emancipation of Western and Central European Jewry, writing was neither a genteel avocation nor a function of scholarship. It was a sword—wielded now gracefully, now clumsily, but ever energetically, in his struggle to establish in America a liberal, progressive Judaism, an *American* Judaism which, though not antipathetic to the age-old Jewish tradition of Old World provenance, should be warmly responsive to the changing needs and splendid promise of Jewish life in the United States. Hardly a littérateur in the usual sense of the word, Wise was, none the less, certainly among the most effective writers ever to put pen to paper in American Jewish annals. All of present-day America's 5,000,000 Jews, not only the 1,000,000 Reform Jews who today own themselves his followers, are in his debt. The sense of goal and purpose, the capacity for organized endeavor characteristic of the various facets of the American Jewish community today—these testify to the effect of Isaac Mayer Wise's pen. Who was this man whose works were such that he is easily to be accounted the most distinguished American Jewish personality of the nineteenth century and indeed one of America's outstanding religious leaders? Isaac Mayer Wise was not a native American; born in Hapsburg-dominated Bohemia, he was well acquainted with the antiliberal, Judeophobic spirit that reigned in Central Europe after the fall of Napoleon. A rebel by nature, he was not content to remain forever an imperial-royal *Schutzjude,* a second-class subject of the bigoted Hapsburg monarchy. After a brief rabbinical tenure in Radnitz, Bohemia, he emigrated to the United States in 1846. Not long after his arrival in New York, he was elected rabbi of Albany's Congregation Beth El, where, with little delay but with much opposition, he commenced the task of religious reform. The reformist ideas he had imbibed in Europe soon aroused the ire of a number of his tradition-minded Albany congregants. His insistence on departures from the traditional norm, which he felt to be anomalous in America, won him some friends but more enemies. Wise would write in later years that "the desire to reform the world is a sickness which some people cannot avoid; it is part and parcel of their spiritual make-up. . . . They are the poorly paid servants of Providence . . . that any and every wretch may make the object of pursuit; but they must, because otherwise mankind would become stupid, stagnate, and decay." This applied in particular, he believed, to Judaism whose future in America was to be assured only by its becoming "reconciled with the spirit of the age and the opinions prevalent in the new fatherland." To secure that future, Wise was prepared to brave obloquy, charges of heresy, threats of excommunication, and the loss of his Albany pulpit. Controversy continued to embitter his ministry at the Beth El Congregation until that position became untenable. By 1850, however, he had gained enough support in Albany to establish a new congregation, a Reform synagogue called *Anshe Emet* (Men of Truth). It was his first substantial victory. As the early 1850s dawned, Wise's reputation spread far beyond the confines of Albany. His writings in journals like the *Asmonean,* a weekly Jewish newspaper published in New York by Robert Lyons, increasingly engaged the attention of his detractors and of his followers; and the publication of his rationalistic *History of the Israelitish Nation,* a bulky 600-page work which appeared in 1853, won praise from Boston's Unitarian preacher Theodore Parker and from Horace Greeley. Wise was particularly pleased, for "these two men were the only Americans known to [him] who were familiar with German philosophical literature." In 1854 Cincinnati's twelve-year-old Bene Jeshurun Congregation, whose "members were young South Germans, mostly from Bavaria, and belonged to the better element," unanimously elected him its rabbi for life; and Wise left Albany for the Queen City of the West, as burgeoning Cincinnati was known. There, on the banks of the Ohio, until his death 46 years later, the ardent reformer would find a warm response to his conviction that "we must be not only American citizens, but become Americans through and through, outside of the synagogue." True, at his new congregation "everything was still officially Orthodox, but the leaders of Orthodoxy were weak and . . . in a short time they even became [his] friends, for they found that [he] was not as bad as was [his] reputation." Wise had scarcely arrived in Cincinnati when he set about founding an organ for the propagation of his views. The establishment of *The Israelite* in 1854 and of *Die Deborah* a year later ensured him a substantial following among both the English-speaking and the German-speaking Jewish settlers of the Ohio and Mississippi Valleys. American Jewish life, on Wise's arrival in the United States, was a wilderness, but Wise could not rest content with that situation. He had not been the first to perceive American Jewry's need for higher religious and cultural standards and for organization on a nation-wide basis, but by dint of his own prodigious industry and the unifactory forces unleashed generally in American life at the conclusion of the Civil War, Wise was to achieve unprecedented success. In

1873, after two decades of laborious pleading and preaching, one of Wise's great dreams came close to fulfillment with the establishment under his inspiration of the Union of American Hebrew Congregations, today the great lay arm of American Reform Judaism. Two years later, in 1875, the Union established in Cincinnati under Wise's presidency the Hebrew Union College, America's first successful rabbinical seminary and now the scholastic center of American—and world—liberal Judaism. "No one who failed to see the embryonic college," Wise wrote in later years, "can imagine how ridiculous was this little hole-in-the-wall of a school, in its not-too-bright cellar [at Cincinnati's Bene Israel Temple], carrying the pompous name of a college . . . each evening the whole library was locked up in a two-and-one-half-foot box, not because of thieves, but because of mice." Wise was never discouraged, however, and at his death 25 years later there was no longer anything "ridiculous" about the growing Hebrew Union College, already recognized as one of American Jewry's major intellectual institutions. Another of Wise's fondest dreams came to fruition in 1889, when the alumni of the college and a number of other liberal rabbis joined to establish the Central Conference of American Rabbis. Wise's influence in this institution, too, was pre-eminent. Some of Wise's admirers have described him as a prophet. That he was not is clear from his unrelenting antagonism to the Biblical criticism, which has become an important concern of liberal Jewish scholarship and from his angry opposition to Zionism, today so potent a source of spiritual and philanthropic edification for American Jewry. It is apparent also in the fact that he was not particularly sympathetic to the East European immigrants whose sons and grandsons have since played so creative and productive a role in American life. As is often the case with great men, Wise cherished great prejudices. He was quite blind to the possibilities of Biblical criticism and of Zionism; he was unable to appreciate the potential value of the massive East European immigration of his day. No prophet, Wise *was* a pioneer, and if in the years that have followed his death prophets were able to arise in American Judaism, it is to Wise and his tireless pioneering efforts that the credit belongs in great measure. No significant sector of the American Jewish community—be it Reform, Conservative, or Orthodox—has remained unaffected by his work and his idealism.

Stanley F. Chyet

History of the Israelitish Nation . . . , Albany, N. Y., 1853.
The Essence of Judaism . . . , Cincinnati, 1861.
Hymns, Psalms & Prayers . . . , (with others), Cincinnati, [1868].
The Martyrdom of Jesus of Nazareth . . . , Cincinnati, [1874].
The Cosmic God . . . , Cincinnati, 1876.
History of the Hebrews' Second Commonwealth . . . , Cincinnati, 1880.
Selected Writings . . . , Cincinnati, 1900.
Reminiscences . . . , (David Philipson, ed. and trans.), Cincinnati, 1901.

WISE, JOSH. Pseud. See John W. Raper.

WISEMAN, CHARLES M. L. (Jan. 15, 1829–Feb. 27, 1904), was born near New Salem, Fairfield County. After teaching in district schools, he was a traveling book salesman for C. W. James of Cincinnati for four years. In 1855 he moved to Lancaster, where he was postmaster for thirteen years.

Centennial History of Lancaster . . . , Lancaster, 1898.
Pioneer Period and Pioneer People of Fairfield County . . . , Columbus, 1901.

WISH, HARVEY (Sept. 4, 1909–), educator, born in Chicago, has been professor of history at Western Reserve University since 1945. He has published several influential historical studies, e.g., *Contemporary America . . .* , New York, [1945]. WW 30

WISHARD, JOHN G. (Sept. 19, 1863–July 15, 1940), physician, born in Danville, Ind., lived and practiced in Wooster from 1910 until his death. He wrote articles and a book about Persia, where he was a medical missionary, 1899–1909, and an autobiographical work: *Reminiscences of a Doctor . . .* , [Wooster, 1935]. WWW 1

WISHART, CHARLES FREDERICK (Sept. 3, 1870–April 11, 1960), clergyman and educator, was born in Ontario, Richland County. After graduating from Monmouth College in 1894 and Pittsburgh Theological Seminary in 1897, he was ordained to the ministry of the United Presbyterian Church. He served churches in Pittsburgh, 1897–1910, and Chicago, 1914–19, was on the faculty of Pittsburgh Seminary, 1910–14, and was president of the College of Wooster, 1919–44. He published a number of books on religious and educational themes, e.g., *The Range Finders, a Message to the Ministry,* Philadelphia, 1921. WW 26

WISHART, JOHN ELLIOTT (Nov. 29, 1866–Dec. 23, 1940), Presbyterian clergyman and educator, brother of Charles F. Wishart (q.v.), was born in New Athens, Harrison County. He graduated from Monmouth College in 1889 and Allegheny Seminary in 1892. He served pastorates in various states and was on the faculty of Xenia Theological Seminary, 1905–23. His writings include *The Spirits of Just Men Made Perfect . . .*, Oberlin, [1916]. WWW 1

WITTENMYER, ANNIE TURNER (Aug. 26, 1827–Feb. 2, 1900), was born in Sandy Springs, Adams County. She married William Wittenmyer in 1847 and three years later moved to Keokuk, Iowa. She worked with the Sanitary Commission during the Civil War and was a nurse with Iowa troops. After the war she lectured and wrote in behalf of temperance and women's rights. Frances Willard wrote an introduction for the first volume below, and Mrs. U. S. Grant wrote an introduction for the second.

History of the Woman's Christian Temperance Crusade . . ., Boston, 1882.
Under the Guns . . ., Boston, 1895.

WITTKE, CARL FREDERICK (Nov. 13, 1892–), educator, was born in Columbus, Franklin County. He graduated from Ohio State University in 1913 and Harvard University (Ph.D.) in 1921. He served on the Ohio State University history faculty, 1916–37, and the Oberlin College faculty, 1937–48. Since 1948 he has been dean of the Western Reserve University Graduate School. He has written numerous historical articles, edited a five-volume history of Ohio (1941-44), and published a number of significant studies of American culture, e.g., *Tambo and Bones; A History of the American Minstrel Stage*, Durham, N. C., 1930. WW 30

WOELLNER, FREDRIC PHILIP (Feb. 18, 1890–), educator, was born in Cincinnati, Hamilton County. He graduated from the University of Cincinnati in 1912 and Columbia University (Ph.D.) in 1923. He taught in the Cincinnati schools, 1912–14, and at Buffalo State Teachers College, 1915–21. He served on the education faculty of the University of California at Los Angeles, 1925–56. A prolific writer, he published numerous articles, textbooks, and other books on various subjects, e.g., *The Highlands of the Mind; A Psychological Analysis of the Sermon on the Mount*, Pasadena, Calif., 1930. WW 30

WOLDMAN, ALBERT ALEXANDER (Jan. 1, 1897–), lawyer, born in Russia, was brought to America when he was one year old. He graduated from Western Reserve University in 1917 and from the law school in 1918. He worked on the Cleveland *Press* and on the *Plain Dealer*, 1917–19, was admitted to the Ohio bar and began practice in 1919, began teaching at John Marshall Law School in 1936, and since 1953 has been judge of the Cuyahoga County juvenile court. He has published several books, e.g., *Lawyer Lincoln*, Boston, 1936. WW 30

WOLF, EDITH ANISFIELD (Aug. 2, 1889–), was born in Cleveland, Cuyahoga County. She graduated from Western Reserve University and also studied at the Cleveland School of Art. Her poems have appeared in various newspapers and magazines and in several collections, e.g., *Balance; A Bookful of Little Thoughts*, Cleveland, 1942. BDCP

WOLF, HOWARD (Aug. 3, 1902–Aug. 4, 1955), journalist, was born in Akron, Summit County. He worked on the Cleveland *News* and on the editorial staff of the Akron *Beacon-Journal*. At the time of his death he was an advertising executive in Columbus. Besides a book on the rubber industry, he wrote in collaboration with his wife, Gertrude A. Wolf, a collection of poems: *The World, the Flesh, and the Holy Ghosts*, Caldwell, Idaho, 1933.

WOLF, MORRIS HERBERT (1888–), lawyer, born in Russia, came to Cleveland when he was eighteen and, since being admitted to the bar, has practiced in that city. He wrote a trilogy of novels, the first of which was *Hank Miller*, New York, [1928].

WOLF, SIMON (Oct. 28, 1836–June 4, 1923), lawyer, born in Bavaria, was brought to America in 1848. He worked for an uncle at Uhrichsville for a time, studied law, and was graduated from Ohio Law College, Cleveland, in 1861. He practiced for a year in New Philadelphia and then moved to Washington, D. C., where he spent the remainder of his life. He knew every President from Lincoln to Harding, and worked actively to persuade each of them to protect the rights of Jewish minorities throughout the world. He was also active in philanthropic organizations. He wrote many articles in periodicals, and several books and pamphlets, e.g., *Mordecai Manuel Noah: A Biographical Sketch*, Philadelphia, 1897. A collection of his addresses and papers was published posthumously in 1926.

WOLFE, ALBERT BENEDICT (Aug. 23, 1876–), educator, born in Arlington, Ill., was on the Oberlin College faculty, 1907–14. After teaching at the University of Texas, 1914–23, he returned to Ohio as a member of the department of economics, Ohio State University, 1923–46. Since his retirement he has continued to live in Columbus. His writings include *Conservatism, Radicalism, and Scientific Method . . .*, New York, 1923. WW 25

WOLFE, HENRY CUTLER (Jan. 11, 1898–), journalist, was born in Newcomerstown, Tuscarawas County. He served with an American ambulance unit in Italy in 1918, was with the American Relief Administration in Russia in 1922, and with the International Red Cross mission to Greece in 1923. He has written and lectured widely on international relations. During the 1930s he wrote a regular feature, "The European Scene," for the Columbus *Sunday Dispatch*. He has published several books on foreign relations, e.g., *The German Octopus; Hitler Bids for World Power*, New York, 1938. WW 30

WOLFE, NAPOLEON BONAPARTE (Dec. 25, 1823– ?), physician, was born in Columbia, Pa. As a young man he taught school, worked as a plasterer and as a printer, and in 1842 began to study medicine. After practicing in Pennsylvania and in St. Louis, Mo., he settled in Cincinnati in 1857. He published two technical works on respiratory diseases, his medical specialty. A believer in spiritualism, he wrote in the book below about his experiences with mediums.

Startling Facts in Modern Spiritualism, Cincinnati, 1874.

WOLFE, ROLLAND EMERSON (Feb. 25, 1902–), educator, was born in Hartville, Stark County. He graduated from Manchester College, Ind., in 1924, from Oberlin Seminary in 1928, and from Harvard University (Ph.D.) in 1933. He served as pastor of Congregational churches in Ohio and Massachusetts, 1926–39, was on the faculty of Tufts College, 1934–46, and has been on the faculty of Western Reserve University since 1946. He has published a number of articles and books on religious themes, e.g., *Meet Amos and Hosea . . .*, New York, [1945]. WW 30

WOLFE, WILLIAM G. (Feb. 26, 1874–Nov. 13, 1947), educator, was born and reared in Quaker City, Guernsey County. He attended Ohio Northern University, taught school in Quaker City, and was superintendent of the Guernsey County schools, 1914–35. Altogether, he spent 43 years in educational work. He published *Stories of Guernsey County . . .*, Cambridge, 1943.

WOLFENSTEIN, MARTHA (Aug. 5, 1869–March, 1906), was born in Insterberg, Prussia, but was brought to America as a small child and lived until 1878 in St. Louis, Mo., where her father was a rabbi. In 1878 he became superintendent of the Jewish Orphan Asylum, Cleveland, and she spent the remainder of her life in that city. She published at least two collections of stories, e.g., a book about Jewish life in an Austrian village: *Idylls of the Gass*, Philadelphia, [1901].

WOOD, AARON (Oct. 15, 1802– ?), clergyman, born in Virginia, was brought to southern Ohio in 1805. He served as an itinerant Methodist minister in Ohio, Indiana, and Illinois until he was 23, after which he lived in Indiana. Besides the pamphlet below, some of his addresses and sermons were published.

Sketches of Things and Peoples in Indiana . . ., Indianapolis, 1883.

WOOD, CHARLES SEELY (April 19, 1845–Nov. 20, 1912), clergyman, was born in Cincinnati, Hamilton County. After graduating from Miami University in 1866, he was ordained to the Presbyterian ministry and served until 1876, when he retired because of ill health. He died in Urbana.

Alice and Her Two Friends, Philadelphia, 1896.

On the Frontier with St. Clair . . ., Boston, [1902].

The Sword of Wayne . . ., Boston, [1903].

Camp-fires on the Scioto . . ., Boston, 1905.

Christmas at Big Moose Falls, Boston, [1911].

"Don't Give Up the Ship!", New York, 1912.

WOOD, DAVID WESLEY (Sept. 11, 1844–Nov. 24, 1922), lawyer, was born in Pleasant Township, Knox County. He enlisted in the 20th O.V.I. at Columbus in Sept., 1861, and served until July, 1865. After the war he lived in Mount Vernon until 1880. He practiced law in Chicago and Washington, D. C. He died in Pocatello, Idaho.

History of the 20th O.V.V.I. Regiment . . ., Columbus, 1876.

WOOD, ESTHER (1905–), born in Akron, N. Y., lived in Mansfield for about fifteen years. Her address in 1951 was Upper Montclair, N. J. She has written a number of books for younger readers, e.g., *Belinda Blue,* New York, [1940]. JBA

WOOD, EUGENE (March 11, 1860–Feb. 25, 1923), was born near Bellefontaine, Logan County. He attended Ohio Wesleyan University, 1876–80. His writings include *Back Home,* New York, 1905. WWW 1

WOOD, FRANCIS MARION (June 23, 1834–April 11, 1911), clergyman, was born in Fairton, N. J. After graduating from Princeton University in 1858 and from the seminary in 1861, he was ordained to the Presbyterian ministry. He served several churches in Ohio, including the church at Carlisle, Warren County, 1862–68, a history of which he wrote. He later served in North Dakota and as a missionary in South Africa.

The New Jersey Church . . . , Cincinnati, 1868.

WOOD, FREDERICK MARCUS (Oct. 19, 1872–Sept. 26, 1952), educator, was born in Cincinnati, Hamilton County. After graduating from Western Reserve University in 1897, he taught in the secondary schools of Lake County for many years. He published a book of memories of his college days: *In the Consulship of Plancus,* Painesville, 1941, and also a book of verse: *Rhythmically Speaking,* Painesville, 1945.

WOOD, GEORGE L. (1837–Sept. 14, 1867), lawyer, was born in Chardon, Geauga County. He read law in Warren and practiced there after his admission to the bar. He served in the 7th O.V.I. until discharged as a result of a wound received at Port Republic, Va., June 9, 1862. In 1864 he enlisted in the 125th O.V.I. and served until the end of the war.

The Seventh Regiment: A Record, New York, 1865.

WOOD, JAMES CRAVEN (Jan. 11, 1858–Aug. 29, 1948), gynecologist, was born in Wood County. He graduated from Ohio Wesleyan University and the University of Michigan, served on the faculty of the University of Michigan Homeopathic Medical College, 1885–94, and later practiced in Cleveland while serving on the faculty of Cleveland-Pulte Medical College. He wrote numerous medical articles and textbooks; a play, *Then and Now;* and an autobiography, *An Old Doctor of the New School,* Caldwell, Idaho, 1942. WWW 2

WOOD, SHERIDAN FRANZELL (July 16, 1867–), clergyman, was born in Guernsey County. He became a minister in 1889 and served churches in McConnelsville, Akron, Youngstown, and Cleveland. In 1942 he was living near Wooster. He published a book of verse: *Blossoms from the Clay,* [West Lafayette, 1917], and a novel about the Civil War: *Creston Meadows; A Story of Love and Daring,* Philadelphia, [1927].

WOOD-ALLEN, MARY (Oct. 19, 1841–1908), physician, was born in Delta, Fulton County. She graduated from Ohio Wesleyan University in 1861, studied medicine in Austria, and graduated in medicine from the University of Michigan in 1875. She practiced in Newark, N. J., and was active in the work of the W.C.T.U. Many of her books and leaflets were published by the Wood-Allen Publishing Co., Ann Arbor, Mich. She wrote a number of pamphlets in the "American Motherhood" series and other booklets relating to sex instruction, not all of which are listed below.

Almost a Man, Ann Arbor, [1895].

The Marvels of our Bodily Dwelling . . . , Ann Arbor, 1895.

Almost a Woman, Ann Arbor, [1897].

What a Young Girl Ought to Know, Philadelphia, 1897.

Baby's Firsts, Ann Arbor, [1898].

What a Young Woman Ought to Know, Philadelphia, [1898].

Marriage, Its Duties and Privileges . . . , Chicago, 1901.

WOODHULL, VICTORIA C. See Victoria C. W. Martin.

WOODMAN, JAY JOSHUA (April 14, 1871–June 18, 1945), was born on a farm near Orangeville, Mich. After spending several years in California, he settled in Napoleon, Henry County, where he spent the remainder of his life. He was a building contractor and collected Indian relics as a hobby. He lectured on Indians and wrote a book: *Indian Legends . . . ,* Boston, 1924.

WOODMANSEE, JAMES (1814–Dec. 1887), was born on a farm in Liberty Township, Butler County. Except for a few months with a company of actors in Louisville, Ky., he spent his entire life on the farm. An eccentric who called himself "the Bard of Sugar Valley," he published a volume containing the first six books of a projected volume to be entitled *Religion: A Poem in Twelve Books.* At the end of the first book appears the query "Does the World want the other Six Books?" Since the other six books were never published, we must assume that the World had seen enough.

The Closing Scene; A Vision . . . , Cincinnati, 1857.

Wrinkles; From the Brow of Experience, and Other Poems, Cincinnati, 1860.

WOODROW, NANCY MANN WADDEL (1870–Sept. 7, 1935), was born in Chillicothe, Ross County. In 1900 she moved to New York City and contributed verse and fiction to various national magazines. She died in New York City and is buried in Chillicothe. Often using the pen names Jane Wade and Mrs. Wilson Woodrow, she published a number of novels, e.g., *The Beauty,* Indianapolis, [1910]. WWW 1

WOODROW, MRS. WILSON. See Nancy M. W. Woodrow.

WOODS, HENRY McKEE (Aug. 14, 1857–Dec. 2, 1943), clergyman, was born in Columbus, Franklin County. After graduating from Union Theological Seminary in Virginia, he was ordained to the Presbyterian ministry. He served as a missionary in China, 1883–1925, and after his return to the United States, he lived in Ventnor, N. J. He edited *A Chinese Bible Encyclopedia,* published numerous articles, and wrote a book contrasting Protestantism and Roman Catholicism: *Our Priceless Heritage,* London, [1934].

WOODS, JOSEPH THATCHER (March 16, 1828–Aug. 5, 1911), physician, was born in Columbiana County of a pioneer family. In 1835 his father moved to Portage County, where Joseph was reared on the family farm. He was largely self-educated, except for study under local physicians, until he went to the University of Michigan, 1853–55. After his graduation he practiced medicine in Williamstown, Hancock County. He volunteered as a surgeon in 1862 and served with the 96th O.V.I. throughout the war. After practicing three years in Findlay, he moved to Toledo, where he practiced for the remainder of his life.

Services of the Ninety-sixth Ohio Volunteers, Toledo, 1874.

Steedman and his Men at Chickamauga, Toledo, 1876.

The Exile of the Acadians, the People of Longfellow's 'Evangeline,' Toledo, 1887.

WOODS, PERRY DANIEL (Jan. 30, 1881–Jan. 9, 1950), educator, was born in Piqua, Miami County. He graduated from Denison University in 1905, Colgate-Rochester Divinity School in 1926, and the University of Oregon (Ph.D.) in 1932. He taught in Puerto Rico and at several universities, including Rio Grande College, 1919–27, and Ohio State University, 1927–29. After 1929 he lived in Oregon. He wrote *The First Fifty Years of Rio Grande College,* [Gallipolis, 1926]. DAS 1

WOODS, VIRNA (April 26, 1864–March 6, 1903), was born in Wilmington, Clinton County, but when she was two years old her parents moved to Zanesville, where she was reared and educated. In 1883 she went to California. She used California materials for the local color of the verse and stories which she contributed to various periodicals. She died in Sacramento, Calif.

The Amazons; A Lyrical Drama, Meadville, Pa., 1891.

A Modern Magdalene, Boston, 1894.

An Elusive Lover, New York, 1898.

WOODWARD, MARY CROOK SLOAN (July 3, 1833–Aug. 16, 1916), was born in Lycoming County, Pa., but was brought to Montgomery County when three years old. She was married, Nov. 11, 1856, to Samuel Franklin Woodward, a prosperous farmer of Osborn, Greene County. She began writing poetry around 1880 and afterward published two collections.

Roses and Thorns, Dayton, 1894.

Darkness and Dawn, Dayton, 1903.

WOODWARD, ROBERT CHRISTIE (June 3, 1829–July 24, 1896), librarian, was born in Springfield, Clark County, and passed his entire life in that community. He was librarian of Warder Public Library for many years.

Sketches of Springfield, Springfield, 1852.

WOODWARD, S. M. Pseud. See Miles W. Smith.

WOOLLEY, CELIA PARKER (June 14, 1848–March 9, 1918), was born in Toledo, Lucas County, but while she was a child her parents moved to Michigan. In 1868 she married Dr. J. H. Woolley, and they moved to Chicago in 1876. She was Chicago correspondent of the *Christian Register* for eight years and served as president of the Chicago Woman's Club. She also was pastor of the Unitarian Church at Geneva, Ill., 1893–96.

Love and Theology; A Novel, Boston, 1887.

A Girl Graduate, New York, 1889.

Roger Hunt, New York, 1892.

The Western Slope, Evanston, 1903.
The Angel at the Gate . . . , [Chicago], 1919.

WOOLLEY, JOHN GRANVILLE (Feb. 15, 1850–Aug. 13, 1922), lawyer and prohibitionist, was born in Collinsville, Butler County. He graduated from Ohio Wesleyan University in 1871 and from the University of Michigan law school in 1873. He practiced law in Paris, Ill., Minneapolis, Minn., and New York City. A confirmed drunkard, he suddenly reformed in 1888, and from that time until his death he devoted himself to the cause of prohibition. He lectured against liquor in many parts of the world, ran for President on the Prohibition ticket in 1900, and edited the *New Voice,* 1899–1906. Besides the titles below, many of his speeches and articles were reprinted in pamphlet form.

Seed Number One Hard; Six Speeches, New York, 1893.
The Christian Citizen, Chicago, [1900].
Temperance Progress in the Century, (with William E. Johnson), Philadelphia, 1903.
South Sea Letters, (with Mary V. Woolley), Chicago, 1906.
Civic Sermons, 8 vols., Westerville, 1911.

WOOLLEY, SOLOMON JACKSON (Jan. 12, 1828– ?), was born near Zanesville, Muskingum County. He moved to Hocking County at an early age. After traveling through southern Ohio selling books and clocks, he became a daguerreotypist and traveled to the lower Mississippi country; during the Civil War, he took pictures of Union troops in West Virginia. In 1858 he had acquired a farm near Hilliards, Franklin County, and in 1870 he settled there and conducted a factory for the manufacture of drain tile. He contributed numerous articles to agricultural publications, principally on the subject of drainage. His autobiography is not without interest, especially for its account of his travels in southern Ohio. The last third of the book is devoted to an account of litigation in which he had become involved.

Life Recollections and Opinions of Solomon Jackson Woolley. An Autobiography, Columbus, 1881.

WOOLSEY, SARAH CHAUNCEY (Jan. 29, 1835–April 9, 1905), was born in Cleveland, Cuyahoga County, and attended private schools there; she was also a student at Mrs. Hubbard's Boarding School, Hanover, N. H. When she was about twenty, her family moved to New Haven, Conn. She did hospital work during the Civil War. Around 1872 her family moved to Newport, R. I., where she lived for the rest of her life. She was one of the most popular juvenile writers of her day. Her pen name was Susan Coolidge.

The New-year's Bargain, Boston, 1872.
What Katy Did, Boston, 1872.
Mischief's Thanksgiving, and Other Stories, Boston, 1874.
What Katy Did at School, Boston, 1874.
Nine Little Goslings, Boston, 1875.
Eyebright, Boston, 1879.
Verses, Boston, 1880.
Cross Patch, and Other Stories . . . , Boston, 1881.
A Guernsey Lily . . . , Boston, 1881.
A Round Dozen, Boston, 1883.
A Little Country Girl, Boston, 1885.
What Katy Did Next, Boston, 1886.
A Short History of the City of Philadelphia . . . , Boston, 1887.
Clover, Boston, 1888.
A Few More Verses, Boston, 1889.
Just Sixteen, Boston, 1889.
For Summer Afternoons, Boston, 1890.
Verses, Boston, 1890.
In the High Valley . . . , Boston, 1891.
Rhymes and Ballads for Girls and Boys, Boston, 1892.
The Barberry Bush, and Eight Other Stories . . . , Boston, 1893.
Not Quite Eighteen, Boston, 1894.
An Old Convent School in Paris, and Other Papers, Boston, 1895.
Curly Locks, Boston, [1899].
A Little Knight of Labor, Boston, [1899].
Little Tommy Tucker, Boston, 1900.
Two Girls, Boston, [1900].
Little Bo-Peep, Boston, [1901].
Uncle and Aunt, Boston, [1901].
The Rule of Three, Philadelphia, [1904].
Last Verses, Boston, 1906.
A Sheaf of Stories, Boston, 1906.

WOOLSON, ABBA LOUISA GOOLD (April 30, 1838–Feb. 6, 1921), born in Windham, Maine, taught for a short time at Mount Auburn Ladies' Institute, Cincinnati. She wrote and lectured for women's rights and also published a number of essays and sketches, e.g., *Browsing among Books . . . ,* Boston, 1881.

WOOLSON, CONSTANCE FENIMORE (March 5, 1840–Jan. 24, 1894), was born in Claremont, N. H. A critic for the Boston *Globe* once suggested that she "may easily become the novelist laureate" of her period, a fanciful idea springing from Miss Woolson's wide range of diverse scenes. Between 1869 and 1894 she wrote nine volumes of fiction for adults, and she was extraordinarily sensitive to regional life extending from Mackinac to Florida. She was one of our earliest and most authentic "local colorists," writing of the Lake Superior country, Ohio, Virginia, the Blue Ridge, and the Deep South, both inland and along the eastern coast from Charleston to Florida. Later she became a transatlantic author, treating of Americans in Italy. Henry James admired her work, and William Dean Howells, when he turned against her, erred grievously. One volume of her short stories, *Castle Nowhere: Lake-Country Sketches* (1875), depicts the Wine Islands of Lake Erie, Separatists in northern Ohio, settlers in the St. Clair Flats, and the French, Indians, English, and Americans on the shores and islands of Lake Superior. Another, *Rodman the Keeper: Southern Sketches* (1880), illuminates lives and customs in the war-torn South and in Spanish Florida. Two volumes of short stories, *The Front Yard, and Other Italian Stories* (1895) and *Dorothy, and Other Italian Stories* (1896), spring from her observations of Americans in Italy. All of her five novels were written in Italy, but treat of life in the United States. *Anne* (1882), her first, is laid in Mackinac and New York; *For the Major* (1883), *East Angels* (1886), *Jupiter Lights* (1889), and *Horace Chase* (1894) bear largely on Southern life. *Jupiter Lights* contains some of her best writing, but *Horace Chase*—an account of a self-made man who marries a girl of a younger generation—is her highest achievement in long fiction. Miss Woolson was never married. Her fiction, though mostly of a woman's world, is not maternal. Her romantic heroines are not beautiful, but they possess distinction of character; her wives are frequently self-centered and greedy. She made close studies of widows, both young and old, of young wives too selfish to establish families, and of elder, unmarried sisters. Like Hawthorne and James, she delved in minds distorted by frustration; she was psychological in her approach, and she centered her attention on individuals. Her short stories exhibit her extraordinary power to fuse period, place, and character; they may be more enduring than her novels. Family sorrows determined Miss Woolson's far-flung residences. Her mother, a niece of James Fenimore Cooper, noted in her diary: ". . . in the early days of March [1840] came Number Six [Constance]. . . . When she was but two days old, scarlet fever appeared in the family, and in three short weeks, three of our dear little ones entered Paradise." Only Connie and the two eldest survived. The family moved to Cleveland, where Constance came under the literary influence of Miss Lucinda (Linda) Guilford (q.v.). She also attended Madame Chegary's school in New York City. In Cleveland both of her elder sisters died, and Constance—born sixth—became the eldest living child. Her father, a manufacturer and merchant, took his family on long vacations to the Lake Superior region and to various places in northern Ohio and the Tuscarawas Valley. After her father's death in 1869, Miss Woolson began her literary career, using materials of the Great Lakes country and of interior Ohio. Following the death of her sister Clara's husband, Miss Woolson and her mother lived in the South: in the summer there was Asheville, N. C.; in the winter, St. Augustine, Fla. There were also periods of residence in Charleston, S. C., in Tennessee, and in Georgia. In 1879 her mother died, and Miss Woolson and her sister, Clara Benedict, sailed for Europe. Miss Woolson chose Italy for her residence —Florence, Rome, and finally Venice, with long periods in Switzerland, Germany, and England. She died in Venice. In letters to her nephew, Samuel Mather, of Cleveland, and to other relatives (first printed in the *South Atlantic Quarterly*, January, 1940), Miss Woolson revealed the painstaking care she gave to her work: ". . . each page of my novels," she once wrote, "is thought of, literally, for years before it is written out for the final time." And in another letter she described her life in Venice: "I am called at 4½ a.m. I take a cup of tea, & go out to walk at 5. Come in at 6, or soon after. Bath; breakfast; cool linen attire. Then my stand-up desk, where I remain until 7 p.m. with a half an hour's rest at noon. . . . At evening, dinner; . . . & the evening is spent on my high-up terrace, under the splendid stars, & overlooking the wide view."

Lyon N. Richardson

The Old Stone House, (Pseud., Anne March), Boston, 1873.

Castle Nowhere: Lake Country Sketches, Boston, 1875.

Two Women: 1862. A Poem, New York, 1877.

Rodman the Keeper: Southern Sketches, New York, 1880.

Anne; A Novel, New York, 1882.

For the Major, a Novelette, New York, 1883.

East Angels, a Novel, New York, [1886].

Jupiter Lights: A Novel, New York, 1889.

Horace Chase: A Novel, New York, 1894.

The Front Yard, and Other Italian Stories, New York, 1895.

Dorothy and Other Italian Stories, New York, 1896.
Mentone, Cairo and Corfu, New York, 1896.

WORCESTER, ELWOOD (May 16, 1862–July 19, 1940), clergyman, was born in Massillon, Stark County, but grew up in Rochester, N. Y., where his parents moved while he was a child. He graduated from Columbia University in 1886, General Theological Seminary in 1887, and the University of Leipzig (Ph.D.) in 1889. Ordained an Episcopal deacon in 1890 and a priest in 1891, he was on the faculty of Lehigh University, 1890–96, rector of St. Stephen's Church, Philadelphia, 1896–1904, and rector of Emmanuel Church, Boston, 1904–29. In Boston he worked in close cooperation with physicians and psychiatrists, and the "Emmanuel Movement" aroused great interest in America and Europe. He published articles and books on religion and psychotherapy and an autobiography, *Life's Adventure . . . ,* New York, 1932. DAB 22

WORDEN, WILBERTINE TETERS (June, 1870–April 27, 1949), was born in Caldwell, Noble County, and lived there for the first nine years of her life. A graduate of Colorado State University, she married Charles G. Worden, who died in 1898. She was later married to the author Harry Leon Wilson, but after being divorced from him resumed the name of her first husband. She wrote for numerous magazines and newspapers.

The Snows of Yester-year; A Novel, Boston, 1895.

WORK, EDGAR WHITTAKER (Nov. 20, 1862–April 17, 1934), clergyman, was born in Logan, Hocking County. He graduated from University of Wooster in 1884 and from Lane Theological Seminary in 1887. He served Presbyterian pastorates in Van Wert, 1887–90, and Dayton, 1895–1902, and was on the Wooster faculty, 1890–95. He later served churches in New York and Colorado. His writings include *Study to Be Quiet,* Chicago, 1904. WWW 1

WORK, F. ERNEST (Jan. 22, 1877–Oct. 26, 1957), educator, was born in Indiana County, Pa. He earned his doctorate in history at Ohio State University and served for 24 years on the faculty of Muskingum College. At the suggestion of Ethiopian students who had been in his classes, Emperor Haile Selassie invited him to Ethiopia to organize the educational system. He also helped write the constitution of Ethiopia. He was decorated by the Emperor. He wrote *Ethiopia, a Pawn in European Diplomacy,* New Concord, [1935].

WORKMAN, CHARLES HANSON (April 23, 1859–April 29, 1945), educator and lawyer, was born in Holmes County. He graduated from Ohio Northern University in 1882 and from the law school in 1884. He taught history at Ohio Northern, 1883–91. After being admitted to the bar in 1894, he practiced in Mansfield.

Lincoln in Debate, Ada, 1893.
A Visit to St. Gauden's [sic] Lincoln, [Mansfield, 1926].

WORKMAN, MARY CHRISTIANIA SHEEDY (Nov. 12, 1859–March 12, 1926), was born in Cincinnati, Hamilton County. After attending Ohio Northern University and studying in Paris, she taught school in southwestern Ohio for eleven years. After marrying Charles H. Workman (q.v.), she lived in Mansfield. Under the name Mrs. Hanson Workman, she wrote a privately printed novel: *An American Singer in Paris . . . ,* Cincinnati, 1908.

WORTH, GORHAM A. (1783–1856), banker, was born in New York State. He was a banker in Cincinnati for a number of years and later lived in New York City and Albany. His *American Bards,* an imitation of Byronic satire, has erroneously been called the first book of original verse published west of the mountains—an honor rightfully due Thomas Johnson of Kentucky. Worth's poems were published anonymously; the *Sketches* are signed "O.P.Q."; and *Random Recollections* contains a note to the publisher signed Ignatius Jones.

A New-Year's Lay . . . , [Cincinnati, 1816].
American Bards . . . , [Cincinnati], 1819.
Sketches of the Character of the New-York Press, New York, 1844.
Random Recollections of Albany . . . , Albany, 1849.
Recollections of Cincinnati . . . , Albany, 1851.

WORTHINGTON, EDWARD WILLIAM (May 10, 1854–April 15, 1906), Episcopal clergyman, born in Batavia, N. Y., was pastor of Grace Church, Cleveland, from 1887 until his death.

Ember Days and Other Papers, Milwaukee, 1897.
The Holy Eucharist Devotionally Considered, New York, [1901].

WORTHINGTON, THOMAS (March 18, 1807–Feb. 23, 1884), soldier, son of Governor Thomas Worthington, was born at Adena, Ross County. He graduated from the U. S. Military Academy in 1827, served in the Mexican War, and was colonel of the 46th O.V.I. in the Civil War. Besides the titles below, he published a military manual for volunteers in 1861. He was convinced that both Grant and Sherman held personal grudges against him and therefore blocked his promotion; this conviction underlies all of his writings on the war. The first title was announced for six parts, but only the first appeared.

The Blunders of the Rebellion and Their Dead Sea Fruit . . ., Washington, D. C., 1869.
Shiloh . . ., Washington, D. C., 1872.
Brief History of the 46th Ohio Volunteers, [Washington, D. C.?, 1878?].
Col. Worthington Vindicated . . ., Washington, D. C., 1878.
A Correct History of Grant at the Battle of Shiloh . . ., Washington, D. C., 1880.
A Correct History of Pope, McDowell, and Fitz John Porter at the Second Battle of Bull Run . . ., Washington, D. C., 1880.
Report on the Flank March to Join McClernand's Right . . ., Washington, D. C., 1880.

WORTS, GEORGE FRANK (March 16, 1892–), was born in Toledo, Lucas County. He was a radio operator on the Great Lakes and the Pacific, 1910–14, studied at Columbia University, 1914–15, and has since been a free-lance writer. Since 1941 he has lived in Hawaii. He has written a number of motion-picture scripts and novels, e.g., *Dangerous Young Man,* New York, 1940, and under the pen name Loring Brent, *No More a Corpse,* New York, [1932]. WW 30

WRIGHT, CHARLES (Aug. 27, 1834–July 10, 1902), was born near Oxford, Butler County. In Aug., 1861, he enlisted in the 81st O.V.I. and served for three years until discharged for a hip injury. He later served as Oxford Township clerk for 22 years and as clerk of the board of education.

A Corporal's Story. Experiences in the Ranks of Company C, 81st Ohio Volunteer Infantry . . ., Philadelphia, 1887.

WRIGHT, CHARLES BAKER (Oct. 5, 1859–April 24, 1942), educator, was born in Cleveland, Cuyahoga County. He graduated from Buchtel College in 1880. From 1885 to 1920 he was on the faculty of Middlebury College. He published several books, including *A Teacher's Avocations,* Middlebury, [Vt.], 1925, and a collection of poetry: *Verses in Varying Mood,* Middlebury, Vt., 1931. WWW 2

WRIGHT, D. THEW (Nov. 25, 1825–Sept. 11, 1912), lawyer, was born in Cincinnati, Hamilton County. He attended Woodward College, graduated from Yale University in 1847 and Harvard Law School in 1849, and was admitted to the Ohio bar in 1850. He served on the state supreme court bench, 1873–76. His only novel was based on a protracted Cincinnati law case, Young *vs.* Dagneaux *et al.*

Miss Armington's Ward; Or, the Inferior Sex, Boston, 1874.

WRIGHT, EDWARD E. (April 23, 1859– ?), was born in Harrisville, Harrison County. He wrote *Everard and Eulalia* when he was eighteen years old and was teaching school in Harrison County. He later became the amanuensis of Robert J. Burdette (q.v.) in Burlington, Iowa. He practiced law in Council Bluffs, Iowa, and later lived in Brooklyn, N. Y.

Everard and Eulalia, Council Bluffs, Iowa, [1886].
The Lightning's Flash . . ., Council Bluffs, Iowa, [1892].

WRIGHT, EDWARD STAGER (Feb. 20, 1862 Aug. 16, 1910), journalist, was born in Cleveland, Cuyahoga County. He worked on various newspapers in Cleveland and other cities and wrote a travel book: *Westward 'Round the World,* New York, [1908].

WRIGHT, ELEAZER. Pseud. See Richard McNemar.

WRIGHT, ELIZUR (Feb. 12, 1804–Nov. 21, 1885), was born in South Canaan, Conn. When he was six years old, his family moved to Tallmadge, and he grew up in that community. After graduating from Yale University in 1826, he joined the faculty of Western Reserve College at Hudson. Dissension over the conservative position of the college on the antislavery question caused several faculty members, including Wright, to resign in 1833. He became corresponding secretary of the American Anti-Slavery Society in 1833, edited many of the society's tracts, and was editor of the *Quarterly Anti-Slavery Magazine.* He later broke with the abolitionist leaders, and in 1841 he published a translation of La Fontaine's *Fables* which he sold from door to door. In 1846 he founded a newspaper in Boston, the *Weekly Chronotype,* in which he began to tilt against life insurance companies, with the result that he was employed by several companies to set up sound tables. For the rest of his life he continued his "lobby for the widow and the orphan" and also was employed as an actuary by several insurance companies. Known as the "father of life insurance," he actually was a censor whose efforts had much to do with the establishment of sound standards for insurance. He published a number of actuarial tables and similar compilations not listed below.

The Sin of Slavery, and Its Remedy . . ., New York, 1833.
The District School, According to the Lancasterian [sic] Method of Teaching, Oberlin, 1843.
An Eye-Opener for the Wide Awakes, Boston, 1860.
The Programme of Peace, Boston, 1862.
A Curiosity of Law . . ., Boston, 1866.
Savings-Banks Life Insurance . . ., Boston, 1872.
Politics and Mysteries of Life Insurance, Boston, 1873.
Elements of Life Insurance . . ., Boston, 1876.
Traps Baited with Orphans . . ., Boston, 1877.
The Necessity of Reform in Life Insurance, [Boston, 1878].
Insurance and Self-insurance . . ., Boston, 1880.
Myron Holley; And What He Did for Liberty and True Religion, Boston, 1882.

WRIGHT, FRANCES. See Frances Wright D'Arusmont.

WRIGHT, GEORGE ERNEST (Sept. 5, 1909–), educator, was born in Zanesville, Muskingum County. He graduated from the College of Wooster in 1931, from McCormick Theological Seminary in 1934, and Johns Hopkins University (Ph.D.) in 1936. He has been on the faculty of McCormick Seminary since 1939. He has written several articles and books on archaeology and religion, e.g., *The Old Testament against Its Environment,* Chicago, 1950. WW 30

WRIGHT, GEORGE FREDERICK (Jan. 22, 1838–April 20, 1921), clergyman and educator, was born in Whitehall, N. Y. After graduating from Oberlin College in 1859 and Oberlin Seminary in 1862, he served Congregational churches in New England, 1862–81. While serving a church in Andover, Mass., his observations of a gravel bank near his parsonage became the turning point in his career. His theory that it was of glacial rather than marine origin brought him widespread attention from geologists. His theories as to the antiquity of man were closely related to his theological and geological interests. He was a member of the Oberlin faculty, 1881–1907, and was editor of *Biblotheca Sacra,* 1883–1921. In 1901 he made a journey across Asia and through Turkestan. Besides his books he wrote nearly 600 magazine articles.

The Logic of Christian Evidences, Andover, [Mass.], 1880.
An Inquiry Concerning the Relation of Death to Probation, Boston, [1882].
Studies in Science and Religion, Andover, Mass., 1882.
The Glacial Boundary in Ohio, Indiana and Kentucky, Cleveland, 1884.
The Ice Age in North America and Its Bearings upon the Antiquity of Man, New York, 1889.
The Muir Glacier, Alaska, Philadelphia, [1889].
Charles Grandison Finney, New York, 1891.
Man and the Glacial Period, New York, 1892.
Greenland Ice Fields and Life in the North Atlantic . . ., New York, 1896.
Memorial of Charles Candee Baldwin . . ., Cleveland, 1896.
Asiatic Russia, 2 vols., New York, 1902.
Scientific Confirmation of Old Testament History, Oberlin, 1906.
Origin and Antiquity of Man, Oberlin, 1912.
See Ohio First . . ., Oberlin, [1915].
A Standard History of Lorain County . . ., 2 vols., Chicago, 1916.
Story of My Life and Work, Oberlin, 1916.
Scientific Aspects of the Christian Religion, New York, [n.d.].

WRIGHT, HENRY COLLIER (Aug. 29, 1868–Oct. 24, 1935), was born in Leroy, Medina County. After graduating from Ohio Wesleyan University in 1892, he was director of the Citizens' Party, Cincinnati, an investigator for the Russell Sage Foundation, and a commissioner of the Department of Public Charities of New York City. He lectured and wrote articles on social work and also published a book, largely devoted to an attack on George B. Cox: *Bossism in Cincinnati,* Cincinnati, 1905. WWW 1

WRIGHT, HOWELL (Jan. 21, 1882–Nov. 3, 1954), born in Swansea, Mass., graduated from Yale University in 1906 and in 1912 came to Cleveland as superintendent of Cleveland Associated Charities. He later was public utilities director for the city. His writings include *Public Ownership, Promises and Results . . .* , Cleveland, [1936].

WRIGHT, ISAAC (1859–Jan. 31, 1929), journalist, was born in Stockport, England, but his parents settled in Toledo while he was still a young boy. From 1873 until his death he wrote for various Toledo newspapers.

The East Side, Past and Present, [Toledo, 1894].

WRIGHT, JOHN A. (Aug. 27, 1854–Aug. 22, 1929), physician, was born in Portland, Maine, but his family moved to Toledo in 1868. After attending the University of Michigan, he graduated from Miami Medical College, Cincinnati, in 1877 and immediately afterward began practice in Toledo. He taught at Toledo Medical College and was first president of the Toledo Medical Society. He published medical articles and a book about a pilgrimage to Rome: *The Story of a Modern Pilgrim,* Toledo, 1926.

WRIGHT, JOHN FLAVEL (1795–Sept. 13, 1879), clergyman, was a pastor in Cincinnati in the 1820s and also was an official of the Methodist Book Concern, 1832–44.

Sketches of the Life and Labors of James Quinn . . . , Cincinnati, 1851.

WRIGHT, LOUIS CLINTON (Feb. 3, 1879–Feb. 10, 1953), clergyman and educator, was born in Virgil, N. Y. He graduated from Syracuse University in 1904, Boston University School of Theology in 1907, and Boston University (Ph.D.) in 1917. He was pastor of Epworth-Euclid Church, Cleveland, 1920–34, and president of Baldwin-Wallace College, 1934–48. He published *Trails for Climbing Youth,* New York, [1939]. WW 26

WRIGHT, LOUISE C. (May 9, 1866–Oct. 3, 1953), educator, born in Princeton, N. J., taught in the Cleveland school system, 1916–40. A graduate of Neff College of Physical Education, Philadelphia, she taught at Fort Edward Collegiate Institution, N. Y., for several years before coming to Cleveland. She died in Elyria, where she had lived since her retirement from teaching. She wrote a book for children: *Story Plays,* New York, 1923.

WRIGHT, MARMADUKE BURR (Nov. 10, 1803–Aug. 15, 1879), physician and educator, was born in Pemberton, N. J. In 1823, after graduating in medicine from the University of Pennsylvania, he settled in Columbus. He served on the faculty of the Medical College of Ohio in various capacities from 1838 until his retirement in 1868. He contributed many professional papers to medical journals and delivered numerous addresses that were reprinted in pamphlet form. Otto Juettner described him as "a great obstetrician, splendid and honest medical politician, brilliant teacher, man of affairs and versatile medical writer." He died in Cincinnati.

Incidents of Professional Life, Cincinnati, 1841.

The Science of Medicine as a Compilation of Truths, Cincinnati, 1843.

The Memorial of M. B. Wright in Relation to the Medical College of Ohio . . . , Columbus, 1851.

Historical Reminiscences of the Professors of the Medical College of Ohio, Cincinnati, 1861.

The Idolatry of Our People; Or, the Rebellion in Its Medical Aspects, Cincinnati, 1862.

WRIGHT, MARY TAPPAN (Dec., 1851–Aug. 28, 1916), was born in Steubenville, Jefferson County. Her father was a professor at Kenyon College. In 1879 she married John H. Wright. She lived for many years in Cambridge, Mass., and her death occurred in that community.

A Truce, and Other Stories, New York, 1895.

Aliens, New York, 1902.

The Test, New York, 1904.

The Tower, New York, 1906.

The Charioteers, New York, 1912.

WRIGHT, NATHANIEL (Jan. 28, 1789–May 20, 1875), clergyman, was born in Hanover, N. H. He graduated from Dartmouth College in 1811, read law, and began practicing in Cincinnati in 1817. He retired in 1842. His *Memorial Address* was delivered April 28, 1872, in the Second Presbyterian Church just after the church building was sold. It contains many reminiscences of early Cincinnati.

Memorial Address . . . , Cincinnati, 1873.

WRIGHT, PHILIP GREEN (Oct. 3, 1861–Sept. 4, 1934), born in Boston, Mass., taught mathematics at Buchtel College, 1884–86. Remarkably versatile, he worked as a civil engineer, taught a variety of subjects, wrote several technical studies of tariff laws, and published three volumes of poetry, e.g., *The Dial of the Heart,* Boston, 1905. DAB 20

WRIGHT, THOMAS LEE (Aug. 7, 1825–1893), physician, was born in Windham, Portage County. After attending Miami University, he graduated from Ohio Medical College in 1846. He then went to Kansas, where he was adopted into the Wyandot tribe of Indians and practiced among them until 1854. In 1856 he returned to Ohio and practiced in Bellefontaine.

Notes on the Theory of Human Existence, Cincinnati, 1848.
A Disquisition on the Ancient History of Medicine . . . , Cincinnati, 1855.
Medico-Legal: An Inquiry . . . , Columbus, 1860.
Science and Revelation, Bellefontaine, 1878.
Responsibility Restricted by Insane Delusion, [Cincinnati, 1879].
The Quality of Mental Operations Debased by the Use of Alcohol . . . , St. Louis, Mo., 1881.
Inebriism, a Pathological and Psychological Study, Columbus, 1885.

WRIGHT, WILLIAM (May 9, 1829–March 16, 1898), journalist, was born in Ohio of Quaker parents. In 1847 he went to Iowa, where he lived for ten years, writing for Iowa newspapers and *Graham's Magazine.* He went to the Sierra Nevadas in 1857, and while wandering from one mining camp to another wrote humorous sketches for various newspapers that he signed Dan De-Quille, the name by which he is generally known. In 1861 he became editor of the Virginia City *Daily Territorial Enterprise.* He is best remembered in literary history for his relationship with Mark Twain, who was on the staff, 1862–64. The two men remained lifelong friends. He died in West Lafayette, Iowa.

History of the Big Bonanza . . . , San Francisco, 1876.
A History of the Comstock Silver Lode & Mines . . . , Virginia [City], Nevada, [1889].

WRIGHT, WILLIAM BURNET (April 15, 1838–May 2, 1924), clergyman, was born in Cincinnati, Hamilton County. He graduated from Dartmouth College in 1857 and Andover Theological Seminary in 1860. After his ordination to the Congregational ministry, he served churches in Boston, Mass., and Buffalo, N. Y. He was a popular lecturer on history, literature, and biography. He died in Buffalo.

Ancient Cities from the Dawn to the Daylight, Boston, 1886.
The World to Come, Boston, 1887.
Master and Men; Or, the Sermon on the Mount Practiced on the Plain, Boston, 1894.
Cities of Paul . . . , Boston, 1905.
The Heart of the Master, Boston, 1911.

WRIGHT, WILLIAM HEERMANS (July 18, 1900–April 23, 1952), merchant, was born in Cadiz, Harrison County. He graduated from Ohio State University in 1922, married Margaret Aikin in 1926, and for a number of years operated a department store in Warren, Pa. He wrote a column in the Warren *Times-Mirror,* a number of short stories, two historical dramas in verse, and numerous poems. He published a collection of verse: *But Not for the Knight,* [Warren, Pa.], 1935.

WUNDER, CLINTON (Dec. 17, 1892–), clergyman, was born in Cincinnati, Hamilton County. He graduated from the University of Cincinnati in 1914, spent several years in Y.M.C.A. work, and graduated from Rochester Theological Seminary in 1922. He was pastor of Baptist Temple, Rochester, 1921–29, was a lecturer and broadcaster, and was a Dale Carnegie Institute instructor. He published a handbook on church methods: *"Crowds of Souls" for the Church and the Kingdom,* New York, [1926]. WW 30

WUNKER, PEGGY (Aug. 15, 1910–), was born in Danville, Ky. She attended Kentucky public schools and the University of Cincinnati. She has written book reviews for the Cincinnati *Enquirer* and has published poems in various periodicals and anthologies. In 1932 she married Howard Wunker and has since lived in Cincinnati. She has published *Poems,* New York, 1939.

WYER, SAMUEL S. (Feb. 18, 1879–Nov. 30, 1955), engineer, was born in Wayne County. He graduated from Ohio State University in 1903 and began practicing as a consulting engineer in Columbus in 1905. He also lectured widely on social and industrial problems and published books and pamphlets on utilities and resources, e.g., *Regulation, Valuation and Depreciation of Public Utilities,* Columbus, [1913]. WWW 3

WYLIE, DAVID GOURLEY (May 15, 1857–Aug. 26, 1930), clergyman, was born in New Richland, Logan County. He graduated from Geneva College in 1879, Union Theological Seminary in 1883, and New York University (Ph.D.) in 1888. He afterward served as pastor of various Presbyterian churches in New York State.

A Visit to Europe, 1895.
The Minister's Companion, 1910.

WYLIE, EDNA EDWARDS (April 17, 1876–Nov. 25, 1907), born in Sibley, Iowa, spent her last years in Cleveland, where her husband, E. M. Wylie, was a clergyman. She published several works of fiction, e.g., *The Ward of the Sewing-Circle,* Boston, 1905. WWW 1

WYLIE, RICHARD CAMERON (Aug. 27, 1846–July 31, 1928), clergyman and educator, was born near Zanesville, Muskingum County. He graduated from Muskingum College in 1870 and Allegheny Seminary in 1875. In 1908 he joined the faculty of Allegheny Seminary. His writings include *Sabbath Laws in the United States,* Pittsburgh, Pa., 1905. WWW 1

WYMAN, MARY ELIZABETH TISDEL (March 26, 1845–May 11, 1926), was born in Madison, Lake County. In 1868 she married Don Lloyd Wyman, author of a number of stories for children. After living in Nebraska for a number of years, they returned to Ohio and settled in Painesville. She published a genealogical work and *The New Dealers of 1776,* Painesville, 1935.

WYMAN, WILLIAM H. (July 21, 1831–Oct. 7, 1911), insurance executive, was born in Canton, N. Y. In 1850 he entered the Cincinnati office of the Protection Company as a junior clerk, and as time went by he became one of the leading insurance underwriters in the region. During his business career he became absorbed in the Bacon-Shakespeare controversy and compiled his annotated bibliography, one of the least known yet one of the most valuable contributions to the subject. In 1890 he moved to Omaha, Neb., where he spent the remainder of his life.

Bibliography of the Bacon-Shakespeare Controversy, with Notes and Extracts, Cincinnati, 1884.

WYRICK, DAVID (? – ?), was born in Ohio, probably in Newark, Licking County. Largely self-educated, he had decided abilities in some fields, especially mathematics, and served for some years as county surveyor until the condition of his legs, swollen by elephantiasis, forced him to retire. In 1860–61 he perpetrated one of the most amusing hoaxes in the history of Ohio archaeology. On June 29, 1860, he appeared on the streets of Newark exhibiting with great exultation the stone afterward known as the "Newark Holy Stone," as proof of his contention that the Hebrews were the builders of the earthworks of the Midwest. He claimed to have discovered it while excavating in the earthworks near Newark. Bearing on each of its four sides an inscription in Hebrew, it was a sensational discovery; it soon became the property of the Ethnological Society of New York and was the subject of much speculation among the distinguished members of that society. Had Wyrick rested on his laurels, his fame might have remained secure. But in November of the next year, he produced a second stone and published his pamphlet describing his discoveries. The second stone carried a likeness of a somewhat pugnacious Moses with his name in Hebrew above his head. This was too much for even the most gullible archaeologists, and the imposition was discovered. Wyrick died soon afterward, and among his effects was found a Hebrew Bible and evidence that it had been a secret study for years.

Ernest J. Wessen

A Representation of the Two Stones with the Characters Inscribed upon Them, That Were Found by D. Wyrick, during the Summer of 1860, Near Newark, Ohio, Newark, [1861?].

WYSNER, GLORA MAY, teacher and missionary, born in Anderson, Ind., lived in Ohio for about ten years. She taught in Ohio schools, 1917–21, attended Ohio University, and was a social worker in Cleveland, 1923–26. Ordained to the Methodist ministry, she served as a missionary in Algeria, 1926–39, and as secretary of the International Missionary Council. She has published magazine articles, pamphlets, and books, e.g., *Near East Panorama,* New York, [1950]. WWAW 1

Y

YATES, EMMA HAYDEN EAMES (Haydie) (c.1897–July 1, 1950), was born in Bar Harbor, Maine. Her father was an automobile manufacturer in Cleveland, and she spent her girlhood in that city and Hagerstown, Md. She was on the staff of *The New Yorker* during its early years. She died in Naples, Fla. She lived on a Wyoming ranch,

1927–34, and later wrote an account of her experiences: *70 Miles from a Lemon,* Boston, 1947.

YATES, SARAH ANNIE (Feb. 15, 1850–Dec. 3, 1933), was born in Troy, N. Y. She lived in England during part of her girlhood and afterward lived in the Dakotas. After the death of her husband, she attended Metaphysical College of Illinois and Cincinnati Eclectic College. In 1887 she settled in Cincinnati, where she founded Cincinnati Metaphysical College the following year. She wrote a book of recollections which also includes her views on "mental therapy": *Leaves from the Autumn of a Busy Life,* [Cincinnati, 1929].

YOCUM, EDITH EBERLE. See Edith Eberle.

YORICK. Pseud. See James W. Ward.

YOUMANS, ELEANOR (Sept. 7, 1876–), was born in Maxville, Mo., but her parents moved to Licking County in 1881. She married Briggs M. Youmans in 1900. Her last known address is Pataskala, Licking County. She has written a number of books for children, e.g., *Skitter Cat,* Indianapolis, [1925].

YOUNG, AGNES BROOKS (Nov. 18, 1898–), was born in Cleveland, Cuyahoga County. After studying art in Cleveland, New York, and Paris, she married George B. Young. She was costume director of the Cleveland Playhouse, 1923–27, was with the Yale University Theatre, 1928–29, and taught at Western Reserve University, 1930–32. She has written and lectured on fashions and the stage. Under the pen name Agatha Young, she has also published several novels; the first was a story of Cleveland in the 1870s: *Light in the Sky,* [1948]. WW 30

YOUNG, ALLYN ABBOTT (Sept. 19, 1876–March 7, 1929), educator, was born in Kenton, Hardin County. He graduated from Hiram College in 1894 and the University of Wisconsin (Ph.D.) in 1902. After teaching at Western Reserve University from 1902 to 1904, he served at various other institutions. He was teaching at the London School of Economics at the time of his death. His publications were largely technical papers in the field of economics. A collection of his addresses and essays was published: *Economic Problems, New and Old,* New York, 1927. DAB 20

YOUNG, CALVIN M. (May 6, 1851–Dec. 29, 1918), was born in Darke County. After attending district schools, he operated a farm and made archaeological research and local history his avocation. He wrote *Little Turtle . . . ,* [Indianapolis], 1917.

YOUNG, CATHERINE (Aug. 21, 1900–), was born in Akron, Summit County. After graduating from Akron West High School in 1917, she attended Smith College and after her graduation taught at Hunter College for a time. She is now Mrs. Jack Masters, Sea Island City, N. J. While spending a year in southern France, she wrote *A Lady Who Loved Herself . . . ,* New York, 1930.

YOUNG, CHARLES VAN PATTEN (Nov. 30, 1876–), educator, was born in Middletown, Butler County. He graduated from Cornell University in 1899 and Princeton Theological Seminary in 1902. He was a member of the Cornell physical education department, 1904–44. He has written books on rowing and on Cornell, and a history of athletics: *How Men Have Lived,* Boston, 1931. WW 26

YOUNG, DAN (April 7, 1783–March 30, 1867), was born in Grafton County, N. H. At the age of 22 he became a Methodist minister and preached in several New England states. In 1820 he formed a company which he led to Ohio. They moved down the Allegheny River on flatboats to the Ohio and landed at Hayport (Wheelersburg), Scioto County, where Young built a cotton mill. He later organized the Ohio Iron Company and built several furnaces in southern Ohio.

Autobiography of Dan Young, a New England Preacher of the Olden Time, New York, 1860.

YOUNG, DAVID (March 19, 1776–Sept. 15, 1859), clergyman, was born in Allegheny County, Pa. After being licensed as a Methodist preacher in 1801, he settled in Shelby County, Ky., and in 1806 he preached on the Marietta circuit. After preaching in several Southern states, he returned to Ohio in 1812 and served there until 1856.

Autobiography of a Pioneer . . . , Cincinnati, 1857.

YOUNG, JEREMIAH SIMEON (Sept. 9, 1866–Dec. 30, 1947), educator, was born in Wellston, Jackson County. After graduating from Kansas College in 1890, he taught in Colorado, 1891–97, and was school superintendent in Fostoria, 1898–1900. He earned his doctorate at the University of Chicago in 1902, taught for several years in Midwestern public schools, and served on the University of Minnesota faculty, 1909–37. He wrote numerous textbooks and articles, and *The Government of the People of the State of Minnesota,* New York, [1906]. WWW 2

YOUNG, JESSE BOWMAN (July 5, 1844–July 30, 1914), Methodist clergyman, born in Berwick, Pa., was pastor of Walnut Hills Church, Cincinnati, 1900–08. He published numerous books, most of them on religious subjects, and a book for young readers concerning his experiences in the Civil War: *What a Boy Saw in the Army . . . ,* Cincinnati, 1888.

YOUNG, LOUISE MERWIN (Sept. 5, 1903–), was born in East Palestine, Columbiana County. She graduated from Ohio Wesleyan University in 1925 and the University of Pennsylvania (Ph.D.) in 1939. A resident of Washington, D. C., she has been active in civic affairs, has lectured at American University, and has written books and articles on history and politics, e.g., *Understanding Politics; A Practical Guide for Women,* New York, [1950]. WWAW 1

YOUNGS, BENJAMIN SETH (Sept. 17, 1774–March, 1855), Shaker, was born in New Lebanon, N. Y. He was one of the three missionaries who arrived in Turtle Creek in 1805 and converted Richard McNemar (q.v.). He was recalled to New York in 1836. The *Testimony,* often called the Shaker Bible, was unsigned, but it is generally regarded as being largely from Young's pen. Thomas Jefferson is said to have called it the best ecclesiastical history ever written.

The Testimony of Christ's Second Appearing . . . , Lebanon, 1808.

Transactions of the Ohio Mob, Called in the Public Papers "An Expedition Against the Shakers," [n.p., 1810].

YOUTZ, HERBERT ALDEN (April 28, 1867–March 20, 1943), clergyman, born in Commerce, Iowa, was on the faculty of Oberlin Graduate School of Theology, 1918–32. He published several books on religious themes, e.g., *The Enlarging Conception of God,* New York, 1914. WW 20

Z

ZACHOS, JOHN CELIVERGOS (Dec. 20, 1820–March 20, 1898), was born in Constantinople, Turkey, of Greek parentage. His father, a general in the Greek army, died in battle in 1824; in 1830 the boy was brought to America by Dr. Samuel Gridley Howe and placed in a preparatory school at Amherst, Mass. He graduated from Kenyon College in 1840 and attended the medical school of Miami University but did not graduate. His first writings appeared in periodicals published by L. A. Hines (q.v.). He was associate principal of the Cooper Female Seminary, Dayton, 1851–54, and taught at Antioch College, 1854–57. He lived in Ohio from 1836 until the outbreak of the Civil War, when he joined the Union army as an assistant surgeon. After the war he was pastor of a Unitarian church in Meadville, Pa., and taught at Meadville Seminary. In 1871 he moved to New York City, where he was a curator at Cooper Union and a teacher of literature and oratory. He published several textbooks in oratory and elocution. Some of his addresses on the tariff were published separately as pamphlets under the pen name Cadmus.

A Sketch of the Life and Opinions of Mr. Peter Cooper . . . , New York, 1876.

The Political and Financial Opinions of Peter Cooper . . . , New York, 1877.

The Fiscal Problem of All Civilized Nations, New York, 1881.

ZAHM, ALBERT FRANCIS (Jan. 5, 1862–July 23, 1954), educator, was born in New Lexington, Perry County. He graduated from the University of Notre Dame in 1883 and Johns Hopkins University (Ph.D.) in 1898. He taught at Notre Dame and at Catholic University of America, was director of the Aerodynamical Laboratory of the U. S. Navy, and was in charge of the aeronautical division of the Library of Congress. He published a number of scientific monographs and *Aerial Navigation; A Popular Treatise . . . ,* New York, 1911. WWW 3

ZAHM, JOHN AUGUSTINE (Sept. 14, 1851–Nov. 10, 1921), clergyman, brother of Albert F. Zahm (q.v.), was born in New Lexington, Perry County. His family moved to Huntington, Ind., in 1863. After graduating from the University of Notre Dame in 1871, he entered the Congregation of the Holy Cross and was ordained to the priesthood in 1875. His life was spent teaching, lecturing, and writing. A prodigious worker, he contributed many articles to the *American Ecclesiastical Review, Outlook,* and other periodicals. Some of his lectures were printed as pamphlets. He occasionally used as a pen name J. H. Mozans.

The Catholic Church and Modern Science, Notre Dame, Ind., 1883.
Letters from the Hawaiian Islands, Notre Dame, Ind., 1886.
Sound and Music, Chicago, 1892.
Catholic Science and Catholic Scientists, Philadelphia, 1893.
Bible, Science and Faith, Baltimore, 1894.
Evolution and Dogma, Chicago, 1896.
Science and the Church, Chicago, 1896.
Scientific Theory and Catholic Doctrine, Chicago, 1896.
Following the Conquistadores . . . , 3 vols., New York, 1910–16.
Woman in Science . . . , New York, 1913.
Great Inspirers, New York, 1917.
The Quest of El Dorado . . . , New York, 1917.
From Berlin to Bagdad and Babylon, New York, 1922.

ZANGERLE, JOHN A. (April 12, 1866–Oct. 1, 1956), lawyer, was born in Cleveland, Cuyahoga County. He was admitted to the Ohio bar in 1890, practiced in Cleveland, and achieved a wide reputation as a tax expert. In 1912 he was named auditor of Cuyahoga County, a post he held for more than thirty years. Besides books on real-estate appraisal and taxation, he published *Rockefeller before a Jury,* Cleveland, 1906. WW 25

ZARTMAN, RUFUS CALVIN (Nov. 10, 1856–May 14, 1946), clergyman, was born in Hopewell Township, Perry County. After graduating from Heidelberg College (1881) and Seminary (1883), he was ordained to the ministry of the Reformed Church and served pastorates in Wooster, 1883–88, Akron, 1888–91, and Philadelphia, 1891–1921. In 1921 he became Superintendent of Evangelism in the Reformed Church. He died in Springfield, Mass. He published a family history, sermons, and books on religious themes, e.g., *Eternal Life,* Philadelphia, 1901. WWC 1

ZEISBERGER, DAVID (April 11, 1721–Nov. 17, 1808), missionary, was born in Moravia. His parents were sent to a Moravian colony in Georgia by Count Zinzendorf in 1838, and David joined them there shortly afterward. The family later moved to Bethlehem, Pa. After 1745 David lived on the frontier as a missionary to the Indians. He accompanied the Delawares when they were pushed westward, and in May, 1772, he established the settlement at Schoenbrunn in the Tuscarawas Valley. In October of the same year he established Gnadenhutton, later the scene of the most notorious massacre on the Ohio frontier. To Zeisberger belongs the distinction of founding the first church and the first school in the Ohio territory. In 1781 he was taken as a prisoner to Detroit, and the Schoenbrunn settlement was dispersed. In 1798 he settled at Goshen, Tuscarawas County, where he spent the rest of his life. He wrote hymns and translated religious works into the Delaware language. He also wrote a textbook, the first book written in what is now Ohio: *Essays of a Delaware-Indian and English Spelling-Book . . . ,* Philadelphia, 1776.

ZELIGS, ROSE, educator and psychologist, was born in Cincinnati, Hamilton County. A graduate of the University of Cincinnati (A.B., 1925; Ed.D., 1937), she taught in the Cincinnati public schools, 1925–48, and is now a psychological counselor in Sherman Oaks, Calif. She has written many articles for professional and popular magazines and *Glimpses into Child Life . . . ,* New York, 1942. WWAW 1

ZENNER, PHILIP (May 17, 1852–June 25, 1956), physician, was born in Cincinnati, Hamilton County. He graduated from Ohio University in 1870 and Miami Medical College in 1875. He also studied in Europe and taught neurology and psychiatry at the University of Cincinnati Medical School, 1900–10. At the time of his retirement in 1947, he had practiced in Cincinnati for more than sixty years. He died at the age of 104 in Cincinnati. He published *Mind Cure and Other Essays,* Cincinnati, 1912. WW 26

ZERBE, ALVIN SYLVESTER (Oct. 27, 1847–March 21, 1935), clergyman and educator, was born in Reading, Pa. After attending Ohio Wesleyan University, he graduated from Heidelberg College in 1871 and was ordained as a clergyman of the Reformed Church in 1873. He served on the faculties of Ursinus College, Heidelberg College, Heidelberg Seminary, and Central Theological Seminary, Dayton. He died in Dayton.

Europe through American Eyes . . . , Dayton, 1886.

The Antiquity of Hebrew Writing and Literature . . . , Cleveland, 1911.
Christianity and False Evolutionism, Cleveland, [1925].
Evolution in a Nutshell . . . , Chicago, [1926].
The Karl Barth Theology . . . , Cleveland, [1930].

ZEYDEL, EDWIN HERMANN (Dec. 31, 1893–), educator, born in Brooklyn, N. Y., has been in the German department, University of Cincinnati, since 1926. He has published German textbooks, professional articles, and literary and critical works, e.g., *Ludwig Tieck, the German Romanticist* . . . , Princeton, [N. J.], 1931. WW 30

ZIG. Pseud. See Eliza A. Conner.

ZIMMERMAN, SARAH A. (July 18, 1904–), was born in Xenia, Greene County, but grew up in Bellbrook, where her parents moved when she was a year old. A graduate of Western College, she taught English at Fairview High School, Dayton, until 1954, when she joined the staff of the Dayton *Daily News.* Under the pen name Henry John Colyton, she has published stories in national magazines and a novel: *Sir Pagan* . . . , New York, 1947.

ZINK, HAROLD (May 15, 1901–), educator, was born in Roswell, N. M. He graduated from the University of Denver in 1921 and Harvard University (Ph.D.) in 1926. He taught political science at DePauw University, 1925–48, and since 1948 has been a member of the Ohio State University faculty. He has written articles and books on politics and government, e.g., *City Bosses in the United States* . . . , Durham, N. C., 1930. WW 30

ZIPPERLIN, ADOLPH (1818–Feb. 28, 1905), physician, was born in Germany. He graduated in medicine from the University of Tübingen in 1841 and came to America in 1848. He practiced in Weinsburg, Canal Fulton, and Akron, and during the Civil War served as a surgeon with the 108th O.V.I. After the war he settled in Cincinnati, where he practiced until his death. He was an enthusiastic naturalist and a vigorous supporter of the Zoological Gardens.

Geschichtlicher Abriss der Entstehung und Entwickelung der Zoologischen Garten . . . , Cincinnati, 1880.

ZOLLARS, ELY VAUGHN (Sept. 19, 1847–Feb. 10, 1916), educator, was born in Lower Salem, Washington County. After graduating from Bethany College in 1875, he served as president of several institutions: Kentucky Classical and Business College, 1877–84, Girard Female College, 1884–85, Hiram College, 1888–1902, and Texas Christian University, 1902–06. In 1906 he founded Phillips University in Enid, Okla. He published several volumes of sermons not listed below.

The Great Salvation, Cincinnati, [1895].
College Endowment among the Disciples . . . , Cincinnati, 1900.
A Creed That Needs No Revision, Cincinnati, 1900.
Hebrew Prophecy, Cincinnati, [1907].
The Word of Truth . . . , Cincinnati, [1910].
The King of Kings, Cincinnati, 1911.
The Commission Executed . . . , Cincinnati, 1912.
The Abrahamic Prophecies Fulfilled . . . , Cincinnati, 1913.

ZOOK, GEORGE FREDERICK (April 22, 1885–Aug. 17, 1951), educator, born in Fort Scott, Kan., was president of the University of Akron, 1925–33. He published a number of articles and reports on educational questions and a series of lectures: *America at War* . . . , [Washington, D. C., 1918]. WWW 3

ZORBAUGH, CHARLES LOUIS (Jan. 8, 1867–Aug. 17, 1943), clergyman, was born in Iowa. After graduating from Parsons College, Iowa, in 1887 and McCormick Seminary in 1894, he was ordained as a Presbyterian clergyman. He was pastor of Windermere Church, Cleveland, 1896–1911, superintendent of church extension, 1911–24, and executive secretary of the Synod of Ohio, 1924–37. He published articles, pamphlets, and a collection of poems: *Vagabond Verse,* Cleveland, 1942. WWW 2

ZORBAUGH, HARVEY WARREN (Sept. 20, 1896–), educator, was born in East Cleveland, Cuyahoga County, the son of Charles L. Zorbaugh (q.v.). He studied at Oberlin College, 1915–17, graduated from Vanderbilt University in 1922, and did graduate work at the University of Chicago. He is on the faculty of New York University. He has published a sociological study: *Gold Coast and Slum* . . . , Chicago, [1929]. WW 30

ZORMAN, IVAN (April 28, 1889–Aug. 4, 1957), was born in Yugoslavia, but was brought to Cleveland when he was four years old and spent his life in that city. He studied at Western Reserve University and taught at Central Institute. An accomplished musician, he was a church organist for many years and trained several choral groups. He published several books of original poems and translated Slovene poetry, e.g., *Pesmi,* Cleveland, 1922.

ZORN, CARL M. (March 18, 1846–July 12, 1928), clergyman, born in Germany, was pastor of Zion Evangelical Lutheran Church, Cleveland, 1881–1917. He died in East Cleveland. He published several books in German and in English, e.g., *Eunice. Letters of a Fatherly Friend to a Young Christian Mother . . . ,* St. Louis, Mo., 1921.

ZURCHER, ARNOLD JOHN (Oct. 20, 1902–), educator, was born in South Amherst, Lorain County. He graduated from Oberlin College in 1924 and Princeton University (Ph.D.) in 1928. He has been on the faculty of New York University since 1928. He has published textbooks in political science and other books on economics and government, e.g., *The Experiment with Democracy in Central Europe . . . ,* New York, 1933. WW 30

ZYBURA, JOHN STANISLAUS (d.1934), clergyman, was born in Cleveland, Cuyahoga County. After studying in the United States and Italy, he was ordained to the Roman Catholic priesthood in 1898. From 1917 until his death in a Columbus sanitarium, he suffered from tuberculosis. His writings include *Contemporary Godlessness . . . ,* St. Louis, Mo., 1924.

ZYLYFF. Pseud. See Thomas H. Tibbles.

APPENDIX A

The Martha Kinney Cooper Ohioana Library Association

THE OHIOANA LIBRARY collection was established in 1929 by Martha Kinney Cooper, while her husband, the late Myers Y. Cooper, was serving as Governor of Ohio. The library, which was later named in honor of its founder, was developed by Mrs. Depew Head, who served as its Director until her retirement in 1953. The present Director is Walter Rumsey Marvin. Mrs. Cooper's original collection of books was housed in the Governor's Mansion; it has now expanded to comprise more than 15,000 books and brochures by Ohioans or about Ohio, clippings, photographs, radio and television scripts, and a file of biographical data for more than 9,000 authors and composers, and occupies quarters in the Ohio Departments Building, Columbus. The general purposes of the Association are to encourage literature, music, and art in Ohio today and to preserve the cultural heritage of the past. Regular activities include an annual spring pilgrimage to a point of interest in Ohio, recognition of Ohio authors and composers at an annual fall luncheon, and publication of a quarterly magazine, *Ohioana: Of Ohio and Ohioans,* and two annuals.

Much of the success of Ohioana activities is the result of its county-based organization; chairmen in most of Ohio's eighty-eight counties work diligently to carry out the various projects sponsored by the Association. The chairmen for 1961, listed below, and their predecessors over the past ten years have assisted greatly in the preparation of this volume by suggesting names of authors and by searching out information on authors whose files were incomplete.

ADAMS COUNTY
Mrs. A. C. Palmer, Peebles

ALLEN COUNTY
Mrs. Karl F. Ritter, Lima
Mrs. William Baumberger, Jr., Lima

ASHLAND COUNTY
Mrs. J. Frank McClure, Loudonville

ASHTABULA COUNTY
Mrs. W. B. Hubbard, Ashtabula

ATHENS COUNTY
Mrs. H. L. Atkinson, Athens

BELMONT COUNTY
Mrs. Fred R. Graves, Barnesville

BROWN COUNTY
Mrs. John Markley, Georgetown

BUTLER COUNTY
Mrs. Louis H. Frechtling, Hamilton
Mrs. Willard W. Spencer, Oxford

CARROLL COUNTY
Miss Mary E. Martin, Carrollton
Mrs. Velma Griffin, Dellroy

CHAMPAIGN COUNTY
Miss Helen Krout, Mechanicsburg

CLARK COUNTY
Miss Mary L. Spining, Springfield

CLERMONT COUNTY
Mrs. Thomas Longworth, Felicity

CLINTON COUNTY
Miss Alice Mills, Worthington

COLUMBIANA COUNTY
Mrs. Charles E. Goodman, East Liverpool

COSHOCTON COUNTY
Miss Waive B. Ripple, West Lafayette
Mrs. Fred C. Karr, Coshocton

CRAWFORD COUNTY
Mrs. Ernest G. Hesser, Crestline
Mrs. Paul Schieber, Galion

CUYAHOGA COUNTY
Miss Donna Root, Cleveland
Mrs. Ferral C. Shons, Bedford

DARKE COUNTY
Mrs. Martin D. Pluess, Greenville

DEFIANCE COUNTY
Mrs. Lester S. Ivins, Defiance

DELAWARE COUNTY
Mrs. Harley Dennis, Ashley
Miss Sarah Stevenson, Delaware

ERIE COUNTY
Mr. Paul F. Laning, Sandusky

FAIRFIELD COUNTY
Mrs. Gerald Spitler, Baltimore
Mrs. Perrin Hazleton, Lancaster

FAYETTE COUNTY
Mrs. Frank Mayo, Washington Court House

FRANKLIN COUNTY
Mrs. Fred Ellsperman, Columbus

FULTON COUNTY
Mrs. Merril Bernath, Wauseon

GALLIA COUNTY
Mrs. W. A. Lewis, Rio Grande
Mrs. Nellie Scarberry, Gallipolis

GREENE COUNTY
Mrs. Asa C. Messenger, Xenia

GUERNSEY COUNTY
Mrs. Rose S. Henderson, Cambridge
Miss Helen Sunnafrank, Cambridge

HAMILTON COUNTY
Mrs. F. L. Woodbridge, Cincinnati

HANCOCK COUNTY
Mr. R. L. Heminger, Findlay

HARRISON COUNTY
Mrs. H. B. McConnell, Cadiz

HIGHLAND COUNTY
Miss Violet Morgan, Hillsboro

HOCKING COUNTY
Mrs. Ruth DeWitt Nixon, Logan

HURON COUNTY
Mr. and Mrs. Rex Bracy, Norwalk

JACKSON COUNTY
Mrs. Charles Bruny, Jackson

JEFFERSON
Mr. J. W. Preble, Steubenville

KNOX COUNTY
Mrs. E. V. Queen, Mount Vernon
Miss Louise Adams, Gambier

LAKE COUNTY
Mrs. Harold A. Furlong, Painesville

LAWRENCE COUNTY
Mrs. Ralph Mittendorf, Ironton

LOGAN COUNTY
Mrs. Vern Campbell, Bellefontaine

LORAIN COUNTY
Miss Lelia Holloway, Oberlin

LUCAS COUNTY
Mrs. Robert E. Walker, Toledo

MADISON COUNTY
Mrs. Mark S. Taylor, London
Mrs. B. L. Adair, London

MAHONING COUNTY
Mrs. I. M. Brown, Youngstown

MARION COUNTY
Miss Pansy K. Rauhauser, Marion

MEIGS COUNTY
Mrs. Everett R. Hayes, Portland

MIAMI COUNTY
Mr. Leonard U. Hill, Piqua
Mrs. A. Lynn Paschall, Troy

MONROE COUNTY
Miss Eva Moffatt, Woodsfield

MONTGOMERY COUNTY
Mrs. Katharine Kennedy Brown, Dayton
Miss Elizabeth Faries, Dayton

MORGAN COUNTY
Mrs. C. F. Ott, McConnelsville
Mrs. Charles Dougan, McConnelsville

MORROW COUNTY
Mrs. Elizabeth Dunham, Cardington

MUSKINGUM COUNTY
Mr. Norris F. Schneider, Zanesville

OTTAWA COUNTY
Mrs. George A. Bredehoft, Oak Harbor

PERRY COUNTY
Mrs. Ronald Shoup, New Lexington

PICKAWAY COUNTY
Mrs. John W. Eshelman, III, Circleville

PIKE COUNTY
Mrs. Harold McCormick, Waverly

PORTAGE COUNTY
Mrs. W. I. Parmelee, Sr., Ravenna

PUTNAM COUNTY
Mrs. Elmer B. Unverferth, Ottawa

RICHLAND COUNTY
Mr. R. M. Wilkinson, Shelby

SANDUSKY COUNTY
Mrs. Hallie Grimes, Fremont

SCIOTO COUNTY
Mr. John Johnley, Portsmouth

SENECA COUNTY
Mrs. Earl Adams, Bloomville
Mrs. Ralph Summers, Tiffin

SHELBY COUNTY
Mrs. Marion Russell, Sidney

STARK COUNTY
Mrs. Oliver Kuhn, Hartville

SUMMIT COUNTY
Mrs. Thomas C. Gray, Akron
Miss Dorothy Whittington, Akron

UNION COUNTY
Miss Ferne Mills, Marysville

VAN WERT COUNTY
Miss Elisabeth Rex, Van Wert

VINTON COUNTY
Mrs. Jeannette C. Grim, McArthur

WARREN COUNTY
Mrs. Hazel Phillips, Lebanon
Mrs. Harry G. Noble, Lebanon

WASHINGTON COUNTY
Mrs. Sophia Russell, Marietta
Mrs. Raymond G. Guthrie, Marietta

WAYNE COUNTY
Mrs. Walter J. Buss, Wooster

WILLIAMS COUNTY
Mrs. R. K. Ameter, Bryan

WOOD COUNTY
Dr. Walter A. Zaugg, Bowling Green

WYANDOT COUNTY
Mr. Harry E. Kinley, Upper Sandusky

APPENDIX B

Index of Contributors

THE NAMES of contributors who are also subjects of entries in this volume are starred.

*Altick, Richard D. (Delia S. Bacon)
Professor of English, Ohio State University

Anderson, Yeatman, III (Ormsby M. Mitchel, John S. Williams)
Curator of Rare Books, Cincinnati Public Library

Bettman, Iphigene (Clara L. de Chambrun)
Cincinnati *Enquirer*

*Bevis, Alma M. (Harriet E. B. Stowe)
Columbus

Bevis, Howard L. (Harlan H. Hatcher)
President Emeritus, Ohio State University

Blanck, Jacob (John Bennett, Martha Finley)
Editor, *Bibliography of American Literature*

*Bruce, Mary Hoge (Jervis Cutler)
Cincinnati

Buell, Ellen Lewis (Lois Lenski)
Editor of Children's Books, New York *Times*

Chapman, Paul H. (Jim Tully)
Professor of English, Mount Union College

Chesnutt, Helen M. (Charles Chesnutt)
Educator, Cleveland Public Schools

Chyet, Stanley F. (Isaac M. Wise)
Research Fellow, Hebrew Union College

Cox, Marion and Ella (George D. Hunt, Lysander M. Stanley)
Cave Creek, Arizona

*Dickoré, Marie (Charles Reemelin)
Genealogist, Cincinnati

DiSalle, Michael V. (Samuel M. Jones)
Mayor of Toledo, 1948–50; Governor of Ohio, 1958–

Duffy, Charles (Ambrose G. Bierce, Edward R. Sill)
Professor of English, University of Akron

Eberstadt, Charles (Hubert H. Bancroft, Lansford W. Hastings)
Antiquarian Bookseller, New York City

Fischer, Karl W. (Francis W. Shepardson)
Journalist, Indianapolis, Ind.

Flanagan, John T. (James Hall)
Professor of English, University of Illinois
Foerster, Norman (Irving Babbitt)
Professor of English, Emeritus, University of Iowa
Frederick, John T. (Walter Havighurst)
Professor of English, University of Notre Dame
Frohman, Charles E. (Daniel Frohman)
Attorney, Sandusky
Gee, Clarence S. (Joseph Badger)
Retired Presbyterian Clergyman, Lockport, N. Y.
Gehlke, Charles E. (Charles F. Thwing)
Professor of Sociology, Emeritus, Western Reserve University
Haber, Tom Burns (William D. Gallagher)
Associate Professor of English, Ohio State University
Hall, Virginius C. (Moses Dawson)
Late Director, Historical and Philosophical Society
Hamilton, William (Benjamin F. Ells)
Director Emeritus, Dayton Public Library
*Harper, Robert S. (Murat Halstead)
Editor and Author, Washington Court House
*Havighurst, Walter (William D. Howells)
Professor of English, Miami University
Hazen, Gladys F. (William R. Harper)
Columbus
Head, Florence M. (Ben Ames Williams)
Director Emeritus, Ohioana Library
Henderson, Robert W. (John S. Rarey)
Bibliographer of American Sports, New York City
Horine, Emmet F. (Daniel Drake)
Retired Physician, Brooks, Ky.
*Jones, W. Powell (George P. Krapp)
Professor of English, Western Reserve University
Keagy, W. R. (Lafcadio Hearn)
Public Utilities Executive, Cincinnati
King, J. L. (Minnie H. Moody)
Professor of English, Denison University
Knepper, George W. (Lucius V. Bierce)
Professor of History, University of Akron
Lattimer, David W. (Washington Gladden)
Late Professor of History, Denison University
Lindsay, Howard (Russel Crouse)
Playwright, New York City
*Lydenberg, Harry M. (Paul L. Dunbar)
Late Director, New York Public Library
Marchman, Watt P. (David R. Locke)
Director, Hayes Memorial Library
Marvin, Walter R. (Frank M. Hubbard)
Director, Ohioana Library

McConnell, H. B. (Robert P. Scott, David Christy, Percy Hammond, Charles A. Hanna, William H. Holmes)
Late Editor, Cadiz *Republican*

*McDonald, Gerald D. (Adna H. Lightner, Jeremiah N. Reynolds, Addison P. Russell, Oliver J. Thatcher)
Chief, American History Division, New York Public Library

*McKay, George L. (Harry M. Lydenberg)
Librarian, New York City

Miller, Ernest I. (Frances W. D'Arusmont, Timothy Flint, John U. Lloyd)
Director, Cincinnati Public Library

*Nicola, Milton G. (Edwin M. Robinson)
Clergyman, Titusville, Pa.

*Orians, G. Harrison (John J. Piatt, Edith M. Thomas)
Professor of American Literature, University of Toledo

Overman, William D. (Samuel A. Lane)
Director, Library and Archives, Firestone Tire & Rubber Co.

Parker, Wyman W. (Margaret Coxe, Edwin H. Davis, Peter Neff, James H. Perkins)
Director, Wesleyan University Library, Middlebury, Conn.

*Pollard, James E. (James Thurber)
Professor of Journalism, Ohio State University

Price, Robert (Mary H. Catherwood)
Professor of English, Otterbein College

Ravitz, Abe C. (Clarence Darrow)
Associate Professor of English, Hiram College

*Richardson, Lyon N. (Constance R. Woolson)
Professor of English and Director of Libraries, Western Reserve University

Rigney, Eugene (Burton E. Stevenson)
President, Ross County Historical Society, Chillicothe

Roberts, Katherine S. (Katherine M. B. Sherwood)
La Jolla, Calif.

*Rodabaugh, James H. (Louis Bromfield, William H. McGuffey, William H. Smith)
Head, History and Science Division, Ohio Historical Society

*Rodgers, Andrew D. (Charles L. Lesquereux, William S. Sullivant)
Attorney, Columbus

Sagmaster, Joseph (William H. Venable)
Cincinnati *Enquirer*

Salomon, R. G. (Philander Chase)
Professor of Ecclesiastical History, Bexley Hall, Kenyon College

*Schneider, Norris F. (Zane Grey, Charles D. Stewart)
Educator and Historian, Zanesville

Seltzer, Louis B. (Lowell J. Thomas)
Editor, Cleveland *Press*

*Shaw, Archer H. (Charles F. Browne)
Retired Editor, Cleveland *Plain Dealer*

Shaw, Henry K. (Burke A. Hinsdale)
Librarian, Christian Theological Seminary, Indianapolis, Ind.
*Siberell, Lloyd E. (Dard Hunter)
Railway Executive, Columbus
*Smith, Ophia D. (Cynthia C. M. Clark)
Oxford
Southwick, Erman D. (Samuel P. Hildreth)
Associate Editor, Marietta *Daily Times*
*Southworth, James S. (Jean S. Untermeyer)
Professor of English, University of Toledo
Stevenson, Adlai E. (Arthur M. Schlesinger, Jr.)
U. S. Ambassador to the United Nations
Sutcliffe, Denham (Sherwood Anderson)
Professor of English, Kenyon College
Templeton, Lee (Eber D. Howe, Norman M. Thomas)
Researcher and Writer, Milwaukee, Wis.
* Thornton, Willis (Herman Fetzer, Albert G. Riddle)
Director, Western Reserve University Press
*Thurber, James (Elliott Nugent)
New York City
*Untermeyer, Jean S. (Frederic Ridgely Torrence)
New York City
*Utter, William T. (Joseph M. Bimeler)
Professor of History, Emeritus, Denison University
Vitz, Carl (Henry F. Farny, Henry Howe)
Director Emeritus, Cincinnati Public Library
Walters, Everett (Joseph B. Foraker)
Dean, Graduate School, Ohio State University
Warner, Landon (Brand Whitlock)
Professor of History, Kenyon College
*Welch, Herbert (Francis J. McConnell)
Retired Bishop, Methodist Episcopal Church
Welsh, E. G. (Clarence E. N. Macartney)
Chairman, Committee on History, Synod of Ohio, Presbyterian Church, U. S. A.
West, Susannah R. (Albion W. Tourgee)
Teacher, Toledo Public Schools
*Wittke, Carl (Arthur M. Schlesinger)
Dean, Graduate School, Western Reserve University
Zorn, Roman J. (James F. Rhodes)
Associate Professor of History, University of Wisconsin

APPENDIX C

Native Ohio Authors

ADAMS COUNTY
Collison, Wilson
Connelly, Thomas W.
Doyle, Edwin A.
Jones, John W.
Kerr, John G.
Lawrance, Uriah M.
Lawrance, William I.
Morrison, Marion
Murphy, David A.
Prather, John
Ramsay, William W.
Smith, Joseph P.
Stableton, John K.
Steen, Moses D. A.
Storer, Elroy T.
Vance, Virginia E. L.
Wilson, John B.
Wittenmyer, Annie T.

ALLEN COUNTY
Baker, Naaman R.
Baxter, Samuel A.
Beiler, Irwin R.
Binkley, Wilfred E.
Burkhardt, Franklin A.
Cable, John L.
Dunne, Gerald W. E.
Eastman, Fred
Fenneman, Nevin M.
Fess, Simeon D.
Knoble, Cliff
Reese, Marie
Rudy, Jacob M.
Rusler, William
Tate, Jane B.

ASHLAND COUNTY
Adams, James A.
Bailey, Rae
Diffendorfer, Ralph E.
Duff, William A.
Grosscup, Peter S.
Long, Simon P.
Newell, William R.
Percival, Milton O.
Rice, Rosella
Robinson, Henry M.
Ross, Edmund G.
Ryall, Lydia J.
Swineford, Alfred P.
White, Wilbert W.

ASHTABULA COUNTY
Andrews, Clarence L.
Babcock, Bernie
Baldwin, Alpha W.
Baldwin, Harman A.
Bell, Archie
Blanchard, Charles E.
Brewer, Annette F.
Brown, Edward
Burton, Theodore E.
Cadwell, Clara G.
Chafer, Lewis S.
Cheney, Frank J.
Colby, June R.
Ellis, Edward S.
Gilchrist, Rosetta L.
Graves, Adelia C. S.
Grover, Delo C.
Hall, Francis I.
Holcomb, Carlysle H.
Howard, John H.
Howland, Charles R.
Hunt, Harrison R.
Lampson, Edward C.
McClelland, Stewart W.
Montgomery, Helen B.
Peck, Walter E.
Picket, Joseph W.
Randall, Pauline B.
Read, Matthew C.
Reed, Sarah A.
Richardson, Lyon N.
SeCheverell, John H.
Sperry, Paul
Streeter, John W.
Thayer, Frank
Titus, John H.
Tourgee, Albion W.
Wade, Decius S.
Wheeler, William W.
Wight, Francis A.

ATHENS COUNTY
Adney, Edwin T.
Ballard, Harlan H.
Bean, Elijah H.
Bond, Lewis H.
Cranston, Earl
DeVelling, Charles T.
Doan, Frank C.
Hoyt, Elizabeth
Kerr, Alvah M.
Lightner, Adna H.
McGill, Mary R.
Matthews, Charles G.
Miller, Samuel A.
Minturn, Joseph A.
Moore, David H.
Naylor, Charles W.
Pilcher, Elijah H.
Rood, John
Stanley, John
True, Hiram L.
Walker, Charles M.
Weethee, Jonathan P.

AUGLAIZE COUNTY
Baker, Arthur M.
Bryan, John
Hoorman, Ferdinand
Howell, Joseph M.
Katterhenry, Edwin A.
Kelley, Francis B.
Morris, Charles E.
Nichols, Robert M.
Shawan, Jacob A.
Smith, Arthur H.
Taeusch, Carl F.
Tully, Jim

BELMONT COUNTY
Ahrendts, Marinda B.
Alexander, Robert
Barnes, Walter
Beazell, William P.
Cochran, John S.
Cochran, Negley D.
Daggett, Mary S.
Darrah, David H.
Edgerton, Jesse
Elliott, Harrison S.
Fritz, John H. C.
Gallaher, Wallace W.
Genin, Sylvester
Giffen, John K.
Glasier, Jessie
Gray, Elisha

Gregg, Thomas
Harrold, Charles F.
Hays, Ebenezer Z.
Howells, William D.
Lee, Alfred E.
Ludey, Charles A.
McPherson, Lydia S.
Matson, Nehemiah
Matthews, Essie C.
Pancoast, Chalmers L.
Peddicord, Kelion F.
Ransom, Reverdy C.
Rider, William H.
Scott, Henry D.
Sharp, Robert L.
Sherwood, Robert E.
Spencer, Edna E. C.
Thoburn, Isabella
Thoburn, James M.
Thoburn, Joseph B.
Thompson, George W.
Thompson, Hugh H.
Vail, Isaac N.
Ver Beck, William F.
Wallace, Francis
Walton, Joseph
Warden, Lewis C.
Welsh, Isaac
Wilson, Erasmus

BROWN COUNTY

Ammen, Daniel
Evans, Nelson W.
Gregg, Frank M.
Hayes, Doremus A.
Humphreys, Mary G.
Keyt, Alonzo T.
Kincheloe, Samuel C.
McLain, John S.
Peake, Elmore E.
Rogers, Joseph M.
Stivers, Emmons B.
Swiggett, Howard
Thornton, George B.
Williams, Bertye Y.

BUTLER COUNTY

Augspurger, Marie M.
Baker, James H.
Barrett, Fred W.
Beaver, Robert P.
Byrne, Thomas S.
Campbell, Edwin R.
Clark, George R.
Cooper, Jacob
Cox, James M.
Crooks, James
DeLeeuw, Adèle L.
DeLeeuw, Cateau
Demoret, Alfred
Elliott, Joseph T.
Flickinger, Daniel K.
Fréchette, Annie T. H.
Gray, William C.
Greene, James H.
Greer, Carl R.
Halstead, Murat
Hamilton, Jay B.
Heaton, David
Heiser, Karl W.
Hurst, Fannie
Kaser, Margaret K.
Keil, Frederick W.
Landis, Frederick
Lenski, Gerhard E.
Liebman, Joshua L.
Longley, Alcander
Longley, Elias
McCloskey, Robert
MacCracken, Henry M.
Martin, John B.
Mason, Carl H.
Meeker, Ezra
Merz, Charles H.
Miller, Elizabeth K.
Oglesby, William D.
Peake, Thomas D.
Peters, William E.
Pierce, Squier L.
Sharkey, Donald C.
Sharts, Joseph W.
Shaw, Albert
Sheehan, Murray
Smith, Louis P.
Stabler, Alvin K.
Taylor, Stella W.
Voorhees, Daniel W.
Wilder, Lucy B.
Woodmansee, James
Woolley, John G.
Wright, Charles
Young, Charles V.

CARROLL COUNTY

Atkinson, Matthew
Tope, Hildred
Tope, Homer W.
Tope, Melancthon
Vail, Theodore N.
Weaver, Jonathan
Weir, William F.

CHAMPAIGN COUNTY

Boyd, Louise E. V.
Brown, Mary E. A.
Clark, Edna M.
Cretcher, Mack
Darrow, Benjamin H.
Eastman, Ephraim R.
Goodwin, Elijah
Houston, William
McAdams, Francis M.
McFarland, Robert W.
Miller, Charles G.
Prince, Benjamin F.
Riker, Ben H.
Schiff, Bessie I.
Seibert, Benjamin E.
Steiner, Jesse F.
Stover, Ross H.
Swisher, James
Ward, May A.
Ware, Joseph
Whitlock, Brand
Williams, Kenneth P.

CLARK COUNTY

Barr, Granville W.
Brain, Belle M.
Braine, Robert D.
Burnett, William R.
Busbey, Hamilton
Canfield, Mary G. W.
Champney, Elizabeth W.
Coffin, Elijah
Coleman, Mary L. R.
Collins, Elijah T.
Colvin, David L.
Funk, Charles E.
Funston, Frederick
Grisso, Forrest W.
Henderson, Elliott B.
Hubbell, George A.
Kauffman, Catherine
Keifer, Joseph W.
Keller, Albert G.
Lamme, Benjamin G.
Lenski, Lois
MacConnell, Sarah A. W.
McKinney, Arthur L.
Macpherson, Georgia H.
Mattox, Absolom H.
Miller, Samuel S.
Mitchell, Charles A.
Newbrough, John B.
Olds, Helen D.
Paschall, Alma
Pearce, Liston H.
Pearson, Francis B.
Plagemann, William W. J.
Pringle, Mary P.
Reeder, Albert
Renick, Marion L.
Rice, Harry E.
Rockel, William M.
Rogers, William A.
Root, Edward T.
Rust, Orton J.
Scholl, John W.
Shepherd, William G.
Shull, James M.
Shull, Lena M. L.
Smith, Jennie
Stephens, David S.
Taylor, Archibald A. E.
Tittle, Ernest E.

Tittle, Walter E.
Toulmin, Harry A.
Wildman, Edward E.
Wilson, Gilbert L.
Woodward, Robert C.

CLERMONT COUNTY
Ashburn, Percy M.
Ashburn, Thomas Q.
Baer, Libbie C.
Bryan, Jennie M.
Chipman, Norton P.
Connor, Eliza A.
Cushing, George H.
Fagley, Frederick L.
Fee, William I.
Fishback, William P.
Foster, Randolph S.
Grant, Ulysses S.
Hall, Charles G.
Hancock, John
Haywood, Harry L.
Hunter, George
Jenkins, Oliver P.
McGehean, Thomas
Makin, John J.
Malone, J. Walter
Melish, John H.
Pemberton, Lovell B.
Robb, Charles
Shields, George O.
Swing, Albert T.
Titus, Murray T.
Wiggins, Lida K.
Williams, Byron

CLINTON COUNTY
Antrim, Joshua
Austin, George M.
Backus, Edwin B.
Bentley, William P.
Conner, Jacob E.
Doane, Robert R.
Dwiggins, William A.
Harvey, William P.
Heiser, Alta H.
Hiatt, Verna W.
Hughes, Jasper S.
Hunt, George M.
Janney, Russell D.
Kile, Orville M.
McDonald, Gerald D.
McKay, Lucinda E.
McVey, Frank L.
McVey, William E.
Moon, Carl
Morris, Alvin M.
Murch, James D.
Russell, Addison P.
Sayrs, William C.
Starbuck, John C.
Thatcher, Oliver J.

Welch, L. B.
Woods, Virna

COLUMBIANA COUNTY
Adams, Charles J.
Atkinson, Robert J.
Atwater, George P.
Barth, Harold B.
Bartholomew, Paul C.
Billingsley, Amos S.
Bradshaw, Marion J.
Bray, Frank C.
Buchanan, John J.
Burson, William
Campbell, Walter L.
Cavanaugh, John W.
Clarke, John H.
Crawford, Mary
Cunningham, Wallace M.
Emeny, Brooks
Firestone, Clark B.
Firestone, Harvey S.
Fisher, George A.
Galbreath, Charles B.
Gilson, John H.
Gould, Charles N.
Hanna, Marcus A.
Holloway, Ephraim S.
Jeffreys, Raymond J.
Johnston, Julia H.
McCook, Henry C.
McCook, John J.
McIntosh, Burr W.
Mendenhall, Thomas C.
Moffat, James D.
Munk, Joseph A.
Reid, Hiram A.
Rogers, Volney
Scott, Daniel F.
Searight, Frank T.
Stookesbury, Sina E.
Stratton, Jennie M.
Tomlinson, William W.
Vallandigham, Clement L.
Vallandigham, James L.
Van Fossan, William H.
Woods, Joseph T.
Young, Louise M.

COSHOCTON COUNTY
Bahmer, William J.
Corlett, William T.
Crawford, Charles
Crile, George W.
Dailey, William M.
Elliott, Blanche
Gamertsfelder, Solomon J.
Green, William
Hardin, Willet L.
Hemler, Opal T.
Kirkpatrick, George R.
McCuskey, Dorothy

Maston, Darius E.
Shaw, William W.
Wheeler, Ada M.

CRAWFORD COUNTY
Beer, Samuel H.
Black, Effie S.
Cowden, Robert
Flick, Alexander C.
Kendall, Carol S.
Krohn, William O.
Michelfelder, Sylvester C.
Monnette, Orra E.
Nave, Orville J.
Reid, Dorothy E.
Robinson, John B.
Schuh, Lewis H.
Sears, Paul B.
Shafer, Boyd C.
Stern, Herman I.
Tunison, Joseph S.

CUYAHOGA COUNTY
Abbey, Everett L.
Allen, James T.
Allyn, Eunice E. G.
Amsbary, Mary A.
Anderson, Dwight
Angell, Ernest
Angell, Hildegarde
Ashburn, Joseph N.
Bacher, Otto H.
Bainbridge, Lucy S.
Baldwin, Elbert F.
Ballard, Willis T.
Bauder, Levi F.
Bauer, Mary T.
Bayer, Eleanor R.
Bayer, Leo G.
Bebenroth, Charlotta M.
Bedell, Mary C.
Bender, Eric J.
Bender, George H.
Berger, Elmer
Bittinger, Lucy F.
Black, Glenn G.
Boardman, Mabel T.
Bohn, Frank
Bolton, Charles K.
Bourjaily, Vance N.
Bowen, Dana T.
Brandt, Herbert W.
Breuer, Elizabeth
Brooks, Alden
Brooks, Charles S.
Brooks, Wililam K.
Brown, Albert M.
Brush, Dorothy H.
Burnett, Charles C.
Burrell, George A.
Burstein, Abraham
Burton, Katherine

Butler, Margaret M.
Campbell, Oscar J.
Carrighar, Sally
Case, Leonard
Chalmers, Allen K.
Chandler, Charles D.
Chesnutt, Charles W.
Ciraci, Norma
Clark, Fred G.
Coates, William R.
Colver, Anne
Copeland, Thomas W.
Cox, Jacob D.
Crehore, William W.
Crile, Grace M.
Crowell, Benedict
Crowell, Chester T.
Curtiss, Phebe A.
Cushing, Harvey W.
Cutter, Orlando P.
Davis, Harry E.
DeCapite, Michael
Dietz, David H.
Dorr, Nell B.
Duncan, John A.
Dykstra, Clarence A.
Elliott, Henry W.
Eyssen, Marguerite F.
Falkner, Leonard
Farmer, Elihu J.
Farmer, James E.
Ferris, Theodore N., Jr.
Fiske, Asa S.
Foote, Edward Bliss
Foote, Edward Bond
Foster, Edwin J.
Foster, Hanna A.
Foster, Henry E.
Foster, Leonard G.
Frayer, Ihna T.
Friedel, Francis J.
Frisbie, Robert D.
Fritchman, Stephen H.
Garfield, James A.
Garis, Lillian C.
Gehring, Albert
Gehring, John G.
Gifford, Fannie S. D.
Gouvy, Gertrude
Gunn, Alexander
Hamilton, Edwin T.
Handerson, Henry E.
Hanford, Ben
Hanscom, Alice E.
Haydn, Hiram C.
Hayes, Jeff W.
Heiner, Marie H.
Henkle, Henrietta
Hensey, Andrew F.
Herman, William
Herrick, Clay, Jr.
Hibben, Frank C.
Hills, Norman E.
Hocking, William E.
Holbrook, Reginald H.
Holzworth, John M.
Hopkins, Arthur M.
Hopwood, Avery
Housum, Robert
Hoyt, James H.
Hoyt, Wayland
Huddilston, John H.
Hudson, Jay W.
Hughes, Adella P.
Hutchinson, Veronica S.
Hutchison, Hazel C.
Ireland, Thomas S.
Jones, Howard E.
Kenly, Julie W. T. C.
Kennedy, William S.
Kepler, William M.
Ketchum, Alton H.
Kiener, Mother Mary A.
King, Agnes B.
Kitchen, Karl K.
Knittle, Rhea M.
Knowlton, Donald S.
Knowlton, William A.
Krock, George L.
Lamprecht, Sterling P.
Lawrence, Alberta E. I. C.
Lawrence, Jerome K.
Lewis, Alfred H.
Linderman, Frank B.
Loring, John A.
Loveman, Robert
Luedy, Arthur E.
Lyttle, Charles H.
Mabie, Louise K.
Manak, Roberta
Martin, Charles A.
Mather, Amasa S.
Mather, Frederick G.
Meeker, Nathan C.
Menke, Frank G.
Miller, Dayton C.
Miner, John T.
Mlakar, Frank
Moley, Ramond
Moody, Helen W.
Mooney, James D.
Morrow, Elizabeth R. C.
Munn, Hiran H.
Nasmyth, George W.
Newberry, Arthur S.
Newcomb, Alan H.
Newman, Edward M.
Newman, Gertrude A.
Norton, Alice M.
Norton, Jessie
Nye, Margaret F.
Olmsted, Millicent
Pack, Arthur N.
Packard, Roy D.
Paddock, Buckley B.
Painter, Lydia E. F.
Palmer, Frances L.
Parsons, Julia S.
Peet, Stephen D.
Perkins, Edna B.
Perry, Oliver H.
Picard, George H.
Piercy, Caroline B.
Poese, William
Post, Charles A.
Prentiss, Harriet D. M.
Price, Warwick, J.
Quigley, Martin J.
Raddatz, William J.
Redinger, Ruby V.
Rhodes, Harrison G.
Rhodes, James F.
Roach, Corwin C.
Rockefeller, John D., Jr.
Rorimer, James J.
Rose, William G.
Rourke, Constance M.
Rowell, Adelaide C.
Schaefer, Jack W.
Schauffler, Grace L.
Schneider, Herbert W.
Sethman, William C.
Severance, Mark S.
Seymour, Flora W.
Shackleton, Elizabeth F.
Siedel, Frank
Smart, Charles A.
Smith, Henry L.
Splan, John
Stearns, Lucy P.
Stearns, Theodore
Stearns, Wallace N.
Street, Elwood V.
Stuart, Graham H.
Taylor, Katherine K.
Thompson, Ruth L.
Thornton, Willis
Tildes, Olga A.
Toon, Gladys E.
Townsend, Edward W.
Umbstaetter, Herman D.
Van Kirk, Walter W.
Vincent, Beatrice M.
Vokoun, Frank J.
Waldman, Milton
Walter, Eugene
Webster, Marjorie E.
Wedel, Lois
Weidenthal, Leo
Weston, Asa M.
Wheeler, Edward J.
Whitman, Howard
Whittern, Charles S.
Wiborg, Frank B.
Wilbur, James B.
Wilcox, Frank N.

Williams, Nathan W.
Wolf, Edith A.
Woolsey, Sarah C.
Wright, Charles B.
Wright, Edward S.
Young, Agnes B.
Zangerle, John A.
Zorbaugh, Harvey W.
Zybura, John S.

DARKE COUNTY

Baker, May A.
Charlesworth, Ruby H.
Commons, John R.
Eppse, Merl R.
Gould, Jean R.
Heck, Earl L. W.
Henderson, Joseph F.
Katzenberger, Frances I.
Koch, Katharine I.
Perry, Robert E.
Reck, Waldo E.
Royer, Homer L.
Swartout, Annie F.
Thomas, Lowell J.
Wilson, Frazer E.
Wilson, Grove
Young, Calvin M.

DEFIANCE COUNTY

Boyd, Thomas A.
Chapman, Ervin S.
Clark, Walter E.
Dilworth, Hiram P.
Hootman, George W.
Knight, Ruth A.
Prueser, Sara V.
Royce, Charles C.
Weisenberger, Francis P.
Wilhelm, Donald G.

DELAWARE COUNTY

Allen, Horace N.
Andrews, J. Cutler
Aumann, Francis R.
Campbell, Daisy R.
Canfield, James H.
Evans, Lawrence B.
Hannum, Alberta P.
Hayes, Rutherford B.
Hughes, Thomas J.
Keen, Samuel A.
Kester, Paul
Kyrk, Hazel
Livingston, Miriam D.
Lowry, Robert E.
Neff, Emery E.
Nettleton, Alfred B.
Newcomb, Robert T.
Parlette, Ralph A.
Patterson, Anne V. S.
Paul, Nannette B.
Powell, Thomas E.
Powell, Warren T.
Rhodes, Charles D.
Rose, Martha E. P.
Schuette, Walter E.
Short, John T.
Watts, Mary S.
Wintermute, Martha V. D.

ERIE COUNTY

Anderson, Marjorie
Armstrong, Moses K.
Barker, Laura E. C.
Barringer, Edwin C.
Beatty, John
Butler, Jay C.
Cravath, Paul D.
Davis, Lemuel C.
Emerson, John
Everett, Homer
Everson, Florence M.
Fish, Williston
Frohman, Daniel
Frye, Burton J. C.
Gilchrist, Marie E.
Green, Charles R.
Hathaway, William E.
Hine, Lucius A.
Judson, Phoebe N. G.
Macchetta, Blanche R. T.
MacMillan, Mary L.
Mann, William D.
Merz, Charles
Otis, Philo A.
Parsons, Albert R.
Ruggles, Kent P.
Ryan, James A.
Savage, Ann P.
Silver, Debbie H.
Tillinghast, Henry B.
Tuttle, Hudson
Victor, Orville J.
Ward, William G.
Whitney, Lorenenzo H. L.

FAIRFIELD COUNTY

Bareis, George F.
Brenneman, Henry B.
Clymer, Albert
Ewing, Hugh B.
Giesy, Samuel H.
Griswold, Latta
Hastings, Rosetta B.
Hebble, Charles R.
Hilles, Frederick W.
Hyde, Solon
Killits, John M.
Leonard, Henry
Loucks, Michael
Lytle, James R.
Miller, Charles C.
Neibling, C. C.
Outcault, Richard F.
Reber, George
Sherman, John
Sherman, William T.
Shetrone, Henry C.
Snider, Van A.
Snow, Jane E.
Watson, Amelia B.
Waugh, Alice G.
Weist, Carl S.
Wells, Edmund
Williams, Alfred
Wiseman, Charles M. L.

FAYETTE COUNTY

Allen, Hugh
Baker, Magdalena D. H.
Crispin, William F.
Daugherty, Harry M.
Duffee, May M.
Fitzgerald, Pitt L.
Gillespie, Samuel L.
Gunning, William D.
Hill, John W.
Kirk, Grayson L.
Martin, Lawrence A.
Sanderson, Eugene C.
Savage, Thomas J.
Winchester, Marie M.

FRANKLIN COUNTY

Albaugh, Dorothy P.
Alberry, Faxon F. D.
Blaney, Charles E.
Boylan, Marguerite T.
Brown, Sara L.
Buck, Paul H.
Byers, Joseph P.
Carrington, Margaret I. S.
Carson, Julia M. H.
Cless, George H.
Coit, Stanton
Coulter, Ernest K.
Cox, George C.
Dobyns, Fletcher
Doherty, Henry L.
Donaldson, Thomas C.
Doney, Carl G.
Drake, Emily H.
Dun, John D.
Dyer, John L.
Eaton, Jeannette
Evans, Daniel L.
Felch, William F.
Ferril, Helen R.
Fippin, Elmer O.
Frankenberg, Theodore T.
Frings, Ketti
Gardner, Robert E.
Gill, Wilson L.
Gilliam, Charles F.
Gilmore, Florence

Glenn, James S.
Graebner, Walter A.
Graham, Albert A.
Hack, Gwendolyn D. K.
Haig, Robert M.
Harding, Warren G., II
Horton, Joshua H.
House, Erwin
Hoyt, John W.
Hull, Alexander
Humphries, Adelaide M.
Huntington, Webster P.
Hutchinson, Frank H.
Jackson, Jesse
Janis, Elsie
Jenkins, Hermon D.
Jenney, Mary P.
Kellor, Frances A.
Knopf, Carl S.
LaMonte, John L.
Lawrence, James C.
Leckliter, Grace D.
LeSourd, Leonard E.
McCabe, Lida R.
McClure, Robert E.
McClure, Samuel G., Jr.
McCombs, Ralph L. F.
McElwaine, Ethyl
Mees, Arthur
Mees, Theophilus M. K.
Mills, William S.
Morehead, Lavinia M. E.
Myers, Joseph S.
Newfang, Oscar
Newsom, William M.
Nicholas, Edward
Norris, Emory
O'Kane, Walter C.
Paterson, Robert G.
Platt, Cyrus
Platt, Rutherford H.
Price, Emerson
Rarey, John S.
Reiser, Oliver L.
Richards, Joseph H. C.
Richardson, Will S.
Rickenbacker, Edward V.
Ripley, Roswell S.
Rodgers, Anthony D., III
Schenck, Earl
Schlesinger, Arthur M., Jr.
Schwarzwalder, John
Sherman, Christopher E.
Siebert, Wilbur H.
Sigler, Pearl N.
Smith, Lucy H. K.
Smith, Robert P.
Spahr, Charles B.
Stagg, Abraham
Starling, William
Stewart, Donald O.
Stewart, George B.
Studer, Jacob H.
Sullivant, Joseph
Sullivant, William S.
Tallant, Edith
Taylor, Edward L.
Thomas, Eleanor
Thurber, James G.
Thurston, Edward
Trautman, Milton B.
Vance, Rowland B.
Vaughan, Charles R.
Walker, Rollin H.
Wallis, Louis
Waltz, Elizabeth C.
Wheaton, John M.
Williams, Beryl
Williams, Edward T.
Wilson, John A.
Wittke, Carl F.
Woods, Henry M.

FULTON COUNTY

Aldrich, Fred H.
Alwood, William B.
Bullard, Frederic L.
Derby, Roswell, Jr.
Drennan, Marie
Johnson, Davis B.
Johnson, Solomon
Reighard, Frank H.
Wood-Allen, Mary

GALLIA COUNTY

Agee, Alva
Ball, Eustace H.
Bell, James M.
Coffeen, Henry A.
Dahlgren, Sarah M. V. G.
Evans, William R.
Ewing, Elmore E.
Harding, Arthur R.
Holcombe, Return I.
Love, Jeanette F.
Lucas, Eliza S.
Maddy, Homer B.
Nida, William L.
Shade, William H. T.
Thomas, Ruth
Wickline, William A.

GEAUGA COUNTY

Converse, Julius O.
Denton, Franklin E.
Dodge, Homer J.
Dodge, Martin H.
Henry, Frederick A.
Ludlow, Arthur C.
Luther, Clair F.
Matson, Clarence H.
Stocking, Amer M.
Wood, George L.

GREENE COUNTY

Barrett, Don C.
Benson, Henry C.
Boteler, Mattie M.
Browder, Uriah M.
Campbell, Elsie J. C.
Clemans, Sarah I. C.
Davie, Oliver
Drees, Charles W.
Dunlap, E. K.
Fleming, Daniel J.
Foster, Finley M.
Funk, Isaac K.
Galloway, William A.
George, Andrew M.
Hyslop, James H.
Johnston, Howard A.
Kelly, Fred C.
Lawrance, William V.
McMillan, Homer
Meredith, L. P.
Nesbit, Wilbur D.
Newton, Frances H.
Orr, Charles H.
Owens, Ira S.
Paullin, Charles O.
Paxson, William A.
Peale, Norman V.
Quinn, Daniel
Reid, James H.
Reid, Whitelaw
Rife, David C.
Robinson, George F.
Schlesinger, Arthur M.
Scott, Hervey
Thorne, Charles E.
Torrence, Frederic R.
Walker, Thomas B.
Wike, Murlie B.
Zimmerman, Sarah A.

GUERNSEY COUNTY

Campbell, Mary E.
Carnes, Sidney C.
Eagleson, Hodge M.
Fleming, Wallace B.
Glenn, Emma L. P.
Harris, Leon R.
Heiner, Jessie M.
Jefferson, Charles E.
Lawyer, James P.
Luccock, George N.
Luccock, Naphtali
McFarland, Jeannette
McVicker, Daphne A.
Maple, Joseph C.
Miller, Sadie M.
Neubeck, Mary C.
Oldham, Samuel
Peacock, Thomas B.
Sarchet, Cyrus P. B.
Shimp, Ellis H.

Slaughter, Gertrude E. T.
Spaythe, Jacob A.
Springer, Walter G.
Stewart, Nixon B.
Stranathan, May
Wilson, Joseph G.
Wolfe, William G.
Wood, Sheridan F.

HAMILTON COUNTY

Addington, Sarah
Agger, Eugene E.
Allen, Emory A.
Allen, Ethan
Allen, Hans V. N.
Allen, Lee
Anderson, Bessie W.
Anderson, Edward L.
Anderson, Richard C.
Anspacher, Louis K.
Athens, Ida G.
Backus, Emma H. S.
Baldus, Simon A.
Ball, Alice E.
Banta, Melissa E. R.
Bardon, Minna F.
Beard, Daniel C.
Beard, James C.
Beard, Mary C.
Beard, Thomas F.
Beauchamp, Lou J.
Behrman, Ethel K.
Benedict, Agnes E.
Best, Susie M.
Bevis, Alma D.
Bickham, William D.
Biles, Roy E.
Black, Robert L.
Bodley, Rachel L.
Bonte, George W.
Boyland, George H.
Branham, Charles A.
Brannan, William P.
Brewster, Stanley F.
Brooks, Jennie
Brotherton, John W.
Brown, Frederic
Browning, Charles H.
Bugbee, Lucius H.
Bunker, John J. L.
Burnet, Frank D.
Burrows, Millar
Burt, Pitts H.
Byer, Herbert
Cady, John H.
Carey, Charles H.
Carrier, Warren P.
Carter, Alfred G. W.
Carver, George
Cary, Alice
Cary, Phoebe
Cary, Samuel F.
Chase, Jessie A.
Chester, George R.
Chipman, H. G.
Cist, Henry M.
Clark, Mazie E.
Clarke, Peter E.
Cleveland, Grace E. M.
Clopper, Edward N.
Collins, Clinton
Comegys, Charles G.
Cone, Stephen D.
Cooper, Dorothy
Cooper, William C.
Coyle, Robert M.
Crafts, Sara J.
Craig, John D.
Cranmer, Gibson L.
Cranston, Lucie M.
Crapsey, Algernon S.
Crippen, William G.
Culbertson, Henry C.
Dandridge, Raymond G.
Davis, William B.
Day, Sarah J.
Deasy, Mary M.
DeCamp, Ellis O.
de Chambrun, Clara L.
Dessar, Leo C.
Dexter, Charles
Dickoré, Marie P.
Diebold, Janet H.
Drake, Charles D.
DuBois, Frances H.
Dunbar, Seymour
Dunlevy, Anthony H.
Durham, E. Samuel
Eckstein, Gustav
Eddy, Thomas M.
Elam, Charles M.
Ellard, Harry G.
Ellard, Virginia G.
Eustis, Helen
Eversull, Harry K.
Faison, Mabel H.
Farny, Margaret W.
Field, Sara B.
Fillmore, Parker H.
Finkelstein, Louis
Fisher, George J.
Flash, Henry L.
Fleischmann, Julius
Fletcher, Robert H.
Flowers, Montaville
Fosdick, William W.
Friedrich, Ralph
Fullerton, Kemper
Gamble, Sidney D.
Garey, Thomas A.
Garrard, Lewis H.
Garrison, Elisha E.
Gatchell, Charles
Gavin, Frank S. B.
Gerard, Clinton W.
Glueck, Nelson
Graydon, Thomas H.
Greve, Charles T.
Groesbeck, Telford
Groff, William N.
Groom, Charlotte L.
Hall, Edward H.
Hammel, Mamie L.
Handy, William H.
Hargrave, Catherine P.
Harris, Norman D.
Harrison, Benjamin
Henri, Robert
Herzog, Margaret G.
Hesing, Washington
Hessler, Iola O.
Hexter, Maurice B.
Hoffman, Charles W.
Holmes, Arthur
Hopkins, Charles E.
Hornback, Florence M.
Horton, Thomas C.
Hubbard, Lucius L.
Hubert, Philip G.
Hugentabler, Robert C.
Humble, Henry W.
Hunt, Samuel F.
Huston, Paul G.
Ingalls, Fay
Isaacs, Nathan
Isham, Mary K.
Israel, Edward L.
Jacobs, Anne M.
James, Alice A. S.
James, Francis B.
Jarnagin, Dorothy G.
Jenkins, Edward L.
Jewett, John B.
Kaiser, Ramona
Kates, Philip
Kellogg, Elizabeth R.
Kemper, Andrew C.
Kemper, Frederick A.
Kitchell, Joseph G.
Kittredge, Daniel W.
Koch, Felix J.
Kohler, Julilly H.
Kramer, Stella
Krapp, George P.
Kronenberger, Louis
Kuechler, Otto
Lacey, Margaret E.
Lacey, Thomas J.
Lamott, John H.
Lamson, Peggy F.
Leonard, Adna W.
Levi, Harry
Longworth, Nicholas
Lord, John K.
Lowry, Robert
Lucas, Anna M.

Ludwig, Charles
Lupton, Dilworth
Lytle, William H.
McAllister, Anna S.
McCann, Sister Mary A.
McGiffert, Arthur C., Jr.
McGrane, Reginald C.
McGroarty, William B.
McLaughlin, George
McLaughlin, Mary L.
MacMillan, Marion T.
Maddux, Berton J.
Mallon, Guy W.
Matthews, Mother Eva L.
Matthews, Stanley
Matthews, Thomas S.
Maxwell, James A.
May, Max B.
Mayer, Albert I.
Meeker, Jotham
Meyer, Hugo R.
Minor, Thomas C.
Mitchel, Frederick A.
Mitchell, Daniel H.
Mitchell, Stewart
Moerlein, George
Morgan, Arthur E.
Morgan, William Y.
Morrison, Charles C.
Movius, Anne M.
Neff, Cornelius
Neff, Peter
Nelson, Helen L.
Newhall, Robert D.
Nichols, William T.
Ninde, Edward S.
Nolen, Eleanor W.
Oakes, George W. O.
Ogden, George C.
O'Hara, Julie C.
Oliver, Wade W.
Owen, William M.
Parry, Emma L.
Patterson, Ernest M.
Paver, John M.
Payler, Esther M.
Peck, John W.
Peck, Nelle W.
Pendleton, Edmund
Pendleton, George H.
Perry, Elizabeth W.
Piatt, Donn
Piatt, Louise K.
Posegate, Mabel
Pummill, James
Rains, Paul B.
Ransohoff, Joseph
Raymond, Rossiter W.
Reeves, Arthur M.
Rettig, John
Richardson, Leander
Riker, John F.
Rimanoczy, Richard S.
Risley, Samuel D.
Robinson, Chalfant
Rodabaugh, James H.
Rogers, Lebbeus H.
Rogers, Margaret D.
Ross, Denman W.
Royse, Noble K.
Ruess, Stella K.
Rust, John B.
Ryan, Daniel J.
Ryan, Walter A.
Sampson, Martin W.
Santmyer, Helen H.
Sattler, Eric E.
Sauer, Louis W.
Saunders, David B.
Schevill, Ferdinand
Schevill, Rudolph
Schulze, Mildred E.
Scott, William B.
Scudder, John M.
Sears, Angeline B.
Seasongood, Murray
Self, Margaret C.
Selwyn, Edgar
Sheehan, Perley P.
Shepardson, Francis W.
Shepardson, George D.
Shields, Pauline R.
Shiels, William E.
Shriner, Charles A.
Shuey, Edwin L.
Siewers, Sarah M.
Simrall, Margaret M.
Slater, Mary W.
Smith, George T.
Smith, Miles W.
Smith, Oberlin
Smith, Preserved
Smith, Vincent E.
Sparkes, Boyden
Steep, Thomas
Stephenson, Henry T.
Stephenson, Nathaniel W.
Sternberger, Estelle M.
Stevens, George E.
Steward, Ann
Stewart Anna B.
Stewart, Thomas M.
Storer, Bellamy
Storer, Maria L. N.
Strauss, Joseph B.
Swing, David
Tackenberg, Charles W.
Taft, Charles P.
Taft, Helen H.
Taft, Henry W.
Taft, Horace D.
Taft, Robert A.
Taft, William H.
Tait, John R.
Thomas, Rolla L.
Thompson, Aaron B.
Thompson, Clara A.
Thompson, David D.
Thompson, Priscilla J.
Thomson, Peter G.
Thomson, William M.
Thuma, Helen D.
Tibbals, Seymour S.
Tiffany, Nina M.
Tomlinson, Athelia M.
Tressler, Donald K.
Turner, Lida W.
Turpie, David
Tuttle, Margaretta M.
Underwood, Charlotte W.
Urner, Mabel H.
Urner, Nathan D.
Venable, Emerson
Venable, William M.
Voss, Elizabeth N.
Wald, Lillian D.
Wallington, Nellie U.
Walton, George E.
Wambaugh, Sarah
Washburne, Heluiz C.
White, John W.
Whittaker, James T.
Williams, John F.
Williamson, Horace G.
Wilshire, Henry G.
Wilson, Samuel R.
Woellner, Fredric P.
Wood, Charles S.
Wood, Frederick M.
Workman, Mary C. S.
Wright, D. Thew
Wright, William B.
Wunder, Clinton
Zeligs, Rose
Zenner, Philip

HANCOCK COUNTY

Adams, Jacob
Ascham, John B.
Cole, Ralph D.
Crouse, Russel
Dukes, Harriet E. G.
Fowler, Mary B.
Grose, Parlee C.
Guise, Cedric H.
Heminger, Isaac N.
Hower, Frank L.
Kershner, Glenn R.
Keyser, Cassius J.
McCaughey, Maretta R.
Palmer, John R.
Vance, J. Wilson
Welty, J. Jerome

HARDIN COUNTY

Allen, Abel L.
Benton, Guy P.

Blue, Herbert T. O.
Campbell, Lily B.
Conrard, George H. A.
Freeman, Martin J.
Garwood, Irving
Hale, William J.
Helms, Elmer E.
Kennedy, Sarah L.
Machetanz, Frederick
McMillen, Wheeler
Melhorn, Nathan R.
Shockey, Samuel W.
Stevenson, Louis L.
Thomas, Daniel D.
Young, Allyn A.

HARRISON COUNTY
Akeley, Mary J.
Burtoft, Lavina A. H. J.
Cowen, Benjamin R.
Crawford, Thomas R.
Custer, George A.
Garst, Laura D.
Hammond, Percy H.
Hanna, Charles A.
Harding, John M.
Harrison, Joseph T.
Holmes, James T.
Holmes, William H.
Hough, Lynn H.
Hunter, William H.
Irwin, Demaris
Johnston, Nathan R.
Kyle, Melvin G.
Longsworth, Basil N.
McAdam, Dunlap J.
McGavran, Samuel B.
Nevin, William C.
Petty, Orville A.
Ralston, Chester F.
Ramsay, Janet
Ryder, Melvin
Sawvel, Franklin B.
Schilling, Robert W.
Scott, Robert P.
Shepfer, Harold R.
Shotwell, Walter G.
Simpson, Matthew
Slaughter, Linda W.
Smith, James P.
Tipton, Thomas W.
Vincent, Thomas M.
Welch, Anthony C.
Welch, John
Wishart, John E.
Wright, Edward E.
Wright, William H.

HENRY COUNTY
Brennan, John P.
Brown, Joe E.
DeLong, Arthur H.
Margrat, Mae E.
Redhead, Alice C.
Rothenburger, William R.
Schwiebert, Ernest G.

HIGHLAND COUNTY
Allison, David P.
Ayres, Atlee B.
Bering, John
Beveridge, Albert J.
Bonner, David F.
Brewster, William N.
Caniff, Milton A.
Carlisle, Walter E.
Cornetet, Noah E.
Crothers, Samuel D.
Curry, Otway
Davis, Edwin H.
Doggett, Henry S.
Faris, Lillie A.
Foraker, Joseph B.
Foster, Caroline H. W.
Fullerton, Hugh S.
Harper, Robert S.
Haynes, Roy A.
Honline, Moses A.
Huggins, William L.
Hunter, Cora W.
Irwin, William H. H.
McNicol, Hugh S.
Martin, Renwick H.
Miller, Thurman
Montgomery, Thomas
Moore, David W.
Morgan, Violet
Neff, Elizabeth H.
Parker, Caroline H.
Pike, James
Rives, Marie T.
Scott, Samuel P.
Thompson, Eliza J. T.
Tuttle, Mary M. T.

HOCKING COUNTY
Biddle, Horace P.
McCarty, Ida H. D.
Rodeheaver, Homer A.
Salmans, Levi B.
Webb, Tessa S.
Work, Edgar W.

HOLMES COUNTY
Ballou, Elsie A.
Fortune, Alonza W.
Given, Welker
Harris, Adah M. G.
Laylander, Orange J.
McCulloch, Roscoe C.
McDowell, William F.
Manatt, James I.
Moore, Ambrose B.
Officer, Morris
Pennell, William W.
Uhl, Lemon L.
Welshimer, Helen L.
Williams, Albert B.
Winter, Nevin O.
Workman, Charles H.

HURON COUNTY
Brooks, Eliphalet
Cowles, Julia D.
Culbertson, Hugh E.
Curran, Grace W.
French, Elsie J.
Haas, William H.
Henry, William A.
Jennings, Otto E.
Keesy, William A.
Kennan, George
Kinney, Bruce
Laning, Jay F.
Lisle, William M.
Luxon, Norval N.
Mead, George W.
Miller, Ellen B. R.
Newman, Joseph S.
Noble, Cyrus W.
Osborn, Hartwell
Reed, Fannie K.
Rennelson, Clara H. M.
Ries, William F.
Smith, Abbie N.
Spears, Raymond S.
States, Fannie M.
Waggoner, Clark
Wildman, Marion W.
Williams, Albert R.
Williams, Charles D.

JACKSON COUNTY
Baker, Cornelia
Davies, John T.
Foraker, Julia B.
Gillilan, James D.
Gillilan, Strickland
Isham, Asa B. L.
Jones, Ira L.
Kinnison, Charles S.
Lively, James M.
Long, Fanny F.
Mackley, John H.
Maurer, David W.
Miller, H. C.
Patterson, James H.
Ray, E. S.
Rowe, Frank H.
Williams, Daniel W.
Wilmore, Augustus C.
Young, Jeremiah S.

JEFFERSON COUNTY
Adams, James B.
Bartley, Thomas W.

Bates, David H.
Chapin, Henry D.
Clark, Alexander
Doyle, Joseph B.
Dundass, Samuel R.
Erskine, Dorothy B.
Fisher, Benjamin F.
Geer, Ney N.
Gray, Oliver C.
Hunter, Dard
Lawrence, Lou
Lawrence, William
Leavitt, John M.
McGrew, Thomas F.
Means, Stewart
Merrill, Stephen M.
Mills, William
Milner, Duncan C.
Morgan, Thomas B.
Newton, Joseph H.
Pittenger, William
Riggs, Stephen R.
Roberts, Charles H.
Scott, John
Sloane, William M.
Smith, Byron C.
Todd, Walter E. C.
Updegraff, David B.
Van Kirk, James W.
Wright, Mary T.

KNOX COUNTY
Ames, Delano
Barker, John M.
Bates, Ernest S.
Best, Nolan R.
Beum, Robert L.
Blackledge, Celize F.
Chambers, Merritt M.
Colerick, Edward F.
Gates, Josephine S.
Hastings, Lansford W.
Herrick, Sophia M. B.
Hervey, Henry M.
James, Fleming
Lathrop, Lorin A.
Lee, James
Levering, Robert W.
Lhamon, William J.
Lybarger, Lee F.
Norton, Anthony B.
Scribner, Harvey
Sockman, Ralph W.
Squier, Lee W.
Welker, Martin
Wood, David W.

LAKE COUNTY
Adams, William L.
Barnes, Lemuel C.
Beard, Adelia B.
Beard, William H.
Branch, Edward P.
Carrel, Cora G.
Carrel, Minnie E. B.
Conger, Sarah P.
Curtis, Anna L.
Kellogg, Charlotte
Ladd, George T.
Lincoln, James F.
Mathews, Alfred
Norton, William H.
Olin, Saul C.
Opper, Emma A.
Opper, Frederick B.
Paine, Bayard H.
Shankland, Frank N.
Smith, Joseph
Smith, Percy K.
Warner, Horace E.
Wellman, Walter
Wyman, Mary E. T.

LAWRENCE COUNTY
Fry, Susanna M. D.
Hatcher, Harlan H.
Holliday, Carl
Knepper, Mamie C.
Lampton, William J.
McConn, Charles M.
Moore, Edward E.
Porter, Will
Richards, John T.
Rightmire, George W.
Ryan, Don
Sutton, Joseph J.

LICKING COUNTY
Andorn, Sidney
Ashbrook, William A.
Baird, Samuel J.
Bancroft, Hubert H.
Bates, Miner S.
Beardsley, D. B.
Beecher, Edward N.
Besse, Henry
Bricker, Garland A.
Brown, Harry M.
Bryant, Lorinda M.
Burns, James J.
Burton, Ernest D.
Bushnell, Henry
Catherwood, Mary H.
Clark, Neil M.
Clifton, John L.
Coman, Katharine
Conard, Howard L.
Cook, Tennessee C. C.
Coomes, Oliver
Cooperrider, George T.
Cunningham, William M.
Dorsey, George A.
Elliott, George
Foster, Ethel F.
Gilliam, Davis T.
Hayes, Ellen
Hooper, Osman C.
Hoover, Guy I.
Howard, James Q.
Hunter, Robbins
Lawrence, Eda H.
Legler, Mary F.
Long, Mason
Martin, Victoria C. W.
Metz, Walter C.
Moody, Minnie H.
Murray, Lois L. A.
Myers, Jay A.
Nash, Henry S.
Northrop, Stephen A.
Park, Samuel
Price, Ira M.
Rosecrans, Sylvester H.
Schaff, Morris
Scott, Joseph M.
Scott, Milton R.
Shepardson, Daniel
Simkins, Joshua D.
Smythe, Brandt G.
Spangler, Helen K.
Sparks, Edwin E.
Sprague, Marshall
Sprague, Mary A.
Stevens, Isaac N.
Sturgeon, Molly B.
White, Charles B.
Whitehead, John
Wilder, Margaret B.
Wilson, Edward S.
Wyrick, David

LOGAN COUNTY
Anderson, George W.
Campbell, Marion
Chambers, James J.
Edwards, Donald E.
Fuller, Emily G.
Gladding, Effie P.
Grabiel, Zephaniah
Herskovits, Melville J.
Hopkins, Livingston
Hubbard, Frank M.
Hubbard-Kernan, Will
Johnston, John B.
Kiplinger, Willard M.
Kuhns, William T.
Long, Julius W.
Macartney, Clarence E. N.
McClain, Naomi S.
McGinnis, Frederick A.
Paterson, Robert
Porter, James A.
Shultz, Joseph S.
Smith, Walter G.
Thornton, Edwin W.
Williams, John C.
Wood, Eugene
Wylie, David G.

LORAIN COUNTY
Allen, Frederick D.
Barton, Fred B.
Biddle, Jacob A.
Bragdon, Claude F.
Cathcart, William H.
Chamberlain, Ernest B.
Cochran, William C.
Curtiss, George L.
Cushman, Clarissa W. F.
Dodd, Henry M.
Eastman, Linda A.
Ely, Charles A.
Fairchild, George T.
Freeman, Julia S. W.
Frost, Stanley
Frost, Wesley
Gillmore, Quincy A.
Gittings, Ella P. B.
Haskell, Henry J.
Herrick, Myron T.
Horr, Alfred R.
Hudson, James F.
Jackson, Eva E.
Jewell, Louise P.
Lee, Robert D.
Leighton, Margaret C.
Magoun, F. Alexander
Miner, Luella
Monteith, John
Morgan, Anne E. F.
Parks, L. K.
Pierce, Ernest P.
Rawson, Clayton
Ryder, Arthur W.
Ryder, Robert O.
Shaw, Archer H.
Siddall, John M.
Tenney, Luman H.
Thomas, Katharine G.
Vietzen, Raymond C.
Vincent, John M.
Walden, Robert L.
Warner, Henry E.
Weeks, Frank E.
Westervelt, William D.
Zurcher, Arnold J.

LUCAS COUNTY
Alter, Karl J.
Andrews, Gertrude N.
Ashley, Charles S.
Bartelle, J. P.
Beach, Edward L.
Berdan, John M.
Bliss, Sylvia H.
Brinkerhoff, Robert M.
Brown, Oril
Brownlee, Jane A.
Calisch, Edward N.
Campbell, Louis W.
Colton, Olive A.
Condon, Frank
Corey, Herbert
Cosgrove, Maynard G.
Davis, Lyman E.
Dean, Corinne
Donovan, Joseph W.
Drago, Harry S.
Dunlap, Maurice P.
Effler, Louis R.
Follet, Margaret W.
Ford, Collin
Gilmore, Elsie
Guild, Ella J. P.
Guitteau, William B.
Harpster, Hilda T.
Hollington, Richard D.
Hosmer, John A.
Huberich, Charles H.
Johnson, Wendell F.
Ketcham, Wilmot A.
Larson, Alice
Lawrance, Harold G.
Loban, Ethel H.
MacCracken, Henry N.
MacGowan, Alice
MacVey, William P.
Morse, Robert
Munn, Glenn G.
Niess, Sister Mary Vera
O'Toole, George B.
Pargellis, Stanley M.
Rorick, Isabel S.
Sanger, Margot
Sibley, Edward C.
Smythe, George F.
Taylor, Frederick W.
Tippett, Edwin J.
Wason, Robert A.
Weed, Clarence M.
Wickenden, Arthur C.
Williams, Caroline L. R.
Williams, Egerton R.
Woolley, Celia P.
Worts, George F.

MADISON COUNTY
Beach, John N.
Byers, William N.
Cheseldine, Raymond M.
Crawford, Benjamin F.
Freeman, Winfield
Hickernell, Warren F.
Jeffries, James G.
Johnson, Edward W.
Lane, Etta F.
McGaffey, Ernest
Moriarty, Helen L.
Strain, Rodney
Watson, David K.

MAHONING COUNTY
Aley, Howard C.
Baldwin, William H.
Barker, Mary L.
Bunts, Frank E.
Burnett, Henry L.
Burt, John S.
Butler, Henry A.
Campbell, Mary R.
DeFord, Sara W.
Elser, Donald
Evans, Frederick N.
Fisk, George M.
Galaida, Edward
Gaul, Harriette L. A.
Hamilton, Edmond M.
Hayden, Amos S.
Hutchins, Frank W.
Kemp, Harry H.
Kirtland, Lucian S.
Leonard, Adna B.
Mansfield, Ira F.
Matson, Henry
Moore, Ernest C.
Ott, Edward A.
Packard, Jasper
Schumann, Mary K.
Sherwood, Katherine M. B.
Stanley, Lysander M.
Taylor, Charles B.
Wanamaker, Reuben M.
Whiteleather, Melvin K.

MARION COUNTY
Conklin, Edwin G.
Dix, Fred K.
Fite, Emerson D.
Hahn, Benjamin D.
Hipsher, Edward E.
Keeler, Clyde E.
McNeal, Thomas A.
Orians, George H.
Search, Preston W.
Thomas, Norman M.
Warwick, Frank M.
Weeks, Oliver D.

MEDINA COUNTY
Adams, William E.
Alden, Carroll S.
Aldrich, Julia C.
Alger, Russell A.
Ambler, Henry L.
Barone, Allen G.
Brinkerhoff, Henry R.
Dowd, Quincy L.
Hinsdale, Burke A.
Hinsdale, Wilbert B.
Kingsley, Florence M.
Lewis, Charles B.
Loomis, Elisha S.
Lowrie, Donald A.
Mead, Edward S.
Pond, Mariam B.
Root, Ernest R.

Ross, W. W.
Strong, Sidney D.
Thomas, Edith M.
Treffinger, Carolyn E.
Walters, Zelia M.
Webber, Amos R.
Wieand, Albert C.
Wilcox, Alanson
Wright, Henry C.

MEIGS COUNTY
Andrews, Martin R.
Arnold, Nelson E.
Barrett, Selah H.
Barton, Thomas H.
Bicknell, Emeline L.
Bierce, Ambrose G.
Campbell, James E.
Doerner, Celia
Dunn, Waldo H.
Holliday, George H.
Horton, Samuel D.
Hoyt, Wilbur F.
Larkin, Stillman C.
Poffenbarger, Livia N. S.
Price, Merle
Sibley, William G.
Washburne, Harry R.
Wilder, Theodore

MERCER COUNTY
Dull, Paul P.
Duncan, Marion H.
Frazier, Ida M. H.
Hodder, Alfred
Oswald, John C.
Schockman, Carl S.
Scranton, Stafford S.
Volz, J. Albert
Wilson, Earl

MIAMI COUNTY
Albaugh, Benjamin F.
Albaugh, Noah H.
Beery, Jesse
Bellaw, Americus W.
Brooks, Robert C.
Clark, George G.
Culbertson, James C.
Davis, Arthur N.
DeWeese, Truman A.
Furnas, Boyd E.
Galloway, Julia R.
Gates, Lawrence G.
Green, Asa T.
Jenkinson, Isaac
Kerr, Alva M.
Kinsey, Samuel
Marshall, Thomas B.
Mayo-Smith, Richmond
O'Ferrall, Kirk B.
Pemberton, Benjamin A.
Rollins, Horace J.
Shook, Chester R.
Smiley, Jerome C.
Smith, Ernest A.
Smith, Henry P.
Spengler, Joseph J.
Wells, Bertram W.
Wells, Sarah F.
Widney, Joseph P.
Woods, Perry D.

MONROE COUNTY
Anshutz, Edward
Brewer, Abraham T.
Davidson, Wilbur L.
Fisher, Stokely S.
Harris, Merriman C.
Johnson, William H.
MacMaster, Homer E.
Martin, Harry E.
Martin, Sylvester M.
Parry, Ward H.
Rapking, Aaron H.
Steward, Samuel M.
Taylor, Mary A. M.
Thornbury, Delmar L.
Williams, William A.

MONTGOMERY COUNTY
Albee, Helen R.
Antrim, Doron K.
Antrim, Ernest I.
Argow, Wendelin
Arnold, James O.
Artz, Frederick B.
Babbitt, Irving
Bell, Bernard I.
Black, Margaret S.
Bonser, Thomas A.
Brooks, Nellie S.
Burnet, David S.
Carney, Aubrey T.
Chancellor, William E.
Coan, Charles F.
Coates, Archie A.
Comstock, Daniel W.
Conover, Charlotte R.
Conover, Frank
Creager, Charles E.
Crook, George
Cunningham, Virginia
Dale, Christopher
Daniels, Winthrop M.
Delp, Irwin W.
Denton, Sherman F.
DeRan, Edna S.
Devine, George B.
Dickman, Joseph T.
Dickson, Arthur P.
Doan, Edward N.
Drake, William A.
Dunbar, Paul L.
Edgar, John F.
Eldridge, Charlotte B.
Evans, Virginia M.
Flannery, M. Jay
Fleischmann, Maximilian C.
Frizell, Martha G.
Frizell, William G.
Gates, Elmer
Grimes, Edward B.
Grose, William
Gunckel, John E.
Harper, Fowler V.
Hochwalt, Albert F.
Houk, Eliza P. T.
Hultman, Helen J.
Jenkins, Charles F.
Lecklider, John T.
Louttit, George M.
Lydenberg, Harry M.
Lytle, John H.
McConnaughey, James P.
McCormick, Frank J.
MacDonald, Susanne K. R.
McKee, Philip J.
Marletto, Charlotte L.
Maxwell, Sidney D.
Miller, Louise K.
Mills, William C.
Minnich, Harvey E.
More, Enoch A.
More, James B.
Noffsinger, John S.
Olt, George R.
Parrott, Thomas M.
Patterson, Frederick B.
Payne, Philip
Peterson, Florence
Pollard, Edwina O.
Potts, Frank E.
Pryor, Helen S.
Reeve, Sidney A.
Richards, Clarice E.
Richardson, Jonathan M.
Richmond, Cecil J.
Rockey, Carroll J.
Rudy, Stella M.
Sabine, George H.
Sayler, Harry L.
Scott, William F.
Shinn, Roger L.
Shuey, William J.
Smith, George B.
Steele, Mary D.
Steele, Robert W.
Thomas, Thomas H.
Thruston, Gates P.
Von Engeln, Oskar
Weaver, James B.
Werthner, William B.
Whitlock, William F.
Williams, Susan M.

MORGAN COUNTY
Addis, Hugh
Berry, Elwood S.
Coler, Cyphron S.
Crew Fleming H.
Dawes, Rufus R.
Dellenbaugh, Frederick S.
Elliott, Charles B.
Gall, Alice C.
Garretson, Arthur S.
Naylor, James B.
Pierce, Silas C.
Sprague, William C.
Tannehill, Ivan R.

MORROW COUNTY
Furbay, John H.
Gunsaulus, Frank W.
Hall, John A.
Harding, Warren G.
McGaughy, James R.
Pepper, Charles M.
Powell, Dawn
Sharp, William G.
Snider, Denton J.
Stockham, Alice B.
Williams, Frankwood E.

MUSKINGUM COUNTY
Bevis, Sophia C. H.
Bloomer, James M.
Brush, Albert M.
Brush, Edmund C.
Corbin, Charles R.
Cox, Samuel S.
Cox, William V.
Culbertson, Anne V.
Curran, George E.
Downs, Edward
DuBois, Constance G.
Elson, Henry W.
Fauley, Wilber F.
Findley, Samuel
Fink, Ollie E.
Foley, Louis
Gabriel, Joel C.
Gates, Willey F.
Granger, Alfred H.
Granger, Moses M.
Grey, Zane
Hamilton, Franklin E. E.
Hamilton, Gilbert V. T.
Harkness, Donna J.
Harper, William R.
Kelley, Samuel W.
Kelly, Melville C.
King, William F.
Latta, Samuel A.
Lyons, John F.
McConnell, Francis J.
Maginnis, Sister Mary J.
Maginnis, Sister Monica
Marshall, Carrington T.
Montgomery, Rena W.
Moorehead, William G.
Munhall, Leander W.
Safford, James M.
Stevenson, Thomas M.
Stewart, Charles D.
Swingle, Emma F.
Turner, Lucy M.
Untermeyer, Jean S.
Wiley, Hugh
Woolley, Solomon J.
Wright, George E.
Wylie, Richard C.

NOBLE COUNTY
Allen, William A.
Archer, William C.
Bussenius, Luellen T.
Danford, Harry E.
Long, Lindley G.
Marquis, Samuel S.
Parrish, Rob Roy M.
Wells, A. Wade
Worden, Wilbertine T.

OTTAWA COUNTY
Beardslee, John W.
Chapman, Rose W.
Kelly, Amy
Macelwane, James B.
Peter, William W.
Rice, Augustus E.
Rossiter, Frederick M.

PERRY COUNTY
Birkhimer, William E.
Brandt, John L.
Brown, Rollo W.
Burkett, Charles W.
Conner, James R.
Cookson, Charles W.
Crook, Isaac
Doyle, John H.
Duffy, Herbert S.
Greiner, Henry C.
Helser, Albert D.
Johnson, Edith C.
MacGahan, Januarius A.
Martzolff, Clement L.
Park, Clyde W.
Rockwell, Vera C.
Spencer, Charles E.
Taylor, William A.
Williamson, Charles W.
Wilson, Milton L.
Zahm, Albert F.
Zahm, John A.
Zartman, Rufus C.

PICKAWAY COUNTY
Abernethy, Wealtha V.
Botkin, Charles W.
Brobeck, Florence
Crook, Alja R.
Darst, Lillie C.
Dick, Samuel M.
Dunton, James G.
Greiner, Clark N.
Greve, Jeanette S.
Holman, Mary V.
Kellerman, William A.
Lutz, Harry E.
Lutz, Ralph H.
McPherson, Logan G.
Marfield, Dwight S.
Myers, Allen O.
Page, Henry F.
Swoyer, Grover E.
Taylor, Joseph R.
Victor, Sarah M.

PIKE COUNTY
Duckworth, Sophie H.
Duke, John K.
Moore, Thomas E.
Stewart, Eliza D.
Turner, Harriet M.

PORTAGE COUNTY
Benedict, Hester A.
Bissell, Walter L.
Bradford, Ward
Brewster, H. Pomeroy
Carlton, Frank T.
Crane, Hart
Davison, Henry M.
Fairchild, Lucius
Ferguson, Charles D.
Hall, Harlan P.
Hartzell, Josiah
Hayden, Morgan P.
Hayden, Warren L.
Holbrook, Martin L.
Hood, Edmund L.
Hudson, Thomson J.
Kent, Marvin
Laughlin, James L.
Lee, George H.
Lord, Louis E.
McManus, Silas B.
Mason, Edward C.
Nicola, Milton G.
Peckham, Harry H.
Pinney, Nelson A.
Plimpton, Florus B.
Pounds, Jessie H. B.
Price, Junius L.
Smalley, Eugene V.
Snow, Lorenzo
Swift, Edgar J.
Taylor, Alta
Thompson, William T.
Upton, Harriet T.
White, Ralph J.
Wright, Thomas L.

PREBLE COUNTY
Anderson, Sherwood
Brooke, Mary G.
Byford, William H.
Collins, Paul V.
Corson, Ella M. J.
Corson, Oscar T.
Day, Albert E.
Ellis, Edgar W.
Farquhar, Ross
Ferguson, John B.
Fornshell, Marvin H.
Fox, Henry C.
Hawes, George E.
Kercheval, Albert R.
Kerr, Myra W.
McDill, David
Miller, Marion M.
Neff, William B.
Northrop, Evelyn
Pryor, William C.
Sloan, Richard E.
Talbert, Ernest L.
Upham, Alfred H.

PUTNAM COUNTY
Bowman, John C.
Hicks, Lewis E.
Hill, John W.
McKay, George L.
Miller, Nolan
Needels, Emma E.
Newton, Benjamin G.
Reese, Lloyd W.
Rowe, Edna B.

RICHLAND COUNTY
Altgeld, Emma F.
Anderson, Olive S. L.
Angle, Paul M.
Ashley, Frederick W.
Bates, Ralph Orr
Baughman, Abraham J.
Bell, Alvin E.
Bergen, Fanny D.
Blymyer, William H.
Bromfield, Annette M. C.
Bromfield, Louis
Carpenter, Frank G.
Day, Lewis W.
Dowling, Levi H.
Fraser, Herbert
Garber, Clark M.
Gass, Sherlock B.
Harris, William L.
Hartmann, Raye
Heindel, Augusta F.
Hinman, Walter F.
Ingham, Mary B.
Kerr, Winfield S.
Lawrence, Ida E.
Linham, Helen L.
Love, John W.
McBride, Robert W.
McKinley, Charles F.
Miller, John H.
Mills, Job S.
Olin, John M.
Porter, William T.
Reed, James A.
Reed, Verner Z.
Santley, Mary M.
Sawyer, Franklin
Thompson, Adele E.
Tracy, Russel L.
Wheeler, Olin D.
Williams, Whiting
Wishart, Charles F.

ROSS COUNTY
Anderson, Thomas M.
Bennett, Henry H.
Bennett, John
Bookwalter, Lewis
Brown, John P.
Chamberlin, William H.
Cooke, Flora J.
Crouse, David E.
Dumond, Dwight L.
Erdmann, Myrtle H.
Finley, Martha
Freeman, Albert D.
Galbraith, Robert C.
Galland, Isaac
Garvin, Hugh C.
Giesy, John U.
Gilmore, William E.
Hollyday, Robert H.
Hurst, Samuel H.
Jones, Nelson E.
Kelly, Thomas R.
King, Rufus
Kleeman, Rita S. H.
Lutz, Harley L.
McClintick, William T.
McGinnis, Ralph J.
McKell, David M.
McLandburgh, Florence
Massie, David M.
Mercer, James K.
Monette, John W.
Mowery, William B.
Nelson, Roberta B.
Nipgen, Alvin P.
Patterson, Nellie
Perkins, George
Raper, Howard R.
Renick, William
Rinkliff, George L.
Safford, William E.
Sibberell, Lloyd E.
Stevenson, Burton E.
Taylor, Robert S.
Thomas, Charles C.
Van Deman, Esther B.
Vincent, Clarence A.
Waddell, Charles C.
Waddle, Angus L.
Williams, Samuel W.
Williams, William G.
Woodrow, Nancy M. W.
Worthington, Thomas

SANDUSKY COUNTY
Abernethy, Alonzo
Bates, Margaret H. E.
Bernard, Florence S.
Bradford, George W.
Brayton, Matthew
Bushnell, Edward
Greene, John W.
Hafford, Ferris S.
Keeler, Lucy Elliott
Kuhlman, John H.
Norris, George W.
Remsburg, John E.
Ross, Harry H.
Stair, Grace
Vickery, Willis
Wilson, Henry H.

SCIOTO COUNTY
Bannon, Henry T.
Crabtree, James W.
Finney, Burnham
Geist, Edna Evelyn
Graham, Lucile
Herms, William B.
Horchow, Reuben
Johnson, William S.
Lacroix, John P.
Liebhardt, Louise
Lowry, Howard F.
Mark, Mary L.
Romig, Edna D.
Sauer, McKinley H.
Searl, Fernando C.
Stephenson, Geneva

SENECA COUNTY
Bell, Corydon W.
Black, Forrest R.
Cressey, George B.
Daley, Edith
Houck, Frederick A.
Houck, George F.
Hunsinger, Clarence S.
Ink, Evangeline
Jones, Mabel C.
Krout, John A.
Leahy, Richard P.
McClung, David W.
Myers, Burton D.
Neikirk, Mabel E.
Quinn, John
Seitz, Isaac
Welsh, Alfred H.

SHELBY COUNTY
Albright, Evelyn M.
Edgerton, James A.
Fisher, George C.
Miller, Henry R.
Robinson, Jennie M.
Roman, Frederick W.
Shaw, A. Vere
Stewart, Robert
Stipp, Joseph A.
Wierwille, Victor P.
Wiley, Farida A.

STARK COUNTY
Allardice, James B.
Allensworth, Carl
Becker, Henry J.
Belden, Henry S.
Bow, Frank T.
Casselman, Arthur V.
Clemens, William M.
Cohen, Armond E.
Coy, Martin
Culler, Arthur J.
Danner, John
Day, Stephen A.
Dick, Gertrude M.
Fogle, Richard H.
Frease, Harry
Freitag, George
Gaskill, Joseph W.
Gerwig, George W.
Herbruck, Edward
Herbruck, Emil P.
Higley, Louis A.
Hilles, Howard
Huntley, Florence C.
Jones, Alice D.
Kay, Gertrude A.
Kimbel, Harry M.
Klippart, John H.
Kurtz, Daniel W.
Leet, Lewis D.
Lenz, Ellis C.
Lorenz, Daniel E.
Lorenz, Edmund S.
Macauley, Charles R.
Maline, William A.
Marlett, Melba B.
Miller, Leo F.
Nash, Jay B.
Pease, Abraham P. L.
Piero, Elda Mae
Plum, William R.
Richardson, Anna S. S.
Schwertner, Thomas M.
Sheatsley, Clarence V.
Sheatsley, Jacob
Sherlock, Herbert A.
Silver, Jesse F.
Skinner, Robert P.
Stuhldreher, Harry A.
Sullivan, Oscar M.
Willenborg, Lee L.
Wolfe, Rolland E.
Worcester, Elwood

SUMMIT COUNTY
Bacon, Delia S.
Ball, Frank C.
Bartlett, Edwin J.
Braden, James A.
Britton, Rollin J.
Conger, Arthur L.
Conger, Emily B.
Curtis, William E.
Dales, George S.
Dobbs, Catherine R. B.
Dudley, Lucy M. B.
Fetzer, Herman
Fieberger, Gustave J.
Finley, Ruth E.
Forrest, Albertina M. A.
Goodhue, Willis M.
Gould, Dayton T.
Green, Francis M.
Greenwood, Gertrude S.
Grismer, Karl H.
Haynes, William B.
Hickenlooper, Andrew
Jackson, Thomas W.
Kolbe, Parke R.
Lewis, Tracy H.
Mallory, Herbert S.
Mario, Queena
Nelan, Charles
Nida, Stella H.
Osmun, Thomas E.
Palmer, William F.
Pelikan, Jaroslav J., Jr.
Pixley, Frank
Pockock, Arthur F.
Poda, John
Polsky, Thomas
Randall, Emilius O.
Rempel, Ruth F. W.
Rowe, Frederick L.
Seymour, Thomas D.
Smith, Hariette K.
Sprigle, Ray
Stark, J. C.
Upton, William T.
Vickers, Leonard B.
Waite, Frederick C.
West, John D.
Wetmore, Claude H.
Wolf, Howard
Young, Catherine

TRUMBULL COUNTY
Anderson, Ethel T.
Biggers, Earl D.
Braden, Clark
Busbey, L. White
Case, Alden B.
Christy, Wilbur A.
Collins, James H.
Colvin, Mary M.
Cox, Kenyon
Darrow, Clarence
Darsie, Charles
Davis, Harold E.
Diehl, Henry A.
Elwell, John J.
French, Asel B.
Gates, Errett
Gause, Isaac
Harshman, Samuel R.
Hart, Hastings H.
Hutchins, Louise C. J.
Johnson, Homer U.
Kennedy, Charles E.
Kennedy, James H.
Kinsman, Frederick J.
Lewis, Hiram W.
Lytle, Katherine W.
McKinley, William
McMahon, Amos P.
McNamara, James R.
Mason, Frank H.
Miller, C. Locke
Miller, Ethel H.
Morgan, Libbie S. C.
Nugent, John C.
Olds, Robert
Peck, Harvey W.
Pennell, Orrin H.
Perkins, Jacob B.
Roberts, Clark
Smith, Clayton C.
Spencer, Abbie K.
Towne, Robert D.
Tuttle, Emma R.
Wilson, Lawrence
Wilson, Robert F.

TUSCARAWAS COUNTY
Barrett, Edna D.
Beall, Emma J. R.
Belden, George P.
Budgett, F. E. J.
Callaghan, J. Dorsey
Daulton, Agnes W. M.
Dice, Charles A.
Donahey, James H.
Donahey, Vic
Donahey, William
Helwig, John B.
Huebner, Francis C.
Karn, Esther N.
Keyser, Leander S.
Kohr, Herbert O.
Markham, William C.
Nixon, Anna
Nolan, Preston M.
Nugent, Elliott

Oakley, Imogen B.
Oliver, George F.
Raff, George W.
Ream, Michael V.
Reed, Orville S.
Richardson, Julius M.
Rickert, Martha E.
Robinson, Ben C.
Schulze, Edward C.
Shepfer, William H.
Shutter, Marion D.
Smith, Ella M. D.
Welty, Edwin A.
Wilkin, Robert N.
Wolfe, Henry C.

UNION COUNTY
Bigelow, Maurice A.
Carpenter, Flora L.
Curry, William L.
Field, Jasper N.
Grove, Harriet P.
Harris, DeWitt H.
Heistand, Henry O. S.
Lee, Ella D.
Michael, William H.
Moses, Jasper T.
Sabine, Wallace C. W.
Sanders, James H.
Welshimer, Pearl H.
Williams, Walter R.
Winget, DeWitt H.

VAN WERT COUNTY
Boole, Ella A.
Engle, Trall
Finlayson, Grace M. R.
Grant, James J.
Hankins, Frank H.
Hartzog, William B.
Hinton, Walter
Michael, Bertha I.
Morse, Florence V.
Pollock, Arlo D.
Running, Corinne
Smith, Don
Smith, Donnal V.
Spears, John R.
Weisman, Russell

VINTON COUNTY
Beecher, Willis J.
Biggs, Louise O.
Cherington, Ernest H.
Hibbard, David S.
Raper, John W.
Sisson, Herbert G.
Sowers, Della

WARREN COUNTY
Armstrong, William J.
Brenner, Robert W.
Brown, John F.
Burnet, Whittier
Collett, Mary S. T.
Earhart, Will
Eldridge, Harry C.
Evans, Bergen
Evans, John
Ham, Marion F.
Johnson, Franklin
Keever, Edward W.
Ketcham, Bryan E.
McKay, Martha N.
MacLean, John P.
Merton, Holmes W.
Monfort, Joseph G.
Morrow, Josiah
Morrow, Marco
Patchen, Kenneth
Pauly, Karl B.
Ream, Laura
Reeder, Rudolph R.
Robinson, Edward S.
Roe, Edward R.
Rosenthal, Miriam
Rowley, Charles E.
Schenck, Lucetta
Schenck, Robert C.
Schurz, William L.
Thirkfield, Wilbur P.
Tichenor, William C.
Van Horne, Thomas B.
Venable, William H.
Whitacre, Donald D.

WASHINGTON COUNTY
Addis, H. A. Noureddin
Ambler, Charles H.
Archbold, Ann
Beach, Arthur G.
Bosworth, Francke H.
Boyd, Ellen B.
Carter, John H.
Cheffey, Jessie A.
Cone, Mary
Cotton, Willia D.
Crewson, Evander A.
Cutler, Julia P.
Dale, Sophia D.
Dawes, Charles G.
Dawes, Rufus C.
Devol, George H.
Dumont, Julia L. C.
Dyar, Muriel C.
Emerson, William D.
Ewart, Frank C.
Gage, Frances D. B.
Gilman, Chandler R.
Green, Jonathan H.
Hanford, Helen E.
Havighurst, Marion B.
McCabe, Lorenzo D.
Owen, Elizabeth T.
Powers, Stephen
Putnam, Albigence W.
Rhodes, Dudley W.
Roland, Charles
Schneider, Norris F.
Schramm, Wilbur L.
Shafer, Claude
Speary, Nellie B.
Stille, Samuel H.
Tibbles, Thomas H.
Warren, Manly
Waters, Wilson
Wing, Conway P.
Zollars, Ely V.

WAYNE COUNTY
Alexander, John R.
Amstutz, Peter B.
Brown, William M.
Clark, Charles T.
Compton, Arthur H.
Compton, Karl T.
Compton, Wilson M.
Douglass, Ben
Downing, Edward C.
Gault, Franklin B.
Geissinger, James A.
Gerig, Orie B.
Heyward, Dorothy K.
Hoff, Emanuel B.
Hotchkiss, Willis R.
Jamison, Alcinous B.
Lawrence, John
Lybarger, Edwin L.
McCauley, William F.
McConohay, Augustus P.
Morgan, Florence H.
Notestein, Lucy L.
Notestein, Wallace
Palmer, Edward E.
Sanders, Thomas J.
Schmutz, George S.
Spreng, Samuel P.
Stoll, Elmer E.
Weltmer, Sidney A.
White, John C.
Williams, Edward I. F.
Wyer, Samuel S.

WILLIAMS COUNTY
Bowersox, Charles A.
Caldwell, Howard W.
Eberle, Edith
Ewing, Max A.
Pratt, Cornelia A.
Shinn, William H.
Siple, Paul A.
Stough, Henry W.
Thomas, Lewis F.
Wickey, Harry H.

WOOD COUNTY
Butler, Joseph M.
Canfield, Dwight R.
Cooke, Grace M.
Doud, Harriet E.
Evers, Charles W.
Hamlin, Howard E.
Keeler, Ralph O.
Seitz, Don C.
Slosser, Gaius J.
Thurstin, Wesley S.
Van Tassel, Charles S.
Westerfield, Ray B.
White, Charles E.
Wood, James C.

WYANDOT COUNTY
Cole, Merl B.
Kinney, Muriel
Vogt, Paul L.